STATUTORY SUPPLEMENT TO

CLOSELY HELD BUSINESS ORGANIZATIONS

CASES, MATERIALS, AND PROBLEMS

By

Robert A. Ragazzo
University of Houston Law Foundation Professor of Law
University of Houston Law Center

Douglas K. Moll
Beirne, Maynard & Parsons, L.L.P. Professor of Law
University of Houston Law Center

AMERICAN CASEBOOK SERIES®

THOMSON
™
WEST

Mat #40439601

Thomson/West have created this publication to provide you with accurate and authoritative information concerning the subject matter covered. However, this publication was not necessarily prepared by persons licensed to practice law in a particular jurisdiction. Thomson/West are not engaged in rendering legal or other professional advice, and this publication is not a substitute for the advice of an attorney. If you require legal or other expert advice, you should seek the services of a competent attorney or other professional.

610 Opperman Drive
P.O. Box 64526
St. Paul, MN 55164–0526
1–800–328–9352

Printed in the United States of America

ISBN–13: 978–0–314–16696–8
ISBN–10: 0–314–16696–3

TEXT IS PRINTED ON 10% POST CONSUMER RECYCLED PAPER

Preface

This statutory supplement is designed for use in law school courses covering agency, partnerships, corporations, and other limited liability entities. In particular, the supplement compiles the statutes and comments needed for the use of our casebook, Closely Held Business Organizations: Cases, Materials, and Problems.

In general, the materials included in this supplement are presented in one of three manners. First, for state or federal statutes and rules that have no accompanying comments, the statutory text is reprinted in its entirety. Examples of such materials include the Delaware General Corporation Law, the Delaware Limited Liability Company Act, and selected sections of the New York Business Corporation Law. Second, for some uniform or model statutes, the statutory text and comments are reprinted in their entirety. Such materials include the Revised Uniform Partnership Act (1997), the Revised Uniform Limited Partnership Act (1976 with 1985 amendments), the Uniform Limited Partnership Act (2001), and the Uniform Limited Liability Company Act (1996). Third, for Restatements and some uniform or model statutes, the statutory text is reprinted in its entirety, but only selected comments are included. Examples of such materials include the Second and Third Restatements of Agency (as well as the tentative drafts of the Third Restatement), the Uniform Partnership Act (1914), and the Model Business Corporation Act.

A special note on the Third Restatement of Agency: the final Restatement was completed in the summer of 2006 after the casebook had gone to press. Thus, the casebook was prepared using the latest drafts of the Third Restatement that were available at the time. This supplement includes the tentative drafts that were used in the preparation of the casebook as well as the final version of the Third Restatement. Although there were not many changes between the tentative drafts and the final version, you should be aware that a small number of cited sections and comments in the casebook may be slightly off when consulting the final Restatement (Third) of Agency (2006).

We very much welcome your feedback on this statutory supplement. Please call or e-mail us with any comments, suggestions, or insights. If you notice errors or omissions, please bring them to our attention as well. We'll incorporate as much as we can into the next edition.

Robert A. Ragazzo
Douglas K. Moll

October 2006

*

Acknowledgements

Several students provided us with invaluable research assistance during the preparation of this statutory supplement: Maria Carminati-Garbino (Houston 2008), David Dean (Houston 2008), and Beth Lloyd (Houston 2007). In addition, we are truly grateful for permission to use the following works:

THE MODEL BUSINESS CORPORATION ACT. Copyright 2005 by the American Bar Association. Reprinted with permission.

RESTATEMENT, SECOND, AGENCY. Copyright 1958 by The American Law Institute. All rights reserved. Reprinted with permission.

RESTATEMENT, THIRD, AGENCY. Copyright 2006 by The American Law Institute. All rights reserved. Reprinted with permission.

RESTATEMENT, THIRD, AGENCY, Tentative Draft No. 2. Copyright 2001 by The American Law Institute. All rights reserved. Reprinted with permission.

RESTATEMENT, THIRD, AGENCY, Tentative Draft No. 3. Copyright 2002 by The American Law Institute. All rights reserved. Reprinted with permission.

RESTATEMENT, THIRD, AGENCY, Tentative Draft No. 4. Copyright 2003 by The American Law Institute. All rights reserved. Reprinted with permission.

RESTATEMENT, THIRD, AGENCY, Tentative Draft No. 5. Copyright 2004 by The American Law Institute. All rights reserved. Reprinted with permission.

RESTATEMENT, THIRD, AGENCY, Tentative Draft No. 6. Copyright 2005 by The American Law Institute. All rights reserved. Reprinted with permission.

REVISED UNIFORM LIMITED PARTNERSHIP ACT (1976 with 1985 amendments). Copyright 1985 by the National Conference of Commissioners on Uniform State Laws. Reprinted with permission.

REVISED UNIFORM PARTNERSHIP ACT (1997). Copyright 1997 by the National Conference of Commissioners on Uniform State Laws. Reprinted with permission.

UNIFORM LIMITED LIABILITY COMPANY ACT (1996). Copyright 1996 by the National Conference of Commissioners on Uniform State Laws. Reprinted with permission.

UNIFORM LIMITED PARTNERSHIP ACT (2001). Copyright 2001 by the National Conference of Commissioners on Uniform State Laws. Reprinted with permission.

UNIFORM PARTNERSHIP ACT (1914). Copyright 1914 by the National Conference of Commissioners on Uniform State Laws. Reprinted with permission.

Table of Contents

*

STATUTORY SUPPLEMENT TO
CLOSELY HELD BUSINESS ORGANIZATIONS
CASES, MATERIALS, AND PROBLEMS

*

RESTATEMENT (SECOND) OF AGENCY (1958)

Table of Sections

Chapter 1
INTRODUCTORY MATTERS

TOPIC 1. DEFINITIONS

TOPIC 2. KNOWLEDGE AND NOTICE

TOPIC 3. ESSENTIAL CHARACTERISTICS OF RELATION

TOPIC 4. AGENCY DISTINGUISHED FROM OTHER RELATIONS

TOPIC 2. INTERPRETATION OF AUTHORITY AND APPARENT AUTHORITY

TITLE A. AUTHORITY

TITLE B. INTERPRETATION OF APPARENT AUTHORITY

TOPIC 3. INTERPRETATION OF PARTICULAR AUTHORIZATIONS

TITLE A. AUTHORIZATION TO CONTRACT

TITLE B. AUTHORIZATION TO BUY OR TO SELL

TOPIC 2. DISCLOSED OR PARTIALLY DISCLOSED PRINCIPAL

TITLE A. CREATION OF LIABILITY BY AUTHORIZED ACTS

TITLE B. INTERPRETATION OF WRITTEN INSTRUMENTS AS TO PARTIES

TITLE C. CREATION OF LIABILITY BY UNAUTHORIZED ACTS

TITLE C. DEFENSES AND LIABILITY AFFECTED BY SUBSEQUENT EVENTS

Section

Chapter 7

LIABILITY OF PRINCIPAL TO THIRD PERSON; TORTS

TOPIC 1. LIABILITY FOR PERSONAL VIOLATION OF DUTY

TOPIC 2. LIABILITY FOR AUTHORIZED CONDUCT OR CONDUCT INCIDENTAL THERETO

TITLE A. IN GENERAL

TITLE B. TORTS OF SERVANTS

WHO IS A SERVANT

TOPIC 5. EFFECT OF RATIFICATION

Chapter 11

LIABILITY OF AGENT TO THIRD PERSONS

TOPIC 1. CONTRACTS AND CONVEYANCES

TITLE A. AGENT A PARTY TO A TRANSACTION CONDUCTED BY HIMSELF

TITLE B. AGENT NOT PARTY TO TRANSACTION CONDUCTED BY HIMSELF

TITLE C. DEFENSES AND EFFECTS OF SUBSEQUENT EVENTS

TOPIC 2. THINGS RECEIVED FROM OR FOR PRINCIPAL

TITLE A. THINGS RECEIVED FROM THIRD PERSON

TITLE B. THINGS RECEIVED FROM PRINCIPAL

TOPIC 3. TORTS

TOPIC 4. SUBSEQUENT EVENTS

TOPIC 5. SERVANTS, SUBSERVANTS AND OTHER SUBAGENTS

Chapter 12

LIABILITY OF THIRD PERSON TO AGENT

TOPIC 1. ACTIONS BY AGENT ON BEHALF OF PRINCIPAL

TITLE A. WHEN AGENT CAN SUE IN HIS OWN NAME

TITLE B. DEFENSES

TITLE B. REMEDIES OF AGENT

TITLE C. DEFENSES

INTRODUCTORY MATTERS

TOPIC 1. DEFINITIONS

§ 1. Agency; Principal; Agent

(1) Agency is the fiduciary relation which results from the manifestation of consent by one person to another that the other shall act on his behalf and subject to his control, and consent by the other so to act.

(2) The one for whom action is to be taken is the principal.

(3) The one who is to act is the agent.

Comment b. Agency a legal concept. Agency is a legal concept which depends upon the existence of required factual elements: the manifestation by the principal that the agent shall act for him, the agent's acceptance of the undertaking and the understanding of the parties that the principal is to be in control of the undertaking. The relation which the law calls agency does not depend upon the intent of the parties to create it, nor their belief that they have done so. To constitute the relation, there must be an agreement, but not necessarily a contract, between the parties; if the agreement results in the factual relation between them to which are attached the legal consequences of agency, an agency exists although the parties did not call it agency and did not intend the legal consequences of the relation to follow. Thus, when one who asks a friend to do a slight service for him, such as to return for credit goods recently purchased from a store, neither one may have any realization that they are creating an agency relation or be aware of the legal obligations which would result from performance of the service. On the other hand, one may believe that he has created an agency when in fact the relation is that of seller and buyer. See § 14J. The distinction between agency and other relations, such as those of trust, buyer and seller, and others are stated in Sections 14A to 14O. The distinction between the kind of agent called a servant and a non-servant agent is stated in Section 2.

When it is doubtful whether a representative is the agent of one or the other of two contracting parties, the function of the court is to ascertain the factual relation of the parties to each other and in so doing can properly disregard a statement in the agreement that the agent is to be the agent of one rather than of the other, or a statement by the parties as to the legal relations which are thereby created. See § 14L. The agency relation results if, but only if, there is an understanding between the parties which, as interpreted by the court, creates a fiduciary relation in which the fiduciary is subject to the directions of the one on whose account he acts. It is the element of continuous subjection to the will of the principal which distinguishes the agent from other fiduciaries and the agency agreement from other agreements. The characteristics which tend to indicate an agency or a non-agency relation are stated in Sections 12 to 14O.

§ 2. Master; Servant; Independent Contractor

(1) A master is a principal who employs an agent to perform service in his affairs and who controls or has the right to control the physical conduct of the other in the performance of the service.

(2) A servant is an agent employed by a master to perform service in his affairs whose physical conduct in the performance of the service is controlled or is subject to the right to control by the master.

(3) An independent contractor is a person who contracts with another to do something for him but who is not controlled by the other nor subject to the other's right to control with respect to his physical conduct in the performance of the undertaking. He may or may not be an agent.

Comment a. Servants and non-servant agents. A master is a species of principal, and a servant is a species of agent. The words "master" and "servant" are herein used to indicate the relation from which arises both the liability of an employer for the physical harm caused to third persons by the tort of an employee (see §§ 219–249) and the special duties and immunities of an employer to the employee. See §§ 473–528. Although for brevity the definitions in this Section refer only to the control or right to control the physical conduct of the servant, there are many factors which are considered by the courts in defining the relation. These factors which distinguish a servant from an independent contractor are stated in Section 220. The distinction between servants and agents who are not servants is of importance for the purposes of the Sections referred to. Statements made in the Restatement of this Subject as applicable to principals or agents are, unless otherwise stated, applicable to masters and servants. The rules as to liability of a principal for the torts of agents who are not servants are stated in Sections 250–267, and those with respect to his liability in tort to such agents in Sections 470–472. The duties of servants to masters and their liabilities to third persons are in general the same as those of agents who are not servants. However, servants may have only custody, as distinguished from possession of goods entrusted to them by the master (see § 339, Comment *g* and § 349), and a servant, because of his position, may not be responsible for mistakes made by him as to facts upon which his authority depends, whereas an agent who is not a servant would be responsible. See Comment *c* on § 383.

§ 3. General Agent; Special Agent

(1) A general agent is an agent authorized to conduct a series of transactions involving a continuity of service.

(2) A special agent is an agent authorized to conduct a single transaction or a series of transactions not involving continuity of service.

§ 4. Disclosed Principal; Partially Disclosed Principal; Undisclosed Principal

(1) If, at the time of a transaction conducted by an agent, the other party thereto has notice that the agent is acting for a principal and of the principal's identity, the principal is a disclosed principal.

(2) If the other party has notice that the agent is or may be acting for a principal but has no notice of the principal's identity, the principal for whom the agent is acting is a partially disclosed principal.

(3) If the other party has no notice that the agent is acting for a principal, the one for whom he acts is an undisclosed principal.

§ 5. Subagents and Subservants

(1) A subagent is a person appointed by an agent empowered to do so, to perform functions undertaken by the agent for the principal, but for whose conduct the agent agrees with the principal to be primarily responsible.

(2) A subservant is a person appointed by a servant empowered to do so, to perform functions undertaken by the servant for the master and subject to the control as to his physical conduct both by the master and by the servant, but for whose conduct the servant agrees with the principal to be primarily responsible.

Comment a. An agent may be authorized to appoint another person to perform for the principal an act which the agent is authorized to perform or to have performed. The agreement may be that upon the appointment of such a person the agent's function as agent is performed, and that thereafter the person so appointed is not to be the representative of the agent but is to act solely on account of the principal, in which case the one so appointed is an agent and not a subagent. On the other hand, the agreement may be that the appointing agent is to undertake the performance of the authorized act either by himself or by someone else and that the person so appointed while doing the act on account of the principal is also, in so doing, to be the agent of the appointing agent, who consequently will have the responsibility of a principal with respect to such person. If this is the agreement, the person so appointed is a subagent. What the agreement is depends, as do other agreements, upon the manifestations of the parties as interpreted by the usages between them, the customs of business, and all other circumstances. See §§ 77–81.

A person may be a subagent although the appointing agent has no authority to appoint him. This is so if the agent has apparent authority to make the appointment, or if he otherwise has power to bind the principal, as where he is a general agent and the appointment of a subagent is an ordinary incident of his position, although forbidden in the particular instance. See §§ 161, 194.

b. Reasons for distinguishing "agent" from "subagent". A subagent, as defined herein, is a person for whose conduct the appointing agent is responsible to the principal (see § 406), and in some cases is responsible to the person with whom the subagent deals. See § 362. These legal consequences do not follow when the appointing agent's function is merely to appoint a person to act for the principal, in which case the appointing agent is liable only if negligent in making the appointment. See § 405. In such a case, the person so appointed is not different from any other agent of the principal, and the fact that he was appointed by a superior agent rather than by the principal becomes immaterial. It is useful, therefore, to have a term which applies solely to the special type of relation where the appointed person is both an agent of the principal and an agent of the superior, appointing agent.

The courts have sometimes used the term subagent to describe both subagents as defined herein and also persons who, although appointed by superior agents, are not agents of such superior agents. This difference in usage has not resulted in improper decisions, but it has made the problem of citation difficult, since in noting cases in digests and encyclopedias the cases have to be read carefully to be sure that the court was referring to the kind of person described in this Section as a subagent.

Where an agent has no power to bind P by an appointment of a subagent, the one so appointed is the agent of the agent only, and the latter is responsible both to the principal for any improper delegation or/and to third persons for his agent's conduct. As to the authority to appoint an agent or subagent see Sections 77–81.

Comment e. Subagents in series. There may be a series of subagents, as where an attorney, authorized to collect a debt and appoint a subagent, sends it to a correspondent with a request for him to appoint another for whose conduct the correspondent is to be responsible.

§ 6. Power

A power is an ability on the part of a person to produce a change in a given legal relation by doing or not doing a given act.

§ 7. Authority

Authority is the power of the agent to affect the legal relations of the principal by acts done in accordance with the principal's manifestations of consent to him.

§ 8. Apparent Authority

Apparent authority is the power to affect the legal relations of another person by transactions with third persons, professedly as agent for the other, arising from and in accordance with the other's manifestations to such third persons.

§ 8A. Inherent Agency Power

Inherent agency power is a term used in the restatement of this subject to indicate the power of an agent which is derived not from authority, apparent authority or estoppel, but solely from the agency relation and exists for the protection of persons harmed by or dealing with a servant or other agent.

§ 8B. Estoppel; Change of Position

(1) A person who is not otherwise liable as a party to a transaction purported to be done on his account, is nevertheless subject to liability to persons who have changed their positions because of their belief that the transaction was entered into by or for him, if

(a) he intentionally or carelessly caused such belief, or

(b) knowing of such belief and that others might change their positions because of it, he did not take reasonable steps to notify them of the facts.

(2) An owner of property who represents to third persons that another is the owner of the property or who permits the other so to represent, or who realizes that third persons believe that another is the owner of the property, and that he could easily inform the third persons of the facts, is subject to the loss of the property if the other disposes of it to third persons who, in ignorance of the facts, purchase the property or otherwise change their position with reference to it.

(3) Change of position, as the phrase is used in the restatement of this subject, indicates payment of money, expenditure of labor, suffering a loss or subjection to legal liability.

§ 8C. Restitution

A person who has been unjustly enriched at the expense of another is required to make restitution to the other.

§ 8D. Reformation

If by mistake of fact as to the contents of a written agreement or conveyance, or by mistake of law as to its legal effect, the writing does not conform to the agreement of the parties to it, the writing can be reformed to accord with the agreement.

TOPIC 2. KNOWLEDGE AND NOTICE

§ 9. Notice

(1) A person has notice of a fact if he knows the fact, has reason to know it, should know it, or has been given notification of it.

(2) A person is given notification of a fact by another if the latter

(a) informs him of the fact by adequate or specified means or of other facts from which he has reason to know or should know the facts: or

(b) does an act which, under the rules applicable to the transaction, has the same effect on the legal relations of the parties as the acquisition of knowledge or reason to know.

(3) A person has notice of a fact if his agent has knowledge of the fact, reason to know it or should know it, or has been given a notification of it, under circumstances coming within the rules applying to the liability of a principal because of notice to his agent.

Comment d. Reason to know. A person has reason to know of a fact if he has information from which a person of ordinary intelligence, or of the superior intelligence which such person may have, would infer that the fact in question exists or that there is such a substantial chance of its existence that, if exercising reasonable care with reference to the matter in question, his action would be predicated upon the assumption of its possible existence. The inference drawn need not be that the fact exists; it is sufficient that the likelihood of its existence is so great that a person of ordinary intelligence, or of the superior intelligence which the person in question has, would, if exercising ordinary prudence under the circumstances, govern his conduct as if the fact existed, until he could ascertain its existence or non-existence. The words "reason to know" do not necessarily import the existence of a duty to others to ascertain facts; the words are used both where the actor has a duty to another and where he would not be acting adequately in the protection of his own interests were he not to act with reference to the facts which he has reason to know. One may have reason to know a fact although he does not make the inference of its existence which would be made by a reasonable person in his position and with his knowledge, whether his failure to make such inference is due to inferior intelligence or to a failure properly to exercise such intelligence as he has. A person of superior intelligence or training has reason to know a fact if a person with his mental capacity and attainments would draw such an inference from the facts known to him. On the other hand, "reason to know" imports no duty to ascertain facts not to be deduced as inferences from facts already known; one has reason to know a fact only if a reasonable person in his position would infer such fact from other facts already known to him.

Further, a person has reason to know facts only if the circumstances are such that any unconscious knowledge would be made conscious if such person were to meet the required standards with reference to memory, consideration for the interests of others, or, in some instances, consideration for one's own interests. Thus, one who had no reason to remember facts once known would not at a later time have reason to know the facts. See Sections 276 and 277, which deal with situations in which this distinction may be crucial in determining the liability of the principal because of what an agent has reason to know.

§ 10. Knowledge Which Principal or Agent Should Have Inter Se

Unless the parties have otherwise agreed, a principal or agent, with respect to the other, should know what a person of ordinary experience and intelligence would know, and in addition, what he would know if, having the knowledge and intelligence which he has or which he purports to have, he were to use due care in the performance of his duties to the other.

§ 11. Notification by Principal or Agent to the Other

Unless otherwise agreed, there is a notification of a fact by the principal to the agent or by the agent to the principal:

(a) when one of them states such fact to the other; or

(b) when a reasonable time has elapsed after a writing stating such fact has been delivered

(i) to the other personally,

(ii) to the other's place of business,

(iii) to a place designated by the other as a place for the receipt of business communications, or

(iv) to a place which, in view of business customs or the relations between the parties, is reasonably believed to be the place for the receipt of such communications by the other.

TOPIC 3. ESSENTIAL CHARACTERISTICS OF RELATION

§ 12. Agent as Holder of a Power

An agent or apparent agent holds a power to alter the legal relations between the principal and third persons and between the principal and himself.

§ 13. Agent as a Fiduciary

An agent is a fiduciary with respect to matters within the scope of his agency.

§ 14. Control by Principal

A principal has the right to control the conduct of the agent with respect to matters entrusted to him.

Comment a. The right of control by the principal may be exercised by prescribing what the agent shall or shall not do before the agent acts, or at the time when he acts, or at both times. The principal's right to control is continuous and continues as long as the agency relation exists, even though the principal agreed that he would not exercise it. Thus, the agent is subject to a duty not to act contrary to the principal's directions, although the principal has agreed not to give such directions. See § 33. Further, the principal has power to revoke the agent's authority, although this would constitute a breach of his contract with him. See

§ 118. The agent cannot obtain specific performance of the principal's agreement. If the agent has notice of facts from which he should infer that the principal does not wish him to act as originally specified, the agent's authority is terminated, suspended, or modified accordingly. See § 108. The control of the principal does not, however, include control at every moment; its exercise may be very attenuated and, as where the principal is physically absent, may be ineffective.

The extent of the right to control the physical acts of the agent is an important factor in determining whether or not a master-servant relation between them exists. See § 220.

Comment b. If it is otherwise clear that there is an agency relation, as in the case of recognized agents such as attorneys at law, factors, or auctioneers, the principal, although he has contracted with the agent not to exercise control and to permit the agent the free exercise of his discretion, nevertheless has power to give lawful directions which the agent is under a duty to obey if he continues to act as such. See § 385. If the existence of an agency relation is not otherwise clearly shown, as where the issue is whether a trust or an agency has been created, the fact that it is understood that the person acting is not to be subject to the control of the other as to the manner of performance determines that the relation is not that of agency. See § 14B.

TOPIC 4. AGENCY DISTINGUISHED FROM OTHER RELATIONS

§ 14A. Agent and Partner

A partnership is an association of two or more persons to carry on as co-owners a business for profit.

§ 14B. Agency and Trust

One who has title to property which he agrees to hold for the benefit and subject to the control of another is an agent-trustee and is subject to the rules of agency.

§ 14C. Agent or Director

Neither the board of directors nor an individual director of a business is, as such, an agent of the corporation or of its members.

§ 14D. Agent or Escrow Holder

An escrow holder is not as such an agent of either party to the transaction until the event occurs which terminates the escrow relation.

§ 14E. Agent and Interpreter or Amanuensis

Interpreters and amanuenses are agents for those who have employed them to interpret or to write; if selected by both or neither of the parties to a transaction, they are agents of neither.

§ 14F. Judicially Appointed Fiduciaries

A person appointed by a court to manage the affairs of others is not an agent of the others.

§ 14G. Agent or Assignee

An assignee of a claim is an agent of the assignor only if the latter retains an interest in, and control over, the claim.

§ 14H. Agents or Holders of a Power Given for Their Benefit

One who holds a power created in the form of an agency authority, but given for the benefit of the power holder or of a third person, is not an agent of the one creating the power.

§ 14I. Agent or Holder of a Restitutional Power

A person who has a power created by law to subject another to liability for the protection of the other's person or property or for the performance of the other's obligations is not an agent but is the holder of a power to create restitutional rights.

§ 14J. Agent or Buyer

One who receives goods from another for resale to a third person is not thereby the other's agent in the transaction: whether he is an agent for this purpose or is himself a buyer depends upon whether the parties agree that his duty is to act primarily for the benefit of the one delivering the goods to him or is to act primarily for his own benefit.

§ 14K. Agent or Supplier

One who contracts to acquire property from a third person and convey it to another is the agent of the other only if it is agreed that he is to act primarily for the benefit of the other and not for himself.

Comment a. Typical situations to which the rule stated in this Section apply are the purchase of shares in a corporation through a dealer or the purchase of land through a broker. Factors indicating that the one who is to acquire the property and transfer it to the other is selling to, and not acting as agent for, the other are: (1) That he is to receive a fixed price for the property, irrespective of the price paid by him. This is the most important. (2) That he acts in his own name and receives the title to the property which he thereafter is to transfer. (3) That he has an independent business in buying and selling similar property. None of these factors is conclusive. The question arises in a variety of ways. Thus the issue may be whether or not the supplier is entitled to keep the difference between what he paid for the goods and what it was agreed he should receive from the transferee; if there is an agency, normally this amount must be accounted for. However, a principal may agree that his buying agent is to retain the amount. The issue may arise because of the Statute of Frauds, because an oral order to an agent is not within the Statute, whereas an oral order to a seller, if above the statutory amount, must be in writing. Comment *c* on Section 14J states a number of other ways in which it may be important to determine whether a transaction creates a contract of sale or an agency relation.

§ 14L. Ambiguous Principal

(1) A person who conducts a transaction between two others may be an agent of both of them in the transaction, or the agent of one of them only, although the agent of the other for other transactions, or the agent of one for part of the transaction and the agent of the other for the remainder.

(2) Unless otherwise agreed, one who has received money or other property from another to be paid or transferred to a creditor of the other is the agent of the other and not of the creditor.

§ 14M. Corporate Subsidiaries

A corporation does not become an agent of another corporation merely because a majority of its voting shares is held by the other.

§ 14N. Agent and Independent Contractor

One who contracts to act on behalf of another and subject to the other's control except with respect to his physical conduct is an agent and also an independent contractor.

§ 14O. Security Holder Becoming a Principal

A creditor who assumes control of his debtor's business for the mutual benefit of himself and his debtor, may become a principal, with liability for the acts and transactions of the debtor in connection with the business.

Comment a. A security holder who merely exercises a veto power over the business acts of his debtor by preventing purchases or sales above specified amounts does not thereby become a principal. However, if he takes over the management of the debtor's business either in person or through an agent, and directs what contracts may or may not be made, he becomes a principal, liable as any principal for the obligations incurred thereafter in the normal course of business by the debtor who has now become his general agent. The point at which the creditor becomes a principal is that at which he assumes de facto control over the conduct of his debtor, whatever the terms of the formal contract with his debtor may be.

Where there is an assignment for the benefit of creditors, the latter may become the principals of the assignee if they exercise control over transactions entered into by him on their behalf.

Chapter 2

CREATION OF RELATION

TOPIC 1. MUTUAL CONSENT AND CONSIDERATION

§ 15. Manifestations of Consent

An agency relation exists only if there has been a manifestation by the principal to the agent that the agent may act on his account, and consent by the agent so to act.

§ 16. Consideration

The relation of principal and agent can be created although neither party receives consideration.

TOPIC 2. DELEGABLE ACTS AND POWERS

§ 17. What Acts are Delegable

A person privileged, or subject to a duty, to perform an act or accomplish a result can properly appoint an agent to perform the act or accomplish the result, unless public policy or the agreement with another requires personal performance; if personal performance is required, the doing of the act by another on his behalf does not constitute performance by him.

§ 18. Delegation of Powers Held by Agent

Unless otherwise agreed, an agent cannot properly delegate to another the exercise of discretion in the use of a power held for the benefit of the principal.

§ 19. Appointment to Perform Illegal Acts

The appointment of an agent to do an act is illegal if an agreement to do such an act or the doing of the act itself would be criminal, tortious, or otherwise opposed to public policy.

TOPIC 3. CAPACITY OF PARTIES TO RELATION

§ 20. Capacity of Principal

A person who has capacity to affect his legal relations by giving consent to a delegable act or transaction has capacity to authorize an agent to do such act or to conduct such transaction for him with the same effect as if he were to act in person.

§ 21. Capacity of Agent; In General

(1) Any person has capacity to hold a power to act on behalf of another.

(2) The extent to which the person holding such power is a fiduciary and is subject to duties and liabilities to the principal depends upon his capacity.

§ 22. Husband and Wife as Principal and Agent

A husband or wife can be authorized to act for the other party to the marital relation.

§ 23. Agent Having Interests Adverse to Principal

One whose interests are adverse to those of another can be authorized to act on behalf of the other; it is a breach of duty for him so to act without revealing the existence and extent of such adverse interests.

§ 24. Adverse Party to Transaction as Agent

One party to a transaction can be authorized to act as agent for the other party thereto, except for the purpose of satisfying the requirements of the Statute of Frauds.

TOPIC 4. MASTER AND SERVANT

§ 25. Applicability of General Agency Rules

The rules applicable generally to principal and agent as to the creation of the relation, delegability and capacity of the parties apply to master and servant.

Chapter 3

CREATION AND INTERPRETATION OF AUTHORITY AND APPARENT AUTHORITY

TOPIC 1. METHODS OF MANIFESTING CONSENT

§ 26. Creation of Authority; General Rule

Except for the execution of instruments under seal or for the performance of transactions required by statute to be authorized in a particular way, authority to do an act can be created by written or spoken words or other conduct of the principal which, reasonably interpreted, causes the agent to believe that the principal desires him so to act on the principal's account.

§ 27. Creation of Apparent Authority: General Rule

Except for the execution of instruments under seal or for the conduct of transactions required by statute to be authorized in a particular way, apparent authority to do an act is created as to a third person by written or spoken words or any other conduct of the principal which, reasonably interpreted, causes the third person to believe that the principal consents to have the act done on his behalf by the person purporting to act for him.

§ 28. Authority to Execute Sealed Instruments

(1) Except as stated in Subsection (2), an instrument executed by an agent as a sealed instrument does not operate as such unless authority or apparent authority to execute it has been conferred by an instrument under seal.

(2) Sealed authority is not necessary to execute an instrument under seal where:

(a) the instrument is executed in the principal's presence and by his direction;

(b) the instrument is authorized by a corporation or partnership in accordance with the rules relating to the authorization of such instruments by such associations; or

(c) a statute deprives seals of their legal significance.

§ 29. Defectively Authorized Deed as Memorandum of Contract

(1) Where a statute requires a memorandum of a transaction to be evidenced by the signature of a party to be charged, a sealed instrument signed by an agent, ineffective as a deed because the agent's authority was not under seal, satisfies the requirements of the statute if the instrument is sufficiently definite and the agent is otherwise properly authorized.

(2) A sealed instrument incapable of taking effect as a covenant because made by an agent not authorized under seal is effective as a simple contract if the agent is otherwise authorized and the elements of a simple contract are present.

§ 30. Authority to Execute Writings

(1) Unless so provided by statute, a written authorization is not necessary for the execution of a writing.

(2) A statutory requirement that a memorandum of a transaction be signed by the parties in order to make it effective does not of itself impose a requirement of written authorization to execute such a memorandum.

§ 31. Estoppel to Deny Authorization

(1) A person who manifests to a third person that he has authorized an agent by an instrument under seal or by other formality is subject to liability to such third person as if the authorization had been by such means, if the third person changes his position in reasonable reliance upon the manifestation.

(2) If a principal entrusts to an agent an executed document containing blanks, and the agent fills the blanks without authority and delivers the document to a third person, who changes his position in reliance thereon without notice that the principal did not fill the blanks before execution of the instrument, the principal is subject to liability to the third person as if the instrument had been completed by the principal or by an agent properly authorized to fill the blanks.

TOPIC 2. INTERPRETATION OF AUTHORITY AND APPARENT AUTHORITY

TITLE A. AUTHORITY

§ 32. Applicability of Rules for Interpretation of Agreements

Except to the extent that the fiduciary relation between principal and agent requires special rules, the rules for the interpretation of contracts apply to the interpretation of authority.

§ 33. General Principle of Interpretation

An agent is authorized to do, and to do only, what it is reasonable for him to infer that the principal desires him to do in the light of the principal's manifestations and the facts as he knows or should know them at the time he acts.

§ 34. Circumstances Considered in Interpreting Authority

An authorization is interpreted in light of all accompanying circumstances, including among other matters:

(a) the situation of the parties, their relations to one another, and the business in which they are engaged;

(b) the general usages of business, the usages of trades or employments of the kind to which the authorization relates, and the business methods of the principal;

(c) facts of which the agent has notice respecting the objects which the principal desires to accomplish;

(d) the nature of the subject matter, the circumstances under which the act is to be performed and the legality or illegality of the act; and

(e) the formality or informality, and the care, or lack of it, with which an instrument evidencing the authority is drawn.

§ 35. When Incidental Authority is Inferred

Unless otherwise agreed, authority to conduct a transaction includes authority to do acts which are incidental to it, usually accompany it, or are reasonably necessary to accomplish it.

§ 36. Usage in Interpretation of Authority

Unless otherwise agreed, an agent is authorized to comply with relevant usages of business if the principal has notice that usages of such a nature may exist.

§ 37. General Expressions and Particularized Authorizations

(1) Unless otherwise agreed, general expressions used in authorizing an agent are limited in application to acts done in connection with the act or business to which the authority primarily relates.

(2) The specific authorization of particular acts tends to show that a more general authority is not intended.

§ 38. Interpretation as to Duration of Authority

Authority exists only during the period in which, from the manifestations of the principal and the happening of events of which the agent has notice, the agent reasonably believes that the principal desires him to act.

§ 39. Inference That Agent is to Act Only for Principal's Benefit

Unless otherwise agreed, authority to act as agent includes only authority to act for the benefit of the principal.

§ 40. Inference as to Authority to Disclose Principal

Unless otherwise agreed, an agent is authorized to disclose the existence and identity of his principal; if, as the agent should know, nondisclosure of the principal's existence or identity would subject the principal to disadvantage, the agent has authority only if he makes the proper disclosure.

§ 41. Interpretation of Authority Where Principals or Agents are Joint

(1) Unless otherwise agreed, authority given by two or more principals jointly includes only authority to act for their joint account.

(2) Unless otherwise agreed, authority given in one authorization to two or more persons to act as agents includes only authority to act jointly, except in the execution of a properly delegable authority.

§ 42. Interpretation by the Parties

If the authorization is ambiguous, the interpretation acted upon by the parties controls.

§ 43. Acquiescence by Principal in Agent's Conduct

(1) Acquiescence by the principal in conduct of an agent whose previously conferred authorization reasonably might include it, indicates that the conduct was authorized; if clearly not included in the authorization, acquiescence in it indicates affirmance.

(2) Acquiescence by the principal in a series of acts by the agent indicates authorization to perform similar acts in the future.

§ 44. Interpretation of Ambiguous Instructions

If an authorization is ambiguous because of facts of which the agent has no notice, he has authority to act in accordance with what he reasonably believes to be the intent of the principal although this is contrary to the principal's intent; if the agent should realize its ambiguity, his authority, except in the case of an emergency, is only to act in accordance with the principal's intent. If an authorization is not ambiguous, the agent is authorized to act only in accordance with its reasonable interpretation.

§ 45. Mistake by Agent as to Facts Upon Which Authority Depends

If authority is stated to be conditioned upon the existence of specified facts, whether or not the agent is authorized to act when he reasonably believes that such facts exist, depends upon the agreement of the parties as to whether the agent or the principal shall bear the risk of mistake.

§ 46. Inference of Authority to Disclose Facts Upon Which Authority Depends

Unless otherwise agreed, authority to enter into transactions with third persons includes authority to disclose to them such documents or facts indicating authority as it is reasonable for the principal to anticipate they will desire to see or know of for their own protection.

§ 47. Inference of Authority to Act in an Emergency

Unless otherwise agreed, if after the authorization is given, an unforeseen situation arises for which the terms of the authorization make no provision and it is impracticable for the agent to communicate with the principal, he is authorized to do what he reasonably believes to be necessary in order to prevent substantial loss to the principal with respect to the interests committed to his charge.

§ 48. Parol Evidence Rule

The rules applicable to the contradiction or alteration of an integrated contract by extrinsic evidence apply to an integrated agreement between principal and agent as to the agent's authority.

TITLE B. INTERPRETATION OF APPARENT AUTHORITY

§ 49. Interpretation of Apparent Authority Compared with Interpretation of Authority

The rules applicable to the interpretation of authority are applicable to the interpretation of apparent authority except that:

(a) manifestations of the principal to the other party to the transaction are interpreted in light of what the other party knows or should know instead of what the agent knows or should know, and

(b) if there is a latent ambiguity in the manifestations of the principal for which he is not at fault, the interpretation of apparent authority is based on the facts known to the principal.

TOPIC 3. INTERPRETATION OF PARTICULAR AUTHORIZATIONS

TITLE A. AUTHORIZATION TO CONTRACT

§ 50. When Authority to Contract Inferred

Unless otherwise agreed, authority to make a contract is inferred from authority to conduct a transaction, if the making of such a contract is incidental to the transaction, usually accompanies such a transaction, or is reasonably necessary to accomplish it.

§ 51. Authority Inferred From Authorizing Making of Contract

Unless otherwise agreed, authority to make a specified contract includes authority:

(a) to make it in a usual form and with usual terms or, if there are no usual forms or terms, in an appropriate way; and

(b) to do other acts incidental to its making which are usually done or which, if not usually done, are reasonably necessary for making it.

TITLE B. AUTHORIZATION TO BUY OR TO SELL

§ 52. When Authority to Buy or to Sell Inferred

Unless otherwise agreed, authority to buy property for the principal or to sell his property is inferred from authority to conduct transactions for the principal, if such purchase or sale is incidental to such transactions, usually accompanies them, or is reasonably necessary in accomplishing them.

§ 53. Meanings of "to Buy" and "to Sell"

Authorization "to buy" or "to sell" may be interpreted as meaning that the agent shall:

(a) find a seller or a purchaser from whom or to whom the principal may buy or sell;

(b) make a contract for purchase or sale; or

(c) accept or make a conveyance for the principal.

§ 54. Authority to Find Seller or Purchaser

Unless otherwise agreed, it is inferred that authority to find a seller or a purchaser includes authority to state the terms upon which the principal is willing to buy or to sell; to solicit offers in accordance therewith; and, in the case of agents to sell, to describe the subject matter.

§ 55. Authority to Contract for Purchase or Sale

Unless otherwise agreed, authority to contract for a purchase or sale includes authority to enter into negotiations for and to complete the purchase or sale, including therein usual or other appropriate terms, and, if a writing is required or is usual, to execute such writing.

§ 56. Authority to Acquire Property by Purchase, or to Convey

Unless otherwise agreed, authority to acquire property for the principal by purchase or to transfer the principal's property by sale includes authority to agree upon the terms; to demand or to make the usual representations and warranties; to receive or execute instruments required for the transfer or manifesting it in the usual form; to pay or receive so much of the purchase price as is to be paid at the time of the transfer; and to receive possession of the subject matter or the documents of title, or, in case of a selling agent, to surrender possession if he has been entrusted with it.

§ 57. Limitation of Authority to Identified Subject Matter

(1) Authority to buy or to sell is limited to authority to deal with a subject matter which is sufficiently described to be identified with reasonable certainty by the agent in the light of facts of which he has notice, or which the principal intended to describe.

(2) Unless otherwise agreed, authority to buy or sell a particular thing includes authority to buy or sell that which is appurtenant to it.

§ 58. Authority to Make Unspecified Terms

Unless otherwise agreed, the specification of particular terms in an authorization to buy or to sell does not exclude authority to make additional terms not inconsistent with those prescribed, nor terms which diminish the duties or increase the rights of the principal beyond those specified.

§ 59. Duration of Authority to Buy or to Sell

Authority to buy or to sell exists only when, from the manifestations of the principal or from the happening of events of which the agent has notice, the agent reasonably believes that the principal desires him to buy or to sell.

§ 60. Authorized Methods of Buying or Selling

Unless otherwise agreed, authority to sell includes only authority to sell at private sale and not at auction; authority to purchase includes authority to purchase at private sale or auction.

§ 61. Amount of Price to be Paid or Received

(1) Unless otherwise agreed, authority to buy or sell with no price specified in terms includes authority to buy or sell at the market price if any; otherwise at a reasonable price.

(2) Unless the agent has notice that the principal has a fixed-price policy or unless other facts indicate that the principal's directions are to be followed implicitly, an agent authorized to buy or sell at a fixed price or at the market price is authorized to buy or sell at a price more advantageous to the principal.

§ 62. Authority to Pay or to Receive Purchase Price

(1) Unless otherwise agreed, authority to contract for a purchase or sale or to make or to receive a conveyance on terms by which part or all of the price is payable at the time when the contract or conveyance is

made includes authority to pay or to receive so much of the price as is payable at such time.

(2) Unless otherwise agreed, authority to purchase chattels or choses in action includes authority to pay for them if, but only if, the agent is authorized to receive possession of them or of the documents representing them; authority to sell chattels or choses in action does not include authority to receive the purchase price unless the agent has been entrusted with them or with the documents representing them.

§ 63. Authority to Warrant or to Represent

(1) Unless otherwise agreed, authority to sell includes authority to make such promises operating as warranties, and only such, as are usual in such a transaction; authority to buy is limited to purchases accompanied by such warranties.

(2) Unless otherwise agreed, authority to sell includes authority to make such, and only such, representations as the agent reasonably believes to be true and as are usual with reference to such a subject matter or, in the absence of usage, representations concerning qualities of the subject matter which, at the time, are not open to inspection and as to which the principal has reason to know the buyer will desire to be informed; authority to buy on credit includes authority to make such representations concerning the credit of the buyer as the buyer has reason to know will be required by the seller.

§ 64. Employment of Assistants

Unless otherwise agreed, it is inferred that authority to buy or to sell includes authority to secure such professional or other assistants as the proper performance of the transaction requires.

§ 65. Giving or Receiving Cash or Credit

(1) Unless otherwise agreed, authority to sell includes only authority to sell for money or the customary medium of payment, payable at the time of the transfer of title.

(2) Unless otherwise agreed, authority to purchase includes:

(a) authority to buy for money only and not on credit if the principal supplies the funds: or

(b) authority to pledge the principal's credit upon usual or reasonable terms if the principal does not supply the funds.

§ 66. Authority After Purchase or Sale

Unless otherwise agreed, authority to buy or to sell does not include authority to rescind or modify the terms of the sale after its completion nor to act further with reference to the subject matter except to undo fraud or to correct mistake.

TITLE C. AUTHORIZATION TO LEASE

§ 67. When Authority to Lease is Inferred

(1) Unless otherwise agreed, authority to lease land or chattels is inferred from authority to manage the subject matter if leasing is the usual method of dealing with it or if, in view of the principal's business and other circumstances, leasing is a reasonable method of dealing with it.

(2) Authority to lease land or chattels is not inferred merely from an authority to sell the subject matter, to take charge of it, or to receive rents from it.

§ 68. Authority Inferred From Authority to Lease

The rules of interpretation which are applicable to authority to sell are applicable to authority to lease.

TITLE D. AUTHORIZATION TO TAKE CHARGE OF LAND, CHATTELS, OR INVESTMENTS

§ 69. Authority of Agent in Charge of Things

Unless otherwise agreed, authority to take charge of land, chattels, or securities includes authority to take reasonable measures appropriate to the subject matter, to protect the subject matter against destruction or loss, to keep it in reasonable repair, to recover it if lost or stolen, and, if the subject matter is ordinarily insured by owners, to insure it.

§ 70. Authority to Make Investments

Unless otherwise agreed, an agent authorized to make or manage investments is authorized to invest in, and only in, such securities as would be obtained by a prudent man for his own account, having regard both to safety and income considering his means and purposes; and, if the agent's duties include management, to change investments in accordance with changes in the security of the investments, or the condition of the principal sum.

TITLE E. AUTHORIZATION TO RECEIVE PAYMENT

§ 71. When Authority is Inferred

Unless otherwise agreed, authority to receive payment is inferred from authority to conduct a transaction if the receipt of payment is incidental to such a transaction, usually accompanies it, or is a reasonably necessary means for accomplishing it.

§ 72. Authority Inferred From Authority to Receive Payment

Unless otherwise agreed, authority to receive payment includes authority:

(a) to receive payment in full in money or other customary medium of exchange when the debt is due; and

(b) to surrender to the payer any security for or evidence of the debt to which he is entitled and to give him such receipt as it is usual to give

TITLE F. INTERPRETATION OF AUTHORIZATION TO MANAGE A BUSINESS

§ 73. What Authority is Inferred

Unless otherwise agreed, authority to manage a business includes authority:

(a) to make contracts which are incidental to such business, are usually made in it, or are reasonably necessary in conducting it;

(b) to procure equipment and supplies and to make repairs reasonably necessary for the proper conduct of the business;

(c) to employ, supervise, or discharge employees as the course of business may reasonably require;

(d) to sell or otherwise dispose of goods or other things in accordance with the purposes for which the business is operated;

(e) to receive payment of sums due the principal and to pay debts due from the principal arising out of the business enterprise; and

(f) to direct the ordinary operations of the business.

TITLE G. AUTHORIZATION TO BORROW

§ 74. When Authority is Inferred

Unless otherwise agreed, an agent is not authorized to borrow unless such borrowing is usually incident to the performance of acts which he is authorized to perform for the principal.

§ 75. Authority Inferred From Authority to Borrow

Unless otherwise agreed, authority to borrow includes authority:

(a) to borrow from any lender, for delivery to or for the use of the principal, a reasonable amount in view of the purposes of the borrowing if no amount is specified, upon the terms which are usual, if any, or otherwise upon reasonable terms; if no time is specified, for a reasonable time;

(b) to execute in the name of the principal such evidences of debt as are usually given; and

(c) to make reasonably necessary representations concerning the credit of the principal which the agent reasonably believes to be true.

TITLE H. AUTHORIZATION TO MAKE NEGOTIABLE INSTRUMENTS

§ 76. When Authority is Inferred

Unless otherwise agreed, an agent is not authorized to execute or to endorse negotiable paper unless such execution or endorsement is usually incident to the performance of the acts which he is authorized to perform for the principal.

TITLE I. AUTHORIZATION TO DELEGATE OR TO APPOINT AGENTS AND SUBAGENTS

§ 77. General Rule

The authority to appoint agents, subagents or subservants of the principal can be conferred in the same manner as authority to do other acts for the principal, and the interpretation of the manifestations of the principal is governed by the rules generally applicable to the interpretation of authority.

§ 78. Inference as to Authority to Delegate Authority

Unless otherwise agreed, authority to conduct a transaction does not include authority to delegate to another the performance of acts incidental thereto which involve discretion or the agent's special skill; such authority, however, includes authority to delegate to a subagent the performance of incidental mechanical and ministerial acts.

§ 79. When Authority to Appoint an Agent is Inferred

Unless otherwise agreed, an agent is authorized to appoint another agent for the principal if:

(a) the agent is appointed to a position which, in view of business customs, ordinarily includes authority to appoint other agents; or

(b) the proper conduct of the principal's business in the contemplated manner reasonably requires the employment of other agents; or

(c) the agent is employed to act at a place where or in a business in which it is customary to employ other agents for the performance of such acts; or

(d) an unforeseen contingency arises making it impracticable to communicate with the principal and making such an appointment reasonably necessary for the protection of the interests of the principal entrusted to the agent.

§ 80. When Authority to Appoint a Subagent is Inferred

Unless otherwise agreed, authority to appoint a subagent is inferred from authority to conduct a transaction for the principal for the performance of which the agent is to be responsible to the principal if:

(a) the authorized transaction cannot lawfully be performed by the agent in person;

(b) the agent is a corporation, partnership or other organization;

(c) the business is of such a nature or is to be conducted in such a place that it is impracticable for the agent to perform it in person;

(d) the appointment of subagents for the performance of such transactions is usual, or the principal has reason to know that the agent employs subagents; or

(e) an unforeseen contingency arises in which it is impracticable to communicate with the principal and in which such an appointment is necessary in order to protect the interests of the principal entrusted to the agent.

§ 81. Authority of Servant to Delegate

(1) A servant is not authorized to permit, or to employ another, to perform acts of service which he is employed to perform unless it is so agreed between the master and the servant.

(2) The master and the servant may agree that

(a) the servant is to employ another for the master, or that

(b) the servant is to employ a subservant for whose conduct the servant is responsible to the master, or that

(c) the servant is to employ an independent contractor.

Chapter 4

RATIFICATION

TOPIC 1. DEFINITIONS

§ 82. Ratification

Ratification is the affirmance by a person of a prior act which did not bind him but which was done or professedly done on his account, whereby the act, as to some or all persons, is given effect as if originally authorized by him.

Comment c. A unique concept. The concept of ratification is not a legal fiction, but denotes the legal consequences which result from a series of events beginning with a transaction inoperative as to the principal, and ending in an act of validation. The statement that there is a relation back to the time of the original act is fictitious in form, but in effect, it is a statement of liabilities. The concept is unique. It does not conform to the rules of contracts, since it can be accomplished without consideration to or manifestation by the purported principal and without fresh consent by the other party. Further, it operates as if the transaction were complete at the time and place of the first event, rather than the last, as in the normal case of offer and acceptance. It does not conform to the rules of torts, since the ratifier may become responsible for a harm which was not caused by him, his property or his agent. It can not be justified on a theory of restitution, since the ratifier may not have received a benefit, nor the third person a deprivation. Nor is ratification dependent upon a doctrine of estoppel, since there may be ratification although neither the agent nor the other party suffer a loss resulting from a statement of affirmance or a failure to disavow. However, in some cases in which ratification is claimed, the principal's liability can be based upon unjust enrichment or estoppel, either in addition to or as alternative to his liability based on ratification. See §§ 103, 104.

§ 83. Affirmance

Affirmance is either

(a) a manifestation of an election by one on whose account an unauthorized act has been done to treat the act as authorized, or

(b) conduct by him justifiable only if there were such an election.

TOPIC 2. WHEN AFFIRMANCE RESULTS IN RATIFICATION

§ 84. What Acts Can be Ratified

(1) An act which, when done, could have been authorized by a purported principal, or if an act of service by an intended principal, can be ratified if, at the time of affirmance, he could authorize such an act.

(2) An act which, when done, the purported or intended principal could not have authorized, he cannot ratify, except an act affirmed by a legal representative whose appointment relates back to or before the time of such act.

§ 85. Purporting to Act as Agent as a Requisite for Ratification

(1) Ratification does not result from the affirmance of a transaction with a third person unless the one acting purported to be acting for the ratifier.

(2) An act of service not involving a transaction with a third person is subject to ratification if, but only if, the one doing the act intends or purports to perform it as the servant of another.

§ 86. Illegality or Lack of Capacity at Time of Affirmance

(1) A transaction capable of ratification can be ratified if, but only if, the purported principal can authorize such a transaction at the time of affirmance, except as stated in Subsection (2).

(2) If, by a change in law, a transaction, lawful when done, has become so unlawful that an attempt thereafter to authorize it would be void, the transaction can nevertheless be ratified if it is not against the present public policy to enforce rights resulting from it.

§ 87. Who Can Affirm

To become effective as ratification, the affirmance must be by the person identified as the principal at the time of the original act or, if no person was then identified, by the one for whom the agent intended to act.

§ 88. Affirmance After Withdrawal of Other Party or Other Termination of Original Transaction

To constitute ratification, the affirmance of a transaction must occur before the other party has manifested his withdrawal from it either to the purported principal or to the agent, and before the offer or agreement has otherwise terminated or been discharged.

§ 89. Affirmance After Change of Circumstances

If the affirmance of a transaction occurs at a time when the situation has so materially changed that it would be inequitable to subject the other party to liability thereon, the other party has an election to avoid liability.

§ 90. Affirmance After Rights Have Crystallized

If an act to be effective in creating a right against another or to deprive him of a right must be performed before a specific time, an affirmance is not effective against the other unless made before such time.

§ 91. Knowledge of Principal at Time of Affirmance

(1) If, at the time of affirmance, the purported principal is ignorant of material facts involved in the original transaction, and is unaware of his ignorance, he can thereafter avoid the effect of the affirmance.

(2) Material facts are those which substantially affect the existence or extent of the obligations involved in the transaction, as distinguished from those which affect the values or inducements involved in the transaction.

§ 92. Events not Required for and not Preventing Ratification

An affirmance by the principal of a transaction with a third person is not prevented from resulting in ratification by the fact:

(a) that the other does not give fresh consent to the transaction at or after the affirmance, or does not change his position because of it; or

(b) that the purported principal, before affirming, had repudiated the transaction, if the other party has not acted or has failed to act in reliance upon the repudiation; or

(c) that the other party had a cause of action against the agent because of a breach of warranty or a misrepresentation by the agent as to his authority to conduct the original transaction; or

(d) that the agent conducting the transaction has died or lost capacity; or

(e) that the principal is subject to liability without receiving consideration; or

(f) that the agent or the other party knew the agent to be unauthorized; or

(g) that the principal does not communicate with anyone.

TOPIC 3. WHAT CONSTITUTES AFFIRMANCE

§ 93. Methods and Formalities of Affirmance

(1) Except as stated in Subsection (2), affirmance can be established by any conduct of the purported principal manifesting that he consents to be a party to the transaction, or by conduct justifiable only if there is ratification.

(2) Where formalities are requisite for the authorization of an act, its affirmance must be by the same formalities in order to constitute a ratification.

(3) The affirmance can be made by an agent authorized so to do.

§ 94. Failure to Act as Affirmance

An affirmance of an unauthorized transaction can be inferred from a failure to repudiate it.

§ 95. Necessity of Communicating Manifestation of Affirmance

The manifestation of a definitive election by the principal constitutes affirmance without communication to the agent, to the other party, or to other persons.

§ 96. Effect of Affirming Part of a Transaction

A contract or other single transaction must be affirmed in its entirety in order to effect its ratification.

§ 97. Bringing Suit or Basing Defense as Affirmance

There is affirmance if the purported principal, with knowledge of the facts, in an action in which the third person or the purported agent is an adverse party:

(a) brings suit to enforce promises which were part of the unauthorized transaction or to secure interests which were the fruit of such transaction and to which he would be entitled only if the act had been authorized; or

(b) bases a defense upon the unauthorized transaction as though it were authorized; or

(c) continues to maintain such suit or base such defense.

§ 98. Receipt of Benefits as Affirmance

The receipt by a purported principal, with knowledge of the facts, of something to which he would not be entitled unless an act purported to be done for him were affirmed, and to which he makes no claim except through such act, constitutes an affirmance unless at the time of such receipt he repudiates the act. If he repudiates the act, his receipt of benefits constitutes an affirmance at the election of the other party to the transaction.

§ 99. Retention of Benefits as Affirmance

The retention by a purported principal, with knowledge of the facts and before he has changed his position, of something which he is not entitled to retain unless an act purported to be done on his account is affirmed, and to which he makes no claim except through such act, constitutes an affirmance unless at the time of such retention he repudiates the act. Even if he repudiates the act, his retention constitutes an affirmance at the election of the other party to the transaction.

TOPIC 4. LIABILITIES

§ 100. Effect of Ratification; In General

Except as stated in Section 101, the liabilities resulting from ratification are the same as those resulting from authorization if, between the time when the original act was performed and when it was affirmed, there has been no change in the capacity of the principal or third person or in the legality of authorizing or performing the original act.

§ 100A. Relation Back in Time and Place

The liabilities of the parties to a ratified act or contract are determined in accordance with the law governing the act or contract at the time and place it was done or made. Whether the conduct of the purported principal is an affirmance depends upon the law at the time and place when and where the principal consents or acts.

§ 101. Exceptions to Normal Effect of Ratification

Ratification is not effective:

(a) in favor of a person who, by misrepresentation or duress, has caused the affirmance;

(b) in favor of the agent against the principal if the principal is obliged to affirm in order to protect his own interests; or

(c) in diminution of the rights or other interests of persons not parties to the transaction which were acquired in the subject matter before affirmance.

§ 102. Revocability of Ratification

An affirmance not voidable for fraud, duress, illegality, or lack of capacity; and which cannot be avoided by the principal for lack of knowledge, or by the other party because of a change of position or other similar cause, is not affected by the subsequent attempted withdrawal of either party; an agreement between the principal and the other party to rescind the affirmance does not affect the rights of the agent, and such an agreement between the principal and agent does not affect the rights of the other party.

§ 103. Estoppel to Deny Ratification

A person may be estopped to deny that he has ratified an act or transaction.

§ 104. Liability Because of Adoption, Novation, or Restitution

Although there is no ratification, a person on whose account another acts or purports to act may become a party to a transaction similar to the original transaction by manifesting consent, or he may become subject to liability for the value of benefits received as a result of the original transaction.

Chapter 5

TERMINATION OF AGENCY POWERS

TOPIC 1. TERMINATION OF AUTHORITY

TITLE A. INFERRED FROM ORIGINAL MANIFESTATION IN LIGHT OF SUBSEQUENT EVENTS

§ 105. Lapse of Time

Authority conferred for a specified time terminates at the expiration of that period; if no time is specified, authority terminates at the end of a reasonable period.

§ 106. Accomplishment of Authorized Act

The authority of an agent to perform a specified act or to accomplish a specified result terminates when the act is done or the result is accomplished by the agent or by another, except that if the act is done or the result is accomplished by a person other than the agent, the manifestations of the principal to the agent determine whether the authority terminates at once or when the agent has notice of it.

§ 107. Happening of Specified Events

If the terms of the authorization specifically provide that an authority is to continue until a specified event happens or during the continuance of specified conditions, whether the authority terminates at once upon the happening of the event or the cessation of the condition or only when the agent has notice of such happening or cessation depends upon the interpretation of the principal's manifestation in light of all circumstances.

§ 108. Happening of Unspecified Events or Changes; In General

(1) The authority of an agent terminates or is suspended when the agent has notice of the happening of an event or of a change in circumstances from which he should reasonably infer that the principal does not consent to the further exercise of authority or would not consent if he knew the facts.

(2) The agent's authority revives upon the restoration of the original situation within a reasonable time if the agent has no notice that the principal's position has been changed.

§ 109. Change in Value or Business Conditions

The authority of an agent terminates or is suspended when he has notice of a change in value of the subject matter or a change in business conditions from which he should infer that the principal, if he knew of it, would not consent to the further exercise of the authority.

§ 110. Loss or Destruction of Subject Matter

Unless otherwise agreed, the loss or destruction of the subject matter of the authority or the termination of the principal's interest therein terminates the agent's authority to deal with reference to it, either at once or when the agent has notice of it, dependent upon the manifestation of the principal to the agent.

§ 111. Loss of Qualification of Principal or Agent

The loss of or failure to acquire a qualification by the agent without which it is illegal to do an authorized act, or a similar loss or failure by the principal, of which the agent has notice, terminates the agent's authority to act if thereafter he should infer that the principal, if he knew the facts, would not consent to the further exercise of the authority.

§ 112. Disloyalty of Agent

Unless otherwise agreed, the authority of an agent terminates if, without knowledge of the principal, he acquires adverse interests or if he is otherwise guilty of a serious breach of loyalty to the principal.

§ 113. Bankruptcy of Agent

The bankruptcy or insolvency of an agent terminates his authority to conduct transactions in which the state of his credit would so affect the interests of the principal that the agent should infer that the principal, if he knew the facts, would not consent to the further exercise of the authority.

§ 114. Bankruptcy of Principal

The bankruptcy or the substantial impairment of the assets of the principal, of which the agent has notice, terminates his authority as to transactions which he should infer the principal no longer consents to have conducted for him.

§ 115. War

The outbreak of a war of which the agent has notice terminates his authority if the conditions are thereby so changed that he should infer that the principal, if he knew the facts, would not consent to the further exercise of the authority.

§ 116. Change of Law

A change of law of which the agent has notice and which causes the execution of his authority to be illegal, or which otherwise materially changes the effect of its execution, terminates his authority, if he should infer that the principal, if he knew the circumstances, would not consent to the further exercise of the authority.

TITLE B. TERMINATION BY MUTUAL CONSENT, REVOCATION, OR RENUNCIATION

§ 117. Mutual Consent

The authority of an agent terminates in accordance with the terms of an agreement between the principal and agent so to terminate it.

§ 118. Revocation or Renunciation

Authority terminates if the principal or the agent manifests to the other dissent to its continuance.

§ 119. Manner of Revocation or Renunciation

Authority created in any manner terminates when either party in any manner manifests to the other dissent to its continuance or, unless otherwise agreed, when the other has notice of dissent.

TITLE C. LOSS OF CAPACITY AND IMPOSSIBILITY

§ 120. Death of Principal

(1) The death of the principal terminates the authority of the agent without notice to him, except as stated in subsections (2) and (3) and in the caveat.

(2) Until notice of a depositor's death, a bank has authority to pay checks drawn by him or by agents authorized by him before death.

(3) Until notice of the death of the holder of a check deposited for collection, the bank in which it is deposited and those to which the check is sent for collection have authority to go forward with the process of collection.

Caveat:

No inference is to be drawn from the rule stated in this Section that an agent does not have power to bind the estate of a deceased principal in transactions dependent upon a special relation between the agent and the principal, such as trustee and beneficiary, or in transactions in which special rules are applicable, as in dealings with negotiable instruments.

§ 121. Death of Agent

The death of the agent terminates the authority.

§ 122. Loss of Capacity of Principal or Agent

(1) Except as stated in the caveat, the loss of capacity by the principal has the same effect upon the authority of the agent during the period of incapacity as has the principal's death.

(2) The agent's loss of capacity to do an act for the principal terminates or suspends his authority.

Caveat:

The Institute expresses no opinion as to the effect of the principal's temporary incapacity due to a mental disease.

§ 123. Death or Loss of Capacity of Joint Principals or Agents

The death or loss of capacity of one of two or more joint principals terminates the authority of an agent to act on their joint account to the same extent as the loss of capacity of a single principal. The death or loss of capacity of one of two or more agents authorized to act only jointly terminates the authority of the survivor.

§ 124. Impossibility

There is a termination of the agent's authority:

(a) to create interests in or otherwise deal with a particular subject matter, when it is destroyed;

(b) to affect the interests of the principal in a particular subject matter, when the principal has lost his interests in it;

(c) to enter into transactions with particular persons when they die or lose capacity to become parties to such transactions; or

(d) to effectuate results when, by a change of law or other circumstances, the transactions which the agent is authorized to conduct do not effectuate such results.

TITLE D. EFFECT OF TERMINATION OF AUTHORITY

§ 124A. Effect of Termination of Authority Upon Apparent Authority and Other Powers

The termination of authority does not thereby terminate apparent authority. All other powers of the agent resulting from the relation terminate except powers necessary for the protection of his interests or of those of the principal.

TOPIC 2. TERMINATION OF APPARENT AUTHORITY

§ 125. By Notice of Termination of Authority, or of Principal's Consent, or of a Basic Error

Apparent authority, not otherwise terminated, terminates when the third person has notice of:

(a) the termination of the agent's authority;

(b) a manifestation by the principal that he no longer consents; or

(c) facts, the failure to reveal which, were the transaction with the principal in person, would be ground for rescission by the principal.

Comment b. Apparent authority can exist only as long as the third person, to whom the principal has made a manifestation of authority, continues reasonably to believe that the agent is authorized. He does not have this reasonable belief if he has reason to know that the principal has revoked, or that the agent has renounced the authority, or that such time has elapsed or such events have happened after the authorization as to require the reasonable inference that the agent's authority has terminated. If the authority terminated only because the agent has notice of the happening of an event, the apparent authority may not terminate although the third person has notice of the event (see Comment *d*); it is terminated, however, if he knows that the agent has notice of it. In such case, it would be a breach of duty to the principal for the agent to act, and a third person having notice of this can acquire no rights against the principal by thereafter dealing with the agent. The third person has notice of the termination of authority, although he does not know the facts, if he has reason to know them or if, knowing the facts, he would, if reasonable, draw the inference that the authority is terminated, although in fact he unreasonably infers that it is not. He is also bound by a notification given him by the principal in accordance with the rules stated in Section 136.

§ 126. Apparent Authority Conditioned by Time or Events

Apparent authority conditioned as to time or the happening of events terminates when the time has elapsed or the events have happened, either at once or when the third person has notice thereof, dependent upon the manifestation of the principal to him.

§ 127. Apparent Authority of General Agent

Unless otherwise agreed, if the principal has manifested that an agent is a general agent, the apparent authority thereby created is not terminated by the termination of the agent's authority by a cause other than incapacity or impossibility, unless the third person has notice thereof.

§ 128. Apparent Authority of Specially Accredited Agent

Unless otherwise agreed, if the principal has specially accredited an agent to a third person, the apparent authority thereby created is not terminated by the termination of the agent's authority by causes other than incapacity or impossibility, unless the third person has notice thereof.

§ 129. Apparent Authority of Agent Who Has Begun to Deal

Unless otherwise agreed, if the agent properly begins to deal with a third person and the principal has notice of this, the apparent authority to conduct the transaction is not terminated by the termination of the agent's authority by a cause other than incapacity or impossibility, unless the third person has notice of it.

§ 130. Apparent Authority of Agent Having Indicia of Authority

If the principal entrusts to the agent a power of attorney or other writing which manifests that the agent has authority and which is intended to be shown to third persons, and this is retained by the agent and exhibited to third persons, the termination of the agent's authority by causes other than incapacity or impossibility does not prevent him from having apparent authority as to persons to whom he exhibits the document and who have no notice of the termination of the authority.

§ 131. Agent Has Apparent Authority to Represent Nonexistence of Terminating Events

If, as a third person has notice, the agent's authority terminates upon the happening of an event other than the occurrence of incapacity or impossibility, the occurrence of the event does not terminate apparent authority if the agent is apparently authorized to represent its nonoccurrence and so represents to the third person, who has no notice that the event has occurred.

§ 132. Apparent Authority of Special Agent

Unless otherwise agreed, if the principal has manifested to the third person that the agent is to do a single act or perform a single transaction, the apparent authority terminates with the termination of the agent's authority, unless:

(a) the principal has specially accredited the agent to the third person;

(b) the agent has begun to deal with the third person as the principal has notice;

(c) the agent is in possession of indicia of authority entrusted to him by the principal and shown by him to the third person; or

(d) the principal has manifested that the agent has authority to represent the nonexistence of the terminating event and the agent does so represent.

§ 133. Incapacity of Parties or Other Impossibility

The apparent authority of an agent terminates upon the happening of an event which destroys the capacity of the principal to give the power, or an event which otherwise makes the authorized transaction impossible.

TOPIC 3. NOTICE OF TERMINATION OF AUTHORITY AND APPARENT AUTHORITY

§ 134. When Principal or Agent Has Notice of Termination of Authority

Unless the parties have manifested otherwise to each other, a principal or agent has notice that authority to do an act has terminated or is suspended if he knows, has reason to know, should know, or has been given a notification of the occurrence of an event from which the inference reasonably would be drawn:

(a) by the principal, that the agent does not consent to act;

(b) by the agent, that the principal does not consent to the act or would not if he knew the facts;

(c) by either, that the transaction has become impossible of execution because of incapacity of the parties, destruction of the subject matter, or illegality.

§ 135. When Third Persons Have Notice of Termination of Authority

A third person to whom a principal has manifested that an agent has authority to do an act has notice of the termination of authority when he knows, has reason to know, should know, or has been given a notification of the occurrence of an event from which, if reasonable, he would draw the inference that the principal does not consent to have the agent so act for him, that the agent does not consent so to act for the principal, or that the transaction has become impossible of execution.

§ 136. Notification Terminating Apparent Authority

(1) Unless otherwise agreed, there is a notification by the principal to the third person of revocation of an agent's authority or other fact indicating its termination:

(a) when the principal states such fact to the third person; or

(b) when a reasonable time has elapsed after a writing stating such fact has been delivered by the principal

(i) to the other personally;

(ii) to the other's place of business;

(iii) to a place designated by the other as one in which business communications are received; or

(iv) to a place which, in view of the business customs or relations between the parties is reasonably believed to be the place for the receipt of such communications by the other.

(2) Unless otherwise agreed, a notification to be effective in terminating apparent authority must be given by the means stated in Subsection (1) with respect to a third person:

(a) who has previously extended credit to or received credit from the principal through the agent in reliance upon a manifestation from the principal of continuing authority in the agent;

(b) to whom the agent has been specially accredited;

(c) with whom the agent has begun to deal, as the principal should know; or

(d) who relies upon the possession by the agent of indicia of authority entrusted to him by the principal.

(3) Except as to the persons included in Subsection (2), the principal can properly give notification of the termination of the agent's authority by:

(a) advertising the fact in a newspaper of general circulation in the place where the agency is regularly carried on; or

(b) giving publicity by some other method reasonably adapted to give the information to such third person.

TOPIC 4. SUBAGENTS

§ 137. Termination of Powers of Subagents

The principles applicable to the termination of an agent's authority or apparent authority are applicable also to the termination of the authority or apparent authority of a subagent or subservant.

Comment b. Notice to agent or subagent. If, in situations not involving subagency, authority would terminate because the agent has knowledge of facts or should know of them (see §§ 105–116), the authority of a subagent terminates under similar circumstances when either he or the intermediate agent acquires knowledge of or should know of such facts; except that where such knowledge is acquired by the intermediate agent it does not become operative as to the subagent until the agent has had time to communicate with him, and except that the agent may have apparent authority or other power to continue to authorize him to act for the principal. The agent and subagent are not, however, to be charged with their combined knowledge, if the knowledge had by each is not sufficient to create an inference of termination, unless the agent has failed in his duty to the principal to communicate to the subagent the knowledge which he has, or the subagent has failed in his duty to communicate facts to the agent. If, in situations not involving subagency, the authority of an agent terminates by notification by the principal to him, the authority of a subagent under similar circumstances terminates by notification by the principal either to the agent or the subagent. If the notification is given to the agent, the subagent's authority terminates only when the agent has had an opportunity to communicate with him. If the notification is to the subagent, it is ineffective if the subagent does not know that he is transacting the principal's business, as would be true when he is employed by an agent for an undisclosed principal, unless the principal can reasonably satisfy the subagent of his identification with the transaction. After the agent's authority to authorize a subagent to act for the principal has terminated, he may have apparent authority or other power to do so. If he has this and continues to direct the subagent to act, the latter's authority does not terminate.

The authority of the subagent may terminate because of the death or incapacity of the principal, the agent, or himself. In accordance with the rules generally applicable to agents (see §§ 120–123), no notice of such death or incapacity is necessary for the termination of authority or apparent authority, except as stated in Section 120. If the subagent continues to act after the death of the agent, he alone is responsible to the principal; the estate of the agent is not liable for his unauthorized acts, unless it had been so agreed between the principal and agent. His authority terminates without notice when the authorized act becomes impossible of execution. See § 124.

TOPIC 5. TERMINATION OF POWERS GIVEN AS SECURITY

§ 138. Definition

A power given as security is a power to affect the legal relations of another, created in the form of an agency authority, but held for the benefit of the power holder or a third person and given to secure the performance of a duty or to protect a title, either legal or equitable, such power being given when the duty or title is created or given for consideration.

§ 139. Termination of Powers Given as Security

(1) Unless otherwise agreed, a power given as security is not terminated by:

(a) revocation by the creator of the power;

(b) surrender by the holder of the power, if he holds for the benefit of another;

(c) the loss of capacity during the lifetime of either the creator of the power or the holder of the power; or

(d) the death of the holder of the power, or, if the power is given as security for a duty which does not terminate at the death of the creator of the power, by his death.

(2) A power given as security is terminated by its surrender by the beneficiary, if of full capacity; or by the happening of events which, by its terms, discharges the obligations secured by it, or which makes its execution illegal or impossible.

Chapter 6

LIABILITY OF PRINCIPAL TO THIRD PERSONS; CONTRACTS AND CONVEYANCES

TOPIC 1. GENERAL PRINCIPLES

§ 140. Liability Based Upon Agency Principles

The liability of the principal to a third person upon a transaction conducted by an agent, or the transfer of his interests by an agent, may be based upon the fact that:

(a) the agent was authorized;

(b) the agent was apparently authorized; or

(c) the agent had a power arising from the agency relation and not dependent upon authority or apparent authority.

§ 141. Liability Based on Other Than Agency Principles

A principal, although not subject to liability because of principles of agency, may be liable to a third person on account of a transaction with an agent, because of the principles of estoppel, restitution or negotiability.

§ 142. Liability for Acts of Servants and Subagents

The rules as to the power of an agent to subject the principal to liability are applicable to the power of a servant and of a subservant or other subagent.

§ 143. Effect of Ratification

Upon ratification with knowledge of the material facts, the principal becomes responsible for contracts and conveyances made for him by one purporting to act on his account as if the transaction had been authorized, if there has been no supervening loss of capacity by the principal or change in the law which would render illegal the authorization or performance of such a transaction.

TOPIC 2. DISCLOSED OR PARTIALLY DISCLOSED PRINCIPAL

TITLE A. CREATION OF LIABILITY BY AUTHORIZED ACTS

§ 144. General Rule

A disclosed or partially disclosed principal is subject to liability upon contracts made by an agent acting within his authority if made in proper form and with the understanding that the principal is a party.

§ 145. Authorized Representations

In actions brought upon a contract or to rescind a contract or conveyance to which he is a party, a disclosed or partially disclosed principal is responsible for authorized representations of an agent made in connection with it as if made by himself, subject to the rules as to the effect of knowledge of, and notifications given to, the agent.

§ 146. Manifestations by Agent Determining Parties

If an agent of a disclosed or partially disclosed principal makes an authorized contract with a third person, the liability of the principal thereon depends upon the agreement between the agent and the other party as to the parties to the transaction.

§ 147. Inference that Principal is a Party; Simple Contracts

Unless otherwise agreed, a disclosed or partially disclosed principal is a party to a contract, if not negotiable or sealed, made by his agent within his authority.

§ 148. Orders of Several Principals Combined

Unless otherwise agreed between the principal and the agent, no one of two or more disclosed or partially disclosed principals, each of whom independently authorizes the same agent to make a contract, is liable upon a single contract made by the agent which combines the orders of the principals and calls for a single performance.

§ 149. Written Contracts not Containing Principal's Name

A disclosed or partially disclosed principal is subject to liability upon an authorized contract in writing, if not negotiable or sealed, although it purports to be the contract of the agent, unless the principal is excluded as a party by the terms of the instrument or by the agreement of the parties.

§ 150. Contracts Specifically Including or Excluding Principal

If an integrated contract by its specific terms excludes the principal as a party, extrinsic evidence is inadmissible to show that he is a party; if the integrated contract by its specific terms makes the principal a party, extrinsic evidence is not admissible to show that it was agreed that he should not become a party.

§ 151. Sealed Instruments

In the absence of statute, a disclosed or partially disclosed principal is not a covenantor or grantor in a sealed contract or conveyance unless he appears upon the instrument to be such.

§ 152. Negotiable Instruments

A disclosed or partially disclosed principal is not liable as a party to a negotiable instrument in which he is not named.

§ 153. Transactions Required to be in Writing

For the purpose of satisfying the provisions of a statute requiring a note or memorandum to be signed by the party to be charged or by his agent, a memorandum signed by a properly authorized agent with or without indication of the existence or identity of the principal is sufficient to charge the principal.

TITLE B. INTERPRETATION OF WRITTEN INSTRUMENTS AS TO PARTIES

§ 154. General Rule

In determining the parties to an integrated contract made by an agent on account of his principal, the rules dealing with interpretation stated in the Restatement of Contracts apply.

§ 155. Instrument in Which Principal Appears as Such

In the absence of manifestations to the contrary therein, an unsealed written instrument is interpreted as the instrument of the principal and not of the agent if, from a consideration of it as a whole, it appears that the agent is acting as agent for a principal whose name appears therein as such.

§ 156. Instrument in Which Fact of Agency or Name of Principal Appears

In the absence of a manifestation to the contrary therein, an unsealed written instrument is interpreted as the instrument of the principal and not of the agent if, in the signature or description of the parties, the name of the principal and agent both appear, the agent indicating his agency. The addition of the word "agent" to the signature or description of the signer does not of itself prevent the inference that such person is a party to the contract.

§ 157. Instrument in Which Agency Shown Only in One Part

An unsealed written instrument, in one portion of which there is a manifestation that the agent is acting only for the principal, is interpreted as the instrument of the principal and not of the agent, although in other portions of the instrument or in the signature the agent's name appears without designation.

§ 158. Interpretation of Sealed Instruments as to Parties

The rules which determine the interpretation of unseated instruments as to parties, are applicable to the interpretation of sealed instruments as to parties, except that:

(a) in order that a person should be bound as a covenantor or grantor in a sealed instrument he must be named as such therein, and the instrument must purport to be sealed by him; and

(b) in order that a person should be a covenantee or grantee in a sealed instrument he must appear as such in the instrument.

TITLE C. CREATION OF LIABILITY BY UNAUTHORIZED ACTS

§ 159. Apparent Authority

A disclosed or partially disclosed principal is subject to liability upon contracts made by an agent acting within his apparent authority if made in proper form and with the understanding that the apparent principal is a party. The rules as to the liability of a principal for authorized acts, are applicable to unauthorized acts which are apparently authorized.

§ 160. Violation of Secret Instructions

A disclosed or partially disclosed principal authorizing an agent to make a contract, but imposing upon him limitations as to incidental terms intended not to be revealed, is subject to liability upon a contract made in violation of such limitations with a third person who has no notice of them.

§ 161. Unauthorized Acts of General Agent

A general agent for a disclosed or partially disclosed principal subjects his principal to liability for acts done on his account which usually accompany or are incidental to transactions which the agent is authorized to conduct if, although they are forbidden by the principal, the other party reasonably believes that the agent is authorized to do them and has no notice that he is not so authorized.

§ 161A. Unauthorized Acts of Special Agents

A special agent for a disclosed or partly disclosed principal has no power to bind his principal by contracts or conveyances which he is not authorized or apparently authorized to make, unless the principal is estopped, or unless:

(a) the agent's only departure from his authority or apparent authority is

(i) in naming or disclosing the principal, or

(ii) in having an improper motive, or

(iii) in being negligent in determining the facts upon which his authority is based, or

(iv) in making misrepresentations; or

(b) the agent is given possession of goods or commercial documents with authority to deal with them.

§ 162. Unauthorized Representations

Except as to statements with relation to the agent's authority, in actions brought upon a contract or to rescind a contract, a disclosed or partially disclosed principal is responsible for unauthorized representations of the agent made incidental to it, if the contract is otherwise authorized and if true representations as to the same matter are within the authority or the apparent authority of the agent, unless the other party thereto has notice that the representations are untrue or unauthorized.

§ 163. Disobedience as to Naming or Disclosing Principal

(1) A principal who directs an agent to make a contract in the principal's name is subject to liability upon such a contract although made in the agent's name, unless the principal is excluded from it by its form or terms.

(2) If a principal directs the agent to make a contract in the agent's name, concealing the existence or identity of the principal, he is subject to liability upon such a contract although the agent discloses the existence or identity of the principal or makes the contract in his name, except as stated in the Caveat.

Caveat:

No statement is made as to the principal's liability if the disclosure of his existence or identity may defeat his purposes.

§ 164. Contracts Unauthorized in Part

(1) Except as stated in subsection (2), an agent for a disclosed or partially disclosed principal who exceeds his powers in making an unauthorized contract with a third person does not bind the principal either by the contract as made or by the contract as it would have been made had he acted in accordance with his authority.

(2) Where the only difference between the contract as authorized and the contract as made is a difference as to amount, or the inclusion or exclusion of a separable part, the principal is liable upon the contract as it was authorized to be made, provided that the other party seasonably manifests his willingness to accept the contract as it was authorized.

§ 165. Agent Acts for Improper Purpose

A disclosed or partially disclosed principal is subject to liability upon a contract purported to be made on his account by an agent authorized to make it for the principal's benefit, although the agent acts for his own or other improper purposes, unless the other party has notice that the agent is not acting for the principal's benefit.

§ 165A. Mistaken Exercise of Conditional Authority

If the authority of an agent of a disclosed or partially disclosed principal is stated to be conditioned upon determination by the agent of specified facts, the principal is bound by such determination although the agent was negligent in making it.

§ 166. Persons Having Notice of Limitations of Agent's Authority

A person with notice of a limitation of an agent's authority cannot subject the principal to liability upon a transaction with the agent if he should know that the agent is acting improperly.

§ 167. Persons Having Notice of Limitations of Written Authorizations

If a person dealing with an agent has notice that the agent's authority is created or described in a writing which is intended for his inspection, he is affected by limitations upon the authority contained in the writing, unless misled by conduct of the principal.

§ 168. Power of Agent as to Statements of His Authority

A disclosed or partially disclosed principal is not thereby subject to liability because of untrue representations by an agent as to the existence or extent of his authority or the facts upon which it depends.

§ 169. Agent Authorized to Disclose Terms

A disclosed or partially disclosed principal who invites third persons to deal with the agent on terms to be disclosed by the agent is subject to liability upon contracts made with them by the agent, although the terms are not within the authority of the agent, unless they have notice that the terms are not authorized.

§ 170. Agent's Statements of Facts on Which His Authority Depends

A disclosed or partially disclosed principal who invites third persons to rely upon the representation of an agent as to the happening of a contingency upon which the authority of the agent depends is subject to liability upon contracts made with the agent by such third persons in reasonable reliance upon unauthorized and untrue representations of the agent that the contingency has happened.

§ 171. Authority Dependent on Facts Within Agent's Peculiar Knowledge

Unless otherwise agreed, a disclosed or partially disclosed principal who manifests to third persons that a general agent is authorized to make a contract if an event happens or if a specified fact exists, the happening or existence of which is peculiarly within the agent's knowledge, is subject to liability as a party to a contract made with such persons who rely upon the untruthful representations of the agent that the event has happened or that the fact exists; unless otherwise agreed, the principal is not subject to liability for such statements by a special agent.

§ 172. General Agent Authorized to Issue Commercial Documents

Unless otherwise agreed, a disclosed or partially disclosed principal who authorizes a general agent in the regular course of his employment to issue documents representing chattels or choses in action if an event happens or a specified fact exists, the happening or existence of which is peculiarly within the knowledge of the agent, is subject to liability to purchasers of such documents who have no notice that the agent has improperly issued them.

§ 173. Unauthorized Issue of Negotiable Instrument

A disclosed or partially disclosed principal who employs a general agent in a position in which it is usual for such agents to issue negotiable instruments is subject to liability to a holder in due course of such an instrument issued by the agent in the name of the principal, although contrary to the principal's directions, as if the instrument were authorized.

§ 174. Agent Entrusted with Possession of a Chattel

Aside from statute, a disclosed or partially disclosed principal who entrusts an agent with the possession of a chattel, other than a commercial document representing a chattel or chose in action, but who does not authorize him to sell it, display it for sale, or otherwise affect the principal's interest in it, is not thereby bound by an unauthorized transaction with reference to the chattel between the agent and a third person.

§ 175. Agent Authorized to Deal with Chattel Entrusted to Him

(1) Apart from statute, and except as stated in Subsection (3), the interests of a disclosed or partially disclosed principal who entrusts an agent with the possession of a chattel, other than a commercial document representing a chattel or chose in action, with directions to deal with it in a particular manner, as by sale, barter, pledge or mortgage, are not thereby affected by a transaction of a kind different from that authorized.

(2) The interests of the principal are affected by an unauthorized transaction of the same kind as that authorized, if conducted by an agent with one who reasonably believes him to be authorized and who pays value.

(3) If the principal delivers a chattel to a dealer in such chattels to be sold or exhibited for sale, an unauthorized sale of the chattel in accordance with the normal business practices to one who reasonably believes the dealer to be authorized to sell the chattel, binds the owner although the dealer was not authorized to sell it without the consent of the owner, or was not authorized to sell it to the person to whom it was sold, or at the price at which it was sold.

§ 176. Agent Entrusted with Commercial Document

A disclosed or partially disclosed principal who entrusts an agent with possession of, and a limited authority to deal with, a document representing a chattel or a chose in action in such form that possession of it is commonly regarded as indicating a general power to dispose of it, is subject to the loss of his interests in it by the agent's unauthorized disposition of it if it comes to the hands of a purchaser without notice that the agent was not authorized to dispose of it.

§ 177. Agent Entrusted with Negotiable Instruments

A disclosed or partially disclosed principal who entrusts an agent with the possession of a negotiable instrument not payable to bearer or endorsed to the agent is not thereby subject to the loss of his interests therein by the collection of the claim or the transfer of the document by the agent.

§ 177A. Agent Authorized to Fill Blanks

Where a principal entrusts an agent with an executed document containing blanks with authority to fill the blanks, and the agent fills the blanks in an unauthorized way, a person receiving the document from the agent

(a) is not entitled to hold the principal thereon, if he had notice that the agent filled the blanks.

(b) is entitled to hold the principal, if without notice that the blanks were unfilled when given to the agent.

§ 178. Agent Authorized to Collect a Debt

(1) If an agent, authorized to receive only money in payment of a debt, receives a check or other thing from the debtor and obtains the amount of the debt from the negotiation or sale of the thing received, the debt is paid.

(2) If an agent who is authorized to receive a check payable to the principal as conditional payment forges the principal's endorsement to such a check, the maker is relieved of liability to the principal if the drawee bank pays the check and charges the amount to the maker.

(3) An agent authorized to state to a debtor the amount of a debt, the amount of which is ordinarily determined or ascertained by the creditor, binds the principal by the receipt of a larger amount than that due resulting from the agent's misrepresentation.

§ 178A. Where Agent Authorized to Pay Debts Makes a Mistaken Payment

An agent authorized to pay his principal's debts binds the principal by a mistaken payment, whether of fact or law, to the same extent as if the principal had made the payment.

TITLE D. DEFENSES AND LIABILITY AFFECTED BY SUBSEQUENT EVENTS

§ 179. Rights Between Third Person and Agent

Unless otherwise agreed, the liability of a disclosed or partially disclosed principal is not affected by any rights or liabilities existing between the other party and the agent at the time the contract is made.

§ 180. Defenses of Principal; In General

A disclosed or partially disclosed principal is entitled to all defenses arising out of a transaction between his agent and a third person. He is not entitled to defenses which are personal to the agent.

§ 181. Subsequent Dealings Between Agent and Other Party

Where an agent for a disclosed or partially disclosed principal has entered into a transaction on behalf of the principal, subsequent dealings between the agent and the other party:

(a) may increase or diminish the principal's liability because of the further exercise of the agent's power, or

(b) may diminish the principal's liability because the dealings are in derogation of the principal's rights.

§ 182. Performance by Other Party Believing Agent Authorized

A disclosed or partially disclosed principal on whose account an agent purports to make a contract does not become liable as a party to the contract by reason of the fact that the other party performs the contract believing that the agent is authorized nor, unless there is ratification, by reason of the fact that the principal receives a benefit as the result of such a performance.

§ 183. Settlement with Agent by Principal

A disclosed or partially disclosed principal is not discharged from liability to the other party to a transaction conducted by an agent by payment to, or settlement of accounts with, the agent, unless he does so in reasonable reliance upon conduct of the other party which is not induced by the agent's misrepresentations and which indicates that the agent has settled the account.

§ 184. Judgment for or Against Agent

(1) Recovery of judgment against the agent of a disclosed or partially disclosed principal for failure of performance of a contract to which

the agent is a party does not thereby discharge the principal unless the agent and principal were joint contractors.

(2) The existence and extent of the liability of a disclosed or partially disclosed principal upon a contract to which the agent is a party may be determined by a judgment for or against the agent in an action between the agent and the other party to the contract, in accordance with the rules of res judicata.

§ 184A. Joinder of Principal and Agent

If a disclosed or partially disclosed principal and his agent are joined in an action on a contract to which both are parties and a judgment on the merits is rendered for one and against the other, or a judgment for a larger amount is rendered against one than against the other, the judgments are erroneous.

§ 185. Satisfaction of Claim by Agent

A disclosed or partially disclosed principal ceases to be liable to the other party upon a contract to the extent that the claim against him has been satisfied by an agent who has been authorized to do so or who is a party to the contract.

TOPIC 3. UNDISCLOSED PRINCIPAL

TITLE A. CREATION OF LIABILITY BY AUTHORIZED ACTS

§ 186. General Rule

An undisclosed principal is bound by contracts and conveyances made on his account by an agent acting within his authority, except that the principal is not bound by a contract which is under seal or which is negotiable, or upon a contract which excludes him.

§ 187. Orders of Several Principals Combined

Unless otherwise agreed between the principals and the agent, no one of two or more undisclosed principals, each of whom independently authorizes the same agent to make a contract, is liable upon a single contract made by the agent which combines the orders of the principals and calls for a single performance.

§ 188. Authorized Representations

In actions brought upon a contract or to rescind a contract or conveyance made by an agent for an undisclosed principal, the principal is responsible for authorized representations of the agent made in connection therewith as if made by himself, subject to the rules with regard to notice to the principal because of notifications given to the agent or of his knowledge of facts.

§ 189. Contracts Specifically Excluding Principal

An undisclosed principal does not become liable upon a contract which provides that he or any undisclosed principal shall not be a party to it.

§ 190. Simple Contracts in Writing

An undisclosed principal may be liable upon a simple contract in writing, although it purports to be the contract of the agent.

§ 191. Sealed Instruments

In the absence of statute, an undisclosed principal is not liable as a party to a sealed instrument.

§ 192. Negotiable Instruments

An undisclosed principal is not liable as a party to a negotiable instrument.

§ 193. Transactions Required to be in Writing

For the purpose of satisfying the provisions of a statute requiring a note or memorandum to be signed by the party to be charged or by his agent, a memorandum signed by a properly authorized agent on account of an undisclosed principal is sufficient to charge the principal.

TITLE B. CREATION OF LIABILITY BY UNAUTHORIZED ACTS

§ 194. Acts of General Agents

A general agent for an undisclosed principal authorized to conduct transactions subjects his principal to liability for acts done on his account, if usual or necessary in such transactions, although forbidden by the principal to do them.

§ 195. Acts of Manager Appearing to be Owner

An undisclosed principal who entrusts an agent with the management of his business is subject to liability to third persons with whom the agent enters into transactions usual in such businesses and on the principal's account, although contrary to the directions of the principal.

§ 195A. Unauthorized Acts of Special Agents

A special agent for an undisclosed principal has no power to bind his principal by contracts or conveyances which he is not authorized to make unless:

(a) the agent's only departure from his authority is

(i) in not disclosing his principal, or

(ii) in having an improper motive, or

(iii) in being negligent in determining the facts upon which his authority is based, or

(iv) in making misrepresentations; or

(b) the agent is given possession of goods or commercial documents with authority to deal with them.

§ 196. Unauthorized Representations

In actions brought upon a contract or to rescind a contract, an undisclosed principal is subject to liability for unauthorized representations of the agent made incidental to it, if the contract is otherwise authorized and if true representations as to the same matter are within the authority of the agent, unless the other party has reason to know that they are untrue.

§ 196A. Mistaken Exercise of Conditional Authority

If the authority of an agent of an undisclosed principal is stated to be conditioned upon the determination by the agent of specific facts, the principal is bound by such determination although the agent was negligent in making it.

§ 197. Disobedience as to Disclosing Principal

A principal who directs an agent to make a contract in the principal's name or to reveal the principal's existence becomes liable upon the contract although made by the agent in his own name with another who has no reason to know that a principal exists, if the contract is one to which an undisclosed principal can be a party.

§ 198. Contracts Unauthorized in Part

(1) Except as stated in Subsection (2), an agent for an undisclosed principal who exceeds his powers in making an unauthorized contract with a third person does not bind the principal either by the contract as made or by the contract as it would have been had the agent acted in accordance with his authority.

(2) Where the only difference between the contract as authorized and the contract as made is a difference as to amount or the inclusion or exclusion of a separable part, the principal is liable upon the contract as it was authorized to be made, if the other party seasonably manifests his willingness to accept the contract as it was authorized.

Caveat:

The rule stated herein does not include the situation in which the agent, in making the unauthorized terms, intends to act in fraud of the principal, as to which no statement is made.

§ 199. Acts not on Account of Principal or Done with an Improper Motive

An undisclosed principal who authorizes an agent to make a particular contract on his account and in his business is not liable upon such contract if the agent makes the very contract authorized but does not intend to act on account of the principal. If the agent intends to act for the principal, the fact that he has an improper motive does not prevent the principal from being liable.

§ 200. Agent Entrusted with Possession of a Chattel

Apart from statute, an undisclosed principal who entrusts an agent with the possession of a chattel, other than a commercial document representing a chattel or chose in action, but who does not authorize him to sell it, display it for sale or otherwise affect the principal's interest in it, is not thereby bound by a transaction with respect to the chattel between the agent and a third person who believes the agent to be the owner.

§ 201. Agent Authorized to Deal with Chattel Entrusted to Him

(1) Apart from statute and except as stated in Subsection (3), the interests of an undisclosed principal who entrusts an agent with a chattel other than a commercial document representing a chattel or chose in action with directions to deal with it in a particular way, as by sale, barter, pledge or mortgage, is not thereby affected by a transaction of a kind different from that authorized.

(2) The interests of the principal are affected by an unauthorized transaction of the same kind as that authorized if it is conducted in the usual and ordinary course of business by an agent with one who reasonably believes the agent to be the owner and who pays value.

(3) If the principal delivers a chattel to a dealer in such chattels to be sold or exhibited for sale, an unauthorized sale of the chattel by such dealer in accordance with the normal business practices to one who reasonably believes the dealer to be the owner, binds the owner, although the dealer was not authorized to sell it without the consent of the owner or was not authorized to sell it to the person to whom it was sold or at the price at which it was sold.

§ 202. Agent Entrusted with Commercial Document

An undisclosed principal who entrusts an agent with possession of, and a limited authority to deal with, a document representing a chattel or a chose in action in such form that the possession thereof is commonly regarded as indicating a general power to dispose of it is subject to the loss of his interests therein by the agent's unauthorized disposition of it if it comes to the hands of a purchaser who takes it, reasonably believing that the agent is the owner.

TITLE C. DEFENSES AND LIABILITY AFFECTED BY SUBSEQUENT EVENTS

§ 203. Defenses of Undisclosed Principal; In General

An undisclosed principal is entitled to all defenses arising out of a transaction with an agent, but not defenses which are personal to the agent.

§ 204. Notice to Principal or Agent

The liability of an undisclosed principal is affected by the knowledge which he acquires or by notification given to him which is relevant to his liability, and also by knowledge acquired or notification given to the agent with which he is chargeable.

§ 205. Power of Agent to Modify Contract Before Disclosure of Principal

Until the existence of the principal is disclosed, an agent who has made a contract for an undisclosed principal has power to cancel the contract and to modify it with binding effect upon the principal if the contract or conveyance, as modified, is authorized or is within the inherent power of the agent to make.

§ 206. Power of Agent as to Performance of or Defaults in Contract Before Disclosure of Principal

Until his existence is disclosed, the principal is affected by performance rendered by the third person to the agent, by notifications given to the agent with respect to the contract, and by the performance or default of the agent.

§ 207. Dealings Between Other Party and Agent After Disclosure of Principal

Dealings between the agent of an undisclosed principal and the other party to a transaction subsequent to the disclosure of the existence or identity of the principal:

(a) may increase or diminish the principal's liability because of the further exercise of the agent's power; or

(b) may diminish the principal's liability because the dealings are in derogation of the principal's rights.

§ 208. Settlement with Agent by Principal

An undisclosed principal is not discharged from liability to the other party to a transaction conducted by an agent by payment to, or settlement of accounts with, the agent, unless he does so in reasonable reliance upon conduct of the other party which is not induced by the agent's misrepresentations and which indicates that the agent has settled the account.

§ 209. Choice by Third Person to Look Only to Agent

An undisclosed principal is not discharged from liability upon a contract made for him by an agent by the fact that, after the discovery of his existence or identity, the other party looks only to the agent for payment or performance.

§ 210. Judgment for or Against Agent

(1) An undisclosed principal is discharged from liability upon a contract if, with knowledge of the identity of the principal, the other party recovers judgment against the agent who made the contract, for breach of the contract.

(2) The principal is not discharged by a recovery of judgment against the agent by the other party before knowledge of the identity of the principal.

(3) The existence and extent of the liability of an undisclosed principal upon a contract made by an agent may be determined by a judgment for or against the agent in an action between the agent and the other party in accordance with the rules of res judicata stated in the Restatement of Judgments.

§ 210A. Joinder of Undisclosed Principal and Agent

A principal, initially undisclosed, and his agent can properly be joined in one action based upon a contract made by the agent; but if either defendant objects, the plaintiff can secure judgment only against the one whom he elects to hold.

§ 211. Satisfaction of Claim by Agent

An undisclosed principal ceases to be liable upon a contract made on his account by an agent if the claim of the other party against the agent has been satisfied.

Chapter 7

LIABILITY OF PRINCIPAL TO THIRD PERSON; TORTS

TOPIC 1. LIABILITY FOR PERSONAL VIOLATION OF DUTY

§ 212. Principal Intends Conduct or Consequences

A person is subject to liability for the consequences of another's conduct which results from his directions as he would be for his own personal conduct if, with knowledge of the conditions, he intends the conduct, or if he intends its consequences, unless the one directing or the one acting has a privilege or immunity not available to the other.

§ 213. Principal Negligent or Reckless

A person conducting an activity through servants or other agents is subject to liability for harm resulting from his conduct if he is negligent or reckless:

(a) in giving improper or ambiguous orders of in failing to make proper regulations; or

(b) in the employment of improper persons or instrumentalities in work involving risk of harm to others:

(c) in the supervision of the activity; or

(d) in permitting, or failing to prevent, negligent or other tortious conduct by persons, whether or not his servants or agents, upon premises or with instrumentalities under his control.

§ 214. Failure of Principal to Perform Non-Delegable Duty

A master or other principal who is under a duty to provide protection for or to have care used to protect others or their property and who confides the performance of such duty to a servant or other person is subject to liability to such others for harm caused to them by the failure of such agent to perform the duty.

TOPIC 2. LIABILITY FOR AUTHORIZED CONDUCT OR CONDUCT INCIDENTAL THERETO

TITLE A. IN GENERAL

§ 215. Conduct Authorized but Unintended by Principal

A master or other principal who unintentionally authorizes conduct of a servant or other agent which constitutes a tort to a third person is subject to liability to such person.

§ 216. Unauthorized Tortious Conduct

A master or other principal may be liable to another whose interests have been invaded by the tortious conduct of a servant or other agent, although the principal does not personally violate a duty to such other or authorize the conduct of the agent causing the invasion.

§ 217. Where Principal or Agent Has Immunity or Privilege

In an action against a principal based on the conduct of a servant in the course of employment:

(a) The principal has a defense if:

(i) he had an immunity from liability to the person harmed, or

(ii) he had a delegable privilege so to act, or

(iii) the agent had a privilege which he properly exercised on his principal's behalf, or

(iv) the agent did not fall below the duty of care owed by the principal to the third person.

(b) The principal has no defense because of the fact that:

(i) he had a non-delegable privilege to do the act, or

(ii) the agent had an immunity from civil liability as to the act.

§ 217A. Dealings and Actions Between Injured Party and Agent

The liability of a principal for the tort of a servant or other agent may be affected by:

(a) dealings between the injured party and the agent, or

(b) a judgment for or against the agent in an action between the injured party and the agent.

§ 217B. Joinder of Principal and Agent

(1) Principal and agent can be joined in an action for a wrong resulting from the tortious conduct of an agent or that of agent and principal, and a judgment can be rendered against each.

(2) If the action is based solely upon the tortious conduct of the agent, judgments on the merits for the agent and against the principal, or judgments of varying amounts for compensatory damages are erroneous.

§ 217C. Punitive Damages

Punitive damages can properly be awarded against a master or other principal because of an act by an agent if, but only if:

(a) the principal authorized the doing and the manner of the act, or

(b) the agent was unfit and the principal was reckless in employing him, or

(c) the agent was employed in a managerial capacity and was acting in the scope of employment, or

(d) the principal or a managerial agent of the principal ratified or approved the act.

§ 217D. Penalties

A principal may be subject to penalties enforced under the rules of the criminal law, for acts done by a servant or other agent.

§ 218. Effect of Ratification

Upon ratification, a purported master or other principal becomes subject to liability for injuries caused by the tortious act of one acting or purporting to act as his agent as if the act had been authorized, if there has been no loss of capacity by the principal.

TITLE B. TORTS OF SERVANTS

§ 219. When Master is Liable for Torts of His Servants

(1) A master is subject to liability for the torts of his servants committed while acting in the scope of their employment.

(2) A master is not subject to liability for the torts of his servants acting outside the scope of their employment, unless:

(a) the master intended the conduct or the consequences, or

(b) the master was negligent or reckless, or

(c) the conduct violated a non-delegable duty of the master, or

(d) the servant purported to act or to speak on behalf of the principal and there was reliance upon apparent authority, or he was aided in accomplishing the tort by the existence of the agency relation.

WHO IS A SERVANT

§ 220. Definition of Servant

(1) A servant is a person employed to perform services in the affairs of another and who with respect to the physical conduct in the performance of the services is subject to the other's control or right to control.

(2) In determining whether one acting for another is a servant or an independent contractor, the following matters of fact, among others, are considered:

(a) the extent of control which, by the agreement, the master may exercise over the details of the work;

(b) whether or not the one employed is engaged in a distinct occupation or business;

(c) the kind of occupation, with reference to whether, in the locality, the work is usually done under the direction of the employer or by a specialist without supervision;

(d) the skill required in the particular occupation;

(e) whether the employer or the workman supplies the instrumentalities, tools, and the place of work for the person doing the work;

(f) the length of time for which the person is employed;

(g) the method of payment, whether by the time or by the job;

(h) whether or not the work is a part of the regular business of the employer;

(i) whether or not the parties believe they are creating the relation of master and servant; and

(j) whether the principal is or is not in business.

§ 221. Master's Consent to Service

To constitute the relation of master and servant, the one for whom the service is rendered must consent or manifest his consent to receive the services as a master.

§ 222. Servants of Agent of Undisclosed Principal

An undisclosed principal is subject to liability to third persons for conduct within the scope of employment of servants and of subservants employed for him by a servant or other agent empowered to employ them.

§ 223. Servant Required to be Taken From a Limited Class

The relation of master and servant may exist although the law requires the selection of persons for the particular work to be made from a limited class irrespective of how limited the class is, and the master is subject to liability for torts committed within the scope of employment by servants selected from such a class.

§ 224. Persons Compelled to Serve

One compelled by law or duress to render services to another has power to subject the other to liability as if there were a master and servant relation.

§ 225. Person Serving Gratuitously

One who volunteers services without an agreement for or expectation of reward may be a servant of the one accepting such services.

§ 226. Servant Acting for Two Masters

A person may be the servant of two masters, not joint employers, at one time as to one act, if the service to one does not involve abandonment of the service to the other.

§ 227. Servant Lent to Another Master

A servant directed or permitted by his master to perform services for another may become the servant of such other in performing the services. He may become the other's servant as to some acts and not as to others.

SCOPE OF EMPLOYMENT

§ 228. General Statement

(1) Conduct of a servant is within the scope of employment if, but only if:

(a) it is of the kind he is employed to perform;

(b) it occurs substantially within the authorized time and space limits;

(c) it is actuated, at least in part, by a purpose to serve the master; and

(d) if force is intentionally used by the servant against another, the use of force is not unexpectable by the master.

(2) Conduct of a servant is not within the scope of employment if it is different in kind from that authorized, far beyond the authorized time or space limits, or too little actuated by a purpose to serve the master.

§ 229. Kind of Conduct Within Scope of Employment

(1) To be within the scope of the employment, conduct must be of the same general nature as that authorized, or incidental to the conduct authorized.

(2) In determining whether or not the conduct, although not authorized, is nevertheless so similar to or incidental to the conduct

authorized as to be within the scope of employment, the following matters of fact are to be considered:

(a) whether or not the act is one commonly done by such servants;

(b) the time, place and purpose of the act;

(c) the previous relations between the master and the servant;

(d) the extent to which the business of the master is apportioned between different servants;

(e) whether or not the act is outside the enterprise of the master or, if within the enterprise, has not been entrusted to any servant;

(f) whether or not the master has reason to expect that such an act will be done;

(g) the similarity in quality of the act done to the act authorized;

(h) whether or not the instrumentality by which the harm is done has been furnished by the master to the servant;

(i) the extent of departure from the normal method of accomplishing an authorized result; and

(j) whether or not the act is seriously criminal.

Comment a. As stated in Section 212, a master is responsible for an act or result which he intends the servant to perform or achieve if the servant acts because of his directions. Also, as stated in Section 215, a master is responsible for authorized but unintended conduct. Thus, a servant is authorized to do anything which is reasonably regarded as incidental to the work specifically directed or which is usually done in connection with such work. The scope of employment includes not only such acts but also other acts which, as between the master and servant, the servant is not privileged to do. The limits of the scope of employment are dependent upon the facts of the particular case, and no more definite statement can profitably be made concerning them than that made in Subsection (2). Since the phrase "scope of the employment," is used for the purpose of determining the liability of the master for the conduct of servants, the ultimate question is whether or not it is just that the loss resulting from the servant's acts should be considered as one of the normal risks to be borne by the business in which the servant is employed.

The factors here stated have primary reference to the physical activities of servants. The special rules which deal with situations in which the master may be liable for deceit, false arrest or attachment and similar matters are stated in Sections 246–264.

§ 230. Forbidden Acts

An act, although forbidden, or done in a forbidden manner, may be within the scope of employment.

§ 231. Criminal or Tortious Acts

An act may be within the scope of employment although consciously criminal or tortious.

§ 232. Failure to Act

The failure of a servant to act may be conduct within the scope of employment.

§ 233. Time of Service

Conduct of a servant is within the scope of employment only during a period which has a reasonable connection with the authorized period.

§ 234. Area of Service

Conduct is within the scope of employment only in the authorized area or in a locality not unreasonably distant from it.

§ 235. Conduct not for Purpose of Serving Master

An act of a servant is not within the scope of employment if it is done with no intention to perform it as a part of or incident to a service on account of which he is employed.

§ 236. Conduct Actuated by Dual Purpose

Conduct may be within the scope of employment, although done in part to serve the purposes of the servant or of a third person.

§ 237. Re-entry into Employment

A servant who has temporarily departed in space or time from the scope of employment does not re-enter it until he is again reasonably near the authorized space and time limits and is acting with the intention of serving his master's business.

USE OF INSTRUMENTALITIES BY SERVANTS

§ 238. Instrumentalities not Used in Employment

Except where he is at fault or fails to perform a nondelegable duty, a master is not liable for harm caused by the use of instrumentalities entrusted by him to a servant when they are not used in the scope of employment.

§ 239. Use of Unauthorized Instrumentality

A master is not liable for injuries caused by the negligence of a servant in the use of an instrumentality which if of a substantially different kind from that authorized as a means of performing the master's service, or over the use of which it is understood that the master is to have no right of control.

§ 240. Servant Leaves Instrumentality in Dangerous Situation

A master is subject to liability for the resulting harm if his servant, entrusted with the possession of an instrumentality, leaves it while within the scope of employment under such circumstances that an undue risk of harm to third persons is created, although the servant leaves it to serve some purpose of his own.

§ 241. Unauthorized Transfer of Custody of Instrumentality

A master who has entrusted a servant with an instrumentality is subject to liability for harm caused by its negligent management by one to whom the servant entrusts its custody to do the work the servant was employed to perform, if the servant should realize that there is an undue risk that such person will harm others by its management.

§ 242. Liability to Invitee of Servant

A master is not subject to liability for the conduct of a servant towards a person harmed as the result of accepting or soliciting from the servant an invitation, not binding upon the master, to enter or remain upon the master's premises or vehicle, although the conduct which immediately causes the harm is within the scope of the servant's employment.

SPECIFIC TORTS OF SERVANTS

§ 243. Negligence

A master is subject to liability for physical harm caused by the negligent conduct of servants within the scope of employment.

§ 244. Trespass and Conversion

A master is subject to liability for a trespass or a conversion caused by an act done by a servant within the scope of employment.

§ 245. Use of Force

A master is subject to liability for the intended tortious harm by a servant to the person or things of another by an act done in connection with the servant's employment, although the act was unauthorized, if the act was not unexpectable in view of the duties of the servant.

§ 246. Tortious Institution or Conduct of Legal Proceedings

A master is subject to liability for the tortious institution or conduct of legal proceedings by a servant acting within the scope of employment.

§ 247. Defamation

A master is subject to liability for defamatory statements made by a servant acting within the scope of his employment, or, as to those hearing or reading the statement, within his apparent authority.

§ 248. Interference with Business Relations

A master is subject to liability to third persons injured in their business relations by the tortious conduct of a servant acting within the scope of employment or, if apparent authority is relevant, acting within his apparent authority.

§ 249. Misrepresentations

A master is subject to liability for the misrepresentations of a servant causing pecuniary loss as he is for the misrepresentations of an agent who is not a servant.

TITLE C. AGENTS' TORTS; LIABILITY NOT DEPENDENT UPON RELATION OF MASTER AND SERVANT

IN GENERAL

§ 250. Non–Liability for Physical Harm by Non–Servant Agents

A principal is not liable for physical harm caused by the negligent physical conduct of a non-servant agent during the performance of the principal's business, if he neither intended nor authorized the result nor the manner of performance, unless he was under a duty to have the act performed with due care.

§ 251. Liability for Physical Harm Caused by a Servant or a Non-Servant Agent

A principal is subject to liability for physical harm to the person or the tangible things of another caused by the negligence of a servant or a non-servant agent:

(a) in the performance of an act which the principal is under a duty to have performed with care; and

(b) in the making of a representation which the agent is authorized or apparently authorized to make or which is within the power of the agent to make for the principal.

§ 252. Mistaken Action by Agents

If a servant or other agent, authorized to do an act provided certain conditions exist, and to determine whether or not such conditions exist, does the act in the erroneous belief that such conditions do exist and thereby commits a tort, the principal is subject to liability for the act.

§ 253. Tortious Institution or Conduct of Legal Proceedings

A principal who authorizes a servant or other agent to institute or conduct such legal proceedings as in his judgment are lawful and desirable for the protection of the principal's interests is subject to liability to a person against whom proceedings reasonably adapted to accomplish the principal's purposes are tortiously brought by the agent.

§ 254. Defamation

A principal is subject to liability for a defamatory statement by a servant or other agent if the agent was authorized, or if, as to the person to whom he made the statement, he was apparently authorized to make it.

§ 255. Acts of Subservants and Other Subagents

The rules applicable to the liability of a principal for the acts of agents, are applicable to his liability for subservants and other subagents insofar as their conduct has relation to the principal's affairs.

MISREPRESENTATIONS

§ 256. Knowledge of Principal When Agent Innocently Makes a Misrepresentation

If a principal knows facts unknown to a servant or other agent and which are relevant to a transaction which the agent is authorized to conduct, and, because of his justifiable ignorance, the agent makes a material misstatement of facts, the principal:

(a) is subject to liability for an intentional misrepresentation, if he believed the agent would make the statement, or for a negligent misrepresentation, if he had reason to know the agent would make the statement.

(b) is not subject to liability in tort if he had no reason to know that the agent would enter into such a transaction, or if, after acquiring the information, he had no way of communicating with the agent.

§ 257. Misrepresentations; In General

A principal is subject to liability for loss caused to another by the other's reliance upon a tortious representation of a servant or other agent, if the representation is:

(a) authorized;

(b) apparently authorized; or

(c) within the power of the agent to make for the principal.

Comment g. Physical harm. The rule stated in this Section applies to physical harm resulting from the misrepresentation, as well as to economic loss. Thus, an agent authorized to direct travelers causes his employer to be liable if he negligently directs them to a dangerous place in which they are harmed.

§ 258. Incidental Misrepresentations

In the absence of an exculpatory agreement, a principal authorizing a servant or other agent to enter into negotiations to which representations concerning the subject matter thereof are usually incident is subject to liability for loss caused to the other party to the transaction by tortious misrepresentations of the agent upon matters which the principal might reasonably expect would be the subject of representations, provided the other party has no notice that the representations are unauthorized.

§ 259. Rescission of Transaction for Misrepresentations of Agent

(1) A transaction into which one is induced to enter by reliance upon untrue and material representations as to the subject matter, made by a servant or other agent entrusted with its preliminary or final negotiations, is subject to rescission at the election of the person deceived.

(2) Change of position by the principal:

(a) is a defense if the agent has no power to bind the principal by the misrepresentations;

(b) is not a defense if the principal was liable for the misrepresentations.

Caveat:

No statement is made as to the defense of change of position if the misrepresentation, although within the power of the agent to make for the principal, was not tortious.

§ 260. Contracts Limiting Liability for Agent's Misrepresentations

(1) An innocent principal can, by contract with another, relieve himself of liability for deceit because of unauthorized fraud by a servant or other agent upon the other party.

(2) A contract with, or a conveyance to, the principal obtained by his agent through misrepresentations can be rescinded by the other party to the contract or conveyance prior to a change of position by the principal, even though the contract provides that "it shall not be affected by misrepresentations not contained therein" and includes a statement that the agent has made no representations.

Caveat:

The rule stated in Subsection (2) is not intended to deny the possibility that the principal and the other party can make a binding agreement that the other party shall not be able to avoid the transaction because of his reliance upon misrepresentations made by the agent.

§ 261. Agent's Position Enables Him to Deceive

A principal who puts a servant or other agent in a position which enables the agent, while apparently acting within his authority, to commit a fraud upon third persons is subject to liability to such third persons for the fraud.

Comment a. The principal is subject to liability under the rule stated in this Section although he is entirely innocent, has received no benefit from the transaction, and, as stated in Section 262, although the agent acted solely for his own purposes. Liability is based upon the fact that the agent's position facilitates the consummation of the fraud, in that from the point of view of the third person the transaction seems regular on its face and the agent appears to be acting in the ordinary course of the business confided to him.

§ 262. Agent Acts for His Own Purposes

A person who otherwise would be liable to another for the misrepresentations of one apparently acting for him is not relieved from liability by the fact that the servant or other agent acts entirely for his own purposes, unless the other has notice of this.

§ 263. Property Acquired for Principal by Fraud of Agent

Unless he has changed his position, a principal whose servant or other agent has fraudulently acquired property for him, holds it subject to the interests of the defrauded person. If the principal is liable in tort for the fraud of the agent, his change of position after acquiring the property is not a defense.

§ 264. Misrepresentations by Subservants and Other Subagents

The rules applicable to representations by servants and other agents are applicable to representations by subservants and other subagents made in connection with transactions conducted for the principal.

TITLE D. CONDUCT WITHIN APPARENT AUTHORITY OR EMPLOYMENT

§ 265. General Rule

(1) A master or other principal is subject to liability for torts which result from reliance upon, or belief in, statements or other conduct within an agent's apparent authority.

(2) Unless there has been reliance, the principal is not liable in tort for conduct of a servant or other agent merely because it is within his apparent authority or apparent scope of employment.

§ 266. Physical Harm Caused by Reliance Upon Representations

A purported master or other principal is subject to liability for physical harm caused to others or to their belongings by their reasonable reliance upon the tortious representations of one acting within his apparent authority or apparent scope of employment.

§ 267. Reliance Upon Care or Skill of Apparent Servant or Other Agent

One who represents that another is his servant or other agent and thereby causes a third person justifiably to rely upon the care or skill of such apparent agent is subject to liability to the third person for harm caused by the lack of care or skill of the one appearing to be a servant or other agent as if he were such.

Chapter 8

LIABILITY OF PRINCIPAL TO THIRD PERSONS; NOTICE THROUGH AGENT

TOPIC 1. NOTIFICATION TO OR BY AGENTS

§ 268. General Rule

(1) Unless the notifier has notice that the agent has an interest adverse to the principal, a notification given to an agent is notice to the principal if it is given:

(a) to an agent authorized to receive it;

(b) to an agent apparently authorized to receive it;

(c) to an agent authorized to conduct a transaction, with respect to matters connected with it as to which notice is usually given to such an agent, unless the one giving the notification has notice that the agent is not authorized to receive it;

(d) to an agent to whom by the terms of a contract notification is to be given, with reference to matters in connection with the contract; or

(e) to the agent of an unidentified or undisclosed principal with reference to transactions entered into by such agent within his powers, until discovery of the identity of the principal; thereafter as in the case of a disclosed principal.

(2) The rules as to the giving of notification to an agent apply to the giving of notification by an agent.

§ 269. Time When Notification Must be Given

To be effective as notice, a notification must be given to or by an agent during the time when the agent I as power to affect his principal by giving or receiving such notification.

§ 270. Time When Notice Results

Notice results when the act or event constituting notification is performed or happens.

§ 271. Notification; Agent's Interests Adverse to Principal's

A notification by or to a third person to or by an agent is not prevented from being notice to or by the principal because of the fact that the agent, when receiving or giving the notification, is acting adversely to the principal, unless the third person has notice of the agent's adverse purposes.

TOPIC 2. KNOWLEDGE OF AGENTS

§ 272. General Rule

In accordance with and subject to the rules stated in this Topic, the liability of a principal is affected by the knowledge of an agent concerning a matter as to which he acts within his power to bind the principal or upon which it is his duty to give the principal information.

Comment b. Where agent has reason to know or should know. In situations in which knowledge of a particular fact is relevant to the legal liability of participants in an event, their liability is often affected by their having knowledge of other facts from which persons of ordinary intelligence and prudence would infer the existence of the fact in question or would be led to make such inquiries as would give them knowledge of it. In such cases they have reason to know the fact in question or they should know of it. The Comment on Section 9 indicates the meaning of these phrases and gives illustrations of situations in which knowledge is important in a variety of situations. If an agent has reason to know or should know a particular fact, the principal is affected as if the circumstances were such that the principal would have reason to know or should know the fact, subject to the rules stated in Sections 274–282.

§ 273. Agent Having Apparent Authority

Except where there is reliance upon the appearance of agency, a principal is not bound by knowledge of an agent concerning matters as to which he has only apparent authority.

§ 274. Agent Acquiring Property for Principal

The knowledge of an agent who acquires property for his principal affects the interests of his principal in the subject matter to the same extent as if the principal had acquired it with the same knowledge, except where the agent is privileged not to disclose or to act upon the knowledge, or a change in conditions makes it inequitable thus to affect the principal.

§ 275. Agent Having Duty to Reveal Knowledge

Except where the agent is acting adversely to the principal or where knowledge as distinguished from reason to know is important, the principal is affected by the knowledge which an agent has a duty to disclose to the principal or to another agent of the principal to the same extent as if the principal had the information.

§ 276. Time, Place or Manner of Acquisition of Agent's Knowledge

Except for knowledge acquired confidentially, the time, place, or manner in which knowledge is acquired by a servant or other agent is immaterial in determining the liability of his principal because of it.

§ 277. Agent Who Should, but Does not, Have Knowledge

The principal is not affected by the knowledge which an agent should have acquired in the performance of the agent's duties to the principal or to others, except where the principal or master has a duty to others that care shall be exercised in obtaining information.

§ 278. Time When Agent's Knowledge Affects Principal

The principal is affected by the knowledge which the agent has when acting for him or, if it is the duty of the agent to communicate the information and not otherwise to act, the principal is affected after the lapse of such time as is reasonable for its communication.

§ 279. Agent Dealing with Principal as Adverse Party

The principal is not affected by the knowledge of an agent as to matters involved in a transaction in which the agent deals with the principal or another agent of the principal as, or on account of, an adverse party.

§ 280. Agent's Knowledge of His Own Unauthorized Acts

If an agent has done an unauthorized act or intends to do one, the principal is not affected by the agent's knowledge that he has done or intends to do the act.

§ 281. Agent Privileged not to Disclose Knowledge

A principal is not affected by the knowledge of an agent who is privileged not to disclose or act upon it and who does not disclose or act upon it.

§ 282. Agent Acting Adversely to Principal

(1) A principal is not affected by the knowledge of an agent in a transaction in which the agent secretly is acting adversely to the principal and entirely for his own or another's purposes, except as stated in Subsection (2).

(2) The principal is affected by the knowledge of an agent who acts adversely to the principal:

(a) if the failure of the agent to act upon or to reveal the information results in a violation of a contractual or relational duty of the principal to a person harmed thereby;

(b) if the agent enters into negotiations within the scope of his powers and the person with whom he deals reasonably believes him to be authorized to conduct the transaction; or

(c) if, before he has changed his position, the principal knowingly retains a benefit through the act of the agent which otherwise he would not have received.

TOPIC 3. SERVANTS AND SUBAGENTS

§ 283. General Rule

The rules stated in this chapter which state the rules which apply to the liability of a principal because of notice through an agent apply to the liability:

(a) of a master or other principal because of the knowledge of, or notification to, a servant, subservant or other subagent which the servant or subagent had a duty to act upon or to communicate to the agent or to the principal because of his employment or apparent employment.

(b) of a master or other principal because of a notification given by a servant, subservant or other subagent.

Chapter 9

ADMISSIBILITY IN EVIDENCE OF STATEMENTS OF AGENTS

§ 284. Operative and Relevant Statements

In actions between the principal and third persons, evidence of a statement by an agent is admissible for or against either party for the purpose of proving that such statement was made, if the fact that the statement was made constitutes, or is relevant in the proof of, one of the ultimate facts required to be established in order to maintain a cause of action or defense.

§ 285. Statements as to Authority

Evidence of a statement by an agent concerning the existence or extent of his authority is not admissible against the principal to prove its existence or extent, unless it appears by other evidence that the making of such statement was within the authority of the agent or, as to persons dealing with the agent, within the apparent authority or other power of the agent.

§ 286. Statement to Third Persons Constituting Admissions

In an action between the principal and a third person, statements of an agent to a third person are admissible in evidence against the principal to prove the truth of facts asserted in them as though made by the principal, if the agent was authorized to make the statement or was authorized to make, on the principal's behalf, any statements concerning the subject matter.

§ 287. Reports to Principal

Statements by an agent to the principal or to another agent of the principal are not admissible against the principal as admissions; such statements may be admissible in evidence under other rules of evidence.

§ 288. When Agent Has Authority to Make Statements

(1) The general rules concerning the interpretation of authority are applicable in determining whether an agent has authority to make statements concerning operative or other facts.

(2) Authority to do an act or to conduct a transaction does not of itself include authority to make statements concerning the act or transaction.

(3) Authority to make statements of fact does not of itself include authority to make statements admitting liability because of such facts.

§ 289. Statements Admissible Under General Rules of Evidence

Evidence of statements of agents, whether or not such statements are authorized, is admissible in favor of and against the principal, if admissible under the general rules of evidence as to the admissibility of such statements by persons not agents.

§ 290. Ratification of Agent's Statements

If a statement would be admissible in evidence because made in the course of authorized conduct, such a statement made by a person purporting to act for another or intending to serve another, is admissible if the person on whose behalf the statement was made or was purported to have been made, ratifies the conduct.

§ 291. Statements of Servants and Subagents

The rules dealing with the admissibility of statements by agents apply to the admissibility of statements by servants, subservants and other subagents with reference to transactions conducted for the principal by them.

Chapter 10

LIABILITY OF THIRD PERSON TO PRINCIPAL

TOPIC 1. CONTRACTS; DISCLOSED AGENCY

§ 292. General Rule

The other party to a contract made by an agent for a disclosed or partially disclosed principal, acting within his authority, apparent authority or other agency power, is liable to the principal as if he had contracted directly with the principal, unless the principal is excluded as a party by the form or terms of the contract.

§ 293. Principal Excluded From Transaction

The other party to a contract made by an agent on behalf of a disclosed or partially disclosed principal does not become liable to such principal upon it in an action at law if the principal is excluded as a party by the form or terms of the contract.

§ 294. Orders of Several Principals Combined

Unless otherwise agreed between the principals and the agent, the other party to a contract made by an agent who has been authorized by several disclosed or partially disclosed principals to act for them separately, but who combines their orders and purports to contract for them jointly, is not liable in an action at law brought upon the contract by one of them alone.

§ 295. Negotiable Instruments

An obligor upon a negotiable instrument given to an agent on account of a principal not named or described therein is not liable to the principal in an action at law upon the instrument, unless the principal is an endorsee or otherwise becomes a holder.

§ 296. Sealed Instruments

In the absence of statute, an obligor named in a sealed instrument given to an agent on behalf of the principal is not liable to the principal upon it in an action at law unless the principal appears therein as a covenantee.

§ 297. Interpretation of Written Instruments as to Parties

The rules with respect to the interpretation of written instruments as to the parties to them in actions brought against the principal by the person with whom the agent dealt are applicable in actions brought by the principal against the third person.

§ 298. Defenses of Other Party

The other party to a contract made by an agent on behalf of a disclosed or partially disclosed principal has all the defenses which he would have had against the principal if the principal had made the contract under the same circumstances.

§ 299. Rights Between Other Party and Agent

Unless otherwise agreed, the liability of the other party to a disclosed or partially disclosed principal upon a contract made by an agent is not affected by any rights or liabilities then existing between the other party and the agent.

§ 300. Dealings and Actions Between Agent and Other Party Subsequent to the Transaction

The liability of one who has contracted with an agent for a disclosed or partially disclosed principal is affected by:

(a) subsequent dealings between him and the agent

(i) which bind the principal because of the agent's authority or other power, or

(ii) which are in derogation of the principal's rights as a contracting party.

(b) a judgment in an action between him and the agent.

§ 301. Unauthorized Assignment of Contract by Agent

If a document evidencing a contract which an agent has made with another on behalf of the principal is in such form that the principal has reason to believe that third persons may reasonably believe the agent to be the owner of the contract or to have power of disposition of it, and if the agent had power to bind the principal by a contract in that form, the claim of the principal against the other party is destroyed by the agent's unauthorized transfer to a bona fide purchaser of the rights against the other party under the contract.

TOPIC 2. CONTRACTS; UNDISCLOSED AGENCY

§ 302. General Rule

A person who makes a contract with an agent of an undisclosed principal, intended by the agent to be on account of his principal and within the power of such agent to bind his principal, is liable to the principal as if the principal himself had made the contract with him, unless he is excluded by the form or terms of the contract, unless his existence is fraudulently concealed or unless there is set-off or a similar defense against the agent.

§ 303. Principal Excluded From Transaction

A person with whom an agent makes a contract on account of an undisclosed principal is not liable in an action at law brought upon the contract by such principal:

(a) if the contract is in the form of a sealed or negotiable instrument; or

(b) if the terms of the contract exclude liability to any undisclosed principal or to the particular principal.

§ 304. Agent Misrepresents Existence of Principal

A person with whom an agent contracts on account of an undisclosed principal can rescind the contract if he was induced to enter into it by a representation that the agent was not acting for a principal and if, as the agent or principal had notice, he would not have dealt with the principal.

§ 305. Orders of Several Principals Combined

Unless otherwise agreed between the principal and the agent, the other party to a contract made by an agent for several undisclosed principals who have not jointly authorized him is not liable in an action at law upon the contract brought by one of them alone.

§ 306. Rights Between Other Party and Agent

(1) If the agent has been authorized to conceal the existence of the principal, the liability to an undisclosed principal of a person dealing with the agent within his power to bind the principal is diminished by any claim which such person may have against the agent at the time of making the contract and until the existence of the principal becomes known to him, if he could set off such claim in an action against the agent.

(2) If the agent is authorized only to contract in the principal's name, the other party does not have set-off for a claim due him from the agent unless the agent has been entrusted with the possession of chattels which he disposes of as directed or unless the principal has otherwise misled the third person into extending credit to the agent.

§ 307. Dealings and Actions Between Agent and Other Party Subsequent to Transaction

(1) When an agent has made a contract for an undisclosed principal:

(a) until the existence of the principal is known, the agent has power to rescind, perform and receive performance of the contract and to modify it with binding effect, if the contract or conveyance, as modified, is within his agency powers.

(b) after the principal's existence is known, the agent has the same powers with reference to the contract as if the principal had been originally disclosed or partially disclosed.

(2) A judgment for or against the agent either before or after the principal's existence is known may increase, decrease or terminate the claim of the principal.

§ 307A. Unauthorized Assignment by Agent

If an agent assigns an assignable contract which he has made for an undisclosed principal to one who pays value and has no notice of the principal's interests, the transferee is entitled to the contract.

§ 308. Defenses of Other Party

In an action by an undisclosed principal against the other party to a contract, the other party has all the defenses, except those of a purely procedural nature:

(a) which he would have had against the principal if the principal had made the contract under the same circumstances,

(b) which he had against the agent until the discovery of the principal, unless the agent was authorized to contract only in the principal's name.

§ 309. Principal Cannot or Does not Give Required Performance

Acts done or offered to be done by an undisclosed principal which, if performed by a person other than the agent, are not substantially those which the contract contemplates, are not effective as a performance or as a tender of performance of the contract.

§ 310. When Performance Must be Rendered to Principal

An undisclosed principal upon whose account an agent has acted within his power to bind the principal in making a contract, unless he is excluded by its terms, can require the other party to render performance to him instead of to the agent, except in the case of personal services or where performance to the principal would subject the other to a substantially different liability from that contemplated.

TOPIC 3. NON-CONTRACTUAL LIABILITY

§ 311. Mistaken Dealing with Unauthorized Agent

A person with whom an agent deals in excess of his power to subject the principal to liability or to affect the principal's interests is not relieved from liability to the principal for interference with the principal's interests by such dealing because of a reasonable belief that the agent was authorized or was the owner of the subject matter.

§ 312. Intentionally Causing or Assisting Agent to Violate Duty

A person who, without being privileged to do so, intentionally causes or assists an agent to violate a duty to his principal is subject to liability to the principal.

§ 313. Adversely Employing Agent of Another

(1) A person who, knowing that the other party to a transaction has employed an agent to conduct a transaction for him, employs the agent on his own account in such transaction is subject to liability to the other party, unless he reasonably believes that the other party acquiesces in the double employment.

(2) If without knowledge of the common agency, two persons employ the same agent to conduct a transaction between them, the transaction is voidable at the election of either.

§ 314. Restitutional Liability

A person who receives the principal's property from an agent of another, with notice that the agent is thereby committing a breach of fiduciary duty to the principal, holds the property thus acquired as a constructive trustee, or at the election of the principal, is subject to liability for its value; one who receives such property, non-tortiously and without notice, but who is not a bona fide purchaser, is subject to liability to the extent to which he has been unjustly enriched.

§ 315. Third Person Fraudulent

A person who fraudulently obtains a contract through, or enters into a transaction with, an agent acting within the scope of his power to bind the principal, or who by fraud causes the agent to do what would be a violation of his duty to the principal if the agent knew the facts, is subject to liability to the principal whether the fraud is practiced upon the agent or upon the principal.

§ 316. Interference with, or Harm Caused to, Servants or Other Agents

(1) A person who, not being privileged to do so, intentionally interferes with the performance of the principal's business by the agent is subject to liability to the principal for the harm thereby caused to him.

(2) A person who tortiously causes physical harm to an agent not a servant is not thereby liable to the principal for the harm thereby caused to him.

§ 317. Contributory Negligence of Agent

The contributory negligence of an agent acting within the scope of his power to bind his principal by his conduct bars the principal from recovery against a third person to the same extent as if the principal had been negligent.

§ 317A. Indemnity and Contribution From Another Principal

(1) Unless otherwise agreed between them, one of two principals who has made expenditures because of the conduct of a common agent is entitled to

(a) contribution from the other principal if, as between the two, each was equally responsible for the agent's conduct, or

(b) indemnity from the other principal if the agent's conduct was the result of a breach of duty to the plaintiff by the other principal.

(2) If the negligence or fraud of two servants or other agents of different principals unites in causing injury to a third person, one of the principals is entitled to indemnity or contribution from the other for amounts paid in compensation for the injury, in accordance with the rules stated in the Restatement of Restitution.

TOPIC 4. SERVANTS, SUBSERVANTS AND OTHER SUBAGENTS

§ 318. General Rule

The rules which apply to the liability of a third person to principals generally are applicable to his liability to a master or other principal on whose account a servant, subservant or other subagent has acted or purported to act.

TOPIC 5. EFFECT OF RATIFICATION

§ 319. General Rule

Where a purported servant or other agent has entered into a transaction with a third person, its ratification by the purported master or other principal has the same effect upon the liabilities of the third person to the principal as an original authorization.

Chapter 11

LIABILITY OF AGENT TO THIRD PERSONS

TOPIC 1. CONTRACTS AND CONVEYANCES

TITLE A. AGENT A PARTY TO A TRANSACTION CONDUCTED BY HIMSELF

§ 320. Principal Disclosed

Unless otherwise agreed, a person making or purporting to make a contract with another as agent for a disclosed principal does not become a party to the contract.

§ 321. Principal Partially Disclosed

Unless otherwise agreed, a person purporting to make a contract with another for a partially disclosed principal is a party to the contract.

§ 322. Principal Undisclosed

An agent purporting to act upon his own account, but in fact making a contract on account of an undisclosed principal, is a party to the contract.

§ 323. Integrated Contracts

(1) If it appears unambiguously in an integrated contract that the agent is a party or is not a party, extrinsic evidence is not admissible to show a contrary intent, except for the purpose of reforming the contract.

(2) If the fact of agency appears in an integrated contract, not sealed or negotiable, and there is no unambiguous expression of an intention either to make the agent a party thereto or not to make him a party thereto, extrinsic evidence can be introduced to show the intention of the parties.

(3) If the fact of agency does not appear in an integrated contract, an agent who appears to be a party thereto can not introduce extrinsic evidence to show that he is not a party, except:

(a) for the purpose of reforming the contract; or

(b) to establish that his name was signed as the business name of the principal and that it was so agreed by the parties.

§ 324. Negotiable Instruments

(1) In the absence of reformation, an agent signing a negotiable instrument in his own name is a party to it although the fact of agency appears upon it, unless the name of the principal also appears.

(2) An agent is not liable as a party to a negotiable instrument on which the name of the principal appears if it is interpreted as being executed by the agent only on behalf of such principal and if the agent has power to bind the principal.

(3) If the name of the principal appears upon a negotiable instrument and the agent does not appear unambiguously as a party, extrinsic evidence of an understanding that the agent shall not be a party to it is admissible as against any holder of the instrument who has notice of the agreement or who is not a holder in due course.

§ 325. Sealed Instruments

An agent is not liable as a party to a sealed instrument unless he is named as covenantor in the instrument which also purports to be sealed by him. If these facts appear unambiguously, extrinsic evidence is not admissible to show that it was agreed that he should be a party, except for the purpose of reforming the instrument.

§ 326. Principal Known to be Nonexistent or Incompetent

Unless otherwise agreed, a person who, in dealing with another, purports to act as agent for a principal whom both know to be nonexistent or wholly incompetent, becomes a party to such a contract.

§ 327. Interpretation of Written Instruments as to Parties

The rules with respect to the interpretation of written instruments as to the parties thereto in actions brought against the principal by the third person are applicable in actions brought by the third person against the agent.

TITLE B. AGENT NOT PARTY TO TRANSACTION CONDUCTED BY HIMSELF

§ 328. Liability of Authorized Agent for Performance of Contract

An agent, by making a contract only on behalf of a competent disclosed or partially disclosed principal whom he has power so to bind, does not thereby become liable for its nonperformance.

§ 329. Agent Who Warrants Authority

A person who purports to make a contract, conveyance or representation on behalf of another who has full capacity but whom he has no power to bind, thereby becomes subject to liability to the other party thereto upon an implied warranty of authority, unless he has manifested that he does not make such warranty or the other party knows that the agent is not so authorized.

§ 330. Liability for Misrepresentation of Authority

A person who tortiously misrepresents to another that he has authority to make a contract, conveyance, or representation on behalf of a principal whom he has no power to bind, is subject to liability to the other in an action of tort for loss caused by reliance upon such misrepresentation.

§ 331. Agent Making No Warranty or Representation of Authority

A person who purports to make a contract, conveyance or representation on behalf of a principal whom he has no power to bind thereby is not subject to liability to the other party thereto if he sufficiently manifests that he does not warrant his authority and makes no tortious misrepresentation.

§ 332. Agent of Partially Incompetent Principal

An agent making a contract for a disclosed principal whose contracts are voidable because of lack of full capacity to contract, or for a principal who, although having capacity to contract generally, is incompetent to enter into the particular transaction, is not thereby liable to the other party. He does not become liable by reason of the failure of the principal to perform, unless he contracts or represents that the principal has capacity or unless he has reason to know of the principal's lack of capacity and of the other party's ignorance thereof.

TITLE C. DEFENSES AND EFFECTS OF SUBSEQUENT EVENTS

§ 333. Rights Between Other Party and Principal

Unless otherwise agreed, the liability of an agent upon a contract between a third person and the principal to which the agent is a party is not affected by any rights or liabilities existing between the third person and the principal not arising from the transaction, except that, with the consent of the principal, the agent can set off a claim which the principal would have in an action brought against him.

§ 334. Defenses of Agent; In General

In an action against an agent upon a contract between a third person and the principal to which the agent is a party, the agent has all the defenses which arise out of the transaction itself and also those which he has personally against the third person; defenses which are personal to the principal are not available to the agent.

§ 335. Agent Surety for Principal

In an action brought against an agent upon a contract to which the agent is a party but under which the primary duty of performance rests upon the principal, the agent has the defenses available to a surety.

§ 336. Election by Other Party to Hold Principal; Agency Disclosed

Unless otherwise agreed, the agent of a disclosed or partially disclosed principal who is a party to a contract made by another with such principal is not relieved from liability upon the contract by the determination of the other party to look to the principal alone, nor, unless the agent and the principal are joint contractors, by the fact that the other gets a judgment against the principal. He is relieved from liability to the extent that he is prejudiced thereby if he changes his position in justifiable reliance upon a manifestation of the other that he will look solely to the principal for performance.

§ 337. Election by Other Party to Hold Principal; Agency Undisclosed

An agent who has made a contract on behalf of an undisclosed principal is not relieved from liability by the determination of the other party thereto to look to the principal alone for the performance of the contract. He is discharged from liability if the other obtains a judgment against the principal, or, to the extent that he is prejudiced thereby, if he changes his position in justifiable reliance upon the other's manifestation that he will look solely to the principal for payment.

§ 338. Effect of Ratification

Ratification by a principal of a contract which an agent without authority purported to make for the principal terminates the liability of the agent to the other party for the breach of warranty or misrepresentation of authority.

TOPIC 2. THINGS RECEIVED FROM OR FOR PRINCIPAL

TITLE A. THINGS RECEIVED FROM THIRD PERSON

§ 339. Other Party Rescinds for Cause Existing at Time of Transaction; Principal Disclosed or Partially Disclosed

An agent who has received things from another for a disclosed or partially disclosed principal in a transaction conducted by him has a duty to return them or their proceeds if the other rescinds the transaction for a cause existing at the time of their receipt, to the extent that the agent has not, before notice of rescission and in good faith, changed his position.

§ 340. Other Party Rescinds for Cause Arising After Transaction; Principal Disclosed or Partially Disclosed

If an agent receives things on behalf of a disclosed or partially disclosed principal by a transaction to which he is not a party and the other party rescinds the transaction for a cause arising after the things have been received, the agent does not thereby have a duty to return them.

§ 341. Other Party Rescinds; Principal Undisclosed

An agent who has received things from another on behalf of an undisclosed principal has a duty to return them or their proceeds upon rescission of the transaction, under the same circumstances as if the agent had acted upon his own account, except that payment by the agent to the principal does not constitute such a change of position as relieves the agent from liability to the other.

TITLE B. THINGS RECEIVED FROM PRINCIPAL

§ 342. General Rule

(1) An agent who receives money or other thing from his principal to pay or transfer to another person is not thereby liable to the other.

(2) An agent whose promise to pay is primarily for the benefit of a third person may be liable in an action of contract to the third person for his failure to perform his promise.

(3) If an agent receives money in trust from the principal for the benefit of another, the agent is liable as a trustee to the other.

TOPIC 3. TORTS

§ 343. General Rule

An agent who does an act otherwise a tort is not relieved from liability by the fact that he acted at the command of the principal or on account of the principal, except where he is exercising a privilege of the principal, or a privilege held by him for the protection of the principal's interests, or where the principal owes no duty or less than the normal duty of care to the person harmed.

§ 344. Liability for Directed Conduct or Consequences

An agent is subject to liability, as he would be for his own personal conduct, for the consequences of another's conduct which results from his directions if, with knowledge of the circumstances, he intends the conduct, or its consequences, except where the agent or the one acting has a privilege or immunity not available to the other.

§ 345. Agent Exercising Privileges of Principal

An agent is privileged to do what otherwise would constitute a tort if his principal is privileged to have an agent do it and has authorized the agent to do it.

§ 346. Privilege to Protect Principal's Interests

An agent is privileged to give such protection to the person or property of his principal as is authorized by the principal to the same extent as the principal is privileged to act in the protection of himself or his property.

§ 347. Immunities and Standard of Care of Principal

(1) An agent does not have the immunities of his principal although acting at the direction of the principal.

(2) Where, because of his relation to a third person, a master owes no duty, or a diminished duty, of care, a servant in the performance of his master's work owes no greater duty, unless there has been reliance by the master or by a third person upon a greater undertaking by the servant.

§ 348. Fraud and Duress

An agent who fraudulently makes representations, uses duress, or knowingly assists in the commission of tortious fraud or duress by his principal or by others is subject to liability in tort to the injured person although the fraud or duress occurs in a transaction on behalf of the principal.

§ 348A. Trespass to Land

An agent who enters the land of another is not relieved from liability for trespass by the fact that he acted on account of the principal and reasonably believed that the principal had possession or the right to possession of the land, or the right to authorize the agent to enter.

§ 349. Conversion

An agent who does acts which would otherwise constitute trespass to or conversion of a chattel is not relieved from liability by the fact that he acts on account of his principal and reasonably, although mistakenly, believes that the principal is entitled to possession of the chattels.

§ 350. Negligent Action

An agent is subject to liability if, by his acts, he creates an unreasonable risk of harm to the interests of others protected against negligent invasion.

§ 351. Directing or Permitting Negligent Conduct of Others

An agent who directs or permits conduct of another under such circumstances that he should realize that there is an unreasonable risk of physical harm to others or to their belongings is subject to liability for harm resulting from a risk which his direction or permission creates.

§ 352. Agent's Failure to Perform Duties to Principal; In General

An agent is not liable for harm to a person other than his principal because of his failure adequately to perform his duties to his principal, unless physical harm results from reliance upon performance of the duties by the agent, or unless the agent has taken control of land or other tangible things.

§ 353. Failure to Act Intending to Cause Physical Harm

An agent entrusted by his principal with a duty to act for the protection of others or their tangible things is subject to liability to such others for physical harm caused to them or to their things by his assumption of duty and subsequent unprivileged failure so to act intending harm to result, if the result would not have happened but for his assumption of the duty.

§ 354. Agent's Negligent Failure After Undertaking Protection of Others

An agent who, by promise or otherwise, undertakes to act for his principal under such circumstances that some action is necessary for the protection of the person or tangible things of another, is subject to liability to the other for physical harm to him or to his things caused by the reliance of the principal or of the other upon his undertaking and his subsequent unexcused failure to act, if such failure creates an unreasonable risk of harm to him and the agent should so realize.

Caveat:

If the agent has not entered upon performance, it is not clear that liability will result from the agent's subsequent failure of performance.

§ 355. Agent as Custodian

An agent who has the custody of land or chattels and who should realize that there is an undue risk that their condition will cause harm to the person, land, or chattels of others is subject to liability for such harm caused during the continuance of his custody, by his failure to use care to take such reasonable precautions as he is authorized to take.

§ 356. Agent in Control of Third Persons

An agent who has taken control over the conduct of another who, as he should realize, is likely to cause physical harm to the person or tangible belongings of third persons unless the conduct of the other is controlled, is under a duty to use reasonable care to take such measures of control as he is authorized to take.

§ 357. Conduct Causing Harm to Pecuniary Interests of Third Persons

An agent who intentionally or negligently fails to perform duties to his principal is not thereby liable to a person whose economic interests are thereby harmed.

§ 358. Liability for Conduct of Other Agents

(1) The agent of a disclosed or partially disclosed principal is not subject to liability for the conduct of other agents unless he is at fault in appointing, supervising, or cooperating with them.

(2) An agent employing servants or other agents for the principal not revealing to them the existence of the principal, is subject to liability to third persons for their torts as is any other principal; if he reveals the existence of a principal to them, but not to third persons, he is subject to liability for their torts only to persons who have dealt with such agents in reliance upon their apparent employment.

§ 359. Liability to Other Agents

The liability of a servant or other agent to a fellow servant or other agent employed by the employer is the same as to third persons.

§ 359A. Liability of Agents for Crimes

A servant or other agent is not relieved from criminal liability for conduct otherwise a crime because of a command by his principal.

TOPIC 4. SUBSEQUENT EVENTS

§ 359B. Dealings and Actions Between Injured Party and Principal

The liability of an agent for tortious conduct for which his principal is liable may be affected by:

(a) dealings between the injured party and the principal, or

(b) a judgment for or against the principal.

§ 359C. Joinder of Principal and Agent

(1) Principal and agent can be joined in one action for a wrong resulting from the tortious conduct of an agent or that of agent and principal, and a judgment can issue against each.

(2) If the action is based solely upon the tortious conduct of the agent, a judgment on the merits for the agent and against the principal, or a smaller judgment for compensatory damages against the agent than against the principal, is erroneous.

§ 360. Effect of Ratification

Ratification releases a purported agent from liability to a third person for conduct which was tortious with respect to him only because the agent had no power to bind the principal thereby; ratification does not release the agent from liability for conduct which would have been tortious although authorized.

TOPIC 5. SERVANTS, SUBSERVANTS AND OTHER SUBAGENTS

§ 361. Liability of Servants, Subservants and Other Subagents

The rules as to the liability of agents to third persons are applicable to the liability of servants, subservants and other subagents.

§ 362. Liability of Agent for Conduct of Servants, Subservants and Other Subagents

The liability of an agent to third persons for the conduct of his servants, subservants and other subagents is the same as that of a master or other principal for the conduct of his servants and other agents.

Chapter 12

LIABILITY OF THIRD PERSON TO AGENT

TOPIC 1. ACTIONS BY AGENT ON BEHALF OF PRINCIPAL

TITLE A. WHEN AGENT CAN SUE IN HIS OWN

§ 363. Contracts; General Rule

An agent who makes a contract on behalf of a principal cannot maintain an action thereon in his own name on behalf of the principal although authorized by the principal to bring suit, unless the agent is a promisee or transferee.

§ 364. Contracts; Agent a Party Promisee

A person with whom an agent makes a contract on behalf of a principal is subject to liability in an action brought thereon by the agent in his own name on behalf of the principal if the agent is a party promisee.

§ 365. Agent as Transferee of Contract

Subject to defenses, an agent to whom a negotiable instrument or other contract has been transferred can maintain an action upon it for the principal's benefit as any other transferee can do, unless this is prevented by statutes providing that only the real party in interest can maintain an action.

§ 366. Rescission or Reformation of Contracts

The other party to a contract of which the agent is a party promisee is subject to liability in an action brought by the agent in his own name on behalf of the principal for its rescission or reformation, or in other actions based upon its rescission.

§ 367. Possessory Actions

A person who tortiously interferes with the possession or right to possession of chattels held by an agent on behalf of his principal is subject to liability in an action brought by the agent in his own name.

§ 367A. Misdelivery by Agent

An agent authorized to deliver goods for his principal to a third person and who by mistake delivers them to one not entitled to them can maintain an action against such person for their recovery or value.

TITLE B. DEFENSES

§ 368. General Rule

In an action brought by an agent in his own name on behalf of his principal, the other party to the contract has all the defenses which would be available to him if the action were brought by the principal, except procedural defenses based upon the personal inability of the principal to maintain the action or, in the case of contracts, defenses based upon the fact that the principal is excluded as a party thereto by its form or terms.

§ 369. Agent Who Has Acted Without Authority

A person who, without power to do so, purports to bind a disclosed or partially disclosed principal as a party to a contract cannot, even though he is a party thereto and offers to perform it, maintain an action thereon against the other party to it, unless the purported principal ratifies it.

§ 370. Agent Without Authority to Maintain Suit

In an action upon a contract brought by an agent for the benefit of the principal, it is a defense that the agent does not have authority from the principal to sue or to continue the action.

§ 371. Set-Off Against Agent

In an action upon a contract brought by an agent for the benefit of a disclosed or partially disclosed principal, the other party to the contract can set off claims which he could set off against the principal if the action were brought by him; and only such claims.

TOPIC 2. ACTIONS BY AGENT ON HIS OWN BEHALF

§ 372. Agent as Owner of Contract Right

(1) Unless otherwise agreed, an agent who has or who acquires an interest in a contract which he makes on behalf of his principal can,

although not a promisee, maintain such action thereon as might a transferee having a similar interest.

(2) An agent does not have such an interest in a contract as to entitle him to maintain an action at law upon it in his own name merely because he is entitled to a portion of the proceeds as compensation for making it or because he is liable for its breach.

§ 373. Actions for Restitution

A person to whom an agent delivers money or goods belonging to his principal, or on account of his principal, is subject to liability to the agent for their retention if such person is thereby unjustly enriched at the expense of the agent.

§ 374. Actions of Tort by Agents Against Third Persons

(1) The fact that an act, otherwise a tort upon an agent, is committed by another while the agent is conducting the affairs of the principal, or because of the agency relation, does not prevent the agent from maintaining an action against the other on his own account.

(2) A servant or other agent has no action of tort because another has tortiously harmed the principal or destroyed his business, unless the other acted for the purpose of harming the agent's interests.

(3) A servant or other agent has a cause of action against one who, without privilege, purposely causes the principal not to perform his contract of employment or not to continue the employment.

§ 375. Defenses

(1) An agent who acquires the beneficial interest in a contract which he has made or purported to make for a principal is subject to the same defenses by the other party thereto, as is any assignee of such contract.

(2) The agreement of an agent with another, in violation of his duties of loyalty to his principal, is unenforceable.

Chapter 13

DUTIES AND LIABILITIES OF AGENT TO PRINCIPAL

TOPIC 1. DUTIES

TITLE A. EFFECT OF MANIFESTATIONS OF CONSENT BETWEEN PRINCIPAL AND AGENT

§ 376. General Rule

The existence and extent of the duties of the agent to the principal are determined by the terms of the agreement between the parties, interpreted in light of the circumstances under which it is made, except to the extent that fraud, duress, illegality, or the incapacity of one or both of the parties to the agreement modifies it or deprives it of legal effect.

TITLE B. DUTIES OF SERVICE AND OBEDIENCE

§ 377. Contractual Duties

A person who makes a contract with another to perform services as an agent for him is subject to a duty to act in accordance with his promise.

§ 378. Gratuitous Undertakings

One who, by a gratuitous promise or other conduct which he should realize will cause another reasonably to rely upon the performance of definite acts of service by him as the other's agent, causes the other to refrain from having such acts done by other available means is subject to a duty to use care to perform such service or, while other means are available, to give notice that he will not perform.

Caveat:

When the gratuitous agent has not entered upon performance, it is not clear that liability will be imposed.

§ 379. Duty of Care and Skill

(1) Unless otherwise agreed, a paid agent is subject to a duty to the principal to act with standard care and with the skill which is standard in the locality for the kind of work which he is employed to perform and, in addition, to exercise any special skill that he has.

(2) Unless otherwise agreed, a gratuitous agent is under a duty to the principal to act with the care and skill which is required of persons not agents performing similar gratuitous undertakings for others.

§ 380. Duty of Good Conduct

Unless otherwise agreed, an agent is subject to a duty not to conduct himself with such impropriety that he brings disrepute upon the principal or upon the business in which he is engaged. If the service involves personal relations, he has a duty not to act in such a way as to make continued friendly relations with the principal impossible.

§ 381. Duty to Give Information

Unless otherwise agreed, an agent is subject to a duty to use reasonable efforts to give his principal information which is relevant to affairs entrusted to him and which, as the agent has notice, the principal would desire to have and which can be communicated without violating a superior duty to a third person.

§ 382. Duty to Keep and Render Accounts

Unless otherwise agreed, an agent is subject to a duty to keep, and render to his principal, an account of money or other things which he has received or paid out on behalf of the principal.

§ 383. Duty to Act Only as Authorized

Except when he is privileged to protect his own or another's interests, an agent is subject to a duty to the principal not to act in the principal's affairs except in accordance with the principal's manifestation of consent.

§ 384. Duty not to Attempt the Impossible or Impracticable

Unless otherwise agreed, an agent is subject to a duty to the principal not to continue to render service which subjects the principal to risk of expense if it reasonably appears to him to be impossible or impracticable for him to accomplish the objects of the principal and if he cannot communicate with the principal.

§ 385. Duty to Obey

(1) Unless otherwise agreed, an agent is subject to a duty to obey all reasonable directions in regard to the manner of performing a service that he has contracted to perform.

(2) Unless he is privileged to protect his own or another's interests, an agent is subject to a duty not to act in matters entrusted to him on account of the principal contrary to the directions of the principal, even though the terms of the employment prescribe that such directions shall not be given.

§ 386. Duties After Termination of Authority

Unless otherwise agreed, an agent is subject to a duty not to act as such after the termination of his authority.

TITLE C. DUTIES OF LOYALTY

§ 387. General Principle

Unless otherwise agreed, an agent is subject to a duty to his principal to act solely for the benefit of the principal in all matters connected with his agency.

§ 388. Duty to Account for Profits Arising Out of Employment

Unless otherwise agreed, an agent who makes a profit in connection with transactions conducted by him on behalf of the principal is under a duty to give such profit to the principal.

§ 389. Acting as Adverse Party Without Principal's Consent

Unless otherwise agreed, an agent is subject to a duty not to deal with his principal as an adverse party in a transaction connected with his agency without the principal's knowledge.

§ 390. Acting as Adverse Party with Principal's Consent

An agent who, to the knowledge of the principal, acts on his own account in a transaction in which he is employed has a duty to deal fairly with the principal and to disclose to him all facts which the agent knows or should know would reasonably affect the principal's judgment, unless the principal has manifested that he knows such facts or that he does not care to know them.

§ 391. Acting for Adverse Party Without Principal's Consent

Unless otherwise agreed, an agent is subject to a duty to his principal not to act on behalf of an adverse party in a transaction connected with his agency without the principal's knowledge.

Comment b. Where act not inconsistent with agent's duty. An agent can properly deal with the other party to a transaction if such dealing is not inconsistent with his duties to the principal. Thus, an agent employed to sell can properly lend money to the buyer to complete the purchase or he may "split" his commission with the buyer, unless because of business policy or otherwise it is understood that he is not to do so.

§ 392. Acting for Adverse Party with Principal's Consent

An agent who, to the knowledge of two principals, acts for both of them in a transaction between them, has a duty to act with fairness to each and to disclose to each all facts which he knows or should know would reasonably affect the judgment of each in permitting such dual agency, except as to a principal who has manifested that he knows such facts or does not care to know them.

§ 393. Competition as to Subject Matter of Agency

Unless otherwise agreed, an agent is subject to a duty not to compete with the principal concerning the subject matter of his agency.

§ 394. Acting for One with Conflicting Interests

Unless otherwise agreed, an agent is subject to a duty not to act or to agree to act during the period of his agency for persons whose interests conflict with those of the principal in matters in which the agent is employed.

§ 395. Using or Disclosing Confidential Information

Unless otherwise agreed, an agent is subject to a duty to the principal not to use or to communicate information confidentially given him by the principal or acquired by him during the course of or on account of his agency or in violation of his duties as agent, in competition with or to the injury of the principal, on his own account or on behalf of another, although such information does not relate to the transaction in which he is then employed, unless the information is a matter of general knowledge.

§ 396. Using Confidential Information After Termination of Agency

Unless otherwise agreed, after the termination of the agency, the agent:

(a) has no duty not to compete with the principal;

(b) has a duty to the principal not to use or to disclose to third persons, on his own account or on account of others, in competition with the principal or to his injury, trade secrets, written lists of names, or other similar confidential matters given to him only for the principal's use or acquired by the agent in violation of duty. The agent is entitled to use general information concerning the method of business of the principal and the names of the customers retained in his memory, if not acquired in violation of his duty as agent;

(c) has a duty to account for profits made by the sale or use of trade secrets and other confidential information, whether or not in competition with the principal;

(d) has a duty to the principal not to take advantage of a still subsisting confidential relation created during the prior agency relation.

§ 397. When Agent Has Right to Patents

Unless otherwise agreed, a person employed by another to do noninventive work is entitled to patents which are the result of his invention although the invention is due to the work for which he is employed.

§ 398. Confusing or Appearing to Own Principal's Things

Unless otherwise agreed, an agent receiving or holding things on behalf of the principal is subject to a duty to the principal not to receive or deal with them so that they will appear to be his own, and not so to mingle them with his own things as to destroy their identity.

TOPIC 2. LIABILITIES

§ 399. Remedies of Principal

A principal whose agent has violated or threatens to violate his duties has an appropriate remedy for such violation. Such remedy may be:

(a) an action on the contract of service;

(b) an action for losses and for the misuse of property;

(c) an action in equity to enforce the provisions of an express trust undertaken by the agent;

(d) an action for restitution, either at law or in equity;

(e) an action for an accounting;

(f) an action for an injunction;

(g) set-off or counterclaim;

(h) causing the agent to be made party to an action brought by a third person against the principal;

(i) self-help;

(j) discharge; or

(k) refusal to pay compensation or rescission of the contract of employment.

§ 400. Liability for Breach of Contract

An agent who commits a breach of his contract with his principal is subject to liability to the principal in accordance with the principles stated in the Restatement of Contracts.

§ 401. Liability for Loss Caused

An agent is subject to liability for loss caused to the principal by any breach of duty.

§ 402. Liability for Misuse of Principal's Property

(1) An agent is subject to liability to the principal for the value of a chattel, a chose in action, or money which he holds for the principal and to the immediate possession of which the principal is entitled, together with interest thereon if the amount is liquidated, or damages, if the agent:

(a) intentionally or negligently destroys it or causes its loss;

(b) uses it for his own purposes under an adverse claim;

(c) unreasonably refuses to surrender it on demand;

(d) manifests that he will not surrender it except on conditions which he is not privileged to exact;

(e) makes delivery of it to a person to whom he is not authorized to deliver it;

(f) improperly causes the title or indicia of title to be placed in his own name, if either this is done in bad faith or the thing substantially depreciates in value while the title is so held because of his wrongful conduct;

(g) deviates substantially from his authority in its transfer to a third person in a sale or purchase; or

(h) intentionally and substantially deviates from his authority in dealing with the possession of the thing, and the chattel suffers substantial harm during the course of such wrongful dealing or because of it.

(2) An agent who deviates substantially from his authority in the transfer of land belonging to the principal or who, in bad faith, causes the title of such land to be placed in his own name, is subject to liability to the principal for the value of the land.

§ 403. Liability for Things Received in Violation of Duty of Loyalty

If an agent receives anything as a result of his violation of a duty of loyalty to the principal, he is subject to a liability to deliver it, its value, or its proceeds, to the principal.

§ 404. Liability for Use of Principal's Assets

An agent who, in violation of duty to his principal, uses for his own purposes or those of a third person assets of the principal's business is subject to liability to the principal for the value of the use. If the use predominates in producing a profit he is subject to liability, at the principal's election, for such profit; he is not, however, liable for profits made by him merely by the use of time which he has contracted to devote to the principal unless he violates his duty not to act adversely or in competition with the principal.

§ 404A. Restitutional Liability of Agent to Principal

Although the agent has committed no breach of duty to the principal, he is liable in an action for restitution for any enrichment which it is unjust for him to retain.

§ 405. Liability for Conduct of Other Agents

(1) Except as stated in Subsections (2) and (3), an agent is not subject to liability to the principal for the conduct of other agents who are not his subagents.

(2) An agent is subject to liability to the principal if, having a duty to appoint or to supervise other agents, he has violated his duty through lack of care or otherwise in the appointment or supervision, and harm thereby results to the principal in a foreseeable manner. He is also subject to liability if he directs, permits, or otherwise takes part in the improper conduct of other agents.

(3) An agent is subject to liability to a principal for the failure of another agent to perform a service which he and such other have jointly contracted to perform for the principal.

§ 406. Liability for Conduct of Subagent

Unless otherwise agreed, an agent is responsible to the principal for the conduct of a subservant or other subagent with reference to the principal's affairs entrusted to the subagent, as the agent is for his own conduct; and as to other matters, as a principal is for the conduct of a servant or other agent.

Comment b. An agent who employs a subagent is the latter's principal and is responsible both to third persons (see § 362) and to his principal for the subagent's derelictions. Thus the agent is subject to liability to the principal for harm to the principal's property or business caused by the subagent's negligence or other wrong to the principal's interests. The agent is also under a duty to indemnify the principal for payments made by the latter to third persons resulting from the agent's misrepresentations or other tortious conduct or from transactions binding the principal but beyond the authority of the subagent.

§ 407. Principal's Choice of Remedies

(1) If an agent has received a benefit as a result of violating his duty of loyalty, the principal is entitled to recover from him what he has so received, its value, or its proceeds, and also the amount of damage thereby caused; except that, if the violation consists of the wrongful disposal of the principal's property, the principal cannot recover its value and also what the agent received in exchange therefor.

(2) A principal who has recovered damages from a third person because of an agent's violation of his duty of loyalty is entitled nevertheless to obtain from the agent any profit which the agent improperly received as a result of the transaction.

§ 408. Liability Created by Principal's Ratification

The ratification of the act of a purported agent subjects him to liability to account to the person for whom he intended or purported to act for profits made by him to which the purported principal would have been entitled if the act had been authorized.

§ 409. When Principal Can Properly Terminate Employment; Condonation

(1) A principal is privileged to discharge before the time fixed by the contract of employment an agent who has committed such a violation of duty that his conduct constitutes a material breach of contract or who, without committing a violation of duty, fails to perform or reasonably appears to be unable to perform a material part of the promised service, because of physical or mental disability.

(2) The election by the principal not to discharge the agent for a breach of duty does not of itself release the agent from liability for loss caused by the breach nor, if the agent commits subsequent breaches of duty, is the principal prevented from electing subsequently to treat the first breach as cause for discharge.

TOPIC 3. DEFENSES

§ 410. Incapacity of Agent

Whether or not an agent who lacks full capacity is subject to liability to the principal for conduct which, but for such lack of capacity, would be a breach of duty, depends upon the extent of his incapacity and the character of his conduct.

§ 411. Illegality as a Defense for Nonperformance of Service

In accordance with and subject to the conditions stated in the Restatement of Contracts, one who undertakes to perform service as the agent of another is not liable for failing to perform such service if, at the time of the undertaking or of performance, such service is illegal.

§ 412. Criminality as Defense for Failure to Account

(1) Except as stated in Subsections (2) and (3), the fact that money or other thing received by the agent from or on behalf of the principal is the proceeds of a crime by the principal or by another, or was given to

the agent to accomplish an unlawful purpose, does not relieve the agent from a duty to account for it or its proceeds.

(2) An agent who has received money or other thing from or on behalf of the principal is under no duty to deliver the same to the principal or to account for the use thereof:

(a) if the delivery to the principal would be, or would aid in, the commission of a criminal act; or

(b) if the thing was obtained by the agent without his fraud, duress, or undue influence, and

(i) the thing was given for the purpose of accomplishing a very serious crime, or

(ii) a crime involving more than a minor offense has been accomplished by the delivery to the agent of the thing or by its use.

(3) An agent who has received the proceeds or profits of an act committed by him on behalf of and at the direction of the principal and for which the principal is criminally responsible is under no duty to deliver them to the principal if the crime is more than a minor offense.

§ 413. Impossibility as Defense

Subject to and in accordance with the rules stated in the Restatement of Contracts, an agent is under no duty to render services, the performance of which is impossible or impracticable if, when he promises to perform them, he has no reason to know that they are then impossible or impracticable or to anticipate that they will become such before the time for performance.

§ 414. Statutes of Frauds as Defense

(1) If a statute provides that no action shall be brought upon an agreement not capable of performance within a year unless the promise is in writing signed by the party to be charged, a person who orally promises to act as an agent for a period which cannot terminate within a year from the promise is not thereby subject to liability in an action upon the agreement for a failure to perform it.

(2) Although a statute requires the creation of a trust in land or other thing to be manifested and proved by a writing signed by the party to be charged, an agent who is authorized and who agrees orally to acquire such thing for the principal, and who acquires it in his own name, holds the thing thus acquired upon a constructive or resulting trust for the principal.

(3) If the principal is not bound to compensate the agent for his services because the principal has not signed a memorandum as required by a statute, the agent is not liable for failing to render promised

services if, having been requested to do so, the principal refuses to sign a memorandum.

§ 415. Principal's Contributory Fault as Defense

The liability of the agent to the principal can be avoided, terminated, or reduced by a breach of contract by the principal, his contributory fault, or his failure to mitigate damages.

§ 416. Ratification or Affirmance as Defense

The ratification or other affirmance by the principal of an unauthorized act done by an agent acting in excess of his power to bind the principal releases the agent from liability in damages to the principal for having violated a duty to him, except when the principal:

(a) is obliged to affirm the act in order to protect his own interests; or

(b) is caused to ratify by the misrepresentation or duress of the agent.

§ 417. Rights of Third Persons as Defense

An agent who has received anything on account of his principal cannot defeat the claim of the principal upon the ground that a third person has a right superior to the principal's unless:

(a) the agent has been divested of it by, or has delivered it to, the holder of the paramount title; or

(b) the title of the principal has terminated after receipt by the agent, by a voluntary transfer or otherwise; or

(c) the agent interpleads the third person.

§ 418. Privilege of Agent to Protect His Own Interests

An agent is privileged to protect interests of his own which are superior to those of the principal, even though he does so at the expense of the principal's interests or in disobedience to his orders.

§ 419. Discharge by Release or Contract

An agent who has committed a breach of duty to the principal is discharged from liability by an effective release given by the principal or a contract with the principal having the effect of a discharge.

§ 420. Judicial Declaration of Insolvency or Bankruptcy of Agent

(1) The agent's bankruptcy or a judicial declaration of insolvency may discharge him from liability to the principal.

(2) The rights of the principal in property held for him by the agent or held by the agent in breach of trust are not affected by the agent's bankruptcy or discharge in insolvency proceedings.

§ 421. Set–Off and Counterclaim

Rights of set-off or counterclaim may be available to an agent in an action brought against him by the principal.

§ 421A. Other Events Terminating or Diminishing Agent's Liability

The principal's cause of action against the agent may be terminated or diminished because of:

(a) the rules as to the effect of judgments;

(b) the discharge of or satisfaction of a claim against a co-obligor;

(c) the statute of limitations; or

(d) laches.

TOPIC 4. DUTIES AND LIABILITIES OF PARTICULAR KINDS OF AGENTS

§ 422. Agents in Charge of Land or Chattels

Unless otherwise agreed, an agent who has charge of land or chattels for his principal is subject to a duty to the principal to use reasonable care in their protection, to use them only in accordance with the directions of the principal and for his benefit, and to surrender them upon demand or upon the termination of the agency.

§ 423. Agents Holding a Title

Unless otherwise agreed, an agent who holds the title to something for the principal is subject to a duty to the principal to use reasonable care in the protection of the title which he so holds, to act in accordance with the directions of the principal, to use it only for the principal's benefit, and to transfer it upon demand or upon the termination of the agency.

§ 424. Agents to Buy or to Sell

Unless otherwise agreed, an agent employed to buy or to sell is subject to a duty to the principal, within the limits set by the principal's directions, to be loyal to the principal's interests and to use reasonable care to obtain terms which best satisfy the manifested purposes of the principal.

§ 425. Agents to Make Investments

Unless otherwise agreed, an agent employed to make or to manage investments has a duty to the principal:

(a) to use care to invest promptly;

(b) to invest only in such securities as would be obtained by a prudent investor for his own account, having in view both safety and income, in the light of the principal's means and purposes; and

(c) to change investments in accordance with changes in the security of the investments or the condition of the principal, if his duties include management.

§ 426. Agents to Make Collections

Unless otherwise agreed, an agent employed to collect from others goods or money due the principal has a duty of using reasonable care and skill in making such collections in accordance with the directions of the principal.

§ 427. Agents Who Have Made Collections

Unless otherwise agreed, an agent who has received goods or money for the principal has a duty to use care to keep them safely until they are remitted or delivered to the principal, and to deliver them to the principal upon his demand when the amount due him has been ascertained. The agent may also have a duty to use care to notify the principal of the collection, or to remit the goods or money to him within a reasonable time.

§ 428. Subservants and Other Subagents

(1) Unless otherwise agreed, a subagent who knows of the existence of the ultimate principal owes him the duties owed by an agent to a principal, except the duties dependent upon the existence of a contract.

(2) Unless otherwise agreed, a subagent owes the agent the duties of an agent to his principal.

(3) The rules stated in Subsections (1) and (2) apply to a subservant.

Comment b. Loyalty to principal and agent. The subagent is subject to a duty, as is the agent (see § 385), not to act contrary to what he knows to be the principal's orders. Although he has a duty of loyalty and obedience to the agent who is his immediate principal, the subagent is subject to liability to the ultimate principal for participating in a breach of duty by the agent to the principal if he has notice that the agent's conduct constitutes a breach of duty. He also may be subject to liability for unauthorized dealing with the principal's lands or chattels under the rule stated in Section 402; his justifiable mistake as to the power of his superior, the agent, to bind the principal does not necessarily excuse him.

The subagent has the delegable privileges of the agent, so that, in a conflict of interests between the agent and the principal, the subagent is both entitled and required to prefer the interests of the agent if, under the circumstances, the agent would be entitled to prefer his own interests to those of the principal.

§ 429. Servants

The rules as to the duties and liabilities to the principal of agents who are not servants apply to servants.

§ 430. Purported Agents

One who, without the consent or manifestation of consent of another, purports to act as the agent for such other is subject to liability for loss occasioned to the other by such conduct or for the value of anything belonging to the purported principal which he has improperly used. If the other ratifies, the liability of the purported agent to the other is the same as if he originally had been an agent who had acted without authority and whose conduct the principal ratified.

§ 431. Agents and Subagents Employed for Undisclosed Principal

(1) If an agent employs another agent for an undisclosed principal, the person so employed is subject to liability to the principal for a failure to perform duties due to the employing agent, in accordance with the rules generally applicable to undisclosed principals.

(2) If an agent employs a subagent to perform services for an undisclosed principal, the subagent is as subject to liability to the principal for his conduct as if the principal were disclosed, except that, until his discovery of the principal's existence, conduct which is privileged as to the agent is privileged as to the principal.

(3) The rules stated in Subsections (1) and (2) as to agents and subagents apply to servants and subservants employed by the agent.

Chapter 14

DUTIES AND LIABILITIES OF PRINCIPAL TO AGENT

TOPIC 1. CONTRACTUAL AND RESTITUTIONAL DUTIES AND LIABILITIES

TITLE A. INTERPRETATION OF CONTRACTS AND LIABILITIES THEREUNDER

§ 432. Duty to Perform Contract

A principal is subject to a duty to an agent to perform the contract which he has made with the agent.

§ 433. Duty to Furnish Opportunity for Work

A principal does not, by contracting to employ an agent, thereby promise to provide him with an opportunity for work, but the circumstances under which the agreement for employment is made or the nature of the employment may warrant an inference of such a promise.

§ 434. Duty not to Interfere with Agent's Work

A principal who has contracted to afford an agent an opportunity to work has a duty to refrain from unreasonably interfering with his work.

§ 435. Duty to Give Agent Information

Unless otherwise agreed, it is inferred that a principal contracts to use care to inform the agent of risks of physical harm or pecuniary loss which, as the principal has reason to know, exist in the performance of authorized acts and which he has reason to know are unknown to the agent. His duty to give other information depends upon the agreement between them.

§ 436. Duty to Keep and Render Accounts

Unless otherwise agreed, a master has a duty to keep and render accounts of the amount due from him to a servant; whether principals of other agents have such a duty depends upon the method of compensation, the fact that the agent operates or does not operate an independent enterprise, the customs of business and other similar factors.

§ 437. Duty of Good Conduct

Unless otherwise agreed, a principal who has contracted to employ an agent has a duty to conduct himself so as not to harm the agent's reputation nor to make it impossible for the agent, consistently with his reasonable self-respect or personal safety, to continue in the employment.

§ 438. Duty of Indemnity; The Principle

(1) A principal is under a duty to indemnify the agent in accordance with the terms of the agreement with him.

(2) In the absence of terms to the contrary in the agreement of employment, the principal has a duty to indemnify the agent where the agent

(a) makes a payment authorized or made necessary in executing the principal's affairs or, unless he is officious, one beneficial to the principal, or

(b) suffers a loss which, because of their relation, it is fair that the principal should bear.

§ 439. When Duty of Indemnity Exists

Unless otherwise agreed, a principal is subject to a duty to exonerate an agent who is not barred by the illegality of his conduct to indemnify him for:

(a) authorized payments made by the agent on behalf of the principal;

(b) payments upon contracts upon which the agent is authorized to make himself liable, and upon obligations arising from the possession or ownership of things which he is authorized to hold on account of the principal;

(c) payments of damages to third persons which he is required to make on account of the authorized performance of an act which constitutes a tort or a breach of contract;

(d) expenses of defending actions by third persons brought because of the agent's authorized conduct, such actions being unfounded but not brought in bad faith; and

(e) payments resulting in benefit to the principal, made by the agent under such circumstances that it would be inequitable for indemnity not to be made.

§ 440. When No Duty of Indemnity

Unless otherwise agreed, the principal is not subject to a duty to indemnify an agent:

(a) for pecuniary loss or other harm, not of benefit to the principal, arising from the performance of unauthorized acts or resulting solely from the agent's negligence or other fault; or

(b) if the principal has otherwise performed his duties to the agent, for physical harm caused by the performance of authorized acts, for harm suffered as a result of torts, other than the tortious institution of suits, committed upon the agent by third persons because of his employment, or for harm suffered by the refusal of third persons to deal with him; or

(c) if the agent's loss resulted from an enterprise which he knew to be illegal.

§ 441. Duty to Pay Compensation

Unless the relation of the parties, the triviality of the services, or other circumstances, indicate that the parties have agreed otherwise, it is inferred that a person promises to pay for services which he requests or permits another to perform for him as his agent.

§ 442. Period of Employment

Unless otherwise agreed, mutual promises by principal and agent to employ and to serve create obligations to employ and to serve which are terminable upon notice by either party; if neither party terminates the employment, it may terminate by lapse of time or by supervening events.

§ 442A. Death or Incapacity of Principal or Agent

(1) Unless otherwise agreed, the death of either principal or agent terminates the liabilities for nonperformance of a contract of employment.

(2) Unless otherwise agreed, the mental incapacity of the principal, or the mental or physical incapacity of the agent, to perform services, terminates the liabilities for nonperformance of a contract of employment.

§ 443. Amount of Compensation

If the contract of employment provides for compensation to the agent, he is entitled to receive for the full performance of the agreed service:

(a) the definite amount agreed upon and no more, if the agreement is definite as to amount; or

(b) the fair value of his services, if there is no agreement for a definite amount.

§ 444. Compensation for Extra Services

If an agent is employed for specified hours or for specified work at a specified rate, and upon request he performs services outside of the agreed hours or performs other than the agreed services, it is inferred that he is not to receive compensation for such additional services, unless his compensation is based upon the number of his working hours, or for such different services, unless his compensation is based upon the results which he accomplishes.

§ 445. Compensation Dependent Upon Specified Result

Except where there is revocation in bad faith, an agent whose compensation is conditional upon the performance by him of specified services, or his accomplishment of a specified result, is not entitled to the agreed compensation unless he renders the specified services or achieves the result.

§ 446. Compensation Dependent Upon Specified Result in Limited Time

An agent whose compensation is conditional upon his performance of specified services or his accomplishment of a specified result within a specified time is not entitled to the agreed compensation unless he renders the services or achieves the result within such time, unless the principal, in bad faith, has prevented him from doing so.

§ 447. Compensation Dependent Upon Securing Specified Price or Other Terms

An agent whose compensation is conditional upon procuring a transaction on specified terms is not entitled to such compensation if, as a result of his efforts, a transaction is effected on different or modified terms, although the principal thereby benefits.

§ 448. Compensation; Agent as Effective Cause

An agent whose compensation is conditional upon his accomplishment of a specified result is entitled to the agreed compensation if, and only if, he is the effective cause of accomplishing the result.

§ 449. Compensation When Principal Competes

The principal does not, by contracting to pay compensation contingent upon the agent's success in accomplishing a definite result, thereby promise that he will not compete either personally or through another agent.

§ 450. Duty not to Terminate Employment

A principal has a duty not to repudiate or terminate the employment in violation of the contract of employment.

§ 451. Compensation and Indemnity for Acts Performed After Termination

Unless otherwise agreed, upon termination of the agency relation, whether or not in breach of contract by either party, the principal has no duty to compensate the agent for subsequent services or to indemnify him for obligations subsequently assumed, unless otherwise the principal would be unjustly enriched.

§ 452. Compensation Upon Termination Without Breach by Either Party; Services Part of Agreed Exchange

Unless otherwise agreed, if the principal has contracted to pay the agent for his services and the relation terminates without breach of contract by either party, the principal is subject to liability to pay to the agent for services previously performed and which are part of the agreed exchange:

(a) the agreed compensation for services for which compensation is apportioned in the contract; and

(b) the value, not exceeding the agreed ratable compensation, of services for which the compensation is not apportioned.

§ 453. Compensation Upon Termination Without Breach by Either Party; Services Not Part of Agreed Exchange

(1) Unless otherwise agreed, an agent whose compensation is dependent upon the accomplishment of a specified result is not entitled to compensation for services rendered in an unsuccessful effort to accomplish that result before the rightful termination of the agency, although the principal is thereby benefited, if the services are not part of the agreed exchange.

(2) If the agent's compensation is not proportioned to the extent of his efforts in successfully accomplishing the result, it is inferred that his services are not part of the agreed exchange.

§ 454. Revocation in Bad Faith of Offer of Compensation

An agent to whom the principal has made a revocable offer of compensation if he accomplishes a specified result is entitled to the promised amount if the principal, in order to avoid payment of it, revokes the offer and thereafter the result is accomplished as the result of the agent's prior efforts.

§ 455. Damages Where Termination Results From Principal's Breach of Contract

If in violation of the contract of employment, the principal terminates or repudiates the employment, or the agent properly terminates it because of breach of contract by the principal, the agent is entitled at his election to receive either:

(a) the amount of the net losses caused and gains prevented by the principal's breach or, if there are no such losses or gains, a small sum as nominal damages; or

(b) the reasonable value of the services previously rendered the principal, not limited by the contract price, except that for services for which a price is apportioned by the terms of the contract he is entitled to receive the contract price and no more.

§ 456. Revocation for Breach of Contract or Renunciation in Breach of Contract

If a principal properly discharges an agent for breach of contract, or the agent wrongfully renounces the employment, the principal is subject to liability to pay to the agent, with a deduction for the loss caused the principal by the breach of contract:

(a) the agreed compensation for services properly rendered for which the compensation is apportioned in the contract, whether or not the agent's breach is wilful and deliberate; and

(b) the value, not exceeding the agreed ratable compensation, of services properly rendered for which the compensation is not apportioned if, but only if, the agent's breach is not wilful and deliberate.

§ 457. Restitutional Liability Where No Contract or Voidable Contract

A principal for whom an agent has performed services in accordance with a voidable contract which is avoided by one of the parties, or for whom an agent or purported agent has performed services without a promise by the principal to pay, is subject to liability to the agent to the extent that he has been unjustly enriched by such services.

§ 458. Liability of Principal to Subagent

The authorized employment of a subservant or other subagent does not thereby subject the principal to contractual liability to the subagent but the principal is subject to the same tort liability and has the same duty of indemnity to him as to agents directly employed.

§ 459. Liability of Agents to Subagents

An agent who employs a subservant or other subagent has the duties and liabilities of a principal to him.

§ 460. Liability of Undisclosed Principal and Agent to Person Employed by Agent

(1) A principal on whose behalf an agent employs other agents and subagents without disclosing the principal's existence is liable to those thus employed in accordance with the rules which determine the liability of an undisclosed principal to third persons.

(2) The employing agent has the same liabilities to those employed as he would have if acting on his own account.

§ 461. Servants and Subservants

(1) A master as to his servants, and a servant as to his subservants are subject to the same contractual and restitutional duties as to their agents who are not servants.

(2) A master is not subject to contractual liability to a subservant, but he has the same tort and restitutional liability to a subservant as to his other servants.

§ 462. Effect of Ratification

Upon ratification, an agent or other person who without power to bind the principal, has purported to do so is entitled to the same rights against the principal as if the act had been authorized, unless the principal:

(a) is induced to affirm by the misrepresentation or duress of the agent; or

(b) is obliged to affirm in order to protect his own interests.

TITLE B. REMEDIES OF AGENT

§ 463. General Rule

An agent whose principal violates or threatens to violate a contractual or restitutional duty to him has an appropriate remedy. He can, in a proper case:

(a) maintain an action at law;

(b) obtain a decree for an accounting or other equitable relief;

(c) maintain a claim to a set-off or a counterclaim in an action brought by the principal;

(d) refuse to render further services;

(e) exercise the rights of a lien holder; or

(f) stop in transit goods shipped to the principal.

§ 464. When Agent Has Lien

Unless he undertakes duties inconsistent with such a right or otherwise agrees that it is not to exist:

(a) an agent has a right to retain possession of money, goods, or documents of the principal, of which he has gained possession in the proper execution of his agency, until he is paid the amount due him from the principal as compensation for services performed or as indemnity for money advanced or liability incurred by him in connection with such things;

(b) a factor, banker, or attorney-at-law has the further right to retain possession of money, goods, or documents until he is paid the amount due him upon the general balance of accounts created by transactions conducted by him as such factor, banker, or attorney;

(c) a factor who has made advances or incurred liability with respect to goods received by him for sale has a right to sell them contrary to directions of the principal, after notice to the principal, if the reasonable protection of the factor's interest so requires;

(d) an agent to whom goods have been consigned but not received, and who advances money in anticipation of their receipt, has a right to their possession and thereafter, under the circumstances stated in Clauses (a), (b), and (c), to the rights therein stated; and

(e) an attorney of record who has obtained a judgment has an interest therein, as security for his fees in the case and for proper payments made and liabilities incurred during the course of the proceedings.

§ 465. When Subagent Has Lien

(1) Against the agent who employed him, a subagent has a lien under the circumstances under which other agents have liens, subject, however, to the rights of the principal.

(2) Unless otherwise agreed, the lien of a subagent on things of a disclosed or partially disclosed principal is limited to the rights between the principal and the agent, except where the agent bound the principal by a transaction with the subagent in excess of his authority.

(3) Against an undisclosed principal, a subagent has a lien under the same circumstances as if the agent were the principal, except where the agent has acted in excess of his authority.

§ 466. When Agent Has Right of Stoppage in Transit

Unless otherwise agreed, an agent who has a security interest in goods of the principal because of money paid by him for them, liability incurred in their purchase, or advances made to the principal upon their security, is entitled to stop them when in transit to the principal upon learning of the principal's insolvency.

TITLE C. DEFENSES

§ 467. Illegality as Defense

An agent who makes an illegal agreement with the principal to act for him, or whose services for the principal are illegal under the rules stated in the Restatement of Contracts, is entitled neither to compensation for his services nor indemnity for losses sustained by him in performing them, except as therein stated.

§ 468. Statutes of Frauds as Defense

(1) If a statute provides that no action shall be brought upon an agreement not capable of performance within a year unless the promise is in writing signed by the party to be charged, a person who, by a bilateral contract, orally promises to employ another as an agent for such a period that the contract is not capable of performance within a year from the time of the promise, is not thereby liable in an action upon the agreement for failure to perform it.

(2) If a statute provides that a person employing another for a specified purpose shall not be liable to the other for compensation although the other renders the promised performance, unless the employer has signed a memorandum in writing, a person has no duty to pay to another whom he orally employs for such purpose either the promised compensation or the reasonable value of services rendered.

(3) Except as stated in Subsection (2), an agent who has partially or fully performed a contract which is not enforceable because a memorandum thereof has not been signed is entitled to the fair value of services rendered if the principal refuses to perform the contract or to sign a memorandum.

§ 469. Disloyalty or Insubordination as Defense

An agent is entitled to no compensation for conduct which is disobedient or which is a breach of his duty of loyalty; if such conduct constitutes a wilful and deliberate breach of his contract of service, he is not entitled to compensation even for properly performed services for which no compensation is apportioned.

§ 469A. Other Events Terminating or Diminishing Agent's Claim

The claim of the agent against the principal may be terminated or diminished because of:

(a) discharge or release by contract with the principal,

(b) the discharge of the principal in bankruptcy,

(c) set-off or counterclaim,

(d) the rules as to the effect of judgments,

(e) the discharge or satisfaction of claim against a co-obligor,

(f) the statute of limitations,

(g) laches.

TOPIC 2. LIABILITY IN TORT FOR HIS OWN MISCONDUCT

§ 470. General Rule

A principal is subject to the same liability to an agent for his own conduct as he is to third persons for similar conduct, except that a master has nondelegable duties of care with respect to working conditions of his servants.

§ 471. Duty of Warning

A principal is subject to liability in an action of tort for failing to use care to warn an agent of an unreasonable risk involved in the employment, if the principal should realize that it exists and that the agent is likely not to become aware of it, thereby suffering harm.

TOPIC 3. LIABILITY TO AGENTS NOT SERVANTS FOR TORTS OF SERVANTS, OTHER AGENTS, AND CONTRACTORS

§ 472. General Rule

A principal is subject to the same liability to an agent who is not a servant for damage caused by the tortious conduct of his servants, of other agents, and of other persons doing work for him, as he is to third persons.

TOPIC 4. LIABILITY TO SERVANTS FOR TORTS OF SERVANTS, OTHER AGENTS, AND CONTRACTORS

TITLE A. GENERAL RULE

§ 473. Statement of Rule

A master is subject to the same liability to a servant for damage caused by the tortious conduct of his other servants, of his agents who are not servants, and of other persons doing work for him, as he is to third persons, except where he is not liable for the conduct of fellow servants, in accordance with the fellow servant rule and except that he has non-delegable duties of care to servants acting in the scope of employment.

TITLE B. THE FELLOW SERVANT RULE

§ 474. Statement of Rule

A master is not liable to a servant or subservant who, while acting within the scope of his employment or in connection therewith, is injured solely by the negligence of a fellow servant in the performance of acts not involving a violation of the master's non-delegable duties, unless the servant was coerced or deceived into serving, was too young to appreciate the risks, or was employed in violation of statute.

§ 475. Definition of Fellow Servant

Fellow servants are servants employed by the same master in the same enterprise or household and so related in their labor that, because of proximity or otherwise, there is a special risk of harm to one of them if the other is negligent.

§ 476. Fellow Servant Rule; Different Masters

Two servants employed by different masters are not fellow servants, although both servants are engaged upon the same piece of work and are subject to special risks from the negligence of each other.

§ 477. Fellow Servant Rule; Same Enterprise

Servants of the same master are fellow servants only if they are employed in the same enterprise or household.

§ 478. Fellow Servant Rule; Separate Departments

Servants employed in the same enterprise by the same master are not fellow servants unless they are so related in their labor that they are regularly or are likely to be in proximity to each other, or there is a special risk of harm to one of them if the other is negligent; but one may be a fellow servant of another even though the other is employed in a separate department.

§ 479. Fellow Servant Rule; Difference in Rank

One may be a fellow servant of another although the other is a superior or inferior servant.

§ 480. Fellow Servant Rule; Different Services

One may be a fellow servant of another although the two are performing different kinds of work.

§ 481. Fellow Servant Rule; Persons Compelled to Serve

(1) A servant compelled by law or by duress to enter the employment is not subject to the disabilities created by the fellow servant rule.

(2) Compulsion of law to continue in an employment voluntarily entered does not prevent the disabilities of the fellow servant rule from applying.

§ 482. Fellow Servant Rule; Non-Disclosure of Master or of Common Employment

(1) The fellow servant rule does not prevent a servant from having a cause of action against a master for an injury caused by the conduct of another servant employed by the same master if the injured servant, as the master should know, reasonably believes that the person injuring him is employed by a different master.

(2) Servants employed by the agent of an undisclosed principal are subject to the disabilities of the fellow servant rule in actions against the principal for the negligence of other servants employed in the same enterprise.

§ 483. Fellow Servant Rule; Illegal Employment

A servant employed in violation of a statute passed for the protection of the class to which he belongs against the risks arising from the conduct of fellow servants is not subject to the disabilities created by the fellow servant rule.

§ 484. Fellow Servant Rule; Incapacity of Servant

(1) A person too young to appreciate the risks of the employment is not subject to the disabilities created by the fellow servant rule.

(2) The fact that a person does not have capacity to contract does not prevent the application of the fellow servant rule.

§ 485. Fellow Servant Rule; Volunteer Assistants

A person who, without the consent of the master, acts as a servant in assisting a servant to perform the master's business primarily for the purpose of aiding the servant or the business of the master is subject to the disabilities created by the fellow servant rule.

§ 486. Fellow Servant Rule; Time and Place

The immunity of the master from liability to a servant for conduct of a fellow servant continues while the servant:

(a) is acting within the scope of his employment or in connection therewith; or

(b) is upon the premises or vehicle of his master, in connection with the work for which he is employed.

§ 487. Fellow Servant Rule; Assaults

A master is subject to liability to a servant for the unprivileged use of force directed against him, or for defamation, by another servant of the same master, acting within the scope of his authority in the enforcement of commands or in the protection of the principal's interests.

§ 488. Fellow Servant Rule; Belongings of Servants

The immunity created by the fellow servant rule applies not only to physical harm suffered by a servant, but also to damage to implements supplied by and used by him within the scope of his employment.

§ 489. Fellow Servant Rule; Families of Servants

Except in an action by members of a servant's family based upon an injury to him, the disabilities created by the fellow servant rule do not extend to the members of a servant's family who are harmed by another servant of the same master or by such servant himself.

§ 490. Fellow Servant Rule; Third Persons Suffering Loss

(1) The disabilities of the fellow servant rule apply to a person suffering pecuniary loss from harm to a servant caused by a fellow

servant, except a parent of an unemancipated minor employed without the parent's consent.

(2) A parent who has consented to the illegal employment of his minor child cannot recover for harm to the child caused by his fellow servants even though the minor could recover.

§ 491. Fellow Servant Rule; Statutory Modifications

The immunity of the master from liability for the conduct of fellow servants may be diminished or terminated by statute.

TITLE C. NON-DELEGABLE DUTIES OF MASTER

§ 492. General Rule

A master is subject to a duty that care be used either to provide working conditions which are reasonably safe for his servants and subservants, considering the nature of the employment, or to warn them of risks of unsafe conditions which he should realize they may not discover by the exercise of due care.

Caveat:

No opinion is expressed as to whether or not the master is subject to liability to a servant harmed by the intentional failure of a person to whom the master has entrusted the duty of making working conditions safe, if the failure to make safe results from the intention of such person to cause harm.

§ 493. Extent of Duty of Care

In creating and maintaining the conditions of employment, the master has a duty to his servants to have precautions taken which reasonable care, intelligence, and regard for the safety of his servants require.

§ 494. Duty of Care to Children

Except as provided by statute, the standard of care as to working conditions with respect to children is the same as that with respect to adults, but in the application of the standard, the youth and inexperience of the child are considered.

§ 495. Knowledge Which Master is Required to Have

A master is subject to a duty to his servants to conduct his business in the light of knowledge which he has, and of such knowledge as to the conditions likely to harm his servants as persons experienced in the business and having special acquaintance with the subject matter have.

§ 496. Notice to Master of Dangerous Conditions

For the purpose of determining whether or not due care has been used in the performance of the non-delegable duties of the master to his servants, the master has notice of facts affecting the safety of his servants if notice of such facts comes to him, or to a servant or other person whose duty it is to act upon them in the performance of the master's duty to protect his servants.

§ 497. Time When and Place Where Duty Exists

The duty of the master to a servant to furnish reasonably safe conditions exists only while the servant is properly acting within the scope of his employment or while, in connection therewith, he is in a place or vehicle in the control of the master in which he is then required to be by reason of his employment or which has been provided for use incidental to his employment.

§ 498. Applicability of Tort Principles as to Risk and Causation

A master is not subject to liability to a servant harmed by the negligent breach of the master's duty to his servants, unless:

(a) the servant harmed is one to whom the master owed the duty of care;

(b) the harm suffered is within the risk created by the breach of duty; and

(c) the negligent conduct is the responsible cause of the harm.

§ 499. Risks Inherent in Enterprise

A master who has performed his duties of care is not liable to a servant harmed by a risk incident to the nature of the work.

§ 500. Transitory Dangers

The master's liability for unsafe working conditions does not extend to temporary dangerous conditions of which the conduct of fellow servants in the performance of operative details of the work is the sole responsible cause.

§ 501. Structures or Instrumentalities Made by Master

A master who, by his servants, erects structures or manufactures instrumentalities for use in his business is subject to liability to his servants who subsequently occupy or use them in their employment and who are harmed by defects therein which care in the erection or manufacture would have prevented.

§ 502. Structures, Instrumentalities, or Materials Acquired From Others

A master who uses in his business a completed structure, instrumentality, or materials not made by his servants:

(a) is subject to liability for harm caused to his servants by a failure to use reasonable care in the purchase or inspection thereof;

(b) is not subject to liability for harm caused to his servants by unknown defects due to negligence in manufacture or upkeep prior to the time of purchase which reasonable care in the acquisition or inspection thereof would not reveal.

§ 503. Maintenance, Inspection, and Repair

The duty of a master as to working conditions extends to the maintenance, inspection, and repair of the premises in his control upon which his servants are employed and of the implements which they use, and to the control of the conduct of fellow servants with whom they work.

§ 504. Harm Caused by Third Persons or Upon Premises not in Master's Control

The master's duty as to working conditions does not extend to the condition of premises not in his control, or to the conduct of third persons with whom the servants are to be brought into contact during the course of the work, except that he has a duty to disclose dangerous conditions of which he should know.

§ 505. Number and Quality of Servants

The duty of the master as to working conditions includes a duty of care to provide a sufficient number of competent fellow servants so that the conditions of employment are not unreasonably dangerous.

§ 506. General Plan of Work

The duty of the master as to working conditions includes a duty of care so to plan the work that the servants employed therein are not subjected to unreasonable risks.

§ 507. Duty to Provide Supervisors

The duty of the master as to working conditions includes a duty of care to supply competent supervisors of the operative details of the business where this is reasonably necessary to prevent undue risk of harm to his servants in the performance of such details.

§ 508. Duty to Make and Enforce Rules

In work dangerous to servants employed in it unless rules are made for its conduct, the duty of the master as to working conditions includes a duty that care be used to promulgate and enforce suitable rules.

§ 509. Liability for Improper Orders

The duty of the master as to working conditions includes a duty of care as to orders given as acts of management and not in connection with the operative details of the work.

§ 510. Duties to Instruct, Warn, and Give Suitable Work to Servant

The master's duty as to working conditions includes a duty that care be used to give such instruction to servants employed by him as, from what the master should know concerning them and the work they are employed to do, is necessary to prevent unreasonable risk to them and to other servants during the progress of the work, and to give them work suitable to their apparent capacities.

§ 511. Liability for Harm From Forces of Nature

The master's duty as to working conditions includes a duty that care be used to guard against reasonably foreseeable harm from natural forces against which he should know the servants cannot protect themselves.

§ 512. Duty to Protect Endangered or Hurt Employee

(1) If a servant, while acting within the scope of his employment, comes into a position of imminent danger of serious harm and this is known to the master or to a person who has duties of management, the master is subject to liability for a failure by himself or by such person to exercise reasonable care to avert the threatened harm.

(2) If a servant is hurt and thereby becomes helpless when acting within the scope of employment and this is known to the master or to a person having duties of management, the master is subject to liability for his negligent failure or that of such person to give first aid to the servant and to care for him until he can be cared for by others.

§ 513. Liability to Servants Having Duty of Inspection

A master who has satisfied his duties as to warning and the selection of fellow servants is not liable to servants employed to make an inspection for harm caused during such employment by the condition which they were employed to discover.

§ 514. Liability to Servants Completing Things

A servant engaged in continuing the process of manufacture of a structure, instrumentality, or other thing does not have a cause of action against the master because of the negligence of a fellow servant in the prior construction or inspection of such thing, if the master has performed his duties of care as to materials, organization, and the selection of fellow servants.

§ 515. Liability to Servants Manufacturing Their Own Instrumentalities

If a master supplies a group of servants with carefully selected materials out of which they manufacture a structure or appliance to be used by them for temporary construction purposes, the master is not liable to one of them for harm caused during such use by the negligence of another member of the group in its construction, if the master has performed his duties of care as to planning, supervision, and the selection of fellow servants.

§ 516. Liability to Volunteer Assistants of Servants and to Servants of Independent Contractors

The duties of a master to his servants do not extend to those who assist his servants in the performance of the master's work, but who are not his servants.

§ 517. Liability to Lent Servants

A servant knowing that he has been lent by his master to serve another as his servant has the rights of a servant against the second master but not those of a servant against the first.

§ 518. Liability of Apparent Master and Undisclosed Master

(1) One who employs another as his servant is subject to liability to him for unsafe working conditions although the employment is on behalf of an undisclosed principal.

(2) An undisclosed principal is subject to liability for unsafe working conditions to a servant or subservant employed for him by a servant or other agent empowered to employ such servant or subservant.

§ 519. Liability of Master Required to Employ Servants From a Specified Class

The master's liability for unsafe working conditions does not extend to conditions of which the responsible cause is the negligence of a person to whom he is required to confide the control of such conditions and over whose directions he has no control, unless the master has notice of the conditions or of the incompetency of such person.

§ 520. Statutory Duties

A master is subject to liability to his servants for harm caused to them by his failure to perform duties imposed upon him by statute for their protection.

TITLE D. DEFENSES

§ 521. Servant's Assumption of Risk

In the absence of a statute or an agreement to the contrary, a master is not liable to a servant for harm caused by the unsafe state of the premises or other conditions of the employment, if the servant, with knowledge of the facts and understanding of the risks, voluntarily enters or continues in the employment.

§ 522. Assumption of Risk; Master Promises to Make Safe

Unless otherwise agreed, if a master manifests his intention to remedy dangerous conditions of employment for which he would be responsible to servants having no notice of them, he is subject to liability to a servant harmed by such conditions who reasonably believes that the conditions will be made safe, until such time as the servant has reason to believe that the conditions will not be changed.

§ 523. Assumption of Risk; Service Coerced

Although a servant enters or continues in his employment with the knowledge that the conditions of his employment are unsafe, he is not barred from recovery for harm caused by the failure of the employer to make the conditions safe if, at the time when he so enters or remains, he is compelled by law to do so, or if he is coerced to act in the protection of his own interests or of the interests of others by a situation created through a breach of the master's duty.

§ 524. Servant's Assumption of Risks Within Protection of Statutes

Whether or not a servant is barred from recovery against his master because the servant voluntarily encounters a known risk from which a statute requires the master to protect him depends upon the construction placed upon the statute.

§ 525. Servant's Contributory Negligence

A servant harmed by a violation of the master's duty of care is subject to the defense of contributory negligence if his own negligence is a contributing cause of the harm.

§ 526. Servant's Disobedience of Orders

Unless a statute provides otherwise, a servant harmed by the concurrence of his own wilful and unjustified violation of orders and the negligence of the master has no cause of action against his master for such harm.

§ 527. Illegal Employment

A servant knowingly assisting in an illegal enterprise conducted by the master is barred from recovery against the master for harm received as the result of a failure by the master to perform what would otherwise be his non-delegable duties, under the conditions which bar any person assisting another in the commission of illegal acts from recovery for the harmful conduct of the other.

§ 528. Workmen's Compensation Acts

The freedom of a master from liability to a servant for the conduct of a fellow servant, his liability for personal fault, and his liability for failure to perform his non-delegable duties may be diminished or terminated by statutes providing for compensation to be paid to servants for harm arising out of and in the course of their employment, irrespective of fault.

RESTATEMENT (THIRD) OF AGENCY TENTATIVE DRAFTS NOS. 2–6

Table of Sections

Chapter 1

INTRODUCTORY MATTERS

TOPIC 1. DEFINITIONS AND TERMINOLOGY

Chapter 2

PRINCIPLES OF ATTRIBUTION

TOPIC 1. ACTUAL AUTHORITY

TOPIC 2. APPARENT AUTHORITY

TOPIC 3. RESPONDEAT SUPERIOR

TOPIC 4. RELATED DOCTRINES

Chapter 3

CREATION AND TERMINATION OF AUTHORITY AND AGENCY RELATIONSHIPS

TOPIC 1. CREATING AND EVIDENCING ACTUAL AUTHORITY

TOPIC 2. CREATING APPARENT AUTHORITY

TOPIC 3. CAPACITY TO ACT AS PRINCIPAL OR AGENT

TOPIC 4. TERMINATION OF AGENT'S POWER

TITLE A. TERMINATION OF ACTUAL AUTHORITY

TITLE B. TERMINATION OF APPARENT AUTHORITY

TITLE C. IRREVOCABLE POWERS

TOPIC 5. AGENTS WITH MULTIPLE PRINCIPALS

Chapter 4

RATIFICATION

Chapter 5

NOTIFICATIONS AND NOTICE

Chapter 1

INTRODUCTORY MATTERS

TOPIC 1. DEFINITIONS AND TERMINOLOGY

§ 1.01 Agency Defined

Agency is the fiduciary relationship that arises when one person (a "principal") manifests assent to another person (an "agent") that the agent shall act on the principal's behalf and subject to the principal's control, and the agent manifests assent or otherwise consents so to act.

Comment f(1). Principal's power and right of interim control—in general. An essential element of agency is the principal's right to control the agent's actions. Control is a concept that embraces a wide spectrum of meanings, but within any relationship of agency the principal initially states what the agent shall and shall not do, in specific or general terms. Additionally, a principal has the right to give interim instructions or directions to the agent once the relationship is established. Within an organization the right to control its agents is essential to the organization's ability to function, regardless of its size, structure, or degree of hierarchy or complexity. In an organization, it is often another agent, one holding a supervisory position, who gives the directions. A principal may exercise influence over an agent's actions in other ways as well. Incentive structures that reward the agent for achieving results affect the agent's actions. In an organization, assigning a specified function with a functionally descriptive title to a person tends to control activity because it manifests what types of activity are approved by the principal to all who know of the function and title, including their holder.

A relationship of agency is not present unless the person on whose behalf action is taken has the right to control the actor. Thus, if a person is appointed by a court to act as a receiver, the receiver is not the agent of the person whose affairs the receiver manages because the appointing court retains the power to control the receiver.

A principal's control over an agent will as a practical matter be incomplete because no agent is an automaton who mindlessly but perfectly executes commands. A principal's power to give instructions, created by the agency relationship, does not mean that all instructions the principal gives are rightful. The agent's duty of obedience does not require the agent to obey instructions to commit a crime or a tort or to violate established professional standards. See § 8.09(2). Moreover, the agent's duty of obedience does not supersede the agent's power to resign and terminate the agency relationship. See § 3.10.

The power to give interim instructions distinguishes principals in agency relationships from those who contract to receive services provided by persons who are not agents. In many agreements to provide services, the agreement between the service provider and the recipient specifies terms and conditions creating contractual obligations that, if enforceable, prescribe or delimit the choices that the service provider has the right to make. In particular, if the service provider breaches a contractual obligation, the service recipient has a claim for breach of contract. The service provider may be constrained by both the existence of such an obligation and the prospect of remedies for breach of contract. The fact that such an agreement imposes constraints on the service provider does not mean that the service recipient has an interim right to give instructions to the provider. Thus, setting standards in an agreement for acceptable service quality does not of itself create a right of control. If a service provider is retained to give an independent assessment, the expectation of independence is in tension with a right of control in the service recipient.

To the extent the parties have created a relationship of agency, however, the principal has a power of control even if the principal has previously agreed with the agent that the principal will not give interim instructions to the agent or will not otherwise interfere in the agent's exercise of discretion. However, a principal who has made such an agreement but then subsequently exercises its power of control may breach contractual duties owed to the agent, and the agent may have remedies available for the breach.

If an agent disregards or contravenes an instruction, the doctrine of actual authority, defined in § 2.01, governs the consequences as between the principal and the agent. The rights and obligations of the third party with whom the agent interacts are governed by the doctrines of actual authority and apparent authority. Doctrines of estoppel, restitution, and ratification are also relevant under some circumstances. See §§ 2.03, 2.05–2.07, and 4.01–.08.

The principal's right of control in an agency relationship is a narrower and more sharply defined concept than domination or influence more generally. Many positions and relationships give one person the ability to dominate or influence other persons but not the right to control their actions. Family ties, friendship, perceived expertise, and religious beliefs are often the source of influence or dominance, as are the variety of circumstances that create a strong position in bargaining. A position of dominance or influence does not in itself mean that a person is a principal in a relationship of agency with the person over whom dominance or influence may be exercised. The relationship is one of agency only if the person susceptible to dominance or influence has consented to act on behalf of the other and the other has a right of control, not simply an ability to bring influence to bear. Thus, a debtor does not become a creditor's agent when a loan agreement gives the creditor veto rights over decisions the debtor may make, because the debtor has not consented to act on behalf of the creditor as opposed to acting in its own interests.

The principal's right of control presupposes that the principal retains the capacity throughout the relationship to assess the agent's performance, provide instructions to the agent, and terminate the agency relationship by revoking the agent's authority. See § 3.10 as to the principal's power to revoke authority. Under the common law of agency, a durable agency power, one that survives the principal's loss of mental competence, was not feasible because of the loss of control by the principal. State statutes now permit the creation of durable powers, which enable an agent to act on behalf of a principal incapable of exercising control. Legitimating the power does not eliminate the risks for the principal that are inherent when the agent is not subject to direction or termination by the principal. Durable powers of attorney are discussed further in §§ 3.07(2)(b) and 3.12.

Comment f(2). Principal's power and right of interim control—corporate context. Many questions testing the nature of the right of control arise as a result of the legal consequences of incorporating or creating a juridical or legal person distinct from its shareholders, its governing body, and its agents. A corporation's agents are its own because it is a distinct legal person; they are not the agents of other affiliated corporations unless, separately, an agency relation has been created between the agents and the affiliated corporation. Similarly, the hierarchical link between a local union and its international affiliate does not by itself create a relationship of agency between the local and the international.

Although a corporation's shareholders elect its directors and may have the right to remove directors once elected, the directors are neither the shareholders' nor the corporation's agents as defined in this section, given the treatment of directors within contemporary corporation law in the United States. Directors' powers originate as the legal consequence of their election and are not conferred or delegated by shareholders. Although corporation statutes require shareholder approval for specific fundamental transactions, corporation law generally invests managerial authority over corporate affairs in the board of directors, not in shareholders, providing that management shall occur by or under the directors. Thus, shareholders ordinarily do not have a right to control directors by giving binding instructions to them. If the statute under which the corporation has been incorporated so permits, shareholders may be allocated power to give binding instructions to directors through a provision in the corporation's articles or through a validly adopted shareholder agreement. The fact that a corporation statute may refer to directors as the corporation's "agents" for a particular purpose does not place directors in an agency relationship with shareholders for purposes of the common law of agency. In any event, directors' ability to bind the corporation is invested in the directors as a board, not in individual directors acting unilaterally. A director may, of course, also be an employee or officer (who may or may not be an employee) of the corporation, giving the director an additional and separate conventional position or role as an agent. Fellow directors may, with that director's consent, appoint a director as an agent to act on behalf of the corporation in some respect or matter.

Comment g. Acting on behalf of. The common-law definition of agency requires as an essential element that the agent consent to act on the principal's behalf, as well as subject to the principal's control. From the standpoint of the principal, this is the purpose of creating the relationship. The common law of agency encompasses employment as well as nonemployment relations. Employee and nonemployee agents who represent their principal in transactions with third parties act on the principal's account and behalf. Employee-agents whose work does not involve transactional interactions with third parties also act "on behalf of" their employer-principal. By consenting to act on behalf of the principal, an agent who is an employee consents to do the work that the employer directs and to do it subject to the employer's instructions. In either case, actions "on behalf of" the principal do not necessarily entail that the principal benefits as a result.

In any relationship created by contract, the parties contemplate a benefit to be realized through the other party's performance. Performing a duty created by contract may well benefit the other party, but the performance is that of an agent only if the elements of agency are present. A person is not "acting on behalf of" a supplier in a distribution relationship in which goods are purchased from the supplier for resale. A purchaser who resells goods supplied by another is acting as a principal, not an agent. However, some courts treat a trademark licensee as the agent of the licensor in some situations, with the result that the licensor is liable to third parties for defective goods produced by licensees.

An actor who acts under the immediate control of another person is not that person's agent unless the actor has agreed to act on the person's behalf. For example, a foreman or supervisor in charge of a crew of laborers exercises full and detailed control over the laborers' work activities. The relationship between the foreman and the laborers is not an agency relationship despite the foreman's full control, nor is their relationship one of subagency. Section 1.04(9) defines subagency. The foreman and the laborers are co-agents of a common employer who occupy different strata within an organizational hierarchy; the foreman's role of direction, defined by the organization, does not make the laborers the foreman's own agents. The laborers act on behalf of the common employer, not the foreman. Likewise, the captain of a ship and its crew are co-agents, hierarchically stratified, who have consented to act on behalf of their common principal, the ship's owner.

It is possible to create a power to affect a person's legal relations to be exercised for the benefit of the holder of the power. Such powers typically are created as security for the interests of the holder or otherwise to benefit a person other than the person who creates the power. Consequently, the holder of such a power is not an agent as defined in this section, even though the power has the form of agency and, if exercised, will result in some of agency's legal consequences. The creator does not have a right to control the power holder's use of the power, and the power holder is not under a duty to use it in the interests of the creator. Sections 3.12–.13 specifically treat powers given as security.

Relationships of agency are a subset of the larger family of relationships in which one person acts on behalf of another and is subject to fiduciary obligations. Agency is not antithetical to these other relationships, and whether a fiduciary is, additionally, an agent of another depends on the circumstances of the particular relationship. For example, as defined in Restatement Third, Trusts § 2 (Tentative Draft No. 1, 1996), a trust is a fiduciary relationship with respect to property that arises as a result of a manifestation of intention to create that relationship; a trustee is not an agent of the settlor or beneficiaries unless the terms of the trust subject the trustee to the control of either the settlor or the beneficiaries. Principals in agency relationships have power to terminate authority, and thus remove the agent; trust beneficiaries, in contrast, do not have power to remove the trustee.

As agents, all employees owe duties of loyalty to their employers. The specific implications vary with the position the employee occupies, the nature of the employer's assets to which the employee has access, and the degree of discretion that the employee's work requires. However ministerial or routinized the work assignment may be, no agent, whether or not an employee, is simply a pair of hands, legs, or eyes. All are sentient, and, capable of disloyal action, all have the duty to act loyally.

§ 1.02 Parties' Labelling and Popular Usage not Controlling

An agency relationship arises only when the elements stated in § 1.01 are present. Whether a relationship is characterized as agency in an agreement between parties or in the context of industry or popular usage is not controlling.

§ 1.03 Manifestation

A person manifests assent or intention through written or spoken words or other conduct.

§ 1.04 Terminology

(1) *Co-agents.* Co-agents have agency relationships with the same principal. A co-agent may be appointed by the principal or by another agent actually or apparently authorized by the principal to do so.

(2) Disclosed, undisclosed, and unidentified principals.

(a) *Disclosed principal.* A principal is disclosed if, when an agent and a third party interact, the third party has notice that the agent is acting for a principal and has notice of the principal's identity.

(b) *Undisclosed principal.* A principal is undisclosed if, when an agent and a third party interact, the third party has no notice that the agent is acting for a principal.

(c) *Unidentified principal.* A principal is unidentified if, when an agent and a third party interact, the third party has notice that the agent is acting for a principal but does not have notice of the principal's identity.

(3) *Dual agent; joint principals.* A dual agent acts on behalf of more than one principal with regard to the same transaction. Such principals are joint principals.

(4) *Gratuitous agent.* A gratuitous agent acts without a right to compensation.

(5) *Notice.* A person has notice of a fact if the person knows the fact, has reason to know the fact, has received an effective notification of the fact, or should know the fact to fulfill a duty owed to another person. Notice of a fact that an agent knows or has reason to know is imputed to the principal as stated in §§ 5.03 and 5.04. A notification given to an agent is effective as notice to the principal as stated in § 5.02 (1).

(6) *Person.* A person is (a) an individual; (b) an organization or association that has legal capacity to possess rights and incur obligations; (c) a government, political subdivision, or instrumentality or entity created by government; or (d) any other entity that has legal capacity to possess rights and incur obligations.

(7) *Power given as security.* A power given as security is a power to affect the legal relations of its creator that is created in the form of a manifestation of actual authority and held for the benefit of the holder or a third person. It is given to protect a legal or equitable title or to secure the performance of a duty apart from any duties owed the holder of the power by its creator that are incident to a relationship of agency under § 1.01.

(8) *Power of attorney.* A power of attorney is an instrument that states an agent's authority.

(9) *Subagent.* A subagent is a person appointed by an agent to perform functions that the agent has consented to perform on behalf of the agent's principal.

(10) *Superior and subordinate co-agents.* A superior co-agent has the right, conferred by the principal, to direct a subordinate co-agent.

(11) *Trustee and agent-trustee.* A trustee is a holder of property who is subject to fiduciary duties to deal with the property for the benefit of charity or for one or more persons, at least one of whom is not the sole trustee. An agent-trustee is a trustee subject to the control of the settlor or of one or more beneficiaries.

Chapter 2

PRINCIPLES OF ATTRIBUTION

TOPIC 1. ACTUAL AUTHORITY

§ 2.01 Actual Authority

An agent acts with actual authority when, at the time of taking action that has legal consequences for the principal, the agent reasonably believes, in accordance with the principal's manifestations to the agent, that the principal wishes the agent so to act.

Comment b. Terminology. As defined in this section, "actual authority" is a synonym for "true authority," a term used in some opinions. The definition in this section does not attempt to classify different types of actual authority on the basis of the degree of detail in the principal's manifestation, which may consist of written or spoken words or other conduct. See § 1.03. As commonly used, the term "express authority" often means actual authority that the principal has stated in very specific or detailed language.

The term "implied authority" has more than one meaning. "Implied authority" is often used to mean actual authority either (1) to do what is necessary, usual, and proper to accomplish or perform the agent's express responsibilities or (2) to act in a manner in which the agent believes the principal wishes the agent to act based on the agent's reasonable interpretation of the principal's manifestation in light of the principal's objectives and other facts known to the agent. These meanings are not mutually exclusive. Both fall within the definition of actual authority. Section 2.02, which delineates the scope of actual authority, subsumes the practical consequences of implied authority.

The term "inherent agency power," used in the Restatement Second of Agency and defined therein by § 8A, is not used in this Restatement. Inherent agency power is defined as "a term used ... to indicate the power of an agent which is derived not from authority, apparent authority or estoppel, but solely from the agency relation and exists for the protection of persons named by or dealing with a servant or agent." Other doctrines stated in this Restatement encompass the justifications underpinning § 8A, including the importance of interpretation by the agent in the agent's relationship with the principal, as well as the doctrines of apparent authority, estoppel, and restitution.

§ 2.02 Scope of Actual Authority

(1) An agent has actual authority to take action designated or implied in the principal's manifestations and acts necessary or incidental to achieving the principal's objectives, as the agent reasonably understands them when the agent determines how to act.

(2) An agent's interpretation of the principal's manifestations is reasonable if it reflects any meaning known by the agent to be ascribed by the principal and, in the absence of any meaning known to the agent, as a reasonable person in the agent's position would interpret the manifestations in light of the context, including circumstances of which the agent has notice and the agent's fiduciary duty to the principal.

(3) An agent's understanding of the principal's objectives is reasonable if it accords with the principal's manifestations and the inferences that a reasonable person in the agent's position would draw from the circumstances creating the agency.

TOPIC 2. APPARENT AUTHORITY

§ 2.03 Apparent Authority

Apparent authority is the power held by an agent or other actor to affect a principal's legal relations with third parties when a third party reasonably believes the actor has authority to act on behalf of the principal and that belief is traceable to the principal's manifestations.

TOPIC 3. RESPONDEAT SUPERIOR

§ 2.04 Respondeat Superior

An employer is liable for torts committed by employees while acting in the scope of their employment.

TOPIC 4. RELATED DOCTRINES

§ 2.05 Estoppel to Deny Existence of Agency Relationship

A person who has not made a manifestation that an actor has authority as an agent and who is not otherwise liable as a party to a transaction purportedly done by the actor on that person's account is liable to a third party who justifiably is induced to make a detrimental change in position because the transaction is believed to be on the person's account, if

(1) the person intentionally or carelessly caused such belief, or

(2) having notice of such belief and that it might induce others to change their positions, the person did not take reasonable steps to notify them of the facts.

§ 2.06 Estoppel of Undisclosed Principal

An undisclosed principal may not rely on instructions given an agent that qualify or reduce the agent's authority to less than the authority a third party would reasonably believe the agent to have under the same circumstances if the principal had been disclosed.

Comment c. Rationale. The principle stated in this section will result in liability in a relatively small number of cases. Liability will result only when a third party deals with an agent but has no notice that the agent represents the interests of another and when the third party would not have reason to inquire into the scope of the agent's authority if the third party knew the agent acted on behalf of a principal. If both of these conditions are met, the principal may not deny the agent's authority to prejudice the third party. The principal may not rely on qualifications or reductions to the agent's authority, when the doctrine of apparent authority would make the qualification or restriction ineffective as to an agent acting on behalf of a disclosed or an unidentified principal. The principal has in such cases chosen to place the agent in a position in which it is reasonable for third parties to believe that the agent has authority consistent with the position.

The rule stated in this section, like the doctrine of apparent authority, protects third parties by backstopping actual authority when circumstances might otherwise permit the principal opportunistically to speculate at the expense of third parties. See § 2.03, Comment *c*. Apparent authority does not arise when a principal is undisclosed because no manifestation has been made that the actor with whom the third party interacts has authority to act as an agent. If the agent operates a business under the agent's name, the appearance to the third party may be that the agent owns the business and that its assets will be available to satisfy business-related obligations incurred by the agent. The opportunity for speculation provided the principal would emerge when the principal has limited the agent's authority, and the agent enters into a contract that exceeds the agent's actual authority. Then, if the contract is advantageous to the principal, neither the principal nor the agent will raise the agent's lack of authority, and the third party will lack reason to know of it. On the other hand, if the contract then is disadvantageous to the principal, the principal may assert lack of authority as a defense.

The doctrine allocates to the principal the risk that the agent will deviate from the principal's instructions and do acts that are consistent with the position the agent occupies, which are acts that third parties would anticipate an agent in such a position would have authority to do and may well be acts that are foreseeable to the principal. Such acts are especially likely to be foreseeable when they are consistent with the agent's position although they contravene the principal's instructions.

It is true that a third party who deals with an actor, lacking notice that the actor is someone's agent, does not expect the liability of any person in addition to the immediate actor with whom the third party deals. Estoppel's perspective is broader, if less well defined. The question is whether it is unjust, in particular circumstances, to permit a principal who has chosen to deal through an agent but to remain undisclosed to have the benefit of restrictions on the agent's authority. In the instance in which the rule is applicable, it is unlikely that the third party will inquire into the status of the immediate actor or seek to identify the existence of restrictions on that actor's right to interact with legal consequences for the third party. The need to make such inquiries, in the circumstances to which this doctrine applies, is unlikely to occur to a reasonable third party, and making the inquiry may be difficult or its cost may seem excessive relative to the magnitude of the particular transaction. When the third party previously dealt with the agent as the owner of the business now managed by the agent, the third party may assume that inquiry is unnecessary for transactions similar to prior transactions. Separately, if an undisclosed principal has notice of an agent's unauthorized actions and notice that a third party will as a consequence be induced to make a detrimental change in position, the undisclosed principal may be estopped to deny the agent's authority. The undisclosed principal may avoid the estoppel by disclosing the agent's status and the extent of the agent's authority.

The doctrine encompasses deviations from actual authority of a sort that would not lead a reasonable third party to make separate inquiry into the scope of the agent's authority. Such deviations are foreseeable to the principal and are likely not to be contested by any principal, whether or not undisclosed, when they appear likely to benefit the principal.

§ 2.07 Restitution of Benefit

A principal who is unjustly enriched by the action of an agent or a person who appears to be an agent must make restitution.

Chapter 3

CREATION AND TERMINATION OF AUTHORITY AND AGENCY RELATIONSHIPS

TOPIC 1. CREATING AND EVIDENCING ACTUAL AUTHORITY

§ 3.01 Creation of Actual Authority

Actual authority, as defined in § 2.01, is created by a principal's manifestation to an agent that, as reasonably understood by the agent, expresses the principal's assent that the agent take action on the principal's behalf.

§ 3.02 Formal Requirements

If the law requires a writing or record signed by the principal to evidence an agent's authority to bind a principal to a contract or other transaction, the principal is not bound in the absence of such a writing or record. A principal may be estopped to assert the lack of such a writing or record when a third party has been induced to make a detrimental change in position by the reasonable belief that an agent has authority to bind the principal that is traceable to a manifestation made by the principal.

Comment b. Equal Dignity requirements. Creating actual authority under § 3.01 does not require a writing or other formality. However, legislation in many states imposes what is often termed an "equal dignity" requirement for the creation of authority or agency applicable to specific types of agreements. As with the Statute of Frauds more generally, the purpose is to prevent fraud and perjury by safeguarding the principal against agreements made by an agent who lacks authority. Under an equal dignity rule, if a transaction is unenforceable unless the party to be charged has agreed in writing to be bound, an agent's authority to enter into such a transaction on behalf of a principal must likewise be in writing. Such rules also apply to ratification. See § 4.02, Comment *e*. If an agent acted with apparent authority as defined in § 2.03 but no writing or record evidences the agent's authority, the principal is not bound to contracts or other transactions to which an equal dignity rule applies.

A writing includes "any intentional reduction to written form," see Restatement Second, Contracts § 131 Comment *d* (1982). A record includes an electronic record that is given the legal effect of a writing. Electronic records are given the legal effect of paper and ink writings by legislation, including the Uniform Electronic Transactions Act § 7 (1999) and the federal Electronic Signatures in Global and National Commerce Act § 101(a) (2000). A writing is signed by the principal by affixing a symbol that evidences intention to authenticate the writing. See Restatement Second, Contracts § 134. Similarly, an electronic record is signed by attaching to it an electronic sound, symbol or process that is adopted with the intention of signing the record. See Uniform Electronic Transactions Act § 2(8).

Equal dignity rules are either elements in a statute of frauds or are stated in separate statutes. Equal dignity rules apply when a statute of frauds requires the underlying agreement to be evidenced by a writing signed by the party to be charged, including agreements for the sale or lease of land and suretyship agreements. On the scope of contracts to which Statutes of Frauds apply, see Restatement Second, Contracts § 110 (1981). Equal dignity rules are inapplicable when a writing is required by agreement but not by law. However, a contract may not be binding when in and of itself a contractual provision requires the principal to sign personally.

Equal dignity rules have been applied with some stringency. For example, when one spouse acts as the agent of the other who owns property, or as an agent when both spouses own property jointly, the equal dignity rule requires the agent-spouse's authorization to be in writing. If a principal executes a contract but leaves blanks that are completed by the agent, the contract may not be enforceable against the principal if the third party has notice that the agent may fill in the blanks only when the agent is authorized in writing to do so.

Nevertheless, the application of equal dignity rules should not outrun their purpose. Equal dignity rules do not apply when an action on the contract is brought by the principal against the third party. An equal dignity rule may be satisfied by a writing or record executed by a principal following the agent's execution of the contract or transaction. Moreover, if an agent has acted without actual authority, as well as without prior written authorization, the principal would be able to ratify the transaction by a signed writing, see § 4.01, Comment *e*, so long as the principal ratifies prior to a manifestation from the third party that the third party has withdrawn from the transaction, see § 4.05(1). Additionally, an equal dignity rule does not create a defense that an agent may assert against the third party, such as when the agent misrepresents authority. See §§ 6.10–6.11.

TOPIC 2. CREATING APPARENT AUTHORITY

§ 3.03 Creation of Apparent Authority

Apparent authority, as defined in § 2.03, is created by a person's manifestation that another has authority to act with legal consequences for the person who makes the manifestation, if a third party reasonably believes the actor to be authorized and the belief is traceable to the manifestation.

TOPIC 3. CAPACITY TO ACT AS PRINCIPAL OR AGENT

§ 3.04 Capacity to Act as Principal

(1) An individual person has capacity to act as principal in a relationship of agency as defined in § 1.01 as to acts and transactions for which the individual would have capacity if acting in person at the time the agent takes action.

(2) Whether a person that is not an individual has capacity to be a principal in a relationship of agency as defined in § 1.01, together with the effect of the person's lack or loss of capacity on those who interact with it, is governed by the law applicable to the person.

(3) If performance of an act is not delegable, its performance by an agent does not constitute performance by the principal.

§ 3.05 Capacity to Act as Agent

Any person may be empowered to act so as to affect the legal relations of another. The actor's capacity governs the extent to which, by so acting, the actor becomes subject to duties and liabilities to the person whose legal relations are affected or to third parties.

TOPIC 4. TERMINATION OF AGENT'S POWER

TITLE A. TERMINATION OF ACTUAL AUTHORITY

§ 3.06 Termination of Actual Authority—In General

An agent's actual authority may be terminated by:

(1) the agent's death, cessation of existence, or suspension of powers as stated in § 3.07(1) and (3);

(2) the principal's death, cessation of existence, or suspension of powers as stated in § 3.07(2) and (4);

(3) the principal's loss of capacity, as stated in § 3.08(1) and (3);

(4) an agreement between the agent and principal, as stated in § 3.09; and

(5) a manifestation of revocation by the principal to the agent, or of renunciation by the agent to the principal, as stated in § 3.10(1).

Comment b. Agreement between principal and agent and changes in circumstances. The basis for actual authority is a manifestation of assent made by the principal to the agent. When the manifestation is embodied in an agreement that specifies circumstances under which the agent's actual authority shall terminate, occurrence of a specified circumstance reflects termination of the principal's expressed assent. Regardless of whether the initial agreement contains a termination provision, mutual agreement to terminate the agency relationship is always effective to terminate the agent's actual authority.

Following the principal's manifestation of assent to an agent, circumstances may change such that, at the time the agent takes action, it is not reasonable for the agent to believe that the principal at that time consents to the action being taken on the principal's behalf even though the principal has not manifested dissent to the action by that time. For example, the agent may become insolvent and have notice that it is important to the principal to be represented by a solvent agent. The agent may lose capacity to bind itself by a contract or to become subject to other obligations and have notice that it is important to the principal that the agent retain such capacity. Events that are totally outside the control of the agent or the principal may also make it unreasonable for the agent to believe that the principal consents to the agent's action. For example, if the principal retains the agent to sell goods in a particular geographically-defined market, the occurrence of war or widespread civil unrest may so impair the value of the agent's efforts to the principal that the agent would not be reasonable in believing the principal wishes the agent to sell into the territory. The agent then lacks actual authority so to act, but the agent would have acted with actual authority had the agent acted prior to the change in circumstances. The focal point for determining whether an agent acted with actual authority is the time of action, not the time of the principal's manifestation, which may be earlier. See §§ 2.01 and 2.02.

An alternate analysis of the impact of changed circumstances, as set forth in Restatement Second, Agency, requires the use of at least two distinct focal points. First, it is posited that an agent has actual authority up until the agent receives notice of the changed circumstances. Notice that circumstances have changed, beyond those operative when the principal manifested consent to the agent, then implicitly modifies either the principal's manifestation of consent or the actual authority it engenders on the basis of the agent's reasonable belief in the principal's consent. See Restatement Second, Agency, Introductory Note to Chapter 5. Moreover, if circumstances thereafter revert to those present originally, the agent's actual authority, having once existed but thereafter having been terminated, is again revived. See id. § 108(2). This Restatement does not follow this alternate pattern of analysis because it is unnecessary in light of the nature of actual authority and the rules that determine whether an agent acted with actual authority. See §§ 2.01–2.02.

§ 3.07 Death, Cessation of Existence, and Suspension of Powers

(1) The death of an individual agent terminates the agent's actual authority.

(2) The death of an individual principal terminates the agent's actual authority. The termination is effective only when the agent has notice of the principal's death. The termination is also effective as against a third party with whom the agent deals when the third party has notice of the principal's death.

(3) When an agent that is not an individual ceases to exist or commences a process that will lead to cessation of existence, or when its powers are suspended, the agent's actual authority terminates, except as provided by law.

(4) When a principal that is not an individual ceases to exist or commences a process that will lead to cessation of its existence, or when its powers are suspended, the agent's actual authority terminates except as provided by law.

§ 3.08 Loss of Capacity

(1) An individual principal's loss of capacity to do an act terminates the agent's actual authority to do the act. The termination is effective only when the agent has notice that the principal's loss of capacity is permanent or that the principal has been adjudicated to lack capacity. The termination is also effective as against a third party with whom the agent deals when the third party has notice that the principal's loss of capacity is permanent or that the principal has been adjudicated to lack capacity.

(2) A written instrument that complies with applicable legislation may make an agent's actual authority effective upon a principal's loss of capacity, or confer it irrevocably regardless of such loss.

(3) If a principal that is not an individual loses capacity to do an act, its agent's actual authority to do the act is terminated.

§ 3.09 Termination by Agreement

An agent's actual authority terminates as agreed by the agent and the principal, subject to the provisions of § 3.10.

§ 3.10 Manifestation Terminating Actual Authority

(1) Notwithstanding any agreement between principal and agent, an agent's actual authority terminates if the agent renounces it by a manifestation to the principal, or if the principal revokes the agent's actual authority by a manifestation to the agent. A revocation or a renunciation is effective when the other party has notice of it.

(2) A principal's manifestation of revocation is, unless otherwise agreed, ineffective to terminate a power given as security, or to terminate a proxy to vote securities or other membership or ownership interests that is made irrevocable in compliance with applicable legislation. See §§ 3.12–3.13.

TITLE B. TERMINATION OF APPARENT AUTHORITY

§ 3.11 Termination of Apparent Authority

(1) The termination of actual authority does not by itself end any apparent authority held by the agent.

(2) Apparent authority ends when it is no longer reasonable for the third party with whom the agent deals to believe that the agent continues to act with actual authority.

TITLE C. IRREVOCABLE POWERS

§ 3.12 Power Given as Security; Irrevocable Proxy

(1) A power given as security is a power to affect the legal relations of its creator that is created in the form of a manifestation of actual authority and held for the benefit of the holder or a third person. This power is given to protect a legal or equitable title, or to secure the performance of a duty apart from any duties owed the holder of the power by its creator that are incident to a relationship of agency under § 1.01. It is given upon the creation of the duty or title or for consideration. It is distinct from actual authority that the holder may exercise if the holder is an agent of the creator of the power.

(2) A power to exercise voting rights associated with securities or a membership interest may be conferred on a proxy through a manifestation of actual authority. The power may be given as security under (1) and it may be made irrevocable in compliance with applicable legislation.

§ 3.13 Termination of Power Given as Security or Irrevocable Proxy

(1) A power given as security or an irrevocable proxy is terminated by an event that

(a) discharges the obligation secured by the power or terminates the interest secured or supported by the proxy,

(b) makes its execution illegal or impossible, or

(c) constitutes an effective surrender of the power or proxy by the person for whose benefit it was created or conferred.

(2) Unless otherwise agreed, neither a power given as security nor a proxy made irrevocable as provided in § 3.12(2) is terminated by:

(a) a manifestation revoking the power or proxy made by the person who created it;

(b) surrender of the power or proxy by its holder if it is held for the benefit of another person, unless that person consents;

(c) loss of capacity by the creator or the holder of the power or proxy;

(d) death of the holder of the power or proxy, unless the holder's death terminates the interest secured or supported by the power or proxy; or

(e) death of the creator of the power or proxy, if the power or proxy is given as security for the performance of a duty that does not terminate with the death of its creator.

TOPIC 5. AGENTS WITH MULTIPLE PRINCIPALS

§ 3.14 Agents with Multiple Principals

An agent acting in the same transaction or matter on behalf of more than one principal may be one or both of the following:

(a) a subagent, as stated in § 3.15; or

(b) an agent for co-principals, as stated in § 3.16.

§ 3.15 Subagency

(1) A subagent is a person appointed by an agent to perform functions that the agent has consented to perform on behalf of the agent's principal.

(2) In appointing a subagent, an agent may act with actual or apparent authority.

Comment b. Subagency contrasted with co-agency. Agency creates a personal relationship between principal and agent; an agent's delegation of power to another person to act on behalf of the principal is inconsistent with the undertaking made when a person consents to act as agent on behalf of a principal. However, a principal may empower an agent to appoint another agent to act on the principal's behalf. The second agent may be a subagent or a co-agent. See Comment *d* for discussion of the consequences that follow if the second agent is characterized as a subagent.

An agent who appoints a subagent delegates to the subagent power to act on behalf of the principal that the principal has conferred on the agent. A subagent acts subject to the control of the appointing agent, and the principal's legal position is affected by action taken by the subagent as if the action had been taken by the appointing agent. Thus, a subagent has two principals, the appointing agent and that agent's principal. Although an appointing agent has the right and duty to control a subagent, the interests and instructions of the appointing agent's principal are paramount. See Comment *d*.

In contrast, an agent who appoints a co-agent does not delegate power held by the agent to the co-agent. By empowering an agent to appoint a co-agent, the principal creates a mechanism through which to generate additional relationships of agency between the principal and persons chosen by the agent. Co-agents, although they may occupy dominant and subordinate positions within an organizational hierarchy, share a common principal.

A person appointed by an agent to act on behalf of the agent's principal is a subagent if the appointing agent has agreed with the principal that the appointing agent shall be responsible to the principal for the agent's conduct. Such agreement may be express or implied. For example, employees of an appointing agent whom the agent designates to act on behalf of the appointing agent's principal are presumed to be subagents, not co-agents of the appointing agent. When an agent is itself a corporation or other legal person, its officers, employees, partners, or members who are designated to work on the principal's account are subagents. In contrast, when a manager within an organization hires persons as employees of the organization, those hired are presumed to be the hiring manager's co-agents and not subagents. Employees of a single organization are presumed to be co-agents of that organization, not subagents.

Comment c. Creation of subagency. An agent has actual authority to create a relationship of subagency when the agent reasonably believes, based on a manifestation from the principal, that the principal consents to the appointment of a subagent. For the definition of actual authority, see § 2.01. For the means by which a principal creates it, see § 3.01.

A principal's consent to the appointment of a subagent may be express or implied. For example, a principal's consent to the appointment of subagents may be implied when the principal retains an individual as agent to carry out a number of transactions and has notice that the amount of work involved exceeds the agent's individual capability or requires action that the agent may not legally perform, such as action for which the law requires a license. Implied consent to appoint subagents is also present when an agent is itself a person that is not an individual, such as a corporation.

Subagents may be appointed in series. This would occur when a subagent has actual or apparent authority to appoint another for whose conduct the appointing subagent is responsible.

An agent may have apparent authority to appoint a subagent if the principal has made a manifestation to third parties that the agent has such authority. Section 1.03 defines manifestation. Section 2.03 defines apparent authority; § 3.03 states how it is created. A principal may make a manifestation that an agent has actual authority to appoint subagents by placing the agent in a position in which agents customarily have such authority without notice to third parties that the agent's authority does not include the appointment of subagents. A subagent appointed by an agent acting with only apparent authority may act on behalf of the principal with actual authority. See Comment *d*.

If an agent acts without actual or apparent authority in purporting to appoint a subagent, the person so appointed is the agent solely of the appointing agent and is not the principal's subagent unless the principal ratifies the appointment.

In emergencies and other unforeseen circumstances, when communication between agent and principal is not feasible, an agent's actual authority to take action to protect the principal's interests may permit the agent to appoint a subagent although the principal has not previously manifested consent to the agent to make such an appointment. See § 2.02, Comment *d*.

A person may be appointed as a subagent even though the person does not expect to be compensated for actions taken.

Comment d. Consequences of subagency. As between a principal and third parties, it is immaterial that an action was taken by a subagent as opposed to an agent directly appointed by the principal. In this respect, subagency is governed by a principle of transparency that looks from the subagent to the principal and through the appointing agent. As to third parties, an action taken by a subagent carries the legal consequences for the principal that would follow were the action instead taken by the appointing agent....

When a subagent works on a principal's account, notifications received by the subagent are effective as notifications to the principal to the same extent as if the principal had appointed the subagent directly. Likewise, notice of facts the subagent knows or has reason to know is imputed to the principal to the same extent as if the principal had appointed the subagent directly....

As among a principal, an appointing agent, and a subagent, the fact that action is taken by a subagent may carry different or additional legal consequences than if the action were taken directly by the appointing agent or by a co-agent of the appointing agent. The legal consequences of subagency reflect the distinct significance of (1) the relationship between an appointing agent and a subagent; (2) the relationship between a principal and an appointing agent; and (3) the relationship between a principal and a subagent. An appointing agent is responsible to the principal for the subagent's conduct. This may subject an appointing agent to liability for loss incurred by the principal as a consequence of misconduct by a subagent. In contrast, an agent is subject to liability stemming from a co-agent's conduct only as stated in § 7.01, Comments *b* and *d*.

Statutes may change the results that would otherwise follow when a subagent takes action. For example, under U.C.C. Article 4, when the owner of an item deposits it with a bank for collection, the depositary bank is treated as the agent of the item's owner. If the depositary bank sends the item for collection to another bank, the collecting bank is treated as the owner's subagent. See U.C.C. § 4–201(a). However, under U.C.C. § 4–202, although a depositary bank has a duty to use ordinary care in selecting intermediaries and in giving proper instructions to them, it is not liable for another bank's "insolvency, neglect, misconduct, mistake, or default. . . ."

Although an appointing agent is responsible for a subagent's action and has the right and duty to control the subagent, the principal's interests and instructions are nonetheless paramount. Several specific doctrines reflect this general point. If a subagent acts without actual or apparent authority, only the principal may ratify the subagent's action; ratification by an appointing agent is effective only when the principal has authorized the appointing agent to ratify on its behalf. Moreover, a subagent is a fiduciary, as is any agent. See § 1.01. A subagent owes fiduciary duties to the principal as well as to the appointing agent. See §§ 8.01–8.06, which state the specifics of these duties. A subagent owes a duty of obedience to the principal as well as to the appointing agent. See § 8.09(2). However, the principal's rights as to the subagent are superior to rights of the appointing agent, even in the event of conflict or disagreement between principal and appointing agent. . . .

If a subagent is appointed by an agent who acts with only apparent authority, the subagent is privileged to act on behalf of the principal because the subagent, on the basis of the principal's manifestation, reasonably believes that the appointing agent acted with the principal's consent in appointing the subagent. As a consequence, the principal is subject to liability to the subagent to indemnify the subagent as stated in § 8.14. The appointing agent, having acted without actual authority in appointing the subagent, is subject to liability to the principal as stated in § 8.09(1). The subagent is not subject to liability to third parties on the basis that the subagent breached warranties of authority. See § 6.10.

A principal's duties to a subagent are those owed to any agent, but the principal is not subject to duties created by agreement between the appointing agent and the subagent, including the appointing agent's agreement to compensate the subagent. See § 8.13, Comment *d*. A subagent may have set-off rights against the principal. See § 6.06.

Comment e. Termination of subagent's actual and apparent authority. Whether a subagent acts with actual authority depends on three separate consensual relationships: (1) between principal and appointing agent; (2) between appointing agent and subagent; and (3) between principal and subagent. A subagent's actual authority terminates upon notice to the subagent that any of these relationships is severed.

Additionally, circumstances that terminate an agent's actual authority by operation of law likewise terminate a subagent's authority. Thus, notice of the death of a principal or of an appointing agent terminates a subagent's actual authority, as does notice that the principal has revoked an appointing agent's actual authority. See §§ 3.07(2) and 3.10(1). If the relationship between an appointing agent and a subagent is severed, for example by notice of the appointing agent's death or loss of capacity, the subagent no longer acts under the control of the appointing agent who had responsibility for the subagent's acts. If a subagent is a lawyer who represents a client having diminished capacity, the lawyer's duties are as stated in Restatement of the Law Governing Lawyers § 24 (2000).

Additionally, a principal may terminate a subagent's actual authority by making a manifestation of revocation directly to the subagent or to the appointing agent. A manifestation revoking a subagent's actual authority made by the principal to the appointing agent should not be effective, in most circumstances, as to the subagent until the subagent has notice of it. A principal has rights and responsibilities of ultimate control, including ultimate control over chains of command and channels of communication. A principal may choose how best to communicate with a subagent, including how best to convey notice that the subagent's actual authority has been revoked. If the principal chooses to rely exclusively on the appointing agent as the channel of communication with the subagent, the principal at least ordinarily should bear the risk that the appointing agent will not duly deliver notice of revocation to the subagent.

In contrast, under the rule stated in Restatement Second, Agency § 137, Comment *b*, when a principal terminates a subagent's authority by giving notice of termination to the appointing agent, "the subagent's authority terminates only when the agent has had an opportunity to communicate with him." If the agent, having had the opportunity to communicate with the subagent, does not do so, or does not do so effectively, the rule as stated in Restatement Second allocates to the subagent the risk of acting without actual authority, although the subagent lacks notice that the principal wishes to terminate the subagent's authority. The notice requirement stated in this Restatement instead allocates to the principal the risk that notice of revocation communicated only to the appointing agent may not reach the subagent. So allocating the risk is supported by a well-reasoned case in the real-estate context. The principal should bear this risk because the principal has consented to the appointment of subagents and because a subagent should be under no greater risk than is an agent of unwittingly taking an unauthorized action following the termination of actual authority.

A subagent may continue to act with apparent authority following termination of the subagent's actual authority when third parties reasonably believe that the subagent continues to act with actual authority on the basis of manifestations traceable to the appointing agent or the principal. See § 3.11.

Comment f. Transactions in real estate. Under the common-law rule in most states, a real-estate broker or salesperson associated with a broker who successfully markets property to a prospective buyer (hereinafter the "showing broker") is treated as the subagent of the broker with whom a prospective seller has listed the property (hereinafter the "listing broker"), even if the showing broker is not the listing broker's employee or associate. Conventional terminology applies the term "broker" or "real-estate broker" to a person holding a license to provide brokerage services. A broker may use the services of salespeople, who may be employees of the broker or the broker's nonemployee associates. Except where the context otherwise requires, the remainder of this Comment refers to all as "brokers."

The better rule, followed in a minority of states, characterizes a showing broker as the agent of the prospective buyer, and not the seller's subagent, when the terms of the relationship between the showing broker and the prospective buyer reasonably reflect the buyer's expectation that the showing broker represents the buyer. The minority rule is consistent with the policy reflected in legislation in a majority of states that explicitly permits a prospective buyer to appoint a real-estate broker to act as the buyer's agent.

A showing broker may be characterized as: (1) the seller's subagent, regardless of whether the broker has a relationship with the buyer that constitutes a relationship of agency as defined by § 1.01; (2) the buyer's agent when the relationship between buyer and broker constitutes a relationship of agency as defined by § 1.01; or (3) neither the agent nor the subagent of buyer or seller. If a showing broker is characterized as acting as agent for both buyer and seller, or as agent for buyer and subagent for seller, the agent is in a position of dual agency.

As the seller's subagent, the showing broker is presumed not to have a relationship of agency with the buyer and does not owe an agent's fiduciary duties to the buyer. It is well-settled, as a matter of industry practice and regulation as well as common-law agency, that a broker in a single real-estate transaction may not represent both buyer and seller unless both know of and consent to the dual representation. Unless such consent is given, a broker who represents both buyer and seller may forfeit any commission otherwise payable to the broker. See § 8.03. In a transaction involving the same property, buyer and seller have interests that are adverse. The benefit that a seller will receive through a higher sales price will be paid by the buyer. Moreover, a broker who represents a prospective seller or buyer of property may have material information that, if disclosed to the other party, will disadvantage the broker's client. For example, information about the seller's reservation price—the lowest price at which the seller may be willing to sell—is material to price negotiations between the seller and prospective buyers. For further treatment of dual agency, see § 8.03.

The mechanism through which a relationship of subagency arises is an offer of a unilateral contract of subagency, made by the listing broker to showing brokers, that is accepted by the showing broker who produces a buyer able and willing to purchase the property at the listing price and terms or at other terms acceptable to the seller. Such an offer is often made when a listing broker lists property with a multiple listing service ("MLS"). A multiple listing service is an agreement among brokers in a particular geographic market to pool information about their listings. A showing broker may also become a subagent in the absence of MLS participation through a relationship of co-operation with the listing broker. When a showing broker produces an offer from a buyer to purchase at the seller's stated listing price and on terms otherwise consistent with the listing agreement, conventional MLS terms require that the listing broker split the commission to be paid by the seller with the successful showing broker.

The legal consequences of how a showing broker is characterized carry corresponding advantages as well as disadvantages from the standpoint of buyers and sellers of real estate. Characterizing a showing broker as the seller's subagent orients the showing broker's duties exclusively to the seller, with the implication that the broker must disclose to the seller all material information the broker learns about the buyer. This disadvantages a buyer if the showing broker discloses information the buyer has provided to the seller or the listing broker, such as the maximum price the buyer is willing to pay to acquire property. However, this characterization may be advantageous to the buyer if the showing broker induces the buyer to purchase a property through fraud because the buyer may rescind the transaction. See Restatement Second, Contracts § 164(1). To be sure, a seller may not perceive this consequence to be fair when the seller has had no contact with a showing broker who induces a purchase through fraud. In contrast, if a showing broker acts as a buyer's agent, the buyer will be limited to remedies against the broker if the seller has not participated in the fraud. See Restatement Second, Contracts § 164(2). Neither buyer nor seller benefits if a showing broker is not characterized as either the seller's subagent or the buyer's agent because the duties of a non-agent showing broker are indeterminate. However, principals in real-estate transactions may benefit if non-agent showing brokers charge lower commissions than brokers who act as agents and subagents.

The common-law rule applicable to agency relationships in this context should reflect the reasonable expectations of prospective buyers and sellers of property and the real-estate professionals who act on their behalf. If a broker has agreed to assist a prospective buyer, it is reasonable for the prospective buyer to expect that the broker does not owe duties of loyalty to the seller of property that the buyer purchases. Treating a showing broker as the seller's subagent is likely to conflict with the expectations of a buyer to whom the showing broker has given guidance and, in many instances, advice. Moreover, a seller may reasonably expect that, as the seller's subagent, the showing broker will be loyal to the seller's interests and will not compromise them through advice or information that the showing broker may share with buyers. If a showing broker is treated as a buyer's agent, although the buyer loses the availability of rescission as a remedy in some situations, the buyer gains the advantages of representation by a professional whom the buyer is free to choose. Real-estate professionals are best served by rules that clarify the identity of parties to whom particular duties are owed and that do not create the risk of inadvertently acting as a dual agent for buyer and seller.

Empirical results confirm the significance to buyers of retaining the services of an agent who has clearly-defined duties to represent the buyer, even when the agent is compensated by splitting a commission that will be payable from the proceeds of a sale and that will be augmented the greater the sale price. In Georgia, following the enactment of a statute that encourages buyers to retain their own agents, the average time required to sell a house fell, as did reported sale prices of expensive houses. Additionally, a large majority of buyers chose to be represented by their own agent.

Statutes in about four-fifths of the states expressly permit prospective buyers to retain licensed real-estate brokers as agents. Since 1993, the Realtors' Association has permitted listing brokers to offer showing brokers, as an alternative to a relationship of subagency, a relationship of "cooperation and compensation" that is compatible both with a showing broker who acts as a buyer's agent as well as with a showing broker who acts as the seller's subagent.

Unless a statute so requires, a writing should not be necessary to establish that a prospective buyer and a real-estate broker have consented to create a relationship of agency. See § 3.02, Comment *e*, for discussion of statutes that impose a writing requirement on agreements to pay commissions to brokers. Statutes in some states require a written agreement to create a relationship of agency with either a listing broker or a buyer's agent.

If a prospective buyer does not create a relationship of agency as defined in § 1.01 with a showing broker, the showing broker should be treated as the seller's subagent if the seller has expressly or impliedly consented to the appointment of subagents by the listing broker. The showing broker should not be treated as the buyer's agent when no relationship of agency as defined in § 1.01 has been created between the buyer and the showing broker, nor should the showing broker be treated as an intermediary who acts as no one's agent, unless a statute so requires.

If a prospective buyer consents to a relationship of agency as defined in § 1.01 with a particular real-estate broker, it is incompatible with the duties thereby created for that broker additionally to act as subagent for the seller of property that the buyer purchases unless the buyer knows of the subagency and consents to it and unless the seller knows of and consents to the broker's relationship with the buyer. A broker retained by a prospective buyer would become a dual agent if the broker also acts as subagent on behalf of the seller of the property purchased by the buyer who is represented by the broker. This would occur if the property's owner lists it with the buyer's broker or if the buyer's broker is also characterized as the subagent of the property's owner. If the property in which a buyer is interested is listed in MLS under terms that designate a successful showing broker as the seller's subagent, that designation should not be operative without the consent of a buyer who has previously retained the showing broker as the buyer's agent.

However, an agent is not a dual agent if there is no substantial risk that the agent's action on behalf of one principal will materially and adversely affect the agent's action on behalf of another principal. See § 8.03. An agent retained by a buyer does not become a dual agent by taking ministerial actions on behalf of a seller. Dual agency, as noted above, results when the broker whom a buyer has retained to act as the buyer's agent also serves as listing agent for the property purchased by the buyer, whether at the outset of the buyer's relationship with the broker or thereafter if the owner of the property lists it for sale with that broker. Under the common-law rule in most states, a broker has a relationship of agency with each of the broker's clients although the clients have agreed to be represented by individuals among the broker's cohort of employees and associates. Thus, a broker would be characterized as a dual agent when one employee or associate serves as the designated agent of a buyer and another serves as the seller's designated agent. Statutes in some states explicitly permit the practice of designated dual agency and impose specific writing and disclosure requirements. In contrast, a few statutes categorically prohibit dual agency in transactions but permit the use of nonagent intermediaries, as described below.

Relationships among brokers, sellers, and buyers have been recharacterized by statutes enacted by many states since the late 1980's. Statutes in about four-fifths of the states expressly permit prospective buyers to retain licensed real-estate brokers to act as their agents. However, these statutes are disparate in specifying the default rule that characterizes a showing broker when the buyer has not appointed that broker as agent. Several statutes provide that subagency shall not be deemed to be created automatically or through participation in a MLS. Some statutes provide that if no written agreement establishes a relationship of agency or subagency, a broker is treated as a "transaction broker," "transaction coordinator," or "facilitator" who does not act as either party's agent or subagent. Some statutes that permit the use of such nonagent intermediaries specify the duties owed by the intermediary. Many statutes make subagency the default characterization, either explicitly or implicitly by not specifying an alternative. Other statutes require specific types of disclosure, such as disclosure to a prospective buyer that a seller's agent represents the seller. Several statutes permit the parties to create a relationship of "designated dual agency" not subject to the usual consequences of dual agency, in which one sales associate in a real-estate brokerage represents the seller of a property and the other its buyer. Some statutes characterize such brokers as "limited agents," specifying their duties. Some statutes explicitly prohibit "designated dual agency." Statutes in a few states explicitly abrogate the common law of agency.

§ 3.16 Agent for Co-principals

Two or more persons may as co-principals appoint an agent to act for them in the same transaction or matter.

Chapter 4

RATIFICATION

§ 4.01 Ratification Defined

(1) A person may ratify a prior act done by another without actual or apparent authority.

(2) A person ratifies an act by

(a) manifesting assent that the act shall affect the person's legal relations, or

(b) conduct that is justifiable only on the assumption that the person so consents.

(3) Ratification does not occur unless

(a) the act is ratifiable as stated in § 4.03,

(b) the person ratifying has capacity as stated in § 4.04,

(c) the ratification is timely as stated in § 4.05, and

(d) the ratification encompasses the act in its entirety as stated in § 4.07.

Comment b. The nature and effect of ratification. As the term is used in agency law, ratification is both an act and a set of effects. The act of ratification consists of an externally-observable assent to be bound by the prior act of another person. When the prior act did not otherwise affect the legal relations of the ratifier, ratification provides the basis on which the ratifier's legal relations are affected by the act. The set of effects that ratification creates are the consequences of actual authority. That is, when a person ratifies another's act, the legal consequence is that the person's legal relations are affected as they would have been had the actor been an agent acting with actual authority at the time of the act.

In most jurisdictions, ratification may create a relationship of agency when none existed between the actor and the ratifier at the time of the act. It is necessary that the actor have acted or purported to act on behalf of the ratifier. See § 4.03. This limits the range of ratifiable acts to those done by an actor who is an agent, or who is not an agent but pretends to be.

Ratification often serves the function of clarifying situations of ambiguous or uncertain authority. A principal's ratification confirms or validates the agent's right to have acted as the agent did. That is, an agent's action may have been effective to bind the principal to the third party, and the third party to the principal, because the agent acted with apparent authority. See § 2.03. If the principal ratifies the agent's act, it is thereafter not necessary to establish that the agent acted with apparent authority. Moreover, by replicating the effects of actual authority, the principal's ratification eliminates claims the principal would otherwise have against the agent for acting without actual authority. See § 8.09, Comment *b*. The principal's ratification may also eliminate claims that third parties could assert against the agent when the agent has purported to have authority to bind the principal but the principal is not bound. See § 6.10. Ratification is effective even when the third party knew that the agent lacked authority to bind the principal but nonetheless dealt with the agent.

Much of the doctrine applicable to ratification either determines the validity and significance of the principal's assent or makes ratification unavailable or limits its effects when unfair consequences otherwise would follow. Although ratification creates the legal effects of actual authority, it reverses in time the sequence between an agent's conduct and the principal's manifestation of assent. If the principal ratifies, the relevant time for determining legal consequences is the time of the agent's act. See § 4.02, Comment *b*. Thus, if the agent purported to commit the principal to a transaction, the principal and third party become bound as of the time of the agent's commitment when the principal ratifies. If the agent's act constituted a tort, the time of the act is the time as of which the principal becomes vicariously liable, if the principal ratifies the agent's act. If the agent receives a notification, or learns information relevant to the action the agent takes, the notification is effective as to the principal, and the information is imputed to the principal, as of the time of the agent's act if the principal ratifies it. See § 5.02.

The sole requirement for ratification is a manifestation of assent or other conduct indicative of consent by the principal. To be effective as a ratification, the principal's assent need not be communicated to the agent or to third parties whose legal relations will be affected by the ratification. See Comment *d*. The principal is not bound by a ratification made without knowledge of material facts about the agent's act, unless the principal chose to ratify with awareness that such knowledge was lacking. See § 4.06. When there are two or more co-principals, each must ratify to be bound. In most cases in which the outcome turns on whether a principal has ratified, the claim of ratification is asserted by a third party who seeks to bind the principal in the absence of other bases to attribute the legal consequences of the agent's act to the principal. It is fair to hold the principal to such consequences when the principal has, after the fact, assented to the agent's act. The principal's ability to ratify also enables the principal to create a clear basis on which to hold the third party to transactions that are desirable from the principal's perspective. The doctrines stated in §§ 4.05, 4.07 and 4.08 deny the principal the power to ratify when the result of ratification would be unfair. Absent such circumstances, it is not unfair to bind the third party when the principal elects to ratify a transaction because the result binds the third party only as originally anticipated or hoped, which is to the terms of a transaction with the principal.

The effects of the principal's ratification are also fair to the agent because by assenting to the agent's act the principal usually eliminates claims that the principal or the third party might otherwise assert against the agent. Ratification is an all-or-nothing proposition in two basic respects. First, in most cases, by ratifying the principal eliminates claims the principal might otherwise have against the agent for acting without actual authority. See § 4.02(2) for exceptions to this general principle. Were the doctrine otherwise, the principal could speculate at the agent's expense by ratifying a transaction as against the third party, but holding the agent accountable if, after the time of ratification, the transaction turned out to be a losing proposition for the principal. Second, a principal must ratify a single transaction in its entirety, thereby becoming subject to its burdens as well as enjoying its benefits. See § 4.07.

§ 4.02 Effect of Ratification

(1) Subject to the exceptions stated in subsection (2), ratification creates the effects of actual authority after the fact.

(2) Ratification is not effective:

(a) in favor of a person who causes it by misrepresentation or other conduct that would make a contract voidable;

(b) in favor of an agent against a principal when the principal ratifies to avoid a loss; or

(c) to diminish the rights or other interests of persons, not parties to the transaction, that were acquired in the subject matter prior to the ratification.

§ 4.03 Acts That May be Ratified

A person may ratify an act if the actor acted or purported to act as an agent on the person's behalf.

§ 4.04 Capacity to Ratify

(1) A person may ratify an act if

(a) the person existed at the time of the act, and

(b) the person had capacity as defined in § 3.04 at the time of ratifying the act.

(2) At a later time, a principal may avoid a ratification made earlier when the principal lacked capacity as defined in § 3.04.

§ 4.05 Timing of Ratification

A ratification of a transaction is not effective unless it precedes the occurrence of circumstances that would cause the ratification to have adverse and inequitable effects on the rights of third parties. These circumstances include:

(1) any manifestation of intention to withdraw from the transaction made by the third party;

(2) any material change in circumstances that would make it inequitable to bind the third party, unless the third party chooses to be bound; and

(3) a specific time that determines whether a third party is deprived of a right or subjected to a liability.

§ 4.06 Knowledge Requisite to Ratification

A person is not bound by a ratification made without knowledge of material facts involved in the original act when the person was unaware of such lack of knowledge.

§ 4.07 No Partial Ratification

A ratification is not effective unless it encompasses the entirety of an act, contract, or other single transaction.

§ 4.08 Estoppel to Deny Ratification

If a person makes a manifestation that the person has ratified another's act, and the manifestation, as reasonably understood by a third party, induces the third party to make a detrimental change in position, the person may be estopped to deny the ratification.

Chapter 5

NOTIFICATIONS AND NOTICE

§ 5.01 Notifications and Notice—In General

(1) A notification is a manifestation that is made in the form required by agreement among parties or applicable law, or in a reason-

able manner in the absence of any agreement or applicable law, with the intention of affecting the legal rights and duties of the notifier in relation to rights and duties of persons to whom the notification is given.

(2) A notification given to or by an agent is effective as notice to the principal as stated in § 5.02.

(3) A person has notice of a fact if the person knows the fact, has reason to know the fact, has received an effective notification of the fact, or should know the fact to fulfill a duty owed to another person.

(4) Notice of a fact that an agent knows or has reason to know is imputed to the principal as stated in §§ 5.03 and 5.04.

§ 5.02 Notification Given by or to an Agent

(1) A notification given to an agent is effective as notice to the principal if the agent has actual or apparent authority to receive the notification, unless the person who gives the notification knows or has reason to know that the agent is acting adversely to the principal as defined in § 5.04(2).

(2) A notification given by an agent is effective as notification given by the principal if the agent has actual or apparent authority to give the notification, unless the person who receives the notification knows or has reason to know that the agent is acting adversely to the principal as defined in § 5.04(2).

§ 5.03 Imputation of Notice of Fact to Principal

For purposes of determining a principal's legal relations with a third party, notice of a fact that an agent knows or has reason to know is imputed to the principal if knowledge of the fact is material to the agent's duties to the principal, unless the agent

(a) acts adversely to the principal as stated in § 5.04, or

(b) is subject to a duty to another not to disclose the fact to the principal.

Comment c. Imputation within organizational principals. Imputation doctrines, like common-law agency in general, treat a juridical person that is an organization as one legal person. Organizations generally function by subdividing work or activities into specific functions that are assigned to different people. See § 1.03, Comment *c*. Within an organization, the work done by some agents consists of obtaining information on the basis of which co-agents take action. Imputation recognizes that an organization constitutes one legal person and that its link to the external world is through its agents, including those whose assigned function is to receive, collect, report, or record information for organizational purposes. . . .

The nature and scope of the duties assigned to an agent are key to imputation within an organization. . . .

An organization's large size does not in itself defeat imputation, nor does the fact that an organization has structured itself internally into separate departments or divisions. Organizations are treated as possessing the collective knowledge of their employees and other agents, when that knowledge is material to the agents' duties, however the organization may have configured itself or its internal practices for transmission of information.

If an agent has learned a fact under circumstances that impose a duty on the agent not to reveal it to a principal, notice of that fact is not imputed to that principal. Thus, notice of a fact that an agent learns in confidence from one principal is not imputed to another principal. For further discussion, see Comment *e*.

An organization may put in place internal restrictions on how information is handled and transmitted to assist in fulfilling duties of confidentiality owed to its clients. Such restrictions are common in multi-function financial firms.

If information is communicated within an organization contrary to a prohibition imposed by an internal barrier on communication, the firm is charged with notice of the information.... Prior communications that contravene an organization's internal barrier call the barrier's general effectiveness into question. A barrier is not likely to be effective or to appear credible when personnel who possess nonpublic information work on shared projects with personnel whose job functions involve trading or other activity that would be aided by access to nonpublic information. Indicia of commitment to the barrier at an organization's highest levels enhance its credibility, as does consistent imposition of sanctions when violations are known to have occurred. A barrier's credibility will also be enhanced by regular review of its efficacy by a suitable organ of internal governance, such as an internal audit or regulatory department or an independent audit or other committee of a board of directors.

Barriers on intra-organization transmission of nonpublic information may also be strongly encouraged or required by law or regulation, which evolves as circumstances require. For example, the SEC's Rule 14e–3(b), promulgated under § 14(e) of the Securities Exchange Act, provides that a person (other than a natural person) will not be subject to liability for trading on the basis of nonpublic information about an impending tender offer if the person has established reasonable policies to ensure that individuals who make decisions to trade in securities of the target corporation do not receive information about the bid possessed by other individuals within the same firm. Such barriers may also be required by law. For example, the Insider Trading and Securities Fraud Enforcement Act of 1988 requires broker-dealers and investment advisers to establish and maintain written procedures to prevent misuse of inside information. See 15 U.S.C. § 78o(f). National banks are required by the Office of the Comptroller of the Currency to use internal barriers to prevent bank trust departments from unlawfully obtaining nonpublic information from other bank departments. See 12 C.F.R. § 9.5.

An internal barrier on communication of nonpublic information does not provide a defense to the legal consequences of a failure to take action in light of information that is otherwise freely available. . . .

§ 5.04 An Agent Who Acts Adversely to a Principal

For purposes of determining a principal's legal relations with a third party, notice of a fact that an agent knows or has reason to know is not imputed to the principal if the agent acts adversely to the principal in a transaction or matter, intending to act solely for the agent's own purposes or those of another person. Nevertheless, notice is imputed

(a) when necessary to protect the rights of a third party who dealt with the principal in good faith; or

(b) when the principal has ratified or knowingly retained a benefit from the agent's action.

A third party who deals with a principal through an agent, knowing or having reason to know that the agent acts adversely to the principal, does not deal in good faith for this purpose.

Comment b. Exception to imputation—in general. The doctrine stated in this section is an exception to the general rule, stated in § 5.03, that notice is imputed to a principal of a fact that an agent knows or has reason to know if knowledge of the fact is material to the agent's duties to the principal and to the principal's legal relations with third parties. The exception stated in this section is often termed the "adverse interest" exception. There is no imputation if the agent acts adversely to the principal. The adverse interest exception is subject to two exclusions or exceptions. First, as stated in subsection (a), notice is imputed to the principal of facts that an agent who acts adversely knows or has reason to know when necessary to protect the rights of a third party who has dealt with the principal in good faith. Second, as stated in subsection (b), notice is imputed to a principal when the principal ratifies the agent's action or knowingly retains a benefit from the agent's action, although the agent acted adversely to the principal.

A third party who knows or has reason to know that an agent acts adversely to the principal, and who deals with the principal through the agent, has not dealt in good faith and may not rely on the adverse interest exception Thus, imputation protects innocent third parties but not those who know or have reason to know that an agent is not likely to transmit material information to the principal.

The rule stated in this section, like the rule stated in § 5.03, is applicable only for purposes of determining a principal's legal relations with a third party. Thus, notice is not imputed for purposes of determining rights and liabilities as between principal and agent. As a consequence, imputation does not furnish a basis on which an agent may defend against a claim by the principal.

If a principal ratifies action taken by an agent, the principal is bound by the legal consequences of that action as if the principal had knowledge of all the facts known by the agent. Section 4.01(2) states how a principal may ratify an agent's action, including by retaining a benefit produced by the agent's action. See Comment *d* for further discussion.

This section states a well-established doctrine. Partnership legislation has long incorporated the principle that a partnership is not charged with the knowledge of a partner who acts adversely to it. Under § 12 of the Uniform Partnership Act (1914) and § 102(f) of the Uniform Partnership Act (1997), a partnership is charged with a partner's knowledge, "except in the case of a fraud on the partnership committed by or with the consent of that partner."

However, as stated above, in order to protect third parties who dealt with the principal in good faith, common-law agency doctrine encompasses exclusions to the exception to imputation when an agent acts adversely. As stated in subsection (a), the adverse-interest exception to imputation does not defeat the rights of a third party who dealt in good faith with the principal through an agent. Common-law agency also recognizes that a principal may elect to ratify the actions of an adversely-acting agent. Taken as a whole, the common-law doctrine reflects a balance among factors that, if pressed in isolation to their respective extremes, would lead to divergent outcomes.

Ordinarily an agent's failure to disclose a material fact to a principal does not defeat imputation, nor does the fact that the agent's action otherwise constitutes a breach of a duty owed the principal. See § 5.03, Comment *b*. A principal's opportunity to monitor an agent and create incentives for the proper handling of information warrant imputing an agent's knowledge to the principal even when the agent has breached duties of disclosure to the principal. Moreover, imputation does not rest on an identification between principal and agent but rather on the fact that a principal's agents link it to the external world for purposes of obtaining and conveying information as well as taking action.

When an agent acts for the agent's own purposes or those of another person, the principal may be subject to liability to third parties because the agent may reasonably appear to be acting as the principal's representative with actual authority. See § 2.03. Likewise, notice of material facts known to an agent is imputed to the principal when the agent deals with a third party who reasonably believes the agent to be authorized so to act for the principal. However, this section does not protect a third party who knows or has reason to know that an agent acts adversely to the principal. If the third party colludes with the agent against the principal or otherwise knows or has reason to know that the agent is acting adversely to the principal, the third party should not expect that the agent will fulfill duties of disclosure owed to the principal.

Chapter 6

CONTRACTS AND OTHER TRANSACTIONS WITH THIRD PARTIES

TOPIC 1. PARTIES TO CONTRACTS

§ 6.01 Agent for Disclosed Principal

When an agent acting with actual or apparent authority makes a contract on behalf of a disclosed principal,

(1) the principal and the third party are parties to the contract; and

(2) the agent is not a party to the contract unless the agent and third party agree otherwise.

§ 6.02 Agent for Unidentified Principal

When an agent acting with actual or apparent authority makes a contract on behalf of an unidentified principal,

(1) the principal and the third party are parties to the contract; and

(2) the agent is a party to the contract unless the agent and the third party agree otherwise.

§ 6.03 Agent for Undisclosed Principal

When an agent acting with actual authority makes a contract on behalf of an undisclosed principal,

(1) unless excluded by the contract, the principal is a party;

(2) the agent and the third party are parties to the contract; and

(3) the principal, if a party to the contract, and the third party have the same rights, liabilities, and defenses against each other as if the principal made the contract personally, subject to §§ 6.05–.09.

d. Circumstances that affect rights or liabilities of undisclosed principal; contract excluding undisclosed principal as party. An undisclosed principal does not become a party to a contract if the contract excludes the principal. An explicit exclusion limits the third party's manifestation of assent to be bound. An undisclosed principal is not excluded from a contract by language stating that the contract is not assignable. In contrast, an undisclosed principal and an agent may agree that the agent alone shall be liable on a contract. An agreement between an undisclosed principal and an agent cannot effectively exclude the principal as a party to the contract because the third party has not assented to such exclusion.

By dealing on behalf of an undisclosed principal, an agent does not implicitly represent that the agent is not acting for a principal. This is because it is usually not material to a third party whether the person with whom the third party deals, and who becomes subject to liability on contracts made with the third party, acts as an agent for an undisclosed principal. See § 6.11, Comment *d*. If an agent falsely represents that the agent does not act on behalf of a principal, the third party may avoid a contract made with the agent under the circumstances stated in § 6.11(4). A third party may avoid a contract made by an agent acting for an undisclosed principal if the agent or the principal know or have reason to know that the third party would not have dealt with the principal as a party to the contract. See id. See also § 6.02, Comment *c*.

The nature of the performance that a contract requires determines whether performance by an undisclosed principal will be effective as performance under the contract and whether an undisclosed principal can require that the third party render performance to the principal. Performance by an undisclosed principal is not effective as performance under a contract if the third party has a substantial interest in receiving performance from the agent who made the contract. This limit corresponds to the limit on delegability of performance of a duty as stated in Restatement Second, Contracts § 318(2).

The nature of the performance that a contract requires from a third party determines whether an undisclosed principal is entitled to receive that performance. An undisclosed principal may not require that a third party render performance to the principal if rendering performance to the principal would materially change the nature of the third party's duty, materially increase the burden or risk imposed on the third party, or materially impair the third party's chance of receiving return performance. These limits correspond to the limits imposed on assignment of a contractual right. See Restatement Second, Contracts § 317(2).

§ 6.04 Principal Does not Exist or Lacks Capacity

If a person who, purporting to act as an agent on behalf of a principal, makes a contract with a third party and knows or has reason to know that the purported principal does not exist or lacks capacity to be a party to a contract, the purported agent is a party to the contract unless the third party agrees otherwise.

TOPIC 2. RIGHTS, LIABILITIES, AND DEFENSES

TITLE A. GENERAL

§ 6.05 Contract That is Unauthorized in Part or that Combines Orders of Several Principals

(1) If an agent makes a contract with a third party that differs from the contract that the agent had actual or apparent authority to make only in an amount or by the inclusion or exclusion of a separable part, the principal is subject to liability to the third party to the extent of the contract that the agent had actual or apparent authority to make if

(a) the third party seasonably makes a manifestation to the principal of willingness to be bound; and

(b) the principal has not changed position in reasonable reliance on the belief that no contract bound the principal and the third party.

(2) Two or more principals may authorize the same agent to make separate contracts for them. If the agent makes a single contract with a third party on the principals' behalves that combines the principals' separate orders or interests and calls for a single performance by the third party,

(a) if the principals are unidentified or undisclosed, the third party and the agent are the only parties to the combined contract; and

(b) if the agent purports to make the combined contract on behalf of disclosed principals, the agent is subject to liability to the third party for breach of the agent's warranty of authority as stated in § 6.10, unless the separate principals are bound by the combined contract.

Unless the agent acted with actual or apparent authority to bind each of the principals to the combined contract, and subject to (1), none of the separate principals is subject to liability on the combined contract, and the third party is not subject to liability on the combined contract to any of the separate principals.

§ 6.06 Setoff

(1) When an agent makes a contract on behalf of a disclosed or unidentified principal, unless the principal and the third party agree otherwise,

(a) the third party may not set off any amount that the agent owes the third party against an amount the third party owes the principal under the contract; and

(b) the principal may not set off any amount that the third party owes the agent against an amount the principal owes the third party under the contract.

(2) When an agent makes a contract on behalf of an undisclosed principal,

(a) until the third party has notice that the agent acts on behalf of a principal, the third party may set off any amount that the agent owes the third party against an amount the third party owes the principal under the contract;

(b) after the third party has notice that the agent acts on behalf of a principal, the third party may not set off any amount that the agent thereafter comes to owe the third party against an amount the third party owes the principal under the contract unless the principal consents; and

(c) the principal may not set off any amount that the third party owes the agent against an amount that the principal owes the third party under the contract, unless the principal and the third party agree otherwise.

(3) Unless otherwise agreed, an agent who is a party to a contract may not set off any amount that the principal owes the agent against an amount that the agent owes the third party under the contract. However, with the principal's consent, the agent may set off any amount that the principal could set off against an amount that the principal owes the third party under the contract.

TITLE B. SUBSEQUENT DEALINGS BETWEEN THIRD PARTY AND PRINCIPAL OR AGENT

§ 6.07 Settlement with Agent by Principal or Third Party

(1) A principal's payment to or settlement of accounts with an agent discharges the principal's liability to a third party with whom the agent has made a contract on the principal's behalf only when the principal acts in reasonable reliance on a manifestation by the third party, not induced by misrepresentation by the agent, that the agent has settled the account with the third party.

(2) A third party's payment to or settlement of accounts with an agent discharges the third party's liability to the principal if the agent acts with actual or apparent authority in accepting the payment or settlement.

(3) When an agent has made a contract on behalf of an undisclosed principal,

(a) the third party's payment to or settlement of accounts with the agent discharges the third party's liability to the principal until the third party has notice of the principal's existence;

(b) after the third party has notice of the principal's existence, the third party's payment to or settlement of accounts with the agent discharges the third party's liability to the principal if the agent acts with actual or apparent authority in accepting the payment or settlement; and

(c) after receiving notice of the principal's existence, the third party may demand reasonable proof of the principal's identity and relationship to the agent. Until such proof is received, the third party's payment to or settlement of accounts in good faith with the agent discharges the third party's duty to the principal.

§ 6.08 Other Subsequent Dealings Between Third Party and Agent

(1) When an agent has made a contract with a third party on behalf of a disclosed or unidentified principal, subsequent dealings between the agent and the third person may increase or diminish the principal's liability to the third person if the agent acts with actual or apparent authority or the principal ratifies the agent's action.

(2) When an agent has made a contract with a third party on behalf of an undisclosed principal,

(a) unless the third party has notice of the principal's existence, subsequent dealings between the third party and the agent may increase or diminish the liability of the principal to the third party if the agent acts with actual authority, or the principal ratifies the agent's action; and

(b) after the third party has notice of the principal's existence, subsequent dealings between the third party and the agent may increase or decrease the principal's liability to the third party if the agent acts with actual or apparent authority or the principal ratifies the agent's action.

§ 6.09 Effect of Judgment Against Agent or Principal

When an agent has made a contract with a third party on behalf of a principal, unless the contract provides otherwise,

(1) the liability of the principal or the agent is not discharged if the third party obtains a judgment against the other; and

(2) the liability of the principal or the agent is discharged to the extent a judgment against the other is satisfied.

TITLE C. AGENT'S WARRANTIES AND REPRESENTATIONS

§ 6.10 Agent's Implied Warranty of Authority

A person who purports to make a contract, representation, or conveyance on behalf of another person, lacking power to bind that person, gives an implied warranty of authority to the third party, and is subject to liability for damages for loss caused by breach of that warranty, including loss of the benefit expected from performance by the principal, unless

(1) the person who purports to make the contract, conveyance, or representation makes a manifestation to the third party that no warranty of authority is given; or

(2) the third party knows that the person who purports to make the contract, conveyance or representation acts without actual authority.

§ 6.11 Agent's Representations

(1) When an agent for a disclosed or undisclosed principal makes a false representation about the agent's authority to a third party, the principal is not subject to liability unless the principal has made a manifestation to the third party that, reasonably interpreted, causes the third party to rely on the agent's representation and the third party does not have notice that the agent's representation is false.

(2) A representation by an agent made incident to a contract or conveyance is attributed to a disclosed or unidentified principal as if the principal made the representation directly when the agent had actual or apparent authority to make the contract or conveyance, unless the third party knew or had reason to know that the representation was untrue or that the agent acted without actual authority in making it.

(3) A representation by an agent made incident to a contract or conveyance is attributed to an undisclosed principal as if the principal made the representation directly when

(a) the agent acted with actual authority in making the representation, or

(b) the agent acted without actual authority in making the representation but had actual authority to make true representations about the same matter.

The agent's representation is not attributed to the principal when the third party knew or had reason to know it was untrue.

(4) When an agent who makes a contract or conveyance on behalf of an undisclosed principal falsely represents to the third party that the agent does not act on behalf of a principal, the third party may avoid the contract or conveyance if the principal or agent had notice that the third party would not have dealt with the principal.

Chapter 7

TORTS—LIABILITY OF AGENT AND PRINCIPAL

TOPIC 1. AGENT'S LIABILITY

§ 7.01 Agent's Liability to Third Party

An agent is subject to liability to a third party harmed by the agent's tortious conduct. Conduct otherwise tortious is not privileged simply because an actor acts as an agent or an employee, with actual or apparent authority, or within the scope of employment.

§ 7.02 Duty to Principal; Duty to Third Party

An agent's breach of a duty owed to the principal is not an independent basis for an agent's tort liability to a third party. An agent is subject to tort liability to a third party harmed by the agent's conduct only when the agent's conduct breaches a duty that the agent owes to the third party.

TOPIC 2. PRINCIPAL'S LIABILITY

§ 7.03 Principal's Liability—In General

A principal is subject to liability to a third party harmed by an agent's conduct when

(1) as stated in § 7.04 the agent acts with actual authority or the principal ratifies the agent's conduct and

(a) the agent's conduct is tortious, or

(b) the agent's conduct, if that of the principal, would subject the principal to tort liability; or

(2) as stated in § 7.05, the principal is negligent in selecting, supervising, or otherwise controlling the agent; or

(3) as stated in § 7.06, the principal delegates performance of a duty to use care to protect other persons or their property to an agent who fails to perform the duty; or

(4) as stated in § 7.07, the agent is an employee who commits a tort while acting within the scope of employment; or

(5) as stated in § 7.08, the agent commits a tort when acting with apparent authority in dealing with a third party on or purportedly on behalf of the principal.

Comment d. Agents with multiple principals. An agent who commits a tort may have more than one principal for at least some purposes. On agents with multiple principals in general, see Chapter 3, Topic 5. In the context of a principal's liability on the basis of an agent's tort, it is helpful to distinguish among three different types of relationships: (1) subagency; (2) employees who are "borrowed" by one employer from another employer; and (3) officers of inter-related entities.

Comment d(1). Subagency. A subagent is a person appointed by an agent to perform functions that the agent has consented to perform on behalf of the principal. See § 3.15(1). For general discussion of the consequences of subagency, see id. Comment *d.* A subagent may be an employee of the appointing agent. When a subagent is an employee, as defined in § 7.07(3), of the appointing agent, the appointing agent is subject to vicarious liability for torts committed by the subagent within the scope of employment. See § 7.07. Both the appointing agent and the principal are subject to vicarious liability when a subagent acts with apparent authority in committing a tort, as stated in § 7.08. An appointing agent may be subject to liability for torts of a subagent who is not an employee. For example, when a law firm assigns work on behalf of a client to a "temporary" lawyer who is neither a member of the firm nor its employee, the firm creates a relationship of subagency with the "temporary" lawyer that subjects it to liability to its client for acts and omissions of the "temporary" lawyer. See Restatement Third, The Law Governing Lawyers § 58, Comment *e* (2000).

A relationship of subagency does not result when an agent appoints a co-agent. Co-agents share a common principal, although they may occupy dominant and subordinate positions in an organizational hierarchy. See § 3.15, Comment *b*. An agent who has authority to hire a co-agent is not subject to vicarious liability for the co-agent's tortious conduct.

Comment d(2). "Lent employees," or "borrowed servants." When work requires specialized skills or equipment, or requires that an actor perform a task on less than a full-time basis, it is not unusual that the actor who performs the work is employed by a firm that contracts to provide the actor's services to another firm. The types of actors who work through such arrangements vary greatly, as does the nature of the work they do. These arrangements span the range of highly skilled professionals, including nurses, lawyers and other members of licensed professions; office workers; skilled construction workers; and unskilled manual laborers. The risks of injury to third parties posed by such work vary, as do the settings in which work is performed. Moreover, the specifics of such arrangements vary in several respects. These include the duration of an actor's placement in a particular workplace and the provision of supervision, training, and tools needed to perform work. An actor's employer may provide requisite training, furnish the actor with specialized equipment needed for work, and reassign the actor with frequency. Alternatively, the actor may work on a long-term basis within a particular firm using tools and receiving training provided by that firm.

When an actor negligently injures a third party while performing work for the firm that has contracted for the actor's services, the question is whether that firm (often termed the "special employer") or the initial employer (often termed the "general employer"), or both, should be subject to liability to the third party. Liability should be allocated to the employer in the best position to take measures to prevent the injury suffered by the third party. An employer is in that position if the employer has the right to control an employee's conduct. When both a general and special employer have the right to control an employee's conduct, the practical history of direction may establish that one employer in fact ceded its right of control to the other, whether through its failure to exercise the right or otherwise.

It is a question of fact whether a general or a special employer, or both, have the right to control an employee's conduct. Factors that a court may consider in making this determination include the extent of control that an employer may exercise over the details of an employee's work and the timing of the work; the relationship between the employee's work and the nature of the special employer's business; the nature of the employee's work, the skills required to perform it, and the degree of supervision customarily associated with the work; the duration of the employee's work in the special employer's firm; the identity of the employer who furnishes equipment or other instrumentalities requisite to performing the work; and the method of payment for the work.

Many cases allocate liability in this context on the basis that a general employer has an exclusive right of control over employees assigned to work for clients of the general employer. This presupposes that ties between a general employer and an assigned employee will remain strong despite the employee's emplacement in the special employer's workplace where the employee's performance will often be subject to some degree of direction and monitoring by members of the special employer's management. It may also reflect assumptions about links between the general employer and the risk that third parties will be injured when work is done in a special employer's workplace. A general employer is in a position to screen prospective employees to determine their general aptitude and fitness; a general employer may also provide training to those it selects for employment. If a general employer assigns an employee and furnishes the employee with equipment to use in performing assigned work, the general employer is also in a position to impose requirements for the proper usage and maintenance of the equipment. A general employer may also be in a better position to provide insurance coverage for an employee's actions. Any presumption that a general employer has the right to control an employee may be rebutted by proving factual indicia that the right has been assumed by a special employer. Even within the same jurisdiction, it may be difficult to predict whether a given set of indicia will demonstrate that a special employer has assumed the right of control.

However, a significant number of cases allocate liability to a special employer on the basis of its right and ability to direct a borrowed employee's specific actions in its workplace. A justification for this approach is that a borrowed employee may retain only formal ties to a general employer, depending on the duration and nature of the borrowed employee's relationship with the special employer, which weakens the likelihood that the general employer retains any practical capacity to control the borrowed employee's conduct. This approach also reflects the possibility that a special employer may in fact be in the best position to exercise control in a manner that reduces the risk of injury to third parties. This possibility may be especially likely when the nature of a borrowed employee's work requires co-ordinated effort as part of a skilled team and close direction or supervision by the team's leader. Some cases allocate liability to both general and special employer on the basis that both exercised control over the employee and both benefited in some degree from the employee's work.

A related question, arising when the third party injured by an actor's negligence is an employee of the special employer, is the applicability of worker's compensation insurance law to the employee's claims.

Although these questions may often be related as a practical matter, worker's compensation questions are beyond the scope of this Restatement.

Comment d(3). Officers of inter-related entities. The fact that a corporation or other entity owns a majority of the voting equity in another entity does not create a relationship of agency between them or between each entity and the other's agents. Likewise, common ownership of multiple entities does not create relationships of agency among them. See § 1.01, Comment *(f)(2)*. An entity becomes the agent of another entity, and an individual becomes an entity's agent, only when they are linked by the elements of an agency relationship as stated in § 1.01.

Within a related group of corporations or other entities the same individuals may serve as officers or directors of more than one entity. An overlapping cast in multiple organizational roles does not in itself create relationships of agency that are not otherwise present.

When the same individuals serve multiple entities as their officers, directors, or employees, it may become necessary to determine the entity to which an individual's conduct should be attributed. There is a general presumption that contracts and other transactions entered into by a shared officer are attributed to the entity for which the officer purports to be acting. A rationale for this presumption is that the identity of the party who will be bound by a contract or transaction is often material to the other party to the contract or transaction. See § 6.01, Comment *b*. This rationale does not support applying the same presumption when a shared officer's conduct is tortious, especially when the party injured by the conduct has not chosen to engage in a transaction conducted by the shared officer. Moreover, that an officer purports to act on behalf of a particular entity does not create a basis for attribution that corresponds to policies and objectives that underlie contemporary tort law. When harm is caused negligently, these objectives include achieving fairness by rectifying an injustice that has been inflicted on a plaintiff by a defendant and providing a defendant with appropriate safety incentives. See Restatement Third, Torts: Liability for Physical Harm (Basic Principles) § 6, Comment *b*. On harm that is caused intentionally, see id. § 5, Comment *a*. Likewise, the contract-based presumption is inapt when a shared officer's conduct violates a statute that proscribes or regulates conduct, particularly conduct outside a transactional context.

§ 7.04 Agent Acts with Actual Authority

A principal is subject to liability to a third party harmed by an agent's conduct when the agent's conduct is within the scope of the agent's actual authority or the principal ratifies it; and

(1) the agent's conduct is tortious, or

(2) the agent's conduct, if that of the principal, would subject the principal to tort liability.

§ 7.05 Principal's Negligence in Conducting Activity Through Agent; Principal's Special Relationship with Another Person

(1) A principal who conducts an activity through an agent is subject to liability for harm to a third party caused by the agent's conduct if the harm was caused by the principal's negligence in selecting, training, retaining, supervising, or otherwise controlling the agent.

(2) When a principal has a special relationship with another person, the principal owes that person a duty of reasonable care with regard to risks arising out of the relationship, including the risk that agents of the principal will harm the person with whom the principal has such a special relationship.

§ 7.06 Failure in Performance of Principal's Duty of Protection

A principal required by law to protect another cannot avoid liability by delegating performance of the duty to another, whether or not the delegate is an agent.

§ 7.07 Employee Acting Within Scope of Employment

(1) An employer is subject to vicarious liability for a tort committed by its employee acting within the scope of employment.

(2) An employee acts within the scope of employment when performing work assigned by the employer or engaging in a course of conduct subject to the employer's control. An employee's act is not within the scope of employment when it occurs within an independent course of conduct not intended by the employee to serve any purpose of the employer.

(3) For purposes of this section,

(a) an employee is an agent whose principal controls or has the right to control the manner and means of the agent's performance of work, and

(b) the fact that work is performed gratuitously does not relieve a principal of liability.

Comment c. Conduct in the performance of work and scope of employment. An employee's conduct is within the scope of employment when it constitutes performance of work assigned to the employee by the employer. The fact that the employee performs the work carelessly does not take the employee's conduct outside the scope of employment, nor does the fact that the employee otherwise makes a mistake in performing the work. Likewise, conduct is not outside the scope of employment merely because an employee disregards the employer's instructions.

. . . An employee may believe that the employer wishes the employee to disregard an inconvenient constraint when the employee fears that compliance would jeopardize completing the employee's assigned mission at all or completing it on or ahead of schedule. Although the employee's belief may be mistaken, it is compatible with acting in an assigned role to do an assigned task. However, the character or extreme nature of an employee's actions may demonstrate that the employee's course of conduct is independent of performing work assigned by the employer and intended solely to further the employee's own purposes.

An employee's failure to take action may also be conduct within the scope of employment. For example, an employee's failure to do work assigned by the employer, when harm to a third party results, under some circumstances may constitute negligence. A negligent action "frequently involves a failure to take a reasonable precaution . . . which can be described as an omission, and it hence can be said that the omission in itself is negligent." Restatement Third, Torts: Liability for Physical Harm (Basic Principles) § 3, Comment *c* (Tentative Draft No. 1, 2001).

An employee's assigned work may include tasks that contemplate the necessity of using physical force to complete the assigned work, as in Illustrations 1 and 2. An employee's assigned duties may also place the employee in situations in which physical consequences may follow in an uninterrupted sequence from verbal exchanges with third parties. An escalation in the pitch of an employee's conduct does not by itself transform the conduct into an independent course of conduct that represents a departure not within the scope of employment. It is a question of fact what motivated an employee's conduct as verbal exchanges escalate or when an employee's use of physical force becomes more pronounced.

In determining whether an employee's tortious conduct is within the scope of employment, the nature of the tort is relevant, as is whether the conduct also constitutes a criminal act. An employee's intentionally criminal conduct may indicate a departure from conduct within the scope of employment, not a single escalation. . . .

The determinative question is whether the course of conduct in which the tort occurred is within the scope of employment. Intentional torts and other intentional wrongdoing may be within the scope of employment. For example, if an employee's job duties include determining the prices at which the employer's output will be sold to customers, the employee's agreement with a competitor to fix prices is within the scope of employment unless circumstances establish a departure from the scope of employment. Likewise, when an employee's job duties include making statements to prospective customers to induce them to buy from the employer, intentional misrepresentations made by the employee are within the scope of employment unless circumstances establish that the employee has departed from it.

An employee may engage in conduct, part of which is within the scope of employment and part of which is not. . . .

When an employee's tortious conduct is outside the scope of employment, alternate theories of liability may be available against the employer. . . .

§ 7.08 Agent Acts with Apparent Authority

A principal is subject to vicarious liability for a tort committed by an agent in dealing or communicating with a third party on or purportedly on behalf of the principal and actions taken by the agent with apparent authority constitute the tort or enable the agent to conceal its commission.

Chapter 8

DUTIES OF AGENT AND PRINCIPAL TO EACH OTHER

TOPIC 1. AGENT'S DUTIES TO PRINCIPAL

TITLE A. GENERAL FIDUCIARY PRINCIPLE

§ 8.01 General Fiduciary Principle

An agent has a fiduciary duty to act loyally for the principal's benefit in all matters connected with the agency relationship.

TITLE B. DUTIES OF LOYALTY

§ 8.02 Material Benefit Arising Out of Position

An agent has a duty not to acquire a material benefit from a third party in connection with transactions conducted or other actions taken on behalf of the principal or otherwise through the agent's use of the agent's position.

Comment e. Remedies. When an agent breaches the duty stated in this section, the principal may recover monetary relief from the agent and, in appropriate circumstances, from any third party who participated in the agent's breach. A principal may avoid a contract entered into by the agent with a third party who participates in the agent's breach of duty. The principal may recover any material benefit received by the agent through the agent's breach, the value of the benefit, or proceeds of the benefit retained by the agent. The principal may also recover damages for any harm caused by the agent's breach. If an agent's breach of duty involves a wrongful disposal of assets of the principal, the principal cannot recover both the value of the asset and what the agent received in exchange. If a principal recovers damages from a third party as a consequence of an agent's breach of fiduciary duty, the principal remains entitled to recover from the agent any benefit that the agent improperly received from the transaction.

If a principal seeks to recover a material benefit received by an agent, the value of the benefit, or its proceeds, the principal's recovery is not subject to a deduction for expenses incurred by the agent to induce a third party to confer the benefit on the agent.

However, if an agent breaches the agent's fiduciary duty by taking personal advantage of a business opportunity as discussed in Comment *d*, the principal may recover property that the agent acquired through the breach only if the principal reimburses the agent. The amount of reimbursement is either the amount paid by the agent for the property or the amount for which the principal could have obtained the property, whichever is less. See Restatement of Restitution §§ 194, 195; Principles of Corporate Governance: Analysis and Recommendations, Comment to § 5.05(e) and Illustration 13.

§ 8.03 Acting as or on Behalf of an Adverse Party

An agent has a duty not to deal with the principal as or on behalf of an adverse party in a transaction connected with the agency relationship.

Comment b. Rationale. As a fiduciary, an agent has a duty to the principal to act loyally in the principal's interest in all matters in connection with the agency relationship. See § 8.01. The rule stated in this section is a specific application of this general principle. When an agent deals with the principal on the agent's own account, the agent's own interests are irreconcilably in tension with the principal's interests because the interest of each is furthered by action—negotiating a higher or a lower price, for example—that is incompatible with the interests of the other. If an agent acts on behalf of the principal in a transaction with the agent, the agent's duty to act loyally in the principal's interest conflicts with the agent's self-interest. Even if the agent's divided loyalty does not result in demonstrable harm to the principal, the agent has breached the agent's duty of undivided loyalty. Likewise, an agent who acts on behalf of more than one principal in a transaction between or among the principals has breached the agent's duty of loyalty to each principal through undertaking service to multiple principals that divides the agent's loyalty.

A principal may consent to conduct by an agent that would otherwise constitute a breach of the agent's duty. See § 8.06. On consent by multiple principals when an agent conducts a transaction between or among the principals, see § 8.06(2).

The duty stated in this section is formulated broadly. So long as the transaction in which an agent acts as or on behalf of an adverse party is connected with the agency relationship, the agent is subject to the duty although the agent does not have direct or indirect responsibility for conducting the transaction on behalf of the principal. The breadth of this formulation requires that an agent disclose adverse interests to the principal so that the principal may evaluate, as only the principal is situated to do, how best to protect its interests in light of the agent's interest. See § 8.06. The breadth of the formulation also makes it unnecessary for a principal to prescribe its agents' duties and prohibit outside interests that its agents may have or acquire with great specificity in formulating the initial terms of its relationship with its agents.

A principal's knowledge that an agent deals as or on behalf of an adverse party does not relieve the agent of duties to the principal in connection with that transaction. Under the rule stated in § 8.06, the agent has a duty to deal fairly with the principal and to disclose to the principal all facts of which the agent has notice that are reasonably relevant to the principal's exercise of judgment, unless the principal has manifested that the principal already knows them or does not wish to know them. Thus, a principal's knowledge that its agent acts as or on behalf of an adverse party does not convert the relationship between principal and agent into an arms-length relationship. Moreover, as stated in § 8.11, an agent has a duty to use reasonable effort to furnish information to the principal although the agent does not deal as or on behalf of an adverse party.

It is, of course, possible that an agent may assume an adverse position in which the agent may not legally discharge the duties of disclosure that the agent owes to the principal because the agent owes a duty to another person not to disclose a fact that §§ 8.06 and 8.11 require be disclosed to the principal. . . .

However, an agent whose acts on behalf of a party consist solely of ministerial acts that require no exercise of discretion, judgment, or skill does not act on behalf of that party for purposes of determining whether the agent acts adversely to another principal. Thus, one principal's agent who performs only ministerial acts for another does not become a dual agent.

A custom in an industry that permits self-dealing by agents, if unknown to the principal, does not relieve the agent of the duty to refrain from self-dealing. If an agreement between principal and agent grants the agent discretion to take such adverse action, the agent is subject to a contract-law duty of good faith and fair dealing in exercising the discretion. See § 8.01, Comment *b*.

Many business-organization statutes contain provisions that address self-dealing conduct on the part of specified organizational actors. Under contemporary partnership legislation, a partner has a duty to "refrain from dealing with the partnership in the conduct or winding up of the partnership business as or on behalf of a party having an interest adverse to the partnership. . . ." Rev. Unif. Partnership Act § 404 (b)(2). Similarly, a manager of a limited liability company (LLC) has a comparable duty, as does a member of a member-managed LLC. See Unif. Limited Liability Company Act § 409 (b)(2). Many corporation statutes have provisions applicable to transactions between a corporation and a director, or between a corporation and an officer, in which mechanisms are specified through which the director or officer may fulfill duties owed to the corporation in connection with the transaction. See Principles of Corporate Governance: Analysis and Recommendations § 5.02 (1994).

§ 8.04 Competition

Throughout the duration of an agency relationship, an agent has a duty to refrain from competing with the principal and from taking action on behalf of or otherwise assisting the principal's competitors. During that time, an agent may take action, not otherwise wrongful, to prepare for competition following termination of the agency relationship.

§ 8.05 Use of Principal's Property; Use of Confidential Information

An agent has a duty

(1) not to use property of the principal for the agent's own purposes or those of a third party; and

(2) not to use or communicate confidential information of the principal for the agent's own purposes or those of a third party.

§ 8.06 Principal's Consent

(1) Conduct by an agent that would otherwise constitute a breach of duty as stated in §§ 8.01, 8.02, 8.03, 8.04 and 8.05 does not constitute a breach of duty if the principal consents to the conduct, provided that

(a) in obtaining the principal's consent, the agent

(i) acts in good faith,

(ii) discloses all material facts that the agent knows, has reason to know, or should know would reasonably affect the principal's judgment unless the principal has manifested that such facts are already known by the principal or that the principal does not wish to know them, and

(iii) otherwise deals fairly with the principal; and

(b) the principal's consent concerns either a specific act or transaction, or acts or transactions of a specified type that could reasonably be expected to occur in the ordinary course of the agency relationship.

(2) An agent who acts for more than one principal in a transaction between or among them has a duty

(a) to deal in good faith with each principal,

(b) to disclose to each principal

(i) the fact that the agent acts for the other principal or principals, and

(ii) all other facts that the agent knows, has reason to know, or should know would reasonably affect the principal's judgment unless the principal has manifested that such facts are already known by the principal or that the principal does not wish to know them, and

(c) otherwise to deal fairly with each principal.

TITLE C. DUTIES OF PERFORMANCE

§ 8.07 Duty Created by Contract

An agent has a duty to act in accordance with the express and implied terms of any contract between the agent and the principal.

§ 8.08 Duties of Care, Competence, and Diligence

Subject to any agreement with the principal, an agent has a duty to the principal to act with the care, competence, and diligence normally exercised by agents in similar circumstances. Special skills or knowledge of an agent are circumstances to be taken in account in determining whether the agent acted with due care and diligence.

Comment b. Common-law and statutory duties of care; regulatory duties. A principal and an agent may establish benchmarks or other measures for the effort and skill to be expected from the agent. For example, a contract between principal and agent may specify measures for the effort that the agent has a duty to expend in pursuing the principal's objectives. An agent may also, by contract, guarantee that the agent's work will be successful in achieving an objective or that the agent's work will be satisfactory to the principal. On conditions that an obligor be satisfied with an obligee's performance, see Restatement Second, Contracts § 228 (1979). A contract may also, in appropriate circumstances, raise or lower the standard of performance to be expected of an agent or specify the remedies or mechanisms of dispute resolution available to the principal. Regardless of their content, contractually-shaped or contractually-created duties are grounded in the mutual assent of agent and principal.

In contrast to § 8.06, the rule stated in this section articulates a broader role for general agreements that a principal and an agent may make in advance. If an agreement between principal and agent is otherwise enforceable, it may define the standard of performance applicable to the agent across the board in general terms and without the specificity required under § 8.06(1)(b) for consent by a principal to conduct by an agent that would otherwise breach a duty of loyalty owed to the principal under §§ 8.01, 8.02, 8.03, 8.04, or 8.05. Moreover, a principal's consent under § 8.06 is ineffective unless in obtaining the consent the agent acted consistently with the requirements stated in § 8.06 (1)(a) or (2).

The duties stated in this section will often overlap with an agent's duties of performance that are express or implied terms of a contract between principal and agent. However, the duties stated in this section are tort-law duties because they "denote the fact that the actor is required to conduct himself in a particular manner at the risk that if he does not do so he becomes subject to liability to another to whom the duty is owed for any injury sustained by such other, of which that actor's conduct is a legal cause." Restatement Second, Torts § 4 (1964). Tort law imposes duties of care on an agent because the agent undertakes to act on behalf of the principal, because the principal's reliance on that undertaking is foreseeable by the agent, and because it is often socially useful that an agent fulfill the agent's undertaking to the principal. See Restatement Second, Torts § 323; Restatement Third, Torts: Liability for Physical Harm (Basic Principles) § 43 (Tentative Draft No. 4, 2004).

The overlap between duties derived from tort law and from an agent's contract with the principal will often provide the principal with alternative remedies when a breach of duty subjects the agent to liability. In particular, an agent is subject to liability to the principal for all harm, whether past, present, or prospective, caused the principal by the agent's breach of the duties stated in this section. See Restatement Second, Torts § 910. The agent's liability includes an obligation to indemnify the principal when a wrongful act by the agent subjects the principal to vicarious liability to a third person. See §§ 7.07 and 7.08. One agent's breach of the duties stated in this section does not bar an innocent principal from recovery against another agent who is also subject to liability.

Statutory provisions may also be relevant in determining the duties of care owed by an agent. For example, some organizational statutes establish standards of conduct for officers and others who act on behalf of an organization. Under § 8.42(a)(2) of the Model Business Corporation Act, an officer must act, in performing the officer's duties, "with the care that a person in like position would reasonably exercise under similar circumstances. . . ." The Revised Uniform Partnership Act states that a partner owes a duty of care to the partnership and to other partners "in the conduct and winding up of the partnership business" that is limited to "refraining from engaging in grossly negligent or reckless conduct, intentional misconduct, or a knowing violation of law." Rev. Unif. Partnership Act § 404 (c). The Uniform Limited Liability Company Act imposes a comparable standard on an LLC's managers and members who are also managers. Unif. Limited Liability Co. Act § 409 (c) and (h)(2).

An agent's conduct may be subject to regulation by statutes, administrative rules, or rules of a particular profession. An agent's violation of such a statute or rule does not in itself establish that the agent breached the agent's duty to the principal stated in this section. If the statute or rule is designed to protect persons in the principal's position, the trier of fact may consider the agent's violation of the statute in defining and applying the standard stated in this section.

§ 8.09 Duty to Act Only Within Scope of Actual Authority and to Comply with Principal's Reasonable Instructions

(1) An agent has a duty to take action only within the scope of the agent's actual authority.

(2) An agent has a duty to comply with all lawful instructions received from the principal and persons designated by the principal concerning the agent's actions on behalf of the principal.

§ 8.10 Duty of Good Conduct

An agent has a duty, within the scope of the agency relationship, to act reasonably and, unless consistent with a reasonable interpretation of manifestations made by the principal, to refrain from conduct that is likely to damage the principal's enterprise.

§ 8.11 Duty to Provide Information

An agent has a duty to use reasonable effort to provide the principal with facts that the agent knows, has reason to know, or should know when

(1) the agent knows or has reason to know that the principal would wish to have the facts; or, subject to any manifestation by the principal, the facts are material to the agent's duties to the principal; and

(2) the facts can be provided to the principal without violating a duty owed by the agent to another person.

§ 8.12 Duties Regarding Principal's Property—Segregation, Record–Keeping, and Accounting

An agent has a duty, subject to any agreement with the principal,

(1) not to deal with the principal's property so that it appears to be the agent's property;

(2) not to mingle the principal's property with anyone else's; and

(3) to keep and render accounts to the principal of money or other property received or paid out on the principal's account.

TOPIC 2. PRINCIPAL'S DUTIES TO AGENT

§ 8.13 Duty Created by Contract

A principal has a duty to act in accordance with the express and implied terms of any contract between the principal and the agent.

Comment d. Compensation—other issues. Unless an agreement between a principal and an agent indicates otherwise, a principal has a duty to pay compensation to an agent for services that the agent provides. An agreement that an agent will not have a right to compensation for services provided may be implied from the agent's relationship to the principal or from the trivial nature of the services requested. The amount of compensation due may be determined by the terms of agreement between principal and agent and may be fixed in amount or made contingent on whether the agent achieves stated outcomes or on other criteria. An agreement between a principal and an agent may also set the agent's right to compensation at an amount or rate that is standard or customary in a particular industry. If an agent has a right to be paid compensation by a principal but the amount due cannot be determined on the basis of the terms of the parties's agreement, the agent is entitled to the value of the services provided by the agent.

A principal's duty to pay compensation to an agent does not extend to fulfilling an agent's duties to pay compensation to subagents engaged by the agent, unless the principal so agrees. See § 3.15, Comment *d* for an extended discussion of the consequences of subagency relationships. Thus, unless a principal agrees otherwise, the principal is not a guarantor of obligations undertaken by its agent to pay subagents appointed by the agent. Were the rule otherwise, a principal would bear the risk that an appointing agent would make generous arrangements with a subagent in exchange for payments by the subagent or would be tempted for other reasons to disregard the principal's interests in making arrangements with a subagent.

In contrast, a principal's duties of indemnity extend to subagents appointed by agents of the principal. See § 8.14, Comment *b*.

§ 8.14 Duty to Indemnify

A principal has a duty to indemnify an agent

(1) in accordance with the terms of any contract between them; and

(2) unless otherwise agreed,

(a) when the agent makes a payment

(i) within the scope of the agent's actual authority, or

(ii) that is beneficial to the principal, unless the agent acts officiously in making the payment; or

(b) when the agent suffers a loss that fairly should be borne by the principal in light of their relationship.

§ 8.15 Principal's Duty to Deal Fairly and in Good Faith

A principal has a duty to deal with the agent fairly and in good faith, including a duty to provide the agent with information about risks of physical harm or pecuniary loss that the principal knows, has reason to know, or should know are present in the agent's work but unknown to the agent.

Comment d. Duty to refrain from conduct likely to injure agent's business reputation or reasonable self-respect. This duty is the reciprocal of an agent's duty of good conduct as stated in § 8.10. Although a principal is not subject to a duty of loyalty to an agent, the principal's duty to deal with an agent fairly and in good faith requires that the principal refrain from conduct that is likely to injure the agent's business reputation through the agent's association with the principal. Likewise, a principal has a duty to refrain from conduct that will injure the agent's reasonable self-respect if the association continues.

The nature of the agent's work and other circumstances of the relationship between principal and agent are relevant to whether a principal's conduct breaches this duty.

*

RESTATEMENT (THIRD) OF AGENCY (2006)

Table of Sections

Chapter 1

INTRODUCTORY MATTERS

TOPIC 1. DEFINITIONS AND TERMINOLOGY

Chapter 2

PRINCIPLES OF ATTRIBUTION

TOPIC 1. ACTUAL AUTHORITY

TOPIC 2. APPARENT AUTHORITY

TOPIC 3. RESPONDEAT SUPERIOR

TOPIC 4. RELATED DOCTRINES

Chapter 3

CREATION AND TERMINATION OF AUTHORITY AND AGENCY RELATIONSHIPS

TOPIC 1. CREATING AND EVIDENCING ACTUAL AUTHORITY

Section

TOPIC 2. CREATING APPARENT AUTHORITY

TOPIC 3. CAPACITY TO ACT AS PRINCIPAL OR AGENT

TOPIC 4. TERMINATION OF AGENT'S POWER

TITLE A. TERMINATION OF ACTUAL AUTHORITY

TITLE B. TERMINATION OF APPARENT AUTHORITY

TITLE C. IRREVOCABLE POWERS

TOPIC 5. AGENTS WITH MULTIPLE PRINCIPALS

Chapter 4

RATIFICATION

Chapter 1

INTRODUCTORY MATTERS

TOPIC 1. DEFINITIONS AND TERMINOLOGY

§ 1.01 Agency Defined

Agency is the fiduciary relationship that arises when one person (a "principal") manifests assent to another person (an "agent") that the agent shall act on the principal's behalf and subject to the principal's control, and the agent manifests assent or otherwise consents so to act.

Comment f. Principal's power and right of interim control

(1). Principal's power and right of interim control—in general. An essential element of agency is the principal's right to control the agent's actions. Control is a concept that embraces a wide spectrum of meanings, but within any relationship of agency the principal initially states what the agent shall and shall not do, in specific or general terms. Additionally, a principal has the right to give interim instructions or directions to the agent once their relationship is established. Within an organization the right to control its agents is essential to the organization's ability to function, regardless of its size, structure, or degree of hierarchy or complexity. In an organization, it is often another agent, one holding a supervisory position, who gives the directions. For definitions of the terms "superior" and "subordinate" coagents, see § 1.04(9). A principal may exercise influence over an agent's actions in other ways as well. Incentive structures that reward the agent for achieving results affect the agent's actions. In an organization, assigning a specified function with a functionally descriptive title to a person tends to control activity because it manifests what types of activity are approved by the principal to all who know of the function and title, including their holder.

A relationship of agency is not present unless the person on whose behalf action is taken has the right to control the actor. Thus, if a person is appointed by a court to act as a receiver, the receiver is not the agent of the person whose affairs the receiver manages because the appointing court retains the power to control the receiver.

A principal's control over an agent will as a practical matter be incomplete because no agent is an automaton who mindlessly but perfectly executes commands. A principal's power to give instructions, created by the agency relationship, does not mean that all instructions the principal gives are proper. An agent's duty of obedience does not require the agent to obey instructions to commit a crime or a tort or to violate established professional standards. See § 8.09(2). Moreover, an agent's duty of obedience does not supersede the agent's power to resign and terminate the agency relationship. See § 3.10.

The power to give interim instructions distinguishes principals in agency relationships from those who contract to receive services provided by persons who are not agents. In many agreements to provide services, the agreement between the service provider and the recipient specifies terms and conditions creating contractual obligations that, if enforceable, prescribe or delimit the choices that the service provider has the right to make. In particular, if the service provider breaches a contractual obligation, the service recipient has a claim for breach of contract. The service provider may be constrained by both the existence of such an obligation and the prospect of remedies for breach of contract. The fact that such an agreement imposes constraints on the service provider does not mean that the service recipient has an interim right to give instructions to the provider. Thus, setting standards in an agreement for acceptable service quality does not of itself create a right of control. Additionally, if a service provider is retained to give an independent assessment, the expectation of independence is in tension with a right of control in the service recipient.

To the extent the parties have created a relationship of agency, however, the principal has a power of control even if the principal has previously agreed with the agent that the principal will not give interim instructions to the agent or will not otherwise interfere in the agent's exercise of discretion. However, a principal who has made such an agreement but then subsequently exercises its power of control may breach contractual duties owed to the agent, and the agent may have remedies available for the breach.

If an agent disregards or contravenes an instruction, the doctrine of actual authority, defined in § 2.01, governs the consequences as between the principal and the agent. Section 8.09 states an agent's duties to act only within the scope of actual authority and to comply with lawful instructions. The rights and obligations of the third party with whom the agent interacts are governed by the doctrines of actual authority and apparent authority. Doctrines of estoppel, restitution, and ratification are also relevant under some circumstances. See §§ 2.03, 2.05–2.07, and 4.01–4.08.

The principal's right of control in an agency relationship is a narrower and more sharply defined concept than domination or influence more generally. Many positions and relationships give one person the ability to dominate or influence other persons but not the right to control their actions. Family ties, friendship, perceived expertise, and religious beliefs are often the source of influence or dominance, as are the variety of circumstances that create a strong position in bargaining. A position of dominance or influence does not in itself mean that a person is a principal in a relationship of agency with the person over whom dominance or influence may be exercised. A relationship is one of agency only if the person susceptible to dominance or influence has consented to act on behalf of the other and the other has a right of control, not simply an ability to bring influence to bear.

The right to veto another's decisions does not by itself create the right to give affirmative directives that action be taken, which is integral to the right of control within common-law agency. Thus, a debtor does not become a creditor's agent when a loan agreement gives the creditor veto rights over decisions the debtor may make. Moreover, typically a debtor does not consent to act on behalf of the creditor as opposed to acting in its own interests.

The principal's right of control presupposes that the principal retains the capacity throughout the relationship to assess the agent's performance, provide instructions to the agent, and terminate the agency relationship by revoking the agent's authority. See § 3.10 on the principal's power to revoke authority. Under the common law of agency, as stated in Restatement Second, Agency § 122(1), a durable agency power, one that survives the principal's loss of mental competence, was not feasible because of the loss of control by the principal. Section 3.08(2), like statutes in all states, recognizes the efficacy of durable powers, which enable an agent to act on behalf of a principal incapable of exercising control. Legitimating the power does not eliminate the risks for the principal that are inherent when the agent is not subject to direction or termination by the principal.

(2). Principal's power and right of interim control—corporate context. Many questions testing the nature of the right of control arise as a result of the legal consequences of incorporating or creating a juridical or legal person distinct from its shareholders, its governing body, and its agents. A corporation's agents are its own because it is a distinct legal person; they are not the agents of other affiliated corporations unless, separately, an agency relation has been created between the agents and the affiliated corporation. Similarly, the hierarchical link between a local union and its international affiliate does not by itself create a relationship of agency between the local and the international.

Although a corporation's shareholders elect its directors and may have the right to remove directors once elected, the directors are neither the shareholders' nor the corporation's agents as defined in this section, given the treatment of directors within contemporary corporation law in the United States. Directors' powers originate as the legal consequence of their election and are not conferred or delegated by shareholders. Although corporation statutes require shareholder approval for specific fundamental transactions, corporation law generally invests managerial authority over corporate affairs in a board of directors, not in shareholders, providing that management shall occur by or under the board of directors. Thus, shareholders ordinarily do not have a right to control directors by giving binding instructions to them. If the statute under which a corporation has been incorporated so permits, shareholders may be allocated power to give binding instructions to directors through a provision in the corporation's articles or through a validly adopted shareholder agreement. The fact that a corporation statute may refer to directors as the corporation's "agents" for a particular purpose does not place directors in an agency relationship with shareholders for purposes of the common law of agency. In any event, directors' ability to bind the corporation is invested in the directors as a board, not in individual directors acting unilaterally. A director may, of course, also be an employee or officer (who may or may not be an employee) of the corporation, giving the director an additional and separate conventional position or role as an agent. Fellow directors may, with that director's consent, appoint a director as an agent to act on behalf of the corporation in some respect or matter.

Comment g. Acting on behalf of. The common-law definition of agency requires as an essential element that the agent consent to act on the principal's behalf, as well as subject to the principal's control. From the standpoint of the principal, this is the purpose for creating the relationship. The common law of agency encompasses employment as well as nonemployment relations. Employee and nonemployee agents who represent their principal in transactions with third parties act on the principal's account and behalf. Employee-agents whose work does not involve transactional interactions with third parties also act "on behalf of" their employer-principal. By consenting to act on behalf of the principal, an agent who is an employee consents to do the work that the employer directs and to do it subject to the employer's instructions. In either case, actions "on behalf of" a principal do not necessarily entail that the principal will benefit as a result.

In any relationship created by contract, the parties contemplate a benefit to be realized through the other party's performance. Performing a duty created by contract may well benefit the other party but the performance is that of an agent only if the elements of agency are present. A purchaser is not "acting on behalf of" a supplier in a distribution relationship in which goods are purchased from the supplier for resale. A purchaser who resells goods supplied by another is acting as a principal, not an agent. However, courts may treat a trademark licensee as the agent of the licensor in certain situations, with the result that the licensor is liable to third parties for defective goods produced by licensees.

An actor who acts under the immediate control of another person is not that person's agent unless the actor has agreed to act on the person's behalf. For example, a foreman or supervisor in charge of a crew of laborers exercises full and detailed control over the laborers' work activities. The relationship between the foreman and the laborers is not an agency relationship despite the foreman's full control, nor is their relationship one of subagency. Section 1.04(8) defines subagency. The foreman and the laborers are coagents of a common employer who occupy different strata within an organizational hierarchy. See § 1.04(9), which defines "superior" and "subordinate" coagents. The foreman's role of direction, defined by the organization, does not make the laborers the foreman's own agents. The laborers act on behalf of their common employer, not the foreman. Likewise, the captain of a ship and its crew are coagents, hierarchically stratified, who have consented to act on behalf of their common principal, the ship's owner.

It is possible to create a power to affect a person's legal relations to be exercised for the benefit of the holder of the power. Such powers typically are created as security for the interests of the holder or otherwise to benefit a person other than the person who creates the power. Consequently, the holder of such a power is not an agent as defined in this section, even though the power has the form of agency and, if exercised, will result in some of agency's legal consequences. The creator does not have a right to control the power holder's use of the power, and the power holder is not under a duty to use it in the interests of the creator. Sections 3.12–3.13 specifically treat powers given as security.

Relationships of agency are among the larger family of relationships in which one person acts to further the interests of another and is subject to fiduciary obligations. Agency is not antithetical to these other relationships, and whether a fiduciary is, additionally, an agent of another depends on the circumstances of the particular relationship. For example, as defined in Restatement Third, Trusts § 2, a trust is a fiduciary relationship with respect to property that arises from a manifestation of intention to create that relationship; a trustee is not an agent of the settlor or beneficiaries unless the terms of the trust subject the trustee to the control of either the settlor or the beneficiaries. Principals in agency relationships have power to terminate authority and thus remove the agent; trust beneficiaries, in contrast, do not have power to remove the trustee.

As agents, all employees owe duties of loyalty to their employers. The specific implications vary with the position the employee occupies, the nature of the employer's assets to which the employee has access, and the degree of discretion that the employee's work requires. However ministerial or routinized a work assignment may be, no agent, whether or not an employee, is simply a pair of hands, legs, or eyes. All are sentient and, capable of disloyal action, all have the duty to act loyally. For further discussion of the scope of fiduciary duty, see § 8.01, Comment *c*.

§ 1.02 Parties' Labeling and Popular Usage not Controlling

An agency relationship arises only when the elements stated in § 1.01 are present. Whether a relationship is characterized as agency in an agreement between parties or in the context of industry or popular usage is not controlling.

§ 1.03 Manifestation

A person manifests assent or intention through written or spoken words or other conduct.

§ 1.04 Terminology

(1) *Coagents.* Coagents have agency relationships with the same principal. A coagent may be appointed by the principal or by another agent actually or apparently authorized by the principal to do so.

(2) *Disclosed, undisclosed, and unidentified principals.*

(a) *Disclosed principal.* A principal is disclosed if, when an agent and a third party interact, the third party has notice that the agent is acting for a principal and has notice of the principal's identity.

(b) *Undisclosed principal.* A principal is undisclosed if, when an agent and a third party interact, the third party has no notice that the agent is acting for a principal.

(c) *Unidentified principal.* A principal is unidentified if, when an agent and a third party interact, the third party has notice that the agent is acting for a principal but does not have notice of the principal's identity.

(3) *Gratuitous agent.* A gratuitous agent acts without a right to compensation.

(4) *Notice.* A person has notice of a fact if the person knows the fact, has reason to know the fact, has received an effective notification of the fact, or should know the fact to fulfill a duty owed to another person. Notice of a fact that an agent knows or has reason to know is imputed to the principal as stated in §§ 5.03 and 5.04. A notification given to or by an agent is effective as notice to or by the principal as stated in § 5.02.

(5) *Person.* A person is (a) an individual; (b) an organization or association that has legal capacity to possess rights and incur obligations; (c) a government, political subdivision, or instrumentality or entity created by government; or (d) any other entity that has legal capacity to possess rights and incur obligations.

(6) *Power given as security.* A power given as security is a power to affect the legal relations of its creator that is created in the form of a manifestation of actual authority and held for the benefit of the holder or a third person. It is given to protect a legal or equitable title or to secure the performance of a duty apart from any duties owed the holder of the power by its creator that are incident to a relationship of agency under § 1.01.

(7) *Power of attorney.* A power of attorney is an instrument that states an agent's authority.

(8) *Subagent.* A subagent is a person appointed by an agent to perform functions that the agent has consented to perform on behalf of the agent's principal and for whose conduct the appointing agent is responsible to the principal. The relationship between an appointing agent and a subagent is one of agency, created as stated in § 1.01.

(9) *Superior and subordinate coagents.* A superior coagent has the right, conferred by the principal, to direct a subordinate coagent.

(10) *Trustee and agent-trustee.* A trustee is a holder of property who is subject to fiduciary duties to deal with the property for the benefit of charity or for one or more persons, at least one of whom is not the sole trustee. An agent-trustee is a trustee subject to the control of the settlor or of one or more beneficiaries.

Chapter 2

PRINCIPLES OF ATTRIBUTION

TOPIC 1. ACTUAL AUTHORITY

§ 2.01 Actual Authority

An agent acts with actual authority when, at the time of taking action that has legal consequences for the principal, the agent reasonably believes, in accordance with the principal's manifestations to the agent, that the principal wishes the agent so to act.

Comment b. Terminology. As defined in this section, "actual authority" is a synonym for "true authority," a term used in some opinions. The definition in this section does not attempt to classify different types of actual authority on the basis of the degree of detail in the principal's manifestation, which may consist of written or spoken words or other conduct. See § 1.03. As commonly used, the term "express authority" often means actual authority that a principal has stated in very specific or detailed language.

The term "implied authority" has more than one meaning. "Implied authority" is often used to mean actual authority either (1) to do what is necessary, usual, and proper to accomplish or perform an agent's express responsibilities or (2) to act in a manner in which an agent believes the principal wishes the agent to act based on the agent's reasonable interpretation of the principal's manifestation in light of the principal's objectives and other facts known to the agent. These meanings are not mutually exclusive. Both fall within the definition of actual authority. Section 2.02, which delineates the scope of actual authority, subsumes the practical consequences of implied authority.

The term "inherent agency power," used in Restatement Second, Agency, and defined therein by § 8A, is not used in this Restatement. Inherent agency power is defined as "a term used ... to indicate the power of an agent which is derived not from authority, apparent authority or estoppel, but solely from the agency relation and exists for the protection of persons harmed by or dealing with a servant or other agent." Other doctrines stated in this Restatement encompass the justifications underpinning § 8A, including the importance of interpretation by the agent in the agent's relationship with the principal, as well as the doctrines of apparent authority, estoppel, and restitution.

§ 2.02 Scope of Actual Authority

(1) An agent has actual authority to take action designated or implied in the principal's manifestations to the agent and acts necessary or incidental to achieving the principal's objectives, as the agent reasonably understands the principal's manifestations and objectives when the agent determines how to act.

(2) An agent's interpretation of the principal's manifestations is reasonable if it reflects any meaning known by the agent to be ascribed by the principal and, in the absence of any meaning known to the agent, as a reasonable person in the agent's position would interpret the manifestations in light of the context, including circumstances of which the agent has notice and the agent's fiduciary duty to the principal.

(3) An agent's understanding of the principal's objectives is reasonable if it accords with the principal's manifestations and the inferences that a reasonable person in the agent's position would draw from the circumstances creating the agency.

TOPIC 2. APPARENT AUTHORITY

§ 2.03 Apparent Authority

to 3rd Party

Apparent authority is the power held by an agent or other actor to affect a principal's legal relations with third parties when a third party reasonably believes the actor has authority to act on behalf of the principal and that belief is traceable to the principal's manifestations.

TOPIC 3. RESPONDEAT SUPERIOR

§ 2.04 Respondeat Superior

An employer is subject to liability for torts committed by employees while acting within the scope of their employment.

TOPIC 4. RELATED DOCTRINES

§ 2.05 Estoppel to Deny Existence of Agency Relationship

A person who has not made a manifestation that an actor has authority as an agent and who is not otherwise liable as a party to a transaction purportedly done by the actor on that person's account is subject to liability to a third party who justifiably is induced to make a detrimental change in position because the transaction is believed to be on the person's account, if

(1) the person intentionally or carelessly caused such belief, or

(2) having notice of such belief and that it might induce others to change their positions, the person did not take reasonable steps to notify them of the facts.

§ 2.06 Liability of Undisclosed Principal

(1) An undisclosed principal is subject to liability to a third party who is justifiably induced to make a detrimental change in position by an agent acting on the principal's behalf and without actual authority if the principal, having notice of the agent's conduct and that it might induce

others to change their positions, did not take reasonable steps to notify them of the facts.

(2) An undisclosed principal may not rely on instructions given an agent that qualify or reduce the agent's authority to less than the authority a third party would reasonably believe the agent to have under the same circumstances if the principal had been disclosed.

Inherent authority (undiscl. princip.)

Comment c. Rationale. The principle stated in this section will result in liability in a relatively small number of cases in which a third party deals with an agent but has no notice that the agent represents the interests of another. Under subsection (1), a principal is subject to liability to a third party who is justifiably induced to make a detrimental change in position by the conduct of an agent acting without actual authority when the principal has notice of the agent's conduct and its likely impact on third parties and fails to take reasonable steps to inform them of the facts. The underlying principle is consistent with the estoppel doctrine stated in § 2.05. Under subsection (2), a principal is subject to liability to a third party when the third party would have no reason to inquire into the scope of the agent's authority if the third party knew the agent acted on behalf of a principal. The principal may not rely on qualifications or reductions to the agent's authority when the doctrine of apparent authority would make the qualification or restriction ineffective as to an agent acting on behalf of a disclosed or an unidentified principal. In such cases, the principal has chosen to place the agent in a position in which it is reasonable for third parties to believe that the agent has authority consistent with the position.

The rule stated in this section, like the doctrine of apparent authority, protects third parties by backstopping actual authority when circumstances might otherwise permit the principal opportunistically to speculate at the expense of third parties. See § 2.03, Comment *c*. Apparent authority does not arise when a principal is undisclosed because no manifestation has been made that the actor with whom the third party interacts has authority to act as an agent.

policy

A further rationale for the doctrine stated in this section is protection of the reasonable expectations of third parties who deal with an ongoing enterprise following an undisclosed sale to a new owner, whether or not affiliated in some manner with the former owner, when the former owner continues to operate the enterprise as agent on behalf of the new owner. The enterprise's new owner, as undisclosed principal, would or reasonably should expect that third parties will continue to deal with the now-agent as if no change had occurred. If the agent operates a business under the agent's name, the appearance to the third party may be that the agent owns the business and that its assets will be available to satisfy business-related obligations incurred by the agent. The opportunity for speculation provided the principal would emerge when the principal has limited the agent's authority and the agent enters into a contract that exceeds the agent's actual authority. Then, if the contract is advantageous to the principal, neither the principal nor the agent will raise the agent's lack of authority and the third party will not know of it. On the other hand, if the contract then is disadvantageous to the principal, the principal may assert lack of authority as a defense.

The doctrine allocates to the principal the risk that the agent will deviate from the principal's instructions while doing acts that are consistent with the apparent position the agent occupies, which are acts that third parties would anticipate an agent in such a position would have authority to do and may well be acts that are foreseeable to the principal. Such acts are especially likely to be foreseeable when they are consistent with the agent's position although they contravene the principal's instructions.

A third party who deals with an actor, lacking notice that the actor is someone's agent, does not expect the liability of any person in addition to the immediate actor with whom the third party deals. Estoppel's perspective is broader but less well defined. The question is whether it is unjust, in particular circumstances, to permit a principal who has chosen to deal through an agent but to remain undisclosed to have the benefit of restrictions on the agent's authority. In the instance in which the rule is applicable, it is unlikely that the third party will inquire into the status of the immediate actor or seek to identify the existence of restrictions on that actor's right to interact with legal consequences for the third party. The need to make such inquiries, in the circumstances to which this doctrine applies, is unlikely to occur to a reasonable third party, and making the inquiry may be difficult or its cost may seem excessive relative to the magnitude of the particular transaction. When a third party previously dealt with the agent as the owner of the business now managed by the agent, the third party may assume that inquiry is unnecessary for transactions similar to prior transactions. Separately, if an undisclosed principal has notice of an agent's unauthorized actions and notice that a third party will as a consequence be induced to make a detrimental change in position, the undisclosed principal may be estopped to deny the agent's authority. The undisclosed principal may avoid estoppel by disclosing the agent's status and the extent of the agent's authority.

The doctrine encompasses deviations from actual authority of a sort that would not lead a reasonable third party to inquire separately into the scope of the agent's authority. Such deviations are foreseeable to the principal and are likely not to be contested by any principal, whether or not undisclosed, when they appear likely to benefit the principal.

§ 2.07 Restitution of Benefit

If a principal is unjustly enriched at the expense of another person by the action of an agent or a person who appears to be an agent, the principal is subject to a claim for restitution by that person.

Chapter 3

CREATION AND TERMINATION OF AUTHORITY AND AGENCY RELATIONSHIPS

TOPIC 1. CREATING AND EVIDENCING ACTUAL AUTHORITY

§ 3.01 Creation of Actual Authority

Actual authority, as defined in § 2.01, is created by a principal's manifestation to an agent that, as reasonably understood by the agent, expresses the principal's assent that the agent take action on the principal's behalf.

§ 3.02 Formal Requirements

If the law requires a writing or record signed by the principal to evidence an agent's authority to bind a principal to a contract or other transaction, the principal is not bound in the absence of such a writing or record. A principal may be estopped to assert the lack of such a writing or record when a third party has been induced to make a detrimental change in position by the reasonable belief that an agent has authority to bind the principal that is traceable to a manifestation made by the principal.

Comment b. Equal-dignity requirements. Creating actual authority under § 3.01 does not require a writing or other formality. However, legislation in many states imposes what is often termed an "equal dignity" requirement for the creation of authority or agency applicable to specific types of agreements. As with the Statute of Frauds more generally, the purpose is to prevent fraud and perjury by safeguarding the principal against agreements made by an agent who lacks authority. Under an equal-dignity rule, if a transaction is unenforceable unless the party to be charged has agreed in writing to be bound, an agent's authority to enter into such a transaction on behalf of a principal must likewise be in writing. Such rules also apply to ratification. See § 4.02, Comment *e*. If an agent acted with apparent authority as defined in § 2.03 but no writing or record evidences the agent's authority, the principal is not bound to contracts or other transactions to which an equal-dignity rule applies.

A writing includes "any intentional reduction to tangible form," see Restatement Second, Contracts § 131, Comment *d*. A record includes an electronic record that is given the legal effect of a writing. Electronic records are given the legal effect of paper-and-ink writings by legislation, including the Uniform Electronic Transactions Act § 7 (1999) and the federal Electronic Signatures in Global and National Commerce Act § 101(a) (2000). A writing is signed by the principal by affixing a symbol that evidences intention to authenticate the writing. See Restatement

Second, Contracts § 134. Similarly, an electronic record is signed by attaching to it an electronic sound, symbol, or process that is adopted with the intention of signing the record. See Uniform Electronic Transactions Act § 2(8).

Equal-dignity rules are either elements in a statute of frauds or are stated in separate statutes. Equal-dignity rules apply when a statute of frauds requires the underlying agreement to be evidenced by a writing signed by the party to be charged, including agreements for the sale or lease of land and suretyship agreements. On the scope of contracts to which statutes of frauds apply, see Restatement Second, Contracts § 110. Equal-dignity rules are inapplicable when a writing is required by agreement but not by law. However, a contract may not be binding when a contractual provision itself requires that the principal sign personally.

Equal-dignity rules have been applied with some stringency. For example, when one spouse acts as the agent of the other who owns property, or as an agent when both spouses own property jointly, the equal-dignity rule requires the agent-spouse's authorization to be in writing. If a principal executes a contract but leaves blanks that are completed by the agent, the contract may not be enforceable against the principal if the third party has notice that the agent may fill in the blanks only when the agent is authorized in writing to do so.

Nevertheless, the application of equal-dignity rules should not outrun their purpose. Equal-dignity rules do not apply when an action on a contract is brought by the principal against a third party. An equal-dignity rule may be satisfied by a writing or record executed by a principal following the agent's execution of the contract or transaction. Moreover, if an agent has acted without actual authority, as well as without prior written authorization, the principal would be able to ratify the transaction by a signed writing, see § 4.01, Comment *e*, so long as the principal ratifies prior to a manifestation from the third party that the third party has withdrawn from the transaction, see § 4.05(1). Additionally, an equal-dignity rule does not create a defense that an agent may assert against the third party, such as when the agent misrepresents authority. On an agent's warranties of authority, see § 6.10. On an agent's representations, see § 6.11.

TOPIC 2. CREATING APPARENT AUTHORITY

§ 3.03 Creation of Apparent Authority

Apparent authority, as defined in § 2.03, is created by a person's manifestation that another has authority to act with legal consequences for the person who makes the manifestation, when a third party reasonably believes the actor to be authorized and the belief is traceable to the manifestation.

TOPIC 3. CAPACITY TO ACT AS PRINCIPAL OR AGENT

§ 3.04 Capacity to Act as Principal

(1) An individual has capacity to act as principal in a relationship of agency as defined in § 1.01 if, at the time the agent takes action, the individual would have capacity if acting in person.

(2) The law applicable to a person that is not an individual governs whether the person has capacity to be a principal in a relationship of agency as defined in § 1.01, as well as the effect of the person's lack or loss of capacity on those who interact with it.

(3) If performance of an act is not delegable, its performance by an agent does not constitute performance by the principal.

§ 3.05 Capacity to Act as Agent

Any person may ordinarily be empowered to act so as to affect the legal relations of another. The actor's capacity governs the extent to which, by so acting, the actor becomes subject to duties and liabilities to the person whose legal relations are affected or to third parties.

TOPIC 4. TERMINATION OF AGENT'S POWER

TITLE A. TERMINATION OF ACTUAL AUTHORITY

§ 3.06 Termination of Actual Authority—In General

An agent's actual authority may be terminated by:

(1) the agent's death, cessation of existence, or suspension of powers as stated in § 3.07(1) and (3); or

(2) the principal's death, cessation of existence, or suspension of powers as stated in § 3.07(2) and (4); or

(3) the principal's loss of capacity, as stated in § 3.08(1) and (3); or

(4) an agreement between the agent and the principal or the occurrence of circumstances on the basis of which the agent should reasonably conclude that the principal no longer would assent to the agent's taking action on the principal's behalf, as stated in § 3.09; or

(5) a manifestation of revocation by the principal to the agent, or of renunciation by the agent to the principal, as stated in § 3.10(1); or

(6) the occurrence of circumstances specified by statute.

Comment b. Agreement between principal and agent and changes in circumstances. The basis for actual authority is a manifestation of assent made by a principal to an agent. See § 3.01. When the manifestation is embodied in an agreement that specifies circumstances under which the agent's actual authority shall terminate, occurrence of a specified circumstance effects termination of the principal's expressed assent. Regardless of whether the initial agreement contains a termination provision, mutual agreement to terminate the agency relationship is always effective to terminate the agent's actual authority. See § 3.09.

Following the principal's manifestation of assent to an agent, circumstances may change such that, at the time the agent takes action, it is not reasonable for the agent to believe that the principal at that time consents to the action being taken on the principal's behalf even though the principal has not manifested dissent to the action by that time. For example, the agent may become insolvent and have notice that it is important to the principal to be represented by a solvent agent. The agent may lose capacity to bind itself by a contract or to become subject to other obligations and have notice that it is important to the principal that the agent retain such capacity. Events that are totally outside the control of the agent or the principal may also make it unreasonable for the agent to believe that the principal consents to the agent's action. For example, if the principal retains the agent to sell goods in a particular geographically defined market, the occurrence of war or widespread civil unrest may so impair the value of the agent's efforts to the principal that the agent would not be reasonable in believing the principal wishes the agent to sell into the territory. The agent then lacks actual authority so to act but would have acted with actual authority had the agent acted prior to the change in circumstances. The focal point for determining whether an agent acted with actual authority is the time of action, not the time of the principal's manifestation, which may be earlier. See §§ 2.01 and 2.02.

An alternate analysis of the impact of changed circumstances, as set forth in Restatement Second, Agency, requires the use of at least two distinct focal points. First, it is posited that an agent has actual authority up until the agent receives notice of the changed circumstances. Notice that circumstances have changed, beyond those operative when the principal manifested consent to the agent, then implicitly modifies either the principal's manifestation of consent or the actual authority it engenders on the basis of the agent's reasonable belief in the principal's consent. See Restatement Second, Agency, Introductory Note to Chapter 5. Moreover, if circumstances thereafter revert to those present originally, the agent's actual authority, having once existed but thereafter having been terminated, is again revived. See Restatement Second, Agency § 108(2). This Restatement does not follow this alternate pattern of analysis because it is unnecessary in light of the nature of actual authority and the rules that determine whether an agent acted with actual authority. See §§ 2.01–2.02.

§ 3.07 Death, Cessation of Existence, and Suspension of Powers

(1) The death of an individual agent terminates the agent's actual authority.

(2) The death of an individual principal terminates the agent's actual authority. The termination is effective only when the agent has notice of the principal's death. The termination is also effective as against a third party with whom the agent deals when the third party has notice of the principal's death.

(3) When an agent that is not an individual ceases to exist or commences a process that will lead to cessation of existence or when its powers are suspended, the agent's actual authority terminates except as provided by law.

(4) When a principal that is not an individual ceases to exist or commences a process that will lead to cessation of its existence or when its powers are suspended, the agent's actual authority terminates except as provided by law.

§ 3.08 Loss of Capacity

(1) An individual principal's loss of capacity to do an act terminates the agent's actual authority to do the act. The termination is effective only when the agent has notice that the principal's loss of capacity is permanent or that the principal has been adjudicated to lack capacity. The termination is also effective as against a third party with whom the agent deals when the third party has notice that the principal's loss of capacity is permanent or that the principal has been adjudicated to lack capacity.

(2) A written instrument may make an agent's actual authority effective upon a principal's loss of capacity, or confer it irrevocably regardless of such loss.

(3) If a principal that is not an individual loses capacity to do an act, its agent's actual authority to do the act is terminated.

§ 3.09 Termination by Agreement or by Occurrence of Changed Circumstances

An agent's actual authority terminates (1) as agreed by the agent and the principal, subject to the provisions of § 3.10; or (2) upon the occurrence of circumstances on the basis of which the agent should reasonably conclude that the principal no longer would assent to the agent's taking action on the principal's behalf.

§ 3.10 Manifestation Terminating Actual Authority

(1) Notwithstanding any agreement between principal and agent, an agent's actual authority terminates if the agent renounces it by a manifestation to the principal or if the principal revokes the agent's actual authority by a manifestation to the agent. A revocation or a renunciation is effective when the other party has notice of it.

(2) A principal's manifestation of revocation is, unless otherwise agreed, ineffective to terminate a power given as security or to terminate a proxy to vote securities or other membership or ownership interests that is made irrevocable in compliance with applicable legislation. See §§ 3.12–3.13.

TITLE B. TERMINATION OF APPARENT AUTHORITY

§ 3.11 Termination of Apparent Authority

(1) The termination of actual authority does not by itself end any apparent authority held by an agent.

(2) Apparent authority ends when it is no longer reasonable for the third party with whom an agent deals to believe that the agent continues to act with actual authority.

TITLE C. IRREVOCABLE POWERS

§ 3.12 Power Given as Security; Irrevocable Proxy

(1) A power given as security is a power to affect the legal relations of its creator that is created in the form of a manifestation of actual authority and held for the benefit of the holder or a third person. This power is given to protect a legal or equitable title or to secure the performance of a duty apart from any duties owed the holder of the power by its creator that are incident to a relationship of agency under § 1.01. It is given upon the creation of the duty or title or for consideration. It is distinct from actual authority that the holder may exercise if the holder is an agent of the creator of the power.

(2) A power to exercise voting rights associated with securities or a membership interest may be conferred on a proxy through a manifestation of actual authority. The power may be given as security under (1) and may be made irrevocable in compliance with applicable legislation.

§ 3.13 Termination of Power Given as Security or Irrevocable Proxy

(1) A power given as security or an irrevocable proxy is terminated by an event that

(a) discharges the obligation secured by the power or terminates the interest secured or supported by the proxy, or

(b) makes its execution illegal or impossible, or

(c) constitutes an effective surrender of the power or proxy by the person for whose benefit it was created or conferred.

(2) Unless otherwise agreed, neither a power given as security nor a proxy made irrevocable as provided in § 3.12(2) is terminated by:

(a) a manifestation revoking the power or proxy made by the person who created it; or

(b) surrender of the power or proxy by its holder if it is held for the benefit of another person, unless that person consents; or

(c) loss of capacity by the creator or the holder of the power or proxy; or

(d) death of the holder of the power or proxy, unless the holder's death terminates the interest secured or supported by the power or proxy; or

(e) death of the creator of the power or proxy, if the power or proxy is given as security for the performance of a duty that does not terminate with the death of its creator.

TOPIC 5. AGENTS WITH MULTIPLE PRINCIPALS

§ 3.14 Agents with Multiple Principals

An agent acting in the same transaction or matter on behalf of more than one principal may be one or both of the following:

(a) a subagent, as stated in § 3.15; or

(b) an agent for coprincipals, as stated in § 3.16.

§ 3.15 Subagency

(1) A subagent is a person appointed by an agent to perform functions that the agent has consented to perform on behalf of the agent's principal and for whose conduct the appointing agent is responsible to the principal. The relationships between a subagent and the appointing agent and between the subagent and the appointing agent's principal are relationships of agency as stated in § 1.01.

(2) An agent may appoint a subagent only if the agent has actual or apparent authority to do so.

Comment b. Subagency contrasted with coagency. Agency creates a personal relationship between principal and agent; an agent's delegation of power to another person to act on behalf of the principal is inconsistent with the undertaking made when a person consents to act as agent on behalf of a principal. However, a principal may empower an agent to appoint another agent to act on the principal's behalf. The second agent may be a subagent or a coagent. See Comment *d* for discussion of the consequences that follow if the second agent is characterized as a subagent.

An agent who appoints a subagent delegates to the subagent power to act on behalf of the principal that the principal has conferred on the agent. A subagent acts subject to the control of the appointing agent, and the principal's legal position is affected by action taken by the subagent as if the action had been taken by the appointing agent. Thus, a subagent has two principals, the appointing agent and that agent's principal. Although an appointing agent has the right and duty to control a subagent, the interests and instructions of the appointing agent's principal are paramount. See Comment *d*.

In contrast, an agent who appoints a coagent does not delegate power held by the agent to the coagent. By empowering an agent to appoint a coagent, the principal creates a mechanism through which to generate additional relationships of agency between the principal and persons chosen by the agent. Coagents, although they may occupy dominant and subordinate positions within an organizational hierarchy, share a common principal.

A person appointed by an agent to act on behalf of the agent's principal is a subagent if the appointing agent has agreed with the principal that the appointing agent shall be responsible to the principal for the agent's conduct. Such agreement may be express or implied. For example, employees of an appointing agent whom the agent designates to act on behalf of the appointing agent's principal are presumed to be subagents, not coagents of the appointing agent. When an agent is itself a corporation or other legal person, its officers, employees, partners, or members who are designated to work on the principal's account are subagents. In contrast, when a manager within an organization hires persons as employees of the organization, those hired are presumed to be the hiring manager's coagents and not subagents. Employees of a single organization are presumed to be coagents of that organization, not subagents.

Comment c. Creation of subagency. An agent has actual authority to create a relationship of subagency when the agent reasonably believes, based on a manifestation from the principal, that the principal consents to the appointment of a subagent. For the definition of actual authority, see § 2.01. For the means by which a principal creates it, see § 3.01.

A principal's consent to the appointment of a subagent may be express or implied. For example, a principal's consent to the appointment of subagents may be implied when the principal retains an individual as agent to carry out a number of transactions and has notice that the amount of work involved exceeds the agent's individual capability or requires action that the agent may not legally perform, such as action for which the law requires a license. Implied consent to appoint subagents is also present when an agent is itself a person that is not an individual, such as a corporation.

Subagents may be appointed in series. This would occur when a subagent has actual or apparent authority to appoint another for whose conduct the appointing subagent is responsible.

An agent may have apparent authority to appoint a subagent if the principal has made a manifestation to third parties that the agent has such authority. Section 1.03 defines manifestation. Section 2.03 defines apparent authority; § 3.03 states how it is created. A principal may make a manifestation that an agent has actual authority to appoint subagents by placing the agent in a position in which agents customarily have such authority without notice to third parties that the agent's authority does not include the appointment of subagents. A subagent appointed by an agent acting with only apparent authority may act on behalf of the principal with actual authority. See Comment *d*.

If an agent acts without actual or apparent authority in purporting to appoint a subagent, the person so appointed is the agent solely of the appointing agent and is not the principal's subagent unless the principal ratifies the appointment. On the requisites for ratification, see Chapter 4.

In emergencies and other unforeseen circumstances, when communication between agent and principal is not feasible, an agent's actual authority to take action to protect the principal's interests may permit the agent to appoint a subagent although the principal has not previously manifested consent to the agent to make such an appointment. See § 2.02, Comment *d*.

A person may be appointed as a subagent even though the person does not expect to be compensated for actions taken.

Comment d. Consequences of subagency. As between a principal and third parties, it is immaterial that an action was taken by a subagent as opposed to an agent directly appointed by the principal. In this respect, subagency is governed by a principle of transparency that looks from the subagent to the principal and through the appointing agent. As to third parties, an action taken by a subagent carries the legal consequences for the principal that would follow were the action instead taken by the appointing agent. . . .

When a subagent works on a principal's account, notifications received by the subagent are effective as notifications to the principal to the same extent as if the principal had appointed the subagent directly. Likewise, notice of facts the subagent knows or has reason to know is imputed to the principal to the same extent as if the principal had appointed the subagent directly. . . .

As among a principal, an appointing agent, and a subagent, the fact that action is taken by a subagent may carry different or additional legal consequences than if the action were taken directly by the appointing agent or by a coagent of the appointing agent. The legal consequences of subagency reflect the distinct significance of (1) the relationship between an appointing agent and a subagent; (2) the relationship between a principal and an appointing agent; and (3) the relationship between a principal and a subagent. An appointing agent is responsible to the principal for the subagent's conduct. This may subject an appointing agent to liability for loss incurred by the principal as a consequence of misconduct by a subagent. A contract between the principal and the appointing agent that requires or permits the appointment of subagents will often delineate the extent of the appointing agent's liability and will require indemnification by the principal of the appointing agent. In contrast, an agent is subject to liability stemming from a coagent's conduct only when the agent's own conduct subjects the agent to liability. See § 7.01, Comments *b* and *d*.

Statutes may change the results that would otherwise follow when a subagent takes action. For example, under Article 4 of the Uniform Commercial Code, when the owner of an item deposits it with a bank for collection, the depositary bank is treated as the agent of the item's owner. If the depositary bank sends the item for collection to another bank, the collecting bank is treated as the owner's subagent. See U.C.C. § 4–201(a). However, under U.C.C. § 4–202, although a depositary bank has a duty to use ordinary care in selecting intermediaries and in giving proper instructions to them, it is not liable for another bank's "insolvency, neglect, misconduct, mistake, or default...."

Although an appointing agent is responsible for a subagent's action and has the right and duty to control the subagent, the principal's interests and instructions are nonetheless paramount. Several specific doctrines reflect this general point. If a subagent acts without actual or apparent authority, only the principal may ratify the subagent's action; ratification by an appointing agent is effective only when the principal has authorized the appointing agent to ratify on its behalf. Moreover, a subagent is a fiduciary, as is any agent. See § 1.01. A subagent owes duties of loyalty to the principal as well as to the appointing agent. See §§ 8.01–8.06, which state the specifics of these duties. A subagent owes a duty of obedience to the principal as well as to the appointing agent. See § 8.09(2). However, the principal's rights as to the subagent are superior to rights of the appointing agent, even in the event of conflict or disagreement between principal and appointing agent.

If a subagent is appointed by an agent who acts with only apparent authority, the subagent is privileged to act on behalf of the principal because the subagent, on the basis of the principal's manifestation, reasonably believes that the appointing agent acted with the principal's consent in appointing the subagent. As a consequence, the principal is subject to liability to the subagent to indemnify the subagent as stated in § 8.14. The appointing agent, having acted without actual authority in appointing the subagent, is subject to liability to the principal as stated in § 8.09(1). The subagent is not subject to liability to third parties on the basis that the subagent breached warranties of authority. See § 6.10.

A principal's duties to a subagent are those owed to any agent, but the principal is not subject to duties created by agreement between the appointing agent and the subagent, including the appointing agent's agreement to compensate the subagent. See § 8.13, Comment *d*. A subagent may have set-off rights against the principal. See § 6.06.

Comment e. Termination of subagent's actual and apparent authority. Whether a subagent acts with actual authority depends on three separate consensual relationships: (1) between principal and appointing agent; (2) between appointing agent and subagent; and (3) between principal and subagent. A subagent's actual authority terminates upon notice to the subagent that any of these relationships is severed.

Additionally, circumstances that terminate an agent's actual authority by operation of law likewise terminate a subagent's authority. Thus, notice of the death of a principal or of an appointing agent terminates a subagent's actual authority, as does notice that the principal has revoked an appointing agent's actual authority. See §§ 3.07(2) and 3.10(1). If the relationship between an appointing agent and a subagent is severed, for example by notice of the appointing agent's death or loss of capacity, the subagent no longer acts under the control of the appointing agent who had responsibility for the subagent's acts. If a subagent is a lawyer who represents a client having diminished capacity, the lawyer's duties are as stated in Restatement Third, The Law Governing Lawyers § 24.

Additionally, a principal may terminate a subagent's actual authority by making a manifestation of revocation directly to the subagent or to the appointing agent. A manifestation revoking a subagent's actual authority made by the principal to the appointing agent should not be effective, in most circumstances, as to the subagent until the subagent has notice of it. A principal has rights and responsibilities of ultimate control, including ultimate control over chains of command and channels of communication. A principal may choose how best to communicate with a subagent, including how best to convey notice that the subagent's actual authority has been revoked. If the principal chooses to rely exclusively on the appointing agent as the channel of communication with the subagent, the principal at least ordinarily should bear the risk that the appointing agent will not duly deliver notice of revocation to the subagent.

In contrast, under the rule stated in Restatement Second, Agency § 137, Comment *b*, when a principal terminates a subagent's authority by giving notice of termination to the appointing agent, "the subagent's authority terminates only when the agent has had an opportunity to communicate with him." If the appointing agent, having had the opportunity to communicate with the subagent, does not do so, or does not do so effectively, the rule as stated in Restatement Second allocates to the subagent the risk of acting without actual authority, although the subagent lacks notice that the principal wishes to terminate the subagent's authority. The notice requirement stated in this Restatement instead allocates to the principal the risk that notice of revocation communicated only to the appointing agent may not reach the subagent. So allocating the risk is supported by a well-reasoned case in the real-estate context. The principal should bear this risk because the principal has consented to the appointment of subagents and because a subagent should be under no greater risk than is an agent of unwittingly taking an unauthorized action following the termination of actual authority.

A subagent may continue to act with apparent authority following termination of the subagent's actual authority when third parties reasonably believe that the subagent continues to act with actual authority on the basis of manifestations traceable to the appointing agent or the principal. See § 3.11.

Comment f. Transactions in real estate. Under the common-law rule in most states, a real-estate broker or salesperson associated with a broker who successfully markets property to a prospective buyer (hereinafter the "showing broker") is treated as the subagent of the broker with whom a prospective seller has listed the property (hereinafter the "listing broker"), even if the showing broker is not the listing broker's employee or associate. Conventional terminology applies the term "broker" or "real-estate broker" to a person holding a license to provide brokerage services. A broker may use the services of salespeople, who may be employees of the broker or the broker's nonemployee associates. Except where the context otherwise requires, the remainder of this Comment refers to all as "brokers."

The better rule, followed in a minority of states, characterizes a showing broker as the agent of the prospective buyer, and not the seller's subagent, when the terms of the relationship between the showing broker and the prospective buyer reasonably reflect the buyer's expectation that the showing broker represents the buyer. The minority rule is consistent with the policy reflected in legislation in a majority of states that explicitly permits a prospective buyer to appoint a real-estate broker to act as the buyer's agent.

A showing broker may be characterized as: (1) the seller's subagent, regardless of whether the broker has a relationship with the buyer that constitutes a relationship of agency as defined by § 1.01; (2) the buyer's agent when the relationship between buyer and broker constitutes a relationship of agency as defined by § 1.01; or (3) neither the agent nor the subagent of buyer or seller. If a showing broker is characterized as acting as agent for both buyer and seller, or as agent for buyer and subagent for seller, the agent is in a position of dual agency because the showing broker represents adverse parties to the same transaction. See § 8.03.

As the seller's subagent, a showing broker is presumed not to have a relationship of agency with the buyer and does not owe an agent's fiduciary duties to the buyer. It is well-settled, as a matter of industry practice and regulation as well as common-law agency, that a broker in a single real-estate transaction may not represent both buyer and seller unless both know of and consent to the dual representation. Unless such consent is given, a broker who represents both buyer and seller may forfeit any commission otherwise payable to the broker. See § 8.03, Comment *d*. In a transaction involving the same property, buyer and seller have interests that are adverse. The benefit that a seller will receive through a higher sales price will be paid by the buyer. Moreover, a broker who represents a prospective seller or buyer of property may have material information that, if disclosed to the other party, will disadvantage the broker's client. For example, information about the seller's reservation price—the lowest price at which the seller may be willing to sell—is material to price negotiations between the seller and prospective buyers. For further treatment of dual agency, see § 8.03.

The mechanism through which a relationship of subagency arises is an offer of a unilateral contract of subagency, made by the listing broker to showing brokers, that is accepted by the showing broker who produces a buyer able and willing to purchase the property at the listing price and terms or at other terms acceptable to the seller. Such an offer is often made when a listing broker lists property with a multiple listing service ("MLS"). A multiple listing service is an agreement among brokers in a particular geographic market to pool information about their listings. A showing broker may also become a subagent in the absence of MLS participation through a relationship of cooperation with the listing broker. When a showing broker produces an offer from a buyer to purchase at the seller's stated listing price and on terms otherwise consistent with the listing agreement, conventional MLS terms require that the listing broker split the commission to be paid by the seller with the successful showing broker.

The legal consequences of how a showing broker is characterized carry corresponding advantages as well as disadvantages from the standpoint of buyers and sellers of real estate. Characterizing a showing broker as the seller's subagent orients the showing broker's duties exclusively to the seller, with the implication that the broker must disclose to the seller all material information the broker learns about the buyer. This disadvantages a buyer if the showing broker discloses information the buyer has provided to the seller or the listing broker, such as the maximum price the buyer is willing to pay to acquire property. However, this characterization may be advantageous to the buyer if the showing broker induces the buyer to purchase a property through fraud because the buyer may rescind the transaction. For the circumstances under which a misrepresentation makes a contract voidable, see Restatement Second, Contracts § 164(1). To be sure, a seller may not perceive this consequence to be fair when the seller has had no contact with a showing broker who induces a purchase through fraud. In contrast, if a showing broker acts as a buyer's agent, the buyer will be limited to remedies against the broker if the seller is innocent of the fraud and has in good faith given value or changed position in reliance on the transaction. See Restatement Second, Contracts § 164(2). Neither buyer nor seller benefits if a showing broker is not characterized as either the seller's subagent or the buyer's agent because the duties of a nonagent showing broker are indeterminate. However, principals in real-estate transactions may benefit if nonagent showing brokers charge lower commissions than brokers who act as agents and subagents.

The common-law rule applicable to agency relationships in this context should reflect the reasonable expectations of prospective buyers and sellers of property and the real-estate professionals who act on their behalf. If a broker has agreed to assist a prospective buyer, it is reasonable for the prospective buyer to expect that the broker does not owe duties of loyalty to the seller of property that the buyer purchases. Treating a showing broker as the seller's subagent is likely to conflict with the expectations of a buyer to whom the showing broker has given guidance and, in many instances, advice. Moreover, a seller may reasonably expect that, as the seller's subagent, the showing broker will be loyal to the seller's interests and will not compromise them through advice or information that the showing broker may share with buyers. If a showing broker is treated as a buyer's agent, although the buyer loses the availability of rescission as a remedy in some situations, the buyer gains the advantages of representation by a professional whom the buyer is free to choose. Real-estate professionals are best served by rules that clarify the identity of parties to whom particular duties are owed and that do not create the risk of inadvertently acting as a dual agent for buyer and seller.

Empirical results confirm the significance to buyers of retaining the services of an agent who has clearly defined duties to represent the buyer, even when the agent is compensated by splitting a commission that will be payable from the proceeds of a sale and that will be augmented the greater the sale price. In Georgia, following the enactment of a statute that encourages buyers to retain their own agents, the average time required to sell a house fell, as did reported sale prices of expensive houses. Additionally, a large majority of buyers chose to be represented by their own agent.

Statutes in many states expressly permit prospective buyers to retain licensed real-estate brokers as agents. Since 1993, the Realtors' Association has permitted listing brokers to offer showing brokers, as an alternative to a relationship of subagency, a relationship of "cooperation and compensation" that is compatible both with a showing broker who acts as a buyer's agent as well as with a showing broker who acts as the seller's subagent.

Unless a statute so requires, a writing should not be necessary to establish that a prospective buyer and a real-estate broker have consented to create a relationship of agency. See § 3.02, Comment *e*, for discussion of statutes that impose a writing requirement on agreements to pay commissions to brokers. Statutes in some states require a written agreement to create a relationship of agency with either a listing broker or a buyer's agent.

If a prospective buyer does not create a relationship of agency as defined in § 1.01 with a showing broker, the showing broker should be treated as the seller's subagent if the seller has expressly or impliedly consented to the appointment of subagents by the listing broker. The showing broker should not be treated as the buyer's agent when no relationship of agency as defined in § 1.01 has been created between the buyer and the showing broker, nor should the showing broker be treated as an intermediary who acts as no one's agent, unless a statute so requires.

If a prospective buyer consents to a relationship of agency as defined in § 1.01 with a particular real-estate broker, it is incompatible with the duties thereby created for that broker additionally to act as subagent for the seller of property that the buyer purchases unless the buyer knows of the subagency and consents to it and unless the seller knows of and consents to the broker's relationship with the buyer. On consent by a principal to conduct by an agent that would otherwise breach the agent's duties of loyalty to the principal, see § 8.06. A broker retained by a prospective buyer would become a dual agent if the broker also acts as subagent on behalf of the seller of the property purchased by the buyer who is represented by the broker. This would occur if the property's owner lists it with the buyer's broker or if the buyer's broker is also characterized as the subagent of the property's owner. If the property in which a buyer is interested is listed in a MLS under terms that designate a successful showing broker as the seller's subagent, that designation should not be operative without the consent of a buyer who has previously retained the showing broker as the buyer's agent.

However, an agent is not a dual agent if there is no substantial risk that the agent's action on behalf of one principal will materially and adversely affect the agent's action on behalf of another principal. See § 8.03. An agent retained by a buyer does not become a dual agent by taking ministerial actions on behalf of a seller. Dual agency, as noted above, results when the broker whom a buyer has retained to act as the buyer's agent also serves as listing agent for the property purchased by the buyer, whether at the outset of the buyer's relationship with the broker or thereafter if the owner of the property lists it for sale with that broker. Under the common-law rule in most states, a broker has a relationship of agency with each of the broker's clients although the clients have agreed to be represented by individuals among the broker's cohort of employees and associates. Thus, a broker would be characterized as a dual agent when one employee or associate serves as the designated agent of a buyer and another serves as the seller's designated agent. Statutes in some states explicitly permit the practice of designated dual agency and impose specific writing and disclosure requirements. In contrast, a few statutes categorically prohibit dual agency in transactions but permit the use of nonagent intermediaries, as described below.

Relationships among brokers, sellers, and buyers have been recharacterized by statutes enacted by many states since the late 1980s. Statutes in many states expressly permit prospective buyers to retain licensed real-estate brokers to act as their agents. However, these statutes are disparate in specifying the default rule that characterizes a showing broker when a buyer has not appointed that broker as agent. Several statutes provide that subagency shall not be deemed to be created automatically or through participation in a MLS. Some statutes provide that, if no written agreement establishes a relationship of agency or subagency, a broker is treated as a "transaction broker," "transaction coordinator," or "facilitator" who does not act as either party's agent or subagent. Some statutes that permit the use of such nonagent intermediaries specify the duties owed by the intermediary. Many statutes make subagency the default characterization, either explicitly or implicitly by not specifying an alternative. Other statutes require specific types of disclosure, such as disclosure to a prospective buyer that a seller's agent represents the seller. Several statutes permit the parties to create a relationship of "designated dual agency" not subject to the usual consequences of dual agency, in which one sales associate in a real-estate brokerage represents the seller of a property and the other its buyer. Some statutes characterize such brokers as "limited agents," specifying their duties. Some statutes explicitly prohibit "designated dual agency." Statutes in a few states explicitly abrogate the common law of agency.

§ 3.16 Agent for Coprincipals

Two or more persons may as coprincipals appoint an agent to act for them in the same transaction or matter.

Chapter 4

RATIFICATION

§ 4.01 Ratification Defined

(1) Ratification is the affirmance of a prior act done by another, whereby the act is given effect as if done by an agent acting with actual authority.

(2) A person ratifies an act by

(a) manifesting assent that the act shall affect the person's legal relations, or

(b) conduct that justifies a reasonable assumption that the person so consents.

(3) Ratification does not occur unless

(a) the act is ratifiable as stated in § 4.03,

(b) the person ratifying has capacity as stated in § 4.04,

(c) the ratification is timely as stated in § 4.05, and

(d) the ratification encompasses the act in its entirety as stated in § 4.07.

Comment b. The nature and effect of ratification. As the term is used in agency law, ratification is both an act and a set of effects. The act of ratification consists of an externally observable manifestation of assent to be bound by the prior act of another person. When the prior act did not otherwise affect the legal relations of the ratifier, ratification provides the basis on which the ratifier's legal relations are affected by the act. The set of effects that ratification creates are the consequences of actual authority. That is, when a person ratifies another's act, the legal consequence is that the person's legal relations are affected as they would have been had the actor been an agent acting with actual authority at the time of the act.

In most jurisdictions, ratification may create a relationship of agency when none existed between the actor and the ratifier at the time of the act. It is necessary that the actor have acted or purported to act on behalf of the ratifier. See § 4.03. This limits the range of ratifiable acts to those done by an actor who is an agent or who is not an agent but pretends to be.

Ratification often serves the function of clarifying situations of ambiguous or uncertain authority. A principal's ratification confirms or validates an agent's right to have acted as the agent did. That is, an agent's action may have been effective to bind the principal to the third party, and the third party to the principal, because the agent acted with apparent authority. See § 2.03. If the principal ratifies the agent's act, it is thereafter not necessary to establish that the agent acted with apparent authority. Moreover, by replicating the effects of actual authority, the principal's ratification eliminates claims the principal would otherwise have against the agent for acting without actual authority. See § 8.09, Comment *b*. The principal's ratification may also eliminate claims that third parties could assert against the agent when the agent has purported to be authorized to bind the principal but the principal is not bound. See § 6.10. Ratification is effective even when the third party knew that the agent lacked authority to bind the principal but nonetheless dealt with the agent.

Much of the doctrine applicable to ratification either determines the validity and significance of the principal's assent or makes ratification unavailable or limits its effects when unfair consequences otherwise would follow. Although ratification creates the legal effects of actual authority, it reverses in time the sequence between an agent's conduct and the principal's manifestation of assent. If the principal ratifies, the relevant time for determining legal consequences is the time of the agent's act. See § 4.02, Comment *b*. Thus, if the agent purported to commit the principal to a transaction, the principal and third party become bound as of the time of the agent's commitment when the principal ratifies. If the agent's act constituted a tort, the time of the act is the time as of which the principal becomes vicariously liable, if the principal ratifies the agent's act. If the agent receives a notification, or learns information relevant to the action the agent takes, the notification is effective as to the principal, and knowledge of the information is imputed to the principal, as of the time of the agent's act if the principal ratifies it. See § 5.02, which covers notifications.

The sole requirement for ratification is a manifestation of assent or other conduct indicative of consent by the principal. To be effective as a ratification, the principal's assent need not be communicated to the agent or to third parties whose legal relations will be affected by the ratification. See Comment *d*. The principal is not bound by a ratification made without knowledge of material facts about the agent's act unless the principal chose to ratify with awareness that such knowledge was lacking. See § 4.06. When there are two or more coprincipals, each must ratify to be bound. In most cases in which the outcome turns on whether a principal has ratified, the claim of ratification is asserted by a third party who seeks to bind the principal in the absence of other bases to attribute the legal consequences of an agent's act to the principal. It is fair to hold the principal to such consequences when the principal has, after the fact, assented to the agent's act. The principal's ability to ratify also enables the principal to create a clear basis on which to hold the third party to transactions that are desirable from the principal's perspective. The doctrines stated in §§ 4.05, 4.07, and 4.08 deny the principal the power to ratify when the result of ratification would be unfair. Absent such circumstances, it is not unfair to bind the third party when the principal elects to ratify a transaction because the result binds the third party only as originally anticipated or hoped, which is to the terms of a transaction with the principal.

The effects of the principal's ratification are also fair to the agent because by assenting to the agent's act the principal usually eliminates claims that the principal or the third party might otherwise assert against the agent. Ratification is an all-or-nothing proposition in two basic respects. First, in most cases, by ratifying the principal eliminates claims the principal might otherwise have against the agent for acting without actual authority. See § 4.02(2) for exceptions to this general principle. Were the doctrine otherwise, the principal could speculate at the agent's expense by ratifying a transaction as against the third party, but holding the agent accountable if, after the time of ratification, the transaction turned out to be a losing proposition for the principal. Second, a principal must ratify a single transaction in its entirety, thereby becoming subject to its burdens as well as enjoying its benefits. See § 4.07.

§ 4.02 Effect of Ratification

(1) Subject to the exceptions stated in subsection (2), ratification retroactively creates the effects of actual authority.

(2) Ratification is not effective:

(a) in favor of a person who causes it by misrepresentation or other conduct that would make a contract voidable;

(b) in favor of an agent against a principal when the principal ratifies to avoid a loss; or

(c) to diminish the rights or other interests of persons, not parties to the transaction, that were acquired in the subject matter prior to the ratification.

§ 4.03 Acts That May be Ratified

A person may ratify an act if the actor acted or purported to act as an agent on the person's behalf.

§ 4.04 Capacity to Ratify

(1) A person may ratify an act if

(a) the person existed at the time of the act, and

(b) the person had capacity as defined in § 3.04 at the time of ratifying the act.

(2) At a later time, a principal may avoid a ratification made earlier when the principal lacked capacity as defined in § 3.04.

§ 4.05 Timing of Ratification

A ratification of a transaction is not effective unless it precedes the occurrence of circumstances that would cause the ratification to have adverse and inequitable effects on the rights of third parties. These circumstances include:

(1) any manifestation of intention to withdraw from the transaction made by the third party;

(2) any material change in circumstances that would make it inequitable to bind the third party, unless the third party chooses to be bound; and

(3) a specific time that determines whether a third party is deprived of a right or subjected to a liability.

§ 4.06 Knowledge Requisite to Ratification

A person is not bound by a ratification made without knowledge of material facts involved in the original act when the person was unaware of such lack of knowledge.

§ 4.07 No Partial Ratification

A ratification is not effective unless it encompasses the entirety of an act, contract, or other single transaction.

§ 4.08 Estoppel to Deny Ratification

If a person makes a manifestation that the person has ratified another's act and the manifestation, as reasonably understood by a third party, induces the third party to make a detrimental change in position, the person may be estopped to deny the ratification.

Chapter 5

NOTIFICATIONS AND NOTICE

§ 5.01 Notifications and Notice—In General

(1) A notification is a manifestation that is made in the form required by agreement among parties or by applicable law, or in a reasonable manner in the absence of an agreement or an applicable law, with the intention of affecting the legal rights and duties of the notifier in relation to rights and duties of persons to whom the notification is given.

(2) A notification given to or by an agent is effective as notification to or by the principal as stated in § 5.02.

(3) A person has notice of a fact if the person knows the fact, has reason to know the fact, has received an effective notification of the fact, or should know the fact to fulfill a duty owed to another person.

(4) Notice of a fact that an agent knows or has reason to know is imputed to the principal as stated in §§ 5.03 and 5.04.

§ 5.02 Notification Given by or to an Agent

(1) A notification given to an agent is effective as notice to the principal if the agent has actual or apparent authority to receive the notification, unless the person who gives the notification knows or has reason to know that the agent is acting adversely to the principal as stated in § 5.04.

(2) A notification given by an agent is effective as notification given by the principal if the agent has actual or apparent authority to give the notification, unless the person who receives the notification knows or has reason to know that the agent is acting adversely to the principal as stated in § 5.04.

§ 5.03 Imputation of Notice of Fact to Principal

For purposes of determining a principal's legal relations with a third party, notice of a fact that an agent knows or has reason to know is imputed to the principal if knowledge of the fact is material to the agent's duties to the principal, unless the agent

(a) acts adversely to the principal as stated in § 5.04, or

(b) is subject to a duty to another not to disclose the fact to the principal.

Comment c. Imputation within organizational principals. Imputation doctrines, like common-law agency in general, treat a juridical person that is an organization as one legal person. Organizations generally function by subdividing work or activities into specific functions that are assigned to different people. See § 1.03, Comment *c*. Within an organization, the work done by some agents consists of obtaining information on the basis of which coagents take action. Imputation recognizes that an organization constitutes one legal person and that its link to the external world is through its agents, including those whose assigned function is to receive, collect, report, or record information for organizational purposes....

The nature and scope of the duties assigned to an agent are key to imputation within an organization....

An organization's large size does not in itself defeat imputation, nor does the fact that an organization has structured itself internally into separate departments or divisions. Organizations are treated as possessing the collective knowledge of their employees and other agents, when that knowledge is material to the agents' duties, however the organization may have configured itself or its internal practices for transmission of information.

If an agent has learned a fact under circumstances that impose a duty on the agent not to reveal it to a principal, notice of that fact is not imputed to that principal. Thus, notice of a fact that an agent learns in confidence from one principal is not imputed to another principal. For further discussion, see Comment *e*.

An organization may put in place internal restrictions on how information is handled and transmitted to assist in fulfilling duties of confidentiality owed to its clients. Such restrictions are common in multifunction financial-services firms.

If information is communicated within an organization contrary to a prohibition imposed by an internal barrier on communication, the firm is charged with notice of the information.... Prior communications that contravene an organization's internal barrier call the barrier's general effectiveness into question. A barrier is not likely to be effective or to appear credible when personnel who possess nonpublic information work on shared projects with personnel whose job functions involve trading or other activity that would be aided by access to nonpublic information. Indicia of commitment to the barrier at an organization's highest levels enhance its credibility, as does consistent imposition of sanctions when violations are known to have occurred. A barrier's credibility will also be enhanced by regular review of its efficacy by a suitable organ of internal governance, such as an internal audit or regulatory department or an independent audit or other committee of a board of directors.

Barriers on intra-organization transmission of nonpublic information may also be strongly encouraged or required by law or regulation, which evolves as circumstances require. For example, the SEC's Rule 14e–3(b), promulgated under § 14(e) of the Securities Exchange Act, provides that a person (other than a natural person) will not be subject to liability for trading on the basis of nonpublic information about an impending tender offer if the person has established reasonable policies to ensure that individuals who make decisions to trade in securities of the target corporation do not receive information about the bid possessed by other individuals within the same firm. Such barriers may also be required by law. For example, the Insider Trading and Securities Fraud Enforcement Act of 1988 requires broker-dealers and investment advisers to establish and maintain written procedures to prevent misuse of inside information. See 15 U.S.C. § 78o(f). National banks are required by the Office of the Comptroller of the Currency to use internal barriers to prevent bank trust departments from unlawfully obtaining nonpublic information from other bank departments. See 12 C.F.R. § 9.5.

An internal barrier on communication of nonpublic information does not provide a defense to the legal consequences of a failure to take action in light of information that is otherwise freely available. . . .

§ 5.04 An Agent Who Acts Adversely to a Principal

For purposes of determining a principal's legal relations with a third party, notice of a fact that an agent knows or has reason to know is not imputed to the principal if the agent acts adversely to the principal in a transaction or matter, intending to act solely for the agent's own purposes or those of another person. Nevertheless, notice is imputed

(a) when necessary to protect the rights of a third party who dealt with the principal in good faith; or

(b) when the principal has ratified or knowingly retained a benefit from the agent's action.

A third party who deals with a principal through an agent, knowing or having reason to know that the agent acts adversely to the principal, does not deal in good faith for this purpose.

Comment b. Exception to imputation—in general. The doctrine stated in this section is an exception to the general rule, stated in § 5.03, that notice is imputed to a principal of a fact that an agent knows or has reason to know if knowledge of the fact is material to the agent's duties to the principal and to the principal's legal relations with third parties. The exception stated in this section is often termed the "adverse interest" exception. There is no imputation if an agent acts adversely to the principal. The adverse-interest exception is subject to two exclusions or exceptions. First, as stated in subsection (a), notice is imputed to the principal of facts that an agent who acts adversely knows or has reason to know when necessary to protect the rights of a third party who has dealt with the principal in good faith. Second, as stated in subsection (b), notice is imputed to a principal when the principal ratifies the agent's action or knowingly retains a benefit from the agent's action, although the agent acted adversely to the principal.

A third party who knows or has reason to know that an agent acts adversely to the principal, and who deals with the principal through the agent, has not dealt in good faith and may not rely on the adverse-interest exception. Thus, imputation protects innocent third parties but not those who know or have reason to know that an agent is not likely to transmit material information to the principal.

The rule stated in this section, like the rule stated in § 5.03, is applicable only for purposes of determining a principal's legal relations with a third party. Thus, notice is not imputed for purposes of determining rights and liabilities as between principal and agent. As a consequence, imputation does not furnish a basis on which an agent may defend against a claim by the principal.

If a principal ratifies action taken by an agent, the principal is bound by the legal consequences of that action as if the principal had knowledge of all the facts known by the agent. Section 4.01(2) states how a principal may ratify an agent's action, including by retaining a benefit produced by the agent's action. See Comment *d* for further discussion.

This section states a well-established doctrine. Partnership legislation has long incorporated the principle that a partnership is not charged with the knowledge of a partner who acts adversely to it. Under § 12 of the Uniform Partnership Act (1914) and § 102(f) of the Uniform Partnership Act (1997), a partnership is charged with a partner's knowledge, "except in the case of a fraud on the partnership committed by or with the consent of that partner."

However, as stated above, in order to protect third parties who deal with the principal in good faith, common-law agency doctrine encompasses exclusions to the exception to imputation when an agent acts adversely. As stated in subsection (a), the adverse-interest exception to imputation does not defeat the rights of a third party who dealt in good faith with the principal through an agent. Common-law agency also recognizes that a principal may elect to ratify the actions of an adversely acting agent. Taken as a whole, the common-law doctrine reflects a balance among factors that, if pressed in isolation to their respective extremes, would lead to divergent outcomes.

Ordinarily, an agent's failure to disclose a material fact to a principal does not defeat imputation, nor does the fact that the agent's action otherwise constitutes a breach of a duty owed the principal. See § 5.03, Comment *b*. For an agent's duty to provide information to the principal, see § 8.11. A principal's opportunity to monitor an agent and create incentives for the proper handling of information warrant imputing an agent's knowledge to the principal even when the agent has breached duties of disclosure to the principal. Moreover, imputation does not rest on an identification between principal and agent but rather on the fact that a principal's agents link it to the external world for purposes of obtaining and conveying information as well as taking action.

When an agent acts for the agent's own purposes or those of another person, the principal may be subject to liability to third parties because the agent may reasonably appear to be acting as the principal's representative with actual authority. See § 2.03. Likewise, notice of material facts known to an agent is imputed to the principal when the agent deals with a third party who reasonably believes the agent to be authorized so to act for the principal. However, this section does not protect a third party who knows or has reason to know that an agent acts adversely to the principal. If the third party colludes with the agent against the principal or otherwise knows or has reason to know that the agent is acting adversely to the principal, the third party should not expect that the agent will fulfill duties of disclosure owed to the principal.

Chapter 6

CONTRACTS AND OTHER TRANSACTIONS WITH THIRD PARTIES

TOPIC 1. PARTIES TO CONTRACTS

§ 6.01 Agent for Disclosed Principal

When an agent acting with actual or apparent authority makes a contract on behalf of a disclosed principal,

(1) the principal and the third party are parties to the contract; and

(2) the agent is not a party to the contract unless the agent and third party agree otherwise.

§ 6.02 Agent for Unidentified Principal

When an agent acting with actual or apparent authority makes a contract on behalf of an unidentified principal,

(1) the principal and the third party are parties to the contract; and

(2) the agent is a party to the contract unless the agent and the third party agree otherwise.

§ 6.03 Agent for Undisclosed Principal

When an agent acting with actual authority makes a contract on behalf of an undisclosed principal,

(1) unless excluded by the contract, the principal is a party to the contract;

(2) the agent and the third party are parties to the contract; and

(3) the principal, if a party to the contract, and the third party have the same rights, liabilities, and defenses against each other as if the principal made the contract personally, subject to §§ 6.05–6.09.

Comment d. Circumstances that affect rights or liabilities of undisclosed principal; contract excluding undisclosed principal as party. An undisclosed principal does not become a party to a contract if the contract excludes the principal. An explicit exclusion limits the third party's manifestation of assent to be bound. Such an explicit exclusion provides a simple device through which a third party may exclude the interests of persons other than those identified as parties to the contract. An undisclosed principal is not excluded from a contract by language stating that the contract is not assignable.

In contrast, an undisclosed principal and an agent may agree that the agent alone shall be liable on a contract. An agreement between an undisclosed principal and an agent cannot effectively exclude the principal as a party to the contract because the third party has not assented to such exclusion.

By dealing on behalf of an undisclosed principal, an agent does not implicitly represent that the agent is not acting for a principal. This is because it is usually not material to a third party whether the person with whom the third party deals, and who becomes subject to liability on contracts made with the third party, acts as an agent for an undisclosed principal. See § 6.11, Comment *d*. If an agent falsely represents that the agent does not act on behalf of a principal, the third party may avoid a contract made with the agent under the circumstances stated in § 6.11(4). A third party may avoid a contract made by an agent acting for an undisclosed principal if the agent or the principal knows or has reason to know that the third party would not have dealt with the principal as a party to the contract. See id. See also § 6.02, Comment *c*.

The nature of the performance that a contract requires determines whether performance by an undisclosed principal will be effective as performance under the contract and whether an undisclosed principal can require that the third party render performance to the principal. Performance by an undisclosed principal is not effective as performance under a contract if the third party has a substantial interest in receiving performance from the agent who made the contract. This limit corresponds to the limit on delegability of performance of a duty as stated in Restatement Second, Contracts § 318(2).

The nature of the performance that a contract requires from a third party determines whether an undisclosed principal is entitled to receive that performance. An undisclosed principal may not require that a third party render performance to the principal if rendering performance to the principal would materially change the nature of the third party's duty, materially increase the burden or risk imposed on the third party, or materially impair the third party's chance of receiving return performance. These limits correspond to the limits imposed on assignment of a contractual right. See Restatement Second, Contracts § 317(2).

§ 6.04 Principal Does not Exist or Lacks Capacity

Unless the third party agrees otherwise, a person who makes a contract with a third party purportedly as an agent on behalf of a principal becomes a party to the contract if the purported agent knows or has reason to know that the purported principal does not exist or lacks capacity to be a party to a contract.

TOPIC 2. RIGHTS, LIABILITIES, AND DEFENSES

TITLE A. GENERAL

§ 6.05 Contract That is Unauthorized in Part or That Combines Orders of Several Principals

(1) If an agent makes a contract with a third party that differs from the contract that the agent had actual or apparent authority to make only in an amount or by the inclusion or exclusion of a separable part, the principal is subject to liability to the third party to the extent of the contract that the agent had actual or apparent authority to make if

(a) the third party seasonably makes a manifestation to the principal of willingness to be bound; and

(b) the principal has not changed position in reasonable reliance on the belief that no contract bound the principal and the third party.

(2) Two or more principals may authorize the same agent to make separate contracts for them. If the agent makes a single contract with a third party on the principals' behalves that combines the principals' separate orders or interests and calls for a single performance by the third party,

(a) if the agent purports to make the combined contract on behalf of disclosed principals, the agent is subject to liability to the third party for breach of the agent's warranty of authority as stated in § 6.10, unless the separate principals are bound by the combined contract;

(b) if the principals are unidentified or undisclosed, the third party and the agent are the only parties to the combined contract; and

(c) unless the agent acted with actual or apparent authority to bind each of the principals to the combined contract,

(i) subject to (1), none of the separate principals is subject to liability on the combined contract; and

(ii) the third party is not subject to liability on the combined contract to any of the separate principals.

§ 6.06 Setoff

(1) When an agent makes a contract on behalf of a disclosed or unidentified principal, unless the principal and the third party agree otherwise,

(a) the third party may not set off any amount that the agent independently owes the third party against an amount the third party owes the principal under the contract; and

(b) the principal may not set off any amount that the third party independently owes the agent against an amount the principal owes the third party under the contract.

(2) When an agent makes a contract on behalf of an undisclosed principal,

(a) the third party may set off

(i) any amount that the agent independently owed the third party at the time the agent made the contract and

(ii) any amount that the agent thereafter independently comes to owe the third party until the third party has notice that the agent acts on behalf of a principal against an amount the third party owes the principal under the contract;

(b) after the third party has notice that the agent acts on behalf of a principal, the third party may not set off any amount that the agent thereafter independently comes to owe the third party against an amount the third party owes the principal under the contract unless the principal consents; and

(c) the principal may not set off any amount that the third party independently owes the agent against an amount that the principal owes the third party under the contract, unless the principal and the third party agree otherwise.

(3) Unless otherwise agreed, an agent who is a party to a contract may not set off any amount that the principal independently owes the agent against an amount that the agent owes the third party under the contract. However, with the principal's consent, the agent may set off any amount that the principal could set off against an amount that the principal owes the third party under the contract.

TITLE B. SUBSEQUENT DEALINGS BETWEEN THIRD PARTY AND PRINCIPAL OR AGENT

§ 6.07 Settlement with Agent by Principal or Third Party

(1) A principal's payment to or settlement of accounts with an agent discharges the principal's liability to a third party with whom the agent has made a contract on the principal's behalf only when the principal acts in reasonable reliance on a manifestation by the third party, not induced by misrepresentation by the agent, that the agent has settled the account with the third party.

(2) A third party's payment to or settlement of accounts with an agent discharges the third party's liability to the principal if the agent acts with actual or apparent authority in accepting the payment or settlement.

(3) When an agent has made a contract on behalf of an undisclosed principal,

(a) until the third party has notice of the principal's existence, the third party's payment to or settlement of accounts with the agent discharges the third party's liability to the principal;

(b) after the third party has notice of the principal's existence, the third party's payment to or settlement of accounts with the agent discharges the third party's liability to the principal if the agent acts with actual or apparent authority in accepting the payment or settlement; and

(c) after receiving notice of the principal's existence, the third party may demand reasonable proof of the principal's identity and relationship to the agent. Until such proof is received, the third party's payment to or settlement of accounts in good faith with the agent discharges the third party's liability to the principal.

§ 6.08 Other Subsequent Dealings Between Third Party and Agent

(1) When an agent has made a contract with a third party on behalf of a disclosed or unidentified principal, subsequent dealings between the agent and the third party may increase or diminish the principal's rights or liabilities to the third party if the agent acts with actual or apparent authority or the principal ratifies the agent's action.

(2) When an agent has made a contract with a third party on behalf of an undisclosed principal,

(a) until the third party has notice of the principal's existence, subsequent dealings between the third party and the agent may increase or diminish the rights or liabilities of the principal to the third party if the agent acts with actual authority, or the principal ratifies the agent's action; and

(b) after the third party has notice of the principal's existence, subsequent dealings between the third party and the agent may increase or diminish the principal's rights or liabilities to the third party if the agent acts with actual or apparent authority or the principal ratifies the agent's action.

§ 6.09 Effect of Judgment Against Agent or Principal

When an agent has made a contract with a third party on behalf of a principal, unless the contract provides otherwise,

(1) the liability, if any, of the principal or the agent to the third party is not discharged if the third party obtains a judgment against the other; and

(2) the liability, if any, of the principal or the agent to the third party is discharged to the extent a judgment against the other is satisfied.

TITLE C. AGENT'S WARRANTIES AND REPRESENTATIONS

§ 6.10 Agent's Implied Warranty of Authority

A person who purports to make a contract, representation, or conveyance to or with a third party on behalf of another person, lacking power to bind that person, gives an implied warranty of authority to the third party and is subject to liability to the third party for damages for loss caused by breach of that warranty, including loss of the benefit expected from performance by the principal, unless

(1) the principal or purported principal ratifies the act as stated in § 4.01; or

(2) the person who purports to make the contract, representation, or conveyance gives notice to the third party that no warranty of authority is given; or

(3) the third party knows that the person who purports to make the contract, representation, or conveyance acts without actual authority.

§ 6.11 Agent's Representations

(1) When an agent for a disclosed or unidentified principal makes a false representation about the agent's authority to a third party, the principal is not subject to liability unless the agent acted with actual or apparent authority in making the representation and the third party does not have notice that the agent's representation is false.

(2) A representation by an agent made incident to a contract or conveyance is attributed to a disclosed or unidentified principal as if the principal made the representation directly when the agent had actual or apparent authority to make the contract or conveyance unless the third party knew or had reason to know that the representation was untrue or that the agent acted without actual authority in making it.

(3) A representation by an agent made incident to a contract or conveyance is attributed to an undisclosed principal as if the principal made the representation directly when

(a) the agent acted with actual authority in making the representation, or

(b) the agent acted without actual authority in making the representation but had actual authority to make true representations about the same matter.

The agent's representation is not attributed to the principal when the third party knew or had reason to know it was untrue.

(4) When an agent who makes a contract or conveyance on behalf of an undisclosed principal falsely represents to the third party that the agent does not act on behalf of a principal, the third party may avoid the contract or conveyance if the principal or agent had notice that the third party would not have dealt with the principal.

Chapter 7

TORTS—LIABILITY OF AGENT AND PRINCIPAL

TOPIC 1. AGENT'S LIABILITY

§ 7.01 Agent's Liability to Third Party

An agent is subject to liability to a third party harmed by the agent's tortious conduct. Unless an applicable statute provides otherwise, an actor remains subject to liability although the actor acts as an agent or an employee, with actual or apparent authority, or within the scope of employment.

§ 7.02 Duty to Principal; Duty to Third Party

An agent's breach of a duty owed to the principal is not an independent basis for the agent's tort liability to a third party. An agent is subject to tort liability to a third party harmed by the agent's conduct only when the agent's conduct breaches a duty that the agent owes to the third party.

TOPIC 2. PRINCIPAL'S LIABILITY

§ 7.03 Principal's Liability—In General

(1) A principal is subject to direct liability to a third party harmed by an agent's conduct when

(a) as stated in § 7.04, the agent acts with actual authority or the principal ratifies the agent's conduct and

(i) the agent's conduct is tortious, or

(ii) the agent's conduct, if that of the principal, would subject the principal to tort liability; or

(b) as stated in § 7.05, the principal is negligent in selecting, supervising, or otherwise controlling the agent; or

(c) as stated in § 7.06, the principal delegates performance of a duty to use care to protect other persons or their property to an agent who fails to perform the duty.

(2) A principal is subject to vicarious liability to a third party harmed by an agent's conduct when

(a) as stated in § 7.07, the agent is an employee who commits a tort while acting within the scope of employment; or

(b) as stated in § 7.08, the agent commits a tort when acting with apparent authority in dealing with a third party on or purportedly on behalf of the principal.

Comment d. Agents with multiple principals. An agent who commits a tort may have more than one principal for at least some purposes. On agents with multiple principals in general, see Chapter 3, Topic 5. In the context of a principal's liability on the basis of an agent's tort, it is helpful to distinguish among three different types of relationships: (1) subagency; (2) employees who are "borrowed" by one employer from another employer; and (3) officers of interrelated entities.

(1) Subagency. A subagent is a person appointed by an agent to perform functions that the agent has consented to perform on behalf of the principal. See § 3.15(1). For general discussion of the consequences of subagency, see § 3.15, Comment *d.* A subagent may be an employee of the appointing agent. When a subagent is an employee, as defined in § 7.07(3), of the appointing agent, the appointing agent is subject to vicarious liability for torts committed by the subagent within the scope of employment. See § 7.07. Both the appointing agent and the principal are subject to vicarious liability when a subagent acts with apparent authority in committing a tort, as stated in § 7.08. An appointing agent may be subject to liability for torts of a subagent who is not an employee. For example, when a law firm assigns work on behalf of a client to a "temporary" lawyer who is neither a member of the firm nor its employee, the firm creates a relationship of subagency with the "temporary" lawyer that subjects it to liability to its client for acts and omissions of the "temporary" lawyer. See Restatement Third, The Law Governing Lawyers § 58, Comment *e.*

A relationship of subagency does not result when an agent appoints a coagent. Coagents share a common principal, although they may occupy dominant and subordinate positions in an organizational hierarchy. See § 3.15, Comment *b.* An agent who has authority to hire a coagent is not subject to vicarious liability for the coagent's tortious conduct.

(2) "Lent employees," or "borrowed servants." When work requires specialized skills or equipment or requires that an actor perform a task on less than a full-time basis, it is not unusual that the actor who performs the work is employed by a firm that contracts to provide the actor's services to another firm. The types of actors who work through such arrangements vary greatly, as does the nature of the work they do. These arrangements span the range of highly skilled professionals, including nurses, lawyers, and other members of licensed professions; office workers; skilled construction workers; and unskilled manual laborers. The risks of injury to third parties posed by such work vary, as do the settings in which work is performed. Moreover, the specifics of such arrangements vary in several respects. These include the duration of an actor's placement in a particular workplace and the provision of supervision, training, and tools needed to perform work. An actor's employer may provide requisite training, furnish the actor with specialized equipment needed for work, and reassign the actor with frequency. Alternatively, the actor may work on a long-term basis within a particular firm using tools and receiving training provided by that firm.

When an actor negligently injures a third party while performing work for the firm that has contracted for the actor's services, the question is whether that firm (often termed the "special employer") or the initial employer (often termed the "general employer"), or both, should be subject to liability to the third party. Liability should be allocated to the employer in the better position to take measures to prevent the injury suffered by the third party. An employer is in that position if the employer has the right to control an employee's conduct. When both a general and special employer have the right to control an employee's conduct, the practical history of direction may establish that one employer in fact ceded its right of control to the other, whether through its failure to exercise the right or otherwise.

It is a question of fact whether a general or a special employer, or both, have the right to control an employee's conduct. Factors that a court may consider in making this determination include the extent of control that an employer may exercise over the details of an employee's work and the timing of the work; the relationship between the employee's work and the nature of the special employer's business; the nature of the employee's work, the skills required to perform it, and the degree of supervision customarily associated with the work; the duration of the employee's work in the special employer's firm; the identity of the employer who furnishes equipment or other instrumentalities requisite to performing the work; and the method of payment for the work.

Many cases allocate liability in this context on the basis that a general employer has an exclusive right of control over employees assigned to work for clients of the general employer. This presupposes that ties between a general employer and an assigned employee will remain strong despite the employee's emplacement in the special employer's workplace where the employee's performance will often be subject to some degree of direction and monitoring by members of the special employer's management. It may also reflect assumptions about links between the general employer and the risk that third parties will be injured when work is done in a special employer's workplace. A general employer is in a position to screen prospective employees to determine their general aptitude and fitness; a general employer may also provide training to those it selects for employment. If a general employer assigns an employee and furnishes the employee with equipment to use in performing assigned work, the general employer is also in a position to impose requirements for the proper usage and maintenance of the equipment. A general employer may also be in a better position to provide insurance coverage for an employee's actions. Any presumption that a general employer has the right to control an employee may be rebutted by proving factual indicia that the right has been assumed by a special employer. Even within the same jurisdiction, it may be difficult to predict whether a given set of indicia will demonstrate that a special employer has assumed the right of control.

However, a significant number of cases allocate liability to a special employer on the basis of its right and ability to direct a borrowed employee's specific actions in its workplace. A justification for this approach is that a borrowed employee may retain only formal ties to a general employer, depending on the duration and nature of the borrowed employee's relationship with the special employer, which weakens the likelihood that the general employer retains any practical capacity to control the borrowed employee's conduct. This approach also reflects the possibility that a special employer may in fact be in the better position to exercise control in a manner that reduces the risk of injury to third parties. This possibility may be especially likely when the nature of a borrowed employee's work requires coordinated effort as part of a skilled team and close direction or supervision by the team's leader. Some cases allocate liability to both general and special employer on the basis that both exercised control over the employee and both benefited to some degree from the employee's work.

A related question, arising when the third party injured by an actor's negligence is an employee of the special employer, is the applicability of workers'-compensation insurance law to the employee's claims. Although these questions may often be related as a practical matter, workers'-compensation questions are beyond the scope of this Restatement.

(3) Officers of interrelated entities. The fact that a corporation or other entity owns a majority of the voting equity in another entity does not create a relationship of agency between them or between each entity and the other's agents. Likewise, common ownership of multiple entities does not create relationships of agency among them. See § 1.01, Comment *f(2)*. An entity becomes the agent of another entity, and an individual becomes an entity's agent, only when they are linked by the elements of an agency relationship as stated in § 1.01.

Within a related group of corporations or other entities the same individuals may serve as officers or directors of more than one entity. An overlapping cast in multiple organizational roles does not in itself create relationships of agency that are not otherwise present.

When the same individuals serve multiple entities as their officers, directors, or employees, it may become necessary to determine the entity to which an individual's conduct should be attributed. There is a general presumption that contracts and other transactions entered into by a shared officer are attributed to the entity for which the officer purports to be acting. A rationale for this presumption is that the identity of the party who will be bound by a contract or transaction is often material to the other party to the contract or transaction. See § 6.01, Comment *b*. This rationale does not support applying the same presumption when a shared officer's conduct is tortious, especially when the party injured by the conduct has not chosen to engage in a transaction conducted by the shared officer. Moreover, that an officer purports to act on behalf of a particular entity does not create a basis for attribution that corresponds to policies and objectives that underlie contemporary tort law. When harm is caused negligently, these objectives include remedying an injustice that has been inflicted on a plaintiff by a defendant and providing a defendant with appropriate safety incentives. See Restatement Third, Torts: Liability for Physical Harm § 6, Comment *d* (Proposed Final Draft No. 1, 2005). On harm that is caused intentionally, see id. § 5, Comment *a*. Likewise, the contract-based presumption is inapt when a shared officer's conduct violates a statute that proscribes or regulates conduct, particularly conduct outside a transactional context.

§ 7.04 Agent Acts with Actual Authority

A principal is subject to liability to a third party harmed by an agent's conduct when the agent's conduct is within the scope of the agent's actual authority or ratified by the principal; and

(1) the agent's conduct is tortious, or

(2) the agent's conduct, if that of the principal, would subject the principal to tort liability.

§ 7.05 Principal's Negligence in Conducting Activity Through Agent; Principal's Special Relationship with Another Person

(1) A principal who conducts an activity through an agent is subject to liability for harm to a third party caused by the agent's conduct if the harm was caused by the principal's negligence in selecting, training, retaining, supervising, or otherwise controlling the agent.

(2) When a principal has a special relationship with another person, the principal owes that person a duty of reasonable care with regard to risks arising out of the relationship, including the risk that agents of the principal will harm the person with whom the principal has such a special relationship.

§ 7.06 Failure in Performance of Principal's Duty of Protection

A principal required by contract or otherwise by law to protect another cannot avoid liability by delegating performance of the duty, whether or not the delegate is an agent.

§ 7.07 Employee Acting Within Scope of Employment

(1) An employer is subject to vicarious liability for a tort committed by its employee acting within the scope of employment.

(2) An employee acts within the scope of employment when performing work assigned by the employer or engaging in a course of

conduct subject to the employer's control. An employee's act is not within the scope of employment when it occurs within an independent course of conduct not intended by the employee to serve any purpose of the employer.

(3) For purposes of this section,

(a) an employee is an agent whose principal controls or has the right to control the manner and means of the agent's performance of work, and

(b) the fact that work is performed gratuitously does not relieve a principal of liability.

Comment c. Conduct in the performance of work and scope of employment. An employee's conduct is within the scope of employment when it constitutes performance of work assigned to the employee by the employer. The fact that the employee performs the work carelessly does not take the employee's conduct outside the scope of employment, nor does the fact that the employee otherwise makes a mistake in performing the work. Likewise, conduct is not outside the scope of employment merely because an employee disregards the employer's instructions.

. . . [T]he fact that an employee's action violates a generally applicable law, such as a speeding limit, does not by itself place the employee's conduct outside the scope of employment. These results are not surprising. An employee may believe that the employer wishes the employee to disregard an inconvenient constraint when the employee fears that compliance would jeopardize completing the employee's assigned mission at all or completing it on or ahead of schedule. Although the employee's belief may be mistaken, it is compatible with acting in an assigned role to do an assigned task. However, the character, extreme nature, or other circumstances accompanying an employee's actions may demonstrate that the employee's course of conduct is independent of performing work assigned by the employer and intended solely to further the employee's own purposes. . . .

An employee's failure to take action may also be conduct within the scope of employment. For example, an employee's failure to do work assigned by the employer, when harm to a third party results, under some circumstances may constitute negligence. A negligent action "frequently involves a failure to take a reasonable precaution. . . . [which] can be described as an omission, and it hence can be said that the omission is itself negligent." Restatement Third, Torts: Liability for Physical Harm § 3, Comment *c* (Proposed Final Draft No. 1, 2005).

An employee's assigned work may include tasks that contemplate the necessity of using physical force to complete the assigned work. . . . An employee's assigned duties may also place the employee in situations in which physical consequences may follow in an uninterrupted sequence from verbal exchanges with third parties. An escalation in the pitch of an employee's conduct does not by itself transform the conduct into an independent course of conduct that represents a departure not within the scope of employment. It is a question of fact what motivated an employee's conduct as verbal exchanges escalate or when an employee's use of physical force becomes more pronounced.

In determining whether an employee's tortious conduct is within the scope of employment, the nature of the tort is relevant, as is whether the conduct also constitutes a criminal act. An employee's intentionally criminal conduct may indicate a departure from conduct within the scope of employment, not a simple escalation. The nature and magnitude of the conduct are relevant to determining the employee's intention at the time....

The determinative question is whether the course of conduct in which the tort occurred is within the scope of employment. Intentional torts and other intentional wrongdoing may be within the scope of employment. For example, if an employee's job duties include determining the prices at which the employer's output will be sold to customers, the employee's agreement with a competitor to fix prices is within the scope of employment unless circumstances establish a departure from the scope of employment. Likewise, when an employee's job duties include making statements to prospective customers to induce them to buy from the employer, intentional misrepresentations made by the employee are within the scope of employment unless circumstances establish that the employee has departed from it.

An employee may engage in conduct, part of which is within the scope of employment and part of which is not....

When an employee's tortious conduct is outside the scope of employment, alternate theories of liability may be available against the employer....

§ 7.08 Agent Acts with Apparent Authority

A principal is subject to vicarious liability for a tort committed by an agent in dealing or communicating with a third party on or purportedly on behalf of the principal when actions taken by the agent with apparent authority constitute the tort or enable the agent to conceal its commission.

Chapter 8

DUTIES OF AGENT AND PRINCIPAL TO EACH OTHER

TOPIC 1. AGENT'S DUTIES TO PRINCIPAL

TITLE A. GENERAL FIDUCIARY PRINCIPLE

§ 8.01 General Fiduciary Principle

An agent has a fiduciary duty to act loyally for the principal's benefit in all matters connected with the agency relationship.

TITLE B. DUTIES OF LOYALTY

§ 8.02 Material Benefit Arising Out of Position

An agent has a duty not to acquire a material benefit from a third party in connection with transactions conducted or other actions taken on behalf of the principal or otherwise through the agent's use of the agent's position.

Comment e. Remedies. When an agent breaches the duty stated in this section, the principal may recover monetary relief from the agent and, in appropriate circumstances, from any third party who participated in the agent's breach. A principal may avoid a contract entered into by the agent with a third party who participated in the agent's breach of duty. The principal may recover any material benefit received by the agent through the agent's breach, the value of the benefit, or proceeds of the benefit retained by the agent. The principal may also recover damages for any harm caused by the agent's breach. If an agent's breach of duty involves a wrongful disposal of assets of the principal, the principal cannot recover both the value of the asset and what the agent received in exchange. If a principal recovers damages from a third party as a consequence of an agent's breach of fiduciary duty, the principal remains entitled to recover from the agent any benefit that the agent improperly received from the transaction.

If a principal seeks to recover a material benefit received by an agent, the value of the benefit, or its proceeds, the principal's recovery is not subject to a deduction for expenses incurred by the agent to induce a third party to confer the benefit on the agent.

However, if an agent breaches the agent's fiduciary duty by taking personal advantage of a business opportunity as discussed in Comment *d*, the principal may recover property that the agent acquired through the breach only if the principal reimburses the agent. The amount of reimbursement is either the amount paid by the agent for the property or the amount for which the principal could have obtained the property, whichever is less. See Restatement of Restitution §§ 194, 195; Principles of Corporate Governance: Analysis and Recommendations, Comment to § 5.05(e) and Illustration 13.

§ 8.03 Acting as or on Behalf of an Adverse Party

An agent has a duty not to deal with the principal as or on behalf of an adverse party in a transaction connected with the agency relationship.

Comment b. Rationale. As a fiduciary, an agent has a duty to the principal to act loyally in the principal's interest in all matters in connection with the agency relationship. See § 8.01. The rule stated in this section is a specific application of this general principle. When an agent deals with the principal on the agent's own account, the agent's own interests are irreconcilably in tension with the principal's interests because the interest of each is furthered by action—negotiating a higher or a lower price, for example—that is incompatible with the interests of the other. If an agent acts on behalf of the principal in a transaction with the agent, the agent's duty to act loyally in the principal's interest conflicts with the agent's self-interest. Even if the agent's divided loyalty does not result in demonstrable harm to the principal, the agent has breached the agent's duty of undivided loyalty. Likewise, an agent who acts on behalf of more than one principal in a transaction between or among the principals has breached the agent's duty of loyalty to each principal through undertaking service to multiple principals that divides the agent's loyalty.

A principal may consent to conduct by an agent that would otherwise constitute a breach of the agent's duty. See § 8.06. On consent by multiple principals when an agent conducts a transaction between or among the principals, see § 8.06(2).

The duty stated in this section is formulated broadly. So long as the transaction in which an agent acts as or on behalf of an adverse party is connected with the agency relationship, the agent is subject to the duty although the agent does not have direct or indirect responsibility for conducting the transaction on behalf of the principal. The breadth of this formulation requires that an agent disclose adverse interests to the principal so that the principal may evaluate, as only the principal is situated to do, how best to protect its interests in light of the agent's interest. See § 8.06. The breadth of the formulation also makes it unnecessary for a principal to prescribe its agents' duties and prohibit outside interests that its agents may have or acquire with great specificity in formulating the initial terms of its relationship with its agents.

A principal's knowledge that an agent deals as or on behalf of an adverse party does not relieve the agent of duties to the principal in connection with that transaction. Under the rule stated in § 8.06, the agent has a duty to deal fairly with the principal and to disclose to the principal all facts of which the agent has notice that are reasonably relevant to the principal's exercise of judgment, unless the principal has manifested that the principal already knows them or does not wish to know them. Thus, a principal's knowledge that its agent acts as or on behalf of an adverse party does not convert the relationship between principal and agent into an arm's-length relationship. Moreover, as stated in § 8.11, an agent has a duty to use reasonable effort to furnish information to the principal although the agent does not deal as or on behalf of an adverse party.

It is, of course, possible that an agent may assume an adverse position in which the agent may not legally discharge the duties of disclosure that the agent owes to the principal because the agent owes a duty to another person not to disclose a fact that §§ 8.06 and 8.11 require be disclosed to the principal. In Illustration 3, for example, A's duties to T Corporation may prohibit A's disclosure of new product developments to T Corporation's customer, P Corporation. Unless it is possible for T Corporation to shield A from access to facts that A will have a duty to disclose to P Corporation, A's position is not tenable, and consequently A must withdraw as P Corporation's agent.

However, an agent whose acts on behalf of a party consist solely of ministerial acts that require no exercise of discretion, judgment, or skill does not act on behalf of that party for purposes of determining whether the agent acts adversely to another principal. Thus, one principal's agent who performs only ministerial acts for another does not become a dual agent.

A custom in an industry that permits self-dealing by agents, if unknown to the principal, does not relieve the agent of the duty to refrain from self-dealing. If an agreement between principal and agent grants the agent discretion to take such adverse action, the agent is subject to a contract-law duty of good faith and fair dealing in exercising the discretion. See § 8.01, Comment *b*.

Many business-organization statutes contain provisions that address self-dealing conduct on the part of specified organizational actors. Under contemporary partnership legislation, a partner has a duty to "refrain from dealing with the partnership in the conduct or winding up of the partnership business as or on behalf of a party having an interest adverse to the partnership. . . ." Rev. Unif. Partnership Act § 404(b)(2). Similarly, a manager of a limited-liability company (LLC) has a comparable duty, as does a member of a member-managed LLC. See Unif. Limited Liability Company Act § 409(b)(2). Many corporation statutes have provisions applicable to transactions between a corporation and a director, or between a corporation and an officer, in which mechanisms are specified through which the director or officer may fulfill duties owed to the corporation in connection with the transaction. See Principles of Corporate Governance: Analysis and Recommendations § 5.02.

§ 8.04 Competition

Throughout the duration of an agency relationship, an agent has a duty to refrain from competing with the principal and from taking action on behalf of or otherwise assisting the principal's competitors. During that time, an agent may take action, not otherwise wrongful, to prepare for competition following termination of the agency relationship.

§ 8.05 Use of Principal's Property; Use of Confidential Information

An agent has a duty

(1) not to use property of the principal for the agent's own purposes or those of a third party; and

(2) not to use or communicate confidential information of the principal for the agent's own purposes or those of a third party.

§ 8.06 Principal's Consent

(1) Conduct by an agent that would otherwise constitute a breach of duty as stated in §§ 8.01, 8.02, 8.03, 8.04, and 8.05 does not constitute a breach of duty if the principal consents to the conduct, provided that

(a) in obtaining the principal's consent, the agent

(i) acts in good faith,

(ii) discloses all material facts that the agent knows, has reason to know, or should know would reasonably affect the principal's judgment unless the principal has manifested that such facts are already known by the principal or that the principal does not wish to know them, and

(iii) otherwise deals fairly with the principal; and

(b) the principal's consent concerns either a specific act or transaction, or acts or transactions of a specified type that could reasonably be expected to occur in the ordinary course of the agency relationship.

(2) An agent who acts for more than one principal in a transaction between or among them has a duty

(a) to deal in good faith with each principal,

(b) to disclose to each principal

(i) the fact that the agent acts for the other principal or principals, and

(ii) all other facts that the agent knows, has reason to know, or should know would reasonably affect the principal's judgment unless the principal has manifested that such facts are already known by the principal or that the principal does not wish to know them, and

(c) otherwise to deal fairly with each principal.

TITLE C. DUTIES OF PERFORMANCE

§ 8.07 Duty Created by Contract

An agent has a duty to act in accordance with the express and implied terms of any contract between the agent and the principal.

§ 8.08 Duties of Care, Competence, and Diligence

Subject to any agreement with the principal, an agent has a duty to the principal to act with the care, competence, and diligence normally exercised by agents in similar circumstances. Special skills or knowledge possessed by an agent are circumstances to be taken into account in determining whether the agent acted with due care and diligence. If an agent claims to possess special skills or knowledge, the agent has a duty to the principal to act with the care, competence, and diligence normally exercised by agents with such skills or knowledge.

Comment b. Common-law and statutory duties of care; regulatory duties. A principal and an agent may establish benchmarks or other measures for the effort and skill to be expected from the agent. For example, a contract between principal and agent may specify measures for the effort that the agent has a duty to expend in pursuing the principal's objectives. An agent may also guarantee by contract that the agent's work will be successful in achieving an objective or that the agent's work will be satisfactory to the principal. On conditions that an obligor be satisfied with an obligee's performance, see Restatement Second, Contracts § 228. A contract may also, in appropriate circumstances, raise or lower the standard of performance to be expected of an agent or specify the remedies or mechanisms of dispute resolution available to the principal. Regardless of their content, contractually shaped or contractually created duties are grounded in the mutual assent of agent and principal.

In contrast to § 8.06, the rule stated in this section articulates a broader role for general agreements that a principal and an agent may make in advance. If an agreement between principal and agent is otherwise enforceable, it may define the standard of performance applicable to the agent across the board in general terms and without the specificity required under § 8.06(1)(b) for consent by a principal to conduct by an agent that would otherwise breach a duty of loyalty owed to the principal under §§ 8.01, 8.02, 8.03, 8.04, or 8.05. Moreover, a principal's consent under § 8.06 is ineffective unless in obtaining the consent the agent acted consistently with the requirements stated in § 8.06(1)(a) or (2).

The duties stated in this section will often overlap with an agent's duties of performance that are express or implied terms of a contract between principal and agent. However, the duties stated in this section are tort-law duties because they "denote the fact that the actor is required to conduct himself in a particular manner at the risk that if he does not do so he becomes subject to liability to another to whom the duty is owed for any injury sustained by such other, of which that actor's conduct is a legal cause." Restatement Second, Torts § 4. Tort law imposes duties of care on an agent because the agent undertakes to act on behalf of the principal, because the principal's reliance on that undertaking is foreseeable by the agent, and because it is often socially useful that an agent fulfill the agent's undertaking to the principal. See Restatement Second, Torts § 323; Restatement Third, Torts: Liability for Physical Harm § 42 (Proposed Final Draft No. 1, 2005).

The overlap between duties derived from tort law and from an agent's contract with the principal will often provide the principal with alternative remedies when a breach of duty subjects the agent to liability. In particular, an agent is subject to liability to the principal for all harm, whether past, present, or prospective, caused the principal by the agent's breach of the duties stated in this section. See Restatement Second, Torts § 910. The agent's liability includes an obligation to indemnify the principal when a wrongful act by the agent subjects the principal to vicarious liability to a third person. See §§ 7.07 and 7.08. One agent's breach of the duties stated in this section does not bar an innocent principal from recovery against another agent who is also subject to liability.

Statutory provisions may also be relevant in determining the duties of care owed by an agent. For example, some organizational statutes establish standards of conduct for officers and others who act on behalf of an organization. Under § 8.42(a)(2) of the Model Business Corporation Act, an officer must act, in performing the officer's duties, "with the care that a person in like position would reasonably exercise under similar circumstances. . . ." The Revised Uniform Partnership Act states that a partner owes a duty of care to the partnership and to other partners "in the conduct and winding up of the partnership business" that is limited to "refraining from engaging in grossly negligent or reckless conduct, intentional misconduct, or a knowing violation of law." Rev. Unif. Partnership Act § 404(c). The Uniform Limited Liability Company Act imposes a comparable standard on an LLC's managers and members who are also managers. Unif. Limited Liability Co. Act § 409(c) and (h)(2).

An agent's conduct may be subject to regulation by statutes, administrative rules, or rules of a particular profession. An agent's violation of such a statute or rule does not in itself establish that the agent breached the agent's duty to the principal stated in this section. If the statute or rule is designed to protect persons in the principal's position, the trier of fact may consider the agent's violation of the statute in defining and applying the standard stated in this section.

§ 8.09 Duty to Act Only Within Scope of Actual Authority and to Comply with Principal's Lawful Instructions

(1) An agent has a duty to take action only within the scope of the agent's actual authority.

(2) An agent has a duty to comply with all lawful instructions received from the principal and persons designated by the principal concerning the agent's actions on behalf of the principal.

§ 8.10 Duty of Good Conduct

An agent has a duty, within the scope of the agency relationship, to act reasonably and to refrain from conduct that is likely to damage the principal's enterprise.

§ 8.11 Duty to Provide Information

An agent has a duty to use reasonable effort to provide the principal with facts that the agent knows, has reason to know, or should know when

(1) subject to any manifestation by the principal, the agent knows or has reason to know that the principal would wish to have the facts or the facts are material to the agent's duties to the principal; and

(2) the facts can be provided to the principal without violating a superior duty owed by the agent to another person.

§ 8.12 Duties Regarding Principal's Property—Segregation, Record–Keeping, and Accounting

An agent has a duty, subject to any agreement with the principal,

(1) not to deal with the principal's property so that it appears to be the agent's property;

(2) not to mingle the principal's property with anyone else's; and

(3) to keep and render accounts to the principal of money or other property received or paid out on the principal's account.

TOPIC 2. PRINCIPAL'S DUTIES TO AGENT

§ 8.13 Duty Created by Contract

A principal has a duty to act in accordance with the express and implied terms of any contract between the principal and the agent.

Comment d. Compensation—other issues. Unless an agreement between a principal and an agent indicates otherwise, a principal has a duty to pay compensation to an agent for services that the agent provides. An agreement that an agent will not have a right to compensation for services provided may be implied from the agent's relationship to the principal or from the trivial nature of the services requested. The amount of compensation due may be determined by the terms of agreement between principal and agent and may be fixed in amount or made contingent on whether the agent achieves stated outcomes or on other criteria. An agreement between a principal and an agent may also set the agent's right to compensation at an amount or rate that is standard or customary in a particular industry. If an agent has a right to be paid compensation by a principal but the amount due cannot be determined on the basis of the terms of the parties' agreement, the agent is entitled to the value of the services provided by the agent.

A principal's duty to pay compensation to an agent does not extend to fulfilling an agent's duties to pay compensation to subagents engaged by the agent, unless the principal so agrees. See § 3.15, Comment *d*, for an extended discussion of the consequences of subagency relationships. Thus, unless a principal agrees otherwise, the principal is not a guarantor of obligations undertaken by its agent to pay subagents appointed by the agent. Were the rule otherwise, a principal would bear the risk that an appointing agent would make generous arrangements with a subagent in exchange for payments by the subagent or would be tempted for other reasons to disregard the principal's interests in making arrangements with a subagent.

In contrast, a principal's duties of indemnity extend to subagents appointed by agents of the principal. See § 8.14, Comment *b*.

§ 8.14 Duty to Indemnify

A principal has a duty to indemnify an agent

(1) in accordance with the terms of any contract between them; and

(2) unless otherwise agreed,

(a) when the agent makes a payment

(i) within the scope of the agent's actual authority, or

(ii) that is beneficial to the principal, unless the agent acts officiously in making the payment; or

(b) when the agent suffers a loss that fairly should be borne by the principal in light of their relationship.

§ 8.15 Principal's Duty to Deal Fairly and in Good Faith

A principal has a duty to deal with the agent fairly and in good faith, including a duty to provide the agent with information about risks of physical harm or pecuniary loss that the principal knows, has reason to know, or should know are present in the agent's work but unknown to the agent.

Comment d. Duty to refrain from conduct likely to injure agent's business reputation or reasonable self-respect. This duty is the reciprocal of an agent's duty of good conduct as stated in § 8.10. Although a principal is not subject to a duty of loyalty to an agent, the principal's duty to deal with an agent fairly and in good faith requires that the principal refrain from conduct that is likely to injure the agent's business reputation through the agent's association with the principal. Likewise, a principal has a duty to refrain from conduct that will injure the agent's reasonable self-respect if the association continues.

The nature of the agent's work and other circumstances of the relationship between principal and agent are relevant to whether a principal's conduct breaches this duty.

UNIFORM PARTNERSHIP ACT (1914)

Table of Sections

Part I

PRELIMINARY PROVISIONS

Part II

NATURE OF A PARTNERSHIP

Part III

RELATIONS OF PARTNERS TO PERSONS DEALING WITH THE PARTNERSHIP

Part IV

RELATIONS OF PARTNERS TO ONE ANOTHER

Part I

PRELIMINARY PROVISIONS

§ 1. Name of Act

This act may be cited as Uniform Partnership Act.

§ 2. Definition of Terms

In this act, "Court" includes every court and judge having jurisdiction in the case.

"Business" includes every trade, occupation, or profession.

"Person" includes individuals, partnerships, corporations, and other associations.

"Bankrupt" includes bankrupt under the Federal Bankruptcy Act or insolvent under any state insolvent act.

"Conveyance" includes every assignment, lease, mortgage, or encumbrance.

"Real property" includes land and any interest or estate in land.

§ 3. Interpretation of Knowledge and Notice

(1) A person has "knowledge" of a fact within the meaning of this act not only when he has actual knowledge thereof, but also when he has knowledge of such other facts as in the circumstances shows bad faith.

(2) A person has "notice" of a fact within the meaning of this act when the person who claims the benefit of the notice:

(a) States the fact to such person, or

(b) Delivers through the mail, or by other means of communication, a written statement of the fact to such person or to a proper person at his place of business or residence.

§ 4. Rules of Construction

(1) The rule that statutes in derogation of the common law are to be strictly construed shall have no application to this act.

(2) The law of estoppel shall apply under this act.

(3) The law of agency shall apply under this act.

(4) This act shall be so interpreted and construed as to effect its general purpose to make uniform the law of those states which enact it.

(5) This act shall not be construed so as to impair the obligations of any contract existing when the act goes into effect, nor to affect any action or proceedings begun or right accrued before this act takes effect.

§ 5. Rules for Cases not Provided for in this Act

In any case not provided for in this act the rules of law and equity, including the law merchant, shall govern.

Part II

NATURE OF A PARTNERSHIP

§ 6. Partnership Defined

(1) A partnership is an association of two or more persons to carry on as co-owners a business for profit.

(2) But any association formed under any other statute of this state, or any statute adopted by authority, other than the authority of this state, is not a partnership under this act, unless such association would have been a partnership in this state prior to the adoption of this act; but this act shall apply to limited partnerships except in so far as the statutes relating to such partnerships are inconsistent herewith.

Comment

Subdivision (1). Explanation of the Reason for the Words Employed in the Definition. The first inquiry is, Why say a partnership is "an association of two or more persons"? In view of the fact that the word "association" itself implies the acting together of two or more persons, why not merely say that a partnership is an association to carry on business in which the members are co-owners of the business? The word person includes, as stated in section 2, supra, "individuals, partnerships, corporations, and other associations." The definition as worded thus asserts, what would be doubtful if the words "of two or more persons" were omitted, namely, that any one of these associations may become members of a partnership. It is true that if two or more corporations attempt to form a partnership the contract may be ultra vires as to both (Boyd v. American Carbon Black Co., (1897) 37 Atl. 937, 182 Pa.St. 206); but the capacity of corporations to contract is a question of corporation law. Under the present law it appears that a partnership can, as such, be a member of another partnership, if that was the intent of the parties. [Raymond v. Putnam, (1862) 44 N.H. 160; Cheap v. Cramond, (1821), 4 Barn. & Ald. 663, 6 E.C.L. 645; In re Hamilton, (1880) 1 Fed. 800; Riddle v. Whitehill, (1890) 10 S.Ct. 924, 135 U.S. 621, 34 U.S. (L.Ed.) 282.]

The words "to carry on as co-owners a business" remove any doubt in the following case: A and B sign partnership articles and make their agreed contributions to the common fund. A refuses to carry on business as agreed. Is there a partnership to be wound up in accordance with the provisions of Part VI "Dissolution and Winding-up"? The words quoted require an affirmative answer to this question. If the words "carrying on business" had been used, in the case given, no partnership would exist, and Part VI would not apply.

The definition asserts that the associates are "co-owners" of the business. This distinguishes a partnership from an agency—an association of principal and agent. A business is a series of acts directed toward an end. Ownership involves the power of ultimate control. To state that partners are co-owners of a business is to state that they each have the power of ultimate control.

Lastly, the definition asserts that the business is for profit. Partnership is a branch of our commercial law; it has developed in connection with a particular business association, and it is, therefore, essential that the operation of the act should be confined to associations organized for profit.

In view of the many definitions of a partnership which have been proposed, it is desirable to note the reasons for the omission of certain ideas expressed in some of the definitions cited by Lindley in his work on Partnership, pp. 11, 12.

It is not indicated that the association must be a voluntary one. In the domain of private law the term association necessarily involves the idea that the association is voluntary.

To say that the association must be created by contract, is not only unnecessary, but in view of the varied use of the word "contract" in our law, if the word is used an explanation would have to be made as to whether the contract could be implied, and if so, whether it could be implied in law or only implied as a fact. By merely saying that it is an association these difficulties are avoided.

Again, it is not said that the business must be lawful business. The effect of the unlawfulness of the business is dealt with under Part VI "Dissolution and Winding-up." Section 31(3), infra, provides that dissolution is produced "By any event which makes it unlawful for the business of the partnership to be carried on or for the members to carry it on in partnership." If the business is wholly unlawful, then the partnership is dissolved the moment it is created. The omission of the word "lawful" in the definition does not prevent this result. Very often, however, a business may be in part lawful and in part unlawful. Hotel-keepers may run a "dive." Placing the word "lawful" before the word business in the definition would tend to throw a doubt on the propriety of the orderly winding up of such a business as a partnership.

§ 7. Rules for Determining the Existence of a Partnership

In determining whether a partnership exists, these rules shall apply:

(1) Except as provided by section 16 persons who are not partners as to each other are not partners as to third persons.

(2) Joint tenancy, tenancy in common, tenancy by the entireties, joint property, common property, or part ownership does not of itself establish a partnership, whether such co-owners do or do not share any profits made by the use of the property.

(3) The sharing of gross returns does not of itself establish a partnership, whether or not the persons sharing them have a joint or

common right or interest in any property from which the returns are derived.

(4) The receipt by a person of a share of the profits of a business is prima facie evidence that he is a partner in the business, but no such inference shall be drawn if such profits were received in payment:

(a) As a debt by installments or otherwise,

(b) As wages of an employee or rent to a landlord,

(c) As an annuity to a widow or representative of a deceased partner,

(d) As interest on a loan, though the amount of payment vary with the profits of the business,

(e) As the consideration for the sale of the good-will of a business or other property by installments or otherwise.

§ 8. Partnership Property

(1) All property originally brought into the partnership stock or subsequently acquired by purchase or otherwise, on account of the partnership, is partnership property.

(2) Unless the contrary intention appears, property acquired with partnership funds is partnership property.

(3) Any estate in real property may be acquired in the partnership name. Title so acquired can be conveyed only in the partnership name.

(4) A conveyance to a partnership in the partnership name, though without words of inheritance, passes the entire estate of the grantor unless a contrary intent appears.

Part III

RELATIONS OF PARTNERS TO PERSONS DEALING WITH THE PARTNERSHIP

§ 9. Partner Agent of Partnership as to Partnership Business

(1) Every partner is an agent of the partnership for the purpose of its business, and the act of every partner, including the execution in the partnership name of any instrument, for apparently carrying on in the usual way the business of the partnership of which he is a member binds the partnership, unless the partner so acting has in fact no authority to act for the partnership in the particular matter, and the person with whom he is dealing has knowledge of the fact that he has no such authority.

(2) An act of a partner which is not apparently for the carrying on of the business of the partnership in the usual way does not bind the partnership unless authorized by the other partners.

(3) Unless authorized by the other partners or unless they have abandoned the business, one or more but less than all the partners have no authority to:

(a) Assign the partnership property in trust for creditors or on the assignee's promise to pay the debts of the partnership,

(b) Dispose of the good-will of the business,

(c) Do any other act which would make it impossible to carry on the ordinary business of a partnership,

(d) Confess a judgment,

(e) Submit a partnership claim or liability to arbitration or reference.

(4) No act of a partner in contravention of a restriction on authority shall bind the partnership to persons having knowledge of the restriction.

§ 10. Conveyance of Real Property of the Partnership

(1) Where title to real property is in the partnership name, any partner may convey title to such property by a conveyance executed in the partnership name; but the partnership may recover such property unless the partner's act binds the partnership under the provisions of paragraph (1) of section 9, or unless such property has been conveyed by the grantee or a person claiming through such grantee to a holder for value without knowledge that the partner, in making the conveyance, has exceeded his authority.

(2) Where title to real property is in the name of the partnership, a conveyance executed by a partner, in his own name, passes the equitable interest of the partnership, provided the act is one within the authority of the partner under the provisions of paragraph (1) of section 9.

(3) Where title to real property is in the name of one or more but not all the partners, and the record does not disclose the right of the partnership, the partners in whose name the title stands may convey title to such property, but the partnership may recover such property if the partners' act does not bind the partnership under the provisions of paragraph (1) of section 9, unless the purchaser or his assignee, is a holder for value, without knowledge.

(4) Where the title to real property is in the name of one or more or all the partners, or in a third person in trust for the partnership, a conveyance executed by a partner in the partnership name, or in his own name, passes the equitable interest of the partnership, provided the act is one within the authority of the partner under the provisions of paragraph (1) of section 9.

(5) Where the title to real property is in the names of all the partners a conveyance executed by all the partners passes all their rights in such property.

§ 11. Partnership Bound by Admission of Partner

An admission or representation made by any partner concerning partnership affairs within the scope of his authority as conferred by this act is evidence against the partnership.

§ 12. Partnership Charged with Knowledge of or Notice to Partner

Notice to any partner of any matter relating to partnership affairs, and the knowledge of the partner acting in the particular matter, acquired while a partner or then present to his mind, and the knowledge of any other partner who reasonably could and should have communicated it to the acting partner, operate as notice to or knowledge of the partnership, except in the case of a fraud on the partnership committed by or with the consent of that partner.

§ 13. Partnership Bound by Partner's Wrongful Act

Where, by any wrongful act or omission of any partner acting in the ordinary course of the business of the partnership or with the authority of his co-partners, loss or injury is caused to any person, not being a partner in the partnership, or any penalty is incurred, the partnership is liable therefor to the same extent as the partner so acting or omitting to act.

§ 14. Partnership Bound by Partner's Breach of Trust

The partnership is bound to make good the loss:

(a) Where one partner acting within the scope of his apparent authority receives money or property of a third person and misapplies it; and

(b) Where the partnership in the course of its business receives money or property of a third person and the money or property so received is misapplied by any partner while it is in the custody of the partnership.

§ 15. Nature of Partner's Liability

All partners are liable

(a) Jointly and severally for everything chargeable to the partnership under sections 13 and 14.

(b) Jointly for all other debts and obligations of the partnership; but any partner may enter into a separate obligation to perform a partnership contract.

§ 16. Partner by Estoppel

(1) When a person, by words spoken or written or by conduct, represents himself, or consents to another representing him to any one, as a partner in an existing partnership or with one or more persons not actual partners, he is liable to any such person to whom such representation has been made, who has, on the faith of such representation, given credit to the actual or apparent partnership, and if he has made such representation or consented to its being made in a public manner he is liable to such person, whether the representation has or has not been made or communicated to such person so giving credit by or with the knowledge of the apparent partner making the representation or consenting to its being made.

(a) When a partnership liability results, he is liable as though he were an actual member of the partnership.

(b) When no partnership liability results, he is liable jointly with the other persons, if any, so consenting to the contract or representation as to incur liability, otherwise separately.

(2) When a person has been thus represented to be a partner in an existing partnership, or with one or more persons not actual partners, he is an agent of the persons consenting to such representation to bind them to the same extent and in the same manner as though he were a partner in fact, with respect to persons who rely upon the representation. Where all the members of the existing partnership consent to the representation, a partnership act or obligation results; but in all other cases it is the joint act or obligation of the person acting and the persons consenting to the representation.

§ 17. Liability of Incoming Partner

A person admitted as a partner into an existing partnership is liable for all the obligations of the partnership arising before his admission as though he had been a partner when such obligations were incurred, except that this liability shall be satisfied only out of partnership property.

Part IV

RELATIONS OF PARTNERS TO ONE ANOTHER

§ 18. Rules Determining Rights and Duties of Partners

The rights and duties of the partners in relation to the partnership shall be determined, subject to any agreement between them, by the following rules:

(a) Each partner shall be repaid his contributions, whether by way of capital or advances to the partnership property and share equally in the profits and surplus remaining after all liabilities, including those to partners, are satisfied; and must contribute towards the losses, whether of capital or otherwise, sustained by the partnership according to his share in the profits.

(b) The partnership must indemnify every partner in respect of payments made and personal liabilities reasonably incurred by him in the ordinary and proper conduct of its business, or for the preservation of its business or property.

(c) A partner, who in aid of the partnership makes any payment or advance beyond the amount of capital which he agreed to contribute, shall be paid interest from the date of the payment or advance.

(d) A partner shall receive interest on the capital contributed by him only from the date when repayment should be made.

(e) All partners have equal rights in the management and conduct of the partnership business.

(f) No partner is entitled to remuneration for acting in the partnership business, except that a surviving partner is entitled to reasonable compensation for his services in winding up the partnership affairs.

(g) No person can become a member of a partnership without the consent of all the partners.

(h) Any difference arising as to ordinary matters connected with the partnership business may be decided by a majority of the partners; but no act in contravention of any agreement between the partners may be done rightfully without the consent of all the partners.

§ 19. Partnership Books

The partnership books shall be kept, subject to any agreement between the partners, at the principal place of business of the partnership, and every partner shall at all times have access to and may inspect and copy any of them.

§ 20. Duty of Partners to Render Information

Partners shall render on demand true and full information of all things affecting the partnership to any partner or the legal representative of any deceased partner or partner under legal disability.

§ 21. Partner Accountable as a Fiduciary

(1) Every partner must account to the partnership for any benefit, and hold as trustee for it any profits derived by him without the consent of the other partners from any transaction connected with the formation,

conduct, or liquidation of the partnership or from any use by him of its property.

(2) This section applies also to the representatives of a deceased partner engaged in the liquidation of the affairs of the partnership as the personal representatives of the last surviving partner.

§ 22. Right to an Account

Any partner shall have the right to a formal account as to partnership affairs:

(a) If he is wrongfully excluded from the partnership business or possession of its property by his co-partners,

(b) If the right exists under the terms of any agreement,

(c) As provided by section 21,

(d) Whenever other circumstances render it just and reasonable.

§ 23. Continuation of Partnership Beyond Fixed Term

(1) When a partnership for a fixed term or particular undertaking is continued after the termination of such term or particular undertaking without any express agreement, the rights and duties of the partners remain the same as they were at such termination, so far as is consistent with a partnership at will.

(2) A continuation of the business by the partners or such of them as habitually acted therein during the term, without any settlement or liquidation of the partnership affairs, is prima facie evidence of a continuation of the partnership.

Part V

PROPERTY RIGHTS OF A PARTNER

§ 24. Extent of Property Rights of a Partner

The property rights of a partner are (1) his rights in specific partnership property, (2) his interest in the partnership, and (3) his right to participate in the management.

§ 25. Nature of a Partner's Right in Specific Partnership Property

(1) A partner is co-owner with his partners of specific partnership property holding as a tenant in partnership.

(2) The incidents of this tenancy are such that:

(a) A partner, subject to the provisions of this act and to any agreement between the partners, has an equal right with his partners to possess specific partnership property for partnership purposes; but he has no right to possess such property for any other purpose without the consent of his partners.

(b) A partner's right in specific partnership property is not assignable except in connection with the assignment of rights of all the partners in the same property.

(c) A partner's right in specific partnership property is not subject to attachment or execution, except on a claim against the partnership. When partnership property is attached for a partnership debt the partners, or any of them, or the representatives of a deceased partner, cannot claim any right under the homestead or exemption laws.

(d) On the death of a partner his right in specific partnership property vests in the surviving partner or partners, except where the deceased was the last surviving partner, when his right in such property vests in his legal representative. Such surviving partner or partners, or the legal representative of the last surviving partner, has no right to possess the partnership property for any but a partnership purpose.

(e) A partner's right in specific partnership property is not subject to dower, curtesy, or allowances to widows, heirs, or next of kin.

§ 26. Nature of Partner's Interest in the Partnership

A partner's interest in the partnership is his share of the profits and surplus, and the same is personal property.

§ 27. Assignment of Partner's Interest

(1) A conveyance by a partner of his interest in the partnership does not of itself dissolve the partnership, nor, as against the other partners in the absence of agreement, entitle the assignee, during the continuance of the partnership, to interfere in the management or administration of the partnership business or affairs, or to require any information or account of partnership transactions, or to inspect the partnership books; but it merely entitles the assignee to receive in accordance with his contract the profits to which the assigning partner would otherwise be entitled.

(2) In case of a dissolution of the partnership, the assignee is entitled to receive his assignor's interest and may require an account from the date only of the last account agreed to by all the partners.

§ 28. Partner's Interest Subject to Charging Order

(1) On due application to a competent court by any judgment creditor of a partner, the court which entered the judgment, order, or decree, or any other court, may charge the interest of the debtor partner with payment of the unsatisfied amount of such judgment debt with interest thereon; and may then or later appoint a receiver of his share of the profits, and of any other money due or to fall due to him in respect of the partnership, and make all other orders, directions, accounts and inquiries which the debtor partner might have made, or which the circumstances of the case may require.

(2) The interest charged may be redeemed at any time before foreclosure, or in case of a sale being directed by the court may be purchased without thereby causing a dissolution:

(a) With separate property, by any one or more of the partners, or

(b) With partnership property, by any one or more of the partners with the consent of all the partners whose interests are not so charged or sold.

(3) Nothing in this act shall be held to deprive a partner of his right, if any, under the exemption laws, as regards his interest in the partnership.

Part VI

DISSOLUTION AND WINDING UP

§ 29. Dissolution Defined

The dissolution of a partnership is the change in the relation of the partners caused by any partner ceasing to be associated in the carrying on as distinguished from the winding up of the business.

§ 30. Partnership not Terminated by Dissolution

On dissolution the partnership is not terminated, but continues until the winding up of partnership affairs is completed.

§ 31. Causes of Dissolution

Dissolution is caused:

(1) Without violation of the agreement between the partners,

(a) By the termination of the definite term or particular undertaking specified in the agreement,

(b) By the express will of any partner when no definite term or particular undertaking is specified,

(c) By the express will of all the partners who have not assigned their interests or suffered them to be charged for their separate debts, either before or after the termination of any specified term or particular undertaking,

(d) By the expulsion of any partner from the business bona fide in accordance with such a power conferred by the agreement between the partners;

(2) In contravention of the agreement between the partners, where the circumstances do not permit a dissolution under any other provision of this section, by the express will of any partner at any time;

(3) By any event which makes it unlawful for the business of the partnership to be carried on or for the members to carry it on in partnership;

(4) By the death of any partner;

(5) By the bankruptcy of any partner or the partnership;

(6) By decree of court under section 32.

§ 32. Dissolution by Decree of Court

(1) On application by or for a partner the court shall decree a dissolution whenever:

(a) A partner has been declared a lunatic in any judicial proceeding or is shown to be of unsound mind,

(b) A partner becomes in any other way incapable of performing his part of the partnership contract,

(c) A partner has been guilty of such conduct as tends to affect prejudicially the carrying on of the business,

(d) A partner wilfully or persistently commits a breach of the partnership agreement, or otherwise so conducts himself in matters relating to the partnership business that it is not reasonably practicable to carry on the business in partnership with him,

(e) The business of the partnership can only be carried on at a loss,

(f) Other circumstances render a dissolution equitable.

(2) On the application of the purchaser of a partner's interest under sections 27 or 28:

(a) After the termination of the specified term or particular undertaking,

(b) At any time if the partnership was a partnership at will when the interest was assigned or when the charging order was issued.

§ 33. General Effect of Dissolution on Authority of Partner

Except so far as may be necessary to wind up partnership affairs or to complete transactions begun but not then finished, dissolution terminates all authority of any partner to act for the partnership,

(1) With respect to the partners,

(a) When the dissolution is not by the act, bankruptcy or death of a partner; or

(b) When the dissolution is by such act, bankruptcy or death of a partner, in cases where section 34 so requires.

(2) With respect to persons not partners, as declared in section 35.

§ 34. Right of Partner to Contribution From Co-partners After Dissolution

Where the dissolution is caused by the act, death or bankruptcy of a partner, each partner is liable to his co-partners for his share of any liability created by any partner acting for the partnership as if the partnership had not been dissolved unless

(a) The dissolution being by act of any partner, the partner acting for the partnership had knowledge of the dissolution, or

(b) The dissolution being by the death or bankruptcy of a partner, the partner acting for the partnership had knowledge or notice of the death or bankruptcy.

§ 35. Power of Partner to Bind Partnership to Third Persons After Dissolution

(1) After dissolution a partner can bind the partnership except as provided in Paragraph (3).

(a) By any act appropriate for winding up partnership affairs or completing transactions unfinished at dissolution;

(b) By any transaction which would bind the partnership if dissolution had not taken place, provided the other party to the transaction

(i) Had extended credit to the partnership prior to dissolution and had no knowledge or notice of the dissolution; or

(ii) Though he had not so extended credit, had nevertheless known of the partnership prior to dissolution, and, having no knowledge or notice of dissolution, the fact of dissolution had not been advertised in a newspaper of general circulation in the place (or in each place if more than one) at which the partnership business was regularly carried on.

(2) The liability of a partner under Paragraph (1b) shall be satisfied out of partnership assets alone when such partner had been prior to dissolution

(a) Unknown as a partner to the person with whom the contract is made; and

(b) So far unknown and inactive in partnership affairs that the business reputation of the partnership could not be said to have been in any degree due to his connection with it.

(3) The partnership is in no case bound by any act of a partner after dissolution

(a) Where the partnership is dissolved because it is unlawful to carry on the business, unless the act is appropriate for winding up partnership affairs; or

(b) Where the partner has become bankrupt; or

(c) Where the partner has no authority to wind up partnership affairs; except by a transaction with one who

(i) Had extended credit to the partnership prior to dissolution and had no knowledge or notice of his want of authority; or

(ii) Had not extended credit to the partnership prior to dissolution, and; having no knowledge or notice of his want of authority, the fact of his want of authority has not been advertised in the manner provided for advertising the fact of dissolution in Paragraph (1b II).

(4) Nothing in this section shall affect the liability under Section 16 of any person who after dissolution represents himself or consents to another representing him as a partner in a partnership engaged in carrying on business.

§ 36. Effect of Dissolution on Partner's Existing Liability

(1) The dissolution of the partnership does not of itself discharge the existing liability of any partner.

(2) A partner is discharged from any existing liability upon dissolution of the partnership by an agreement to that effect between himself, the partnership creditor and the person or partnership continuing the business; and such agreement may be inferred from the course of dealing between the creditor having knowledge of the dissolution and the person or partnership continuing the business.

(3) Where a person agrees to assume the existing obligations of a dissolved partnership, the partners whose obligations have been assumed shall be discharged from any liability to any creditor of the partnership who, knowing of the agreement, consents to a material alteration in the nature or time of payment of such obligations.

(4) The individual property of a deceased partner shall be liable for all obligations of the partnership incurred while he was a partner but subject to the prior payment of his separate debts.

§ 37. Right to Wind Up

Unless otherwise agreed the partners who have not wrongfully dissolved the partnership or the legal representative of the last surviving partner, not bankrupt, has the right to wind up the partnership affairs; provided, however, that any partner, his legal representative or his assignee, upon cause shown, may obtain winding up by the court.

§ 38. Rights of Partners to Application of Partnership Property

(1) When dissolution is caused in any way, except in contravention of the partnership agreement, each partner, as against his co-partners and all persons claiming through them in respect of their interests in the partnership, unless otherwise agreed, may have the partnership property applied to discharge its liabilities, and the surplus applied to pay in cash the net amount owing to the respective partners. But if dissolution is caused by expulsion of a partner, bona fide under the partnership agreement and if the expelled partner is discharged from all partnership liabilities, either by payment or agreement under section 36(2), he shall receive in cash only the net amount due him from the partnership.

(2) When dissolution is caused in contravention of the partnership agreement the rights of the partners shall be as follows:

(a) Each partner who has not caused dissolution wrongfully shall have,

(i) All the rights specified in paragraph (1) of this section, and

(ii) The right, as against each partner who has caused the dissolution wrongfully, to damages for breach of the agreement.

(b) The partners who have not caused the dissolution wrongfully, if they all desire to continue the business in the same name, either by themselves or jointly with others, may do so, during the agreed term for the partnership and for that purpose may possess the partnership property, provided they secure the payment by bond approved by the court, or pay to any partner who has caused the dissolution wrongfully, the value of his interest in the partnership at the dissolution, less any damages recoverable under clause (2a II) of this section, and in like manner indemnify him against all present or future partnership liabilities.

(c) A partner who has caused the dissolution wrongfully shall have:

(i) If the business is not continued under the provisions of paragraph (2b) all the rights of a partner under paragraph (1), subject to clause (2a II), of this section,

(ii) If the business is continued under paragraph (2b) of this section the right as against his co-partners and all claiming through them in respect of their interests in the partnership, to have the value of his interest in the partnership, less any damages caused to his co-partners by the dissolution, ascertained and paid to him in cash, or the payment secured by bond approved by the court, and to be released from all existing liabilities of the partnership; but in ascertaining the value of the partner's interest the value of the good-will of the business shall not be considered.

§ 39. Rights Where Partnership is Dissolved for Fraud or Misrepresentation

Where a partnership contract is rescinded on the ground of the fraud or misrepresentation of one of the parties thereto, the party entitled to rescind is, without prejudice to any other right, entitled,

(a) To a lien on, or a right of retention of, the surplus of the partnership property after satisfying the partnership liabilities to third persons for any sum of money paid by him for the purchase of an interest in the partnership and for any capital or advances contributed by him; and

(b) To stand, after all liabilities to third persons have been satisfied, in the place of the creditors of the partnership for any payments made by him in respect of the partnership liabilities; and

(c) To be indemnified by the person guilty of the fraud or making the representation against all debts and liabilities of the partnership.

§ 40. Rules for Distribution

In settling accounts between the partners after dissolution, the following rules shall be observed, subject to any agreement to the contrary:

(a) The assets of the partnership are:

(i) The partnership property,

(ii) The contributions of the partners necessary for the payment of all the liabilities specified in clause (b) of this paragraph.

(b) The liabilities of the partnership shall rank in order of payment, as follows:

(i) Those owing to creditors other than partners,

(ii) Those owing to partners other than for capital and profits,

(iii) Those owing to partners in respect of capital,

(iv) Those owing to partners in respect of profits.

(c) The assets shall be applied in the order of their declaration in clause (a) of this paragraph to the satisfaction of the liabilities.

(d) The partners shall contribute, as provided by section 18(a) the amount necessary to satisfy the liabilities; but if any, but not all, of the partners are insolvent, or, not being subject to process, refuse to contribute, the other partners shall contribute their share of the liabilities, and, in the relative proportions in which they share the profits, the additional amount necessary to pay the liabilities.

(e) An assignee for the benefit of creditors or any person appointed by the court shall have the right to enforce the contributions specified in clause (d) of this paragraph.

(f) Any partner or his legal representative shall have the right to enforce the contributions specified in clause (d) of this paragraph, to the extent of the amount which he has paid in excess of his share of the liability.

(g) The individual property of a deceased partner shall be liable for the contributions specified in clause (d) of this paragraph.

(h) When partnership property and the individual properties of the partners are in possession of a court for distribution, partnership creditors shall have priority on partnership property and separate creditors on individual property, saving the rights of lien or secured creditors as heretofore.

(i) Where a partner has become bankrupt or his estate insolvent the claims against his separate property shall rank in the following order:

(i) Those owing to separate creditors,

(ii) Those owing to partnership creditors,

(iii) hose owing to partners by way of contribution.

§ 41. Liability of Persons Continuing the Business in Certain Cases

(1) When any new partner is admitted into an existing partnership, or when any partner retires and assigns (or the representative of the deceased partner assigns) his rights in partnership property to two or more of the partners, or to one or more of the partners and one or more third persons, if the business is continued without liquidation of the partnership affairs, creditors of the first or dissolved partnership are also creditors of the partnership so continuing the business.

(2) When all but one partner retire and assign (or the representative of a deceased partner assigns) their rights in partnership property to the remaining partner, who continues the business without liquidation of partnership affairs, either alone or with others, creditors of the dissolved partnership are also creditors of the person or partnership so continuing the business.

(3) When any partner retires or dies and the business of the dissolved partnership is continued as set forth in paragraphs (1) and (2) of this section, with the consent of the retired partners or the representative of the deceased partner, but without any assignment of his right in partnership property, rights of creditors of the dissolved partnership and of the creditors of the person or partnership continuing the business shall be as if such assignment had been made.

(4) When all the partners or their representatives assign their rights in partnership property to one or more third persons who promise to pay the debts and who continue the business of the dissolved partnership, creditors of the dissolved partnership are also creditors of the person or partnership continuing the business.

(5) When any partner wrongfully causes a dissolution and the remaining partners continue the business under the provisions of section 38(2b), either alone or with others, and without liquidation of the partnership affairs, creditors of the dissolved partnership are also creditors of the person or partnership continuing the business.

(6) When a partner is expelled and the remaining partners continue the business either alone or with others, without liquidation of the partnership affairs, creditors of the dissolved partnership are also creditors of the person or partnership continuing the business.

(7) The liability of a third person becoming a partner in the partnership continuing the business, under this section, to the creditors of the dissolved partnership shall be satisfied out of partnership property only.

(8) When the business of a partnership after dissolution is continued under any conditions set forth in this section the creditors of the dissolved partnership, as against the separate creditors of the retiring or deceased partner or the representative of the deceased partner, have a prior right to any claim of the retired partner or the representative of the deceased partner against the person or partnership continuing the business, on account of the retired or deceased partner's interest in the dissolved partnership or on account of any consideration promised for such interest or for his right in partnership property.

(9) Nothing in this section shall be held to modify any right of creditors to set aside any assignment on the ground of fraud.

(10) The use by the person or partnership continuing the business of the partnership name, or the name of a deceased partner as part thereof, shall not of itself make the individual property of the deceased partner liable for any debts contracted by such person or partnership.

§ 42. Rights of Retiring or Estate of Deceased Partner When the Business is Continued

When any partner retires or dies, and the business is continued under any of the conditions set forth in section 41 (1, 2, 3, 5, 6), or section 38(2b) without any settlement of accounts as between him or his estate and the person or partnership continuing the business, unless otherwise agreed, he or his legal representative as against such persons or partnership may have the value of his interest at the date of dissolution ascertained, and shall receive as an ordinary creditor an amount equal to the value of his interest in the dissolved partnership with interest, or, at his option or at the option of his legal representative, in lieu of interest, the profits attributable to the use of his right in the property of the dissolved partnership; provided that the creditors of the dissolved partnership as against the separate creditors, or the representative of the retired or deceased partner, shall have priority on any claim arising under this section, as provided by section 41(8) of this act.

§ 43. Accrual of Actions

The right to an account of his interest shall accrue to any partner, or his legal representative, as against the winding up partners or the surviving partners or the person or partnership continuing the business, at the date of dissolution, in the absence of any agreement to the contrary.

Part VII

MISCELLANEOUS PROVISIONS

§ 44. When Act Takes Effect

This act shall take effect on the ______ day of ______ one thousand nine hundred and ______.

§ 45. Legislation Repealed

All acts or parts of acts inconsistent with this act are hereby repealed.

*

REVISED UNIFORM PARTNERSHIP ACT (1997)

Table of Sections

Article 1

GENERAL PROVISIONS

Article 2

NATURE OF PARTNERSHIP

Article 3

RELATIONS OF PARTNERS TO PERSONS DEALING WITH PARTNERSHIP

Article 4

RELATIONS OF PARTNERS TO EACH OTHER AND TO PARTNERSHIP

Article 5

TRANSFEREES AND CREDITORS OF PARTNER

Article 6

PARTNER'S DISSOCIATION

Article 7

PARTNER'S DISSOCIATION WHEN BUSINESS NOT WOUND UP

Article 8

WINDING UP PARTNERSHIP BUSINESS

Article 9
CONVERSIONS AND MERGERS

Article 10
LIMITED LIABILITY PARTNERSHIP

Article 11
FOREIGN LIMITED LIABILITY PARTNERSHIP

Article 12
MISCELLANEOUS PROVISIONS

Article 1
GENERAL PROVISIONS

§ 101. Definitions

In this [Act]:

(1) "Business" includes every trade, occupation, and profession.

(2) "Debtor in bankruptcy" means a person who is the subject of:

(i) an order for relief under Title 11 of the United States Code or a comparable order under a successor statute of general application; or

(ii) a comparable order under federal, state, or foreign law governing insolvency.

(3) "Distribution" means a transfer of money or other property from a partnership to a partner in the partner's capacity as a partner or to the partner's transferee.

(4) "Foreign limited liability partnership" means a partnership that:

(i) is formed under laws other than the laws of this State; and

(ii) has the status of a limited liability partnership under those laws.

(5) "Limited liability partnership" means a partnership that has filed a statement of qualification under Section 1001 and does not have a similar statement in effect in any other jurisdiction.

(6) "Partnership" means an association of two or more persons to carry on as co-owners a business for profit formed under Section 202, predecessor law, or comparable law of another jurisdiction.

(7) "Partnership agreement" means the agreement, whether written, oral, or implied, among the partners concerning the partnership, including amendments to the partnership agreement.

(8) "Partnership at will" means a partnership in which the partners have not agreed to remain partners until the expiration of a definite term or the completion of a particular undertaking.

(9) "Partnership interest" or "partner's interest in the partnership" means all of a partner's interests in the partnership, including the partner's transferable interest and all management and other rights.

(10) "Person" means an individual, corporation, business trust, estate, trust, partnership, association, joint venture, government, governmental subdivision, agency, or instrumentality, or any other legal or commercial entity.

(11) "Property" means all property, real, personal, or mixed, tangible or intangible, or any interest therein.

(12) "State" means a State of the United States, the District of Columbia, the Commonwealth of Puerto Rico, or any territory or insular possession subject to the jurisdiction of the United States.

(13) "Statement" means a statement of partnership authority under Section 303, a statement of denial under Section 304, a statement of dissociation under Section 704, a statement of dissolution under Section

805, a statement of merger under Section 907, a statement of qualification under Section 1001, a statement of foreign qualification under Section 1102, or an amendment or cancellation of any of the foregoing.

(14) "Transfer" includes an assignment, conveyance, lease, mortgage, deed, and encumbrance.

Comment

These Comments include the original Comments to the Revised Uniform Partnership Act (RUPA or the Act) and the new Comments to the Limited Liability Partnership Act Amendments to the Uniform Partnership Act (1994). The new Comments regarding limited liability partnerships are integrated into the RUPA Comments.

The RUPA continues the definition of "business" from Section 2 of the Uniform Partnership Act (UPA).

RUPA uses the more contemporary term "debtor in bankruptcy" instead of "bankrupt." The definition is adapted from the new Georgia Partnership Act, Ga. Code Ann. § 14–8–2(1). The definition does not distinguish between a debtor whose estate is being liquidated under Chapter 7 of the Bankruptcy Code and a debtor who is being rehabilitated under Chapter 11, 12, or 13 and includes both. The filing of a voluntary petition under Section 301 of the Bankruptcy Code constitutes an order for relief, but the debtor is entitled to notice and an opportunity to be heard before the entry of an order for relief in an involuntary case under Section 303 of the Code. The term also includes a debtor who is the subject of a comparable order under state or foreign law.

The definition of "distribution" is new and adds precision to the accounting rules established in Sections 401 and 807 and related sections. Transfers to a partner in the partner's capacity as a creditor, lessor, or employee of the partnership, for example, are not "distributions."

The definition of a "foreign limited liability partnership" includes a partnership formed under the laws of another State, foreign country, or other jurisdiction provided it has the status of a limited liability partnership in the other jurisdiction. Since the scope and nature of foreign limited liability partnership liability shields may vary in different jurisdictions, the definition avoids reference to similar or comparable laws. Rather, the definition incorporates the concept of a limited liability partnership in the foreign jurisdiction, however defined in that jurisdiction. The reference to formation "under laws other than the laws of this State" makes clear that the definition includes partnerships formed in foreign countries as well as in another State.

The definition of a "limited liability partnership" makes clear that a partnership may adopt the special liability shield characteristics of a limited liability partnership simply by filing a statement of qualification under Section 1001. A partnership may file the statement in this State regardless of where formed. When coupled with the governing law provisions of Section 106(b), this definition simplifies the choice of law issues applicable to partnerships with multi-state activities and contacts. Once a statement of qualification is filed, a partnership's internal affairs and the liability of its partners are determined by the law of the State where the statement is filed. See Section 106(b). The partnership may not vary this particular requirement. See Section 103(b)(9).

The reference to a "partnership" in the definition of a limited liability partnership makes clear that the RUPA definition of the term rather than the UPA concept controls for purposes of a limited liability partnership. Section 101(6) defines a "partnership" as "an association of two or more persons to carry on as co-owners a business for profit formed under Section 202, predecessor law, or comparable law of another jurisdiction." Section 202(b) further provides that "an association formed under a statute other than this [Act], a predecessor statute, or a comparable statute of another jurisdiction is not a partnership under this [Act]." This language was intended to clarify that a limited partnership is not a RUPA general partnership. It was not intended to preclude the application of any RUPA general partnership rules to limited partnerships where limited partnership law otherwise adopts the RUPA rules. See Comments to Section 202(b) and Prefatory Note.

The effect of these definitions leaves the scope and applicability of RUPA to limited partnerships to limited partnership law, not to sever the linkage between the two Acts in all cases. Certain provisions of RUPA will continue to govern limited partnerships by virtue of Revised Uniform Limited Partnership Act (RULPA) Section 1105 which provides that "in any case not provided for in this [Act] the provisions of the Uniform Partnership Act govern." The RUPA partnership definition includes partnerships formed under the UPA. Therefore, the limited liability partnership rules will govern limited partnerships "in any case not provided for" in RULPA. Since RULPA does not provide for any rules applicable to a limited partnership becoming a limited liability partnership, the limited liability partnership rules should apply to limited partnerships that file a statement of qualification.

Partner liability deserves special mention. RULPA Section 403(b) provides that a general partner of a limited partnership "has the liabilities of a partner in a partnership without limited partners." Thus limited partnership law expressly references general partnership law for general partner liability and does not separately consider the liability of such partners. The liability of a general partner of a limited partnership that becomes a LLLP would therefore be the liability of a general partner in an LLP and would be governed by Section 306. The liability of a limited partner in a LLLP is a more complicated matter. RULPA Section 303(a) separately considers the liability of a limited partner. Unless also a general partner, a limited partner is not liable for the obligations of a limited partnership unless the partner participates in the control of the business and then only to persons reasonably believing the limited partner is a general partner. Therefore, arguably limited partners in a LLLP will have the specific RULPA Section 303(c) liability shield while general partners will have a superior Section 306(c) liability shield. In order to clarify limited partner liability and other linkage issues, States that have adopted RUPA, these limited liability partnership rules, and RULPA may wish to consider an amendment to RULPA. A suggested form of such an amendment is:

SECTION 1107. LIMITED LIABILITY LIMITED PARTNERSHIP.

(a) A limited partnership may become a limited liability partnership by:

(1) obtaining approval of the terms and conditions of the limited partnership becoming a limited liability limited partnership by the vote necessary to amend the limited partnership agreement except, in the case of a limited partnership agreement that expressly considers contribution obligations, the vote necessary to amend those provisions;

(2) filing a statement of qualification under Section 1001(c) of the Uniform Partnership Act (1994); and

(3) complying with the name requirements of Section 1002 of the Uniform Partnership Act (1994).

(b) A limited liability limited partnership continues to be the same entity that existed before the filing of a statement of qualification under Section 1001(c) of the Uniform Partnership Act (1994).

(c) Sections 306(c) and 307(b) of the Uniform Partnership Act (1994) apply to both general and limited partners of a limited liability limited partnership.

"Partnership" is defined to mean an association of two or more persons to carry on as co-owners a business for profit formed under Section 202 (or predecessor law or comparable law of another jurisdiction), that is, a general partnership. Thus, as used in RUPA, the term "partnership" does not encompass limited partnerships, contrary to the use of the term in the UPA. Section 901(3) defines "limited partnership" for the purpose of Article 9, which deals with conversions and mergers of general and limited partnerships.

The definition of "partnership agreement" is adapted from Section 101(9) of RULPA. The RUPA definition is intended to include the agreement among the partners, including amendments, concerning either the affairs of the partnership or the conduct of its business. It does not include other agreements between some or all of the partners, such as a lease or loan agreement. The partnership agreement need not be written; it may be oral or inferred from the conduct of the parties.

Any partnership in which the partners have not agreed to remain partners until the expiration of a definite term or the completion of a particular undertaking is a "partnership at will." The distinction between an "at-will" partnership and a partnership for "a definite term or the completion of a particular undertaking" is important in determining the rights of dissociating and continuing partners following the dissociation of a partner. See Sections 601, 602, 701(b), 801(a), 802(b), and 803.

It is sometimes difficult to determine whether a partnership is at will or is for a definite term or the completion of a particular undertaking. Presumptively, every partnership is an at-will partnership. *See, e.g., Stone v. Stone*, 292 So. 2d 686 (La. 1974); *Frey v. Hauke*, 171 Neb. 852, 108 N.W.2d 228 (1961). To constitute a partnership for a term or a particular undertaking, the partners must agree (i) that the partnership will continue for a definite term or until a particular undertaking is completed and (ii) that they will remain partners until the expiration of the term or the completion of the undertaking. Both are necessary for a term partnership; if the partners have the unrestricted right, as distinguished from the power, to withdraw from a partnership formed for a term or particular undertaking, the partnership is one at will, rather than a term partnership.

To find that the partnership is formed for a definite term or a particular undertaking, there must be clear evidence of an agreement among the partners that the partnership (i) has a minimum or maximum duration or (ii) terminates at the conclusion of a particular venture whose time is indefinite but certain to occur. *See, e.g., Stainton v. Tarantino*, 637 F. Supp. 1051 (E.D. Pa. 1986) (partnership to dissolve no later than December 30, 2020); *Abel v. American Art Analog, Inc.*, 838 F.2d 691 (3d Cir. 1988) (partnership purpose to market an art book); *68th Street Apts., Inc. v. Lauricella*, 362 A.2d 78 (N.J. Super. Ct. 1976) (partnership purpose to construct an apartment building). A partnership to conduct a business which may last indefinitely, however, is an at-will partnership, even though there may be an obligation of the partnership, such as a mortgage, which must be repaid by a certain date, absent a specific agreement that no partner can rightfully withdraw until the obligation is repaid. *See, e.g., Page v. Page*, 55 Cal. 2d. 192, 359 P.2d 41 (1961) (partnership purpose to operate a linen supply business); *Frey v. Hauke, supra* (partnership purpose to contract and operate a bowling alley); *Girard Bank v. Haley*, 460 Pa. 237, 332 A.2d 443 (1975) (partnership purpose to maintain and lease buildings).

"Partnership interest" or "partner's interest in the partnership" is defined to mean all of a partner's interests in the partnership, including the partner's transferable interest and all management and other rights. A partner's "transferable interest" is a more limited concept and means only his share of the profits and losses and right to receive distributions, that is, the partner's economic interests. See Section 502 and Comment. Compare RULPA § 101(10) ("partnership interest" includes partner's economic interests only).

The definition of "person" is the usual definition used by the National Conference of Commissioners on Uniform State Laws (NCCUSL or the Conference). The definition includes other legal or commercial entities such as limited liability companies.

"Property" is defined broadly to include all types of property, as well as any interest in property.

The definition of "State" is the Conference's usual definition.

The definition of "statement" is new and refers to one of the various statements authorized by RUPA to enhance or limit the agency authority of a partner, to deny the authority or status of a partner, or to give notice of certain events, such as the dissociation of a partner or the dissolution of the partnership. See Sections 303, 304, 704, 805, and 907. Generally, Section 105 governs the execution, filing, and recording of all statements. The definition also makes clear that a statement of qualification under Section 1001 and a statement of foreign qualification under Section 1102 are considered statements. Both qualification statements are therefore subject to the execution, filing, and recordation rules of Section 105.

"Transfer" is defined broadly to include all manner of conveyances, including leases and encumbrances.

§ 102. Knowledge and Notice

(a) A person knows a fact if the person has actual knowledge of it.

(b) A person has notice of a fact if the person:

(1) knows of it;

(2) has received a notification of it; or

(3) has reason to know it exists from all of the facts known to the person at the time in question.

(c) A person notifies or gives a notification to another by taking steps reasonably required to inform the other person in ordinary course, whether or not the other person learns of it.

(d) A person receives a notification when the notification:

(1) comes to the person's attention; or

(2) is duly delivered at the person's place of business or at any other place held out by the person as a place for receiving communications.

(e) Except as otherwise provided in subsection (f), a person other than an individual knows, has notice, or receives a notification of a fact for purposes of a particular transaction when the individual conducting the transaction knows, has notice, or receives a notification of the fact, or in any event when the fact would have been brought to the individual's attention if the person had exercised reasonable diligence. The person exercises reasonable diligence if it maintains reasonable routines for communicating significant information to the individual conducting the transaction and there is reasonable compliance with the routines. Reasonable diligence does not require an individual acting for the person to communicate information unless the communication is part of the individual's regular duties or the individual has reason to know of the transaction and that the transaction would be materially affected by the information.

(f) A partner's knowledge, notice, or receipt of a notification of a fact relating to the partnership is effective immediately as knowledge by, notice to, or receipt of a notification by the partnership, except in the case of a fraud on the partnership committed by or with the consent of that partner.

Comment

The concepts and definitions of "knowledge," "notice," and "notification" draw heavily on Section 1–201(25) to (27) of the Uniform Commercial Code (UCC). The UCC text has been altered somewhat to improve clarity and style, but in general no substantive changes are intended from the UCC concepts. "A notification" replaces the UCC's redundant phrase, "a notice or notification," throughout the Act.

A person "knows" a fact only if that person has actual knowledge of it. Knowledge is cognitive awareness. That is solely an issue of fact. This is a change from the UPA Section 3(1) definition of "knowledge" which included the concept of "bad faith" knowledge arising from other known facts.

"Notice" is a lesser degree of awareness than "knows" and is based on a person's: (i) actual knowledge; (ii) receipt of a notification; or (iii) reason to know based on actual knowledge of other facts and the circumstances at the time. The latter is the traditional concept of inquiry notice.

Generally, under RUPA, statements filed pursuant to Section 105 do not constitute constructive knowledge or notice, except as expressly provided in the Act. *See* Section 301(1) (generally requiring knowledge of limitations on partner's apparent authority). Properly recorded statements of limitation on a partner's authority, on the other hand, generally constitute constructive knowledge with respect to the transfer of real property held in the partnership name. *See* Sections 303(d)(1), 303(e), 704(b), and 805(b). The other exceptions are Sections 704(c) (statement of dissociation effective 90 days after filing) and 805(c) (statement of dissolution effective 90 days after filing).

A person "receives" a notification when (i) the notification is delivered to the person's place of business (or other place for receiving communications) or (ii) the recipient otherwise actually learns of its existence.

The sender "notifies" or gives a notification by making an effort to inform the recipient, which is reasonably calculated to do so in ordinary course, even if the recipient does not actually learn of it.

The Official Comment to UCC Section 1–201(26), on which this subsection is based, explains that "notifies" is the word used when the essential fact is the proper dispatch of the notice, not its receipt. When the essential fact is the other party's receipt of the notice, that is stated.

A notification is not required to be in writing. That is a change from UPA Section 3(2)(b). As under the UCC, the time and circumstances under which a notification may cease to be effective are not determined by RUPA.

Subsection (e) determines when an agent's knowledge or notice is imputed to an organization, such as a corporation. In general, only the knowledge or notice of the agent conducting the particular transaction is imputed to the organization. Organizations are expected to maintain reasonable internal routines to insure that important information reaches the individual agent handling a transaction. If, in the exercise of reasonable diligence on the part of the organization, the agent should have known or had notice of a fact, or received a notification of it, the organization is bound. The Official Comment to UCC Section 1–201(27) explains:

> This makes clear that reason to know, knowledge, or a notification, although "received" for instance by a clerk in Department A of an organization, is effective for a transaction conducted in Department B only from the time when it was or should have been communicated to the individual conducting that transaction.

Subsection (e) uses the phrase "person other than an individual" in lieu of the UCC term "organization."

Subsection (f) continues the rule in UPA Section 12 that a partner's knowledge or notice of a fact relating to the partnership is imputed to the partnership, except in the case of fraud on the partnership. Limited partners, however, are not "partners" within the meaning of RUPA. *See* Comment 4 to Section 202. It is anticipated that RULPA will address the issue of whether notice to a limited partner is imputed to a limited partnership.

§ 103. Effect of Partnership Agreement; Nonwaivable Provisions

(a) Except as otherwise provided in subsection (b), relations among the partners and between the partners and the partnership are governed by the partnership agreement. To the extent the partnership agreement does not otherwise provide, this [Act] governs relations among the partners and between the partners and the partnership.

(b) The partnership agreement may not:

(1) vary the rights and duties under Section 105 except to eliminate the duty to provide copies of statements to all of the partners;

(2) unreasonably restrict the right of access to books and records under Section 403(b);

(3) eliminate the duty of loyalty under Section 404(b) or 603(b)(3), but:

(i) the partnership agreement may identify specific types or categories of activities that do not violate the duty of loyalty, if not manifestly unreasonable; or

(ii) all of the partners or a number or percentage specified in the partnership agreement may authorize or ratify, after full disclosure of all material facts, a specific act or transaction that otherwise would violate the duty of loyalty;

(4) unreasonably reduce the duty of care under Section 404(c) or 603(b)(3);

(5) eliminate the obligation of good faith and fair dealing under Section 404(d), but the partnership agreement may prescribe the standards by which the performance of the obligation is to be measured, if the standards are not manifestly unreasonable;

(6) vary the power to dissociate as a partner under Section 602(a), except to require the notice under Section 601(1) to be in writing;

(7) vary the right of a court to expel a partner in the events specified in Section 601(5);

(8) vary the requirement to wind up the partnership business in cases specified in Section 801(4), (5), or (6);

(9) vary the law applicable to a limited liability partnership under Section 106(b); or

(10) restrict rights of third parties under this [Act].

Comment

1. The general rule under Section 103(a) is that relations among the partners and between the partners and the partnership are governed by the partnership agreement. *See* Section 101(5). To the extent that the partners fail to agree upon a contrary rule, RUPA provides the default rule. Only the rights and duties listed in Section 103(b), and implicitly the corresponding liabilities and remedies under Section 405, are mandatory and cannot be waived or varied by agreement beyond what is authorized. Those are the only exceptions to the general principle that the provisions of RUPA with respect to the rights of the partners *inter se* are merely default rules, subject to modification by the partners. All modifications must also, of course, satisfy the general standards of contract validity. See Section 104.

2. Under subsection (b)(1), the partnership agreement may not vary the requirements for executing, filing, and recording statements under Section 105, except the duty to provide copies to all the partners. A statement that is not executed, filed, and recorded in accordance with the statutory requirements will not be accorded the effect prescribed in the Act, except as provided in Section 303(d).

3. Subsection (b)(2) provides that the partnership agreement may not unreasonably restrict a partner or former partner's access rights to books and records under Section 403(b). It is left to the courts to determine what restrictions are reasonable. See Comment 2 to Section 403. Other information rights in Section 403 can be varied or even eliminated by agreement.

4. Subsection (b)(3) through (5) are intended to ensure a fundamental core of fiduciary responsibility. Neither the fiduciary duties of loyalty or care, nor the obligation of good faith and fair dealing, may be eliminated entirely. However, the statutory requirements of each can be modified by agreement, subject to the limitation stated in subsection (b)(3) through (5).

There has always been a tension regarding the extent to which a partner's fiduciary duty of loyalty can be varied by agreement, as contrasted with the other partners' consent to a particular and known breach of duty. On the one hand, courts have been loathe to enforce agreements broadly "waiving" in advance a partner's fiduciary duty of loyalty, especially where there is unequal bargaining power, information, or sophistication. For this reason, a very broad provision in a partnership agreement in effect negating any duty of loyalty, such as a provision giving a managing partner complete discretion to manage the business with no liability except for acts and omissions that constitute willful misconduct, will not likely be enforced. *See, e.g., Labovitz v. Dolan*, 189 Ill. App. 3d 403, 136 Ill. Dec. 780, 545 N.E.2d 304 (1989). On the other hand, it is clear that the remaining partners can "consent" to a particular conflicting interest transaction or other breach of duty, after the fact, provided there is full disclosure.

RUPA attempts to provide a standard that partners can rely upon in drafting exculpatory agreements. It is not necessary that the agreement be restricted to a particular transaction. That would require bargaining over every transaction or opportunity, which would be excessively burdensome. The agreement may be drafted in terms of types or categories of activities or transactions, but it should be reasonably specific.

A provision in a real estate partnership agreement authorizing a partner who is a real estate agent to retain commissions on partnership property bought and sold by that partner would be an example of a "type or category" of activity that is not manifestly unreasonable and thus should be enforceable under the Act. Likewise, a provision authorizing that partner to buy or sell real property for his own account without prior disclosure to the other partners or without first offering it to the partnership would be enforceable as a valid category of partnership activity.

Ultimately, the courts must decide the outer limits of validity of such agreements, and context may be significant. It is intended that the risk of judicial refusal to enforce manifestly unreasonable exculpatory clauses will discourage sharp practices while accommodating the legitimate needs of the parties in structuring their relationship.

5. Subsection (b)(3)(i) permits the partners, in their partnership agreement, to identify specific types or categories of partnership activities that do not violate the duty of loyalty. A modification of the statutory standard must not, however, be manifestly unreasonable. This is intended to discourage overreaching by a partner with superior bargaining power since the courts may refuse to enforce an overly broad exculpatory clause. *See, e.g.*, *Vlases v. Montgomery Ward & Co.*, 377 F.2d 846, 850 (3d Cir. 1967) (limitation prohibits unconscionable agreements); *PPG Industries, Inc. v. Shell Oil Co.*, 919 F.2d 17, 19 (5th Cir. 1990) (apply limitation deferentially to agreements of sophisticated parties).

Subsection (b)(3)(ii) is intended to clarify the right of partners, recognized under general law, to consent to a known past or anticipated violation of duty and to waive their legal remedies for redress of that violation. This is intended to cover situations where the conduct in question is not specifically authorized by the partnership agreement. It can also be used to validate conduct that might otherwise not satisfy the "manifestly unreasonable" standard. Clause (ii) provides that, after full disclosure of all material facts regarding a specific act or transaction that otherwise would violate the duty of loyalty, it may be authorized or ratified by the partners. That authorization or ratification must be unanimous unless a lesser number or percentage is specified for this purpose in the partnership agreement.

6. Under subsection (b)(4), the partners' duty of care may not be unreasonably reduced below the statutory standard set forth in Section 404(d), that is, to refrain from engaging in grossly negligent or reckless conduct, intentional misconduct, or a knowing violation of law.

For example, partnership agreements frequently contain provisions releasing a partner from liability for actions taken in good faith and in the honest belief that the actions are in the best interests of the partnership and indemnifying the partner against any liability incurred in connection with the business of the partnership if the partner acts in a good faith belief that he has authority to act. Many partnership agreements reach this same result by listing various activities and stating that the performance of these activities is deemed not to constitute gross negligence or willful misconduct. These types of provisions are intended to come within the modifications authorized by subsection (b)(4). On the other hand, absolving partners of intentional misconduct is probably unreasonable. As with contractual standards of loyalty, determining the outer limit in reducing the standard of care is left to the courts.

The standard may, of course, be increased by agreement to one of ordinary care or an even higher standard of care.

7. Subsection (b)(5) authorizes the partners to determine the standards by which the performance of the obligation of good faith and fair dealing is to be measured. The language of subsection (b)(5) is based on UCC Section 1–102(3). The partners can negotiate and draft specific contract provisions tailored to their particular needs (*e.g.*, five days notice of a partners' meeting is adequate notice), but blanket waivers of the obligation are unenforceable. *See, e.g., PPG Indus., Inc. v. Shell Oil Co.*, 919 F.2d 17 (5th Cir. 1990); *First Security Bank v. Mountain View Equip. Co.*, 112 Idaho 158, 730 P.2d 1078 (Ct. App. 1986), *aff'd*, 112 Idaho 1078, 739 P.2d 377 (1987); *American Bank of Commerce v. Covolo*, 88 N.M. 405, 540 P.2d 1294 (1975).

8. Section 602(a) continues the traditional UPA Section 31(2) rule that every partner has the power to withdraw from the partnership at any time, which power can not be bargained away. Section 103(b)(6) provides that the partnership agreement may not vary the power to dissociate as a partner under Section 602(a), except to require that the notice of withdrawal under Section 601(1) be in writing. The UPA was silent with respect to requiring a written notice of withdrawal.

9. Under subsection (b)(7), the right of a partner to seek court expulsion of another partner under Section 601(5) can not be waived or varied (e.g., requiring a 90–day notice) by agreement. Section 601(5) refers to judicial expulsion on such grounds as misconduct, breach of duty, or impracticability.

10. Under subsection (b)(8), the partnership agreement may not vary the right of partners to have the partnership dissolved and its business wound up under Section 801(4), (5), or (6). Section 801(4) provides that the partnership must be wound up if its business is unlawful. Section 801(5) provides for judicial winding up in such circumstances as frustration of the firm's economic purpose, partner misconduct, or impracticability. Section 801(6) accords standing to transferees of an interest in the partnership to seek judicial dissolution of the partnership in specified circumstances.

11. Subsection (b)(9) makes clear that a limited liability partnership may not designate the law of a State other than the State where it filed its statement of qualification to govern its internal affairs and the liability of its partners. See Sections 101(5), 106(b), and 202(a). Therefore, the selection of a State within which to file a statement of qualification has important choice of law ramifications, particularly where the partnership was formed in another State. See Comments to Section 106(b).

12. Although stating the obvious, subsection(b)(10) provides expressly that the rights of a third party under the Act may not be restricted by an agreement among the partners to which the third party has not agreed. A non-partner who is a party to an agreement among the partners is, of course, bound. *Cf.* Section 703(c) (creditor joins release).

13. The Article 9 rules regarding conversions and mergers are not listed in Section 103(b) as mandatory. Indeed, Section 907 states expressly that partnerships may be converted and merged in any other manner provided by law. The effect of compliance with Article 9 is to provide a "safe harbor" assuring the legal validity of such conversions and mergers. Although not immune from variation in the partnership agreement, noncompliance with the requirements of Article 9 in effecting a conversion or merger is to deny that "safe harbor" validity to the transaction. In this regard, Sections 903(b) and 905(c)(2) require that the conversion or merger of a limited partnership be approved by all of the partners, notwithstanding a contrary provision in the limited partnership agreement. Thus, in effect, the agreement can not vary the voting requirement without sacrificing the benefits of the "safe harbor."

§ 104. Supplemental Principles of Law

(a) Unless displaced by particular provisions of this [Act], the principles of law and equity supplement this [Act].

(b) If an obligation to pay interest arises under this [Act] and the rate is not specified, the rate is that specified in [applicable statute].

Comment

The principles of law and equity supplement RUPA unless displaced by a particular provision of the Act. This broad statement combines the separate rules contained in UPA Sections 4(2), 4(3), and 5. These supplementary principles encompass not only the law of agency and estoppel and the law merchant mentioned in the UPA, but all of the other principles listed in UCC Section 1–103: the law relative to capacity to contract, fraud, misrepresentation, duress, coercion, mistake, bankruptcy, and other common law validating or invalidating causes, such as unconscionability. No substantive change from either the UPA or the UCC is intended.

It was thought unnecessary to repeat the UPA Section 4(1) admonition that statutes in derogation of the common law are not to be strictly construed. This principle is now so well established that it is not necessary to so state in the Act. No change in the law is intended. See the Comment to RUPA Section 1101.

Subsection (b) is new. It is based on the definition of "interest" in Section 14–8–2(5) of the Georgia act and establishes the applicable rate of interest in the absence of an agreement among the partners. Adopting

States can select the State's legal rate of interest or other statutory interest rate, such as the rate for judgments.

§ 105. Execution, Filing, and Recording of Statements

(a) A statement may be filed in the office of [the Secretary of State]. A certified copy of a statement that is filed in an office in another State may be filed in the office of [the Secretary of State]. Either filing has the effect provided in this [Act] with respect to partnership property located in or transactions that occur in this State.

(b) A certified copy of a statement that has been filed in the office of the [Secretary of State] and recorded in the office for recording transfers of real property has the effect provided for recorded statements in this [Act]. A recorded statement that is not a certified copy of a statement filed in the office of the [Secretary of State] does not have the effect provided for recorded statements in this [Act].

(c) A statement filed by a partnership must be executed by at least two partners. Other statements must be executed by a partner or other person authorized by this [Act]. An individual who executes a statement as, or on behalf of, a partner or other person named as a partner in a statement shall personally declare under penalty of perjury that the contents of the statement are accurate.

(d) A person authorized by this [Act] to file a statement may amend or cancel the statement by filing an amendment or cancellation that names the partnership, identifies the statement, and states the substance of the amendment or cancellation.

(e) A person who files a statement pursuant to this section shall promptly send a copy of the statement to every nonfiling partner and to any other person named as a partner in the statement. Failure to send a copy of a statement to a partner or other person does not limit the effectiveness of the statement as to a person not a partner.

(f) The [Secretary of State] may collect a fee for filing or providing a certified copy of a statement. The [officer responsible for recording transfers of real property] may collect a fee for recording a statement.

Comment

1. Section 105 is new. It mandates the procedural rules for the execution, filing, and recording of the various "statements" (see Section 101(11)) authorized by RUPA. Section 101(13) makes clear that a statement of qualification filed by a partnership to become a limited liability partnership is included in the definition of a statement. Therefore, the execution, filing, and recording rules of this section must be followed except that the decision to file the statement of qualification must be approved by the vote of the partners necessary to amend the

partnership agreement as to contribution requirements. See Section 1001(b) and Comments.

No filings are mandatory under RUPA. In all cases, the filing of a statement is optional and voluntary. A system of mandatory filing and disclosure for partnerships, similar to that required for corporations and limited partnerships, was rejected for several reasons. First, RUPA is designed to accommodate the needs of small partnerships, which often have unwritten or sketchy agreements and limited resources. Furthermore, inadvertent partnerships are also governed by the Act, as the default form of business organization, in which case filing would be unlikely.

The RUPA filing provisions are, however, likely to encourage the voluntary use of partnership statements. There are a number of strong incentives for the partnership or the partners to file statements or for third parties, such as lenders or transferees of partnership property, to compel them to do so.

Only statements that are executed, filed, and, if appropriate (such as the authority to transfer real property), recorded in conformity with Section 105 have the legal consequences accorded statements by RUPA. The requirements of Section 105 cannot be varied in the partnership agreement, except the duty to provide copies of statements to all the partners. *See* Section 103(b)(1).

In most States today, the filing and recording of statements requires written documents. As technology advances, alternatives suitable for filing and recording may be developed. RUPA itself does not impose any requirement that statements be in writing. It is intended that the form or medium for filing and recording be left to the general law of adopting States.

2. Section 105(a) provides for a single, central filing of all statements, as is the case with corporations, limited partnerships, and limited liability companies. The expectation is that most States will assign to the Secretary of State the responsibility of maintaining the filing system for partnership statements. Since a partnership is an entity under RUPA, all statements should be indexed by partnership name, not by the names of the individual partners.

Partnerships transacting business in more than one State will want to file copies of statements in each State because subsection (a) limits the legal effect of filed statements to property located or transactions occurring within the State. The filing of a certified copy of a statement originally filed in another State is permitted, and indeed encouraged, in order to avoid inconsistencies between statements filed in different States.

3. Subsection (b), in effect, mandates the use of certified copies of filed statements for local recording in the real estate records by limiting the legal effect of recorded statements under the Act to those copies. The

reason for recording only certified copies of filed statements is to eliminate the possibility of inconsistencies affecting the title to real property.

Subsection (c) requires that statements filed on behalf of a partnership, that is, the entity, be executed by at least two partners. Individual partners and other persons authorized by the Act to file a statement may execute it on their own behalf. To protect the partners and the partnership from unauthorized or improper filings, an individual who executes a statement as a partner must personally declare under penalty of perjury that the statement is accurate.

The amendment or cancellation of statements is authorized by subsection (d).

As a further safeguard against inaccurate or unauthorized filings, subsection (e) requires that a copy of every statement filed be sent to each partner, although the failure to do so does not limit the effectiveness of the statement. This requirement may, however, be eliminated in the partnership agreement. *See* Section 103(b)(1). Partners may also file a statement of denial under Section 304.

4. A filed statement may be amended or canceled by any person authorized by the Act to file an original statement. The amendment or cancellation must state the name of the partnership so that it can be properly indexed and found, identify the statement being amended or canceled, and the substance of the amendment or cancellation. An amendment generally has the same operative effect as an original statement. A cancellation of extraordinary authority terminates that authority. A cancellation of a limitation on authority revives a previous grant of authority. *See* Section 303(d). The subsequent filing of a statement similar in kind to a statement already of record is treated as an amendment, even if not so denominated. Any substantive conflict between filed statements operates as a cancellation of authority under Section 303.

§ 106. Governing Law

(a) Except as otherwise provided in subsection (b), the law of the jurisdiction in which a partnership has its chief executive office governs relations among the partners and between the partners and the partnership.

(b) The law of this State governs relations among the partners and between the partners and the partnership and the liability of partners for an obligation of a limited liability partnership.

Comment

The subsection (a) internal relations rule is new. *Cf.* RULPA § 901 (internal affairs governed by law of State in which limited partnership organized).

RUPA looks to the jurisdiction in which a partnership's chief executive office is located to provide the law governing the internal relations among the partners and between the partners and the partnership. The concept of the partnership's "chief executive office" is drawn from UCC Section 9–103(3)(d). It was chosen in lieu of the State of organization because no filing is necessary to form a general partnership, and thus the situs of its organization is not always clear, unlike a limited partnership, which is organized in the State where its certificate is filed.

The term "chief executive office" is not defined in the Act, nor is it defined in the UCC. Paragraph 5 of the Official Comment to UCC Section 9–103(3)(d) explains:

> "Chief executive office" . . . means the place from which in fact the debtor manages the main part of his business operations. . . . Doubt may arise as to which is the "chief executive office" of a multi-state enterprise, but it would be rare that there could be more than two possibilities. . . . [The rule] will be simple to apply in most cases. . . .

In the absence of any other clear rule for determining a partnership's legal situs, it seems convenient to use that rule for choice of law purposes as well.

The choice-of-law rule provided by subsection (a) is only a default rule, and the partners may by agreement select the law of another State to govern their internal affairs, subject to generally applicable conflict of laws requirements. For example, where the partners may not resolve a particular issue by an explicit provision of the partnership agreement, such as the rights and duties set forth in Section 103(b), the law chosen will not be applied if the partners or the partnership have no substantial relationship to the chosen State or other reasonable basis for their choice or if application of the law of the chosen State would be contrary to a fundamental policy of a State that has a materially greater interest than the chosen State. *See* Restatement (Second) of Conflict of Laws § 187(2) (1971). The partners must, however, select only one State to govern their internal relations. They cannot select one State for some aspects of their internal relations and another State for others.

Contrasted with the variable choice-of-law rule provided by subsection (a), the law of the State where a limited liability partnership files its statement of qualification applies to such a partnership and may not be varied by the agreement of the partners. See Section 103(b)(9). Also, a partnership that files a statement of qualification in another State is not defined as a limited liability partnership in this State. See Section 101(5). Unlike a general partnership which may be formed without any filing, a partnership may only become a limited liability partnership by filing a statement of qualification. Therefore, the situs of its organization is clear. Because it is often unclear where a general partnership is actually formed, the decision to file a statement of qualification in a particular State constitutes a choice-of-law for the partnership which cannot be altered by the partnership agreement. See Comments to Section 103(b)(9). If the partnership agreement of an existing partnership specifies the law of a particular State as its governing law, and the partnership thereafter files a statement of qualification in another State, the partnership agreement choice is no longer controlling. In such cases, the filing of a statement of qualification "amends" the partnership agreement on this limited matter. Accordingly, if a statement of qualification is revoked or canceled for a limited liability partnership, the law of the State of filing would continue to apply unless the partnership agreement thereafter altered the applicable law rule.

§ 107. Partnership Subject to Amendment or Repeal of [Act]

A partnership governed by this [Act] is subject to any amendment to or repeal of this [Act].

Comment

The reservation of power provision is new. It is adapted from Section 1.02 of the Revised Model Business Corporation Act (RMBCA) and Section 1106 of RULPA.

As explained in the Official Comment to the RMBCA, the genesis of those provisions is *Trustees of Dartmouth College v. Woodward*, 17 U.S. (4 Wheat) 518 (1819), which held that the United States Constitution prohibits the application of newly enacted statutes to existing corporations, while suggesting the efficacy of a reservation of power provision. Its purpose is to avoid any possible argument that a legal entity created pursuant to statute or its members have a contractual or vested right in any specific statutory provision and to ensure that the State may in the future modify its enabling statute as it deems appropriate and require existing entities to comply with the statutes as modified.

Article 2

NATURE OF PARTNERSHIP

§ 201. Partnership as Entity

(a) A partnership is an entity distinct from its partners.

(b) A limited liability partnership continues to be the same entity that existed before the filing of a statement of qualification under Section 1001.

Comment

RUPA embraces the entity theory of the partnership. In light of the UPA's ambivalence on the nature of partnerships, the explicit statement provided by subsection (a) is deemed appropriate as an expression of the increased emphasis on the entity theory as the dominant model. *But see* Section 306 (partners' liability joint and several unless the partnership has filed a statement of qualification to become a limited liability partnership).

Giving clear expression to the entity nature of a partnership is intended to allay previous concerns stemming from the aggregate theory, such as the necessity of a deed to convey title from the "old" partnership to the "new" partnership every time there is a change of cast among the partners. Under RUPA, there is no "new" partnership just because of membership changes. That will avoid the result in cases such as *Fairway Development Co. v. Title Insurance Co.*, 621 F. Supp. 120 (N.D. Ohio 1985), which held that the "new" partnership resulting from a partner's death did not have standing to enforce a title insurance policy issued to the "old" partnership.

Subsection (b) makes clear that the explicit entity theory provided by subsection (a) applies to a partnership both before and after it files a statement of qualification to become a limited liability partnership. Thus, just as there is no "new" partnership resulting from membership changes, the filing of a statement of qualification does not create a "new" partnership. The filing partnership continues to be the same partnership entity that existed before the filing. Similarly, the amendment or cancellation of a statement of qualification under Section 105(d) or the revocation of a statement of qualification under Section 1003(c) does not terminate the partnership and create a "new" partnership. See Section 1003(d). Accordingly, a partnership remains the same entity regardless of a filing, cancellation, or revocation of a statement of qualification.

§ 202. Formation of Partnership

(a) Except as otherwise provided in subsection (b), the association of two or more persons to carry on as co-owners a business for profit forms a partnership, whether or not the persons intend to form a partnership.

(b) An association formed under a statute other than this [Act], a predecessor statute, or a comparable statute of another jurisdiction is not a partnership under this [Act].

(c) In determining whether a partnership is formed, the following rules apply:

(1) Joint tenancy, tenancy in common, tenancy by the entireties, joint property, common property, or part ownership does not by itself establish a partnership, even if the co-owners share profits made by the use of the property.

(2) The sharing of gross returns does not by itself establish a partnership, even if the persons sharing them have a joint or

common right or interest in property from which the returns are derived.

(3) A person who receives a share of the profits of a business is presumed to be a partner in the business, unless the profits were received in payment:

(i) of a debt by installments or otherwise;

(ii) for services as an independent contractor or of wages or other compensation to an employee;

(iii) of rent;

(iv) of an annuity or other retirement or health benefit to a beneficiary, representative, or designee of a deceased or retired partner;

(v) of interest or other charge on a loan, even if the amount of payment varies with the profits of the business, including a direct or indirect present or future ownership of the collateral, or rights to income, proceeds, or increase in value derived from the collateral; or

(vi) for the sale of the goodwill of a business or other property by installments or otherwise.

Comment

1. Section 202 combines UPA Sections 6 and 7. The traditional UPA Section 6(1) "definition" of a partnership is recast as an operative rule of law. No substantive change in the law is intended. The UPA "definition" has always been understood as an operative rule, as well as a definition. The addition of the phrase, "whether or not the persons intend to form a partnership," merely codifies the universal judicial construction of UPA Section 6(1) that a partnership is created by the association of persons whose intent is to carry on as co-owners a business for profit, regardless of their subjective intention to be "partners." Indeed, they may inadvertently create a partnership despite their expressed subjective intention not to do so. The new language alerts readers to this possibility.

As under the UPA, the attribute of co-ownership distinguishes a partnership from a mere agency relationship. A business is a series of acts directed toward an end. Ownership involves the power of ultimate control. To state that partners are co-owners of a business is to state that they each have the power of ultimate control. See Official Comment to UPA § 6(1). On the other hand, as subsection (c)(1) makes clear, passive co-ownership of property by itself, as distinguished from the carrying on of a business, does not establish a partnership.

2. Subsection (b) provides that business associations organized under other statutes are not partnerships. Those statutory associations include corporations, limited partnerships, and limited liability compa-

nies. That continues the UPA concept that general partnership is the residual form of for profit business association, existing only if another form does not.

A limited partnership is not a partnership under this definition. Nevertheless, certain provisions of RUPA will continue to govern limited partnerships because RULPA itself, in Section 1105, so requires "in any case not provided for" in RULPA. For example, the rules applicable to a limited liability partnership will generally apply to limited partnerships. See Comment to Section 101(5) (definition of a limited liability partnership). In light of that RULPA Section 1105, UPA Section 6(2), which provides that limited partnerships are governed by the UPA, is redundant and has not been carried over to RUPA. It is also more appropriate that the applicability of RUPA to limited partnerships be governed exclusively by RULPA. For example, a RULPA amendment may clarify certain linkage questions regarding the application of the limited liability partnership rules to limited partnerships. See Comment to Section 101(5) for a suggested form of such an amendment.

It is not intended that RUPA change any common law rules concerning special types of associations, such as mining partnerships, which in some jurisdictions are not governed by the UPA.

Relationships that are called "joint ventures" are partnerships if they otherwise fit the definition of a partnership. An association is not classified as a partnership, however, simply because it is called a "joint venture."

An unincorporated nonprofit organization is not a partnership under RUPA, even if it qualifies as a business, because it is not a "for profit" organization.

3. Subsection (c) provides three rules of construction that apply in determining whether a partnership has been formed under subsection (a). They are largely derived from UPA Section 7, and to that extent no substantive change is intended. The sharing of profits is recast as a rebuttable presumption of a partnership, a more contemporary construction, rather than as prima facie evidence thereof. The protected categories, in which receipt of a share of the profits is not presumed to create a partnership, apply whether the profit share is a single flat percentage or a ratio which varies, for example, after reaching a dollar floor or different levels of profits.

Like its predecessor, RUPA makes no attempt to answer in every case whether a partnership is formed. Whether a relationship is more properly characterized as that of borrower and lender, employer and employee, or landlord and tenant is left to the trier of fact. As under the UPA, a person may function in both partner and nonpartner capacities.

Paragraph (3)(v) adds a new protected category to the list. It shields from the presumption a share of the profits received in payment of interest or other charges on a loan, "including a direct or indirect present or future ownership in the collateral, or rights to income, proceeds, or increase in value derived from the collateral." The quoted language is taken from Section 211 of the Uniform Land Security Interest Act. The purpose of the new language is to protect shared-appreciation mortgages, contingent or other variable or performance-related mortgages, and other equity participation arrangements by clarifying that contingent payments do not presumptively convert lending arrangements into partnerships.

4. Section 202(e) of the 1993 Act stated that partnerships formed under RUPA are general partnerships and that the partners are general partners. That section has been deleted as unnecessary. Limited partners are not "partners" within the meaning of RUPA, however.

§ 203. Partnership Property

Property acquired by a partnership is property of the partnership and not of the partners individually.

Comment

All property acquired by a partnership, by transfer or otherwise, becomes partnership property and belongs to the partnership as an entity, rather than to the individual partners. This expresses the substantive result of UPA Sections 8(1) and 25.

Neither UPA Section 8(1) nor RUPA Section 203 provides any guidance concerning when property is "acquired by" the partnership. That problem is dealt with in Section 204.

UPA Sections 25(2)(c) and (e) also provide that partnership property is not subject to exemptions, allowances, or rights of a partner's spouse, heirs, or next of kin. Those provisions have been omitted as unnecessary. No substantive change is intended. Those exemptions and rights inure to the property of the partners, and not to partnership property.

§ 204. When Property is Partnership Property

(a) Property is partnership property if acquired in the name of:

(1) the partnership; or

(2) one or more partners with an indication in the instrument transferring title to the property of the person's capacity as a partner or of the existence of a partnership but without an indication of the name of the partnership.

(b) Property is acquired in the name of the partnership by a transfer to:

(1) the partnership in its name; or

(2) one or more partners in their capacity as partners in the partnership, if the name of the partnership is indicated in the instrument transferring title to the property.

(c) Property is presumed to be partnership property if purchased with partnership assets, even if not acquired in the name of the partnership or of one or more partners with an indication in the instrument transferring title to the property of the person's capacity as a partner or of the existence of a partnership.

(d) Property acquired in the name of one or more of the partners, without an indication in the instrument transferring title to the property of the person's capacity as a partner or of the existence of a partnership and without use of partnership assets, is presumed to be separate property, even if used for partnership purposes.

Comment

1. Section 204 sets forth the rules for determining when property is acquired by the partnership and, hence, becomes partnership property. It is based on UPA Section 8(3), as influenced by the recent Alabama and Georgia modifications. The rules govern the acquisition of personal property, as well as real property, that is held in the partnership name. *See* Section 101(9).

2. Subsection (a) governs the circumstances under which property becomes "partnership property," and subsection (b) clarifies the circumstances under which property is acquired "in the name of the partnership." The concept of record title is emphasized, although the term itself is not used. Titled personal property, as well as all transferable interests in real property acquired in the name of the partnership, are covered by this section.

Property becomes partnership property if acquired (1) in the name of the partnership or (2) in the name of one or more of the partners with an indication in the instrument transferring title of either (i) their capacity as partners or (ii) of the existence of a partnership, even if the name of the partnership is not indicated. Property acquired "in the name of the partnership" includes property acquired in the name of one or more partners in their capacity as partners, but only if the name of the partnership is indicated in the instrument transferring title.

Property transferred to a partner is partnership property, even though the name of the partnership is not indicated, if the instrument transferring title indicates either (i) the partner's capacity as a partner or (ii) the existence of a partnership. This is consonant with the entity theory of partnership and resolves the troublesome issue of a conveyance to fewer than all the partners but which nevertheless indicates their partner status.

3. Ultimately, it is the intention of the partners that controls whether property belongs to the partnership or to one or more of the

partners in their individual capacities, at least as among the partners themselves. RUPA sets forth two rebuttable presumptions that apply when the partners have failed to express their intent.

First, under subsection (c), property purchased with partnership funds is presumed to be partnership property, notwithstanding the name in which title is held. The presumption is intended to apply if partnership credit is used to obtain financing, as well as the use of partnership cash or property for payment. Unlike the rule in subsection (b), under which property is deemed to be partnership property if the partnership's name or the partner's capacity as a partner is disclosed in the instrument of conveyance, subsection (c) raises only a presumption that the property is partnership property if it is purchased with partnership assets.

That presumption is also subject to an important caveat. Under Section 302(b), partnership property held in the name of individual partners, without an indication of their capacity as partners or of the existence of a partnership, that is transferred by the partners in whose name title is held to a purchaser without knowledge that it is partnership property is free of any claims of the partnership.

Second, under subsection (d), property acquired in the name of one or more of the partners, without an indication of their capacity as partners and without use of partnership funds or credit, is presumed to be the partners' separate property, even if used for partnership purposes. In effect, it is presumed in that case that only the use of the property is contributed to the partnership.

4. Generally, under RUPA, partners and third parties dealing with partnerships will be able to rely on the record to determine whether property is owned by the partnership. The exception is property purchased with partnership funds without any reference to the partnership in the title documents. The inference concerning the partners' intent from the use of partnership funds outweighs any inference from the State of the title, subject to the overriding reliance interest in the case of a purchaser without notice of the partnership's interest. This allocation of risk should encourage the partnership to eliminate doubt about ownership by putting title in the partnership.

5. UPA Section 8(4) provides, "A transfer to a partnership in the partnership name, even without words of inheritance, passes the entire estate or interest of the grantor unless a contrary intent appears." It has been omitted from RUPA as unnecessary because modern conveyancing law deems all transfers to pass the entire estate or interest of the grantor unless a contrary intent appears.

Article 3

RELATIONS OF PARTNERS TO PERSONS DEALING WITH PARTNERSHIP

§ 301. Partner Agent of Partnership

Subject to the effect of a statement of partnership authority under Section 303:

(1) Each partner is an agent of the partnership for the purpose of its business. An act of a partner, including the execution of an instrument in the partnership name, for apparently carrying on in the ordinary course the partnership business or business of the kind carried on by the partnership binds the partnership, unless the partner had no authority to act for the partnership in the particular matter and the person with whom the partner was dealing knew or had received a notification that the partner lacked authority.

(2) An act of a partner which is not apparently for carrying on in the ordinary course the partnership business or business of the kind carried on by the partnership binds the partnership only if the act was authorized by the other partners.

Comment

1. Section 301 sets forth a partner's power, as an agent of the firm, to bind the partnership entity to third parties. The rights of the partners among themselves, including the right to restrict a partner's authority, are governed by the partnership agreement and by Section 401.

The agency rules set forth in Section 301 are subject to an important qualification. They may be affected by the filing or recording of a statement of partnership authority. The legal effect of filing or recording a statement of partnership authority is set forth in Section 303.

2. Section 301(1) retains the basic principles reflected in UPA Section 9(1). It declares that each partner is an agent of the partnership and that, by virtue of partnership status, each partner has apparent authority to bind the partnership in ordinary course transactions. The effect of Section 301(1) is to characterize a partner as a general managerial agent having both actual and apparent authority co-extensive in scope with the firm's ordinary business, at least in the absence of a contrary partnership agreement.

Section 301(1) effects two changes from UPA Section 9(1). First, it clarifies that a partner's apparent authority includes acts for carrying on in the ordinary course "business of the kind carried on by the partnership," not just the business of the particular partnership in question. The UPA is ambiguous on this point, but there is some authority for an expanded construction in accordance with the so-called English rule. *See, e.g.*, *Burns v. Gonzalez*, 439 S.W.2d 128, 131 (Tex. Civ. App. 1969) (dictum); *Commercial Hotel Co. v. Weeks*, 254 S.W. 521 (Tex. Civ. App. 1923). No substantive change is intended by use of the more customary phrase "carrying on in the ordinary course" in lieu of the UPA phrase "in the usual way." The UPA and the case law use both terms without apparent distinction.

The other change from the UPA concerns the allocation of risk of a partner's lack of authority. RUPA draws the line somewhat differently from the UPA.

Under UPA Section 9(1) and (4), only a person with knowledge of a restriction on a partner's authority is bound by it. Section 301(1) provides that a person who has received a notification of a partner's lack of authority is also bound. The meaning of "receives a notification" is explained in Section 102(d). Thus, the partnership may protect itself from unauthorized acts by giving a notification of a restriction on a partner's authority to a person dealing with that partner. A notification may be effective upon delivery, whether or not it actually comes to the other person's attention. To that extent, the risk of lack of authority is shifted to those dealing with partners.

On the other hand, as used in the UPA, the term "knowledge" embodies the concept of "bad faith" knowledge arising from other known facts. As used in RUPA, however, "knowledge" is limited to actual knowledge. *See* Section 102(a). Thus, RUPA does not expose persons dealing with a partner to the greater risk of being bound by a restriction based on their purported reason to know of the partner's lack of authority from all the facts they did know. Compare Section 102(b)(3) (notice).

With one exception, this result is not affected even if the partnership files a statement of partnership authority containing a limitation on a partner's authority. Section 303(f) makes clear that a person dealing with a partner is not deemed to know of such a limitation merely because it is contained in a filed statement of authority. Under Section 303(e), however, all persons are deemed to know of a limitation on the authority of a partner to transfer real property contained in a recorded statement. Thus, a recorded limitation on authority concerning real property constitutes constructive knowledge of the limitation to the whole world.

3. Section 301(2) is drawn directly from UPA Section 9(2), with conforming changes to mirror the new language of subsection (1). Subsection (2) makes it clear that the partnership is bound by a partner's actual authority, even if the partner has no apparent authority. Section 401(j) requires the unanimous consent of the partners for a grant of authority outside the ordinary course of business, unless the partnership agreement provides otherwise. Under general agency principles, the partners can subsequently ratify a partner's unauthorized act. See Section 104(a).

4. UPA Section 9(3) contains a list of five extraordinary acts that require unanimous consent of the partners before the partnership is bound. RUPA omits that section. That leaves it to the courts to decide the outer limits of the agency power of a partner. Most of the acts listed in UPA Section 9(3) probably remain outside the apparent authority of a partner under RUPA, such as disposing of the goodwill of the business, but elimination of a statutory rule will afford more flexibility in some situations specified in UPA Section 9(3). In particular, it seems archaic that the submission of a partnership claim to arbitration always requires unanimous consent. *See* UPA § 9(3)(e).

5. Section 301(1) fully reflects the principle embodied in UPA Section 9(4) that the partnership is not bound by an act of a partner in contravention of a restriction on his authority known to the other party.

§ 302. Transfer of Partnership Property

(a) Partnership property may be transferred as follows:

(1) Subject to the effect of a statement of partnership authority under Section 303, partnership property held in the name of the partnership may be transferred by an instrument of transfer executed by a partner in the partnership name.

(2) Partnership property held in the name of one or more partners with an indication in the instrument transferring the property to them of their capacity as partners or of the existence of a partnership, but without an indication of the name of the partnership, may be transferred by an instrument of transfer executed by the persons in whose name the property is held.

(3) Partnership property held in the name of one or more persons other than the partnership, without an indication in the instrument transferring the property to them of their capacity as partners or of the existence of a partnership, may be transferred by an instrument of transfer executed by the persons in whose name the property is held.

(b) A partnership may recover partnership property from a transferee only if it proves that execution of the instrument of initial transfer did not bind the partnership under Section 301 and:

(1) as to a subsequent transferee who gave value for property transferred under subsection (a)(1) and (2), proves that the subsequent transferee knew or had received a notification that the person who executed the instrument of initial transfer lacked authority to bind the partnership; or

(2) as to a transferee who gave value for property transferred under subsection (a)(3), proves that the transferee knew or had received a notification that the property was partnership property and that the person who executed the instrument of initial transfer lacked authority to bind the partnership.

(c) A partnership may not recover partnership property from a subsequent transferee if the partnership would not have been entitled to recover the property, under subsection (b), from any earlier transferee of the property.

(d) If a person holds all of the partners' interests in the partnership, all of the partnership property vests in that person. The person may execute a document in the name of the partnership to evidence vesting of the property in that person and may file or record the document.

Comment

1. Section 302 replaces UPA Section 10 and provides rules for the transfer and recovery of partnership property. The language is adapted in part from Section 14–8–10 of the Georgia partnership statute.

2. Subsection (a)(1) deals with the transfer of partnership property held in the name of the partnership and subsection (a)(2) with property held in the name of one or more of the partners with an indication either of their capacity as partners or of the existence of a partnership. Subsection (a)(3) deals with partnership property held in the name of one or more of the partners without an indication of their capacity as partners or of the existence of a partnership. Like the general agency rules in Section 301, the power of a partner to transfer partnership property under subsection (a)(1) is subject to the effect under Section 303 of the filing or recording of a statement of partnership authority. These rules are intended to foster reliance on record title.

UPA Section 10 covers only real property. Section 302, however, also governs the transfer of partnership personal property acquired by instrument and held in the name of the partnership or one or more of the partners.

3. Subsection (b) deals with the right of the partnership to recover partnership property transferred by a partner without authority. Subsection (b)(1) deals with the recovery of property held in either the name of the partnership or the name of one or more of the partners with an indication of their capacity as partners or of the existence of a partnership, while subsection (b)(2) deals with the recovery of property held in the name of one or more persons without an indication of their capacity as partners or of the existence of a partnership.

In either case, a transfer of partnership property may be avoided only if the partnership proves that it was not bound under Section 301 by the execution of the instrument of initial transfer. Under Section 301, the partnership is bound by a transfer in the ordinary course of business, unless the transferee actually knew or had received a notification of the partner's lack of authority. See Section 102(a) and (d). The reference to Section 301, rather than Section 301(1), is intended to clarify that a partner's actual authority is not revoked by Section 302. Compare UPA § 10(1) (refers to partner's authority under Section 9(1)).

The burden of proof is on the partnership to prove the partner's lack of authority and, in the case of a subsequent transferee, the transferee's knowledge or notification thereof. Thus, even if the transfer to the initial transferee could be avoided, the partnership may not recover the property from a subsequent purchaser or other transferee for value unless it also proves that the subsequent transferee knew or had received a notification of the partner's lack of authority with respect to the initial transfer. Since knowledge is required, rather than notice, a remote purchaser has no duty to inquire as to the authority for the initial transfer, even if he knows it was partnership property.

The burden of proof is on the transferee to show that value was given. Value, as used in this context, is synonymous with valuable consideration and means any consideration sufficient to support a simple contract.

The burden of proof on all other issues is allocated to the partnership because it is generally in a better position than the transferee to produce the evidence. Moreover, the partnership may protect itself against unauthorized transfers by ensuring that partnership real property is held in the name of the partnership and that a statement of partnership authority is recorded specifying any limitations on the partners' authority to convey real property. Under Section 303(e), transferees of real property held in the partnership name are conclusively bound by those limitations. On the other hand, transferees can protect themselves by insisting that the partnership record a statement specifying who is authorized to transfer partnership property. Under Section 303(d), transferees for value, without actual knowledge to the contrary, may rely on that grant of authority.

4. Subsection (b)(2) replaces UPA Section 10(3) and provides that partners who hold partnership property in their own names, without an indication in the record of their capacity as partners or of the existence of a partnership, may transfer good title to a transferee for value without knowledge or a notification that it was partnership property. To recover the property under this subsection, the partnership has the burden of proving that the transferee knew or had received a notification of the partnership's interest in the property, as well as of the partner's lack of authority for the initial transfer.

5. Subsection (c) is new and provides that property may not be recovered by the partnership from a remote transferee if any intermediate transferee of the property would have prevailed against the partnership. *Cf.* Uniform Fraudulent Transfer Act, §§ 8(a) (subsequent transferee from bona fide purchaser protected), 8(b)(2) (same).

6. Subsection (d) is new. The UPA does not have a provision dealing with the situation in which all of the partners' interests in the partnership are held by one person, such as a surviving partner or a purchaser of all the other partners' interests. Subsection (d) allows for clear record title, even though the partnership no longer exists as a

technical matter. When a partnership becomes a sole proprietorship by reason of the dissociation of all but one of the partners, title vests in the remaining "partner," although there is no "transfer" of the property. The remaining "partner" may execute a deed or other transfer of record in the name of the non-existent partnership to evidence vesting of the property in that person's individual capacity.

7. UPA Section 10(2) provides that, where title to real property is in the partnership name, a conveyance by a partner in his own name transfers the partnership's equitable interest in the property. It has been omitted as was done in Georgia and Florida. In this situation, the conveyance is clearly outside the chain of title and so should not pass title or any interest in the property. UPA Section 10(2) dilutes, albeit slightly, the effect of record title and is, therefore, inconsistent with RUPA's broad policy of fostering reliance on the record.

UPA Section 10(4) and (5) have also been omitted. Those situations are now adequately covered by Section 302(a).

§ 303. Statement of Partnership Authority

(a) A partnership may file a statement of partnership authority, which:

(1) must include:

(i) the name of the partnership;

(ii) the street address of its chief executive office and of one office in this State, if there is one;

(iii) the names and mailing addresses of all of the partners or of an agent appointed and maintained by the partnership for the purpose of subsection (b); and

(iv) the names of the partners authorized to execute an instrument transferring real property held in the name of the partnership; and

(2) may state the authority, or limitations on the authority, of some or all of the partners to enter into other transactions on behalf of the partnership and any other matter.

(b) If a statement of partnership authority names an agent, the agent shall maintain a list of the names and mailing addresses of all of the partners and make it available to any person on request for good cause shown.

(c) If a filed statement of partnership authority is executed pursuant to Section 105(c) and states the name of the partnership but does not contain all of the other information required by subsection (a), the statement nevertheless operates with respect to a person not a partner as provided in subsections (d) and (e).

(d) Except as otherwise provided in subsection (g), a filed statement of partnership authority supplements the authority of a partner to enter into transactions on behalf of the partnership as follows:

(1) Except for transfers of real property, a grant of authority contained in a filed statement of partnership authority is conclusive in favor of a person who gives value without knowledge to the contrary, so long as and to the extent that a limitation on that authority is not then contained in another filed statement. A filed cancellation of a limitation on authority revives the previous grant of authority.

(2) A grant of authority to transfer real property held in the name of the partnership contained in a certified copy of a filed statement of partnership authority recorded in the office for recording transfers of that real property is conclusive in favor of a person who gives value without knowledge to the contrary, so long as and to the extent that a certified copy of a filed statement containing a limitation on that authority is not then of record in the office for recording transfers of that real property. The recording in the office for recording transfers of that real property of a certified copy of a filed cancellation of a limitation on authority revives the previous grant of authority.

(e) A person not a partner is deemed to know of a limitation on the authority of a partner to transfer real property held in the name of the partnership if a certified copy of the filed statement containing the limitation on authority is of record in the office for recording transfers of that real property.

(f) Except as otherwise provided in subsections (d) and (e) and Sections 704 and 805, a person not a partner is not deemed to know of a limitation on the authority of a partner merely because the limitation is contained in a filed statement.

(g) Unless earlier canceled, a filed statement of partnership authority is canceled by operation of law five years after the date on which the statement, or the most recent amendment, was filed with the [Secretary of State].

Comment

1. Section 303 is new. It provides for an optional statement of partnership authority specifying the names of the partners authorized to execute instruments transferring real property held in the name of the partnership. It may also grant supplementary authority to partners, or limit their authority, to enter into other transactions on behalf of the partnership. The execution, filing, and recording of statements is governed by Section 105.

RUPA follows the lead of California and Georgia in authorizing the optional filing of statements of authority. Filing a statement of partnership authority may be deemed to satisfy the disclosure required by a State's fictitious name statute, if the State so chooses.

Section 105 provides for the central filing of statements, rather than local filing. However, to be effective in connection with the transfer of real property, a statement of partnership authority must also be recorded locally with the land records.

2. The most important goal of the statement of authority is to facilitate the transfer of real property held in the name of the partnership. A statement must specify the names of the partners authorized to execute an instrument transferring that property.

Under subsection (d)(2), a recorded grant of authority to transfer real property held in the name of the partnership is conclusive in favor of a transferee for value without actual knowledge to the contrary. A partner's authority to transfer partnership real property is affected by a recorded statement only if the property is held in the name of the partnership. A recorded statement has no effect on the partners' authority to transfer partnership real property that is held other than in the name of the partnership. In that case, by definition, the record will not indicate the name of the partnership, and thus the partnership's interest would not be disclosed by a title search. *See* Section 204. To be effective, the statement recorded with the land records must be a certified copy of the original statement filed with the Secretary of State. *See* Section 105(b).

The presumption of authority created by subsection (d)(2) operates only so long as and to the extent that a limitation on the partner's authority is not contained in another recorded statement. This is intended to condition reliance on the record to situations where there is no conflict among recorded statements, amendments, or denials of authority. See Section 304. If the record is in conflict regarding a partner's authority, transferees must go outside the record to determine the partners' actual authority. This rule is modified slightly in the case of a cancellation of a limitation on a partner's authority, which revives the previous grant of authority.

Under subsection (e), third parties are deemed to know of a recorded limitation on the authority of a partner to transfer real property held in the partnership name. Since transferees are bound under Section 301 by knowledge of a limitation on a partner's authority, they are bound by such a recorded limitation. Of course, a transferee with actual knowledge of a limitation on a partner's authority is bound under Section 301, whether or not there is a recorded statement of limitation.

3. A statement of partnership authority may have effect beyond the transfer of real property held in the name of the partnership. Under subsection (a)(2), a statement of authority may contain any other matter the partnership chooses, including a grant of authority, or a limitation on the authority, of some or all of the partners to enter into other transactions on behalf of the partnership. Since Section 301 confers

authority on all partners to act for the partnership in ordinary matters, the real import of such a provision is to grant extraordinary authority, or to limit the ordinary authority, of some or all of the partners.

The effect given to such a provision is different from that accorded a provision regarding the transfer of real property. Under subsection (d)(1), a filed grant of authority is binding on the partnership, in favor of a person who gives value without actual knowledge to the contrary, unless limited by another filed statement. That is the same rule as for statements involving real property under subsection 301(d)(2). There is, however, no counterpart to subsection (e) regarding a filed limitation of authority. To the contrary, subsection (f) makes clear that filing a limitation of authority does not operate as constructive knowledge of a partner's lack of authority with respect to non-real property transactions.

Under Section 301, only a third party who knows or has received a notification of a partner's lack of authority in an ordinary course transaction is bound. Thus, a limitation on a partner's authority to transfer personal property or to enter into other non-real property transactions on behalf of the partnership, contained in a filed statement of partnership authority, is effective only against a third party who knows or has received a notification of it. The fact of the statement being filed has no legal significance in those transactions, although the filed statement is a potential source of actual knowledge to third parties.

4. It should be emphasized that Section 303 concerns the authority of partners to bind the partnership to third persons. As among the partners, the authority of a partner to take any action is governed by the partnership agreement, or by the provisions of RUPA governing the relations among partners, and is not affected by the filing or recording of a statement of partnership authority.

5. The exercise of the option to file a statement of partnership authority imposes a further disclosure obligation on the partnership. Under subsection (a)(1), a filed statement must include the street address of its chief executive office and of an office in the State (if any), as well as the names and mailing addresses of all of the partners or, alternatively, of an agent appointed and maintained by the partnership for the purpose of maintaining such a list. If an agent is appointed, subsection (b) provides that the agent shall maintain a list of all of the partners and make it available to any person on request for good cause shown. Under subsection (c), the failure to make all of the required disclosures does not affect the statement's operative effect, however.

6. Under subsection (g), a statement of authority is canceled by operation of law five years after the date on which the statement, or the most recent amendment, was filed.

7. Section 308(c) makes clear that a person does not become a partner solely because he is named as a partner in a statement of

partnership authority filed by another person. See also Section 304 ("person named as a partner" may file statement of denial).

§ 304. Statement of Denial

A partner or other person named as a partner in a filed statement of partnership authority or in a list maintained by an agent pursuant to Section 303(b) may file a statement of denial stating the name of the partnership and the fact that is being denied, which may include denial of a person's authority or status as a partner. A statement of denial is a limitation on authority as provided in Section 303(d) and (e).

Comment

Section 304 is new and complements Section 303. It provides partners (and persons named as partners) an opportunity to deny any fact asserted in a statement of partnership authority, including denial of a person's status as a partner or of another person's authority as a partner. A statement of denial must be executed, filed, and recorded pursuant to the requirements of Section 105.

Section 304 does not address the consequences of a denial of partnership. No adverse inference should be drawn from the failure of a person named as a partner to deny such status, however. See Section 308(c) (person not liable as a partner merely because named in statement as a partner).

A statement of denial operates as a limitation on a partner's authority to the extent provided in Section 303. Section 303(d) provides that a filed or recorded statement of partnership authority is conclusive, in favor of purchasers without knowledge to the contrary, so long as and to the extent that a limitation on that authority is not contained in another filed or recorded statement. A filed or recorded statement of denial operates as such a limitation on authority, thereby precluding reliance on an inconsistent grant of authority. Under Section 303(d), a filed or recorded cancellation of a statement of denial that operates as a limitation on authority revives the previous grant of authority.

Under Section 303(e), a recorded statement of denial of a partner's authority to transfer partnership real property held in the partnership name constitutes constructive knowledge of that limitation.

§ 305. Partnership Liable for Partner's Actionable Conduct

(a) A partnership is liable for loss or injury caused to a person, or for a penalty incurred, as a result of a wrongful act or omission, or other actionable conduct, of a partner acting in the ordinary course of business of the partnership or with authority of the partnership.

(b) If, in the course of the partnership's business or while acting with authority of the partnership, a partner receives or causes the partnership to receive money or property of a person not a partner, and the money or property is misapplied by a partner, the partnership is liable for the loss.

Comment

Section 305(a), which is derived from UPA Section 13, imposes liability on the partnership for the wrongful acts of a partner acting in the ordinary course of the partnership's business or otherwise within the partner's authority. The scope of the section has been expanded by deleting from UPA Section 13, "not being a partner in the partnership." This is intended to permit a partner to sue the partnership on a tort or other theory during the term of the partnership, rather than being limited to the remedies of dissolution and an accounting. See also Comment 2 to Section 405.

The section has also been broadened to cover no-fault torts by the addition of the phrase, "or other actionable conduct."

The partnership is liable for the actionable conduct or omission of a partner acting in the ordinary course of its business or "with the authority of the partnership." This is intended to include a partner's apparent, as well as actual, authority, thereby bringing within Section 305(a) the situation covered in UPA Section 14(a).

The phrase in UPA Section 13, "to the same extent as the partner so acting or omitting to act," has been deleted to prevent a partnership from asserting a partner's immunity from liability. This is consistent with the general agency rule that a principal is not entitled to its agent's immunities. *See* Restatement (Second) of Agency § 217(b) (1957). The deletion is not intended to limit a partnership's contractual rights.

Section 305(b) is drawn from UPA Section 14(b), but has been edited to improve clarity. It imposes strict liability on the partnership for the misapplication of money or property received by a partner in the course of the partnership's business or otherwise within the scope of the partner's actual authority.

§ 306. Partner's Liability

(a) Except as otherwise provided in subsections (b) and (c), all partners are liable jointly and severally for all obligations of the partnership unless otherwise agreed by the claimant or provided by law.

(b) A person admitted as a partner into an existing partnership is not personally liable for any partnership obligation incurred before the person's admission as a partner.

(c) An obligation of a partnership incurred while the partnership is a limited liability partnership, whether arising in contract, tort, or otherwise, is solely the obligation of the partnership. A partner is not personally liable, directly or indirectly, by way of contribution or otherwise, for such an obligation solely by reason of being or so acting as a partner. This subsection applies notwithstanding anything inconsistent in the partnership agreement that existed immediately before the vote required to become a limited liability partnership under Section 1001(b).

LLP

Comment

1. Section 306(a) changes the UPA rule by imposing joint and several liability on the partners for all partnership obligations where the partnership is not a limited liability partnership. Under UPA Section 15, partners' liability for torts is joint and several, while their liability for contracts is joint but not several. About ten States that have adopted the UPA already provide for joint and several liability. The UPA reference to "debts and obligations" is redundant, and no change is intended by RUPA's reference solely to "obligations."

Joint and several liability under RUPA differs, however, from the classic model, which permits a judgment creditor to proceed immediately against any of the joint and several judgment debtors. Generally, Section 307(d) requires the judgment creditor to exhaust the partnership's assets before enforcing a judgment against the separate assets of a partner.

2. RUPA continues the UPA scheme of liability with respect to an incoming partner, but states the rule more clearly and simply. Under Section 306(a), an incoming partner becomes jointly and severally liable, as a partner, for all partnership obligations, except as otherwise provided in subsection (b). That subsection eliminates an incoming partner's personal liability for partnership obligations incurred before his admission as a partner. In effect, a new partner has no personal liability to existing creditors of the partnership, and only his investment in the firm is at risk for the satisfaction of existing partnership debts. That is presently the rule under UPA Sections 17 and 41(7), and no substantive change is intended. As under the UPA, a new partner's personal assets are at risk with respect to partnership liabilities incurred after his admission as a partner.

3. Subsection (c) alters classic joint and several liability of general partners for obligations of a partnership that is a limited liability partnership. Like shareholders of a corporation and members of a limited liability company, partners of a limited liability partnership are not personally liable for partnership obligations incurred while the partnership liability shield is in place solely because they are partners. As with shareholders of a corporation and members of a limited liability company, partners remain personally liable for their personal misconduct.

In cases of partner misconduct, Section 401(c) sets forth a partnership's obligation to indemnify the culpable partner where the partner's liability was incurred in the ordinary course of the partnership's business. When indemnification occurs, the assets of both the partnership and the culpable partner are available to a creditor. However, Sections 306(c), 401(b), and 807(b) make clear that a partner who is not otherwise liable under Section 306(c) is not obligated to contribute assets to the partnership in excess of agreed contributions to share the loss with the culpable partner. (See Comments to Sections 401(b) and 807(b). regarding a slight variation in the context of priority of payment of partnership obligations.) Accordingly, Section 306(c) makes clear that an innocent partner is not personally liable for specified partnership obligations, directly or indirectly, by way of contribution or otherwise.

Although the liability shield protections of Section 306(c) may be modified in part or in full in a partnership agreement (and by way of private contractual guarantees), the modifications must constitute an intentional waiver of the liability protections. See Sections 103(b), 104(a), and 902(b). Since the mere act of filing a statement of qualification reflects the assumption that the partners intend to modify the otherwise applicable partner liability rules, the final sentence of subsection (c) makes clear that the filing negates inconsistent aspects of the partnership agreement that existed immediately before the vote to approve becoming a limited liability partnership. The negation only applies to a partner's personal liability for future partnership obligations. The filing however has no effect as to previously created partner obligations to the partnership in the form of specific capital contribution requirements.

Inter se contribution agreements may erode part or all of the effects of the liability shield. For example, Section 807(f) provides that an assignee for the benefit of creditors of a partnership or a partner may enforce a partner's obligation to contribute to the partnership. The ultimate effect of such contribution obligations may make each partner jointly and severally liable for all partnership obligations—even those incurred while the partnership is a limited liability partnership. Although the final sentence of subsection (c) negates such provisions existing before a statement of qualification is filed, it will have no effect on any amendments to the partnership agreement after the statement is filed.

The connection between partner status and personal liability for partnership obligations is severed only with respect to obligations incurred while the partnership is a limited liability partnership. Partnership obligations incurred before a partnership becomes a limited liability partnership or incurred after limited liability partnership status is revoked or canceled are treated as obligations of an ordinary partnership. See Sections 1001 (filing), 1003 (revocation), and 1006 (cancellation). Obligations incurred by a partnership during the period when its statement of qualification is administratively revoked will be considered as incurred by a limited liability partnership provided the partnership's status as such is reinstated within two years under Section 1003(e). See Section 1003(f).

When an obligation is incurred is determined by other law. See Section 104(a). Under that law, and for the limited purpose of determining when partnership contract obligations are incurred, the reasonable expectations of creditors and the partners are paramount. Therefore, partnership obligations under or relating to a note, contract, or other agreement generally are incurred when the note, contract, or other agreement is made. Also, an amendment, modification, extension, or renewal of a note, contract, or other agreement should not affect or otherwise reset the time at which a partnership obligation under or relating to that note, contract, or other agreement is incurred, even as to a claim that relates to the subject matter of the amendment, modification, extension, or renewal. A note, contract, or other agreement may expressly modify these rules and fix the time a partnership obligation is incurred thereunder.

For the limited purpose of determining when partnership tort obligations are incurred, a distinction is intended between injury and the conduct causing that injury. The purpose of the distinction is to prevent unjust results. Partnership obligations under or relating to a tort generally are incurred when the tort conduct occurs rather than at the time of the actual injury or harm. This interpretation prevents a culpable partnership from engaging in wrongful conduct and then filing a statement of qualification to sever the vicarious responsibility of its partners for future injury or harm caused by conduct that occurred prior to the filing.

§ 307. Actions by and Against Partnership and Partners

(a) A partnership may sue and be sued in the name of the partnership.

(b) An action may be brought against the partnership and, to the extent not inconsistent with Section 306, any or all of the partners in the same action or in separate actions.

(c) A judgment against a partnership is not by itself a judgment against a partner. A judgment against a partnership may not be satisfied from a partner's assets unless there is also a judgment against the partner.

(d) A judgment creditor of a partner may not levy execution against the assets of the partner to satisfy a judgment based on a claim against the partnership unless the partner is personally liable for the claim under Section 306 and:

(1) a judgment based on the same claim has been obtained against the partnership and a writ of execution on the judgment has been returned unsatisfied in whole or in part;

(2) the partnership is a debtor in bankruptcy;

(3) the partner has agreed that the creditor need not exhaust partnership assets;

(4) a court grants permission to the judgment creditor to levy execution against the assets of a partner based on a finding that partnership assets subject to execution are clearly insufficient to satisfy the judgment, that exhaustion of partnership assets is excessively burdensome, or that the grant of permission is an appropriate exercise of the court's equitable powers; or

(5) liability is imposed on the partner by law or contract independent of the existence of the partnership.

(e) This section applies to any partnership liability or obligation resulting from a representation by a partner or purported partner under Section 308.

Comment

1. Section 307 is new. Subsection (a) provides that a partnership may sue and be sued in the partnership name. That entity approach is designed to simplify suits by and against a partnership.

At common law, a partnership, not being a legal entity, could not sue or be sued in the firm name. The UPA itself is silent on this point, so in the absence of another enabling statute, it is generally necessary to join all the partners in an action against the partnership.

Most States have statutes or rules authorizing partnerships to sue or be sued in the partnership name. Many of those statutes, however, are found in the state provisions dealing with civil procedure rather than in the partnership act.

2. Subsection (b) provides that suit generally may be brought against the partnership and any or all of the partners in the same action or in separate actions. It is intended to clarify that the partners need not be named in an action against the partnership. In particular, in an action against a partnership, it is not necessary to name a partner individually in addition to the partnership. This will simplify and reduce the cost of litigation, especially in cases of small claims where there are known to be significant partnership assets and thus no necessity to collect the judgment out of the partners' assets.

Where the partnership is a limited liability partnership, the limited liability partnership rules clarify that a partner not liable for the alleged partnership obligation may not be named in the action against the partnership unless the action also seeks to establish personal liability of the partner for the obligation. See subsections (b) and (d).

3. Subsection (c) provides that a judgment against the partnership is not, standing alone, a judgment against the partners, and it cannot be satisfied from a partner's personal assets unless there is a judgment

against the partner. Thus, a partner must be individually named and served, either in the action against the partnership or in a later suit, before his personal assets may be subject to levy for a claim against the partnership.

RUPA leaves it to the law of judgments, as did the UPA, to determine the collateral effects to be accorded a prior judgment for or against the partnership in a subsequent action against a partner individually. See Section 60 of the Second Restatement of Judgments (1982) and the Comments thereto.

4. Subsection (d) requires partnership creditors to exhaust the partnership's assets before levying on a judgment debtor partner's individual property where the partner is personally liable for the partnership obligation under Section 306. That rule respects the concept of the partnership as an entity and makes partners more in the nature of guarantors than principal debtors on every partnership debt. It is already the law in some States.

As a general rule, a final judgment against a partner cannot be enforced by a creditor against the partner's separate assets unless a writ of execution against the partnership has been returned unsatisfied. Under subsection (d), however, a creditor may proceed directly against the partner's assets if (i) the partnership is a debtor in bankruptcy (see Section 101(2)); (ii) the partner has consented; or (iii) the liability is imposed on the partner independently of the partnership. For example, a judgment creditor may proceed directly against the assets of a partner who is liable independently as the primary tortfeasor, but must exhaust the partnership's assets before proceeding against the separate assets of the other partners who are liable only as partners.

There is also a judicial override provision in subsection (d)(4). A court may authorize execution against the partner's assets on the grounds that (i) the partnership's assets are clearly insufficient; (ii) exhaustion of the partnership's assets would be excessively burdensome; or (iii) it is otherwise equitable to do so. For example, if the partners who are parties to the action have assets located in the forum State, but the partnership does not, a court might find that exhaustion of the partnership's assets would be excessively burdensome.

5. Although subsection (d) is silent with respect to pre-judgment remedies, the law of pre-judgment remedies already adequately embodies the principle that partnership assets should be exhausted before partners' assets are attached or garnished. Attachment, for example, typically requires a showing that the partnership's assets are being secreted or fraudulently transferred or are otherwise inadequate to satisfy the plaintiff's claim. A showing of some exigent circumstance may also be required to satisfy due process. *See Connecticut v. Doehr*, 501 U.S. 1, 16 (1991).

6. Subsection (e) clarifies that actions against the partnership under Section 308, involving representations by partners or purported partners, are subject to Section 307.

§ 308. Liability of Purported Partner

(a) If a person, by words or conduct, purports to be a partner, or consents to being represented by another as a partner, in a partnership or with one or more persons not partners, the purported partner is liable to a person to whom the representation is made, if that person, relying on the representation, enters into a transaction with the actual or purported partnership. If the representation, either by the purported partner or by a person with the purported partner's consent, is made in a public manner, the purported partner is liable to a person who relies upon the purported partnership even if the purported partner is not aware of being held out as a partner to the claimant. If partnership liability results, the purported partner is liable with respect to that liability as if the purported partner were a partner. If no partnership liability results, the purported partner is liable with respect to that liability jointly and severally with any other person consenting to the representation.

(b) If a person is thus represented to be a partner in an existing partnership, or with one or more persons not partners, the purported partner is an agent of persons consenting to the representation to bind them to the same extent and in the same manner as if the purported partner were a partner, with respect to persons who enter into transactions in reliance upon the representation. If all of the partners of the existing partnership consent to the representation, a partnership act or obligation results. If fewer than all of the partners of the existing partnership consent to the representation, the person acting and the partners consenting to the representation are jointly and severally liable.

(c) A person is not liable as a partner merely because the person is named by another in a statement of partnership authority.

(d) A person does not continue to be liable as a partner merely because of a failure to file a statement of dissociation or to amend a statement of partnership authority to indicate the partner's dissociation from the partnership.

(e) Except as otherwise provided in subsections (a) and (b), persons who are not partners as to each other are not liable as partners to other persons.

Comment

Section 308 continues the basic principles of partnership by estoppel from UPA Section 16, now more accurately entitled "Liability of Purported Partner." Subsection (a) continues the distinction between representations made to specific persons and those made in a public manner.

It is the exclusive basis for imposing liability as a partner on persons who are not partners in fact. As under the UPA, there is no duty of denial, and thus a person held out by another as a partner is not liable unless he actually consents to the representation. See the Official Comment to UPA Section 16. Also see Section 308(c) (no duty to file statement of denial) and Section 308(d) (no duty to file statement of dissociation or to amend statement of partnership authority).

Subsection (b) emphasizes that the persons being protected by Section 308 are those who enter into transactions in reliance upon a representation. If all of the partners of an existing partnership consent to the representation, a partnership obligation results. Apart from Section 308, the firm may be bound in other situations under general principles of apparent authority or ratification.

If a partnership liability results under Section 308, the creditor must exhaust the partnership's assets before seeking to satisfy the claim from the partners. See Section 307.

Subsections (c) and (d) are new and deal with potential negative inferences to be drawn from a failure to correct inaccurate or outdated filed statements. Subsection (c) makes clear that an otherwise innocent person is not liable as a partner for failing to deny his partnership status as asserted by a third person in a statement of partnership authority. Under subsection (d), a partner's liability as a partner does not continue after dissociation solely because of a failure to file a statement of dissociation.

Subsection (e) is derived from UPA Section 7(1). It means that only those persons who are partners as among themselves are liable as partners to third parties for the obligations of the partnership, except for liabilities incurred by purported partners under Section 308(a) and (b).

Article 4

RELATIONS OF PARTNERS TO EACH OTHER AND TO PARTNERSHIP

§ 401. Partner's Rights and Duties

(a) Each partner is deemed to have an account that is:

(1) credited with an amount equal to the money plus the value of any other property, net of the amount of any liabilities, the partner contributes to the partnership and the partner's share of the partnership profits; and

(2) charged with an amount equal to the money plus the value of any other property, net of the amount of any liabilities, distributed by the partnership to the partner and the partner's share of the partnership losses.

(b) Each partner is entitled to an equal share of the partnership profits and is chargeable with a share of the partnership losses in proportion to the partner's share of the profits.

(c) A partnership shall reimburse a partner for payments made and indemnify a partner for liabilities incurred by the partner in the ordinary course of the business of the partnership or for the preservation of its business or property.

(d) A partnership shall reimburse a partner for an advance to the partnership beyond the amount of capital the partner agreed to contribute.

(e) A payment or advance made by a partner which gives rise to a partnership obligation under subsection (c) or (d) constitutes a loan to the partnership which accrues interest from the date of the payment or advance.

(f) Each partner has equal rights in the management and conduct of the partnership business.

(g) A partner may use or possess partnership property only on behalf of the partnership.

(h) A partner is not entitled to remuneration for services performed for the partnership, except for reasonable compensation for services rendered in winding up the business of the partnership.

(i) A person may become a partner only with the consent of all of the partners.

(j) A difference arising as to a matter in the ordinary course of business of a partnership may be decided by a majority of the partners. An act outside the ordinary course of business of a partnership and an amendment to the partnership agreement may be undertaken only with the consent of all of the partners.

(k) This section does not affect the obligations of a partnership to other persons under Section 301.

Comment

1. Section 401 is drawn substantially from UPA Section 18. It establishes many of the default rules that govern the relations among partners. All of these rules are, however, subject to contrary agreement of the partners as provided in Section 103.

2. Subsection (a) provides that each partner is deemed to have an account that is credited with the partner's contributions and share of the partnership profits and charged with distributions to the partner and the partner's share of partnership losses. In the absence of another system of partnership accounts, these rules establish a rudimentary system of accounts for the partnership. The rules regarding the settlement of the partners' accounts upon the dissolution and winding up of the partnership business are found in Section 807.

3. Subsection (b) establishes the default rules for the sharing of partnership profits and losses. The UPA Section 18(a) rules that profits are shared equally and that losses, whether capital or operating, are shared in proportion to each partner's share of the profits are continued. Thus, under the default rule, partners share profits per capita and not in proportion to capital contribution as do corporate shareholders or partners in limited partnerships. Compare RULPA Section 504. With respect to losses, the qualifying phrase, "whether capital or operating," has been deleted as inconsistent with contemporary partnership accounting practice and terminology; no substantive change is intended.

If partners agree to share profits other than equally, losses will be shared similarly to profits, absent agreement to do otherwise. That rule, carried over from the UPA, is predicated on the assumption that partners would likely agree to share losses on the same basis as profits, but may fail to say so. Of course, by agreement, they may share losses on a different basis from profits.

The default rules apply, as does UPA Section 18(a), where one or more of the partners contribute no capital, although there is case law to the contrary. *See, e.g., Kovacik v. Reed*, 49 Cal. 2d 166, 315 P.2d 314 (1957); *Becker v. Killarney*, 177 Ill. App. 3d 793, 523 N.E.2d 467 (1988). It may seem unfair that the contributor of services, who contributes little or no capital, should be obligated to contribute toward the capital loss of the large contributor who contributed no services. In entering a partnership with such a capital structure, the partners should foresee that application of the default rule may bring about unusual results and take advantage of their power to vary by agreement the allocation of capital losses.

Subsection (b) provides that each partner "is chargeable" with a share of the losses, rather than the UPA formulation that each partner shall "contribute" to losses. Losses are charged to each partner's account as provided in subsection (a)(2). It is intended to make clear that a partner is not obligated to contribute to partnership losses before his withdrawal or the liquidation of the partnership, unless the partners agree otherwise. In effect, unless related to an obligation for which the partner is not personally liable under Section 306(c), a partner's negative account represents a debt to the partnership unless the partners agree to the contrary. Similarly, each partner's share of the profits is credited to his account under subsection (a)(1). Absent an agreement to the contrary, however, a partner does not have a right to receive a current distribution of the profits credited to his account, the interim distribution of profits being a matter arising in the ordinary course of business to be decided by majority vote of the partners.

However, where a liability to contribute at dissolution and winding up relates to a partnership obligation governed by the limited liability rule of Section 306(c), a partner is not obligated to contribute additional assets even at dissolution and winding up. See Section 807(b). In such a case, although a partner is not personally liable for the partnership obligation, that partner's interest in the partnership remains at risk. See also Comment to Section 401(c) relating to indemnification.

In the case of an operating limited liability partnership, the Section 306 liability shield may be partially eroded where the limited liability partnership incurs both shielded and unshielded liabilities. Where the limited liability partnership uses its assets to pay shielded liabilities before paying unshielded liabilities, each partner's obligation to contribute to the limited liability partnership for that partner's share of the unpaid and unshielded obligations at dissolution and winding up remains intact. The same issue is less likely to occur in the context of the termination of a limited liability partnership since a partner's contribution obligation is based only on that partner's share of unshielded obligations and the partnership will ordinarily use the contributed assets to pay unshielded claims first as they were the basis of the contribution obligations. See Comments to Section 807(b).

4. Subsection (c) is derived from UPA Section 18(b) and provides that the partnership shall reimburse partners for payments made and indemnify them for liabilities incurred in the ordinary course of the partnership's business or for the preservation of its business or property. Reimbursement and indemnification is an obligation of the partnership. Indemnification may create a loss toward which the partners must contribute. Although the right to indemnification is usually enforced in the settlement of accounts among partners upon dissolution and winding up of the partnership business, the right accrues when the liability is incurred and thus may be enforced during the term of the partnership in an appropriate case. *See* Section 405 and Comment. A partner's right to indemnification under this Act is not affected by the partnership becoming a limited liability partnership. Accordingly, partners continue to share partnership losses to the extent of partnership assets.

5. Subsection (d) is based on UPA Section 18(c). It makes explicit that the partnership must reimburse a partner for an advance of funds beyond the amount of the partner's agreed capital contribution, thereby treating the advance as a loan.

6. Subsection (e), which is also drawn from UPA Section 18(c), characterizes the partnership's obligation under subsection (c) or (d) as a loan to the partnership which accrues interest from the date of the payment or advance. See Section 104(b) (default rate of interest).

7. Under subsection (f), each partner has equal rights in the management and conduct of the business. It is based on UPA Section 18(e), which has been interpreted broadly to mean that, absent contrary agreement, each partner has a continuing right to participate in the management of the partnership and to be informed about the partnership business, even if his assent to partnership business decisions is not required. There are special rules regarding the partner vote necessary to

approve a partnership becoming (or canceling its status as) a limited liability partnership. See Section 1001(b).

8. Subsection (g) provides that partners may use or possess partnership property only for partnership purposes. That is the edited remains of UPA Section 25(2)(a), which deals in detail with the incidents of tenancy in partnership. That tenancy is abolished as a consequence of the entity theory of partnerships. *See* Section 501 and Comments.

9. Subsection (h) continues the UPA Section 18(f) rule that a partner is not entitled to remuneration for services performed, except in winding up the partnership. Subsection (h) deletes the UPA reference to a "surviving" partner. That means any partner winding up the business is entitled to compensation, not just a surviving partner winding up after the death of another partner. The exception is not intended to apply in the hypothetical winding up that takes place if there is a buyout under Article 7.

10. Subsection (i) continues the substance of UPA Section 18(g) that no person can become a partner without the consent of all the partners.

11. Subsection (j) continues with one important clarification the UPA Section 18(h) scheme of allocating management authority among the partners. In the absence of an agreement to the contrary, matters arising in the ordinary course of the business may be decided by a majority of the partners. Amendments to the partnership agreement and matters outside the ordinary course of the partnership business require unanimous consent of the partners. Although the text of the UPA is silent regarding extraordinary matters, courts have generally required the consent of all partners for those matters. *See, e.g., Paciaroni v. Crane*, 408 A.2d 946 (Del. Ch. 1989); *Thomas v. Marvin E. Jewell & Co.*, 232 Neb. 261, 440 N.W.2d 437 (1989); *Duell v. Hancock*, 83 A.D.2d 762, 443 N.Y.S.2d 490 (1981).

It is not intended that subsection (j) embrace a claim for an objection to a partnership decision that is not discovered until after the fact. There is no cause of action based on that after-the-fact second-guessing.

12. Subsection (k) is new and was added to make it clear that Section 301 governs partners' agency power to bind the partnership to third persons, while Section 401 governs partners' rights among themselves.

§ 402. Distributions in Kind

A partner has no right to receive, and may not be required to accept, a distribution in kind.

Comment

Section 402 provides that a partner has no right to demand and receive a distribution in kind and may not be required to take a distribution in kind. That continues the "in kind" rule of UPA Section 38(*l*). The new language is suggested by RULPA Section 605.

This section is complemented by Section 807(a) which provides that, in winding up the partnership business on dissolution, any surplus after the payment of partnership obligations must be applied to pay in cash the net amount distributable to each partner.

§ 403. Partner's Rights and Duties with Respect to Information

(a) A partnership shall keep its books and records, if any, at its chief executive office.

(b) A partnership shall provide partners and their agents and attorneys access to its books and records. It shall provide former partners and their agents and attorneys access to books and records pertaining to the period during which they were partners. The right of access provides the opportunity to inspect and copy books and records during ordinary business hours. A partnership may impose a reasonable charge, covering the costs of labor and material, for copies of documents furnished.

(c) Each partner and the partnership shall furnish to a partner, and to the legal representative of a deceased partner or partner under legal disability:

(1) without demand, any information concerning the partnership's business and affairs reasonably required for the proper exercise of the partner's rights and duties under the partnership agreement or this [Act]; and

(2) on demand, any other information concerning the partnership's business and affairs, except to the extent the demand or the information demanded is unreasonable or otherwise improper under the circumstances.

Comment

1. Subsection (a) provides that the partnership's books and records, if any, shall be kept at its chief executive office. It continues the UPA Section 19 rule, modified to include partnership records other than its "books," i.e., financial records. The concept of "chief executive office" comes from UCC Section 9–103(3)(d). See the Comment to Section 106.

Since general partnerships are often informal or even inadvertent, no books and records are enumerated as mandatory, such as that found in RULPA Section 105. Any requirement in UPA Section 19 that the partnership keep books is oblique at best, since it states merely where the books shall be kept, not that they shall be kept. Under RUPA, there is no liability to either partners or third parties for the failure to keep partnership books. A partner who undertakes to keep books, however, must do so accurately and adequately.

In general, a partnership should, at a minimum, keep those books and records necessary to enable the partners to determine their share of the profits and losses, as well as their rights on withdrawal. An action for an accounting provides an adequate remedy in the event adequate records are not kept. The partnership must also maintain any books and records required by state or federal taxing or other governmental authorities.

2. Under subsection (b), partners are entitled to access to the partnership books and records. Former partners are expressly given a similar right, although limited to the books and records pertaining to the period during which they were partners. The line between partners and former partners is not a bright one for this purpose, however, and should be drawn in light of the legitimate interests of a dissociated partner in the partnership. For example, a withdrawing partner's liability is ongoing for pre-withdrawal liabilities and will normally be extended to new liabilities for at least 90 days. It is intended that a former partner be accorded access to partnership books and records as reasonably necessary to protect that partner's legitimate interests during the period his rights and liabilities are being wound down.

The right of access is limited to ordinary business hours, and the right to inspect and copy by agent or attorney is made explicit. The partnership may impose a reasonable charge for furnishing copies of documents. *Accord*, RULPA § 105(b).

A partner's right to inspect and copy the partnership's books and records is not conditioned on the partner's purpose or motive. Compare RMBCA Section 16.02(c)(*l*) (shareholder must have proper purpose to inspect certain corporate records). A partner's unlimited personal liability justifies an unqualified right of access to the partnership books and records. An abuse of the right to inspect and copy might constitute a violation of the obligation of good faith and fair dealing for which the other partners would have a remedy. See Sections 404(d) and 405.

Under Section 103(b)(2), a partner's right of access to partnership books and records may not be unreasonably restricted by the partnership agreement. Thus, to preserve a partner's core information rights despite unequal bargaining power, an agreement limiting a partner's right to inspect and copy partnership books and records is subject to judicial review. Nevertheless, reasonable restrictions on access to partnership books and records by agreement are authorized. For example, a provision in a partnership agreement denying partners access to the compensation of other partners should be upheld, absent any abuse such as fraud or duress.

3. Subsection (c) is a significant revision of UPA Section 20 and provides a more comprehensive, although not exclusive, statement of partners' rights and duties with respect to partnership information other than books and records. Both the partnership and the other partners are obligated to furnish partnership information.

Paragraph (1) is new and imposes an affirmative disclosure obligation on the partnership and partners. There is no express UPA provision imposing an affirmative obligation to disclose any information other than the partnership books. Under some circumstances, however, an affirmative disclosure duty has been inferred from other sections of the Act, as well as from the common law, such as the fiduciary duty of good faith. Under UPA Section 18(e), for example, all partners enjoy an equal right in the management and conduct of the partnership business, absent contrary agreement. That right has been construed to require that every partner be provided with ongoing information concerning the partnership business. See Comment 7 to Section 401. Paragraph (1) provides expressly that partners must be furnished, without demand, partnership information reasonably needed for them to exercise their rights and duties as partners. In addition, a disclosure duty may, under some circumstances, also spring from the Section 404(d) obligation of good faith and fair dealing. See Comment 4 to Section 404.

Paragraph (2) continues the UPA rule that partners are entitled, on demand, to any other information concerning the partnership's business and affairs. The demand may be refused if either the demand or the information demanded is unreasonable or otherwise improper. That qualification is new to the statutory formulation. The burden is on the partnership or partner from whom the information is requested to show that the demand is unreasonable or improper. The UPA admonition that the information furnished be "true and full" has been deleted as unnecessary, and no substantive change is intended.

The Section 403(c) information rights can be waived or varied by agreement of the partners, since there is no Section 103(b) limitation on the variation of those rights as there is with respect to the Section 403(b) access rights to books and records. *See* Section 103(b)(2).

§ 404. General Standards of Partner's Conduct

(a) The only fiduciary duties a partner owes to the partnership and the other partners are the duty of loyalty and the duty of care set forth in subsections (b) and (c).

(b) A partner's duty of loyalty to the partnership and the other partners is limited to the following:

(1) to account to the partnership and hold as trustee for it any property, profit, or benefit derived by the partner in the conduct and winding up of the partnership business or derived from a use by the partner of partnership property, including the appropriation of a partnership opportunity;

(2) to refrain from dealing with the partnership in the conduct or winding up of the partnership business as or on behalf of a party having an interest adverse to the partnership; and

(3) to refrain from competing with the partnership in the conduct of the partnership business before the dissolution of the partnership.

(c) A partner's duty of care to the partnership and the other partners in the conduct and winding up of the partnership business is limited to refraining from engaging in grossly negligent or reckless conduct, intentional misconduct, or a knowing violation of law.

(d) A partner shall discharge the duties to the partnership and the other partners under this [Act] or under the partnership agreement and exercise any rights consistently with the obligation of good faith and fair dealing.

(e) A partner does not violate a duty or obligation under this [Act] or under the partnership agreement merely because the partner's conduct furthers the partner's own interest.

(f) A partner may lend money to and transact other business with the partnership, and as to each loan or transaction the rights and obligations of the partner are the same as those of a person who is not a partner, subject to other applicable law.

(g) This section applies to a person winding up the partnership business as the personal or legal representative of the last surviving partner as if the person were a partner.

Comment

1. Section 404 is new. The title, "General Standards of Partner's Conduct," is drawn from RMBCA Section 8.30. Section 404 is both comprehensive and exclusive. In that regard, it is structurally different from the UPA which touches only sparingly on a partner's duty of loyalty and leaves any further development of the fiduciary duties of partners to the common law of agency. Compare UPA Sections 4(3) and 21.

Section 404 begins by stating that the only fiduciary duties a partner owes to the partnership and the other partners are the duties of loyalty and care set forth in subsections (b) and (c) of the Act. Those duties may not be waived or eliminated in the partnership agreement, but the agreement may identify activities and determine standards for measuring performance of the duties, if not manifestly unreasonable. *See* Sections 103(b)(3)-(5).

Section 404 continues the term "fiduciary" from UPA Section 21, which is entitled "Partner Accountable as a Fiduciary." Arguably, the term "fiduciary" is inappropriate when used to describe the duties of a partner because a partner may legitimately pursue self-interest (see

Section 404(e)) and not solely the interest of the partnership and the other partners, as must a true trustee. Nevertheless, partners have long been characterized as fiduciaries. *See, e.g., Meinhard v. Salmon*, 249 N.Y. 458, 463, 164 N.E. 545, 546 (1928) (Cardozo, J.). Indeed, the law of partnership reflects the broader law of principal and agent, under which every agent is a fiduciary. *See* Restatement (Second) of Agency § 13 (1957).

2. Section 404(b) provides three specific rules that comprise a partner's duty of loyalty. Those rules are exclusive and encompass the entire duty of loyalty.

Subsection (b)(*l*) is based on UPA Section 21(1) and continues the rule that partnership property usurped by a partner, including the misappropriation of a partnership opportunity, is held in trust for the partnership. The express reference to the appropriation of a partnership opportunity is new, but merely codifies case law on the point. *See, e.g., Meinhard v. Salmon, supra*; *Fouchek v. Janicek*, 190 Ore. 251, 225 P.2d 783 (1950). Under a constructive trust theory, the partnership can recover any money or property in the partner's hands that can be traced to the partnership. *See, e.g., Yoder v. Hooper*, 695 P.2d 1182 (Colo. App. 1984), *aff'd*, 737 P.2d 852 (Colo. 1987); *Fortugno v. Hudson Manure Co.*, 51 N.J. Super. 482, 144 A.2d 207 (1958); *Harestad v. Weitzel*, 242 Or. 199, 536 P.2d 522 (1975). As a result, the partnership's claim is greater than that of an ordinary creditor. See Official Comment to UPA Section 21.

UPA Section 21(1) imposes the duty on partners to account for profits and benefits in all transactions connected with "the formation, conduct, or liquidation of the partnership." Reference to the "formation" of the partnership has been eliminated by RUPA because of concern that the duty of loyalty could be inappropriately extended to the pre-formation period when the parties are really negotiating at arm's length. *Compare Herring v. Offutt*, 295 A.2d 876 (Ct. App. Md. 1972), *with Phoenix Mutual Life Ins. Co. v. Shady Grove Plaza Limited Partnership*, 734 F. Supp. 1181 (D. Md. 1990), *aff'd*, 937 F.2d 603 (4th Cir. 1991). Once a partnership is agreed to, each partner becomes a fiduciary in the "conduct" of the business. Pre-formation negotiations are, of course, subject to the general contract obligation to deal honestly and without fraud.

Upon a partner's dissociation, Section 603(b)(3) limits the application of the duty to account for personal profits to those derived from matters arising or events occurring before the dissociation, unless the partner participates in winding up the partnership's business. Thus, after withdrawal, a partner is free to appropriate to his own benefit any new business opportunity thereafter coming to his attention, even if the partnership continues.

Subsection (b)(2) provides that a partner must refrain from dealing with the partnership as or on behalf of a party having an interest adverse to the partnership. This rule is derived from Sections 389 and 391 of the Restatement (Second) of Agency. Comment c to Section 389 explains that the rule is not based upon the harm caused to the principal, but upon avoiding a conflict of opposing interests in the mind of an agent whose duty is to act for the benefit of his principal.

Upon a partner's dissociation, Section 603(b)(3) limits the application of the duty to refrain from representing interests adverse to the partnership to the same extent as the duty to account. Thus, after withdrawal, a partner may deal with the partnership as an adversary with respect to new matters or events.

Section 404(b)(3) provides that a partner must refrain from competing with the partnership in the conduct of its business. This rule is derived from Section 393 of the Restatement (Second) of Agency and is an application of the general duty of an agent to act solely on his principal's behalf.

The duty not to compete applies only to the "conduct" of the partnership business; it does not extend to winding up the business, as do the other loyalty rules. Thus, a partner is free to compete immediately upon an event of dissolution under Section 801, unless the partnership agreement otherwise provides. A partner who dissociates without a winding up of the business resulting is also free to compete, because Section 603(b)(2) provides that the duty not to compete terminates upon dissociation. A dissociated partner is not, however, free to use confidential partnership information after dissociation. *See* Restatement (Second) of Agency § 393 cmt. e (1957). Trade secret law also may apply. See the Uniform Trade Secrets Act.

Under Section 103(b)(3), the partnership agreement may not "eliminate" the duty of loyalty. Section 103(b)(3)(i) expressly empowers the partners, however, to identify specific types or categories of activities that do not violate the duty of loyalty, if not manifestly unreasonable. As under UPA Section 21, the other partners may also consent to a specific act or transaction that otherwise violates one of the rules. For the consent to be effective under Section 103(b)(3)(ii), there must be full disclosure of all material facts regarding the act or transaction and the partner's conflict of interest. See Comment 5 to Section 103.

3. Subsection (c) is new and establishes the duty of care that partners owe to the partnership and to the other partners. There is no statutory duty of care under the UPA, although a common law duty of care is recognized by some courts. *See, e.g., Rosenthal v. Rosenthal*, 543 A.2d 348, 352 (Me. 1988) (duty of care limited to acting in a manner that does not constitute gross negligence or willful misconduct).

The standard of care imposed by RUPA is that of gross negligence, which is the standard generally recognized by the courts. *See, e.g., Rosenthal v. Rosenthal, supra.* Section 103(b)(4) provides that the duty of care may not be eliminated entirely by agreement, but the standard may be reasonably reduced. See Comment 6 to Section 103.

4. Subsection (d) is also new. It provides that partners have an obligation of good faith and fair dealing in the discharge of all their duties, including those arising under the Act, such as their fiduciary duties of loyalty and care, and those arising under the partnership agreement. The exercise of any rights by a partner is also subject to the obligation of good faith and fair dealing. The obligation runs to the partnership and to the other partners in all matters related to the conduct and winding up of the partnership business.

The obligation of good faith and fair dealing is a contract concept, imposed on the partners because of the consensual nature of a partnership. See Restatement (Second) of Contracts § 205 (1981). It is not characterized, in RUPA, as a fiduciary duty arising out of the partners' special relationship. Nor is it a separate and independent obligation. It is an ancillary obligation that applies whenever a partner discharges a duty or exercises a right under the partnership agreement or the Act.

The meaning of "good faith and fair dealing" is not firmly fixed under present law. "Good faith" clearly suggests a subjective element, while "fair dealing" implies an objective component. It was decided to leave the terms undefined in the Act and allow the courts to develop their meaning based on the experience of real cases. Some commentators, moreover, believe that good faith is more properly understood by what it excludes than by what it includes. See Robert S. Summers, *"Good Faith" in General Contract Law and the Sales Provisions of the Uniform Commercial Code*, 54 Va. L. Rev. 195, 262 (1968):

Good faith, as judges generally use the term in matters contractual, is best understood as an "excluder"—a phrase with no general meaning or meanings of its own. Instead, it functions to rule out many different forms of bad faith. It is hard to get this point across to persons used to thinking that every word must have one or more general meanings of its own—must be either univocal or ambiguous.

The UCC definition of "good faith" is honesty in fact and, in the case of a merchant, the observance of reasonable commercial standards of fair dealing in the trade. *See* UCC §§ 1–201(19), 2–103(b). Those definitions were rejected as too narrow or not applicable.

In some situations the obligation of good faith includes a disclosure component. Depending on the circumstances, a partner may have an affirmative disclosure obligation that supplements the Section 403 duty to render information.

Under Section 103(b)(5), the obligation of good faith and fair dealing may not be eliminated by agreement, but the partners by agreement may determine the standards by which the performance of the obligation is to be measured, if the standards are not manifestly unreasonable. See Comment 7 to Section 103.

5. Subsection (e) is new and deals expressly with a very basic issue on which the UPA is silent. A partner as such is not a trustee and is not

held to the same standards as a trustee. Subsection (e) makes clear that a partner's conduct is not deemed to be improper merely because it serves the partner's own individual interest.

That admonition has particular application to the duty of loyalty and the obligation of good faith and fair dealing. It underscores the partner's rights as an owner and principal in the enterprise, which must always be balanced against his duties and obligations as an agent and fiduciary. For example, a partner who, with consent, owns a shopping center may, under subsection (e), legitimately vote against a proposal by the partnership to open a competing shopping center.

6. Subsection (f) authorizes partners to lend money to and transact other business with the partnership and, in so doing, to enjoy the same rights and obligations as a nonpartner. That language is drawn from RULPA Section 107. The rights and obligations of a partner doing business with the partnership as an outsider are expressly made subject to the usual laws governing those transactions. They include, for example, rules limiting or qualifying the rights and remedies of inside creditors, such as fraudulent transfer law, equitable subordination, and the law of avoidable preferences, as well as general debtor-creditor law. The reference to "other applicable law" makes clear that subsection (f) is not intended to displace those laws, and thus they are preserved under Section 104(a).

It is unclear under the UPA whether a partner may, for the partner's own account, purchase the assets of the partnership at a foreclosure sale or upon the liquidation of the partnership. Those purchases are clearly within subsection (f)'s broad approval. It is also clear under that subsection that a partner may purchase partnership assets at a foreclosure sale, whether the partner is the mortgagee or the mortgagee is an unrelated third party. Similarly, a partner may purchase partnership property at a tax sale. The obligation of good faith requires disclosure of the partner's interest in the transaction, however.

7. Subsection (g) provides that the prescribed standards of conduct apply equally to a person engaged in winding up the partnership business as the personal or legal representative of the last surviving partner, as if the person were a partner. This is derived from UPA Section 21(2), but now embraces the duty of care and the obligation of good faith and fair dealing, as well as the duty of loyalty.

§ 405. Actions by Partnership and Partners

(a) A partnership may maintain an action against a partner for a breach of the partnership agreement, or for the violation of a duty to the partnership, causing harm to the partnership.

(b) A partner may maintain an action against the partnership or another partner for legal or equitable relief, with or without an accounting as to partnership business, to:

(1) enforce the partner's rights under the partnership agreement;

(2) enforce the partner's rights under this [Act], including:

(i) the partner's rights under Sections 401, 403, or 404;

(ii) the partner's right on dissociation to have the partner's interest in the partnership purchased pursuant to Section 701 or enforce any other right under Article 6 or 7; or

(iii) the partner's right to compel a dissolution and winding up of the partnership business under Section 801 or enforce any other right under Article 8; or

(3) enforce the rights and otherwise protect the interests of the partner, including rights and interests arising independently of the partnership relationship.

(c) The accrual of, and any time limitation on, a right of action for a remedy under this section is governed by other law. A right to an accounting upon a dissolution and winding up does not revive a claim barred by law.

Comment

1. Section 405(a) is new and reflects the entity theory of partnership. It provides that the partnership itself may maintain an action against a partner for any breach of the partnership agreement or for the violation of any duty owed to the partnership, such as a breach of fiduciary duty.

2. Section 405(b) is the successor to UPA Section 22, but with significant changes. At common law, an accounting was generally not available before dissolution. That was modified by UPA Section 22 which specifies certain circumstances in which an accounting action is available without requiring a partner to dissolve the partnership. Section 405(b) goes far beyond the UPA rule. It provides that, during the term of the partnership, partners may maintain a variety of legal or equitable actions, including an action for an accounting, as well as a final action for an accounting upon dissolution and winding up. It reflects a new policy choice that partners should have access to the courts during the term of the partnership to resolve claims against the partnership and the other partners, leaving broad judicial discretion to fashion appropriate remedies.

Under RUPA, an accounting is not a prerequisite to the availability of the other remedies a partner may have against the partnership or the other partners. That change reflects the increased willingness courts have shown to grant relief without the requirement of an accounting, in derogation of the so-called "exclusivity rule." *See, e.g., Farney v. Hauser*, 109 Kan. 75, 79, 198 Pac. 178, 180 (1921) ("[For] all practical purposes a partnership may be considered as a business entity"); *Auld v. Estridge*,

86 Misc. 2d 895, 901, 382 N.Y.S.2d 897, 901 (1976) ("No purpose of justice is served by delaying the resolution here on empty procedural grounds").

Under subsection (b), a partner may bring a direct suit against the partnership or another partner for almost any cause of action arising out of the conduct of the partnership business. That eliminates the present procedural barriers to suits between partners filed independently of an accounting action. In addition to a formal account, the court may grant any other appropriate legal or equitable remedy. Since general partners are not passive investors like limited partners, RUPA does not authorize derivative actions, as does RULPA Section 1001.

Subsection (b)(3) makes it clear that a partner may recover against the partnership and the other partners for personal injuries or damage to the property of the partner caused by another partner. *See, e.g., Duffy v. Piazza Construction Co.*, 815 P.2d 267 (Wash. App. 1991); *Smith v. Hensley*, 354 S.W.2d 744 (Ky. App.). One partner's negligence is not imputed to bar another partner's action. *See, e.g., Reeves v. Harmon*, 475 P.2d 400 (Okla. 1970); *Eagle Star Ins. Co. v. Bean*, 134 F.2d 755 (9th Cir. 1943) (fire insurance company not subrogated to claim against partners who negligently caused fire that damaged partnership property).

3. Generally, partners may limit or contract away their Section 405 remedies. They may not, however, eliminate entirely the remedies for breach of those duties that are mandatory under Section 103(b). See Comment 1 to Section 103.

4. Section 405(c) replaces UPA Section 43 and provides that other (i.e., non-partnership) law governs the accrual of a cause of action for which subsection (b) provides a remedy. The statute of limitations on such claims is also governed by other law, and claims barred by a statute of limitations are not revived by reason of the partner's right to an accounting upon dissolution, as they were under the UPA. The effect of those rules is to compel partners to litigate their claims during the life of the partnership or risk losing them. Because an accounting is an equitable proceeding, it may also be barred by laches where there is an undue delay in bringing the action. Under general law, the limitations periods may be tolled by a partner's fraud.

5. UPA Section 39 grants ancillary remedies to a person who rescinds his participation in a partnership because it was fraudulently induced, including the right to a lien on surplus partnership property for the amount of that person's interest in the partnership. RUPA has no counterpart provision to UPA Section 39, and leaves it to the general law of rescission to determine the rights of a person fraudulently induced to invest in a partnership. See Section 104(a).

§ 406. Continuation of Partnership Beyond Definite Term or Particular Undertaking

(a) If a partnership for a definite term or particular undertaking is continued, without an express agreement, after the expiration of the term or completion of the undertaking, the rights and duties of the partners remain the same as they were at the expiration or completion, so far as is consistent with a partnership at will.

(b) If the partners, or those of them who habitually acted in the business during the term or undertaking, continue the business without any settlement or liquidation of the partnership, they are presumed to have agreed that the partnership will continue.

Comment

Section 406 continues UPA Section 23, with no substantive change. Subsection (a) provides that, if a term partnership is continued without an express agreement beyond the expiration of its term or the completion of the undertaking, the partners' rights and duties remain the same as they were, so far as is consistent with a partnership at will.

Subsection (b) provides that if the partnership is continued by the partners without any settlement or liquidation of the business, it is presumed that the partners have agreed not to wind up the business. The presumption is rebuttable. If the partnership is continued under this subsection, there is no dissolution under (2)(iii). As a partnership at will, however, the partnership may be dissolved under (1) at any time.

Article 5

TRANSFEREES AND CREDITORS OF PARTNER

§ 501. Partner not Co-owner of Partnership Property

A partner is not a co-owner of partnership property and has no interest in partnership property which can be transferred, either voluntarily or involuntarily.

Comment

Section 501 provides that a partner is not a co-owner of partnership property and has no interest in partnership property that can be transferred, either voluntarily or involuntarily. Thus, the section abolishes the UPA Section 25(1) concept of tenants in partnership and reflects the adoption of the entity theory. Partnership property is owned by the entity and not by the individual partners. See also Section 203, which provides that property transferred to or otherwise acquired by the partnership is property of the partnership and not of the partners individually.

RUPA also deletes the references in UPA Sections 24 and 25 to a partner's "right in specific partnership property," although those rights are largely defined away by the detailed rules of UPA Section 25 itself.

Thus, it is clear that a partner who misappropriates partnership property is guilty of embezzlement the same as a shareholder who misappropriates corporate property.

Adoption of the entity theory also has the effect of protecting partnership property from execution or other process by a partner's personal creditors. That continues the result under UPA Section 25(2)(c). Those creditors may seek a charging order under Section 504 to reach the partner's transferable interest in the partnership.

RUPA does not interfere with a partner's exemption claim in nonpartnership property. As under the UPA, disputes over whether specific property belongs to the partner or to the firm will likely arise in the context of an exemption claim by a partner.

A partner's spouse, heirs, or next of kin are not entitled to allowances or other rights in partnership property. That continues the result under UPA Section 25(2)(e).

§ 502. Partner's Transferable Interest in Partnership

The only transferable interest of a partner in the partnership is the partner's share of the profits and losses of the partnership and the partner's right to receive distributions. The interest is personal property.

Comment

Section 502 continues the UPA Section 26 concept that a partner's only transferable interest in the partnership is the partner's share of profits and losses and right to receive distributions, that is, the partner's financial rights. The term "distribution" is defined in Section 101(3). Compare RULPA Section 101(10) ("partnership interest").

The partner's transferable interest is deemed to be personal property, regardless of the nature of the underlying partnership assets.

Under Section 503(b)(3), a transferee of a partner's transferable interest has standing to seek judicial dissolution of the partnership business.

A partner has other interests in the partnership that may not be transferred, such as the right to participate in the management of the business. Those rights are included in the broader concept of a "partner's interest in the partnership." *See* Section 101(9).

§ 503. Transfer of Partner's Transferable Interest

(a) A transfer, in whole or in part, of a partner's transferable interest in the partnership:

(1) is permissible;

(2) does not by itself cause the partner's dissociation or a dissolution and winding up of the partnership business; and

(3) does not, as against the other partners or the partnership, entitle the transferee, during the continuance of the partnership, to participate in the management or conduct of the partnership business, to require access to information concerning partnership transactions, or to inspect or copy the partnership books or records.

(b) A transferee of a partner's transferable interest in the partnership has a right:

(1) to receive, in accordance with the transfer, distributions to which the transferor would otherwise be entitled;

(2) to receive upon the dissolution and winding up of the partnership business, in accordance with the transfer, the net amount otherwise distributable to the transferor; and

(3) to seek under Section 801(6) a judicial determination that it is equitable to wind up the partnership business.

(c) In a dissolution and winding up, a transferee is entitled to an account of partnership transactions only from the date of the latest account agreed to by all of the partners.

(d) Upon transfer, the transferor retains the rights and duties of a partner other than the interest in distributions transferred.

(e) A partnership need not give effect to a transferee's rights under this section until it has notice of the transfer.

(f) A transfer of a partner's transferable interest in the partnership in violation of a restriction on transfer contained in the partnership agreement is ineffective as to a person having notice of the restriction at the time of transfer.

Comment

1. Section 503 is derived from UPA Section 27. Subsection (a)(1) states explicitly that a partner has the right to transfer his transferable interest in the partnership. The term "transfer" is used throughout RUPA in lieu of the term "assignment." See Section 101(10).

Subsection (a)(2) continues the UPA Section 27(1) rule that an assignment of a partner's interest in the partnership does not of itself cause a winding up of the partnership business. Under Section 601(4)(ii), however, a partner who has transferred substantially all of his partnership interest may be expelled by the other partners.

Subsection (a)(3), which is also derived from UPA Section 27(*l*), provides that a transferee is not, as against the other partners, entitled (i) to participate in the management or conduct of the partnership business; (ii) to inspect the partnership books or records; or (iii) to require any information concerning or an account of partnership transactions.

2. The rights of a transferee are set forth in subsection (b). Under subsection (b)(1), which is derived from UPA Section 27(*l*), a transferee is entitled to receive, in accordance with the terms of the assignment, any distributions to which the transferor would otherwise have been entitled under the partnership agreement before dissolution. After dissolution, the transferee is also entitled to receive, under subsection (b)(2), the net amount that would otherwise have been distributed to the transferor upon the winding up of the business.

Subsection (b)(3) confers standing on a transferee to seek a judicial dissolution and winding up of the partnership business as provided in Section 801(6), thus continuing the rule of UPA Section 32(2).

Section 504(b) accords the rights of a transferee to the purchaser at a sale foreclosing a charging order. The same rule should apply to creditors or other purchasers who acquire partnership interests by pursuing UCC remedies or statutory liens under federal or state law.

3. Subsection (c) is based on UPA Section 27(2). It grants to transferees the right to an account of partnership transactions, limited to the period since the date of the last account agreed to by all of the partners.

4. Subsection (d) is new. It makes clear that unless otherwise agreed the partner whose interest is transferred retains all of the rights and duties of a partner, other than the right to receive distributions. That means the transferor is entitled to participate in the management of the partnership and remains personally liable for all partnership obligations, unless and until he withdraws as a partner, is expelled under Section 601(4)(ii), or is otherwise dissociated under Section 601.

A divorced spouse of a partner who is awarded rights in the partner's partnership interest as part of a property settlement is entitled only to the rights of a transferee. The spouse may instead be granted a money judgment in the amount of the property award, enforceable by a charging order in the same manner as any other money judgment against a partner. In neither case, however, would the spouse become a partner by virtue of the property settlement or succeed to any of the partner's management rights. *See, e.g., Warren v. Warren*, 12 Ark. App. 260, 675 S.W.2d 371 (1984).

5. Subsection (e) is new and provides that the partnership has no duty to give effect to the transferee's rights until the partnership receives notice of the transfer. This is consistent with UCC Section 9–318(3), which provides that an "account debtor" is authorized to pay the assignor until the account debtor receives notification that the amount due or to become due has been assigned and that payment is to be made to the assignee. It further provides that the assignee, on request, must furnish reasonable proof of the assignment.

6. Subsection (f) is new and provides that a transfer of a partner's transferable interest in the partnership in violation of a restriction on transfer contained in a partnership agreement is ineffective as to a person with timely notice of the restriction. Under Section 103(a), the partners may agree among themselves to restrict the right to transfer their partnership interests. Subsection (f) makes explicit that a transfer in violation of such a restriction is ineffective as to a transferee with notice of the restriction. See Section 102(b) for the meaning of "notice." RUPA leaves to general law and the UCC the issue of whether a transfer in violation of a valid restriction is effective as to a transferee without notice of the restriction.

Whether a particular restriction will be enforceable, however, must be considered in light of other law. *See* 11 U.S.C. § 541(c)(1) (property owned by bankrupt passes to trustee regardless of restrictions on transfer); UCC § 9–318(4) (agreement between account debtor and assignor prohibiting creation of security interest in a general intangible or requiring account debtor's consent is ineffective); *Battista v. Carlo*, 57 Misc. 2d 495, 293 N.Y.S.2d 227 (1968) (restriction on transfer of partnership interest subject to rules against unreasonable restraints on alienation of property) (dictum); *Tupper v. Kroc*, 88 Nev. 146, 494 P.2d 1275 (1972) (partnership interest subject to charging order even if partnership agreement prohibits assignments). *Cf. Tu–Vu Drive–In Corp. v. Ashkins*, 61 Cal. 2d 283, 38 Cal. Rptr. 348, 391 P.2d 828 (1964) (restraints on transfer of corporate stock must be reasonable). Even if a restriction on the transfer of a partner's transferable interest in a partnership were held to be unenforceable, the transfer might be grounds for expelling the partner-transferor from the partnership under Section 601(5)(ii).

7. Other rules that apply in the case of transfers include Section 601(4)(ii) (expulsion of partner who transfers substantially all of partnership interest); Section 601(6) (dissociation of partner who makes an assignment for benefit of creditors); and Section 801(6) (transferee has standing to seek judicial winding up).

§ 504. Partner's Transferable Interest Subject to Charging Order

(a) On application by a judgment creditor of a partner or of a partner's transferee, a court having jurisdiction may charge the transferable interest of the judgment debtor to satisfy the judgment. The court may appoint a receiver of the share of the distributions due or to become due to the judgment debtor in respect of the partnership and make all other orders, directions, accounts, and inquiries the judgment debtor might have made or which the circumstances of the case may require.

(b) A charging order constitutes a lien on the judgment debtor's transferable interest in the partnership. The court may order a foreclosure of the interest subject to the charging order at any time. The purchaser at the foreclosure sale has the rights of a transferee.

(c) At any time before foreclosure, an interest charged may be redeemed:

(1) by the judgment debtor;

(2) with property other than partnership property, by one or more of the other partners; or

(3) with partnership property, by one or more of the other partners with the consent of all of the partners whose interests are not so charged.

(d) This [Act] does not deprive a partner of a right under exemption laws with respect to the partner's interest in the partnership.

(e) This section provides the exclusive remedy by which a judgment creditor of a partner or partner's transferee may satisfy a judgment out of the judgment debtor's transferable interest in the partnership.

Comment

1. Section 504 continues the UPA Section 28 charging order as the proper remedy by which a judgment creditor of a partner may reach the debtor's transferable interest in a partnership to satisfy the judgment. Subsection (a) makes the charging order available to the judgment creditor of a transferee of a partnership interest. Under Section 503(b), the transferable interest of a partner or transferee is limited to the partner's right to receive distributions from the partnership and to seek judicial liquidation of the partnership. The court may appoint a receiver of the debtor's share of the distributions due or to become due and make all other orders that may be required.

2. Subsection (b) is new and codifies the case law under the UPA holding that a charging order constitutes a lien on the debtor's transferable interest. The lien may be foreclosed by the court at any time, and the purchaser at the foreclosure sale has the Section 503(b) rights of a transferee. For a general discussion of the charging order remedy, see *I Alan R. Bromberg & Larry E. Ribstein, Partnership* (1988), at 3:69.

3. Subsection (c) continues the UPA Section 28(2) right of the debtor or other partners to redeem the partnership interest before the foreclosure sale. Redemption by the partnership (i.e., with partnership property) requires the consent of all the remaining partners. Neither the UPA nor RUPA provide a statutory procedural framework for the redemption.

4. Subsection (d) provides that nothing in RUPA deprives a partner of his rights under the State's exemption laws. That is essentially the same as UPA Section 28(3).

5. Subsection (e) provides that the charging order is the judgment creditor's exclusive remedy. Although the UPA nowhere states that a charging order is the exclusive process for a partner's individual judgment creditor, the courts have generally so interpreted it. *See, e.g.*,

Matter of Pischke, 11 B.R. 913 (E.D. Va. 1981); *Baum v. Baum*, 51 Cal. 2d 610, 335 P.2d 481 (1959); *Atlantic Mobile Homes, Inc. v. LeFever*, 481 So. 2d 1002 (Fla. App. 1986).

Notwithstanding subsection (e), there may be an exception for the enforcement of family support orders. Some States have unique statutory procedures for the enforcement of support orders. In Florida, for example, a court may issue an "income deduction order" requiring any person or entity providing "income" to the obligor of a support order to remit to the obligee or a depository, as directed by the court, a specified portion of the income. Fla. Stat. § 61.1301 (1993). "Income" is broadly defined to include any form of payment to the obligor, including wages, salary, compensation as an independent contractor, dividends, interest, or other payment, regardless of source. Fla. Stat. § 61.046(4) (1993). That definition includes distributions payable to an obligor partner. A charging order under RUPA would still be necessary to reach the obligor's entire partnership interest, however.

Article 6

PARTNER'S DISSOCIATION

§ 601. Events Causing Partner's Dissociation

A partner is dissociated from a partnership upon the occurrence of any of the following events:

(1) the partnership's having notice of the partner's express will to withdraw as a partner or on a later date specified by the partner;

(2) an event agreed to in the partnership agreement as causing the partner's dissociation;

(3) the partner's expulsion pursuant to the partnership agreement;

(4) the partner's expulsion by the unanimous vote of the other partners if:

(i) it is unlawful to carry on the partnership business with that partner;

(ii) there has been a transfer of all or substantially all of that partner's transferable interest in the partnership, other than a transfer for security purposes, or a court order charging the partner's interest, which has not been foreclosed;

(iii) within 90 days after the partnership notifies a corporate partner that it will be expelled because it has filed a certificate of dissolution or the equivalent, its charter has been revoked, or its right to conduct business has been suspended by the jurisdiction of its incorporation, there is no revocation of the certificate of dissolution or no reinstatement of its charter or its right to conduct business; or

(iv) a partnership that is a partner has been dissolved and its business is being wound up;

(5) on application by the partnership or another partner, the partner's expulsion by judicial determination because:

(i) the partner engaged in wrongful conduct that adversely and materially affected the partnership business;

(ii) the partner willfully or persistently committed a material breach of the partnership agreement or of a duty owed to the partnership or the other partners under Section 404; or

(iii) the partner engaged in conduct relating to the partnership business which makes it not reasonably practicable to carry on the business in partnership with the partner;

(6) the partner's:

(i) becoming a debtor in bankruptcy;

(ii) executing an assignment for the benefit of creditors;

(iii) seeking, consenting to, or acquiescing in the appointment of a trustee, receiver, or liquidator of that partner or of all or substantially all of that partner's property; or

(iv) failing, within 90 days after the appointment, to have vacated or stayed the appointment of a trustee, receiver, or liquidator of the partner or of all or substantially all of the partner's property obtained without the partner's consent or acquiescence, or failing within 90 days after the expiration of a stay to have the appointment vacated;

(7) in the case of a partner who is an individual:

(i) the partner's death;

(ii) the appointment of a guardian or general conservator for the partner; or

(iii) a judicial determination that the partner has otherwise become incapable of performing the partner's duties under the partnership agreement;

(8) in the case of a partner that is a trust or is acting as a partner by virtue of being a trustee of a trust, distribution of the trust's entire transferable interest in the partnership, but not merely by reason of the substitution of a successor trustee;

(9) in the case of a partner that is an estate or is acting as a partner by virtue of being a personal representative of an estate, distribution of the estate's entire transferable interest in the partnership, but not merely by reason of the substitution of a successor personal representative; or

(10) termination of a partner who is not an individual, partnership, corporation, trust, or estate.

Comment

1. RUPA dramatically changes the law governing partnership breakups and dissolution. An entirely new concept, "dissociation," is used in lieu of the UPA term "dissolution" to denote the change in the relationship caused by a partner's ceasing to be associated in the carrying on of the business. "Dissolution" is retained but with a different meaning. See Section 802. The entity theory of partnership provides a conceptual basis for continuing the firm itself despite a partner's withdrawal from the firm.

Under RUPA, unlike the UPA, the dissociation of a partner does not necessarily cause a dissolution and winding up of the business of the partnership. Section 801 identifies the situations in which the dissociation of a partner causes a winding up of the business. Section 701 provides that in all other situations there is a buyout of the partner's interest in the partnership, rather than a windup of the partnership business. In those other situations, the partnership entity continues, unaffected by the partner's dissociation.

A dissociated partner remains a partner for some purposes and still has some residual rights, duties, powers, and liabilities. Although Section 601 determines when a partner is dissociated from the partnership, the consequences of the partner's dissociation do not all occur at the same time. Thus, it is more useful to think of a dissociated partner as a partner for some purposes, but as a former partner for others. For example, see Section 403(b) (former partner's access to partnership books and records). The consequences of a partner's dissociation depend on whether the partnership continues or is wound up, as provided in Articles 6, 7, and 8.

Section 601 enumerates all of the events that cause a partner's dissociation. Section 601 is similar in approach to RULPA Section 402, which lists the events resulting in a general partner's withdrawal from a limited partnership.

2. Section 601(1) provides that a partner is dissociated when the partnership has notice of the partner's express will to withdraw as a partner, unless a later date is specified by the partner. If a future date is specified by the partner, other partners may dissociate before that date; specifying a future date does not bind the others to remain as partners until that date. See also Section 801(2)(i).

Section 602(a) provides that a partner has the power to withdraw at any time. The power to withdraw is immutable under Section 103(b)(6), with the exception that the partners may agree the notice must be in writing. This continues the present rule that a partner has the power to withdraw at will, even if not the right. See UPA Section 31(2). Since no writing is required to create a partner relationship, it was felt unnecessarily formalistic, and a trap for the unwary, to require a writing to end one. If a written notification is given, Section 102(d) clarifies when it is deemed received.

RUPA continues the UPA "express will" concept, thus preserving existing case law. Section 601(1) clarifies existing law by providing that the partnership must have notice of the partner's expression of will before the dissociation is effective. See Section 102(b) for the meaning of "notice."

3. Section 601(2) provides expressly that a partner is dissociated upon an event agreed to in the partnership agreement as causing dissociation. There is no such provision in the UPA, but that result has been assumed.

4. Section 601(3) provides that a partner may be expelled by the other partners pursuant to a power of expulsion contained in the partnership agreement. That continues the basic rule of UPA Section 31(1)(d). The expulsion can be with or without cause. As under existing law, the obligation of good faith under Section 404(d) does not require prior notice, specification of cause, or an opportunity to be heard. *See Holman v. Coie*, 11 Wash. App. 195, 522 P.2d 515, *cert. denied*, 420 U.S. 984 (1974).

5. Section 601(4) empowers the partners, by unanimous vote, to expel a partner for specified causes, even if not authorized in the partnership agreement. This changes the UPA Section 31(1)(d) rule that authorizes expulsion only if provided in the partnership agreement. A partner may be expelled from a term partnership, as well as from a partnership at will. Under Section 103(a), the partnership agreement may change or abolish the partners' power of expulsion.

Subsection (4)(i) is derived from UPA Section 31(3). A partner may be expelled if it is unlawful to carry on the business with that partner. Section 801(4), on the other hand, provides that the partnership itself is dissolved and must be wound up if substantially all of the business is unlawful.

Subsection (4)(ii) provides that a partner may be expelled for transferring substantially all of his transferable interest in the partnership, other than as security for a loan. (He may, however, be expelled upon foreclosure.) This rule is derived from UPA Section 31(1)(c). To avoid the presence of an unwelcome transferee, the remaining partners may dissolve the partnership under Section 801(2)(ii), after first expelling the transferor partner. A transfer of a partner's entire interest may, in some circumstances, evidence the transferor's intention to withdraw under Section 601(1).

Subsection (4)(iii) provides for the expulsion of a corporate partner if it has filed a certificate of dissolution, its charter has been revoked, or its right to conduct business has been suspended, unless cured within 90 days after notice. This provision is derived from RULPA Section 402(9). The cure proviso is important because charter revocation is very common in some States and partner status should not end merely because of a technical noncompliance with corporate law that can easily be cured. Withdrawal of a voluntarily filed notice of dissolution constitutes a cure.

Subsection (4)(iv) is the partnership analogue of paragraph (iii) and is suggested by RULPA Section 402(8). It provides that a partnership that is a partner may be expelled if it has been dissolved and its business is being wound up. It is intended that the right of expulsion not be triggered solely by the dissolution event, but only upon commencement of the liquidation process.

6. Section 601(5) empowers a court to expel a partner if it determines that the partner has engaged in specified misconduct. The enumerated grounds for judicial expulsion are based on the UPA Section 32(1) grounds for judicial dissolution. The application for expulsion may be brought by the partnership or any partner. The phrase "judicial determination" is intended to include an arbitration award, as well as any final court order or decree.

Subsection (5)(i) provides for the partner's expulsion if the court finds that the partner has engaged in wrongful conduct that adversely and materially affected the partnership business. That language is derived from UPA Section 32(1)(c).

Subsection (5)(ii) provides for expulsion if the court determines that the partner willfully or persistently committed a material breach of the partnership agreement or of a duty owed to the partnership or to the other partners under Section 404. That would include a partner's breach of fiduciary duty. Paragraph (ii), together with paragraph (iii), carry forward the substance of UPA Section 32(1)(d).

Subsection (5)(iii) provides for judicial expulsion of a partner who engaged in conduct relating to the partnership business that makes it not reasonably practicable to carry on the business in partnership with that partner. Expulsion for such misconduct makes the partner's dissociation wrongful under Section 602(a)(ii) and may also support a judicial decree of dissolution under Section 801(5)(ii).

7. Section 601(6) provides that a partner is dissociated upon becoming a debtor in bankruptcy or upon taking or suffering other action evidencing the partner's insolvency or lack of financial responsibility.

Subsection (6)(i) is derived from UPA Section 31(5), which provides for dissolution upon a partner's bankruptcy. *Accord* RULPA § 402(4)(ii). There is some doubt as to whether UPA Section 31(1) is limited to so-called "straight bankruptcy" under Chapter 7 or includes other bankruptcy relief, such as Chapter 11. Under RUPA Section 101(2), however, "debtor in bankruptcy" includes a person who files a voluntary petition, or against whom relief is ordered in an involuntary case, under any chapter of the Bankruptcy Code.

Initially, upon the filing of the bankruptcy petition, the debtor partner's transferable interest in the partnership will pass to the bankruptcy trustee as property of the estate under Section 541(a)(1) of the Bankruptcy Code, notwithstanding any restrictions on transfer provided in the partnership agreement. In most Chapter 7 cases, that will result in the eventual buyout of the partner's interest.

The application of various provisions of the federal Bankruptcy Code to Section 601(6)(i) is unclear. In particular, there is uncertainty as to the validity of UPA Section 31(5), and thus its RUPA counterpart, under Sections 365(e) and 541(c)(1) of the Bankruptcy Code. Those sections generally invalidate so-called *ipso facto* laws that cause a termination or modification of the debtor's contract or property rights because of the bankruptcy filing. As a consequence, RUPA Section 601(6)(i), which provides for a partner's dissociation by operation of law upon becoming a debtor in bankruptcy, may be invalid under the Supremacy Clause. *See, e.g., In the Matter of Phillips*, 966 F.2d 926 (5th Cir. 1992); *In re Cardinal Industries, Inc.*, 105 B.R. 385 (Bankr. S.D. Ohio 1989), 116 B.R. 964 (Bankr. S.D. Ohio 1990); *In re Corky Foods Corp.*, 85 B.R. 903 (Bankr. S.D. Fla. 1988). *But see, In re Catron*, 158 B.R. 629 (E.D. Va. 1993) (partnership agreement could not be assumed by debtor under Bankruptcy Code § 365(c)(1) because other partners excused by UPA from accepting performance by or rendering performance to party other than debtor and buyout option not invalid *ipso facto* clause under Code § 365 (e)), *aff'd per curiam*, 25 F.3d 1038 (4th Cir. 1994). RUPA reflects the policy choice, as a matter of state partnership law, that a partner be dissociated upon becoming a debtor in bankruptcy.

Subsection (6)(ii) is new and provides for dissociation upon a general assignment for the benefit of a partner's creditors. The UPA says nothing about an assignment for the benefit of creditors or the appointment of a trustee, receiver, or liquidator. Subsection (6)(iii) and (iv) cover the latter and are based substantially on RULPA Section 402(4) and (5).

8. UPA Section 31(4) provides for the dissolution of a partnership upon the death of any partner, although by agreement the remaining partners may continue the partnership business. RUPA Section 601(7)(i), on the other hand, provides for dissociation upon the death of a partner who is an individual, rather than dissolution of the partnership. That changes existing law, except in those States previously adopting a similar non-uniform provision, such as California, Georgia, and Texas. Normally, under RUPA, the deceased partner's transferable interest in the partnership will pass to his estate and be bought out under Article 7.

Section 601(7)(ii) replaces UPA Section 32(1)(a) and provides for dissociation upon the appointment of a guardian or general conservator for partner who is an individual. The appointment itself operates as the event of dissociation, and no further order of the court is necessary.

Section 601(7)(iii) is based on UPA Section 32(1)(b) and provides for dissociation upon a judicial determination that an individual partner has in any other way become incapable of performing his duties under the partnership agreement. The intent is to include physical incapacity.

9. Section 601(8) is new and provides for the dissociation of a partner that is a trust, or is acting as a partner by virtue of being a trustee of a trust, upon the distribution by the trust of its entire transferable interest in the partnership, but not merely upon the substitution of a successor trustee. The provision is inspired by RULPA Section 402(7).

10. Section 601(9) is new and provides for the dissociation of a partner that is an estate, or is acting as a partner by virtue of being a personal representative of an estate, upon the distribution of the estate's entire transferable interest in the partnership, but not merely the substitution of a successor personal representative. It is based on RULPA Section 402(10). Under Section 601(7), a partner is dissociated upon death, however, and the estate normally becomes a transferee, not a partner.

11. Section 601(10) is new and provides that a partner that is not an individual, partnership, corporation, trust, or estate is dissociated upon its termination. It is the comparable "death" analogue for other types of entity partners, such as a limited liability company.

§ 602. Partner's Power to Dissociate; Wrongful Dissociation

(a) A partner has the power to dissociate at any time, rightfully or wrongfully, by express will pursuant to Section 601(1).

(b) A partner's dissociation is wrongful only if:

(1) it is in breach of an express provision of the partnership agreement; or

(2) in the case of a partnership for a definite term or particular undertaking, before the expiration of the term or the completion of the undertaking:

(i) the partner withdraws by express will, unless the withdrawal follows within 90 days after another partner's dissociation by death or otherwise under Section 601(6) through (10) or wrongful dissociation under this subsection;

(ii) the partner is expelled by judicial determination under Section 601(5);

(iii) the partner is dissociated by becoming a debtor in bankruptcy; or

(iv) in the case of a partner who is not an individual, trust other than a business trust, or estate, the partner is expelled or otherwise dissociated because it willfully dissolved or terminated.

(c) A partner who wrongfully dissociates is liable to the partnership and to the other partners for damages caused by the dissociation. The liability is in addition to any other obligation of the partner to the partnership or to the other partners.

Comment

1. Subsection (a) states explicitly what is implicit in UPA Section 31(2) and RUPA Section 601(1)—that a partner has the power to dissociate at any time by expressing a will to withdraw, even in contravention of the partnership agreement. The phrase "rightfully or wrongfully" reflects the distinction between a partner's power to withdraw in contravention of the partnership agreement and a partner's right to do so. In this context, although a partner can not be enjoined from exercising the power to dissociate, the dissociation may be wrongful under subsection (b).

2. Subsection (b) provides that a partner's dissociation is wrongful only if it results from one of the enumerated events. The significance of a wrongful dissociation is that it may give rise to damages under subsection (c) and, if it results in the dissolution of the partnership, the wrongfully dissociating partner is not entitled to participate in winding up the business under Section 804.

Under subsection (b), a partner's dissociation is wrongful if (1) it breaches an express provision of the partnership agreement or (2), in a term partnership, before the expiration of the term or the completion of the undertaking (i) the partner voluntarily withdraws by express will, except a withdrawal following another partner's wrongful dissociation or dissociation by death or otherwise under Section 601(6) through (10); (ii) the partner is expelled for misconduct under Section 601(5); (iii) the partner becomes a debtor in bankruptcy (see Section 101(2)); or (iv) a partner that is an entity (other than a trust or estate) is expelled or otherwise dissociated because its dissolution or termination was willful. Since subsection (b) is merely a default rule, the partnership agreement may eliminate or expand the dissociations that are wrongful or modify the effects of wrongful dissociation.

The exception in subsection (b)(2)(i) is intended to protect a partner's reactive withdrawal from a term partnership after the premature departure of another partner, such as the partnership's rainmaker or main supplier of capital, under the same circumstances that may result in the dissolution of the partnership under Section 801(2)(i). Under that section, a term partnership is dissolved 90 days after the bankruptcy, incapacity, death (or similar dissociation of a partner that is an entity), or wrongful dissociation of any partner, unless a majority in interest (see Comment 5(i) to Section 801 for a discussion of the term "majority in interest") of the remaining partners agree to continue the partnership. Under Section 602(b)(2)(i), a partner's exercise of the right of withdrawal by express will under those circumstances is rendered "rightful," even if the partnership is continued by others, and does not expose the withdrawing partner to damages for wrongful dissociation under Section 602(c).

A partner wishing to withdraw prematurely from a term partnership for any other reason, such as another partner's misconduct, can avoid being treated as a wrongfully dissociating partner by applying to a court under Section 601(5)(iii) to have the offending partner expelled. Then, the partnership could be dissolved under Section 801(2)(i) or the remaining partners could, by unanimous vote, dissolve the partnership under Section 801(2)(ii).

3. Subsection (c) provides that a wrongfully dissociating partner is liable to the partnership and to the other partners for any damages caused by the wrongful nature of the dissociation. That liability is in addition to any other obligation of the partner to the partnership or to the other partners. For example, the partner would be liable for any damage caused by breach of the partnership agreement or other misconduct. The partnership might also incur substantial expenses resulting from a partner's premature withdrawal from a term partnership, such as replacing the partner's expertise or obtaining new financing. The wrongfully dissociating partner would be liable to the partnership for those and all other expenses and damages that are causally related to the wrongful dissociation.

Section 701(c) provides that any damages for wrongful dissociation may be offset against the amount of the buyout price due to the partner under Section 701(a), and Section 701(h) provides that a partner who wrongfully dissociates from a term partnership is not entitled to payment of the buyout price until the term expires.

Under UPA Section 38(2)(c)(II), in addition to an offset for damages, the goodwill value of the partnership is excluded in determining the value of a wrongfully dissociating partner's partnership interest. Under RUPA, however, unless the partnership's goodwill is damaged by the wrongful dissociation, the value of the wrongfully dissociating partner's interest will include any goodwill value of the partnership. If the firm's goodwill is damaged, the amount of the damages suffered by the partnership and the remaining partners will be offset against the buyout price. See Section 701 and Comments.

§ 603. Effect of Partner's Dissociation

(a) If a partner's dissociation results in a dissolution and winding up of the partnership business, Article 8 applies; otherwise, Article 7 applies.

(b) Upon a partner's dissociation:

(1) the partner's right to participate in the management and conduct of the partnership business terminates, except as otherwise provided in Section 803;

(2) the partner's duty of loyalty under Section 404(b)(3) terminates; and

(3) the partner's duty of loyalty under Section 404(b)(1) and (2) and duty of care under Section 404(c) continue only with regard to matters arising and events occurring before the partner's dissociation, unless the partner participates in winding up the partnership's business pursuant to Section 803.

Comment

1. Section 603(a) is a "switching" provision. It provides that, after a partner's dissociation, the partner's interest in the partnership must be purchased pursuant to the buyout rules in Article 7 unless there is a dissolution and winding up of the partnership business under Article 8. Thus, a partner's dissociation will always result in either a buyout of the dissociated partner's interest or a dissolution and winding up of the business.

By contrast, under the UPA, every partner dissociation results in the dissolution of the partnership, most of which trigger a right to have the business wound up unless the partnership agreement provides otherwise. *See* UPA § 38. The only exception in which the remaining partners have a statutory right to continue the business is when a partner wrongfully dissolves the partnership in breach of the partnership agreement. *See* UPA § 38(2)(b).

2. Section 603(b) is new and deals with some of the internal effects of a partner's dissociation. Subsection (b)(1) makes it clear that one of the consequences of a partner's dissociation is the immediate loss of the right to participate in the management of the business, unless it results in a dissolution and winding up of the business. In that case, Section 804(a) provides that all of the partners who have not wrongfully dissociated may participate in winding up the business.

Subsection (b)(2) and (3) clarify a partner's fiduciary duties upon dissociation. No change from current law is intended. With respect to the duty of loyalty, the Section 404(b)(3) duty not to compete terminates upon dissociation, and the dissociated partner is free immediately to engage in a competitive business, without any further consent. With respect to the partner's remaining loyalty duties under Section 404(b) and duty of care under Section 404(c), a withdrawing partner has a continuing duty after dissociation, but it is limited to matters that arose or events that occurred before the partner dissociated. For example, a partner who leaves a brokerage firm may immediately compete with the firm for new clients, but must exercise care in completing on-going client transactions and must account to the firm for any fees received from the old clients on account of those transactions. As the last clause makes clear, there is no contraction of a dissociated partner's duties under subsection (b)(3) if the partner thereafter participates in the dissolution and winding up the partnership's business.

Article 7

PARTNER'S DISSOCIATION WHEN BUSINESS NOT WOUND UP

§ 701. Purchase of Dissociated Partner's Interest

(a) If a partner is dissociated from a partnership without resulting in a dissolution and winding up of the partnership business under Section 801, the partnership shall cause the dissociated partner's interest in the partnership to be purchased for a buyout price determined pursuant to subsection (b).

(b) The buyout price of a dissociated partner's interest is the amount that would have been distributable to the dissociating partner under Section 807(b) if, on the date of dissociation, the assets of the partnership were sold at a price equal to the greater of the liquidation value or the value based on a sale of the entire business as a going concern without the dissociated partner and the partnership were wound up as of that date. Interest must be paid from the date of dissociation to the date of payment.

(c) Damages for wrongful dissociation under Section 602(b), and all other amounts owing, whether or not presently due, from the dissociated partner to the partnership, must be offset against the buyout price. Interest must be paid from the date the amount owed becomes due to the date of payment.

(d) A partnership shall indemnify a dissociated partner whose interest is being purchased against all partnership liabilities, whether incurred before or after the dissociation, except liabilities incurred by an act of the dissociated partner under Section 702.

(e) If no agreement for the purchase of a dissociated partner's interest is reached within 120 days after a written demand for payment, the partnership shall pay, or cause to be paid, in cash to the dissociated partner the amount the partnership estimates to be the buyout price and accrued interest, reduced by any offsets and accrued interest under subsection (c).

(f) If a deferred payment is authorized under subsection (h), the partnership may tender a written offer to pay the amount it estimates to be the buyout price and accrued interest, reduced by any offsets under subsection (c), stating the time of payment, the amount and type of security for payment, and the other terms and conditions of the obligation.

(g) The payment or tender required by subsection (e) or (f) must be accompanied by the following:

(1) a statement of partnership assets and liabilities as of the date of dissociation;

(2) the latest available partnership balance sheet and income statement, if any;

(3) an explanation of how the estimated amount of the payment was calculated; and

(4) written notice that the payment is in full satisfaction of the obligation to purchase unless, within 120 days after the written notice, the dissociated partner commences an action to determine the buyout price, any offsets under subsection (c), or other terms of the obligation to purchase.

(h) A partner who wrongfully dissociates before the expiration of a definite term or the completion of a particular undertaking is not entitled to payment of any portion of the buyout price until the expiration of the term or completion of the undertaking, unless the partner establishes to the satisfaction of the court that earlier payment will not cause undue hardship to the business of the partnership. A deferred payment must be adequately secured and bear interest.

(i) A dissociated partner may maintain an action against the partnership, pursuant to Section 405(b)(2)(ii), to determine the buyout price of that partner's interest, any offsets under subsection (c), or other terms of the obligation to purchase. The action must be commenced within 120 days after the partnership has tendered payment or an offer to pay or within one year after written demand for payment if no payment or offer to pay is tendered. The court shall determine the buyout price of the dissociated partner's interest, any offset due under subsection (c), and accrued interest, and enter judgment for any additional payment or refund. If deferred payment is authorized under subsection (h), the court shall also determine the security for payment and other terms of the obligation to purchase. The court may assess reasonable attorney's fees and the fees and expenses of appraisers or other experts for a party to the action, in amounts the court finds equitable, against a party that the court finds acted arbitrarily, vexatiously, or not in good faith. The finding may be based on the partnership's failure to tender payment or an offer to pay or to comply with subsection (g).

Comment

1. Article 7 is new and provides for the buyout of a dissociated partner's interest in the partnership when the partner's dissociation does not result in a dissolution and winding up of its business under Article 8. *See* Section 603(a). If there is no dissolution, the remaining partners have a right to continue the business and the dissociated partner has a right to be paid the value of his partnership interest. These rights can, of course, be varied in the partnership agreement. *See*

Section 103. A dissociated partner has a continuing relationship with the partnership and third parties as provided in Sections 603(b), 702, and 703. See also Section 403(b) (former partner's access to partnership books and records).

2. Subsection (a) provides that, if a partner's dissociation does not result in a windup of the business, the partnership shall cause the interest of the dissociating partner to be purchased for a buyout price determined pursuant to subsection (b). The buyout is mandatory. The "cause to be purchased" language is intended to accommodate a purchase by the partnership, one or more of the remaining partners, or a third party.

For federal income tax purposes, a payment to a partner for his interest can be characterized either as a purchase of the partner's interest or as a liquidating distribution. The two have different tax consequences. RUPA permits either option by providing that the payment may come from either the partnership, some or all of the continuing partners, or a third party purchaser.

3. Subsection (b) provides how the "buyout price" is to be determined. The terms "fair market value" or "fair value" were not used because they are often considered terms of art having a special meaning depending on the context, such as in tax or corporate law. "Buyout price" is a new term. It is intended that the term be developed as an independent concept appropriate to the partnership buyout situation, while drawing on valuation principles developed elsewhere.

Under subsection (b), the buyout price is the amount that would have been distributable to the dissociating partner under Section 807(b) if, on the date of dissociation, the assets of the partnership were sold at a price equal to the greater of liquidation value or going concern value without the departing partner. Liquidation value is not intended to mean distress sale value. Under general principles of valuation, the hypothetical selling price in either case should be the price that a willing and informed buyer would pay a willing and informed seller, with neither being under any compulsion to deal. The notion of a minority discount in determining the buyout price is negated by valuing the business as a going concern. Other discounts, such as for a lack of marketability or the loss of a key partner, may be appropriate, however.

Since the buyout price is based on the value of the business at the time of dissociation, the partnership must pay interest on the amount due from the date of dissociation until payment to compensate the dissociating partner for the use of his interest in the firm. Section 104(b) provides that interest shall be at the legal rate unless otherwise provided in the partnership agreement. The UPA Section 42 option of electing a share of the profits in lieu of interest has been eliminated.

UPA Section 38(2)(c)(II) provides that the good will of the business not be considered in valuing a wrongfully dissociating partner's interest.

The forfeiture of good will rule is implicitly rejected by RUPA. See Section 602(c) and Comment 3.

The Section 701 rules are merely default rules. The partners may, in the partnership agreement, fix the method or formula for determining the buyout price and all of the other terms and conditions of the buyout right. Indeed, the very right to a buyout itself may be modified, although a provision providing for a complete forfeiture would probably not be enforceable. *See* Section 104(a).

4. Subsection (c) provides that the partnership may offset against the buyout price all amounts owing by the dissociated partner to the partnership, whether or not presently due, including any damages for wrongful dissociation under Section 602(c). This has the effect of accelerating payment of amounts not yet due from the departing partner to the partnership, including a long-term loan by the partnership to the dissociated partner. Where appropriate, the amounts not yet due should be discounted to present value. A dissociating partner, on the other hand, is not entitled to an add-on for amounts owing to him by the partnership. Thus, a departing partner who has made a long-term loan to the partnership must wait for repayment, unless the terms of the loan agreement provide for acceleration upon dissociation.

It is not intended that the partnership's right of setoff be construed to limit the amount of the damages for the partner's wrongful dissociation and any other amounts owing to the partnership to the value of the dissociated partner's interest. Those amounts may result in a net sum due to the partnership from the dissociated partner.

5. Subsection (d) follows the UPA Section 38 rule and provides that the partnership must indemnify a dissociated partner against all partnership liabilities, whether incurred before or after the dissociation, except those incurred by the dissociated partner under Section 702.

6. Subsection (e) provides that, if no agreement for the purchase of the dissociated partner's interest is reached within 120 days after the dissociated partner's written demand for payment, the partnership must pay, or cause to be paid, in cash the amount it estimates to be the buyout price, adjusted for any offsets allowed and accrued interest. Thus, the dissociating partner will receive in cash within 120 days of dissociation the undisputed minimum value of the partner's partnership interest. If the dissociated partner claims that the buyout price should be higher, suit may thereafter be brought as provided in subsection (i) to have the amount of the buyout price determined by the court. This is similar to the procedure for determining the value of dissenting shareholders' shares under RMBCA Sections 13.20–13.28.

The "cause to be paid" language of subsection (a) is repeated here to permit either the partnership, one or more of the continuing partners, or a third-party purchaser to tender payment of the estimated amount due.

7. Subsection (f) provides that, when deferred payment is authorized in the case of a wrongfully dissociating partner, a written offer stating the amount the partnership estimates to be the purchase price should be tendered within the 120–day period, even though actual payment of the amount may be deferred, possibly for many years. See Comment 8. The dissociated partner is entitled to know at the time of dissociation what amount the remaining partners think is due, including the estimated amount of any damages allegedly caused by the partner's wrongful dissociation that may be offset against the buyout price.

8. Subsection (g) provides that the payment of the estimated price (or tender of a written offer under subsection (f)) by the partnership must be accompanied by (1) a statement of the partnership's assets and liabilities as of the date of the partner's dissociation; (2) the latest available balance sheet and income statement, if the partnership maintains such financial statements; (3) an explanation of how the estimated amount of the payment was calculated; and (4) a written notice that the payment will be in full satisfaction of the partnership's buyout obligation unless the dissociated partner commences an action to determine the price within 120 days of the notice. Subsection (g) is based in part on the dissenters' rights provisions of RMBCA Section 13.25(b).

Those disclosures should serve to identify and narrow substantially the items of dispute between the dissociated partner and the partnership over the valuation of the partnership interest. They will also serve to pin down the parties as to their claims of partnership assets and values and as to the existence and amount of all known liabilities. See Comment 4. Lastly, it will force the remaining partners to consider thoughtfully the difficult and important questions as to the appropriate method of valuation under the circumstances, and in particular, whether they should use going concern or liquidation value. Simply getting that information on the record in a timely fashion should increase the likelihood of a negotiated resolution of the parties' differences during the 120–day period within which the dissociated partner must bring suit.

9. Subsection (h) replaces UPA Section 38(2)(c) and provides a somewhat different rule for payment to a partner whose dissociation before the expiration of a definite term or the completion of a particular undertaking is wrongful under Section 602(b). Under subsection (h), a wrongfully dissociating partner is not entitled to receive any portion of the buyout price before the expiration of the term or completion of the undertaking, unless the dissociated partner establishes to the satisfaction of the court that earlier payment will not cause undue hardship to the business of the partnership. In all other cases, there must be an immediate payment in cash.

10. Subsection (i) provides that a dissociated partner may maintain an action against the partnership to determine the buyout price, any offsets, or other terms of the purchase obligation. The action must be commenced within 120 days after the partnership tenders payment of

the amount it estimates to be due or, if deferred payment is authorized, its written offer. This provision creates a 120–day "cooling off" period. It also allows the parties an opportunity to negotiate their differences after disclosure by the partnership of its financial statements and other required information.

If the partnership fails to tender payment of the estimated amount due (or a written offer, if deferred payment is authorized), the dissociated partner has one year after written demand for payment in which to commence suit.

If the parties fail to reach agreement, the court must determine the buyout price of the partner's interest, any offsets, including damages for wrongful dissociation, and the amount of interest accrued. If payment to a wrongfully dissociated partner is deferred, the court may also require security for payment and determine the other terms of the obligation.

Under subsection (i), attorney's fees and other costs may be assessed against any party found to have acted arbitrarily, vexatiously, or not in good faith in connection with the valuation dispute, including the partnership's failure to tender payment of the estimated price or to make the required disclosures. This provision is based in part on RMBCA Section 13.31(b).

§ 702. Dissociated Partner's Power to Bind and Liability to Partnership

(a) For two years after a partner dissociates without resulting in a dissolution and winding up of the partnership business, the partnership, including a surviving partnership under Article 9, is bound by an act of the dissociated partner which would have bound the partnership under Section 301 before dissociation only if at the time of entering into the transaction the other party:

(1) reasonably believed that the dissociated partner was then a partner;

(2) did not have notice of the partner's dissociation; and

(3) is not deemed to have had knowledge under Section 303(e) or notice under Section 704(c).

(b) A dissociated partner is liable to the partnership for any damage caused to the partnership arising from an obligation incurred by the dissociated partner after dissociation for which the partnership is liable under subsection (a).

Comment

1. Section 702 deals with a dissociated partner's lingering apparent authority to bind the partnership in ordinary course partnership transactions and the partner's liability to the partnership for any loss caused thereby. It also applies to partners who withdraw incident to a merger under Article 9. *See* Section 906(e).

A dissociated partner has no actual authority to act for the partnership. *See* Section 603(b)(1). Nevertheless, in order to protect innocent third parties, Section 702(a) provides that the partnership remains bound, for two years after a partner's dissociation, by that partner's acts that would, before his dissociation, have bound the partnership under Section 301 if, and only if, the other party to the transaction reasonably believed that he was still a partner, did not have notice of the partner's dissociation, and is not deemed to have had knowledge of the dissociation under Section 303(e) or notice thereof under Section 704(c).

Under Section 301, every partner has apparent authority to bind the partnership by any act for carrying on the partnership business in the ordinary course, unless the other party knows that the partner has no actual authority to act for the partnership or has received a notification of the partner's lack of authority. Section 702(a) continues that general rule for two years after a partner's dissociation, subject to three modifications.

After a partner's dissociation, the general rule is modified, first, by requiring the other party to show reasonable reliance on the partner's status as a partner. Section 301 has no explicit reliance requirement, although the partnership is bound only if the partner purports to act on its behalf. Thus, the other party will normally be aware of the partnership and presumably the partner's status as such.

The second modification is that, under Section 702(a), the partnership is not bound if the third party has notice of the partner's dissociation, while under the general rule of Section 301 the partnership is bound unless the third party knows of the partner's lack of authority. Under Section 102(b), a person has "notice" of a fact if he knows or has reason to know it exists from all the facts that are known to him or he has received a notification of it. Thus, the partnership may protect itself by sending a notification of the dissociation to a third party, and a third party may, in any event, have a duty to inquire further based on what is known. That provides the partnership with greater protection from the unauthorized acts of a dissociated partner than from those of partners generally.

The third modification of the general apparent authority rule under Section 702(a) involves the effect of a statement of dissociation. Section 704(c) provides that, for the purposes of Sections 702(a)(3) and 703(b)(3), third parties are deemed to have notice of a partner's dissociation 90 days after the filing of a statement of dissociation. Thus, the filing of a statement operates as constructive notice of the dissociated partner's lack of authority after 90 days, conclusively terminating the dissociated partner's Section 702 apparent authority.

With respect to a dissociated partner's authority to transfer partnership real property, Section 303(e) provides that third parties are deemed to have knowledge of a limitation on a partner's authority to transfer real property held in the partnership name upon the proper recording of a statement containing such a limitation. Section 704(b) provides that a statement of dissociation operates as a limitation on the dissociated partner's authority for the purposes of Section 303(e). Thus, a properly recorded statement of dissociation operates as constructive knowledge of a dissociated partner's lack of authority to transfer real property held in the partnership name, effective immediately upon recording.

Under RUPA, therefore, a partnership should notify all known creditors of a partner's dissociation and may, by filing a statement of dissociation, conclusively limit to 90 days a dissociated partner's lingering agency power. Moreover, under Section 703(b), a dissociated partner's lingering liability for post-dissociation partnership liabilities may be limited to 90 days by filing a statement of dissociation. These incentives should encourage both partnerships and dissociating partners to file statements routinely. Those transacting substantial business with partnerships can protect themselves from the risk of dealing with dissociated partners, or relying on their credit, by checking the partnership records at least every 90 days.

2. Section 702(b) is a corollary to subsection (a) and provides that a dissociated partner is liable to the partnership for any loss resulting from an obligation improperly incurred by the partner under subsection (a). In effect, the dissociated partner must indemnify the partnership for any loss, meaning a loss net of any gain from the transaction. The dissociated partner is also personally liable to the third party for the unauthorized obligation.

§ 703. Dissociated Partner's Liability to Other Persons

(a) A partner's dissociation does not of itself discharge the partner's liability for a partnership obligation incurred before dissociation. A dissociated partner is not liable for a partnership obligation incurred after dissociation, except as otherwise provided in subsection (b).

(b) A partner who dissociates without resulting in a dissolution and winding up of the partnership business is liable as a partner to the other party in a transaction entered into by the partnership, or a surviving partnership under Article 9, within two years after the partner's dissociation, only if the partner is liable for the obligation under Section 306 and at the time of entering into the transaction the other party:

(1) reasonably believed that the dissociated partner was then a partner;

(2) did not have notice of the partner's dissociation; and

(3) is not deemed to have had knowledge under Section 303(e) or notice under Section 704(c).

(c) By agreement with the partnership creditor and the partners continuing the business, a dissociated partner may be released from liability for a partnership obligation.

(d) A dissociated partner is released from liability for a partnership obligation if a partnership creditor, with notice of the partner's dissociation but without the partner's consent, agrees to a material alteration in the nature or time of payment of a partnership obligation.

Comment

Section 703(a) is based on UPA Section 36(1) and continues the basic rule that the departure of a partner does not of itself discharge the partner's liability to third parties for any partnership obligation incurred before dissociation. The word "obligation" is used instead of "liability" and is intended to include broadly both tort and contract liability incurred before dissociation. The second sentence states affirmatively that a dissociating partner is not liable for any partnership obligation incurred after dissociation except as expressly provided in subsection (b).

Section 703(b) is new and deals with the problem of protecting third parties who extend credit to the partnership after a partner's dissociation, believing that he is still a partner. It provides that the dissociated partner remains liable as a partner for transactions entered into by the partnership within two years after departure, if the other party does not have notice of the partner's dissociation and reasonably believes when entering the transaction that the dissociated partner is still a partner. The dissociated partner is not personally liable, however, if the other party is deemed to know of the dissociation under Section 303(e) or to have notice thereof under Section 704(c). Also, a dissociated partner is not personally liable for limited liability partnership obligations for which the partner is not personally liable under Section 306.

Section 703(b) operates similarly to Section 702(a) in that it requires reliance on the departed partner's continued partnership status, as well as lack of notice. Under Section 704(c), a statement of dissociation operates conclusively as constructive notice 90 days after filing for the purposes of Section 703(b)(3) and, under Section 704(b), as constructive knowledge when recorded for the purposes of Section 303(d) and (e).

Section 703(c) continues the rule of UPA Section 36(2) that a departing partner can bargain for a contractual release from personal liability for a partnership obligation, but it requires the consent of both the creditor and the remaining partners.

Section 703(d) continues the rule of UPA Section 36(3) that a dissociated partner is released from liability for a partnership obligation if the creditor, with notice of the partner's departure, agrees to a material alteration in the nature or time of payment, without that partner's consent. This rule covers all partner dissociations and is not limited, as is the UPA rule, to situations in which a third party "agrees to assume the existing obligations of a dissolved partnership."

In general under RUPA, as a result of the adoption of the entity theory, relationships between a partnership and its creditors are not affected by the dissociation of a partner or by the addition of a new partner, unless otherwise agreed. Therefore, there is no need under RUPA, as there is under the UPA, for an elaborate provision deeming the new partnership to assume the liabilities of the old partnership. See UPA Section 41.

The "dual priority" rule in UPA Section 36(4) is eliminated to reflect the abolition of the "jingle rule," providing that separate debts have first claim on separate property, in order to conform to the Bankruptcy Code. See Comment 2 to Section 807. A deceased partner's estate, and thus all of his individual property, remains liable for partnership obligations incurred while he was a partner, however.

§ 704. Statement of Dissociation

(a) A dissociated partner or the partnership may file a statement of dissociation stating the name of the partnership and that the partner is dissociated from the partnership.

(b) A statement of dissociation is a limitation on the authority of a dissociated partner for the purposes of Section 303(d) and (e).

(c) For the purposes of Sections 702(a)(3) and 703(b)(3), a person not a partner is deemed to have notice of the dissociation 90 days after the statement of dissociation is filed.

Comment

Section 704 is new and provides for a statement of dissociation and its effects. Subsection (a) authorizes either a dissociated partner or the partnership to file a statement of dissociation. Like other RUPA filings, the statement of dissociation is voluntary. Both the partnership and the departing partner have an incentive to file, however, and it is anticipated that those filings will become routine upon a partner's dissociation. The execution, filing, and recording of the statement is governed by Section 105.

Filing or recording a statement of dissociation has threefold significance:

(1) It is a statement of limitation on the dissociated partner's authority to the extent provided in Section 303(d) and (e). Under Section 303(d), a filed or recorded limitation on the authority of a partner destroys the conclusive effect of a prior grant of authority to the extent it contradicts the prior grant. Under Section 303(e), nonpartners are conclusively bound by a limitation on the authority of a partner to transfer real property held in the partnership name, if the statement is properly recorded in the real property records.

(2) Ninety days after the statement is filed, nonpartners are deemed to have notice of the dissociation and thus conclusively

bound for purposes of cutting off the partner's apparent authority under Sections 301 and 702(a)(3).

(3) Ninety days after the statement is filed, third parties are conclusively bound for purposes of cutting off the dissociated partner's continuing liability under Section 703(b)(3) for transactions entered into by the partnership after dissociation.

§ 705. Continued Use of Partnership Name

Continued use of a partnership name, or a dissociated partner's name as part thereof, by partners continuing the business does not of itself make the dissociated partner liable for an obligation of the partners or the partnership continuing the business.

Comment

Section 705 is an edited version of UPA Section 41(10) and provides that a dissociated partner is not liable for the debts of the continuing business simply because of continued use of the partnership name or the dissociated partner's name as a part thereof. That prevents forcing the business to forego the good will associated with its name.

Article 8

WINDING UP PARTNERSHIP BUSINESS

§ 801. Events Causing Dissolution and Winding up of Partnership Business

A partnership is dissolved, and its business must be wound up, only upon the occurrence of any of the following events:

(1) in a partnership at will, the partnership's having notice from a partner, other than a partner who is dissociated under Section 601(2) through (10), of that partner's express will to withdraw as a partner, or on a later date specified by the partner;

(2) in a partnership for a definite term or particular undertaking:

(i) within 90 days after a partner's dissociation by death or otherwise under Section 601(6) through (10) or wrongful dissociation under Section 602(b), the express will of at least half of the remaining partners to wind up the partnership business, for which purpose a partner's rightful dissociation pursuant to Section 602(b)(2)(i) constitutes the expression of that partner's will to wind up the partnership business;

(ii) the express will of all of the partners to wind up the partnership business; or

(iii) the expiration of the term or the completion of the undertaking;

(3) an event agreed to in the partnership agreement resulting in the winding up of the partnership business;

(4) an event that makes it unlawful for all or substantially all of the business of the partnership to be continued, but a cure of illegality within 90 days after notice to the partnership of the event is effective retroactively to the date of the event for purposes of this section;

(5) on application by a partner, a judicial determination that:

(i) the economic purpose of the partnership is likely to be unreasonably frustrated;

(ii) another partner has engaged in conduct relating to the partnership business which makes it not reasonably practicable to carry on the business in partnership with that partner; or

(iii) it is not otherwise reasonably practicable to carry on the partnership business in conformity with the partnership agreement; or

(6) on application by a transferee of a partner's transferable interest, a judicial determination that it is equitable to wind up the partnership business:

(i) after the expiration of the term or completion of the undertaking, if the partnership was for a definite term or particular undertaking at the time of the transfer or entry of the charging order that gave rise to the transfer; or

(ii) at any time, if the partnership was a partnership at will at the time of the transfer or entry of the charging order that gave rise to the transfer.

Comment

1. Under UPA Section 29, a partnership is dissolved every time a partner leaves. That reflects the aggregate nature of the partnership under the UPA. Even if the business of the partnership is continued by some of the partners, it is technically a new partnership. The dissolution of the old partnership and creation of a new partnership causes many unnecessary problems.

Under RULPA, limited partnerships dissolve far less readily than do general partnerships under the UPA. A limited partnership does not dissolve on the withdrawal of a limited partner, nor does it necessarily dissolve on the withdrawal of a general partner. *See* RULPA § 801(4).

RUPA's move to the entity theory is driven in part by the need to prevent a technical dissolution or its consequences. Under RUPA, not every partner dissociation causes a dissolution of the partnership. Only certain departures trigger a dissolution. The basic rule is that a partnership is dissolved, and its business must be wound up, only upon the occurrence of one of the events listed in Section 801. All other dissociations result in a buyout of the partner's interest under Article 7 and a continuation of the partnership entity and business by the remaining partners. *See* Section 603(a).

With only three exceptions, the provisions of Section 801 are merely default rules and may by agreement be varied or eliminated as grounds for dissolution. The first exception is dissolution under Section 801(4) resulting from carrying on an illegal business. The other two exceptions cover the power of a court to dissolve a partnership under Section 801(5) on application of a partner and under Section 801(6) on application of a transferee. See Comments 6–8 for further explanation of these provisions.

2. Under RUPA, "dissolution" is merely the commencement of the winding up process. The partnership continues for the limited purpose of winding up the business. In effect, that means the scope of the partnership business contracts to completing work in process and taking such other actions as may be necessary to wind up the business. Winding up the partnership business entails selling its assets, paying its debts, and distributing the net balance, if any, to the partners in cash according to their interests. The partnership entity continues, and the partners are associated in the winding up of the business until winding up is completed. When the winding up is completed, the partnership entity terminates.

3. Section 801 continues two basic rules from the UPA. First, it continues the rule that any member of an at-will partnership has the right to force a liquidation. Second, by negative implication, it continues the rule that the partners who wish to continue the business of a term partnership can not be forced to liquidate the business by a partner who withdraws prematurely in violation of the partnership agreement.

Those rules are gleaned from the separate UPA provisions governing dissolution and its consequences. Under UPA Section 31(1)(b), dissolution is caused by the express will of any partner when no definite term or particular undertaking is specified. UPA Section 38(1) provides that upon dissolution any partner has the right to have the business wound up. That is a default rule and applies only in the absence of an agreement affording the other partners a right to continue the business.

UPA Section 31(2) provides that a term partnership may be dissolved at any time, in contravention of the partnership agreement, by the express will of any partner. In that case, however, UPA Section 38(2)(b) provides that the nonbreaching partners may by unanimous consent continue the business. If the business is continued, they must buy out the breaching partner.

4. Section 801(1) provides that a partnership at will is dissolved and its business must be wound up upon the partnership's having notice

of a partner's express will to withdraw as a partner, unless a later effective date is specified by the partner. A partner at will who has already been dissociated in some other manner, such as a partner who has been expelled, does not thereafter have a right to cause the partnership to be dissolved and its business wound up.

If, after dissolution, none of the partners wants the partnership wound up, Section 802(b) provides that, with the consent of all the partners, including the withdrawing partner, the remaining partners may continue the business. In that event, although there is a technical dissolution of the partnership and, at least in theory, a temporary contraction of the scope of the business, the partnership entity continues and the scope of its business is restored. See Section 802(b) and Comment 2.

5. Section 801(2) provides three ways in which a term partnership may be dissolved before the expiration of the term:

(i) Subsection (2)(i) provides for dissolution after a partner's dissociation by death or otherwise under Section 601(6) to (10) or wrongful dissociation under Section 602(b), if within 90 days after the dissociation at least half of the remaining partners express their will to dissolve the partnership. Thus if a term partnership had six partners and one of the partners dies or wrongfully dissociates before the end of the term, the partnership will, as a result of the dissociation, be dissolved only if three of the remaining five partners affirmatively vote in favor of dissolution within 90 days after the dissociation.* This reactive dissolution of a term partnership protects the remaining partners where the dissociating partner is crucial to the successful continuation of the business. The corresponding UPA Section 38(2)(b) rule requires unanimous consent of the remaining partners to continue the business, thus giving each partner an absolute right to a reactive liquidation. Under UPA 1994, if the partnership is continued by the majority, any dissenting partner who wants to withdraw may do so rightfully under the exception to Section 602(b)(2)(i), in which case his interest in the partnership will be bought out under Article 7. By itself, however, a partner's vote not to continue the business is not necessarily an expression of the partner's will to withdraw, and a dissenting partner may still elect to remain a partner and continue in the business.

* Prior to August 1997, Section 801(2)(i) provided that upon the dissociation of a partner in a term partnership by death or otherwise under Section 601(6) through (10) or wrongful dissociation under 602(b) the partnership would dissolve unless "a majority in interest of the remaining partners (including partners who have rightfully dissociated pursuant to Section 602(b)(2)(i)) agree to continue the partnership." This language was thought to be necessary for a term partnership to lack continuity of life under the Internal Revenue Act tax classification regulations. These regulations were repealed effective January 1, 1997. The current language, approved at the 1997 annual meeting of the National Conference of Commissioners on Uniform State Laws, allows greater continuity in a term partnership than the prior version of this subsection and UPA Section 38(2)(b).

The Section 601 dissociations giving rise to a reactive dissolution are: (6) a partner's bankruptcy or similar financial impairment; (7) a partner's death or incapacity; (8) the distribution by a trust-partner of its entire partnership interest; (9) the distribution by an estate-partner of its entire partnership interest; and (10) the termination of an entity-partner. Any dissociation during the term of the partnership that is wrongful under Section 602(b), including a partner's voluntary withdrawal, expulsion or bankruptcy, also gives rise to a reactive dissolution. Those statutory grounds may be varied by agreement or the reactive dissolution may be abolished entirely.

Under Section 601(6)(i), a partner is dissociated upon becoming a debtor in bankruptcy. The bankruptcy of a partner or of the partnership is not, however, an event of dissolution under Section 801. That is a change from UPA Section 31(5). A partner's bankruptcy does, however, cause dissolution of a term partnership under Section 801(2)(i), unless a majority in interest of the remaining partners thereafter agree to continue the partnership. Affording the other partners the option of buying out the bankrupt partner's interest avoids the necessity of winding up a term partnership every time a partner becomes a debtor in bankruptcy.

Similarly, under Section 801(2)(i), the death of any partner will result in the dissolution of a term partnership, only if at least half of the remaining partners express their will to wind up the partnership's business. If dissolution does occur, the deceased partner's transferable interest in the partnership passes to his estate and must be bought out under Article 7. See Comment 8 to Section 601.

(ii) Section 801(2)(ii) provides that a term partnership may be dissolved and wound up at any time by the express will of all the partners. That is merely an expression of the general rule that the partnership agreement may override the statutory default rules and that the partnership agreement, like any contract, can be amended at any time by unanimous consent.

UPA Section 31(1)(c) provides that a term partnership may be wound up by the express will of all the partners whose transferable interests have not been assigned or charged for a partner's separate debts. That rule reflects the belief that the remaining partners may find transferees very intrusive. This provision has been deleted, however, because the liquidation is easily accomplished under Section 801(2)(ii) by first expelling the transferor partner under Section 601(4)(ii).

(iii) Section 801(2)(iii) is based on UPA Section 31(1)(a) and provides for winding up a term partnership upon the expiration of the term or the completion of the undertaking.

Subsection (2)(iii) must be read in conjunction with Section 406. Under Section 406(a), if the partners continue the business after the expiration of the term or the completion of the undertaking, the partnership will be treated as a partnership at will. Moreover, if the partners continue the business without any settlement or liquidation of the partnership, under Section 406(b) they are presumed to have agreed that the partnership will continue, despite the lack of a formal agreement. The partners may also agree to ratify all acts taken since the end of the partnership's term.

6. Section 801(3) provides for dissolution upon the occurrence of an event specified in the partnership agreement as resulting in the winding up of the partnership business. The partners may, however, agree to continue the business and to ratify all acts taken since dissolution.

7. Section 801(4) continues the basic rule in UPA Section 31(3) and provides for dissolution if it is unlawful to continue the business of the partnership, unless cured. The "all or substantially all" proviso is intended to avoid dissolution for insubstantial or innocent regulatory violations. If the illegality is cured within 90 days after notice to the partnership, it is effective retroactively for purposes of this section. The requirement that an uncured illegal business be wound up cannot be varied in the partnership agreement. *See* Section 103(b)(8).

8. Section 801(5) provides for judicial dissolution on application by a partner. It is based in part on UPA Section 32(1), and the language comes in part from RULPA Section 802. A court may order a partnership dissolved upon a judicial determination that: (i) the economic purpose of the partnership is likely to be unreasonably frustrated; (ii) another partner has engaged in conduct relating to the partnership business which makes it not reasonably practicable to carry on the business in partnership with that partner; or (iii) it is not otherwise reasonably practicable to carry on the partnership business in conformity with the partnership agreement. The court's power to wind up the partnership under Section 801(5) cannot be varied in the partnership agreement. *See* Section 103(b)(8).

RUPA deletes UPA Section 32(1)(e) which provides for dissolution when the business can only be carried on at a loss. That provision might result in a dissolution contrary to the partners' expectations in a start-up or tax shelter situation, in which case "book" or "tax" losses do not signify business failure. Truly poor financial performance may justify dissolution under subsection (5)(i) as a frustration of the partnership's economic purpose.

RUPA also deletes UPA Section 32(1)(f) which authorizes a court to order dissolution of a partnership when "other circumstances render a dissolution equitable." That provision was regarded as too open-ended and, given RUPA's expanded remedies for partners, unnecessary. No significant change in result is intended, however, since the interpretation of UPA Section 32(1)(f) is comparable to the specific grounds expressed in subsection (5). *See, e.g., Karber v. Karber*, 145 Ariz. 293, 701 P.2d 1 (Ct. App. 1985) (partnership dissolved on basis of suspicion and ill will, citing UPA §§ 32(1)(d) and (f)); *Fuller v. Brough*, 159 Colo. 147, 411 P.2d 18 (1966) (not equitable to dissolve partnership for trifling causes or temporary grievances that do not render it impracticable to carry on partnership business); *Lau v. Wong*, 1 Haw. App. 217, 616 P.2d 1031 (1980) (partnership dissolved where business operated solely for benefit of managing partner).

9. Section 801(6) provides for judicial dissolution on application by a transferee of a partner's transferable interest in the partnership, including the purchaser of a partner's interest upon foreclosure of a charging order. It is based on UPA Section 32(2) and authorizes dissolution upon a judicial determination that it is equitable to wind up the partnership business (i) after the expiration of the partnership term or completion of the undertaking or (ii) at any time, if the partnership were a partnership at will at the time of the transfer or when the charging order was issued. The requirement that the court determine that it is equitable to wind up the business is new. The rights of a transferee under this section cannot be varied in the partnership agreement. *See* Section 103(b)(8).

§ 802. Partnership Continues After Dissolution

(a) Subject to subsection (b), a partnership continues after dissolution only for the purpose of winding up its business. The partnership is terminated when the winding up of its business is completed.

(b) At any time after the dissolution of a partnership and before the winding up of its business is completed, all of the partners, including any dissociating partner other than a wrongfully dissociating partner, may waive the right to have the partnership's business wound up and the partnership terminated. In that event:

(1) the partnership resumes carrying on its business as if dissolution had never occurred, and any liability incurred by the partnership or a partner after the dissolution and before the waiver is determined as if dissolution had never occurred; and

(2) the rights of a third party accruing under Section 804(1) or arising out of conduct in reliance on the dissolution before the third party knew or received a notification of the waiver may not be adversely affected.

Comment

1. Section 802(a) is derived from UPA Section 30 and provides that a partnership continues after dissolution only for the purpose of winding up its business, after which it is terminated. RUPA continues the concept of "termination" to mark the completion of the winding up process. Since no filing or other formality is required, the date will often be determined only by hindsight. No legal rights turn on the partnership's termination or the date thereof. Even after termination, if a previously unknown liability is asserted, all of the partners are still liable.

2. Section 802(b) makes explicit the right of the remaining partners to continue the business after an event of dissolution if all of the

partners, including the dissociating partner or partners, waive the right to have the business wound up and the partnership terminated. Only those "dissociating" partners whose dissociation was the immediate cause of the dissolution must waive the right to have the business wound up. The consent of wrongfully dissociating partners is not required.

3. Upon waiver of the right to have the business wound up, Paragraph (1) of the subsection provides that the partnership entity may resume carrying on its business as if dissolution had never occurred, thereby restoring the scope of its business to normal. "Resumes" is intended to mean that acts appropriate to winding up, authorized when taken, are in effect ratified, and the partnership remains liable for those acts, as provided explicitly in paragraph (2).

If the business is continued following a waiver of the right to dissolution, any liability incurred by the partnership or a partner after the dissolution and before the waiver is to be determined as if dissolution had never occurred. That has the effect of validating transactions entered into after dissolution that might not have been appropriate for winding up the business, because, upon waiver, any liability incurred by either the partnership or a partner in those transactions will be determined under Sections 702 and 703, rather than Sections 804 and 806.

As to the liability for those transactions among the partners themselves, the partners by agreement may provide otherwise. Thus, a partner who, after dissolution, incurred an obligation appropriate for winding up, but not appropriate for continuing the business, may protect himself by conditioning his consent to the continuation of the business on the ratification of the transaction by the continuing partners.

Paragraph (2) of the subsection provides that the rights of third parties accruing under Section 804(1) before they knew (or were notified) of the waiver may not be adversely affected by the waiver. That is intended to mean the partnership is bound, notwithstanding a subsequent waiver of dissolution and resumption of its business, by a transaction entered into after dissolution that was appropriate for winding up the partnership business, even if not appropriate for continuing the business. Similarly, any rights of a third party arising out of conduct in reliance on the dissolution are protected, absent knowledge (or notification) of the waiver. Thus, for example, a partnership loan, callable upon dissolution, that has been called is not reinstated by a subsequent waiver. If the loan has not been called before the lender learns (or is notified) of the waiver, however, it may not thereafter be called because of the dissolution. On the other hand, a waiver does not reinstate a lease that is terminated by the dissolution itself.

§ 803. Right to Wind up Partnership Business

(a) After dissolution, a partner who has not wrongfully dissociated may participate in winding up the partnership's business, but on application of any partner, partner's legal representative, or transferee, the [designate the appropriate court], for good cause shown, may order judicial supervision of the winding up.

(b) The legal representative of the last surviving partner may wind up a partnership's business.

(c) A person winding up a partnership's business may preserve the partnership business or property as a going concern for a reasonable time, prosecute and defend actions and proceedings, whether civil, criminal, or administrative, settle and close the partnership's business, dispose of and transfer the partnership's property, discharge the partnership's liabilities, distribute the assets of the partnership pursuant to Section 807, settle disputes by mediation or arbitration, and perform other necessary acts.

Comment

Section 803(a) is drawn from UPA Section 37. It provides that the partners who have not wrongfully dissociated may participate in winding up the partnership business. Wrongful dissociation is defined in Section 602. On application of any partner, a court may for good cause judicially supervise the winding up.

Section 803(b) continues the rule of UPA Section 25(2)(d) that the legal representative of the last surviving partner may wind up the business. It makes clear that the representative of the last surviving partner will not be forced to go to court for authority to wind up the business. On the other hand, the legal representative of a deceased partner, other than the last surviving partner, has only the rights of a transferee of the deceased partner's transferable interest. See Comment 8 to Section 601.

Section 803(c) is new and provides further guidance on the powers of a person who is winding up the business. It is based on Delaware Laws, Title 6, Section 17–803. The powers enumerated are not intended to be exclusive.

Subsection (c) expressly authorizes the preservation of the partnership's business or property as a going concern for a reasonable time. Some courts have reached that result without benefit of statutory authority. *See, e.g., Paciaroni v. Crane*, 408 A.2d 946 (Del. Ch. 1979). An agreement to continue the partnership business in order to preserve its going-concern value until sale is not a waiver of a partner's right to have the business liquidated.

The authorization of mediation and arbitration implements Conference policy to encourage alternative dispute resolution.

A partner's fiduciary duties of care and loyalty under Section 404 extend to winding up the business, except as modified by Section 603(b).

§ 804. Partner's Power to Bind Partnership After Dissolution

Subject to Section 805, a partnership is bound by a partner's act after dissolution that:

(1) is appropriate for winding up the partnership business; or

(2) would have bound the partnership under Section 301 before dissolution, if the other party to the transaction did not have notice of the dissolution.

Comment

Section 804 is the successor to UPA Sections 33(2) and 35, which wind down the authority of partners to bind the partnership to third persons.

Section 804(1) provides that partners have the authority to bind the partnership after dissolution in transactions that are appropriate for winding-up the partnership business. Section 804(2) provides that partners also have the power after dissolution to bind the partnership in transactions that are inconsistent with winding up. The partnership is bound in a transaction not appropriate for winding up, however, only if the partner's act would have bound the partnership under Section 301 before dissolution and the other party to the transaction did not have notice of the dissolution. *See* Section 102(b) (notice). Compare Section 301(1) (partner has apparent authority unless other party knows or has received a notification of lack of authority).

Section 804(2) attempts to balance the interests of the partners to terminate their mutual agency authority against the interests of outside creditors who have no notice of the partnership's dissolution. Even if the partnership is not bound under Section 804, the faithless partner who purports to act for the partnership after dissolution may be liable individually to an innocent third party under the law of agency. See Section 330 of the Restatement (Second) of Agency (agent liable for misrepresentation of authority), applicable under RUPA as provided in Section 104(a).

RUPA eliminates the special and confusing UPA rules limiting the authority of partners after dissolution. The special protection afforded by UPA Section 35(1)(b)(I) to former creditors and the lesser special protection afforded by UPA Section 35(1)(b)(II) to other parties who knew of the partnership before dissolution are both abolished. RUPA eschews these cumbersome notice provisions in favor of the general apparent authority rules of Section 301, subject to the effect of a filed or recorded statement of dissolution under Section 805. This enhances the protection of innocent third parties and imposes liability on the partnership and the partners who choose their fellow partner-agents and are in the best position to protect others by providing notice of the dissolution.

Also deleted are the special rules for unknown partners in UPA Section 35(2) and for certain causes of dissolution in UPA Section 35(3). Those, too, are inconsistent with RUPA's policy of adhering more closely to the general agency rules of Section 301.

Section 804 should be contrasted with Section 702, which winds down the power of a partner being bought out. The power of a dissociating partner is limited to transactions entered into within two years after the partner's dissociation. Section 804 has no time limitation. However, the apparent authority of partners in both situations is now subject to the filing of a statement of dissociation or dissolution, as the case may be, which operates to cut off such authority after 90 days.

§ 805. Statement of Dissolution

(a) After dissolution, a partner who has not wrongfully dissociated may file a statement of dissolution stating the name of the partnership and that the partnership has dissolved and is winding up its business.

(b) A statement of dissolution cancels a filed statement of partnership authority for the purposes of Section 303(d) and is a limitation on authority for the purposes of Section 303(e).

(c) For the purposes of Sections 301 and 804, a person not a partner is deemed to have notice of the dissolution and the limitation on the partners' authority as a result of the statement of dissolution 90 days after it is filed.

(d) After filing and, if appropriate, recording a statement of dissolution, a dissolved partnership may file and, if appropriate, record a statement of partnership authority which will operate with respect to a person not a partner as provided in Section 303(d) and (e) in any transaction, whether or not the transaction is appropriate for winding up the partnership business.

Comment

1. Section 805 is new. Subsection (a) provides that, after an event of dissolution, any partner who has not wrongfully dissociated may file a statement of dissolution on behalf of the partnership. The filing and recording of a statement of dissolution is optional. The execution, filing, and recording of the statement is governed by Section 105. The legal consequences of filing a statement of dissolution are similar to those of a statement of dissociation under Section 704.

2. Subsection (b) provides that a statement of dissolution cancels a filed statement of partnership authority for the purposes of Section 303(d), thereby terminating any extraordinary grant of authority contained in that statement.

A statement of dissolution also operates as a limitation on authority for the purposes of Section 303(e). That section provides that third parties are deemed to know of a limitation on the authority of a partner to transfer real property held in the name of the partnership if a certified copy of the statement containing the limitation is recorded with the real estate records. In effect, a properly recorded statement of dissolution restricts the authority of all partners to real property transfers that are appropriate for winding up the business. Thus, third parties must inquire of the partnership whether a contemplated real property transfer is appropriate for winding up. After dissolution, the partnership may, however, file and record a new statement of authority that will bind the partnership under Section 303(d).

3. Subsection (c) operates in conjunction with Sections 301 and 804 to wind down partners' apparent authority after dissolution. It provides that, for purposes of those sections, 90 days after the filing of a statement of dissolution nonpartners are deemed to have notice of the dissolution and the corresponding limitation on the authority of all partners. Sections 301 and 804 provide that a partner's lack of authority is binding on persons with notice thereof. Thus, after 90 days the statement of dissolution operates as constructive notice conclusively limiting the apparent authority of partners to transactions that are appropriate for winding up the business.

4. Subsection (d) provides that, after filing and, if appropriate, recording a statement of dissolution, the partnership may file and record a new statement of partnership authority that will operate as provided in Section 303(d). A grant of authority contained in that statement is conclusive and may be relied upon by a person who gives value without knowledge to the contrary, whether or not the transaction is appropriate for winding up the partnership business. That makes the partners' record authority conclusive after dissolution, and precludes going behind the record to inquire into whether or not the transaction was appropriate for winding up.

§ 806. Partner's Liability to Other Partners After Dissolution

(a) Except as otherwise provided in subsection (b) and Section 306, after dissolution a partner is liable to the other partners for the partner's share of any partnership liability incurred under Section 804.

(b) A partner who, with knowledge of the dissolution, incurs a partnership liability under Section 804(2) by an act that is not appropriate for winding up the partnership business is liable to the partnership for any damage caused to the partnership arising from the liability.

Comment

Section 806 is the successor to UPA Sections 33(1) and 34, which govern the rights of partners among themselves with respect to post-dissolution liability.

Subsection (a) provides that, except as provided in Section 306(a) and subsection (b), after dissolution each partner is liable to the other partners by way of contribution for his share of any partnership liability incurred under Section 804. That includes not only obligations that are appropriate for winding up the business, but also obligations that are inappropriate if within the partner's apparent authority. Consistent with other provisions of this Act, Section 806(a) makes clear that a partner does not have a contribution obligation with regard to limited liability partnership obligations for which the partner is not liable under Section 306. See Comments to Section 401(b).

Subsection (a) draws no distinction as to the cause of dissolution. Thus, as among the partners, their liability is treated alike in all events of dissolution. That is a change from UPA Section 33(*l*).

Subsection (b) creates an exception to the general rule in subsection (a). It provides that a partner, who with knowledge of the winding up nevertheless incurs a liability binding on the partnership by an act that is inappropriate for winding up the business, is liable to the partnership for any loss caused thereby.

Section 806 is merely a default rule and may be varied in the partnership agreement. *See* Section 103(a).

§ 807. Settlement of Accounts and Contributions Among Partners

CA$H

(a) In winding up a partnership's business, the assets of the partnership, including the contributions of the partners required by this section, must be applied to discharge its obligations to creditors, including, to the extent permitted by law, partners who are creditors. Any surplus must be applied to pay in cash the net amount distributable to partners in accordance with their right to distributions under subsection (b).

(b) Each partner is entitled to a settlement of all partnership accounts upon winding up the partnership business. In settling accounts among the partners, profits and losses that result from the liquidation of the partnership assets must be credited and charged to the partners' accounts. The partnership shall make a distribution to a partner in an amount equal to any excess of the credits over the charges in the partner's account. A partner shall contribute to the partnership an amount equal to any excess of the charges over the credits in the partner's account but excluding from the calculation charges attributable to an obligation for which the partner is not personally liable under Section 306.

(c) If a partner fails to contribute the full amount required under subsection (b), all of the other partners shall contribute, in the proportions in which those partners share partnership losses, the additional amount necessary to satisfy the partnership obligations for which they are personally liable under Section 306. A partner or partner's legal representative may recover from the other partners any contributions the partner makes to the extent the amount contributed exceeds that partner's share of the partnership obligations for which the partner is personally liable under Section 306.

(d) After the settlement of accounts, each partner shall contribute, in the proportion in which the partner shares partnership losses, the amount necessary to satisfy partnership obligations that were not known at the time of the settlement and for which the partner is personally liable under Section 306.

(e) The estate of a deceased partner is liable for the partner's obligation to contribute to the partnership.

(f) An assignee for the benefit of creditors of a partnership or a partner, or a person appointed by a court to represent creditors of a partnership or a partner, may enforce a partner's obligation to contribute to the partnership.

Comment

1. Section 807 provides the default rules for the settlement of accounts and contributions among the partners in winding up the business. It is derived in part from UPA Sections 38(1) and 40.

2. Subsection (a) continues the rule in UPA Section 38(*l*) that, in winding up the business, the partnership assets must first be applied to discharge partnership liabilities to creditors. For this purpose, any required contribution by the partners is treated as an asset of the partnership. After the payment of all partnership liabilities, any surplus must be applied to pay in cash the net amount due the partners under subsection (b) by way of a liquidating distribution.

RUPA continues the "in-cash" rule of UPA Section 38(1) and is consistent with Section 402, which provides that a partner has no right to receive, and may not be required to accept, a distribution in kind, unless otherwise agreed. The in-cash rule avoids the valuation problems that afflict unwanted in-kind distributions.

The partnership must apply its assets to discharge the obligations of partners who are creditors on a parity with other creditors. See Section 404(f) and Comment 6. In effect, that abolishes the priority rules in UPA Section 40(b) and (c) which subordinate the payment of inside debt to outside debt. Both RULPA and the RMBCA do likewise. *See* RULPA § 804; RMBCA §§ 6.40(f), 14.05(a). Ultimately, however, a partner whose "debt" has been repaid by the partnership is personally liable, as a partner, for any outside debt remaining unsatisfied, unlike a limited partner or corporate shareholder. Accordingly, the obligation to contribute sufficient funds to satisfy the claims of outside creditors may result in the equitable subordination of inside debt when partnership assets are insufficient to satisfy all obligations to non-partners.

RUPA in effect abolishes the "dual priority" or "jingle" rule of UPA Section 40(h) and (i). Those sections gave partnership creditors priority as to partnership property and separate creditors priority as to separate property. The jingle rule has already been preempted by the Bankruptcy Code, at least as to Chapter 7 partnership liquidation proceedings. Under Section 723(c) of the Bankruptcy Code, and under RUPA, partnership creditors share pro rata with the partners' individual creditors in the assets of the partners' estates.

3. Subsection (b) provides that each partner is entitled to a settlement of all partnership accounts upon winding up. It also establishes the default rules for closing out the partners' accounts. First, the profits and losses resulting from the liquidation of the partnership assets must be credited or charged to the partners' accounts, according to their respective shares of profits and losses. Then, the partnership must make a final liquidating distribution to those partners with a positive account balance. That distribution should be in the amount of the excess of credits over the charges in the account. Any partner with a negative account balance must contribute to the partnership an amount equal to the excess of charges over the credits in the account provided the excess relates to an obligation for which the partner is personally liable under Section 306. The partners may, however, agree that a negative account does not reflect a debt to the partnership and need not be repaid in settling the partners' accounts.

Section 807(b) makes clear that a partner's contribution obligation to a partnership in dissolution only considers the partner's share of obligations for which the partner was personally liable under Section 306 ("unshielded obligations"). See Comments to Section 401(b) (partner contribution obligation to an operating partnership). Properly determined under this Section, the total required partner contributions will be sufficient to satisfy the partnership's total unshielded obligations. In special circumstances where a partnership has both shielded and unshielded obligations and the partner required contributions are used to first pay shielded partnership obligations, the partners may be required to make further contributions to satisfy the partnership unpaid unshielded obligations. The proper resolution of this matter is left to debtor-creditor law as well as the law governing the fiduciary obligations of the partners. See Section 104(a).

RUPA eliminates the distinction in UPA Section 40(b) between the liability owing to a partner in respect of capital and the liability owing in respect of profits. Section 807(b) speaks simply of the right of a partner to a liquidating distribution. That implements the logic of RUPA Sections 401(a) and 502 under which contributions to capital and shares in profits and losses combine to determine the right to distributions. The partners may, however, agree to share "operating" losses differently from "capital" losses, thereby continuing the UPA distinction.

4. Subsection (c) continues the UPA Section 40(d) rule that solvent partners share proportionately in the shortfall caused by insolvent partners who fail to contribute their proportionate share. The partnership may enforce a partner's obligation to contribute. *See* Section 405(a). A partner is entitled to recover from the other partners any contributions in excess of that partner's share of the partnership's liabilities. *See* Section 405(b)(iii).

5. Subsection (d) provides that, after settling the partners' accounts, each partner must contribute, in the proportion in which he shares losses, the amount necessary to satisfy partnership obligations that were not known at the time of the settlement. That continues the basic rule of UPA Section 40(d) and underscores that the obligation to contribute exists independently of the partnership's books of account. It specifically covers the situation of a partnership liability that was unknown when the partnership books were closed.

6. Under subsection (e), the estate of a deceased partner is liable for the partner's obligation to contribute to partnership losses. That continues the rule of UPA Section 40(g).

7. Subsection (f) provides that an assignee for the benefit of creditors of the partnership or of a partner (or other court appointed creditor representative) may enforce any partner's obligation to contribute to the partnership. That continues the rules of UPA Sections 36(4) and 40(e).

Article 9

CONVERSIONS AND MERGERS

§ 901. Definitions

In this article:

(1) "General partner" means a partner in a partnership and a general partner in a limited partnership.

(2) "Limited partner" means a limited partner in a limited partnership.

(3) "Limited partnership" means a limited partnership created under the [State Limited Partnership Act], predecessor law, or comparable law of another jurisdiction.

(4) "Partner" includes both a general partner and a limited partner.

Comment

1. Article 9 is new. The UPA is silent with respect to the conversion or merger of partnerships, and thus it is necessary under the UPA to structure those types of transactions as asset transfers. RUPA pro-

vides specific statutory authority for conversions and mergers. It provides for continuation of the partnership entity, thereby simplifying those transactions and adding certainty to the legal consequences.

A number of States currently authorize the merger of limited partnerships, and some authorize them to merge with other business entities such as corporations and limited liability companies. A few States currently authorize the merger of a general and a limited partnership or the conversion of a general to a limited partnership.

2. As Section 908 makes clear, the requirements of Article 9 are not mandatory, and a partnership may convert or merge in any other manner provided by law. Article 9 is merely a "safe harbor." If the requirements of the article are followed, the conversion or merger is legally valid. Since most States have no other established procedure for the conversion or merger of partnerships, it is likely that the Article 9 procedures will be used in virtually all cases.

3. Article 9 does not restrict the provisions authorizing conversions and mergers to domestic partnerships. Since no filing is required for the creation of a partnership under RUPA, it is often unclear where a partnership is domiciled. Moreover, a partnership doing business in the State satisfies the definition of a partnership created under this Act since it is an association of two or more co-owners carrying on a business for profit. Even a partnership clearly domiciled in another State could easily amend its partnership agreement to provide that its internal affairs are to be governed by the laws of a jurisdiction that has enacted Article 9 of RUPA. No harm is likely to result from extending to foreign partnerships the right to convert or merge under local law.

4. Because Article 9 deals with the conversion and merger of both general and limited partnerships, Section 901 sets forth four definitions distinguishing between the two types of partnerships solely for the purposes of Article 9. "Partner" includes both general and limited partners, and "general partner" includes general partners in both general and limited partnerships.

§ 902. Conversion of Partnership to Limited Partnership

(a) A partnership may be converted to a limited partnership pursuant to this section.

(b) The terms and conditions of a conversion of a partnership to a limited partnership must be approved by all of the partners or by a number or percentage specified for conversion in the partnership agreement.

(c) After the conversion is approved by the partners, the partnership shall file a certificate of limited partnership in the jurisdiction in which the limited partnership is to be formed. The certificate must include:

(1) a statement that the partnership was converted to a limited partnership from a partnership;

(2) its former name; and

(3) a statement of the number of votes cast by the partners for and against the conversion and, if the vote is less than unanimous, the number or percentage required to approve the conversion under the partnership agreement.

(d) The conversion takes effect when the certificate of limited partnership is filed or at any later date specified in the certificate.

(e) A general partner who becomes a limited partner as a result of the conversion remains liable as a general partner for an obligation incurred by the partnership before the conversion takes effect. If the other party to a transaction with the limited partnership reasonably believes when entering the transaction that the limited partner is a general partner, the limited partner is liable for an obligation incurred by the limited partnership within 90 days after the conversion takes effect. The limited partner's liability for all other obligations of the limited partnership incurred after the conversion takes effect is that of a limited partner as provided in the [State Limited Partnership Act].

Comment

Section 902(a) authorizes the conversion of a "partnership" to a "limited partnership." Section 202(b) limits the usual RUPA definition of "partnership" to general partnerships. That definition is applicable to Article 9. If a limited partnership is contemplated, Article 9 uses the term "limited partnership." See Section 901(3).

Subsection (b) provides that the terms and conditions of the conversion must be approved by all the partners, unless the partnership agreement specifies otherwise for a conversion.

Subsection (c) provides that, after approval, the partnership must file a certificate of limited partnership which includes the requisite information concerning the conversion.

Subsection (d) provides that the conversion takes effect when the certificate is filed, unless a later effective date is specified.

Subsection (e) establishes the partners' liabilities following a conversion. A partner who becomes a limited partner as a result of the conversion remains fully liable as a general partner for any obligation arising before the effective date of the conversion, both to third parties and to other partners for contribution. Third parties who transact business with the converted partnership unaware of a partner's new status as a limited partner are protected for 90 days after the conversion. Since RULPA Section 201(a)(3) requires the certificate of limited partnership to name all of the general partners, and under RUPA Section 902(c) the certificate must also include a statement of the conversion, parties transacting business with the converted partnership can protect themselves by checking the record of the State where the limited partnership is formed (the State where the conversion takes place). A former general partner who becomes a limited partner as a result of the conversion can avoid the lingering 90–day exposure to liability as a general partner by notifying those transacting business with the partnership of his limited partner status.

Although Section 902 does not expressly provide that a partner's withdrawal upon a term partnership's conversion to a limited partnership is rightful, it was assumed that the unanimity requirement for the approval of a conversion would afford a withdrawing partner adequate opportunity to protect his interest as a condition of approval. This question is left to the partnership agreement if it provides for conversion without the approval of all the partners.

§ 903. Conversion of Limited Partnership to Partnership

(a) A limited partnership may be converted to a partnership pursuant to this section.

(b) Notwithstanding a provision to the contrary in a limited partnership agreement, the terms and conditions of a conversion of a limited partnership to a partnership must be approved by all of the partners.

(c) After the conversion is approved by the partners, the limited partnership shall cancel its certificate of limited partnership.

(d) The conversion takes effect when the certificate of limited partnership is canceled.

(e) A limited partner who becomes a general partner as a result of the conversion remains liable only as a limited partner for an obligation incurred by the limited partnership before the conversion takes effect. Except as otherwise provided in Section 306, the partner is liable as a general partner for an obligation of the partnership incurred after the conversion takes effect.

Comment

Section 903(a) authorizes the conversion of a limited partnership to a general partnership.

Subsection (b) provides that the conversion must be approved by all of the partners, even if the partnership agreement provides to the contrary. That includes all of the general and limited partners. *See* Section 901(4). The purpose of the unanimity requirement is to protect a limited partner from exposure to personal liability as a general partner without clear and knowing consent at the time of conversion. Despite a general voting provision to the contrary in the partnership agreement, conversion to a general partnership may never have been contemplated by the limited partner when the partnership investment was made.

Subsection (c) provides that, after approval of the conversion, the converted partnership must cancel its certificate of limited partnership. *See* RULPA § 203.

Subsection (d) provides that the conversion takes effect when the certificate of limited partnership is canceled.

Subsection (e) provides that a limited partner who becomes a general partner is liable as a general partner for all partnership obligations for which a general partner would otherwise be personally liable for if incurred after the effective date of the conversion, but still has only limited liability for obligations incurred before the conversion.

§ 904. Effect of Conversion; Entity Unchanged

(a) A partnership or limited partnership that has been converted pursuant to this article is for all purposes the same entity that existed before the conversion.

(b) When a conversion takes effect:

(1) all property owned by the converting partnership or limited partnership remains vested in the converted entity;

(2) all obligations of the converting partnership or limited partnership continue as obligations of the converted entity; and

(3) an action or proceeding pending against the converting partnership or limited partnership may be continued as if the conversion had not occurred.

Comment

Section 904 sets forth the effect of a conversion on the partnership. Subsection (a) provides that the converted partnership is for all purposes the same entity as before the conversion.

Subsection (b) provides that upon conversion: (1) all partnership property remains vested in the converted entity; (2) all obligations remain the obligations of the converted entity; and (3) all pending legal actions may be continued as if the conversion had not occurred. The term "entity" as used in Article 9 refers to either or both general and limited partnerships as the context requires.

Under subsection (b)(1), title to partnership property remains vested in the converted partnership. As a matter of general property law, title remains vested without further act or deed and without reversion or impairment.

§ 905. Merger of Partnerships

(a) Pursuant to a plan of merger approved as provided in subsection (c), a partnership may be merged with one or more partnerships or limited partnerships.

(b) The plan of merger must set forth:

(1) the name of each partnership or limited partnership that is a party to the merger;

(2) the name of the surviving entity into which the other partnerships or limited partnerships will merge;

(3) whether the surviving entity is a partnership or a limited partnership and the status of each partner;

(4) the terms and conditions of the merger;

(5) the manner and basis of converting the interests of each party to the merger into interests or obligations of the surviving entity, or into money or other property in whole or part; and

(6) the street address of the surviving entity's chief executive office.

(c) The plan of merger must be approved:

(1) in the case of a partnership that is a party to the merger, by all of the partners, or a number or percentage specified for merger in the partnership agreement; and

(2) in the case of a limited partnership that is a party to the merger, by the vote required for approval of a merger by the law of the State or foreign jurisdiction in which the limited partnership is organized and, in the absence of such a specifically applicable law, by all of the partners, notwithstanding a provision to the contrary in the partnership agreement.

(d) After a plan of merger is approved and before the merger takes effect, the plan may be amended or abandoned as provided in the plan.

(e) The merger takes effect on the later of:

(1) the approval of the plan of merger by all parties to the merger, as provided in subsection (c);

(2) the filing of all documents required by law to be filed as a condition to the effectiveness of the merger; or

(3) any effective date specified in the plan of merger.

Comment

Section 905 provides a "safe harbor" for the merger of a general partnership and one or more general or limited partnerships. The surviving entity may be either a general or a limited partnership.

The plan of merger must set forth the information required by subsection (b), including the status of each partner and the manner and basis of converting the interests of each party to the merger into interests or obligations of the surviving entity.

Subsection (c) provides that the plan of merger must be approved: (1) by all the partners of each general partnership that is a party to the merger, unless its partnership agreement specifically provides otherwise for mergers; and (2) by all the partners, including both general and limited partners, of each limited partnership that is a party to the merger, notwithstanding a contrary provision in its partnership agreement, unless specifically authorized by the law of the jurisdiction in which that limited partnership is organized. Like Section 902(b), the purpose of the unanimity requirement is to protect limited partners from exposure to liability as general partners without their clear and knowing consent.

Subsection (d) provides that the plan of merger may be amended or abandoned at any time before the merger takes effect, if the plan so provides.

Subsection (e) provides that the merger takes effect on the later of: (1) approval by all parties to the merger; (2) filing of all required documents; or (3) the effective date specified in the plan. The surviving entity must file all notices and documents relating to the merger required by other applicable statutes governing the entities that are parties to the merger, such as articles of merger or a certificate of limited partnership. It may also amend or cancel a statement of partnership authority previously filed by any party to the merger.

§ 906. Effect of Merger

(a) When a merger takes effect:

(1) the separate existence of every partnership or limited partnership that is a party to the merger, other than the surviving entity, ceases;

(2) all property owned by each of the merged partnerships or limited partnerships vests in the surviving entity;

(3) all obligations of every partnership or limited partnership that is a party to the merger become the obligations of the surviving entity; and

(4) an action or proceeding pending against a partnership or limited partnership that is a party to the merger may be continued as if the merger had not occurred, or the surviving entity may be substituted as a party to the action or proceeding.

(b) The [Secretary of State] of this State is the agent for service of process in an action or proceeding against a surviving foreign partnership or limited partnership to enforce an obligation of a domestic partnership or limited partnership that is a party to a merger. The surviving entity shall promptly notify the [Secretary of State] of the mailing address of its chief executive office and of any change of address. Upon receipt of process, the [Secretary of State] shall mail a copy of the process to the surviving foreign partnership or limited partnership.

(c) A partner of the surviving partnership or limited partnership is liable for:

(1) all obligations of a party to the merger for which the partner was personally liable before the merger;

(2) all other obligations of the surviving entity incurred before the merger by a party to the merger, but those obligations may be satisfied only out of property of the entity; and

(3) except as otherwise provided in Section 306, all obligations of the surviving entity incurred after the merger takes effect, but those obligations may be satisfied only out of property of the entity if the partner is a limited partner.

(d) If the obligations incurred before the merger by a party to the merger are not satisfied out of the property of the surviving partnership or limited partnership, the general partners of that party immediately before the effective date of the merger shall contribute the amount necessary to satisfy that party's obligations to the surviving entity, in the manner provided in Section 807 or in the [Limited Partnership Act] of the jurisdiction in which the party was formed, as the case may be, as if the merged party were dissolved.

(e) A partner of a party to a merger who does not become a partner of the surviving partnership or limited partnership is dissociated from the entity, of which that partner was a partner, as of the date the merger takes effect. The surviving entity shall cause the partner's interest in the entity to be purchased under Section 701 or another statute specifically applicable to that partner's interest with respect to a merger. The surviving entity is bound under Section 702 by an act of a general partner dissociated under this subsection, and the partner is liable under Section 703 for transactions entered into by the surviving entity after the merger takes effect.

Comment

Section 906 states the effect of a merger on the partnerships that are parties to the merger and on the individual partners.

Subsection (a) provides that when the merger takes effect: (1) the separate existence of every partnership that is a party to the merger (other than the surviving entity) ceases; (2) all property owned by the parties to the merger vests in the surviving entity; (3) all obligations of every party to the merger become the obligations of the surviving entity; and (4) all legal actions pending against a party to the merger may be continued as if the merger had not occurred or the surviving entity may be substituted as a party. Title to partnership property vests in the surviving entity without further act or deed and without reversion or impairment.

Subsection (b) makes the Secretary of State the agent for service of process in any action against the surviving entity, if it is a foreign entity, to enforce an obligation of a domestic partnership that is a party to the merger. The purpose of this rule is to make it more convenient for local creditors to sue a foreign surviving entity when the credit was extended to a domestic partnership that has disappeared as a result of the merger.

Subsection (c) provides that a general partner of the surviving entity is liable for (1) all obligations for which the partner was personally liable before the merger; (2) all other obligations of the surviving entity incurred before the merger by a party to the merger, which obligations may be satisfied only out of the surviving entity's partnership property; and (3) all obligations incurred by the surviving entity after the merger, limited to the surviving entity's property in the case of limited partners and also limited to obligations of the partnership for which the partner was personally liable under Section 306.

This scheme of liability is similar to that of an incoming partner under Section 306(b). Only the surviving partnership itself is liable for all obligations, including obligations incurred by every constituent party before the merger. A general partner of the surviving entity is personally liable for obligations of the surviving entity incurred before the merger by the partnership of which he was a partner and those incurred by the surviving entity after the merger. Thus, a general partner of the surviving entity is liable only to the extent of his partnership interest for obligations incurred before the merger by a constituent party of which he was not a general partner.

Subsection (d) requires general partners to contribute the amount necessary to satisfy all obligations for which they were personally liable before the merger, if such obligations are not satisfied out of the partnership property of the surviving entity, in the same manner as provided in Section 807 or the limited partnership act of the applicable jurisdiction, as if the merged party were then dissolved. *See* RULPA §§ 502, 608.

Subsection (e) provides for the dissociation of a partner of a party to the merger who does not become a partner in the surviving entity. The surviving entity must buy out that partner's interest in the partnership under Section 701 or other specifically applicable statute. If the state limited partnership act has a dissenter's rights provision providing a different method of determining the amount due a dissociating limited partner, it would apply, rather than Section 701, since the two statutes should be read *in pari materia*.

Although subsection (e) does not expressly provide that a partner's withdrawal upon the merger of a term partnership is rightful, it was assumed that the unanimity requirement for the approval of a merger would afford a withdrawing partner adequate opportunity to protect his interest as a condition of approval. This question is left to the partnership agreement if it provides for merger without the approval of all the partners.

Under subsection (e), a dissociating general partner's lingering agency power is wound down, pursuant to Section 702, the same as in any other dissociation. Moreover, a dissociating general partner may be liable, under Section 703, for obligations incurred by the surviving entity for up to two years after the merger. A dissociating general partner can, however, limit to 90 days his exposure to liability by filing a statement of dissociation under Section 704.

§ 907. Statement of Merger

(a) After a merger, the surviving partnership or limited partnership may file a statement that one or more partnerships or limited partnerships have merged into the surviving entity.

(b) A statement of merger must contain:

(1) the name of each partnership or limited partnership that is a party to the merger;

(2) the name of the surviving entity into which the other partnerships or limited partnership were merged;

(3) the street address of the surviving entity's chief executive office and of an office in this State, if any; and

(4) whether the surviving entity is a partnership or a limited partnership.

(c) Except as otherwise provided in subsection (d), for the purposes of Section 302, property of the surviving partnership or limited partnership which before the merger was held in the name of another party to the merger is property held in the name of the surviving entity upon filing a statement of merger.

(d) For the purposes of Section 302, real property of the surviving partnership or limited partnership which before the merger was held in the name of another party to the merger is property held in the name of the surviving entity upon recording a certified copy of the statement of merger in the office for recording transfers of that real property.

(e) A filed and, if appropriate, recorded statement of merger, executed and declared to be accurate pursuant to Section 105(c), stating the name of a partnership or limited partnership that is a party to the merger in whose name property was held before the merger and the name of the surviving entity, but not containing all of the other information required by subsection (b), operates with respect to the partnerships or limited partnerships named to the extent provided in subsections (c) and (d).

Comment

Section 907(a) provides that the surviving entity may file a statement of merger. The execution, filing, and recording of the statement are governed by Section 105.

Subsection (b) requires the statement to contain the name of each party to the merger, the name and address of the surviving entity, and whether it is a general or limited partnership.

Subsection (c) provides that, for the purpose of the Section 302 rules regarding the transfer of partnership property, all personal and intangible property which before the merger was held in the name of a party to the merger becomes, upon the filing of the statement of merger with the Secretary of State, property held in the name of the surviving entity.

Subsection (d) provides a similar rule for real property, except that real property does not become property held in the name of the surviving entity until a certified copy of the statement of merger is recorded in the office for recording transfers of that real property under local law.

Subsection (e) is a savings provision in the event a statement of merger fails to contain all of the information required by subsection (b). The statement will have the operative effect provided in subsections (c) and (d) if it is executed and declared to be accurate pursuant to Section 105(e) and correctly states the name of the party to the merger in whose name the property was held before the merger, so that it would be found by someone searching the record. Compare Section 303(c) (statement of partnership authority).

§ 908. Nonexclusive

This article is not exclusive. Partnerships or limited partnerships may be converted or merged in any other manner provided by law.

Comment

Section 908 provides that Article 9 is not exclusive. It is merely a "safe harbor." Partnerships may be converted or merged in any other manner provided by statute or common law. Existing statutes in a few States already authorize the conversion or merger of general partnerships and limited partnerships. See Comment 1 to Section 901. Those procedures may be followed in lieu of Article 9.

Article 10

LIMITED LIABILITY PARTNERSHIP

§ 1001. Statement of Qualification

(a) A partnership may become a limited liability partnership pursuant to this section.

(b) The terms and conditions on which a partnership becomes a limited liability partnership must be approved by the vote necessary to amend the partnership agreement except, in the case of a partnership agreement that expressly considers obligations to contribute to the partnership, the vote necessary to amend those provisions.

(c) After the approval required by subsection (b), a partnership may become a limited liability partnership by filing a statement of qualification. The statement must contain:

(1) the name of the partnership;

(2) the street address of the partnership's chief executive office and, if different, the street address of an office in this State, if any;

(3) if the partnership does not have an office in this State, the name and street address of the partnership's agent for service of process;

(4) a statement that the partnership elects to be a limited liability partnership; and

(5) a deferred effective date, if any.

(d) The agent of a limited liability partnership for service of process must be an individual who is a resident of this State or other person authorized to do business in this State.

(e) The status of a partnership as a limited liability partnership is effective on the later of the filing of the statement or a date specified in the statement. The status remains effective, regardless of changes in the partnership, until it is canceled pursuant to Section 105(d) or revoked pursuant to Section 1003.

(f) The status of a partnership as a limited liability partnership and the liability of its partners is not affected by errors or later changes in the information required to be contained in the statement of qualification under subsection (c).

(g) The filing of a statement of qualification establishes that a partnership has satisfied all conditions precedent to the qualification of the partnership as a limited liability partnership.

(h) An amendment or cancellation of a statement of qualification is effective when it is filed or on a deferred effective date specified in the amendment or cancellation.

Comment

Any partnership may become a limited liability partnership by filing a statement of qualification. See Comments to Sections 101(6) and 202(b) regarding a limited partnership filing a statement of qualification to become a limited liability limited partnership. Section 1001 sets forth the required contents of a statement of qualification. The section also sets forth requirements for the approval of a statement of qualification, establishes the effective date of the filing (and any amendments) which remains effective until canceled or revoked, and provides that the liability of the partners of a limited liability partnership is not affected by errors or later changes in the statement information.

Subsection (b) provides that the terms and conditions on which a partnership becomes a limited liability partnership must be generally be approved by the vote necessary to amend the partnership agreement. This means that the act of becoming a limited liability partnership is equivalent to an amendment of the partnership agreement. Where the partnership agreement is silent as to how it may be amended, the subsection (b) vote requires the approval of every partner. Since the limited liability partnership rules are not intended to increase the vote necessary to amend the partnership agreement, where the partnership agreement specifically sets forth an amendment process, that process may be used. Where a partnership agreement sets forth several amendment procedures depending upon the nature of the amendment, the required vote will be that necessary to amend the contribution obligations of the partners. The specific "contribution" vote is preferred because the filing of the statement directly affects partner contribution obligations. Therefore, the language "considers contribution" should be broadly interpreted to include any amendment vote that indirectly affects any partner's contribution obligation such as a partner's obligation to "indemnify" other partners.

The unanimous vote default rule reflects the significance of a partnership becoming a limited liability partnership. In general, upon such a filing each partner is released from the personal contribution obligation imposed under this Act in exchange for relinquishing the right to enforce the contribution obligations of other partners under this Act. See Comments to Sections 306(c) and 401(b). The wisdom of this bargain will depend on many factors including the relative risks of the partners' duties and the assets of the partnership.

Subsection (c) sets forth the information required in a statement of qualification. The must include the name of the partnership which must comply with Section 1002 to identify the partnership as a limited liability partnership. The statement must also include the address of the partnership's chief executive office and, if different, the street address of any other office in this State. A statement must include the name and street address of an agent for service of process only if it does not have any office in this State.

As with other statements, a statement of qualification must be filed in the office of the Secretary of State. See Sections 101(13) and 105(a). Accordingly, a statement of qualification is executed, filed, and otherwise regarded as a statement under this Act. For example, a copy of a filed statement must be sent to every nonfiling partner unless otherwise provided in the partnership agreement. See Sections 105(e) and 103(b)(1). A statement of qualification must be executed by at least two partners under penalties of perjury that the contents of the statement are accurate. See Section 105(c). A person who files the statement must promptly send a copy of the statement to every nonfiling partner but failure to send the copy does not limit the effectiveness of the filed statement to a nonpartner. Section 105(e). The filing must be accompanied by the fee required by the Secretary of State. Section 105(f).

Subsection (d) makes clear that once a statement is filed and effective, the status of the partnership as a limited liability partnership remains effective until the partnership status is either canceled or revoked "regardless of changes in the partnership." Accordingly, a partnership that dissolves but whose business is continued under a business continuation agreement retains its status as a limited liability partnership without the need to refile a new statement. Also, limited liability partnership status remains even though a partnership may be dissolved, wound up, and terminated. Even after the termination of the partnership, the former partners of a terminated partnership would not be personally liable for partnership obligations incurred while the partnership was a limited liability partnership.

Subsection (d) also makes clear that limited liability partnership status remains effective until actual cancellation under Section 1003 or revocation under Section 105(d). Ordinarily the terms and conditions of becoming a limited liability partnership must be approved by the vote necessary to amend the partnership agreement. See Sections 1001(b), 306(c), and 401(j). Since the statement of cancellation may be filed by a person authorized to file the original statement of qualification, the same vote necessary to approve the filing of the statement of qualification must be obtained to file the statement of cancellation. See Section 105(d).

Subsection (f) provides that once a statement of qualification is executed and filed under subsection (c) and Section 105, the partnership assumes the status of a limited liability partnership. This status is intended to be conclusive with regard to third parties dealing with the partnership. It is not intended to affect the rights of partners. For example, a properly executed and filed statement of qualification conclusively establishes the limited liability shield described in Section 306(c). If the partners executing and filing the statement exceed their authority, the internal abuse of authority has no effect on the liability shield with regard to third parties. Partners may challenge the abuse of authority for purposes of establishing the liability of the culpable partners but may not effect the liability shield as to third parties. Likewise, third parties may not challenge the existence of the liability shield because the decision to file the statement lacked the proper vote. As a result, the filing of the statement creates the liability shield even when the required subsection (b) vote is not obtained.

§ 1002. Name

The name of a limited liability partnership must end with "Registered Limited Liability Partnership", "Limited Liability Partnership", "R.L.L.P.", "L.L.P.", "RLLP," or "LLP".

Comment

The name provisions are intended to alert persons dealing with a limited liability partnership of the presence of the liability shield. Because many jurisdictions have adopted the naming concept of a "registered'' limited liability partnership, this aspect has been retained. These name requirements also distinguish limited partnerships and general partnerships that become limited liability partnerships because the new name must be at the end of and in addition to the general or limited partnership's regular name. See Comments to Section 101(6). Since the name identification rules of this section do not alter the regular name of the partnership, they do not disturb historic notions of apparent authority of partners in both general and limited partnerships.

§ 1003. Annual Report

(a) A limited liability partnership, and a foreign limited liability partnership authorized to transact business in this State, shall file an annual report in the office of the [Secretary of State] which contains:

(1) the name of the limited liability partnership and the State or other jurisdiction under whose laws the foreign limited liability partnership is formed;

(2) the street address of the partnership's chief executive office and, if different, the street address of an office of the partnership in this State, if any; and

(3) if the partnership does not have an office in this State, the name and street address of the partnership's current agent for service of process.

(b) An annual report must be filed between [January 1 and April 1] of each year following the calendar year in which a partnership files a statement of qualification or a foreign partnership becomes authorized to transact business in this State.

(c) The [Secretary of State] may revoke the statement of qualification of a partnership that fails to file an annual report when due or pay the required filing fee. To do so, the [Secretary of State] shall provide the partnership at least 60 days' written notice of intent to revoke the statement. The notice must be mailed to the partnership at its chief executive office set forth in the last filed statement of qualification or annual report. The notice must specify the annual report that has not been filed, the fee that has not been paid, and the effective date of the revocation. The revocation is not effective if the annual report is filed and the fee is paid before the effective date of the revocation.

(d) A revocation under subsection (c) only affects a partnership's status as a limited liability partnership and is not an event of dissolution of the partnership.

(e) A partnership whose statement of qualification has been revoked may apply to the [Secretary of State] for reinstatement within two years after the effective date of the revocation.

The application must state:

(1) the name of the partnership and the effective date of the revocation; and

(2) that the ground for revocation either did not exist or has been corrected.

(f) A reinstatement under subsection (e) relates back to and takes effect as of the effective date of the revocation, and the partnership's status as a limited liability partnership continues as if the revocation had never occurred.

Comment

Section 1003 sets forth the requirements of an annual report that must be filed by all limited liability partnerships and any foreign limited liability partnership authorized to transact business in this State. See Sections 101(5)(definition of a limited liability partnership) and 101(4)(definition of a foreign limited liability partnership). The failure of a limited liability partnership to file an annual report is a basis for the Secretary of State to administratively revoke its statement of qualification. See Section 1003(c). A foreign limited liability partnership that fails to file an annual report may not maintain an action or proceeding in this State. See Section 1103(a).

Subsection (a) generally requires that an annual report contain the same information required in a statement of qualification. Compare Sections 1001(a) and 1003(a). The differences are that the annual report requires disclosure of the State of formation of a foreign limited liability partnership but deletes the delayed effective date and limited liability partnership election statement provisions of a statement of qualification. As such, the annual report serves to update the information required in a statement of qualification. Under subsection (b), the annual report must be filed between January 1 and April 1 of each calendar year following the year in which a statement of qualification was filed or a foreign limited liability partnership becomes authorized to transact business. This timing requirement means that a limited liability partnership must make an annual filing and may not prefile multiple annual reports in a single year.

Subsection (c) sets forth the procedure for the Secretary of State to administratively revoke a partnership's statement of qualification for the failure to file an annual report when due or pay the required filing fee. The Secretary of State must provide a partnership at least 60 days' written notice of the intent to revoke the statement. The notice must be mailed to the partnership at the address of its chief executive office set forth in the last filed statement or annual report and must state the grounds for revocation as well as the effective date of revocation. The revocation is not effective if the stated problem is cured before the stated effective date.

Under subsection (d), a revocation only terminates the partnership's status as a limited liability partnership but is not an event of dissolution of the partnership itself. Where revocation occurs, a partnership may apply for reinstatement under subsection (e) within two years after the effective date of the revocation. The application must state that the grounds for revocation either did not exist or have been corrected. The Secretary of State may grant the application on the basis of the statements alone or require proof of correction. Under subsection (f), when the application is granted, the reinstatement relates back to and takes effect as of the effective date of the revocation. The relation back doctrine prevents gaps in a reinstated partnership's liability shield. See Comments to Section 306(c).

Article 11

FOREIGN LIMITED LIABILITY PARTNERSHIP

§ 1101. Law Governing Foreign Limited Liability Partnership

(a) The law under which a foreign limited liability partnership is formed governs relations among the partners and between the partners and the partnership and the liability of partners for obligations of the partnership.

(b) A foreign limited liability partnership may not be denied a statement of foreign qualification by reason of any difference between the law under which the partnership was formed and the law of this State.

(c) A statement of foreign qualification does not authorize a foreign limited liability partnership to engage in any business or exercise any power that a partnership may not engage in or exercise in this State as a limited liability partnership.

Comment

Section 1101 provides that the laws where a foreign limited liability partnership is formed rather than the laws of this State govern both the internal relations of the partnership and liability of its partners for the obligations of the partnership. See Section 101(4)(definition of a foreign limited liability partnership). Section 106(b) provides that the laws of this State govern the internal relations of a domestic limited liability and the liability of its partners for the obligations of the partnership. See Sections 101(5)(definition of a domestic limited liability partnership). A partnership may therefore chose the laws of a particular jurisdiction by filing a statement of qualification in that jurisdiction. But there are limitations on this choice.

Subsections (b) and (c) together make clear that although a foreign limited liability partnership may not be denied a statement of foreign qualification simply because of a difference between the laws of its foreign jurisdiction and the laws of this State, it may not engage in any business or exercise any power in this State that a domestic limited liability partnership may not engage in or exercise. Under subsection (c), a foreign limited liability partnership that engages in a business or exercises a power in this State that a domestic may not engage in or exercise, does so only as a ordinary partnership without the benefit of the limited liability partnership liability shield set forth in Section 306(c). In this sense, a foreign limited liability partnership is treated the same as a domestic limited liability partnership. Also, the Attorney General may maintain an action to restrain a foreign limited liability partnership from transacting an unauthorized business in this State. See Section 1105.

§ 1102. Statement of Foreign Qualification

(a) Before transacting business in this State, a foreign limited liability partnership must file a statement of foreign qualification. The statement must contain:

(1) the name of the foreign limited liability partnership which satisfies the requirements of the State or other jurisdiction under whose law it is formed and ends with "Registered Limited Liability Partnership", "Limited Liability Partnership", "R.L.L.P.", "L.L.P.", "RLLP," or "LLP";

(2) the street address of the partnership's chief executive office and, if different, the street address of an office of the partnership in this State, if any;

(3) if there is no office of the partnership in this State, the name and street address of the partnership's agent for service of process; and

(4) a deferred effective date, if any.

(b) The agent of a foreign limited liability company for service of process must be an individual who is a resident of this State or other person authorized to do business in this State.

(c) The status of a partnership as a foreign limited liability partnership is effective on the later of the filing of the statement of foreign qualification or a date specified in the statement. The status remains effective, regardless of changes in the partnership, until it is canceled pursuant to Section 105(d) or revoked pursuant to Section 1003.

(d) An amendment or cancellation of a statement of foreign qualification is effective when it is filed or on a deferred effective date specified in the amendment or cancellation.

Comment

Section 1102 provides that a foreign limited liability partnership must file a statement of foreign qualification before transacting business in this State. The section also sets forth the information required in the statement. As with other statements, a statement of foreign qualification must be filed in the office of the Secretary of State. See Sections 101(13), 105(a), and 1001(c). Accordingly, a statement of foreign qualification is executed, filed, and otherwise regarded as a statement under this Act. See Section 101(13)(definition of a statement includes a statement of foreign qualification).

Subsection (a) generally requires the same information in a statement of foreign qualification as is required in a statement of qualification. Compare Section 1001(c). The statement of foreign qualification must include a name that complies with the requirements for domestic limited liability partnership under Section 1002 and must include the address of the partnership's chief executive office and, if different, the street address of any other office in this State. If a foreign limited liability partnership does not have any office in this State, the statement of foreign qualification must include the name and street address of an agent for service of process.

As with a statement of qualification, a statement of foreign qualification (and amendments) is effective when filed or at a later specified filing date. Compare Sections 1102(b) and (c) with Sections 1001(e) and (h). Likewise, a statement of foreign qualification remains effective until canceled by the partnership or revoked by the Secretary of State, regardless of changes in the partnership. See Sections 105(d) (statement cancellation) and Section 1003 (revocation for failure to file annual report or pay annual filing fee) and Compare Sections 1102(b) and 1001(e). Statement of qualification provisions regarding the relationship of the status of a foreign partnership relative to its initial filing of a statement are governed by foreign law and are therefore omitted from this section. See Sections 1001(f)(effect of errors and omissions) and (g)(filing establishes all conditions precedent to qualification).

§ 1103. Effect of Failure to Qualify

(a) A foreign limited liability partnership transacting business in this State may not maintain an action or proceeding in this State unless it has in effect a statement of foreign qualification.

(b) The failure of a foreign limited liability partnership to have in effect a statement of foreign qualification does not impair the validity of a contract or act of the foreign limited liability partnership or preclude it from defending an action or proceeding in this State.

(c) A limitation on personal liability of a partner is not waived solely by transacting business in this State without a statement of foreign qualification.

(d) If a foreign limited liability partnership transacts business in this State without a statement of foreign qualification, the [Secretary of State] is its agent for service of process with respect to a right of action arising out of the transaction of business in this State.

Comment

Section 1103 makes clear that the only consequence of a failure to file a statement of foreign qualification is that the foreign limited liability partnership will not be able to maintain an action or proceeding in this State. The partnership's contracts remain valid, it may defend an action or proceeding, personal liability of the partners is not waived, and the Secretary of State is the agent for service of process with respect to claims arising out of transacting business in this State. Sections 1103(b)-(d). Once a statement of foreign qualification is filed, the Secretary of State may revoke the statement for failure to file an annual report but the partnership has the right to cure the failure for two years. See Section 1003(c) and (e). Since the failure to file a statement of foreign qualification has no impact on the liability shield of the partners, a revocation of a statement of foreign qualification also has no impact on the liability shield created under foreign laws. Compare Sections 1103(c) and 1003(f)(revocation of the statement of qualification of a domestic limited liability partnership removes partner liability shield unless filing problems cured within two years).

§ 1104. Activities not Constituting Transacting Business

(a) Activities of a foreign limited liability partnership which do not constitute transacting business for the purpose of this article include:

(1) maintaining, defending, or settling an action or proceeding;

(2) holding meetings of its partners or carrying on any other activity concerning its internal affairs;

(3) maintaining bank accounts;

(4) maintaining offices or agencies for the transfer, exchange, and registration of the partnership's own securities or maintaining trustees or depositories with respect to those securities;

(5) selling through independent contractors;

(6) soliciting or obtaining orders, whether by mail or through employees or agents or otherwise, if the orders require acceptance outside this State before they become contracts;

(7) creating or acquiring indebtedness, with or without a mortgage, or other security interest in property;

(8) collecting debts or foreclosing mortgages or other security interests in property securing the debts, and holding, protecting, and maintaining property so acquired;

(9) conducting an isolated transaction that is completed within 30 days and is not one in the course of similar transactions; and

(10) transacting business in interstate commerce.

(b) For purposes of this article, the ownership in this State of income-producing real property or tangible personal property, other than property excluded under subsection (a), constitutes transacting business in this State.

(c) This section does not apply in determining the contacts or activities that may subject a foreign limited liability partnership to service of process, taxation, or regulation under any other law of this State.

Comment

Because the Attorney General may restrain a foreign limited liability partnership from transacting an unauthorized business in this State and a foreign partnership may not maintain an action or proceeding in this State, the concept of "transacting business" in this State is important. To provide more certainty, subsection (a) sets forth ten separate categories of activities that do not constitute transacting business. Subsection (c) makes clear that the section only considers the definition of "transacting business" and as no impact on whether a foreign limited liability partnership's activities in this State subject it to service of process, taxation, or regulation under any other law of this State.

§ 1105. Action by [Attorney General]

The [Attorney General] may maintain an action to restrain a foreign limited liability partnership from transacting business in this State in violation of this article.

Comment

Section 1105 makes clear that the Attorney General may restrain a foreign limited liability from transacting an unauthorized business in this State. As a threshold matter, a foreign limited liability partnership must be "transacting business" in this State within the meaning of Section 1104. Secondly, the business transacted in this State must be that which could not be engaged in by a domestic limited liability partnership. See Section 1101(c). The fact that a foreign limited liability partnership has a statement of foreign qualification does not permit it to engage in any unauthorized business in this State or impair the power of the Attorney General to restrain the foreign partnership from engaging in the unauthorized business. See Section 1101(c).

Article 12

MISCELLANEOUS PROVISIONS

§ 1201. Uniformity of Application and Construction

This [Act] shall be applied and construed to effectuate its general purpose to make uniform the law with respect to the subject of this [Act] among States enacting it.

§ 1202. Short Title

This [Act] may be cited as the Uniform Partnership Act (1997).

§ 1203. Severability Clause

If any provision of this [Act] or its application to any person or circumstance is held invalid, the invalidity does not affect other provisions or applications of this [Act] which can be given effect without the invalid provision or application, and to this end the provisions of this [Act] are severable.

§ 1204. Effective Date

This [Act] takes effect . . . .

Comment

The effective date of the Act established by an adopting State has operative effects under Section 1206, which defers mandatory application of the Act to existing partnerships.

§ 1205. Repeals

Effective January 1, 199__, the following acts and parts of acts are repealed: [the State Partnership Act as amended and in effect immediately before the effective date of this [Act]].

Comment

This section repeals the adopting State's present general partnership act. The effective date of the repealer should not be any earlier than the date selected by that State in Section 1206(b) for the application of the Act to all partnerships.

§ 1206. Applicability

(a) Before January 1, 199__, this [Act] governs only a partnership formed:

(1) after the effective date of this [Act], except a partnership that is continuing the business of a dissolved partnership under [Section 41 of the superseded Uniform Partnership Act]; and

(2) before the effective date of this [Act], that elects, as provided by subsection (c), to be governed by this [Act].

(b) On and after January 1, 199___, this [Act] governs all partnerships.

(c) Before January 1, 199___, a partnership voluntarily may elect, in the manner provided in its partnership agreement or by law for amending the partnership agreement, to be governed by this [Act]. The provisions of this [Act] relating to the liability of the partnership's partners to third parties apply to limit those partners' liability to a third party who had done business with the partnership within one year before the partnership's election to be governed by this [Act] only if the third party knows or has received a notification of the partnership's election to be governed by this [Act].

Comment

This section provides for a transition period in the applicability of the Act to existing partnerships, similar to that provided in the revised Texas partnership act. *See* Tex. Rev. Civ. Stat. Ann. art. 6132b–10.03 (Vernon Supp. 1994). Subsection (a) makes application of the Act mandatory for all partnerships formed after the effective date of the Act and permissive, by election, for existing partnerships. That affords existing partnerships and partners an opportunity to consider the changes effected by RUPA and to amend their partnership agreements, if appropriate.

Under subsection (b), application of the Act becomes mandatory for all partnerships, including existing partnerships that did not previously elect to be governed by it, upon a future date to be established by the adopting State. Texas, for example, deferred for five years mandatory compliance by existing partnerships.

Subsection (c) provides that an existing partnership may voluntarily elect to be governed by RUPA in the manner provided for amending its partnership agreement. Under UPA Section 18(h), that requires the consent of all the partners, unless otherwise agreed. Third parties doing business with the partnership must know or be notified of the election before RUPA's rules limiting a partner's liability become effective as to them. Those rules would include, for example, the provisions of Section 704 limiting the liability of a partner 90 days after the filing of a statement of dissociation. Without knowledge of the partnership's election, third parties would not be aware that they must check the record to ascertain the extent of a dissociated partner's personal liability.

§ 1207. Savings Clause

This [Act] does not affect an action or proceeding commenced or right accrued before this [Act] takes effect.

Comment

This section continues the prior law after the effective date of the Act with respect to a pending action or proceeding or a right accrued at the time of the effective date. Since courts generally apply the law that exists at the time an action is commenced, in many circumstances the new law of this Act would displace the old law, but for this section.

Almost all States have general savings statutes, usually as part of their statutory construction acts. These are often very broad. Compare Uniform Statute and Rule Construction Act § 16(a) (narrow savings clause). As RUPA is remedial, the more limited savings provisions in Section 1207 are more appropriate than the broad savings provisions of the usual general savings clause. *See generally*, Comment to Uniform Statute and Rule Construction Act § 16.

Pending "action" refers to a judicial proceeding, while "proceeding" is broader and includes administrative proceedings. Although it is not always clear whether a right has "accrued," the term generally means that a cause of action has matured and is ripe for legal redress. *See, e.g., Estate of Hoover v. Iowa Dept. of Social Services*, 299 Iowa 702, 251 N.W.2d 529 (1977); *Nielsen v. State of Wisconsin*, 258 Wis. 1110, 141 N.W.2d 194 (1966). An inchoate right is not enough, and thus, for example, there is no accrued right under a contract until it is breached.

[Sections 1208 through 1211 are necessary only for jurisdictions adopting Uniform Limited Liability Partnership Act Amendments after previously adopting Uniform Partnership Act (1994)]

§ 1208. Effective Date

These [Amendments] take effect ....

§ 1209. Repeals

Effective January 1, 199__, the following acts and parts of acts are repealed: [the Limited Liability Partnership amendments to the State Partnership Act as amended and in effect immediately before the effective date of these [Amendments]].

§ 1210. Applicability

(a) Before January 1, 199__, these [Amendments] govern only a limited liability partnership formed:

(1) on or after the effective date of these [Amendments], unless that partnership is continuing the business of a dissolved limited liability partnership; and

(2) before the effective date of these [Amendments], that elects, as provided by subsection (c), to be governed by these [Amendments].

(b) On and after January 1, 199__, these [Amendments] govern all partnerships.

(c) Before January 1, 199__, a partnership voluntarily may elect, in the manner provided in its partnership agreement or by law for amending the partnership agreement, to be governed by these [Amendments]. The provisions of these [Amendments] relating to the liability of the partnership's partners to third parties apply to limit those partners' liability to a third party who had done business with the partnership within one year before the partnership's election to be governed by these [Amendments], only if the third party knows or has received a notification of the partnership's election to be governed by these [Amendments].

(d) The existing provisions for execution and filing a statement of qualification of a limited liability partnership continue until either the limited liability partnership elects to have this [Act] apply or January 1, 199__.

§ 1211. Savings Clause

These [Amendments] do not affect an action or proceeding commenced or right accrued before these [Amendments] take effect.

*

DELAWARE GENERAL CORPORATION LAW

(Delaware Code, Title 8, Chapter 1)

Table of Sections

SUBCHAPTER I. FORMATION

SUBCHAPTER II. POWERS

SUBCHAPTER III. REGISTERED OFFICE AND REGISTERED AGENT

SUBCHAPTER VI. STOCK TRANSFERS

SUBCHAPTER VII. MEETINGS, ELECTIONS, VOTING AND NOTICE

SUBCHAPTER VIII. AMENDMENT OF CERTIFICATE OF INCORPORATION; CHANGES IN CAPITAL AND CAPITAL STOCK

Section

SUBCHAPTER IX. MERGER, CONSOLIDATION OR CONVERSION

SUBCHAPTER X. SALE OF ASSETS, DISSOLUTION AND WINDING UP

SUBCHAPTER XI. INSOLVENCY; RECEIVERS AND TRUSTEES

SUBCHAPTER XII. RENEWAL, REVIVAL, EXTENSION AND RESTORATION OF CERTIFICATE OF INCORPORATION OR CHARTER

SUBCHAPTER XIII. SUITS AGAINST CORPORATIONS, DIRECTORS, OFFICERS OR STOCKHOLDERS

SUBCHAPTER XIV. CLOSE CORPORATIONS; SPECIAL PROVISIONS

SUBCHAPTER XV. FOREIGN CORPORATIONS

SUBCHAPTER I. FORMATION

§ 101. Incorporators; How Corporation Formed; Purposes

(a) Any person, partnership, association or corporation, singly or jointly with others, and without regard to such person's or entity's residence, domicile or state of incorporation, may incorporate or organize a corporation under this chapter by filing with the Division of Corporations in the Department of State a certificate of incorporation which shall be executed, acknowledged and filed in accordance with § 103 of this title.

(b) A corporation may be incorporated or organized under this chapter to conduct or promote any lawful business or purposes, except as may otherwise be provided by the Constitution or other law of this State.

(c) Corporations for constructing, maintaining and operating public utilities, whether in or outside of this State, may be organized under this chapter, but corporations for constructing, maintaining and operating public utilities within this State shall be subject to, in addition to this chapter, the special provisions and requirements of Title 26 applicable to such corporations.

§ 102. Contents of Certificate of Incorporation

(a) The certificate of incorporation shall set forth:

(1) The name of the corporation, which (i) shall contain 1 of the words "association," "company," "corporation," "club," "foundation," "fund," "incorporated," "institute," "society," "union," "syndicate," or "limited," (or abbreviations thereof, with or without punctuation), or words (or abbreviations thereof, with or without punctuation) of like import of foreign countries or jurisdictions (provided they are written in roman characters or letters); provided, however, that the Division of Corporations in the Department of State may waive such requirement (unless it determines that such name is, or might otherwise appear to be, that of a natural person) if such corporation executes, acknowledges and files with the Secretary of State in accordance with § 103 of this title a certificate stating that its total assets, as defined in subsection (i) of § 503 of this title, are not less than $10,000,000, (ii) shall be such as to distinguish it upon the records in the office of the Division of Corporations in the Department of State from the names that are reserved on such records and from the names on such records of each other corporation, partnership, limited partnership, limited liability company or statutory trust organized or registered as a domestic or foreign corporation, partnership, limited partnership, limited liability company or statutory trust under the laws of this State, except with the written consent of the person who has reserved such name or such other foreign corporation or domestic or foreign partnership, limited partnership, limited liability company or statutory trust, executed, acknowledged and filed with the Secretary of State in accordance with § 103 of this title and (iii) shall not contain the word "bank," or any variation thereof, except for the name of a bank reporting to and under the supervision of the State Bank Commissioner of this State or a subsidiary of a bank or savings association (as those terms

are defined in the Federal Deposit Insurance Act, as amended, at 12 U.S.C. § 1813), or a corporation regulated under the Bank Holding Company Act of 1956, as amended, 12 U.S.C. § 1841 et seq., or the Home Owners' Loan Act, as amended, 12 U.S.C. § 1461 et seq.; provided, however, that this section shall not be construed to prevent the use of the word "bank," or any variation thereof, in a context clearly not purporting to refer to a banking business or otherwise likely to mislead the public about the nature of the business of the corporation or to lead to a pattern and practice of abuse that might cause harm to the interests of the public or the State as determined by the Division of Corporations in the Department of State;

(2) The address (which shall include the street, number, city and county) of the corporation's registered office in this State, and the name of its registered agent at such address;

(3) The nature of the business or purposes to be conducted or promoted. It shall be sufficient to state, either alone or with other businesses or purposes, that the purpose of the corporation is to engage in any lawful act or activity for which corporations may be organized under the General Corporation Law of Delaware, and by such statement all lawful acts and activities shall be within the purposes of the corporation, except for express limitations, if any;

(4) If the corporation is to be authorized to issue only 1 class of stock, the total number of shares of stock which the corporation shall have authority to issue and the par value of each of such shares, or a statement that all such shares are to be without par value. If the corporation is to be authorized to issue more than 1 class of stock, the certificate of incorporation shall set forth the total number of shares of all classes of stock which the corporation shall have authority to issue and the number of shares of each class and shall specify each class the shares of which are to be without par value and each class the shares of which are to have par value and the par value of the shares of each such class. The certificate of incorporation shall also set forth a statement of the designations and the powers, preferences and rights, and the qualifications, limitations or restrictions thereof, which are permitted by § 151 of this title in respect of any class or classes of stock or any series of any class of stock of the corporation and the fixing of which by the certificate of incorporation is desired, and an express grant of such authority as it may then be desired to grant to the board of directors to fix by resolution or resolutions any thereof that may be desired but which shall not be fixed by the certificate of incorporation. The foregoing provisions of this paragraph shall not apply to corporations which are not to have authority to issue capital stock. In the case of such corporations, the fact that they are not to have authority to issue capital stock shall be stated in the certificate of incorporation. The conditions of membership of such corporations

shall likewise be stated in the certificate of incorporation or the certificate may provide that the conditions of membership shall be stated in the bylaws;

(5) The name and mailing address of the incorporator or incorporators;

(6) If the powers of the incorporator or incorporators are to terminate upon the filing of the certificate of incorporation, the names and mailing addresses of the persons who are to serve as directors until the first annual meeting of stockholders or until their successors are elected and qualify.

(b) In addition to the matters required to be set forth in the certificate of incorporation by subsection (a) of this section, the certificate of incorporation may also contain any or all of the following matters:

(1) Any provision for the management of the business and for the conduct of the affairs of the corporation, and any provision creating, defining, limiting and regulating the powers of the corporation, the directors, and the stockholders, or any class of the stockholders, or the members of a nonstock corporation; if such provisions are not contrary to the laws of this State. Any provision which is required or permitted by any section of this chapter to be stated in the bylaws may instead be stated in the certificate of incorporation;

(2) The following provisions, in haec verba, viz:

"Whenever a compromise or arrangement is proposed between this corporation and its creditors or any class of them and/or between this corporation and its stockholders or any class of them, any court of equitable jurisdiction within the State of Delaware may, on the application in a summary way of this corporation or of any creditor or stockholder thereof or on the application of any receiver or receivers appointed for this corporation under § 291 of Title 8 of the Delaware Code or on the application of trustees in dissolution or of any receiver or receivers appointed for this corporation under § 279 of Title 8 of the Delaware Code order a meeting of the creditors or class of creditors, and/or of the stockholders or class of stockholders of this corporation, as the case may be, to be summoned in such manner as the said court directs. If a majority in number representing three fourths in value of the creditors or class of creditors, and/or of the stockholders or class of stockholders of this corporation, as the case may be, agree to any compromise or arrangement and to any reorganization of this corporation as consequence of such compromise or arrangement, the said compromise or arrangement and the said reorganization shall, if sanctioned by the court to which the said application has been made, be binding on all the creditors or class of creditors, and/or on all the stockholders or class of stockholders, of this corporation, as the case may be, and also on this corporation'';

(3) Such provisions as may be desired granting to the holders of the stock of the corporation, or the holders of any class or series of a class thereof, the preemptive right to subscribe to any or all additional issues of stock of the corporation of any or all classes or series thereof, or to any securities of the corporation convertible into such stock. No stockholder shall have any preemptive right to subscribe to an additional issue of stock or to any security convertible into such stock unless, and except to the extent that, such right is expressly granted to such stockholder in the certificate of incorporation. All such rights in existence on July 3, 1967, shall remain in existence unaffected by this paragraph unless and until changed or terminated by appropriate action which expressly provides for the change or termination;

(4) Provisions requiring for any corporate action, the vote of a larger portion of the stock or of any class or series thereof, or of any other securities having voting power, or a larger number of the directors, than is required by this chapter;

(5) A provision limiting the duration of the corporation's existence to a specified date; otherwise, the corporation shall have perpetual existence;

(6) A provision imposing personal liability for the debts of the corporation on its stockholders or members to a specified extent and upon specified conditions; otherwise, the stockholders or members of a corporation shall not be personally liable for the payment of the corporation's debts except as they may be liable by reason of their own conduct or acts;

(7) A provision eliminating or limiting the personal liability of a director to the corporation or its stockholders for monetary damages for breach of fiduciary duty as a director, provided that such provision shall not eliminate or limit the liability of a director: (i) For any breach of the director's duty of loyalty to the corporation or its stockholders; (ii) for acts or omissions not in good faith or which involve intentional misconduct or a knowing violation of law; (iii) under § 174 of this title; or (iv) for any transaction from which the director derived an improper personal benefit. No such provision shall eliminate or limit the liability of a director for any act or omission occurring prior to the date when such provision becomes effective. All references in this paragraph to a director shall also be deemed to refer (x) to a member of the governing body of a corporation which is not authorized to issue capital stock, and (y) to such other person or persons, if any, who, pursuant to a provision of the certificate of incorporation in accordance with § 141(a) of this title, exercise or perform any of the powers or duties otherwise conferred or imposed upon the board of directors by this title.

(c) It shall not be necessary to set forth in the certificate of incorporation any of the powers conferred on corporations by this chapter.

(d) Except for provisions included pursuant to subdivisions (a)(1), (a)(2), (a)(5), (a)(6), (b)(2), (b)(5), (b)(7) of this section, and provisions included pursuant to subdivision (a)(4) of this section specifying the classes, number of shares, and par value of shares the corporation is authorized to issue, any provision of the certificate of incorporation may be made dependent upon facts ascertainable outside such instrument, provided that the manner in which such facts shall operate upon the provision is clearly and explicitly set forth therein. The term "facts," as used in this subsection, includes, but is not limited to, the occurrence of any event, including a determination or action by any person or body, including the corporation.

(e) The exclusive right to the use of a name that is available for use by a domestic or foreign corporation may be reserved by or on behalf of:

(1) Any person intending to incorporate or organize a corporation with that name under this chapter or contemplating such incorporation or organization;

(2) Any domestic corporation or any foreign corporation qualified to do business in the State of Delaware, in either case, intending to change its name or contemplating such a change;

(3) Any foreign corporation intending to qualify to do business in the State of Delaware and adopt that name or contemplating such qualification and adoption; and

(4) Any person intending to organize a foreign corporation and have it qualify to do business in the State of Delaware and adopt that name or contemplating such organization, qualification and adoption.

The reservation of a specified name may be made by filing with the Secretary of State an application, executed by the applicant, certifying that the reservation is made by or on behalf of a domestic corporation, foreign corporation or other person described in paragraphs (e)(1)-(4) of this section above, and specifying the name to be reserved and the name and address of the applicant. If the Secretary of State finds that the name is available for use by a domestic or foreign corporation, the Secretary shall reserve the name for the use of the applicant for a period of 120 days. The same applicant may renew for successive 120–day periods a reservation of a specified name by filing with the Secretary of State, prior to the expiration of such reservation (or renewal thereof), an application for renewal of such reservation, executed by the applicant, certifying that the reservation is renewed by or on behalf of a domestic corporation, foreign corporation or other person described in paragraphs (e)(1)-(4) of this section above and specifying the name reservation to be renewed and the name and address of the applicant. The right to the exclusive use of a reserved name may be transferred to any other person by filing in the office of the Secretary of State a notice of the transfer, executed by the applicant for whom the name was reserved, specifying the name reservation to be transferred and the name and address of the transferee. The reservation of a specified name may be cancelled by filing with the Secretary of State a notice of cancellation, executed by the applicant or transferee, specifying the name reservation to be cancelled and the name and address of the applicant or transferee. Unless the Secretary of State finds that any application, application for renewal, notice of transfer, or notice of cancellation filed with the Secretary of State as required by this subsection does not conform to law, upon receipt of all filing fees required by law the Secretary of State shall prepare and return to the person who filed such instrument a copy of the filed instrument with a notation thereon of the action taken by the Secretary of State. A fee as set forth in § 391 of this title shall be paid at the time of the reservation of any name, at the time of the renewal of any such reservation and at the time of the filing of a notice of the transfer or cancellation of any such reservation.

§ 103. Execution, Acknowledgment, Filing, Recording and Effective Date of Original Certificate of Incorporation and Other Instruments; Exceptions

(a) Whenever any instrument is to be filed with the Secretary of State or in accordance with this section or chapter, such instrument shall be executed as follows:

(1) The certificate of incorporation, and any other instrument to be filed before the election of the initial board of directors if the initial directors were not named in the certificate of incorporation, shall be signed by the incorporator or incorporators (or, in the case of any such other instrument, such incorporator's or incorporators' successors and assigns). If any incorporator is not available by reason of death, incapacity, unknown address, or refusal or neglect to act, then any such other instrument may be signed, with the same effect as if such incorporator had signed it, by any person for whom or on whose behalf such incorporator, in executing the certificate of incorporation, was acting directly or indirectly as employee or agent, provided that such other instrument shall state that such incorporator is not available and the reason therefor, that such incorporator in executing the certificate of incorporation was acting directly or indirectly as employee or agent for or on behalf of such person, and that such person's signature on such instrument is otherwise authorized and not wrongful.

(2) All other instruments shall be signed:

a. By any authorized officer of the corporation; or

b. If it shall appear from the instrument that there are no such officers, then by a majority of the directors or by such directors as may be designated by the board; or

c. If it shall appear from the instrument that there are no such officers or directors, then by the holders of record, or such of them as may be designated by the holders of record, of a majority of all outstanding shares of stock; or

d. By the holders of record of all outstanding shares of stock.

(b) Whenever this chapter requires any instrument to be acknowledged, such requirement is satisfied by either:

(1) The formal acknowledgment by the person or 1 of the persons signing the instrument that it is such person's act and deed or the act and deed of the corporation, and that the facts stated therein are true. Such acknowledgment shall be made before a person who is authorized by the law of the place of execution to take acknowledgments of deeds. If such person has a seal of office such person shall affix it to the instrument.

(2) The signature, without more, of the person or persons signing the instrument, in which case such signature or signatures shall constitute the affirmation or acknowledgment of the signatory, under penalties of perjury, that the instrument is such person's act and deed or the act and deed of the corporation, and that the facts stated therein are true.

(c) Whenever any instrument is to be filed with the Secretary of State or in accordance with this section or chapter, such requirement means that:

(1) The signed instrument shall be delivered to the office of the Secretary of State;

(2) All taxes and fees authorized by law to be collected by the Secretary of State in connection with the filing of the instrument shall be tendered to the Secretary of State; and

(3) Upon delivery of the instrument, the Secretary of State shall record the date and time of its delivery. Upon such delivery and tender of the required taxes and fees, the Secretary of State shall certify that the instrument has been filed in the Secretary of State's office by endorsing upon the signed instrument the word "Filed", and the date and time of its filing. This endorsement is the "filing date" of the instrument, and is conclusive of the date and time of its filing in the absence of actual fraud. The Secretary of State shall file and index the endorsed instrument. Except as provided in paragraph (4) of this subsection and in subsection (i) of this section, such filing date of an instrument shall be the date and time of delivery of the instrument.

(4) Upon request made upon or prior to delivery, the Secretary of State may, to the extent deemed practicable, establish as the filing date of an instrument a date and time after its delivery. If the Secretary of State refuses to file any instrument due to an error, omission or other imperfection, the Secretary of State may hold such instrument in suspension, and in such event, upon delivery of a replacement instrument in proper form for filing and tender of the required taxes and fees within 5 business days after notice of such suspension is given to the filer, the Secretary of State shall establish as the filing date of such instrument the date and time that would have been the filing date of the rejected instrument had it been accepted for filing. The Secretary of State shall not issue a certificate of good standing with respect to any corporation with an instrument held in suspension pursuant to this subsection. The Secretary of State may establish as the filing date of an instrument the date and time at which information from such instrument is entered pursuant to subdivision (c)(7) of this section if such instrument is delivered on the same date and within 4 hours after such information is entered.

(5) The Secretary of State, acting as agent for the recorders of each of the counties, shall collect and deposit in a separate account established exclusively for that purpose a county assessment fee with respect to each filed instrument and shall thereafter weekly remit from such account to the recorder of each of the said counties the amount or amounts of such fees as provided for in subdivision (c)(5) of this section or as elsewhere provided by law. Said fees shall be for the purposes of defraying certain costs incurred by the counties in merging the information and images of such filed documents with the document information systems of each of the recorder's offices in the counties and in retrieving, maintaining and displaying such information and images in the offices of the recorders and at remote locations in each of such counties. In consideration for its acting as the agent for the recorders with respect to the collection and payment of the county assessment fees, the Secretary of State shall retain and pay over to the General Fund of the State an administrative charge of 1 percent of the total fees collected.

(6) The assessment fee to the counties shall be $24 for each 1-page instrument filed with the Secretary of State in accordance with this section and $9 for each additional page for instruments with more than 1 page. The recorder's office to receive the assessment fee shall be the recorder's office in the county in which the corporation's registered office in this State is, or is to be, located, except that an assessment fee shall not be charged for either a certificate of dissolution qualifying for treatment under § 391(a)(5)b. of this title or a document filed in accordance with Subchapter XV of this chapter.

(7) The Secretary of State, acting as agent, shall collect and deposit in a separate account established exclusively for that purpose a courthouse municipality fee with respect to each filed instrument and shall thereafter monthly remit funds from such account to the treasuries of the municipalities designated in § 301 of Title 10. Said fees shall be for the purposes of defraying certain costs incurred by such municipalities in hosting the primary locations for the Delaware Courts. The fee to such municipalities shall be $20 for each instrument filed with the Secretary of State in accordance with this section. The municipality to receive the fee shall be the municipality designated in § 301 of Title 10 in the county in which the corporation's registered office in this State is, or is to be, located, except that a fee shall not be charged for a certificate of dissolution qualifying for treatment under § 391(a)(5)b. of this title, a resignation of agent without appointment of a successor under § 136 of this title, or a document filed in accordance with Subchapter XV of this chapter.

(8) The Secretary of State shall cause to be entered such information from each instrument as the Secretary of State deems appropriate into the Delaware Corporation Information System or any system which is a successor thereto in the office of the Secretary of State, and such information and a copy of each such instrument shall be permanently maintained as a public record on a suitable medium. The Secretary of State is authorized to grant direct access to such system to registered agents subject to the execution of an operating agreement between the Secretary of State and such registered agent. Any registered agent granted such access shall demonstrate the existence of policies to ensure that information entered into the system accurately reflects the content of instruments in the possession of the registered agent at the time of entry.

(d) Any instrument filed in accordance with subsection (c) of this section shall be effective upon its filing date. Any instrument may provide that it is not to become effective until a specified time subsequent to the time it is filed, but such time shall not be later than a time on the 90th day after the date of its filing. If any instrument filed in accordance with subsection (c) of this section provides for a future effective date or time and if the transaction is terminated or its terms are amended to change the future effective date or time prior to the future effective date or time, the instrument shall be terminated or amended by the filing, prior to the future effective date or time set forth in such instrument, of a certificate of termination or amendment of the original instrument, executed in accordance with subsection (a) of this section, which shall identify the instrument which has been terminated or amended and shall state that the instrument has been terminated or the manner in which it has been amended.

(e) If another section of this chapter specifically prescribes a manner of executing, acknowledging or filing a specified instrument or a time when such instrument shall become effective which differs from the corresponding provisions of this section, then such other section shall govern.

(f) Whenever any instrument authorized to be filed with the Secretary of State under any provision of this title, has been so filed and is an inaccurate record of the corporate action therein referred to, or was defectively or erroneously executed, sealed or acknowledged, the instrument may be corrected by filing with the Secretary of State a certificate of correction of the instrument which shall be executed, acknowledged and filed in accordance with this section. The certificate of correction shall specify the inaccuracy or defect to be corrected and shall set forth the portion of the instrument in corrected form. In lieu of filing a certificate of correction the instrument may be corrected by filing with the Secretary of State a corrected instrument which shall be executed, acknowledged and filed in accordance with this section. The corrected instrument shall be specifically designated as such in its heading, shall specify the inaccuracy or defect to be corrected, and shall set forth the entire instrument in corrected form. An instrument corrected in accordance with this section shall be effective as of the date the original instrument was filed, except as to those persons who are substantially and adversely affected by the correction and as to those persons the instrument as corrected shall be effective from the filing date.

(g) Notwithstanding that any instrument authorized to be filed with the Secretary of State under this title is when filed inaccurately, defectively or erroneously executed, sealed or acknowledged, or otherwise defective in any respect, the Secretary of State shall have no liability to any person for the preclearance for filing, the acceptance for filing or the filing and indexing of such instrument by the Secretary of State.

(h) Any signature on any instrument authorized to be filed with the Secretary of State under this title may be a facsimile, a conformed signature or an electronically transmitted signature.

(i)(1) If:

a. Together with the actual delivery of an instrument and tender of the required taxes and fees, there is delivered to the Secretary of State a separate affidavit (which in its heading shall be designated as an "affidavit of extraordinary condition") attesting, on the basis of personal knowledge of the affiant or a reliable source of knowledge identified in the affidavit, that an earlier effort to deliver such instrument and tender such taxes and fees was made in good faith, specifying the nature, date and time of such good faith effort and requesting that the Secretary of State establish such date and time as the filing date of such instrument; or

b. Upon the actual delivery of an instrument and tender of the required taxes and fees, the Secretary of State in the Secretary's discretion provides a written waiver of the requirement for such an affidavit stating that it appears to the Secretary of State that an earlier effort to deliver such instrument and tender such taxes and fees was made in good faith and specifying the date and time of such effort; and

c. The Secretary of State determines that an extraordinary condition existed at such date and time, that such earlier effort was unsuccessful as a result of the existence of such extraordinary condition, and that such actual delivery and tender were made within a reasonable period (not to exceed 2 business days) after the cessation of such extraordinary condition,

then the Secretary of State may establish such date and time as the filing date of such instrument. No fee shall be paid to the Secretary of State for receiving an affidavit of extraordinary condition.

(2) For purposes of this subsection, an "extraordinary condition" means: any emergency resulting from an attack on, invasion or occupation by foreign military forces of, or disaster, catastrophe, war or other armed conflict, revolution or insurrection, or rioting or civil commotion in, the United States or a locality in which the Secretary of State conducts its business or in which the good faith effort to deliver the instrument and tender the required taxes and fees is made, or the immediate threat of any of the foregoing; or any malfunction or outage of the electrical or telephone service to the Secretary of State's office, or weather or other condition in or about a locality in which the Secretary of State conducts its business, as a result of which the Secretary of State's office is not open for the purpose of the filing of instruments under this chapter or such filing cannot be effected without extraordinary effort. The Secretary of State may require such proof as it deems necessary to make the determination required under paragraph (1)c. of this subsection, and any such determination shall be conclusive in the absence of actual fraud.

(3) If the Secretary of State establishes the filing date of an instrument pursuant to this subsection, the date and time of delivery of the affidavit of extraordinary condition or the date and time of the Secretary of State's written waiver of such affidavit shall be endorsed on such affidavit or waiver and such affidavit or waiver, so endorsed, shall be attached to the filed instrument to which it relates. Such filed instrument shall be effective as of the date and time established as the filing date by the Secretary of State pursuant to this subsection, except as to those persons who are substantially and adversely affected by such establishment and, as to those persons, the instrument shall be effective from the date and time endorsed on the affidavit of extraordinary condition or written waiver attached thereto.

§ 104. Certificate of Incorporation; Definition

The term "certificate of incorporation," as used in this chapter, unless the context requires otherwise, includes not only the original certificate of incorporation filed to create a corporation but also all other certificates, agreements of merger or consolidation, plans of reorganization, or other instruments, howsoever designated, which are filed pursuant to §§ 102, 133–136, 151, 241–243, 245, 251–258, 263–264, 303, or any other section of this title, and which have the effect of amending or supplementing in some respect a corporation's original certificate of incorporation.

§ 105. Certificate of Incorporation and Other Certificates; Evidence

A copy of a certificate of incorporation, or a restated certificate of incorporation, or of any other certificate which has been filed in the office of the Secretary of State as required by any provision of this title shall, when duly certified by the Secretary of State, be received in all courts, public offices and official bodies as prima facie evidence of:

(1) Due execution, acknowledgment and filing of the instrument;

(2) Observance and performance of all acts and conditions necessary to have been observed and performed precedent to the instrument becoming effective; and

(3) Any other facts required or permitted by law to be stated in the instrument.

§ 106. Commencement of Corporate Existence

Upon the filing with the Secretary of State of the certificate of incorporation, executed and acknowledged in accordance with § 103 of this title, the incorporator or incorporators who signed the certificate, and such incorporator's or incorporators' successors and assigns, shall, from the date of such filing, be and constitute a body corporate, by the name set forth in the certificate, subject to subsection (d) of § 103 of this title and subject to dissolution or other termination of its existence as provided in this chapter.

§ 107. Powers of Incorporators

If the persons who are to serve as directors until the first annual meeting of stockholders have not been named in the certificate of incorporation, the incorporator or incorporators, until the directors are elected, shall manage the affairs of the corporation and may do whatever is necessary and proper to perfect the organization of the corporation, including the adoption of the original bylaws of the corporation and the election of directors.

§ 108. Organization Meeting of Incorporators or Directors Named in Certificate of Incorporation

(a) After the filing of the certificate of incorporation an organization meeting of the incorporator or incorporators, or of the board of directors if the initial directors were named in the certificate of incorporation, shall be held, either within or without this State, at the call of a majority of the incorporators or directors, as the case may be, for the purposes of adopting bylaws, electing directors (if the meeting is of the incorporators) to serve or hold office until the first annual meeting of stockholders or until their successors are elected and qualify, electing officers if the meeting is of the directors, doing any other or further acts to perfect the organization of the corporation, and transacting such other business as may come before the meeting.

(b) The persons calling the meeting shall give to each other incorporator or director, as the case may be, at least 2 days' written notice thereof by any usual means of communication, which notice shall state the time, place and purposes of the meeting as fixed by the persons calling it. Notice of the meeting need not be given to anyone who attends the meeting or who signs a waiver of notice either before or after the meeting.

(c) Any action permitted to be taken at the organization meeting of the incorporators or directors, as the case may be, may be taken without a meeting if each incorporator or director, where there is more than 1, or the sole incorporator or director where there is only 1, signs an instrument which states the action so taken.

§ 109. Bylaws

(a) The original or other bylaws of a corporation may be adopted, amended or repealed by the incorporators, by the initial directors if they were named in the certificate of incorporation, or, before a corporation has received any payment for any of its stock, by its board of directors. After a corporation has received any payment for any of its stock, the power to adopt, amend or repeal bylaws shall be in the stockholders entitled to vote, or, in the case of a nonstock corporation, in its members entitled to vote; provided, however, any corporation may, in its certificate of incorporation, confer the power to adopt, amend or repeal bylaws upon the directors or, in the case of a nonstock corporation, upon its governing body by whatever name designated. The fact that such power has been so conferred upon the directors or governing body, as the case may be, shall not divest the stockholders or members of the power, nor limit their power to adopt, amend or repeal bylaws.

(b) The bylaws may contain any provision, not inconsistent with law or with the certificate of incorporation, relating to the business of the corporation, the conduct of its affairs, and its rights or powers or the rights or powers of its stockholders, directors, officers or employees.

§ 110. Emergency Bylaws and Other Powers in Emergency

(a) The board of directors of any corporation may adopt emergency bylaws, subject to repeal or change by action of the stockholders, which shall notwithstanding any different provision elsewhere in this chapter or in Chapters 3 and 5 of Title 26, or in Chapter 7 of Title 5, or in the certificate of incorporation or bylaws, be operative during any emergency resulting from an attack on the United States or on a locality in which the corporation conducts its business or customarily holds meetings of its board of directors or its stockholders, or during any nuclear or atomic disaster, or during the existence of any catastrophe, or other similar emergency condition, as a result of which a quorum of the board of directors or a standing committee thereof cannot readily be convened for action. The emergency bylaws may make any provision that may be practical and necessary for the circumstances of the emergency, including provisions that:

(1) A meeting of the board of directors or a committee thereof may be called by any officer or director in such manner and under such conditions as shall be prescribed in the emergency bylaws;

(2) The director or directors in attendance at the meeting, or any greater number fixed by the emergency bylaws, shall constitute a quorum; and

(3) The officers or other persons designated on a list approved by the board of directors before the emergency, all in such order of priority and subject to such conditions and for such period of time (not longer than reasonably necessary after the termination of the emergency) as may be provided in the emergency bylaws or in the resolution approving the list, shall, to the extent required to provide a quorum at any meeting of the board of directors, be deemed directors for such meeting.

(b) The board of directors, either before or during any such emergency, may provide, and from time to time modify, lines of succession in the event that during such emergency any or all officers or agents of the corporation shall for any reason be rendered incapable of discharging their duties.

(c) The board of directors, either before or during any such emergency, may, effective in the emergency, change the head office or designate several alternative head offices or regional offices, or authorize the officers so to do.

(d) No officer, director or employee acting in accordance with any emergency bylaws shall be liable except for wilful misconduct.

(e) To the extent not inconsistent with any emergency bylaws so adopted, the bylaws of the corporation shall remain in effect during any emergency and upon its termination the emergency bylaws shall cease to be operative.

(f) Unless otherwise provided in emergency bylaws, notice of any meeting of the board of directors during such an emergency may be given only to such of the directors as it may be feasible to reach at the time and by such means as may be feasible at the time, including publication or radio.

(g) To the extent required to constitute a quorum at any meeting of the board of directors during such an emergency, the officers of the corporation who are present shall, unless otherwise provided in emergency bylaws, be deemed, in order of rank and within the same rank in order of seniority, directors for such meeting.

(h) Nothing contained in this section shall be deemed exclusive of any other provisions for emergency powers consistent with other sections of this title which have been or may be adopted by corporations created under this chapter.

§ 111. Jurisdiction to Interpret, Apply, Enforce or Determine the Validity of Corporate Instruments and Provisions of this Title

(a) Any civil action to interpret, apply, enforce or determine the validity of the provisions of:

(1) The certificate of incorporation or the bylaws of a corporation;

(2) Any instrument, document or agreement by which a corporation creates or sells, or offers to create or sell, any of its stock, or any rights or options respecting its stock;

(3) Any written restrictions on the transfer, registration of transfer or ownership of securities under § 202 of this title;

(4) Any proxy under § 212 or 215 of this title;

(5) Any voting trust or other voting agreement under § 218 of this title;

(6) Any agreement or certificate of merger or consolidation governed by § 251–253, 255–258, 263 or 264 of this title;

(7) Any certificate of conversion under § 265 or 266 of this title;

(8) Any certificate of domestication, transfer or continuance under § 388, 389 or 390 of this title; or

(9) Any other instrument, document, agreement, or certificate required by any provision of this title;

May be brought in the Court of Chancery, except to the extent that a statute confers exclusive jurisdiction on a court, agency or tribunal other than the Court of Chancery.

(b) Any civil action to interpret, apply or enforce any provision of this title may be brought in the Court of Chancery.

SUBCHAPTER II. POWERS

§ 121. General Powers

(a) In addition to the powers enumerated in § 122 of this title, every corporation, its officers, directors and stockholders shall possess and may exercise all the powers and privileges granted by this chapter or by any other law or by its certificate of incorporation, together with any powers incidental thereto, so far as such powers and privileges are necessary or convenient to the conduct, promotion or attainment of the business or purposes set forth in its certificate of incorporation.

(b) Every corporation shall be governed by the provisions and be subject to the restrictions and liabilities contained in this chapter.

§ 122. Specific Powers

Every corporation created under this chapter shall have power to:

(1) Have perpetual succession by its corporate name, unless a limited period of duration is stated in its certificate of incorporation;

(2) Sue and be sued in all courts and participate, as a party or otherwise, in any judicial, administrative, arbitrative or other proceeding, in its corporate name;

(3) Have a corporate seal, which may be altered at pleasure, and use the same by causing it or a facsimile thereof, to be impressed or affixed or in any other manner reproduced;

(4) Purchase, receive, take by grant, gift, devise, bequest or otherwise, lease, or otherwise acquire, own, hold, improve, employ, use and otherwise deal in and with real or personal property, or any interest therein, wherever situated, and to sell, convey, lease, exchange, transfer or otherwise dispose of, or mortgage or pledge, all or any of its property and assets, or any interest therein, wherever situated;

(5) Appoint such officers and agents as the business of the corporation requires and to pay or otherwise provide for them suitable compensation;

(6) Adopt, amend and repeal bylaws;

(7) Wind up and dissolve itself in the manner provided in this chapter;

(8) Conduct its business, carry on its operations and have offices and exercise its powers within or without this State;

(9) Make donations for the public welfare or for charitable, scientific or educational purposes, and in time of war or other national emergency in aid thereof;

(10) Be an incorporator, promoter or manager of other corporations of any type or kind;

(11) Participate with others in any corporation, partnership, limited partnership, joint venture or other association of any kind, or in any transaction, undertaking or arrangement which the participating corporation would have power to conduct by itself, whether or not such participation involves sharing or delegation of control with or to others;

(12) Transact any lawful business which the corporation's board of directors shall find to be in aid of governmental authority;

(13) Make contracts, including contracts of guaranty and suretyship, incur liabilities, borrow money at such rates of interest as the corporation may determine, issue its notes, bonds and other obligations, and secure any of its obligations by mortgage, pledge or other encumbrance of all or any of its property, franchises and income, and make contracts of guaranty and suretyship which are necessary or convenient to the conduct, promotion or attainment of the business of (a) a corporation all of the outstanding stock of which is owned, directly or indirectly, by the contracting corporation, or (b) a corporation which owns, directly or indirectly, all of the outstanding stock of the contracting corporation, or (c) a corporation all of the outstanding stock of which is owned, directly or indirectly, by a corporation which owns, directly or indirectly, all of the outstanding stock of the contracting corporation, which contracts of guaranty and suretyship shall be deemed to be necessary or convenient to the conduct, promotion or attainment of the business of the contracting corporation, and make other contracts of guaranty and suretyship which are necessary or convenient to the conduct, promotion or attainment of the business of the contracting corporation;

(14) Lend money for its corporate purposes, invest and reinvest its funds, and take, hold and deal with real and personal property as security for the payment of funds so loaned or invested;

(15) Pay pensions and establish and carry out pension, profit sharing, stock option, stock purchase, stock bonus, retirement, benefit, incentive and compensation plans, trusts and provisions for any or all of its directors, officers and employees, and for any or all of the directors, officers and employees of its subsidiaries;

(16) Provide insurance for its benefit on the life of any of its directors, officers or employees, or on the life of any stockholder for

the purpose of acquiring at such stockholder's death shares of its stock owned by such stockholder.

(17) Renounce, in its certificate of incorporation or by action of its board of directors, any interest or expectancy of the corporation in, or in being offered an opportunity to participate in, specified business opportunities or specified classes or categories of business opportunities that are presented to the corporation or 1 or more of its officers, directors or stockholders.

§ 123. Powers Respecting Securities of Other Corporations or Entities

Any corporation organized under the laws of this State may guarantee, purchase, take, receive, subscribe for or otherwise acquire; own, hold, use or otherwise employ; sell, lease, exchange, transfer or otherwise dispose of; mortgage, lend, pledge or otherwise deal in and with, bonds and other obligations of, or shares or other securities or interests in, or issued by, any other domestic or foreign corporation, partnership, association or individual, or by any government or agency or instrumentality thereof. A corporation while owner of any such securities may exercise all the rights, powers and privileges of ownership, including the right to vote.

§ 124. Effect of Lack of Corporate Capacity or Power; Ultra Vires

No act of a corporation and no conveyance or transfer of real or personal property to or by a corporation shall be invalid by reason of the fact that the corporation was without capacity or power to do such act or to make or receive such conveyance or transfer, but such lack of capacity or power may be asserted:

(1) In a proceeding by a stockholder against the corporation to enjoin the doing of any act or acts or the transfer of real or personal property by or to the corporation. If the unauthorized acts or transfer sought to be enjoined are being, or are to be, performed or made pursuant to any contract to which the corporation is a party, the court may, if all of the parties to the contract are parties to the proceeding and if it deems the same to be equitable, set aside and enjoin the performance of such contract, and in so doing may allow to the corporation or to the other parties to the contract, as the case may be, such compensation as may be equitable for the loss or damage sustained by any of them which may result from the action of the court in setting aside and enjoining the performance of such contract, but anticipated profits to be derived from the performance of the contract shall not be awarded by the court as a loss or damage sustained;

Stockholder v. Corp

(2) In a proceeding by the corporation, whether acting directly or through a receiver, trustee or other legal representative, or through stockholders in a representative suit, against an incumbent or former officer or director of the corporation, for loss or damage due to such incumbent or former officer's or director's unauthorized act;

(3) In a proceeding by the Attorney General to dissolve the corporation, or to enjoin the corporation from the transaction of unauthorized business.

§ 125. Conferring Academic or Honorary Degrees

No corporation organized after April 18, 1945, shall have power to confer academic or honorary degrees unless the certificate of incorporation or an amendment thereof shall so provide and unless the certificate of incorporation or an amendment thereof prior to its being filed in the office of the Secretary of State shall have endorsed thereon the approval of the Department of Education of this State. No corporation organized before April 18, 1945, any provision in its certificate of incorporation to the contrary notwithstanding, shall possess the power aforesaid without first filing in the office of the Secretary of State a certificate of amendment so providing, the filing of which certificate of amendment in the office of the Secretary of State shall be subject to prior approval of the Department of Education, evidenced as hereinabove provided. Approval shall be granted only when it appears to the reasonable satisfaction of the Department of Education that the corporation is engaged in conducting a bona fide institution of higher learning, giving instructions in arts and letters, science or the professions, or that the corporation proposes, in good faith, to engage in that field and has or will have the resources, including personnel, requisite for the conduct of an institution of higher learning. Upon dissolution, all such corporations shall comply with § 8530 of Title 14. Notwithstanding any provision herein to the contrary, no corporation shall have the power to conduct a private business or trade school unless the certificate of incorporation or an amendment thereof, prior to its being filed in the office of the Secretary of State, shall have endorsed thereon the approval of the Department of Education pursuant to Chapter 85 of Title 14.

Notwithstanding the foregoing provisions, any corporation conducting a law school, which has its principal place of operation in Delaware, and which intends to meet the standards of approval of the American Bar Association, may, after it has been in actual operation for not less than 1 year, retain at its own expense a dean or dean emeritus of a law school fully approved by the American Bar Association to make an on-site inspection and report concerning the progress of the corporation toward meeting the standards for approval by the American Bar Association. Such dean or dean emeritus shall be chosen by the Attorney General from a panel of 3 deans whose names are presented to the Attorney General as being willing to serve. One such dean on this panel shall be nominated by the trustees of said law school corporation; another dean shall be nominated by a committee of the Student Bar Association of said law school; and the other dean shall be nominated by a committee of lawyers who are parents of students attending such law school. If any of the above-named groups cannot find a dean, it may substitute 2 full professors of accredited law schools for the dean it is entitled to nominate, and in such a case if the Attorney General chooses 1 of such professors, such professor shall serve the function of a dean as herein prescribed. If the dean so retained shall report in writing that, in such dean's professional judgment, the corporation is attempting, in good faith, to comply with the standards for approval of the American Bar Association and is making reasonable progress toward meeting such standards, the corporation may file a copy of the report with the Secretary of Education and with the Attorney General. Any corporation which complies with these provisions by filing such report shall be deemed to have temporary approval from the State and shall be entitled to amend its certificate of incorporation to authorize the granting of standard academic law degrees. Thereafter, until the law school operated by the corporation is approved by the American Bar Association, the corporation shall file once during each academic year a new report, in the same manner as the first report. If, at any time, the corporation fails to file such a report, or if the dean retained to render such report states that, in such dean's opinion, the corporation is not continuing to make reasonable progress toward accreditation, the Attorney General, at the request of the Secretary of Education, may file a complaint in the Court of Chancery to suspend said temporary approval and degree-granting power until a further report is filed by a dean or dean emeritus of an accredited law school that the school has resumed its progress towards meeting the standards for approval. Upon approval of the law school by the American Bar Association, temporary approval shall become final, and shall no longer be subject to suspension or vacation under this section.

§ 126. Banking Power Denied

(a) No corporation organized under this chapter shall possess the power of issuing bills, notes, or other evidences of debt for circulation as money, or the power of carrying on the business of receiving deposits of money.

(b) Corporations organized under this chapter to buy, sell and otherwise deal in notes, open accounts and other similar evidences of debt, or to loan money and to take notes, open accounts and other similar evidences of debt as collateral security therefor, shall not be deemed to be engaging in the business of banking.

§ 127. Private Foundation; Powers and Duties

A corporation of this State which is a private foundation under the United States internal revenue laws and whose certificate of incorporation does not expressly provide that this section shall not apply to it is required to act or to refrain from acting so as not to subject itself to the taxes imposed by 26 U.S.C. § 4941 (relating to taxes on self-dealing), 4942 (relating to taxes on failure to distribute income), 4943 (relating to taxes on excess business holdings), 4944 (relating to taxes on investments which jeopardize charitable purpose), or 4945 (relating to taxable expenditures), or corresponding provisions of any subsequent United States internal revenue law.

SUBCHAPTER III. REGISTERED OFFICE AND REGISTERED AGENT

§ 131. Registered Office in State; Principal Office or Place of Business in State

(a) Every corporation shall have and maintain in this State a registered office which may, but need not be, the same as its place of business.

(b) Whenever the term "corporation's principal office or place of business in this State" or "principal office or place of business of the corporation in this State," or other term of like import, is or has been used in a corporation's certificate of incorporation, or in any other document, or in any statute, it shall be deemed to mean and refer to, unless the context indicates otherwise, the corporation's registered office required by this section; and it shall not be necessary for any corporation to amend its certificate of incorporation or any other document to comply with this section.

§ 132. Registered Agent in State; Resident Agent [Effective Until Jan. 1, 2007]

(a) Every corporation shall have and maintain in this State a registered agent, which agent may be any of (i) the corporation itself, (ii) an individual resident in this State, (iii) a domestic corporation (other than the corporation itself), a domestic limited partnership, a domestic limited liability company or a domestic statutory trust or (iv) a foreign corporation, a foreign limited partnership or a foreign limited liability company authorized to transact business in this State, in each case, having a business office identical with the office of such registered agent which generally is open during normal business hours to accept service of process and otherwise perform the functions of a registered agent.

(b) Whenever the term "resident agent" or "resident agent in charge of a corporation's principal office or place of business in this State," or other term of like import which refers to a corporation's agent required by statute to be located in this State, is or has been used in a corporation's certificate of incorporation, or in any other document, or in any statute, it shall be deemed to mean and refer to, unless the context indicates otherwise, the corporation's registered agent required by this section; and it shall not be necessary for any corporation to amend its certificate of incorporation or any other document to comply with this section.

§ 132. Registered Agent in State; Resident Agent [Effective Jan. 1, 2007]

(a) Every corporation shall have and maintain in this State a registered agent, which agent may be any of:

(1) The corporation itself;

(2) An individual resident in this State;

(3) A domestic corporation (other than the corporation itself), a domestic partnership (whether general (including a limited liability partnership) or limited (including a limited liability limited partnership)), a domestic limited liability company or a domestic statutory trust; or

(4) A foreign corporation, a foreign partnership (whether general (including a limited liability partnership) or limited (including a limited liability limited partnership)), a foreign limited liability company or a foreign statutory trust.

(b) Every registered agent shall:

(1) If an entity, maintain a business office in this State which is generally open, or if an individual, be generally present at a designated location in this State, at sufficiently frequent times to accept service of process and otherwise perform the functions of a registered agent;

(2) If a foreign entity, be authorized to transact business in this State;

(3) Accept service of process and other communications directed to the corporations for which it serves as registered agent and forward same to the corporation to which the service or communication is directed; and

(4) Forward to the corporations for which it serves as registered agent the annual report required by § 502 of this title or an electronic notification of same in a form satisfactory to the Secretary of State ("Secretary").

(c) Any registered agent who at any time serves as registered agent for more than 50 entities (a "commercial registered agent"), whether domestic or foreign, shall satisfy and comply with the following qualifications.

(1) A natural person serving as a commercial registered agent shall:

a. Maintain a principal residence or a principal place of business in this State;

b. Maintain a Delaware business license;

c. Be generally present at a designated location within this State during normal business hours to accept service of process and otherwise perform the functions of a registered agent as specified in subsection (b) of this section; and

d. Provide the Secretary upon request with such information identifying and enabling communication with such commercial registered agent as the Secretary shall require;

(2) A domestic or foreign corporation, a domestic or foreign partnership (whether general (including a limited liability partnership) or limited (including a limited liability limited partnership)), a domestic or foreign limited liability company, or a domestic or foreign statutory trust serving as a commercial registered agent shall:

a. Have a business office within this State which is generally open during normal business hours to accept service of process and otherwise perform the functions of a registered agent as specified in subsection (b) of this section;

b. Maintain a Delaware business license;

c. Have generally present at such office during normal business hours an officer, director or managing agent who is a natural person; and

d. Provide the Secretary upon request with such information identifying and enabling communication with such commercial registered agent as the Secretary shall require.

(3) For purposes of this subsection and paragraph (f)(2)a. of this section, a commercial registered agent shall also include any registered agent which has an officer, director or managing agent in common with any other registered agent or agents if such registered agents at any time during such common service as officer, director or managing agent collectively served as registered agents for more than 50 entities, whether domestic or foreign.

(d) Every corporation formed under the laws of this State or qualified to do business in this State shall provide to its registered agent and update from time to time as necessary the name, business address and business telephone number of a natural person who is an officer, director, employee, or designated agent of the corporation, who is then authorized to receive communications from the registered agent. Such person shall be deemed the communications contact for the corporation. Every registered agent shall retain (in paper or electronic form) the above information concerning the current communications contact for each corporation for which he, she or it serves as a registered agent. If the corporation fails to provide the registered agent with a current communications contact, the registered agent may resign as the registered agent for such corporation pursuant to § 136 of this title.

(e) The Secretary is authorized to issue such rules and regulations as may be necessary or appropriate to carry out the enforcement of subsections (b), (c) and (d) of this section, and to take actions reasonable and necessary to assure registered agents' compliance with subsections (b), (c) and (d) of this section. Such actions may include refusal to file documents submitted by a registered agent.

(f) Upon application of the Secretary, the Court of Chancery may enjoin any person or entity from serving as a registered agent or as an officer, director or managing agent of a registered agent.

(1) Upon the filing of a complaint by the Secretary pursuant to this section, the Court may make such orders respecting such proceeding as it deems appropriate, and may enter such orders granting interim or final relief as it deems proper under the circumstances.

(2) Any one or more of the following grounds shall be a sufficient basis to grant an injunction pursuant to this section:

a. With respect to any registered agent who at any time within 1 year immediately prior to the filing of the Secretary's complaint is a commercial registered agent, failure after notice and warning to comply with the qualifications set forth in subsection (b) of this section and/or the requirements of subsection (c) or (d) of this section above;

b. The person serving as a registered agent, or any person who is an officer, director or managing agent of an entity registered agent, has been convicted of a felony or any crime which includes an element of dishonesty or fraud or involves moral turpitude;

c. The registered agent has engaged in conduct in connection with acting as a registered agent that is intended to or likely to deceive or defraud the public.

(3) With respect to any order the court enters pursuant to this section with respect to an entity that has acted as a registered agent, the court may also direct such order to any person who has served as an officer, director, or managing agent of such registered agent. Any person who, on or after January 1, 2007, serves as an officer, director, or managing agent of an entity acting as a registered agent in this State shall be deemed thereby to have consented to the appointment of such registered agent as agent upon whom service of process may be made in any action brought pursuant to this section, and service as an officer, director, or managing agent of an entity acting as a registered agent in this State shall be a signification of the consent of such person that any process when so served shall be of the same legal force and validity as if served upon such person within this State, and such appointment of the registered agent shall be irrevocable.

(4) Upon the entry of an order by the Court enjoining any person or entity from acting as a registered agent, the Secretary shall mail or deliver notice of such order to each affected corporation at the address of its principal place of business as specified in its most recent franchise tax report or other record of the Secretary. If such corporation is a domestic corporation and fails to obtain and designate a new registered agent within 30 days after such notice is given, the Secretary shall declare the charter of such corporation forfeited. If such corporation is a foreign corporation, and fails to obtain and designate a new registered agent within 30 days after such notice is given, the Secretary shall forfeit its qualification to do business in this State. If the court enjoins a person or entity from acting as a registered agent as provided in this section and no new registered agent shall have been obtained and designated in the time and manner aforesaid, service of legal process against the corporation for which the registered agent had been acting shall thereafter be upon the Secretary in accordance with § 321 of this title. The Court of Chancery may, upon application of the Secretary on notice to the former registered agent, enter such orders as it deems appropriate to give the Secretary access to information in the former registered agent's possession in order to facilitate communication with the corporations the former registered agent served.

(g) The Secretary is authorized to make a list of registered agents available to the public, and to establish such qualifications and issue such rules and regulations with respect to such listing as the Secretary deems necessary or appropriate.

(h) Whenever the term "resident agent" or "resident agent in charge of a corporation's principal office or place of business in this State," or other term of like import which refers to a corporation's agent required by statute to be located in this State, is or has been used in a corporation's certificate of incorporation, or in any other document, or in any statute, it shall be deemed to mean and refer to, unless the context indicates otherwise, the corporation's registered agent required by this section; and it shall not be necessary for any corporation to amend its certificate of incorporation or any other document to comply with this section.

§ 133. Change of Location of Registered Office; Change of Registered Agent

Any corporation may, by resolution of its board of directors, change the location of its registered office in this State to any other place in this State. By like resolution, the registered agent of a corporation may be changed to any other person or corporation including itself. In either such case, the resolution shall be as detailed in its statement as is required by § 102(a)(2) of this title. Upon the adoption of such a resolution, a certificate certifying the change shall be executed, acknowledged, and filed in accordance with § 103 of this title.

§ 134. Change of Address or Name of Registered Agent

(a) A registered agent may change the address of the registered office of the corporation or corporations for which the agent is a registered agent to another address in this State by filing with the Secretary of State a certificate, executed and acknowledged by such registered agent, setting forth the address at which such registered agent has maintained the registered office for each of the corporations for which it is a registered agent, and further certifying to the new address to which each such registered office will be changed on a given day, and at which new address such registered agent will thereafter maintain the registered office for each of the corporations for which it is a registered agent. Thereafter, or until further change of address, as authorized by law, the registered office in this State of each of the corporations for which the agent is a registered agent shall be located at the new address of the registered agent thereof as given in the certificate.

(b) In the event of a change of name of any person or corporation acting as registered agent in this State, such registered agent shall file with the Secretary of State a certificate, executed and acknowledged by such registered agent, setting forth the new name of such registered agent, the name of such registered agent before it was changed, and the address at which such registered agent has maintained the registered office for each of the corporations for which it acts as a registered agent. A change of name of any person or corporation acting as a registered agent as a result of a merger or consolidation of the registered agent, with or into another person or corporation which succeeds to its assets by operation of law, shall be deemed a change of name for purposes of this section.

§ 135. Resignation of Registered Agent Coupled with Appointment of Successor

The registered agent of 1 or more corporations may resign and appoint a successor registered agent by filing a certificate with the Secretary of State, stating the name and address of the successor agent, in accordance with § 102(a)(2) of this title. There shall be attached to such certificate a statement of each affected corporation ratifying and approving such change of registered agent. Each such statement shall be executed and acknowledged in accordance with § 103 of this title. Upon such filing, the successor registered agent shall become the registered agent of such corporations as have ratified and approved such substitution and the successor registered agent's address, as stated in such certificate, shall become the address of each such corporation's registered office in this State. The Secretary of State shall then issue a certificate that the successor registered agent has become the registered agent of the corporations so ratifying and approving such change and setting out the names of such corporations.

§ 136. Resignation of Registered Agent not Coupled with Appointment of Successor

(a) The registered agent of 1 or more corporations may resign without appointing a successor by filing a certificate of resignation with the Secretary of State, but such resignation shall not become effective until 30 days after the certificate is filed. The certificate shall be executed and acknowledged by the registered agent, shall contain a statement that written notice of resignation was given to each affected corporation at least 30 days prior to the filing of the certificate by mailing or delivering such notice to the corporation at its address last known to the registered agent and shall set forth the date of such notice.

(b) After receipt of the notice of the resignation of its registered agent, provided for in subsection (a) of this section, the corporation for which such registered agent was acting shall obtain and designate a new registered agent to take the place of the registered agent so resigning in the same manner as provided in § 133 of this title for change of registered agent. If such corporation, being a corporation of this State, fails to obtain and designate a new registered agent as aforesaid prior to the expiration of the period of 30 days after the filing by the registered agent of the certificate of resignation, the Secretary of State shall declare the charter of such corporation forfeited. If such corporation, being a foreign corporation, fails to obtain and designate a new registered agent as aforesaid prior to the expiration of the period of 30 days after the filing by the registered agent of the certificate of resignation, the Secretary of State shall forfeit its authority to do business in this State.

(c) After the resignation of the registered agent shall have become effective as provided in this section and if no new registered agent shall have been obtained and designated in the time and manner aforesaid, service of legal process against the corporation for which the resigned registered agent had been acting shall thereafter be upon the Secretary of State in accordance with § 321 of this title.

SUBCHAPTER IV. DIRECTORS AND OFFICERS

§ 141. Board of Directors; Powers; Number, Qualifications, Terms and Quorum; Committees; Classes of Directors; Nonprofit Corporations; Reliance Upon Books; Action Without Meeting; Removal

(a) The business and affairs of every corporation organized under this chapter shall be managed by or under the direction of a board of directors, except as may be otherwise provided in this chapter or in its certificate of incorporation. If any such provision is made in the certificate of incorporation, the powers and duties conferred or imposed upon the board of directors by this chapter shall be exercised or performed to such extent and by such person or persons as shall be provided in the certificate of incorporation.

(b) The board of directors of a corporation shall consist of 1 or more members, each of whom shall be a natural person. The number of directors shall be fixed by, or in the manner provided in, the bylaws, unless the certificate of incorporation fixes the number of directors, in which case a change in the number of directors shall be made only by amendment of the certificate. Directors need not be stockholders unless so required by the certificate of incorporation or the bylaws. The certificate of incorporation or bylaws may prescribe other qualifications for directors. Each director shall hold office until such director's successor is elected and qualified or until such director's earlier resignation or removal. Any director may resign at any time upon notice given in writing or by electronic transmission to the corporation. A resignation is effective when the resignation is delivered unless the resignation specifies a later effective date or an effective date determined upon the happening of an event or events. A resignation which is conditioned upon the director failing to receive a specified vote for reelection as a director may provide that it is irrevocable. A majority of the total number of directors shall constitute a quorum for the transaction of business unless the certificate of incorporation or the bylaws require a greater number. Unless the certificate of incorporation provides otherwise, the bylaws may provide that a number less than a majority shall constitute a quorum which in no case shall be less than 1/3 of the total number of directors except that when a board of 1 director is authorized under this section, then 1 director shall constitute a quorum. The vote of the majority of the directors present at a meeting at which a quorum is present shall be the act of the board of directors unless the certificate of incorporation or the bylaws shall require a vote of a greater number.

(c)(1) All corporations incorporated prior to July 1, 1996, shall be governed by paragraph (1) of this subsection, provided that any such corporation may by a resolution adopted by a majority of the whole board elect to be governed by paragraph (2) of this subsection, in which case paragraph (1) of this subsection shall not apply to such corporation. All corporations incorporated on or after July 1, 1996, shall be governed by paragraph (2) of this subsection. The board of directors may, by resolution passed by a majority of the whole board, designate 1 or more committees, each committee to consist of 1 or more of the directors of the corporation. The board may designate 1 or more directors as alternate members of any committee, who may replace any absent or disqualified member at any meeting of the committee. The bylaws may provide that in the absence or disqualification of a member of a committee, the member or members present at any meeting and not disqualified from voting, whether or not the member or members present constitute a quorum, may unanimously appoint another member of the board of directors to act at the meeting in the place of any such absent or disqualified member. Any such committee, to the extent provided in the resolution of the board of directors, or in the bylaws of the corporation, shall have and may exercise all the powers and authority of the board of directors in the management of the business and affairs of the corporation, and may authorize the seal of the corporation to be affixed to all papers which may require it; but no such committee shall have the power or authority in reference to amending the certificate of incorporation (except that a committee may, to the extent authorized in the resolution or resolutions providing for the issuance of shares of stock adopted by the board of directors as provided in subsection (a) of § 151 of this title, fix the designations and any of the preferences or rights of such shares relating to dividends, redemption, dissolution, any distribution of assets of the corporation or the conversion into, or the exchange of such shares for, shares of any other class or classes or any other series of the same or any other class or classes of stock of the corporation or fix the number of shares of any series of stock or authorize the increase or decrease of the shares of any series), adopting an agreement of merger or consolidation under § 251, § 252, § 254, § 255, § 256, § 257, § 258, § 263 or § 264 of this title, recommending to the stockholders the sale, lease or exchange of all or substantially all of the corporation's property and assets, recommending to the stockholders a dissolution of the corporation or a revocation of a dissolution, or amending the bylaws of the corporation; and, unless the resolution, bylaws or certificate of incorporation expressly so provides, no such committee shall have the power or authority to declare a dividend, to authorize the issuance of stock or to adopt a certificate of ownership and merger pursuant to § 253 of this title.

(2) The board of directors may designate 1 or more committees, each committee to consist of 1 or more of the directors of the corporation. The board may designate 1 or more directors as alternate members of any committee, who may replace any absent or disqualified member at any meeting of the committee. The bylaws may provide that in the absence or disqualification of a member of a committee, the member or members present at any meeting and not disqualified from voting, whether or not such member or members constitute a quorum, may unanimously appoint another member of the board of directors to act at the meeting in the place of any such absent or disqualified member. Any such committee, to the extent provided in the resolution of the board of directors, or in the bylaws of the corporation, shall have and may exercise all the powers and authority of the board of directors in the management of the business and affairs of the corporation, and may authorize the seal of the corporation to be affixed to all papers which may require it; but no such committee shall have the power or authority in refer-

ence to the following matter: (i) approving or adopting, or recommending to the stockholders, any action or matter (other than the election or removal of directors) expressly required by this chapter to be submitted to stockholders for approval or (ii) adopting, amending or repealing any bylaw of the corporation.

(3) Unless otherwise provided in the certificate of incorporation, the bylaws or the resolution of the board of directors designating the committee, a committee may create 1 or more subcommittees, each subcommittee to consist of 1 or more members of the committee, and delegate to a subcommittee any or all of the powers and authority of the committee.

(d) The directors of any corporation organized under this chapter may, by the certificate of incorporation or by an initial bylaw, or by a bylaw adopted by a vote of the stockholders, be divided into 1, 2 or 3 classes; the term of office of those of the first class to expire at the first annual meeting held after such classification becomes effective; of the second class 1 year thereafter; of the third class 2 years thereafter; and at each annual election held after such classification becomes effective, directors shall be chosen for a full term, as the case may be, to succeed those whose terms expire. The certificate of incorporation or bylaw provision dividing the directors into classes may authorize the board of directors to assign members of the board already in office to such classes at the time such classification becomes effective. The certificate of incorporation may confer upon holders of any class or series of stock the right to elect 1 or more directors who shall serve for such term, and have such voting powers as shall be stated in the certificate of incorporation. The terms of office and voting powers of the directors elected separately by the holders of any class or series of stock may be greater than or less than those of any other director or class of directors. In addition, the certificate of incorporation may confer upon 1 or more directors, whether or not elected separately by the holders of any class or series of stock, voting powers greater than or less than those of other directors. If the certificate of incorporation provides that 1 or more directors shall have more or less than 1 vote per director on any matter, every reference in this chapter to a majority or other proportion of the directors shall refer to a majority or other proportion of the votes of the directors.

(e) A member of the board of directors, or a member of any committee designated by the board of directors, shall, in the performance of such member's duties, be fully protected in relying in good faith upon the records of the corporation and upon such information, opinions, reports or statements presented to the corporation by any of the corporation's officers or employees, or committees of the board of directors, or by any other person as to matters the member reasonably believes are within such other person's professional or expert competence and who has been selected with reasonable care by or on behalf of the corporation.

(f) Unless otherwise restricted by the certificate of incorporation or bylaws, any action required or permitted to be taken at any meeting of the board of directors or of any committee thereof may be taken without a meeting if all members of the board or committee, as the case may be, consent thereto in writing, or by electronic transmission and the writing or writings or electronic transmission or transmissions are filed with the minutes of proceedings of the board, or committee. Such filing shall be in paper form if the minutes are maintained in paper form and shall be in electronic form if the minutes are maintained in electronic form.

(g) Unless otherwise restricted by the certificate of incorporation or bylaws, the board of directors of any corporation organized under this chapter may hold its meetings, and have an office or offices, outside of this State.

(h) Unless otherwise restricted by the certificate of incorporation or bylaws, the board of directors shall have the authority to fix the compensation of directors.

(i) Unless otherwise restricted by the certificate of incorporation or bylaws, members of the board of directors of any corporation, or any committee designated by the board, may participate in a meeting of such board, or committee by means of conference telephone or other communications equipment by means of which all persons participating in the meeting can hear each other, and participation in a meeting pursuant to this subsection shall constitute presence in person at the meeting.

(j) The certificate of incorporation of any corporation organized under this chapter which is not authorized to issue capital stock may provide that less than 1/3 of the members of the governing body may constitute a quorum thereof and may otherwise provide that the business and affairs of the corporation shall be managed in a manner different from that provided in this section. Except as may be otherwise provided by the certificate of incorporation, this section shall apply to such a corporation, and when so applied, all references to the board of directors, to members thereof, and to stockholders shall be deemed to refer to the governing body of the corporation, the members thereof and the members of the corporation, respectively.

(k) Any director or the entire board of directors may be removed, with or without cause, by the holders of a majority of the shares then entitled to vote at an election of directors, except as follows:

(1) Unless the certificate of incorporation otherwise provides, in the case of a corporation whose board is classified as provided in subsection (d) of this section, shareholders may effect such removal only for cause; or

(2) In the case of a corporation having cumulative voting, if less than the entire board is to be removed, no director may be removed without cause if the votes cast against such director's removal would be sufficient to elect such director if then cumulatively voted at an

election of the entire board of directors, or, if there be classes of directors, at an election of the class of directors of which such director is a part.

Whenever the holders of any class or series are entitled to elect 1 or more directors by the certificate of incorporation, this subsection shall apply, in respect to the removal without cause of a director or directors so elected, to the vote of the holders of the outstanding shares of that class or series and not to the vote of the outstanding shares as a whole.

§ 142. Officers; Titles, Duties, Selection, Term; Failure to Elect; Vacancies

(a) Every corporation organized under this chapter shall have such officers with such titles and duties as shall be stated in the bylaws or in a resolution of the board of directors which is not inconsistent with the bylaws and as may be necessary to enable it to sign instruments and stock certificates which comply with §§ 103(a)(2) and 158 of this title. One of the officers shall have the duty to record the proceedings of the meetings of the stockholders and directors in a book to be kept for that purpose. Any number of offices may be held by the same person unless the certificate of incorporation or bylaws otherwise provide.

(b) Officers shall be chosen in such manner and shall hold their offices for such terms as are prescribed by the bylaws or determined by the board of directors or other governing body. Each officer shall hold office until such officer's successor is elected and qualified or until such officer's earlier resignation or removal. Any officer may resign at any time upon written notice to the corporation.

(c) The corporation may secure the fidelity of any or all of its officers or agents by bond or otherwise.

(d) A failure to elect officers shall not dissolve or otherwise affect the corporation.

(e) Any vacancy occurring in any office of the corporation by death, resignation, removal or otherwise, shall be filled as the bylaws provide. In the absence of such provision, the vacancy shall be filled by the board of directors or other governing body.

§ 143. Loans to Employees and Officers; Guaranty of Obligations of Employees and Officers

Any corporation may lend money to, or guarantee any obligation of, or otherwise assist any officer or other employee of the corporation or of its subsidiary, including any officer or employee who is a director of the corporation or its subsidiary, whenever, in the judgment of the directors, such loan, guaranty or assistance may reasonably be expected to benefit the corporation. The loan, guaranty or other assistance may be with or without interest, and may be unsecured, or secured in such manner as the board of directors shall approve, including, without limitation, a pledge of shares of stock of the corporation. Nothing in this section contained shall be deemed to deny, limit or restrict the powers of guaranty or warranty of any corporation at common law or under any statute.

§ 144. Interested Directors; Quorum

(a) No contract or transaction between a corporation and 1 or more of its directors or officers, or between a corporation and any other corporation, partnership, association, or other organization in which 1 or more of its directors or officers, are directors or officers, or have a financial interest, shall be void or voidable solely for this reason, or solely because the director or officer is present at or participates in the meeting of the board or committee which authorizes the contract or transaction, or solely because any such director's or officer's votes are counted for such purpose, if:

(1) The material facts as to the director's or officer's relationship or interest and as to the contract or transaction are disclosed or are known to the board of directors or the committee, and the board or committee in good faith authorizes the contract or transaction by the affirmative votes of a majority of the disinterested directors, even though the disinterested directors be less than a quorum; or

(2) The material facts as to the director's or officer's relationship or interest and as to the contract or transaction are disclosed or are known to the shareholders entitled to vote thereon, and the contract or transaction is specifically approved in good faith by vote of the shareholders; or

(3) The contract or transaction is fair as to the corporation as of the time it is authorized, approved or ratified, by the board of directors, a committee or the shareholders.

(b) Common or interested directors may be counted in determining the presence of a quorum at a meeting of the board of directors or of a committee which authorizes the contract or transaction.

§ 145. Indemnification of Officers, Directors, Employees and Agents; Insurance

(a) A corporation shall have power to indemnify any person who was or is a party or is threatened to be made a party to any threatened, pending or completed action, suit or proceeding, whether civil, criminal, administrative or investigative (other than an action by or in the right of the corporation) by reason of the fact that the person is or was a director, officer, employee or agent of the corporation, or is or was serving at the request of the corporation as a director, officer, employee or agent of another corporation, partnership, joint venture, trust or other enterprise, against expenses (including attorneys' fees), judgments, fines and amounts paid in settlement actually and reasonably incurred by the person in connection with such action, suit or proceeding if the person acted in good faith and in a manner the person reasonably believed to be in or not opposed to the best interests of the corporation, and, with respect to any criminal action or proceeding, had no reasonable cause to believe the person's conduct was unlawful. The termination of any action, suit or proceeding by judgment, order, settlement, conviction, or upon a plea of nolo contendere or its equivalent, shall not, of itself, create a presumption that the person did not act in good faith and in a manner which the person reasonably believed to be in or not opposed to the best interests of the corporation, and, with respect to any criminal action or proceeding, had reasonable cause to believe that the person's conduct was unlawful.

(b) A corporation shall have power to indemnify any person who was or is a party or is threatened to be made a party to any threatened, pending or completed action or suit by or in the right of the corporation to procure a judgment in its favor by reason of the fact that the person is or was a director, officer, employee or agent of the corporation, or is or was serving at the request of the corporation as a director, officer, employee or agent of another corporation, partnership, joint venture, trust or other enterprise against expenses (including attorneys' fees) actually and reasonably incurred by the person in connection with the defense or settlement of such action or suit if the person acted in good faith and in a manner the person reasonably believed to be in or not opposed to the best interests of the corporation and except that no indemnification shall be made in respect of any claim, issue or matter as to which such person shall have been adjudged to be liable to the corporation unless and only to the extent that the Court of Chancery or the court in which such action or suit was brought shall determine upon application that, despite the adjudication of liability but in view of all the circumstances of the case, such person is fairly and reasonably entitled to indemnity for such expenses which the Court of Chancery or such other court shall deem proper.

(c) To the extent that a present or former director or officer of a corporation has been successful on the merits or otherwise in defense of any action, suit or proceeding referred to in subsections (a) and (b) of this section, or in defense of any claim, issue or matter therein, such person shall be indemnified against expenses (including attorneys' fees) actually and reasonably incurred by such person in connection therewith.

(d) Any indemnification under subsections (a) and (b) of this section (unless ordered by a court) shall be made by the corporation only as authorized in the specific case upon a determination that indemnification of the present or former director, officer, employee or agent is proper in the circumstances because the person has met the applicable standard of conduct set forth in subsections (a) and (b) of this section. Such determination shall be made, with respect to a person who is a director or officer at the time of such determination, (1) by a majority vote of the directors who are not parties to such action, suit or proceeding, even though less than a quorum, or (2) by a committee of such directors designated by majority vote of such directors, even though less than a quorum, or (3) if there are no such directors, or if such directors so direct, by independent legal counsel in a written opinion, or (4) by the stockholders.

(e) Expenses (including attorneys' fees) incurred by an officer or director in defending any civil, criminal, administrative or investigative action, suit or proceeding may be paid by the corporation in advance of the final disposition of such action, suit or proceeding upon receipt of an undertaking by or on behalf of such director or officer to repay such amount if it shall ultimately be determined that such person is not entitled to be indemnified by the corporation as authorized in this section. Such expenses (including attorneys' fees) incurred by former directors and officers or other employees and agents may be so paid upon such terms and conditions, if any, as the corporation deems appropriate.

(f) The indemnification and advancement of expenses provided by, or granted pursuant to, the other subsections of this section shall not be deemed exclusive of any other rights to which those seeking indemnification or advancement of expenses may be entitled under any bylaw, agreement, vote of stockholders or disinterested directors or otherwise, both as to action in such person's official capacity and as to action in another capacity while holding such office.

(g) A corporation shall have power to purchase and maintain insurance on behalf of any person who is or was a director, officer, employee or agent of the corporation, or is or was serving at the request of the corporation as a director, officer, employee or agent of another corporation, partnership, joint venture, trust or other enterprise against any liability asserted against such person and incurred by such person in any such capacity, or arising out of such person's status as such, whether or not the corporation would have the power to indemnify such person against such liability under this section.

(h) For purposes of this section, references to "the corporation" shall include, in addition to the resulting corporation, any constituent corporation (including any constituent of a constituent) absorbed in a consolidation or merger which, if its separate existence had continued, would have had power and authority to indemnify its directors, officers, and employees or agents, so that any person who is or was a director, officer, employee or agent of such constituent corporation, or is or was serving at the request of such constituent corporation as a director, officer, employee or agent of another corporation, partnership, joint venture, trust or other enterprise, shall stand in the same position under this section with respect to the resulting or surviving corporation as such person would have with respect to such constituent corporation if its separate existence had continued.

(i) For purposes of this section, references to "other enterprises" shall include employee benefit plans; references to "fines" shall include any excise taxes assessed on a person with respect to any employee benefit plan; and references to "serving at the request of the corporation" shall include any service as a director, officer, employee or agent of the corporation which imposes duties on, or involves services by, such director, officer, employee or agent with respect to an employee benefit plan, its participants or beneficiaries; and a person who acted in good faith and in a manner such person reasonably believed to be in the interest of the participants and beneficiaries of an employee benefit plan shall be deemed to have acted in a manner "not opposed to the best interests of the corporation" as referred to in this section.

(j) The indemnification and advancement of expenses provided by, or granted pursuant to, this section shall, unless otherwise provided when authorized or ratified, continue as to a person who has ceased to be a director, officer, employee or agent and shall inure to the benefit of the heirs, executors and administrators of such a person.

(k) The Court of Chancery is hereby vested with exclusive jurisdiction to hear and determine all actions for advancement of expenses or indemnification brought under this section or under any bylaw, agreement, vote of stockholders or disinterested directors, or otherwise. The Court of Chancery may summarily determine a corporation's obligation to advance expenses (including attorneys' fees).

§ 146. Submission of Matters for Stockholder Vote

A corporation may agree to submit a matter to a vote of its stockholders whether or not the board of directors determines at any time subsequent to approving such matter that such matter is no longer advisable and recommends that the stockholders reject or vote against the matter.

SUBCHAPTER V. STOCK AND DIVIDENDS

§ 151. Classes and Series of Stock; Redemption; Rights

(a) Every corporation may issue 1 or more classes of stock or 1 or more series of stock within any class thereof, any or all of which classes may be of stock with par value or stock without par value and which classes or series may have such voting powers, full or limited, or no voting powers, and such designations, preferences and relative, participating, optional or other special rights, and qualifications, limitations or restrictions thereof, as shall be stated and expressed in the certificate of incorporation or of any amendment thereto, or in the resolution or resolutions providing for the issue of such stock adopted by the board of directors pursuant to authority expressly vested in it by the provisions of its certificate of incorporation. Any of the voting powers, designations, preferences, rights and qualifications, limitations or restrictions of any such class or series of stock may be made dependent upon facts ascertainable outside the certificate of incorporation or of any amendment thereto, or outside the resolution or resolutions providing for the issue of such stock adopted by the board of directors pursuant to authority expressly vested in it by its certificate of incorporation, provided that the manner in which such facts shall operate upon the voting powers, designations, preferences, rights and qualifications, limitations or restrictions of such class or series of stock is clearly and expressly set forth in the certificate of incorporation or in the resolution or resolutions providing for the issue of such stock adopted by the board of directors. The term "facts," as used in this subsection, includes, but is not limited to, the occurrence of any event, including a determination or action by any person or body, including the corporation. The power to increase or decrease or otherwise adjust the capital stock as provided in this chapter shall apply to all or any such classes of stock.

(b) Any stock of any class or series may be made subject to redemption by the corporation at its option or at the option of the holders of such stock or upon the happening of a specified event; provided however, that immediately following any such redemption the corporation shall have outstanding 1 or more shares of 1 or more classes or series of stock, which share, or shares together, shall have full voting powers. Notwithstanding the limitation stated in the foregoing proviso:

(1) Any stock of a regulated investment company registered under the Investment Company Act of 1940 [15 U.S.C. § 80 a–1 et seq.], as heretofore or hereafter amended, may be made subject to redemption by the corporation at its option or at the option of the holders of such stock.

(2) Any stock of a corporation which holds (directly or indirectly) a license or franchise from a governmental agency to conduct its business or is a member of a national securities exchange, which license, franchise or membership is conditioned upon some or all of the holders of its stock possessing prescribed qualifications, may be made subject to redemption by the corporation to the extent necessary to prevent the loss of such license, franchise or membership or to reinstate it.

Any stock which may be made redeemable under this section may be redeemed for cash, property or rights, including securities of the same or another corporation, at such time or times, price or prices, or rate or rates, and with such adjustments, as shall be stated in the certificate of incorporation or in the resolution or resolutions providing for the issue of such stock adopted by the board of directors pursuant to subsection (a) of this section.

(c) The holders of preferred or special stock of any class or of any series thereof shall be entitled to receive dividends at such rates, on such conditions and at such times as shall be stated in the certificate of incorporation or in the resolution or resolutions providing for the issue of such stock adopted by the board of directors as hereinabove provided, payable in preference to, or in such relation to, the dividends payable on any other class or classes or of any other series of stock, and cumulative or noncumulative as shall be so stated and expressed. When dividends upon the preferred and special stocks, if any, to the extent of the preference to which such stocks are entitled, shall have been paid or declared and set apart for payment, a dividend on the remaining class or classes or series of stock may then be paid out of the remaining assets of the corporation available for dividends as elsewhere in this chapter provided.

(d) The holders of the preferred or special stock of any class or of any series thereof shall be entitled to such rights upon the dissolution of, or upon any distribution of the assets of, the corporation as shall be stated in the certificate of incorporation or in the resolution or resolutions providing for the issue of such stock adopted by the board of directors as hereinabove provided.

(e) Any stock of any class or of any series thereof may be made convertible into, or exchangeable for, at the option of either the holder or the corporation or upon the happening of a specified event, shares of any other class or classes or any other series of the same or any other class or classes of stock of the corporation, at such price or prices or at such rate or rates of exchange and with such adjustments as shall be stated in the certificate of incorporation or in the resolution or resolutions providing for the issue of such stock adopted by the board of directors as hereinabove provided.

(f) If any corporation shall be authorized to issue more than 1 class of stock or more than 1 series of any class, the powers, designations, preferences and relative, participating, optional, or other special rights of each class of stock or series thereof and the qualifications, limitations or restrictions of such preferences and/or rights shall be set forth in full or summarized on the face or back of the certificate which the corporation shall issue to represent such class or series of stock, provided that, except as otherwise provided in § 202 of this title, in lieu of the foregoing requirements, there may be set forth on the face or back of the certificate which the corporation shall issue to represent such class or series of stock, a statement that the corporation will furnish without charge to each stockholder who so requests the powers, designations, preferences and relative, participating, optional, or other special rights of each class of stock or series thereof and the qualifications, limitations or restrictions of such preferences and/or rights. Within a reasonable time after the issuance or transfer of uncertificated stock, the corporation shall send to the registered owner thereof a written notice containing the information required to be set forth or stated on certificates pursuant to this section or § 156, 202(a) or 218(a) of this title or with respect to this section a statement that the corporation will furnish without charge to each stockholder who so requests the powers, designations, preferences and relative participating, optional or other special rights of each class of stock or series thereof and the qualifications, limitations or restrictions of such preferences and/or rights. Except as otherwise expressly provided by law, the rights and obligations of the holders of uncertificated stock and the rights and obligations of the holders of certificates representing stock of the same class and series shall be identical.

(g) When any corporation desires to issue any shares of stock of any class or of any series of any class of which the powers, designations, preferences and relative, participating, optional or other rights, if any, or the qualifications, limitations or restrictions thereof, if any, shall not have been set forth in the certificate of incorporation or in any amendment thereto but shall be provided for in a resolution or resolutions adopted by the board of directors pursuant to authority expressly vested in it by the certificate of incorporation or any amendment thereto, a certificate of designations setting forth a copy of such resolution or resolutions and the number of shares of stock of such class or series as to which the resolution or resolutions apply shall be executed, acknowledged, filed and shall become effective, in accordance with § 103 of this title. Unless otherwise provided in any such resolution or resolutions, the number of shares of stock of any such series to which such resolution or resolutions apply may be increased (but not above the total number of authorized shares of the class) or decreased (but not below the number of shares thereof then outstanding) by a certificate likewise executed, acknowledged and filed setting forth a statement that a specified increase or decrease therein had been authorized and directed by a resolution or resolutions likewise adopted by the board of directors. In case the number of such shares shall be decreased the number of shares so specified in the certificate shall resume the status which they had prior to the adoption of the first resolution or resolutions. When no shares of any such class or series are outstanding, either because none were issued or because no issued shares of any such class or series remain outstanding, a certificate setting forth a resolution or resolutions adopted by the board of directors that none of the authorized shares of such class or series are outstanding, and that none will be issued subject to the certificate of designations previously filed with respect to such class or series, may be executed, acknowledged and filed in accordance with § 103 of this title and, when such certificate becomes effective, it shall have the effect of eliminating from the certificate of incorporation all matters set forth in the certificate of designations with respect to such class or series of stock. Unless otherwise provided in the certificate of incorporation, if no shares of stock have been issued of a class or series of stock established by a resolution of the board of directors, the voting powers, designations, preferences and relative, participating, optional or other rights, if any, or the qualifications, limitations or restrictions thereof, may be amended by a resolution or resolutions adopted by the board of directors. A certificate which (1) states that no shares of the class or series have been issued, (2) sets forth a copy of the resolution or resolutions and (3) if the designation of the class or series is being changed, indicates the original designation and the new designation, shall be executed, acknowledged and filed and shall become effective, in accordance with § 103 of this title. When any certificate filed under this subsection becomes effective, it shall have the effect of amending the certificate of incorporation; except that neither the filing of such certificate nor the filing of a restated certificate of incorporation pursuant to § 245 of this title shall prohibit the board of directors from subsequently adopting such resolutions as authorized by this subsection.

§ 152. Issuance of Stock; Lawful Consideration; Fully Paid Stock

The consideration, as determined pursuant to subsections (a) and (b) of § 153 of this title, for subscriptions to, or the purchase of, the capital stock to be issued by a corporation shall be paid in such form and in such manner as the board of directors shall determine. The board of directors may authorize capital stock to be issued for consideration consisting of cash, any tangible or intangible property or any benefit to the corporation, or any combination thereof. In the absence of actual fraud in the transaction, the judgment of the directors as to the value of such consideration shall be conclusive. The capital stock so issued shall be deemed to be fully paid and nonassessable stock upon receipt by the corporation of such consideration; provided, however, nothing contained herein shall prevent the board of directors from issuing partly paid shares under § 156 of this title.

§ 153. Consideration for Stock

(a) Shares of stock with par value may be issued for such consideration, having a value not less than the par value thereof, as determined from time to time by the board of directors, or by the stockholders if the certificate of incorporation so provides.

(b) Shares of stock without par value may be issued for such consideration as is determined from time to time by the board of directors, or by the stockholders if the certificate of incorporation so provides.

(c) Treasury shares may be disposed of by the corporation for such consideration as may be determined from time to time by the board of directors, or by the stockholders if the certificate of incorporation so provides.

(d) If the certificate of incorporation reserves to the stockholders the right to determine the consideration for the issue of any shares, the stockholders shall, unless the certificate requires a greater vote, do so by a vote of a majority of the outstanding stock entitled to vote thereon.

§ 154. Determination of Amount of Capital; Capital, Surplus and Net Assets Defined

Any corporation may, by resolution of its board of directors, determine that only a part of the consideration which shall be received by the corporation for any of the shares of its capital stock which it shall issue from time to time shall be capital; but, in case any of the shares issued shall be shares having a par value, the amount of the part of such consideration so determined to be capital shall be in excess of the aggregate par value of the shares issued for such consideration having a par value, unless all the shares issued shall be shares having a par value, in which case the amount of the part of such consideration so determined to be capital need be only equal to the aggregate par value of such shares. In each such case the board of directors shall specify in dollars the part of such consideration which shall be capital. If the board of directors shall not have determined (1) at the time of issue of any shares of the capital stock of the corporation issued for cash or (2) within 60 days after the issue of any shares of the capital stock of the corporation issued for consideration other than cash what part of the consideration for such shares shall be capital, the capital of the corporation in respect of such shares shall be an amount equal to the aggregate par value of such shares having a par value, plus the amount of the consideration for such shares without par value. The amount of the consideration so determined to be capital in respect of any shares without par value shall be the stated capital of such shares. The capital of the corporation may be increased from time to time by resolution of the board of directors directing that a portion of the net assets of the corporation in excess of the amount so determined to be capital be transferred to the capital account. The board of directors may direct that the portion of such net assets so transferred shall be treated as capital in respect of any shares of the corporation of any designated class or classes. The excess, if any, at any given time, of the net assets of the corporation over the amount so determined to be capital shall be surplus. Net assets means the amount by which total assets exceed total liabilities. Capital and surplus are not liabilities for this purpose.

§ 155. Fractions of Shares

A corporation may, but shall not be required to, issue fractions of a share. If it does not issue fractions of a share, it shall (1) arrange for the disposition of fractional interests by those entitled thereto, (2) pay in cash the fair value of fractions of a share as of the time when those entitled to receive such fractions are determined or (3) issue scrip or warrants in registered form (either represented by a certificate or uncertificated) or in bearer form (represented by a certificate) which shall entitle the holder to receive a full share upon the surrender of such scrip or warrants aggregating a full share. A certificate for a fractional share or an uncertificated fractional share shall, but scrip or warrants shall not unless otherwise provided therein, entitle the holder to exercise voting rights, to receive dividends thereon and to participate in any of the assets of the corporation in the event of liquidation. The board of directors may cause scrip or warrants to be issued subject to the conditions that they shall become void if not exchanged for certificates representing the full shares or uncertificated full shares before a specified date, or subject to the conditions that the shares for which scrip or warrants are exchangeable may be sold by the corporation and the proceeds thereof distributed to the holders of scrip or warrants, or subject to any other conditions which the board of directors may impose.

§ 156. Partly Paid Shares

Any corporation may issue the whole or any part of its shares as partly paid and subject to call for the remainder of the consideration to be paid therefor. Upon the face or back of each stock certificate issued to represent any such partly paid shares, or upon the books and records of the corporation in the case of uncertificated partly paid shares, the total amount of the consideration to be paid therefor and the amount paid thereon shall be stated. Upon the declaration of any dividend on fully paid shares, the corporation shall declare a dividend upon partly paid shares of the same class, but only upon the basis of the percentage of the consideration actually paid thereon.

§ 157. Rights and Options Respecting Stock

(a) Subject to any provisions in the certificate of incorporation, every corporation may create and issue, whether or not in connection with the issue and sale of any shares of stock or other securities of the corporation, rights or options entitling the holders thereof to acquire from the corporation any shares of its capital stock of any class or classes, such rights or options to be evidenced by or in such instrument or instruments as shall be approved by the board of directors.

(b) The terms upon which, including the time or times which may be limited or unlimited in duration, at or within which, and the consideration (including a formula by which such consideration may be determined) for which any such shares may be acquired from the corporation upon the exercise of any such right or option, shall be such as shall be stated in the certificate of incorporation, or in a resolution adopted by the board of directors providing for the creation and issue of such rights or options, and, in every case, shall be set forth or incorporated by reference in the instrument or instruments evidencing such rights or options. In the absence of actual fraud in the transaction, the judgment of the directors as to the consideration for the issuance of such rights or options and the sufficiency thereof shall be conclusive.

(c) The board of directors may, by a resolution adopted by the board, authorize 1 or more officers of the corporation to do 1 or both of the following: (i) designate officers and employees of the corporation or of any of its subsidiaries to be recipients of such rights or options created by the corporation, and (ii) determine the number of such rights or options to be received by such officers and employees; provided, however, that the resolution so authorizing such officer or officers shall specify the total number of rights or options such officer or officers may so award. The board of directors may not authorize an officer to designate himself or herself as a recipient of any such rights or options.

(d) In case the shares of stock of the corporation to be issued upon the exercise of such rights or options shall be shares having a par value, the consideration so to be received therefor shall have a value not less than the par value thereof. In case the shares of stock so to be issued shall be shares of stock without par value, the consideration therefor shall be determined in the manner provided in § 153 of this title.

§ 158. Stock Certificates; Uncertificated Shares

The shares of a corporation shall be represented by certificates, provided that the board of directors of the corporation may provide by resolution or resolutions that some or all of any or all classes or series of its stock shall be uncertificated shares. Any such resolution shall not apply to shares represented by a certificate until such certificate is surrendered to the corporation. Every holder of stock represented by certificates shall be entitled to have a certificate signed by, or in the name of the corporation by the chairperson or vice-chairperson of the board of directors, or the president or vice-president, and by the treasurer or an assistant treasurer, or the secretary or an assistant secretary of such corporation representing the number of shares registered in certificate form. Any or all the signatures on the certificate may be a facsimile. In case any officer, transfer agent or registrar who has signed or whose facsimile signature has been placed upon a certificate shall have ceased to be such officer, transfer agent or registrar before such certificate is issued, it may be issued by the corporation with the same effect as if such person were such officer, transfer agent or registrar at the date of issue. A corporation shall not have power to issue a certificate in bearer form.

§ 159. Shares of Stock; Personal Property, Transfer and Taxation

The shares of stock in every corporation shall be deemed personal property and transferable as provided in Article 8 of subtitle I of Title 6. No stock or bonds issued by any corporation organized under this chapter shall be taxed by this State when the same shall be owned by non-residents of this State, or by foreign corporations. Whenever any transfer of shares shall be made for collateral security, and not absolutely, it shall be so expressed in the entry of transfer if, when the certificates are presented to the corporation for transfer or uncertificated shares are requested to be transferred, both the transferor and transferee request the corporation to do so.

§ 160. Corporation's Powers Respecting Ownership, Voting, etc., of its Own Stock; Rights of Stock Called for Redemption

(a) Every corporation may purchase, redeem, receive, take or otherwise acquire, own and hold, sell, lend, exchange, transfer or otherwise dispose of, pledge, use and otherwise deal in and with its own shares; provided, however, that no corporation shall:

(1) Purchase or redeem its own shares of capital stock for cash or other property when the capital of the corporation is impaired or when such purchase or redemption would cause any impairment of the capital of the corporation, except that a corporation may purchase or redeem out of capital any of its own shares which are entitled upon any distribution of its assets, whether by dividend or in liquidation, to a preference over another class or series of its stock, or, if no shares entitled to such a preference are outstanding, any of its own shares, if such shares will be retired upon their acquisition and the capital of the corporation reduced in accordance with §§ 243 and 244 of this title. Nothing in this subsection shall invalidate or otherwise affect a note, debenture or other obligation of a corporation given by it as consideration for its acquisition by purchase, redemption or exchange of its shares of stock if at the time such note, debenture or obligation was delivered by the corporation its capital was not then impaired or did not thereby become impaired;

(2) Purchase, for more than the price at which they may then be redeemed, any of its shares which are redeemable at the option of the corporation; or

(3) Redeem any of its shares unless their redemption is authorized by subsection (b) of § 151 of this title and then only in accordance with such section and the certificate of incorporation.

(b) Nothing in this section limits or affects a corporation's right to resell any of its shares theretofore purchased or redeemed out of surplus and which have not been retired, for such consideration as shall be fixed by the board of directors.

(c) Shares of its own capital stock belonging to the corporation or to another corporation, if a majority of the shares entitled to vote in the election of directors of such other corporation is held, directly or indirectly, by the corporation, shall neither be entitled to vote nor be counted for quorum purposes. Nothing in this section shall be construed as limiting the right of any corporation to vote stock, including but not limited to its own stock, held by it in a fiduciary capacity.

(d) Shares which have been called for redemption shall not be deemed to be outstanding shares for the purpose of voting or determining the total number of shares entitled to vote on any matter on and after the date on which written notice of redemption has been sent to holders thereof and a sum sufficient to redeem such shares has been irrevocably deposited or set aside to pay the redemption price to the holders of the shares upon surrender of certificates therefor.

§ 161. Issuance of Additional Stock; When and by Whom

The directors may, at any time and from time to time, if all of the shares of capital stock which the corporation is authorized by its certificate of incorporation to issue have not been issued, subscribed for, or otherwise committed to be issued, issue or take subscriptions for additional shares of its capital stock up to the amount authorized in its certificate of incorporation.

§ 162. Liability of Stockholder or Subscriber for Stock not Paid in Full

(a) When the whole of the consideration payable for shares of a corporation has not been paid in, and the assets shall be insufficient to satisfy the claims of its creditors, each holder of or subscriber for such shares shall be bound to pay on each share held or subscribed for by such holder or subscriber the sum necessary to complete the amount of the unpaid balance of the consideration for which such shares were issued or are to be issued by the corporation.

(b) The amounts which shall be payable as provided in subsection (a) of this section may be recovered as provided in § 325 of this title, after a writ of execution against the corporation has been returned unsatisfied as provided in said § 325.

(c) Any person becoming an assignee or transferee of shares or of a subscription for shares in good faith and without knowledge or notice that the full consideration therefor has not been paid shall not be personally liable for any unpaid portion of such consideration, but the transferor shall remain liable therefor.

(d) No person holding shares in any corporation as collateral security shall be personally liable as a stockholder but the person pledging such shares shall be considered the holder thereof and shall be so liable. No executor, administrator, guardian, trustee or other fiduciary shall be personally liable as a stockholder, but the estate or funds held by such executor, administrator, guardian, trustee or other fiduciary in such fiduciary capacity shall be liable.

(e) No liability under this section or under § 325 of this title shall be asserted more than 6 years after the issuance of the stock or the date of the subscription upon which the assessment is sought.

(f) In any action by a receiver or trustee of an insolvent corporation or by a judgment creditor to obtain an assessment under this section, any stockholder or subscriber for stock of the insolvent corporation may appear and contest the claim or claims of such receiver or trustee.

§ 163. Payment for Stock not Paid in Full

The capital stock of a corporation shall be paid for in such amounts and at such times as the directors may require. The directors may, from time to time, demand payment, in respect of each share of stock not fully paid, of such sum of money as the necessities of the business may, in the judgment of the board of directors, require, not exceeding in the whole the balance remaining unpaid on said stock, and such sum so demanded shall be paid to the corporation at such times and by such installments as the directors shall direct. The directors shall give written notice of the time and place of such payments, which notice shall be mailed at least 30 days before the time for such payment, to each holder of or subscriber for stock which is not fully paid at such holder's or subscriber's last known post-office address.

§ 164. Failure to Pay for Stock; Remedies

When any stockholder fails to pay any installment or call upon such stockholder's stock which may have been properly demanded by the directors, at the time when such payment is due, the directors may collect the amount of any such installment or call or any balance thereof remaining unpaid, from the said stockholder by an action at law, or they shall sell at public sale such part of the shares of such delinquent stockholder as will pay all demands then due from such stockholder with interest and all incidental expenses, and shall transfer the shares so sold to the purchaser, who shall be entitled to a certificate therefor.

Notice of the time and place of such sale and of the sum due on each share shall be given by advertisement at least 1 week before the sale, in a newspaper of the county in this State where such corporation's registered office is located, and such notice shall be mailed by the corporation to such delinquent stockholder at such stockholder's last known post-office address, at least 20 days before such sale.

If no bidder can be had to pay the amount due on the stock, and if the amount is not collected by an action at law, which may be brought within the county where the corporation has its registered office, within 1 year from the date of the bringing of such action at law, the said stock and the amount previously paid in by the delinquent stockholder on the stock shall be forfeited to the corporation.

§ 165. Revocability of Preincorporation Subscriptions

Unless otherwise provided by the terms of the subscription, a subscription for stock of a corporation to be formed shall be irrevocable, except with the consent of all other subscribers or the corporation, for a period of 6 months from its date.

§ 166. Formalities Required of Stock Subscriptions

A subscription for stock of a corporation, whether made before or after the formation of a corporation, shall not be enforceable against a subscriber, unless in writing and signed by the subscriber or by such subscriber's agent.

§ 167. Lost, Stolen or Destroyed Stock Certificates; Issuance of New Certificate or Uncertificated Shares

A corporation may issue a new certificate of stock or uncertificated shares in place of any certificate theretofore issued by it, alleged to have been lost, stolen or destroyed, and the corporation may require the owner of the lost, stolen or destroyed certificate, or such owner's legal representative to give the corporation a bond sufficient to indemnify it against any claim that may be made against it on account of the alleged loss, theft or destruction of any such certificate or the issuance of such new certificate or uncertificated shares.

§ 168. Judicial Proceedings to Compel Issuance of New Certificate or Uncertificated Shares

(a) If a corporation refuses to issue new uncertificated shares or a new certificate of stock in place of a certificate theretofore issued by it, or by any corporation of which it is the lawful successor, alleged to have been lost, stolen or destroyed, the owner of the lost, stolen or destroyed certificate or such owner's legal representatives may apply to the Court of Chancery for an order requiring the corporation to show cause why it should not issue new uncertificated shares or a new certificate of stock in place of the certificate so lost, stolen or destroyed. Such application shall be by a complaint which shall state the name of the corporation, the number and date of the certificate, if known or ascertainable by the plaintiff, the number of shares of stock represented thereby and to whom issued, and a statement of the circumstances attending such loss, theft or destruction. Thereupon the court shall make an order requiring the corporation to show cause at a time and place therein designated, why it should not issue new uncertificated shares or a new certificate of stock in place of the one described in the complaint. A copy of the complaint and order shall be served upon the corporation at least 5 days before the time designated in the order.

(b) If, upon hearing, the court is satisfied that the plaintiff is the lawful owner of the number of shares of capital stock, or any part thereof, described in the complaint, and that the certificate therefor has been lost, stolen or destroyed, and no sufficient cause has been shown why new uncertificated shares or a new certificate should not be issued in place thereof, it shall make an order requiring the corporation to issue and deliver to the plaintiff new uncertificated shares or a new certificate for such shares. In its order the court shall direct that, prior to the issuance and delivery to the plaintiff of such new uncertificated shares or a new certificate, the plaintiff give the corporation a bond in such form and with such security as to the court appears sufficient to indemnify the corporation against any claim that may be made against it on account of the alleged loss, theft or destruction of any such certificate or the issuance of such new uncertificated shares or new certificate. No corporation which has issued uncertificated shares or a certificate pursuant to an order of the court entered hereunder shall be liable in an amount in excess of the amount specified in such bond.

§ 169. Situs of Ownership of Stock

For all purposes of title, action, attachment, garnishment and jurisdiction of all courts held in this State, but not for the purpose of taxation, the situs of the ownership of the capital stock of all corporations existing under the laws of this State, whether organized under this chapter or otherwise, shall be regarded as in this State.

§ 170. Dividends; Payment; Wasting Asset Corporations

(a) The directors of every corporation, subject to any restrictions contained in its certificate of incorporation, may declare and pay dividends upon the shares of its capital stock, or to its members if the corporation is a nonstock corporation, either (1) out of its surplus, as defined in and computed in accordance with §§ 154 and 244 of this title, or (2) in case there shall be no such surplus, out of its net profits for the fiscal year in which the dividend is declared and/or the preceding fiscal year. If the capital of the corporation, computed in accordance with §§ 154 and 244 of this title, shall have been diminished by depreciation in the value of its property, or by losses, or otherwise, to an amount less than the aggregate amount of the capital represented by the issued and outstanding stock of all classes having a preference upon the distribution of assets, the directors of such corporation shall not declare and pay out of such net profits any dividends upon any shares of any classes of its capital stock until the deficiency in the amount of capital represented by the issued and outstanding stock of all classes having a preference upon the distribution of assets shall have been repaired. Nothing in this subsection shall invalidate or otherwise affect a note, debenture or other obligation of the corporation paid by it as a dividend on shares of its stock, or any payment made thereon, if at the time such note, debenture or obligation was delivered by the corporation, the corporation had either surplus or net profits as provided in clause (1) or (2) of this subsection from which the dividend could lawfully have been paid.

(b) Subject to any restrictions contained in its certificate of incorporation, the directors of any corporation engaged in the exploitation of wasting assets (including but not limited to a corporation engaged in the exploitation of natural resources or other wasting assets, including patents, or engaged primarily in the liquidation of specific assets) may determine the net profits derived from the exploitation of such wasting assets or the net proceeds derived from such liquidation without taking into consideration the depletion of such assets resulting from lapse of time, consumption, liquidation or exploitation of such assets.

§ 171. Special Purpose Reserves

The directors of a corporation may set apart out of any of the funds of the corporation available for dividends a reserve or reserves for any proper purpose and may abolish any such reserve.

§ 172. Liability of Directors and Committee Members as to Dividends or Stock Redemption

A member of the board of directors, or a member of any committee designated by the board of directors, shall be fully protected in relying in good faith upon the records of the corporation and upon such information, opinions, reports or statements presented to the corporation by any of its officers or employees, or committees of the board of directors, or by any other person as to matters the director reasonably believes are within such other person's professional or expert competence and who has been selected with reasonable care by or on behalf of the corporation, as to the value and amount of the assets, liabilities and/or net profits of the corporation or any other facts pertinent to the existence and amount of surplus or other funds from which dividends might properly be declared and paid, or with which the corporation's stock might properly be purchased or redeemed.

§ 173. Declaration and Payment of Dividends

No corporation shall pay dividends except in accordance with this chapter. Dividends may be paid in cash, in property, or in shares of the corporation's capital stock. If the dividend is to be paid in shares of the corporation's theretofore unissued capital stock the board of directors shall, by resolution, direct that there be designated as capital in respect of such shares an amount which is not less than the aggregate par value of par value being declared as a dividend and, in the case of shares without par value being declared as a dividend, such amount as shall be determined by the board of directors. No such designation as capital shall be necessary if shares are being distributed by a corporation pursuant to a split-up or division of its stock rather than as payment of a dividend declared payable in stock of the corporation.

§ 174. Liability of Directors for Unlawful Payment of Dividend or Unlawful Stock Purchase or Redemption; Exoneration From Liability; Contribution Among Directors; Subrogation

(a) In case of any wilful or negligent violation of § 160 or 173 of this title, the directors under whose administration the same may happen shall be jointly and severally liable, at any time within 6 years after paying such unlawful dividend or after such unlawful stock purchase or redemption, to the corporation, and to its creditors in the event of its dissolution or insolvency, to the full amount of the dividend unlawfully paid, or to the full amount unlawfully paid for the purchase or redemption of the corporation's stock, with interest from the time such liability accrued. Any director who may have been absent when the same was done, or who may have dissented from the act or resolution by which the same was done, may be exonerated from such liability by causing his or her dissent to be entered on the books containing the minutes of the proceedings of the directors at the time the same was done, or immediately after such director has notice of the same.

(b) Any director against whom a claim is successfully asserted under this section shall be entitled to contribution from the other directors who voted for or concurred in the unlawful dividend, stock purchase or stock redemption.

(c) Any director against whom a claim is successfully asserted under this section shall be entitled, to the extent of the amount paid by such director as a result of such claim, to be subrogated to the rights of the corporation against stockholders who received the dividend on, or assets for the sale or redemption of, their stock with knowledge of facts indicating that such dividend, stock purchase or redemption was unlawful under this chapter, in proportion to the amounts received by such stockholders respectively.

SUBCHAPTER VI. STOCK TRANSFERS

§ 201. Transfer of Stock, Stock Certificates and Uncertificated Stock

Except as otherwise provided in this chapter, the transfer of stock and the certificates of stock which represent the stock or uncertificated stock shall be governed by Article 8 of subtitle I of Title 6. To the extent that any provision of this chapter is inconsistent with any provision of subtitle I of Title 6, this chapter shall be controlling.

§ 202. Restrictions on Transfer and Ownership of Securities

(a) A written restriction or restrictions on the transfer or registration of transfer of a security of a corporation, or on the amount of the corporation's securities that may be owned by any person or group of persons, if permitted by this section and noted conspicuously on the certificate or certificates representing the security or securities so restricted or, in the case of uncertificated shares, contained in the notice or notices sent pursuant to § 151(f) of this title, may be enforced against the holder of the restricted security or securities or any successor or transferee of the holder including an executor, administrator, trustee, guardian or other fiduciary entrusted with like responsibility for the person or estate of the holder. Unless noted conspicuously on the certificate or certificates representing the security or securities so restricted or, in the case of uncertificated shares, contained in the notice or notices sent pursuant to § 151(f) of this title, a restriction, even though permitted by this section, is ineffective except against a person with actual knowledge of the restriction.

(b) A restriction on the transfer or registration of transfer of securities of a corporation, or on the amount of a corporation's securities that may be owned by any person or group of persons, may be imposed by the certificate of incorporation or by the bylaws or by an agreement among any number of security holders or among such holders and the corporation. No restrictions so imposed shall be binding with respect to securities issued prior to the adoption of the restriction unless the holders of the securities are parties to an agreement or voted in favor of the restriction.

(c) A restriction on the transfer or registration of transfer of securities of a corporation or on the amount of such securities that may be owned by any person or group of persons is permitted by this section if it:

(1) Obligates the holder of the restricted securities to offer to the corporation or to any other holders of securities of the corporation or to any other person or to any combination of the foregoing, a prior opportunity, to be exercised within a reasonable time, to acquire the restricted securities; or

(2) Obligates the corporation or any holder of securities of the corporation or any other person or any combination of the foregoing, to purchase the securities which are the subject of an agreement respecting the purchase and sale of the restricted securities; or

(3) Requires the corporation or the holders of any class or series of securities of the corporation to consent to any proposed transfer of the restricted securities or to approve the proposed transferee of the restricted securities, or to approve the amount of securities of the corporation that may be owned by any person or group of persons; or

(4) Obligates the holder of the restricted securities to sell or transfer an amount of restricted securities to the corporation or to any other holders of securities of the corporation or to any other person or to any combination of the foregoing, or causes or results in the automatic sale or transfer of an amount of restricted securities to the corporation or to any other holders of securities of the corporation or to any other person or to any combination of the foregoing; or

(5) Prohibits or restricts the transfer of the restricted securities to, or the ownership of restricted securities by, designated persons

or classes of persons or groups of persons, and such designation is not manifestly unreasonable.

(d) Any restriction on the transfer or the registration of transfer of the securities of a corporation, or on the amount of securities of a corporation that may be owned by a person or group of persons, for any of the following purposes shall be conclusively presumed to be for a reasonable purpose:

(1) Maintaining any local, state, federal or foreign tax advantage to the corporation or its stockholders, including without limitation:

a. Maintaining the corporation's status as an electing small business corporation under subchapter S of the United States Internal Revenue Code [26 U.S.C. § 1371 et seq.], or

b. Maintaining or preserving any tax attribute (including without limitation net operating losses), or

c. Qualifying or maintaining the qualification of the corporation as a real estate investment trust pursuant to the United States Internal Revenue Code or regulations adopted pursuant to the United States Internal Revenue Code, or

(2) Maintaining any statutory or regulatory advantage or complying with any statutory or regulatory requirements under applicable local, state, federal or foreign law.

(e) Any other lawful restriction on transfer or registration of transfer of securities, or on the amount of securities that may be owned by any person or group of persons, is permitted by this section.

§ 203. Business Combinations with Interested Stockholders

(a) Notwithstanding any other provisions of this chapter, a corporation shall not engage in any business combination with any interested stockholder for a period of 3 years following the time that such stockholder became an interested stockholder, unless:

(1) Prior to such time the board of directors of the corporation approved either the business combination or the transaction which resulted in the stockholder becoming an interested stockholder;

(2) Upon consummation of the transaction which resulted in the stockholder becoming an interested stockholder, the interested stockholder owned at least 85% of the voting stock of the corporation outstanding at the time the transaction commenced, excluding for purposes of determining the voting stock outstanding (but not the outstanding voting stock owned by the interested stockholder) those shares owned (i) by persons who are directors and also officers and (ii) employee stock plans in which employee participants do not

have the right to determine confidentially whether shares held subject to the plan will be tendered in a tender or exchange offer; or

(3) At or subsequent to such time the business combination is approved by the board of directors and authorized at an annual or special meeting of stockholders, and not by written consent, by the affirmative vote of at least 66 2/3% of the outstanding voting stock which is not owned by the interested stockholder.

(b) The restrictions contained in this section shall not apply if:

(1) The corporation's original certificate of incorporation contains a provision expressly electing not to be governed by this section;

(2) The corporation, by action of its board of directors, adopts an amendment to its bylaws within 90 days of February 2, 1988, expressly electing not to be governed by this section, which amendment shall not be further amended by the board of directors;

(3) The corporation, by action of its stockholders, adopts an amendment to its certificate of incorporation or bylaws expressly electing not to be governed by this section; provided that, in addition to any other vote required by law, such amendment to the certificate of incorporation or bylaws must be approved by the affirmative vote of a majority of the shares entitled to vote. An amendment adopted pursuant to this paragraph shall be effective immediately in the case of a corporation that both (i) has never had a class of voting stock that falls within any of the 3 categories set out in subsection (b)(4) hereof, and (ii) has not elected by a provision in its original certificate of incorporation or any amendment thereto to be governed by this section. In all other cases, an amendment adopted pursuant to this paragraph shall not be effective until 12 months after the adoption of such amendment and shall not apply to any business combination between such corporation and any person who became an interested stockholder of such corporation on or prior to such adoption. A bylaw amendment adopted pursuant to this paragraph shall not be further amended by the board of directors;

(4) The corporation does not have a class of voting stock that is: (i) Listed on a national securities exchange; (ii) authorized for quotation on The NASDAQ Stock Market; or (iii) held of record by more than 2,000 stockholders, unless any of the foregoing results from action taken, directly or indirectly, by an interested stockholder or from a transaction in which a person becomes an interested stockholder;

(5) A stockholder becomes an interested stockholder inadvertently and (i) as soon as practicable divests itself of ownership of sufficient shares so that the stockholder ceases to be an interested stockholder; and (ii) would not, at any time within the 3-year period immediately prior to a business combination between the corpora-

tion and such stockholder, have been an interested stockholder but for the inadvertent acquisition of ownership;

(6) The business combination is proposed prior to the consummation or abandonment of and subsequent to the earlier of the public announcement or the notice required hereunder of a proposed transaction which (i) constitutes one of the transactions described in the 2nd sentence of this paragraph; (ii) is with or by a person who either was not an interested stockholder during the previous 3 years or who became an interested stockholder with the approval of the corporation's board of directors or during the period described in paragraph (7) of this subsection (b); and (iii) is approved or not opposed by a majority of the members of the board of directors then in office (but not less than 1) who were directors prior to any person becoming an interested stockholder during the previous 3 years or were recommended for election or elected to succeed such directors by a majority of such directors. The proposed transactions referred to in the preceding sentence are limited to (x) a merger or consolidation of the corporation (except for a merger in respect of which, pursuant to § 251(f) of this title, no vote of the stockholders of the corporation is required); (y) a sale, lease, exchange, mortgage, pledge, transfer or other disposition (in 1 transaction or a series of transactions), whether as part of a dissolution or otherwise, of assets of the corporation or of any direct or indirect majority-owned subsidiary of the corporation (other than to any direct or indirect wholly-owned subsidiary or to the corporation) having an aggregate market value equal to 50% or more of either that aggregate market value of all of the assets of the corporation determined on a consolidated basis or the aggregate market value of all the outstanding stock of the corporation; or (z) a proposed tender or exchange offer for 50% or more of the outstanding voting stock of the corporation. The corporation shall give not less than 20 days' notice to all interested stockholders prior to the consummation of any of the transactions described in clause (x) or (y) of the 2nd sentence of this paragraph; or

(7) The business combination is with an interested stockholder who became an interested stockholder at a time when the restrictions contained in this section did not apply by reason of any of paragraphs (1) through (4) of this subsection (b), provided, however, that this paragraph (7) shall not apply if, at the time such interested stockholder became an interested stockholder, the corporation's certificate of incorporation contained a provision authorized by the last sentence of this subsection (b).

Notwithstanding paragraphs (1), (2), (3) and (4) of this subsection, a corporation may elect by a provision of its original certificate of incorporation or any amendment thereto to be governed by this section; provided that any such amendment to the certificate of incorporation shall not apply to restrict a business combination between the corporation and an interested stockholder of the corporation if the interested stockholder became such prior to the effective date of the amendment.

(c) As used in this section only, the term:

(1) "Affiliate" means a person that directly, or indirectly through 1 or more intermediaries, controls, or is controlled by, or is under common control with, another person.

(2) "Associate," when used to indicate a relationship with any person, means: (i) Any corporation, partnership, unincorporated association or other entity of which such person is a director, officer or partner or is, directly or indirectly, the owner of 20% or more of any class of voting stock; (ii) any trust or other estate in which such person has at least a 20% beneficial interest or as to which such person serves as trustee or in a similar fiduciary capacity; and (iii) any relative or spouse of such person, or any relative of such spouse, who has the same residence as such person.

(3) "Business combination," when used in reference to any corporation and any interested stockholder of such corporation, means:

(i) Any merger or consolidation of the corporation or any direct or indirect majority-owned subsidiary of the corporation with (A) the interested stockholder, or (B) with any other corporation, partnership, unincorporated association or other entity if the merger or consolidation is caused by the interested stockholder and as a result of such merger or consolidation subsection (a) of this section is not applicable to the surviving entity;

(ii) Any sale, lease, exchange, mortgage, pledge, transfer or other disposition (in 1 transaction or a series of transactions), except proportionately as a stockholder of such corporation, to or with the interested stockholder, whether as part of a dissolution or otherwise, of assets of the corporation or of any direct or indirect majority-owned subsidiary of the corporation which assets have an aggregate market value equal to 10% or more of either the aggregate market value of all the assets of the corporation determined on a consolidated basis or the aggregate market value of all the outstanding stock of the corporation;

(iii) Any transaction which results in the issuance or transfer by the corporation or by any direct or indirect majority-owned subsidiary of the corporation of any stock of the corporation or of such subsidiary to the interested stockholder, except: (A) Pursuant to the exercise, exchange or conversion of securities exercisable for, exchangeable for or convertible into stock of such corporation or any such subsidiary which securities were outstanding prior to the time that the interested stockholder became such; (B) pursuant to a merger under § 251(g) of this title; (C) pursuant to a dividend or distribution paid or made, or the exercise, exchange or conversion of securities exercisable for, exchangeable for or convertible into stock of such corporation or any such subsidiary which security is distributed, pro rata to all holders of a class or series of stock of such corporation subsequent to the time the interested stockholder became such; (D) pursuant to an exchange offer by the corporation to purchase stock made on the same terms to all holders of said stock; or (E) any issuance or transfer of stock by the corporation; provided however, that in no case under items (C)-(E) of this subparagraph shall there be an increase in the interested stockholder's proportionate share of the stock of any class or series of the corporation or of the voting stock of the corporation;

(iv) Any transaction involving the corporation or any direct or indirect majority-owned subsidiary of the corporation which has the effect, directly or indirectly, of increasing the proportionate share of the stock of any class or series, or securities convertible into the stock of any class or series, of the corporation or of any such subsidiary which is owned by the interested stockholder, except as a result of immaterial changes due to fractional share adjustments or as a result of any purchase or redemption of any shares of stock not caused, directly or indirectly, by the interested stockholder; or

(v) Any receipt by the interested stockholder of the benefit, directly or indirectly (except proportionately as a stockholder of such corporation), of any loans, advances, guarantees, pledges or other financial benefits (other than those expressly permitted in subparagraphs (i)-(iv) of this paragraph) provided by or through the corporation or any direct or indirect majority-owned subsidiary.

(4) "Control," including the terms "controlling," "controlled by" and "under common control with," means the possession, directly or indirectly, of the power to direct or cause the direction of the management and policies of a person, whether through the ownership of voting stock, by contract or otherwise. A person who is the owner of 20% or more of the outstanding voting stock of any corporation, partnership, unincorporated association or other entity shall be presumed to have control of such entity, in the absence of proof by a preponderance of the evidence to the contrary; Notwithstanding the foregoing, a presumption of control shall not apply where such person holds voting stock, in good faith and not for the purpose of circumventing this section, as an agent, bank, broker, nominee, custodian or trustee for 1 or more owners who do not individually or as a group have control of such entity.

(5) "Interested stockholder" means any person (other than the corporation and any direct or indirect majority-owned subsidiary of the corporation) that (i) is the owner of 15% or more of the outstanding voting stock of the corporation, or (ii) is an affiliate or associate of the corporation and was the owner of 15% or more of the outstanding voting stock of the corporation at any time within the 3-year period immediately prior to the date on which it is sought to be determined whether such person is an interested stockholder, and the affiliates and associates of such person; provided, however, that the term "interested stockholder" shall not include (x) any person who (A) owned shares in excess of the 15% limitation set forth herein as of, or acquired such shares pursuant to a tender offer commenced prior to, December 23, 1987, or pursuant to an exchange offer announced prior to the aforesaid date and commenced within 90 days thereafter and either (I) continued to own shares in excess of such 15% limitation or would have but for action by the corporation or (II) is an affiliate or associate of the corporation and so continued (or so would have continued but for action by the corporation) to be the owner of 15% or more of the outstanding voting stock of the corporation at any time within the 3-year period immediately prior to the date on which it is sought to be determined whether such a person is an interested stockholder or (B) acquired said shares from a person described in item (A) of this paragraph by gift, inheritance or in a transaction in which no consideration was exchanged; or (y) any person whose ownership of shares in excess of the 15% limitation set forth herein is the result of action taken solely by the corporation; provided that such person shall be an interested stockholder if thereafter such person acquires additional shares of voting stock of the corporation, except as a result of further corporate action not caused, directly or indirectly, by such person. For the purpose of determining whether a person is an interested stockholder, the voting stock of the corporation deemed to be outstanding shall include stock deemed to be owned by the person through application of paragraph (9) of this subsection but shall not include any other unissued stock of such corporation which may be issuable pursuant to any agreement, arrangement or understanding, or upon exercise of conversion rights, warrants or options, or otherwise.

(6) "Person" means any individual, corporation, partnership, unincorporated association or other entity.

(7) "Stock" means, with respect to any corporation, capital stock and, with respect to any other entity, any equity interest.

(8) "Voting stock" means, with respect to any corporation, stock of any class or series entitled to vote generally in the election of directors and, with respect to any entity that is not a corporation, any equity interest entitled to vote generally in the election of the governing body of such entity. Every reference to a percentage of

voting stock shall refer to such percentage of the votes of such voting stock.

(9) "Owner," including the terms "own" and "owned," when used with respect to any stock, means a person that individually or with or through any of its affiliates or associates:

(i) Beneficially owns such stock, directly or indirectly; or

(ii) Has (A) the right to acquire such stock (whether such right is exercisable immediately or only after the passage of time) pursuant to any agreement, arrangement or understanding, or upon the exercise of conversion rights, exchange rights, warrants or options, or otherwise; provided, however, that a person shall not be deemed the owner of stock tendered pursuant to a tender or exchange offer made by such person or any of such person's affiliates or associates until such tendered stock is accepted for purchase or exchange; or (B) the right to vote such stock pursuant to any agreement, arrangement or understanding; provided, however, that a person shall not be deemed the owner of any stock because of such person's right to vote such stock if the agreement, arrangement or understanding to vote such stock arises solely from a revocable proxy or consent given in response to a proxy or consent solicitation made to 10 or more persons; or

(iii) Has any agreement, arrangement or understanding for the purpose of acquiring, holding, voting (except voting pursuant to a revocable proxy or consent as described in item (B) of subparagraph (ii) of this paragraph), or disposing of such stock with any other person that beneficially owns, or whose affiliates or associates beneficially own, directly or indirectly, such stock.

(d) No provision of a certificate of incorporation or bylaw shall require, for any vote of stockholders required by this section, a greater vote of stockholders than that specified in this section.

(e) The Court of Chancery is hereby vested with exclusive jurisdiction to hear and determine all matters with respect to this section.

SUBCHAPTER VII. MEETINGS, ELECTIONS, VOTING AND NOTICE

§ 211. Meetings of Stockholders

(a)(1) Meetings of stockholders may be held at such place, either within or without this State as may be designated by or in the manner provided in the certificate of incorporation or bylaws, or if not so designated, as determined by the board of directors. If, pursuant to this paragraph or the certificate of incorporation or the bylaws of the corporation, the board of directors is authorized to determine the place of a meeting of stockholders, the board of directors may, in its sole discretion, determine that the meeting shall not be held at any place, but may instead be held solely by means of remote communication as authorized by paragraph (a)(2) of this section.

(2) If authorized by the board of directors in its sole discretion, and subject to such guidelines and procedures as the board of directors may adopt, stockholders and proxyholders not physically present at a meeting of stockholders may, by means of remote communication:

a. Participate in a meeting of stockholders; and

b. Be deemed present in person and vote at a meeting of stockholders, whether such meeting is to be held at a designated place or solely by means of remote communication, provided that (i) the corporation shall implement reasonable measures to verify that each person deemed present and permitted to vote at the meeting by means of remote communication is a stockholder or proxyholder, (ii) the corporation shall implement reasonable measures to provide such stockholders and proxyholders a reasonable opportunity to participate in the meeting and to vote on matters submitted to the stockholders, including an opportunity to read or hear the proceedings of the meeting substantially concurrently with such proceedings, and (iii) if any stockholder or proxyholder votes or takes other action at the meeting by means of remote communication, a record of such vote or other action shall be maintained by the corporation.

(b) Unless directors are elected by written consent in lieu of an annual meeting as permitted by this subsection, an annual meeting of stockholders shall be held for the election of directors on a date and at a time designated by or in the manner provided in the bylaws. Stockholders may, unless the certificate of incorporation otherwise provides, act by written consent to elect directors; provided, however, that, if such consent is less than unanimous, such action by written consent may be in lieu of holding an annual meeting only if all of the directorships to which directors could be elected at an annual meeting held at the effective time of such action are vacant and are filled by such action. Any other proper business may be transacted at the annual meeting.

(c) A failure to hold the annual meeting at the designated time or to elect a sufficient number of directors to conduct the business of the corporation shall not affect otherwise valid corporate acts or work a forfeiture or dissolution of the corporation except as may be otherwise specifically provided in this chapter. If the annual meeting for election of directors is not held on the date designated therefor or action by written consent to elect directors in lieu of an annual meeting has not been taken, the directors shall cause the meeting to be held as soon as is convenient. If there be a failure to hold the annual meeting or to take action by written consent to elect directors in lieu of an annual meeting for a period of 30 days after the date designated for the annual meeting, or if no date has been designated, for a period of 13 months after the latest to occur of the organization of the corporation, its last annual meeting or the last action by written consent to elect directors in lieu of an annual meeting, the Court of Chancery may summarily order a meeting to be held upon the application of any stockholder or director. The shares of stock represented at such meeting, either in person or by proxy, and entitled to vote thereat, shall constitute a quorum for the purpose of such meeting, notwithstanding any provision of the certificate of incorporation or bylaws to the contrary. The Court of Chancery may issue such orders as may be appropriate, including, without limitation, orders designating the time and place of such meeting, the record date for determination of stockholders entitled to vote, and the form of notice of such meeting.

(d) Special meetings of the stockholders may be called by the board of directors or by such person or persons as may be authorized by the certificate of incorporation or by the bylaws.

(e) All elections of directors shall be by written ballot unless otherwise provided in the certificate of incorporation; if authorized by the board of directors, such requirement of a written ballot shall be satisfied by a ballot submitted by electronic transmission, provided that any such electronic transmission must either set forth or be submitted with information from which it can be determined that the electronic transmission was authorized by the stockholder or proxy holder.

§ 212. Voting Rights of Stockholders; Proxies; Limitations

(a) Unless otherwise provided in the certificate of incorporation and subject to § 213 of this title, each stockholder shall be entitled to 1 vote for each share of capital stock held by such stockholder. If the certificate of incorporation provides for more or less than 1 vote for any share, on any matter, every reference in this chapter to a majority or other proportion of stock, voting stock or shares shall refer to such majority or other proportion of the votes of such stock, voting stock or shares.

(b) Each stockholder entitled to vote at a meeting of stockholders or to express consent or dissent to corporate action in writing without a meeting may authorize another person or persons to act for such stockholder by proxy, but no such proxy shall be voted or acted upon after 3 years from its date, unless the proxy provides for a longer period.

(c) Without limiting the manner in which a stockholder may authorize another person or persons to act for such stockholder as proxy pursuant to subsection (b) of this section, the following shall constitute a valid means by which a stockholder may grant such authority:

(1) A stockholder may execute a writing authorizing another person or persons to act for such stockholder as proxy. Execution may be accomplished by the stockholder or such stockholder's au-

thorized officer, director, employee or agent signing such writing or causing such person's signature to be affixed to such writing by any reasonable means including, but not limited to, by facsimile signature.

(2) A stockholder may authorize another person or persons to act for such stockholder as proxy by transmitting or authorizing the transmission of a telegram, cablegram, or other means of electronic transmission to the person who will be the holder of the proxy or to a proxy solicitation firm, proxy support service organization or like agent duly authorized by the person who will be the holder of the proxy to receive such transmission, provided that any such telegram, cablegram or other means of electronic transmission must either set forth or be submitted with information from which it can be determined that the telegram, cablegram or other electronic transmission was authorized by the stockholder. If it is determined that such telegrams, cablegrams or other electronic transmissions are valid, the inspectors or, if there are no inspectors, such other persons making that determination shall specify the information upon which they relied.

(d) Any copy, facsimile telecommunication or other reliable reproduction of the writing or transmission created pursuant to subsection (c) of this section may be substituted or used in lieu of the original writing or transmission for any and all purposes for which the original writing or transmission could be used, provided that such copy, facsimile telecommunication or other reproduction shall be a complete reproduction of the entire original writing or transmission.

(e) A duly executed proxy shall be irrevocable if it states that it is irrevocable and if, and only as long as, it is coupled with an interest sufficient in law to support an irrevocable power. A proxy may be made irrevocable regardless of whether the interest with which it is coupled is an interest in the stock itself or an interest in the corporation generally.

§ 213. Fixing Date for Determination of Stockholders of Record

(a) In order that the corporation may determine the stockholders entitled to notice of or to vote at any meeting of stockholders or any adjournment thereof, the board of directors may fix a record date, which record date shall not precede the date upon which the resolution fixing the record date is adopted by the board of directors, and which record date shall not be more than 60 nor less than 10 days before the date of such meeting. If no record date is fixed by the board of directors, the record date for determining stockholders entitled to notice of or to vote at a meeting of stockholders shall be at the close of business on the day next preceding the day on which notice is given, or, if notice is waived, at the close of business on the day next preceding the day on which the meeting is held. A determination of stockholders of record entitled to notice of or to vote at a meeting of stockholders shall apply to any adjournment of the meeting; provided, however, that the board of directors may fix a new record date for the adjourned meeting.

(b) In order that the corporation may determine the stockholders entitled to consent to corporate action in writing without a meeting, the board of directors may fix a record date, which record date shall not precede the date upon which the resolution fixing the record date is adopted by the board of directors, and which date shall not be more than 10 days after the date upon which the resolution fixing the record date is adopted by the board of directors. If no record date has been fixed by the board of directors, the record date for determining stockholders entitled to consent to corporate action in writing without a meeting, when no prior action by the board of directors is required by this chapter, shall be the first date on which a signed written consent setting forth the action taken or proposed to be taken is delivered to the corporation by delivery to its registered office in this State, its principal place of business or an officer or agent of the corporation having custody of the book in which proceedings of meetings of stockholders are recorded. Delivery made to a corporation's registered office shall be by hand or by certified or registered mail, return receipt requested. If no record date has been fixed by the board of directors and prior action by the board of directors is required by this chapter, the record date for determining stockholders entitled to consent to corporate action in writing without a meeting shall be at the close of business on the day on which the board of directors adopts the resolution taking such prior action.

(c) In order that the corporation may determine the stockholders entitled to receive payment of any dividend or other distribution or allotment of any rights or the stockholders entitled to exercise any rights in respect of any change, conversion or exchange of stock, or for the purpose of any other lawful action, the board of directors may fix a record date, which record date shall not precede the date upon which the resolution fixing the record date is adopted, and which record date shall be not more than 60 days prior to such action. If no record date is fixed, the record date for determining stockholders for any such purpose shall be at the close of business on the day on which the board of directors adopts the resolution relating thereto.

§ 214. Cumulative Voting

The certificate of incorporation of any corporation may provide that at all elections of directors of the corporation, or at elections held under specified circumstances, each holder of stock or of any class or classes or of a series or series thereof shall be entitled to as many votes as shall equal the number of votes which (except for such provision as to cumulative voting) such holder would be entitled to cast for the election of directors with respect to such holder's shares of stock multiplied by the number of directors to be elected by such holder, and that such holder may cast all of such votes for a single director or may distribute them among the number to be voted for, or for any 2 or more of them as such holder may see fit.

§ 215. Voting Rights of Members of Nonstock Corporations; Quorum; Proxies

(a) Sections 211 through 214 and 216 of this title shall not apply to corporations not authorized to issue stock, except that § 211(a) of this title and § 212(c) and (d) of this title shall apply to such corporations, and, when so applied, all references therein to stockholders and to the board of directors shall be deemed to refer to the members and the governing body of a nonstock corporation, respectively.

(b) Unless otherwise provided in the certificate of incorporation of a nonstock corporation, each member shall be entitled at every meeting of members to 1 vote in person or by proxy, but no proxy shall be voted on after 3 years from its date, unless the proxy provides for a longer period.

(c) Unless otherwise provided in this chapter, the certificate of incorporation or bylaws of a nonstock corporation may specify the number of members having voting power who shall be present or represented by proxy at any meeting in order to constitute a quorum for, and the votes that shall be necessary for, the transaction of any business. In the absence of such specification in the certificate of incorporation or bylaws of a nonstock corporation:

(1) One-third of the members of such corporation shall constitute a quorum at a meeting of such members;

(2) In all matters other than the election of the governing body of such corporation, the affirmative vote of a majority of such members present in person or represented by proxy at the meeting and entitled to vote on the subject matter shall be the act of the members, unless the vote of a greater number is required by this chapter; and

(3) Members of the governing body shall be elected by a plurality of the votes of the members of the corporation present in person or represented by proxy at the meeting and entitled to vote thereon.

(d) If the election of the governing body of any nonstock corporation shall not be held on the day designated by the bylaws, the governing body shall cause the election to be held as soon thereafter as convenient. The failure to hold such an election at the designated time shall not work any forfeiture or dissolution of the corporation, but the Court of Chancery may summarily order such an election to be held upon the application of any member of the corporation. At any election pursuant to such order the persons entitled to vote in such election who shall be present at such meeting, either in person or by proxy, shall constitute a quorum for such meeting, notwithstanding any provision of the certificate of incorporation or the bylaws of the corporation to the contrary.

(e) If authorized by the governing body, any requirement of a written ballot shall be satisfied by a ballot submitted by electronic transmission, provided that any such electronic transmission must either set forth or be submitted with information from which it can be determined that the electronic transmission was authorized by the member or proxy holder.

§ 216. Quorum and Required Vote for Stock Corporations

Subject to this chapter in respect of the vote that shall be required for a specified action, the certificate of incorporation or bylaws of any corporation authorized to issue stock may specify the number of shares and/or the amount of other securities having voting power the holders of which shall be present or represented by proxy at any meeting in order to constitute a quorum for, and the votes that shall be necessary for, the transaction of any business, but in no event shall a quorum consist of less than one-third of the shares entitled to vote at the meeting, except that, where a separate vote by a class or series or classes or series is required, a quorum shall consist of no less than one-third of the shares of such class or series or classes or series. In the absence of such specification in the certificate of incorporation or bylaws of the corporation:

(1) A majority of the shares entitled to vote, present in person or represented by proxy, shall constitute a quorum at a meeting of stockholders;

(2) In all matters other than the election of directors, the affirmative vote of the majority of shares present in person or represented by proxy at the meeting and entitled to vote on the subject matter shall be the act of the stockholders;

(3) Directors shall be elected by a plurality of the votes of the shares present in person or represented by proxy at the meeting and entitled to vote on the election of directors; and

(4) Where a separate vote by a class or series or classes or series is required, a majority of the outstanding shares of such class or series or classes or series, present in person or represented by proxy, shall constitute a quorum entitled to take action with respect to that vote on that matter and the affirmative vote of the majority of shares of such class or series or classes or series present in person or represented by proxy at the meeting shall be the act of such class or series or classes or series.

A bylaw amendment adopted by stockholders which specifies the votes that shall be necessary for the election of directors shall not be further amended or repealed by the board of directors.

§ 217. Voting Rights of Fiduciaries, Pledgors and Joint Owners of Stock

(a) Persons holding stock in a fiduciary capacity shall be entitled to vote the shares so held. Persons whose stock is pledged shall be entitled to vote, unless in the transfer by the pledgor on the books of the corporation such person has expressly empowered the pledgee to vote thereon, in which case only the pledgee, or such pledgee's proxy, may represent such stock and vote thereon.

(b) If shares or other securities having voting power stand of record in the names of 2 or more persons, whether fiduciaries, members of a partnership, joint tenants, tenants in common, tenants by the entirety or otherwise, or if 2 or more persons have the same fiduciary relationship respecting the same shares, unless the secretary of the corporation is given written notice to the contrary and is furnished with a copy of the instrument or order appointing them or creating the relationship wherein it is so provided, their acts with respect to voting shall have the following effect:

(1) If only 1 votes, such person's act binds all;

(2) If more than 1 vote, the act of the majority so voting binds all;

(3) If more than 1 vote, but the vote is evenly split on any particular matter, each faction may vote the securities in question proportionally, or any person voting the shares, or a beneficiary, if any, may apply to the Court of Chancery or such other court as may have jurisdiction to appoint an additional person to act with the persons so voting the shares, which shall then be voted as determined by a majority of such persons and the person appointed by the Court. If the instrument so filed shows that any such tenancy is held in unequal interests, a majority or even split for the purpose of this subsection shall be a majority or even split in interest.

§ 218. Voting Trusts and Other Voting Agreements

(a) One stockholder or 2 or more stockholders may by agreement in writing deposit capital stock of an original issue with or transfer capital stock to any person or persons, or entity or entities authorized to act as trustee, for the purpose of vesting in such person or persons, entity or entities, who may be designated voting trustee, or voting trustees, the right to vote thereon for any period of time determined by such agreement, upon the terms and conditions stated in such agreement. The agreement may contain any other lawful provisions not inconsistent with such purpose. After the filing of a copy of the agreement in the registered office of the corporation in this State, which copy shall be open to the inspection of any stockholder of the corporation or any beneficiary of the trust under the agreement daily during business hours, certificates of stock or uncertificated stock shall be issued to the voting trustee or trustees to represent any stock of an original issue so deposited with such voting trustee or trustees, and any certificates of stock or uncertificated stock so transferred to the voting trustee or trustees shall be surrendered and cancelled and new certificates or uncertificated stock shall be issued therefore to the voting trustee or trustees. In the certificate so issued, if any, it shall be stated that it is issued pursuant to such agreement, and that fact shall also be stated in the stock ledger of the corporation. The voting trustee or trustees may vote the stock so issued or transferred during the period specified in the agreement. Stock standing in the name of the voting trustee or trustees may be voted either in person or by proxy, and in voting the stock, the voting trustee or trustees shall incur no responsibility as stockholder, trustee or otherwise, except for their own individual malfeasance. In any case where 2 or more persons or entities are designated as voting trustees, and the right and method of voting any stock standing in their names at any meeting of the corporation are not fixed by the agreement appointing the trustees, the right to vote the stock and the manner of voting it at the meeting shall be determined by a majority of the trustees, or if they be equally divided as to the right and manner of voting the stock in any particular case, the vote of the stock in such case shall be divided equally among the trustees.

(b) Any amendment to a voting trust agreement shall be made by a written agreement, a copy of which shall be filed in the registered office of the corporation in this State.

(c) An agreement between 2 or more stockholders, if in writing and signed by the parties thereto, may provide that in exercising any voting rights, the shares held by them shall be voted as provided by the agreement, or as the parties may agree, or as determined in accordance with a procedure agreed upon by them.

(d) This section shall not be deemed to invalidate any voting or other agreement among stockholders or any irrevocable proxy which is not otherwise illegal.

§ 219. List of Stockholders Entitled to Vote; Penalty for Refusal to Produce; Stock Ledger

(a) The officer who has charge of the stock ledger of a corporation shall prepare and make, at least 10 days before every meeting of stockholders, a complete list of the stockholders entitled to vote at the meeting, arranged in alphabetical order, and showing the address of each stockholder and the number of shares registered in the name of each stockholder. Nothing contained in this section shall require the corporation to include electronic mail addresses or other electronic contact information on such list. Such list shall be open to the examination of any stockholder for any purpose germane to the meeting for a period of at least 10 days prior to the meeting: (i) on a reasonably accessible electronic network, provided that the information required to gain access to such list is provided with the notice of the meeting, or (ii) during ordinary business hours, at the principal place of business of the corporation. In the event that the corporation determines to make the list available on an electronic network, the corporation may take reasonable steps to ensure that such information is available only to stockholders of the corporation. If the meeting is to be held at a place, then the list shall be produced and kept at the time and place of the meeting during the whole time thereof and may be inspected by any stockholder who is present. If the meeting is to be held solely by means of remote communication, then the list shall also be open to the examination of any stockholder during the whole time of the meeting on a reasonably accessible electronic network, and the information required to access such list shall be provided with the notice of the meeting.

(b) Upon the wilful neglect or refusal of the directors to produce such a list at any meeting for the election of directors held at a place, or to open such a list to examination on a reasonably accessible electronic network during any meeting for the election of directors held solely by means of remote communication, they shall be ineligible for election to any office at such meeting.

(c) The stock ledger shall be the only evidence as to who are the stockholders entitled by this section to examine the list required by this section or to vote in person or by proxy at any meeting of stockholders.

§ 220. Inspection of Books and Records

(a) As used in this section:

(1) "List of stockholders" includes lists of members in a nonstock corporation.

(2) "Stockholder" means a holder of record of stock in a stock corporation, or a person who is the beneficial owner of shares of such stock held either in a voting trust or by a nominee on behalf of such person, and also a member of a nonstock corporation as reflected on the records of the nonstock corporation.

(3) "Subsidiary" means any entity directly or indirectly owned, in whole or in part, by the corporation of which the stockholder is a stockholder and over the affairs of which the corporation directly or indirectly exercises control, and includes, without limitation, corporations, partnerships, limited partnerships, limited liability partnerships, limited liability companies, statutory trusts and/or joint ventures.

(4) "Under oath" includes statements the declarant affirms to be true under penalty of perjury under the laws of the United States or any state.

(b) Any stockholder, in person or by attorney or other agent, shall, upon written demand under oath stating the purpose thereof, have the right during the usual hours for business to inspect for any proper purpose, and to make copies and extracts from:

(1) The corporation's stock ledger, a list of its stockholders, and its other books and records; and

(2) A subsidiary's books and records, to the extent that:

a. The corporation has actual possession and control of such records of such subsidiary; or

b. The corporation could obtain such records through the exercise of control over such subsidiary, provided that as of the date of the making of the demand:

1. The stockholder inspection of such books and records of the subsidiary would not constitute a breach of an agreement between the corporation or the subsidiary and a person or persons not affiliated with the corporation; and

2. The subsidiary would not have the right under the law applicable to it to deny the corporation access to such books and records upon demand by the corporation.

In every instance where the stockholder is other than a record holder of stock in a stock corporation or a member of a nonstock corporation, the demand under oath shall state the person's status as a stockholder, be accompanied by documentary evidence of beneficial ownership of the stock, and state that such documentary evidence is a true and correct copy of what it purports to be. A proper purpose shall mean a purpose reasonably related to such person's interest as a stockholder. In every instance where an attorney or other agent shall be the person who seeks the right to inspection, the demand under oath shall be accompanied by a power of attorney or such other writing which authorizes the attorney or other agent to so act on behalf of the stockholder. The demand under oath shall be directed to the corporation at its registered office in this State or at its principal place of business.

(c) If the corporation, or an officer or agent thereof, refuses to permit an inspection sought by a stockholder or attorney or other agent acting for the stockholder pursuant to subsection (b) of this section or does not reply to the demand within 5 business days after the demand has been made, the stockholder may apply to the Court of Chancery for an order to compel such inspection. The Court of Chancery is hereby vested with exclusive jurisdiction to determine whether or not the person seeking inspection is entitled to the inspection sought. The Court may summarily order the corporation to permit the stockholder to inspect the corporation's stock ledger, an existing list of stockholders, and its other books and records, and to make copies or extracts therefrom; or the Court may order the corporation to furnish to the stockholder a list of its stockholders as of a specific date on condition that the stockholder first pay to the corporation the reasonable cost of obtaining and furnishing such list and on such other conditions as the Court deems appropriate.

Where the stockholder seeks to inspect the corporation's books and records, other than its stock ledger or list of stockholders, such stockholder shall first establish that:

(1) Such stockholder is a stockholder;

(2) Such stockholder has complied with this section respecting the form and manner of making demand for inspection of such documents; and

(3) The inspection such stockholder seeks is for a proper purpose.

Where the stockholder seeks to inspect the corporation's stock ledger or list of stockholders and establishes that such stockholder is a stockholder and has complied with this section respecting the form and manner of making demand for inspection of such documents, the burden of proof shall be upon the corporation to establish that the inspection such stockholder seeks is for an improper purpose. The Court may, in its discretion, prescribe any limitations or conditions with reference to the inspection, or award such other or further relief as the Court may deem just and proper. The Court may order books, documents and records, pertinent extracts therefrom, or duly authenticated copies thereof, to be brought within this State and kept in this State upon such terms and conditions as the order may prescribe.

(d) Any director (including a member of the governing body of a nonstock corporation) shall have the right to examine the corporation's stock ledger, a list of its stockholders and its other books and records for a purpose reasonably related to the director's position as a director. The Court of Chancery is hereby vested with the exclusive jurisdiction to determine whether a director is entitled to the inspection sought. The Court may summarily order the corporation to permit the director to inspect any and all books and records, the stock ledger and the list of stockholder's and to make copies or extracts therefrom. The burden of proof shall be upon the corporation to establish that the inspection such director seeks is for an improper purpose. The Court may, in its discretion, prescribe any limitations or conditions with reference to the inspection, or award such other and further relief as the Court may deem just and proper.

§ 221. Voting, Inspection and Other Rights of Bondholders and Debenture Holders

Every corporation may in its certificate of incorporation confer upon the holders of any bonds, debentures or other obligations issued or to be issued by the corporation the power to vote in respect to the corporate affairs and management of the corporation to the extent and in the manner provided in the certificate of incorporation and may confer upon such holders of bonds, debentures or other obligations the same right of inspection of its books, accounts and other records, and also any other rights, which the stockholders of the corporation have or may have by reason of this chapter or of its certificate of incorporation. If the certificate of incorporation so provides, such holders of bonds, debentures or other obligations shall be deemed to be stockholders, and their bonds, debentures or other obligations shall be deemed to be shares of stock, for the purpose of any provision of this chapter which requires the vote of stockholders as a prerequisite to any corporate action and the certificate of incorporation may divest the holders of capital stock, in whole or in part, of their right to vote on any corporate matter whatsoever, except as set forth in paragraph (2) of subsection (b) of § 242 of this title.

§ 222. Notice of Meetings and Adjourned Meetings

(a) Whenever stockholders are required or permitted to take any action at a meeting, a written notice of the meeting shall be given which shall state the place, if any, date and hour of the meeting, the means of remote communications, if any, by which stockholders and proxy holders may be deemed to be present in person and vote at such meeting, and, in the case of a special meeting, the purpose or purposes for which the meeting is called.

(b) Unless otherwise provided in this chapter, the written notice of any meeting shall be given not less than 10 nor more than 60 days before the date of the meeting to each stockholder entitled to vote at such meeting. If mailed, notice is given when deposited in the United States mail, postage prepaid, directed to the stockholder at such stockholder's address as it appears on the records of the corporation. An affidavit of the secretary or an assistant secretary or of the transfer agent or other agent of the corporation that the notice has been given shall, in the absence of fraud, be prima facie evidence of the facts stated therein.

(c) When a meeting is adjourned to another time or place, unless the bylaws otherwise require, notice need not be given of the adjourned meeting if the time, place, if any, thereof, and the means of remote communications, if any, by which stockholders and proxy holders may be deemed to be present in person and vote at such adjourned meeting are announced at the meeting at which the adjournment is taken. At the adjourned meeting the corporation may transact any business which might have been transacted at the original meeting. If the adjournment is for more than 30 days, or if after the adjournment a new record date is fixed for the adjourned meeting, a notice of the adjourned meeting shall be given to each stockholder of record entitled to vote at the meeting.

§ 223. Vacancies and Newly Created Directorships

(a) Unless otherwise provided in the certificate of incorporation or bylaws:

(1) Vacancies and newly created directorships resulting from any increase in the authorized number of directors elected by all of

the stockholders having the right to vote as a single class may be filled by a majority of the directors then in office, although less than a quorum, or by a sole remaining director;

(2) Whenever the holders of any class or classes of stock or series thereof are entitled to elect 1 or more directors by the certificate of incorporation, vacancies and newly created directorships of such class or classes or series may be filled by a majority of the directors elected by such class or classes or series thereof then in office, or by a sole remaining director so elected.

If at any time, by reason of death or resignation or other cause, a corporation should have no directors in office, then any officer or any stockholder or an executor, administrator, trustee or guardian of a stockholder, or other fiduciary entrusted with like responsibility for the person or estate of a stockholder, may call a special meeting of stockholders in accordance with the certificate of incorporation or the bylaws, or may apply to the Court of Chancery for a decree summarily ordering an election as provided in § 211 of this title.

(b) In the case of a corporation the directors of which are divided into classes, any directors chosen under subsection (a) of this section shall hold office until the next election of the class for which such directors shall have been chosen, and until their successors shall be elected and qualified.

(c) If, at the time of filling any vacancy or any newly created directorship, the directors then in office shall constitute less than a majority of the whole board (as constituted immediately prior to any such increase), the Court of Chancery may, upon application of any stockholder or stockholders holding at least 10 percent of the voting stock at the time outstanding having the right to vote for such directors, summarily order an election to be held to fill any such vacancies or newly created directorships, or to replace the directors chosen by the directors then in office as aforesaid, which election shall be governed by § 211 of this title as far as applicable.

(d) Unless otherwise provided in the certificate of incorporation or bylaws, when 1 or more directors shall resign from the board, effective at a future date, a majority of the directors then in office, including those who have so resigned, shall have power to fill such vacancy or vacancies, the vote thereon to take effect when such resignation or resignations shall become effective, and each director so chosen shall hold office as provided in this section in the filling of other vacancies.

§ 224. Form of Records

Any records maintained by a corporation in the regular course of its business, including its stock ledger, books of account, and minute books, may be kept on, or by means of, or be in the form of, any information storage device, or method provided that the records so kept can be converted into clearly legible paper form within a reasonable time. Any corporation shall so convert any records so kept upon the request of any person entitled to inspect such records pursuant to any provision of this chapter. When records are kept in such manner, a clearly legible paper form produced from or by means of the information storage device or method shall be admissible in evidence, and accepted for all other purposes, to the same extent as an original paper record of the same information would have been, provided the paper form accurately portrays the record.

§ 225. Contested Election of Directors; Proceedings to Determine Validity

(a) Upon application of any stockholder or director, or any officer whose title to office is contested, or any member of a corporation without capital stock, the Court of Chancery may hear and determine the validity of any election, appointment, removal or resignation of any director, member of the governing body, or officer of any corporation, and the right of any person to hold or continue to hold such office, and, in case any such office is claimed by more than 1 person, may determine the person entitled thereto; and to that end make such order or decree in any such case as may be just and proper, with power to enforce the production of any books, papers and records of the corporation relating to the issue. In case it should be determined that no valid election has been held, the Court of Chancery may order an election to be held in accordance with § 211 or 215 of this title. In any such application, service of copies of the application upon the registered agent of the corporation shall be deemed to be service upon the corporation and upon the person whose title to office is contested and upon the person, if any, claiming such office; and the registered agent shall forward immediately a copy of the application to the corporation and to the person whose title to office is contested and to the person, if any, claiming such office, in a postpaid, sealed, registered letter addressed to such corporation and such person at their post-office addresses last known to the registered agent or furnished to the registered agent by the applicant stockholder. The Court may make such order respecting further or other notice of such application as it deems proper under the circumstances.

(b) Upon application of any stockholder or any member of a corporation without capital stock, the Court of Chancery may hear and determine the result of any vote of stockholders or members, as the case may be, upon matters other than the election of directors, officers or members of the governing body. Service of the application upon the registered agent of the corporation shall be deemed to be service upon the corporation, and no other party need be joined in order for the Court to adjudicate the result of the vote. The Court may make such order respecting notice of the application as it deems proper under the circumstances.

§ 226. Appointment of Custodian or Receiver of Corporation on Deadlock or for Other Cause

(a) The Court of Chancery, upon application of any stockholder, may appoint 1 or more persons to be custodians, and, if the corporation is insolvent, to be receivers, of and for any corporation when:

(1) At any meeting held for the election of directors the stockholders are so divided that they have failed to elect successors to directors whose terms have expired or would have expired upon qualification of their successors; or

(2) The business of the corporation is suffering or is threatened with irreparable injury because the directors are so divided respecting the management of the affairs of the corporation that the required vote for action by the board of directors cannot be obtained and the stockholders are unable to terminate this division; or

(3) The corporation has abandoned its business and has failed within a reasonable time to take steps to dissolve, liquidate or distribute its assets.

(b) A custodian appointed under this section shall have all the powers and title of a receiver appointed under § 291 of this title, but the authority of the custodian is to continue the business of the corporation and not to liquidate its affairs and distribute its assets, except when the Court shall otherwise order and except in cases arising under paragraph (3) of subsection (a) of this section or paragraph (2) of subsection (a) of § 352 of this title.

§ 227. Powers of Court in Elections of Directors

(a) The Court of Chancery, in any proceeding instituted under § 211, 215 or 225 of this title may determine the right and power of persons claiming to own stock, or in the case of a corporation without capital stock, of the persons claiming to be members, to vote at any meeting of the stockholders or members.

(b) The Court of Chancery may appoint a Master to hold any election provided for in § 211, 215 or 225 of this title under such orders and powers as it deems proper; and it may punish any officer or director for contempt in case of disobedience of any order made by the Court; and, in case of disobedience by a corporation of any order made by the Court, may enter a decree against such corporation for a penalty of not more than $5,000.

§ 228. Consent of Stockholders or Members in Lieu of Meeting

(a) Unless otherwise provided in the certificate of incorporation, any action required by this chapter to be taken at any annual or special meeting of stockholders of a corporation, or any action which may be taken at any annual or special meeting of such stockholders, may be taken without a meeting, without prior notice and without a vote, if a consent or consents in writing, setting forth the action so taken, shall be signed by the holders of outstanding stock having not less than the minimum number of votes that would be necessary to authorize or take such action at a meeting at which all shares entitled to vote thereon were present and voted and shall be delivered to the corporation by delivery to its registered office in this State, its principal place of business or an officer or agent of the corporation having custody of the book in which proceedings of meetings of stockholders are recorded. Delivery made to a corporation's registered office shall be by hand or by certified or registered mail, return receipt requested.

(b) Unless otherwise provided in the certificate of incorporation, any action required by this chapter to be taken at a meeting of the members of a nonstock corporation, or any action which may be taken at any meeting of the members of a nonstock corporation, may be taken without a meeting, without prior notice and without a vote, if a consent or consents in writing, setting forth the action so taken, shall be signed by members having not less than the minimum number of votes that would be necessary to authorize or take such action at a meeting at which all members having a right to vote thereon were present and voted and shall be delivered to the corporation by delivery to its registered office in this State, its principal place of business or an officer or agent of the corporation having custody of the book in which proceedings of meetings of members are recorded. Delivery made to a corporation's registered office shall be by hand or by certified or registered mail, return receipt requested.

(c) Every written consent shall bear the date of signature of each stockholder or member who signs the consent, and no written consent shall be effective to take the corporate action referred to therein unless, within 60 days of the earliest dated consent delivered in the manner required by this section to the corporation, written consents signed by a sufficient number of holders or members to take action are delivered to the corporation by delivery to its registered office in this State, its principal place of business or an officer or agent of the corporation having custody of the book in which proceedings of meetings of stockholders or members are recorded. Delivery made to a corporation's registered office shall be by hand or by certified or registered mail, return receipt requested.

(d)(1) A telegram, cablegram or other electronic transmission consenting to an action to be taken and transmitted by a stockholder, member or proxyholder, or by a person or persons authorized to act for a stockholder, member or proxyholder, shall be deemed to be written, signed and dated for the purposes of this section, provided that any such telegram, cablegram or other electronic transmission sets forth or is delivered with information from which the corporation can determine

(A) that the telegram, cablegram or other electronic transmission was transmitted by the stockholder, member or proxyholder or by a person or persons authorized to act for the stockholder, member or proxyholder and (B) the date on which such stockholder, member or proxyholder or authorized person or persons transmitted such telegram, cablegram or electronic transmission. The date on which such telegram, cablegram or electronic transmission is transmitted shall be deemed to be the date on which such consent was signed. No consent given by telegram, cablegram or other electronic transmission shall be deemed to have been delivered until such consent is reproduced in paper form and until such paper form shall be delivered to the corporation by delivery to its registered office in this State, its principal place of business or an officer or agent of the corporation having custody of the book in which proceedings of meetings of stockholders or members are recorded. Delivery made to a corporation's registered office shall be made by hand or by certified or registered mail, return receipt requested. Notwithstanding the foregoing limitations on delivery, consents given by telegram, cablegram or other electronic transmission, may be otherwise delivered to the principal place of business of the corporation or to an officer or agent of the corporation having custody of the book in which proceedings of meetings of stockholders or members are recorded if, to the extent and in the manner provided by resolution of the board of directors or governing body of the corporation.

(2) Any copy, facsimile or other reliable reproduction of a consent in writing may be substituted or used in lieu of the original writing for any and all purposes for which the original writing could be used, provided that such copy, facsimile or other reproduction shall be a complete reproduction of the entire original writing.

(e) Prompt notice of the taking of the corporate action without a meeting by less than unanimous written consent shall be given to those stockholders or members who have not consented in writing and who, if the action had been taken at a meeting, would have been entitled to notice of the meeting if the record date for such meeting had been the date that written consents signed by a sufficient number of holders or members to take the action were delivered to the corporation as provided in subsection (c) of this section. In the event that the action which is consented to is such as would have required the filing of a certificate under any other section of this title, if such action had been voted on by stockholders or by members at a meeting thereof, the certificate filed under such other section shall state, in lieu of any statement required by such section concerning any vote of stockholders or members, that written consent has been given in accordance with this section.

§ 229. Waiver of Notice

Whenever notice is required to be given under any provision of this chapter or the certificate of incorporation or bylaws, a written waiver, signed by the person entitled to notice, or a waiver by electronic transmission by the person entitled to notice, whether before or after the time stated therein, shall be deemed equivalent to notice. Attendance of a person at a meeting shall constitute a waiver of notice of such meeting, except when the person attends a meeting for the express purpose of objecting at the beginning of the meeting, to the transaction of any business because the meeting is not lawfully called or convened. Neither the business to be transacted at, nor the purpose of, any regular or special meeting of the stockholders, directors or members of a committee of directors need be specified in any written waiver of notice or any waiver by electronic transmission unless so required by the certificate of incorporation or the bylaws.

§ 230. Exception to Requirements of Notice

(a) Whenever notice is required to be given, under any provision of this chapter or of the certificate of incorporation or bylaws of any corporation, to any person with whom communication is unlawful, the giving of such notice to such person shall not be required and there shall be no duty to apply to any governmental authority or agency for a license or permit to give such notice to such person. Any action or meeting which shall be taken or held without notice to any such person with whom communication is unlawful shall have the same force and effect as if such notice had been duly given. In the event that the action taken by the corporation is such as to require the filing of a certificate under any of the other sections of this title, the certificate shall state, if such is the fact and if notice is required, that notice was given to all persons entitled to receive notice except such persons with whom communication is unlawful.

(b) Whenever notice is required to be given, under any provision of this title or the certificate of incorporation or bylaws of any corporation, to any stockholder or, if the corporation is a nonstock corporation, to any member, to whom (1) notice of 2 consecutive annual meetings, and all notices of meetings or of the taking of action by written consent without a meeting to such person during the period between such 2 consecutive annual meetings, or (2) all, and at least 2, payments (if sent by first-class mail) of dividends or interest on securities during a 12–month period, have been mailed addressed to such person at such person's address as shown on the records of the corporation and have been returned undeliverable, the giving of such notice to such person shall not be required. Any action or meeting which shall be taken or held without notice to such person shall have the same force and effect as if such notice had been duly given. If any such person shall deliver to the corporation a written notice setting forth such person's then current address, the requirement that notice be given to such person shall be reinstated. In the event that the action taken by the corporation is such as to require the filing of a certificate under any of the other sections of this title, the certificate need not state that notice was not given to persons to whom notice was not required to be given pursuant to this subsection.

(c) The exception in paragraph (b)(1) of this section to the requirement that notice be given shall not be applicable to any notice returned as undeliverable if the notice was given by electronic transmission.

§ 231. Voting Procedures and Inspectors of Elections

(a) The corporation shall, in advance of any meeting of stockholders, appoint 1 or more inspectors to act at the meeting and make a written report thereof. The corporation may designate 1 or more persons as alternate inspectors to replace any inspector who fails to act. If no inspector or alternate is able to act at a meeting of stockholders, the person presiding at the meeting shall appoint 1 or more inspectors to act at the meeting. Each inspector, before entering upon the discharge of the duties of inspector, shall take and sign an oath faithfully to execute the duties of inspector with strict impartiality and according to the best of such inspector's ability.

(b) The inspectors shall:

(1) Ascertain the number of shares outstanding and the voting power of each;

(2) Determine the shares represented at a meeting and the validity of proxies and ballots;

(3) Count all votes and ballots;

(4) Determine and retain for a reasonable period a record of the disposition of any challenges made to any determination by the inspectors; and

(5) Certify their determination of the number of shares represented at the meeting, and their count of all votes and ballots.

The inspectors may appoint or retain other persons or entities to assist the inspectors in the performance of the duties of the inspectors.

(c) The date and time of the opening and the closing of the polls for each matter upon which the stockholders will vote at a meeting shall be announced at the meeting. No ballot, proxies or votes, nor any revocations thereof or changes thereto, shall be accepted by the inspectors after the closing of the polls unless the Court of Chancery upon application by a stockholder shall determine otherwise.

(d) In determining the validity and counting of proxies and ballots, the inspectors shall be limited to an examination of the proxies, any envelopes submitted with those proxies, any information provided in accordance with § 211(e) or § 212(c)(2) of this title, or any information provided pursuant to § 211(a)(2)(B)(i) or (iii) of this title, ballots and the regular books and records of the corporation, except that the inspectors may consider other reliable information for the limited purpose of reconciling proxies and ballots submitted by or on behalf of banks, brokers, their nominees or similar persons which represent more votes than the holder of a proxy is authorized by the record owner to cast or more votes than the stockholder holds of record. If the inspectors consider other reliable information for the limited purpose permitted herein, the inspectors at the time they make their certification pursuant to subsection (b)(5) of this section shall specify the precise information considered by them including the person or persons from whom they obtained the information, when the information was obtained, the means by which the information was obtained and the basis for the inspectors' belief that such information is accurate and reliable.

(e) Unless otherwise provided in the certificate of incorporation or bylaws, this section shall not apply to a corporation that does not have a class of voting stock that is:

(1) Listed on a national securities exchange;

(2) Authorized for quotation on an interdealer quotation system of a registered national securities association; or

(3) Held of record by more than 2,000 stockholders.

§ 232. Notice by Electronic Transmission

(a) Without limiting the manner by which notice otherwise may be given effectively to stockholders, any notice to stockholders given by the corporation under any provision of this chapter, the certificate of incorporation, or the bylaws shall be effective if given by a form of electronic transmission consented to by the stockholder to whom the notice is given. Any such consent shall be revocable by the stockholder by written notice to the corporation. Any such consent shall be deemed revoked if (1) the corporation is unable to deliver by electronic transmission 2 consecutive notices given by the corporation in accordance with such consent and (2) such inability becomes known to the secretary or an assistant secretary of the corporation or to the transfer agent, or other person responsible for the giving of notice; provided, however, the inadvertent failure to treat such inability as a revocation shall not invalidate any meeting or other action.

(b) Notice given pursuant to subsection (a) of this section shall be deemed given: (1) if by facsimile telecommunication, when directed to a number at which the stockholder has consented to receive notice; (2) if by electronic mail, when directed to an electronic mail address at which the stockholder has consented to receive notice; (3) if by a posting on an electronic network together with separate notice to the stockholder of such specific posting, upon the later of (A) such posting and (B) the giving of such separate notice; and (4) if by any other form of electronic transmission, when directed to the stockholder. An affidavit of the secretary or an assistant secretary or of the transfer agent or other agent of the corporation that the notice has been given by a form of electronic transmission shall, in the absence of fraud, be prima facie evidence of the facts stated therein.

(c) For purposes of this chapter, "electronic transmission" means any form of communication, not directly involving the physical transmission of paper, that creates a record that may be retained, retrieved and reviewed by a recipient thereof, and that may be directly reproduced in paper form by such a recipient through an automated process.

(d) This section shall apply to a corporation organized under this chapter that is not authorized to issue capital stock, and when so applied, all references to stockholders shall be deemed to refer to members of such a corporation.

(e) This section shall not apply to § 164, 296, 311, 312, or 324 of this title.

§ 233. Notice to Stockholders Sharing an Address

(a) Without limiting the manner by which notice otherwise may be given effectively to stockholders, any notice to stockholders given by the corporation under any provision of this chapter, the certificate of incorporation, or the bylaws shall be effective if given by a single written notice to stockholders who share an address if consented to by the stockholders at that address to whom such notice is given. Any such consent shall be revocable by the stockholder by written notice to the corporation.

(b) Any stockholder who fails to object in writing to the corporation, within 60 days of having been given written notice by the corporation of its intention to send the single notice permitted under subsection (a) of this section, shall be deemed to have consented to receiving such single written notice.

(c) This section shall apply to a corporation organized under this chapter that is not authorized to issue capital stock, and when so applied, all references to stockholders shall be deemed to refer to members of such a corporation.

(d) This section shall not apply to § 164, 296, 311, 312 or 324 of this chapter.

SUBCHAPTER VIII. AMENDMENT OF CERTIFICATE OF INCORPORATION; CHANGES IN CAPITAL AND CAPITAL STOCK

§ 241. Amendment of Certificate of Incorporation Before Receipt of Payment for Stock

(a) Before a corporation has received any payment for any of its stock, it may amend its certificate of incorporation at any time or times, in any and as many respects as may be desired, so long as its certificate of incorporation as amended would contain only such provisions as it would be lawful and proper to insert in an original certificate of incorporation filed at the time of filing the amendment.

(b) The amendment of a certificate of incorporation authorized by this section shall be adopted by a majority of the incorporators, if directors were not named in the original certificate of incorporation or have not yet been elected, or, if directors were named in the original certificate of incorporation or have been elected and have qualified, by a majority of the directors. A certificate setting forth the amendment and certifying that the corporation has not received any payment for any of its stock and that the amendment has been duly adopted in accordance with this section shall be executed, acknowledged and filed in accordance with § 103 of this title. Upon such filing, the corporation's certificate of incorporation shall be deemed to be amended accordingly as of the date on which the original certificate of incorporation became effective, except as to those persons who are substantially and adversely affected by the amendment and as to those persons the amendment shall be effective from the filing date.

§ 242. Amendment of Certificate of Incorporation After Receipt of Payment for Stock; Nonstock Corporations

(a) After a corporation has received payment for any of its capital stock, it may amend its certificate of incorporation, from time to time, in any and as many respects as may be desired, so long as its certificate of incorporation as amended would contain only such provisions as it would be lawful and proper to insert in an original certificate of incorporation filed at the time of the filing of the amendment; and, if a change in stock or the rights of stockholders, or an exchange, reclassification, subdivision, combination or cancellation of stock or rights of stockholders is to be made, such provisions as may be necessary to effect such change, exchange, reclassification, subdivision, combination or cancellation. In particular, and without limitation upon such general power of amendment, a corporation may amend its certificate of incorporation, from time to time, so as:

(1) To change its corporate name; or

(2) To change, substitute, enlarge or diminish the nature of its business or its corporate powers and purposes; or

(3) To increase or decrease its authorized capital stock or to reclassify the same, by changing the number, par value, designations, preferences, or relative, participating, optional, or other special rights of the shares, or the qualifications, limitations or restrictions of such rights, or by changing shares with par value into shares without par value, or shares without par value into shares with par value either with or without increasing or decreasing the number of shares, or by subdividing or combining the outstanding shares of any class or series of a class of shares into a greater or lesser number of outstanding shares; or

(4) To cancel or otherwise affect the right of the holders of the shares of any class to receive dividends which have accrued but have not been declared; or

(5) To create new classes of stock having rights and preferences either prior and superior or subordinate and inferior to the stock of any class then authorized, whether issued or unissued; or

(6) To change the period of its duration.

Any or all such changes or alterations may be effected by 1 certificate of amendment.

(b) Every amendment authorized by subsection (a) of this section shall be made and effected in the following manner:

(1) If the corporation has capital stock, its board of directors shall adopt a resolution setting forth the amendment proposed, declaring its advisability, and either calling a special meeting of the stockholders entitled to vote in respect thereof for the consideration of such amendment or directing that the amendment proposed be considered at the next annual meeting of the stockholders. Such special or annual meeting shall be called and held upon notice in accordance with § 222 of this title. The notice shall set forth such amendment in full or a brief summary of the changes to be effected thereby, as the directors shall deem advisable. At the meeting a vote of the stockholders entitled to vote thereon shall be taken for and against the proposed amendment. If a majority of the outstanding stock entitled to vote thereon, and a majority of the outstanding stock of each class entitled to vote thereon as a class has been voted in favor of the amendment, a certificate setting forth the amendment and certifying that such amendment has been duly adopted in accordance with this section shall be executed, acknowledged and filed and shall become effective in accordance with § 103 of this title.

(2) The holders of the outstanding shares of a class shall be entitled to vote as a class upon a proposed amendment, whether or not entitled to vote thereon by the certificate of incorporation, if the amendment would increase or decrease the aggregate number of authorized shares of such class, increase or decrease the par value of the shares of such class, or alter or change the powers, preferences, or special rights of the shares of such class so as to affect them adversely. If any proposed amendment would alter or change the powers, preferences, or special rights of 1 or more series of any class so as to affect them adversely, but shall not so affect the entire class, then only the shares of the series so affected by the amendment shall be considered a separate class for the purposes of this paragraph. The number of authorized shares of any such class or classes of stock may be increased or decreased (but not below the number of shares thereof then outstanding) by the affirmative vote of the holders of a majority of the stock of the corporation entitled to vote

irrespective of this subsection, if so provided in the original certificate of incorporation, in any amendment thereto which created such class or classes of stock or which was adopted prior to the issuance of any shares of such class or classes of stock, or in any amendment thereto which was authorized by a resolution or resolutions adopted by the affirmative vote of the holders of a majority of such class or classes of stock.

(3) If the corporation has no capital stock, then the governing body thereof shall adopt a resolution setting forth the amendment proposed and declaring its advisability. If a majority of all the members of the governing body shall vote in favor of such amendment, a certificate thereof shall be executed, acknowledged and filed and shall become effective in accordance with § 103 of this title. The certificate of incorporation of any such corporation without capital stock may contain a provision requiring any amendment thereto to be approved by a specified number or percentage of the members or of any specified class of members of such corporation in which event such proposed amendment shall be submitted to the members or to any specified class of members of such corporation without capital stock in the same manner, so far as applicable, as is provided in this section for an amendment to the certificate of incorporation of a stock corporation; and in the event of the adoption thereof by such members, a certificate evidencing such amendment shall be executed, acknowledged and filed and shall become effective in accordance with § 103 of this title.

(4) Whenever the certificate of incorporation shall require for action by the board of directors, by the holders of any class or series of shares or by the holders of any other securities having voting power the vote of a greater number or proportion than is required by any section of this title, the provision of the certificate of incorporation requiring such greater vote shall not be altered, amended or repealed except by such greater vote.

(c) The resolution authorizing a proposed amendment to the certificate of incorporation may provide that at any time prior to the effectiveness of the filing of the amendment with the Secretary of State, notwithstanding authorization of the proposed amendment by the stockholders of the corporation or by the members of a nonstock corporation, the board of directors or governing body may abandon such proposed amendment without further action by the stockholders or members.

§ 243. Retirement of Stock

(a) A corporation, by resolution of its board of directors, may retire any shares of its capital stock that are issued but are not outstanding.

(b) Whenever any shares of the capital stock of a corporation are retired, they shall resume the status of authorized and unissued shares of the class or series to which they belong unless the certificate of incorporation otherwise provides. If the certificate of incorporation prohibits the reissuance of such shares, or prohibits the reissuance of such shares as a part of a specific series only, a certificate stating that reissuance of the shares (as part of the class or series) is prohibited identifying the shares and reciting their retirement shall be executed, acknowledged and filed and shall become effective in accordance with § 103 of this title. When such certificate becomes effective, it shall have the effect of amending the certificate of incorporation so as to reduce accordingly the number of authorized shares of the class or series to which such shares belong or, if such retired shares constitute all of the authorized shares of the class or series to which they belong, of eliminating from the certificate of incorporation all reference to such class or series of stock.

(c) If the capital of the corporation will be reduced by or in connection with the retirement of shares, the reduction of capital shall be effected pursuant to § 244 of this title.

§ 244. Reduction of Capital

(a) A corporation, by resolution of its board of directors, may reduce its capital in any of the following ways:

(1) By reducing or eliminating the capital represented by shares of capital stock which have been retired;

(2) By applying to an otherwise authorized purchase or redemption of outstanding shares of its capital stock some or all of the capital represented by the shares being purchased or redeemed, or any capital that has not been allocated to any particular class of its capital stock;

(3) By applying to an otherwise authorized conversion or exchange of outstanding shares of its capital stock some or all of the capital represented by the shares being converted or exchanged, or some or all of any capital that has not been allocated to any particular class of its capital stock, or both, to the extent that such capital in the aggregate exceeds the total aggregate par value or the stated capital of any previously unissued shares issuable upon such conversion or exchange; or

(4) By transferring to surplus (i) some or all of the capital not represented by any particular class of its capital stock; (ii) some or all of the capital represented by issued shares of its par value capital stock, which capital is in excess of the aggregate par value of such shares; or (iii) some of the capital represented by issued shares of its capital stock without par value.

(b) Notwithstanding the other provisions of this section, no reduction of capital shall be made or effected unless the assets of the corporation remaining after such reduction shall be sufficient to pay any debts of the corporation for which payment has not been otherwise provided. No reduction of capital shall release any liability of any stockholder whose shares have not been fully paid.

(c) [Repealed.]

§ 245. Restated Certificate of Incorporation

(a) A corporation may, whenever desired, integrate into a single instrument all of the provisions of its certificate of incorporation which are then in effect and operative as a result of there having theretofore been filed with the Secretary of State 1 or more certificates or other instruments pursuant to any of the sections referred to in § 104 of this title, and it may at the same time also further amend its certificate of incorporation by adopting a restated certificate of incorporation.

(b) If the restated certificate of incorporation merely restates and integrates but does not further amend the certificate of incorporation, as theretofore amended or supplemented by any instrument that was filed pursuant to any of the sections mentioned in § 104 of this title, it may be adopted by the board of directors without a vote of the stockholders, or it may be proposed by the directors and submitted by them to the stockholders for adoption, in which case the procedure and vote required by § 242 of this title for amendment of the certificate of incorporation shall be applicable. If the restated certificate of incorporation restates and integrates and also further amends in any respect the certificate of incorporation, as theretofore amended or supplemented, it shall be proposed by the directors and adopted by the stockholders in the manner and by the vote prescribed by § 242 of this title or, if the corporation has not received any payment for any of its stock, in the manner and by the vote prescribed by § 241 of this title.

(c) A restated certificate of incorporation shall be specifically designated as such in its heading. It shall state, either in its heading or in an introductory paragraph, the corporation's present name, and, if it has been changed, the name under which it was originally incorporated, and the date of filing of its original certificate of incorporation with the Secretary of State. A restated certificate shall also state that it was duly adopted in accordance with this section. If it was adopted by the board of directors without a vote of the stockholders (unless it was adopted pursuant to § 241 of this title), it shall state that it only restates and integrates and does not further amend the provisions of the corporation's certificate of incorporation as theretofore amended or supplemented, and that there is no discrepancy between those provisions and the provisions of the restated certificate. A restated certificate of incorporation may omit (a) such provisions of the original certificate of incorporation which named the incorporator or incorporators, the initial board of directors and the original subscribers for shares, and (b) such provisions contained in any amendment to the certificate of incorporation as were necessary to effect a change, exchange, reclassification, subdivision, combination or cancellation of stock, if such change, exchange, reclassification, subdivision, combination or cancellation has become effective. Any such omissions shall not be deemed a further amendment.

(d) A restated certificate of incorporation shall be executed, acknowledged and filed in accordance with § 103 of this title. Upon its filing with the Secretary of State, the original certificate of incorporation, as theretofore amended or supplemented, shall be superseded; thenceforth, the restated certificate of incorporation, including any further amendments or changes made thereby, shall be the certificate of incorporation of the corporation, but the original date of incorporation shall remain unchanged.

(e) Any amendment or change effected in connection with the restatement and integration of the certificate of incorporation shall be subject to any other provision of this chapter, not inconsistent with this section, which would apply if a separate certificate of amendment were filed to effect such amendment or change.

§ 246. [Reserved]

SUBCHAPTER IX. MERGER, CONSOLIDATION OR CONVERSION

§ 251. Merger or Consolidation of Domestic Corporations and Limited Liability Company

(a) Any 2 or more corporations existing under the laws of this State may merge into a single corporation, which may be any 1 of the constituent corporations or may consolidate into a new corporation formed by the consolidation, pursuant to an agreement of merger or consolidation, as the case may be, complying and approved in accordance with this section.

(b) The board of directors of each corporation which desires to merge or consolidate shall adopt a resolution approving an agreement of merger or consolidation and declaring its advisability. The agreement shall state: (1) The terms and conditions of the merger or consolidation; (2) the mode of carrying the same into effect; (3) in the case of a merger, such amendments or changes in the certificate of incorporation of the surviving corporation as are desired to be effected by the merger, or, if no such amendments or changes are desired, a statement that the certificate of incorporation of the surviving corporation shall be its certificate of incorporation; (4) in the case of a consolidation, that the certificate of incorporation of the resulting corporation shall be as is set forth in an attachment to the agreement; (5) the manner, if any, of converting the shares of each of the constituent corporations into shares or other securities of the corporation surviving or resulting from the merger or consolidation, or of cancelling some or all of such shares, and, if any shares of any of the constituent corporations are not to remain outstanding, to be converted solely into shares or other securities of the surviving or resulting corporation or to be cancelled, the cash, property, rights or securities of any other corporation or entity which the holders of such shares are to receive in exchange for, or upon conversion of such shares and the surrender of any certificates evidencing them, which cash, property, rights or securities of any other corporation or entity may be in addition to or in lieu of shares or other securities of the surviving or resulting corporation; and (6) such other details or provisions as are deemed desirable, including, without limiting the generality of the foregoing, a provision for the payment of cash in lieu of the issuance or recognition of fractional shares, interests or rights, or for any other arrangement with respect thereto, consistent with § 155 of this title. The agreement so adopted shall be executed and acknowledged in accordance with § 103 of this title. Any of the terms of the agreement of merger or consolidation may be made dependent upon facts ascertainable outside of such agreement, provided that the manner in which such facts shall operate upon the terms of the agreement is clearly and expressly set forth in the agreement of merger or consolidation. The term "facts," as used in the preceding sentence, includes, but is not limited to, the occurrence of any event, including a determination or action by any person or body, including the corporation.

(c) The agreement required by subsection (b) of this section shall be submitted to the stockholders of each constituent corporation at an annual or special meeting for the purpose of acting on the agreement. Due notice of the time, place and purpose of the meeting shall be mailed to each holder of stock, whether voting or nonvoting, of the corporation at the stockholder's address as it appears on the records of the corporation, at least 20 days prior to the date of the meeting. The notice shall contain a copy of the agreement or a brief summary thereof, as the directors shall deem advisable. At the meeting, the agreement shall be considered and a vote taken for its adoption or rejection. If a majority of the outstanding stock of the corporation entitled to vote thereon shall be voted for the adoption of the agreement, that fact shall be certified on the agreement by the secretary or assistant secretary of the corporation. If the agreement shall be so adopted and certified by each constituent corporation, it shall then be filed and shall become effective, in accordance with § 103 of this title. In lieu of filing the agreement of merger or consolidation required by this section, the surviving or resulting corporation may file a certificate of merger or consolidation, executed in accordance with § 103 of this title, which states:

(1) The name and state of incorporation of each of the constituent corporations;

(2) That an agreement of merger or consolidation has been approved, adopted, certified, executed and acknowledged by each of the constituent corporations in accordance with this section;

(3) The name of the surviving or resulting corporation;

(4) In the case of a merger, such amendments or changes in the certificate of incorporation of the surviving corporation as are desired to be effected by the merger, or, if no such amendments or changes are desired, a statement that the certificate of incorporation of the surviving corporation shall be its certificate of incorporation;

(5) In the case of a consolidation, that the certificate of incorporation of the resulting corporation shall be as set forth in an attachment to the certificate;

(6) That the executed agreement of consolidation or merger is on file at an office of the surviving corporation, stating the address thereof; and

(7) That a copy of the agreement of consolidation or merger will be furnished by the surviving corporation, on request and without cost, to any stockholder of any constituent corporation.

(d) Any agreement of merger or consolidation may contain a provision that at any time prior to the time that the agreement (or a certificate in lieu thereof) filed with the Secretary of State becomes effective in accordance with § 103 of this title, the agreement may be terminated by the board of directors of any constituent corporation notwithstanding approval of the agreement by the stockholders of all or any of the constituent corporations; in the event the agreement of merger or consolidation is terminated after the filing of the agreement (or a certificate in lieu thereof) with the Secretary of State but before the agreement (or a certificate in lieu thereof) has become effective, a certificate of termination or merger or consolidation shall be filed in accordance with § 103 of this title. Any agreement of merger or consolidation may contain a provision that the boards of directors of the constituent corporations may amend the agreement at any time prior to the time that the agreement (or a certificate in lieu thereof) filed with the Secretary of State becomes effective in accordance with § 103 of this title, provided that an amendment made subsequent to the adoption of the agreement by the stockholders of any constituent corporation shall not (1) alter or change the amount or kind of shares, securities, cash, property and/or rights to be received in exchange for or on conversion of all or any of the shares of any class or series thereof of such constituent corporation, (2) alter or change any term of the certificate of incorporation of the surviving corporation to be effected by the merger or consolidation, or (3) alter or change any of the terms and conditions of the agreement if such alteration or change would adversely affect the holders of any class or series thereof of such constituent corporation; in the event the agreement of merger or consolidation is amended after the filing thereof with the Secretary of State but before the agreement has become effective, a certificate of amendment of merger or consolidation shall be filed in accordance with § 103 of this title.

(e) In the case of a merger, the certificate of incorporation of the surviving corporation shall automatically be amended to the extent, if any, that changes in the certificate of incorporation are set forth in the agreement of merger.

(f) Notwithstanding the requirements of subsection (c) of this section, unless required by its certificate of incorporation, no vote of stockholders of a constituent corporation surviving a merger shall be necessary to authorize a merger if (1) the agreement of merger does not amend in any respect the certificate of incorporation of such constituent corporation, (2) each share of stock of such constituent corporation outstanding immediately prior to the effective date of the merger is to be an identical outstanding or treasury share of the surviving corporation after the effective date of the merger, and (3) either no shares of common stock of the surviving corporation and no shares, securities or obligations convertible into such stock are to be issued or delivered under the plan of merger, or the authorized unissued shares or the treasury shares of common stock of the surviving corporation to be issued or delivered under the plan of merger plus those initially issuable upon conversion of any other shares, securities or obligations to be issued or delivered under such plan do not exceed 20% of the shares of common stock of such constituent corporation outstanding immediately prior to the effective date of the merger. No vote of stockholders of a constituent corporation shall be necessary to authorize a merger or consolidation if no shares of the stock of such corporation shall have been issued prior to the adoption by the board of directors of the resolution approving the agreement of merger or consolidation. If an agreement of merger is adopted by the constituent corporation surviving the merger, by action of its board of directors and without any vote of its stockholders pursuant to this subsection, the secretary or assistant secretary of that corporation shall certify on the agreement that the agreement has been adopted pursuant to this subsection and, (1) if it has been adopted pursuant to the first sentence of this subsection, that the conditions specified in that sentence have been satisfied, or (2) if it has been adopted pursuant to the second sentence of this subsection, that no shares of stock of such corporation were issued prior to the adoption by the board of directors of the resolution approving the agreement of merger or consolidation. The agreement so adopted and certified shall then be filed and shall become effective, in accordance with § 103 of this title. Such filing shall constitute a representation by the person who executes the agreement that the facts stated in the certificate remain true immediately prior to such filing.

(g) Notwithstanding the requirements of subsection (c) of this section, unless expressly required by its certificate of incorporation, no vote of stockholders of a constituent corporation shall be necessary to authorize a merger with or into a single direct or indirect wholly-owned subsidiary of such constituent corporation if: (1) such constituent corporation and the direct or indirect wholly-owned subsidiary of such constituent corporation are the only constituent entities to the merger; (2) each share or fraction of a share of the capital stock of the constituent corporation outstanding immediately prior to the effective time of the merger is converted in the merger into a share or equal fraction of share of capital stock of a holding company having the same designations, rights, powers and preferences, and the qualifications, limitations and restrictions thereof, as the share of stock of the constituent corporation being converted in the merger; (3) the holding company and the constituent corporation are corporations of this State and the direct or indirect wholly-owned subsidiary that is the other constituent entity to the merger is a corporation or limited liability company of this State; (4) the certificate of incorporation and by-laws of the holding company immediately following the effective time of the merger contain provisions identical to the certificate of incorporation and by-laws of the constituent corporation immediately prior to the effective time of the merger (other than provisions, if any, regarding the incorporator or incorporators, the corporate name, the registered office and agent, the initial board of directors and the initial subscribers for shares and such provisions contained in any amendment to the certificate of incorporation as were necessary to effect a change, exchange, reclassification, subdivision, combination or cancellation of stock, if such change, exchange, reclassification, subdivision, combination, or cancellation has become effective); (5) as a result of the merger the constituent corporation or its successor becomes or remains a direct or indirect wholly-owned subsidiary of the holding company; (6) the directors of the constituent corporation become or remain the directors of the holding company upon the effective time of the merger; (7) the organizational documents of the surviving entity immediately following the effective time of the merger contain provisions identical to the certificate of incorporation of the constituent corporation immediately prior to the effective time of the merger (other than provisions, if any, regarding the incorporator or incorporators, the corporate or entity name, the registered office and agent, the initial board of directors and the initial subscribers for shares, references to members rather than stockholders or shareholders, references to interests, units or the like rather than stock or shares, references to managers, managing members or other members of the governing body rather than directors and such provisions contained in any amendment to the certificate of incorporation as were necessary to effect a change, exchange, reclassification, subdivision, combination or cancellation of stock, if such change, exchange, reclassification, subdivision, combination or cancellation has become effective); provided, however, that (i) if the organizational documents of the surviving entity do not contain the following provisions, they shall be amended in the merger to contain provisions requiring that (A) any act or transaction by or involving the surviving entity, other than the election or removal of directors or managers, managing members or other members of the governing body of the surviving entity, that requires for its adoption under this chapter or its organizational documents the approval of the stockholders or members of the surviving entity shall, by specific reference to this subsection, require, in addition, the approval of the stockholders of the holding company (or any successor by merger), by the same vote as is required by this chapter and/or by the organizational documents of the surviving entity; provided, however, that for purposes of this clause (i)(A), any surviving entity that is not a corporation shall include in such amendment a requirement that the approval of the stockholders of the holding company be obtained for any act or transaction by or involving the surviving entity, other than the election or removal of directors or managers, managing members or other members of the governing body of the surviving entity, which would require the approval of the stockholders of the surviving entity if the surviving entity were a corporation subject to this chapter; (B) any amendment of the organizational documents of a surviving entity that is not a corporation, which amendment would, if adopted by a corporation subject to this chapter, be required to be included in the certificate of incorporation of such corporation, shall, by specific reference to this subsection, require, in addition, the approval of the stockholders of the holding company (or any successor by merger), by the same vote as is required by this chapter and/or by the organizational documents of the surviving entity; and (C) the business and affairs of a surviving entity that is not a corporation shall be managed by or under the direction of a board of directors, board of managers or other governing body consisting of individuals who are subject to the same fiduciary duties applicable to, and who are liable for breach of such duties to the same extent as, directors of a corporation subject to this chapter; and (ii) the organizational documents of the surviving entity may be amended in the merger (A) to reduce the number of classes and shares of capital stock or other equity interests or units that the surviving entity is authorized to issue and (B) to eliminate any provision authorized by subsection (d) of § 141 of this title; and (8) the stockholders of the constituent corporation do not recognize gain or loss for United States federal income tax purposes as determined by the board of directors of the constituent corporation. Neither subdivision (g)(7)(i) of this section nor any provision of a surviving entity's organizational documents required by subdivision (g)(7)(i) shall be deemed or construed to require approval of the stockholders of the holding company to elect or remove directors or managers, managing members or other members of the governing body of the surviving entity. The term "organizational documents", as used in subdivision (g)(7) and in the preceding sentence, shall, when used in reference to a corporation, mean the certificate of incorporation of such corporation, and when used in reference to a limited liability company, mean the limited liability company agreement of such limited liability company.

As used in this subsection only, the term "holding company" means a corporation which, from its incorporation until consummation of a merger governed by this subsection, was at all times a direct or indirect wholly-owned subsidiary of the constituent corporation and whose capital stock is issued in such merger. From and after the effective time of a merger adopted by a constituent corporation by action of its board of directors and without any vote of stockholders pursuant to this subsection: (i) to the extent the restrictions of § 203 of this title applied to the constituent corporation and its stockholders at the effective time of the merger, such restrictions shall apply to the holding company and its stockholders immediately after the effective time of the merger as though it were the constituent corporation, and all shares of stock of the holding company acquired in the merger shall for purposes of § 203 of this title be deemed to have been acquired at the time that the shares of stock of the constituent corporation converted in the merger were acquired, and provided further that any stockholder who immediately prior to the effective time of the merger was not an interested stockholder within the meaning of § 203 of this title shall not solely by reason of the merger become an interested stockholder of the holding company, (ii) if the corporate name of the holding company immediately following the effective time of the merger is the same as the corporate name of the constituent corporation immediately prior to the effective time of the merger, the shares of capital stock of the holding company into which the shares of capital stock of the constituent corporation are converted in the merger shall be represented by the stock certificates that previously represented shares of capital stock of the constituent corporation capital stock of the constituent corporation and (iii) to the extent a stockholder of the constituent corporation immediately prior to the merger had standing to institute or maintain derivative litigation on behalf of the constituent corporation, nothing in this section shall be deemed to limit or extinguish such standing. If an agreement of merger is adopted by a constituent corporation by action of its board of directors and without any vote of stockholders pursuant to this subsection, the secretary or assistant secretary of the constituent corporation shall certify on the agreement that the agreement has been adopted pursuant to this subsection and that the conditions specified in the first sentence of this subsection have been satisfied. The agreement so adopted and certified shall then be filed and become effective, in accordance with § 103 of this title. Such filing shall constitute a representation by the person who executes the agreement that the facts stated in the certificate remain true immediately prior to such filing.

§ 252. Merger or Consolidation of Domestic and Foreign Corporations; Service of Process Upon Surviving or Resulting Corporation

(a) Any 1 or more corporations of this State may merge or consolidate with 1 or more other corporations of any other state or states of the United States, or of the District of Columbia if the laws of the other state or states, or of the District permit a corporation of such jurisdiction to merge or consolidate with a corporation of another jurisdiction. The constituent corporations may merge into a single corporation, which may be any 1 of the constituent corporations, or they may consolidate into a new corporation formed by the consolidation, which may be a corporation of the state of incorporation of any 1 of the constituent corporations, pursuant to an agreement of merger or consolidation, as the case may be, complying and approved in accordance with this section. In addition, any 1 or more corporations existing under the laws of this State may merge or consolidate with 1 or more corporations organized under the laws of any jurisdiction other than 1 of the United States if the laws under which the other corporation or corporations are organized permit a corporation of such jurisdiction to merge or consolidate with a corporation of another jurisdiction.

(b) All the constituent corporations shall enter into an agreement of merger or consolidation. The agreement shall state: (1) The terms and conditions of the merger or consolidation; (2) the mode of carrying the same into effect; (3) the manner, if any, of converting the shares of each of the constituent corporations into shares or other securities of the corporation surviving or resulting from the merger or consolidation, or of cancelling some or all of such shares, and, if any shares of any of the constituent corporations are not to remain outstanding, to be converted solely into shares or other securities of the surviving or resulting corporation or to be cancelled, the cash, property, rights or securities of any other corporation or entity which the holders of such shares are to receive in exchange for, or upon conversion of, such shares and the surrender of any certificates evidencing them, which cash, property, rights or securities of any other corporation or entity may be in addition to or in lieu of the shares or other securities of the surviving or resulting corporation; (4) such other details or provisions as are deemed desirable, including, without limiting the generality of the foregoing, a provision for the payment of cash in lieu of the issuance or recognition of fractional shares of the surviving or resulting corporation or of any other corporation the securities of which are to be received in the merger or consolidation, or for some other arrangement with respect thereto consistent with § 155 of this title; and (5) such other provisions or facts as shall be required to be set forth in certificates of incorporation by the laws of the state which are stated in the agreement to be the laws that shall govern the surviving or resulting corporation and that can be stated in the case of a merger or consolidation. Any of the terms of the agreement of merger or consolidation may be made dependent upon facts ascertainable outside of such agreement, provided that the manner in which such facts shall operate upon the terms of the agreement is clearly and expressly set forth in the agreement of merger or consolidation. The term "facts," as used in the preceding sentence, includes, but is not limited to, the occurrence of any event, including a determination or action by any person or body, including the corporation.

(c) The agreement shall be adopted, approved, certified, executed and acknowledged by each of the constituent corporations in accordance with the laws under which it is formed, and, in the case of a Delaware corporation, in the same manner as is provided in § 251 of this title. The agreement shall be filed and shall become effective for all purposes of the laws of this State when and as provided in § 251 of this title with respect to the merger or consolidation of corporations of this State. In lieu of filing the agreement of merger or consolidation, the surviving or resulting corporation may file a certificate of merger or consolidation, executed in accordance with § 103 of this title, which states:

(1) The name and state or jurisdiction of incorporation of each of the constituent corporations;

(2) That an agreement of merger or consolidation has been approved, adopted, certified, executed and acknowledged by each of the constituent corporations in accordance with this subsection;

(3) The name of the surviving or resulting corporation;

(4) In the case of a merger, such amendments or changes in the certificate of incorporation of the surviving corporation as are desired to be effected by the merger, or, if no such amendments or changes are desired, a statement that the certificate of incorporation of the surviving corporation shall be its certificate of incorporation;

(5) In the case of a consolidation, that the certificate of incorporation of the resulting corporation shall be as is set forth in an attachment to the certificate;

(6) That the executed agreement of consolidation or merger is on file at an office of the surviving corporation and the address thereof;

(7) That a copy of the agreement of consolidation or merger will be furnished by the surviving corporation, on request and without cost, to any stockholder of any constituent corporation;

(8) If the corporation surviving or resulting from the merger or consolidation is to be a corporation of this State, the authorized capital stock of each constituent corporation which is not a corporation of this State; and

(9) The agreement, if any, required by subsection (d) of this section.

(d) If the corporation surviving or resulting from the merger or consolidation is to be governed by the laws of the District of Columbia or any state or jurisdiction other than this State, it shall agree that it may be served with process in this State in any proceeding for enforcement of any obligation of any constituent corporation of this State, as well as for enforcement of any obligation of the surviving or resulting corporation arising from the merger or consolidation, including any suit or other proceeding to enforce the right of any stockholders as determined in appraisal proceedings pursuant to § 262 of this title, and shall irrevocably appoint the Secretary of State as its agent to accept service of process in any such suit or other proceedings and shall specify the address to which a copy of such process shall be mailed by the Secretary of State. In the event of such service upon the Secretary of State in accordance with this subsection, the Secretary of State shall forthwith notify such surviving or resulting corporation thereof by letter, certified mail, return receipt requested, directed to such surviving or resulting corporation at its address so specified, unless such surviving or resulting corporation shall have designated in writing to the Secretary of State a different address for such purpose, in which case it shall be mailed to the last address so designated. Such letter shall enclose a copy of the process and any other papers served on the Secretary of State pursuant to this subsection. It shall be the duty of the plaintiff in the event of such service to serve process and any other papers in duplicate, to notify the Secretary of State that service is being effected pursuant to this subsection and to pay the Secretary of State the sum of $50 for the use of the State, which sum shall be taxed as part of the costs in the proceeding, if the plaintiff shall prevail therein. The Secretary of State shall maintain an alphabetical record of any such service setting forth the name of the plaintiff and the defendant, the title, docket number and nature of the proceeding in which process has been served, the fact that service has been effected pursuant to this subsection, the return date thereof, and the day and hour service was made. The Secretary of State shall not be required to retain such information longer than 5 years from receipt of the service of process.

(e) Subsection (d) and the second sentence of subsection (c) of § 251 of this title shall apply to any merger or consolidation under this section; subsection (e) of § 251 of this title shall apply to a merger under this section in which the surviving corporation is a corporation of this State; subsection (f) of § 251 of this title shall apply to any merger under this section.

§ 253. Merger of Parent Corporation and Subsidiary or Subsidiaries

(a) In any case in which at least 90% of the outstanding shares of each class of the stock of a corporation or corporations (other than a corporation which has in its certificate of incorporation the provision required by § 251(g)(7)(i) of this title), of which class there are outstanding shares that, absent this subsection, would be entitled to vote on such merger, is owned by another corporation and 1 of the corporations is a corporation of this State and the other or others are corporations of this State, or any other state or states, or the District of Columbia and the laws of the other state or states, or the District permit a corporation of such jurisdiction to merge with a corporation of another jurisdiction, the corporation having such stock ownership may either merge the other corporation or corporations into itself and assume all of its or their obligations, or merge itself, or itself and 1 or more of such other corporations, into 1 of the other corporations by executing, acknowledging and filing, in accordance with § 103 of this title, a certificate of such ownership and merger setting forth a copy of the resolution of its board of directors to so merge and the date of the adoption; provided, however, that in case the parent corporation shall not own all the outstanding stock of all the subsidiary corporations, parties to a merger as aforesaid, the resolution of the board of directors of the parent corporation shall state the terms and conditions of the merger, including the securities, cash, property, or rights to be issued, paid, delivered or granted by the surviving corporation upon surrender of each share of the subsidiary corporation or corporations not owned by the parent corporation, or the cancellation of some or all of such shares. Any of the terms of the resolution of the board of directors to so merge may be made dependent upon facts ascertainable outside of such resolution, provided that the manner in which such facts shall operate upon the terms of the resolution is clearly and expressly set forth in the resolution. The term "facts," as used in the preceding sentence, includes, but is not limited to, the occurrence of any event, including a determination or action by any person or body, including the corporation. If the parent corporation be not the surviving corporation, the resolution shall include provision for the pro rata issuance of stock of the surviving corporation to the holders of the stock of the parent corporation on surrender of any certificates therefor, and the certificate of ownership and merger shall state that the proposed merger has been approved by a majority of the outstanding stock of the parent corporation entitled to vote thereon at a meeting duly called and held after 20 days' notice of the purpose of the meeting mailed to each such stockholder at the stockholder's address as it appears on the records of the corporation if the parent corporation is a corporation of this State or state that the proposed merger has been adopted, approved, certified, executed and acknowledged by the parent corporation in accordance with the laws under which it is organized if the parent corporation is not a corporation of this State. If the surviving corporation exists under the laws of the District of Columbia or any state or jurisdiction other than this State, subsection (d) of § 252 of this title shall also apply to a merger under this section.

(b) If the surviving corporation is a Delaware corporation, it may change its corporate name by the inclusion of a provision to that effect in the resolution of merger adopted by the directors of the parent corporation and set forth in the certificate of ownership and merger, and upon the effective date of the merger, the name of the corporation shall be so changed.

(c) Subsection (d) of § 251 of this title shall apply to a merger under this section, and subsection (e) of § 251 of this title shall apply to a merger under this section in which the surviving corporation is the subsidiary corporation and is a corporation of this State. References to "agreement of merger" in subsections (d) and (e) of § 251 of this title shall mean for purposes of this subsection the resolution of merger adopted by the board of directors of the parent corporation. Any merger which effects any changes other than those authorized by this section or made applicable by this subsection shall be accomplished under § 251 or § 252 of this title. Section 262 of this title shall not apply to any merger effected under this section, except as provided in subsection (d) of this section.

(d) In the event all of the stock of a subsidiary Delaware corporation party to a merger effected under this section is not owned by the parent corporation immediately prior to the merger, the stockholders of the subsidiary Delaware corporation party to the merger shall have appraisal rights as set forth in § 262 of this title.

(e) A merger may be effected under this section although 1 or more of the corporations parties to the merger is a corporation organized under the laws of a jurisdiction other than 1 of the United States; provided that the laws of such jurisdiction permit a corporation of such jurisdiction to merge with a corporation of another jurisdiction.

§ 254. Merger or Consolidation of Domestic Corporation and Joint-Stock or Other Association

(a) The term "joint-stock association" as used in this section, includes any association of the kind commonly known as a joint-stock association or joint-stock company and any unincorporated association, trust or enterprise having members or having outstanding shares of stock or other evidences of financial or beneficial interest therein, whether formed by agreement or under statutory authority or otherwise, but does not include a corporation, partnership or limited liability company. The term "stockholder" as used in this section, includes every member of such joint-stock association or holder of a share of stock or other evidence of financial or beneficial interest therein.

(b) Any 1 or more corporations of this State may merge or consolidate with 1 or more joint-stock associations, except a joint-stock association formed under the laws of a state which forbids such merger or consolidation. Such corporation or corporations and such 1 or more joint-stock associations may merge into a single corporation, or joint-stock association, which may be any one of such corporations or joint-stock associations, or they may consolidate into a new corporation or joint-stock association of this State, pursuant to an agreement of merger or consolidation, as the case may be, complying and approved in accordance with this section. The surviving or resulting entity may be organized for profit or not organized for profit, and if the surviving or resulting entity is a corporation, it may be a stock corporation or a nonstock corporation.

(c) Each such corporation and joint-stock association shall enter into a written agreement of merger or consolidation. The agreement shall state: (1) The terms and conditions of the merger or consolidation; (2) the mode of carrying the same into effect; (3) the manner, if any, of converting the shares of stock of each stock corporation, the interest of members of each nonstock corporation, and the shares, membership or financial or beneficial interests in each of the joint-stock associations into shares or other securities of a stock corporation or membership interests of a nonstock corporation or into shares, memberships or financial or beneficial interests of the joint-stock association surviving or resulting from such merger or consolidation, or of cancelling some or all of such shares, memberships or financial or beneficial interests, and, if any shares of any such stock corporation, any membership interests of any such nonstock corporation or any shares, memberships or financial or beneficial interests in any such joint-stock association are not to remain outstanding, to be converted solely into shares or other securities of the stock corporation or membership interests of the nonstock corporation or into shares, memberships or financial or beneficial interests of the joint-stock association surviving or resulting from such merger or consolidation or to be cancelled, the cash, property, rights or securities of any other corporation or entity which the holders of shares of any such stock corporation, membership interests of any such nonstock corporation, or shares, memberships or financial or beneficial interests of any such joint-stock association are to receive in exchange for, or upon conversion of such shares, membership interests or shares, memberships or financial or beneficial interests, and the surrender of any certificates evidencing them, which cash, property, rights or securities of any other corporation or entity may be in addition to or in lieu of shares or other securities of the stock corporation or membership interests of the nonstock corporation or shares, memberships or financial or beneficial interests of the joint-stock association surviving or resulting from such merger or consolidation; and (4) such other details or provisions as are deemed desirable, including, without limiting the generality of the foregoing, a provision for the payment of cash in lieu of the issuance of fractional shares where the surviving or resulting entity is a corporation. There shall also be set forth in the agreement such other matters or provisions as shall then be required to be set forth in certificates of incorporation or documents required to establish and maintain a joint-stock association by the laws of this State and that can be stated in the case of such merger or consolidation. Any of the terms of the agreement of merger or consolidation may be made dependent upon facts ascertainable outside of such agreement, provided that the manner in which such facts shall operate upon the terms of the agreement is clearly and expressly set forth in the agreement of merger or consolidation. The term "facts," as used in the preceding sentence, includes, but is not limited to, the occurrence of any event, including a determination or action by any person or body, including the corporation.

(d) The agreement required by subsection (c) of this section shall be adopted, approved, certified, executed and acknowledged by each of the stock or nonstock corporations in the same manner as is provided in § 251 or § 255 of this title, respectively, and in the case of the joint-stock associations in accordance with their articles of association or other instrument containing the provisions by which they are organized or regulated or in accordance with the laws of the state under which they are formed, as the case may be. Where the surviving or resulting entity is a corporation, the agreement shall be filed and shall become effective for all purposes of the laws of this State when and as provided in § 251 of this title with respect to the merger or consolidation of corporations of this State. In lieu of filing the agreement of merger or consolidation, where the surviving or resulting entity is a corporation it may file a certificate of merger or consolidation, executed in accordance with § 103 of this title, which states:

(1) The name and state of domicile of each of the constituent entities;

(2) That an agreement of merger or consolidation has been approved, adopted, certified, executed and acknowledged by each of the constituent entities in accordance with this subsection;

(3) The name of the surviving or resulting corporation;

(4) In the case of a merger, such amendments or changes in the certificate of incorporation of the surviving corporation as are desired to be effected by the merger, or, if no such amendments or changes are desired, a statement that the certificate of incorporation of the surviving corporation shall be its certificate of incorporation;

(5) In the case of a consolidation, that the certificate of incorporation of the resulting corporation shall be as is set forth in an attachment to the certificate;

(6) That the executed agreement of consolidation or merger is on file at an office of the surviving corporation and the address thereof; and

(7) That a copy of the agreement of consolidation or merger will be furnished by the surviving corporation, on request and without cost, to any stockholder of any constituent entity.

Where the surviving or resulting entity is a joint-stock association, the agreement shall be filed and shall be effective for all purposes when filed in accordance with the laws regulating the creation of joint-stock associations.

(e) Sections 251(d), 251(e), 251(f), 252(d), 259 through 262 and 328 of this title shall, insofar as they are applicable, apply to mergers or consolidations between corporations and joint-stock associations; the word "corporation" where applicable, as used in those sections, being deemed to include joint-stock associations as defined herein. The second sentence of § 251(c) of this title shall be applicable to any merger or consolidation under this section. Where the surviving or resulting entity is a corporation, the personal liability, if any, of any stockholder of a joint-stock association existing at the time of such merger or consolidation shall not thereby be extinguished, shall remain personal to such stockholder and shall not become the liability of any subsequent transferee of any share of stock in such surviving or resulting corporation or of any other stockholder of such surviving or resulting corporation.

(f) Nothing in this section shall be deemed to authorize the merger of a charitable nonstock corporation or charitable joint-stock association into a stock corporation or joint-stock association if the charitable status of such nonstock corporation or joint-stock association would be thereby lost or impaired, but a stock corporation or joint-stock association may be merged into a charitable nonstock corporation or charitable joint-stock association which shall continue as the surviving corporation or joint-stock association.

§ 255. Merger or Consolidation of Domestic Nonstock Corporations

(a) Any 2 or more nonstock corporations of this State, whether or not organized for profit, may merge into a single corporation, which may be any 1 of the constituent corporations, or they may consolidate into a new nonstock corporation, whether or not organized for profit, formed by the consolidation, pursuant to an agreement of merger or consolidation, as the case may be, complying and approved in accordance with this section.

(b) The governing body of each corporation which desires to merge or consolidate shall adopt a resolution approving an agreement of merger or consolidation. The agreement shall state: (1) The terms and conditions of the merger or consolidation; (2) the mode of carrying the same into effect; (3) such other provisions or facts required or permitted by this chapter to be stated in a certificate of incorporation for nonstock corporations as can be stated in the case of a merger or consolidation, stated in such altered form as the circumstances of the case require; (4) the manner, if any, of converting the memberships of each of the constituent corporations into memberships of the corporation surviving or resulting from the merger or consolidation, or of cancelling some or all of such membership interests; and (5) such other details or provisions as are deemed desirable. Any of the terms of the agreement of merger or consolidation may be made dependent upon facts ascertainable outside of such agreement, provided that the manner in which such facts shall operate upon the terms of the agreement is clearly and expressly set forth in the agreement of merger or consolidation. The term "facts," as used in the preceding sentence, includes, but is not limited to, the occurrence of any event, including a determination or action by any person or body, including the corporation.

(c) The agreement shall be submitted to the members of each constituent corporation who have the right to vote for the election of the members of the governing body of their corporation, at an annual or special meeting thereof for the purpose of acting on the agreement. Due notice of the time, place and purpose of the meeting shall be mailed to each member of each such corporation who has the right to vote for the election of the members of the governing body of the corporation, at the member's address as it appears on the records of the corporation, at least

20 days prior to the date of the meeting. The notice shall contain a copy of the agreement or a brief summary thereof, as the governing body shall deem advisable. At the meeting the agreement shall be considered and a vote by ballot, in person or by proxy, taken for the adoption or rejection of the agreement. If a majority of the voting power of members of each such corporation who have the voting power above mentioned shall be for the adoption of the agreement, then that fact shall be certified on the agreement by the officer of each such corporation performing the duties ordinarily performed by the secretary or assistant secretary of a corporation. The agreement so adopted and certified shall be executed, acknowledged and filed, and shall become effective, in accordance with § 103 of this title. The provisions set forth in the last sentence of subsection (c) of § 251 shall apply to a merger under this section, and the reference therein to "stockholder" shall be deemed to include "member" hereunder.

(d) If, under the certificate of incorporation of any 1 or more of the constituent corporations, there shall be no members who have the right to vote for the election of the members of the governing body of the corporation other than the members of that body themselves, the agreement duly entered into as provided in subsection (b) of this section shall be submitted to the members of the governing body of such corporation or corporations, at a meeting thereof. Notice of the meeting shall be mailed to the members of the governing body in the same manner as is provided in the case of a meeting of the members of a corporation. If at the meeting two thirds of the total number of members of the governing body shall vote by ballot, in person, for the adoption of the agreement, that fact shall be certified on the agreement in the same manner as is provided in the case of the adoption of the agreement by the vote of the members of a corporation and thereafter the same procedure shall be followed to consummate the merger or consolidation.

(e) Subsection (e) of § 251 shall apply to a merger under this section.

(f) Nothing in this section shall be deemed to authorize the merger of a charitable nonstock corporation into a nonstock corporation if such charitable nonstock corporation would thereby have its charitable status lost or impaired; but a nonstock corporation may be merged into a charitable nonstock corporation which shall continue as the surviving corporation.

§ 256. Merger or Consolidation of Domestic and Foreign Nonstock Corporations; Service of Process Upon Surviving or Resulting Corporation

(a) Any 1 or more nonstock corporations of this State may merge or consolidate with 1 or more other nonstock corporations of any other state or states of the United States, or of the District of Columbia if the laws of such other state or states or of the District permit a corporation of such jurisdiction to merge with a corporation of another jurisdiction. The constituent corporations may merge into a single corporation, which may be any 1 of the constituent corporations, or they may consolidate into a new nonstock corporation formed by the consolidation, which may be a corporation of the state of incorporation of any 1 of the constituent corporations, pursuant to an agreement of merger or consolidation, as the case may be, complying and approved in accordance with this section. In addition, any 1 or more nonstock corporations organized under the laws of any jurisdiction other than 1 of the United States may merge or consolidate with 1 or more nonstock corporations of this State if the surviving or resulting corporation will be a corporation of this State, and if the laws under which the other corporation or corporations are formed permit a corporation of such jurisdiction to merge with a corporation of another jurisdiction.

(b) All the constituent corporations shall enter into an agreement of merger or consolidation. The agreement shall state: (1) The terms and conditions of the merger or consolidation; (2) the mode of carrying the same into effect; (3) the manner, if any, of converting the memberships of each of the constituent corporations into memberships of the corporation surviving or resulting from such merger or consolidation or of cancelling some or all of such memberships; (4) such other details and provisions as shall be deemed desirable; and (5) such other provisions or facts as shall then be required to be stated in a certificate of incorporation by the laws of the state which are stated in the agreement to be the laws that shall govern the surviving or resulting corporation and that can be stated in the case of a merger or consolidation. Any of the terms of the agreement of merger or consolidation may be made dependent upon facts ascertainable outside of such agreement, provided that the manner in which such facts shall operate upon the terms of the agreement is clearly and expressly set forth in the agreement of merger or consolidation. The term "facts," as used in the preceding sentence, includes, but is not limited to, the occurrence of any event, including a determination or action by any person or body, including the corporation.

(c) The agreement shall be adopted, approved, certified, executed and acknowledged by each of the constituent corporations in accordance with the laws under which it is formed and, in the case of a Delaware corporation, in the same manner as is provided in § 255 of this title. The agreement shall be filed and shall become effective for all purposes of the laws of this State when and as provided in § 255 of this title with respect to the merger of nonstock corporations of this State. Insofar as they may be applicable, the provisions set forth in the last sentence of subsection (c) of § 252 of this title shall apply to a merger under this section, and the reference therein to "stockholder" shall be deemed to include "member" hereunder.

(d) If the corporation surviving or resulting from the merger or consolidation is to be governed by the laws of any state other than this State, it shall agree that it may be served with process in this State in any proceeding for enforcement of any obligation of any constituent corporation of this State, as well as for enforcement of any obligation of the surviving or resulting corporation arising from the merger or consolidation and shall irrevocably appoint the Secretary of State as its agent to accept service of process in any suit or other proceedings and shall specify the address to which a copy of such process shall be mailed by the Secretary of State. In the event of such service upon the Secretary of State in accordance with this subsection, the Secretary of State shall forthwith notify such surviving or resulting corporation thereof by letter, certified mail, return receipt requested, directed to such corporation at its address so specified, unless such surviving or resulting corporation shall have designated in writing to the Secretary of State a different address for such purpose, in which case it shall be mailed to the last address so designated. Such letter shall enclose a copy of the process and any other papers served upon the Secretary of State. It shall be the duty of the plaintiff in the event of such service to serve process and any other papers in duplicate, to notify the Secretary of State that service is being made pursuant to this subsection, and to pay the Secretary of State the sum of $50 for the use of the State, which sum shall be taxed as a part of the costs in the proceeding if the plaintiff shall prevail therein. The Secretary of State shall maintain an alphabetical record of any such service setting forth the name of the plaintiff and defendant, the title, docket number and nature of the proceeding in which process has been served upon the Secretary of State, the fact that service has been effected pursuant to this subsection, the return date thereof, and the day and hour when the service was made. The Secretary of State shall not be required to retain such information for a period longer than 5 years from receipt of the service of process.

(e) Subsection (e) of § 251 of this title shall apply to a merger under this section if the corporation surviving the merger is a corporation of this State.

§ 257. Merger or Consolidation of Domestic Stock and Nonstock Corporations

(a) Any 1 or more nonstock corporations of this State, whether or not organized for profit, may merge or consolidate with 1 or more stock corporations of this State, whether or not organized for profit. The constituent corporations may merge into a single corporation, which may be any 1 of the constituent corporations, or they may consolidate into a new corporation formed by the consolidation, pursuant to an agreement of merger or consolidation, as the case may be, complying and approved in accordance with this section. The surviving constituent corporation or the new corporation may be organized for profit or not organized for profit and may be a stock corporation or a nonstock corporation.

(b) The board of directors of each stock corporation which desires to merge or consolidate and the governing body of each nonstock corporation which desires to merge or consolidate shall adopt a resolution approving an agreement of merger or consolidation. The agreement shall state: (1) The terms and conditions of the merger or consolidation; (2) the mode of carrying the same into effect; (3) such other provisions or facts required or permitted by this chapter to be stated in a certificate of incorporation as can be stated in the case of a merger or consolidation, stated in such altered form as the circumstances of the case require; (4) the manner, if any, of converting the shares of stock of a stock corporation and the interests of the members of a nonstock corporation into shares or other securities of a stock corporation or membership interests of a nonstock corporation surviving or resulting from such merger or consolidation or of cancelling some or all of such shares or interests, and, if any shares of any such stock corporation or membership interests of any such nonstock corporation are not to remain outstanding, to be converted solely into shares or other securities of the stock corporation or membership interests of the nonstock corporation surviving or resulting from such merger or consolidation or to be cancelled, the cash, property, rights or securities of any other corporation or entity which the holders of shares of any such stock corporation or membership interests of any such nonstock corporation are to receive in exchange for, or upon conversion of such shares or membership interests, and the surrender of any certificates evidencing them, which cash, property, rights or securities of any other corporation or entity may be in addition to or in lieu of shares or other securities of any stock corporation or membership interests of any nonstock corporation surviving or resulting from such merger or consolidation; and (5) such other details or provisions as are deemed desirable. In such merger or consolidation the interests of members of a constituent nonstock corporation may be treated in various ways so as to convert such interests into interests of value, other than shares of stock, in the surviving or resulting stock corporation or into shares of stock in the surviving or resulting stock corporation, voting or nonvoting, or into creditor interests or any other interests of value equivalent to their membership interests in their nonstock corporation. The voting rights of members of a constituent nonstock corporation need not be considered an element of value in measuring the reasonable equivalence of the value of the interests received in the surviving or resulting stock corporation by members of a constituent nonstock corporation, nor need the voting rights of shares of stock in a constituent stock corporation be considered as an element of value in measuring the reasonable equivalence of the value of the interests in the surviving or resulting nonstock corporations received by stockholders of a constituent stock corporation, and the voting or nonvoting shares of a stock corporation may be converted into voting or nonvoting regular, life, general, special or other type of membership, however designated, creditor interests or participating interests, in the nonstock corporation surviving or resulting from such merger or consolidation of a stock corporation and a nonstock corporation. Any of the terms of the agreement of merger or consolidation may be made dependent upon facts ascertainable outside of such agreement, provided that the manner in which such facts shall operate upon the terms of the agreement is clearly and expressly set forth in the agreement of merger or consolidation. The term "facts," as used in the preceding sentence, includes, but is not limited to, the occurrence of any event, including a determination or action by any person or body, including the corporation.

(c) The agreement required by subsection (b) of this section, in the case of each constituent stock corporation, shall be adopted, approved, certified, executed and acknowledged by each constituent corporation in the same manner as is provided in § 251 of this title and, in the case of each constituent nonstock corporation, shall be adopted, approved, certified, executed and acknowledged by each of said constituent corporations in the same manner as is provided in § 255 of this title. The agreement shall be filed and shall become effective for all purposes of the laws of this State when and as provided in § 251 of this title with respect to the merger of stock corporations of this State. Insofar as they may be applicable, the provisions set forth in the last sentence of subsection (c) of § 251 of this title shall apply to a merger under this section, and the reference therein to "stockholder" shall be deemed to include "member" hereunder.

(d) Subsection (e) of § 251 of this title shall apply to a merger under this section, if the surviving corporation is a corporation of this State; subsection (d) and the second sentence of subsection (c) of § 251 of this title shall apply to any constituent stock corporation participating in a merger or consolidation under this section; and subsection (f) of § 251 of this title shall apply to any constituent stock corporation participating in a merger under this section.

(e) Nothing in this section shall be deemed to authorize the merger of a charitable nonstock corporation into a stock corporation, if the charitable status of such nonstock corporation would thereby be lost or impaired; but a stock corporation may be merged into a charitable nonstock corporation which shall continue as the surviving corporation.

§ 258. Merger or Consolidation of Domestic and Foreign Stock and Nonstock Corporations

(a) Any 1 or more corporations of this State, whether stock or nonstock corporations and whether or not organized for profit, may merge or consolidate with 1 or more other corporations of any other state or states of the United States or of the District of Columbia whether stock or nonstock corporations and whether or not organized for profit, if the laws under which the other corporation or corporations are formed shall permit such a corporation of such jurisdiction to merge with a corporation of another jurisdiction. The constituent corporations may merge into a single corporation, which may be any 1 of the constituent corporations, or they may consolidate into a new corporation formed by the consolidation, which may be a corporation of the place of incorporation of any 1 of the constituent corporations, pursuant to an agreement of merger or consolidation, as the case may be, complying and approved in accordance with this section. The surviving or new corporation may be either a stock corporation or a membership corporation, as shall be specified in the agreement of merger required by subsection (b) of this section.

(b) The method and procedure to be followed by the constituent corporations so merging or consolidating shall be as prescribed in § 257 of this title in the case of Delaware corporations. The agreement of merger or consolidation shall also set forth such other matters or provisions as shall then be required to be set forth in certificates of incorporation by the laws of the state which are stated in the agreement to be the laws which shall govern the surviving or resulting corporation and that can be stated in the case of a merger or consolidation. The agreement, in the case of foreign corporations, shall be adopted, approved, executed and acknowledged by each of the constituent foreign corporations in accordance with the laws under which each is formed.

(c) The requirements of subsection (d) of § 252 of this title as to the appointment of the Secretary of State to receive process and the manner of serving the same in the event the surviving or new corporation is to be governed by the laws of any other state shall also apply to mergers or consolidations effected under this section. Subsection (e) of § 251 of this title shall apply to mergers effected under this section if the surviving corporation is a corporation of this State; subsection (d) of § 251 of this title shall apply to any constituent stock corporation participating in a merger or consolidation under this section; and subsection (f) of § 251 of this title shall apply to any constituent stock corporation participating in a merger under this section.

(d) Nothing in this section shall be deemed to authorize the merger of a charitable nonstock corporation into a stock corporation, if the charitable status of such nonstock corporation would thereby be lost or impaired; but a stock corporation may be merged into a charitable nonstock corporation which shall continue as the surviving corporation.

§ 259. Status, Rights, Liabilities, of Constituent and Surviving or Resulting Corporations Following Merger or Consolidation

(a) When any merger or consolidation shall have become effective under this chapter, for all purposes of the laws of this State the separate existence of all the constituent corporations, or of all such constituent corporations except the one into which the other or others of such constituent corporations have been merged, as the case may be, shall cease and the constituent corporations shall become a new corporation, or be merged into 1 of such corporations, as the case may be, possessing all the rights, privileges, powers and franchises as well of a public as of a private nature, and being subject to all the restrictions, disabilities and duties of each of such corporations so merged or consolidated; and all and singular, the rights, privileges, powers and franchises of each of said corporations, and all property, real, personal and mixed, and all debts due to any of said constituent corporations on whatever account, as well for stock subscriptions as all other things in action or belonging to each of such corporations shall be vested in the corporation surviving or resulting from such merger or consolidation; and all property, rights, privileges, powers and franchises, and all and every other interest shall be thereafter as effectually the property of the surviving or resulting corporation as they were of the several and respective constituent corporations, and the title to any real estate vested by deed or otherwise, under the laws of this State, in any of such constituent corporations, shall not revert or be in any way impaired by reason of this chapter; but all rights of creditors and all liens upon any property of any of said constituent corporations shall be preserved unimpaired, and all debts, liabilities and duties of the respective constituent corporations shall thenceforth attach to said surviving or resulting corporation, and may be enforced against it to the same extent as if said debts, liabilities and duties had been incurred or contracted by it.

(b) In the case of a merger of banks or trust companies, without any order or action on the part of any court or otherwise, all appointments, designations, and nominations, and all other rights and interests as trustee, executor, administrator, registrar of stocks and bonds, guardian of estates, assignee, receiver, trustee of estates of persons mentally ill and in every other fiduciary capacity, shall be automatically vested in the corporation resulting from or surviving such merger; provided, however, that any party in interest shall have the right to apply to an appropriate court or tribunal for a determination as to whether the surviving corporation shall continue to serve in the same fiduciary capacity as the merged corporation, or whether a new and different fiduciary should be appointed.

§ 260. Powers of Corporation Surviving or Resulting From Merger or Consolidation; Issuance of Stock, Bonds or Other Indebtedness

When 2 or more corporations are merged or consolidated, the corporation surviving or resulting from the merger may issue bonds or other obligations, negotiable or otherwise, and with or without coupons or interest certificates thereto attached, to an amount sufficient with its capital stock to provide for all the payments it will be required to make, or obligations it will be required to assume, in order to effect the merger or consolidation. For the purpose of securing the payment of any such bonds and obligations, it shall be lawful for the surviving or resulting corporation to mortgage its corporate franchise, rights, privileges and property, real, personal or mixed. The surviving or resulting corporation may issue certificates of its capital stock or uncertificated stock if authorized to do so and other securities to the stockholders of the constituent corporations in exchange or payment for the original shares, in such amount as shall be necessary in accordance with the terms of the agreement of merger or consolidation in order to effect such merger or consolidation in the manner and on the terms specified in the agreement.

§ 261. Effect of Merger Upon Pending Actions

Any action or proceeding, whether civil, criminal or administrative, pending by or against any corporation which is a party to a merger or consolidation shall be prosecuted as if such merger or consolidation had not taken place, or the corporation surviving or resulting from such merger or consolidation may be substituted in such action or proceeding.

§ 262. Appraisal Rights

(a) Any stockholder of a corporation of this State who holds shares of stock on the date of the making of a demand pursuant to subsection (d) of this section with respect to such shares, who continuously holds such shares through the effective date of the merger or consolidation, who has otherwise complied with subsection (d) of this section and who has neither voted in favor of the merger or consolidation nor consented thereto in writing pursuant to § 228 of this title shall be entitled to an appraisal by the Court of Chancery of the fair value of the stockholder's shares of stock under the circumstances described in subsections (b) and (c) of this section. As used in this section, the word "stockholder" means a holder of record of stock in a stock corporation and also a member of record of a nonstock corporation; the words "stock" and "share" mean and include what is ordinarily meant by those words and also membership or membership interest of a member of a nonstock corporation; and the words "depository receipt" mean a receipt or other instrument issued by a depository representing an interest in one or more shares, or fractions thereof, solely of stock of a corporation, which stock is deposited with the depository.

(b) Appraisal rights shall be available for the shares of any class or series of stock of a constituent corporation in a merger or consolidation to be effected pursuant to § 251 (other than a merger effected pursuant to § 251(g) of this title), § 252, § 254, § 257, § 258, § 263 or § 264 of this title:

(1) Provided, however, that no appraisal rights under this section shall be available for the shares of any class or series of stock, which stock, or depository receipts in respect thereof, at the record date fixed to determine the stockholders entitled to receive notice of and to vote at the meeting of stockholders to act upon the agree-

ment of merger or consolidation, were either (i) listed on a national securities exchange or designated as a national market system security on an interdealer quotation system by the National Association of Securities Dealers, Inc. or (ii) held of record by more than 2,000 holders; and further provided that no appraisal rights shall be available for any shares of stock of the constituent corporation surviving a merger if the merger did not require for its approval the vote of the stockholders of the surviving corporation as provided in subsection (f) of § 251 of this title.

(2) Notwithstanding paragraph (1) of this subsection, appraisal rights under this section shall be available for the shares of any class or series of stock of a constituent corporation if the holders thereof are required by the terms of an agreement of merger or consolidation pursuant to §§ 251, 252, 254, 257, 258, 263 and 264 of this title to accept for such stock anything except:

a. Shares of stock of the corporation surviving or resulting from such merger or consolidation, or depository receipts in respect thereof;

b. Shares of stock of any other corporation, or depository receipts in respect thereof, which shares of stock (or depository receipts in respect thereof) or depository receipts at the effective date of the merger or consolidation will be either listed on a national securities exchange or designated as a national market system security on an interdealer quotation system by the National Association of Securities Dealers, Inc. or held of record by more than 2,000 holders;

c. Cash in lieu of fractional shares or fractional depository receipts described in the foregoing subparagraphs a. and b. of this paragraph; or

d. Any combination of the shares of stock, depository receipts and cash in lieu of fractional shares or fractional depository receipts described in the foregoing subparagraphs a., b. and c. of this paragraph.

(3) In the event all of the stock of a subsidiary Delaware corporation party to a merger effected under § 253 of this title is not owned by the parent corporation immediately prior to the merger, appraisal rights shall be available for the shares of the subsidiary Delaware corporation.

(c) Any corporation may provide in its certificate of incorporation that appraisal rights under this section shall be available for the shares of any class or series of its stock as a result of an amendment to its certificate of incorporation, any merger or consolidation in which the corporation is a constituent corporation or the sale of all or substantially all of the assets of the corporation. If the certificate of incorporation contains such a provision, the procedures of this section, including those set forth in subsections (d) and (e) of this section, shall apply as nearly as is practicable.

(d) Appraisal rights shall be perfected as follows:

(1) If a proposed merger or consolidation for which appraisal rights are provided under this section is to be submitted for approval at a meeting of stockholders, the corporation, not less than 20 days prior to the meeting, shall notify each of its stockholders who was such on the record date for such meeting with respect to shares for which appraisal rights are available pursuant to subsection (b) or (c) hereof that appraisal rights are available for any or all of the shares of the constituent corporations, and shall include in such notice a copy of this section. Each stockholder electing to demand the appraisal of such stockholder's shares shall deliver to the corporation, before the taking of the vote on the merger or consolidation, a written demand for appraisal of such stockholder's shares. Such demand will be sufficient if it reasonably informs the corporation of the identity of the stockholder and that the stockholder intends thereby to demand the appraisal of such stockholder's shares. A proxy or vote against the merger or consolidation shall not constitute such a demand. A stockholder electing to take such action must do so by a separate written demand as herein provided. Within 10 days after the effective date of such merger or consolidation, the surviving or resulting corporation shall notify each stockholder of each constituent corporation who has complied with this subsection and has not voted in favor of or consented to the merger or consolidation of the date that the merger or consolidation has become effective; or

(2) If the merger or consolidation was approved pursuant to § 228 or § 253 of this title, then either a constituent corporation before the effective date of the merger or consolidation or the surviving or resulting corporation within 10 days thereafter shall notify each of the holders of any class or series of stock of such constituent corporation who are entitled to appraisal rights of the approval of the merger or consolidation and that appraisal rights are available for any or all shares of such class or series of stock of such constituent corporation, and shall include in such notice a copy of this section. Such notice may, and, if given on or after the effective date of the merger or consolidation, shall, also notify such stockholders of the effective date of the merger or consolidation. Any stockholder entitled to appraisal rights may, within 20 days after the date of mailing of such notice, demand in writing from the surviving or resulting corporation the appraisal of such holder's shares. Such demand will be sufficient if it reasonably informs the corporation of the identity of the stockholder and that the stockholder intends thereby to demand the appraisal of such holder's shares. If such notice did not notify stockholders of the effective date of the merger or consolidation, either (i) each such constituent corporation shall

send a second notice before the effective date of the merger or consolidation notifying each of the holders of any class or series of stock of such constituent corporation that are entitled to appraisal rights of the effective date of the merger or consolidation or (ii) the surviving or resulting corporation shall send such a second notice to all such holders on or within 10 days after such effective date; provided, however, that if such second notice is sent more than 20 days following the sending of the first notice, such second notice need only be sent to each stockholder who is entitled to appraisal rights and who has demanded appraisal of such holder's shares in accordance with this subsection. An affidavit of the secretary or assistant secretary or of the transfer agent of the corporation that is required to give either notice that such notice has been given shall, in the absence of fraud, be prima facie evidence of the facts stated therein. For purposes of determining the stockholders entitled to receive either notice, each constituent corporation may fix, in advance, a record date that shall be not more than 10 days prior to the date the notice is given, provided, that if the notice is given on or after the effective date of the merger or consolidation, the record date shall be such effective date. If no record date is fixed and the notice is given prior to the effective date, the record date shall be the close of business on the day next preceding the day on which the notice is given.

(e) Within 120 days after the effective date of the merger or consolidation, the surviving or resulting corporation or any stockholder who has complied with subsections (a) and (d) hereof and who is otherwise entitled to appraisal rights, may file a petition in the Court of Chancery demanding a determination of the value of the stock of all such stockholders. Notwithstanding the foregoing, at any time within 60 days after the effective date of the merger or consolidation, any stockholder shall have the right to withdraw such stockholder's demand for appraisal and to accept the terms offered upon the merger or consolidation. Within 120 days after the effective date of the merger or consolidation, any stockholder who has complied with the requirements of subsections (a) and (d) hereof, upon written request, shall be entitled to receive from the corporation surviving the merger or resulting from the consolidation a statement setting forth the aggregate number of shares not voted in favor of the merger or consolidation and with respect to which demands for appraisal have been received and the aggregate number of holders of such shares. Such written statement shall be mailed to the stockholder within 10 days after such stockholder's written request for such a statement is received by the surviving or resulting corporation or within 10 days after expiration of the period for delivery of demands for appraisal under subsection (d) hereof, whichever is later.

(f) Upon the filing of any such petition by a stockholder, service of a copy thereof shall be made upon the surviving or resulting corporation, which shall within 20 days after such service file in the office of the

Register in Chancery in which the petition was filed a duly verified list containing the names and addresses of all stockholders who have demanded payment for their shares and with whom agreements as to the value of their shares have not been reached by the surviving or resulting corporation. If the petition shall be filed by the surviving or resulting corporation, the petition shall be accompanied by such a duly verified list. The Register in Chancery, if so ordered by the Court, shall give notice of the time and place fixed for the hearing of such petition by registered or certified mail to the surviving or resulting corporation and to the stockholders shown on the list at the addresses therein stated. Such notice shall also be given by 1 or more publications at least 1 week before the day of the hearing, in a newspaper of general circulation published in the City of Wilmington, Delaware or such publication as the Court deems advisable. The forms of the notices by mail and by publication shall be approved by the Court, and the costs thereof shall be borne by the surviving or resulting corporation.

(g) At the hearing on such petition, the Court shall determine the stockholders who have complied with this section and who have become entitled to appraisal rights. The Court may require the stockholders who have demanded an appraisal for their shares and who hold stock represented by certificates to submit their certificates of stock to the Register in Chancery for notation thereon of the pendency of the appraisal proceedings; and if any stockholder fails to comply with such direction, the Court may dismiss the proceedings as to such stockholder.

(h) After determining the stockholders entitled to an appraisal, the Court shall appraise the shares, determining their fair value exclusive of any element of value arising from the accomplishment or expectation of the merger or consolidation, together with a fair rate of interest, if any, to be paid upon the amount determined to be the fair value. In determining such fair value, the Court shall take into account all relevant factors. In determining the fair rate of interest, the Court may consider all relevant factors, including the rate of interest which the surviving or resulting corporation would have had to pay to borrow money during the pendency of the proceeding. Upon application by the surviving or resulting corporation or by any stockholder entitled to participate in the appraisal proceeding, the Court may, in its discretion, permit discovery or other pretrial proceedings and may proceed to trial upon the appraisal prior to the final determination of the stockholder entitled to an appraisal. Any stockholder whose name appears on the list filed by the surviving or resulting corporation pursuant to subsection (f) of this section and who has submitted such stockholder's certificates of stock to the Register in Chancery, if such is required, may participate fully in all proceedings until it is finally determined that such stockholder is not entitled to appraisal rights under this section.

(i) The Court shall direct the payment of the fair value of the shares, together with interest, if any, by the surviving or resulting corporation to the stockholders entitled thereto. Interest may be simple or compound, as the Court may direct. Payment shall be so made to each such stockholder, in the case of holders of uncertificated stock forthwith, and the case of holders of shares represented by certificates upon the surrender to the corporation of the certificates representing such stock. The Court's decree may be enforced as other decrees in the Court of Chancery may be enforced, whether such surviving or resulting corporation be a corporation of this State or of any state.

(j) The costs of the proceeding may be determined by the Court and taxed upon the parties as the Court deems equitable in the circumstances. Upon application of a stockholder, the Court may order all or a portion of the expenses incurred by any stockholder in connection with the appraisal proceeding, including, without limitation, reasonable attorney's fees and the fees and expenses of experts, to be charged pro rata against the value of all the shares entitled to an appraisal.

(k) From and after the effective date of the merger or consolidation, no stockholder who has demanded appraisal rights as provided in subsection (d) of this section shall be entitled to vote such stock for any purpose or to receive payment of dividends or other distributions on the stock (except dividends or other distributions payable to stockholders of record at a date which is prior to the effective date of the merger or consolidation); provided, however, that if no petition for an appraisal shall be filed within the time provided in subsection (e) of this section, or if such stockholder shall deliver to the surviving or resulting corporation a written withdrawal of such stockholder's demand for an appraisal and an acceptance of the merger or consolidation, either within 60 days after the effective date of the merger or consolidation as provided in subsection (e) of this section or thereafter with the written approval of the corporation, then the right of such stockholder to an appraisal shall cease. Notwithstanding the foregoing, no appraisal proceeding in the Court of Chancery shall be dismissed as to any stockholder without the approval of the Court, and such approval may be conditioned upon such terms as the Court deems just.

(l) The shares of the surviving or resulting corporation to which the shares of such objecting stockholders would have been converted had they assented to the merger or consolidation shall have the status of authorized and unissued shares of the surviving or resulting corporation.

§ 263. Merger or Consolidation of Domestic Corporation and Partnerships

(a) Any 1 or more corporations of this State may merge or consolidate with 1 or more partnerships (whether general (including a limited liability partnership) or limited (including a limited liability limited partnership)), of this State or of any other state or states of the United States, or of the District of Columbia, unless the laws of such other state or states or the District of Columbia forbid such merger or consolidation. Such corporation or corporations and such 1 or more partnerships may merge with or into a corporation, which may be any 1 of such corporations, or they may merge with or into a partnership, which may be any 1 of such partnerships, or they may consolidate into a new corporation or partnership formed by the consolidation, which shall be a corporation or partnership of this State or any other state of the United States, or the District of Columbia, which permits such merger or consolidation, pursuant to an agreement of merger or consolidation, as the case may be, complying and approved in accordance with this section.

(b) Each such corporation and partnership shall enter into a written agreement of merger or consolidation. The agreement shall state: (1) The terms and conditions of the merger or consolidation; (2) the mode of carrying the same into effect; (3) the manner, if any, of converting the shares of stock of each such corporation and the partnership interests of each such partnership into shares, partnership interests or other securities of the entity surviving or resulting from such merger or consolidation or of cancelling some or all of such shares or interests, and if any shares of any such corporation or any partnership interests of any such partnership are not to remain outstanding, to be converted solely into shares, partnership interests or other securities of the entity surviving or resulting from such merger or consolidation or to be cancelled, the cash, property, rights or securities of any other corporation or entity which the holders of such shares or partnership interests are to receive in exchange for, or upon conversion of such shares or partnership interests and the surrender of any certificates evidencing them, which cash, property, rights or securities of any other corporation or entity may be in addition to or in lieu of shares, partnership interests or other securities of the entity surviving or resulting from such merger or consolidation; and (4) such other details or provisions as are deemed desirable, including, without limiting the generality of the foregoing, a provision for the payment of cash in lieu of the issuance of fractional shares or interests of the surviving or resulting corporation or partnership. Any of the terms of the agreement of merger or consolidation may be made dependent upon facts ascertainable outside of such agreement, provided that the manner in which such facts shall operate upon the terms of the agreement is clearly and expressly set forth in the agreement of merger or consolidation. The term "facts," as used in the preceding sentence, includes, but is not limited to, the occurrence of any event, including a determination or action by any person or body, including the corporation.

(c) The agreement required by subsection (b) of this section shall be adopted, approved, certified, executed and acknowledged by each of the corporations in the same manner as is provided in § 251 of this title and, in the case of the partnerships, in accordance with their partnership agreements and in accordance with the laws of the state under which they are formed, as the case may be. If the surviving or resulting entity is a partnership, in addition to any other approvals, each stockholder of a merging corporation who will become a general partner of the surviving or resulting partnership must approve the agreement of merger or consolidation. The agreement shall be filed and shall become effective for all purposes of the laws of this State when and as provided in § 251 of this title with respect to the merger or consolidation of corporations of this State. In lieu of filing the agreement of merger or consolidation, the surviving or resulting corporation or partnership may file a certificate of merger or consolidation, executed in accordance with § 103 of this title, if the surviving or resulting entity is a corporation, or by a general partner, if the surviving or resulting entity is a partnership, which states: (1) The name and state of domicile of each of the constituent entities; (2) that an agreement of merger or consolidation has been approved, adopted, certified, executed and acknowledged by each of the constituent entities in accordance with this subsection; (3) the name of the surviving or resulting corporation or partnership; (4) in the case of a merger in which a corporation is the surviving entity, such amendments or changes in the certificate of incorporation of the surviving corporation as are desired to be effected by the merger, or, if no such amendments or changes are desired, a statement that the certificate of incorporation of the surviving corporation shall be its certificate of incorporation; (5) in the case of a consolidation in which a corporation is the resulting entity, that the certificate of incorporation of the resulting corporation shall be as is set forth in an attachment to the certificate; (6) that the executed agreement of consolidation or merger is on file at an office of the surviving corporation or partnership and the address thereof; (7) that a copy of the agreement of consolidation or merger will be furnished by the surviving or resulting entity, on request and without cost, to any stockholder of any constituent corporation or any partner of any constituent partnership; and (8) the agreement, if any, required by subsection (d) of this section.

(d) If the entity surviving or resulting from the merger or consolidation is to be governed by the laws of the District of Columbia or any state other than this State, it shall agree that it may be served with process in this State in any proceeding for enforcement of any obligation of any constituent corporation or partnership of this State, as well as for enforcement of any obligation of the surviving or resulting corporation or partnership arising from the merger or consolidation, including any suit or other proceeding to enforce the right of any stockholders as determined in appraisal proceedings pursuant to § 262 of this title, and shall irrevocably appoint the Secretary of State as its agent to accept service of process in any such suit or other proceedings and shall specify the address to which a copy of such process shall be mailed by the Secretary of State. In the event of such service upon the Secretary of State in accordance with this subsection, the Secretary of State shall forthwith notify such surviving or resulting corporation or partnership thereof by letter, certified mail, return receipt requested, directed to such surviving or resulting corporation or partnership at its address so specified, unless such surviving or resulting corporation or partnership shall have designated in writing to the Secretary of State a different address for such purpose, in which case it shall be mailed to the last address so designated. Such letter shall enclose a copy of the process and any other papers served on the Secretary of State pursuant to this subsection. It shall be the duty of the plaintiff in the event of such service to serve process and any other papers in duplicate, to notify the Secretary of State that service is being effected pursuant to this subsection and to pay the Secretary of State the sum of $50 for the use of the State, which sum shall be taxed as part of the costs in the proceeding, if the plaintiff shall prevail therein. The Secretary of State shall maintain an alphabetical record of any such service setting forth the name of the plaintiff and the defendant, the title, docket number and nature of the proceeding in which process has been served upon the Secretary of State, the fact that service has been effected pursuant to this subsection, the return date thereof, and the day and hour service was made. The Secretary of State shall not be required to retain such information longer than 5 years from receipt of the service of process.

(e) Sections 251(c) (second sentence) and (d)-(f), 259–261 and 328 of this title shall, insofar as they are applicable, apply to mergers or consolidations between corporations and partnerships.

§ 264. Merger or Consolidation of Domestic Corporation and Limited Liability Company

(a) Any 1 or more corporations of this State may merge or consolidate with 1 or more limited liability companies, of this State or of any other state or states of the United States, or of the District of Columbia, unless the laws of such other state or states or the District of Columbia forbid such merger or consolidation. Such corporation or corporations and such 1 or more limited liability companies may merge with or into a corporation, which may be any 1 of such corporations, or they may merge with or into a limited liability company, which may be any 1 of such limited liability companies, or they may consolidate into a new corporation or limited liability company formed by the consolidation, which shall be a corporation or limited liability company of this State or any other state of the United States, or the District of Columbia, which permits such merger or consolidation, pursuant to an agreement of merger or consolidation, as the case may be, complying and approved in accordance with this section.

(b) Each such corporation and limited liability company shall enter into a written agreement of merger or consolidation. The agreement shall state:

(1) The terms and conditions of the merger or consolidation;

(2) The mode of carrying the same into effect;

(3) The manner, if any, of converting the shares of stock of each such corporation and the limited liability company interests of each

such limited liability company into shares, limited liability company interests or other securities of the entity surviving or resulting from such merger or consolidation or of cancelling some or all of such shares or interests, and if any shares of any such corporation or any limited liability company interests of any such limited liability company are not to remain outstanding, to be converted solely into shares, limited liability company interests or other securities of the entity surviving or resulting from such merger or consolidation or to be cancelled, the cash, property, rights or securities of any other corporation or entity which the holders of such shares or limited liability company interests are to receive in exchange for, or upon conversion of such shares or limited liability company interests and the surrender of any certificates evidencing them, which cash, property, rights or securities of any other corporation or entity may be in addition to or in lieu of shares, limited liability company interests or other securities of the entity surviving or resulting from such merger or consolidation; and

(4) Such other details or provisions as are deemed desirable, including, without limiting the generality of the foregoing, a provision for the payment of cash in lieu of the issuance of fractional shares or interests of the surviving or resulting corporation or limited liability company. Any of the terms of the agreement of merger or consolidation may be made dependent upon facts ascertainable outside of such agreement, provided that the manner in which such facts shall operate upon the terms of the agreement is clearly and expressly set forth in the agreement of merger or consolidation. The term "facts," as used in the preceding sentence, includes, but is not limited to, the occurrence of any event, including a determination or action by any person or body, including the corporation.

(c) The agreement required by subsection (b) shall be adopted, approved, certified, executed and acknowledged by each of the corporations in the same manner as is provided in § 251 of this title and, in the case of the limited liability companies, in accordance with their limited liability company agreements and in accordance with the laws of the state under which they are formed, as the case may be. The agreement shall be filed and shall become effective for all purposes of the laws of this State when and as provided in § 251 of this title with respect to the merger or consolidation of corporations of this State. In lieu of filing the agreement of merger or consolidation, the surviving or resulting corporation or limited liability company may file a certificate of merger or consolidation, executed in accordance with § 103 of this title, if the surviving or resulting entity is a corporation, or by an authorized person, if the surviving or resulting entity is a limited liability company, which states:

(1) The name and state of domicile of each of the constituent entities;

(2) That an agreement of merger or consolidation has been approved, adopted, certified, executed and acknowledged by each of the constituent entities in accordance with this subsection;

(3) The name of the surviving or resulting corporation or limited liability company;

(4) In the case of a merger in which a corporation is the surviving entity, such amendments or changes in the certificate of incorporation of the surviving corporation as are desired to be effected by the merger, or, if no such amendments or changes are desired, a statement that the certificate of incorporation of the surviving corporation shall be its certificate of incorporation;

(5) In the case of a consolidation in which a corporation is the resulting entity, that the certificate of incorporation of the resulting corporation shall be as is set forth in an attachment to the certificate;

(6) That the executed agreement of consolidation or merger is on file at an office of the surviving corporation or limited liability company and the address thereof;

(7) That a copy of the agreement of consolidation or merger will be furnished by the surviving or resulting entity, on request and without cost, to any stockholder of any constituent corporation or any member of any constituent limited liability company; and

(8) The agreement, if any, required by subsection (d) of this section.

(d) If the entity surviving or resulting from the merger or consolidation is to be governed by the laws of the District of Columbia or any state other than this State, it shall agree that it may be served with process in this State in any proceeding for enforcement of any obligation of any constituent corporation or limited liability company of this State, as well as for enforcement of any obligation of the surviving or resulting corporation or limited liability company arising from the merger or consolidation, including any suit or other proceeding to enforce the right of any stockholders as determined in appraisal proceedings pursuant to the provisions of § 262 of this title, and shall irrevocably appoint the Secretary of State as its agent to accept service of process in any such suit or other proceedings and shall specify the address to which a copy of such process shall be mailed by the Secretary of State. In the event of such service upon the Secretary of State in accordance with this subsection, the Secretary of State shall forthwith notify such surviving or resulting corporation or limited liability company thereof by letter, certified mail, return receipt requested, directed to such surviving or resulting corporation or limited liability company at its address so specified, unless such surviving or resulting corporation or limited liability company shall have designated in writing to the Secretary of State a different address for such purpose, in which case it shall be mailed to the last address so designated. Such letter shall enclose a copy of the process and any other papers served on the Secretary of State pursuant to this subsection. It shall be the duty of the plaintiff in the event of such service to serve process and any other papers in duplicate, to notify the Secretary of State that service is being effected pursuant to this subsection and to pay the Secretary of State the sum of $50 for the use of the State, which sum shall be taxed as part of the costs in the proceeding, if the plaintiff shall prevail therein. The Secretary of State shall maintain an alphabetical record of any such service setting forth the name of the plaintiff and the defendant, the title, docket number and nature of the proceeding in which process has been served upon the Secretary of State, the fact that service has been effected pursuant to this subsection, the return date thereof, and the day and hour service was made. The Secretary of State shall not be required to retain such information longer than 5 years from receipt of the service of process.

(e) Sections 251(c) (second sentence) and (d)-(f), 259–261 and 328 of this title shall, insofar as they are applicable, apply to mergers or consolidations between corporations and limited liability companies.

§ 265. Conversion of Other Entities to a Domestic Corporation

(a) As used in this section, the term "other entity" means a limited liability company, statutory trust, business trust or association, real estate investment trust, common-law trust or any other unincorporated business including a partnership (whether general (including a limited liability partnership) or limited (including a limited liability limited partnership)), or a foreign corporation.

(b) Any other entity may convert to a corporation of this State by complying with subsection (h) of this section and filing in the office of the Secretary of State:

(1) A certificate of conversion to corporation that has been executed in accordance with subsection (i) of this section and filed in accordance with § 103 of this title; and

(2) A certificate of incorporation that has been executed, acknowledged and filed in accordance with § 103 of this title.

(c) The certificate of conversion to corporation shall state:

(1) The date on which and jurisdiction where the other entity was first created, incorporated, formed or otherwise came into being and, if it has changed, its jurisdiction immediately prior to its conversion to a domestic corporation;

(2) The name of the other entity immediately prior to the filing of the certificate of conversion to corporation; and

(3) The name of the corporation as set forth in its certificate of incorporation filed in accordance with subsection (b) of this section.

(4) [Repealed.]

(d) Upon the effective time of the certificate of conversion to corporation and the certificate of incorporation, the other entity shall be converted to a corporation of this State and the corporation shall thereafter be subject to all of the provisions of this title, except that notwithstanding § 106 of this title, the existence of the corporation shall be deemed to have commenced on the date the other entity commenced its existence in the jurisdiction in which the other entity was first created, formed, incorporated or otherwise came into being.

(e) The conversion of any other entity to a corporation of this State shall not be deemed to affect any obligations or liabilities of the other entity incurred prior to its conversion to a corporation of this State or the personal liability of any person incurred prior to such conversion.

(f) When an other entity has been converted to a corporation of this State pursuant to this section, the corporation of this State shall, for all purposes of the laws of the State of Delaware, be deemed to be the same entity as the converting other entity. When any conversion shall have become effective under this section, for all purposes of the laws of the State of Delaware, all of the rights, privileges and powers of the other entity that has converted, and all property, real, personal and mixed, and all debts due to such other entity, as well as all other things and causes of action belonging to such other entity, shall remain vested in the domestic corporation to which such other entity has converted and shall be the property of such domestic corporation and the title to any real property vested by deed or otherwise in such other entity shall not revert or be in any way impaired by reason of this chapter; but all rights of creditors and all liens upon any property of such other entity shall be preserved unimpaired, and all debts, liabilities and duties of the other entity that has converted shall remain attached to the corporation of this State to which such other entity has converted, and may be enforced against it to the same extent as if said debts, liabilities and duties had originally been incurred or contracted by it in its capacity as a corporation of this State. The rights, privileges, powers and interests in property of the other entity, as well as the debts, liabilities and duties of the other entity, shall not be deemed, as a consequence of the conversion, to have been transferred to the domestic corporation to which such other entity has converted for any purpose of the laws of the State of Delaware.

(g) Unless otherwise agreed for all purposes of the laws of the State of Delaware or as required under applicable non-Delaware law, the converting other entity shall not be required to wind up its affairs or pay its liabilities and distribute its assets, and the conversion shall not be deemed to constitute a dissolution of such other entity and shall constitute a continuation of the existence of the converting other entity in the form of a corporation of this State.

(h) Prior to filing a certificate of conversion to corporation with the office of the Secretary of State, the conversion shall be approved in the manner provided for by the document, instrument, agreement or other writing, as the case may be, governing the internal affairs of the other entity and the conduct of its business or by applicable law, as appropriate, and a certificate of incorporation shall be approved by the same authorization required to approve the conversion.

(i) The certificate of conversion to corporation shall be signed by any person who is authorized to sign the certificate of conversion to corporation on behalf of the other entity.

(j) In connection with a conversion hereunder, rights or securities of, or interests in, the other entity which is to be converted to a corporation of this State may be exchanged for or converted into cash, property, or shares of stock, rights or securities of such corporation of this State or, in addition to or in lieu thereof, may be exchanged for or converted into cash, property, or shares of stock, rights or securities of or interests in another domestic corporation or other entity or may be cancelled.

§ 266. Conversion of a Domestic Corporation to Other Entities

(a) A corporation of this State may, upon the authorization of such conversion in accordance with this section, convert to a limited liability company, statutory trust, business trust or association, real estate investment trust, common-law trust or any other unincorporated business including a partnership (whether general (including a limited liability partnership) or limited (including a limited liability limited partnership)) or a foreign corporation.

(b) The board of directors of the corporation which desires to convert under this section shall adopt a resolution approving such conversion, specifying the type of entity into which the corporation shall be converted and recommending the approval of such conversion by the stockholders of the corporation. Such resolution shall be submitted to the stockholders of the corporation at an annual or special meeting. Due notice of the time, and purpose of the meeting shall be mailed to each holder of stock, whether voting or nonvoting, of the corporation at the address of the stockholder as it appears on the records of the corporation, at least 20 days prior to the date of the meeting. At the meeting, the resolution shall be considered and a vote taken for its adoption or rejection. If all outstanding shares of stock of the corporation, whether voting or nonvoting, shall be voted for the adoption of the resolution, the conversion shall be authorized.

(1)-(4) [Repealed.]

(c) If a corporation shall convert in accordance with this section to another entity organized, formed or created under the laws of a jurisdiction other than the State of Delaware, the corporation shall file with the

Secretary of State a certificate of conversion executed in accordance with § 103 of this title, which certifies:

(1) The name of the corporation, and if it has been changed, the name under which it was originally incorporated;

(2) The date of filing of its original certificate of incorporation with the Secretary of State;

(3) The name and jurisdiction of the entity to which the corporation shall be converted;

(4) That the conversion has been approved in accordance with the provisions of this section;

(5) The agreement of the corporation that it may be served with process in the State of Delaware in any action, suit or proceeding for enforcement of any obligation of the corporation arising while it was a corporation of this State, and that it irrevocably appoints the Secretary of State as its agent to accept service of process in any such action, suit or proceeding; and

(6) The address to which a copy of the process referred to in subsection (c)(5) of this section shall be mailed to it by the Secretary of State. In the event of such service upon the Secretary of State in accordance with subsection (c)(5) of this section, the Secretary of State shall forthwith notify such corporation that has converted out of the State of Delaware by letter, certified mail, return receipt requested, directed to such corporation that has converted out of the State of Delaware at the address so specified, unless such corporation shall have designated in writing to the Secretary of State a different address for such purpose, in which case it shall be mailed to the last address designated. Such letter shall enclose a copy of the process and any other papers served on the Secretary of State pursuant to this subsection. It shall be the duty of the plaintiff in the event of such service to serve process and any other papers in duplicate, to notify the Secretary of State that service is being effected pursuant to this subsection and to pay the Secretary of State the sum of $50 for the use of the State, which sum shall be taxed as part of the costs in the proceeding, if the plaintiff shall prevail therein. The Secretary of State shall maintain an alphabetical record of any such service setting forth the name of the plaintiff and the defendant, the title, docket number and nature of the proceeding in which process has been served, the fact that service has been effected pursuant to this subsection, the return date thereof, and the day and hour service was made. The Secretary of State shall not be required to retain such information longer than 5 years from receipt of the service of process.

(d) Upon the filing in the Office of the Secretary of State of a certificate of conversion to non-Delaware entity in accordance with subsection (c) of this section or upon the future effective date or time of the certificate of conversion to non-Delaware entity and payment to the Secretary of State of all fees prescribed under this title, the Secretary of State shall certify that the corporation has filed all documents and paid all fees required by this title, and thereupon the corporation shall cease to exist as a corporation of this State at the time the certificate of conversion becomes effective in accordance with § 103 of this title. Such certificate of the Secretary of State shall be prima facie evidence of the conversion by such corporation out of the State of Delaware.

(e) The conversion of a corporation out of the State of Delaware in accordance with this section and the resulting cessation of its existence as a corporation of this State pursuant to a certificate of conversion to non-Delaware entity shall not be deemed to affect any obligations or liabilities of the corporation incurred prior to such conversion or the personal liability of any person incurred prior to such conversion, nor shall it be deemed to affect the choice of law applicable to the corporation with respect to matters arising prior to such conversion.

(f) Unless otherwise provided in a resolution of conversion adopted in accordance with this section, the converting corporation shall not be required to wind up its affairs or pay its liabilities and distribute its assets, and the conversion shall not constitute a dissolution of such corporation.

(g) In connection with a conversion of a domestic corporation to another entity pursuant to this section, shares of stock, of the corporation of this State which is to be converted may be exchanged for or converted into cash, property, rights or securities of, or interests in, the entity to which the corporation of this State is being converted or, in addition to or in lieu thereof, may be exchanged for or converted into cash, property, shares of stock, rights or securities of, or interests in, another domestic corporation or other entity or may be cancelled.

(h) When a corporation has been converted to another entity or business form pursuant to this section, the other entity or business form shall, for all purposes of the laws of the State of Delaware, be deemed to be the same entity as the corporation. When any conversion shall have become effective under this section, for all purposes of the laws of the State of Delaware, all of the rights, privileges and powers of the corporation that has converted, and all property, real, personal and mixed, and all debts due to such corporation, as well as all other things and causes of action belonging to such corporation, shall remain vested in the other entity or business form to which such corporation has converted and shall be the property of such other entity or business form, and the title to any real property vested by deed or otherwise in such corporation shall not revert or be in any way impaired by reason of this chapter; but all rights of creditors and all liens upon any property of such corporation shall be preserved unimpaired, and all debts, liabilities and duties of the corporation that has converted shall remain attached to the other entity or business form to which such corporation has converted, and may be enforced against it to the same extent as if said debts, liabilities and duties had originally been incurred or contracted by it in its capacity as such other entity or business form. The rights, privileges, powers and interest in property of the corporation that has converted, as well as the debts, liabilities and duties of such corporation, shall not be deemed, as a consequence of the conversion, to have been transferred to the other entity or business form to which such corporation has converted for any purpose of the laws of the State of Delaware.

(i) No vote of stockholders of a corporation shall be necessary to authorize a conversion if no shares of the stock of such corporation shall have been issued prior to the adoption by the board of directors of the resolution approving the conversion.

SUBCHAPTER X. SALE OF ASSETS, DISSOLUTION AND WINDING UP

§ 271. Sale, Lease or Exchange of Assets; Consideration; Procedure

(a) Every corporation may at any meeting of its board of directors or governing body sell, lease or exchange all or substantially all of its property and assets, including its goodwill and its corporate franchises, upon such terms and conditions and for such consideration, which may consist in whole or in part of money or other property, including shares of stock in, and/or other securities of, any other corporation or corporations, as its board of directors or governing body deems expedient and for the best interests of the corporation, when and as authorized by a resolution adopted by the holders of a majority of the outstanding stock of the corporation entitled to vote thereon or, if the corporation is a nonstock corporation, by a majority of the members having the right to vote for the election of the members of the governing body, at a meeting duly called upon at least 20 days' notice. The notice of the meeting shall state that such a resolution will be considered.

(b) Notwithstanding authorization or consent to a proposed sale, lease or exchange of a corporation's property and assets by the stockholders or members, the board of directors or governing body may abandon such proposed sale, lease or exchange without further action by the stockholders or members, subject to the rights, if any, of third parties under any contract relating thereto.

(c) For purposes of this section only, the property and assets of the corporation include the property and assets of any subsidiary of the corporation. As used in this subsection, "subsidiary" means any entity wholly-owned and controlled, directly or indirectly, by the corporation and includes, without limitation, corporations, partnerships, limited partnerships, limited liability partnerships, limited liability companies, and/or statutory trusts. Notwithstanding subsection (a) of this section, except to the extent the certificate of incorporation otherwise provides, no resolution by stockholders or members shall be required for a sale, lease or exchange of property and assets of the corporation to a subsidiary.

§ 272. Mortgage or Pledge of Assets

The authorization or consent of stockholders to the mortgage or pledge of a corporation's property and assets shall not be necessary, except to the extent that the certificate of incorporation otherwise provides.

§ 273. Dissolution of Joint Venture Corporation Having 2 Stockholders

(a) If the stockholders of a corporation of this State, having only 2 stockholders each of which own 50% of the stock therein, shall be engaged in the prosecution of a joint venture and if such stockholders shall be unable to agree upon the desirability of discontinuing such joint venture and disposing of the assets used in such venture, either stockholder may, unless otherwise provided in the certificate of incorporation of the corporation or in a written agreement between the stockholders, file with the Court of Chancery a petition stating that it desires to discontinue such joint venture and to dispose of the assets used in such venture in accordance with a plan to be agreed upon by both stockholders or that, if no such plan shall be agreed upon by both stockholders, the corporation be dissolved. Such petition shall have attached thereto a copy of the proposed plan of discontinuance and distribution and a certificate stating that copies of such petition and plan have been transmitted in writing to the other stockholder and to the directors and officers of such corporation. The petition and certificate shall be executed and acknowledged in accordance with § 103 of this title.

(b) Unless both stockholders file with the Court of Chancery (1) within 3 months of the date of the filing of such petition, a certificate similarly executed and acknowledged stating that they have agreed on such plan, or a modification thereof, and (2) within 1 year from the date of the filing of such petition, a certificate similarly executed and acknowledged stating that the distribution provided by such plan had been completed, the Court of Chancery may dissolve such corporation and may by appointment of 1 or more trustees or receivers with all the powers and title of a trustee or receiver appointed under § 279 of this title, administer and wind up its affairs. Either or both of the above periods may be extended by agreement of the stockholders, evidenced by a certificate similarly executed, acknowledged and filed with the Court of Chancery prior to the expiration of such period.

§ 274. Dissolution Before Issuance of Shares or Beginning of Business; Procedure

If a corporation has not issued shares or has not commenced the business for which the corporation was organized, a majority of the incorporators, or, if directors were named in the certificate of incorporation or have been elected, a majority of the directors, may surrender all of the corporation's rights and franchises by filing in the office of the Secretary of State a certificate, executed and acknowledged by a majority of the incorporators or directors, stating that no shares of stock have been issued or that the business or activity for which the corporation was organized has not been begun; that no part of the capital of the corporation has been paid, or, if some capital has been paid, that the amount actually paid in for the corporation's shares, less any part thereof disbursed for necessary expenses, has been returned to those entitled thereto; that if the corporation has begun business but it has not issued shares, all debts of the corporation have been paid; that if the corporation has not begun business but has issued stock certificates, all issued stock certificates, if any, have been surrendered and cancelled; and that all rights and franchises of the corporation are surrendered. Upon such certificate becoming effective in accordance with § 103 of this title, the corporation shall be dissolved.

§ 275. Dissolution Generally; Procedure

(a) If it should be deemed advisable in the judgment of the board of directors of any corporation that it should be dissolved, the board, after the adoption of a resolution to that effect by a majority of the whole board at any meeting called for that purpose, shall cause notice to be mailed to each stockholder entitled to vote thereon of the adoption of the resolution and of a meeting of stockholders to take action upon the resolution.

(b) At the meeting a vote shall be taken upon the proposed dissolution. If a majority of the outstanding stock of the corporation entitled to vote thereon shall vote for the proposed dissolution, a certification of dissolution shall be filed with the Secretary of State pursuant to subsection (d) of this section.

(c) Dissolution of a corporation may also be authorized without action of the directors if all the stockholders entitled to vote thereon shall consent in writing and a certificate of dissolution shall be filed with the Secretary of State pursuant to subsection (d) of this section.

(d) If dissolution is authorized in accordance with this section, a certificate of dissolution shall be executed, acknowledged and filed, and shall become effective, in accordance with § 103 of this title. Such certificate of dissolution shall set forth:

(1) The name of the corporation;

(2) The date dissolution was authorized;

(3) That the dissolution has been authorized by the board of directors and stockholders of the corporation, in accordance with subsections (a) and (b) of this section, or that the dissolution has been authorized by all of the stockholders of the corporation entitled

to vote on a dissolution, in accordance with subsection (c) of this section; and

(4) The names and addresses of the directors and officers of the corporation.

(e) The resolution authorizing a proposed dissolution may provide that notwithstanding authorization or consent to the proposed dissolution by the stockholders, or the members of a nonstock corporation pursuant to § 276 of this title, the board of directors or governing body may abandon such proposed dissolution without further action by the stockholders or members.

(f) Upon a certificate of dissolution becoming effective in accordance with § 103 of this title, the corporation shall be dissolved.

§ 276. Dissolution of Nonstock Corporation; Procedure

(a) Whenever it shall be desired to dissolve any corporation having no capital stock, the governing body shall perform all the acts necessary for dissolution which are required by § 275 of this title to be performed by the board of directors of a corporation having capital stock. If the members of a corporation having no capital stock are entitled to vote for the election of members of its governing body, they shall perform all the acts necessary for dissolution which are required by § 275 of this title to be performed by the stockholders of a corporation having capital stock. If there is no member entitled to vote thereon, the dissolution of the corporation shall be authorized at a meeting of the governing body, upon the adoption of a resolution to dissolve by the vote of a majority of members of its governing body then in office. In all other respects, the method and proceedings for the dissolution of a corporation having no capital stock shall conform as nearly as may be to the proceedings prescribed by § 275 of this title for the dissolution of corporations having capital stock.

(b) If a corporation having no capital stock has not commenced the business for which the corporation was organized, a majority of the governing body or, if none, a majority of the incorporators may surrender all of the corporation rights and franchises by filing in the office of the Secretary of State a certificate, executed and acknowledged by a majority of the incorporators or governing body, conforming as nearly as may be to the certificate prescribed by § 274 of this title.

§ 277. Payment of Franchise Taxes Before Dissolution or Merger

No corporation shall be dissolved or merged under this chapter until all franchise taxes due to or assessable by the State including all franchise taxes due or which would be due or assessable for the entire calendar month during which the dissolution or merger becomes effective have been paid by the corporation.

§ 278. Continuation of Corporation After Dissolution for Purposes of Suit and Winding Up Affairs

All corporations, whether they expire by their own limitation or are otherwise dissolved, shall nevertheless be continued, for the term of 3 years from such expiration or dissolution or for such longer period as the Court of Chancery shall in its discretion direct, bodies corporate for the purpose of prosecuting and defending suits, whether civil, criminal or administrative, by or against them, and of enabling them gradually to settle and close their business, to dispose of and convey their property, to discharge their liabilities and to distribute to their stockholders any remaining assets, but not for the purpose of continuing the business for which the corporation was organized. With respect to any action, suit or proceeding begun by or against the corporation either prior to or within 3 years after the date of its expiration or dissolution, the action shall not abate by reason of the dissolution of the corporation; the corporation shall, solely for the purpose of such action, suit or proceeding, be continued as a body corporate beyond the 3–year period and until any judgments, orders or decrees therein shall be fully executed, without the necessity for any special direction to that effect by the Court of Chancery.

§ 279. Trustees or Receivers for Dissolved Corporations; Appointment; Powers; Duties

When any corporation organized under this chapter shall be dissolved in any manner whatever, the Court of Chancery, on application of any creditor, stockholder or director of the corporation, or any other person who shows good cause therefor, at any time, may either appoint 1 or more of the directors of the corporation to be trustees, or appoint 1 or more persons to be receivers, of and for the corporation, to take charge of the corporation's property, and to collect the debts and property due and belonging to the corporation, with power to prosecute and defend, in the name of the corporation, or otherwise, all such suits as may be necessary or proper for the purposes aforesaid, and to appoint an agent or agents under them, and to do all other acts which might be done by the corporation, if in being, that may be necessary for the final settlement of the unfinished business of the corporation. The powers of the trustees or receivers may be continued as long as the Court of Chancery shall think necessary for the purposes aforesaid.

§ 280. Notice to Claimants; Filing of Claims

(a)(1) After a corporation has been dissolved in accordance with the procedures set forth in this chapter, the corporation or any successor entity may give notice of the dissolution, requiring all persons having a claim against the corporation other than a claim against the corporation in a pending action, suit or proceeding to which the corporation is a party to present their claims against the corporation in accordance with such notice. Such notice shall state:

a. That all such claims must be presented in writing and must contain sufficient information reasonably to inform the corporation or successor entity of the identity of the claimant and the substance of the claim;

b. The mailing address to which such a claim must be sent;

c. The date by which such a claim must be received by the corporation or successor entity, which date shall be no earlier than 60 days from the date thereof; and

d. That such claim will be barred if not received by the date referred to in subparagraph c. of this subsection; and

e. That the corporation or a successor entity may make distributions to other claimants and the corporation's stockholders or persons interested as having been such without further notice to the claimant; and

f. The aggregate amount, on an annual basis, of all distributions made by the corporation to its stockholders for each of the 3 years prior to the date the corporation dissolved.

Such notice shall also be published at least once a week for 2 consecutive weeks in a newspaper of general circulation in the county in which the office of the corporation's last registered agent in this State is located and in the corporation's principal place of business and, in the case of a corporation having $10,000,000 or more in total assets at the time of its dissolution, at least once in all editions of a daily newspaper with a national circulation. On or before the date of the first publication of such notice, the corporation or successor entity shall mail a copy of such notice by certified or registered mail, return receipt requested, to each known claimant of the corporation including persons with claims asserted against the corporation in a pending action, suit or proceeding to which the corporation is a party.

(2) Any claim against the corporation required to be presented pursuant to this subsection is barred if a claimant who was given actual notice under this subsection does not present the claim to the dissolved corporation or successor entity by the date referred to in subparagraph (1)c. of this subsection.

(3) A corporation or successor entity may reject, in whole or in part, any claim made by a claimant pursuant to this subsection by mailing notice of such rejection by certified or registered mail, return receipt requested, to the claimant within 90 days after receipt of such claim and, in all events, at least 150 days before the

expiration of the period described in § 278 of this title; provided however, that in the case of a claim filed pursuant to § 295 of this title against a corporation or successor entity for which a receiver or trustee has been appointed by the Court of Chancery the time period shall be as provided in § 296 of this title, and the 30–day appeal period provided for in § 296 of this title shall be applicable. A notice sent by a corporation or successor entity pursuant to this subsection shall state that any claim rejected therein will be barred if an action, suit or proceeding with respect to the claim is not commenced within 120 days of the date thereof, and shall be accompanied by a copy of §§ 278–283 of this title and, in the case of a notice sent by a court-appointed receiver or trustee and as to which a claim has been filed pursuant to § 295 of this title, copies of §§ 295 and 296 of this title.

(4) A claim against a corporation is barred if a claimant whose claim is rejected pursuant to paragraph (3) of this subsection does not commence an action, suit or proceeding with respect to the claim no later than 120 days after the mailing of the rejection notice.

(b)(1) A corporation or successor entity electing to follow the procedures described in subsection (a) of this section shall also give notice of the dissolution of the corporation to persons with contractual claims contingent upon the occurrence or nonoccurrence of future events or otherwise conditional or unmatured, and request that such persons present such claims in accordance with the terms of such notice. Provided however, that as used in this section and in § 281 of this title, the term "contractual claims" shall not include any implied warranty as to any product manufactured, sold, distributed or handled by the dissolved corporation. Such notice shall be in substantially the form, and sent and published in the same manner, as described in subsection (a)(1) of this section.

(2) The corporation or successor entity shall offer any claimant on a contract whose claim is contingent, conditional or unmatured such security as the corporation or successor entity determines is sufficient to provide compensation to the claimant if the claim matures. The corporation or successor entity shall mail such offer to the claimant by certified or registered mail, return receipt requested, within 90 days of receipt of such claim and, in all events, at least 150 days before the expiration of the period described in § 278 of this title. If the claimant offered such security does not deliver in writing to the corporation or successor entity a notice rejecting the offer within 120 days after receipt of such offer for security, the claimant shall be deemed to have accepted such security as the sole source from which to satisfy the claim against the corporation.

(c)(1) A corporation or successor entity which has given notice in accordance with subsection (a) of this section shall petition the Court of Chancery to determine the amount and form of security that will be reasonably likely to be sufficient to provide compensation for any claim against the corporation which is the subject of a pending action, suit or proceeding to which the corporation is a party other than a claim barred pursuant to subsection (a) of this section.

(2) A corporation or successor entity which has given notice in accordance with subsections (a) and (b) of this section shall petition the Court of Chancery to determine the amount and form of security that will be sufficient to provide compensation to any claimant who has rejected the offer for security made pursuant to subsection (b)(2) of this section.

(3) A corporation or successor entity which has given notice in accordance with subsection (a) of this section shall petition the Court of Chancery to determine the amount and form of security which will be reasonably likely to be sufficient to provide compensation for claims that have not been made known to the corporation or that have not arisen but that, based on facts known to the corporation or successor entity, are likely to arise or to become known to the corporation or successor entity within 5 years after the date of dissolution or such longer period of time as the Court of Chancery may determine not to exceed 10 years after the date of dissolution. The Court of Chancery may appoint a guardian ad litem in respect of any such proceeding brought under this subsection. The reasonable fees and expenses of such guardian, including all reasonable expert witness fees, shall be paid by the petitioner in such proceeding.

(d) The giving of any notice or making of any offer pursuant to this section shall not revive any claim then barred or constitute acknowledgment by the corporation or successor entity that any person to whom such notice is sent is a proper claimant and shall not operate as a waiver of any defense or counterclaim in respect of any claim asserted by any person to whom such notice is sent.

(e) As used in this section, the term "successor entity" shall include any trust, receivership or other legal entity governed by the laws of this State to which the remaining assets and liabilities of a dissolved corporation are transferred and which exists solely for the purposes of prosecuting and defending suits, by or against the dissolved corporation, enabling the dissolved corporation to settle and close the business of the dissolved corporation, to dispose of and convey the property of the dissolved corporation, to discharge the liabilities of the dissolved corporation and to distribute to the dissolved corporation's stockholders any remaining assets, but not for the purpose of continuing the business for which the dissolved corporation was organized.

(f) The time periods and notice requirements of this section shall, in the case of a corporation or successor entity for which a receiver or trustee has been appointed by the Court of Chancery, be subject to variation by, or in the manner provided in, the Rules of the Court of Chancery.

§ 281. Payment and Distribution to Claimants and Stockholders

(a) A dissolved corporation or successor entity which has followed the procedures described in § 280 of this title:

(1) Shall pay the claims made and not rejected in accordance with § 280(a) of this title,

(2) Shall post the security offered and not rejected pursuant to § 280(b)(2) of this title,

(3) Shall post any security ordered by the Court of Chancery in any proceeding under § 280(c) of this title, and

(4) Shall pay or make provision for all other claims that are mature, known and uncontested or that have been finally determined to be owing by the corporation or such successor entity.

Such claims or obligations shall be paid in full and any such provision for payment shall be made in full if there are sufficient assets. If there are insufficient assets, such claims and obligations shall be paid or provided for according to their priority, and, among claims of equal priority, ratably to the extent of assets legally available therefor. Any remaining assets shall be distributed to the stockholders of the dissolved corporation; provided, however, that such distribution shall not be made before the expiration of 150 days from the date of the last notice of rejections given pursuant to § 280(a)(3) of this title. In the absence of actual fraud, the judgment of the directors of the dissolved corporation or the governing persons of such successor entity as to the provision made for the payment of all obligations under paragraph (4) of this subsection shall be conclusive.

(b) A dissolved corporation or successor entity which has not followed the procedures described in § 280 of this title shall, prior to the expiration of the period described in § 278 of this title, adopt a plan of distribution pursuant to which the dissolved corporation or successor entity (i) shall pay or make reasonable provision to pay all claims and obligations, including all contingent, conditional or unmatured contractual claims known to the corporation or such successor entity, (ii) shall make such provision as will be reasonably likely to be sufficient to provide compensation for any claim against the corporation which is the subject of a pending action, suit or proceeding to which the corporation is a party and (iii) shall make such provision as will be reasonably likely to be sufficient to provide compensation for claims that have not been made known to the corporation or that have not arisen but that, based on facts known to the corporation or successor entity, are likely to arise or to become known to the corporation or successor entity within 10 years after the date of dissolution. The plan of distribution shall provide that such claims shall be paid in full and any such provision for payment made shall be made in full if there are sufficient assets. If there are insufficient assets, such plan shall provide that such claims and obligations shall be paid or provided for according to their priority and, among claims of equal priority, ratably to the extent of assets legally available therefor. Any remaining assets shall be distributed to the stockholders of the dissolved corporation.

(c) Directors of a dissolved corporation or governing persons of a successor entity which has complied with subsection (a) or (b) of this section shall not be personally liable to the claimants of the dissolved corporation.

(d) As used in this section, the term "successor entity" has the meaning set forth in § 280(e) of this title.

(e) The term "priority," as used in this section, does not refer either to the order of payments set forth in subsection (a)(1)-(4) of this section or to the relative times at which any claims mature or are reduced to judgment.

§ 282. Liability of Stockholders of Dissolved Corporations

(a) A stockholder of a dissolved corporation the assets of which were distributed pursuant to § 281(a) or (b) of this title shall not be liable for any claim against the corporation in an amount in excess of such stockholder's pro rata share of the claim or the amount so distributed to such stockholder, whichever is less.

(b) A stockholder of a dissolved corporation the assets of which were distributed pursuant to § 281(a) of this title shall not be liable for any claim against the corporation on which an action, suit or proceeding is not begun prior to the expiration of the period described in § 278 of this title.

(c) The aggregate liability of any stockholder of a dissolved corporation for claims against the dissolved corporation shall not exceed the amount distributed to such stockholder in dissolution.

§ 283. Jurisdiction

The Court of Chancery shall have jurisdiction of any application prescribed in this subchapter and of all questions arising in the proceedings thereon, and may make such orders and decrees and issue injunctions therein as justice and equity shall require.

§ 284. Revocation or Forfeiture of Charter; Proceedings

(a) The Court of Chancery shall have jurisdiction to revoke or forfeit the charter of any corporation for abuse, misuse or nonuse of its corporate powers, privileges or franchises. The Attorney General shall, upon the Attorney General's own motion or upon the relation of a proper party, proceed for this purpose by complaint in the county in which the registered office of the corporation is located.

(b) The Court of Chancery shall have power, by appointment of receivers or otherwise, to administer and wind up the affairs of any corporation whose charter shall be revoked or forfeited by any court under any section of this title or otherwise, and to make such orders and decrees with respect thereto as shall be just and equitable respecting its affairs and assets and the rights of its stockholders and creditors.

(c) No proceeding shall be instituted under this section for nonuse of any corporation's powers, privileges or franchises during the first 2 years after its incorporation.

§ 285. Dissolution or Forfeiture of Charter by Decree of Court; Filing

Whenever any corporation is dissolved or its charter forfeited by decree or judgment of the Court of Chancery, the decree or judgment shall be forthwith filed by the Register in Chancery of the county in which the decree or judgment was entered, in the office of the Secretary of State, and a note thereof shall be made by the Secretary of State on the corporation's charter or certificate of incorporation and on the index thereof.

SUBCHAPTER XI. INSOLVENCY; RECEIVERS AND TRUSTEES

§ 291. Receivers for Insolvent Corporations; Appointment and Powers

Whenever a corporation shall be insolvent, the Court of Chancery, on the application of any creditor or stockholder thereof, may, at any time, appoint 1 or more persons to be receivers of and for the corporation, to take charge of its assets, estate, effects, business and affairs, and to collect the outstanding debts, claims, and property due and belonging to the corporation, with power to prosecute and defend, in the name of the corporation or otherwise, all claims or suits, to appoint an agent or agents under them, and to do all other acts which might be done by the corporation and which may be necessary or proper. The powers of the receivers shall be such and shall continue so long as the Court shall deem necessary.

§ 292. Title to Property; Filing Order of Appointment; Exception

(a) Trustees or receivers appointed by the Court of Chancery of and for any corporation, and their respective survivors and successors, shall, upon their appointment and qualification or upon the death, resignation or discharge of any cotrustee or coreceiver, be vested by operation of law and without any act or deed, with the title of the corporation to all of its property, real, personal or mixed of whatsoever nature, kind, class or description, and wheresoever situate, except real estate situate outside this State.

(b) Trustees or receivers appointed by the Court of Chancery shall, within 20 days from the date of their qualification, file in the office of the recorder in each county in this State, in which any real estate belonging to the corporation may be situated, a certified copy of the order of their appointment and evidence of their qualification.

(c) This section shall not apply to receivers appointed pendente lite.

§ 293. Notices to Stockholders and Creditors

All notices required to be given to stockholders and creditors in any action in which a receiver or trustee for a corporation was appointed shall be given by the Register in Chancery, unless otherwise ordered by the Court of Chancery.

§ 294. Receivers or Trustees; Inventory; List of Debts and Report

Trustees or receivers shall, as soon as convenient, file in the office of the Register in Chancery of the county in which the proceeding is pending, a full and complete itemized inventory of all the assets of the corporation which shall show their nature and probable value, and an account of all debts due from and to it, as nearly as the same can be ascertained. They shall make a report to the Court of their proceedings, whenever and as often as the Court shall direct.

§ 295. Creditors' Proofs of Claims; When Barred; Notice

All creditors shall make proof under oath of their respective claims against the corporation, and cause the same to be filed in the office of the Register in Chancery of the county in which the proceeding is pending within the time fixed by and in accordance with the procedure established by the Rules of the Court of Chancery. All creditors and claimants failing to do so, within the time limited by this section, or the time prescribed by the order of the Court, may, by direction of the Court, be barred from participating in the distribution of the assets of the corporation. The Court may also prescribe what notice, by publication or otherwise, shall be given to the creditors of the time fixed for the filing and making proof of claims.

§ 296. Adjudication of Claims; Appeal

(a) The Register in Chancery, immediately upon the expiration of the time fixed for the filing of claims, in compliance with § 295 of this title, shall notify the trustee or receiver of the filing of the claims, and the trustee or receiver, within 30 days after receiving the notice, shall inspect the claims, and if the trustee or receiver or any creditor shall not be satisfied with the validity or correctness of the same, or any of them, the trustee or receiver shall forthwith notify the creditors whose claims are disputed of such trustee's or receiver's decision. The trustee or receiver shall require all creditors whose claims are disputed to submit themselves to such examination in relation to their claims as the trustee or receiver shall direct, and the creditors shall produce such books and papers relating to their claims as shall be required. The trustee or receiver shall have power to examine, under oath or affirmation, all witnesses produced before such trustee or receiver touching the claims, and shall pass upon and allow or disallow the claims, or any part thereof, and notify the claimants of such trustee's or receiver's determination.

(b) Every creditor or claimant who shall have received notice from the receiver or trustee that such creditor's or claimant's claim has been disallowed in whole or in part may appeal to the Court of Chancery within 30 days thereafter. The Court, after hearing, shall determine the rights of the parties.

§ 297. Sale of Perishable or Deteriorating Property

Whenever the property of a corporation is at the time of the appointment of a receiver or trustee encumbered with liens of any character, and the validity, extent or legality of any lien is disputed or brought in question, and the property of the corporation is of a character which will deteriorate in value pending the litigation respecting the lien, the Court of Chancery may order the receiver or trustee to sell the property of the corporation, clear of all encumbrances, at public or private sale, for the best price that can be obtained therefor, and pay the net proceeds arising from the sale thereof after deducting the costs of the sale into the Court, there to remain subject to the order of the Court, and to be disposed of as the Court shall direct.

§ 298. Compensation, Costs and Expenses of Receiver or Trustee

The Court of Chancery, before making distribution of the assets of a corporation among the creditors or stockholders thereof, shall allow a reasonable compensation to the receiver or trustee for such receiver's or trustee's services, and the costs and expenses incurred in and about the execution of such receiver's or trustee's trust, and the costs of the proceedings in the Court, to be first paid out of the assets.

§ 299. Substitution of Trustee or Receiver as Party; Abatement of Actions

A trustee or receiver, upon application by such receiver or trustee in the court in which any suit is pending, shall be substituted as party plaintiff in the place of the corporation in any suit or proceeding which was so pending at the time of such receiver's or trustee's appointment. No action against a trustee or receiver of a corporation shall abate by reason of such receiver's or trustee's death, but, upon suggestion of the facts on the record, shall be continued against such receiver's or trustee's successor or against the corporation in case no new trustee or receiver is appointed.

§ 300. Employee's Lien for Wages When Corporation Insolvent

Whenever any corporation of this State, or any foreign corporation doing business in this State, shall become insolvent, the employees doing labor or service of whatever character in the regular employ of the corporation, shall have a lien upon the assets thereof for the amount of the wages due to them, not exceeding 2 months' wages respectively, which shall be paid prior to any other debt or debts of the corporation. The word "employee" shall not be construed to include any of the officers of the corporation.

§ 301. Discontinuance of Liquidation

The liquidation of the assets and business of an insolvent corporation may be discontinued at any time during the liquidation proceedings when it is established that cause for liquidation no longer exists. In such event the Court of Chancery in its discretion, and subject to such condition as it may deem appropriate, may dismiss the proceedings and direct the receiver or trustee to redeliver to the corporation all of its remaining property and assets.

§ 302. Compromise or Arrangement Between Corporation and Creditors or Stockholders

(a) Whenever the provision permitted by paragraph (2) of subsection (b) of § 102 of this title is included in the original certificate of incorporation of any corporation, all persons who become creditors or stockholders thereof shall be deemed to have become such creditors or stockholders subject in all respects to that provision and the same shall be absolutely binding upon them. Whenever that provision is inserted in the certificate of incorporation of any such corporation by an amendment of its certificate all persons who become creditors or stockholders of such corporation after such amendment shall be deemed to have become such creditors or stockholders subject in all respects to that provision and the same shall be absolutely binding upon them.

(b) The Court of Chancery may administer and enforce any compromise or arrangement made pursuant to the provision contained in paragraph (2) of subsection (b) of § 102 of this title and may restrain, pendente lite, all actions and proceedings against any corporation with respect to which the Court shall have begun the administration and enforcement of that provision and may appoint a temporary receiver for such corporation and may grant the receiver such powers as it deems proper, and may make and enforce such rules as it deems necessary for the exercise of such jurisdiction.

§ 303. Proceeding Under the Federal Bankruptcy Code of the United States; Effectuation

(a) Any corporation of this State, an order for relief with respect to which has been entered pursuant to the Federal Bankruptcy Code, 11 U.S.C. § 101 et seq., or any successor statute, may put into effect and carry out any decrees and orders of the court or judge in such bankruptcy proceeding and may take any corporate action provided or directed by such decrees and orders, without further action by its directors or stockholders. Such power and authority may be exercised, and such corporate action may be taken, as may be directed by such decrees or orders, by the trustee or trustees of such corporation appointed or elected in the bankruptcy proceeding (or a majority thereof), or if none be appointed or elected and acting, by designated officers of the corporation, or by a representative appointed by the court or judge, with like effect as if exercised and taken by unanimous action of the directors and stockholders of the corporation.

(b) Such corporation may, in the manner provided in subsection (a) of this section, but without limiting the generality or effect of the foregoing, alter, amend or repeal its bylaws; constitute or reconstitute and classify or reclassify its board of directors, and name, constitute or appoint directors and officers in place of or in addition to all or some of the directors or officers then in office; amend its certificate of incorporation, and make any change in its capital or capital stock, or any other amendment, change, or alteration, or provision, authorized by this chapter; be dissolved, transfer all or part of its assets, merge or consolidate as permitted by this chapter, in which case, however, no stockholder shall have any statutory right of appraisal of such stockholder's stock; change the location of its registered office, change its registered agent, and remove or appoint any agent to receive service of process; authorize and fix the terms, manner and conditions of, the issuance of bonds, debentures or other obligations, whether or not convertible into stock of any class, or bearing warrants or other evidences of optional rights to purchase or subscribe for stock of any class; or lease its property and franchises to any corporation, if permitted by law.

(c) A certificate of any amendment, change or alteration, or of dissolution, or any agreement of merger or consolidation, made by such corporation pursuant to the foregoing provisions, shall be filed with the Secretary of State in accordance with § 103 of this title, and, subject to subsection (d) of said § 103 of this title, shall thereupon become effective in accordance with its terms and the provisions hereof. Such certificate, agreement of merger or other instrument shall be made, executed and acknowledged, as may be directed by such decrees or orders, by the trustee or trustees appointed or elected in the bankruptcy proceeding (or a majority thereof), or, if none be appointed or elected and acting, by the officers of the corporation, or by a representative appointed by the court or judge, and shall certify that provision for the making of such certificate, agreement or instrument is contained in a decree or order of a court or judge having jurisdiction of a proceeding under such Federal Bankruptcy Code or successor statute.

(d) This section shall cease to apply to such corporation upon the entry of a final decree in the bankruptcy proceeding closing the case and discharging the trustee or trustees, if any; provided however, that the closing of a case and discharge of trustee or trustees, if any, will not affect the validity of any act previously performed pursuant to subsections (a) through (c) of this section.

(e) On filing any certificate, agreement, report or other paper made or executed pursuant to this section, there shall be paid to the Secretary of State for the use of the State the same fees as are payable by corporations not in bankruptcy upon the filing of like certificates, agreements, reports or other papers.

SUBCHAPTER XII. RENEWAL, REVIVAL, EXTENSION AND RESTORATION OF CERTIFICATE OF INCORPORATION OR CHARTER

§ 311. Revocation of Voluntary Dissolution

(a) At any time prior to the expiration of 3 years following the dissolution of a corporation pursuant to § 275 of this title, or, at any time prior to the expiration of such longer period as the Court of Chancery may have directed pursuant to § 278 of this title, a corporation may revoke the dissolution theretofore effected by it in the following manner:

(1) For purposes of this section, the term "stockholders" shall mean the stockholders of record on the date the dissolution became effective.

(2) The board of directors shall adopt a resolution recommending that the dissolution be revoked and directing that the question of the revocation be submitted to a vote at a special meeting of stockholders;

(3) Notice of the special meeting of stockholders shall be given in accordance with § 222 of this title to each of the stockholders.

(4) At the meeting a vote of the stockholders shall be taken on a resolution to revoke the dissolution. If a majority of the stock of the corporation which was outstanding and entitled to vote upon a dissolution at the time of its dissolution shall be voted for the resolution, a certificate of revocation of dissolution shall be executed, and acknowledged in accordance with § 103 of this title, which shall state:

a. The name of the corporation;

b. The names and respective addresses of its officers;

c. The names and respective addresses of its directors;

d. That a majority of the stock of the corporation which was outstanding and entitled to vote upon a dissolution at the time of its dissolution have voted in favor of a resolution to revoke the dissolution; or, if it be the fact, that, in lieu of a meeting and vote of stockholders, the stockholders have given their written consent to the revocation in accordance with § 228 of this title.

(b) Upon the filing in the office of the Secretary of State of the certificate of revocation of dissolution, the Secretary of State, upon being satisfied that the requirements of this section have been complied with, shall issue a certificate that the dissolution has been revoked. Upon the issuance of such certificate by the Secretary of the State, the revocation of the dissolution shall become effective and the corporation may again carry on its business.

(c) Upon the issuance of the certificate by the Secretary of State to which subsection (b) of this section refers, the provisions of § 211(c) of this title shall govern, and the period of time the corporation was in dissolution shall be included within the calculation of the 30–day and 13–month periods to which § 211(c) of this title refers. An election of directors, however, may be held at the special meeting of stockholders to which subsection (a) of this section refers, and in that event, that meeting of stockholders shall be deemed an annual meeting of stockholders for purposes of § 211(c) of this title.

(d) If after the dissolution became effective any other corporation organized under the laws of this State shall have adopted the same name as the corporation, or shall have adopted a name so nearly similar thereto as not to distinguish it from the corporation, or any foreign corporation shall have qualified to do business in this State under the same name as the corporation or under a name so nearly similar thereto as not to distinguish it from the corporation, then, in such case, the corporation shall not be reinstated under the same name which it bore when its dissolution became effective, but shall adopt and be reinstated under some other name, and in such case the certificate to be filed under this section shall set forth the name borne by the corporation at the time its dissolution became effective and the new name under which the corporation is to be reinstated.

(e) Nothing in this section shall be construed to affect the jurisdiction or power of the Court of Chancery under § 279 or 280 of this title.

§ 312. Renewal, Revival, Extension and Restoration of Certificate of Incorporation [Effective Until Jan. 1, 2007]

(a) As used in this section, the term "certificate of incorporation" includes the charter of a corporation organized under any special act or any law of this State.

(b) Any corporation may, at any time before the expiration of the time limited for its existence and any corporation whose certificate of incorporation has become inoperative by law for nonpayment of taxes and any corporation whose certificate of incorporation has been forfeited pursuant to § 136(b) of this title and any corporation whose certificate of incorporation has expired by reason of failure to renew it or whose certificate of incorporation has been renewed, but, through failure to comply strictly with the provisions of this chapter, the validity of whose renewal has been brought into question, may at any time procure an extension, restoration, renewal or revival of its certificate of incorporation, together with all the rights, franchises, privileges and immunities and subject to all of its duties, debts and liabilities which had been secured or imposed by its original certificate of incorporation and all amendments thereto.

(c) The extension, restoration, renewal or revival of the certificate of incorporation may be procured by executing, acknowledging and filing a certificate in accordance with § 103 of this title.

(d) The certificate required by subsection (c) of this section shall state:

(1) The name of the corporation, which shall be the existing name of the corporation or the name it bore when its certificate of incorporation expired, except as provided in subsection (f) of this section, and the date of filing of its original certificate of incorporation with the Secretary of State;

(2) The address (which shall include the street, city and county) of the corporation's registered office in this State and the name of its registered agent at such address;

(3) Whether or not the renewal, restoration or revival is to be perpetual and if not perpetual the time for which the renewal, restoration or revival is to continue and, in case of renewal before the expiration of the time limited for its existence, the date when the renewal is to commence, which shall be prior to the date of the expiration of the old certificate of incorporation which it is desired to renew;

(4) That the corporation desiring to be renewed or revived and so renewing or reviving its certificate of incorporation was organized under the laws of this State;

(5) The date when the certificate of incorporation would expire, if such is the case, or such other facts as may show that the certificate of incorporation has been forfeited pursuant to § 136(b) of this title, or has become inoperative or void or that the validity of any renewal has been brought into question;

(6) That the certificate for renewal or revival is filed by authority of those who were directors or members of the governing body of the corporation at the time its certificate of incorporation expired or who were elected directors or members of the governing body of the corporation as provided in subsection (h) of this section.

(e) Upon the filing of the certificate in accordance with § 103 of this title the corporation shall be renewed and revived with the same force and effect as if its certificate of incorporation had not been forfeited pursuant to § 136(b) of this title, or inoperative and void, or had not expired by limitation. Such reinstatement shall validate all contracts, acts, matters and things made, done and performed within the scope of its certificate of incorporation by the corporation, its officers and agents during the time when its certificate of incorporation was forfeited pursuant to § 136(b) of this title, or was inoperative or void or after its expiration by limitation, with the same force and effect and to all intents and purposes as if the certificate of incorporation had at all times remained in full force and effect. All real and personal property, rights and credits, which belonged to the corporation at the time its certificate of incorporation became forfeited pursuant to § 136(b) of this title, or inoperative or void, or expired by limitation and which were not disposed of prior to the time of its revival or renewal shall be vested in the corporation, after its revival and renewal, as fully and amply as they were held by the corporation at and before the time its certificate of incorporation became forfeited pursuant to § 136(b) of this title, inoperative or void, or expired by limitation, and the corporation after its renewal and revival shall be as exclusively liable for all contracts, acts, matters and things made, done or performed in its name and on its behalf by its officers and agents prior to its reinstatement, as if its certificate of incorporation had at all times remained in full force and effect.

(f) If, since the certificate of incorporation become forfeited pursuant to § 136(b) of this title, or inoperative or void for nonpayment of taxes, or expired by limitation, any other corporation organized under the laws of this State shall have adopted the same name as the corporation sought to be renewed or revived or shall have adopted a name so nearly similar thereto as not to distinguish it from the corporation to be renewed or revived or any foreign corporation qualified in accordance with § 371 of this title shall have adopted the same name as the corporation sought to be renewed or revived or shall have adopted a name so nearly similar thereto as not to distinguish it from the corporation to be renewed or revived, then in such case the corporation to be renewed or revived shall not be renewed under the same name which it bore when its certificate of incorporation became forfeited pursuant to § 136(b) of this title, inoperative or void, or expired but shall adopt or be renewed under some other name and in such case the certificate to be filed under the provisions of this section shall set forth the name borne by the corporation at the time its certificate of incorporation became forfeited pursuant to § 136(b) of this title, inoperative or void, or expired and the new name under which the corporation is to be renewed or revived.

(g) Any corporation that renews or revives its certificate of incorporation under this chapter shall pay to this State a sum equal to all franchise taxes, penalties and interest thereon due at the time its certificate of incorporation became forfeited pursuant to § 136(b) of this title, inoperative and void for nonpayment of taxes, or expired by limitation or otherwise; provided, however, that any corporation that renews or revives its certificate of incorporation under this chapter whose certificate of incorporation has been forfeited, void or expired for more than 5 years shall, in lieu of the payment of the franchise taxes and penalties otherwise required by this subsection, pay a sum equal to 3 times the amount of the annual franchise tax that would be due and payable by such corporation for the year in which the renewal or revival is effected, computed at the then current rate of taxation. No payment made pursuant to this subsection shall reduce the amount of franchise tax due under Chapter 5 of this title for the year in which the renewal or revival is effected.

(h) If a sufficient number of the last acting officers of any corporation desiring to renew or revive its certificate of incorporation are not available by reason of death, unknown address or refusal or neglect to act, the directors of the corporation or those remaining on the board, even if only 1, may elect successors to such officers. In any case where there shall be no directors of the corporation available for the purposes aforesaid, the stockholders may elect a full board of directors, as provided by the bylaws of the corporation, and the board shall then elect such officers as are provided by law, by the certificate of incorporation or by the bylaws to carry on the business and affairs of the corporation. A special meeting of the stockholders for the purposes of electing directors may be called by any officer, director or stockholder upon notice given in accordance with § 222 of this title.

(i) After a renewal or revival of the certificate of incorporation of the corporation shall have been effected, the provisions of § 211(c) of this title shall govern and the period of time the certificate of incorporation of the corporation was forfeited pursuant to § 136(b) of this title, or was inoperative or void, or after its expiration by limitation, shall be included within the calculation of the 30–day and 13–month periods to which § 211(c) of this title refers. A special meeting of stockholders held in accordance with subsection (h) of this section shall be deemed an annual meeting of stockholders for purposes of § 211(c) of this title.

(j) Whenever it shall be desired to renew or revive the certificate of incorporation of any corporation organized under this chapter not for profit and having no capital stock, the governing body shall perform all the acts necessary for the renewal or revival of the charter of the corporation which are performed by the board of directors in the case of a corporation having capital stock. The members of any corporation not for profit and having no capital stock who are entitled to vote for the election of members of its governing body, shall perform all the acts necessary for the renewal or revival of the certificate of incorporation of the corporation which are performed by the stockholders in the case of a corporation having capital stock. In all other respects, the procedure for the renewal or revival of the certificate of incorporation of a corporation not for profit or having no capital stock shall conform, as nearly as may be applicable, to the procedure prescribed in this section for the renewal or revival of the certificate of incorporation of a corporation having capital stock.

§ 312. Renewal, Revival, Extension and Restoration of Certificate of Incorporation [Effective Jan. 1, 2007]

(a) As used in this section, the term "certificate of incorporation" includes the charter of a corporation organized under any special act or any law of this State.

(b) Any corporation may, at any time before the expiration of the time limited for its existence and any corporation whose certificate of incorporation has become forfeited or void pursuant to this title and any corporation whose certificate of incorporation has expired by reason of failure to renew it or whose certificate of incorporation has been renewed, but, through failure to comply strictly with the provisions of this chapter, the validity of whose renewal has been brought into question, may at any time procure an extension, restoration, renewal or revival of its certificate of incorporation, together with all the rights, franchises, privileges and immunities and subject to all of its duties, debts and liabilities which had been secured or imposed by its original certificate of incorporation and all amendments thereto.

(c) The extension, restoration, renewal or revival of the certificate of incorporation may be procured by executing, acknowledging and filing a certificate in accordance with § 103 of this title.

(d) The certificate required by subsection (c) of this section shall state:

(1) The name of the corporation, which shall be the existing name of the corporation or the name it bore when its certificate of

incorporation expired, except as provided in subsection (f) of this section, and the date of filing of its original certificate of incorporation with the Secretary of State;

(2) The address (which shall include the street, city and county) of the corporation's registered office in this State and the name of its registered agent at such address;

(3) Whether or not the renewal, restoration or revival is to be perpetual and if not perpetual the time for which the renewal, restoration or revival is to continue and, in case of renewal before the expiration of the time limited for its existence, the date when the renewal is to commence, which shall be prior to he date of the expiration of the old certificate of incorporation which it is desired to renew;

(4) That the corporation desiring to be renewed or revived and so renewing or reviving its certificate of incorporation was organized under the laws of this State;

(5) The date when the certificate of incorporation would expire, if such is the case, or such other facts as may show that the certificate of incorporation has become forfeited or void pursuant to this title, or that the validity of any renewal has been brought into question;

(6) That the certificate for renewal or revival is filed by authority of those who were directors or members of the governing body of the corporation at the time its certificate of incorporation expired or who were elected directors or members of the governing body of the corporation as provided in subsection (h) of this section.

(e) Upon the filing of the certificate in accordance with § 103 of this title the corporation shall be renewed and revived with the same force and effect as if its certificate of incorporation had not been forfeited or void pursuant to this title, or had not expired by limitation. Such reinstatement shall validate all contracts, acts, matters and things made, done and performed within the scope of its certificate of incorporation by the corporation, its officers and agents during the time when its certificate of incorporation was forfeited or void pursuant to this title, or after its expiration by limitation, with the same force and effect and to all intents and purposes as if the certificate of incorporation had at all times remained in full force and effect. All real and personal property, rights and credits, which belonged to the corporation at the time its certificate of incorporation became forfeited or void pursuant to this title, or expired by limitation and which were not disposed of prior to the time of its revival or renewal shall be vested in the corporation, after its revival and renewal, as fully and amply as they were held by the corporation at and before the time its certificate of incorporation became forfeited or void pursuant to this title, or expired by limitation, and the corporation after its renewal and revival shall be as exclusively liable for all contracts, acts, matters and things made, done or performed in its name and on its behalf by its officers and agents prior to its reinstatement, as if its certificate of incorporation had at all times remained in full force and effect.

(f) If, since the certificate of incorporation became forfeited or void pursuant to this title, or expired by limitation, any other corporation organized under the laws of this State shall have adopted the same name as the corporation sought to be renewed or revived or shall have adopted a name so nearly similar thereto as not to distinguish it from the corporation to be renewed or revived or any foreign corporation qualified in accordance with § 371 of this title shall have adopted the same name as the corporation sought to be renewed or revived or shall have adopted a name so nearly similar thereto as not to distinguish it from the corporation to be renewed or revived, then in such case the corporation to be renewed or revived shall not be renewed under the same name which it bore when its certificate of incorporation became forfeited or void pursuant to this title, or expired but shall adopt or be renewed under some other name and in such case the certificate to be filed under the provisions of this section shall set forth the name borne by the corporation at the time its certificate of incorporation became forfeited or void pursuant to this title, or expired and the new name under which the corporation is to be renewed or revived.

(g) Any corporation that renews or revives its certificate of incorporation under this chapter shall pay to this State a sum equal to all franchise taxes, penalties and interest thereon due at the time its certificate of incorporation became forfeited or void pursuant to this title, or expired by limitation or otherwise; provided, however, that any corporation that renews or revives its certificate of incorporation under this chapter whose certificate of incorporation has been forfeited, void or expired for more than 5 years shall, in lieu of the payment of the franchise taxes and penalties otherwise required by this subsection, pay a sum equal to 3 times the amount of the annual franchise tax that would be due and payable by such corporation for the year in which the renewal or revival is effected, computed at the then current rate of taxation. No payment made pursuant to this subsection shall reduce the amount of franchise tax due under Chapter 5 of this title for the year in which the renewal or revival is effected.

(h) If a sufficient number of the last acting officers of any corporation desiring to renew or revive its certificate of incorporation are not available by reason of death, unknown address or refusal or neglect to act, the directors of the corporation or those remaining on the board, even if only 1, may elect successors to such officers. In any case where there shall be no directors of the corporation available for the purposes aforesaid, the stockholders may elect a full board of directors, as provided by the bylaws of the corporation, and the board shall then elect such officers as are provided by law, by the certificate of incorporation or by the bylaws to carry on the business and affairs of the corporation. A special meeting of the stockholders for the purposes of electing directors may be called by any officer, director or stockholder upon notice given in accordance with § 222 of this title.

(i) After a renewal or revival of the certificate of incorporation of the corporation shall have been effected, the provisions of § 211(c) of this title shall govern and the period of time the certificate of incorporation of the corporation was forfeited pursuant to this title, or after its expiration by limitation, shall be included within the calculation of the 30–day and 13–month periods to which § 211(c) of this title refers. A special meeting of stockholders held in accordance with subsection (h) of this section shall be deemed an annual meeting of stockholders for purposes of § 211(c) of this title.

(j) Whenever it shall be desired to renew or revive the certificate of incorporation of any corporation organized under this chapter not for profit and having no capital stock, the governing body shall perform all the acts necessary for the renewal or revival of the charter of the corporation which are performed by the board of directors in the case of a corporation having capital stock. The members of any corporation not for profit and having no capital stock who are entitled to vote for the election of members of its governing body, shall perform all the acts necessary for the renewal or revival of the certificate of incorporation of the corporation which are performed by the stockholders in the case of a corporation having capital stock. In all other respects, the procedure for the renewal or revival of the certificate of incorporation of a corporation not for profit or having no capital stock shall conform, as nearly as may be applicable, to the procedure prescribed in this section for the renewal or revival of the certificate of incorporation of a corporation having capital stock.

§ 313. Renewal of Certificate of Incorporation or Charter of Religious, Charitable, Educational, Etc., Corporations

(a) Every religious corporation, and every purely charitable or educational association, and every company, association or society, which by its certificate of incorporation, had, at the time its certificate of incorporation or charter became void by operation of law, for its object the assistance of sick, needy or disabled members, or the defraying of funeral expenses of deceased members, or to provide for the wants of the widows and families after death of its members, whose certificate of incorporation or charter has become inoperative and void, by operation of § 510 of this title for failure to file annual franchise tax reports required, and for failure to pay taxes or penalties from which it would have been exempt if the reports had been filed, shall be deemed to have filed all the reports and be relieved of all the taxes and penalties, upon satisfactory proof submitted to the Secretary of State of its right to be classified under any of the classifications set out in this subsection, and upon filing with the Secretary of State a certificate of renewal and revival in manner and form as required by § 312 of this title.

(b) Upon the filing by the corporation of the proof of classification as required by subsection (a) of this section, the filing of the certificate of renewal and revival and payment of the required filing fees, the Secretary of State shall issue a certificate that the corporation's certificate of incorporation or charter has been renewed and revived as of the date of the certificate and the corporation shall be renewed and revived with the same force and effect as provided in § 312(e) of this title for other corporations.

(c) Nothing contained in this section relieves any corporation of any of the classifications set out in subsection (a) of this section from filing the annual report required by § 502 of this title.

§ 314. Status of Corporation

Any corporation desiring to renew, extend and continue its corporate existence, shall upon complying with applicable constitutional provisions of this State, continue for the time stated in its certificate of renewal, a corporation and shall, in addition to the rights, privileges and immunities conferred by its charter, possess and enjoy all the benefits of this chapter, which are applicable to the nature of its business, and shall be subject to the restrictions and liabilities by this chapter imposed on such corporations.

SUBCHAPTER XIII. SUITS AGAINST CORPORATIONS, DIRECTORS, OFFICERS OR STOCKHOLDERS

§ 321. Service of Process on Corporations

(a) Service of legal process upon any corporation of this State shall be made by delivering a copy personally to any officer or director of the corporation in this State, or the registered agent of the corporation in this State, or by leaving it at the dwelling house or usual place of abode in this State of any officer, director or registered agent (if the registered agent be an individual), or at the registered office or other place of business of the corporation in this State. If the registered agent be a corporation, service of process upon it as such agent may be made by serving, in this State, a copy thereof on the president, vice-president, secretary, assistant secretary or any director of the corporate registered agent. Service by copy left at the dwelling house or usual place of abode of any officer, director or registered agent, or at the registered office or other place of business of the corporation in this State, to be effective must be delivered thereat at least 6 days before the return date of the process, and in the presence of an adult person, and the officer serving the process shall distinctly state the manner of service in such person's return thereto. Process returnable forthwith must be delivered personally to the officer, director or registered agent.

(b) In case the officer whose duty it is to serve legal process cannot by due diligence serve the process in any manner provided for by subsection (a) of this section, it shall be lawful to serve the process against the corporation upon the Secretary of State, and such service shall be as effectual for all intents and purposes as if made in any of the ways provided for in subsection (a) hereof. In the event that service is effected through the Secretary of State in accordance with this subsection, the Secretary of State shall forthwith notify the corporation by letter, certified mail, return receipt requested, directed to the corporation at its principal place of business as it appears on the records relating to such corporation on file with the Secretary of State or, if no such address appears, at its last registered office. Such letter shall enclose a copy of the process and any other papers served on the Secretary of State pursuant to this subsection. It shall be the duty of the plaintiff in the event of such service to serve process and any other papers in duplicate, to notify the Secretary of State that service is being effected pursuant to this subsection, and to pay the Secretary of State the sum of $50 for the use of the State, which sum shall be taxed as part of the costs in the proceeding if the plaintiff shall prevail therein. The Secretary of State shall maintain an alphabetical record of any such service setting forth the name of the plaintiff and defendant, the title, docket number and nature of the proceeding in which process has been served upon the Secretary of State, the fact that service has been effected pursuant to this subsection, the return date thereof, and the day and hour when the service was made. The Secretary of State shall not be required to retain such information for a period longer than 5 years from receipt of the service of process.

(c) Service upon corporations may also be made in accordance with § 3111 of Title 10 or any other statute or rule of court.

§ 322. Failure of Corporation to Obey Order of Court; Appointment of Receiver

Whenever any corporation shall refuse, fail or neglect to obey any order or decree of any court of this State within the time fixed by the court for its observance, such refusal, failure or neglect shall be a sufficient ground for the appointment of a receiver of the corporation by the Court of Chancery. If the corporation be a foreign corporation, such refusal, failure or neglect shall be a sufficient ground for the appointment of a receiver of the assets of the corporation within this State.

§ 323. Failure of Corporation to Obey Writ of Mandamus; Quo Warranto Proceedings for Forfeiture of Charter

If any corporation fails to obey the mandate of any peremptory writ of mandamus issued by a court of competent jurisdiction of this State for a period of 30 days after the serving of the writ upon the corporation in any manner as provided by the laws of this State for the service of writs, any party in interest in the proceeding in which the writ of mandamus issued may file a statement of such fact prepared by such party or such party's attorney with the Attorney General of this State, and it shall thereupon be the duty of the Attorney General to forthwith commence proceedings of quo warranto against the corporation in a court of competent jurisdiction, and the court, upon competent proof of such state of facts and proper proceedings had in such proceeding in quo warranto, shall decree the charter of the corporation forfeited.

§ 324. Attachment of Shares of Stock or any Option, Right or Interest Therein; Procedure; Sale; Title Upon Sale; Proceeds

(a) The shares of any person in any corporation with all the rights thereto belonging, or any person's option to acquire the shares, or such person's right or interest in the shares, may be attached under this section for debt, or other demands, if such person appears on the books of the corporation to hold or own such shares, option, right or interest. So many of the shares, or so much of the option, right or interest therein may be sold at public sale to the highest bidder, as shall be sufficient to satisfy the debt, or other demand, interest and costs, upon an order issued therefor by the court from which the attachment process issued, and after such notice as is required for sales upon execution process. Except as to an uncertificated security as defined in § 8–102 of Title 6, the attachment is not laid and no order of sale shall issue unless § 8–112 of Title 6 has been satisfied. No order of sale shall be issued until after final judgment shall have been rendered in any case. If the debtor lives out of the county, a copy of the order shall be sent by registered or certified mail, return receipt requested, to such debtor's last known address, and shall also be published in a newspaper published in the county of such debtor's last known residence, if there be any, 10 days before the sale; and if the debtor be a nonresident of this State shall be mailed as aforesaid and published at least twice for 2 successive weeks, the last publication to be at least 10 days before the sale, in a newspaper published in the county where the attachment process issued. If the shares of stock or any of them or the option to acquire shares or any such right or interest in shares, or any part of them, be so sold, any assignment, or transfer thereof, by the debtor, after attachment, shall be void.

(b) When attachment process issues for shares of stock, or any option to acquire such or any right or interest in such, a certified copy of the process shall be left in this State with any officer or director, or with the registered agent of the corporation. Within 20 days after service of the process, the corporation shall serve upon the plaintiff a certificate of the number of shares held or owned by the debtor in the corporation, with the number or other marks distinguishing the same, or in the case the debtor appears on the books of the corporation to have an option to acquire shares of stock or any right or interest in any shares of stock of the corporation, there shall be served upon the plaintiff within 20 days after service of the process a certificate setting forth any such option, right or interest in the shares of the corporation in the language and form in which the option, right or interest appears on the books of the corporation, anything in the certificate of incorporation or bylaws of the corporation to the contrary notwithstanding. Service upon a corporate registered agent may be made in the manner provided in § 321 of this title.

(c) If, after sale made and confirmed, a certified copy of the order of sale and return and the stock certificate, if any, be left with any officer or director or with the registered agent of the corporation, the purchaser shall be thereby entitled to the shares or any option to acquire shares or any right or interest in shares so purchased, and all income, or dividends which may have been declared, or become payable thereon since the attachment laid. Such sale, returned and confirmed, shall transfer the shares or the option to acquire shares or any right or interest in shares sold to the purchaser, as fully as if the debtor, or defendant, had transferred the same to such purchaser according to the certificate of incorporation or bylaws of the corporation, anything in the certificate of incorporation or bylaws to the contrary notwithstanding. The court which issued the levy and confirmed the sale shall have the power to make an order compelling the corporation, the shares of which were sold, to issue new certificates or uncertificated shares to the purchaser at the sale and to cancel the registration of the shares attached on the books of the corporation upon the giving of an open end bond by such purchaser adequate to protect such corporation.

(d) The money arising from the sale of the shares or from the sale of the option or right or interest shall be applied and paid, by the public official receiving the same, as by law is directed as to the sale of personal property in cases of attachment.

§ 325. Actions Against Officers, Directors or Stockholders to Enforce Liability of Corporation; Unsatisfied Judgment Against Corporation

(a) When the officers, directors or stockholders of any corporation shall be liable by the provisions of this chapter to pay the debts of the corporation, or any part thereof, any person to whom they are liable may have an action, at law or in equity, against any 1 or more of them, and the complaint shall state the claim against the corporation, and the ground on which the plaintiff expects to charge the defendants personally.

(b) No suit shall be brought against any officer, director or stockholder for any debt of a corporation of which such person is an officer, director or stockholder, until judgment be obtained therefor against the corporation and execution thereon returned unsatisfied.

§ 326. Action by Officer, Director or Stockholder Against Corporation for Corporate Debt Paid

When any officer, director or stockholder shall pay any debt of a corporation for which such person is made liable by the provisions of this chapter, such person may recover the amount so paid in an action against the corporation for money paid for its use, and in such action only the property of the corporation shall be liable to be taken, and not the property of any stockholder.

§ 327. Stockholder's Derivative Action; Allegation of Stock Ownership

In any derivative suit instituted by a stockholder of a corporation, it shall be averred in the complaint that the plaintiff was a stockholder of the corporation at the time of the transaction of which such stockholder complains or that such stockholder's stock thereafter devolved upon such stockholder by operation of law.

§ 328. Effect of Liability of Corporation on Impairment of Certain Transactions

The liability of a corporation of this State, or the stockholders, directors or officers thereof, or the rights or remedies of the creditors thereof, or of persons doing or transacting business with the corporation, shall not in any way be lessened or impaired by the sale of its assets, or by the increase or decrease in the capital stock of the corporation, or by its merger or consolidation with 1 or more corporations or by any change or amendment in its certificate of incorporation.

§ 329. Defective Organization of Corporation as Defense

(a) No corporation of this State and no person sued by any such corporation shall be permitted to assert the want of legal organization as a defense to any claim.

(b) This section shall not be construed to prevent judicial inquiry into the regularity or validity of the organization of a corporation, or its lawful possession of any corporate power it may assert in any other suit or proceeding where its corporate existence or the power to exercise the corporate rights it asserts is challenged, and evidence tending to sustain the challenge shall be admissible in any such suit or proceeding.

§ 330. Usury; Pleading by Corporation

No corporation shall plead any statute against usury in any court of law or equity in any suit instituted to enforce the payment of any bond, note or other evidence of indebtedness issued or assumed by it.

SUBCHAPTER XIV. CLOSE CORPORATIONS; SPECIAL PROVISIONS

§ 341. Law Applicable to Close Corporation

(a) This subchapter applies to all close corporations, as defined in § 342 of this title. Unless a corporation elects to become a close corporation under this subchapter in the manner prescribed in this subchapter, it shall be subject in all respects to this chapter, except this subchapter.

(b) This chapter shall be applicable to all close corporations, as defined in § 342 of this title, except insofar as this subchapter otherwise provides.

§ 342. Close Corporation Defined; Contents of Certificate of Incorporation

(a) A close corporation is a corporation organized under this chapter whose certificate of incorporation contains the provisions required by § 102 of this title and, in addition, provides that:

(1) All of the corporation's issued stock of all classes, exclusive of treasury shares, shall be represented by certificates and shall be held of record by not more than a specified number of persons, not exceeding 30; and

(2) All of the issued stock of all classes shall be subject to 1 or more of the restrictions on transfer permitted by § 202 of this title; and

(3) The corporation shall make no offering of any of its stock of any class which would constitute a "public offering" within the meaning of the United States Securities Act of 1933 [15 U.S.C. § 77a et seq.] as it may be amended from time to time.

(b) The certificate of incorporation of a close corporation may set forth the qualifications of stockholders, either by specifying classes of persons who shall be entitled to be holders of record of stock of any class, or by specifying classes of persons who shall not be entitled to be holders of stock of any class or both.

(c) For purposes of determining the number of holders of record of the stock of a close corporation, stock which is held in joint or common tenancy or by the entireties shall be treated as held by 1 stockholder.

§ 343. Formation of a Close Corporation

A close corporation shall be formed in accordance with §§ 101, 102 and 103 of this title, except that:

(1) Its certificate of incorporation shall contain a heading stating the name of the corporation and that it is a close corporation; and

(2) Its certificate of incorporation shall contain the provisions required by § 342 of this title.

§ 344. Election of Existing Corporation to Become a Close Corporation

Any corporation organized under this chapter may become a close corporation under this subchapter by executing, acknowledging and filing, in accordance with § 103 of this title, a certificate of amendment of its certificate of incorporation which shall contain a statement that it elects to become a close corporation, the provisions required by § 342 of this title to appear in the certificate of incorporation of a close corporation, and a heading stating the name of the corporation and that it is a close corporation. Such amendment shall be adopted in accordance with the requirements of § 241 or 242 of this title, except that it must be approved by a vote of the holders of record of at least two thirds of the shares of each class of stock of the corporation which are outstanding.

§ 345. Limitations on Continuation of Close Corporation Status

A close corporation continues to be such and to be subject to this subchapter until:

(1) It files with the Secretary of State a certificate of amendment deleting from its certificate of incorporation the provisions required or permitted by § 342 of this title to be stated in the certificate of incorporation to qualify it as a close corporation; or

(2) Any 1 of the provisions or conditions required or permitted by § 342 of this title to be stated in a certificate of incorporation to qualify a corporation as a close corporation has in fact been breached and neither the corporation nor any of its stockholders takes the steps required by § 348 of this title to prevent such loss of status or to remedy such breach.

§ 346. Voluntary Termination of Close Corporation Status by Amendment of Certificate of Incorporation; Vote Required

(a) A corporation may voluntarily terminate its status as a close corporation and cease to be subject to this subchapter by amending its certificate of incorporation to delete therefrom the additional provisions required or permitted by § 342 of this title to be stated in the certificate of incorporation of a close corporation. Any such amendment shall be adopted and shall become effective in accordance with § 242 of this title, except that it must be approved by a vote of the holders of record of at least two-thirds of the shares of each class of stock of the corporation which are outstanding.

(b) The certificate of incorporation of a close corporation may provide that on any amendment to terminate its status as a close corporation, a vote greater than two-thirds or a vote of all shares of any class shall be required; and if the certificate of incorporation contains such a provision, that provision shall not be amended, repealed or modified by any vote less than that required to terminate the corporation's status as a close corporation.

§ 347. Issuance or Transfer of Stock of a Close Corporation in Breach of Qualifying Conditions

(a) If stock of a close corporation is issued or transferred to any person who is not entitled under any provision of the certificate of incorporation permitted by subsection (b) of § 342 of this title to be a holder of record of stock of such corporation, and if the certificate for such stock conspicuously notes the qualifications of the persons entitled to be holders of record thereof, such person is conclusively presumed to have notice of the fact of such person's ineligibility to be a stockholder.

(b) If the certificate of incorporation of a close corporation states the number of persons, not in excess of 30, who are entitled to be holders of record of its stock, and if the certificate for such stock conspicuously states such number, and if the issuance or transfer of stock to any person would cause the stock to be held by more than such number of persons, the person to whom such stock is issued or transferred is conclusively presumed to have notice of this fact.

(c) If a stock certificate of any close corporation conspicuously notes the fact of a restriction on transfer of stock of the corporation, and the restriction is one which is permitted by § 202 of this title, the transferee of the stock is conclusively presumed to have notice of the fact that such person has acquired stock in violation of the restriction, if such acquisition violates the restriction.

(d) Whenever any person to whom stock of a close corporation has been issued or transferred has, or is conclusively presumed under this section to have, notice either (1) that such person is a person not eligible to be a holder of stock of the corporation, or (2) that transfer of stock to such person would cause the stock of the corporation to be held by more than the number of persons permitted by its certificate of incorporation to hold stock of the corporation, or (3) that the transfer of stock is in violation of a restriction on transfer of stock, the corporation may, at its option, refuse to register transfer of the stock into the name of the transferee.

(e) Subsection (d) of this section shall not be applicable if the transfer of stock, even though otherwise contrary to subsection (a), (b) or (c), of this section has been consented to by all the stockholders of the close corporation, or if the close corporation has amended its certificate of incorporation in accordance with § 346 of this title.

(f) The term "transfer," as used in this section, is not limited to a transfer for value.

(g) The provisions of this section do not in any way impair any rights of a transferee regarding any right to rescind the transaction or to recover under any applicable warranty express or implied.

§ 348. Involuntary Termination of Close Corporation Status; Proceeding to Prevent Loss of Status

(a) If any event occurs as a result of which 1 or more of the provisions or conditions included in a close corporation's certificate of incorporation pursuant to § 342 of this title to qualify it as a close corporation has been breached, the corporation's status as a close corporation under this subchapter shall terminate unless:

(1) Within 30 days after the occurrence of the event, or within 30 days after the event has been discovered, whichever is later, the corporation files with the Secretary of State a certificate, executed and acknowledged in accordance with § 103 of this title, stating that a specified provision or condition included in its certificate of incorporation pursuant to § 342 of this title to qualify it as a close corporation has ceased to be applicable, and furnishes a copy of such certificate to each stockholder; and

(2) The corporation concurrently with the filing of such certificate takes such steps as are necessary to correct the situation which threatens its status as a close corporation, including, without limitation, the refusal to register the transfer of stock which has been wrongfully transferred as provided by § 347 of this title, or a proceeding under subsection (b) of this section.

(b) The Court of Chancery, upon the suit of the corporation or any stockholder, shall have jurisdiction to issue all orders necessary to prevent the corporation from losing its status as a close corporation, or to restore its status as a close corporation by enjoining or setting aside any act or threatened act on the part of the corporation or a stockholder which would be inconsistent with any of the provisions or conditions required or permitted by § 342 of this title to be stated in the certificate of incorporation of a close corporation, unless it is an act approved in accordance with § 346 of this title. The Court of Chancery may enjoin or set aside any transfer or threatened transfer of stock of a close corporation which is contrary to the terms of its certificate of incorporation or of any transfer restriction permitted by § 202 of this title, and may enjoin any public offering, as defined in § 342 of this title, or threatened public offering of stock of the close corporation.

§ 349. Corporate Option Where a Restriction on Transfer of a Security is Held Invalid

If a restriction on transfer of a security of a close corporation is held not to be authorized by § 202 of this title, the corporation shall nevertheless have an option, for a period of 30 days after the judgment setting aside the restriction becomes final, to acquire the restricted security at a price which is agreed upon by the parties, or if no agreement is reached as to price, then at the fair value as determined by the Court of Chancery. In order to determine fair value, the Court may appoint an appraiser to receive evidence and report to the Court such appraiser's findings and recommendation as to fair value.

§ 350. Agreements Restricting Discretion of Directors

A written agreement among the stockholders of a close corporation holding a majority of the outstanding stock entitled to vote, whether solely among themselves or with a party not a stockholder, is not invalid, as between the parties to the agreement, on the ground that it so relates to the conduct of the business and affairs of the corporation as to restrict or interfere with the discretion or powers of the board of directors. The effect of any such agreement shall be to relieve the directors and impose upon the stockholders who are parties to the agreement the liability for managerial acts or omissions which is imposed on directors to the extent and so long as the discretion or powers of the board in its management of corporate affairs is controlled by such agreement.

§ 351. Management by Stockholders

The certificate of incorporation of a close corporation may provide that the business of the corporation shall be managed by the stockholders of the corporation rather than by a board of directors. So long as this provision continues in effect:

(1) No meeting of stockholders need be called to elect directors;

(2) Unless the context clearly requires otherwise, the stockholders of the corporation shall be deemed to be directors for purposes of applying provisions of this chapter; and

(3) The stockholders of the corporation shall be subject to all liabilities of directors.

Such a provision may be inserted in the certificate of incorporation by amendment if all incorporators and subscribers or all holders of record of all of the outstanding stock, whether or not having voting power, authorize such a provision. An amendment to the certificate of incorporation to delete such a provision shall be adopted by a vote of the holders of a majority of all outstanding stock of the corporation, whether or not otherwise entitled to vote. If the certificate of incorporation contains a provision authorized by this section, the existence of such provision shall be noted conspicuously on the face or back of every stock certificate issued by such corporation.

§ 352. Appointment of Custodian for Close Corporation

(a) In addition to § 226 of this title respecting the appointment of a custodian for any corporation, the Court of Chancery, upon application of any stockholder, may appoint 1 or more persons to be custodians, and, if the corporation is insolvent, to be receivers, of any close corporation when:

(1) Pursuant to § 351 of this title the business and affairs of the corporation are managed by the stockholders and they are so divided that the business of the corporation is suffering or is threatened with irreparable injury and any remedy with respect to such deadlock provided in the certificate of incorporation or bylaws or in any written agreement of the stockholders has failed; or

(2) The petitioning stockholder has the right to the dissolution of the corporation under a provision of the certificate of incorporation permitted by § 355 of this title.

(b) In lieu of appointing a custodian for a close corporation under this section or § 226 of this title the Court of Chancery may appoint a provisional director, whose powers and status shall be as provided in § 353 of this title if the Court determines that it would be in the best interest of the corporation. Such appointment shall not preclude any subsequent order of the Court appointing a custodian for such corporation.

§ 353. Appointment of a Provisional Director in Certain Cases

(a) Notwithstanding any contrary provision of the certificate of incorporation or the bylaws or agreement of the stockholders, the Court of Chancery may appoint a provisional director for a close corporation if the directors are so divided respecting the management of the corporation's business and affairs that the votes required for action by the board of directors cannot be obtained with the consequence that the business and affairs of the corporation can no longer be conducted to the advantage of the stockholders generally.

(b) An application for relief under this section must be filed (1) by at least one half of the number of directors then in office, (2) by the holders of at least one third of all stock then entitled to elect directors, or, (3) if there be more than 1 class of stock then entitled to elect 1 or more directors, by the holders of two thirds of the stock of any such class; but the certificate of incorporation of a close corporation may provide that a lesser proportion of the directors or of the stockholders or of a class of stockholders may apply for relief under this section.

(c) A provisional director shall be an impartial person who is neither a stockholder nor a creditor of the corporation or of any subsidiary or affiliate of the corporation, and whose further qualifications, if any, may be determined by the Court of Chancery. A provisional director is not a receiver of the corporation and does not have the title and powers of a custodian or receiver appointed under §§ 226 and 291 of this title. A provisional director shall have all the rights and powers of a duly elected director of the corporation, including the right to notice of and to vote at meetings of directors, until such time as such person shall be removed by order of the Court of Chancery or by the holders of a majority of all shares then entitled to vote to elect directors or by the holders of two thirds of the shares of that class of voting shares which filed the application for appointment of a provisional director. A provisional director's compensation shall be determined by agreement between such person and the corporation subject to approval of the Court of Chancery, which may fix such person's compensation in the absence of agreement or in the event of disagreement between the provisional director and the corporation.

(d) Even though the requirements of subsection (b) of this section relating to the number of directors or stockholders who may petition for appointment of a provisional director are not satisfied, the Court of Chancery may nevertheless appoint a provisional director if permitted by subsection (b) of § 352 of this title.

§ 354. Operating Corporation as Partnership

No written agreement among stockholders of a close corporation, nor any provision of the certificate of incorporation or of the bylaws of the corporation, which agreement or provision relates to any phase of the affairs of such corporation, including but not limited to the management of its business or declaration and payment of dividends or other division of profits or the election of directors or officers or the employment of stockholders by the corporation or the arbitration of disputes, shall be invalid on the ground that it is an attempt by the parties to the agreement or by the stockholders of the corporation to treat the corporation as if it were a partnership or to arrange relations among the stockholders or between the stockholders and the corporation in a manner that would be appropriate only among partners.

§ 355. Stockholders' Option to Dissolve Corporation

(a) The certificate of incorporation of any close corporation may include a provision granting to any stockholder, or to the holders of any specified number or percentage of shares of any class of stock, an option to have the corporation dissolved at will or upon the occurrence of any specified event or contingency. Whenever any such option to dissolve is exercised, the stockholders exercising such option shall give written notice thereof to all other stockholders. After the expiration of 30 days following the sending of such notice, the dissolution of the corporation shall proceed as if the required number of stockholders having voting power had consented in writing to dissolution of the corporation as provided by § 228 of this title.

(b) If the certificate of incorporation as originally filed does not contain a provision authorized by subsection (a) of this section, the certificate may be amended to include such provision if adopted by the affirmative vote of the holders of all the outstanding stock, whether or not entitled to vote, unless the certificate of incorporation specifically authorizes such an amendment by a vote which shall be not less than two thirds of all the outstanding stock whether or not entitled to vote.

(c) Each stock certificate in any corporation whose certificate of incorporation authorizes dissolution as permitted by this section shall conspicuously note on the face thereof the existence of the provision. Unless noted conspicuously on the face of the stock certificate, the provision is ineffective.

§ 356. Effect of this Subchapter on Other Laws

This subchapter shall not be deemed to repeal any statute or rule of law which is or would be applicable to any corporation which is organized under this chapter but is not a close corporation.

SUBCHAPTER XV. FOREIGN CORPORATIONS

§ 371. Definition; Qualification to do Business in State; Procedure

(a) As used in this chapter, the words "foreign corporation" mean a corporation organized under the laws of any jurisdiction other than this State.

(b) No foreign corporation shall do any business in this State, through or by branch offices, agents or representatives located in this State, until it shall have paid to the Secretary of State of this State for the use of this State, $80, and shall have filed in the office of the Secretary of State:

(1) A certificate issued by an authorized officer of the jurisdiction of its incorporation evidencing its corporate existence. If such certificate is in a foreign language, a translation thereof, under oath of the translator, shall be attached thereto;

(2) A statement executed by an authorized officer of each corporation setting forth (i) the name and address of its registered agent

in this State, which agent shall be either an individual resident in this State when appointed or another corporation authorized to transact business in this State, (ii) a statement, as of a date not earlier than 6 months prior to the filing date, of the assets and liabilities of the corporation, and (iii) the business it proposes to do in this State, and a statement that it is authorized to do that business in the jurisdiction of its incorporation. The statement shall be acknowledged in accordance with § 103 of this title.

(c) The certificate of the Secretary of State, under seal of office, of the filing of the certificates required by subsection (b) of this section, shall be delivered to the registered agent upon the payment to the Secretary of State of the fee prescribed for such certificates, and the certificate shall be prima facie evidence of the right of the corporation to do business in this State; provided, that the Secretary of State shall not issue such certificate unless the name of the corporation is such as to distinguish it upon the records in the office of the Division of Corporations in the Department of State from the names that are reserved on such records and from the names on such records of each other corporation, partnership, limited partnership, limited liability company or statutory trust organized or registered as a domestic or foreign corporation, partnership, limited partnership, limited liability company or statutory trust under the laws of this State, except with the written consent of the person who has reserved such name or such other corporation, partnership, limited partnership, limited liability company or statutory trust, executed, acknowledged and filed with the Secretary of State in accordance with § 103 of this title. If the name of the foreign corporation conflicts with the name of a corporation, partnership, limited partnership, limited liability company or statutory trust organized under the laws of this State, or a name reserved for a corporation, partnership, limited partnership, limited liability company or statutory trust to be organized under the laws of this State, or a name reserved or registered as that of a foreign corporation, partnership, limited partnership, limited liability company or statutory trust under the laws of this State, the foreign corporation may qualify to do business if it adopts an assumed name which shall be used when doing business in this State as long as the assumed name is authorized for use by this section.

§ 372. Additional Requirements in Case of Change of Name, Change of Business Purpose or Merger or Consolidation

(a) Every foreign corporation admitted to do business in this State which shall change its corporate name, or enlarge, limit or otherwise change the business which it proposes to do in this State, shall, within 30 days after the time said change becomes effective, file with the Secretary of State a certificate, which shall set forth:

(1) The name of the foreign corporation as it appears on the records of the Secretary of State of this State;

(2) The jurisdiction of its incorporation;

(3) The date it was authorized to do business in this State;

(4) If the name of the foreign corporation has been changed, a statement of the name relinquished, a statement of the new name and a statement that the change of name has been effected under the laws of the jurisdiction of its incorporation and the date the change was effected;

(5) If the business it proposes to do in this State is to be enlarged, limited or otherwise changed, a statement reflecting such change and a statement that it is authorized to do in the jurisdiction of its incorporation the business which it proposes to do in this State.

(b) Whenever a foreign corporation authorized to transact business in this State shall be the survivor of a merger permitted by the laws of the state or country in which it is incorporated, it shall, within 30 days after the merger becomes effective, file a certificate, issued by the proper officer of the state or country of its incorporation, attesting to the occurrence of such event. If the merger has changed the corporate name of such foreign corporation or has enlarged, limited or otherwise changed the business it proposes to do in this State, it shall also comply with subsection (a) of this section.

(c) Whenever a foreign corporation authorized to transact business in this State ceases to exist because of a statutory merger or consolidation, it shall comply with § 381 of this title.

(d) The Secretary of State shall be paid, for the use of the State, $50 for filing and indexing each certificate required by subsection (a) or (b) of this section, and in the event of a change of name an additional $20 shall be paid for a certificate to be issued as evidence of filing the change of name.

§ 373. Exceptions to Requirements

(a) No foreign corporation shall be required to comply with §§ 371 and 372 of this title, under any of the following conditions:

(1) If it is in the mail order or a similar business, merely receiving orders by mail or otherwise in pursuance of letters, circulars, catalogs or other forms of advertising, or solicitation, accepting the orders outside this State, and filling them with goods shipped into this State;

(2) If it employs salespersons, either resident or traveling, to solicit orders in this State, either by display of samples or otherwise (whether or not maintaining sales offices in this State), all orders being subject to approval at the offices of the corporation without

this State, and all goods applicable to the orders being shipped in pursuance thereof from without this State to the vendee or to the seller or such seller's agent for delivery to the vendee, and if any samples kept within this State are for display or advertising purposes only, and no sales, repairs or replacements are made from stock on hand in this State;

(3) If it sells, by contract consummated outside this State, and agrees, by the contract, to deliver into this State, machinery, plants or equipment, the construction, erection or installation of which within this State requires the supervision of technical engineers or skilled employees performing services not generally available, and as a part of the contract of sale agrees to furnish such services, and such services only, to the vendee at the time of construction, erection or installation;

(4) If its business operations within this State, although not falling within the terms of paragraphs (1), (2) and (3) of this subsection or any of them, are nevertheless wholly interstate in character;

(5) If it is an insurance company doing business in this State;

(6) If it creates, as borrower or lender, or acquires, evidences of debt, mortgages or liens on real or personal property;

(7) If it secures or collects debts or enforces any rights in property securing the same.

(b) This section shall have no application to the question of whether any foreign corporation is subject to service of process and suit in this State under § 382 of this title or any other law of this State.

§ 374. Annual Report

On or before the 30th day of June in each year, a foreign corporation doing business in this State shall file a report with the Secretary of State. The report shall be made on behalf of the corporation by its president, secretary, treasurer or other officer duly authorized so to act, or by any 2 of its directors, or by any incorporator in the event its board of directors shall not have been elected. The fact that an individual's name is signed on a certification attached to a corporate report shall be prima facie evidence that such individual is authorized to certify the report on behalf of the corporation; however the official title or position of the individual signing the corporate report shall be designated. The report shall be on a calendar year basis and shall state the address (which shall include the street, number, city and county) of its registered office in this State; the name of its registered agent at such address upon whom service of process against the corporation may be served; the address (which shall include the street, number, city, state or foreign country) of the main or headquarters place of business of the corporation without this State; the names and addresses of all the directors and officers of the corporation and when the term of each expires; the date appointed for the next annual meeting of the stockholders for the election of directors; the number of shares of each class of its capital stock which it is authorized to issue, if any, and the par value thereof when applicable; and the number of shares of each class of the capital stock actually issued, if any; the amount of capital invested in real estate and other property in this State, and the tax paid thereon; and, if exempt from taxation in this State for any cause, the specific facts entitling the corporation to such exemption from taxation.

§ 375. Failure to File Report

Upon the failure, neglect or refusal of any foreign corporation to file an annual report as required by § 374 of this title, the Secretary of State may, in the Secretary of State's discretion, investigate the reasons therefor and shall terminate the right of the foreign corporation to do business within this State upon failure of the corporation to file an annual report within any 2–year period.

§ 376. Service of Process Upon Qualified Foreign Corporations

(a) All process issued out of any court of this State, all orders made by any court of this State, all rules and notices of any kind required to be served on any foreign corporation which has qualified to do business in this State may be served on the registered agent of the corporation designated in accordance with § 371 of this title, or, if there be no such agent, then on any officer, director or other agent of the corporation then in this State.

(b) In case the officer whose duty it is to serve legal process cannot by due diligence serve the process in any manner provided for by subsection (a) of this section, it shall be lawful to serve the process against the corporation upon the Secretary of State and such service shall be as effectual for all intents and purposes as if made in any of the ways provided for in subsection (a) of this section. In the event of service upon the Secretary of State pursuant to this subsection, the Secretary of State shall forthwith notify the corporation by letter, certified mail, return receipt requested, directed to the corporation at its principal place of business as it appears on the last annual report filed pursuant to § 374 of this title or, if no such address appears, at its last registered office. Such letter shall enclose a copy of the process and any other papers served upon the Secretary of State pursuant to this subsection. It shall be the duty of the plaintiff in the event of such service to serve process and any other papers in duplicate, to notify the Secretary of State that service is being effected pursuant to this subsection, and to pay the Secretary of State the sum of $50 for the use of the State, which sum shall be taxed as a part of the costs in the proceeding if the plaintiff shall prevail therein. The Secretary of State shall maintain an alphabetical record of any such service setting forth the name of the plaintiff and the defendant, the title, docket number and nature of the proceeding in which process has been served upon the Secretary of State, the fact that service has been effected pursuant to this subsection, the return date thereof, and the day and hour when the service was made. The Secretary of State shall not be required to retain such information for a period longer than 5 years from receipt of such service.

§ 377. Change of Registered Agent

(a) Any foreign corporation, which has qualified to do business in this State, may change its registered agent and substitute another registered agent by filing a certificate with the Secretary of State, acknowledged in accordance with § 103 of this title, setting forth: (1) The name and address of its registered agent designated in this State upon whom process directed to said corporation may be served; and (2) a revocation of all previous appointments of agent for such purposes. Such registered agent shall be either an individual residing in this State when appointed or a corporation authorized to transact business in this State.

(b) Any individual or corporation designated by a foreign corporation as its registered agent for service of process may resign by filing with the Secretary of State a signed statement that the registered agent is unwilling to continue to act as the registered agent of the corporation for service of process, including in the statement the post-office address of the main or headquarters office of the foreign corporation, but such resignation shall not become effective until 30 days after the statement is filed. The statement shall be acknowledged by the registered agent and shall contain a representation that written notice of resignation was given to the corporation at least 30 days prior to the filing of the statement by mailing or delivering such notice to the corporation at its address given in the statement.

(c) If any agent designated and certified as required by § 371 of this title shall die or remove from this State, or resign, then the foreign corporation for which the agent had been so designated and certified shall, within 10 days after the death, removal or resignation of its agent, substitute, designate and certify to the Secretary of State, the name of another registered agent for the purposes of this subchapter, and all process, orders, rules and notices mentioned in § 376 of this title may be served on or given to the substituted agent with like effect as is prescribed in that section.

§ 378. Penalties for Noncompliance

Any foreign corporation doing business of any kind in this State without first having complied with any section of this subchapter applicable to it, shall be fined not less than $200 nor more than $500 for each such offense. Any agent of any foreign corporation that shall do any business in this State for any foreign corporation before the foreign corporation has complied with any section of this subchapter applicable to it, shall be fined not less than $100 nor more than $500 for each such offense.

§ 379. Banking Powers Denied

(a) No foreign corporation shall, within the limits of this State, by any implication or construction, be deemed to possess the power of discounting bills, notes or other evidence of debt, of receiving deposits, of buying and selling bills of exchange, or of issuing bills, notes or other evidences of debt upon loan for circulation as money, anything in its charter or articles of incorporation to the contrary notwithstanding, except as otherwise provided in subchapter VII of Chapter 7 or in Chapter 14 of Title 5.

(b) All certificates issued by the Secretary of State under § 371 of this title shall expressly set forth the limitations and restrictions contained in this section.

§ 380. Foreign Corporation as Fiduciary in this State

A corporation organized and doing business under the laws of the District of Columbia or of any state of the United States other than Delaware, duly authorized by its certificate of incorporation or bylaws so to act, may be appointed by any last will and testament or other testamentary writing, probated within this State, or by a deed of trust, mortgage or other agreement, as executor, guardian, trustee or other fiduciary, and may act as such within this State, when and to the extent that the laws of the District of Columbia or of the state in which the foreign corporation is organized confer like powers upon corporations organized and doing business under the laws of this State.

§ 381. Withdrawal of Foreign Corporation From State; Procedure; Service of Process on Secretary of State

(a) Any foreign corporation which shall have qualified to do business in this State under § 371 of this title, may surrender its authority to do business in this State and may withdraw therefrom by filing with the Secretary of State:

(1) A certificate executed in accordance with § 103 of this title, stating that it surrenders its authority to transact business in the state and withdraws therefrom; and stating the address to which the Secretary of State may mail any process against the corporation that may be served upon the Secretary of State, or

(2) A copy of a certificate of dissolution issued by the proper official of the State or other jurisdiction of its incorporation, certified to be a true copy under the hand and official seal of the official,

together with a certificate, which shall be executed in accordance with paragraph (1) of this subsection, stating the address to which the Secretary of State may mail any process against the corporation that may be served upon the Secretary of State; or

(3) A copy of an order or decree of dissolution made by any court of competent jurisdiction or other competent authority of the State or other jurisdiction of its incorporation, certified to be a true copy under the hand of the clerk of the court or other official body, and the official seal of the court or official body or clerk thereof, together with a certificate executed in accordance with paragraph (1) of this subsection, stating the address to which the Secretary of State may mail any process against the corporation that may be served upon the Secretary of State.

(b) The Secretary of State shall, upon payment to the Secretary of State of the fees prescribed in § 391 of this title, issue a sufficient number of certificates, under the Secretary of State's hand and official seal, evidencing the surrender of the authority of the corporation to do business in this State and its withdrawal therefrom. One of the certificates shall be furnished to the corporation withdrawing and surrendering its right to do business in this State; 1 certificate shall be delivered to the agent of the corporation designated as such immediately prior to the withdrawal.

(c) Upon the issuance of the certificates by the Secretary of State, the appointment of the registered agent of the corporation in this State, upon whom process against the corporation may be served, shall be revoked, and the corporation shall be deemed to have consented that service of process in any action, suit or proceeding based upon any cause of action arising in this State, during the time the corporation was authorized to transact business in this State, may thereafter be made by service upon the Secretary of State.

(d) In the event of service upon the Secretary of State in accordance with subsection (c) of this section, the Secretary of State shall forthwith notify the corporation by letter, certified mail, return receipt requested, directed to the corporation at the address stated in the certificate which was filed by the corporation with the Secretary of State pursuant to subsection (a) of this section. Such letter shall enclose a copy of the process and any other papers served upon the Secretary of State. It shall be the duty of the plaintiff in the event of such service to serve process and any other papers in duplicate, to notify the Secretary of State that service is being made pursuant to this subsection, and to pay the Secretary of State the sum of $50 for the use of the State, which sum shall be taxed as part of the cost of the action, suit or proceeding if the plaintiff shall prevail therein. The Secretary of State shall maintain an alphabetical record of such service setting forth the name of the plaintiff and defendant, the title, docket number and nature of the proceeding in which the process has been served upon the Secretary of State, the fact that service has been effected pursuant to this subsection, the return date thereof, and the day and hour when the service was made. The Secretary of State shall not be required to retain such information for a period longer than 5 years from receipt of the service of process.

§ 382. Service of Process on Nonqualifying Foreign Corporations

(a) Any foreign corporation which shall transact business in this State without having qualified to do business under § 371 of this title shall be deemed to have thereby appointed and constituted the Secretary of State of this State its agent for the acceptance of legal process in any civil action, suit or proceeding against it in any state or federal court in this State arising or growing out of any business transacted by it within this State. The transaction of business in this State by such corporation shall be a signification of the agreement of such corporation that any such process when so served shall be of the same legal force and validity as if served upon an authorized officer or agent personally within this State.

(b) Section 373 of this title shall not apply in determining whether any foreign corporation is transacting business in this State within the meaning of this section; and "the transaction of business" or "business transacted in this State," by any such foreign corporation, whenever those words are used in this section, shall mean the course or practice of carrying on any business activities in this State, including, without limiting the generality of the foregoing, the solicitation of business or orders in this State. This section shall not apply to any insurance company doing business in this State.

(c) In the event of service upon the Secretary of State in accordance with subsection (a) of this section, the Secretary of State shall forthwith notify the corporation thereof by letter, certified mail, return receipt requested, directed to the corporation at the address furnished to the Secretary of State by the plaintiff in such action, suit or proceeding. Such letter shall enclose a copy of the process and any other papers served upon the Secretary of State. It shall be the duty of the plaintiff in the event of such service to serve process and any other papers in duplicate, to notify the Secretary of State that service is being made pursuant to this subsection, and to pay the Secretary of State the sum of $50 for the use of the State, which sum shall be taxed as a part of the costs in the proceeding if the plaintiff shall prevail therein. The Secretary of State shall maintain an alphabetical record of any such process setting forth the name of the plaintiff and defendant, the title, docket number and nature of the proceeding in which process has been served upon the Secretary of State, the fact that service has been effected pursuant to this subsection, the return date thereof, and the day and hour when the service was made. The Secretary of State shall not be required to retain such information for a period longer than 5 years from receipt of the service of process.

§ 383. Actions by and Against Unqualified Foreign Corporations

(a) A foreign corporation which is required to comply with §§ 371 and 372 of this title and which has done business in this State without authority shall not maintain any action or special proceeding in this State unless and until such corporation has been authorized to do business in this State and has paid to the State all fees, penalties and franchise taxes for the years or parts thereof during which it did business in this State without authority. This prohibition shall not apply to any successor in interest of such foreign corporation.

(b) The failure of a foreign corporation to obtain authority to do business in this State shall not impair the validity of any contract or act of the foreign corporation or the right of any other party to the contract to maintain any action or special proceeding thereon, and shall not prevent the foreign corporation from defending any action or special proceeding in this State.

§ 384. Foreign Corporations Doing Business Without Having Qualified; Injunctions

The Court of Chancery shall have jurisdiction to enjoin any foreign corporation, or any agent thereof, from transacting any business in this State if such corporation has failed to comply with any section of this subchapter applicable to it or if such corporation has secured a certificate of the Secretary of State under § 371 of this title on the basis of false or misleading representations. The Attorney General shall, upon the Attorney General's own motion or upon the relation of proper parties, proceed for this purpose by complaint in any county in which such corporation is doing business.

§ 385. Filing of Certain Instruments with Recorder of Deeds not Required

No instrument that is required to be filed with the Secretary of State of this State by this subchapter need be filed with the Recorder of Deeds of any county of this State in order to comply with this subchapter.

SUBCHAPTER XVI. DOMESTICATION AND TRANSFER

§ 388. Domestication of non-United States Entities

(a) As used in this section, the term:

(1) "Foreign jurisdiction" means any foreign country or other foreign jurisdiction (other than the United States, any state, the

District of Columbia, or any possession or territory of the United States); and

(2) "Non–United States entity" means a corporation, a limited liability company, a statutory trust, a business trust or association, a real estate investment trust, a common-law trust, or any other unincorporated business or entity, including a partnership (whether general (including a limited liability partnership) or limited (including a limited liability limited partnership)), formed, incorporated, created or that otherwise came into being under the laws of any foreign jurisdiction.

(b) Any non-United States entity may become domesticated as a corporation in this State by complying with subsection (h) of this section and filing with the Secretary of State:

(1) A certificate of corporate domestication which shall be executed in accordance with subsection (g) of this section and filed in accordance with § 103 of this title; and

(2) A certificate of incorporation, which shall be executed, acknowledged and filed in accordance with § 103 of this title.

(c) The certificate of corporate domestication shall certify:

(1) The date on which and jurisdiction where the non-United States entity was first formed, incorporated, created or otherwise came into being;

(2) The name of the non-United States entity immediately prior to the filing of the certificate of corporate domestication;

(3) The name of the corporation as set forth in its certificate of incorporation filed in accordance with subsection (b) of this section; and

(4) The jurisdiction that constituted the seat, siege social, or principal place of business or central administration of the non-United States entity or any other equivalent thereto under applicable law, immediately prior to the filing of the certificate of corporate domestication; and

(5) That the domestication has been approved in the manner provided for by the document, instrument, agreement or other writing, as the case may be, governing the internal affairs of the non-United States entity and the conduct of its business or by applicable non-Delaware law, as appropriate.

(d) Upon the certificate of corporate domestication and the certificate of incorporation becoming effective in accordance with § 103 of this title, the non-United States entity shall be domesticated as a corporation in this State and the corporation shall thereafter be subject to all of the provisions of this title, except that notwithstanding § 106 of this title, the existence of the corporation shall be deemed to have commenced on the date the non-United States entity commenced its existence in the jurisdiction in which the non-United States entity was first formed, incorporated, created or otherwise came into being.

(e) The domestication of any non-United States entity as a corporation in this State shall not be deemed to affect any obligations or liabilities of the non-United States entity incurred prior to its domestication as a corporation in this State, or the personal liability of any person therefor.

(f) The filing of a certificate of corporate domestication shall not affect the choice of law applicable to the non-United States entity, except that, from the effective time of the domestication, the law of the State of Delaware, including this title, shall apply to the non-United States entity to the same extent as if the non-United States entity had been incorporated as a corporation of this State on that date.

(g) The certificate of corporate domestication shall be signed by any person who is authorized to sign the certificate of corporate domestication on behalf of the non-United States entity.

(h) Prior to the filing of a certificate of corporate domestication with the Secretary of State, the domestication shall be approved in the manner provided for by the document, instrument, agreement or other writing, as the case may be, governing the internal affairs of the non-United States entity and the conduct of its business or by applicable non-Delaware law, as appropriate, and the certificate of incorporation shall be approved by the same authorization required to approve the domestication.

(i) When a non-United States entity has become domesticated as a corporation pursuant to this section, for all purposes of the laws of the State of Delaware, the corporation shall be deemed to be the same entity as the domesticating non-United States entity and the domestication shall constitute a continuation of the existence of the domesticating non-United States entity in the form of a corporation of this State. When any domestication shall have become effective under this section, for all purposes of the laws of the State of Delaware, all of the rights, privileges and powers of the non-United States entity that has been domesticated, and all property, real, personal and mixed, and all debts due to such non-United States entity, as well as all other things and causes of action belonging to such non-United States entity, shall remain vested in the corporation to which such non-United States entity has been domesticated (and also in the non-United States entity, if and for so long as the non-United States entity continues its existence in the foreign jurisdiction in which it was existing immediately prior to the domestication) and shall be the property of such corporation (and also of the non-United States entity, if and for so long as the non-United States entity continues its existence in the foreign jurisdiction in which it was existing immediately prior to the domestication), and the title to any real property vested by deed or otherwise in such non-United States entity shall not revert or be in any way impaired by reason of this title; but all rights of creditors and all liens upon any property of such non-United States entity shall be preserved unimpaired, and all debts, liabilities and duties of the non-United States entity that has been domesticated shall remain attached to the corporation to which such non-United States entity has been domesticated (and also to the non-United States entity, if and for so long as the non-United States entity continues its existence in the foreign jurisdiction in which it was existing immediately prior to the domestication), and may be enforced against it to the same extent as if said debts, liabilities and duties had originally been incurred or contracted by it in its capacity as such corporation. The rights, privileges, powers and interests in property of the non-United States entity, as well as the debts, liabilities and duties of the non-United States entity, shall not be deemed, as a consequence of the domestication, to have been transferred to the corporation to which such non-United States entity has domesticated for any purpose of the laws of the State of Delaware.

(j) Unless otherwise agreed or otherwise required under applicable non-Delaware law, the domesticating non-United States entity shall not be required to wind up its affairs or pay its liabilities and distribute its assets, and the domestication shall not be deemed to constitute a dissolution of such non-United States entity. If, following domestication, a non-United States entity that has become domesticated as a corporation of this State continues its existence in the foreign jurisdiction in which it was existing immediately prior to domestication, the corporation and such non-United States entity shall, for all purposes of the laws of the State of Delaware, constitute a single entity formed, incorporated, created or otherwise having come into being, as applicable, and existing under the laws of the State of Delaware and the laws of such foreign jurisdiction.

(k) In connection with a domestication under this section, shares of stock, rights or securities of, or interests in, the non-United States entity that is to be domesticated as a corporation of this State may be exchanged for or converted into cash, property, or shares of stock, rights or securities of such corporation or, in addition to or in lieu thereof, may be exchanged for or converted into cash, property, or shares of stock, rights or securities of, or interests in, another corporation or other entity or may be cancelled.

§ 389. Temporary Transfer of Domicile into this State

(a) As used in this section:

(1) The term "foreign jurisdiction" and the term "non-United States entity" shall have the same meanings as set forth in § 388(a) of this title.

(2) The terms "officers" and "directors" include, in addition to such persons, trustees, managers, partners and all other persons performing functions equivalent to those of officers and directors, however named or described in any relevant instrument.

(3) The term "emergency condition" shall be deemed to include but not be limited to any of the following:

a. War or other armed conflict;

b. Revolution or insurrection;

c. Invasion or occupation by foreign military forces;

d. Rioting or civil commotion of an extended nature;

e. Domination by a foreign power;

f. Expropriation, nationalization or confiscation of a material part of the assets or property of the non-United States entity;

g. Impairment of the institution of private property (including private property held abroad);

h. The taking of any action under the laws of the United States whereby persons resident in the jurisdiction, the law of which governs the internal affairs of the non-United States entity, might be treated as "enemies" or otherwise restricted under laws of the United States relating to trading with enemies of the United States;

i. The immediate threat of any of the foregoing; and

j. Such other event which, under the law of the jurisdiction governing the internal affairs of the non-United States entity, permits the non-United States entity to transfer its domicile.

(b) Any non-United States entity may, subject to and upon compliance with this section, transfer its domicile (which term, as used in this section, shall be deemed to refer in addition to the seat, siege social or principal place of business or central administration of such entity, or any other equivalent thereto under applicable law) into this State, and may perform the acts described in this section, so long as the law by which the internal affairs of such entity are governed does not expressly prohibit such transfer.

(c) Any non-United States entity that shall propose to transfer its domicile into this State shall submit to the Secretary of State for the Secretary of State's review, at least 30 days prior to the proposed transfer of domicile, the following:

(1) A copy of its certificate of incorporation and bylaws (or the equivalent thereof under applicable law), certified as true and correct by the appropriate director, officer or government official;

(2) A certificate issued by an authorized official of the jurisdiction the law of which governs the internal affairs of the non-United States entity evidencing its existence;

(3) A list indicating the person or persons who, in the event of a transfer pursuant to this section, shall be the authorized officers and directors of the non-United States entity, together with evidence of their authority to act and their respective executed agreements in writing regarding service of process as set out in subsection (j) of this section;

(4) A certificate executed by the appropriate officer or director of the non-United States entity, setting forth:

a. The name and address of its registered agent in this State;

b. A general description of the business in which it is engaged;

c. That the filing of such certificate has been duly authorized by any necessary action and does not violate the certificate of incorporation or bylaws (or equivalent thereof under applicable law) or any material agreement or instrument binding on such entity;

d. A list indicating the person or persons authorized to sign the written communications required by subsection (e) of this section;

e. An affirmance that such transfer is not expressly prohibited under the law by which the internal affairs of the non-United States entity are governed; and

f. An undertaking that any transfer of domicile into this State will take place only in the event of an emergency condition in the jurisdiction the law of which governs the internal affairs of the non-United States entity and that such transfer shall continue only so long as such emergency condition, in the judgment of the non-United States entity's management, so requires; and

(5) The examination fee prescribed under § 391 of this title.

If any of the documents referred to in paragraphs (1)-(5) of this subsection are not in English, a translation thereof, under oath of the translator, shall be attached thereto. If such documents satisfy the requirements of this section, and if the name of the non-United States entity meets the requirements of § 102(a)(1) of this title, the Secretary of State shall notify the non-United States entity that such documents have been accepted for filing, and the records of the Secretary of State shall reflect such acceptance and such notification. In addition, the Secretary of State shall enter the name of the non-United States entity on the Secretary of State's reserved list to remain there so long as the non-United States entity is in compliance with this section. No document submitted under this subsection shall be available for public inspection pursuant to Chapter 100 of Title 29 until, and unless, such entity effects a transfer of its domicile as provided in this section. The Secretary of State may waive the 30–day period and translation requirement provided for in this subsection upon request by such entity, supported by facts (including, without limitation, the existence of an emergency condition) justifying such waiver.

(d) On or before March 1 in each year, prior to the transfer of its domicile as provided for in subsection (e) of this section, during any such transfer and, in the event that it desires to continue to be subject to a transfer of domicile under this section, after its domicile has ceased to be in this State, the non-United States entity shall file a certificate executed by an appropriate officer or director of the non-United States entity, certifying that the documents submitted pursuant to this section remain in full force and effect or attaching any amendments or supplements thereto and translated as required in subsection (c) of this section, together with the filing fee prescribed under § 391 of this title. In the event that any non-United States entity fails to file the required certificate on or before March 1 in each year, all certificates and filings made pursuant to this section shall become null and void on March 2 in such year, and any proposed transfer thereafter shall be subject to all of the required submissions and the examination fee set forth in subsection (c) of this section.

(e) If the Secretary of State accepts the documents submitted pursuant to subsection (c) of this section for filing, such entity may transfer its domicile to this State at any time by means of a written communication to such effect addressed to the Secretary of State, signed by 1 of the persons named on the list filed pursuant to subparagraph d. of paragraph (4) of subsection (c) of this section, and confirming that the statements made pursuant to paragraph (4) of subsection (c) of this section remain true and correct; provided, that if emergency conditions have affected ordinary means of communication, such notification may be made by telegram, telex, telecopy or other form of writing so long as a duly signed duplicate is received by the Secretary of State within 30 days thereafter. The records of the Secretary of State shall reflect the fact of such transfer. Upon the payment to the Secretary of State of the fee prescribed under § 391 of this title, the Secretary of State shall certify that the non-United States entity has filed all documents and paid all fees required by this title. Such certificate of the Secretary of State shall be prima facie evidence of transfer by such non-United States entity of its domicile into this State.

(f) Except to the extent expressly prohibited by the laws of this State, from and after the time that a non-United States entity transfers its domicile to this State pursuant to this section, the non-United States entity shall have all of the powers which it had immediately prior to such transfer under the law of the jurisdiction governing its internal affairs and the directors and officers designated pursuant to paragraph (3) of subsection (c) of this section, and their successors, may manage the business and affairs of the non-United States entity in accordance with the laws of such jurisdiction. Any such activity conducted pursuant to this section shall not be deemed to be doing business within this State for purposes of § 371 of this title. Any reference in this section to the law of the jurisdiction governing the internal affairs of a non-United States entity which has transferred its domicile into this State shall be deemed to be a reference to such law as in effect immediately prior to the transfer of domicile.

(g) For purposes of any action in the courts of this State, no non-United States entity which has obtained the certificate of the Secretary of State referred to in subsection (e) of this section shall be deemed to be an "enemy" person or entity for any purpose, including, without limitation, in relation to any claim of title to its assets, wherever located, or to its ability to institute suit in said courts.

(h) The transfer by any non-United States entity of its domicile into this State shall not be deemed to affect any obligations or liabilities of such non-United States entity incurred prior to such transfer.

(i) The directors of any non-United States entity which has transferred its domicile into this State may withhold from any holder of equity interests in such entity any amounts payable to such holder on account of dividends or other distributions, if the directors shall determine that such holder will not have the full benefit of such payment, so long as the directors shall make provision for the retention of such withheld payment in escrow or under some similar arrangement for the benefit of such holder.

(j) All process issued out of any court of this State, all orders made by any court of this State and all rules and notices of any kind required to be served on any non-United States entity which has transferred its domicile into this State may be served on the non-United States entity pursuant to § 321 of this title in the same manner as if such entity were a corporation of this State. The directors of a non-United States entity which has transferred its domicile into this State shall agree in writing that they will be amenable to service of process by the same means as, and subject to the jurisdiction of the courts of this State to the same extent as are directors of corporations of this State, and such agreements shall be submitted to the Secretary of State for filing before the respective directors take office.

(k) Any non-United States entity which has transferred its domicile into this State may voluntarily return to the jurisdiction the law of which governs its internal affairs by filing with the Secretary of State an application to withdraw from this State. Such application shall be accompanied by a resolution of the directors of the non-United States entity authorizing such withdrawal and by a certificate of the highest diplomatic or consular official of such jurisdiction accredited to the United States indicating the consent of such jurisdiction to such withdrawal. The application shall also contain, or be accompanied by, the agreement of the non-United States entity that it may be served with process in this State in any proceeding for enforcement of any obligation of the non-United States entity arising prior to its withdrawal from this State, which agreement shall include the appointment of the Secretary of State as the agent of the non-United States entity to accept service of process in any such proceeding and shall specify the address to which a copy of process served upon the Secretary of State shall be mailed. Upon the payment of any fees and taxes owed to this State, the Secretary of State shall file the application and the non-United States entity's domicile shall, as of the time of filing, cease to be in this State.

§ 390. Transfer, Domestication or Continuance of Domestic Corporations

(a) Upon compliance with the provisions of this section, any corporation existing under the laws of this State may transfer to or domesticate or continue in any foreign jurisdiction and, in connection therewith, may elect to continue its existence as a corporation of this State. As used in this section, the term:

(1) "Foreign jurisdiction" means any foreign country, or other foreign jurisdiction (other than the United States, any state, the District of Columbia, or any possession or territory of the United States); and

(2) "Resulting entity" means the entity formed, incorporated, created or otherwise coming into being as a consequence of the transfer of the corporation to, or its domestication or continuance in, a foreign jurisdiction pursuant to this section.

(b) The board of directors of the corporation which desires to transfer to or domesticate or continue in a foreign jurisdiction shall adopt a resolution approving such transfer, domestication or continuance specifying the foreign jurisdiction to which the corporation shall be transferred or in which the corporation shall be domesticated or continued and, if applicable, that in connection with such transfer, domestication or continuance the corporation's existence as a corporation of this State is to continue and recommending the approval of such transfer or domestication or continuance by the stockholders of the corporation. Such resolution shall be submitted to the stockholders of the corporation at an annual or special meeting. Due notice of the time, place and purpose of the meeting shall be mailed to each holder of stock, whether voting or nonvoting, of the corporation at the address of the stockholder as it appears on the records of the corporation, at least 20 days prior to the date of the meeting. At the meeting, the resolution shall be considered and a vote taken for its adoption or rejection. If all outstanding shares of stock of the corporation, whether voting or nonvoting, shall be voted for the adoption of the resolution, the corporation shall file with the Secretary of State a certificate of transfer if its existence as a corporation of this State is to cease or a certificate of transfer and domestic continuance if its existence as a corporation of this State is to continue, executed in accordance with § 103 of this title, which certifies:

(1) The name of the corporation, and if it has been changed, the name under which it was originally incorporated.

(2) The date of filing of its original certificate of incorporation with the Secretary of State.

(3) The foreign jurisdiction to which the corporation shall be transferred or in which it shall be domesticated or continued and the name of the resulting entity.

(4) That the transfer, domestication or continuance of the corporation has been approved in accordance with the provisions of this section.

(5) In the case of a certificate of transfer, (i) that the existence of the corporation as a corporation of this State shall cease when the certificate of transfer becomes effective, and (ii) the agreement of the corporation that it may be served with process in this State in any proceeding for enforcement of any obligation of the corporation arising while it was a corporation of this State which shall also irrevocably appoint the Secretary of State as its agent to accept service of process in any such proceeding and specify the address to which a copy of such process shall be mailed by the Secretary of State.

(6) In the case of a certificate of transfer and domestic continuance, that the corporation will continue to exist as a corporation of this State after the certificate of transfer and domestic continuance becomes effective.

(c) Upon the filing of a certificate of transfer in accordance with subsection (b) of this section and payment to the Secretary of State of all fees prescribed under this title, the Secretary of State shall certify that the corporation has filed all documents and paid all fees required by this title, and thereupon the corporation shall cease to exist as a corporation of this State at the time the certificate of transfer becomes effective in accordance with § 103 of this title. Such certificate of the Secretary of State shall be prima facie evidence of the transfer, domestication or continuance by such corporation out of this State.

(d) The transfer, domestication or continuance of a corporation out of this State in accordance with this section and the resulting cessation of its existence as a corporation of this State pursuant to a certificate of transfer shall not be deemed to affect any obligations or liabilities of the corporation incurred prior to such transfer, domestication or continuance, the personal liability of any person incurred prior to such transfer, domestication or continuance, or the choice of law applicable to the corporation with respect to matters arising prior to such transfer, domestication or continuance. Unless otherwise agreed or otherwise provided in the certificate of incorporation, the transfer, domestication or continuance of a corporation out of the State of Delaware in accordance with this section shall not require such corporation to wind up its affairs or pay its liabilities and distribute its assets under this title and shall not be deemed to constitute a dissolution of such corporation.

(e) If a corporation files a certificate of transfer and domestic continuance, after the time the certificate of transfer and domestic continuance becomes effective, the corporation shall continue to exist as a corporation of this State, and the law of the State of Delaware, including this title, shall apply to the corporation to the same extent as prior to such time. So long as a corporation continues to exist as a corporation of the State of Delaware following the filing of a certificate of transfer and domestic continuance, the continuing corporation and the resulting entity shall, for all purposes of the laws of the State of Delaware, constitute a single entity formed, incorporated, created or otherwise having come into being, as applicable, and existing under the laws of the State of Delaware and the laws of the foreign jurisdiction.

(f) When a corporation has transferred, domesticated or continued pursuant to this section, for all purposes of the laws of the State of Delaware, the resulting entity shall be deemed to be the same entity as the transferring, domesticating or continuing corporation and shall constitute a continuation of the existence of such corporation in the form of the resulting entity. When any transfer, domestication or continuance shall have become effective under this section, for all purposes of the laws of the State of Delaware, all of the rights, privileges and powers of the corporation that has transferred, domesticated or continued, and all property, real, personal and mixed, and all debts due to such corporation, as well as all other things and causes of action belonging to such corporation, shall remain vested in the resulting entity (and also in the corporation that has transferred, domesticated or continued, if and for so long as such corporation continues its existence as a corporation of this State) and shall be the property of such resulting entity (and also of the corporation that has transferred, domesticated or continued, if and for so long as such corporation continues its existence as a corporation of this State), and the title to any real property vested by deed or otherwise in such corporation shall not revert or be in any way impaired by reason of this title; but all rights of creditors and all liens upon any property of such corporation shall be preserved unimpaired, and all debts, liabilities and duties of such corporation shall remain attached to the resulting entity (and also to the corporation that has transferred, domesticated or continued, if and for so long as such corporation continues its existence as a corporation of this State), and may be enforced against it to the same extent as if said debts, liabilities and duties had originally been incurred or contracted by it in its capacity as such resulting entity. The rights, privileges, powers and interests in property of the corporation, as well as the debts, liabilities and duties of the corporation, shall not be deemed, as a consequence of the transfer, domestication or continuance, to have been transferred to the resulting entity for any purpose of the laws of the State of Delaware.

(g) In connection with a transfer, domestication or continuance under this section, shares of stock of the transferring, domesticating or continuing corporation may be exchanged for or converted into cash, property, or shares of stock, rights or securities of, or interests in, the resulting entity or, in addition to or in lieu thereof, may be exchanged for or converted into cash, property, or shares of stock, rights or securities of, or interests in, another corporation or other entity or may be cancelled.

(h) No vote of the stockholders of a corporation shall be necessary to authorize a transfer, domestication or continuance if no shares of the stock of such corporation shall have been issued prior to the adoption by the board of directors of the resolution approving the transfer, domestication or continuance.

SUBCHAPTER XVII. MISCELLANEOUS PROVISIONS

§ 391. Taxes and Fees Payable to Secretary of State Upon Filing Certificate or Other Paper

(a) The following taxes and fees shall be collected by and paid to the Secretary of State, for the use of the State:

(1) Upon the receipt for filing of an original certificate of incorporation, the tax shall be computed on the basis of 2 cents for each share of authorized capital stock having par value up to and including 20,000 shares, 1 cent for each share in excess of 20,000 shares up to and including 200,000 shares, and two-fifths of a cent for each share in excess of 200,000 shares; 1 cent for each share of authorized capital stock without par value up to and including 20,000 shares, one-half of a cent for each share in excess of 20,000 shares up to and including 2,000,000 shares, and two-fifths of a cent for each share in excess of 2,000,000 shares. In no case shall the amount paid be less than $15. For the purpose of computing the tax on par value stock each $100 unit of the authorized capital stock shall be counted as 1 taxable share.

(2) Upon the receipt for filing of a certificate of amendment of certificate of incorporation, or a certificate of amendment of certificate of incorporation before payment of capital, or a restated certificate of incorporation, increasing the authorized capital stock of a corporation, the tax shall be an amount equal to the difference between the tax computed at the foregoing rates upon the total

authorized capital stock of the corporation including the proposed increase, and the tax computed at the foregoing rates upon the total authorized capital stock excluding the proposed increase. In no case shall the amount paid be less than $30.

(3) Upon the receipt for filing of a certificate of amendment of certificate of incorporation before payment of capital and not involving an increase of authorized capital stock, or an amendment to the certificate of incorporation not involving an increase of authorized capital stock, or a restated certificate of incorporation not involving an increase of authorized capital stock, or a certificate of retirement of stock, the tax to be paid shall be $30. For all other certificates relating to corporations, not otherwise provided for, the tax to be paid shall be $5. In case of corporations created solely for religious or charitable purposes no tax shall be paid.

(4) Upon the receipt for filing of a certificate of merger or consolidation of 2 or more corporations, the tax shall be an amount equal to the difference between the tax computed at the foregoing rates upon the total authorized capital stock of the corporation created by the merger or consolidation, and the tax so computed upon the aggregate amount of the total authorized capital stock of the constituent corporations. In no case shall the amount paid be less than $75. The foregoing tax shall be in addition to any tax or fee required under any other law of this State to be paid by any constituent entity that is not a corporation in connection with the filing of the certificate of merger or consolidation.

(5) Upon the receipt for filing of a certificate of dissolution, there shall be paid to and collected by the Secretary of State a tax of:

a. Forty dollars ($40); or

b. Ten dollars ($10) in the case of a certificate of dissolution which certifies that:

1. The corporation has no assets and has ceased transacting business; and

2. The corporation, for each year since its incorporation in this State, has been required to pay only the minimum franchise tax then prescribed by § 503 of this title; and

3. The corporation has paid all franchise taxes and fees due to or assessable by this State through the end of the year in which said certificate of dissolution is filed.

(6) Upon the receipt for filing of a certificate or other paper of surrender and withdrawal from the State by a foreign corporation, there shall be collected by and paid to the Secretary of State a tax of $10.

(7) For receiving and filing and/or indexing any certificate, affidavit, agreement or any other paper provided for by this chapter, for which no different fee is specifically prescribed, a fee of $50 in each case shall be paid to the Secretary of State. The fee in the case of a certificate of incorporation filed as required by § 102 of this title shall be $25. For entering information from each instrument into the Delaware Corporation Information System in accordance with § 103(c)(7) of this title, the fee shall be $5.

a. A certificate of dissolution which meets the criteria stated in paragraph (5)b. of this subsection shall not be subject to such fee; and

b. A certificate of incorporation filed in accordance with § 102 of this title shall be subject to a fee of $25.

(8) For receiving and filing and/or indexing the annual report of a foreign corporation doing business in this State, a fee of $60 shall be paid. In the event of neglect, refusal or failure on the part of any foreign corporation to file the annual report with the Secretary of State on or before the 30th day of June each year, the corporation shall pay a penalty of $100.

(9) For recording and indexing articles of association and other papers required by this chapter to be recorded by the Secretary of State, a fee computed on the basis of 1 cent a line shall be paid.

(10) For certifying copies of any paper on file provided by this chapter, a fee of $30 shall be paid for each copy certified. In addition, a fee of $2 per page shall be paid in each instance where the Secretary of State provides the copies of the document to be certified.

(11) For issuing any certificate of the Secretary of State other than a certification of a copy under paragraph (10) of this subsection, or a certificate that recites all of a corporation's filings with the Secretary of State, a fee of $30 shall be paid for each certificate. For issuing any certificate of the Secretary of State that recites all of a corporation's filings with the Secretary of State, a fee of $125 shall be paid for each certificate.

(12) For filing in the office of the Secretary of State any certificate of change of location or change of registered agent, as provided in § 133 of this title, there shall be collected by and paid to the Secretary of State a fee of $50, plus the same fees for receiving, filing, indexing, copying and certifying the same as are charged in the case of filing a certificate of incorporation.

(13) For filing in the office of the Secretary of State any certificate of change of address or change of name of registered agent, as provided in § 134 of this title, there shall be collected by and paid to the Secretary of State a fee of $50, plus the same fees for

receiving, filing, indexing, copying and certifying the same as are charged in the case of filing a certificate of incorporation.

(14) For filing in the office of the Secretary of State any certificate of resignation of a registered agent and appointment of a successor, as provided in § 135 of this title, there shall be collected by and paid to the Secretary of State a fee of $50 and a further fee of $2 for each corporation whose registered agent is changed by such certificate.

(15) For filing in the office of the Secretary of State, any certificate of resignation of a registered agent without appointment of a successor, as provided in §§ 136 and 377 of this title, there shall be collected by and paid to the Secretary of State a fee of $2.50 for each corporation whose registered agent has resigned by such certificate.

(16) For preparing and providing a written report of a record search, a fee of $30 shall be paid.

(17) For preclearance of any document for filing, a fee of $250 shall be paid.

(18) For receiving and filing and/or indexing an annual franchise tax report of a corporation provided for by § 502 of this title, a fee of $25 shall be paid.

(19) For receiving and filing and/or indexing by the Secretary of State of a certificate of domestication and certificate of incorporation prescribed in § 388(d) of this title, a fee of $100, plus the tax and fee payable upon the receipt for filing of an original certificate of incorporation, shall be paid.

(20) For receiving, reviewing and filing and/or indexing by the Secretary of State of the documents prescribed in § 389(c) of this title, a fee of $10,000 shall be paid.

(21) For receiving, reviewing and filing and/or indexing by the Secretary of State of the documents prescribed in § 389(d) of this title, an annual fee of $2,500 shall be paid.

(22) Except as provided in this section, the fees of the Secretary of State shall be as provided for in § 2315 of Title 29.

(23) In the case of nonstock corporations and of religious, charitable or other nonprofit corporations organized under the laws of the State, the total fees payable to the Secretary of State upon the filing of a Certificate of Change of Registered Agent and/or Registered Office shall be $5.

(24) For accepting a corporate name reservation application, an application for renewal of a corporate name reservation, or a notice of transfer or cancellation of a corporate name reservation, there shall be collected by and paid to the Secretary of State a fee of up to $75.

(25) For receiving and filing and/or indexing by the Secretary of State of a certificate of transfer or a certificate of continuance prescribed in § 390 of this title, a fee of $1,000 shall be paid.

(26) For receiving and filing and/or indexing by the Secretary of State of a certificate of conversion and certificate of incorporation prescribed in § 265 of this title, a fee of $50, plus the tax and fee payable upon the receipt for filing of an original certificate of incorporation, shall be paid.

(27) For receiving and filing and/or indexing by the Secretary of State of a certificate of conversion prescribed in § 266 of this title, a fee of $100 shall be paid.

(b)(1) For the purpose of computing the taxes prescribed in paragraphs (1), (2) and (4) of subsection (a) of this section the authorized capital stock of a corporation shall be considered to be the total number of shares which the corporation is authorized to issue, whether or not the total number of shares that may be outstanding at any one time be limited to a less number.

(2) For the purpose of computing the taxes prescribed in paragraphs (2) and (3) of subsection (a) of this section, a certificate of amendment of certificate of incorporation, or an amended certificate of incorporation before payment of capital, or a restated certificate of incorporation, shall be considered as increasing the authorized capital stock of a corporation provided it involves an increase in the number of shares, or an increase in the par value of shares, or a change of shares with par value into shares without par value, or a change of shares without par value into shares with par value, or any combination of 2 or more of the above changes, and provided further that the tax computed at the rates set forth in paragraph (1) of subsection (a) of this section upon the total authorized capital stock of the corporation including the proposed change or changes exceeds the tax so computed upon the total authorized stock of the corporation excluding such change or changes.

(c) The Secretary of State may issue photocopies or electronic image copies of instruments on file, as well as instruments, documents and other papers not on file, and for all such photocopies or electronic image copies which are not certified by the Secretary of State, a fee of $10 shall be paid for the first page and $2 for each additional page. The Secretary of State may also issue microfiche copies of instruments on file as well as instruments, documents and other papers not on file, and for each such microfiche a fee of $2 shall be paid therefor. Notwithstanding Delaware's Freedom of Information Act or other provision of this Code granting access to public records, the Secretary of State shall issue only photocopies, microfiche or electronic image copies of records in exchange for the fees described above.

(d) No fees for the use of the State shall be charged or collected from any corporation incorporated for the drainage and reclamation of lowlands or for the amendment or renewal of the charter of such corporation.

(e) The Secretary of State may in the Secretary of State's discretion permit the extension of credit for the taxes or fees required by this section upon such terms as the Secretary of State shall deem to be appropriate.

(f) The Secretary of State shall retain from the revenue collected from the taxes or fees required by this section a sum sufficient to provide at all times a fund of at least $500, but not more than $1,500, from which the Secretary of State may refund any payment made pursuant to this section to the extent that it exceeds the taxes or fees required by this section. The fund shall be deposited in the financial institution which is the legal depository of state moneys to the credit of the Secretary of State and shall be disbursable on order of the Secretary of State.

(g) The Secretary of State may in the Secretary of State's discretion charge a fee of $60 for each check received for payment of any fee or tax under Chapter 1 or Chapter 6 of this title that is returned due to insufficient funds or as the result of a stop payment order.

(h) In addition to those fees charged under subsections (a) and (c) of this section, there shall be collected by and paid to the Secretary of State the following:

(1) For all services described in subsections (a) and (c) of this section that are requested to be completed within 1 hour on the same day as the day of the request, an additional sum of up to $1,000 and for all services described in subsections (a) and (c) of this section that are requested to be completed within 2 hours on the same day as the day of the request, an additional sum of up to $200; and

(2) For all services described in subsections (a) and (c) of this section that are requested to be completed within the same day as the day of the request, an additional sum of up to $200; and

(3) For all services described in subsections (a) and (c) of this section that are requested to be completed within a 24–hour period from the time of the request, an additional sum of up to $100.

The Secretary of State shall establish (and may from time to time alter or amend) a schedule of specific fees payable pursuant to this subsection.

(i) A domestic corporation or a foreign corporation registered to do business in this State that files with the Secretary of State any instrument or certificate, and in connection therewith, neglects, refuses or fails to pay any fee or tax under Chapter 1 or Chapter 6 of this title shall, after written demand therefor by the Secretary of State by mail addressed to such domestic corporation or foreign corporation in care of its registered agent in this State, cease to be in good standing as a domestic corporation or registered as a foreign corporation in this State on the 90th day following the date of mailing of such demand, unless such fee or tax and, if applicable, the fee provided for in subsection (g) of this section are paid in full prior to the 90th day following the date of mailing of such demand. A domestic corporation that has ceased to be in good standing or a foreign corporation that has ceased to be registered by reason of the neglect, refusal or failure to pay any such fee or tax shall be restored to and have the status of a domestic corporation in good standing or a foreign corporation that is registered in this State upon the payment of the fee or tax which such domestic corporation or foreign corporation neglected, refused or failed to pay together with the fee provided for in subsection (g) of this section, if applicable. The Secretary of State shall not accept for filing any instrument authorized to be filed with the Secretary of State under this title in respect of any domestic corporation that is not in good standing or any foreign corporation that has ceased to be registered by reason of the neglect, refusal or failure to pay any such fee or tax, and shall not issue any certificate of good standing with respect to such domestic corporation or foreign corporation, unless and until such domestic corporation or foreign corporation shall have been restored to and have the status of a domestic corporation in good standing or a foreign corporation duly registered in this State.

§ 392. [Reserved]

§ 393. Rights, Liabilities and Duties Under Prior Statutes

All rights, privileges and immunities vested or accrued by and under any laws enacted prior to the adoption or amendment of this chapter, all suits pending, all rights of action conferred, and all duties, restrictions, liabilities and penalties imposed or required by and under laws enacted prior to the adoption or amendment of this chapter, shall not be impaired, diminished or affected by this chapter.

§ 394. Reserved Power of State to Amend or Repeal Chapter; Chapter Part of Corporation's Charter or Certificate of Incorporation

This chapter may be amended or repealed, at the pleasure of the General Assembly, but any amendment or repeal shall not take away or impair any remedy under this chapter against any corporation or its officers for any liability which shall have been previously incurred. This chapter and all amendments thereof shall be a part of the charter or certificate of incorporation of every corporation except so far as the same are inapplicable and inappropriate to the objects of the corporation.

§ 395. Corporations Using "Trust" in Name, Advertisements and Otherwise; Restrictions; Violations and Penalties; Exceptions

(a) Every corporation of this State using the word "trust" as part of its name, except a corporation regulated under the Bank Holding Company Act of 1956, 12 U.S.C. § 1841 et seq., or the Savings and Loan Holding Company Act, 12 U.S.C. § 1730a et seq., as those statutes shall from time to time be amended, shall be under the supervision of the State Bank Commissioner of this State and shall make not less than 2 reports during each year to the Commissioner, according to the form which shall be prescribed by the Commissioner, verified by the oaths or affirmations of the president or vice-president, and the treasurer or secretary of the corporation, and attested by the signatures of at least 3 directors.

(b) No corporation of this State shall use the word "trust" as part of its name, except a corporation reporting to and under the supervision of the State Bank Commissioner of this State or a corporation regulated under the Bank Holding Company Act of 1956, 12 U.S.C. § 1841 et seq., or the Savings and Loan Holding Company Act, 12 U.S.C. § 1730a et seq., as those statutes shall from time to time be amended. The name of any such corporation shall not be amended so as to include the word "trust" unless such corporation shall report to and be under the supervision of the Commissioner, or unless it is regulated under the Bank Holding Company Act of 1956 or the Savings and Loan Holding Company Act.

(c) No corporation of this State, except corporations reporting to and under the supervision of the State Bank Commissioner of this State or corporations regulated under the Bank Holding Company Act of 1956, 12 U.S.C. § 1841 et seq., or the Savings and Loan Holding Company Act, 12 U.S.C. § 1730a et seq., as those statutes shall from time to time be amended, shall advertise or put forth any sign as a trust company, or in any way solicit or receive deposits or transact business as a trust company, or use the word "trust" as a part of such corporation's name.

§ 396. Publication of Chapter by Secretary of State; Distribution

The Secretary of State may have printed, from time to time as the Secretary of State deems necessary, pamphlet copies of this chapter, and the Secretary of State shall dispose of the copies to persons and corporations desiring the same for a sum not exceeding the cost of printing. The money received from the sale of the copies shall be disposed of as are other fees of the office of the Secretary of State. Nothing in this section shall prevent the free distribution of single pamphlet copies of this chapter by the Secretary of State, for the printing of which provision is made from time to time by joint resolution of the General Assembly.

§ 397. Penalty for Unauthorized Publication of Chapter

Whoever prints or publishes this chapter without the authority of the Secretary of State of this State, shall be fined not more than $500 or imprisoned not more than 3 months, or both.

§ 398. Short Title

This chapter shall be known and may be identified and referred to as the "General Corporation Law of the State of Delaware."

MODEL BUSINESS CORPORATION ACT

Table of Sections

CHAPTER 1. GENERAL PROVISIONS

Subchapter A. Short Title and Reservation of Power

Subchapter B. Filing Documents

Subchapter C. Secretary of State

Subchapter D. Definitions

CHAPTER 2. INCORPORATION

CHAPTER 7. SHAREHOLDERS

Subchapter A. Meetings

Subchapter B. Voting

Subchapter C. Voting Trusts and Agreements

Subchapter D. Derivative Proceedings

CHAPTER 8. DIRECTORS AND OFFICERS

Subchapter A. Board of Directors

CHAPTER 9. DOMESTICATION AND CONVERSION

Subchapter A. Preliminary Provisions

Subchapter B. Domestication

Subchapter C. Nonprofit Conversion

Subchapter D. Foreign Nonprofit Domestication and Conversion

Subchapter E. Entity Conversion

CHAPTER 10. AMENDMENT OF ARTICLES OF INCORPORATION AND BYLAWS

Subchapter A. Amendment of Articles of Incorporation

CHAPTER 1

GENERAL PROVISIONS

Subchapter A. Short Title and Reservation of Power

§ 1.01 Short Title

This Act shall be known and may be cited as the "[name of state] Business Corporation Act."

§ 1.02 Reservation of Power to Amend or Repeal

The [name of state legislature] has power to amend or repeal all or part of this Act at any time and all domestic and foreign corporations subject to this Act are governed by the amendment or repeal.

Subchapter B. Filing Documents

§ 1.20 Requirements for Documents; Extrinsic Facts

(a) A document must satisfy the requirements of this section, and of any other section that adds to or varies these requirements, to be entitled to filing by the secretary of state.

(b) This Act must require or permit filing the document in the office of the secretary of state.

(c) The document must contain the information required by this Act. It may contain other information as well.

(d) The document must be typewritten or printed or, if electronically transmitted, it must be in a format that can be retrieved or reproduced in typewritten or printed form.

(e) The document must be in the English language. A corporate name need not be in English if written in English letters or Arabic or Roman numerals, and the certificate of existence required of foreign corporations need not be in English if accompanied by a reasonably authenticated English translation.

(f) The document must be executed:

(1) by the chairman of the board of directors of a domestic or foreign corporation, by its president, or by another of its officers;

(2) if directors have not been selected or the corporation has not been formed, by an incorporator; or

(3) if the corporation is in the hands of a receiver, trustee, or other court-appointed fiduciary, by that fiduciary.

(g) The person executing the document shall sign it and state beneath or opposite his signature his name and the capacity in which he signs. The document may but need not contain a corporate seal, attestation, acknowledgment or verification.

(h) If the secretary of state has prescribed a mandatory form for the document under section 1.21, the document must be in or on the prescribed form.

(i) The document must be delivered to the office of the secretary of state for filing. Delivery may be made by electronic transmission if and to the extent permitted by the secretary of state. If it is filed in typewritten or printed form and not transmitted electronically, the secretary of state may require one exact or conformed copy to be delivered with the document (except as provided in sections 5.03 and 15.09).

(j) When the document is delivered to the office of the secretary of state for filing, the correct filing fee, and any franchise tax, license fee, or penalty required to be paid therewith by this Act or other law must be paid or provision for payment made in a manner permitted by the secretary of state.

(k) Whenever a provision of this Act permits any of the terms of a plan or a filed document to be dependent on facts objectively ascertainable outside the plan or filed document, the following provisions apply:

(1) The manner in which the facts will operate upon the terms of the plan or filed document shall be set forth in the plan or filed document.

(2) The facts may include, but are not limited to:

(i) any of the following that is available in a nationally recognized news or information medium either in print or electronically: statistical or market indices, market prices of any security or group of securities, interest rates, currency exchange rates, or similar economic or financial data;

(ii) a determination or action by any person or body, including the corporation or any other party to a plan or filed document; or

(iii) the terms of, or actions taken under, an agreement to which the corporation is a party, or any other agreement or document.

(3) As used in this subsection:

(i) "filed document" means a document filed with the secretary of state under any provision of this Act except chapter 15 or section 16.21; and

(ii) "plan" means a plan of domestication, nonprofit conversion, entity conversion, merger or share exchange.

(4) The following provisions of a plan or filed document may not be made dependent on facts outside the plan or filed document:

(i) The name and address of any person required in a filed document.

(ii) The registered office of any entity required in a filed document.

(iii) The registered agent of any entity required in a filed document.

(iv) The number of authorized shares and designation of each class or series of shares.

(v) The effective date of a filed document.

(vi) Any required statement in a filed document of the date on which the underlying transaction was approved or the manner in which that approval was given.

(5) If a provision of a filed document is made dependent on a fact ascertainable outside of the filed document, and that fact is not

ascertainable by reference to a source described in subsection (k)(2)(i) or a document that is a matter of public record, or the affected shareholders have not received notice of the fact from the corporation, then the corporation shall file with the secretary of state articles of amendment setting forth the fact promptly after the time when the fact referred to is first ascertainable or thereafter changes. Articles of amendment under this subsection (k)(5) are deemed to be authorized by the authorization of the original filed document or plan to which they relate and may be filed by the corporation without further action by the board of directors or the shareholders.

§ 1.21 Forms

(a) The secretary of state may prescribe and furnish on request forms for: (1) an application for a certificate of existence, (2) a foreign corporation's application for a certificate of authority to transact business in this state, (3) a foreign corporation's application for a certificate of withdrawal, and (4) the annual report. If the secretary of state so requires, use of these forms is mandatory.

(b) The secretary of state may prescribe and furnish on request forms for other documents required or permitted to be filed by this Act but their use is not mandatory.

§ 1.22 Filing, Service, and Copying Fees

(a) The secretary of state shall collect the following fees when the documents described in this subsection are delivered to him for filing:

	Document	Fee
(1)	Articles of incorporation	$______.
(2)	Application for use of indistinguishable name	$______.
(3)	Application for reserved name	$______.
(4)	Notice of transfer of reserved name	$______.
(5)	Application for registered name	$______.
(6)	Application for renewal of registered name	$______.
(7)	Corporation's statement of change of registered agent or registered office or both	$______.
(8)	Agent's statement of change of registered office for each affected corporation not to exceed a total of ______	$______.
(9)	Agent's statement of resignation	No fee.
(9A)	Articles of domestication	$______.
(9B)	Articles of charter surrender	$______.
(9C)	Articles of nonprofit conversion	$______.
(9D)	Articles of domestication and conversion	$______.
(9E)	Articles of entity conversion	$______.
(10)	Amendment of articles of incorporation	$______.

	Document	Fee
(11)	Restatement of articles of incorporation with amendment of articles	$______.
(12)	Articles of merger or share exchange	$______.
(13)	Articles of dissolution	$______.
(14)	Articles of revocation of dissolution	$______.
(15)	Certificate of administrative dissolution	No fee.
(16)	Application for reinstatement following administrative dissolution	$______.
(17)	Certificate of reinstatement	No fee.
(18)	Certificate of judicial dissolution	No fee.
(19)	Application for certificate of authority	$______.
(20)	Application for amended certificate of authority	$______.
(21)	Application for certificate of withdrawal	$______.
(21A)	Application for transfer of authority	$______.
(22)	Certificate of revocation of authority to transact business	No fee.
(23)	Annual report	$______.
(24)	Articles of correction	$______.
(25)	Application for certificate of existence or authorization	$______.
(26)	Any other document required or permitted to be filed by this Act	$______.

(b) The secretary of state shall collect a fee of $______ each time process is served on him under this Act. The party to a proceeding causing service of process is entitled to recover this fee as costs if he prevails in the proceeding.

(c) The secretary of state shall collect the following fees for copying and certifying the copy of any filed document relating to a domestic or foreign corporation:

(1) $______ a page for copying; and

(2) $______ for the certificate.

§ 1.23 Effective Time and Date of Document

(a) Except as provided in subsection (b) and section 1.24(c), a document accepted for filing is effective:

(1) at the date and time of filing, as evidenced by such means as the secretary of state may use for the purpose of recording the date and time of filing; or

(2) at the time specified in the document as its effective time on the date it is filed.

(b) A document may specify a delayed effective time and date, and if it does so the document becomes effective at the time and date specified. If a delayed effective date but no time is specified, the document is effective at the close of business on that date. A delayed effective date for a document may not be later than the 90th day after the date it is filed.

§ 1.24 Correcting Filed Document

(a) A domestic or foreign corporation may correct a document filed by the secretary of state if (1) the document contains an inaccuracy, or (2) the document was defectively executed, attested, sealed, verified or acknowledged, or (3) the electronic transmission was defective.

(b) A document is corrected:

(1) by preparing articles of correction that

(i) describe the document (including its filing date) or attach a copy of it to the articles,

(ii) specify the inaccuracy or defect to be corrected, and

(iii) correct the inaccuracy or defect; and

(2) by delivering the articles to the secretary of state for filing.

(c) Articles of correction are effective on the effective date of the document they correct except as to persons relying on the uncorrected document and adversely affected by the correction. As to those persons, articles of correction are effective when filed.

§ 1.25 Filing Duty of Secretary of State

(a) If a document delivered to the office of the secretary of state for filing satisfies the requirements of section 1.20, the secretary of state shall file it.

(b) The secretary of state files a document by recording it as filed on the date and time of receipt. After filing a document, except as provided in sections 5.03 and 15.10, the secretary of state shall deliver to the domestic or foreign corporation or its representative a copy of the document with an acknowledgement of the date and time of filing.

(c) If the secretary of state refuses to file a document, he shall return it to the domestic or foreign corporation or its representative within five days after the document was delivered, together with a brief, written explanation of the reason for his refusal.

(d) The secretary of state's duty to file documents under this section is ministerial. His filing or refusing to file a document does not:

(1) affect the validity or invalidity of the document in whole or part;

(2) relate to the correctness or incorrectness of information contained in the document;

(3) create a presumption that the document is valid or invalid or that information contained in the document is correct or incorrect.

§ 1.26 Appeal From Secretary of State's Refusal to File Document

(a) If the secretary of state refuses to file a document delivered to his office for filing, the domestic or foreign corporation may appeal the refusal within 30 days after the return of the document to the [name or describe] court [of the county where the corporation's principal office (or, if none in this state, its registered office) is or will be located] [of ______ county]. The appeal is commenced by petitioning the court to compel filing the document and by attaching to the petition the document and the secretary of state's explanation of his refusal to file.

(b) The court may summarily order the secretary of state to file the document or take other action the court considers appropriate.

(c) The court's final decision may be appealed as in other civil proceedings.

§ 1.27 Evidentiary Effect of Copy of Filed Document

A certificate from the secretary of state delivered with a copy of a document filed by the secretary of state, is conclusive evidence that the original document is on file with the secretary of state.

§ 1.28 Certificate of Existence

(a) Anyone may apply to the secretary of state to furnish a certificate of existence for a domestic corporation or a certificate of authorization for a foreign corporation.

(b) A certificate of existence or authorization sets forth:

(1) the domestic corporation's corporate name or the foreign corporation's corporate name used in this state;

(2) that

(i) the domestic corporation is duly incorporated under the law of this state, the date of its incorporation, and the period of its duration if less than perpetual; or

(ii) that the foreign corporation is authorized to transact business in this state;

(3) that all fees, taxes, and penalties owed to this state have been paid, if

(i) payment is reflected in the records of the secretary of state and

(ii) nonpayment affects the existence or authorization of the domestic or foreign corporation;

(4) that its most recent annual report required by section 16.21 has been delivered to the secretary of state;

(5) that articles of dissolution have not been filed; and

(6) other facts of record in the office of the secretary of state that may be requested by the applicant.

(c) Subject to any qualification stated in the certificate, a certificate of existence or authorization issued by the secretary of state may be relied upon as conclusive evidence that the domestic or foreign corporation is in existence or is authorized to transact business in this state.

§ 1.29 Penalty for Signing False Document

(a) A person commits an offense if he signs a document he knows is false in any material respect with intent that the document be delivered to the secretary of state for filing.

(b) An offense under this section is a [_______] misdemeanor [punishable by a fine of not to exceed $_______].

Subchapter C. Secretary of State

§ 1.30 Powers

The secretary of state has the power reasonably necessary to perform the duties required of him by this Act.

Subchapter D. Definitions

§ 1.40 Act Definitions

In this Act:

(1) "Articles of incorporation" means the original articles of incorporation, all amendments thereof, and any other documents permitted or required to be filed by a domestic business corporation with the secretary of state under any provision of this Act except section 16.21. If an amendment of the articles or any other document filed under this Act restates the articles in their entirety, thenceforth the "articles" shall not include any prior documents.

(2) "Authorized shares" means the shares of all classes a domestic or foreign corporation is authorized to issue.

(3) "Conspicuous" means so written that a reasonable person against whom the writing is to operate should have noticed it. For example, printing in italics or boldface or contrasting color, or typing in capitals or underlined, is conspicuous.

(4) "Corporation," "domestic corporation" or "domestic business corporation" means a corporation for profit, which is not a foreign

corporation, incorporated under or subject to the provisions of this Act.

(5) "Deliver" or "delivery" means any method of delivery used in conventional commercial practice, including delivery by hand, mail, commercial delivery, and electronic transmission.

(6) "Distribution" means a direct or indirect transfer of money or other property (except its own shares) or incurrence of indebtedness by a corporation to or for the benefit of its shareholders in respect of any of its shares. A distribution may be in the form of a declaration or payment of a dividend; a purchase, redemption, or other acquisition of shares; a distribution of indebtedness; or otherwise.

(6A) "Domestic unincorporated entity" means an unincorporated entity whose internal affairs are governed by the laws of this state.

(7) "Effective date of notice" is defined in section 1.41.

(7A) "Electronic transmission" or "electronically transmitted" means any process of communication not directly involving the physical transfer of paper that is suitable for the retention, retrieval, and reproduction of information by the recipient.

(7B) "Eligible entity" means a domestic or foreign unincorporated entity or a domestic or foreign nonprofit corporation.

(7C) "Eligible interests" means interests or memberships.

(8) "Employee" includes an officer but not a director. A director may accept duties that make him also an employee.

(9) "Entity" includes domestic and foreign business corporation; domestic and foreign nonprofit corporation; estate; trust; domestic and foreign unincorporated entity; and state, United States, and foreign government.

(9A) The phrase "facts objectively ascertainable" outside of a filed document or plan is defined in section 1.20(k).

(9B) "Filing entity" means an unincorporated entity that is of a type that is created by filing a public organic document.

(10) "Foreign corporation" means a corporation incorporated under a law other than the law of this state; which would be a business corporation if incorporated under the laws of this state.

(10A) "Foreign nonprofit corporation" means a corporation incorporated under a law other than the law of this state, which would be a nonprofit corporation if incorporated under the laws of this state.

(10B) "Foreign unincorporated entity" means an unincorporated entity whose internal affairs are governed by an organic law of a jurisdiction other than this state.

(11) "Governmental subdivision" includes authority, county, district, and municipality.

(12) "Includes" denotes a partial definition.

(13) "Individual" means a natural person.

(13A) "Interest" means either or both of the following rights under the organic law of an unincorporated entity:

(i) the right to receive distributions from the entity either in the ordinary course or upon liquidation; or

(ii) the right to receive notice or vote on issues involving its internal affairs, other than as an agent, assignee, proxy or person responsible for managing its business and affairs.

(13B) "Interest holder" means a person who holds of record an interest.

(14) "Means" denotes an exhaustive definition.

(14A) "Membership" means the rights of a member in a domestic or foreign nonprofit corporation.

(14B) "Nonfiling entity" means an unincorporated entity that is of a type that is not created by filing a public organic document.

(14C) "Nonprofit corporation" or "domestic nonprofit corporation" means a corporation incorporated under the laws of this state and subject to the provisions of the [*Model Nonprofit Corporation Act*].

(15) "Notice" is defined in section 1.41.

(15A) "Organic document" means a public organic document or a private organic document.

(15B) "Organic law" means the statute governing the internal affairs of a domestic or foreign business or nonprofit corporation or unincorporated entity.

(15C) "Owner liability" means personal liability for a debt, obligation or liability of a domestic or foreign business or nonprofit corporation or unincorporated entity that is imposed on a person:

(i) solely by reason of the person's status as a shareholder, member or interest holder; or

(ii) by the articles of incorporation, bylaws or an organic document under a provision of the organic law of an entity authorizing the articles of incorporation, bylaws or an organic document to make one or more specified shareholders, members or interest holders liable in their capacity as shareholders, members or interest holders for all or specified debts, obligations or liabilities of the entity.

(16) "Person" includes an individual and an entity.

(17) "Principal office" means the office (in or out of this state) so designated in the annual report where the principal executive offices of a domestic or foreign corporation are located.

(17A) "Private organic document" means any document (other than the public organic document, if any) that determines the internal governance of an unincorporated entity. Where a private organic document has been amended or restated, the term means the private organic document as last amended or restated.

(17B) "Public organic document" means the document, if any, that is filed of public record to create an unincorporated entity. Where a public organic document has been amended or restated, the term means the public organic document as last amended or restated.

(18) "Proceeding" includes civil suit and criminal, administrative, and investigatory action.

(18A) "Public corporation" means a corporation that has shares listed on a national securities exchange or regularly traded in a market maintained by one or more members of a national securities association.

(18B) "Qualified director" is defined in section 1.43.

(19) "Record date" means the date established under chapter 6 or 7 on which a corporation determines the identity of its shareholders and their shareholdings for purposes of this Act. The determinations shall be made as of the close of business on the record date unless another time for doing so is specified when the record date is fixed.

(20) "Secretary" means the corporate officer to whom the board of directors has delegated responsibility under section 8.40(c) for custody of the minutes of the meetings of the board of directors and of the shareholders and for authenticating records of the corporation.

(21) "Shareholder" means the person in whose name shares are registered in the records of a corporation or the beneficial owner of shares to the extent of the rights granted by a nominee certificate on file with a corporation.

(22) "Shares" means the units into which the proprietary interests in a corporation are divided.

(22A) "Sign" or "signature" includes any manual, facsimile, conformed or electronic signature.

(23) "State," when referring to a part of the United States, includes a state and commonwealth (and their agencies and governmental subdivisions) and a territory and insular possession (and their agencies and governmental subdivisions) of the United States.

(24) "Subscriber" means a person who subscribes for shares in a corporation, whether before or after incorporation.

(24A) "Unincorporated entity" means an organization or artificial legal person that either has a separate legal existence or has the power to acquire an estate in real property in its own name and that is not any of the following: a domestic or foreign business or nonprofit corporation, an estate, a trust, a state, the United States, or a foreign government. The term includes a general partnership, limited liability company, limited partnership, business trust, joint stock association and unincorporated nonprofit association.

(25) "United States" includes district, authority, bureau, commission, department, and any other agency of the United States.

(26) "Voting group" means all shares of one or more classes or series that under the articles of incorporation or this Act are entitled to vote and be counted together collectively on a matter at a meeting of shareholders. All shares entitled by the articles of incorporation or this Act to vote generally on the matter are for that purpose a single voting group.

(27) "Voting power" means the current power to vote in the election of directors.

§ 1.41 Notice

(a) Notice under this Act must be in writing unless oral notice is reasonable under the circumstances. Notice by electronic transmission is written notice.

(b) Notice may be communicated in person; by mail or other method of delivery; or by telephone, voice mail or other electronic means. If these forms of personal notice are impracticable, notice may be communicated by a newspaper of general circulation in the area where published, or by radio, television, or other form of public broadcast communication.

(c) Written notice by a domestic or foreign corporation to its shareholder, if in a comprehensible form, is effective (i) upon deposit in the United States mail, if mailed postpaid and correctly addressed to the shareholder's address shown in the corporation's current record of shareholders, or (ii) when electronically transmitted to the shareholder in a manner authorized by the shareholder.

(d) Written notice to a domestic or foreign corporation (authorized to transact business in this state) may be addressed to its registered agent at its registered office or to the corporation or its secretary at its principal office shown in its most recent annual report or, in the case of a foreign corporation that has not yet delivered an annual report, in its application for a certificate of authority.

(e) Except as provided in subsection (c), written notice, if in a comprehensible form, is effective at the earliest of the following:

(1) when received;

(2) five days after its deposit in the United States Mail, if mailed postpaid and correctly addressed;

(3) on the date shown on the return receipt, if sent by registered or certified mail, return receipt requested, and the receipt is signed by or on behalf of the addressee.

(f) Oral notice is effective when communicated, if communicated in a comprehensible manner.

(g) If this Act prescribes notice requirements for particular circumstances, those requirements govern. If articles of incorporation or bylaws prescribe notice requirements, not inconsistent with this section or other provisions of this Act, those requirements govern.

§ 1.42 Number of Shareholders

(a) For purposes of this Act, the following identified as a shareholder in a corporation's current record of shareholders constitutes one shareholder:

(1) three or fewer co-owners;

(2) a corporation, partnership, trust, estate, or other entity;

(3) the trustees, guardians, custodians, or other fiduciaries of a single trust, estate, or account.

(b) For purposes of this Act, shareholdings registered in substantially similar names constitute one shareholder if it is reasonable to believe that the names represent the same person.

§ 1.43 Qualified Director

(a) A "qualified director" is a director who, at the time action is to be taken under:

(1) section 7.44, does not have (i) a material interest in the outcome of the proceeding, or (ii) a material relationship with a person who has such an interest;

(2) section 8.53 or 8.55, (i) is not a party to the proceeding, (ii) is not a director as to whom a transaction is a director's conflicting interest transaction or who sought a disclaimer of the corporation's interest in a business opportunity under section 8.70, which transaction or disclaimer is challenged in the proceeding, and (iii) does not have a material relationship with a director described in either clause (i) or clause (ii) of this subsection (a)(2);

(3) section 8.62, is not a director (i) as to whom the transaction is a director's conflicting interest transaction, or (ii) who has a material relationship with another director as to whom the transaction is a director's conflicting interest transaction; or

(4) section 8.70, would be a qualified director under subsection (a)(3) if the business opportunity were a director's conflicting interest transaction.

(b) For purposes of this section,

(1) "material relationship" means a familial, financial, professional, employment or other relationship that would reasonably be

expected to impair the objectivity of the director's judgment when participating in the action to be taken; and

(2) "material interest" means an actual or potential benefit or detriment (other than one which would devolve on the corporation or the shareholders generally) that would reasonably be expected to impair the objectivity of the director's judgment when participating in the action to be taken.

(c) The presence of one or more of the following circumstances shall not automatically prevent a director from being a qualified director:

(1) nomination or election of the director to the current board by any director who is not a qualified director with respect to the matter (or by any person that has a material relationship with that director), acting alone or participating with others;

(2) service as a director of another corporation of which a director who is not a qualified director with respect to the matter (or any individual who has a material relationship with that director), is or was also a director; or

(3) with respect to action to be taken under section 7.44, status as a named defendant, as a director against whom action is demanded, or as a director who approved the conduct being challenged.

CHAPTER 2

INCORPORATION

§ 2.01 Incorporators

One or more persons may act as the incorporator or incorporators of a corporation by delivering articles of incorporation to the secretary of state for filing.

§ 2.02 Articles of Incorporation

(a) The articles of incorporation must set forth:

(1) a corporate name for the corporation that satisfies the requirements of section 4.01;

(2) the number of shares the corporation is authorized to issue;

(3) the street address of the corporation's initial registered office and the name of its initial registered agent at that office; and

(4) the name and address of each incorporator.

(b) The articles of incorporation may set forth:

(1) the names and addresses of the individuals who are to serve as the initial directors;

(2) provisions not inconsistent with law regarding:

(i) the purpose or purposes for which the corporation is organized;

(ii) managing the business and regulating the affairs of the corporation;

(iii) defining, limiting, and regulating the powers of the corporation, its board of directors, and shareholders;

(iv) a par value for authorized shares or classes of shares;

(v) the imposition of personal liability on shareholders for the debts of the corporation to a specified extent and upon specified conditions;

(3) any provision that under this Act is required or permitted to be set forth in the bylaws;

(4) a provision eliminating or limiting the liability of a director to the corporation or its shareholders for money damages for any action taken, or any failure to take any action, as a director, except liability for (A) the amount of a financial benefit received by a director to which he is not entitled; (B) an intentional infliction of harm on the corporation or the shareholders; (C) a violation of section 8.33; or (D) an intentional violation of criminal law; and

(5) a provision permitting or making obligatory indemnification of a director for liability (as defined in section 8.50(5)) to any person for any action taken, or any failure to take any action, as a director, except liability for (A) receipt of a financial benefit to which he is not entitled, (B) an intentional infliction of harm on the corporation or its shareholders, (C) a violation of section 8.33, or (D) an intentional violation of criminal law.

(c) The articles of incorporation need not set forth any of the corporate powers enumerated in this Act.

(d) Provisions of the articles of incorporation may be made dependent upon facts objectively ascertainable outside the articles of incorporation in accordance with section 1.20(k).

OFFICIAL COMMENT

1. Introduction

Section 2.02(a) sets forth the minimum mandatory requirements for all articles of incorporation while section 2.02(b) describes optional provisions that may be included. A corporation that is formed solely pursuant to the mandatory requirements will generally have the broadest powers and least restrictions on activities permitted by the Model Act. The Model Act thus permits the creation of a "standard" corporation by a simple and easily prepared one-page document.

No reference is made in section 2.02(a) either to the period of duration of the corporation or to its purposes. A corporation formed under these provisions will automatically have perpetual duration under section 3.02(1) unless a special provision is included providing a shorter period. Similarly, a corporation formed without reference to a purpose clause will automatically have the purpose of engaging in any lawful business under section 3.01(a). The option of providing a narrower purpose clause is also preserved in sections 2.02(b)(2) and 3.01, with the effect described in the Official Comment to section 3.01.

. . . .

3. Optional Provisions

Section 2.02(b) describes specific options that may be elected by the draftsman and contains general authorization to include other provisions relevant to the authority of the corporation, its officers and board of directors, or to the management of the corporation's internal affairs. These provisions include:

. . . .

e. Shareholder liability

The basic tenet of modern corporation law is that shareholders are not liable for the corporation's debts by reason of their status as shareholders. Section 2.02(b)(2)(v) nevertheless permits a corporation to impose that liability under specified circumstances if that is desirable. If no provision of this type is included shareholders have no liability for corporate debts except to the extent they become liable by reason of their own conduct or acts. See section 6.22(b).

. . . .

i. Director liability

Section 2.02(b)(4) authorizes the inclusion of a provision in the articles of incorporation eliminating or limiting, with certain exceptions, the liability of the directors to the corporation or its shareholders for money damages. This grant of authority to the shareholders is consistent with the more general authorization of section 2.02(b)(2) for the articles to include a wide range of provisions regulating various matters affecting the corporation, including allocating power between the directors and the shareholders. Developments in the mid-and late 1980s highlighted the need to permit reasonable protection of directors from exposure to personal liability, in addition to indemnification, so that directors would not be discouraged from fully and freely carrying out their duties, including responsible entrepreneurial risk-taking. These developments included increased costs and reduced availability of director and officer liability insurance, the decision of the Delaware Supreme Court in *Smith v. Van Gorkom*, 488 A.2d 858 (1985), and the resulting reluctance of qualified individuals to serve as directors.

So long as any such liability-limitation provision does not extend to liability to third parties, shareholders should be permitted—except when important societal values are at stake—to decide how to allocate the economic risk of the directors' conduct between the corporation and the directors. Shareholders of one corporation may view the issue substantially differently than shareholders of another corporation. Accordingly, section 2.02(b)(4) is optional rather than self-executing. In addition, it follows the path of virtually all the states that have adopted charter option statutes and is applicable only to money damages and not to equitable relief. Likewise, nothing in section 2.02(b)(4) in any way affects the right of the shareholders to remove directors, under section 8.08(a), with or without cause.

The language "any action taken, or any failure to take any action, as a director" parallels section 8.30(d). It is recognized that in the case of individuals who are both directors and officers it will often not be clear in which capacity the individual is acting. The phrase "as a director" emphasizes that section 2.02(b)(4) applies to a director's actions or failures to take action in his capacity as a director and not in any other capacity, such as officer, employee, or controlling shareholder. However, it is not intended to exclude coverage of conduct by individuals, even though they are officers, when they are acting in their capacity as directors.

Because adoption of a liability-limitation provision is left to the decision of the shareholders, they are given considerable latitude in the extent to which they are permitted to limit directors' liability. Accordingly, the exceptions to the statute are few and narrow. As important as validating the shareholders' right to determine for themselves the extent of the directors' liability is stating the limits of this right in terms promoting a clear understanding of the conduct which is and which is not included in the limitation of liability. Terms such as "duty of loyalty," "good faith," "bad faith," and "recklessness" seem no more precise than (and therefore as potentially expansive as) "gross negligence." All of these formulations are characterizations of conduct rather than definitions of it. Characterizations by nature tend to be more elastic than definitions.

Directors should be afforded reasonable predictability; they are entitled to know whether a contemplated course of action will result in personal liability for money damages. Limits on their exculpation from liability are appropriate but should be expressed in terms that minimize the opportunity for after-the-fact second-guessing.

The language of the exceptions to section 2.02(b)(4) is intended to express the parameters of the shareholders' right to limit the directors' liability in terms that will promote predictability. First, some types of improper conduct are so clearly without any societal benefit that the law should not appear to endorse such conduct, especially in the case of a state-created entity such as a corporation. Second, any liability limitation will be prospective and, therefore, by definition, the shareholders will not be able to know in advance the exact nature or extent of any claims that they may be giving up. Third, the public has an interest in encouraging good corporate governance. While the exceptions to the shareholders' right to limit liability are few and narrow, they validate important standards of conduct. Finally, in many cases, there will be shareholders who do not vote in favor of the liability limitation. For these shareholders, there should be an irreducible core of protection, especially in view of the fact that in some cases the votes of the directors themselves as shareholders may be sufficient to approve adoption of the provision.

Financial Benefit

Permitting limitation of the liability of a director for receipt of a financial benefit to which the director is not entitled would validate conduct in which the director could realize a personal gain. Corporate law has long subjected transactions from which a director could benefit personally to special scrutiny. The exception is limited, however, to the amount of the benefit actually received. Thus, liability for punitive damages could be eliminated. However, punitive damages are not eliminated in either the exception for infliction of harm or for violation of criminal law and, thus, in a particular case (for example, theft), punitive damages may be available. The benefit must be financial rather than in less easily measurable and more conjectural forms, such as business goodwill, personal reputation, or social ingratiation. The phrase "received by a director" is not intended to be a "bright line." As a director's conduct moves toward the edge of what may be exculpated, he should bear the risk of miscalculation. Depending upon the circumstances, a director may be deemed to have received a benefit that he caused to be directed to another person, for example, a relative, friend, or affiliate.

What constitutes a financial benefit "to which [the director] is not entitled" is left to judicial development. For example, a director is clearly entitled to reasonable compensation for the performance of services or to an increase in the value of stock or stock options held by him; just as clearly, a director is not entitled to a bribe, a kick-back, or the profits from a corporate opportunity improperly taken by the director.

Intentional Infliction of Harm

There may be situations in which a director intentionally causes harm to the corporation even though he does not receive any improper benefit. The use of the word "intentional," rather than a less precise term such as "knowing," is meant to refer to the specific intent to perform, or fail to perform, the acts with actual knowledge that the director's action, or failure to act, will cause harm, rather than a general intent to perform the acts which cause the harm. No public policy should permit the shareholders to eliminate or limit the liability of directors for conduct intended to cause harm to the corporation.

Unlawful Distributions

Section 8.33(a) indicates a strong policy in favor of liability for unlawful distributions approved by directors who have not complied with the standards of conduct of section 8.30. Many states have similar provisions, which originated, along with other legal capital statutes, out of a concern for creditors. Accordingly, the exception prohibits the shareholders from eliminating or limiting the liability of directors for a violation of section 8.33.

Intentional Violation of Criminal Law

Historically, the criminal law has represented society's statement of the conduct that it most emphatically rejects. Accordingly, even though a director committing a crime may intend to benefit the corporation, the shareholders should not be permitted to exculpate him for any harm caused by his crime, including, for example, fines and legal expenses of the corporation in defending a criminal prosecution. The use of the word "intentional," rather than a less precise term such as "knowing," is meant to refer to the specific intent to perform, or fail to perform, the acts with actual knowledge that the director's action, or failure to act, constitutes a violation of criminal law.

In order to recover for conduct included within any of the exceptions, the plaintiff will continue to be required to establish causation, damages, and other elements imposed by applicable law.

An amendment authorized by section 2.02(b)(4) will become effective in the manner provided by section 1.23 generally for amendments to the articles of incorporation. In addition, in accordance with section 10.09, an amendment under section 2.02(b)(4) will not affect a cause of action existing in favor of the corporation against any directors at the effective time of the amendment.

j. Indemnification

Section 2.02(b)(5) permits a corporation to include in its articles of incorporation a provision authorizing permissible or mandatory indemnification of a director in accordance with section 8.51(a)(2). Section 2.02(b)(5) specifically excepts liability arising out of improper financial benefit received by a director, an intentional infliction of harm on the corporation or the shareholders, an unlawful distribution or an intentional violation of criminal law. These excepted liabilities parallel those a corporation is not permitted to limit or eliminate under section 2.02(b)(4). See "Director liability," above. Officers are not included in the language of section 2.02(b)(5) because, as provided in section 8.56, mandatory indemnification of officers does not require a provision in the articles of incorporation.

. . . .

§ 2.03 Incorporation

(a) Unless a delayed effective date is specified, the corporate existence begins when the articles of incorporation are filed.

(b) The secretary of state's filing of the articles of incorporation is conclusive proof that the incorporators satisfied all conditions precedent to incorporation except in a proceeding by the state to cancel or revoke the incorporation or involuntarily dissolve the corporation.

§ 2.04 Liability for Preincorporation Transactions

All persons purporting to act as or on behalf of a corporation, knowing there was no incorporation under this Act, are jointly and severally liable for all liabilities created while so acting.

§ 2.05 Organization of Corporation

(a) After incorporation:

(1) if initial directors are named in the articles of incorporation, the initial directors shall hold an organizational meeting, at the call of a majority of the directors, to complete the organization of the corporation by appointing officers, adopting bylaws, and carrying on any other business brought before the meeting;

(2) if initial directors are not named in the articles, the incorporator or incorporators shall hold an organizational meeting at the call of a majority of the incorporators:

(i) to elect directors and complete the organization of the corporation; or

(ii) to elect a board of directors who shall complete the organization of the corporation.

(b) Action required or permitted by this Act to be taken by incorporators at an organizational meeting may be taken without a meeting if the action taken is evidenced by one or more written consents describing the action taken and signed by each incorporator.

(c) An organizational meeting may be held in or out of this state.

§ 2.06 Bylaws

(a) The incorporators or board of directors of a corporation shall adopt initial bylaws for the corporation.

(b) The bylaws of a corporation may contain any provision for managing the business and regulating the affairs of the corporation that is not inconsistent with law or the articles of incorporation.

§ 2.07 Emergency Bylaws

(a) Unless the articles of incorporation provide otherwise, the board of directors of a corporation may adopt bylaws to be effective only in an emergency defined in subsection (d). The emergency bylaws, which are subject to amendment or repeal by the shareholders, may make all provisions necessary for managing the corporation during the emergency, including:

(1) procedures for calling a meeting of the board of directors;

(2) quorum requirements for the meeting; and

(3) designation of additional or substitute directors.

(b) All provisions of the regular bylaws consistent with the emergency bylaws remain effective during the emergency. The emergency bylaws are not effective after the emergency ends.

(c) Corporate action taken in good faith in accordance with the emergency bylaws:

(1) binds the corporation; and

(2) may not be used to impose liability on a corporate director, officer, employee, or agent.

(d) An emergency exists for purposes of this section if a quorum of the corporation's directors cannot readily be assembled because of some catastrophic event.

CHAPTER 3

PURPOSES AND POWERS

§ 3.01 Purposes

(a) Every corporation incorporated under this Act has the purpose of engaging in any lawful business unless a more limited purpose is set forth in the articles of incorporation.

(b) A corporation engaging in a business that is subject to regulation under another statute of this state may incorporate under this Act only if permitted by, and subject to all limitations of, the other statute.

§ 3.02 General Powers

Unless its articles of incorporation provide otherwise, every corporation has perpetual duration and succession in its corporate name and has the same powers as an individual to do all things necessary or convenient to carry out its business and affairs, including without limitation power:

(1) to sue and be sued, complain and defend in its corporate name;

(2) to have a corporate seal, which may be altered at will, and to use it, or a facsimile of it, by impressing or affixing it or in any other manner reproducing it;

(3) to make and amend bylaws, not inconsistent with its articles of incorporation or with the laws of this state, for managing the business and regulating the affairs of the corporation;

(4) to purchase, receive, lease, or otherwise acquire, and own, hold, improve, use, and otherwise deal with, real or personal property, or any legal or equitable interest in property, wherever located;

(5) to sell, convey, mortgage, pledge, lease, exchange, and otherwise dispose of all or any part of its property;

(6) to purchase, receive, subscribe for, or otherwise acquire; own, hold, vote, use, sell, mortgage, lend, pledge, or otherwise dispose of; and deal in and with shares or other interests in, or obligations of, any other entity;

(7) to make contracts and guarantees, incur liabilities, borrow money, issue its notes, bonds, and other obligations (which may be convertible into or include the option to purchase other securities of the corporation), and secure any of its obligations by mortgage or pledge of any of its property, franchises, or income;

(8) to lend money, invest and reinvest its funds, and receive and hold real and personal property as security for repayment;

(9) to be a promoter, partner, member, associate, or manager of any partnership, joint venture, trust, or other entity;

(10) to conduct its business, locate offices, and exercise the powers granted by this Act within or without this state;

(11) to elect directors and appoint officers, employees, and agents of the corporation, define their duties, fix their compensation, and lend them money and credit;

(12) to pay pensions and establish pension plans, pension trusts, profit sharing plans, share bonus plans, share option plans, and benefit or incentive plans for any or all of its current or former directors, officers, employees, and agents;

(13) to make donations for the public welfare or for charitable, scientific, or educational purposes;

(14) to transact any lawful business that will aid governmental policy;

(15) to make payments or donations, or do any other act, not inconsistent with law, that furthers the business and affairs of the corporation.

§ 3.03 Emergency Powers

(a) In anticipation of or during an emergency defined in subsection (d), the board of directors of a corporation may:

(1) modify lines of succession to accommodate the incapacity of any director, officer, employee, or agent; and

(2) relocate the principal office, designate alternative principal offices or regional offices, or authorize the officers to do so.

(b) During an emergency defined in subsection (d), unless emergency bylaws provide otherwise:

(1) notice of a meeting of the board of directors need be given only to those directors whom it is practicable to reach and may be

given in any practicable manner, including by publication and radio; and

(2) one or more officers of the corporation present at a meeting of the board of directors may be deemed to be directors for the meeting, in order of rank and within the same rank in order of seniority, as necessary to achieve a quorum.

(c) Corporate action taken in good faith during an emergency under this section to further the ordinary business affairs of the corporation:

(1) binds the corporation; and

(2) may not be used to impose liability on a corporate director, officer, employee, or agent.

(d) An emergency exists for purposes of this section if a quorum of the corporation's directors cannot readily be assembled because of some catastrophic event.

§ 3.04 Ultra Vires

(a) Except as provided in subsection (b), the validity of corporate action may not be challenged on the ground that the corporation lacks or lacked power to act.

(b) A corporation's power to act may be challenged:

(1) in a proceeding by a shareholder against the corporation to enjoin the act;

(2) in a proceeding by the corporation, directly, derivatively, or through a receiver, trustee, or other legal representative, against an incumbent or former director, officer, employee, or agent of the corporation; or

(3) in a proceeding by the attorney general under section 14.30.

(c) In a shareholder's proceeding under subsection (b)(1) to enjoin an unauthorized corporate act, the court may enjoin or set aside the act, if equitable and if all affected persons are parties to the proceeding, and may award damages for loss (other than anticipated profits) suffered by the corporation or another party because of enjoining the unauthorized act.

CHAPTER 4

NAME

§ 4.01 Corporate Name

(a) A corporate name:

(1) must contain the word "corporation," "incorporated," "company," or "limited," or the abbreviation "corp.," "inc.," "co.," or

"ltd.," or words or abbreviations of like import in another language; and

(2) may not contain language stating or implying that the corporation is organized for a purpose other than that permitted by section 3.01 and its articles of incorporation.

(b) Except as authorized by subsections (c) and (d), a corporate name must be distinguishable upon the records of the secretary of state from:

(1) the corporate name of a corporation incorporated or authorized to transact business in this state;

(2) a corporate name reserved or registered under section 4.02 or 4.03;

(3) the fictitious name adopted by a foreign corporation authorized to transact business in this state because its real name is unavailable; and

(4) the corporate name of a not-for-profit corporation incorporated or authorized to transact business in this state.

(c) A corporation may apply to the secretary of state for authorization to use a name that is not distinguishable upon his records from one or more of the names described in subsection (b). The secretary of state shall authorize use of the name applied for if:

(1) the other corporation consents to the use in writing and submits an undertaking in form satisfactory to the secretary of state to change its name to a name that is distinguishable upon the records of the secretary of state from the name of the applying corporation; or

(2) the applicant delivers to the secretary of state a certified copy of the final judgment of a court of competent jurisdiction establishing the applicant's right to use the name applied for in this state.

(d) A corporation may use the name (including the fictitious name) of another domestic or foreign corporation that is used in this state if the other corporation is incorporated or authorized to transact business in this state and the proposed user corporation

(1) has merged with the other corporation;

(2) has been formed by reorganization of the other corporation; or

(3) has acquired all or substantially all of the assets, including the corporate name, of the other corporation.

(e) This Act does not control the use of fictitious names.

§ 4.02 Reserved Name

(a) A person may reserve the exclusive use of a corporate name, including a fictitious name for a foreign corporation whose corporate name is not available, by delivering an application to the secretary of state for filing. The application must set forth the name and address of the applicant and the name proposed to be reserved. If the secretary of state finds that the corporate name applied for is available, he shall reserve the name for the applicant's exclusive use for a nonrenewable 120–day period.

(b) The owner of a reserved corporate name may transfer the reservation to another person by delivering to the secretary of state a signed notice of the transfer that states the name and address of the transferee.

§ 4.03 Registered Name

(a) A foreign corporation may register its corporate name, or its corporate name with any addition required by section 15.06, if the name is distinguishable upon the records of the secretary of state from the corporate names that are not available under section 4.01(b).

(b) A foreign corporation registers its corporate name, or its corporate name with any addition required by section 15.06, by delivering to the secretary of state for filing an application:

(1) setting forth its corporate name, or its corporate name with any addition required by section 15.06, the state or country and date of its incorporation, and a brief description of the nature of the business in which it is engaged; and

(2) accompanied by a certificate of existence (or a document of similar import) from the state or country of incorporation.

(c) The name is registered for the applicant's exclusive use upon the effective date of the application.

(d) A foreign corporation whose registration is effective may renew it for successive years by delivering to the secretary of state for filing a renewal application, which complies with the requirements of subsection (b), between October 1 and December 31 of the preceding year. The renewal application when filed renews the registration for the following calendar year.

(e) A foreign corporation whose registration is effective may thereafter qualify as a foreign corporation under the registered name or consent in writing to the use of that name by a corporation thereafter incorporated under this Act or by another foreign corporation thereafter authorized to transact business in this state. The registration terminates when the domestic corporation is incorporated or the foreign corporation qualifies or consents to the qualification of another foreign corporation under the registered name.

CHAPTER 5

OFFICE AND AGENT

§ 5.01 Registered Office and Registered Agent

Each corporation must continuously maintain in this state:

(1) a registered office that may be the same as any of its places of business; and

(2) a registered agent, who may be:

(i) an individual who resides in this state and whose business office is identical with the registered office;

(ii) a domestic corporation or not-for-profit domestic corporation whose business office is identical with the registered office; or

(iii) a foreign corporation or not-for-profit foreign corporation authorized to transact business in this state whose business office is identical with the registered office.

§ 5.02 Change of Registered Office or Registered Agent

(a) A corporation may change its registered office or registered agent by delivering to the secretary of state for filing a statement of change that sets forth:

(1) the name of the corporation;

(2) the street address of its current registered office;

(3) if the current registered office is to be changed, the street address of the new registered office;

(4) the name of its current registered agent;

(5) if the current registered agent is to be changed, the name of the new registered agent and the new agent's written consent (either on the statement or attached to it) to the appointment; and

(6) that after the change or changes are made, the street addresses of its registered office and the business office of its registered agent will be identical.

(b) If a registered agent changes the street address of his business office, he may change the street address of the registered office of any corporation for which he is the registered agent by notifying the corporation in writing of the change and signing (either manually or in facsimile) and delivering to the secretary of state for filing a statement that complies with the requirements of subsection (a) and recites that the corporation has been notified of the change.

§ 5.03 Resignation of Registered Agent

(a) A registered agent may resign his agency appointment by signing and delivering to the secretary of state for filing the signed original and two exact or conformed copies of a statement of resignation. The statement may include a statement that the registered office is also discontinued.

(b) After filing the statement the secretary of state shall mail one copy to the registered office (if not discontinued) and the other copy to the corporation at its principal office.

(c) The agency appointment is terminated, and the registered office discontinued if so provided, on the 31st day after the date on which the statement was filed.

§ 5.04 Service on Corporation

(a) A corporation's registered agent is the corporation's agent for service of process, notice, or demand required or permitted by law to be served on the corporation.

(b) If a corporation has no registered agent, or the agent cannot with reasonable diligence be served, the corporation may be served by registered or certified mail, return receipt requested, addressed to the secretary of the corporation at its principal office. Service is perfected under this subsection at the earliest of:

(1) the date the corporation receives the mail;

(2) the date shown on the return receipt, if signed on behalf of the corporation; or

(3) five days after its deposit in the United States Mail, as evidenced by the postmark, if mailed postpaid and correctly addressed.

(c) This section does not prescribe the only means, or necessarily the required means of serving a corporation.

CHAPTER 6

SHARES AND DISTRIBUTIONS

Subchapter A. Shares

§ 6.01 Authorized Shares

(a) The articles of incorporation must set forth any classes of shares and series of shares within a class, and the number of shares of each class and series, that the corporation is authorized to issue. If more than one class or series of shares is authorized, the articles of incorporation must prescribe a distinguishing designation for each class or series and must describe, prior to the issuance of shares of a class or series, the terms, including the preferences, rights, and limitations, of that class or series. Except to the extent varied as permitted by this section, all shares of a class or series must have terms, including preferences, rights and limitations, that are identical with those of other shares of the same class or series.

(b) The articles of incorporation must authorize:

(1) one or more classes or series of shares that together have unlimited voting rights, and

(2) one or more classes or series of shares (which may be the same class or classes as those with voting rights) that together are entitled to receive the net assets of the corporation upon dissolution.

(c) The articles of incorporation may authorize one or more classes or series of shares that:

(1) have special, conditional, or limited voting rights, or no right to vote, except to the extent otherwise provided by this Act;

(2) are redeemable or convertible as specified in the articles of incorporation:

(i) at the option of the corporation, the shareholder, or another person or upon the occurrence of a specified event;

(ii) for cash, indebtedness, securities, or other property; and

(iii) at prices and in amounts specified, or determined in accordance with a formula;

(3) entitle the holders to distributions calculated in any manner, including dividends that may be cumulative, noncumulative, or partially cumulative; or

(4) have preference over any other class or series of shares with respect to distributions, including distributions upon the dissolution of the corporation.

(d) Terms of shares may be made dependent upon facts objectively ascertainable outside the articles of incorporation in accordance with section 1.20(k).

(e) Any of the terms of shares may vary among holders of the same class or series so long as such variations are expressly set forth in the articles of incorporation.

(f) The description of the preferences, rights and limitations of classes or series of shares in subsection (c) is not exhaustive.

§ 6.02 Terms of Class or Series Determined by Board of Directors

(a) If the articles of incorporation so provide, the board of directors is authorized, without shareholder approval, to:

(1) classify any unissued shares into one or more classes or into one or more series within a class,

(2) reclassify any unissued shares of any class into one or more classes or into one or more series within one or more classes, or

(3) reclassify any unissued shares of any series of any class into one or more classes or into one or more series within a class.

(b) If the board of directors acts pursuant to subsection (a), it must determine the terms, including the preferences, rights and limitations, to the same extent permitted under section 6.01, of:

(1) any class of shares before the issuance of any shares of that class, or

(2) any series within a class before the issuance of any shares of that series.

(c) Before issuing any shares of a class or series created under this section, the corporation must deliver to the secretary of state for filing articles of amendment setting forth the terms determined under subsection (a).

§ 6.03 Issued and Outstanding Shares

(a) A corporation may issue the number of shares of each class or series authorized by the articles of incorporation. Shares that are issued are outstanding shares until they are reacquired, redeemed, converted, or cancelled.

(b) The reacquisition, redemption, or conversion of outstanding shares is subject to the limitations of subsection (c) of this section and to section 6.40.

(c) At all times that shares of the corporation are outstanding, one or more shares that together have unlimited voting rights and one or more shares that together are entitled to receive the net assets of the corporation upon dissolution must be outstanding.

§ 6.04 Fractional Shares

(a) A corporation may:

(1) issue fractions of a share or pay in money the value of fractions of a share;

(2) arrange for disposition of fractional shares by the shareholders;

(3) issue scrip in registered or bearer form entitling the holder to receive a full share upon surrendering enough scrip to equal a full share.

(b) Each certificate representing scrip must be conspicuously labeled "scrip" and must contain the information required by section 6.25(b).

(c) The holder of a fractional share is entitled to exercise the rights of a shareholder, including the right to vote, to receive dividends, and to participate in the assets of the corporation upon liquidation. The holder of scrip is not entitled to any of these rights unless the scrip provides for them.

(d) The board of directors may authorize the issuance of scrip subject to any condition considered desirable, including:

(1) that the scrip will become void if not exchanged for full shares before a specified date; and

(2) that the shares for which the scrip is exchangeable may be sold and the proceeds paid to the scripholders.

Subchapter B. Issuance of Shares

§ 6.20 Subscription for Shares Before Incorporation

(a) A subscription for shares entered into before incorporation is irrevocable for six months unless the subscription agreement provides a longer or shorter period or all the subscribers agree to revocation.

(b) The board of directors may determine the payment terms of subscription for shares that were entered into before incorporation, unless the subscription agreement specifies them. A call for payment by the board of directors must be uniform so far as practicable as to all shares of the same class or series, unless the subscription agreement specifies otherwise.

(c) Shares issued pursuant to subscriptions entered into before incorporation are fully paid and nonassessable when the corporation receives the consideration specified in the subscription agreement.

(d) If a subscriber defaults in payment of money or property under a subscription agreement entered into before incorporation, the corporation may collect the amount owed as any other debt. Alternatively, unless the subscription agreement provides otherwise, the corporation may rescind the agreement and may sell the shares if the debt remains unpaid for more than 20 days after the corporation sends written demand for payment to the subscriber.

(e) A subscription agreement entered into after incorporation is a contract between the subscriber and the corporation subject to section 6.21.

§ 6.21 Issuance of Shares

(a) The powers granted in this section to the board of directors may be reserved to the shareholders by the articles of incorporation.

(b) The board of directors may authorize shares to be issued for consideration consisting of any tangible or intangible property or benefit to the corporation, including cash, promissory notes, services performed, contracts for services to be performed, or other securities of the corporation.

(c) Before the corporation issues shares, the board of directors must determine that the consideration received or to be received for shares to be issued is adequate. That determination by the board of directors is conclusive insofar as the adequacy of consideration for the issuance of shares relates to whether the shares are validly issued, fully paid, and nonassessable.

(d) When the corporation receives the consideration for which the board of directors authorized the issuance of shares, the shares issued therefor are fully paid and nonassessable.

(e) The corporation may place in escrow shares issued for a contract for future services or benefits or a promissory note, or make other arrangements to restrict the transfer of the shares, and may credit distributions in respect of the shares against their purchase price, until the services are performed, the note is paid, or the benefits received. If the services are not performed, the note is not paid, or the benefits are not received, the shares escrowed or restricted and the distributions credited may be cancelled in whole or part.

(f) (1) An issuance of shares or other securities convertible into or rights exercisable for shares, in a transaction or a series of integrated transactions, requires approval of the shareholders, at a meeting at which a quorum consisting of at least a majority of the votes entitled to be cast on the matter exists, if:

(i) the shares, other securities, or rights are issued for consideration other than cash or cash equivalents, and

(ii) the voting power of shares that are issued and issuable as a result of the transaction or series of integrated transactions will comprise more than 20 percent of the voting power of the shares of the corporation that were outstanding immediately before the transaction.

(2) In this subsection:

(i) For purposes of determining the voting power of shares issued and issuable as a result of a transaction or series of integrated transactions, the voting power of shares shall be the greater of (A) the voting power of the shares to be issued, or (B) the voting power of the shares that would be outstanding after giving effect to the conversion of convertible shares and other securities and the exercise of rights to be issued.

(ii) A series of transactions is integrated if consummation of one transaction is made contingent on consummation of one or more of the other transactions.

§ 6.22 Liability of Shareholders

(a) A purchaser from a corporation of its own shares is not liable to the corporation or its creditors with respect to the shares except to pay the consideration for which the shares were authorized to be issued (section 6.21) or specified in the subscription agreement (section 6.20).

(b) Unless otherwise provided in the articles of incorporation, a shareholder of a corporation is not personally liable for the acts or debts of the corporation except that he may become personally liable by reason of his own acts or conduct.

§ 6.23 Share Dividends

(a) Unless the articles of incorporation provide otherwise, shares may be issued pro rata and without consideration to the corporation's shareholders or to the shareholders of one or more classes or series. An issuance of shares under this subsection is a share dividend.

(b) Shares of one class or series may not be issued as a share dividend in respect of shares of another class or series unless (1) the articles of incorporation so authorize, (2) a majority of the votes entitled to be cast by the class or series to be issued approve the issue, or (3) there are no outstanding shares of the class or series to be issued.

(c) If the board of directors does not fix the record date for determining shareholders entitled to a share dividend, it is the date the board of directors authorizes the share dividend.

§ 6.24 Share Options

(a) A corporation may issue rights, options, or warrants for the purchase of shares or other securities of the corporation. The board of directors shall determine (i) the terms upon which the rights, options, or warrants are issued and (ii) the terms, including the consideration for which the shares or other securities are to be issued. The authorization by the board of directors for the corporation to issue such rights, options, or warrants constitutes authorization of the issuance of the shares or other securities for which the rights, options or warrants are exercisable.

(b) The terms and conditions of such rights, options or warrants, including those outstanding on the effective date of this section, may include, without limitation, restrictions or conditions that:

  (1) preclude or limit the exercise, transfer or receipt of such rights, options or warrants by any person or persons owning or offering to acquire a specified number or percentage of the outstanding shares or other securities of the corporation or by any transferee or transferees of any such person or persons, or

  (2) invalidate or void such rights, options or warrants held by any such person or persons or any such transferee or transferees.

§ 6.25 Form and Content of Certificates

(a) Shares may but need not be represented by certificates. Unless this Act or another statute expressly provides otherwise, the rights and obligations of shareholders are identical whether or not their shares are represented by certificates.

(b) At a minimum each share certificate must state on its face:

(1) the name of the issuing corporation and that it is organized under the law of this state;

(2) the name of the person to whom issued; and

(3) the number and class of shares and the designation of the series, if any, the certificate represents.

(c) If the issuing corporation is authorized to issue different classes of shares or different series within a class, the designations, relative rights, preferences, and limitations applicable to each class and the variations in rights, preferences, and limitations determined for each series (and the authority of the board of directors to determine variations for future series) must be summarized on the front or back of each certificate. Alternatively, each certificate may state conspicuously on its front or back that the corporation will furnish the shareholder this information on request in writing and without charge.

(d) Each share certificate (1) must be signed (either manually or in facsimile) by two officers designated in the bylaws or by the board of directors and (2) may bear the corporate seal or its facsimile.

(e) If the person who signed (either manually or in facsimile) a share certificate no longer holds office when the certificate is issued, the certificate is nevertheless valid.

§ 6.26 Shares Without Certificates

(a) Unless the articles of incorporation or bylaws provide otherwise, the board of directors of a corporation may authorize the issue of some or all of the shares of any or all of its classes or series without certificates. The authorization does not affect shares already represented by certificates until they are surrendered to the corporation.

(b) Within a reasonable time after the issue or transfer of shares without certificates, the corporation shall send the shareholder a written statement of the information required on certificates by section 6.25(b) and (c), and, if applicable, section 6.27.

§ 6.27 Restriction on Transfer of Shares and Other Securities

(a) The articles of incorporation, bylaws, an agreement among shareholders, or an agreement between shareholders and the corporation may impose restrictions on the transfer or registration of transfer of shares of the corporation. A restriction does not affect shares issued before the restriction was adopted unless the holders of the shares are parties to the restriction agreement or voted in favor of the restriction.

(b) A restriction on the transfer or registration of transfer of shares is valid and enforceable against the holder or a transferee of the holder if the restriction is authorized by this section and its existence is noted conspicuously on the front or back of the certificate or is contained in the information statement required by section 6.26(b). Unless so noted, a restriction is not enforceable against a person without knowledge of the restriction.

(c) A restriction on the transfer or registration of transfer of shares is authorized:

(1) to maintain the corporation's status when it is dependent on the number or identity of its shareholders;

(2) to preserve exemptions under federal or state securities law;

(3) for any other reasonable purpose.

(d) A restriction on the transfer or registration of transfer of shares may:

(1) obligate the shareholder first to offer the corporation or other persons (separately, consecutively, or simultaneously) an opportunity to acquire the restricted shares;

(2) obligate the corporation or other persons (separately, consecutively, or simultaneously) to acquire the restricted shares;

(3) require the corporation, the holders of any class of its shares, or another person to approve the transfer of the restricted shares, if the requirement is not manifestly unreasonable;

(4) prohibit the transfer of the restricted shares to designated persons or classes of persons, if the prohibition is not manifestly unreasonable.

(e) For purposes of this section, "shares" includes a security convertible into or carrying a right to subscribe for or acquire shares.

§ 6.28 Expense of Issue

A corporation may pay the expenses of selling or underwriting its shares, and of organizing or reorganizing the corporation, from the consideration received for shares.

Subchapter C. Subsequent Acquisition of Shares by Shareholders and Corporation

§ 6.30 Shareholders' Preemptive Rights

(a) The shareholders of a corporation do not have a preemptive right to acquire the corporation's unissued shares except to the extent the articles of incorporation so provide.

(b) A statement included in the articles of incorporation that "the corporation elects to have preemptive rights" (or words of similar import) means that the following principles apply except to the extent the articles of incorporation expressly provide otherwise:

(1) The shareholders of the corporation have a preemptive right, granted on uniform terms and conditions prescribed by the board of directors to provide a fair and reasonable opportunity to exercise the right, to acquire proportional amounts of the corporation's unissued shares upon the decision of the board of directors to issue them.

(2) A shareholder may waive his preemptive right. A waiver evidenced by a writing is irrevocable even though it is not supported by consideration.

(3) There is no preemptive right with respect to:

(i) shares issued as compensation to directors, officers, agents, or employees of the corporation, its subsidiaries or affiliates:

(ii) shares issued to satisfy conversion or option rights created to provide compensation to directors, officers, agents, or employees of the corporation, its subsidiaries or affiliates;

(iii) shares authorized in articles of incorporation that are issued within six months from the effective date of incorporation;

(iv) shares sold otherwise than for money.

(4) Holders of shares of any class without general voting rights but with preferential rights to distributions or assets have no preemptive rights with respect to shares of any class.

(5) Holders of shares of any class with general voting rights but without preferential rights to distributions or assets have no preemptive rights with respect to shares of any class with preferential rights to distributions or assets unless the shares with preferential rights are convertible into or carry a right to subscribe for or acquire shares without preferential rights.

(6) Shares subject to preemptive rights that are not acquired by shareholders may be issued to any person for a period of one year after being offered to shareholders at a consideration set by the board of directors that is not lower than the consideration set for the exercise of preemptive rights. An offer at a lower consideration or after the expiration of one year is subject to the shareholders' preemptive rights.

(c) For purposes of this section, "shares" includes a security convertible into or carrying a right to subscribe for or acquire shares.

§ 6.31 Corporation's Acquisition of its Own Shares

(a) A corporation may acquire its own shares, and shares so acquired constitute authorized but unissued shares.

(b) If the articles of incorporation prohibit the reissue of the acquired shares, the number of authorized shares is reduced by the number of shares acquired.

Subchapter D. Distributions

§ 6.40 Distributions to Shareholders

(a) A board of directors may authorize and the corporation may make distributions to its shareholders subject to restriction by the articles of incorporation and the limitation in subsection (c).

(b) If the board of directors does not fix the record date for determining shareholders entitled to a distribution (other than one involving a purchase, redemption, or other acquisition of the corporation's shares), it is the date the board of directors authorizes the distribution.

(c) No distribution may be made if, after giving it effect:

(1) the corporation would not be able to pay its debts as they become due in the usual course of business; or

(2) the corporation's total assets would be less than the sum of its total liabilities plus (unless the articles of incorporation permit otherwise) the amount that would be needed, if the corporation were to be dissolved at the time of the distribution, to satisfy the preferential rights upon dissolution of shareholders whose preferential rights are superior to those receiving the distribution.

(d) The board of directors may base a determination that a distribution is not prohibited under subsection (c) either on financial statements prepared on the basis of accounting practices and principles that are reasonable in the circumstances or on a fair valuation or other method that is reasonable in the circumstances.

(e) Except as provided in subsection (g), the effect of a distribution under subsection (c) is measured:

(1) in the case of distribution by purchase, redemption, or other acquisition of the corporation's shares, as of the earlier of (i) the date money or other property is transferred or debt incurred by the corporation or (ii) the date the shareholder ceases to be a shareholder with respect to the acquired shares;

(2) in the case of any other distribution of indebtedness, as of the date the indebtedness is distributed; and

(3) in all other cases, as of (i) the date the distribution is authorized if the payment occurs within 120 days after the date of authorization or (ii) the date the payment is made if it occurs more than 120 days after the date of authorization.

(f) A corporation's indebtedness to a shareholder incurred by reason of a distribution made in accordance with this section is at parity with the corporation's indebtedness to its general, unsecured creditors except to the extent subordinated by agreement.

(g) Indebtedness of a corporation, including indebtedness issued as a distribution, is not considered a liability for purposes of determinations under subsection (c) if its terms provide that payment of principal and interest are made only if and to the extent that payment of a distribution to shareholders could then be made under this section. If the indebtedness is issued as a distribution, each payment of principal or interest is treated as a distribution, the effect of which is measured on the date the payment is actually made.

(h) This section shall not apply to distributions in liquidation under chapter 14.

CHAPTER 7

SHAREHOLDERS

Subchapter A. Meetings

§ 7.01 Annual Meeting

(a) A corporation shall hold a meeting of shareholders annually at a time stated in or fixed in accordance with the bylaws.

(b) Annual shareholders' meetings may be held in or out of this state at the place stated in or fixed in accordance with the bylaws. If no place is stated in or fixed in accordance with the bylaws, annual meetings shall be held at the corporation's principal office.

(c) The failure to hold an annual meeting at the time stated in or fixed in accordance with a corporation's bylaws does not affect the validity of any corporate action.

§ 7.02 Special Meeting

(a) A corporation shall hold a special meeting of shareholders:

(1) on call of its board of directors or the person or persons authorized to do so by the articles of incorporation or bylaws; or

(2) if the holders of at least 10 percent of all the votes entitled to be cast on an issue proposed to be considered at the proposed special meeting sign, date, and deliver to the corporation one or more written demands for the meeting describing the purpose or purposes for which it is to be held, provided that the articles of incorporation may fix a lower percentage or a higher percentage not exceeding 25 percent of all the votes entitled to be cast on any issue proposed to be considered. Unless otherwise provided in the articles of incorporation, a written demand for a special meeting may be revoked by a writing to that effect received by the corporation prior to the receipt by the corporation of de-

mands sufficient in number to require the holding of a special meeting.

(b) If not otherwise fixed under section 7.03 or 7.07, the record date for determining shareholders entitled to demand a special meeting is the date the first shareholder signs the demand.

(c) Special shareholders' meetings may be held in or out of this state at the place stated in or fixed in accordance with the bylaws. If no place is stated or fixed in accordance with the bylaws, special meetings shall be held at the corporation's principal office.

(d) Only business within the purpose or purposes described in the meeting notice required by section 7.05(c) may be conducted at a special shareholders' meeting.

§ 7.03 Court–Ordered Meeting

(a) The [name or describe] court of the county where a corporation's principal office (or, if none in this state, its registered office) is located may summarily order a meeting to be held:

(1) on application of any shareholder of the corporation entitled to participate in an annual meeting if an annual meeting was not held within the earlier of 6 months after the end of the corporation's fiscal year or 15 months after its last annual meeting; or

(2) on application of a shareholder who signed a demand for a special meeting valid under section 7.02, if:

(i) notice of the special meeting was not given within 30 days after the date the demand was delivered to the corporation's secretary; or

(ii) the special meeting was not held in accordance with the notice.

(b) The court may fix the time and place of the meeting, determine the shares entitled to participate in the meeting, specify a record date for determining shareholders entitled to notice of and to vote at the meeting, prescribe the form and content of the meeting notice, fix the quorum required for specific matters to be considered at the meeting (or direct that the votes represented at the meeting constitute a quorum for action on those matters), and enter other orders necessary to accomplish the purpose or purposes of the meeting.

§ 7.04 Action Without Meeting

(a) Action required or permitted by this Act to be taken at a shareholders' meeting may be taken without a meeting if the action is taken by all the shareholders entitled to vote on the action. The action must be evidenced by one or more written consents bearing the date of signature and describing the action taken, signed by all the shareholders entitled to vote on the action, and delivered to the corporation for inclusion in the minutes or filing with the corporate records.

(b) If not otherwise fixed under section 7.03 or 7.07, the record date for determining shareholders entitled to take action without a meeting is the date the first shareholder signs the consent under subsection (a). No written consent shall be effective to take the corporate action referred to therein unless, within 60 days of the earliest date appearing on a consent delivered to the corporation in the manner required by this section, written consents signed by all shareholders entitled to vote on the action are received by the corporation. A written consent may be revoked by a writing to that effect received by the corporation prior to receipt by the corporation of unrevoked written consents sufficient in number to take corporate action.

(c) A consent signed under this section has the effect of a meeting vote and may be described as such in any document.

(d) If this Act requires that notice of proposed action be given to nonvoting shareholders and the action is to be taken by unanimous consent of the voting shareholders, the corporation must give its nonvoting shareholders written notice of the proposed action at least 10 days before the action is taken. The notice must contain or be accompanied by the same material that, under this Act, would have been required to be sent to nonvoting shareholders in a notice of meeting at which the proposed action would have been submitted to the shareholders for action.

§ 7.05 Notice of Meeting

(a) A corporation shall notify shareholders of the date, time, and place of each annual and special shareholders' meeting no fewer than 10 nor more than 60 days before the meeting date. Unless this Act or the articles of incorporation require otherwise, the corporation is required to give notice only to shareholders entitled to vote at the meeting.

(b) Unless this Act or the articles of incorporation require otherwise, notice of an annual meeting need not include a description of the purpose or purposes for which the meeting is called.

(c) Notice of a special meeting must include a description of the purpose or purposes for which the meeting is called.

(d) If not otherwise fixed under section 7.03 or 7.07, the record date for determining shareholders entitled to notice of and to vote at an annual or special shareholders' meeting is the day before the first notice is delivered to shareholders.

(e) Unless the bylaws require otherwise, if an annual or special shareholders' meeting is adjourned to a different date, time, or place, notice need not be given of the new date, time, or place if the new date, time, or place is announced at the meeting before adjournment.

If a new record date for the adjourned meeting is or must be fixed under section 7.07, however, notice of the adjourned meeting must be given under this section to persons who are shareholders as of the new record date.

§ 7.06 Waiver of Notice

(a) A shareholder may waive any notice required by this Act, the articles of incorporation, or bylaws before or after the date and time stated in the notice. The waiver must be in writing, be signed by the shareholder entitled to the notice, and be delivered to the corporation for inclusion in the minutes or filing with the corporate records.

(b) A shareholder's attendance at a meeting:

(1) waives objection to lack of notice or defective notice of the meeting, unless the shareholder at the beginning of the meeting objects to holding the meeting or transacting business at the meeting;

(2) waives objection to consideration of a particular matter at the meeting that is not within the purpose or purposes described in the meeting notice, unless the shareholder objects to considering the matter when it is presented.

§ 7.07 Record Date

(a) The bylaws may fix or provide the manner of fixing the record date for one or more voting groups in order to determine the shareholders entitled to notice of a shareholders' meeting, to demand a special meeting, to vote, or to take any other action. If the bylaws do not fix or provide for fixing a record date, the board of directors of the corporation may fix a future date as the record date.

(b) A record date fixed under this section may not be more than 70 days before the meeting or action requiring a determination of shareholders.

(c) A determination of shareholders entitled to notice of or to vote at a shareholders' meeting is effective for any adjournment of the meeting unless the board of directors fixes a new record date, which it must do if the meeting is adjourned to a date more than 120 days after the date fixed for the original meeting.

(d) If a court orders a meeting adjourned to a date more than 120 days after the date fixed for the original meeting, it may provide that the original record date continues in effect or it may fix a new record date.

§ 7.08 Conduct of the Meeting

(a) At each meeting of shareholders, a chair shall preside. The chair shall be appointed as provided in the bylaws or, in the absence of such provision, by the board.

(b) The chair, unless the articles of incorporation or bylaws provide otherwise, shall determine the order of business and shall have the authority to establish rules for the conduct of the meeting.

(c) Any rules adopted for, and the conduct of, the meeting shall be fair to shareholders.

(d) The chair of the meeting shall announce at the meeting when the polls close for each matter voted upon. If no announcement is made, the polls shall be deemed to have closed upon the final adjournment of the meeting. After the polls close, no ballots, proxies or votes nor any revocations or changes thereto may be accepted.

Subchapter B. Voting

§ 7.20 Shareholders' List for Meeting

(a) After fixing a record date for a meeting, a corporation shall prepare an alphabetical list of the names of all its shareholders who are entitled to notice of a shareholders' meeting. The list must be arranged by voting group (and within each voting group by class or series of shares) and show the address of and number of shares held by each shareholder.

(b) The shareholders' list must be available for inspection by any shareholder, beginning two business days after notice of the meeting is given for which the list was prepared and continuing through the meeting, at the corporation's principal office or at a place identified in the meeting notice in the city where the meeting will be held. A shareholder, his agent, or attorney is entitled on written demand to inspect and, subject to the requirements of section 16.02(c), to copy the list, during regular business hours and at his expense, during the period it is available for inspection.

(c) The corporation shall make the shareholders' list available at the meeting, and any shareholder, his agent, or attorney is entitled to inspect the list at any time during the meeting or any adjournment.

(d) If the corporation refuses to allow a shareholder, his agent, or attorney to inspect the shareholders' list before or at the meeting (or copy the list as permitted by subsection (b)), the [name or describe] court of the county where a corporation's principal office (or, if none in this state, its registered office) is located, on application of the shareholder, may summarily order the inspection or copying at the corporation's expense and may postpone the meeting for which the list was prepared until the inspection or copying is complete.

(e) Refusal or failure to prepare or make available the shareholders' list does not affect the validity of action taken at the meeting.

§ 7.21 Voting Entitlement of Shares

(a) Except as provided in subsections (b) and (d) or unless the articles of incorporation provide otherwise, each outstanding share, regardless of class, is entitled to one vote on each matter voted on at a shareholders' meeting. Only shares are entitled to vote.

(b) Absent special circumstances, the shares of a corporation are not entitled to vote if they are owned, directly or indirectly, by a second corporation, domestic or foreign, and the first corporation owns, directly or indirectly, a majority of the shares entitled to vote for directors of the second corporation.

(c) Subsection (b) does not limit the power of a corporation to vote any shares, including its own shares, held by it in a fiduciary capacity.

(d) Redeemable shares are not entitled to vote after notice of redemption is mailed to the holders and a sum sufficient to redeem the shares has been deposited with a bank, trust company, or other financial institution under an irrevocable obligation to pay the holders the redemption price on surrender of the shares.

§ 7.22 Proxies

(a) A shareholder may vote his shares in person or by proxy.

(b) A shareholder or his agent or attorney-in-fact may appoint a proxy to vote or otherwise act for the shareholder by signing an appointment form, or by an electronic transmission. An electronic transmission must contain or be accompanied by information from which one can determine that the shareholder, the shareholder's agent, or the shareholder's attorney-in-fact authorized the transmission.

(c) An appointment of a proxy is effective when a signed appointment form or an electronic transmission of the appointment is received by the inspector of election or the officer or agent of the corporation authorized to tabulate votes. An appointment is valid for 11 months unless a longer period is expressly provided in the appointment form.

(d) An appointment of a proxy is revocable unless the appointment form or electronic transmission states that it is irrevocable and the appointment is coupled with an interest. Appointments coupled with an interest include the appointment of:

(1) a pledgee;

(2) a person who purchased or agreed to purchase the shares;

(3) a creditor of the corporation who extended it credit under terms requiring the appointment;

(4) an employee of the corporation whose employment contract requires the appointment; or

(5) a party to a voting agreement created under section 7.31.

(e) The death or incapacity of the shareholder appointing a proxy does not affect the right of the corporation to accept the proxy's authority unless notice of the death or incapacity is received by the secretary or other officer or agent authorized to tabulate votes before the proxy exercises his authority under the appointment.

(f) An appointment made irrevocable under subsection (d) is revoked when the interest with which it is coupled is extinguished.

(g) A transferee for value of shares subject to an irrevocable appointment may revoke the appointment if he did not know of its existence when he acquired the shares and the existence of the irrevocable appointment was not noted conspicuously on the certificate representing the shares or on the information statement for shares without certificates.

(h) Subject to section 7.24 and to any express limitation on the proxy's authority stated in the appointment form or electronic transmission, a corporation is entitled to accept the proxy's vote or other action as that of the shareholder making the appointment.

§ 7.23 Shares Held by Nominees

(a) A corporation may establish a procedure by which the beneficial owner of shares that are registered in the name of a nominee is recognized by the corporation as the shareholder. The extent of this recognition may be determined in the procedure.

(b) The procedure may set forth:

(1) the types of nominees to which it applies;

(2) the rights or privileges that the corporation recognizes in a beneficial owner;

(3) the manner in which the procedure is selected by the nominee;

(4) the information that must be provided when the procedure is selected;

(5) the period for which selection of the procedure is effective; and

(6) other aspects of the rights and duties created.

§ 7.24 Corporation's Acceptance of Votes

(a) If the name signed on a vote, consent, waiver, or proxy appointment corresponds to the name of a shareholder, the corporation if acting in good faith is entitled to accept the vote, consent, waiver, or proxy appointment and give it effect as the act of the shareholder.

(b) If the name signed on a vote, consent, waiver, or proxy appointment does not correspond to the name of its shareholder, the corporation if acting in good faith is nevertheless entitled to accept the vote, consent, waiver, or proxy appointment and give it effect as the act of the shareholder if:

(1) the shareholder is an entity and the name signed purports to be that of an officer or agent of the entity;

(2) the name signed purports to be that of an administrator, executor, guardian, or conservator representing the shareholder and, if the corporation requests, evidence of fiduciary status acceptable to the corporation has been presented with respect to the vote, consent, waiver, or proxy appointment;

(3) the name signed purports to be that of a receiver or trustee in bankruptcy of the shareholder and, if the corporation requests, evidence of this status acceptable to the corporation has been presented with respect to the vote, consent, waiver, or proxy appointment;

(4) the name signed purports to be that of a pledgee, beneficial owner, or attorney-in-fact of the shareholder and, if the corporation requests, evidence acceptable to the corporation of the signatory's authority to sign for the shareholder has been presented with respect to the vote, consent, waiver, or proxy appointment;

(5) two or more persons are the shareholder as co-tenants or fiduciaries and the name signed purports to be the name of at least one of the co-owners and the person signing appears to be acting on behalf of all the co-owners.

(c) The corporation is entitled to reject a vote, consent, waiver, or proxy appointment if the secretary or other officer or agent authorized to tabulate votes, acting in good faith, has reasonable basis for doubt about the validity of the signature on it or about the signatory's authority to sign for the shareholder.

(d) The corporation and its officer or agent who accepts or rejects a vote, consent, waiver, or proxy appointment in good faith and in accordance with the standards of this section or section 7.22(b) are not liable in damages to the shareholder for the consequences of the acceptance or rejection.

(e) Corporate action based on the acceptance or rejection of a vote, consent, waiver, or proxy appointment under this section is valid unless a court of competent jurisdiction determines otherwise.

§ 7.25 Quorum and Voting Requirements for Voting Groups

(a) Shares entitled to vote as a separate voting group may take action on a matter at a meeting only if a quorum of those shares exists with respect to that matter. Unless the articles of incorporation provides otherwise, a majority of the votes entitled to be cast on the matter by the voting group constitutes a quorum of that voting group for action on that matter.

(b) Once a share is represented for any purpose at a meeting, it is deemed present for quorum purposes for the remainder of the meeting and for any adjournment of that meeting unless a new record date is or must be set for that adjourned meeting.

(c) If a quorum exists, action on a matter (other than the election of directors) by a voting group is approved if the votes cast within the voting group favoring the action exceed the votes cast opposing the action, unless the articles of incorporation require a greater number of affirmative votes.

(d) An amendment of articles of incorporation adding, changing, or deleting a quorum or voting requirement for a voting group greater than specified in subsection (a) or (c) is governed by section 7.27.

(e) The election of directors is governed by section 7.28.

§ 7.26 Action by Single and Multiple Voting Groups

(a) If the articles of incorporation or this Act provide for voting by a single voting group on a matter, action on that matter is taken when voted upon by that voting group as provided in section 7.25.

(b) If the articles of incorporation or this act provide for voting by two or more voting groups on a matter, action on that matter is taken only when voted upon by each of those voting groups counted separately as provided in section 7.25. Action may be taken by one voting group on a matter even though no action is taken by another voting group entitled to vote on the matter.

§ 7.27 Greater Quorum or Voting Requirements

(a) The articles of incorporation may provide for a greater quorum or voting requirement for shareholders (or voting groups of shareholders) than is provided for by this Act.

(b) An amendment to the articles of incorporation that adds, changes, or deletes a greater quorum or voting requirement must meet the same quorum requirement and be adopted by the same vote and voting groups required to take action under the quorum and voting requirements then in effect or proposed to be adopted, whichever is greater.

§ 7.28 Voting for Directors; Cumulative Voting

(a) Unless otherwise provided in the articles of incorporation, directors are elected by a plurality of the votes cast by the shares entitled to vote in the election at a meeting at which a quorum is present.

(b) Shareholders do not have a right to cumulate their votes for directors unless the articles of incorporation so provide.

(c) A statement included in the articles of incorporation that "[all] [a designated voting group of] shareholders are entitled to cumulate their votes for directors" (or words of similar import) means that the shareholders designated are entitled to multiply the number of votes they are entitled to cast by the number of directors for whom they are entitled to vote and cast the product for a single candidate or distribute the product among two or more candidates.

(d) Shares otherwise entitled to vote cumulatively may not be voted cumulatively at a particular meeting unless:

(1) the meeting notice or proxy statement accompanying the notice states conspicuously that cumulative voting is authorized; or

(2) a shareholder who has the right to cumulate his votes gives notice to the corporation not less than 48 hours before the time set for the meeting of his intent to cumulate his votes during the meeting, and if one shareholder gives this notice all other shareholders in the same voting group participating in the election are entitled to cumulate their votes without giving further notice.

§ 7.29 Inspectors of Election

(a) A public corporation shall, and any other corporation may, appoint one or more inspectors to act at a meeting of shareholders and make a written report of the inspectors' determinations. Each inspector shall take and sign an oath faithfully to execute the duties of inspector with strict impartiality and according to the best of the inspector's ability.

(b) The inspectors shall

(1) ascertain the number of shares outstanding and the voting power of each;

(2) determine the shares represented at a meeting;

(3) determine the validity of proxies and ballots;

(4) count all votes; and

(5) determine the result.

(c) An inspector may be an officer or employee of the corporation.

Subchapter C. Voting Trusts and Agreements

§ 7.30 Voting Trusts

(a) One or more shareholders may create a voting trust, conferring on a trustee the right to vote or otherwise act for them, by signing an agreement setting out the provisions of the trust (which may include anything consistent with its purpose) and transferring their shares to the trustee. When a voting trust agreement is signed, the trustee shall prepare a list of the names and addresses of all owners of beneficial interests in the trust, together with the number and class of shares each transferred to the trust, and deliver copies of the list and agreement to the corporation's principal office.

(b) A voting trust becomes effective on the date the first shares subject to the trust are registered in the trustee's name. A voting trust is valid for not more than 10 years after its effective date unless extended under subsection (c).

(c) All or some of the parties to a voting trust may extend it for additional terms of not more than 10 years each by signing written consent to the extension. An extension is valid for 10 years from the date the first shareholder signs the extension agreement. The voting trustee must deliver copies of the extension agreement and list of beneficial owners to the corporation's principal office. An extension agreement binds only those parties signing it.

§ 7.31 Voting Agreements

(a) Two or more shareholders may provide for the manner in which they will vote their shares by signing an agreement for that purpose. A voting agreement created under this section is not subject to the provisions of section 7.30.

(b) A voting agreement created under this section is specifically enforceable.

§ 7.32 Shareholder Agreements

(a) An agreement among the shareholders of a corporation that complies with this section is effective among the shareholders and the corporation even though it is inconsistent with one or more other provisions of this Act in that it:

(1) eliminates the board of directors or restricts the discretion or powers of the board of directors;

(2) governs the authorization or making of distributions whether or not in proportion to ownership of shares, subject to the limitations in section 6.40;

(3) establishes who shall be directors or officers of the corporation, or their terms of office or manner of selection or removal;

(4) governs, in general or in regard to specific matters, the exercise or division of voting power by or between the shareholders and directors or by or among any of them, including use of weighted voting rights or director proxies;

(5) establishes the terms and conditions of any agreement for the transfer or use of property or the provision of services between the corporation and any shareholder, director, officer or employee of the corporation or among any of them;

(6) transfers to one or more shareholders or other persons all or part of the authority to exercise the corporate powers or to manage the business and affairs of the corporation, including the

resolution of any issue about which there exists a deadlock among directors or shareholders;

(7) requires dissolution of the corporation at the request of one or more of the shareholders or upon the occurrence of a specified event or contingency; or

(8) otherwise governs the exercise of the corporate powers or the management of the business and affairs of the corporation or the relationship among the shareholders, the directors and the corporation, or among any of them, and is not contrary to public policy.

(b) An agreement authorized by this section shall be:

(1) set forth (A) in the articles of incorporation or bylaws and approved by all persons who are shareholders at the time of the agreement or (B) in a written agreement that is signed by all persons who are shareholders at the time of the agreement and is made known to the corporation;

(2) subject to amendment only by all persons who are shareholders at the time of the amendment, unless the agreement provides otherwise; and

(3) valid for 10 years, unless the agreement provides otherwise.

(c) The existence of an agreement authorized by this section shall be noted conspicuously on the front or back of each certificate for outstanding shares or on the information statement required by section 6.26(b). If at the time of the agreement the corporation has shares outstanding represented by certificates, the corporation shall recall the outstanding certificates and issue substitute certificates that comply with this subsection. The failure to note the existence of the agreement on the certificate or information statement shall not affect the validity of the agreement or any action taken pursuant to it. Any purchaser of shares who, at the time of purchase, did not have knowledge of the existence of the agreement shall be entitled to rescission of the purchase. A purchaser shall be deemed to have knowledge of the existence of the agreement if its existence is noted on the certificate or information statement for the shares in compliance with this subsection and, if the shares are not represented by a certificate, the information statement is delivered to the purchaser at or prior to the time of purchase of the shares. An action to enforce the right of rescission authorized by this subsection must be commenced within the earlier of 90 days after discovery of the existence of the agreement or two years after the time of purchase of the shares.

(d) An agreement authorized by this section shall cease to be effective when the corporation becomes a public corporation. If the agreement ceases to be effective for any reason, the board of directors may, if the agreement is contained or referred to in the corporation's articles of incorporation or bylaws, adopt an amendment to the articles of incorporation or bylaws, without shareholder action, to delete the agreement and any references to it.

(e) An agreement authorized by this section that limits the discretion or powers of the board of directors shall relieve the directors of, and impose upon the person or persons in whom such discretion or powers are vested, liability for acts or omissions imposed by law on directors to the extent that the discretion or powers of the directors are limited by the agreement.

(f) The existence or performance of an agreement authorized by this section shall not be a ground for imposing personal liability on any shareholder for the acts or debts of the corporation even if the agreement or its performance treats the corporation as if it were a partnership or results in failure to observe the corporate formalities otherwise applicable to the matters governed by the agreement.

(g) Incorporators or subscribers for shares may act as shareholders with respect to an agreement authorized by this section if no shares have been issued when the agreement is made.

Subchapter D. Derivative Proceedings

§ 7.40 Subchapter Definitions

In this subchapter:

(1) "Derivative proceeding" means a civil suit in the right of a domestic corporation or, to the extent provided in section 7.47, in the right of a foreign corporation.

(2) "Shareholder" includes a beneficial owner whose shares are held in a voting trust or held by a nominee on the beneficial owner's behalf.

§ 7.41 Standing

A shareholder may not commence or maintain a derivative proceeding unless the shareholder:

(1) was a shareholder of the corporation at the time of the act or omission complained of or became a shareholder through transfer by operation of law from one who was a shareholder at that time; and

(2) fairly and adequately represents the interests of the corporation in enforcing the right of the corporation.

§ 7.42 Demand

No shareholder may commence a derivative proceeding until:

(1) a written demand has been made upon the corporation to take suitable action; and

(2) 90 days have expired from the date the demand was made unless the shareholder has earlier been notified that the demand has been rejected by the corporation or unless irreparable injury to the corporation would result by waiting for the expiration of the 90–day period.

OFFICIAL COMMENT

. . . .

2. Upon Whom Demand Should Be Made

Section 7.42 states that demand shall be made upon the corporation. Reference is not made specifically to the board of directors as in previous section 7.40(b) since there may be instances such as a decision to sue a third party for an injury to the corporation, in which the taking of, or refusal to take, action would fall within the authority of an officer of the corporation. Nevertheless, it is expected that in most cases the board of directors will be the appropriate body to review the demand.

To ensure that the demand reaches the appropriate person for review, it should be addressed to the board of directors, chief executive officer, or corporate secretary of the corporation at its principal office.

. . . .

§ 7.43 Stay of Proceedings

If the corporation commences an inquiry into the allegations made in the demand or complaint, the court may stay any derivative proceeding for such period as the court deems appropriate.

§ 7.44 Dismissal

(a) A derivative proceeding shall be dismissed by the court on motion by the corporation if one of the groups specified in subsection (b) or subsection (e) has determined in good faith, after conducting a reasonable inquiry upon which its conclusions are based, that the maintenance of the derivative proceeding is not in the best interests of the corporation.

(b) Unless a panel is appointed pursuant to subsection (e), the determination in subsection (a) shall be made by:

(1) a majority vote of qualified directors present at a meeting of the board of directors if the qualified directors constitute a quorum; or

(2) a majority vote of a committee consisting of two or more qualified directors appointed by majority vote of qualified directors present at a meeting of the board of directors, regardless of whether such qualified directors constitute a quorum.

(c) If a derivative proceeding is commenced after a determination has been made rejecting a demand by a shareholder, the complaint shall allege with particularity facts establishing either (1) that a majority of the board of directors did not consist of qualified directors at the time the determination was made or (2) that the requirements of subsection (a) have not been met.

(d) If a majority of the board of directors consisted of qualified directors at the time the determination was made, the plaintiff shall have the burden of proving that the requirements of subsection (a) have not been met; if not, the corporation shall have the burden of proving that the requirements of subsection (a) have been met.

(e) Upon motion by the corporation, the court may appoint a panel of one or more individuals to make a determination whether the maintenance of the derivative proceeding is in the best interests of the corporation. In such case, the plaintiff shall have the burden of proving that the requirements of subsection (a) have not been met.

§ 7.45 Discontinuance or Settlement

A derivative proceeding may not be discontinued or settled without the court's approval. If the court determines that a proposed discontinuance or settlement will substantially affect the interests of the corporation's shareholders or a class of shareholders, the court shall direct that notice be given to the shareholders affected.

§ 7.46 Payment of Expenses

On termination of the derivative proceeding the court may:

(1) order the corporation to pay the plaintiff's reasonable expenses (including counsel fees) incurred in the proceeding if it finds that the proceeding has resulted in a substantial benefit to the corporation;

(2) order the plaintiff to pay any defendant's reasonable expenses (including counsel fees) incurred in defending the proceeding if it finds that the proceeding was commenced or maintained without reasonable cause or for an improper purpose; or

(3) order a party to pay an opposing party's reasonable expenses (including counsel fees) incurred because of the filing of a pleading, motion or other paper, if it finds that the pleading, motion or other paper was not well grounded in fact, after reasonable inquiry, or warranted by existing law or a good faith argument for the extension, modification or reversal of existing law and was interposed for an improper purpose, such as to harass or cause unnecessary delay or needless increase in the cost of litigation.

§ 7.47 Applicability to Foreign Corporations

In any derivative proceeding in the right of a foreign corporation, the matters covered by this subchapter shall be governed by the laws of the jurisdiction of incorporation of the foreign corporation except for sections 7.43, 7.45, and 7.46.

CHAPTER 8

DIRECTORS AND OFFICERS

Subchapter A. Board of Directors

§ 8.01 Requirement for and Functions of Board of Directors

(a) Except as provided in section 7.32, each corporation must have a board of directors.

(b) All corporate powers shall be exercised by or under the authority of the board of directors of the corporation, and the business and affairs of the corporation shall be managed by or under the direction, and subject to the oversight, of its board of directors, subject to any limitation set forth in the articles of incorporation or in an agreement authorized under section 7.32.

(c) In the case of a public corporation, the board's oversight responsibilities include attention to:

(1) business performance and plans;

(2) major risks to which the corporation is or may be exposed;

(3) the performance and compensation of senior officers;

(4) policies and practices to foster the corporation's compliance with law and ethical conduct;

(5) preparation of the corporation's financial statements;

(6) the effectiveness of the corporation's internal controls;

(7) arrangements for providing adequate and timely information to directors; and

(8) the composition of the board and its committees, taking into account the important role of independent directors.

§ 8.02 Qualifications of Directors

The articles of incorporation or bylaws may prescribe qualifications for directors. A director need not be a resident of this state or a shareholder of the corporation unless the articles of incorporation or bylaws so prescribe.

§ 8.03 Number and Election of Directors

(a) A board of directors must consist of one or more individuals, with the number specified in or fixed in accordance with the articles of incorporation or bylaws.

(b) The number of directors may be increased or decreased from time to time by amendment to, or in the manner provided in, the articles of incorporation or the bylaws.

(c) Directors are elected at the first annual shareholders' meeting and at each annual meeting thereafter unless their terms are staggered under section 8.06.

§ 8.04 Election of Directors by Certain Classes of Shareholders

If the articles of incorporation authorize dividing the shares into classes, the articles may also authorize the election of all or a specified number of directors by the holders of one or more authorized classes of shares. A class (or classes) of shares entitled to elect one or more directors is a separate voting group for purposes of the election of directors.

§ 8.05 Terms of Directors Generally

(a) The terms of the initial directors of a corporation expire at the first shareholders' meeting at which directors are elected.

(b) The terms of all other directors expire at the next annual shareholders' meeting following their election unless their terms are staggered under section 8.06.

(c) A decrease in the number of directors does not shorten an incumbent director's term.

(d) The term of a director elected to fill a vacancy expires at the next shareholders' meeting at which directors are elected.

(e) Despite the expiration of a director's term, he continues to serve until his successor is elected and qualifies or until there is a decrease in the number of directors.

§ 8.06 Staggered Terms for Directors

The articles of incorporation may provide for staggering the terms of directors by dividing the total number of directors into two or three groups, with each group containing one-half or one-third of the total, as near as may be. In that event, the terms of directors in the first group expire at the first annual shareholders' meeting after their election, the terms of the second group expire at the second annual shareholders' meeting after their election, and the terms of the third group, if any, expire at the third annual shareholders' meeting after their election. At each annual shareholders' meeting held thereafter, directors shall be chosen for a term of two years or three years, as the case may be, to succeed those whose terms expire.

§ 8.07 Resignation of Directors

(a) A director may resign at any time by delivering written notice to the board of directors, its chairman, or to the corporation.

(b) A resignation is effective when the notice is delivered unless the notice specifies a later effective date.

§ 8.08 Removal of Directors by Shareholders

(a) The shareholders may remove one or more directors with or without cause unless the articles of incorporation provide that directors may be removed only for cause.

(b) If a director is elected by a voting group of shareholders, only the shareholders of that voting group may participate in the vote to remove him.

(c) If cumulative voting is authorized, a director may not be removed if the number of votes sufficient to elect him under cumulative voting is voted against his removal. If cumulative voting is not authorized, a director may be removed only if the number of votes cast to remove him exceeds the number of votes cast not to remove him.

(d) A director may be removed by the shareholders only at a meeting called for the purpose of removing him and the meeting notice must state that the purpose, or one of the purposes, of the meeting is removal of the director.

§ 8.09 Removal of Directors by Judicial Proceeding

(a) The [name or describe] court of the county where a corporation's principal office (or, if none in this state, its registered office) is located may remove a director of the corporation from office in a proceeding commenced by or in the right of the corporation if the court finds that (1) the director engaged in fraudulent conduct with respect to the corporation or its shareholders, grossly abused the position of director, or intentionally inflicted harm on the corporation; and (2) considering the director's course of conduct and the inadequacy of other available remedies, removal would be in the best interest of the corporation.

(b) A shareholder proceeding on behalf of the corporation under subsection (a) shall comply with all of the requirements of sub-chapter 7D, except section 7.41(1).

(c) The court, in addition to removing the director, may bar the director from reelection for a period prescribed by the court.

(d) Nothing in this section limits the equitable powers of the court to order other relief.

§ 8.10 Vacancy on Board

(a) Unless the articles of incorporation provide otherwise, if a vacancy occurs on a board of directors, including a vacancy resulting from an increase in the number of directors:

(1) the shareholders may fill the vacancy;

(2) the board of directors may fill the vacancy; or

(3) if the directors remaining in office constitute fewer than a quorum of the board, they may fill the vacancy by the affirmative vote of a majority of all the directors remaining in office.

(b) If the vacant office was held by a director elected by a voting group of shareholders, only the holders of shares of that voting group are entitled to vote to fill the vacancy if it is filled by the shareholders.

(c) A vacancy that will occur at a specific later date (by reason of a resignation effective at a later date under section 8.07(b) or otherwise) may be filled before the vacancy occurs but the new director may not take office until the vacancy occurs.

§ 8.11 Compensation of Directors

Unless the articles of incorporation or bylaws provide otherwise, the board of directors may fix the compensation of directors.

Subchapter B. Meetings and Action of the Board

§ 8.20 Meetings

(a) The board of directors may hold regular or special meetings in or out of this state.

(b) Unless the articles of incorporation or bylaws provide otherwise, the board of directors may permit any or all directors to participate in a regular or special meeting by, or conduct the meeting through the use of, any means of communication by which all directors participating may simultaneously hear each other during the meeting. A director participating in a meeting by this means is deemed to be present in person at the meeting.

§ 8.21 Action Without Meeting

(a) Except to the extent that the articles of incorporation or bylaws require that action by the board of directors be taken at a meeting, action required or permitted by this Act to be taken by the board of directors may be taken without a meeting if each director signs a consent describing the action to be taken and delivers it to the corporation.

(b) Action taken under this section is the act of the board of directors when one or more consents signed by all the directors are delivered to the corporation. The consent may specify the time at which the action taken thereunder is to be effective. A director's consent may be withdrawn by a revocation signed by the director and delivered to the corporation prior to delivery to the corporation of unrevoked written consents signed by all the directors.

(c) A consent signed under this section has the effect of action taken at a meeting of the board of directors and may be described as such in any document.

§ 8.22 Notice of Meeting

(a) Unless the articles of incorporation or bylaws provide otherwise, regular meetings of the board of directors may be held without notice of the date, time, place, or purpose of the meeting.

(b) Unless the articles of incorporation or bylaws provide for a longer or shorter period, special meetings of the board of directors must be preceded by at least two days' notice of the date, time, and place of the meeting. The notice need not describe the purpose of the special meeting unless required by the articles of incorporation or bylaws.

§ 8.23 Waiver of Notice

(a) A director may waive any notice required by this Act, the articles of incorporation, or bylaws before or after the date and time stated in the notice. Except as provided by subsection (b), the waiver must be in writing, signed by the director entitled to the notice, and filed with the minutes or corporate records.

(b) A director's attendance at or participation in a meeting waives any required notice to him of the meeting unless the director at the beginning of the meeting (or promptly upon his arrival) objects to holding the meeting or transacting business at the meeting and does not thereafter vote for or assent to action taken at the meeting.

§ 8.24 Quorum and Voting

(a) Unless the articles of incorporation or bylaws require a greater number or unless otherwise specifically provided in this Act, a quorum of a board of directors consists of:

(1) a majority of the fixed number of directors if the corporation has a fixed board size; or

(2) a majority of the number of directors prescribed, or if no number is prescribed the number in office immediately before the meeting begins, if the corporation has a variable-range size board.

(b) The articles of incorporation or bylaws may authorize a quorum of a board of directors to consist of no fewer than one-third of the fixed or prescribed number of directors determined under subsection (a).

(c) If a quorum is present when a vote is taken, the affirmative vote of a majority of directors present is the act of the board of directors unless the articles of incorporation or bylaws require the vote of a greater number of directors.

(d) A director who is present at a meeting of the board of directors or a committee of the board of directors when corporate action is taken is deemed to have assented to the action taken unless: (1) he objects at the beginning of the meeting (or promptly upon his arrival) to holding it or transacting business at the meeting; (2) his dissent or abstention from the action taken is entered in the minutes of the meeting; or (3) he delivers written notice of his dissent or abstention to the presiding officer of the meeting before its adjournment or to the corporation immediately after adjournment of the meeting. The right of dissent or abstention is not available to a director who votes in favor of the action taken.

§ 8.25 Committees

(a) Unless this Act, the articles of incorporation or the bylaws provide otherwise, a board of directors may create one or more committees and appoint one or more members of the board of directors to serve on any such committee.

(b) Unless this Act otherwise provides, the creation of a committee and appointment of members to it must be approved by the greater of (1) a majority of all the directors in office when the action is taken or (2) the number of directors required by the articles of incorporation or bylaws to take action under section 8.24.

(c) Sections 8.20 through 8.24 apply both to committees of the board and to their members.

(d) To the extent specified by the board of directors or in the articles of incorporation or bylaws, each committee may exercise the powers of the board of directors under section 8.01.

(e) A committee may not, however:

(1) authorize or approve distributions, except according to a formula or method, or within limits, prescribed by the board of directors;

(2) approve or propose to shareholders action that this Act requires be approved by shareholders;

(3) fill vacancies on the board of directors or, subject to subsection (g), on any of its committees; or

(4) adopt, amend, or repeal bylaws.

(f) The creation of, delegation of authority to, or action by a committee does not alone constitute compliance by a director with the standards of conduct described in section 8.30.

(g) The board of directors may appoint one or more directors as alternate members of any committee to replace any absent or disqualified member during the member's absence or disqualification. Unless the articles of incorporation or the bylaws or the resolution creating the committee provide otherwise, in the event of the absence or disqualification of a member of a committee, the member or members present at any meeting and not disqualified from voting, unanimously, may appoint another director to act in place of the absent or disqualified member.

Subchapter C. Directors

§ 8.30 Standards of Conduct for Directors

(a) Each member of the board of directors, when discharging the duties of a director, shall act: (1) in good faith, and (2) in a manner the director reasonably believes to be in the best interests of the corporation.

(b) The members of the board of directors or a committee of the board, when becoming informed in connection with their decision-making function or devoting attention to their oversight function, shall discharge their duties with the care that a person in a like position would reasonably believe appropriate under similar circumstances.

(c) In discharging board or committee duties a director shall disclose, or cause to be disclosed, to the other board or committee members information not already known by them but known by the director to be material to the discharge of their decision-making or oversight functions, except that disclosure is not required to the extent that the director reasonably believes that doing so would violate a duty imposed under law, a legally enforceable obligation of confidentiality, or a professional ethics rule.

(d) In discharging board or committee duties a director who does not have knowledge that makes reliance unwarranted is entitled to rely on the performance by any of the persons specified in subsection (f)(1) or subsection (f)(3) to whom the board may have delegated, formally or informally by course of conduct, the authority or duty to perform one or more of the board's functions that are delegable under applicable law.

(e) In discharging board or committee duties a director who does not have knowledge that makes reliance unwarranted is entitled to rely on information, opinions, reports or statements, including financial statements and other financial data, prepared or presented by any of the persons specified in subsection (f).

(f) A director is entitled to rely, in accordance with subsection (d) or (e), on:

(1) one or more officers or employees of the corporation whom the director reasonably believes to be reliable and competent in the functions performed or the information, opinions, reports or statements provided;

(2) legal counsel, public accountants, or other persons retained by the corporation as to matters involving skills or expertise the director reasonably believes are matters (i) within the particular person's professional or expert competence or (ii) as to which the particular person merits confidence; or

(3) a committee of the board of directors of which the director is not a member if the director reasonably believes the committee merits confidence.

OFFICIAL COMMENT

Section 8.30 defines the general standards of conduct for directors. Under subsection (a), each board member must always perform a director's duties in good faith and in a manner reasonably believed to be in the best interests of the corporation. Although each director also has a duty to comply with its requirements, the focus of subsection (b) is on the discharge of those duties by the board as a collegial body. Under subsection (b), the members of the board or a board committee are to perform their duties with the care that a person in a like position would reasonably believe appropriate under similar circumstances. This standard of conduct is often characterized as a duty of care. Subsection (c) sets out the responsibility of each director, in discharging board or committee duties, to disclose or cause to be disclosed to the other members of the board or board committee information, of which they are unaware, known by the director to be material to their decision-making or oversight responsibilities, subject to countervailing confidentiality duties and appropriate action with respect thereto.

Section 8.30 sets forth the standards of conduct for directors by focusing on the manner in which directors perform their duties, not the correctness of the decisions made. These standards of conduct are based on former section 35 of the 1969 Model Act, a number of state statutes and on judicial formulations of the standards of conduct applicable to directors. Section 8.30 should be read in light of the basic role of directors set forth in section 8.01(b), which provides that the "business and affairs of a corporation shall be managed by or under the direction and subject to the oversight of" the board, as supplemented by various provisions of the Act assigning specific powers or responsibilities to the board. Relevant thereto, directors often act collegially in performing their functions and discharging their duties. If the observance of the directors' conduct is called into question, courts will typically evaluate the conduct of the entire board (or committee). Deficient performance of section 8.30 duties on the part of a particular director may be overcome, absent unusual circumstances, by acceptable conduct (meeting, for example, subsection (b)'s standard of care) on the part of other directors sufficient in number to perform the function or discharge the duty in question. While not thereby remedied, the deficient performance becomes irrelevant in any evaluation of the action taken. (This contrasts with a director's duties of loyalty, fair dealing and disclosure which will be evaluated on an individual basis and will also implicate discharge of the director's duties under subsection (a).) Further relevant thereto, the board may delegate or assign to appropriate officers, employees or agents of the corporation the authority or duty to exercise powers that the law does not require it to retain. Since the directors are entitled to rely thereon absent knowledge making reliance unwarranted, deficient performance of the directors' section 8.30 duties will not result from their delegatees' actions or omissions so long as the board acted in good faith and complied with the other standards of conduct set forth in section 8.30 in delegating responsibility and, where appropriate, monitoring performance of the duties delegated.

In earlier versions of the Model Act the duty of care element was included in subsection (a), with the text reading: "[a] director shall discharge his duties . . . with the care an ordinarily prudent person in a like position would exercise under similar circumstances." The use of the phrase "ordinarily prudent person" in a basic guideline for director conduct, suggesting caution or circumspection vis-à-vis danger or risk, has long been problematic given the fact that risk-taking decisions are central to the directors' role. When coupled with the exercise of "care," the prior text had a familiar resonance long associated with the field of tort law. See the Official Comment to section 8.31. The further coupling with the phrasal verb "shall discharge" added to the inference that former section 8.30(a)'s standard of conduct involved a negligence standard, with resultant confusion. In order to facilitate its understanding and analysis, independent of the other general standards of conduct for directors, the duty of care element has been set forth as a separate standard of conduct in subsection (b).

Long before statutory formulations of directors' standards of conduct, courts would invoke the business judgment rule in evaluating directors' conduct and determining whether to impose liability in a particular case. The elements of the business judgment rule and the circumstances for its application are continuing to be developed by the courts. Section 8.30 does not try to codify the business judgment rule or to delineate the differences between that defensive rule and the section's standards of director conduct. Section 8.30 deals only with standards of conduct—the level of performance expected of every director entering into the service of a corporation and undertaking the role and responsibilities of the office of director. The section does not deal directly with the liability of a director—although exposure to liability will usually result from a failure to honor the standards of conduct required to be observed by subsection (a). See section 8.31(a)(1) and clauses (i) and (ii)(A) of section 8.31(a)(2). The issue of directors' liability is addressed in sections 8.31 and 8.33 of this subchapter. Section 8.30 does, however, play an important role in evaluating a director's conduct and the effectiveness of board action. It has relevance in assessing, under section 8.31, the reasonableness of a director's belief. Similarly, it has relevance in assessing a director's timely attention to appropriate inquiry when particular facts and circumstances of significant concern materialize. It serves as a frame of reference for determining, under section 8.33(a), liability for an unlawful distribution. Finally, section 8.30 compliance may have a direct bearing on a court's analysis where transactional justification (*e.g.*, a suit to enjoin a pending merger) is at issue.

A director complying with the standard of care expressed in subsection (b) is entitled to rely (under subsection (c)) upon board functions performed pursuant to delegated authority by, and to rely (under subsection (d)) upon information, opinions, reports or statements, including financial statements and other financial data, provided by, the persons or committees specified in the relevant parts of subsection (e). Within this authorization, the right to rely applies to the entire range of matters for which the board of directors is responsible. However, a director so relying must be without knowledge that would cause that reliance to be unwarranted. Section 8.30 expressly prevents a director from "hiding his or her head in the sand" and relying on the delegation of board functions, or on information, opinions reports or statements, when the director has actual knowledge that makes (or has a measure of knowledge that would cause a person, in a like position under similar circumstances, to undertake reasonable inquiry that would lead to information making) reliance unwarranted. Subsection (a)'s standards of good faith and reasonable belief in the best interests of the corporation also apply to a director's reliance under subsections (d), (e) and (f).

1. Section 8.30(a)

Section 8.30(a) establishes the basic standards of conduct for all directors. Its command is to be understood as peremptory—its obligations are to be observed by every director—and at the core of the subsection's mandate is the requirement that, when performing directors' duties, a director shall act in good faith coupled with conduct reasonably believed to be in the best interests of the corporation. This mandate governs all aspects of directors' duties: the duty of care, the duty to become informed, the duty of inquiry, the duty of informed judgment, the duty of attention, the duty of disclosure, the duty of loyalty, the duty of fair dealing and, finally, the broad concept of fiduciary duty that the courts often use as a frame of reference when evaluating a director's conduct. These duties do not necessarily compartmentalize and, in fact, tend to overlap. For example, the duties of care, inquiry, becoming informed, attention, disclosure and informed judgment all relate to the board's decision-making function, whereas the duties of attention, disclosure, becoming informed and inquiry relate to the board's oversight function.

Two of the phrases chosen to specify the manner in which a director's duties are to be discharged deserve further comment:

(1) The phrase "reasonably believes" is both subjective and objective in character. Its first level of analysis is geared to what the

particular director, acting in good faith, actually believes—not what objective analysis would lead another director (in a like position and acting in similar circumstances) to conclude. The second level of analysis is focused specifically on "reasonably." While a director has wide discretion in marshalling the evidence and reaching conclusions, whether a director's belief is reasonable (*i.e.*, could—not would—a reasonable person in a like position and acting in similar circumstances have arrived at that belief) ultimately involves an overview that is objective in character.

(2) The phrase "best interests of the corporation" is key to an explication of a director's duties. The term "corporation" is a surrogate for the business enterprise as well as a frame of reference encompassing the shareholder body. In determining the corporation's "best interests," the director has wide discretion in deciding how to weigh near-term opportunities versus long-term benefits as well as in making judgments where the interests of various groups within the shareholder body or having other cognizable interests in the enterprise may differ.

As a generalization, section 8.30 operates as a "baseline" principle governing director conduct "when discharging the [ongoing] duties of a director" in circumstances uncomplicated by self-interest taint. The Model Act recognizes, however, that directors' personal interests may not always align with the corporation's best interests and provides procedures by which interest-conflict transactions can be processed. See subchapter D (derivative proceedings) of chapter 7, subchapter E (indemnification), subchapter F (directors' conflicting interest transactions), and subchapter G (business opportunities) of this chapter 8. Those procedures generally contemplate that the interested director will not be involved in taking action on the interest-conflict transaction. And the common law has recognized that other interest-conflict situations may arise which do not entail a "transaction" by or with the corporation. See subchapter G of this chapter 8 (discussing the corporate opportunity doctrine). The interested director is relieved of the duty to act in connection with the matter on behalf of the corporation (specifically, the traditional mandate to act in the corporation's best interests), given the inherent conflict. However, the interested director is still expected to act in good faith, and that duty is normally discharged by observing the obligation of fair dealing. In the case of interest-conflict transactions, where there is a conflicting interest with respect to the corporation under section 8.60(1), the interested director's conduct is governed by subchapter F of this chapter 8. The duty of fair dealing is embedded in the subsection 8.60(4) provision calling for the interested director to make the required disclosure as to the conflicting interest and the transaction and, if one of the two safe harbor procedures is not properly observed, the interested director must prove the fairness (*i.e.*, procedure, involving good faith among other aspects, as well as price) of the transaction to the corporation. In other cases, Section 8.30's standards of conduct are overlaid by various components of the duty to act fairly, the particular thrusts of which will depend upon the kind of interested director's conduct at issue and the circumstances of the case. As a general rule, the duty of fair dealing is normally discharged by the interested director through appropriate disclosure to the other directors considering the matter followed by abstention from participation in any decision-making relevant thereto. If and to the extent that the interested director's action respecting the matter goes further, the reasonableness of the director's belief as to the corporation's best interests, in respect of the action taken, should be evaluated on the basis of not only the director's honest and good faith belief but also on considerations bearing on the fairness of the transaction or conduct to the corporation.

2. Section 8.30(b)

Section 8.30(b) establishes a general standard of care for directors in the context of their dealing with the board's decision-making and oversight functions. While certain aspects will involve individual conduct (*e.g.*, preparation for meetings), these functions are generally performed by the board through collegial action, as recognized by the reference in subsection (b) to board and committee "members" and "their duties." In contrast with subsection (a)'s individual conduct mandate, section 8.30(b) has a two-fold thrust: it provides a standard of conduct for individual action and, more broadly, it states a conduct obligation—"shall discharge their duties"—concerning the degree of care to be collegially used by the directors when performing those functions. It provides that directors have a duty to exercise "the care that a person in a like position would reasonably believe appropriate under similar circumstances."

The traditional formulation for a director's standard (or duty) of care has been geared to the "ordinarily prudent person." For example, the Model Act's prior formulation (in former section 8.30(a)(2)) referred to "the care an ordinarily prudent person in a like position would exercise under similar circumstances," and almost all state statutes that include a standard of care reflect parallel language. The phrase "ordinarily prudent person" constitutes a basic frame of reference grounded in the field of tort law and provides a primary benchmark for determining negligence. For this reason, its use in the standard of care for directors, suggesting that negligence is the proper determinant for measuring deficient (and thus actionable) conduct, has caused confusion and misunderstanding. Accordingly, the phrase "ordinarily prudent person" has been removed from the Model Act's standard of care and in its place "a person in a like position" has been substituted. The standard is not what care a particular director might believe appropriate in the circumstances but what a person—in a like position and acting under similar circumstances—would reasonably believe to be appropriate. Thus, the degree of care that directors should employ, under subsection (b), involves an objective standard.

Some state statutes have used the words "diligence," "care," and "skill" to define the duty of care. There is very little authority as to what "skill" and "diligence," as distinguished from "care," can be required or properly expected of corporate directors in the performance of their duties. "Skill," in the sense of technical competence in a particular field, should not be a qualification for the office of director. The concept of "diligence" is sufficiently subsumed within the concept of "care." Accordingly, the words "diligence" and "skill" are not used in section 8.30's standard of care.

The process by which a director becomes informed, in carrying out the decision-making and oversight functions, will vary. Relevant thereto, the directors' decision-making function is established in large part by various sections of the Act: the issuance of shares (6.21); distributions (6.40); dismissal of derivative proceedings (7.44); indemnification (8.55); interested-transaction authorization (8.62); articles of incorporation amendments (10.02 and 10.03); bylaw amendments (10.20); mergers (11.01); share exchanges (11.02); asset dispositions and mortgages (12.01 and 12.02); and dissolution (14.02). The directors' oversight function is established under section 8.01. In relying on the performance by management of delegated or assigned section 8.01 duties (including, for example, matters of law and legal compliance), as authorized by subsection (d), directors may depend upon the presumption of regularity absent knowledge or notice to the contrary. In discharging the section 8.01 duties associated with the board's oversight function, the standard of care entails primarily a duty of attention. In contrast with the board's decision-making function, which generally involves informed action at a point in time, the oversight function is concerned with a continuum and the duty of attention accordingly involves participatory performance over a period of time.

Several of the phrases chosen to define the standard of conduct in section 8.30(b) deserve specific mention:

(1) The phrase "becoming informed," in the context of the decision-making function, refers to the process of gaining sufficient familiarity with the background facts and circumstances in order to make an informed judgment. Unless the circumstances would permit a reasonable director to conclude that he or she is already sufficiently informed, the standard of care requires every director to take steps to become informed about the background facts and circumstances before taking action on the matter at hand. The process typically involves review of written materials provided before or at the meeting and attention to/participation in the deliberations leading up to a vote. It can involve consideration of information and data generated by persons other than legal counsel, public accountants, etc., retained by the corporation, as contemplated by subsection (e)(2); for example, review of industry studies or research articles prepared by unrelated parties could be very useful. It can also involve direct communications, outside of the boardroom, with members of management or other directors. There is no one way for "becoming informed," and both the method and measure—"how to" and

"how much"—are matters of reasonable judgment for the director to exercise.

(2) The phrase "devoting attention," in the context of the oversight function, refers to concern with the corporation's information and reporting systems and not to proactive inquiry searching out system inadequacies or noncompliance. While directors typically give attention to future plans and trends as well as current activities, they should not be expected to anticipate the problems which the corporation may face except in those circumstances where something has occurred to make it obvious to the board that the corporation should be addressing a particular problem. The standard of care associated with the oversight function involves gaining assurances from management and advisers that systems believed appropriate have been established coupled with ongoing monitoring of the systems in place, such as those concerned with legal compliance or internal controls—followed up with a proactive response when alerted to the need for inquiry.

(3) The reference to "person," without embellishment, is intended to avoid implying any qualifications, such as specialized expertise or experience requirements, beyond the basic director attributes of common sense, practical wisdom, and informed judgment.

(4) The phrase "reasonably believe appropriate" refers to the array of possible options that a person possessing the basic director attributes of common sense, practical wisdom and informed judgment would recognize to be available, in terms of the degree of care that might be appropriate, and from which a choice by such person would be made. The measure of care that such person might determine to be appropriate, in a given instance, would normally involve a selection from the range of options and any choice within the realm of reason would be an appropriate decision under the standard of care called for under subsection (b). However, a decision that is so removed from the realm of reason, or is so unreasonable, that it falls outside the permissible bounds of sound discretion, and thus an abuse of discretion, will not satisfy the standard.

(5) The phrase "in a like position" recognizes that the "care" under consideration is that which would be used by the "person" if he or she were a director of the particular corporation.

(6) The combined phrase "in a like position ... under similar circumstances" is intended to recognize that (a) the nature and extent of responsibilities will vary, depending upon such factors as the size, complexity, urgency, and location of activities carried on by the particular corporation, (b) decisions must be made on the basis of the information known to the directors without the benefit of hindsight, and (c) the special background, qualifications, and management responsibilities of a particular director may be relevant in evaluating that director's compliance with the standard of care. Even though the combined phrase is intended to take into account the special background, qualifications and

management responsibilities of a particular director, it does not excuse a director lacking business experience or particular expertise from exercising the basic director attributes of common sense, practical wisdom, and informed judgment.

3. Section 8.30(c)

A duty to disclose information that a director knows to be material to the oversight or decision-making functions of the board or committee has always been embraced in the standards of conduct set forth in subsections (a) and (b). Subsection (c) makes explicit this existing duty of disclosure among directors. Thus, for example, when a member of the board knows information that the director recognizes is material to a decision by the board to approve financial statements of the corporation, the director is obligated to see to it that such information is provided to the other members of the board. So long as that disclosure is accomplished, the action required of the director can occur through direct statements in meetings of the board, or by any other timely means, including, for example, communicating the information to the chairman of the board or the chairman of a committee, or to the corporation's general counsel, and requesting that the recipient inform the other board or committee members of the disclosed information.

Subsection (c) recognizes that a duty of confidentiality can override a director's obligation to share with other directors information pertaining to a current corporate matter and that a director is not required to make such disclosure to the extent the director reasonably believes that such a duty of confidentiality prohibits it. In some circumstances, a duty of confidentiality may even prohibit disclosure of the nature or the existence of the duty itself. Ordinarily, however, a director who withholds material information based on a reasonable belief that a duty of confidentiality prohibits disclosure should advise the other directors of the existence and nature of that duty. Under the standards of conduct set forth in section 8.30(a), the director may also be required to take other action in light of the confidentiality restraint. The precise nature of that action must, of necessity, depend on the specific circumstances. Depending on the nature of the material information and of the matter before the board of directors or committee of the board, such action may include abstention or absence from all or a portion of the other directors' deliberation or vote on the matter to which the undisclosed information is material, or even resignation as a director. See Official Comment to section 8.62. Finally, a duty of confidentiality may not form the basis for the limitation on disclosure unless it is entered into and relied upon in good faith.

The required disclosure (as defined in section 8.60(7)) that must be made under section 8.62(a) in connection with a director's conflicting interest transaction, and the exceptions to the required disclosure in that context under section 8.62(b), have elements that parallel the disclosure obligation of directors under section 8.30(c). The demands of section

8.62, however, are more detailed and specific. They apply to just one situation—a director's conflict of interest transaction—while the requirements of section 8.30(c) apply generally to all other decision-making and oversight functions. For example, the specific requirements of section 8.62(a)(1) for a deliberation and vote outside the presence of the conflicted director are not imposed universally for all decision-making matters or for oversight matters that do not involve a decision. To the extent they may be different from the generally applicable provisions of section 8.30(c), the specific provisions of subchapter F control and are exclusive with respect to director conflicting interest transactions.

4. Section 8.30(d)

The delegation of authority and responsibility under subsection (d) may take the form of (i) formal action through a board resolution, (ii) implicit action through the election of corporate officers (*e.g.*, chief financial officer or controller) or the appointment of corporate managers (e.g., credit manager), or (iii) informal action through a course of conduct (*e.g.*, involvement through corporate officers and managers in the management of a significant 50%-owned joint venture). A director may properly rely on those to whom authority has been delegated pursuant to subsection (d) respecting particular matters calling for specific action or attention in connection with the directors' decision-making function as well as matters on the board's continuing agenda, such as legal compliance and internal control, in connection with the directors' oversight function. Delegation should be carried out in accordance with the standard of care set forth in section 8.30(b).

By identifying those upon whom a director may rely in connection with the discharge of duties, section 8.30(d) does not limit the ability of directors to delegate their powers under section 8.01(b) except where delegation is expressly prohibited by the Act or otherwise by applicable law (see, *e.g.*, section 8.25(e) and § 11 of the Securities Act of 1933). See section 8.25 and its Official Comment for detailed consideration of delegation to board committees of the authority of the board under section 8.01 and the duty to perform one or more of the board's functions. And by employing the concept of delegation, section 8.30(d) does not limit the ability of directors to establish baseline principles as to management responsibilities. Specifically, section 8.01(b) provides that "all corporate powers shall be exercised by or under the authority of" the board, and a basic board function involves the allocation of management responsibilities and the related assignment (or delegation) of corporate powers. For example, a board can properly decide to retain a third party to assume responsibility for the administration of designated aspects of risk management for the corporation (*e.g.*, health insurance or disability claims). This would involve the directors in the exercise of judgment in connection with the decision-making function pursuant to subsection (b) (*i.e.*, the assignment of authority to exercise corporate powers to an agent). See the Official Comment to section 8.01. It would not entail impermissible delegation-to a person specified in subsection (f)(2) pursuant to subsection (d) of a board function for which the directors by law have a duty to perform. They have the corporate power (under section 8.01(b)) to perform the task but administration of risk management is not a board function coming within the ambit of directors' duties; together with many similar management responsibilities, they may assign the task in the context of the allocation of corporate powers exercised under the authority of the board. This illustration highlights the distinction between delegation of a board function and assignment of authority to exercise corporate powers.

Although the board may delegate the authority or duty to perform one or more of its functions, reliance on delegation under subsection (d) may not alone constitute compliance with section 8.30 and reliance on the action taken by the delegatee may not alone constitute compliance by the directors or a noncommittee board member with section 8.01 responsibilities. On the other hand, should the board committee or the corporate officer or employee performing the function delegated fail to meet section 8.30's standard of care, noncompliance by the board with section 8.01 will not automatically result. Factors to be considered, in this regard, will include the care used in the delegation to and supervision over the delegatee, and the amount of knowledge regarding the particular matter which is available to the particular director. Care in delegation and supervision includes appraisal of the capabilities and diligence of the delegatee in light of the subject and its relative importance and may be facilitated, in the usual case, by receipt of reports concerning the delegatee's activities. The enumeration of these factors is intended to emphasize that directors may not abdicate their responsibilities and avoid accountability simply by delegating authority to others. Rather, a director charged with accountability based upon acts of others will fulfill the director's duties if the standards contained in section 8.30 are met.

5. Section 8.30(e)

Reliance under subsection (e) on a report, statement, opinion, or other information is permitted only if the director has read the information, opinion, report or statement in question, or was present at a meeting at which it was orally presented, or took other steps to become generally familiar with it. A director must comply with the general standard of care of section 8.30(b) in making a judgment as to the reliability and competence of the source of information upon which the director proposes to rely or, as appropriate, that it otherwise merits confidence.

6. Section 8.30(f)

Reliance on one or more of the corporation's officers or employees, pursuant to the intracorporate frame of reference of subsection (f)(1), is conditioned upon a reasonable belief as to the reliability and competence of those who have undertaken the functions performed or who prepared or communicated the information, opinions, reports or statements presented. In determining whether a person is "reliable," the director would typically consider (i) the individual's background experience and scope of responsibility within the corporation in gauging the individual's familiarity and knowledge respecting the subject matter and (ii) the individual's record and reputation for honesty, care and ability in discharging responsibilities which he or she undertakes. In determining whether a person is "competent," the director would normally take into account the same considerations and, if expertise should be relevant, the director would consider the individual's technical skills as well. Recognition in the statute of the right of one director to rely on the expertise and experience of another director, in the context of board or committee deliberations, is unnecessary, for the group's reliance on shared experience and wisdom is an implicit underpinning of director conduct. In relying on another member of the board, a director would quite properly take advantage of the colleague's knowledge and experience in becoming informed about the matter at hand before taking action; however, the director would be expected to exercise independent judgment when it comes time to vote.

Subsection (f)(2), which has an extracorporate frame of reference, permits reliance on outside advisers retained by the corporation, including persons specifically engaged to advise the board or a board committee. Possible advisers include not only those in the professional disciplines customarily supervised by state authorities, such as lawyers, accountants, and engineers, but also those in other fields involving special experience and skills, such as investment bankers, geologists, management consultants, actuaries, and real estate appraisers. The adviser could be an individual or an organization, such as a law firm. Reliance on a nonmanagement director, who is specifically engaged (and, normally, additionally compensated) to undertake a special assignment or a particular consulting role, would fall within this outside adviser frame of reference. The concept of "expert competence" embraces a wide variety of qualifications and is not limited to the more precise and narrower recognition of experts under the Securities Act of 1933. In this respect, subsection (f)(2) goes beyond the reliance provision found in many existing state business corporation acts. In addition, a director may also rely on outside advisers where skills or expertise of a technical nature is not a prerequisite, or where the person's professional or expert competence has not been established, so long as the director reasonably believes the person merits confidence. For example, a board might choose to assign to a private investigator the duty of inquiry (*e.g.*, follow upon rumors about a senior executive's "grand lifestyle") and properly rely on the private investigator's report. And it would be entirely appropriate for a director to rely on advice concerning highly technical aspects of environmental compliance from a corporate lawyer in the corporation's outside law firm, without due inquiry concerning that particular lawyer's technical competence, where the director reasonably believes the lawyer giving the advice is appropriately informed (by reason of resources known to be available from that adviser's legal organization or through other means and therefore merits confidence).

Subsection (f)(3) permits reliance on a board committee when it is submitting recommendations for action by the full board of directors as well as when it is performing supervisory or other functions in instances where neither the full board of directors nor the committee takes dispositive action. For example, the compensation committee typically reviews proposals and makes recommendations for action by the full board of directors. In contrast, there may be reliance upon an investigation undertaken by a board committee and reported to the full board, which form the basis for a decision by the board of directors not to take dispositive action. Another example is reliance on a committee of the board of directors, such as a corporate audit committee with respect to the board's ongoing role of oversight of the accounting and auditing functions of the corporation. In addition where reliance on information or materials prepared or presented by a board committee is not involved, in connection with board action, a director may properly rely on oversight monitoring or dispositive action by a board committee (of which the director is not a member) empowered to act pursuant to authority delegated under section 8.25 or acting with the acquiescence of the board of directors. See the Official Comment to section 8.25. A director may similarly rely on committees not created under section 8.25 which have nondirector members. In parallel with subsection (f)(2)(ii), the concept of "confidence" is substituted for "competence" in order to avoid any inference that technical skills are a prerequisite. In the usual case, the appointment of committee members or the reconstitution of the membership of a standing committee (*e.g.*, the audit committee), following an annual shareholders' meeting, would alone manifest the noncommittee members' belief that the committee "merits confidence." However, the reliance contemplated by subsection (f)(3) is geared to the point in time when the board takes action or the period of time over which a committee is engaged in an oversight function; consequently, the judgment to be made (*i.e.*, whether a committee "merits confidence") will arise at varying points in time. After making an initial judgment that a committee (of which a director is not a member) merits confidence, the director may depend upon the presumption of regularity absent knowledge or notice to the contrary.

7. Application to Officers

Section 8.30 generally deals only with directors. Section 8.42 and its Official Comment explain the extent to which the provisions of section 8.30 apply to officers.

§ 8.31 Standards of Liability for Directors

(a) A director shall not be liable to the corporation or its shareholders for any decision to take or not to take action, or any failure to take any action, as a director, unless the party asserting liability in a proceeding establishes that:

(1) no defense interposed by the director based on (i) any provision in the articles of incorporation authorized by section 2.02(b)(4) or, (ii) the protection afforded by section 8.61 (for action taken in compliance with section 8.62 or section 8.63), or (iii) the protection afforded by section 8.70, precludes liability; and

(2) the challenged conduct consisted or was the result of:

(i) action not in good faith; or

(ii) a decision

(A) which the director did not reasonably believe to be in the best interests of the corporation, or

(B) as to which the director was not informed to an extent the director reasonably believed appropriate in the circumstances; or

(iii) a lack of objectivity due to the director's familial, financial or business relationship with, or a lack of independence due to the director's domination or control by, another person having a material interest in the challenged conduct

(A) which relationship or which domination or control could reasonably be expected to have affected the director's judgment respecting the challenged conduct in a manner adverse to the corporation, and

(B) after a reasonable expectation to such effect has been established, the director shall not have established that the challenged conduct was reasonably believed by the director to be in the best interests of the corporation; or

(iv) a sustained failure of the director to devote attention to ongoing oversight of the business and affairs of the corporation, or a failure to devote timely attention, by making (or causing to be made) appropriate inquiry, when particular facts and circumstances of significant concern materialize that would alert a reasonably attentive director to the need therefore; or

(v) receipt of a financial benefit to which the director was not entitled or any other breach of the director's duties to deal fairly with the corporation and its shareholders that is actionable under applicable law.

(b) The party seeking to hold the director liable:

(1) for money damages, shall also have the burden of establishing that:

(i) harm to the corporation or its shareholders has been suffered, and

(ii) the harm suffered was proximately caused by the director's challenged conduct; or

(2) for other money payment under a legal remedy, such as compensation for the unauthorized use of corporate assets, shall also have whatever persuasion burden may be called for to establish that the payment sought is appropriate in the circumstances; or

(3) for other money payment under an equitable remedy, such as profit recovery by or disgorgement to the corporation, shall also have whatever persuasion burden may be called for to establish that the equitable remedy sought is appropriate in the circumstances.

(c) Nothing contained in this section shall (1) in any instance where fairness is at issue, such as consideration of the fairness of a transaction to the corporation under section 8.61(b)(3), alter the burden of proving the fact or lack of fairness otherwise applicable, (2) alter the fact or lack of liability of a director under another section of this Act, such as the provisions governing the consequences of an unlawful distribution under section 8.33 or a transactional interest under section 8.61, or (3) affect any rights to which the corporation or a shareholder may be entitled under another statute of this state or the United States.

OFFICIAL COMMENT

Subsections (a) and (b) of section 8.30 establish standards of conduct that are central to the role of directors. Section 8.30(b)'s standard of conduct is frequently referred to as a director's duty of care. The employment of the concept of "care," if considered in the abstract, suggests a tort-law/negligence-based analysis looking toward a finding of fault and damage recovery where the duty of care has not been properly observed and loss has been suffered. But the Model Act's desired level of director performance, with its objectively-based standard of conduct ("the care that a person in a like position would reasonably believe appropriate under similar circumstances"), does not carry with it the same type of result-oriented liability analysis. The courts recognize that boards of directors and corporate managers make numerous decisions that involve the balancing of risks and benefits for the enterprise. Although some decisions turn out to be unwise or the result of a mistake of judgment, it is not reasonable to reexamine an unsuccessful decision with the benefit of hindsight. As observed in *Joy v. North*, 692 F.2d 880, 885 (2d Cir. 1982): "Whereas an automobile driver who makes a mistake in judgment as to speed or distance injuring a pedestrian will likely be called upon to respond in damages, a corporate [director or] officer who makes a mistake in judgment as to economic conditions, consumer tastes or production line efficiency will rarely, if ever, be found liable for damages suffered by the corporation." Therefore, as a general rule, a director is not exposed to personal liability for injury or damage caused by an unwise decision. While a director is not personally responsible for unwise decisions or mistakes of judgment—and conduct conforming with the standards of section 8.30 will almost always be protected—a director can be held liable for misfeasance or nonfeasance in performing the duties of a director. And while a director whose performance meets the standards of section 8.30 should have no liability, the fact that a director's performance fails to reach that level does not automatically establish personal liability for damages that the corporation may have suffered as a consequence.

* * *

Note on Directors' Liability

A director's financial risk exposure (*e.g.*, in a lawsuit for money damages suffered by the corporation or its shareholders claimed to have resulted from misfeasance or nonfeasance in connection with the performance of the director's duties) can be analyzed as follows:

1. *Articles of incorporation limitation.* If the corporation's articles of incorporation contain a provision eliminating its directors' liability to the corporation or its shareholders for money damages, adopted pursuant to section 2.02(b)(4), there is no liability unless the director's conduct involves one of the prescribed exceptions that preclude the elimination of liability. See section 2.02 and its Official Comment.

2. *Director's conflicting interest transaction safe harbor.* If the matter at issue involves a director's conflicting interest transaction (as defined in section 8.60(2)) and a safe harbor procedure under section 8.61 involving action taken in compliance with section 8.62 or 8.63 has been properly implemented, there is no liability for the interested director arising out of the transaction. See subchapter F of this chapter 8.

3. *Business opportunities safe harbor.* Similarly, if the matter involves a director's taking of a business opportunity and a safe harbor procedure under section 8.70 has been properly implemented, there is no liability for the director arising out of the taking of the business opportunity. See subchapter G of this chapter 8.

4. *Business judgment rule.* If an articles of incorporation provision adopted pursuant to section 2.02 or a safe harbor procedure under section 8.61 does not shield the director's conduct from liability, this standard of judicial review for director conduct—deeply rooted in the case law—presumes that, absent self-dealing or other breach of the duty of loyalty, directors' decision-making satisfies the applicable legal requirements. A plaintiff challenging the director's conduct in connection with a corporate decision, and asserting liability by reason thereof, encounters certain procedural barriers. In the first instance, many jurisdictions have special pleading requirements that condition the ability to pursue the challenge on the plaintiff's bringing forward specific factual allegations that put in question the availability of the business

judgment presumption. Assuming the suit survives a motion to dismiss for failure to state (in satisfaction of such a condition) an actionable claim, the plaintiff has the burden of overcoming that presumption of regularity.

5. *Damages and proximate cause.* If the business judgment rule does not shield the directors' decision-making from liability, as a general rule it must be established that money damages were suffered by the corporation or its shareholders and those damages resulted from and were legally caused by the challenged act or omission of the director.

6. *Other liability for money payment.* Aside from a claim for damages, the director may be liable to reimburse the corporation pursuant to a claim under *quantum meruit* (the reasonable value of services) or *quantum valebant* (the reasonable value of goods and materials) if corporate resources have been used without proper authorization. In addition, the corporation may be entitled to short-swing profit recovery, stemming from the director's trading in its securities, under § 16(b) of the Securities Exchange Act of 1934.

7. *Equitable profit recovery or disgorgement.* An equitable remedy compelling the disgorgement of the director's improper financial gain or entitling the corporation to profit recovery, where directors' duties have been breached, may require the payment of money by the director to the corporation.

8. *Corporate indemnification.* If the court determines that the director is liable, the director may be indemnified by the corporation for any payments made and expenses incurred, depending upon the circumstances, if a third-party suit is involved. If the proceeding is by or in the right of the corporation, the director may be reimbursed for reasonable expenses incurred in connection with the proceeding if ordered by a court under section 8.54(a)(3).

9. *Insurance.* To the extent that corporate indemnification is not available, the director may be reimbursed for the money damages for which the director is accountable, together with proceeding-related expenses, if the claim/grounds for liability come within the coverage under directors' and officers' liability insurance that has been purchased by the corporation pursuant to section 8.57.

* * *

Section 8.31 includes steps (1) through (6) in the analysis of a director's liability exposure set forth in the above Note. In establishing general standards of director liability under the Model Act, the section also serves the important purpose of providing clarification that the general standards of conduct set forth in section 8.30 are not intended to codify the business judgment rule—a point as to which there has been confusion on the part of some courts (notwithstanding a disclaimer of that purpose and effect in the prior Official Comment to section 8.30). For example, one court viewed the standard of care set forth in Washington's business corporation act (a provision based upon and almost identical to the prior section 8.30(a)—which read "A director shall discharge his duties as a director . . . : (1) in good faith; (2) with the care an ordinarily prudent person in a like position would exercise under similar circumstances; and (3) in a manner he reasonably believes to be in the best interests of the corporation") as having codified the business judgment rule. See *Seafirst Corp. v. Jenkins,* 644 F. Supp. 1152, 1159 (W.D. Wash. 1986). (A later court characterized this view as a mistaken assumption and recognized the disclaimer made in section 8.30's Official Comment. See *Shinn v. Thrust IV Inc.*, 786 P. 2d 285, 290 n.1 (Wash. App. 1990).) Another court declared "Section 309 *[a standard of conduct almost identical to the prior section 8.30(a)]* codifies California's business judgment rule." See *Gaillard v. Natomas Co.,* 208 Cal. App. 3d 1250, 1264 (1989). The Court of Appeals of New York referred to that state's statutory standard of care for directors, a formulation set forth in NYBCL § 717 that is similar to the prior section 8.30(a), as "New York's business judgment rule." See *Lindner Fund, Inc. v. Waldbaum, Inc.*, 624 N.E. 2d 160, 161 (1993). In contrast, another court considering New York's conduct standard observed:

> A board member's obligation to a corporation and its shareholders has two prongs, generally characterized as the duty of care and the duty of loyalty. The duty of care refers to the responsibility of a corporate fiduciary to exercise, in the performance of his tasks, the care that a reasonably prudent person in a similar position would use under similar circumstances. See NYBCL § 717. In evaluating a manager's compliance with the duty of care, New York courts adhere to the business judgment rule, which "bars judicial inquiry into actions of corporate directors taken in good faith and in the exercise of honest judgment in the lawful and legitimate furtherance of corporate purposes." *Norlin Corp. v. Rooney, Pace Inc.*, 744 F.2d 255, 264 (2d Cir. 1984) [quoting *Auerbach v. Bennett*, 47 N.Y. 2d 619, 629 (1979)].

Sections 8.30 and 8.31 adopt the approach to director conduct and director liability taken in the *Norlin* decision. See section 8.30 and its Official Comment with respect to the standards of conduct for directors. For a detailed analysis of how and why standards of conduct and standards of liability diverge in corporate law, see Melvin A. Eisenberg, *The Divergence of Standards of Conduct and Standards of Review in Corporate Law,* 62 Fordham L. Rev. 437 (1993).

The Model Act does not undertake to prescribe detailed litigation procedures. However, it does deal with requirements applicable to shareholder derivative suits (see sections 7.40–7.47) and section 8.31 builds on those requirements. If any of (i) a liability-eliminating provision included in the corporation's articles of incorporation, pursuant to section 2.02(b)(4), (ii) protection for a director's conflicting interest transaction afforded by section 8.61(b)(1) or section 8.61(b)(2), or (iii) protection for a disclaimer of the corporation's interest in a business opportunity afforded by section 8.70 is interposed by a defendant director as a bar to the challenge of his or her conduct, the plaintiff's role in satisfying the requirement of subsection (a)(1)—*i.e.*, establishing that the articles of incorporation provision or the safe harbor provision interposed does not apply—would be governed by the court's procedural rules. Parenthetically, where fairness of a director's conflicting interest transaction can be established, protection from liability is also afforded by section 8.61(b)(3). If it is asserted by a defendant director as a defense, it is important to note that subsection (a)(2)(v) rather than subsection (a)(1) would be implicated and the burden of establishing that the transaction was fair to the corporation—and, therefore, no improper financial benefit was received—is placed on the interested director under section 8.61(b)(3). Similarly, the local pleading and other rules would govern the plaintiff's effort to satisfy subsection (a)(2)'s requirements. Consistent with the general rules of civil procedure, the plaintiff generally has the burden under subsection (b) of proving that the director's deficient conduct caused harm resulting in monetary damage or calls for monetary reimbursement; in the alternative, the circumstances may justify or require an equitable remedy.

1. Section 8.31(a)

If a provision in the corporation's articles of incorporation (adopted pursuant to section 2.02(b)(4)) shelters the director from liability for money damages, or if a safe harbor provision, under subsection (b)(1) or (b)(2) of section 8.61 or section 8.70, shelters the director's conduct in connection with a conflicting interest transaction or the taking of a business opportunity, and such defense applies to all claims in plaintiff's complaint, there is no need to consider further the application of section 8.31's standards of liability. In that event, the court would presumably grant the defendant director's motion for dismissal or summary judgment (or the equivalent) and the proceeding would be ended. If the defense applies to some but not all of plaintiff's claims, defendant is entitled to dismissal or summary judgment with respect to those claims. Termination of the proceeding or dismissal of claims on the basis of an articles of incorporation provision or safe harbor will not automatically follow, however, if the party challenging the director's conduct can assert any of the valid bases for contesting the availability of the liability shelter. Absent such a challenge, the relevant shelter provision is self-executing and the individual director's exoneration from liability is automatic. Further, under both section 8.61 and section 8.70, the directors approving the conflicting interest transaction or the director's taking of the business opportunity will presumably be protected as well, for compliance with the relevant standards of conduct under section 8.30 is important for their action to be effective and, as noted above, conduct meeting section 8.30's standards will almost always be protected.

If a claim of liability arising out of a challenged act or omission of a director is not resolved and disposed of under subsection (a)(1), subsection (a)(2) provides the basis for evaluating whether the conduct in question can be challenged.

* * *

Note on the Business Judgment Rule

Over the years, the courts have developed a broad common law concept geared to business judgment. In basic principle, a board of directors enjoys a presumption of sound business judgment and its decisions will not be disturbed (by a court substituting its own notions of what is or is not sound business judgment) if they can be attributed to any rational business purpose. See *Sinclair Oil Corp. v. Levien*, 280 A.2d 717, 720 (Del. 1971). Relatedly, it is presumed that, in making a business decision, directors act in good faith, on an informed basis, and in the honest belief that the action taken is in the best interests of the corporation. See *Aronson v. Lewis*, 473 A.2d 805, 812 (Del. 1983). When applied, this principle operates both as a procedural rule of evidence and a substantive rule of law, in that if the plaintiff fails to rebut the presumption that the directors acted in good faith, in the corporation's best interest and on an informed basis, the business judgment standard protects both the directors and the decisions they make. See *Citron v. Fairchild Camera & Instrument Corp.*, 569 A. 2d 53, 64 (Del. 1989).

Some have suggested that, within the business judgment standard's broad ambit, a distinction might usefully be drawn between that part which protects directors from personal liability for the decision they make and the part which protects the decision itself from attack. See *Revlon, Inc. v. MacAndrews & Forbes Holdings, Inc.*, 506 A. 2d 173, 180 n.10 (Del. 1986). While these two objects of the business judgment standard's protection are different, and judicial review might result in the decision being enjoined but no personal liability (or vice versa), their operative elements are identical (*i.e.,* good faith, disinterest, informed judgment and "best interests"). As a consequence, the courts have not observed any distinction in terminology and have generally followed the practice of referring only to the business judgment rule, whether dealing with personal liability issues or transactional justification matters.

While, in substance, the operative elements of the standard of judicial review commonly referred to as the business judgment rule have been widely recognized, courts have used a number of different word formulations to articulate the concept. The formulation adopted in § 4.01(c) of The American Law Institute's PRINCIPLES OF CORPORATE GOVERNANCE: ANALYSIS AND RECOMMENDATIONS (1994) provides that a director who makes a business judgment **in good faith** (an obvious prerequisite) fulfills the duty of care standard if the director:

(1) is not interested *[as defined]* in the subject of the business judgment;

(2) is informed with respect to the subject of the business judgment to the extent the director ... reasonably believes to be appropriate under the circumstances; and

(3) rationally believes that the business judgment is in the best interests of the corporation.

Referring to clause (2) above, the decision-making process is to be reviewed on a basis that is to a large extent individualized in nature ("informed ... to the extent the director ... reasonably believes to be appropriate under the circumstances")—as contrasted with the traditional objectively-based duty-of-care standard (*e.g.*, the prior section 8.30(a)'s "care ... an ordinarily prudent person ... would exercise"). An "ordinarily prudent person" might do more to become better informed, but if a director believes, in good faith, that the director can make a sufficiently informed business judgment, the director will be protected so long as that belief is within the bounds of reason. Referring to clause (3) above, the phrase "rationally believes" is stated in the PRINCIPLES to be a term having "both an objective and subjective content. A director ... must actually believe that the business judgment is in the best interests of the corporation and that belief must be rational," 1 PRINCIPLES, at 179. Others see that aspect to be primarily geared to the process employed by a director in making the decision as opposed to the substantive content of the board decision made. See *Aronson v. Lewis, supra,* at 812 ("The business judgment rule is ... a presumption that in making a business decision the directors of a corporation acted on an informed basis, in good faith and in the honest belief that the action taken was in the best interests of the company.... Absent an abuse of discretion, that judgment will be respected by the courts.") In practical application, an irrational belief would in all likelihood constitute an abuse of discretion. *Compare In re Caremark International Inc. Derivative Litigation* (September 25, 1996) (1996 Del. Ch. LEXIS 125 at p. 27: "whether a judge or jury considering the matter after the fact ... believes a decision substantively wrong, or degrees of wrong extending through 'stupid' to 'egregious' or 'irrational', provides no ground for director liability, so long as the court determines that the process employed was either rational or employed in a good faith effort to advance corporate interests ... the business judgment rule is process oriented and informed by a deep respect for all good faith board decisions.")

* * *

Section 8.31 does not codify the business judgment rule as a whole. The section recognizes the common law doctrine and provides guidance as to its application in dealing with director liability claims. Because the elements of the business judgment rule and the circumstances for its application are continuing to be developed by the courts, it would not be desirable to freeze the concept in a statute. For example, in recent years the Delaware Supreme Court has established novel applications of the concept to various transactional justification matters, such as the role of special litigation committees and change-of-control situations. See *Zapata Corporation v. Maldonado*, 430 A. 2d 779 (1981), and *Unocal Corp. v. Mesa Petroleum Co.*, 493 A. 2d 946 (1985), respectively. Under *Zapata*, a rule that applies where there is no disinterested majority on the board appointing the special litigation committee, there is no presumption of regularity and the corporation must bear the burden of proving the independence of the committee, the reasonableness of its investigation, and the reasonableness of the bases of its determination that dismissal of the derivative litigation is in the best interests of the corporation. Under *Unocal*, the board must first establish reasonable grounds for believing an unsolicited takeover bid poses a danger to corporate policy and effectiveness, and a reasonable relationship of defensive measures taken to the threat posed, before the board's action will be entitled to the business judgment presumptions. The business judgment concept has been employed in countless legal decisions and is a topic that has received a great deal of scholarly attention. For an exhaustive treatment of the subject, see D. Block, N. Barton & S. Radin, *The Business Judgment Rule: Fiduciary Duties of Corporate Directors* (4th ed. 1993 & Supp. 1995). While codification of the business judgment rule in section 8.31 is expressly disclaimed, its principal elements, relating to personal liability issues, are embedded in subsection (a)(2).

a. Good faith

The expectation that a director's conduct will be in good faith is an overarching element of his or her baseline duties. Relevant thereto, it has been stated that a lack of good faith is presented where a board "lacked an actual intention to advance corporate welfare" and "bad faith" is presented where "a transaction . . . is authorized for some purpose other than a genuine attempt to advance corporate welfare or is known to constitute a violation of applicable positive law." See *Gagliardi v. TriFoods Int'l Inc.*, 683 A.2d 1049 (Del. Ch. 1996). If a director's conduct can be successfully challenged pursuant to other clauses of subsection (a)(2), there is a substantial likelihood that the conduct in question will also present an issue of good faith implicating clause 2(i). Conduct involving knowingly illegal conduct that exposes the corporation to harm will constitute action not in good faith, and belief that decisions made (in connection with such conduct) were in the best interests of the corporation will be subject to challenge as well. If subsection (a)(2) included only clause 2(i), much of the conduct with which the other clauses are concerned could still be considered pursuant to the subsection, on the basis that such conduct evidenced the actor's lack of good faith. Accordingly, the canon of construction known as *eiusdem generis* has substantial relevance in understanding the broad overlap of the good faith element with the various other subsection (a)(2) clauses. Where conduct has not been found deficient on other grounds, decision-making outside the bounds of reasonable judgment—an abuse of discretion perhaps explicable on no other basis—can give rise to an inference of bad faith. That form of conduct (characterized by the court as "constructive fraud" or "reckless indifference" or "deliberate disregard" in the relatively few case precedents) giving rise to an inference of bad faith will also raise a serious question whether the director could have reasonably believed that the best interests of the corporation would be served. If a director's conflicting interest transaction is determined to be manifestly unfavorable to the corporation, giving rise to an inference of bad faith tainting the directors' action approving the transaction under section 8.62, the safe harbor protection afforded by section 8.61 for both the transaction and the conflicted director would be in jeopardy. See the Official Comment to section 8.61. Depending on the facts and circumstances, the directors who approve a director's conflicting interest transaction that is manifestly unfavorable to the corporation may be at risk under clause (2)(i).

b. Reasonable belief

A director should reasonably believe that his or her decision will be in the best interests of the corporation and a director should become sufficiently informed, with respect to any action taken or not taken, to the extent he or she reasonably believes appropriate in the circumstances. In each case, the director's reasonable belief calls for a subjective belief and, so long as it is his or her honest and good faith belief, a director has wide discretion. However, in the rare case where a decision respecting the corporation's best interests is so removed from the realm of reason (*e.g.*, corporate waste), or a belief as to the sufficiency of the director's preparation to make an informed judgment is so unreasonable as to fall outside the permissible bounds of sound discretion (*e.g.*, a clear case is presented if the director has undertaken no preparation and is woefully uninformed), the director's judgment will not be sustained.

c. Lack of objectivity or independence

If a director has a familial, financial or business relationship with another person having a material interest in a transaction or other conduct involving the corporation, or if the director is dominated or controlled by another person having such a material interest, there is a potential for that conflicted interest or divided loyalty to affect the director's judgment. If the matter at issue involves a director's transactional interest, such as a "director's conflicting interest transaction" (see section 8.60(2)) in which a "related person" (see section 8.60(3)) is involved, it will be governed by section 8.61; otherwise, the lack of objectivity due to a relationship's influence on the director's judgment will be evaluated, in the context of the pending conduct challenge, under section 8.31. If the matter at issue involves lack of independence, the proof of domination or control and its influence on the director's judgment will typically entail different (and perhaps more convincing) evidence than what may be involved in a lack of objectivity case. The variables are manifold, and the facts must be sorted out and weighed on a case-by-case basis. If that other person is the director's spouse or employer, the concern that the director's judgment might be improperly influenced would be substantially greater than if that person is the spouse of the director's step-grandchild or the director's partner in a vacation time-share. When the party challenging the director's conduct can establish that the relationship or the domination or control in question could reasonably be expected to affect the director's judgment respecting the matter at issue in a manner adverse to the corporation, the director will then have the opportunity to establish that the action taken by him or her was reasonably believed to be in the best interests of the corporation. The reasonableness of the director's belief as to the corporation's best interests, in respect of the action taken, should be evaluated on the basis of not only the director's honest and good faith belief but also on considerations bearing on the fairness to the corporation of the transaction or other conduct involving the corporation that is at issue.

d. Improper financial benefit

Subchapter F of chapter 8 of the Model Act deals in detail with directors' transactional interests. Its coverage of those interests is exclusive and its safe harbor procedures for directors' conflicting interest transactions (as defined)—providing shelter from legal challenges based on interest conflicts, when properly observed—will establish a director's entitlement to any financial benefit gained from the transactional event. A director's conflicting interest transaction that is not protected by the fairness standard set forth in section 8.61(b)(3), pursuant to which the conflicted director may establish the transaction to have been fair to the corporation, would often involve receipt of a financial benefit to which the director was not entitled (*i.e.*, the transaction was not "fair" to the corporation). Unauthorized use of corporate assets, such as aircraft or hotel suites, would also provide a basis for the proper challenge of a director's conduct. There can be other forms of improper financial benefit not involving a transaction with the corporation or use of its facilities, such as where a director profits from unauthorized use of proprietary information.

e. Financial benefit/material interest

A director is expected to observe an obligation of undivided loyalty to the corporation and, while the law will not concern itself with trifling deviations (*de minimis non curat lex*), there is no materiality threshold that applies to a financial benefit to which a director is not properly entitled. The Model Act observes this principle in several places (*e.g.*, the exception to liability elimination prescribed in section 2.02(b)(4)(A) and the indemnification restriction in section 8.51(d)(2), as well as the liability standard in subsection (a)(2)(v)). In contrast, there is a materiality threshold for the interest of another in a transaction or conduct where a director's lack of objectivity or lack of independence has been asserted under subsection (a)(2)(iii). In the typical case, analysis of another's interest would first consider the materiality of the transaction or conduct at issue—in most cases, any transaction or other action involving the attention of the board or one of its committees will cross the materiality threshold, but not always—and would then consider the materiality of that person's interest therein. The possibility that another's interest in a transaction or conduct that is not material, or that an immaterial interest of another in a transaction or conduct, would adversely affect a director's judgment is sufficiently remote that it should not be made subject to judicial review.

f. Sustained inattention

The director's role involves two fundamental components: the decision-making function and the oversight function. In contrast with the decision-making function, which generally involves action taken at a point in time, the oversight function under section 8.01(b) involves ongoing monitoring of the corporation's business and affairs over a period of time. This involves the duty of ongoing attention, when actual knowledge of particular facts and circumstances arouse suspicions which indicate a need to make inquiry. As observed by the Supreme Court of New Jersey in *Francis v. United Jersey Bank*, 432 A.2d 814, 822 (Sup. Ct. 1981):

> Directors are under a continuing obligation to keep informed about the activities of the corporation.... Directors may not shut their eyes to corporate misconduct and then claim that because they did not see the misconduct, they did not have a duty to look. The sentinel asleep at his post contributes nothing to the enterprise he is charged to protect.... Directorial management does not require a detailed inspection of day-to-day activities, but rather a general monitoring of corporate affairs and policies.

While the facts will be outcome-determinative, deficient conduct involving a sustained failure to exercise oversight—where found actionable—has typically been characterized by the courts in terms of abdication and continued neglect of a director's duty of attention, not a brief distraction or temporary interruption. However, embedded in the oversight function is the need to inquire when suspicions are aroused. This duty is not a component of ongoing oversight, and does not entail proactive vigilance, but arises when, and only when, particular facts and circumstances of material concern (*e.g.*, evidence of embezzlement at a high level or the discovery of significant inventory shortages) suddenly surface.

g. Other breaches of a director's duties

Subsection (a)(2)(v) is, in part, a catchall provision that implements the intention to make section 8.31 a generally inclusive provision but, at the same time, to recognize the existence of other breaches of common-law duties that can give rise to liability for directors. As developed in the case law, these actionable breaches include unauthorized use of corporate property or information, unfair competition with the corporation and taking of a corporate opportunity. In the latter case, the director is alleged to have wrongfully diverted a business opportunity as to which the corporation had a prior right. Section 8.70 provides a safe harbor mechanism for a director who wishes to take advantage of a business opportunity, regardless of whether such opportunity would be characterized as a "corporate opportunity" under existing case law. Note that section 8.70(b) provides that the fact that a director did not employ the safe harbor provisions of section 8.70 does not create an inference that the opportunity should have first been presented to the corporation or alter the burden of proof otherwise applicable to establish a breach of the director's duty to the corporation.

h. Fairness

Pursuant to section 8.61(b)(3), an interested director (or the corporation, if it chooses) can gain protection for a director's conflicting interest transaction by establishing that it was fair to the corporation. (The concept of "fair" and "fairness," in this and various other contexts, can take into account both fair price and fair dealing on the part of the interested director. See the Official Comment to section 8.61.) Under case law, personal liability as well as transactional justification issues will be subject to a fairness standard of judicial review if the plaintiff makes out a credible claim of breach of the duty of loyalty or if the presumptions of the business judgment standard (*e.g.*, an informed judgment) are overcome, with the burden of proof shifting from the plaintiff to the defendant. In this respect, the issue of fairness is relevant to both subsection (a) and subsection (b). Within the ambit of subsection (a)(2), a director can often respond to the challenge that his or her conduct was deficient by establishing that the transaction or conduct at issue was fair to the corporation. See *Kahn v. Lynch Communications Systems, Inc.* 669 A.2d 79 (Del. 1995). *Cf. Cede & Co. v. Technicolor Inc.*, 634 A.2d 345 (Del. 1993) (when the business judgment rule is rebutted—procedurally—the burden shifts to the defendant directors to prove the "entire fairness" of the challenged transaction). It is to be noted, however, that fairness may not be relevant to the matter at issue (see, *e.g.*, clause (iv) of subsection (a)(2)). If the director is successful in establishing fairness, where the issue of fairness is relevant, then it is unlikely that the complainant can establish legal liability or the appropriateness of an equitable remedy under subsection (b).

i. Director conduct

Subsection (a)(2) deals, throughout, with a director's action that is taken or not taken. To the extent that the director's conduct involves a breach of his or her duty of care or duty of attention within the context of collegial action by the board or one of its committees, proper performance of the relevant duty through the action taken by the director's colleagues can overcome the consequences of his or her deficient conduct. For example, where a director's conduct can be challenged under subsection (a)(2)(ii)(B) by reason of having been uninformed about the decision—he or she did not read the merger materials distributed prior to the meeting, arrived late at the board meeting just in time for the vote but, nonetheless, voted for the merger solely because the others were in favor—the favorable action by a quorum of properly informed directors would ordinarily protect the director against liability. When the director's conduct involves the duty of fair dealing within the context of action taken by the board or one of its committees, the wiser choice will usually be for the director not to participate in the collegial action. That is to say, where a director may have a conflicting interest or a divided loyalty, or even where there may be grounds for the issue to be raised, the better course to follow is usually for the director to disclose the conduct-related facts and circumstances posing the possible compromise of his or her independence or objectivity, and then to withdraw from the meeting (or, in the alternative, to abstain from the deliberations and voting). The board members free of any possible taint can then take appropriate action as contemplated by section 8.30. (If a director's conflicting interest transaction is involved, it will be governed by subchapter F of this chapter and the directors' action will be taken pursuant to section 8.62 (or the board can refer the matter for shareholder's action respecting the transaction under section 8.63). In this connection, particular reference is made to the definition of "qualified director" in section 1.43.) If this course is followed, the director's conduct respecting the matter in question will in all likelihood be beyond challenge.

2. Section 8.31(b)

After satisfying the burden of establishing that the conduct of the director is challengeable under subsection (a), the plaintiff, in order to hold the director liable for money damages under clause (b)(1), has the further burden of establishing that: (i) harm (measurable in money damages) has been suffered by the corporation or its shareholders and (ii) the director's challenged conduct was the proximate cause of that harm. The concept of "proximate cause" is a term of art that is basic to tort law, and the cases providing content to the phrase represent well-developed authority to which a court will undoubtedly refer. A useful approach for the concept's application, for purposes of subsection (b)(1), would be that the challenged conduct must have been a "substantial factor in producing the harm." See *Francis v. United Jersey Bank*, supra, 432 A.2d at 829. Similarly, the plaintiff has the burden of establishing money payment is due from the director pursuant to clause (b)(2). If, while challengeable, the conduct at issue caused no harm under clause (b)(1) or does not provide the basis for other legal remedy under clause (b)(2), but may provide the basis for an equitable remedy under clause (b)(3), the plaintiff must satisfy whatever further burden of persuasion may be indicated to establish that imposition of the remedy sought is appropriate in the circumstances. In *Brophy v. Cities Service Co*, 70 A.2d 5, 8 (Del. Ch. 1949), an employee was required to account for profits derived from the use of the corporation's confidential plans to reacquire its securities through open-market purchases. Notwithstanding the fact that harm to the corporation had not been established, the Chancellor observed: "[p]ublic policy will not permit an employee occupying a position of trust and confidence toward his employer to abuse that relation to his own profit, regardless of whether his employer suffers a loss." Once actionable conduct that provides the basis for an equitable remedy under clause (b)(3) has been established, its appropriateness will often be clear and, if so, no further advocacy on the part of the plaintiff will be required.

3. Section 8.31(c)

While section 8.31 addresses director liability to the corporation or its shareholders under the Model Act—and related case law dealing with interpretation by the courts of their states' business corporation acts or dealing with corporate governance concepts coming within the common law's ambit—it does not limit any liabilities or foreclose any rights expressly provided for under other law. For example, directors can have liability (i) to shareholders (as well as former shareholders), who purchased their shares in a registered public offering, under § 11 of the Securities Act of 1933 and (ii) to the corporation, for short-swing profit recovery, under § 16(b) of the Securities Exchange Act of 1934. Subsection (c) merely acknowledges that those rights are unaffected by section 8.31. And directors can have liability to persons other than the corporation and its shareholders, such as (i) employee benefit plan participants and beneficiaries (who may or may not be shareholders), if the directors are determined to be fiduciaries under the Employee Retirement Income Security Act of 1974, 29 U.S.C. §§ 1001–1461 (1988 & Supp. IV 1992), (ii) government agencies for regulatory violations or (iii) individuals claiming damages for injury governed by tort-law concepts (*e.g.*, libel or slander).

As discussed above in the Official Comment to section 8.31(a), the concept of "fairness" is often relevant to whether a director will have liability if his or her conduct is challenged. Specifically, a director can successfully defend a financial interest in a transaction with the corporation by establishing that it was fair to the corporation. See section 8.61 and its Official Comment. More generally, the courts have resorted to a fairness standard of review where the business judgment rule has been inapplicable. See *Weinberger v. UOP, Inc.*, 457 A.2d 701 (Del. 1983). In the usual case, the defendant seeking to justify challenged conduct, on the basis of fairness, has the burden of proving that it was fair to the corporation. Subsection (c) expressly disclaims any intention to shift the burden of proof otherwise applicable where the question of the fairness of a transaction or other challenged conduct is at issue.

Finally, the Model Act deals expressly with certain aspects of director liability in other sections. For example, a director has a duty to observe the limitations on shareholder distributions set forth in section 6.40 and, if a director votes for or assents to a distribution in violation thereof, the director has personal liability as provided in section 8.33. And section 8.61 channels all directors' transactional interests into the exclusive treatment for directors' conflicting interest transactions that is therein provided, rejecting an award of damages or other sanctions for interests that do not come within its conceptual framework. Subsection (c) expressly acknowledges that the liability standard provided in section 8.33 and the exclusive treatment for directors' transactional interests provided in section 8.61 are unaffected by section 8.31.

§ 8.32 [Reserved]

§ 8.33 Directors' Liability for Unlawful Distributions

(a) A director who votes for or assents to a distribution in excess of what may be authorized and made pursuant to section 6.40(a) or 14.09(a) is personally liable to the corporation for the amount of the distribution that exceeds what could have been distributed without violating section 6.40(a) or 14.09(a) if the party asserting liability establishes that when taking the action the director did not comply with section 8.30.

(b) A director held liable under subsection (a) for an unlawful distribution is entitled to:

(1) contribution from every other director who could be held liable under subsection (a) for the unlawful distribution; and

(2) recoupment from each shareholder of the pro-rata portion of the amount of the unlawful distribution the shareholder accepted, knowing the distribution was made in violation of section 6.40(a) or 14.09(a).

(c) A proceeding to enforce:

(1) the liability of a director under subsection (a) is barred unless it is commenced within two years after the date (i) on which the effect of the distribution was measured under section 6.40(e) or (g), (ii) as of which the violation of section 6.40(a) occurred as the consequence of disregard of a restriction in the articles of incorporation or (iii) on which the distribution of assets to Shareholders under section 14.09(a) was made; or

(2) contribution or recoupment under subsection (b) is barred unless it is commenced within one year after the liability of the claimant has been finally adjudicated under subsection (a).

Subchapter D. Officers

§ 8.40 Officers

(a) A corporation has the officers described in its bylaws or appointed by the board of directors in accordance with the bylaws.

(b) The board of directors may elect individuals to fill one or more offices of the corporation. An officer may appoint one or more officers if authorized by the bylaws or the board of directors.

(c) The bylaws or the board of directors shall assign to one of the officers responsibility for preparing the minutes of the directors' and shareholders' meetings and for maintaining and authenticating the records of the corporation required to be kept under sections 16.01(a) and 16.01(e).

(d) The same individual may simultaneously hold more than one office in a corporation.

§ 8.41 Functions of Officers

Each officer has the authority and shall perform the functions set forth in the bylaws or, to the extent consistent with the bylaws, the functions prescribed by the board of directors or by direction of an officer authorized by the board of directors to prescribe the functions of other officers.

§ 8.42 Standards of Conduct for Officers

(a) An officer, when performing in such capacity, has the duty to act:

(1) in good faith;

(2) with the care that a person in a like position would reasonably exercise under similar circumstances; and

(3) in a manner the officer reasonably believes to be in the best interests of the corporation.

(b) The duty of an officer includes the obligation:

(1) to inform the superior officer to whom, or the board of directors or the committee thereof to which, the officer reports of information about the affairs of the corporation known to the officer, within the scope of the officer's functions, and known to the officer to be material to such superior officer, board or committee; and

(2) to inform his or her superior officer, or another appropriate person within the corporation, or the board of directors, or a committee thereof, of any actual or probable material violation of law involving the corporation or material breach of duty to the corporation by an officer, employee, or agent of the corporation, that the officer believes has occurred or is likely to occur.

(c) In discharging his or her duties, an officer who does not have knowledge that makes reliance unwarranted is entitled to rely on:

(1) the performance of properly delegated responsibilities by one or more employees of the corporation whom the officer reasonably believes to be reliable and competent in performing the responsibilities delegated; or

(2) information, opinions, reports or statements, including financial statements and other financial data, prepared or presented by one or more employees of the corporation whom the officer reasonably believes to be reliable and competent in the matters presented or by legal counsel, public accountants, or other persons retained by the corporation as to matters involving skills or expertise the officer reasonably believes are matters (i) within the particular person's professional or expert competence or (ii) as to which the particular person merits confidence.

(d) An officer shall not be liable to the corporation or its shareholders for any decision to take or not to take action, or any failure to take any action, as an officer, if the duties of the office are performed in compliance with this section. Whether an officer who does not comply with this section shall have liability will depend in such instance on applicable law, including those principles of section 8.31 that have relevance.

OFFICIAL COMMENT

Subsection (a) provides that an officer, when performing in such officer's official capacity, shall meet standards of conduct generally similar to those expected of directors under section 8.30. Consistent with the principles of agency, which generally govern the conduct of corporate employees, an officer is expected to observe the duties of obedience and loyalty and to act with the care that a person in a like position would reasonably exercise under similar circumstances. *See* RESTATEMENT (SECOND) OF AGENCY § 379(1) (1958) ("Unless otherwise agreed, a paid agent is subject to a duty to the principal to act with standard care and with the skill which is standard in the locality for the kind of work which he is employed to perform and, in addition, to exercise any special skill that he has"). This section is not intended to modify, diminish or qualify the duties or standards of conduct that may be imposed upon specific officers by other law or regulation.

The common law, including the law of agency, has recognized a duty on the part of officers and key employees to disclose to their superiors material information relevant to the affairs of the agency entrusted to them. *See* RESTATEMENT (SECOND) OF AGENCY § 381; A. Gilchrist Sparks, III & Lawrence A. Hamermesh, *Common Law Duties of Non–Director Corporate Officers*, 48 BUS. LAW. 215, 226–29 (1992). This duty is implicit in, and embraced under, the broader standard of subsection (a). New subsection (b) sets forth explicitly this disclosure obligation by confirming that the officer's duty includes the obligation (i) to keep superior corporate authorities informed of material information within the officer's sphere of functional responsibilities, and (ii) to inform the relevant superior authority, or other appropriate person within the corporation, of violations of law or breaches of duty that the officer believes have occurred or are about to occur (i.e., more likely than not to occur) and are or would be material to the corporation. Subsection (b)(1) specifies that business information shall be transmitted through the officer's regular reporting channels. Subsection (b)(2) specifies the reporting responsibility differently with respect to actual or probable material violations of law or material breaches of duty. The use of the term "appropriate" in subsection (b)(2) is intended to accommodate both the normative standard that may have been set up by the corporation for reporting potential violations of law or duty to a specified person, such as an ombudsperson, ethics officer, internal auditor, general counsel or the like, and situations where there is no designated person but the officer's immediate superior is not appropriate (for example, because the officer believes that individual is complicit in the unlawful activity or breach of duty).

Subsection (b)(1) should not be interpreted so broadly as to discourage efficient delegation of functions. It addresses the flow of information to the board of directors and to superior officers necessary to enable them to perform their decision-making and oversight functions. See the Official Comment to section 8.31. The officer's duties under subsection (b) may not be negated by agreement; however, their scope under subsection (b)(1) may be shaped by prescribing the scope of an officer's functional responsibilities.

With respect to the duties under subsection (b)(2), codes of conduct or codes of ethics, such as those adopted by many large corporations, may prescribe the circumstances in which and mechanisms by which officers and employees may discharge their duty to report material information to superior officers or the board of directors, or to other designated persons.

The term "material" modifying violations of law or breaches of duty in subsection (b)(2) denotes a qualitative as well as quantitative standard. It relates not only to the potential direct financial impact on the corporation, but also to the nature of the violation or breach. For example, an embezzlement of $10,000, or even less, would be material because of the seriousness of the offense, even though the amount involved would not be material to the financial position or results of operations of the corporation.

The duty under subsection (b)(2) is triggered by an officer's subjective belief that a material violation of law or breach of duty actually or probably has occurred or is likely to occur. This duty is not triggered by objective knowledge concepts, such as whether the officer should have concluded that such misconduct was occurring. The subjectivity of the trigger under subsection (b)(2), however, does not excuse officers from their obligations under subsection (a) to act in good faith and with due care in the performance of the functions assigned to them, including oversight duties within their respective areas of responsibility. There may be occasions when the principles applicable under section 8.30(c) limiting the duty of disclosure by directors where a duty of confidentiality is overriding may also apply to officers. See the Official Comment to section 8.30(c).

An officer's ability to rely on others in meeting the standards prescribed in section 8.42 may be more limited, depending upon the circumstances of the particular case, than the measure and scope of reliance permitted a director under section 8.30, in view of the greater obligation the officer may have to be familiar with the affairs of the corporation. The proper delegation of responsibilities by an officer, separate and apart from the exercise of judgment as to the delegatee's reliability and competence, is concerned with the procedure employed. This will involve, in the usual case, sufficient communication to the end that the delegatee understands the scope of the assignment and, in turn, manifests to the officer a willingness and commitment to undertake its performance. The entitlement to rely upon employees assumes that a delegating officer will maintain a sufficient level of communication with the officer's subordinates to fulfill his or her supervisory responsibilities. The definition of "employee" in section 1.40(8) includes an officer; accordingly, section 8.42 contemplates the delegation of responsibilities to other officers as well as to non-officer employees.

It is made clear, in subsection (d), that performance meeting the section's standards of conduct will eliminate an officer's exposure to any liability to the corporation or its shareholders. In contrast, an officer failing to meet its standards will not automatically face liability. Deficient performance of duties by an officer, depending upon the facts and circumstances, will normally be dealt with through intracorporate disciplinary procedures, such as reprimand, compensation adjustment, delayed promotion, demotion or discharge. These procedures may be subject to (and limited by) the terms of an officer's employment agreement. See section 8.44.

In some cases, failure to observe relevant standards of conduct can give rise to an officer's liability to the corporation or its shareholders. A court review of challenged conduct will involve an evaluation of the particular facts and circumstances in light of applicable law. In this connection, subsection (d) recognizes that relevant principles of section 8.31, such as duties to deal fairly with the corporation and its shareholders and the challenger's burden of establishing proximately caused harm, should be taken into account. In addition, the business judgment rule will normally apply to decisions within an officer's discretionary authority. Liability to others can also arise from an officer's own acts or omissions (e.g., violations of law or tort claims) and, in some cases, an officer with supervisory responsibilities can have risk exposure in connection with the acts or omissions of others.

The Official Comment to section 8.30 supplements this Official Comment to the extent that it can be appropriately viewed as generally applicable to officers as well as directors.

§ 8.43 Resignation and Removal of Officers

(a) An officer may resign at any time by delivering notice to the corporation. A resignation is effective when the notice is delivered unless the notice specifies a later effective time. If a resignation is made effective at a later time and the board or the appointing officer accepts the future effective time, the board or the appointing officer may fill the pending vacancy before the effective time if the board or the appointing officer provides that the successor does not take office until the effective time.

(b) An officer may be removed at any time with or without cause by: (i) the board of directors; (ii) the officer who appointed such officer, unless the bylaws or the board of directors provide otherwise; or (iii) any other officer if authorized by the bylaws or the board of directors.

(c) In this section, "appointing officer" means the officer (including any successor to that officer) who appointed the officer resigning or being removed.

§ 8.44 Contract Rights of Officers

(a) The appointment of an officer does not itself create contract rights.

(b) An officer's removal does not affect the officer's contract rights, if any, with the corporation. An officer's resignation does not affect the corporation's contract rights, if any, with the officer.

Subchapter E. Indemnification and Advance for Expenses

§ 8.50 Subchapter Definitions

In this subchapter:

(1) "Corporation" includes any domestic or foreign predecessor entity of a corporation in a merger.

(2) "Director" or "officer" means an individual who is or was a director or officer, respectively, of a corporation or who, while a director or officer of the corporation, is or was serving at the corporation's request as a director, officer, partner, trustee, employee, or agent of another domestic or foreign corporation, partnership, joint venture, trust, employee benefit plan, or other entity. A director or officer is considered to be serving an employee benefit plan at the corporation's request if the individual's duties to the corporation also impose duties on, or otherwise involve services by, the individual to the plan or to participants in or beneficiaries of the plan. "Director" or "officer" includes, unless the context requires otherwise, the estate or personal representative of a director or officer.

(3) "Expenses" includes counsel fees.

(4) "Liability" means the obligation to pay a judgment, settlement, penalty, fine (including an excise tax assessed with respect to an employee benefit plan), or reasonable expenses incurred with respect to a proceeding.

(5) "Official capacity" means: (i) when used with respect to a director, the office of director in a corporation; and (ii) when used with respect to an officer, as contemplated in section 8.56, the office in a corporation held by the officer. "Official capacity" does not include service for any other domestic or foreign corporation or any partnership, joint venture, trust, employee benefit plan, or other entity.

(6) "Party" means an individual who was, is, or is threatened to be made, a defendant or respondent in a proceeding.

(7) "Proceeding" means any threatened, pending, or completed action, suit, or proceeding, whether civil, criminal, administrative, arbitrative, or investigative and whether formal or informal.

OFFICIAL COMMENT

The definitions set forth in section 8.50 apply only to subchapter E and have no application elsewhere in the Model Act (except as set forth in section 2.02(b)(5)). The term "qualified director," which is used in section 8.53 and 8.55, is defined in section 1.43.

1. Corporation

A special definition of "corporation" is included in subchapter E to make it clear that predecessor entities that have been absorbed in mergers are included within the definition. It is probable that the same result would be reached for many transactions under section 11.07(a) (effect of merger), which provides for the assumption of liabilities by operation of law upon a merger. The express responsibility of successor entities for the liabilities of their predecessors under this subchapter is broader than under section 11.07(a) and may impose liability on a successor although section 11.07(a) does not. Section 8.50(1) is thus an essential aspect of the protection provided by this subchapter for persons eligible for indemnification.

2. Director and Officer

A special definition of "director" and "officer" is included in subchapter E to cover individuals who are made parties to proceedings because they are or were directors or officers or, while serving as directors or officers, also serve or served at the corporation's request in another capacity for another entity. The purpose of the latter part of this definition is to give directors and officers the benefits of the protection of this subchapter while serving at the corporation's request in a responsible position for employee benefit plans, trade associations, nonprofit or charitable entities, domestic or foreign entities, or other kinds of profit or nonprofit ventures. To avoid misunderstanding, it is good practice from both the corporation's and director's or officer's viewpoint for this type of request to be evidenced by resolution, memorandum or other writing. The definition covers an individual who is or was either a director or officer so that further references in the remainder of subchapter E to an individual who is a director or officer necessarily include former directors or officers.

The second sentence of section 8.50(2) addresses the question of liabilities arising under the Employee Retirement Income Security Act of 1974 (ERISA). It makes clear that a director or officer who is serving as a fiduciary of an employee benefit plan is automatically viewed for purposes of this subchapter as having been requested by the corporation to act in that capacity. Special treatment is believed necessary because of the broad definition of "fiduciary" and the requirement that a "fiduciary" must discharge his or her duties "solely in the interest" of the participants and beneficiaries of the employee benefit plan. Decisions by a director or officer, who is serving as a fiduciary under the plan on questions regarding (a) eligibility for benefits, (b) investment decisions, or (c) interpretation of plan provisions respecting (i) qualifying service, (ii) years of service, or (iii) retroactivity, are all subject to the protections of this subchapter. See also sections 8.50(4) and 8.51(b) of this subchapter.

The last sentence of section 8.50(2) provides that the estate or personal representative of a director or officer is entitled to the rights of indemnification possessed by that director or officer. The phrase "unless the context requires otherwise" was added to make clear that the estate or personal representative does not have the right to participate in directorial decisions authorized in this subchapter.

3. Expenses

"Expenses" is defined to include counsel fees in order to avoid repeated references to such fees every time "expenses" appears throughout the subchapter. "Expenses" does not include the other items listed in the definition of "liability," such as judgments or amounts paid in settlement.

4. Liability

"Liability" is defined for convenience in order to avoid repeated references to recoverable items throughout the subchapter. Even though the definition of "liability" includes amounts paid in settlement or to satisfy a judgment, indemnification against certain types of settlements and judgments is not allowed under several provisions of subchapter E. For example, indemnification in suits brought by or in the right of the corporation is limited to expenses (see section 8.51(d)(1)), unless indemnification for a settlement is ordered by a court under section 8.54(a)(3).

The definition of "liability" permits the indemnification only of "reasonable expenses incurred." The intention is that any portion of expenses falling outside the perimeter of reasonableness should not be advanced or indemnified. In contrast, unlike earlier versions of the Model Act and statutes of many states, section 8.50(4) provides that amounts paid to settle or satisfy substantive claims are not subject to a reasonableness test. Since payment of these amounts is permissive—mandatory indemnification is available under section 8.52 only where the defendant is "wholly successful"—a special limitation of "reasonableness" for settlements is inappropriate.

"Penalties" and "fines" are expressly included within the definition of "liability" so that, in appropriate cases, these items may also be indemnified. The purpose of this definition is to cover every type of monetary obligation that may be imposed upon a director, including civil penalties, restitution, and obligations to give notice. This definition also expressly includes as a "fine" the levy of excise taxes under the Internal Revenue Code pursuant to ERISA.

5. Official Capacity

The definition of "official capacity" is necessary because the term determines which of the two alternative standards of conduct set forth in section 8.51(a)(1)(ii) applies: If the action was taken in an "official capacity," the individual to be indemnified must have reasonably believed that he or she was acting in the best interests of the corporation. In contrast, if the action in question was not taken in an "official capacity," the individual need only have reasonably believed that the conduct was not opposed to the best interests of the corporation. See also the Official Comment to section 8.51(a).

6. Party

The definition of "party" includes every "individual who was, is, or is threatened to be made, a defendant or respondent in a proceeding." Thus, the definition includes present and former parties in addition to individuals currently or formerly threatened with being made a party. An individual who is only called as a witness is not a "party" within this definition and, as specifically provided in section 8.58(d), payment or reimbursement of his expenses is not limited by this subchapter.

7. Proceeding

The broad definition of "proceeding" ensures that the benefits of this subchapter will be available to directors in new and unexpected, as well as traditional, types of litigation or other adversarial matters, whether civil, criminal, administrative, or investigative. It also includes arbitration and other dispute resolution proceedings, lawsuit appeals and petitions to review administrative actions.

§ 8.51 Permissible Indemnification

(a) Except as otherwise provided in this section, a corporation may indemnify an individual who is a party to a proceeding because he is a director against liability incurred in the proceeding if:

(1) (i) he conducted himself in good faith; and

(ii) he reasonably believed:

(A) in the case of conduct in his official capacity, that his conduct was in the best interests of the corporation; and

(B) in all other cases, that his conduct was at least not opposed to the best interests of the corporation; and

(iii) in the case of any criminal proceeding, he had no reasonable cause to believe his conduct was unlawful; or

(2) he engaged in conduct for which broader indemnification has been made permissible or obligatory under a provision of the articles of incorporation (as authorized by section 2.02(b)(5)).

(b) A director's conduct with respect to an employee benefit plan for a purpose he reasonably believed to be in the interests of the participants in, and the beneficiaries of, the plan is conduct that satisfies the requirement of subsection (a)(1)(ii)(B).

(c) The termination of a proceeding by judgment, order, settlement, or conviction, or upon a plea of nolo contendere or its equivalent, is not, of itself, determinative that the director did not meet the relevant standard of conduct described in this section.

(d) Unless ordered by a court under section 8.54(a)(3), a corporation may not indemnify a director:

(1) in connection with a proceeding by or in the right of the corporation, except for reasonable expenses incurred in connection with the proceeding if it is determined that the director has met the relevant standard of conduct under subsection (a); or

(2) in connection with any proceeding with respect to conduct for which he was adjudged liable on the basis that he received a financial benefit to which he was not entitled, whether or not involving action in his official capacity.

OFFICIAL COMMENT

1. Section 8.51(a)

Subsection 8.51(a) permits, but does not require, a corporation to indemnify directors if the standards of subsection (a)(1) or of a provision of the articles referred to in subsection (a)(2) are met. This authorization is subject to any limitations set forth in the articles of incorporation pursuant to section 8.58(c). Absent any such limitation, the standards for indemnification of directors contained in this subsection define the outer limits for which discretionary indemnification is permitted under the Model Act. Conduct which does not meet one of these standards is not eligible for permissible indemnification under the Model Act, although court-ordered indemnification may be available under section 8.54(a)(3). Conduct that falls within these outer limits does not automatically entitle directors to indemnification, although a corporation may obligate itself to indemnify directors to the maximum extent permitted by applicable law. See section 8.58(a). No such obligation, however, may exceed these outer limits. Absent such an obligatory provision, section 8.52 defines much narrower circumstances in which directors are entitled as a matter of right to indemnification.

Some state statutes provide separate, but usually similarly worded, standards for indemnification in third-party suits and indemnification in suits brought by or in the right of the corporation. Section 8.51 makes clear that the outer limits of conduct for which indemnification is permitted should not be dependent on the type of proceeding in which the claim arises. To prevent circularity in recovery, however, section 8.51(d)(1) limits indemnification in connection with suits brought by or in the right of the corporation to expenses incurred and excludes amounts paid to settle such suits or to satisfy judgments. In addition, to discourage wrongdoing, section 8.51(d)(2) bars indemnification where the director has been adjudged to have received a financial benefit to which the director is not entitled. Nevertheless, a court may order certain relief from these limitations under section 8.54(a)(3).

The standards of conduct described in subsections (a)(1)(i) and (a)(1)(ii)(A) that must be met in order to permit the corporation to indemnify a director are closely related, but not identical, to the standards of conduct imposed by section 8.30 on members of the board of directors when discharging the duties of a director: good faith, reasonable belief that the best interests of the corporation are being served, and appropriate care (i.e., that which a person in a like position would reasonably believe appropriate under similar circumstances). Unless authorized by a charter provision adopted pursuant to subsection (a)(2), it would be difficult to justify indemnifying a director who has not met any of these standards. It would not, however, make sense to require a director to meet all these standards in order to be indemnified because a director who does so would normally have no liability, at least to the corporation or its shareholders, under the terms of section 8.31.

Section 8.51(a) adopts a middle ground by authorizing discretionary indemnification in the case of a failure to meet the appropriate care standard of section 8.30(b) because public policy would not be well served by an absolute bar. A director's potential liability for conduct which does not on each and every occasion satisfy the appropriate care requirement of section 8.30(b), or which with the benefit of hindsight could be so viewed, would in all likelihood deter qualified individuals from serving as directors and inhibit some who serve from taking risks.

Permitting indemnification against such liability tends to counter these undesirable consequences. Accordingly, section 8.51(a) authorizes indemnification at the corporation's option even though section 8.30's appropriate care requirement is not met, but only if the director satisfies the "good faith" and "corporation's best interests" standards. This reflects a judgment that, balancing public policy considerations, the corporation may indemnify a director who does not satisfy the appropriate care test but not one who fails either of the other two standards.

As in the case of section 8.30, where the concept of good faith is also used, no attempt is made in section 8.51 to provide a definition. The concept involves a subjective test, which would permit indemnification for "a mistake of judgment," in the words of the Official Comment to section 8.31, even though made unwisely or negligently by objective standards. Section 8.51 also requires, as does section 8.30, a "reasonable" belief that conduct when acting in the director's official capacity was in the corporation's best interests. It then adds a provision, not found in section 8.30, relating to criminal proceedings that requires the director to have had no "reasonable cause" to believe that the conduct was unlawful. These both involve objective standards applicable to the director's belief concerning the effect of the conduct in question. Conduct includes both acts and omissions.

Section 8.51(a)(1)(ii)(B) requires, if not acting in the director's official capacity, that the action be "at least not opposed to" the corporation's best interests. This standard is applicable to the director when serving another entity at the request of the corporation or when sued simply because of the director's status. The words "at least" qualify "not opposed to" in order to make it clear that this standard is an outer limit for conduct other than in an official capacity. While this subsection is directed at the interests of the indemnifying (i.e., the requesting) corporation, a director serving another entity by request remains subject to the provisions of the law governing service to that entity, including provisions dealing with conflicts of interest. Compare sections 8.60–8.63. Should indemnification from the requesting corporation be sought by a director for acts done while serving another entity, which acts involved breach of the duty of loyalty owed to that entity, nothing in section 8.51(a)(1)(ii)(B) would preclude the requesting corporation from considering, in assessing its own best interests, whether the fact that its director had engaged in a violation of the duty owed to the other entity was in fact "opposed to" the interests of the indemnifying corporation. Receipt of an improper financial benefit from a subsidiary would normally be opposed to the best interests of the parent.

Section 8.51 also permits indemnification in connection with a proceeding involving an alleged failure to satisfy legal standards other than the standards of conduct in section 8.30, e.g., violations of federal securities laws and environmental laws. It should be noted, however, that the Securities and Exchange Commission takes the position that indemnification against liabilities under the Securities Act of 1933 is against public policy and requires that, as a condition for accelerating the effectiveness of a registration statement under the Act, the issuer must undertake that, unless in the opinion of its counsel the matter has been settled by controlling precedent, it will submit to a court the question whether such indemnification is against public policy as expressed in the Act. 17 C.F.R. § 229.512(h) (1993).

In addition to indemnification under section 8.51(a)(1), section 8.51(a)(2) permits indemnification under the standard of conduct set forth in a charter provision adopted pursuant to section 2.02(b)(5). Based on such a charter provision, section 8.51(a)(2) permits indemnification in connection with claims by third parties and, through section 8.56, applies to officers as well as directors. (This goes beyond the scope of a charter provision adopted pursuant to section 2.02(b)(4), which can only limit liability of directors against claims by the corporation or its shareholders.) Section 8.51(a)(2) is subject to the prohibition of subsection (d)(1) against indemnification of settlements and judgments in derivative suits. It is also subject to the prohibition of subsection (d)(2) against indemnification for receipt of an improper financial benefit; however, this prohibition is already subsumed in the exception contained in section 2.02(b)(5)(A).

2. Section 8.51(b)

As discussed in the Official Comment to Section 8.50(2), ERISA requires that a "fiduciary" (as defined in ERISA) discharge the fiduciary's duties "solely in the interest" of the participants in and beneficiaries of an employee benefit plan. Section 8.51(b) makes clear that a director who is serving as a trustee or fiduciary for an employee benefit plan under ERISA meets the standard for indemnification under section 8.51(a) if the director reasonably believes the conduct while serving in that capacity was in the best interests of the participants in and beneficiaries of the plan.

This standard is arguably an exception to the more general standard that conduct not in an official corporate capacity is indemnifiable if it is "at least not opposed to" the best interests of the corporation. However, a corporation that causes a director to undertake fiduciary duties in connection with an employee benefit plan should expect the director to act in the best interests of the plan's beneficiaries or participants. Thus, subsection (b) establishes and provides a standard for indemnification that is consistent with the statutory policies embodied in ERISA. See Official Comment to section 8.50(2).

3. Section 8.51(c)

The purpose of section 8.51(c) is to reject the argument that indemnification is automatically improper whenever a proceeding has been concluded on a basis that does not exonerate the director claiming indemnification. Even though a final judgment or conviction is not automatically determinative of the issue of whether the minimum standard of conduct was met, any judicial determination of substantive liability would in most instances be entitled to considerable weight. By the same token, it is clear that the termination of a proceeding by settlement or plea of nolo contendere should not of itself create a presumption either that conduct met or did not meet the relevant standard of subsection (a) since a settlement or nolo plea may be agreed to for many reasons unrelated to the merits of the claim. On the other hand, a final determination of non-liability (including one based on a liability-limitation provision adopted under section 2.02(b)(4)) or an acquittal in a criminal case automatically entitles the director to indemnification of expenses under section 8.52.

Section 8.51(c) applies to the indemnification of expenses in derivative proceedings (as well as to indemnification in third party suits). The most likely application of this subsection in connection with a derivative proceeding will be to a settlement since a judgment or order would normally result in liability to the corporation and thereby preclude indemnification for expenses under section 8.51(d)(1), unless ordered by a court under section 8.54(a)(3). In the rare event that a judgment or order entered against the director did not include a determination of liability to the corporation, the entry of the judgment or order would not be determinative that the director failed to meet the relevant standard of conduct.

4. Section 8.51(d)

This subsection makes clear that indemnification is not permissible under section 8.51 in two situations: (i) a proceeding brought by or in the right of a corporation that results in a settlement or a judgment against the director and (ii) a proceeding that results in a judgment that an improper financial benefit was received as a result of the director's conduct.

Permitting indemnification of settlements and judgments in derivative proceedings would give rise to a circularity in which the corporation receiving payment of damages by the director in the settlement or judgment (less attorneys' fees) would then immediately return the same amount to the director (including attorneys' fees) as indemnification. Thus, the corporation would be in a poorer economic position than if there had been no proceeding. This situation is most egregious in the case of a judgment against the director. Even in the case of a settlement, however, prohibiting indemnification is not unfair. Under the revised procedures of section 7.44, upon motion by the corporation, the court must dismiss any derivative proceeding which independent directors (or a court-appointed panel) determine in good faith, after a reasonable inquiry, is not in the best interests of the corporation. Furthermore, under section 2.02(b)(4), the directors have the opportunity to propose to shareholders adoption of a provision limiting the liability of directors in derivative proceedings. In view of these considerations, it is unlikely that directors will be unnecessarily exposed to meritless actions. In addition, if directors were to be indemnified for amounts paid in settlement, the dismissal procedures in section 7.44 might not be fully employed since it could be less expensive for the corporation to indemnify the directors immediately for the amount of the claimed damages rather than bear the expense of the inquiry required by section 7.44. The result could increase the filing of meritless derivative proceedings in order to generate small but immediately paid attorneys' fees. Despite the prohibition on indemnification of a settlement or a judgment in a derivative proceeding, subsection (d)(1) permits indemnification of the related reasonable expenses incurred in the proceeding so long as the director meets the relevant standard of conduct set forth in section 8.51(a). In addition, indemnification of derivative proceeding expenses and amounts paid in settlement where the relevant standard was not met may be ordered by a court under section 8.54(a)(3).

Indemnification under section 8.51 is also prohibited if there has been an adjudication that a director received an improper financial benefit (i.e., a benefit to which the director is not entitled), even if, for example, the director acted in a manner not opposed to the best interests of the corporation. For example, improper use of inside information for financial benefit should not be an action for which the corporation may elect to provide indemnification, even if the corporation was not thereby harmed. Given the express language of section 2.02(b)(5) establishing the outer limit of an indemnification provision contained in the articles of incorporation, a director found to have received an improper financial benefit would not be permitted indemnification under subsection (a)(2). Although it is unlikely that a director found to have received an improper financial benefit could meet the standard in subsection (a)(1)(ii)(B), this limitation is made explicit in section 8.51(d)(2). Section 8.54(a)(3) permits a director found liable in a proceeding referred to in subsection (d)(2) to petition a court for a judicial determination of entitlement to indemnification for reasonable expenses. The language of section 8.51(d)(2) is based on section 2.02(b)(4)(A) and, thus, the same standards should be used in interpreting the application of both provisions. Although a settlement may create an obligation to pay money, it should not be construed for purposes of this subchapter as an adjudication of liability.

§ 8.52 Mandatory Indemnification

A corporation shall indemnify a director who was wholly successful, on the merits or otherwise, in the defense of any proceeding to which he was a party because he was a director of the corporation against reasonable expenses incurred by him in connection with the proceeding.

OFFICIAL COMMENT

Section 8.51 determines whether indemnification may be made voluntarily by a corporation if it elects to do so. Section 8.52 determines whether a corporation must indemnify a director for his expenses; in other words, section 8.52 creates a statutory right of indemnification in favor of the director who meets the requirements of that section. Enforcement of this right by judicial proceeding is specifically contemplated by section 8.54(a)(1). Section 8.54(b) gives the director a statutory right to recover expenses incurred by him in enforcing his statutory right to indemnification under section 8.52.

The basic standard for mandatory indemnification is that the director has been "wholly successful, on the merits or otherwise," in the defense of the proceeding. The word "wholly" is added to avoid the argument accepted in *Merritt-Chapman & Scott Corp. v. Wolfson*, 321 A.2d 138 (Del. 1974), that a defendant may be entitled to partial mandatory indemnification if, by plea bargaining or otherwise, he was able to obtain the dismissal of some but not all counts of an indictment. A defendant is "wholly successful" only if the entire proceeding is disposed of on a basis which does not involve a finding of liability. A director who is precluded from mandatory indemnification by this requirement may still be entitled to permissible indemnification under section 8.51(a) or court-ordered indemnification under section 8.54(a)(3).

The language in earlier versions of the Model Act and in many other state statutes that the basis of success may be "on the merits or otherwise" is retained. While this standard may result in an occasional defendant becoming entitled to indemnification because of procedural defenses not related to the merits, e.g., the statute of limitations or disqualification of the plaintiff, it is unreasonable to require a defendant with a valid procedural defense to undergo a possibly prolonged and expensive trial on the merits in order to establish eligibility for mandatory indemnification.

§ 8.53 Advance for Expenses

(a) A corporation may, before final disposition of a proceeding, advance funds to pay for or reimburse the reasonable expenses incurred in connection with the proceeding by an individual who is a party to the proceeding because that individual is a member of the board of directors if the director delivers to the corporation:

(1) a written affirmation of the director's good faith belief that the relevant standard of conduct described in section 8.51 has been met by the director or that the proceeding involves conduct for which liability has been eliminated under a provision of the articles of incorporation as authorized by section 2.02(b)(4); and

(2) a written undertaking of the director to repay any funds advanced if the director is not entitled to mandatory indemnification under section 8.52 and it is ultimately determined under section 8.54 or section 8.55 that the director has not met the relevant standard of conduct described in section 8.51.

(b) The undertaking required by subsection (a)(2) must be an unlimited general obligation of the director but need not be secured and may be accepted without reference to the financial ability of the director to make repayment.

(c) Authorizations under this section shall be made:

(1) by the board of directors:

(i) if there are two or more qualified directors, by a majority vote of all the qualified directors (a majority of whom shall for such purpose constitute a quorum) or by a majority of the members of a committee of two or more qualified directors appointed by such a vote; or

(ii) if there are fewer than two qualified directors, by the vote necessary for action by the board in accordance with section 8.24(c), in which authorization directors who are not qualified directors may participate; or

(2) by the shareholders, but shares owned by or voted under the control of a director who at the time is not a qualified director may not be voted on the authorization.

OFFICIAL COMMENT

Section 8.53 authorizes, but does not require, a corporation to pay for or reimburse, in advance, a director's reasonable expenses if two conditions are met. This authorization is subject to any limitations set forth in the articles of incorporation pursuant to section 8.58(c).

Section 8.53 recognizes an important difference between indemnification and an advance for expenses: indemnification is retrospective and, therefore, enables the persons determining whether to indemnify to do so on the basis of known facts, including the outcome of the proceeding. Advance for expenses is necessarily prospective and the individuals making the decision whether to advance expenses generally have fewer known facts on which to base their decision. Indemnification may include reimbursement for non-advanced expenses.

Section 8.53 reflects a determination that it is sound public policy to permit the corporation to advance (by direct payment or by reimbursement) the defense expenses of a director so long as the director (i) believes in good faith that the director was acting in accordance with the relevant standard for indemnification set forth in section 8.51 or that the proceeding involves conduct for which liability has been eliminated pursuant to section 2.02(b)(4) and (ii) agrees to repay any amounts advanced if it is ultimately determined that the director is not entitled to indemnification. This policy is based upon the view that a person who serves an entity in a representative capacity should not be required to finance his or her own defense. Moreover, adequate legal representation often involves substantial expenses during the course of the proceeding and many individuals are willing to serve as directors only if they have the assurance that the corporation has the power to advance these expenses. In fact, many corporations enter into contractual obligations (*e.g.*, by a provision in the articles or bylaws or by individual agreements) to advance expenses for directors. See section 8.58(a).

Section 8.53(a) requires the director's written affirmation as to the good faith belief that the director has met the relevant standard of conduct necessary for indemnification by the corporation and a written undertaking by the director to repay any funds advanced if it is ultimately determined that such standard of conduct has not been met. A single undertaking may cover all funds advanced from time to time in connection with the proceeding. Under subsection (b), the undertaking need not be secured and financial ability to repay is not a prerequisite. The theory underlying this subsection is that wealthy directors should not be favored over directors whose financial resources are modest. The undertaking must be made by the director and not by a third party. If the director or the corporation wishes some third party to be responsible for the director's obligation in this regard, either is free to make those arrangements separately with the third party.

In the absence of an obligatory provision established pursuant to section 8.58(a), the decision to advance expenses must be made in accordance with subsection (c). Section 8.53 does not address the question of the standard by which the decision to advance expenses is to be made. Accordingly, the standards of section 8.30 should, in general, govern. The conditions for advance for expenses are different from the conditions for indemnification. Directors normally meet the standards of section 8.30 in approving an advance for expenses if they limit their consideration to the financial ability of the corporation to pay the amount in question and do not have actual knowledge of facts sufficient to cause them to believe that the subsection (a)(1) affirmation was not made in good faith. The directors are not required by section 8.30 to make any inquiry into the merits of the proceeding or the good faith of the belief stated in that affirmation. Thus, in the great majority of cases, no special inquiry will be required. The directors acting on a decision to advance expenses may, but are not required to, consider any additional matters they deem appropriate and may condition the advance of expenses upon compliance with any additional requirements they desire to impose.

A corporation may obligate itself pursuant to section 8.58(a) to advance for expenses under section 8.53 by means of a provision set forth in its articles of incorporation or bylaws, by a resolution of its shareholders or board of directors, by a contract or otherwise. However, any such obligatory arrangement must comply with the requirements of subsection (a) regarding furnishing of an affirmation and undertaking. No other procedures are contemplated, although obligatory arrangements may include notice and other procedures in connection with advancement of expenses and indemnification requests.

At least one court has held that a general obligatory provision requiring indemnification to the extent permitted by law does not include advance for expenses if not specifically mentioned. See, e.g., *Advanced Mining Systems, Inc. v. Fricke*, 623 A.2d 82 (Del. 1992). Unless provided otherwise, section 8.58(a) requires the opposite result, unless provided otherwise.

The decision to advance expenses is required to be made only one time with respect to each proceeding rather than each time a request for payment of expenses is received by the corporation. However, the directors are free to reconsider the decision at any time (*e.g.*, upon a change in the financial ability of the corporation to pay the amounts in question). The decision as to the reasonableness of any expenses may be made by any officer or agent of the corporation duly authorized to do so.

The procedures set forth in subsection (c) for authorizing an advance for expenses parallel the procedures set forth in section 8.55(b) for selecting the person or persons to make the determination that indemnification is permissible. If the advance for expenses is not authorized by the shareholders under subsection (c)(2), the procedure specified in subsection (c)(1)(i) must be used. If it is unavailable, then the procedure under subsection (c)(1)(ii) may be used.

Under subsection (c)(1)(i), the vote required when the qualified directors act as a group is an absolute majority of their number. A majority of the qualified directors constitutes a quorum for board action for this purpose.

The committee of two or more qualified directors referred to in subsection (c)(1)(i) may be a committee of the board of directors to which the power to authorize advances for expenses from time to time has been delegated, so long as (1) the committee was appointed by a majority vote of directors who were, at the time of appointment of the committee, qualified directors and (2) each advance is authorized by a majority vote of members of the committee who, at the time of the vote, are qualified directors.

Under subsection (c)(1)(ii), which is available only if subsection (c)(1)(i) is not available, the board's action must be taken in accordance with section 8.20 or section 8.21, as the case may be, and directors who are not qualified directors may participate in the vote. Allowing directors who at the time are not qualified directors to participate in the authorization decision, if there is no or only one qualified director, is a principle of prudence that is based on the concept that, if there are not at least two qualified directors, then it is preferable to return the power to make the decision to the full board (even though it includes non-qualified directors) than to leave it with one qualified director.

Illustration 1: The board consists of 15 directors, four of whom are non-qualified directors. Of the eleven qualified directors, nine are present at the meeting at which the authorization is to be made (or the committee is to be appointed). Under subsection (c)(1)(i), a quorum is present and at least six of the nine qualified directors present at the board meeting must authorize any advance for expenses because six is an absolute majority of the eleven qualified directors. Alternatively, six of the nine qualified directors present at the board meeting may appoint a committee of two or more of the qualified directors (up to all eleven) to decide whether to authorize the advance. Action by the committee would require an absolute majority of the qualified directors appointed as members.

Illustration 2: The board consists of 15 directors, only one of whom is a qualified director. Subsection (c)(1)(i) is not available because the number of qualified directors is less than two. Accordingly, the decision must be made by the board under subsection (c)(1)(ii) (or, as is always permitted, by the shareholders under subsection (c)(2)).

Authorizations by shareholders rather than by directors are permitted by subsection (c)(2), but shares owned by or voted under the control of directors who at the time are not qualified directors may not be voted on the authorizations. This does not affect general rules, as to the required presence of a quorum at the meeting, otherwise governing the authorization.

The fact that there has been an advance for expenses does not determine whether a director is entitled to indemnification. Repayment of any advance is required only if it is ultimately determined that the director did not meet the relevant standard of conduct in section 8.51. A proceeding will often terminate without a judicial or other determination as to whether the director's conduct met that standard. Nevertheless, the board of directors should make, or cause to be made, an affirmative determination of entitlement to indemnification at the conclusion of the proceeding. This decision should be made in accordance with the procedures set forth in section 8.55.

Judicial enforcement of rights granted by or pursuant to section 8.53 is specifically contemplated by section 8.54.

§ 8.54 Court–Ordered Indemnification and Advance for Expenses

(a) A director who is a party to a proceeding because he is a director may apply for indemnification or an advance for expenses to the court conducting the proceeding or to another court of competent jurisdiction. After receipt of an application and after giving any notice it considers necessary, the court shall:

(1) order indemnification if the court determines that the director is entitled to mandatory indemnification under section 8.52;

(2) order indemnification or advance for expenses if the court determines that the director is entitled to indemnification or advance for expenses pursuant to a provision authorized by section 8.58(a); or

(3) order indemnification or advance for expenses if the court determines, in view of all the relevant circumstances, that it is fair and reasonable

(i) to indemnify the director, or

(ii) to advance expenses to the director, even if he has not met the relevant standard of conduct set forth in section 8.51(a), failed to comply with section 8.53 or was adjudged liable in a proceeding referred to in subsection 8.51(d)(1) or (d)(2), but if he was adjudged so liable his indemnification shall be limited to reasonable expenses incurred in connection with the proceeding.

(b) If the court determines that the director is entitled to indemnification under subsection (a)(1) or to indemnification or advance for expenses under subsection (a)(2), it shall also order the corporation to pay the director's reasonable expenses incurred in connection with obtaining court-ordered indemnification or advance for expenses. If the court determines that the director is entitled to indemnification or advance for expenses under subsection (a)(3), it may also order the corporation to pay the director's reasonable expenses to obtain court-ordered indemnification or advance for expenses.

OFFICIAL COMMENT

Section 8.54(a) provides for court-ordered indemnification in three situations:

(1) A director is entitled to mandatory indemnification under section 8.52. If so, the director may enforce that right by judicial proceeding.

(2) A director is entitled to indemnification or advance for expenses pursuant to a provision in the articles or bylaws, board or shareholder resolution, or contract. If so, the director may enforce that right by judicial proceeding. To the extent that these rights are contractual, the corporation may have contractual defenses. If the corporation has contracted to indemnify a director to the fullest extent permitted by law, a court may, nevertheless, deny an advance for expenses if it determines that the director did not have, at the time he delivered the affirmation required by section 8.53(a)(1), a good faith belief that he met the relevant standard of conduct.

(3) A court in its discretion determines that it is fair and reasonable under all the relevant circumstances to order an advance for expenses or indemnification for the amount of a settlement or judgment (in addition to expenses), whether or not the director met the relevant standard of conduct in section 8.51 or is otherwise ineligible for indemnification. However, there are two exceptions: an adverse judgment in a derivative proceeding (section 8.51(d)(1)) and an adverse judgment in a proceeding charging receipt of an improper financial benefit (section 8.51(d)(2)),

although in either case the court may order payment of expenses. Thus, with these exceptions, section 8.54(a)(3) permits a court to order indemnification for amounts paid in settlement of and expenses incurred in connection with a derivative proceeding or a proceeding charging receipt of an improper financial benefit. Section 8.54(a)(3) applies to (a) a situation in which a provision in the articles of incorporation, bylaws, resolution, or contract obligates the corporation to indemnify or to advance expenses but the relevant standard of conduct has not been met and (b) a situation involving a permissive provision pursuant to which the board declines to exercise its authority to indemnify or to advance expenses. However, in determining whether indemnification or expense advance would be "fair and reasonable," a court should give appropriate deference to an informed decision of a board or committee made in good faith and based upon full information. Ordinarily, a court should not determine that it is "fair and reasonable" to order indemnification or expense advance where the director has not met conditions and procedures to which he agreed.

The discretionary authority of the court to order indemnification of a derivative proceeding settlement under section 8.54(a)(3) contrasts with the denial of similar authority under section 145(b) of the Delaware General Corporation Law. A director seeking court-ordered indemnification or expense advance under section 8.54(a)(3) must show that there are facts peculiar to his situation that make it fair and reasonable to both the corporation and to the director to override an intracorporate declination or any otherwise applicable statutory prohibition against indemnification, e.g., sections 8.51(a) or (d).

Aside from the two exceptions noted above and other than the fairness and reasonableness requirement, there are no statutory outer limits on the court's power to order indemnification under section 8.54(a)(3). In an appropriate case, a court may wish to refer to the provisions of section 2.02(b)(4) establishing the outer limits of a liability-limiting charter provision. It would be an extraordinary situation in which a court would want to provide indemnification going beyond the limits of section 2.02(b)(4), but if the court, as the independent decision-maker, finds that it is "fair and reasonable," then the court is permitted to do so. It should be emphasized again, however, that the director seeking indemnification must make a showing of fairness and reasonableness and that exercise of the power granted by section 8.54(a)(3) is committed to the court's discretion.

Among the factors a court may want to consider are the gravity of the offense, the financial impact upon the corporation, the occurrence of a change in control or, in the case of an advance for expenses, the inability of the director to finance his defense. A court may want to give special attention to certain other issues. First, has the corporation joined in the application to the court for indemnification or an advance for expenses? This factor may be particularly important where under section 8.51(d) indemnification is not permitted for an amount paid in settlement of a proceeding brought by or in the right of the corporation. Second, in a case where indemnification would have been available under section 8.51(a)(2) if the corporation had adopted a provision authorized by section 2.02(b)(5), was the decision to adopt such a provision presented to and rejected by the shareholders and, if not, would exculpation of the director's conduct have resulted under a section 2.02(b)(4) provision? Third, in connection with considering indemnification for expenses under section 8.51(d)(2) in a proceeding in which a director was adjudged liable for receiving a financial benefit to which he was not entitled, was such financial benefit insubstantial—particularly in relation to the other aspects of the transaction involved—and what was the degree of the director's involvement in the transaction and the decision to participate?

Under section 8.54(b), if a director successfully sues to enforce his right to indemnification of expenses under subsection (a)(1) or to indemnification or advance for expenses under subsection (a)(2), then the court must order the corporation to pay the director's expenses in the enforcement proceeding. However, if a director successfully sues for indemnification or advance for expenses under subsection (a)(3), then the court may (but is not required to) order the corporation to pay the director's expenses in the proceeding under subsection (a)(3). The basis for the distinction is that the corporation breached its obligation in the first two cases but not in the third.

Application for indemnification under section 8.54 may be made either to the court in which the proceeding was heard or to another court of appropriate jurisdiction. For example, a defendant in a criminal proceeding who has been convicted but believes that indemnification would be proper could apply either to the court which heard the criminal proceeding or bring an action against the corporation in another forum.

A decision by the board of directors not to oppose the request for indemnification is governed by the general standards of conduct of section 8.30. Even if the corporation decided not to oppose the request, the court must satisfy itself that the person seeking indemnification is deserving of receiving it under section 8.54.

As provided in section 8.58(c), a corporation may limit the rights of a director under section 8.54 by a provision in its articles of incorporation. In the absence of such a provision, the court has general power to exercise the authority granted under this section.

§ 8.55 Determination and Authorization of Indemnification

(a) A corporation may not indemnify a director under section 8.51 unless authorized for a specific proceeding after a determination has been made that indemnification is permissible because the director has met the relevant standard of conduct set forth in section 8.51.

(b) The determination shall be made:

(1) if there are two or more qualified directors, by the board of directors by a majority vote of all the qualified directors (a majority of whom shall for such purpose constitute a quorum), or by a majority of the members of a committee of two or more qualified directors appointed by such a vote;

(2) by special legal counsel:

(i) selected in the manner prescribed in subdivision (1); or

(ii) if there are fewer than two qualified directors, selected by the board of directors (in which selection directors who are not qualified directors may participate); or

(3) by the shareholders, but shares owned by or voted under the control of a director who at the time is not a qualified director may not be voted on the determination.

(c) Authorization of indemnification shall be made in the same manner as the determination that indemnification is permissible except that if there are fewer than two qualified directors, or if the determination is made by special legal counsel, authorization of indemnification shall be made by those entitled to select special legal counsel under subsection (b)(2)(ii).

OFFICIAL COMMENT

Section 8.55 provides the method for determining whether a corporation should indemnify a director under section 8.51. In this section a distinction is made between a "determination" and an "authorization." A "determination" involves a decision whether under the circumstances the person seeking indemnification has met the relevant standard of conduct under section 8.51 and is therefore eligible for indemnification. This decision may be made by the individuals or groups described in section 8.55(b). In addition, after a favorable "determination" has been made, the corporation must decide whether to "authorize" indemnification except to the extent that an obligatory provision under section 8.58(a) is applicable. This decision includes a review of the reasonableness of the expenses, the financial ability of the corporation to make the payment, and the judgment whether the limited financial resources of the corporation should be devoted to this or some other use. While special legal counsel may make the "determination" of eligibility for indemnification, counsel may not "authorize" the indemnification. A pre-existing obligation under section 8.58(a) to indemnify if the director is eligible for indemnification dispenses with the second-step decision to "authorize" indemnification.

Section 8.55(b) establishes procedures for selecting the person or persons who will make the determination of permissibility of indemnification. As indicated in the Official Comment to section 8.53(c), the committee of qualified directors referred to in subsection (b)(*l*) may include a committee of the board to which has been delegated the power to determine whether to indemnify a director so long as the appointment and composition of the committee members comply with subsection (b)(*l*). In selecting special legal counsel under subsection (b)(2), directors who are parties to the proceeding may participate in the decision if there are insufficient qualified directors to satisfy subsection (b)(*l*). Directors who are not eligible to act as qualified directors may also participate in the decision to "authorize" indemnification on the basis of a favorable "determination" if necessary to permit action by the board of directors. The authorization of indemnification is the decision that results in payment of any amounts to be indemnified. This limited participation of interested directors in the authorization decision is justified by the principle of necessity.

Under subsection (b)(1), the vote required when the qualified directors act as a group is an absolute majority of their number. A majority of the qualified directors constitutes a quorum for board action for this purpose. If there are not at least two qualified directors, then the determination of entitlement to indemnification must be made by special legal counsel or by the shareholders.

Legal counsel authorized to make the required determination is referred to as "special legal counsel." In earlier versions of the Model Act, and in the statutes of many states, reference is made to "independent" legal counsel. The word "special" is felt to be more descriptive of the role to be performed; it is intended that the counsel selected should be independent in accordance with governing legal precepts. "Special legal counsel" normally should be counsel having no prior professional relationship with those seeking indemnification, should be retained for the specific purpose, and should not be or have been either inside counsel or regular outside counsel to the corporation. Special legal counsel also should not have any familial, financial or other relationship with any of those seeking indemnification that would, in the circumstances, reasonably be expected to exert an influence on counsel in making the determination. It is important that the process be sufficiently flexible to permit selection of counsel in light of the particular circumstances and so that unnecessary expense may be avoided. Hence the phrase "special legal counsel" is not defined in the statute.

Determinations by shareholders, rather than by directors or special legal counsel, are permitted by subsection (b)(3), but shares owned by or voted under the control of directors who at the time are not qualified directors may not be voted on the determination of eligibility for indemnification. This does not affect general rules as to the required presence of a quorum at the meeting in order for the determination to be made.

Section 8.55 is subject to section 8.58(a), which authorizes an arrangement obligating the corporation in advance to provide indemnification or to advance expenses.

§ 8.56 Indemnification of Officers

(a) A corporation may indemnify and advance expenses under this subchapter to an officer of the corporation who is a party to a proceeding because he is an officer of the corporation

(1) to the same extent as a director; and

(2) if he is an officer but not a director, to such further extent as may be provided by the articles of incorporation, the bylaws, a resolution of the board of directors, or contract except for

(A) liability in connection with a proceeding by or in the right of the corporation other than for reasonable expenses incurred in connection with the proceeding or

(B) liability arising out of conduct that constitutes

(i) receipt by him of a financial benefit to which he is not entitled,

(ii) an intentional infliction of harm on the corporation or the shareholders, or

(iii) an intentional violation of criminal law.

(b) The provisions of subsection (a)(2) shall apply to an officer who is also a director if the basis on which he is made a party to the proceeding is an act or omission solely as an officer.

(c) An officer of a corporation who is not a director is entitled to mandatory indemnification under section 8.52, and may apply to a court under section 8.54 for indemnification or an advance for expenses, in each case to the same extent to which a director may be entitled to indemnification or advance for expenses under those provisions.

OFFICIAL COMMENT

Section 8.56 correlates the general legal principles relating to the indemnification of officers of the corporation with the limitations on indemnification in subchapter E. This correlation may be summarized in general terms as follows.

(1) An officer of a corporation who is *not* a director may be indemnified by the corporation on a discretionary basis to the same extent as though he were a director, and, in addition, may have additional indemnification rights apart from subchapter E, but the outer limits of such rights are specified. See sections 8.56(a)(2) and (c).

(2) An officer who is *also* a director of the corporation is entitled to the indemnification rights of a director and of an officer who is not a director (see preceding paragraph) if his conduct that is the subject of the proceeding was solely in his capacity as an officer. See section 8.56(b).

(3) An *officer* of a corporation who is not a director has the right of mandatory indemnification granted to directors under section 8.52 and the right to apply for court-ordered indemnification under section 8.54. See section 8.56(c).

Section 8.56 does not deal with indemnification of employees and agents because the concerns of self-dealing that arise when directors provide for their own indemnification and expense advance (and sometimes for senior executive officers) are not present when directors (or officers) provide for indemnification and expense advance for employees and agents who are not directors or officers. Moreover, the rights of employees and agents to indemnification and advance for expenses derive from principles of agency, the doctrine of respondeat superior, collective bargaining or other contractual arrangements rather than from a corporation statute. It would be presumptuous for a corporation statute to seek to limit the indemnification bargain that a corporation may wish to make with those it hires or retains. The same standard applicable to directors and officers may not be appropriate for office workers and hazardous waste workers, brokers and custodians, engineers and farm workers. None of their roles or responsibilities are prescribed by the Model Act.

Section 3.02 grants broad powers to corporations, including powers to make contracts, appoint and fix the compensation of employees and agents and to make payments furthering the business and affairs of the corporation. Many corporations provide for the exercise of these powers in the same provisions in the articles, bylaws or otherwise in which they provide for expense advance and indemnification for directors and officers.

Indemnification may also be provided to protect employees or agents from liabilities incurred while serving at a corporation's request as a director, officer, partner, trustee, or agent of another commercial, charitable, or nonprofit venture.

Although employees and agents are not covered by subchapter E, the principles and procedures set forth in the subchapter for indemnification and advance for expenses for directors and officers may be helpful to counsel and courts in dealing with indemnification and expense advance for employees and agents.

Careful consideration should be given to extending mandatory maximum indemnification and expense advance to employees and agents. The same considerations that may favor mandatory maximum indemnification for directors and officers—e.g., encouraging qualified individuals to serve—may not be present in the cases of employees and agents. Many corporations may prefer to retain the discretion to decide, on a case-by-case basis, whether to indemnify and advance expenses to employees and agents (and perhaps even officers, especially nonexecutive officers) rather than binding themselves in advance to do so.

1. Officers Who Are Not Directors

While section 8.56 does not prescribe the standards governing the rights of officers to indemnification, subsection (a) does set outer limits beyond which the corporation may not indemnify. These outer limits for officers (see subsection (a)(2)) are substantially the same as the outer limits on the corporation's power to indemnify directors: (i) in a proceeding by or in the right of the corporation, indemnification is not allowed other than for reasonable expenses incurred in connection therewith and (ii) in any proceeding, indemnification is not allowed in those situations in which directors' liability to the corporation or its shareholders could not be eliminated by a provision included in the articles pursuant to section 2.02(b)(4), i.e., where there has been receipt of a financial benefit to which he is not entitled, intentional infliction of harm on the corporation or shareholders or intentional violation of criminal law. Since officers are held to substantially the same standards of conduct as directors (see section 8.42), there does not appear to be any reasoned basis for granting officers greater indemnification rights as a substantive matter. Procedurally, however, there is an important difference. To permit greater flexibility, officers may be indemnified (within the above-mentioned outer limits) with respect to conduct that does not meet the standards set by section 8.51(a)(1) simply by authorization of the board of directors, whereas directors' indemnification can reach beyond those standards, as contemplated by section 8.51(a)(2), only with a shareholder-approved provision included in the articles pursuant to section 2.02(b)(5). This procedural difference reflects the reduced risk of self-dealing as to officers.

Section 8.56(c) grants nondirector officers the same rights to mandatory indemnification under section 8.52 and to apply to a court for indemnification under section 8.54 as are granted to directors. Since their substantive rights to indemnification are essentially the same as those of directors, it is appropriate to grant officers the same affirmative procedural rights to judicial relief as are provided to directors.

The broad authority in section 8.56(a)(2) to grant indemnification may be limited by appropriate provisions in the articles of incorporation. See section 8.58(c).

2. Officers Who Are Also Directors

Subsection (b) provides, in effect, that an officer of the corporation who is also a director is subject to the same standards of indemnification as other directors and cannot avail himself of the provisions of subsection (a) unless he can establish that the act or omission that is the subject of the proceeding was committed solely in his capacity as officer. Thus, a vice president for sales who is also a director and whose actions failed to meet section 8.51(a) standards could be indemnified provided that his conduct was within the outer limits of subsection (a)(2) and involved only his officer capacity.

This more flexible approach for situations where the individual is not acting as a director seems appropriate as a matter of fairness. There are many instances where officers who also serve as directors assume responsibilities and take actions in their nondirector capacities. It is hard to justify a denial of indemnification to an officer who failed to meet a standard applicable only to directors when the officer can establish that he did not act as a director. Nor are there likely to be complications or difficulties because some directors are treated differently than others where the high burden of proof—solely as officer—is met. Obviously, the burden will be especially difficult to meet where the roles of officer and director are closely intertwined, as is often the case with a chief executive officer.

For a director-officer to be indemnified under section 8.51 for conduct in his capacity as a director when he has not satisfied the standards of section 8.51(a), a provision in the articles under section 2.02(b)(5) is required. If such a provision is included in the articles, the standards for indemnification are those specified in section 2.02(b)(5). For a director-officer to be indemnified for conduct solely in his capacity as an officer, even though the director-officer has not satisfied the standards of section 8.56(a), only a resolution of the board authorizing such indemnification is required, rather than a provision in the articles. If such a resolution is adopted, the standards for indemnification are those specified in subsection (a)(2). However, when a director-officer seeks indemnification or expense advance under subsections (b) and (a)(2) on the basis of having acted solely in his capacity as an officer, indemnification or expense advance must be approved through the same procedures as set forth in sections 8.55 or 8.53(c), as the case may be, for approval of indemnification or expense advance for a director when acting in his capacity as a director.

§ 8.57 Insurance

A corporation may purchase and maintain insurance on behalf of an individual who is a director or officer of the corporation, or who, while a director or officer of the corporation, serves at the corporation's request as a director, officer, partner, trustee, employee, or agent of another domestic or foreign corporation, partnership, joint venture, trust, employee benefit plan, or other entity, against liability asserted against or incurred by him in that capacity or arising from his status as a director or officer, whether or not the corporation would have power to indemnify or advance expenses to him against the same liability under this subchapter.

OFFICIAL COMMENT

Section 8.57 authorizes a corporation to purchase and maintain insurance on behalf of directors and officers against liabilities imposed on them by reason of actions in their official capacity, or their status as such, or arising from their service to the corporation or another entity at the corporation's request. Insurance is not limited to claims against which a corporation is entitled to indemnify under this subchapter. This insurance, usually referred to as "D & O liability insurance," provides protection to directors and officers in addition to the rights of indemnification created by or pursuant to this subchapter (as well as typically protecting the individual insureds against the corporation's failure to pay indemnification required or permitted by this subchapter) and provides a source of reimbursement for corporations which indemnify directors and others for conduct covered by the insurance. On the other hand, policies typically do not cover uninsurable matters, such as actions involving dishonesty, self-dealing, bad faith, knowing violations of the securities acts, or other willful misconduct. Johnston, "Corporate Indemnification and Liability Insurance for Directors and Officers," 33 Bus. Law. 1993, 2024–29 (1978). See also Knepper & Bailey, *Liability of Corporate Officers and Directors,* section 21.07 (4th ed. 1988).

Although this section does not include employees and agents for the reasons stated in the Official Comment to section 8.56, the corporation has the power under section 3.02 to purchase and maintain insurance on their behalf. This power is confirmed in section 8.58(d).

This section is not intended to set the outer limits on the type of insurance which a corporation may maintain or the persons to be covered. Rather, it is included to remove "any doubt as to the power to carry insurance and to maintain it on behalf of directors, officers, employees and agents." Sebring, "Recent Legislative Changes in the Law of Indemnification of Directors, Officers and Others," 23 Bus. Law. 95, 106 (1967).

§ 8.58 Variation by Corporate Action; Application of Subchapter

(a) A corporation may, by a provision in its articles of incorporation or bylaws or in a resolution adopted or a contract approved by its board of directors or shareholders, obligate itself in advance of the act or omission giving rise to a proceeding to provide indemnification in accordance with section 8.51 or advance funds to pay for or reimburse expenses in accordance with section 8.53. Any such obligatory provision shall be deemed to satisfy the requirements for authorization referred to in section 8.53(c) and in section 8.55(c). Any such provision that obligates the corporation to provide indemnification to the fullest extent permitted by law shall be deemed to obligate the corporation to advance funds to pay for or reimburse expenses in accordance with section 8.53 to the fullest extent permitted by law, unless the provision specifically provides otherwise.

(b) Any provision pursuant to subsection (a) shall not obligate the corporation to indemnify or advance expenses to a director of a predecessor of the corporation, pertaining to conduct with respect to the predecessor, unless otherwise specifically provided. Any provision for indemnification or advance for expenses in the articles of incorporation, bylaws, or a resolution of the board of directors or shareholders of a predecessor of the corporation in a merger or in a contract to which the predecessor is a party, existing at the time the merger takes effect, shall be governed by section 11.07(a)(4).

(c) A corporation may, by a provision in its articles of incorporation, limit any of the rights to indemnification or advance for expenses created by or pursuant to this subchapter.

(d) This subchapter does not limit a corporation's power to pay or reimburse expenses incurred by a director or an officer in connection with his appearance as a witness in a proceeding at a time when he is not a party.

(e) This subchapter does not limit a corporation's power to indemnify, advance expenses to or provide or maintain insurance on behalf of an employee or agent.

OFFICIAL COMMENT

Section 8.58(a) authorizes a corporation to make obligatory the permissive provisions of subchapter E in advance of the conduct giving rise to the request for assistance. Many corporations have adopted such provisions, often with shareholder approval. An obligatory provision satisfies the requirements for authorization in subsection (c) of sections 8.53 and 8.55, but compliance would still be required with subsections (a) and (b) of these sections.

Section 8.58(a) further provides that a provision requiring indemnification to the fullest extent permitted by law shall be deemed, absent an express statement to the contrary, to include an obligation to advance expenses under section 8.53. This provision of the statute is intended to avoid a decision such as that of the Delaware Supreme Court in *Advanced Mining Systems, Inc. v. Fricke*, 623 A.2d 82 (Del. 1992). If a corporation provides for obligatory indemnification and not for obligatory advance for expenses, the provision should be reviewed to ensure that it properly reflects the intent in light of the third sentence of section 8.58(a). Also, a corporation should consider whether obligatory expense advance is intended for direct suits by the corporation as well as for derivative suits by shareholders in the right of the corporation. In the former case, assuming compliance with subsections (a) and (b) of section 8.53, the corporation could be required to fund the defense of a defendant director even where the board of directors has already concluded that he has engaged in significant wrongdoing. See Official Comment to section 8.53.

Section 8.58(b) provides that an obligatory indemnification provision as authorized by subsection (a) does not, unless specific provision is made to the contrary, bind the corporation with respect to a predecessor.

An obligatory indemnification provision of a predecessor is treated as a liability (to the extent it is one) under section 11.07(a)(4), which governs the effect of a merger.

Section 8.58(c) permits a corporation to limit the right of the corporation to indemnify or advance expenses by a provision in its articles of incorporation. As provided in section 10.09, no such limitation will affect rights in existence when the provision becomes effective pursuant to section 1.23.

Section 8.58(d) makes clear that subchapter E deals only with actual or threatened defendants or respondents in a proceeding, and that expenses incurred by a director in connection with appearance as a witness may be indemnified without regard to the limitations of subchapter E. Indeed, most of the standards described in sections 8.51 and 8.54(a) by their own terms can have no meaningful application to a director whose only connection with a proceeding is that he has been called as a witness.

Subchapter E does not regulate the power of the corporation to indemnify or advance expenses to employees and agents. That subject is governed by the law of agency and related principles and frequently by contractual arrangements between the corporation and the employee or agent. Section 8.58(e) makes clear that, while indemnification, advance for expenses, and insurance for employees and agents are beyond the scope of this subchapter, the elaboration in subchapter E of standards and procedures for indemnification, expense advance, and insurance for directors and officers is not in any way intended to cast doubt on the power of the corporation to indemnify or advance expenses to or purchase and maintain insurance for employees and agents under section 3.02 or otherwise.

§ 8.59 Exclusivity of Subchapter

A corporation may provide indemnification or advance expenses to a director or an officer only as permitted by this subchapter.

OFFICIAL COMMENT

This subchapter is the exclusive source for the power of a corporation to indemnify or advance expenses to a director or an officer.

Section 8.59 does not preclude provisions in articles of incorporation, bylaws, resolutions, or contracts designed to provide procedural machinery in addition to (but not inconsistent with) that provided by this subchapter. For example, a corporation may properly obligate the board of directors to consider and act expeditiously on an application for indemnification or advance for expenses or to cooperate in the procedural steps required to obtain a judicial determination under section 8.54.

Subchapter F. Directors' Conflicting Interest Transactions

§ 8.60 Subchapter Definitions

In this subchapter:

(1) "Director's conflicting interest transaction" means a transaction effected or proposed to be effected by the corporation (or by an entity controlled by the corporation)

(i) to which, at the relevant time, the director is a party; or

(ii) respecting which, at the relevant time, the director had knowledge and a material financial interest known to the director; or

(iii) respecting which, at the relevant time, the director knew that a related person was a party or had a material financial interest.

(2) "Control" (including the term "controlled by") means (i) having the power, directly or indirectly, to elect or remove a majority of the members of the board of directors or other governing body of an entity, whether through the ownership of voting shares or interests, by contract, or otherwise, or (ii) being subject to a majority of the risk of loss from the entity's activities or entitled to receive a majority of the entity's residual returns.

(3) "Relevant time" means (i) the time at which directors' action respecting the transaction is taken in compliance with section 8.62, or (ii) if the transaction is not brought before the board of directors of the corporation (or its committee) for action under section 8.62, at the time the corporation (or an entity controlled by the corporation) becomes legally obligated to consummate the transaction.

(4) "Material financial interest" means a financial interest in a transaction that would reasonably be expected to impair the objectivity of the director's judgment when participating in action on the authorization of the transaction.

(5) "Related person" means:

(i) the director's spouse;

(ii) a child, stepchild, grandchild, parent, step parent, grandparent, sibling, step sibling, half sibling, aunt, uncle, niece or nephew (or spouse of any thereof) of the director or of the director's spouse;

(iii) an individual living in the same home as the director;

(iv) an entity (other than the corporation or an entity controlled by the corporation) controlled by the director or any person specified above in this subdivision (5);

(v) a domestic or foreign (A) business or nonprofit corporation (other than the corporation or an entity controlled by the corporation) of which the director is a director, (B) unincorporated entity of which the director is a general partner or a member of the governing body, or (C) individual, trust or estate for whom or of which the director is a trustee, guardian, personal representative or like fiduciary; or

(vi) a person that is, or an entity that is controlled by, an employer of the director.

(6) "Fair to the corporation" means, for purposes of section 8.61(b)(3), that the transaction as a whole was beneficial to the corporation, taking into appropriate account whether it was (i) fair in terms of the director's dealings with the corporation, and (ii) comparable to what might have been obtainable in an arm's length transaction, given the consideration paid or received by the corporation.

(7) "Required disclosure" means disclosure of (i) the existence and nature of the director's conflicting interest, and (ii) all facts known to the director respecting the subject matter of the transaction that a director free of such conflicting interest would reasonably believe to be material in deciding whether to proceed with the transaction.

OFFICIAL COMMENT

The definitions set forth in section 8.60 apply only to subchapter F's provisions and, except to the extent relevant to subchapter G, have no application elsewhere in the Model Act. (For the meaning and use of certain terms used below, such as "*D*," "*X* Co." and "*Y* Co.", see the Note at the end of the Introductory Comment of subchapter F.)

1. Director's Conflicting Interest Transaction

The definition of "director's conflicting interest transaction" in subdivision (1) is the core concept underlying subchapter F, demarcating the transactional area that lies within—and without—the scope of the subchapter's provisions. The definition operates preclusively in that, as used in section 8.61, it denies the power of a court to invalidate transactions or otherwise to remedy conduct that falls outside the statutory definition of "director's conflicting interest transaction" solely on the ground that the director has a conflict of interest in the transaction. (Nevertheless, as stated in the Introductory Comment, the transaction might be open to attack under rules of law concerning director misbehavior other than rules based solely on the existence of a conflict of interest transaction, as to which subchapter F is preclusive).

a. Transaction

For a director's conflicting interest transaction to arise, there must first be a transaction effected or proposed to be effected by the corporation or an entity controlled by the corporation to which the director or a related person is a party or in which the director or a related person has a material financial interest. As discussed in the Introductory Comment, the provisions of subchapter F do not apply where there is no "transaction" by the corporation—no matter how conflicting the director's interest may be. For example, a corporate opportunity usurped by a director by definition does not involve a transaction by the corporation, and thus is not covered by subchapter F, even though it may be proscribed under fiduciary duty principles.

Moreover, for purposes of subchapter F, "transaction" means (and requires) a bilateral (or multilateral) arrangement to which the corporation or an entity controlled by the corporation is a party. Subchapter F does not apply to transactions to which the corporation is not a party. Thus, a purchase or sale by the director of the corporation's shares on the open market or from or to a third party is not a "director's conflicting interest transaction" within the meaning of subchapter F because the corporation is not a party to the transaction.

b. Party to the transaction—the corporation

In the usual case, the transaction would be effected by *X* Co. Assume, however, that *X* Co. controls the vote for directors of *S* Co. *D* wishes to sell a building *D* owns to *X* Co. and *X* Co. is willing to buy it. As a business matter, it makes no difference to *X* Co. whether it takes the title directly or indirectly through its subsidiary *S* Co. or some other entity that *X* Co. controls. The applicability of subchapter F does not depend upon that formal distinction, because the subchapter includes within its operative framework transactions by entities controlled by *X* Co. Thus, subchapter F would apply to a sale of the building by *D* to *S* Co.

c. Party to the transaction—the director or a related person

To constitute a director's conflicting interest transaction, *D* (the director identified in the subchapter from time to time as a "conflicted director") must, at the relevant time, (i) be a party to the transaction, or (ii) know of the transaction and *D*'s material financial interest in it, or (iii) know that a related person of *D* was a party to the transaction or (iv) know that a related person of *D* has a material financial interest in the transaction. A material financial interest (as defined in subdivision (4)) is one that would reasonably be expected to impair the objectivity of the director's judgment if *D* were to participate in action by the directors (or by a committee thereof) taken on the authorization of the transaction.

Routine business transactions frequently occur between companies with overlapping directors. If *X* Co. and *Y* Co. have routine, frequent business dealings whose terms are dictated by competitive market forces, then even if a director of *X* Co. has a relevant relationship with *Y* Co., the transactions would almost always be defensible, regardless of approval by disinterested directors or shareholders, on the ground that they are "fair." For example, a common transaction involves a purchase of the corporation's product line by *Y* Co., or perhaps by *D* or a related person, at prices normally charged by the corporation. In such circumstances, it usually will not be difficult for *D* to show that the transaction was on arms-length terms and was fair. Even a purchase by *D* of a product of *X* Co. at a usual "employee's discount," while technically assailable as a conflicting interest transaction, would customarily be viewed as a routine incident of the office of director and, thus, "fair" to the corporation.

D can have a conflicting interest in only two ways.

First, a conflicting interest can arise under either subdivision (1)(i) or (ii). This will be the case if, under clause (i), the transaction is between *D* and *X* Co. A conflicting interest also will arise under clause (ii) if *D* is not a party to the transaction, but knows about it and knows that he or she has a material financial interest in it. The personal economic stake of the director must be in the transaction itself—that is, the director's gain must flow directly from the transaction. A remote gain (for example, a future reduction in tax rates in the local community) is not enough to give rise to a conflicting interest under subdivision (1)(ii).

Second, a conflicting interest for *D* can arise under subdivision (1)(iii) from the involvement in the transaction of a "related person" of *D* that is either a party to the transaction or has a "material financial interest" in it. "Related person" is defined in subdivision (5).

Circumstances may arise where a director could have a conflicting interest under more than one clause of subdivision (1). For example, if *Y* Co. is a party to or interested in the transaction with *X* Co. and *Y* Co. is a related person of *D*, the matter would be governed by subdivision (1)(iii), but *D* also may have a conflicting interest under subdivision (1)(ii) if *D*'s economic interest in *Y* Co. is sufficiently material and if the importance of the transaction to *Y* Co. is sufficiently material.

A director may have relationships and linkages to persons and institutions that are not specified in subdivision (1)(iii). Such relationships and linkages fall outside subchapter F because the categories of persons described in subdivision (1)(iii) constitute the exclusive universe for purposes of subchapter F. For example, in a challenged transaction between *X* Co. and *Y* Co., suppose the court confronts the argument that *D* also is a major creditor of *Y* Co. and that creditor status in *Y* Co. gives D a conflicting interest. The court should rule that *D*'s creditor status in *Y* Co. does not fit any category of subdivision (1); and therefore, the conflict of interest claim must be rejected by reason of section 8.61(a). The result would be different if *Y* Co.'s debt to *D* were of such economic significance to *D* that it would either fall under subdivision (1)(ii) or, if it placed *D* in control of *Y* Co., it would fall under subdivision (1)(iii) (because *Y* Co. is a related person of *D* under subdivision (5)(iv)). To explore the example further, if *D* is also a shareholder of *Y* Co., but *D* does not have a material financial interest in the transaction and does not control *Y* Co., no director's conflicting interest transaction arises and the transaction cannot be challenged on conflict of interest grounds. To avoid any appearance of impropriety, *D*, nonetheless, should consider recusal from the other directors' deliberations and voting on the transaction between *X* Co. and *Y* Co.

It should be noted that any director's interest in a transaction that meets the criteria of section 8.60(1) is considered a "director's conflicting interest transaction." If the director's interest satisfies those criteria, subchapter F draws no distinction between a director's interest that clashes with the interests of the corporation and a director's interest that coincides with, or is parallel to, or even furthers the interests of the corporation. In any of these cases, if the director's "interest" is present, a "conflict" will exist.

2. Control

The definition of "control" in subdivision (2) contains two independent clauses. The first clause addresses possession of the voting or other power, directly or indirectly, to elect or remove a majority of the members of an entity's governing body. That power can arise, for example, from articles of incorporation or a shareholders' agreement. The second clause addresses the circumstances where a person is (i) subject to a majority of the risk of loss from the entity's activities, or (ii) entitled to receive a majority of the entity's residual returns. The second clause of the definition includes, among other circumstances, complex financial structures that do not have voting interests or a governing body in the traditional sense, such as special purpose entities. Although the definition of "control" operates independently of the accounting rules adopted by the U.S. accounting profession, it is consistent with the relevant generally accepted accounting principle (made effective in 2003) that governs when an entity must be included in consolidated financial statements.

3. Relevant Time

The definition of director's conflicting interest transaction requires that, except where he or she is a party, the director know of the transaction. It also requires that where not a party, the director know of the transaction either at the time it is brought before the corporation's board of directors or, if it is not brought before the corporation's board of directors (or a committee thereof), at the time the corporation (or an entity controlled by the corporation) becomes legally bound to consummate the transaction. Where the director lacks such knowledge, the risk to the corporation that the director's judgment might be improperly influenced, or the risk of unfair dealing by the director, is not present. In a corporation of significant size, routine transactions in the ordinary course of business, which typically involve decisionmaking at lower management levels, normally will not be known to the director and, if that is the case, will be excluded from the "knowledge" requirement of the definition in subdivision (1)(ii) or (iii).

4. Material Financial Interest

The "interest" of a director or a related person in a transaction can be direct or indirect (*e.g.*, as an owner of an entity or a beneficiary of a trust or estate), but it must be financial for there to exist a "director's conflicting interest transaction." Thus, for example, an interest in a transaction between *X* Co. and a director's alma mater, or any other transaction involving *X* Co. and a party with which *D* might have emotional involvement but no financial interest, would not give rise to a director's conflicting interest transaction. Moreover, whether a financial interest is material does not turn on any assertion by the possibly conflicted director that the interest in question would not impair his or her objectivity if called upon to vote on the authorization of the transaction. Instead, assuming a court challenge asserting the materiality of the financial interest, the standard calls upon the trier of fact to determine whether the objectivity of a reasonable director in similar circumstances would reasonably be expected to have been impaired by the financial interest when voting on the matter. Thus, the standard is objective, not subjective.

Under subdivision (1)(ii), at the relevant time a director must have knowledge of his or her financial interest in the transaction in addition to knowing about the transaction itself. As a practical matter, a director could not be influenced by a financial interest about which that director had no knowledge. For example, the possibly conflicted director might know about *X* Co.'s transaction with *Y* Co., but might not know that his or her money manager recently established a significant position in *Y* Co. stock for the director's portfolio. In such circumstances, the transaction with *Y* Co. would not give the director a "material financial interest", notwithstanding the portfolio investment's significance. Analytically, if the director did not know about the *Y* Co. portfolio investment, it could not reasonably be expected to impair the objectivity of that director's judgment.

Similarly, under subdivision (1)(iii), a director must know about his or her related person's financial interest in the transaction for the matter to give rise to a "material financial interest" under subdivision (4). If there is such knowledge and "interest" (*i.e.*, the financial interest could be expected to influence the director's judgment), then the matter involves a director's conflicting interest transaction under subdivision (1).

5. Related Person

Six categories of "related person" of the director are set out in subdivision (5). These categories are specific, exclusive and preemptive.

The first three categories involve closely related family, or near-family, individuals as specified in clauses (i) through (iii). The clauses are exclusive insofar as family relationships are concerned and include adoptive relationships. The references to a "spouse" include a common law spouse. Clause (iii) covers personal, as opposed to business, relationships; for example, clause (iii) does not cover a lessee.

Regarding the subcategories of persons described in clause (v) from the perspective of *X* Co., certain of *D*'s relationships with other entities and *D*'s fiduciary relationships are always a sensitive concern, separate and apart from whether *D* has a financial interest in the transaction. Clause (v) reflects the policy judgment that *D* cannot escape *D*'s legal obligation to act in the best interests of another person for whom *D* has such a relationship and, accordingly, that such a relationship (without regard to any financial interest on *D*'s part) should cause the relevant entity to have "related person" status.

The term "employer" as used in subdivision (5)(vi) is not separately defined but should be interpreted sensibly in light of the purpose of the subdivision. The relevant inquiry is whether *D*, because of an employment relationship with an employer who has a significant stake in the outcome of the transaction, is likely to be influenced to act in the interest of that employer rather than in the interest of *X* Co.

6. Fair to the Corporation

The term "fair" accords with traditional language in the case law, but for purposes of subchapter F it also has a special meaning. The transaction, viewed as a whole, must have been beneficial to the corporation, in addition to satisfying the traditional "fair price" and "fair dealing" concepts. In determining whether the transaction was beneficial, the consideration and other terms of the transaction and the process (including the conflicted director's dealings with the corporation) are relevant, but whether the transaction advanced the corporation's commercial interests is to be viewed "as a whole."

In considering the "fairness" of the transaction, the court will be required to consider not only the market fairness of the terms of the deal—whether it is comparable to what might have been obtainable in an arm's length transaction—but also (as the board would have been required to do) whether the transaction was one that was reasonably likely to yield favorable results (or reduce detrimental results). Thus, if a manufacturing company that lacks sufficient working capital allocates some of its scarce funds to purchase a sailing yacht owned by one of its directors, it will not be easy to persuade the court that the transaction was "fair" in the sense that it was reasonably made to further the business interests of the corporation. The facts that the price paid for the yacht was a "fair" market price, and that the full measure of disclosures made by the director is beyond challenge, may still not be enough to defend and uphold the transaction.

a. Consideration and other terms of the transaction

The fairness of the consideration and other transaction terms are to be judged at the relevant time. The relevant inquiry is whether the consideration paid or received by the corporation or the benefit expected to be realized by the corporation was adequate in relation to the obligations assumed or received or other consideration provided by or to the corporation. If the issue in a transaction is the "fairness" of a price, "fair" is not to be taken to imply that there is one single "fair" price, all others being "unfair." It is settled law that a "fair" price is any price within a range that an unrelated party might have been willing to pay or willing to accept, as the case may be, for the relevant property, asset, service or commitment, following a normal arm's-length business negotiation. The same approach applies not only to gauging the fairness of price, but also to the fairness evaluation of any other key term of the deal.

Although the "fair" criterion used to assess the consideration under section 8.61(b)(3) is also a range rather than a point, the width of that range may be narrower than would be the case in an arm's-length transaction. For example, the quality and completeness of disclosures, if any, made by the conflicted director that bear upon the consideration in question are relevant in determining whether the consideration paid or received by the corporation, although otherwise commercially reasonable, was "fair" for purposes of section 8.61(b)(3).

b. Process of decision and the director's conduct

In some circumstances, the behavior of the director having the conflicting interest may affect the finding and content of "fairness." Fair dealing requires that the director make required disclosure (per subdivision (7)) at the relevant time (per subdivision (3)) even if the director plays no role in arranging or negotiating the terms of the transaction. One illustration of unfair dealing is the director's failure to disclose fully the director's interest or hidden defects known to the director regarding the transaction. Another illustration would be the exertion by the director of improper pressure upon the other directors or other parties that might be involved with the transaction. Whether a transaction can be successfully challenged by reason of deficient or improper conduct, notwithstanding the fairness of the economic terms, will turn on the court's evaluation of the conduct and its impact on the transaction.

7. Required Disclosure

A critically important element of subchapter F's safe harbor procedures is that those acting for the corporation be able to make an informed judgment. In view of this requirement, subdivision (7) defines "required disclosure" to mean disclosure of all facts known to *D* about the subject of the transaction that a director free of the conflicting interest would reasonably believe to be material to the decision whether to proceed with the transaction. For example, if *D* knows that the land the corporation is proposing to buy from *D* is sinking into an abandoned coal mine, *D* must disclose not only *D*'s interest in the transaction but also that the land is subsiding. As a director of *X* Co., *D* may not invoke caveat emptor. On the other hand, *D* does not have any obligation to reveal the price that *D* paid for the property ten years ago, or the fact that *D* inherited the property, because that information is not material to the board's evaluation of the property and its business decision whether to proceed with the transaction. Further, while material facts respecting the subject of the transaction must be disclosed, *D* is not required to reveal personal or subjective information that bears upon *D*'s negotiating position (such as, for example, *D*'s urgent need for cash, or the lowest price *D* would be willing to accept). This is true even though such information would be highly relevant to the corporation's decision-making in the sense that, if the information were known to the corporation, it could enable the corporation to hold out for more favorable terms.

§ 8.61 Judicial Action

(a) A transaction effected or proposed to be effected by the corporation (or by an entity controlled by the corporation) may not be the subject of equitable relief, or give rise to an award of damages or other sanctions against a director of the corporation, in a proceeding by a shareholder or by or in the right of the corporation, on the ground that the director has an interest respecting the transaction, if it is not a director's conflicting interest transaction.

(b) A director's conflicting interest transaction may not be the subject of equitable relief, or give rise to an award of damages or other sanctions against a director of the corporation, in a proceeding by a shareholder or by or in the right of the corporation, on the ground that the director has an interest respecting the transaction, if:

(1) directors' action respecting the transaction was taken in compliance with section 8.62 at any time; or

(2) shareholders' action respecting the transaction was taken in compliance with section 8.63 at any time; or

(3) the transaction, judged according to the circumstances at the relevant time, is established to have been fair to the corporation.

OFFICIAL COMMENT

Section 8.61 is the operational section of subchapter F, as it prescribes the judicial consequences of the other sections.

Speaking generally:

(i) If the section 8.62 or section 8.63 procedures are complied with, or if it is established that at the relevant time a director's conflicting interest transaction was fair to the corporation, then a director's conflicting interest transaction is immune from attack on the ground of an interest of the director. However, the narrow scope of subchapter F must again be strongly emphasized; if the transaction is vulnerable to attack on some other ground, observance of subchapter F's procedures does not make it less so.

(ii) If a transaction is *not* a director's conflicting interest transaction as defined in section 8.60(1), then the transaction may *not* be enjoined, rescinded, or made the basis of other sanction on the ground of a conflict of interest of a director, whether or not it went through the procedures of subchapter F. In that sense, subchapter F is specifically intended to be both comprehensive and exclusive.

(iii) If a director's conflicting interest transaction that was not at any time the subject of action taken in compliance with section 8.62 or section 8.63 is challenged on grounds of the director's conflicting interest, and is not shown to be fair to the corporation, then the court may take such remedial action as it considers appropriate under the applicable law of the jurisdiction.

1. Section 8.61(a)

As previously noted, section 8.61(a) makes clear that a transaction between a corporation and another person cannot be the subject of equitable relief, or give rise to an award of damages or other sanctions against a director, on the ground that the director has an interest respecting the transaction, unless the transaction falls within the bright-line definition of "director's conflicting interest transaction" in section 8.60. So, for example, a transaction will not constitute a director's conflicting interest transaction and, therefore, will not be subject to judicial review on the ground that a director had an interest in the transaction, where the transaction is made with a relative of a director who is not one of the relatives specified in section 8.60(5), or on the ground of an alleged interest other than a material financial interest, such as a financial interest of the director that is not material, as defined in section 8.60(4), or a nonfinancial interest. (As noted in the Introductory Comment, however, subchapter F does not apply to, and therefore does not preclude, a challenge to such a transaction based on grounds other than the director's interest.)

If there is reason to believe that the fairness of a transaction involving *D* could be questioned, *D* is well advised to subject the transaction to the safe harbor procedures of subchapter F. Sometimes, a director may be uncertain whether a particular person would be held to fall within a related person category, or whether the scale of the financial interest is material as defined in Section 8.60. In such circumstances, the obvious avenue to follow is to clear the matter with qualified directors under section 8.62 or with the holders of qualified shares under section 8.63. If it is later judicially determined that a conflicting interest in the challenged transaction did exist, the director will have safe harbor protection. It may be expected, therefore, that the procedures of section 8.62 (and, to a lesser extent, section 8.63) will probably be used for many transactions that may lie outside the sharp definitions of section 8.60—a result that is healthy and constructive.

It is important to stress that subchapter F deals only with "transactions." If a non-transactional corporate decision is challenged on the ground that *D* has a conflicting personal stake in it, subsection 8.61(a) is irrelevant.

2. Section 8.61(b)

Clause (1) of subsection (b) provides that if a director has a conflicting interest respecting a transaction, neither the transaction nor the director is legally vulnerable on the ground of the director's conflict if the procedures of section 8.62 have been properly followed. If board action under section 8.62(b)(1) is interposed as a defense in a proceeding challenging a director's conflicting interest transaction, the plaintiff then bears the burden of overcoming that defense under section 8.31.

Challenges to that board action may be based on a failure to meet the specific requirements of section 8.62 or to conform with general standards of director conduct. For example, a challenge addressed to section 8.62 compliance might question whether the acting directors were "qualified directors" or might dispute the quality and completeness of the disclosures made by *D* to the qualified directors. If such a challenge is successful, the board action is ineffective for purposes of subsection (b)(1) and both *D* and the transaction may be subject to the full range of remedies that might apply, absent the safe harbor, unless the fairness of the transaction can be established under subsection (b)(3). The fact that a transaction has been nominally passed through safe harbor procedures does not preclude a subsequent challenge based on any failure to meet the requirements of section 8.62. Recognizing the importance of traditional corporate procedures where the economic interests of a fellow director are concerned, a challenge to the effectiveness of board action for purposes of subsection (b)(1) might also assert that, while the conflicted director's conduct in connection with the process of approval by qualified directors may have been consistent with the statute's expectations, the qualified directors dealing with the matter did not act in good faith or on reasonable inquiry. The kind of relief that may be appropriate when qualified directors have approved a transaction but have not acted in good faith or have failed to become reasonably informed—and, again, where the fairness of the transaction has not been established under subsection (b)(3)—will depend heavily on the facts of the individual case; therefore, it must be largely a matter of sound judicial discretion.

Clause (2) of subsection (b) regarding shareholders' approval of the transaction is the matching piece to clause (1) regarding directors' approval.

The language "at any time" in clauses (1) and (2) of subsection (b) permits the directors or the shareholders to ratify a director's conflicting interest transaction after the fact for purposes of subchapter F. However, good corporate practice is to obtain appropriate approval prior to consummation of a director's conflicting interest transaction.

Clause (3) of subsection (b) provides that a director's conflicting interest transaction will be secure against the imposition of legal or equitable relief if it is established that, although neither directors' nor shareholders' action was taken in compliance with section 8.62 or 8.63, the transaction was fair to the corporation within the meaning of section 8.60(6). Under section 8.61(b)(3) the interested director has the burden of establishing that the transaction was fair.

* * *

Note on Directors' Compensation

Directors' fees and other forms of director compensation are typically set by the board and are specially authorized (though not regulated) by sections 8.11 and 8.57 of the Model Act. Although in the usual case a corporation's directors' compensation practices fall within normal patterns and their fairness can be readily established, they do involve a conflicting interest on the part of most if not all of the directors and, in a given case, may be abused. Therefore, while as a matter of practical necessity these practices will normally be generally accepted in principle, it must be kept in mind that board action on directors' compensation and benefits would be subject to judicial sanction if they are not favorably acted upon by shareholders pursuant to section 8.63 or if they are not in the circumstances fair to the corporation pursuant to section 8.61(b)(3).

§ 8.62 Directors' Action

(a) Directors' action respecting a director's conflicting interest transaction is effective for purposes of section 8.61(b)(1) if the transaction has been authorized by the affirmative vote of a majority (but no fewer than two) of the qualified directors who voted on the transaction, after required disclosure by the conflicted director of information not already known by such qualified directors, or after modified disclosure in compliance with subsection (b), provided that:

(1) the qualified directors have deliberated and voted outside the presence of and without the participation by any other director; and

(2) where the action has been taken by a committee, all members of the committee were qualified directors, and either (i) the committee was composed of all the qualified directors on the board of directors or (ii) the members of the committee were appointed by the affirmative vote of a majority of the qualified directors on the board.

(b) Notwithstanding subsection (a), when a transaction is a director's conflicting interest transaction only because a related person described in clause (v) or clause (vi) of section 8.60(5) is a party to or has a material financial interest in the transaction, the conflicted director is not obligated to make required disclosure to the extent that the director reasonably believes that doing so would violate a duty imposed under law, a legally enforceable obligation of confidentiality, or a professional ethics rule, provided that the conflicted director discloses to the qualified directors voting on the transaction:

(1) all information required to be disclosed that is not so violative,

(2) the existence and nature of the director's conflicting interest, and

(3) the nature of the conflicted director's duty not to disclose the confidential information.

(c) A majority (but no fewer than two) of all the qualified directors on the board of directors, or on the committee, constitutes a quorum for purposes of action that complies with this section.

(d) Where directors' action under this section does not satisfy a quorum or voting requirement applicable to the authorization of the transaction by reason of the articles of incorporation, the bylaws or a provision of law, independent action to satisfy those authorization requirements must be taken by the board of directors or a committee, in which action directors who are not qualified directors may participate.

OFFICIAL COMMENT

Section 8.62 provides the procedure for action by the board of directors or by a board committee under subchapter F. In the normal course this section, together with section 8.61(b), will be the key method for addressing directors' conflicting interest transactions. Any discussion of section 8.62 must be conducted in light of the overarching requirements that directors act in good faith and on reasonable inquiry. Director action that does not comply with those requirements, even if otherwise in compliance with section 8.62, will be subject to challenge and not be given effect under section 8.62. See the Official Comment to section 8.61(b).

1. Section 8.62(a)

The safe harbor for directors' conflicting interest transactions will be effective under section 8.62 if and only if it is authorized by qualified directors. (For the definition of "qualified director," see section 1.43 and the related official comment.) Obviously, safe harbor protection cannot be provided by fellow directors who themselves are not qualified directors; only qualified directors can do so under subsection (a). The definition of "qualified director" in section 1.43 excludes a conflicted director but its exclusions go significantly further, i.e., beyond the persons specified in the categories of section 8.60(5) for purposes of the "related person" definition. For example, if any familial or financial connection or employment or professional relationship with *D* would be likely to impair the objectivity of the director's judgment when participating in a vote on the transaction, that director would not be a qualified director.

Action by the board of directors is effective for purposes of section 8.62 if the transaction is approved by the affirmative vote of a majority (but not less than two) of the qualified directors on the board. Action may also be taken by a duly authorized committee of the board but, for the action to be effective, all members of the committee must be qualified directors and the committee must either be composed of all of the qualified directors on the board or must have been appointed by the affirmative vote of a majority of the qualified directors on the board. This requirement for effective committee action is intended to preclude the appointment as committee members of a favorably inclined minority from among all the qualified directors. Except to the limited extent found in subsection (b), authorization by the qualified directors acting on the matter must be preceded by required disclosure pursuant to subsection (a) followed by deliberation and voting outside the presence of and without the participation by, any other director. Should there be more than one conflicted director interested in the transaction, the need for required disclosure would apply to each. After the qualified directors have had the opportunity to question the conflicted director about the material facts communicated about the transaction, action complying with subsection (a) may be taken at any time before or after the time it becomes a legal obligation. A written record of the qualified directors' deliberations and action is strongly encouraged.

2. Section 8.62(b)

Subsection (b) is a special provision designed to accommodate, in a practical way, situations where a director who has a conflicting interest is not able to comply fully with the disclosure requirement of subsection (a) because of an extrinsic duty of confidentiality that such director reasonably believes to exist. The director may, for example, be prohibited from making full disclosure because of legal restrictions that happen to apply to the transaction (*e.g.*, grand jury seal or national security statute) or professional canon (*e.g.*, attorney-client privilege). The most frequent use of subsection (b), however, will likely involve common directors who find themselves in a position of dual fiduciary obligations that clash. If *D* is also a director of *Y Co.*, *D* may have acquired privileged information from one or both directorships relevant to a transaction between *X Co.* and *Y Co.*, that *D* cannot reveal to one without violating a fiduciary duty owed to the other. In such circumstances, subsection (b) enables the conflicting interest complication to be presented for consideration under subsection (a), and thereby enables *X*

Co. (and *Y Co.*) and *D* to secure for the transaction the protection afforded by subchapter F even though *D* cannot, by reason of applicable law, confidentiality strictures or a professional ethics rule, make the full disclosure otherwise required.

To comply with subsection (b), *D* must (i) notify the qualified directors who are to vote on the transaction respecting the conflicting interest, (ii) disclose to them all information required to be disclosed that does not violate the duty not to disclose, as the case may be, to which *D* reasonably believes he or she is subject, and (iii) inform them of the nature of the duty (*e.g.*, that the duty arises out of an attorney-client privilege or out of a duty as a director of *Y Co.* that prevents *D* from making required disclosure as otherwise mandated by clause (ii) of section 8.60(7)). *D* must then play no personal role in the board's (or committee's) ultimate deliberations or action. The purpose of subsection (b) is to make it clear that the provisions of subchapter F may be employed to "safe harbor" a transaction in circumstances where a conflicted director cannot, because of enforced fiduciary silence, disclose all the known facts.[3] Of course, if *D* invokes subsection (b) and does not make required disclosure before leaving the meeting, the qualified directors may decline to act on the transaction out of concern that *D* knows (or may know) something they do not. On the other hand, if *D* is subject to an extrinsic duty of confidentiality but has no knowledge of material facts that should otherwise be disclosed, *D* would normally state just that and subsection (b) would be irrelevant. Having disclosed the existence and nature of the conflicting interest, *D* would thereby comply with section 8.60(7).

While subchapter F explicitly contemplates that subsection (b) will apply to the frequently recurring situation where transacting corporations have common directors (or where a director of one party is an officer of the other), it should not otherwise be read as attempting to address the scope, or mandate the consequences, of various silence-privileges. That is a topic reserved for local law.

Subsection (b) is available to *D* if a transaction is a director's conflicting interest transaction only because a related person described in section 8.60(5)(v) or (vi) is a party to or has a material financial interest in the transaction. Its availability is so limited because in those instances a director owes a fiduciary duty to such a related person. If *D* or a related person of *D* other than a related person described in section 8.60(5)(v) or (vi) is a party to or has a material financial interest in the transaction, *D*'s only options are satisfying the required disclosure

3. A director could, of course, encounter the same problem of mandated silence with regard to any matter that comes before the board; that is, the problem of forced silence can arise in situations other than transactions involving a conflicting interest of a director. It could happen that at the same board meeting of *X Co.* at which *D* invokes § 8.62(b), another director who has absolutely no financial interest in the transaction might conclude that under local law he or she is bound to silence (because of attorney-client privilege, for example) and under general principles of sound director conduct would withdraw from participation in the board's deliberations and action.

obligation on an unrestricted basis, abandoning the transaction, or accepting the risk of establishing fairness under section 8.61(b)(3), if the transaction is challenged in a court proceeding.

Whenever a conflicted director proceeds in the manner provided in subsection (b), the other directors should recognize that the conflicted director may have information that in usual circumstances *D* would be required to reveal to the qualified directors who are acting on the transaction—information that could well indicate that the transaction would be either favorable or unfavorable for *X Co.*

3. Section 8.62(c)

Subsection (c) states the special quorum requirement for action by qualified directors to be effective under section 8.62. Obviously, conflicted directors are excluded. Also excluded are board members who, while not conflicted directors, are not eligible to be qualified directors. As stated in subsection (a), the qualified directors taking action respecting a director's conflicting interest transaction are to deliberate and vote outside the presence of, and without participation by, any other member of the board.

4. Section 8.62(d)

This subsection underscores the fact that the directors' voting procedures and requirements set forth in subsections (a) through (c) treat only the director's conflicting interest. A transaction authorized by qualified directors in accordance with subchapter F may still need to satisfy different voting and quorum requirements in order to achieve substantive approval of the transaction under other applicable statutory provisions or provisions contained in *X Co.*'s articles of incorporation or bylaws, and vice versa. Thus, in any case where the quorum and/or voting requirements for substantive approval of a transaction differ from the quorum and/or voting requirements for "safe harbor" protection under section 8.62, the directors may find it necessary to conduct (and record in the minutes of the proceedings) two separate votes—one for section 8.62 purposes and the other for substantive approval purposes.

§ 8.63 Shareholders' Action

(a) Shareholders' action respecting a director's conflicting interest transaction is effective for purposes of section 8.61(b)(2) if a majority of the votes cast by the holders of all qualified shares are in favor of the transaction after (1) notice to shareholders describing the action to be taken respecting the transaction, (2) provision to the corporation of the information referred to in subsection (b), and (3) communication to the shareholders entitled to vote on the transaction of the information that is the subject of required disclosure, to the extent the information is not known by them.

(b) A director who has a conflicting interest respecting the transaction shall, before the shareholders' vote, inform the secretary or other officer or agent of the corporation authorized to tabulate votes, in writing, of the number of shares that the director knows are not qualified shares under subsection (c), and the identity of the holders of those shares.

(c) For purposes of this section: (1) "holder" means and "held by" refers to shares held by both a record shareholder (as defined in section 13.01(7)) and a beneficial shareholder (as defined in section 13.01(2)); and (2) "qualified shares" means all shares entitled to be voted with respect to the transaction except for shares that the secretary or other officer or agent of the corporation authorized to tabulate votes either knows, or under subsection (b) is notified, are held by (A) a director who has a conflicting interest respecting the transaction or (B) a related person of the director (excluding a person described in clause (vi) of Section 8.60(5)).

(d) A majority of the votes entitled to be cast by the holders of all qualified shares constitutes a quorum for purposes of compliance with this section. Subject to the provisions of subsection (e), shareholders' action that otherwise complies with this section is not affected by the presence of holders, or by the voting, of shares that are not qualified shares.

(e) If a shareholders' vote does not comply with subsection (a) solely because of a director's failure to comply with subsection (b), and if the director establishes that the failure was not intended to influence and did not in fact determine the outcome of the vote, the court may take such action respecting the transaction and the director, and may give such effect, if any, to the shareholders' vote, as the court considers appropriate in the circumstances.

(f) Where shareholders' action under this section does not satisfy a quorum or voting requirement applicable to the authorization of the transaction by reason of the articles of incorporation, the bylaws or a provision of law, independent action to satisfy those authorization requirements must be taken by the shareholders, in which action shares that are not qualified shares may participate.

OFFICIAL COMMENT

Section 8.63 provides the machinery for shareholders' action that confers safe harbor protection for a director's conflicting interest transaction, just as section 8.62 provides the machinery for directors' action that confers subchapter F safe harbor protection for such a transaction.

1. Section 8.63(a)

Subsection (a) specifies the procedure required to confer effective safe harbor protection for a director's conflicting interest transaction through a vote of shareholders. In advance of the vote, three steps must be taken: (1) shareholders must be given timely and adequate notice describing the transaction; (2) *D* must disclose the information called for in subsection (b); and (3) disclosure must be made to the shareholders entitled to vote, as required by section 8.60(7). In the case of smaller closely-held corporations, this disclosure shall be presented by the director directly to the shareholders gathered at the meeting place where the vote is to be held, or provided in writing to the secretary of the corporation for transmittal with the notice of the meeting. In the case of larger publicly held corporations where proxies are being solicited, the disclosure is to be made by the director to those responsible for preparing the proxy materials, for inclusion therein. If the holders of a majority of all qualified shares (as defined in subsection (b)) entitled to vote on the matter vote favorably, the safe harbor provision of section 8.61(b)(2) becomes effective. Action that complies with subsection (a) may be taken at any time, before or after the time when the corporation becomes legally obligated to complete the transaction.

Section 8.63 does not contain a "limited disclosure" provision that is comparable to section 8.62(b). Thus, the safe harbor protection of subchapter F is not available through shareholder action under section 8.63 in a case where *D* either remains silent or makes less than required disclosure because of an extrinsic duty of confidentiality. This omission is intentional. While the section 8.62(b) procedure is workable in the collegial setting of the boardroom, that is far less likely in the case of action by the shareholder body, especially in large corporations where there is heavy reliance upon the proxy mechanic. Unlike the dynamic that would normally occur in the boardroom, in most situations no opportunity exists for shareholders to quiz *D* about the confidentiality duty and to discuss the implications of acting without the full benefit of *D*'s knowledge about the conflict transaction. In a case of a closely held corporation where section 8.63 procedures are followed, but with *D* acting in a way that would be permitted by section 8.62(b), a court could attach significance to a favorable shareholder vote in evaluating the fairness of the transaction to the corporation.

2. Section 8.63(b)

In many circumstances, the secretary or other vote tabulator of *X Co.* will have no way to know which of *X Co.'s* outstanding shares should be excluded from the tabulation. Subsection (b) (together with subsection (c)) therefore obligates a director who has a conflicting interest respecting the transaction, as a prerequisite to safe harbor protection by shareholder action, to inform the secretary, or other officer or agent authorized to tabulate votes, of the number and holders of shares known to be held by the director or by a related person described in clauses (i) through (v) of section 8.60(5).

If the tabulator of votes knows, or is notified under subsection (b), that particular shares should be excluded but for some reason fails to exclude them from the count and their inclusion in the vote does not affect its outcome, the shareholders' vote will stand. If the improper inclusion determines the outcome, the shareholders' vote fails because it does not comply with subsection (a). But see subsection (e) as to cases where the notification under subsection (b) is defective but not determinative of the outcome of the vote.

3. Section 8.63(c)

Under subsection (a), only "qualified shares" may be counted in the vote for purposes of safe harbor action under section 8.61(b)(2). Subsection (b) defines "qualified shares" to exclude all shares that, before the vote, the secretary or other tabulator of the vote knows, or is notified under subsection (b), are held by the director who has the conflicting interest, or by any specified related person of that director.

The definition of "qualified shares" excludes shares held by *D* or a "related person" as defined in the first five categories of section 8.60(5). That definition does not exclude shares held by entities or persons described in clause (vi) of section 8.60(5), i.e., a person that is, or is an entity that is controlled by, an employer of *D*. If *D* is an employee of *Y Co.*, that fact does not prevent *Y Co.* from exercising its usual rights to vote any shares it may hold in *X Co. D* may be unaware of, and would not necessarily monitor, whether his or her employer holds *X Co.* shares. Moreover, *D* will typically have no control over his or her employer and how it may vote its *X Co.* shares.

4. Section 8.63(e)

If *D* did not provide the information required under subsection (d), on its face the shareholders' action is not in compliance with subsection (a) and *D* has no safe harbor under subsection (a). In the absence of that safe harbor, *D* can be put to the burden of establishing the fairness of the transaction under section 8.61(b)(3).

That result is proper where *D's* failure to inform was determinative of the vote results or, worse, was part of a deliberate effort on *D's* part to influence the outcome. But if *D's* omission was essentially an act of negligence, if the number of unreported shares if voted would not have been determinative of the outcome of the vote, and if the omission was not motivated by *D's* effort to influence the integrity of the voting process, then the court should be free to fashion an appropriate response to the situation in light of all the considerations at the time of its decision. The court should not, in the circumstances, be automatically forced by the mechanics of subchapter F to a lengthy and retrospective trial on "fairness." Subsection (e) grants the court that discretion in those circumstances and permits it to accord such effect, if any, to the shareholders' vote, or to grant such relief respecting the transaction or *D*, as the court may find appropriate.

Despite the presumption of regularity customarily accorded the secretary's record, a plaintiff may go behind the secretary's record for purposes of subsection (e).

5. Section 8.63(f)

This subsection underscores that the shareholders' voting procedures and requirements set forth in subsections (a) through (e) treat only the director's conflicting interest. A transaction that receives a shareholders' vote that complies with subchapter F may well fail to achieve a different vote or quorum that may be required for substantive approval of the transaction under other applicable statutory provisions or provisions contained in *X Co.*'s articles of incorporation or bylaws, and vice versa. Thus, in any case where the quorum and/or voting requirements for substantive approval of a transaction differ from the quorum and/ or voting requirements for "safe harbor" protection under section 8.63, the corporation may find it necessary to conduct (and record in the minutes of the proceedings) two separate shareholder votes—one for section 8.63 purposes and the other for substantive approval purposes (or, if appropriate, conduct two separate tabulations of one vote).

Subchapter G. Business Opportunities

§ 8.70 Business Opportunities

(a) A director's taking advantage, directly or indirectly, of a business opportunity may not be the subject of equitable relief, or give rise to an award of damages or other sanctions against the director, in a proceeding by or in the right of the corporation on the ground that such opportunity should have first been offered to the corporation, if before becoming legally obligated respecting the opportunity the director brings it to the attention of the corporation and:

(1) action by qualified directors disclaiming the corporation's interest in the opportunity is taken in compliance with the procedures set forth in section 8.62, as if the decision being made concerned a director's conflicting interest transaction, or

(2) shareholders' action disclaiming the corporation's interest in the opportunity is taken in compliance with the procedures set forth in section 8.63, as if the decision being made concerned a director's conflicting interest transaction;

except that, rather than making "required disclosure" as defined in section 8.60, in each case the director shall have made prior disclosure to those acting on behalf of the corporation of all material facts concerning the business opportunity that are then known to the director.

(b) In any proceeding seeking equitable relief or other remedies based upon an alleged improper taking advantage of a business opportunity by a director, the fact that the director did not employ the procedure described in subsection (a) before taking advantage of the opportunity shall not create an inference that the opportunity should have been first presented to the corporation or alter the burden of proof otherwise applicable to establish that the director breached a duty to the corporation in the circumstances.

CHAPTER 9

DOMESTICATION AND CONVERSION

Subchapter A. Preliminary Provisions

§ 9.01 Excluded Transactions

This chapter may not be used to effect a transaction that:

(1) [*converts an insurance company organized on the mutual principle to one organized on a stock-share basis*];

(2)

(3)

§ 9.02 Required Approvals [*Optional*]

(a) If a domestic or foreign business corporation or eligible entity may not be a party to a merger without the approval of the [*attorney general*], the [*department of banking*], the [*department of insurance*] or the [*public utility commission*], the corporation or eligible entity shall not be a party to a transaction under this chapter without the prior approval of that agency.

(b) Property held in trust or for charitable purposes under the laws of this state by a domestic or foreign eligible entity shall not, by any transaction under this chapter, be diverted from the objects for which it was donated, granted or devised, unless and until the eligible entity obtains an order of [*court*] [*the attorney general*] specifying the disposition of the property to the extent required by and pursuant to [*cite state statutory cy pres or other nondiversion statute*].

Subchapter B. Domestication

§ 9.20 Domestication

(a) A foreign business corporation may become a domestic business corporation only if the domestication is permitted by the organic law of the foreign corporation.

(b) A domestic business corporation may become a foreign business corporation if the domestication is permitted by the laws of the foreign jurisdiction. Regardless of whether the laws of the foreign jurisdiction require the adoption of a plan of domestication, the domestication shall be approved by the adoption by the corporation of a plan of domestication in the manner provided in this subchapter.

(c) The plan of domestication must include:

(1) a statement of the jurisdiction in which the corporation is to be domesticated;

(2) the terms and conditions of the domestication;

(3) the manner and basis of reclassifying the shares of the corporation following its domestication into shares or other securities, obligations, rights to acquire shares or other securities, cash, other property, or any combination of the foregoing; and

(4) any desired amendments to the articles of incorporation of the corporation following its domestication.

(d) The plan of domestication may also include a provision that the plan may be amended prior to filing the document required by the laws of this state or the other jurisdiction to consummate the domestication, except that subsequent to approval of the plan by the shareholders the plan may not be amended to change:

(1) the amount or kind of shares or other securities, obligations, rights to acquire shares or other securities, cash, or other property to be received by the shareholders under the plan;

(2) the articles of incorporation as they will be in effect immediately following the domestication, except for changes permitted by section 10.05 or by comparable provisions of the laws of the other jurisdiction; or

(3) any of the other terms or conditions of the plan if the change would adversely affect any of the shareholders in any material respect.

(e) Terms of a plan of domestication may be made dependent upon facts objectively ascertainable outside the plan in accordance with section 1.20(k).

(f) If any debt security, note or similar evidence of indebtedness for money borrowed, whether secured or unsecured, or a contract of any kind, issued, incurred or executed by a domestic business corporation before [*the effective date of this subchapter*] contains a provision applying to a merger of the corporation and the document does not refer to a domestication of the corporation, the provision shall be deemed to apply to a domestication of the corporation until such time as the provision is amended subsequent to that date.

§ 9.21 Action on a Plan of Domestication

In the case of a domestication of a domestic business corporation in a foreign jurisdiction:

(1) The plan of domestication must be adopted by the board of directors.

(2) After adopting the plan of domestication the board of directors must submit the plan to the shareholders for their approval. The board of directors must also transmit to the shareholders a recommendation that the shareholders approve the plan, unless the board of directors makes a determination that because of conflicts of interest or other special circumstances it should not make such a recommendation, in which case the board of directors must transmit to the shareholders the basis for that determination.

(3) The board of directors may condition its submission of the plan of domestication to the shareholders on any basis.

(4) If the approval of the shareholders is to be given at a meeting, the corporation must notify each shareholder, whether or not entitled to vote, of the meeting of shareholders at which the plan of domestication is to be submitted for approval. The notice must state that the purpose, or one of the purposes, of the meeting is to consider the plan and must contain or be accompanied by a copy or summary of the plan. The notice shall include or be accompanied by a copy of the articles of incorporation as they will be in effect immediately after the domestication.

(5) Unless the articles of incorporation, or the board of directors acting pursuant to paragraph (3), requires a greater vote or a greater number of votes to be present, approval of the plan of domestication requires the approval of the shareholders at a meeting at which a quorum consisting of at least a majority of the votes entitled to be cast on the plan exists, and, if any class or series of shares is entitled to vote as a separate group on the plan, the approval of each such separate voting group at a meeting at which a quorum of the voting group consisting of at least a majority of the votes entitled to be cast on the domestication by that voting group exists.

(6) Separate voting by voting groups is required by each class or series of shares that:

(i) are to be reclassified under the plan of domestication into other securities, obligations, rights to acquire shares or other securities, cash, other property, or any combination of the foregoing;

(ii) would be entitled to vote as a separate group on a provision of the plan that, if contained in a proposed amendment to articles of incorporation, would require action by separate voting groups under section 10.04; or

(iii) is entitled under the articles of incorporation to vote as a voting group to approve an amendment of the articles.

(7) If any provision of the articles of incorporation, bylaws or an agreement to which any of the directors or shareholders are parties, adopted or entered into before [*the effective date of this subchapter*], applies to a merger of the corporation and that document does not refer to a domestication of the corporation, the provision shall be deemed to apply to a domestication of the corporation until such time as the provision is amended subsequent to that date.

§ 9.22 Articles of Domestication

(a) After the domestication of a foreign business corporation has been authorized as required by the laws of the foreign jurisdiction, articles of domestication shall be executed by any officer or other duly authorized representative. The articles shall set forth:

(1) the name of the corporation immediately before the filing of the articles of domestication and, if that name is unavailable for use in this state or the corporation desires to change its name in connection with the domestication, a name that satisfies the requirements of section 4.01;

(2) the jurisdiction of incorporation of the corporation immediately before the filing of the articles of domestication and the date the corporation was incorporated in that jurisdiction; and

(3) a statement that the domestication of the corporation in this state was duly authorized as required by the laws of the jurisdiction in which the corporation was incorporated immediately before its domestication in this state.

(b) The articles of domestication shall either contain all of the provisions that section 2.02(a) requires to be set forth in articles of incorporation and any other desired provisions that section 2.02(b) permits to be included in articles of incorporation, or shall have attached articles of incorporation. In either case, provisions that would not be required to be included in restated articles of incorporation may be omitted.

(c) The articles of domestication shall be delivered to the secretary of state for filing, and shall take effect at the effective time provided in section 1.23.

(d) If the foreign corporation is authorized to transact business in this state under chapter 15, its certificate of authority shall be cancelled automatically on the effective date of its domestication.

§ 9.23 Surrender of Charter Upon Domestication

(a) Whenever a domestic business corporation has adopted and approved, in the manner required by this subchapter, a plan of domestication providing for the corporation to be domesticated in a foreign jurisdiction, articles of charter surrender shall be executed on behalf of the corporation by any officer or other duly authorized representative. The articles of charter surrender shall set forth:

(1) the name of the corporation;

(2) a statement that the articles of charter surrender are being filed in connection with the domestication of the corporation in a foreign jurisdiction;

(3) a statement that the domestication was duly approved by the shareholders and, if voting by any separate voting group was required, by each such separate voting group, in the manner required by this Act and the articles of incorporation;

(4) the corporation's new jurisdiction of incorporation.

(b) The articles of charter surrender shall be delivered by the corporation to the secretary of state for filing. The articles of charter surrender shall take effect on the effective time provided in section 1.23.

§ 9.24 Effect of Domestication

(a) When a domestication becomes effective:

(1) the title to all real and personal property, both tangible and intangible, of the corporation remains in the corporation without reversion or impairment;

(2) the liabilities of the corporation remain the liabilities of the corporation;

(3) an action or proceeding pending against the corporation continues against the corporation as if the domestication had not occurred;

(4) the articles of domestication, or the articles of incorporation attached to the articles of domestication, constitute the articles of incorporation of a foreign corporation domesticating in this state;

(5) the shares of the corporation are reclassified into shares, other securities, obligations, rights to acquire shares or other securities, or into cash or other property in accordance with the terms of the domestication, and the shareholders are entitled only to the rights provided by those terms and to any appraisal rights they may have under the organic law of the domesticating corporation; and

(6) the corporation is deemed to:

(i) be incorporated under and subject to the organic law of the domesticated corporation for all purposes;

(ii) be the same corporation without interruption as the domesticating corporation; and

(iii) have been incorporated on the date the domesticating corporation was originally incorporated.

(b) When a domestication of a domestic business corporation in a foreign jurisdiction becomes effective, the foreign business corporation is deemed to:

(1) appoint the secretary of state as its agent for service of process in a proceeding to enforce the rights of shareholders who exercise appraisal rights in connection with the domestication; and

(2) agree that it will promptly pay the amount, if any, to which such shareholders are entitled under chapter 13.

(c) The owner liability of a shareholder in a foreign corporation that is domesticated in this state shall be as follows:

(1) The domestication does not discharge any owner liability under the laws of the foreign jurisdiction to the extent any such owner liability arose before the effective time of the articles of domestication.

(2) The shareholder shall not have owner liability under the laws of the foreign jurisdiction for any debt, obligation or liability of the corporation that arises after the effective time of the articles of domestication.

(3) The provisions of the laws of the foreign jurisdiction shall continue to apply to the collection or discharge of any owner liability preserved by paragraph (1), as if the domestication had not occurred.

(4) The shareholder shall have whatever rights of contribution from other shareholders are provided by the laws of the foreign jurisdiction with respect to any owner liability preserved by paragraph (1), as if the domestication had not occurred.

[*(d) A shareholder who becomes subject to owner liability for some or all of the debts, obligations or liabilities of the corporation as a result of its domestication in this state shall have owner liability only for those debts, obligations or liabilities of the corporation that arise after the effective time of the articles of domestication.*]

§ 9.25 Abandonment of a Domestication

(a) Unless otherwise provided in a plan of domestication of a domestic business corporation, after the plan has been adopted and approved as required by this subchapter, and at any time before the domestication has become effective, it may be abandoned by the board of directors without action by the shareholders.

(b) If a domestication is abandoned under subsection (a) after articles of charter surrender have been filed with the secretary of state but before the domestication has become effective, a statement that the domestication has been abandoned in accordance with this section, executed by an officer or other duly authorized representative, shall be delivered to the secretary of state for filing prior to the effective date of the domestication. The statement shall take effect upon filing and the domestication shall be deemed abandoned and shall not become effective.

(c) If the domestication of a foreign business corporation in this state is abandoned in accordance with the laws of the foreign jurisdiction after articles of domestication have been filed with the secretary of state, a statement that the domestication has been abandoned, executed by an officer or other duly authorized representative, shall be delivered to the secretary of state for filing. The statement shall take effect upon filing and the domestication shall be deemed abandoned and shall not become effective.

Subchapter C. Nonprofit Conversion

§ 9.30 Nonprofit Conversion

(a) A domestic business corporation may become a domestic nonprofit corporation pursuant to a plan of nonprofit conversion.

(b) A domestic business corporation may become a foreign nonprofit corporation if the nonprofit conversion is permitted by the laws of the foreign jurisdiction. Regardless of whether the laws of the foreign jurisdiction require the adoption of a plan of nonprofit conversion, the foreign nonprofit conversion shall be approved by the adoption by the domestic business corporation of a plan of nonprofit conversion in the manner provided in this subchapter.

(c) The plan of nonprofit conversion must include:

(1) the terms and conditions of the conversion;

(2) the manner and basis of reclassifying the shares of the corporation following its conversion into memberships, if any, or securities, obligations, rights to acquire memberships or securities, cash, other property, or any combination of the foregoing;

(3) any desired amendments to the articles of incorporation of the corporation following its conversion; and

(4) if the domestic business corporation is to be converted to a foreign nonprofit corporation, a statement of the jurisdiction in which the corporation will be incorporated after the conversion.

(d) The plan of nonprofit conversion may also include a provision that the plan may be amended prior to filing articles of nonprofit conversion, except that subsequent to approval of the plan by the shareholders the plan may not be amended to change:

(1) the amount or kind of memberships or securities, obligations, rights to acquire memberships or securities, cash, or other property to be received by the shareholders under the plan;

(2) the articles of incorporation as they will be in effect immediately following the conversion, except for changes permitted by section 10.05; or

(3) any of the other terms or conditions of the plan if the change would adversely affect any of the shareholders in any material respect.

(e) Terms of a plan of nonprofit conversion may be made dependent upon facts objectively ascertainable outside the plan in accordance with section 1.20(k).

(f) If any debt security, note or similar evidence of indebtedness for money borrowed, whether secured or unsecured, or a contract of any kind, issued, incurred or executed by a domestic business corporation before [*the effective date of this subchapter*] contains a provision applying to a merger of the corporation and the document does not refer to a nonprofit conversion of the corporation, the provision shall be deemed to apply to a nonprofit conversion of the corporation until such time as the provision is amended subsequent to that date.

§ 9.31 Action on a Plan of Nonprofit Conversion

In the case of a conversion of a domestic business corporation to a domestic or foreign nonprofit corporation:

(1) The plan of nonprofit conversion must be adopted by the board of directors.

(2) After adopting the plan of nonprofit conversion, the board of directors must submit the plan to the shareholders for their approval. The board of directors must also transmit to the shareholders a recommendation that the shareholders approve the plan, unless the board of directors makes a determination that because of conflicts of interest or other special circumstances it should not make such a recommendation, in which case the board of directors must transmit to the shareholders the basis for that determination.

(3) The board of directors may condition its submission of the plan of nonprofit conversion to the shareholders on any basis.

(4) If the approval of the shareholders is to be given at a meeting, the corporation must notify each shareholder of the meeting of shareholders at which the plan of nonprofit conversion is to be submitted for approval. The notice must state that the purpose, or one of the purposes, of the meeting is to consider the plan and must contain or be accompanied by a copy or summary of the plan. The notice shall include or be accompanied by a copy of the articles of incorporation as they will be in effect immediately after the nonprofit conversion.

(5) Unless the articles of incorporation, or the board of directors acting pursuant to paragraph (3), requires a greater vote or a

greater number of votes to be present, approval of the plan of nonprofit conversion requires the approval of each class or series of shares of the corporation voting as a separate voting group at a meeting at which a quorum of the voting group consisting of at least a majority of the votes entitled to be cast on the nonprofit conversion by that voting group exists.

(6) If any provision of the articles of incorporation, bylaws or an agreement to which any of the directors or shareholders are parties, adopted or entered into before [*the effective date of this subchapter*], applies to a merger of the corporation and the document does not refer to a nonprofit conversion of the corporation, the provision shall be deemed to apply to a nonprofit conversion of the corporation until such time as the provision is amended subsequent to that date.

§ 9.32 Articles of Nonprofit Conversion

(a) After a plan of nonprofit conversion providing for the conversion of a domestic business corporation to a domestic nonprofit corporation has been adopted and approved as required by this Act, articles of nonprofit conversion shall be executed on behalf of the corporation by any officer or other duly authorized representative. The articles shall set forth:

(1) the name of the corporation immediately before the filing of the articles of nonprofit conversion and if that name does not satisfy the requirements of [*the Model Nonprofit Corporation Act*], or the corporation desires to change its name in connection with the conversion, a name that satisfies the requirements of [*the Model Nonprofit Corporation Act*];

(2) a statement that the plan of nonprofit conversion was duly approved by the shareholders in the manner required by this Act and the articles of incorporation.

(b) The articles of nonprofit conversion shall either contain all of the provisions that [*the Model Nonprofit Corporation Act*] requires to be set forth in articles of incorporation of a domestic nonprofit corporation and any other desired provisions permitted by [*the Model Nonprofit Corporation Act*], or shall have attached articles of incorporation that satisfy the requirements of [*the Model Nonprofit Corporation Act*]. In either case, provisions that would not be required to be included in restated articles of incorporation of a domestic nonprofit corporation may be omitted.

(c) The articles of nonprofit conversion shall be delivered to the secretary of state for filing, and shall take effect at the effective time provided in section 1.23.

§ 9.33 Surrender of Charter Upon Foreign Nonprofit Conversion

(a) Whenever a domestic business corporation has adopted and approved, in the manner required by this subchapter, a plan of nonprofit conversion providing for the corporation to be converted to a foreign nonprofit corporation, articles of charter surrender shall be executed on behalf of the corporation by any officer or other duly authorized representative. The articles of charter surrender shall set forth:

(1) the name of the corporation;

(2) a statement that the articles of charter surrender are being filed in connection with the conversion of the corporation to a foreign nonprofit corporation;

(3) a statement that the foreign nonprofit conversion was duly approved by the shareholders in the manner required by this Act and the articles of incorporation;

(4) the corporation's new jurisdiction of incorporation.

(b) The articles of charter surrender shall be delivered by the corporation to the secretary of state for filing. The articles of charter surrender shall take effect on the effective time provided in section 1.23.

§ 9.34 Effect of Nonprofit Conversion

(a) When a conversion of a domestic business corporation to a domestic nonprofit corporation becomes effective:

(1) the title to all real and personal property, both tangible and intangible, of the corporation remains in the corporation without reversion or impairment;

(2) the liabilities of the corporation remain the liabilities of the corporation;

(3) an action or proceeding pending against the corporation continues against the corporation as if the conversion had not occurred;

(4) the articles of incorporation of the domestic or foreign nonprofit corporation become effective;

(5) the shares of the corporation are reclassified into memberships, securities, obligations, rights to acquire memberships or securities, or into cash or other property in accordance with the plan of conversion, and the shareholders are entitled only to the rights provided in the plan of nonprofit conversion or to any rights they may have under chapter 13; and

(6) the corporation is deemed to:

(i) be a domestic nonprofit corporation for all purposes;

(ii) be the same corporation without interruption as the corporation that existed prior to the conversion; and

(iii) have been incorporated on the date that it was originally incorporated as a domestic business corporation.

(b) When a conversion of a domestic business corporation to a foreign nonprofit corporation becomes effective, the foreign nonprofit corporation is deemed to:

(1) appoint the secretary of state as its agent for service of process in a proceeding to enforce the rights of shareholders who exercise appraisal rights in connection with the conversion; and

(2) agree that it will promptly pay the amount, if any, to which such shareholders are entitled under chapter 13.

[*(c) The owner liability of a shareholder in a domestic business corporation that converts to a domestic nonprofit corporation shall be as follows:*

(1) The conversion does not discharge any owner liability of the shareholder as a shareholder of the business corporation to the extent any such owner liability arose before the effective time of the articles of nonprofit conversion.

(2) The shareholder shall not have owner liability for any debt, obligation or liability of the nonprofit corporation that arises after the effective time of the articles of nonprofit conversion.

(3) The laws of this state shall continue to apply to the collection or discharge of any owner liability preserved by paragraph (1), as if the conversion had not occurred and the nonprofit corporation were still a business corporation.

(4) The shareholder shall have whatever rights of contribution from other shareholders are provided by the laws of this state with respect to any owner liability preserved by paragraph (1), as if the conversion had not occurred and the nonprofit corporation were still a business corporation.

(d) A shareholder who becomes subject to owner liability for some or all of the debts, obligations or liabilities of the nonprofit corporation shall have owner liability only for those debts, obligations or liabilities of the nonprofit corporation that arise after the effective time of the articles of nonprofit conversion.]

§ 9.35 Abandonment of a Nonprofit Conversion

(a) Unless otherwise provided in a plan of nonprofit conversion of a domestic business corporation, after the plan has been adopted and approved as required by this subchapter, and at any time before the nonprofit conversion has become effective, it may be abandoned by the board of directors without action by the shareholders.

(b) If a nonprofit conversion is abandoned under subsection (a) after articles of nonprofit conversion or articles of charter surrender have been filed with the secretary of state but before the nonprofit conversion has become effective, a statement that the nonprofit conversion has been abandoned in accordance with this section, executed by an officer or other duly authorized representative, shall be delivered to the secretary of state for filing prior to the effective date of the nonprofit conversion. The statement shall take effect upon filing and the nonprofit conversion shall be deemed abandoned and shall not become effective.

Subchapter D. Foreign Nonprofit Domestication and Conversion

§ 9.40 Foreign Nonprofit Domestication and Conversion

A foreign nonprofit corporation may become a domestic business corporation if the domestication and conversion is permitted by the organic law of the foreign nonprofit corporation.

§ 9.41 Articles of Domestication and Conversion

(a) After the conversion of a foreign nonprofit corporation to a domestic business corporation has been authorized as required by the laws of the foreign jurisdiction, articles of domestication and conversion shall be executed by any officer or other duly authorized representative. The articles shall set forth:

(1) the name of the corporation immediately before the filing of the articles of domestication and conversion and, if that name is unavailable for use in this state or the corporation desires to change its name in connection with the domestication and conversion, a name that satisfies the requirements of section 4.01;

(2) the jurisdiction of incorporation of the corporation immediately before the filing of the articles of domestication and conversion and the date the corporation was incorporated in that jurisdiction; and

(3) a statement that the domestication and conversion of the corporation in this state was duly authorized as required by the laws of the jurisdiction in which the corporation was incorporated immediately before its domestication and conversion in this state.

(b) The articles of domestication and conversion shall either contain all of the provisions that section 2.02(a) requires to be set forth in articles of incorporation and any other desired provisions that section 2.02(b) permits to be included in articles of incorporation, or shall have attached articles of incorporation. In either case, provisions that would not be required to be included in restated articles of incorporation may be omitted.

(c) The articles of domestication and conversion shall be delivered to the secretary of state for filing, and shall take effect at the effective time provided in section 1.23.

(d) If the foreign nonprofit corporation is authorized to transact business in this state under [*the foreign qualification provision of the Model Nonprofit Corporation Act*], its certificate of authority shall be cancelled automatically on the effective date of its domestication and conversion.

§ 9.42 Effect of Foreign Nonprofit Domestication and Conversion

(a) When a domestication and conversion of a foreign nonprofit corporation to a domestic business corporation becomes effective:

(1) the title to all real and personal property, both tangible and intangible, of the corporation remains in the corporation without reversion or impairment;

(2) the liabilities of the corporation remain the liabilities of the corporation;

(3) an action or proceeding pending against the corporation continues against the corporation as if the domestication and conversion had not occurred;

(4) the articles of domestication and conversion, or the articles of incorporation attached to the articles of domestication and conversion, constitute the articles of incorporation of the corporation;

(5) shares, other securities, obligations, rights to acquire shares or other securities of the corporation, or cash or other property shall be issued or paid as provided pursuant to the laws of the foreign jurisdiction, so long as at least one share is outstanding immediately after the effective time; and

(6) the corporation is deemed to:

(i) be a domestic corporation for all purposes;

(ii) be the same corporation without interruption as the foreign nonprofit corporation; and

(iii) have been incorporated on the date the foreign nonprofit corporation was originally incorporated.

(b) The owner liability of a member of a foreign nonprofit corporation that domesticates and converts to a domestic business corporation shall be as follows:

(1) The domestication and conversion does not discharge any owner liability under the laws of the foreign jurisdiction to the extent any such owner liability arose before the effective time of the articles of domestication and conversion.

(2) The member shall not have owner liability under the laws of the foreign jurisdiction for any debt, obligation or liability of the corporation that arises after the effective time of the articles of domestication and conversion.

(3) The provisions of the laws of the foreign jurisdiction shall continue to apply to the collection or discharge of any owner liability preserved by paragraph (1), as if the domestication and conversion had not occurred.

(4) The member shall have whatever rights of contribution from other members are provided by the laws of the foreign jurisdiction with respect to any owner liability preserved by paragraph (1), as if the domestication and conversion had not occurred.

[*(c) A member of a foreign nonprofit corporation who becomes subject to owner liability for some or all of the debts, obligations or liabilities of the corporation as a result of its domestication and conversion in this state shall have owner liability only for those debts, obligations or liabilities of the corporation that arise after the effective time of the articles of domestication and conversion.*]

§ 9.43 Abandonment of a Foreign Nonprofit Domestication and Conversion

If the domestication and conversion of a foreign nonprofit corporation to a domestic business corporation is abandoned in accordance with the laws of the foreign jurisdiction after articles of domestication and conversion have been filed with the secretary of state, a statement that the domestication and conversion has been abandoned, executed by an officer or other duly authorized representative, shall be delivered to the secretary of state for filing. The statement shall take effect upon filing and the domestication and conversion shall be deemed abandoned and shall not become effective.

Subchapter E. Entity Conversion

§ 9.50 Entity Conversion Authorized; Definitions

(a) A domestic business corporation may become a domestic unincorporated entity pursuant to a plan of entity conversion.

(b) A domestic business corporation may become a foreign unincorporated entity if the entity conversion is permitted by the laws of the foreign jurisdiction.

(c) A domestic unincorporated entity may become a domestic business corporation. If the organic law of a domestic unincorporated entity does not provide procedures for the approval of an entity conversion, the conversion shall be adopted and approved, and the entity conversion effectuated, in the same manner as a merger of the unincorporated entity. If the organic law of a domestic unincorporated entity does not provide procedures for the approval of either an entity conversion or a merger, a plan of entity conversion shall be adopted and approved, the entity conversion effectuated, and appraisal rights exercised, in accordance with the procedures in this subchapter and chapter 13. Without limiting the provisions of this subsection, a domestic unincorporated entity whose organic law does not provide procedures for the approval of an entity conversion shall be subject to subsection (e) and section 9.52(7). For purposes of applying this subchapter and chapter 13:

(1) the unincorporated entity, its interest holders, interests and organic documents taken together, shall be deemed to be a domestic business corporation, shareholders, shares and articles of incorporation, respectively and vice versa, as the context may require; and

(2) if the business and affairs of the unincorporated entity are managed by a group of persons that is not identical to the interest holders, that group shall be deemed to be the board of directors.

(d) A foreign unincorporated entity may become a domestic business corporation if the organic law of the foreign unincorporated entity authorizes it to become a corporation in another jurisdiction.

(e) If any debt security, note or similar evidence of indebtedness for money borrowed, whether secured or unsecured, or a contract of any kind, issued, incurred or executed by a domestic business corporation before [*the effective date of this subchapter*], applies to a merger of the corporation and the document does not refer to an entity conversion of the corporation, the provision shall be deemed to apply to an entity conversion of the corporation until such time as the provision is amended subsequent to that date.

(f) As used in this subchapter:

(1) "Converting entity" means the domestic business corporation or domestic unincorporated entity that adopts a plan of entity conversion or the foreign unincorporated entity converting to a domestic business corporation.

(2) "Surviving entity" means the corporation or unincorporated entity that is in existence immediately after consummation of an entity conversion pursuant to this subchapter.

§ 9.51 Plan of Entity Conversion

(a) A plan of entity conversion must include:

(1) a statement of the type of other entity the surviving entity will be and, if it will be a foreign other entity, its jurisdiction of organization;

(2) the terms and conditions of the conversion;

(3) the manner and basis of converting the shares of the domestic business corporation following its conversion into interests or other securities, obligations, rights to acquire interests or other securities, cash, other property, or any combination of the foregoing; and

(4) the full text, as they will be in effect immediately after consummation of the conversion, of the organic documents of the surviving entity.

(b) The plan of entity conversion may also include a provision that the plan may be amended prior to filing articles of entity conversion, except that subsequent to approval of the plan by the shareholders the plan may not be amended to change:

(1) the amount or kind of shares or other securities, interests, obligations, rights to acquire shares, other securities or interests, cash, or other property to be received under the plan by the shareholders;

(2) the organic documents that will be in effect immediately following the conversion, except for changes permitted by a provision of the organic law of the surviving entity comparable to section 10.05; or

(3) any of the other terms or conditions of the plan if the change would adversely affect any of the shareholders in any material respect.

(c) Terms of a plan of entity conversion may be made dependent upon facts objectively ascertainable outside the plan in accordance with section 1.20(k).

§ 9.52 Action on a Plan of Entity Conversion

In the case of an entity conversion of a domestic business corporation to a domestic or foreign unincorporated entity:

(1) The plan of entity conversion must be adopted by the board of directors.

(2) After adopting the plan of entity conversion, the board of directors must submit the plan to the shareholders for their approval. The board of directors must also transmit to the shareholders a recommendation that the shareholders approve the plan, unless the board of directors makes a determination that because of conflicts of interest or other special circumstances it should not make such a recommendation, in which

case the board of directors must transmit to the shareholders the basis for that determination.

(3) The board of directors may condition its submission of the plan of entity conversion to the shareholders on any basis.

(4) If the approval of the shareholders is to be given at a meeting, the corporation must notify each shareholder, whether or not entitled to vote, of the meeting of shareholders at which the plan of entity conversion is to be submitted for approval. The notice must state that the purpose, or one of the purposes, of the meeting is to consider the plan and must contain or be accompanied by a copy or summary of the plan. The notice shall include or be accompanied by a copy of the organic documents as they will be in effect immediately after the entity conversion.

(5) Unless the articles of incorporation, or the board of directors acting pursuant to paragraph (3), requires a greater vote or a greater number of votes to be present, approval of the plan of entity conversion requires the approval of each class or series of shares of the corporation voting as a separate voting group at a meeting at which a quorum of the voting group consisting of at least a majority of the votes entitled to be cast on the conversion by that voting group exists.

(6) If any provision of the articles of incorporation, bylaws or an agreement to which any of the directors or shareholders are parties, adopted or entered into before [*the effective date of this subchapter*], applies to a merger of the corporation and the document does not refer to an entity conversion of the corporation, the provision shall be deemed to apply to an entity conversion of the corporation until such time as the provision is subsequently amended.

(7) If as a result of the conversion one or more shareholders of the corporation would become subject to owner liability for the debts, obligations or liabilities of any other person or entity, approval of the plan of conversion shall require the execution, by each such shareholder, of a separate written consent to become subject to such owner liability.

§ 9.53 Articles of Entity Conversion

(a) After the conversion of a domestic business corporation to a domestic unincorporated entity has been adopted and approved as required by this Act, articles of entity conversion shall be executed on behalf of the corporation by any officer or other duly authorized representative. The articles shall:

(1) set forth the name of the corporation immediately before the filing of the articles of entity conversion and the name to which

the name of the corporation is to be changed, which shall be a name that satisfies the organic law of the surviving entity;

(2) state the type of unincorporated entity that the surviving entity will be;

(3) set forth a statement that the plan of entity conversion was duly approved by the shareholders in the manner required by this Act and the articles of incorporation;

(4) if the surviving entity is a filing entity, either contain all of the provisions required to be set forth in its public organic document and any other desired provisions that are permitted, or have attached a public organic document; except that, in either case, provisions that would not be required to be included in a restated public organic document may be omitted.

(b) After the conversion of a domestic unincorporated entity to a domestic business corporation has been adopted and approved as required by the organic law of the unincorporated entity, articles of entity conversion shall be executed on behalf of the unincorporated entity by any officer or other duly authorized representative. The articles shall:

(1) set forth the name of the unincorporated entity immediately before the filing of the articles of entity conversion and the name to which the name of the unincorporated entity is to be changed, which shall be a name that satisfies the requirements of section 4.01;

(2) set forth a statement that the plan of entity conversion was duly approved in accordance with the organic law of the unincorporated entity;

(3) either contain all of the provisions that section 2.02(a) requires to be set forth in articles of incorporation and any other desired provisions that section 2.02(b) permits to be included in articles of incorporation, or have attached articles of incorporation; except that, in either case, provisions that would not be required to be included in restated articles of incorporation of a domestic business corporation may be omitted.

(c) After the conversion of a foreign unincorporated entity to a domestic business corporation has been authorized as required by the laws of the foreign jurisdiction, articles of entity conversion shall be executed on behalf of the foreign unincorporated entity by any officer or other duly authorized representative. The articles shall:

(1) set forth the name of the unincorporated entity immediately before the filing of the articles of entity conversion and the name to which the name of the unincorporated entity is to be changed, which shall be a name that satisfies the requirements of section 4.01;

(2) set forth the jurisdiction under the laws of which the unincorporated entity was organized immediately before the filing of the articles of entity conversion and the date on which the unincorporated entity was organized in that jurisdiction;

(3) set forth a statement that the conversion of the unincorporated entity was duly approved in the manner required by its organic law; and

(4) either contain all of the provisions that section 2.02(a) requires to be set forth in articles of incorporation and any other desired provisions that section 2.02(b) permits to be included in articles of incorporation, or have attached articles of incorporation; except that, in either case, provisions that would not be required to be included in restated articles of incorporation of a domestic business corporation may be omitted.

(d) The articles of entity conversion shall be delivered to the secretary of state for filing, and shall take effect at the effective time provided in section 1.23. Articles of entity conversion filed under section 9.53(a) or (b) may be combined with any required conversion filing under the organic law of the domestic unincorporated entity if the combined filing satisfies the requirements of both this section and the other organic law.

(e) If the converting entity is a foreign unincorporated entity that is authorized to transact business in this state under a provision of law similar to chapter 15, its certificate of authority or other type of foreign qualification shall be cancelled automatically on the effective date of its conversion.

§ 9.54 Surrender of Charter Upon Conversion

(a) Whenever a domestic business corporation has adopted and approved, in the manner required by this subchapter, a plan of entity conversion providing for the corporation to be converted to a foreign unincorporated entity, articles of charter surrender shall be executed on behalf of the corporation by any officer or other duly authorized representative. The articles of charter surrender shall set forth:

(1) the name of the corporation;

(2) a statement that the articles of charter surrender are being filed in connection with the conversion of the corporation to a foreign unincorporated entity;

(3) a statement that the conversion was duly approved by the shareholders in the manner required by this Act and the articles of incorporation;

(4) the jurisdiction under the laws of which the surviving entity will be organized;

(5) if the surviving entity will be a nonfiling entity, the address of its executive office immediately after the conversion.

(b) The articles of charter surrender shall be delivered by the corporation to the secretary of state for filing. The articles of charter surrender shall take effect on the effective time provided in section 1.23.

§ 9.55 Effect of Entity Conversion

(a) When a conversion under this subchapter becomes effective:

(1) the title to all real and personal property, both tangible and intangible, of the converting entity remains in the surviving entity without reversion or impairment;

(2) the liabilities of the converting entity remain the liabilities of the surviving entity;

(3) an action or proceeding pending against the converting entity continues against the surviving entity as if the conversion had not occurred;

(4) in the case of a surviving entity that is a filing entity, its articles of incorporation or public organic document and its private organic document become effective;

(5) in the case of a surviving entity that is a nonfiling entity, its private organic document becomes effective;

(6) the shares or interests of the converting entity are reclassified into shares, interests, other securities, obligations, rights to acquire shares, interests or other securities, or into cash or other property in accordance with the plan of conversion; and the shareholders or interest holders of the converting entity are entitled only to the rights provided to them under the terms of the conversion and to any appraisal rights they may have under the organic law of the converting entity; and

(7) the surviving entity is deemed to:

(i) be incorporated or organized under and subject to the organic law of the converting entity for all purposes;

(ii) be the same corporation or unincorporated entity without interruption as the converting entity; and

(iii) have been incorporated or otherwise organized on the date that the converting entity was originally incorporated or organized.

(b) When a conversion of a domestic business corporation to a foreign other entity becomes effective, the surviving entity is deemed to:

(1) appoint the secretary of state as its agent for service of process in a proceeding to enforce the rights of shareholders who exercise appraisal rights in connection with the conversion; and

(2) agree that it will promptly pay the amount, if any, to which such shareholders are entitled under chapter 13.

(c) A shareholder who becomes subject to owner liability for some or all of the debts, obligations or liabilities of the surviving entity shall be personally liable only for those debts, obligations or liabilities of the surviving entity that arise after the effective time of the articles of entity conversion.

(d) The owner liability of an interest holder in an unincorporated entity that converts to a domestic business corporation shall be as follows:

(1) The conversion does not discharge any owner liability under the organic law of the unincorporated entity to the extent any such owner liability arose before the effective time of the articles of entity conversion.

(2) The interest holder shall not have owner liability under the organic law of the unincorporated entity for any debt, obligation or liability of the corporation that arises after the effective time of the articles of entity conversion.

(3) The provisions of the organic law of the unincorporated entity shall continue to apply to the collection or discharge of any owner liability preserved by paragraph (1), as if the conversion had not occurred.

(4) The interest holder shall have whatever rights of contribution from other interest holders are provided by the organic law of the unincorporated entity with respect to any owner liability preserved by paragraph (1), as if the conversion had not occurred.

§ 9.56 Abandonment of an Entity Conversion

(a) Unless otherwise provided in a plan of entity conversion of a domestic business corporation, after the plan has been adopted and approved as required by this subchapter, and at any time before the entity conversion has become effective, it may be abandoned by the board of directors without action by the shareholders.

(b) If an entity conversion is abandoned after articles of entity conversion or articles of charter surrender have been filed with the secretary of state but before the entity conversion has become effective, a statement that the entity conversion has been abandoned in accordance with this section, executed by an officer or other duly authorized representative, shall be delivered to the secretary of state for filing prior to the effective date of the entity conversion. Upon filing, the statement shall take effect and the entity conversion shall be deemed abandoned and shall not become effective.

CHAPTER 10

AMENDMENT OF ARTICLES OF INCORPORATION AND BYLAWS

Subchapter A. Amendment of Articles of Incorporation

§ 10.01 Authority to Amend

(a) A corporation may amend its articles of incorporation at any time to add or change a provision that is required or permitted in the articles of incorporation as of the effective date of the amendment or to delete a provision that is not required to be contained in the articles of incorporation.

(b) A shareholder of the corporation does not have a vested property right resulting from any provision in the articles of incorporation, including provisions relating to management, control, capital structure, dividend entitlement, or purpose or duration of the corporation.

§ 10.02 Amendment Before Issuance of Shares

If a corporation has not yet issued shares, its board of directors, or its incorporators if it has no board of directors, may adopt one or more amendments to the corporation's articles of incorporation.

§ 10.03 Amendment by Board of Directors and Shareholders

If a corporation has issued shares, an amendment to the articles of incorporation shall be adopted in the following manner:

(a) The proposed amendment must be adopted by the board of directors.

(b) Except as provided in sections 10.05, 10.07, and 10.08, after adopting the proposed amendment the board of directors must submit the amendment to the shareholders for their approval. The board of directors must also transmit to the shareholders a recommendation that the shareholders approve the amendment, unless the board of directors makes a determination that because of conflicts of interest or other special circumstances it should not make such a recommendation, in which case the board of directors must transmit to the shareholders the basis for that determination.

(c) The board of directors may condition its submission of the amendment to the shareholders on any basis.

(d) If the amendment is required to be approved by the shareholders, and the approval is to be given at a meeting, the corporation must notify each shareholder, whether or not entitled to vote, of the meeting of shareholders at which the amendment is to be submitted for approval. The notice must state that the purpose, or one of the purposes, of the meeting is to consider the amendment and must contain or be accompanied by a copy of the amendment.

(e) Unless the articles of incorporation, or the board of directors acting pursuant to subsection (c), requires a greater vote or a greater number of shares to be present, approval of the amendment requires the approval of the shareholders at a meeting at which a quorum consisting of at least a majority of the votes entitled to be cast on the amendment exists, and, if any class or series of shares is entitled to vote as a separate group on the amendment, except as provided in section 10.04(c), the approval of each such separate voting group at a meeting at which a quorum of the voting group consisting of at least a majority of the votes entitled to be cast on the amendment by that voting group exists.

OFFICIAL COMMENT

. . . .

3. Quorum and Voting

Section 10.03(e) provides that approval of an amendment requires approval of the shareholders at a meeting at which a quorum consisting of at least a majority of the votes entitled to be cast on the amendment exists, including, if any class or series of shares is entitled to vote as a separate group on the amendment, the approval of each such separate group, at a meeting at which a similar quorum of the voting group exists. If a quorum exists, then under sections 7.25 and 7.26 the amendment will be approved if more votes are cast in favor of the amendment than against it by the voting group or separate voting groups entitled to vote on the plan. This represents a change from the Act's previous voting rule for amendments, which required approval by a majority of votes cast, with no minimum quorum, for some amendments, and approval by a majority of the votes entitled to be cast by a voting group, for others.

If an amendment would affect the voting requirements on future amendments, it must also be approved by the vote required by section 7.27.

§ 10.04 Voting on Amendments by Voting Groups

(a) If a corporation has more than one class of shares outstanding, the holders of the outstanding shares of a class are entitled to vote as a separate voting group (if shareholder voting is otherwise required by this Act) on a proposed amendment to the articles of incorporation if the amendment would:

(1) effect an exchange or reclassification of all or part of the shares of the class into shares of another class;

(2) effect an exchange or reclassification, or create the right of exchange, of all or part of the shares of another class into shares of the class;

(3) change the rights, preferences, or limitations of all or part of the shares of the class;

(4) change the shares of all or part of the class into a different number of shares of the same class;

(5) create a new class of shares having rights or preferences with respect to distributions or to dissolution that are prior or superior to the shares of the class;

(6) increase the rights, preferences, or number of authorized shares of any class that, after giving effect to the amendment, have rights or preferences with respect to distributions or to dissolution that are prior or superior to the shares of the class;

(7) limit or deny an existing preemptive right of all or part of the shares of the class; or

(8) cancel or otherwise affect rights to distributions that have accumulated but not yet been authorized on all or part of the shares of the class.

(b) If a proposed amendment would affect a series of a class of shares in one or more of the ways described in subsection (a), the holders of shares of that series are entitled to vote as a separate voting group on the proposed amendment.

(c) If a proposed amendment that entitles the holders of two or more classes or series of shares to vote as separate voting groups under this section would affect those two or more classes or series in the same or a substantially similar way, the holders of shares of all the classes or series so affected must vote together as a single voting group on the proposed amendment, unless otherwise provided in the articles of incorporation or required by the board of directors.

(d) A class or series of shares is entitled to the voting rights granted by this section although the articles of incorporation provide that the shares are nonvoting shares.

§ 10.05 Amendment by Board of Directors

Unless the articles of incorporation provide otherwise, a corporation's board of directors may adopt amendments to the corporation's articles of incorporation without shareholder approval:

(1) to extend the duration of the corporation if it was incorporated at a time when limited duration was required by law;

(2) to delete the names and addresses of the initial directors;

(3) to delete the name and address of the initial registered agent or registered office, if a statement of change is on file with the secretary of state;

(4) if the corporation has only one class of shares outstanding:

(a) to change each issued and unissued authorized share of the class into a greater number of whole shares of that class; or

(b) to increase the number of authorized shares of the class to the extent necessary to permit the issuance of shares as a share dividend;

(5) to change the corporate name by substituting the word "corporation," "incorporated," "company," "limited," or the abbreviation "corp.," "inc.," "co.," or "ltd.," for a similar word or abbreviation in the name, or by adding, deleting, or changing a geographical attribution for the name;

(6) to reflect a reduction in authorized shares, as a result of the operation of section 6.31(b), when the corporation has acquired its own shares and the articles of incorporation prohibit the reissue of the acquired shares;

(7) to delete a class of shares from the articles of incorporation, as a result of the operation of section 6.31(b), when there are no remaining shares of the class because the corporation has acquired all shares of the class and the articles of incorporation prohibit the reissue of the acquired shares; or

(8) to make any change expressly permitted by section 6.02(a) or (b) to be made without shareholder approval.

§ 10.06 Articles of Amendment

After an amendment to the articles of incorporation has been adopted and approved in the manner required by this Act and by the articles of incorporation, the corporation shall deliver to the secretary of state, for filing, articles of amendment, which shall set forth:

(1) the name of the corporation;

(2) the text of each amendment adopted, or the information required by section 1.20(k)(5);

(3) if an amendment provides for an exchange, reclassification, or cancellation of issued shares, provisions for implementing the amendment if not contained in the amendment itself, which may be made dependent upon facts objectively ascertainable outside the articles of amendment in accordance with section 1.20(k)(5);

(4) the date of each amendment's adoption; and

(5) if an amendment:

(a) was adopted by the incorporators or board of directors without shareholder approval, a statement that the amendment was duly approved by the incorporators or by the board of directors, as the case may be, and that shareholder approval was not required;

(b) required approval by the shareholders, a statement that the amendment was duly approved by the shareholders in the manner required by this Act and by the articles of incorporation; or

(c) is being filed pursuant to section 1.20(k)(5), a statement to that effect.

§ 10.07 Restated Articles of Incorporation

(a) A corporation's board of directors may restate its articles of incorporation at any time, with or without shareholder approval, to consolidate all amendments into a single document.

(b) If the restated articles include one or more new amendments that require shareholder approval, the amendments must be adopted and approved as provided in section 10.03.

(c) A corporation that restates its articles of incorporation shall deliver to the secretary of state for filing articles of restatement setting forth the name of the corporation and the text of the restated articles of incorporation together with a certificate which states that the restated articles consolidate all amendments into a single document and, if a new amendment is included in the restated articles, which also includes the statements required under section 10.06.

(d) Duly adopted restated articles of incorporation supersede the original articles of incorporation and all amendments thereto.

(e) The secretary of state may certify restated articles of incorporation as the articles of incorporation currently in effect, without including the certificate information required by subsection (c).

§ 10.08 Amendment Pursuant to Reorganization

(a) A corporation's articles of incorporation may be amended without action by the board of directors or shareholders to carry out a plan of reorganization ordered or decreed by a court of competent jurisdiction under the authority of a law of the United States.

(b) The individual or individuals designated by the court shall deliver to the secretary of state for filing articles of amendment setting forth:

(1) the name of the corporation;

(2) the text of each amendment approved by the court;

(3) the date of the court's order or decree approving the articles of amendment;

(4) the title of the reorganization proceeding in which the order or decree was entered; and

(5) a statement that the court had jurisdiction of the proceeding under federal statute.

(c) This section does not apply after entry of a final decree in the reorganization proceeding even though the court retains jurisdiction of the proceeding for limited purposes unrelated to consummation of the reorganization plan.

§ 10.09 Effect of Amendment

An amendment to the articles of incorporation does not affect a cause of action existing against or in favor of the corporation, a proceeding to which the corporation is a party, or the existing rights of persons other than shareholders of the corporation. An amendment changing a corporation's name does not abate a proceeding brought by or against the corporation in its former name.

Subchapter B. Amendment of Bylaws

§ 10.20 Amendment by Board of Directors or Shareholders

(a) A corporation's shareholders may amend or repeal the corporation's bylaws.

(b) A corporation's board of directors may amend or repeal the corporation's bylaws, unless:

(1) the articles of incorporation or section 10.21 reserve that power exclusively to the shareholders in whole or part; or

(2) the shareholders in amending, repealing, or adopting a bylaw expressly provide that the board of directors may not amend, repeal, or reinstate that bylaw.

§ 10.21 Bylaw Increasing Quorum or Voting Requirement for Directors

(a) A bylaw that increases a quorum or voting requirement for the board of directors may be amended or repealed:

(1) if originally adopted by the shareholders, only by the shareholders, unless the bylaw otherwise provides;

(2) if adopted by the board of directors, either by the shareholders or by the board of directors.

(b) A bylaw adopted or amended by the shareholders that increases a quorum or voting requirement for the board of directors may provide that it can be amended or repealed only by a specified vote of either the shareholders or the board of directors.

(c) Action by the board of directors under subsection (a) to amend or repeal a bylaw that changes the quorum or voting requirement for the board of directors must meet the same quorum requirement and be adopted by the same vote required to take action under the quorum and voting requirement then in effect or proposed to be adopted, whichever is greater.

CHAPTER 11

MERGERS AND SHARE EXCHANGES

§ 11.01 Definitions

As used in this chapter:

(a) "Merger" means a business combination pursuant to section 11.02.

(b) "Party to a merger" or "party to a share exchange" means any domestic or foreign corporation or eligible entity that will:

(1) merge under a plan of merger;

(2) acquire shares or eligible interests of another corporation or an eligible entity in a share exchange; or

(3) have all of its shares or eligible interests or all of one or more classes or series of its shares or eligible interests acquired in a share exchange.

(c) "Share exchange" means a business combination pursuant to section 11.03.

(d) "Survivor" in a merger means the corporation or eligible entity into which one or more other corporations or eligible entities are merged. A survivor of a merger may preexist the merger or be created by the merger.

§ 11.02 Merger

(a) One or more domestic business corporations may merge with one or more domestic or foreign business corporations or eligible entities pursuant to a plan of merger, or two or more foreign business corporations or domestic or foreign eligible entities may merge into a new domestic business corporation to be created in the merger in the manner provided in this chapter.

(b) A foreign business corporation, or a foreign eligible entity, may be a party to a merger with a domestic business corporation, or may be created by the terms of the plan of merger, only if the merger is permitted by the foreign business corporation or eligible entity.

(b.1) If the organic law of a domestic eligible entity does not provide procedures for the approval of a merger, a plan of merger may be adopted and approved, the merger effectuated, and appraisal rights exercised in accordance with the procedures in this chapter and chapter 13. For the purposes of applying this chapter and chapter 13:

(1) the eligible entity, its members or interest holders, eligible interests and organic documents taken together shall be deemed

to be a domestic business corporation, shareholders, shares and articles of incorporation, respectively and vice versa as the context may require; and

(2) if the business and affairs of the eligible entity are managed by a group of persons that is not identical to the members or interest holders, that group shall be deemed to be the board of directors.

(c) The plan of merger must include:

(1) the name of each domestic or foreign business corporation or eligible entity that will merge and the name of the domestic or foreign business corporation or eligible entity that will be the survivor of the merger;

(2) the terms and conditions of the merger;

(3) the manner and basis of converting the shares of each merging domestic or foreign business corporation and eligible interests of each merging domestic or foreign eligible entity into shares or other securities, eligible interests, obligations, rights to acquire shares, other securities or eligible interests, cash, other property, or any combination of the foregoing;

(4) the articles of incorporation of any domestic or foreign business or nonprofit corporation, or the organic documents of any domestic or foreign unincorporated entity, to be created by the merger, or if a new domestic or foreign business or nonprofit corporation or unincorporated entity is not to be created by the merger, any amendments to the survivor's articles of incorporation or organic documents; and

(5) any other provisions required by the laws under which any party to the merger is organized or by which it is governed, or by the articles of incorporation or organic document of any such party.

(d) Terms of a plan of merger may be made dependent on facts objectively ascertainable outside the plan in accordance with section 1.20(k).

(e) The plan of merger may also include a provision that the plan may be amended prior to filing articles of merger, but if the shareholders of a domestic corporation that is a party to the merger are required or permitted to vote on the plan, the plan must provide that subsequent to approval of the plan by such shareholders the plan may not be amended to change:

(1) the amount or kind of shares or other securities, eligible interests, obligations, rights to acquire shares, other securities or eligible interests, cash, or other property to be received under the plan by the shareholders of or owners of eligible interests in any party to the merger;

(2) the articles of incorporation of any corporation, or the organic documents of any unincorporated entity, that will survive or be created as a result of the merger, except for changes permitted

by section 10.05 or by comparable provisions of the organic laws of any such foreign corporation or domestic or foreign unincorporated entity; or

(3) any of the other terms or conditions of the plan if the change would adversely affect such shareholders in any material respect.

[*(f) Property held in trust or for charitable purposes under the laws of this state by a domestic or foreign eligible entity shall not be diverted by a merger from the objects for which it was donated, granted or devised, unless and until the eligible entity obtains an order of [court] [the attorney general] specifying the disposition of the property to the extent required by and pursuant to [cite state statutory cy pres or other nondiversion statute].*]

§ 11.03 Share Exchange

(a) Through a share exchange:

(1) a domestic corporation may acquire all of the shares of one or more classes or series of shares of another domestic or foreign corporation, or all of the interests of one or more classes or series of interests of a domestic or foreign other entity, in exchange for shares or other securities, interests, obligations, rights to acquire shares or other securities, cash, other property, or any combination of the foregoing, pursuant to a plan of share exchange, or

(2) all of the shares of one or more classes or series of shares of a domestic corporation may be acquired by another domestic or foreign corporation or other entity, in exchange for shares or other securities, interests, obligations, rights to acquire shares or other securities, cash, other property, or any combination of the foregoing, pursuant to a plan of share exchange.

(b) A foreign corporation or eligible entity, may be a party to a share exchange only if the share exchange is permitted by the corporation or other entity is organized or by which it is governed.

(b.1) If the organic law of a domestic other entity does not provide procedures for the approval of a share exchange, a plan of share exchange may be adopted and approved, and the share exchange effectuated, in accordance with the procedures, if any, for a merger. If the organic law of a domestic other entity does not provide procedures for the approval of either a share exchange or a merger, a plan of share exchange may be adopted and approved, the share exchange effectuated, and appraisal rights exercised, in accordance with the procedures in this chapter and chapter 13. For the purposes of applying this chapter and chapter 13:

(1) the other entity, its interest holders, interests and organic documents taken together shall be deemed to be a domestic

business corporation, shareholders, shares and articles of incorporation, respectively and vice versa as the context may require; and

(2) if the business and affairs of the other entity are managed by a group of persons that is not identical to the interest holders, that group shall be deemed to be the board of directors.

(c) The plan of share exchange must include:

(1) the name of each corporation or other entity whose shares or interests will be acquired and the name of the corporation or other entity that will acquire those shares or interests;

(2) the terms and conditions of the share exchange;

(3) the manner and basis of exchanging shares of a corporation or interests in an other entity whose shares or interests will be acquired under the share exchange into shares or other securities, interests, obligations, rights to acquire shares, other securities, or interests, cash, other property, or any combination of the foregoing; and

(4) any other provisions required by the laws under which any party to the share exchange is organized or by the articles of incorporation or organic document of any such party.

(d) Terms of a plan of share exchange may be made dependent on facts objectively ascertainable outside the plan in accordance with section 1.20(k).

(e) The plan of share exchange may also include a provision that the plan may be amended prior to filing articles of share exchange, but if the shareholders of a domestic corporation that is a party to the share exchange are required or permitted to vote on the plan, the plan must provide that subsequent to approval of the plan by such shareholders the plan may not be amended to change:

(1) the amount or kind of shares or other securities, interests, obligations, rights to acquire shares, other securities or interests, cash, or other property to be issued by the corporation or to be received under the plan by the shareholders of or owners of interests in any party to the share exchange; or

(2) any of the other terms or conditions of the plan if the change would adversely affect such shareholders in any material respect.

(f) Section 11.03 does not limit the power of a domestic corporation to acquire shares of another corporation or interests in another entity in a transaction other than a share exchange.

§ 11.04 Action on a Plan of Merger or Share Exchange

In the case of a domestic corporation that is a party to a merger or share exchange:

(a) The plan of merger or share exchange must be adopted by the board of directors.

(b) Except as provided in subsection (g) and in section 11.05, after adopting the plan of merger or share exchange the board of directors must submit the plan to the shareholders for their approval. The board of directors must also transmit to the shareholders a recommendation that the shareholders approve the plan, unless the board of directors makes a determination that because of conflicts of interest or other special circumstances it should not make such a recommendation, in which case the board of directors must transmit to the shareholders the basis for that determination.

(c) The board of directors may condition its submission of the plan of merger or share exchange to the shareholders on any basis.

(d) If the plan of merger or share exchange is required to be approved by the shareholders, and if the approval is to be given at a meeting, the corporation must notify each shareholder, whether or not entitled to vote, of the meeting of shareholders at which the plan is to be submitted for approval. The notice must state that the purpose, or one of the purposes, of the meeting is to consider the plan and must contain or be accompanied by a copy or summary of the plan. If the corporation is to be merged into an existing corporation or other entity, the notice shall also include or be accompanied by a copy or summary of the articles of incorporation or organizational documents of that corporation or other entity. If the corporation is to be merged into a corporation or other entity that is to be created pursuant to the merger, the notice shall include or be accompanied by a copy or a summary of the articles of incorporation or organizational documents of the new corporation or other entity.

(e) Unless the articles of incorporation, or the board of directors acting pursuant to subsection (c), requires a greater vote or a greater number of votes to be present, approval of the plan of merger or share exchange requires the approval of the shareholders at a meeting at which a quorum consisting of at least a majority of the votes entitled to be cast on the plan exists, and, if any class or series of shares is entitled to vote as a separate group on the plan of merger or share exchange, the approval of each such separate voting group at a meeting at which a quorum of the voting group consisting of at least a majority of the votes entitled to be cast on the merger or share exchange by that voting group is present.

(f) Separate voting by voting groups is required:

(1) on a plan of merger, by each class or series of shares that:

(i) are to be converted under the plan of merger into other securities, interests, obligations, rights to acquire shares, other securities or interests, cash, other property, or any combination of the foregoing; or

(ii) would be entitled to vote as a separate group on a provision in the plan that, if contained in a proposed amendment to articles of incorporation, would require action by separate voting groups under section 10.04;

(2) on a plan of share exchange, by each class or series of shares included in the exchange, with each class or series constituting a separate voting group; and

(3) on a plan of merger or share exchange, if the voting group is entitled under the articles of incorporation to vote as a voting group to approve a plan of merger or share exchange.

(g) Unless the articles of incorporation otherwise provide, approval by the corporation's shareholders of a plan of merger or share exchange is not required if:

(1) the corporation will survive the merger or is the acquiring corporation in a share exchange;

(2) except for amendments permitted by section 10.05, its articles of incorporation will not be changed;

(3) each shareholder of the corporation whose shares were outstanding immediately before the effective date of the merger or share exchange will hold the same number of shares, with identical preferences, limitations, and relative rights, immediately after the effective date of change; and

(4) the issuance in the merger or share exchange of shares or other securities convertible into or rights exercisable for shares does not require a vote under section 6.21(f).

(h) If as a result of a merger or share exchange one or more shareholders of a domestic corporation would become subject to owner liability for the debts, obligations or liabilities of any other person or entity, approval of the plan of merger or share exchange shall require the execution, by each such shareholder, of a separate written consent to become subject to such owner liability.

§ 11.05 Merger Between Parent and Subsidiary or Between Subsidiaries

(a) A domestic parent corporation that owns shares of a domestic or foreign subsidiary corporation that carry at least 90 percent of the voting power of each class and series of the outstanding shares of the subsidiary that have voting power may merge the subsidiary into itself or into another such subsidiary, or merge itself into the subsidiary, without the approval of the board of directors or shareholders of the subsidiary, unless the articles of incorporation of any of the corporations otherwise provide, and unless, in the case of a foreign subsidiary, approval by the subsidiary's board of directors or shareholders is required by the laws under which the subsidiary is organized.

(b) If under subsection (a) approval of a merger by the subsidiary's shareholders is not required, the parent corporation shall, within ten days after the effective date of the merger, notify each of the subsidiary's shareholders that the merger has become effective.

(c) Except as provided in subsections (a) and (b), a merger between a parent and a subsidiary shall be governed by the provisions of chapter 11 applicable to mergers generally.

§ 11.06 Articles of Merger or Share Exchange

(a) After a plan of merger or share exchange has been adopted and approved as required by this Act, articles of merger or share exchange shall be executed on behalf of each party to the merger or share exchange by any officer or other duly authorized representative. The articles shall set forth:

(1) the names of the parties to the merger or share exchange;

(2) if the articles of incorporation of the survivor of a merger are amended, or if a new corporation is created as a result of a merger, the amendments to the survivor's articles of incorporation or the articles of incorporation of the new corporation;

(3) if the plan of merger or share exchange required approval by the shareholders of a domestic corporation that was a party to the merger or share exchange, a statement that the plan was duly approved by the shareholders and, if voting by any separate voting group was required, by each such separate voting group, in the manner required by this Act and the articles of incorporation;

(4) if the plan of merger or share exchange did not require approval by the shareholders of a domestic corporation that was a party to the merger or share exchange, a statement to that effect; and

(5) as to each foreign corporation or eligible entity that was a party to the merger or share exchange, a statement that the participation of the foreign corporation or eligible entity was duly authorized as required by the organic law of the corporation or eligible entity.

(b) Articles of merger or share exchange shall be delivered to the secretary of state for filing by the survivor of the merger or the acquiring corporation in a share exchange, and shall take effect at the effective time provided in section 1.23. Articles of merger or share exchange filed under this section may be combined with any filing required under the organic law of any domestic eligible entity involved in the transaction if the combined filing satisfies the requirements of both this section and the other organic law.

§ 11.07 Effect of Merger or Share Exchange

(a) When a merger becomes effective:

(1) the corporation or eligible entity that is designated in the plan of merger as the survivor continues or comes into existence, as the case may be;

(2) the separate existence of every corporation or eligible entity that is merged into the survivor ceases;

(3) all property owned by, and every contract right possessed by, each corporation or eligible entity that merges into the survivor is vested in the survivor without reversion or impairment;

(4) all liabilities of each corporation or eligible entity that is merged into the survivor are vested in the survivor;

(5) the name of the survivor may, but need not be, substituted in any pending proceeding for the name of any party to the merger whose separate existence ceased in the merger;

(6) the articles of incorporation or organic documents of the survivor are amended to the extent provided in the plan of merger;

(7) the articles of incorporation or organic documents of a survivor that is created by the merger become effective; and

(8) the shares of each corporation that is a party to the merger, and the interests in an eligible entity that is a party to a merger, that are to be converted under the plan of merger into shares, eligible interests, obligations, rights to acquire securities, other securities, or eligible interests, cash, other property, or any combination of the foregoing, are converted, and the former holders of such shares or eligible interests are entitled only to the rights provided to them in the plan of merger or to any rights they may have under chapter 13 or the organic law of the eligible entity.

(b) When a share exchange becomes effective, the shares of each domestic corporation that are to be exchanged for shares or other securities, interests, obligations, rights to acquire shares or other securities, cash, other property, or any combination of the foregoing, are entitled only to the rights provided to them in the plan of share exchange or to any rights they may have under chapter 13.

(c) A person who becomes subject to owner liability for some or all of the debts, obligations or liabilities of any entity as a result of a merger or share exchange shall have owner liability only to the extent provided in the organic law of the entity and only for those debts, obligations and liabilities that arise after the effective time of the articles of merger or share exchange.

(d) Upon a merger becoming effective, a foreign corporation, or a foreign eligible entity, that is the survivor of the merger is deemed to:

(1) appoint the secretary of state as its agent for service of process in a proceeding to enforce the rights of shareholders of each domestic corporation that is a party to the merger who exercise appraisal rights, and

(2) agree that it will promptly pay the amount, if any, to which such shareholders are entitled under chapter 13.

(e) The effect of a merger or share exchange on the owner liability of a person who had owner liability for some or all of the debts, obligations or liabilities of a party to the merger or share exchange shall be as follows:

(1) The merger or share exchange does not discharge any owner liability under the organic law of the entity in which the person was a shareholder or interest holder to the extent any such owner liability arose before the effective time of the articles of merger or share exchange.

(2) The person shall not have owner liability under the organic law of the entity in which the person was a shareholder or interest holder prior to the merger or share exchange for any debt, obligation or liability that arises after the effective time of the articles of merger or share exchange.

(3) The provisions of the organic law of any entity for which the person had owner liability before the merger or share exchange shall continue to apply to the collection or discharge of any owner liability preserved by paragraph (1), as if the merger or share exchange had not occurred.

(4) The person shall have whatever rights of contribution from other persons are provided by the organic law of the entity for which the person had owner liability with respect to any owner liability preserved by paragraph (1), as if the merger or share exchange had not occurred.

§ 11.08 Abandonment of a Merger or Share Exchange

(a) Unless otherwise provided in a plan of merger or share exchange or in the laws under which a foreign business corporation or a domestic or foreign eligible entity that is a party to a merger or a share exchange is organized or by which it is governed, after the plan has been adopted and approved as required by this chapter, and at any time before the merger or share exchange has become effective, it may be abandoned by a domestic business corporation that is a party thereto without action by its shareholders in accordance with any procedures set forth in the plan of merger or share exchange or, if no such procedures are set forth in the plan, in the manner determined by the board of directors, subject to any contractual rights of other parties to the merger or share exchange.

(b) If a merger or share exchange is abandoned under subsection (a) after articles of merger or share exchange have been filed with the secretary of state but before the merger or share exchange has become effective, a statement that the merger or share exchange has been abandoned in accordance with this section, executed on behalf of a party to the merger or share exchange by an officer or other duly authorized representative, shall be delivered to the secretary of state for filing prior to the effective date of the merger or share exchange. Upon filing, the statement shall take effect and the merger or share exchange shall be deemed abandoned and shall not become effective.

CHAPTER 12

DISPOSITION OF ASSETS

§ 12.01 Disposition of Assets not Requiring Shareholder Approval

No approval of the shareholders of a corporation is required, unless the articles of incorporation otherwise provide:

(1) to sell, lease, exchange, or otherwise dispose of any or all of the corporation's assets in the usual and regular course of business;

(2) to mortgage, pledge, dedicate to the repayment of indebtedness (whether with or without recourse), or otherwise encumber any or all of the corporation's assets, whether or not in the usual and regular course of business;

(3) to transfer any or all of the corporation's assets to one or more corporations or other entities all of the shares or interests of which are owned by the corporation; or

(4) to distribute assets pro rata to the holders of one or more classes or series of the corporation's shares.

§ 12.02 Shareholder Approval of Certain Dispositions

(a) A sale, lease, exchange, or other disposition of assets, other than a disposition described in section 12.01, requires approval of the corporation's shareholders if the disposition would leave the corporation without a significant continuing business activity. If a corporation retains a business activity that represented at least 25 percent of total assets at the end of the most recently completed fiscal year, and 25 percent of either income from continuing operations before taxes or revenues from continuing operations for that fiscal year, in each case of the corporation and its subsidiaries on a consolidated basis, the corporation will conclusively be deemed to have retained a significant continuing business activity.

(b) A disposition that requires approval of the shareholders under subsection (a) shall be initiated by a resolution by the board of directors authorizing the disposition. After adoption of such a resolution, the board of directors shall submit the proposed disposition to the shareholders for their approval. The board of directors shall also transmit to the shareholders a recommendation that the shareholders approve the proposed disposition, unless the board of directors makes a determination that because of conflicts of interest or other special circumstances it should not make such a recommendation, in which case the board of directors shall transmit to the shareholders the basis for that determination.

(c) The board of directors may condition its submission of a disposition to the shareholders under subsection (b) on any basis.

(d) If a disposition is required to be approved by the shareholders under subsection (a), and if the approval is to be given at a meeting, the corporation shall notify each shareholder, whether or not entitled to vote, of the meeting of shareholders at which the disposition is to be submitted for approval. The notice shall state that the purpose, or one of the purposes, of the meeting is to consider the disposition and shall contain a description of the disposition, including the terms and conditions thereof and the consideration to be received by the corporation.

(e) Unless the articles of incorporation or the board of directors acting pursuant to subsection (c) requires a greater vote, or a greater number of votes to be present, the approval of a disposition by the shareholders shall require the approval of the shareholders at a meeting at which a quorum consisting of at least a majority of the votes entitled to be cast on the disposition exists.

(f) After a disposition has been approved by the shareholders under subsection (b), and at any time before the disposition has been consummated, it may be abandoned by the corporation without action by the shareholders, subject to any contractual rights of other parties to the disposition.

(g) A disposition of assets in the course of dissolution under chapter 14 is not governed by this section.

(h) The assets of a direct or indirect consolidated subsidiary shall be deemed the assets of the parent corporation for the purposes of this section.

OFFICIAL COMMENT

1. In General

Section 12.02(a) requires shareholder approval for a sale, lease, exchange or other disposition by a corporation that would leave the corporation without a significant continuing business activity. The test employed in section 12.02(a) for whether a disposition of assets requires shareholder approval differs verbally from the test employed in past versions of the Model Act, which centered on whether a sale involves "all or substantially all" of a corporation's assets. The "all or substantially all" test has also been used in most corporate statutes. In practice, however, courts interpreting these statutes have commonly employed a test comparable to that embodied in 12.02(a). For example, in *Gimbel v. Signal Cos.*, 316 A.2d 599 (Del. Ch.), aff'd, 316 A.2d 619 (Del. 1974), the court stated that "While it is true that [the all or substantially all] test does not lend itself to a strict mathematical standard to be applied in every case, the qualitative factor can be defined to some degree.... If the sale is of assets quantitatively vital to the operation of the corporation and is out of the ordinary [course] and substantially affects the existence and purpose of the corporation then it is beyond the power of the Board of Directors." In *Thorpe v. Cerbco, Inc.*, 676 A.2d 436 (Del. 1996), a major issue was whether the sale by a corporation, CERBCO, of one of its subsidiaries, East, would have been a sale of all or substantially all of the corporation's assets, and therefore would have required shareholder approval under the Delaware statute. The court, quoting *Oberly v. Kirby*, 592 A.2d 445 (Del. 1991), stated:

> "[T]he rule announced in *Gimbel v. Signal Cos.,* Del. Ch., 316 A.2d 599, *aff'd,* Del. Supr., 316 A.2d 619 (1974), makes it clear that the need for shareholder ... approval is to be measured not by the size of a sale alone, but also by its qualitative effect upon the corporation. Thus, it is relevant to ask whether a transaction 'is out of the ordinary and substantially affects the existence and purpose of the corporation.' [*Gimbel*, 316 A.2d] at 606."
>
> In the opinion below, the Chancellor determined that the sale of East would constitute a radical transformation of CERBCO. In addition, CERBCO's East stock accounted for 68 [percent] of CERBCO's assets in 1990 and this stock was its primary income generating asset. We therefore affirm the decision that East stock constituted "substantially all" of CERBCO's assets as consistent with Delaware law.

See also *Katz v. Bregman*, 431 A.2d 1274 (Del. Ch.), appeal refused sub nom. *Plant Industries, Inc. v. Katz*, 435 A.2d 1044 (Del. 1981); *Stiles v. Aluminum Products Co.*, 338 Ill. App. 48, 86 N.E.2d 887 (1949); *Campbell v. Vose*, 515 F.2d 256 (10th Cir. 1975); *South End Improvement Group, Inc. v. Mulliken*, 602 So. 2d 1327 (Fla. App. 1992); *Schwadel v. Uchitel*, 455 So. 2d 401 (Fla. App. 1984).

Whether a disposition leaves a corporation with a significant continuing business activity, within the meaning of section 12.02(a), depends primarily on whether the corporation will have a remaining business activity that is significant when compared to the corporation's business prior to the disposition. The addition of a safe harbor, embodied in the second sentence of section 12.02(a), under which a significant business activity exists if the continuing business activity represented at least 25 percent of the total assets and 25 percent of either income from continuing operations before income taxes or revenues from continuing operations, in each case of the company and its subsidiaries on a consolidated basis for the most recent full fiscal year, the corporation will conclusively be deemed to have retained a significant continuing business activity, represents a policy judgment that a greater measure of certainty than is provided by interpretations of the current case law is highly desirable. The application of this bright-line safe-harbor test should, in most cases, produce a reasonably clear result substantially in conformity with the approaches taken in the better case law developing the "quantitative" and "qualitative" analyses. The test is to be applied to assets, revenue, and income for the most recent fiscal year ended immediately before the decision by the board of directors to make the disposition in question.

If a corporation disposes of assets for the purpose of reinvesting the proceeds of the disposition in substantially the same business in a somewhat different form (for example, by selling the corporation's only plant for the purpose of buying or building a replacement plant), the disposition and reinvestment should be treated together, so that the transaction should not be deemed to leave the corporation without a significant continuing business activity.

In determining whether a disposition would leave a corporation without a significant continuing business activity, the term "the corporation" includes subsidiaries that are or should be consolidated with the parent under generally accepted accounting principles. Accordingly, if, for example, a corporation's only significant business is owned by a wholly or almost wholly owned subsidiary, a sale of that business requires approval of the parent's shareholders under section 12.02. See *Schwadel v. Uchitel*, 455 So. 2d 401 (Fla. App. 1984). Correspondingly, if a corporation owns one significant business directly, and several other significant businesses through one or more wholly or almost wholly owned subsidiaries, a sale by the corporation of the single business it owns directly does not require shareholder approval under section 12.02.

If all or a large part of a corporation's assets are held for investment, the corporation actively manages those assets, and it has no other significant business, for purposes of the statute the corporation should be considered to be in the business of investing in such assets, so that a sale of most of those assets without a reinvestment should be considered a sale that would leave the corporation without a significant continuing business activity. In applying the 25 percent tests of section 12.02(a), an issue could arise if a corporation had more than one business activity, one or more of which might be traditional operating activities such as manufacturing or distribution, and another of which might be considered managing investments in other securities or enterprises. If the activity constituting the management of investments is to be a continuing business activity as a result of the active engagement of the management of the corporation in that process, and the 25 percent tests were met upon the disposition of the other businesses, shareholder approval would not be required.

As under section 6.40(d) (determination of whether a dividend is permissible), and for the same reasons, the board of directors may base a determination that a retained continuing business falls within the 25 percent bright-line tests of the safe harbor embodied in the second sentence of section 12.02(a) either on accounting principles and practices that are reasonable in the circumstances or (in applying the asset test) on a fair valuation or other method that is reasonable in the circumstances. See section 6.40(d) and Comment 4 thereto.

The utilization of the term "significant," and the specific 25 percent safe harbor test for purposes of this section, should not be read as implying a standard for the test of significance or materiality for any other purposes under the Act or otherwise.

. . . .

CHAPTER 13

APPRAISAL RIGHTS

Subchapter A. Right to Appraisal and Payment for Shares

§ 13.01 Definitions

In this chapter:

(1) "Affiliate" means a person that directly or indirectly through one or more intermediaries controls, is controlled by, or is under common control with another person or is a senior executive thereof. For purposes of section 13.02(b)(4), a person is deemed to be an affiliate of its senior executives.

(2) "Beneficial shareholder" means a person who is the beneficial owner of shares held in a voting trust or by a nominee on the beneficial owner's behalf.

(3) "Corporation" means the issuer of the shares held by a shareholder demanding appraisal and, for matters covered in sections 13.22–13.31, includes the surviving entity in a merger.

(4) "Fair value" means the value of the corporation's shares determined:

   (i) immediately before the effectuation of the corporate action to which the shareholder objects;

   (ii) using customary and current valuation concepts and techniques generally employed for similar businesses in the context of the transaction requiring appraisal; and

   (iii) without discounting for lack of marketability or minority status except, if appropriate, for amendments to the articles pursuant to section 13.02(a)(5).

(5) "Interest" means interest from the effective date of the corporate action until the date of payment, at the rate of interest on judgments in this state on the effective date of the corporate action.

(6) "Preferred shares" means a class or series of shares whose holders have preference over any other class or series with respect to distributions.

(7) "Record shareholder" means the person in whose name shares are registered in the records of the corporation or the beneficial owner of shares to the extent of the rights granted by a nominee certificate on file with the corporation.

(8) "Senior executive" means the chief executive officer, chief operating officer, chief financial officer, and anyone in charge of a principal business unit or function.

(9) "Shareholder" means both a record shareholder and a beneficial shareholder.

OFFICIAL COMMENT

. . . .

2. Definitions

Section 13.01 contains specialized definitions applicable only to chapter 13.

Beneficial shareholder

The definition of "beneficial shareholder" means a person who owns the beneficial interest in shares; "shares" is defined in section 1.40(22) to include, without limitation, a holder of a depository receipt for shares. Similar definitions are found in section 7.40(2) (derivative proceedings) and section 16.02(f) (inspection of records by a shareholder). In the context of chapter 13, beneficial shareholder means a person having a direct economic interest in the shares. The definition is not intended to adopt the broad definition of beneficial ownership in SEC Rule 13d–2, which includes persons with a right to vote or dispose of the shares even though they have no economic interest in them. However, section 13.02(b)(5) includes the concept of the right to vote in determining whether the event represents a conflict transaction that renders the market exception unavailable.

Corporation

The definition of "corporation" in section 13.01(3) includes, for purposes of the post-transaction matters covered in section 13.22 through 13.31, a successor entity in a merger where the corporation is not the surviving entity. The definition does not include a domestic acquiring corporation in a share exchange or disposition of assets because the corporation whose shares or assets were acquired continues in existence in both of these instances and remains responsible for the appraisal obligations. Whether a foreign corporation or other form of domestic or foreign entity is subject to appraisal rights in connection with any of these transactions depends upon the corporation or other applicable law of the relevant jurisdiction.

Fair value

Subsection (i) of the definition of "fair value" in section 13.01(4) makes clear that fair value is to be determined immediately before the effectuation of the corporate action, rather than, as is the case under most state statutes that address the issue, the date of the shareholders' vote. This comports with the purpose of this chapter to preserve the shareholder's prior rights as a shareholder until the effective date of the corporate action, rather than leaving the shareholder in an ambiguous state with neither rights as a shareholder nor perfected appraisal rights. The corporation and, as relevant, its shares are valued as they exist immediately before the effectuation of the corporate action requiring appraisal. Accordingly, section 13.01(4) permits consideration of changes in the market price of the corporation's shares in anticipation of the transaction, to the extent such changes are relevant. Similarly, in a two-step transaction culminating in a merger, the corporation is valued immediately before the second step merger, taking into account any interim changes in value. *Cf. Cede & Co. v. Technicolor, Inc.*, 684 A.2d 289 (Del. 1996).

The definition of "fair value" in section 13.01(4) makes several changes from the prior version. The 1984 Model Act's definition of "fair value" was silent on how fair value was to be determined, except for a concluding clause that excluded from the valuation "any appreciation or depreciation in anticipation of the corporate action, unless exclusion would be inequitable." The Official Comment provided that the section left to the courts "the details by which 'fair value' is to be determined within the broad outlines of the definition." While the logic of the prior Official Comment continues to apply, the exclusionary clause in the prior Model Act definition, including the qualification for cases where the exclusion would be inequitable, has been deleted. Those provisions have not been susceptible to meaningful judicial interpretation and have been set aside in favor of the broader concept in subsection (ii).

The new formulation in paragraph (ii), which is patterned on section 7.22 of the Principles of Corporate Governance promulgated by the American Law Institute, directs courts to keep the methodology chosen in appraisal proceedings consistent with evolving economic concepts and adopts that part of section 7.22 which provides that fair value should be determined using "customary valuation concepts and techniques generally employed ... for similar businesses in the context of the transaction requiring appraisal." Subsection (ii) adopts the accepted view that different transactions and different contexts may warrant different valuation methodologies. Customary valuation concepts and techniques will typically take into account numerous relevant factors, including assigning a higher valuation to corporate assets that would be more productive if acquired in a comparable transaction but excluding any element of value attributable to the unique synergies of the actual purchaser of the corporation or its assets. For example, if the corporation's assets include undeveloped real estate that is located in a prime commercial area, the court should consider the value that would be attributed to the real estate as commercial development property in a comparable transaction. The court should not, however, assign any additional value based upon the specific plans or special use of the actual purchaser.

Modern valuation methods will normally result in a range of values, not a particular single value. When a transaction falls within that range, "fair value" has been established. Absent unusual circumstances, it is expected that the consideration in an arm's-length transaction will fall within the range of "fair value" for purposes of section 13.01(4). Section 7.22 of the ALI Principles of Corporate Governance also provides that in situations that do not involve certain types of specified conflicts of interest, "the aggregate price accepted by the board of directors of the subject corporation should be presumed to represent the fair value of the corporation, or of the assets sold in the case of an asset sale, unless the plaintiff can prove otherwise by clear and convincing evidence." That presumption has not been included in the definition of "fair value" in section 13.01(4) because the framework of defined types of conflict transactions which is a predicate for the ALI's presumption is not contained in the Model Act. Nonetheless, under section 13.01(4), a court determining fair value should give great deference to the aggregate consideration accepted or approved by a disinterested board of directors for an appraisal-triggering transaction.

Subsection (iii) of the definition of "fair value" establishes that valuation discounts for lack of marketability or minority status are inappropriate in most appraisal actions, both because most transactions that trigger appraisal rights affect the corporation as a whole and because such discounts give the majority the opportunity to take advantage of minority shareholders who have been forced against their will to accept the appraisal-triggering transaction. Subsection (iii), in conjunction with the lead-in language to the definition, is also designed to adopt the more modern view that appraisal should generally award a shareholder his or her proportional interest in the corporation after valuing the corporation as a whole, rather than the value of the shareholder's shares when valued alone. If, however, the corporation voluntarily grants appraisal rights for transactions that do not affect the entire corporation—such as certain amendments to the articles of incorporation—the court should use its discretion in applying discounts if appropriate. As the introductory clause of section 13.01 notes, the definition of "fair value" applies only to chapter 13. See the Official Comment to section 14.34 which recognizes that a minority discount may be appropriate under that section.

Interest

The definition of "interest" in section 13.01(5) is included to apprise the parties of their respective rights and obligations. The right to receive interest is based on the elementary consideration that the corporation, rather than the shareholder demanding appraisal, has the use of the shareholder's money from the effective date of the corporate action (when those shareholders who do not demand appraisal rights have the right to receive their consideration from the transaction) until the date of payment. Section 13.01(5) thus requires interest to be paid at the rate of interest on judgments from the effective date of the corporate action until the date of payment. The specification of the rate of interest on judgments, rather than a more subjective rate, eliminates a possible issue of contention and should facilitate voluntary settlements. Each state determines whether interest is compound or simple.

Senior executive

The definition of "senior executive" in section 13.01(8) encompasses the group of individuals in control of corporate information and the day-to-day operations. An employee of a subsidiary organization is a "senior executive" of the parent if the employee is "in charge of a principal business unit or function" of the parent and its subsidiaries on a combined or consolidated basis.

Shareholder

The definition of "shareholder" in section 13.01(9) for purposes of chapter 13 differs from the definition of that term used elsewhere in the Model Act. Section 1.40(21) defines "shareholder" as used generally in the Act to mean only a "record shareholder"; that term is specifically defined in section 13.01(7). Section 13.01(9), on the other hand, defines "shareholder" to include not only a "record shareholder" but also a "beneficial shareholder," a term that is itself defined in section 13.01(2). The specially defined terms "record shareholder" and "beneficial shareholder" appear primarily in section 13.03, which establishes the manner in which beneficial shareholders, and record shareholders who are acting on behalf of beneficial shareholders, perfect appraisal rights. The word "shareholder" is used generally throughout chapter 13 in order to permit both record and beneficial shareholders to take advantage of the provisions of this chapter, subject to their fulfilling the applicable requirements of this chapter.

§ 13.02 Right to Appraisal

(a) A shareholder is entitled to appraisal rights, and to obtain payment of the fair value of that shareholder's shares, in the event of any of the following corporate actions:

(1) consummation of a merger to which the corporation is a party (i) if shareholder approval is required for the merger by section 11.04 and the shareholder is entitled to vote on the merger, except that appraisal rights shall not be available to any shareholder of the corporation with respect to shares of any class or

series that remain outstanding after consummation of the merger, or (ii) if the corporation is a subsidiary and the merger is governed by section 11.05;

(2) consummation of a share exchange to which the corporation is a party as the corporation whose shares will be acquired if the shareholder is entitled to vote on the exchange, except that appraisal rights shall not be available to any shareholder of the corporation with respect to any class or series of shares of the corporation that is not exchanged;

(3) consummation of a disposition of assets pursuant to section 12.02 if the shareholder is entitled to vote on the disposition;

(4) an amendment of the articles of incorporation with respect to a class or series of shares that reduces the number of shares of a class or series owned by the shareholder to a fraction of a share if the corporation has the obligation or right to repurchase the fractional share so created;

(5) any other amendment to the articles of incorporation, merger, share exchange or disposition of assets to the extent provided by the articles of incorporation, bylaws or a resolution of the board of directors;

(6) consummation of a domestication if the shareholder does not receive shares in the foreign corporation resulting from the domestication that have terms as favorable to the shareholder in all material respects, and represent at least the same percentage interest of the total voting rights of the outstanding shares of the corporation, as the shares held by the shareholder before the domestication;

(7) consummation of a conversion of the corporation to nonprofit status pursuant to subchapter 9C; or

(8) consummation of a conversion of the corporation to an unincorporated entity pursuant to subchapter 9E.

(b) Notwithstanding subsection (a), the availability of appraisal rights under subsections (a)(1), (2), (3), (4), (6) and (8) shall be limited in accordance with the following provisions:

(1) Appraisal rights shall not be available for the holders of shares of any class or series of shares which is:

(i) listed on the New York Stock Exchange or the American Stock Exchange or designated as a national market system security on an interdealer quotation system by the National Association of Securities Dealers, Inc.; or

(ii) not so listed or designated, but has at least 2,000 shareholders and the outstanding shares of such class or series has a market value of at least $20 million (exclusive of the value of such shares held by its subsidiaries, senior executives, directors and beneficial shareholders owning more than 10 percent of such shares).

(2) The applicability of subsection (b)(1) shall be determined as of:

(i) the record date fixed to determine the shareholders entitled to receive notice of, and to vote at, the meeting of shareholders to act upon the corporate action requiring appraisal rights; or

(ii) the day before the effective date of such corporate action if there is no meeting of shareholders.

(3) Subsection (b)(1) shall not be applicable and appraisal rights shall be available pursuant to subsection (a) for the holders of any class or series of shares who are required by the terms of the corporate action requiring appraisal rights to accept for such shares anything other than cash or shares of any class or any series of shares of any corporation, or any other proprietary interest of any other entity, that satisfies the standards set forth in subsection (b)(1) at the time the corporate action becomes effective.

(4) Subsection (b)(1) shall not be applicable and appraisal rights shall be available pursuant to subsection (a) for the holders of any class or series of shares where:

(i) any of the shares or assets of the corporation are being acquired or converted, whether by merger, share exchange or otherwise, pursuant to the corporate action by a person, or by an affiliate of a person, who:

(A) is, or at any time in the one-year period immediately preceding approval by the board of directors of the corporate action requiring appraisal rights was, the beneficial owner of 20 percent or more of the voting power of the corporation, excluding any shares acquired pursuant to an offer for all shares having voting power if such offer was made within one year prior to the corporate action requiring appraisal rights for consideration of the same kind and of a value equal to or less than that paid in connection with the corporate action; or

(B) directly or indirectly has, or at any time in the one-year period immediately preceding approval by the board of directors of the corporation of the corporate action requiring appraisal rights had, the power, contractually or otherwise, to cause the appointment or election of 25 percent or more of the directors to the board of directors of the corporation; or

(ii) any of the shares or assets of the corporation are being acquired or converted, whether by merger, share exchange or otherwise, pursuant to such corporate action by a person, or by an affiliate of a person, who is, or at any time in the one-year period immediately preceding approval by the board of directors of the corporate action requiring appraisal rights was, a senior executive or director of the corporation or a senior executive of any affiliate thereof, and that senior executive or director will receive, as a result of the corporate action, a financial benefit not generally available to other shareholders as such, other than:

(A) employment, consulting, retirement or similar benefits established separately and not as part of or in contemplation of the corporate action; or

(B) employment, consulting, retirement or similar benefits established in contemplation of, or as part of, the corporate action that are not more favorable than those existing before the corporate action or, if more favorable, that have been approved on behalf of the corporation in the same manner as is provided in section 8.62; or

(C) in the case of a director of the corporation who will, in the corporate action, become a director of the acquiring entity in the corporate action or one of its affiliates, rights and benefits as a director that are provided on the same basis as those afforded by the acquiring entity generally to other directors of such entity or such affiliate.

(5) For the purposes of paragraph (4) only, the term "beneficial owner" means any person who, directly or indirectly, through any contract, arrangement, or understanding, other than a revocable proxy, has or shares the power to vote, or to direct the voting of, shares, provided that a member of a national securities exchange shall not be deemed to be a beneficial owner of securities held directly or indirectly by it on behalf of another person solely because such member is the record holder of such securities if the member is precluded by the rules of such exchange from voting without instruction on contested matters or matters that may affect substantially the rights or privileges of the holders of the securities to be voted. When two or more persons agree to act together for the purpose of voting their shares of the corporation, each member of the group formed thereby shall be deemed to have acquired beneficial ownership, as of the date of such agreement, of all voting shares of the corporation beneficially owned by any member of the group.

(c) Notwithstanding any other provision of section 13.02, the articles of incorporation as originally filed or any amendment thereto may limit or eliminate appraisal rights for any class or series of preferred shares, but any such limitation or elimination contained in an amendment to the articles of incorporation that limits or eliminates appraisal rights for any of such shares that are outstanding immediately prior to the effective date of such amendment or that the corporation is or may be required to issue or sell thereafter pursuant to any conversion, exchange or other right existing immediately before the effective date of such amendment shall not apply to any corporate action that becomes effective within one year of that date if such action would otherwise afford appraisal rights.

(d) A shareholder entitled to appraisal rights under this chapter may not challenge a completed corporate action for which appraisal rights are available unless such corporate action:

(1) was not effectuated in accordance with the applicable provisions of chapters 9, 10, 11 or 12, or the corporation's articles of incorporation, by laws or board of directors' resolution authorizing the corporate action; or

(2) was procured as a result of fraud or material misrepresentation.

OFFICIAL COMMENT

. . . .

2. Market Exception to Appraisal Rights

Chapter 13 provides a limited exception to appraisal rights for those situations where shareholders can either accept the consideration offered in the appraisal-triggering transaction or can obtain the fair value of their shares by selling them in the market. This provision is predicated on the theory that where an efficient market exists, the market price will be an adequate proxy for the fair value of the corporation's shares, thus making appraisal unnecessary. Furthermore, after the corporation announces an appraisal-triggering action, the market operates at maximum efficiency with respect to that corporation's shares because interested parties and market professionals evaluate the offer and competing offers may be generated if the original offer is deemed inadequate. Moreover, the market exception reflects an evaluation that the uncertainty, costs and time commitment involved in any appraisal proceeding are not warranted where shareholders can sell their shares in an efficient, fair and liquid market. For these reasons, approximately half of the states have enacted market exceptions to their appraisal statutes.

For purposes of this chapter, the market exception is provided for a class or series if two criteria are met: the market in which the class or series is traded must be "liquid" and the value of the shares established by the appraisal-triggering event must be "reliable." Liquidity is defined in section 13.02(b)(1) and requires the class or series of stock to satisfy either of two requirements: the class or series is either listed on the New York Stock Exchange or the American Stock Exchange or is designated as a national market system security on an interdealer quotation system by the National Association of Securities Dealers, Inc.; or, although not so listed or designated, the class or series has at least 2,000 record or beneficial shareholders, provided that using both concepts does not result in duplication. In this instance, the outstanding class or series must also have a market value of at least $20 million, excluding the value of shares held by the corporation's subsidiaries, senior executives, directors and beneficial shareholders owning more than 10 percent of the class or series.

Because section 13.02(b)(3) excludes from the market exception those transactions that require shareholders to accept anything other than cash or securities that also meet the liquidity tests of section 13.02(b)(1), shareholders are assured of receiving either appraisal rights, cash from the transaction, or shares or other proprietary interests in the survivor entity that are liquid. Section 13.02(b)(2) provides that the corporation generally must satisfy the requirements of section 13.02(b)(1) on the record date for a shareholder vote on the appraisal-triggering transaction. For purposes of subsection 13.02(a)(1)(ii), the requirements of section 13.02(b)(1) must be met as of the day before the corporate action becomes effective.

3. Appraisal Rights in Conflict Transactions

The premise of the market exception is that the market must be liquid and the valuation assigned to the relevant shares must be "reliable." Section 13.02(b)(1) is designed to assure liquidity. For purposes of these provisions, section 13.02(b)(4) is designed to assure reliability by recognizing that the market price of, or consideration for, shares of a corporation that proposes to engage in a section 13.02(a) transaction may be subject to influences where a corporation's management, controlling shareholders or directors have conflicting interests that could, if not dealt with appropriately, adversely affect the consideration that otherwise could have been expected. Section 13.02(b)(4) addresses two groups of conflict transactions: those in clause (i), which involve controlling shareholders; and those in clause (ii), which involve senior executives and directors.

Section 13.02(b)(4)(i) covers two possible conflict situations: subsection (A) covers the acquisition or exchange of shares or assets of the corporation by a shareholder or an affiliate of the shareholder that could be considered controlling by virtue of ownership of a substantial amount of voting stock (20 percent); and subsection (B) covers the acquisition or exchange of shares or assets of the corporation by an individual or group, or by an affiliate of such individual or group, that has the ability to exercise control, through contract, stock ownership, or some other means, over at least one fourth of the board's membership. The definition of "beneficial owner" in section 13.02(b)(5) serves to identify possible conflict situations by deeming each member of a group that agrees to vote in tandem to be a beneficial owner of all the voting shares owned by the group. In contrast, the term "beneficial shareholder," as defined in section 13.01(2), is used to identify those persons entitled to appraisal rights. The last portion of subsection (A) recognizes that an acquisition effected in two steps (a tender offer followed by a merger) within one year, where the two steps are either on the same terms or the second step is on terms that are more favorable to target shareholders, is properly considered a single transaction for purposes of identifying conflict transactions, regardless of whether the second-step merger is governed by sections 11.04 or 11.05.

Section 13.02(b)(4)(ii) covers the acquisition or exchange of shares or assets of the corporation by a person, or an affiliate of a person, who is, or in the year leading up to the transaction was, a senior executive or director of the corporation. The section eliminates the market exception for management buyouts because participation in the buyout group is itself "a financial benefit not available to other shareholders as such." The market exception is also not available for transactions involving other types of economic benefits (in addition to benefits afforded to shareholders generally, as such) afforded to senior executives (as defined in section 13.01(8)) and directors in specified conflict situations, unless specific objective or procedural standards are met. Section 13.01(1) specially defines the term "affiliate" for purposes of section 13.02(b)(4) to include an entity of which a person is a senior executive. Due to this specialized definition, if a senior executive of the corporation is to continue and is to receive enumerated employment and other financial benefits after the transaction, the availability of the market exception will depend on meeting one of the three conditions specified in clauses (A), (B) and (C) of section 13.02(b)(4)(ii).

First, under section 13.02(b)(4)(ii)(A), the market exception is not lost if financial benefits that result from the transaction consist of employment, consulting, retirement or similar benefits established separately and not in contemplation of the transaction. For example, if an individual has an arrangement under which benefits will be triggered on a "change of control," such as accelerated vesting of options, retirement benefits, deferred compensation and similar items, or is afforded the opportunity to retire or leave the employ of the enterprise with more favorable economic results than would be the case absent a change of control, the existence of these arrangements would not disqualify the transaction from the market exception if the arrangements had been established as a general condition of the individual's employment or continued employment, rather than in contemplation of the particular transaction. Second, under section 13.02(b)(4)(ii)(B), if such arrangements are established as part of, or as a condition of, the transaction, the market exception will not be lost if the arrangements are either not more favorable than those already in existence or, if more favorable, are approved by "qualified" directors (*i.e.*, meeting the standard of independence specified in section 8.62(d)), in the same manner as is provided for conflicting interest transactions generally with the corporation under section 8.62. This category would include arrangements with the corporation which have been negotiated as part of, or as a condition of, the transaction or arrangements with the acquiring company or one or more of its other subsidiaries. The third situation, delineated in section 13.02(b)(4)(ii)(C), addresses a person who is a director of the issuer and, in connection with the transaction, is to become a director of the acquiring entity or its parent, or to continue as a director of the corporation when it becomes a subsidiary of the acquiring entity. In this situation, the market exception is not lost as long as that person will not be treated more favorably as a director than are other persons who are serving in the same director positions.

. . . .

5. Exclusivity of Appraisal Rights

With two exceptions, section 13.02(d) provides that the appraisal is the exclusive remedy for corporate action that has been completed. The theory underlying this section is that when a majority of shareholders has approved a corporate change, the corporation should be permitted to proceed even if a minority considers the change unwise or disadvantageous. The very existence of the appraisal remedy recognizes that shareholders may disagree about the value of consequences of a corporate action and that some may hold such strong views that they will want to vindicate them in a judicial proceeding. Since a judicial proceeding is insulated from the dynamics of an actual negotiation, it is not surprising that the two processes could produce different valuations. Accordingly, if such a proceeding results in an award of additional consideration to the shareholders who pursued appraisal, no inference should be drawn that the judgment of the majority was wrong or that compensation is now owed to shareholders who did not seek appraisal. Thus, an exclusivity principle is generally justified. Nevertheless, there may be exceptional circumstances where the process by which the corporate action was approved was so flawed that it is appropriate to provide more general relief on behalf of all affected shareholders. Thus, section 13.02(d)(1) does not preclude challenges to serious procedural defects in approving the action, such as a failure to obtain the votes required by statute or by the corporation's own articles, bylaws, or board resolution authorizing the transaction. Similarly, subsection (2) creates an exception for cases where fraud or material misrepresentation have affected the shareholder vote to such an extent as to have caused the corporate action to be approved mistakenly. The concept of misrepresentation includes the omission of a material fact necessary to make statements made not misleading.

Although section 13.02(d) does not address the question of remedies, such as injunctive relief, that may be available before the corporate action is effected, it should be noted that a complaint based solely on adequacy of consideration is not actionable unless accompanied by credible allegations of wrongdoing. Section 13.02(d) is concerned with challenges only to the corporate action and does not address remedies, if any, that shareholders may have against directors or other persons as a result of the corporate action. See section 8.31 and Official Comment.

§ 13.03 Assertion of Rights by Nominees and Beneficial Owners

(a) A record shareholder may assert appraisal rights as to fewer than all the shares registered in the record shareholder's name but owned by a beneficial shareholder only if the record shareholder objects with respect to all shares of the class or series owned by the beneficial shareholder and notifies the corporation in writing of the name and address of each beneficial shareholder on whose behalf appraisal rights are being asserted. The rights of a record shareholder who asserts appraisal rights for only part of the shares held of record in the record shareholder's name under this subsection shall be determined as if the shares as to which the record shareholder objects and the record shareholder's other shares were registered in the names of different record shareholders.

(b) A beneficial shareholder may assert appraisal rights as to shares of any class or series held on behalf of the shareholder only if such shareholder:

(1) submits to the corporation the record shareholder's written consent to the assertion of such rights no later than the date referred to in section 13.22(b)(2)(ii); and

(2) does so with respect to all shares of the class or series that are beneficially owned by the beneficial shareholder.

Subchapter B. Procedure for Exercise of Appraisal Rights

§ 13.20 Notice of Appraisal Rights

(a) If proposed corporate action described in section 13.02(a) is to be submitted to a vote at a shareholders' meeting, the meeting notice must state that the corporation has concluded that shareholders are, are not or may be entitled to assert appraisal rights under this chapter. If the corporation concludes that appraisal rights are or may be available, a copy of this chapter must accompany the meeting notice sent to those record shareholders entitled to exercise appraisal rights.

(b) In a merger pursuant to section 11.05, the parent corporation must notify in writing all record shareholders of the subsidiary who are entitled to assert appraisal rights that the corporate action became effective. Such notice must be sent within ten days after the corporate action became effective and include the materials described in section 13.22.

§ 13.21 Notice of Intent to Demand Payment

(a) If proposed corporate action requiring appraisal rights under section 13.02 is submitted to a vote at a shareholders' meeting, a shareholder who wishes to assert appraisal rights with respect to any class or series of shares:

(1) must deliver to the corporation before the vote is taken written notice of the shareholder's intent to demand payment if the proposed action is effectuated; and

(2) must not vote, or cause or permit to be voted, any shares of such class or series in favor of the proposed action.

(b) A shareholder who does not satisfy the requirements of subsection (a) is not entitled to payment under this chapter.

§ 13.22 Appraisal Notice and Form

(a) If proposed corporate action requiring appraisal rights under section 13.02(a) becomes effective, the corporation must deliver a written appraisal notice and form required by subsection (b)(1) to all shareholders who satisfied the requirements of section 13.21. In the case of a merger under section 11.05, the parent must deliver a written appraisal notice and form to all record shareholders who may be entitled to assert appraisal rights.

(b) The appraisal notice must be sent no earlier than the date the corporate action became effective and no later than ten days after such date and must:

(1) supply a form that specifies the date of the first announcement to shareholders of the principal terms of the proposed corporate action and requires the shareholder asserting appraisal rights to certify (i) whether or not beneficial ownership of those shares for which appraisal rights are asserted was acquired before that date and (ii) that the shareholder did not vote for the transaction;

(2) state:

(i) where the form must be sent and where certificates for certificated shares must be deposited and the date by which those certificates must be deposited, which date may not be earlier than the date for receiving the required form under subsection (2)(ii);

(ii) a date by which the corporation must receive the form which date may not be fewer than 40 nor more than 60 days after the date the subsection (a) appraisal notice and form are sent, and state that the shareholder shall have waived the right to demand appraisal with respect to the shares unless the form is received by the corporation by such specified date;

(iii) the corporation's estimate of the fair value of the shares;

(iv) that, if requested in writing, the corporation will provide, to the shareholder so requesting, within ten days after the date specified in subsection (2)(ii) the number of shareholders who return the forms by the specified date and the total number of shares owned by them; and

(v) the date by which the notice to withdraw under section 13.23 must be received, which date must be within 20 days after the date specified in subsection (2)(ii); and

(3) be accompanied by a copy of this chapter.

§ 13.23 Perfection of Rights; Right to Withdraw

(a) A shareholder who receives notice pursuant to section 13.22 and who wishes to exercise appraisal rights must certify on the form sent by the corporation whether the beneficial owner of such shares acquired beneficial ownership of the shares before the date required to be set forth in the notice pursuant to section 13.22(b)(1). If a shareholder fails to make this certification, the corporation may elect to treat the shareholder's shares as after-acquired shares under section 13.25. In addition, a shareholder who wishes to exercise appraisal rights must execute and return the form and, in the case of certificated shares, deposit the shareholder's certificates in accordance with the terms of the notice by the date referred to in the notice pursuant to section 13.22(b)(2)(ii). Once a shareholder deposits that shareholder's certificates or, in the case of uncertificated shares, returns the executed forms, that shareholder loses all rights as a shareholder, unless the shareholder withdraws pursuant to subsection (b).

(b) A shareholder who has complied with subsection (a) may nevertheless decline to exercise appraisal rights and withdraw from the appraisal process by so notifying the corporation in writing by the date set forth in the appraisal notice pursuant to section 13.22(b)(2)(v). A shareholder who fails to so withdraw from the appraisal process may not thereafter withdraw without the corporation's written consent.

(c) A shareholder who does not execute and return the form and, in the case of certificated shares, deposit that shareholder's share certificates where required, each by the date set forth in the notice described in section 13.22(b), shall not be entitled to payment under this chapter.

§ 13.24 Payment

(a) Except as provided in section 13.25, within 30 days after the form required by section 13.22(b)(2)(ii) is due, the corporation shall pay in cash to those shareholders who complied with section 13.23(a) the amount the corporation estimates to be the fair value of their shares, plus interest.

(b) The payment to each shareholder pursuant to subsection (a) must be accompanied by:

(1) financial statements of the corporation that issued the shares to be appraised, consisting of a balance sheet as of the end of a fiscal year ending not more than 16 months before the date of payment, an income statement for that year, a statement of changes in shareholders' equity for that year, and the latest available interim financial statements, if any;

(2) a statement of the corporation's estimate of the fair value of the shares, which estimate must equal or exceed the corporation's estimate given pursuant to section 13.22(b)(2)(iii);

(3) a statement that shareholders described in subsection (a) have the right to demand further payment under section 13.26 and that if any such shareholder does not do so within the time period specified therein, such shareholder shall be deemed to have accepted such payment in full satisfaction of the corporation's obligations under this chapter.

§ 13.25 After–Acquired Shares

(a) A corporation may elect to withhold payment required by section 13.24 from any shareholder who did not certify that beneficial ownership of all of the shareholder's shares for which appraisal rights are asserted was acquired before the date set forth in the appraisal notice sent pursuant to section 13.22(b)(1).

(b) If the corporation elected to withhold payment under subsection (a), it must, within 30 days after the form required by section 13.22(b)(2)(ii) is due, notify all shareholders who are described in subsection (a):

(1) of the information required by section 13.24(b)(1);

(2) of the corporation's estimate of fair value pursuant to section 13.24(b)(2);

(3) that they may accept the corporation's estimate of fair value, plus interest, in full satisfaction of their demands or demand appraisal under section 13.26;

(4) that those shareholders who wish to accept such offer must so notify the corporation of their acceptance of the corporation's offer within 30 days after receiving the offer; and

(5) that those shareholders who do not satisfy the requirements for demanding appraisal under section 13.26 shall be deemed to have accepted the corporation's offer.

(c) Within ten days after receiving the shareholder's acceptance pursuant to subsection (b), the corporation must pay in cash the amount it offered under subsection (b)(2) to each shareholder who agreed to accept the corporation's offer in full satisfaction of the shareholder's demand.

(d) Within 40 days after sending the notice described in subsection (b), the corporation must pay in cash the amount it offered to pay under subsection (b)(2) to each shareholder described in subsection (b)(5).

§ 13.26 Procedure if Shareholder Dissatisfied with Payment or Offer

(a) A shareholder paid pursuant to section 13.24 who is dissatisfied with the amount of the payment must notify the corporation in writing of that shareholder's estimate of the fair value of the shares and demand payment of that estimate plus interest (less any payment under section 13.24). A shareholder offered payment under section 13.25 who is dissatisfied with that offer must reject the offer and demand payment of the shareholder's stated estimate of the fair value of the shares plus interest.

(b) A shareholder who fails to notify the corporation in writing of that shareholder's demand to be paid the shareholder's stated estimate of the fair value plus interest under subsection (a) within 30 days after receiving the corporation's payment or offer of payment under section 13.24 or section 13.25, respectively, waives the right to demand payment under this section and shall be entitled only to the payment made or offered pursuant to those respective sections.

Subchapter C. Judicial Appraisal of Shares

§ 13.30 Court Action

(a) If a shareholder makes demand for payment under section 13.26 which remains unsettled, the corporation shall commence a proceeding within 60 days after receiving the payment demand and petition the court to determine the fair value of the shares and accrued interest. If the corporation does not commence the proceeding within the 60–day period, it shall pay in cash to each shareholder the amount the shareholder demanded pursuant to section 13.26 plus interest.

(b) The corporation shall commence the proceeding in the appropriate court of the county where the corporation's principal office (or, if none, its registered office) in this state is located. If the corporation is a foreign corporation without a registered office in this state, it shall commence the proceeding in the county in this state where the principal office or registered office of the domestic corporation merged with the foreign corporation was located at the time of the transaction.

(c) The corporation shall make all shareholders (whether or not residents of this state) whose demands remain unsettled parties to the proceeding as in an action against their shares, and all parties must be served with a copy of the petition. Nonresidents may be served by registered or certified mail or by publication as provided by law.

(d) The jurisdiction of the court in which the proceeding is commenced under subsection (b) is plenary and exclusive. The court may appoint one or more persons as appraisers to receive evidence and recommend a decision on the question of fair value. The appraisers shall have the powers described in the order appointing them, or in any amendment to it. The shareholders demanding appraisal rights are entitled to the same discovery rights as parties in other civil proceedings. There shall be no right to a jury trial.

(e) Each shareholder made a party to the proceeding is entitled to judgment (i) for the amount, if any, by which the court finds the fair value of the shareholder's shares, plus interest, exceeds the amount paid by the corporation to the shareholder for such shares or (ii) for the fair value, plus interest, of the shareholder's shares for which the corporation elected to withhold payment under section 13.25.

§ 13.31 Court Costs and Counsel Fees

(a) The court in an appraisal proceeding commenced under section 13.30 shall determine all costs of the proceeding, including the reasonable compensation and expenses of appraisers appointed by the court. The court shall assess the costs against the corporation, except that the court may assess costs against all or some of the shareholders demanding appraisal, in amounts the court finds equitable, to the extent the court finds such shareholders acted arbitrarily, vexatiously, or not in good faith with respect to the rights provided by this chapter.

(b) The court in an appraisal proceeding may also assess the fees and expenses of counsel and experts for the respective parties, in amounts the court finds equitable:

(1) against the corporation and in favor of any or all shareholders demanding appraisal if the court finds the corporation did not substantially comply with the requirements of sections 13.20, 13.22, 13.24 or 13.25; or

(2) against either the corporation or a shareholder demanding appraisal, in favor of any other party, if the court finds that the party against whom the fees and expenses are assessed acted arbitrarily, vexatiously, or not in good faith with respect to the rights provided by this chapter.

(c) If the court in an appraisal proceeding finds that the services of counsel for any shareholder were of substantial benefit to other shareholders similarly situated, and that the fees for those services should not be assessed against the corporation, the court may award to such counsel reasonable fees to be paid out of the amounts awarded the shareholders who were benefitted.

(d) To the extent the corporation fails to make a required payment pursuant to sections 13.24, 13.25, or 13.26, the shareholder may sue directly for the amount owed and, to the extent successful, shall be entitled to recover from the corporation all costs and expenses of the suit, including counsel fees.

CHAPTER 14

DISSOLUTION

Subchapter A. Voluntary Dissolution

§ 14.01 Dissolution by Incorporators or Initial Directors

A majority of the incorporators or initial directors of a corporation that has not issued shares or has not commenced business may dissolve the corporation by delivering to the secretary of state of state for filing articles of dissolution that set forth:

(1) the name of the corporation;

(2) the date of its incorporation;

(3) either (i) that none of the corporation's shares has been issued or (ii) that the corporation has not commenced business;

(4) that no debt of the corporation remains unpaid;

(5) that the net assets of the corporation remaining after winding up have been distributed to the shareholders, if shares were issued; and

(6) that a majority of the incorporators or initial directors authorized the dissolution.

§ 14.02 Dissolution by Board of Directors and Shareholders

(a) A corporation's board of directors may propose dissolution for submission to the shareholders.

(b) For a proposal to dissolve to be adopted:

(1) the board of directors must recommend dissolution to the shareholders unless the board of directors determines that because of conflict of interest or other special circumstances it should make no recommendation and communicates the basis for its determination to the shareholders; and

(2) the shareholders entitled to vote must approve the proposal to dissolve as provided in subsection (e).

(c) The board of directors may condition its submission of the proposal for dissolution on any basis.

(d) The corporation shall notify each shareholder, whether or not entitled to vote, of the proposed shareholders' meeting. The notice must also state that the purpose, or one of the purposes, of the meeting is to consider dissolving the corporation.

(e) Unless the articles of incorporation or the board of directors acting pursuant to subsection (c) require a greater vote, a greater number of shares to be present, or a vote by voting groups, adoption of the proposal to dissolve shall require the approval of the shareholders at a meeting at which a quorum consisting of at least a majority of the votes entitled to be cast exists.

OFFICIAL COMMENT

Section 14.02(b) requires the board of directors, after approving a proposal to dissolve, to submit the proposal to the shareholders for their approval. When submitting the proposal the board of directors must make a recommendation to the shareholders that the plan be approved, unless the board of directors makes a determination that because of conflicts of interest or other special circumstances it should make no recommendation. For example, the board or directors may make such a determination where there is not a sufficient number of directors free of a conflicting interest to approve the proposal or because the board of directors is evenly divided as to the merits of the proposal but is able to agree that shareholders should be permitted to consider dissolution. If the board of directors makes such a determination, it must describe the conflict of interest or special circumstances, and communicate the basis for the determination, when submitting the proposal to dissolve to the shareholders. The exception for conflicts of interest or other special circumstances is intended to be sparingly available. Generally, shareholders should not be asked to act on a proposal for dissolution in the absence of a recommendation by the board of directors. The exception is not intended to relieve the board of directors of its duty to consider carefully the proposed dissolution and the interests of shareholders.

Section 14.02(c) permits the board of directors to condition its submission of a proposal for dissolution on any basis. Among the conditions that a board might impose are that the proposal will not be deemed approved unless it is approved by a specified vote of the shareholders, or by one or more specified classes or series of shares, voting as a separate voting group, or by a specified percentage of disinterested shareholders. The board of directors is not limited to conditions of these types.

Section 14.02(d) provides that if the proposal is required to be approved by the shareholders, and if the approval is to be given at a meeting, the corporation must notify each shareholder, whether or not entitled to vote, of the meeting of shareholders at which the proposal is to be submitted. Requirements concerning the timing and content of a notice of meeting are set out in section 7.05. Section 14.02(d) does not itself require that notice be given to nonvoting shareholders where the proposal is approved, without a meeting, by unanimous consent. However, that requirement is imposed by section 7.04(d).

Section 14.02(e) provides that approval of a proposal for dissolution requires approval of the shareholders at a meeting at which a quorum consisting of a majority of the votes entitled to be cast on the proposal exists. If a quorum is present, then under sections 7.25 and 7.26 the proposal will be approved if more votes are cast in favor of the proposal than against it by the voting group or separate voting groups entitled to vote on the proposal. This represents a change from the Act's previous voting rule for dissolution, which required approval by a majority of outstanding shares.

The Act does not mandate separate voting by voting groups or appraisal rights in relation to dissolution proposals on the theory that, upon dissolution, the rights or all classes or series of shares are fixed by the articles of incorporation. Of course, group voting rights may be conferred by the articles of incorporation or by the board of directors, acting pursuant to subsection (c).

§ 14.03 Articles of Dissolution

(a) At any time after dissolution is authorized, the corporation may dissolve by delivering to the secretary of state for filing articles of dissolution setting forth:

  (1) the name of the corporation;

  (2) the date dissolution was authorized; and

  (3) if dissolution was approved by the shareholders, a statement that the proposal to dissolve was duly approved by the shareholders in the manner required by this Act and by the articles of incorporation.

(b) A corporation is dissolved upon the effective date of its articles of dissolution.

(c) For purposes of this subchapter, "dissolved corporation" means a corporation whose articles of dissolution have become effective and includes a successor entity to which the remaining assets of the corporation are transferred subject to its liabilities for purposes of liquidation.

§ 14.04 Revocation of Dissolution

(a) A corporation may revoke its dissolution within 120 days of its effective date.

(b) Revocation of dissolution must be authorized in the same manner as the dissolution was authorized unless that authorization permitted revocation by action of the board of directors alone, in which event the board of directors may revoke the dissolution without shareholder action.

(c) After the revocation of dissolution is authorized, the corporation may revoke the dissolution by delivering to the secretary of state for filing articles of revocation of dissolution, together with a copy of its articles of dissolution, that set forth:

(1) the name of the corporation;

(2) the effective date of the dissolution that was revoked;

(3) the date that the revocation of dissolution was authorized;

(4) if the corporation's board of directors (or incorporators) revoked the dissolution, a statement to that effect;

(5) if the corporation's board of directors revoked a dissolution authorized by the shareholders, a statement that revocation was permitted by action by the board of directors alone pursuant to that authorization; and

(6) if shareholder action was required to revoke the dissolution, the information required by section 14.03(a) (3).

(d) Revocation of dissolution is effective upon the effective date of the articles of revocation of dissolution.

(e) When the revocation of dissolution is effective, it relates back to and takes effect as of the effective date of the dissolution and the corporation resumes carrying on its business as if dissolution had never occurred.

§ 14.05 Effect of Dissolution

(a) A dissolved corporation continues its corporate existence but may not carry on any business except that appropriate to wind up and liquidate its business and affairs, including:

(1) collecting its assets;

(2) disposing of its properties that will not be distributed in kind to its shareholders;

(3) discharging or making provision for discharging its liabilities;

(4) distributing its remaining property among its shareholders according to their interests; and

(5) doing every other act necessary to wind up and liquidate its business and affairs.

(b) Dissolution of a corporation does not:

(1) transfer title to the corporation's property;

(2) prevent transfer of its shares or securities, although the authorization to dissolve may provide for closing the corporation's share transfer records;

(3) subject its directors or officers to standards of conduct different from those prescribed in chapter 8;

(4) change quorum or voting requirements for its board of directors or shareholders; change provisions for selection, resignation, or removal of its directors or officers or both; or change provisions for amending its bylaws;

(5) prevent commencement of a proceeding by or against the corporation in its corporate name;

(6) abate or suspend a proceeding pending by or against the corporation on the effective date of dissolution; or

(7) terminate the authority of the registered agent of the corporation.

§ 14.06 Known Claims Against Dissolved Corporation

(a) A dissolved corporation may dispose of the known claims against it by notifying its known claimants in writing of the dissolution at any time after its effective date.

(b) The written notice must:

(1) describe information that must be included in a claim;

(2) provide a mailing address where a claim may be sent;

(3) state the deadline, which may not be fewer than 120 days from the effective date of the written notice, by which the dissolved corporation must receive the claim; and

(4) state that the claim will be barred if not received by the deadline.

(c) A claim against the dissolved corporation is barred:

(1) if a claimant who was given written notice under subsection (b) does not deliver the claim to the dissolved corporation by the deadline; or

(2) if a claimant whose claim was rejected by the dissolved corporation does not commence a proceeding to enforce the claim within 90 days from the effective date of the rejection notice.

(d) For purposes of this section, "claim" does not include a contingent liability or a claim based on an event occurring after the effective date of dissolution.

§ 14.07 Other Claims Against Dissolved Corporation

(a) A dissolved corporation may also publish notice of its dissolution and request that persons with claims against the dissolved corporation present them in accordance with the notice.

(b) The notice must:

(1) be published one time in a newspaper of general circulation in the county where the dissolved corporation's principal office (or, if none in this state, its registered office) is or was last located;

(2) describe the information that must be included in a claim and provide a mailing address where the claim may be sent; and

(3) state that a claim against the dissolved corporation will be barred unless a proceeding to enforce the claim is commenced within three years after the publication of the notice.

(c) If the dissolved corporation publishes a newspaper notice in accordance with subsection (b), the claim of each of the following claimants is barred unless the claimant commences a proceeding to enforce the claim against the dissolved corporation within three years after the publication date of the newspaper notice:

(1) a claimant who was not given written notice under section 14.06;

(2) a claimant whose claim was timely sent to the dissolved corporation but not acted on;

(3) a claimant whose claim is contingent or based on an event occurring after the effective date of dissolution.

(d) A claim that is not barred by section 14.06(c) or section 14.07(c) may be enforced:

(1) against the dissolved corporation, to the extent of its undistributed assets; or

(2) except as provided in section 14.08(d), if the assets have been distributed in liquidation, against a shareholder of the dissolved corporation to the extent of the shareholder's pro rata share of the claim or the corporate assets distributed to the shareholder in liquidation, whichever is less, but a shareholder's total liability for all claims under this section may not exceed the total amount of assets distributed to the shareholder.

§ 14.08 Court Proceedings

(a) A dissolved corporation that has published a notice under section 14.07 may file an application with the [name or describe] court of the county where the dissolved corporation's principal office (or, if none in this state, its registered office) is located for a determination of the amount and form of security to be provided for payment of claims that are contingent or have not been made known to the dissolved corporation or that are based on an event occurring after the effective date of dissolution but that, based on the facts known to the dissolved corporation, are reasonably estimated to arise after the effective date of dissolution. Provision need not be made for any claim that is or is reasonably anticipated to be barred under section 14.07(c).

(b) Within 10 days after the filing of the application, notice of the proceeding shall be given by the dissolved corporation to each claimant holding a contingent claim whose contingent claim is shown on the records of the dissolved corporation.

(c) The court may appoint a guardian ad litem to represent all claimants whose identities are unknown in any proceeding brought under this section. The reasonable fees and expenses of such guardian, including all reasonable expert witness fees, shall be paid by the dissolved corporation.

(d) Provision by the dissolved corporation for security in the amount and the form ordered by the court under section 14.08(a) shall satisfy the dissolved corporation's obligations with respect to claims that are contingent, have not been made known to the dissolved corporation or are based on an event occurring after the effective date of dissolution, and such claims may not be enforced against a shareholder who received assets in liquidation.

§ 14.09 Director Duties

(a) Directors shall cause the dissolved corporation to discharge or make reasonable provision for the payment of claims and make distributions of assets to shareholders after payment or provision for claims.

(b) Directors of a dissolved corporation which has disposed of claims under sections 14.06, 14.07, or 14.08 shall not be liable for breach of section 14.09(a) with respect to claims against the dissolved corporation that are barred or satisfied under sections 14.06, 14.07, or 14.08.

Subchapter B. Administrative Dissolution

§ 14.20 Grounds for Administrative Dissolution

The secretary of state may commence a proceeding under section 14.21 to administratively dissolve a corporation if:

(1) the corporation does not pay within 60 days after they are due any franchise taxes or penalties imposed by this Act or other law;

(2) the corporation does not deliver its annual report to the secretary of state within 60 days after it is due;

(3) the corporation is without a registered agent or registered office in this state for 60 days or more;

(4) the corporation does not notify the secretary of state within 60 days that its registered agent or registered office has been changed, that its registered agent has resigned, or that its registered office has been discontinued; or

(5) the corporation's period of duration stated in its articles of incorporation expires.

§ 14.21 Procedure for and Effect of Administrative Dissolution

(a) If the secretary of state determines that one or more grounds exist under section 14.20 for dissolving a corporation, he shall serve the corporation with written notice of his determination under section 5.04.

(b) If the corporation does not correct each ground for dissolution or demonstrate to the reasonable satisfaction of the secretary of state that each ground determined by the secretary of state does not exist within 60 days after service of the notice is perfected under section 5.04, the secretary of state shall administratively dissolve the corporation by signing a certificate of dissolution that recites the ground or grounds for dissolution and its effective date. The secretary of state shall file the original of the certificate and serve a copy on the corporation under section 5.04.

(c) A corporation administratively dissolved continues its corporate existence but may not carry on any business except that necessary to wind up and liquidate its business and affairs under section 14.05 and notify claimants under sections 14.06 and 14.07.

(d) The administrative dissolution of a corporation does not terminate the authority of its registered agent.

§ 14.22 Reinstatement Following Administrative Dissolution

(a) A corporation administratively dissolved under section 14.21 may apply to the secretary of state for reinstatement within two years after the effective date of dissolution. The application must:

(1) recite the name of the corporation and the effective date of its administrative dissolution;

(2) state that the ground or grounds for dissolution either did not exist or have been eliminated;

(3) state that the corporation's name satisfies the requirements of section 4.01; and

(4) contain a certificate from the [taxing authority] reciting that all taxes owed by the corporation have been paid.

(b) If the secretary of state determines that the application contains the information required by subsection (a) and that the information is correct, he shall cancel the certificate of dissolution and prepare a certificate of reinstatement that recites his determination and the effective date of reinstatement, file the original of the certificate, and serve a copy on the corporation under section 5.04.

(c) When the reinstatement is effective, it relates back to and takes effect as of the effective date of the administrative dissolution and the corporation resumes carrying on its business as if the administrative dissolution had never occurred.

§ 14.23 Appeal From Denial of Reinstatement

(a) If the secretary of state denies a corporation's application for reinstatement following administrative dissolution, he shall serve the corporation under section 5.04 with a written notice that explains the reason or reasons for denial.

(b) The corporation may appeal the denial of reinstatement to the [name or describe] court within 30 days after service of the notice of denial is perfected. The corporation appeals by petitioning the court to set aside the dissolution and attaching to the petition copies of the secretary of state's certificate of dissolution, the corporation's application for reinstatement, and the secretary of state's notice of denial.

(c) The court may summarily order the secretary of state to reinstate the dissolved corporation or may take other action the court considers appropriate.

(d) The court's final decision may be appealed as in other civil proceedings.

Subchapter C. Judicial Dissolution

§ 14.30 Grounds for Judicial Dissolution

The [name or describe court or courts] may dissolve a corporation:

(1) in a proceeding by the attorney general if it is established that:

(i) the corporation obtained its articles of incorporation through fraud; or

(ii) the corporation has continued to exceed or abuse the authority conferred upon it by law;

(2) in a proceeding by a shareholder if it is established that:

(i) the directors are deadlocked in the management of the corporate affairs, the shareholders are unable to break the deadlock, and irreparable injury to the corporation is threatened or being suffered, or the business and affairs of the corporation can no longer be conducted to the advantage of the shareholders generally, because of the deadlock;

(ii) the directors or those in control of the corporation have acted, are acting, or will act in a manner that is illegal, oppressive, or fraudulent;

(iii) the shareholders are deadlocked in voting power and have failed, for a period that includes at least two consecutive annual meeting dates, to elect successors to directors whose terms have expired; or

(iv) the corporate assets are being misapplied or wasted;

(3) in a proceeding by a creditor if it is established that:

(i) the creditor's claim has been reduced to judgment, the execution on the judgment returned unsatisfied, and the corporation is insolvent; or

(ii) the corporation has admitted in writing that the creditor's claim is due and owing and the corporation is insolvent; or

(4) in a proceeding by the corporation to have its voluntary dissolution continued under court supervision.

§ 14.31 Procedure for Judicial Dissolution

(a) Venue for a proceeding by the attorney general to dissolve a corporation lies in [name the county or counties]. Venue for a proceeding brought by any other party named in section 14.30 lies in the county where a corporation's principal office (or, if none in this state, its registered office) is or was last located.

(b) It is not necessary to make shareholders parties to a proceeding to dissolve a corporation unless relief is sought against them individually.

(c) A court in a proceeding brought to dissolve a corporation may issue injunctions, appoint a receiver or custodian pendente lite with all powers and duties the court directs, take other action required to preserve the corporate assets wherever located, and carry on the business of the corporation until a full hearing can be held.

(d) Within 10 days of the commencement of a proceeding under section 14.30(2) to dissolve a corporation that is not a public corporation, the corporation must send to all shareholders, other than the petitioner, a notice stating that the shareholders are entitled to avoid the dissolution of the corporation by electing to purchase the petitioner's shares under section 14.34 and accompanied by a copy of section 14.34.

§ 14.32 Receivership or Custodianship

(a) A court in a judicial proceeding brought to dissolve a corporation may appoint one or more receivers to wind up and liquidate, or one or more custodians to manage, the business and affairs of the corporation. The court shall hold a hearing, after notifying all parties to the proceeding and any interested persons designated by the court, before appointing a receiver or custodian. The court appointing a receiver or custodian has exclusive jurisdiction over the corporation and all of its property wherever located.

(b) The court may appoint an individual or a domestic or foreign corporation (authorized to transact business in this state) as a receiver or custodian. The court may require the receiver or custodian to post bond, with or without sureties, in an amount the court directs.

(c) The court shall describe the powers and duties of the receiver or custodian in its appointing order, which may be amended from time to time. Among other powers:

(1) the receiver (i) may dispose of all or any part of the assets of the corporation wherever located, at a public or private sale, if authorized by the court; and (ii) may sue and defend in his own name as receiver of the corporation in all courts of this state;

(2) the custodian may exercise all of the powers of the corporation, through or in place of its board of directors, to the extent necessary to manage the affairs of the corporation in the best interests of its shareholders and creditors.

(d) The court during a receivership may redesignate the receiver a custodian, and during a custodianship may redesignate the custodian a receiver, if doing so is in the best interests of the corporation, its shareholders, and creditors.

(e) The court from time to time during the receivership or custodianship may order compensation paid and expense disbursements or reimbursements made to the receiver or custodian and his counsel from the assets of the corporation or proceeds from the sale of the assets.

§ 14.33 Decree of Dissolution

(a) If after a hearing the court determines that one or more grounds for judicial dissolution described in section 14.30 exist, it may enter a decree dissolving the corporation and specifying the effective date of the dissolution, and the clerk of the court shall deliver a certified copy of the decree to the secretary of state, who shall file it.

(b) After entering the decree of dissolution, the court shall direct the winding-up and liquidation of the corporation's business and affairs in accordance with section 14.05 and the notification of claimants in accordance with sections 14.06 and 14.07.

§ 14.34 Election to Purchase in Lieu of Dissolution

(a) In a proceeding under section 14.30(2) to dissolve a corporation that is not a public corporation, the corporation may elect or, if it fails to elect, one or more shareholders may elect to purchase all shares owned by the petitioning shareholder at the fair value of the shares. An election pursuant to this section shall be irrevocable unless the court determines that it is equitable to set aside or modify the election.

(b) An election to purchase pursuant to this section may be filed with the court at any time within 90 days after the filing of the petition under section 14.30(2) or at such later time as the court in its discretion may allow. If the election to purchase is filed by one or more shareholders, the corporation shall, within 10 days thereafter, give written notice to all shareholders, other than the petitioner. The notice must state the name and number of shares owned by the petitioner and the name and number of shares owned by each electing shareholder and must advise the recipients of their right to join in the election to purchase shares in accordance with this section. Shareholders who wish to participate must file notice of their intention to join in the purchase no later than 30 days after the effective date of the notice to them. All shareholders who have filed an election or notice of their intention to participate in the election to purchase thereby become parties to the proceeding and shall participate in the purchase in proportion to their ownership of shares as of the date the first election was filed, unless they otherwise agree or the court otherwise directs. After an election has been filed by the corporation or one or more shareholders, the proceeding under section 14.30(2) may not be discontinued or settled, nor may the petitioning shareholder sell or otherwise dispose of his shares, unless the court determines that it would be equitable to the corporation and the shareholders, other than the petitioner, to permit such discontinuance, settlement, sale, or other disposition.

(c) If, within 60 days of the filing of the first election, the parties reach agreement as to the fair value and terms of purchase of the petitioner's shares, the court shall enter an order directing the purchase of petitioner's shares upon the terms and conditions agreed to by the parties.

(d) If the parties are unable to reach an agreement as provided for in subsection (c), the court, upon application of any party, shall stay the section 14.30(2) proceedings and determine the fair value of the petitioner's shares as of the day before the date on which the petition under section 14.30(2) was filed or as of such other date as the court deems appropriate under the circumstances.

(e) Upon determining the fair value of the shares, the court shall enter an order directing the purchase upon such terms and conditions as the court deems appropriate, which may include payment of the purchase price in installments, where necessary in the interests of equity, provision for security to assure payment of the purchase price and any additional costs, fees, and expenses as may have been awarded, and, if the shares are to be purchased by shareholders, the allocation of shares among them. In allocating petitioner's shares among holders of different classes of shares, the court should attempt to preserve the existing distribution of voting rights among holders of different classes insofar as practicable and may direct that holders of a specific class or classes shall not participate in the purchase.

Interest may be allowed at the rate and from the date determined by the court to be equitable, but if the court finds that the refusal of the petitioning shareholder to accept an offer of payment was arbitrary or otherwise not in good faith, no interest shall be allowed. If the court finds that the petitioning shareholder had probable grounds for relief under paragraphs (ii) or (iv) of section 14.30(2), it may award to the petitioning shareholder reasonable fees and expenses of counsel and of any experts employed by him.

(f) Upon entry of an order under subsections (c) or (e), the court shall dismiss the petition to dissolve the corporation under section 14.30, and the petitioning shareholder shall no longer have any rights or status as a shareholder of the corporation, except the right to receive the amounts awarded to him by the order of the court which shall be enforceable in the same manner as any other judgment.

(g) The purchase ordered pursuant to subsection (e) shall be made within 10 days after the date the order becomes final unless before that time the corporation files with the court a notice of its intention to adopt articles of dissolution pursuant to sections 14.02 and 14.03, which articles must then be adopted and filed within 50 days thereafter. Upon filing of such articles of dissolution, the corporation shall be dissolved in accordance with the provisions of sections 14.05 through 14.07, and the order entered pursuant to subsection (e) shall no longer be of any force or effect, except that the court may award the petitioning shareholder reasonable fees and expenses in accordance with the provisions of the last sentence of subsection (e) and the petitioner may continue to pursue any claims previously asserted on behalf of the corporation.

(h) Any payment by the corporation pursuant to an order under subsections (c) or (e), other than an award of fees and expenses pursuant to subsection (e), is subject to the provisions of section 6.40.

OFFICIAL COMMENT

The proceeding for judicial dissolution has become an increasingly important remedy for minority shareholders of closely held corporations who believe that the value of their investment is threatened by reason of circumstances or conduct described in section 14.30(2). If the petitioning shareholder proves one or more grounds under section 14.30(2), he is entitled to some form of relief but many courts have hesitated to award dissolution, the only form of relief explicitly provided, because of its adverse effects on shareholders, employees, and others who may have an interest in the continuation of the business.

Commentators have observed that it is rarely necessary to dissolve the corporation and liquidate its assets in order to provide relief: the rights of the petitioning shareholder are fully protected by liquidating only his interest and paying the fair value of his shares while permitting the remaining shareholders to continue the business. In fact, it appears that most dissolution proceedings result in a buyout of one or another of the disputants' shares either pursuant to a statutory buyout provision or a negotiated settlement. See generally Hetherington & Dooley, "Illiquidity and Exploitation: A Proposed Statutory Solution to the Remaining Close Corporation Problem," 63 VA. L. REV. 1 (1977); Haynsworth, "The Effectiveness of Involuntary Dissolution Suits as a Remedy for Close Corporation Dissension," 35 CLEV. ST. L. REV. 25 (1987). Accordingly, section 14.34 affords an orderly procedure by which a dissolution proceeding under section 14.30(2) can be terminated upon payment of the fair value of the petitioner's shares.

1. Availability

There are three prerequisites to filing an election to purchase under section 14.34. First, a proceeding to dissolve the corporation under section 14.30(2) must have been commenced. Second, the corporation must not be a public corporation as defined in section 1.40(18A). Finally, the election may be made only by the corporation or by shareholders other than the shareholder who is seeking to dissolve the corporation under section 14.30(2).

As a practical matter, the remedy of judicial dissolution under section 14.30(2) is appropriate only for shareholders of closely held firms who have no ready market for their shares. Shareholders of publicly traded firms are protected by their right to sell out if they are dissatisfied with current management or they may seek traditional remedies for breach of fiduciary duty. In contrast, a resort to litigation may result in an irreparable breach of personal relationships among the shareholders of a closely held firm, making it impossible for them to continue in business to their mutual advantage.

2. Effect of Filing

The election to purchase is wholly voluntary, but it can be made as a matter of right within 90 days after the filing of the petition under section 14.30(2). After 90 days, leave of court is required. Once an election is filed:

(i) the election is irrevocable and may not be set aside or modified (as to one or more parties) unless the court determines it is equitable to do so; and

(ii) the dissolution proceeding under section 14.30(2) may not be discontinued or settled and the petitioning shareholder may not dispose of his shares without court approval.

These provisions are intended to reduce the risk that either the dissolution proceeding or the buyout election will be used for strategic purposes. For example, the Official Comment to section 14.30 cautions courts to distinguish between dissolution petitions predicated on "genuine abuse" and those brought for other reasons. Section 14.34 makes strategic use of section 14.30(2) a high-risk proposition for the petitioning shareholder because his shares are, in effect, subject to a "call" for 90 days after commencement of the section 14.30(2) proceeding. The petitioner becomes irrevocably committed to sell his shares pursuant to section 14.34 once an election is filed and may not thereafter discontinue the dissolution proceeding or dispose of his shares outside of section 14.34 without permission of the court, which is specifically directed to consider whether such action would be equitable from the standpoint of the corporation and the other shareholders.

By the same token, if the corporation or the other shareholders fail to elect to purchase the petitioner's shares within the first 90 days, they run the risk that the court will decline to accept a subsequent election and will, instead, allow the dissolution proceeding to go forward. Note also that the dissolution proceeding is not affected by the mere filing of an election; it will be stayed only upon application to the court to determine the fair value of the petitioner's shares after the expiration of the 60–day negotiating period provided for in section 14.34(c).

Once an election is filed, it may be set aside or modified only for reasons that the court finds equitable. If the court sets aside the election, the corporation or the electing shareholders are released from their obligation to purchase the petitioner's shares. Under section 14.34(a), the court also has discretion to "modify" the election by releasing one or more electing shareholders without releasing the others.

3. Election by Corporation or Shareholders

Any change in the allocation of shareholdings in a closely held corporation may upset control or other arrangements that have been previously negotiated by the parties. It is therefore desirable that the purchase of petitioner's shares under section 14.34 be made in ways that are least disruptive of existing arrangements. Accordingly, an election by the corporation is given preference during the 90–day period provided for in section 14.34(b). This preference does not affect the order of filing, and any shareholder may file an election (thus triggering the provisions of subsection (b)) as soon as the dissolution proceeding is commenced. If the corporation thereafter files an election within the 90–day period, its election takes precedence over any previously filed election by shareholders. An election by the corporation after 90 days may be filed only with the court's approval and would not be entitled to the same preemptive weight. Section 14.34 does not affect an agreement between the corporation and the other shareholders to participate jointly in the purchase of the petitioner's shares.

Concern over preserving existing control arrangements makes it inadvisable to extend purchase rights to holders of shares that have only preferential rights to distributions or assets but do not have any right to vote (other than as provided by law). On the other hand, control arrangements are not disturbed if shareholders having voting rights elect to purchase nonvoting shares of a petitioning shareholder, and such elections are permitted. If the election to purchase is made by one or more shareholders, section 14.34(b) requires the corporation to notify all other shareholders of their right to join in the purchase "in proportion to their ownership of shares as of the date the first election was filed." This raises the question of whether shareholders of a class different from the class of shares owned by the petitioner may participate in the purchase. Given the wide variety of capital structures adopted by closely held corporations, it is not possible to state a general rule that would be appropriate in all cases. Any allocation that is agreed to by the electing shareholders controls regardless of whether the other terms and conditions of the purchase are set by the parties' agreement pursuant to subsection (c) or are determined by the court pursuant to subsection (e). If electing shareholders cannot agree, the court, under subsection (e), must determine an allocation.

In making this determination, the court should be guided by the desirability of preserving existing arrangements, so far as that is practicable. Accordingly, holders of shares that carry lesser voting rights than the class owned by the petitioner ordinarily should not be permitted to participate pro rata in the purchase, whereas pro rata participation normally would be appropriate for those persons who own shares of a class having voting rights equivalent to those of the class owned by the petitioner. For example, suppose the corporation's articles provide for a five-member board of directors, with three directors to be elected by Class A and two by Class B. The fact that the two classes have been given separate representation on the board of directors strongly suggests the existence of important differences in interest between them. If the petitioning shareholder owns Class B shares, an election to purchase may be filed by any holder of Class A or Class B under subsection (a), and under subsection (b) notice must be given to all other members of each class and any member of either class may file an election to join in the purchase. If no holder of Class B has elected to purchase, the petitioner's Class B shares should be allocated among the electing holders of Class A, in proportion to their holdings of Class A. If one or more holders of Class B has filed an election, however, the court should allocate all of the petitioner's shares to the electing Class B holders unless the parties otherwise agree.

Ordinarily, there is no reason to prohibit interclass purchases where the classes differ only in their economic attributes and voting control is not in issue. Accordingly, the court should permit common shareholders to participate in the purchase of the petitioner's nonvoting preferred shares unless the economic attributes of the preferred are clearly material to some other arrangement that has been worked out among the parties. This would be the case, for example, where the preferred is held by members of a family group and has dissolution rights providing for the distribution of unique assets such as real estate. In that case, it would be inappropriate to permit common shareholders to participate in the purchase of petitioner's preferred stock even though voting control of the corporation would not be affected.

4. Court Order

a. Voluntary agreement

All shareholders who file an election are joined as parties pursuant to subsection (b). If the parties come to terms within the 60–day negotiating period provided for in subsection (c), their agreement will be incorporated in an order of the court and will thereafter be enforceable as such.

b. Terms set by court

If the parties are unable to reach agreement, any or all terms of the purchase may be set by the court under subsection (d). Section 14.34 does not specify the components of "fair value," and the court may find it useful to consider valuation methods that would be relevant to a judicial appraisal of shares under section 13.30. The two proceedings are not wholly analogous, however, and the court should consider all relevant facts and circumstances of the particular case in determining fair value. For example, liquidating value may be relevant in cases of deadlock but an inappropriate measure in other cases. If the court finds that the value of the corporation has been diminished by the wrongful conduct of controlling shareholders, it would be appropriate to include as an element of fair value the petitioner's proportional claim for any compensable corporate injury. In cases where there is dissension but no evidence of wrongful conduct, "fair value" should be determined with reference to what the petitioner would likely receive in a voluntary sale of shares to a third party, taking into account his minority status. If the parties have previously entered into a shareholders' agreement that defines or provides a method for determining the fair value of shares to be sold, the court should look to such definition or method unless the court decides it would be unjust or inequitable to do so in light of the facts and circumstances of the particular case. The valuation date is set as the day before the filing of the petition under section 14.30, although the court may choose an earlier or later date if appropriate under the circumstances of the particular case.

It is expected that an order pursuant to subsection (e) will ordinarily provide for payment in cash, subject, in the case of any payment by the corporation, to the provisions of section 6.40. However, mindful that cash settlement may sometimes impose hardship on the purchasers, subsection (e) recognizes the court's discretion to provide for payment of the purchase price in installments, but only "where necessary in the interests of equity." In determining whether installment payments are "necessary in the interests of equity," the court should weigh any possible hardship to the purchaser against the petitioner's interest in receiving full and prompt payment of the value of his shares. Accordingly, before ordering payment in installments, the court should be satisfied with the purchaser's ability to meet the scheduled payments and to provide such security as the court deems necessary.

Otherwise, the contents of the order under subsection (e) are entirely subject to the court's discretion. The court may allow discovery to determine "fair value" or to decide if the petitioner is entitled to fees and expenses under the last sentence of subsection (e) or if interest should be withheld by virtue of the second sentence of that subsection.

c. *Effect on petitioning shareholder*

The entry of an order under either subsection (c) or (e) results in a dismissal, with prejudice, of the dissolution proceeding under section 14.30(2) and terminates all rights of the petitioner as a shareholder. Thus, the order also terminates all claims that the petitioner may have had in his capacity as a shareholder, and the value of such claims must either be asserted as part of the "fair value" of the petitioner's shares or forever lost except as provided in subsection (g). Under subsection (f), claims asserted by the petitioner in any nonshareholder capacity, such as claims for back wages or indemnification, are not affected by the entry of an order nor does the order affect any rights the petitioner may have as a creditor with respect to shares pledged as security for the purchase price. Otherwise, the order is enforceable only in the same manner as any other judgment, and the petitioner may not seek to reopen the proceedings in the event of a default.

After the entry of an order under subsections (c) or (e), the petitioner is a creditor with respect to the electing shareholders who participate in the purchase, but any payments to be made by the corporation, other than fees and expenses awarded under subsection (e), are subject to section 6.40.

d. *Appeal and the voluntary dissolution alternative*

In addition to the usual rights of appeal available to any party under the laws of the local jurisdiction, subsection (g) affords the alternative of voluntary dissolution after entry of an order under subsection (e). The purchase ordered pursuant to subsection (e) may be consummated at any time during the 10–day period after the order becomes final and must be consummated on the 10th day unless the corporation has previously filed a notice of its intention to dissolve voluntarily. Articles of dissolution must be adopted and filed within the next 50 days. An appeal of the order to purchase stays the running of both the 10– and 50–day periods until the appeal is disposed of and the order becomes final.

If the corporation elects to adopt and file articles of dissolution, it may not thereafter revoke its dissolution pursuant to section 14.04 but must proceed in accordance with the provisions of sections 14.05–14.07. If the corporation elects to dissolve, the petitioning shareholder will receive his pro rata share of the liquidating proceeds distributed to shareholders without reference to the "value" of his shares as determined by the court under subsection (e). By virtue of subsection (f), the petitioning shareholder would not be entitled to vote on a proposal to adopt articles of dissolution under section 14.02. Once articles of dissolution are filed, however, subsection (g) provides that the order under subsection (e) is "no longer of any force or effect." Accordingly, subsection (f) no longer applies, the petitioner resumes shareholder status and will be entitled to a pro rata share of any liquidating distribution to shareholders. To prevent use of voluntary dissolution to evade responsibilities, subsection (g) further provides that the filing of articles of dissolution does not affect either the court's award of fees and expenses to the petitioner under subsection (e) or the petitioner's standing to pursue derivative claims on behalf of the corporation, provided that the derivative claims had been previously asserted by the petitioner in the section 14.34 proceedings or otherwise.

Subchapter D. Miscellaneous

§ 14.40 Deposit with State Treasurer

Assets of a dissolved corporation that should be transferred to a creditor, claimant, or shareholder of the corporation who cannot be found or who is not competent to receive them shall be reduced to cash and deposited with the state treasurer or other appropriate state official for safekeeping. When the creditor, claimant, or shareholder furnishes satisfactory proof of entitlement to the amount deposited, the state treasurer or other appropriate state official shall pay him or his representative that amount.

CHAPTER 15

FOREIGN CORPORATIONS

Subchapter A. Certificate of Authority

§ 15.01 Authority to Transact Business Required

(a) A foreign corporation may not transact business in this state until it obtains a certificate of authority from the secretary of state.

(b) The following activities, among others, do not constitute transacting business within the meaning of subsection (a):

(1) maintaining, defending, or settling any proceeding;

(2) holding meetings of the board of directors or shareholders or carrying on other activities concerning internal corporate affairs;

(3) maintaining bank accounts;

(4) maintaining offices or agencies for the transfer, exchange, and registration of the corporation's own securities or maintaining trustees or depositaries with respect to those securities;

(5) selling through independent contractors;

(6) soliciting or obtaining orders, whether by mail or through employees or agents or otherwise, if the orders require acceptance outside this state before they become contracts;

(7) creating or acquiring indebtedness, mortgages, and security interests in real or personal property;

(8) securing or collecting debts or enforcing mortgages and security interests in property securing the debts;

(9) owning, without more, real or personal property;

(10) conducting an isolated transaction that is completed within 30 days and that is not one in the course of repeated transactions of a like nature;

(11) transacting business in interstate commerce.

(c) The list of activities in subsection (b) is not exhaustive.

§ 15.02 Consequences of Transacting Business Without Authority

(a) A foreign corporation transacting business in this state without a certificate of authority may not maintain a proceeding in any court in this state until it obtains a certificate of authority.

(b) The successor to a foreign corporation that transacted business in this state without a certificate of authority and the assignee of a cause of action arising out of that business may not maintain a proceeding based on that cause of action in any court in this state until the foreign corporation or its successor obtains a certificate of authority.

(c) A court may stay a proceeding commenced by a foreign corporation, its successor, or assignee until it determines whether the foreign corporation or its successor requires a certificate of authority. If it so determines, the court may further stay the proceeding until the foreign corporation or its successor obtains the certificate.

(d) A foreign corporation is liable for a civil penalty of $______ for each day, but not to exceed a total of $______ for each year, it transacts business in this state without a certificate of authority. The attorney general may collect all penalties due under this subsection.

(e) Notwithstanding subsections (a) and (b), the failure of a foreign corporation to obtain a certificate of authority does not impair the validity of its corporate acts or prevent it from defending any proceeding in this state.

§ 15.03 Application for Certificate of Authority

(a) A foreign corporation may apply for a certificate of authority to transact business in this state by delivering an application to the secretary of state for filing. The application must set forth:

(1) the name of the foreign corporation or, if its name is unavailable for use in this state, a corporate name that satisfies the requirements of section 15.06;

(2) the name of the state or country under whose law it is incorporated;

(3) its date of incorporation and period of duration;

(4) the street address of its principal office;

(5) the address of its registered office in this state and the name of its registered agent at that office; and

(6) the names and usual business addresses of its current directors and officers.

(b) The foreign corporation shall deliver with the completed application a certificate of existence (or a document of similar import) duly authenticated by the secretary of state or other official having custody of corporate records in the state or country under whose law it is incorporated.

§ 15.04 Amended Certificate of Authority

(a) A foreign corporation authorized to transact business in this state must obtain an amended certificate of authority from the secretary of state if it changes:

(1) its corporate name;

(2) the period of its duration; or

(3) the state or country of its incorporation.

(b) The requirements of section 15.03 for obtaining an original certificate of authority apply to obtaining an amended certificate under this section.

§ 15.05 Effect of Certificate of Authority

(a) A certificate of authority authorizes the foreign corporation to which it is issued to transact business in this state subject, however, to the right of the state to revoke the certificate as provided in this Act.

(b) A foreign corporation with a valid certificate of authority has the same but no greater rights and has the same but no greater privileges as, and except as otherwise provided by this Act is subject to the same duties, restrictions, penalties, and liabilities now or later imposed on, a domestic corporation of like character.

(c) This Act does not authorize this state to regulate the organization or internal affairs of a foreign corporation authorized to transact business in this state.

§ 15.06 Corporate Name of Foreign Corporation

(a) If the corporate name of a foreign corporation does not satisfy the requirements of section 4.01, the foreign corporation to obtain or maintain a certificate of authority to transact business in this state:

(1) may add the word "corporation," "incorporated," "company," or "limited," or the abbreviation "corp.," "inc.," "co.," or "ltd.," to its corporate name for use in this state; or

(2) may use a fictitious name to transact business in this state if its real name is unavailable and it delivers to the secretary of state for filing a copy of the resolution of its board of directors, certified by its secretary, adopting the fictitious name.

(b) Except as authorized by subsections (c) and (d), the corporate name (including a fictitious name) of a foreign corporation must be distinguishable upon the records of the secretary of state from:

(1) the corporate name of a corporation incorporated or authorized to transact business in this state;

(2) a corporate name reserved or registered under section 4.02 or 4.03;

(3) the fictitious name of another foreign corporation authorized to transact business in this state; and

(4) the corporate name of a not-for-profit corporation incorporated or authorized to transact business in this state.

(c) A foreign corporation may apply to the secretary of state for authorization to use in this state the name of another corporation (incorporated or authorized to transact business in this state) that is not distinguishable upon his records from the name applied for. The secretary of state shall authorize use of the name applied for if:

(1) the other corporation consents to the use in writing and submits an undertaking in form satisfactory to the secretary of state to change its name to a name that is distinguishable upon the records of the secretary of state from the name of the applying corporation; or

(2) the applicant delivers to the secretary of state a certified copy of a final judgment of a court of competent jurisdiction establishing the applicant's right to use the name applied for in this state.

(d) A foreign corporation may use in this state the name (including the fictitious name) of another domestic or foreign corporation that is used in this state if the other corporation is incorporated or authorized to transact business in this state and the foreign corporation:

(1) has merged with the other corporation;

(2) has been formed by reorganization of the other corporation; or

(3) has acquired all or substantially all of the assets, including the corporate name, of the other corporation.

(e) If a foreign corporation authorized to transact business in this state changes its corporate name to one that does not satisfy the requirements of section 4.01, it may not transact business in this state under the changed name until it adopts a name satisfying the requirements of section 4.01 and obtains an amended certificate of authority under section 15.04.

§ 15.07 Registered Office and Registered Agent of Foreign Corporation

Each foreign corporation authorized to transact business in this state must continuously maintain in this state:

(1) a registered office that may be the same as any of its places of business; and

(2) a registered agent, who may be:

(i) an individual who resides in this state and whose business office is identical with the registered office;

(ii) a domestic corporation or not-for-profit domestic corporation whose business office is identical with the registered office; or

(iii) a foreign corporation or foreign not-for-profit corporation authorized to transact business in this state whose business office is identical with the registered office.

§ 15.08 Change of Registered Office or Registered Agent of Foreign Corporation

(a) A foreign corporation authorized to transact business in this state may change its registered office or registered agent by delivering to the secretary of state for filing a statement of change that sets forth:

(1) its name;

(2) the street address of its current registered office;

(3) if the current registered office is to be changed, the street address of its new registered office;

(4) the name of its current registered agent;

(5) if the current registered agent is to be changed, the name of its new registered agent and the new agent's written consent (either on the statement or attached to it) to the appointment; and

(6) that after the change or changes are made, the street addresses of its registered office and the business office of its registered agent will be identical.

(b) If a registered agent changes the street address of his business office, he may change the street address of the registered office of any foreign corporation for which he is the registered agent by notifying the corporation in writing of the change and signing (either manually or in facsimile) and delivering to the secretary of state for filing a statement of change that complies with the requirements of subsection (a) and recites that the corporation has been notified of the change.

§ 15.09 Resignation of Registered Agent of Foreign Corporation

(a) The registered agent of a foreign corporation may resign his agency appointment by signing and delivering to the secretary of state for filing the original and two exact or conformed copies of a statement of resignation. The statement of resignation may include a statement that the registered office is also discontinued.

(b) After filing the statement, the secretary of state shall attach the filing receipt to one copy and mail the copy and receipt to the registered office if not discontinued. The secretary of state shall mail the other copy to the foreign corporation at its principal office address shown in its most recent annual report.

(c) The agency appointment is terminated, and the registered office discontinued if so provided, on the 31st day after the date on which the statement was filed.

§ 15.10 Service on Foreign Corporation

(a) The registered agent of a foreign corporation authorized to transact business in this state is the corporation's agent for service of process, notice, or demand required or permitted by law to be served on the foreign corporation.

(b) A foreign corporation may be served by registered or certified mail, return receipt requested, addressed to the secretary of the foreign corporation at its principal office shown in its application for a certificate of authority or in its most recent annual report if the foreign corporation:

(1) has no registered agent or its registered agent cannot with reasonable diligence be served;

(2) has withdrawn from transacting business in this state under section 15.20; or

(3) has had its certificate of authority revoked under section 15.31.

(c) Service is perfected under subsection (b) at the earliest of:

(1) the date the foreign corporation receives the mail;

(2) the date shown on the return receipt, if signed on behalf of the foreign corporation; or

(3) five days after its deposit in the United States mail, as evidenced by the postmark, if mailed postpaid and correctly addressed.

(d) This section does not prescribe the only means, or necessarily the required means, of serving a foreign corporation.

Subchapter B. Withdrawal or Transfer of Authority

§ 15.20 Withdrawal of Foreign Corporation

(a) A foreign corporation authorized to transact business in this state may not withdraw from this state until it obtains a certificate of withdrawal from the secretary of state.

(b) A foreign corporation authorized to transact business in this state may apply for a certificate of withdrawal by delivering an application to the secretary of state for filing. The application must set forth:

(1) the name of the foreign corporation and the name of the state or country under whose law it is incorporated;

(2) that it is not transacting business in this state and that it surrenders its authority to transact business in this state;

(3) that it revokes the authority of its registered agent to accept service on its behalf and appoints the secretary of state as its agent for service of process in any proceeding based on a cause of action arising during the time it was authorized to transact business in this state;

(4) a mailing address to which the secretary of state may mail a copy of any process served on him under subdivision (3); and

(5) a commitment to notify the secretary of state in the future of any change in its mailing address.

(c) After the withdrawal of the corporation is effective, service of process on the secretary of state under this section is service on the foreign corporation. Upon receipt of process, the secretary of state shall mail a copy of the process to the foreign corporation at the mailing address set forth under subsection (b).

§ 15.21 Automatic Withdrawal Upon Certain Conversions

A foreign business corporation authorized to transact business in this state that converts to a domestic nonprofit corporation or any form of domestic filing entity shall be deemed to have withdrawn on the effective date of the conversion.

§ 15.22 Withdrawal Upon Conversion to a Nonfiling Entity

(a) A foreign business corporation authorized to transact business in this state that converts to a domestic or foreign nonfiling entity shall apply for a certificate of withdrawal by delivering an application to the secretary of state for filing. The application must set forth:

(1) the name of the foreign business corporation and the name of the state or country under whose law it was incorporated before the conversion;

(2) that it surrenders its authority to transact business in this state as a foreign business corporation;

(3) the type of unincorporated entity to which it has been converted and the jurisdiction whose laws govern its internal affairs;

(4) if it has been converted to a foreign unincorporated entity:

(i) that it revokes the authority of its registered agent to accept service on its behalf and appoints the secretary of state as its agent for service of process in any proceeding based on a cause of action arising during the time it was authorized to transact business in this state;

(ii) a mailing address to which the secretary of state may mail a copy of any process served on him under paragraph (i); and

(iii) a commitment to notify the secretary of state in the future of any change in its mailing address.

(b) After the withdrawal under this section of a corporation that has converted to a foreign unincorporated entity is effective, service of process on the secretary of state is service on the foreign unincorporated entity. Upon receipt of process, the secretary of state shall mail a copy of the process to the foreign unincorporated entity at the mailing address set forth under subsection (a)(4).

(c) After the withdrawal under this section of a corporation that has converted to a domestic unincorporated entity is effective, service of process shall be made on the unincorporated entity in accordance with the regular procedures for service of process on the form of unincorporated entity to which the corporation was converted.

§ 15.23 Transfer of Authority

(a) A foreign business corporation authorized to transact business in this state that converts to a foreign nonprofit corporation or to any form of foreign unincorporated entity that is required to obtain a certificate of authority or make a similar type of filing with the secretary of state if it transacts business in this state shall file with the secretary of state an application for transfer of authority executed by any officer or other duly authorized representative. The application shall set forth:

(1) the name of the corporation;

(2) the type of unincorporated entity to which it has been converted and the jurisdiction whose laws govern its internal affairs;

(3) any other information that would be required in a filing under the laws of this state by an unincorporated entity of the type the

corporation has become seeking authority to transact business in this state.

(b) The application for transfer of authority shall be delivered to the secretary of state for filing and shall take effect at the effective time provided in section 1.23.

(c) Upon the effectiveness of the application for transfer of authority, the authority of the corporation under this chapter to transact business in this state shall be transferred without interruption to the converted entity which shall thereafter hold such authority subject to the provisions of the laws of this state applicable to that type of unincorporated entity.

Subchapter C. Revocation of Certificate of Authority

§ 15.30 Grounds for Revocation

The secretary of state may commence a proceeding under section 15.31 to revoke the certificate of authority of a foreign corporation authorized to transact business in this state if:

(1) the foreign corporation does not deliver its annual report to the secretary of state within 60 days after it is due;

(2) the foreign corporation does not pay within 60 days after they are due any franchise taxes or penalties imposed by this Act or other law;

(3) the foreign corporation is without a registered agent or registered office in this state for 60 days or more;

(4) the foreign corporation does not inform the secretary of state under section 15.08 or 15.09 that its registered agent or registered office has changed, that its registered agent has resigned, or that its registered office has been discontinued within 60 days of the change, resignation, or discontinuance;

(5) an incorporator, director, officer, or agent of the foreign corporation signed a document he knew was false in any material respect with intent that the document be delivered to the secretary of state for filing;

(6) the secretary of state receives a duly authenticated certificate from the secretary of state or other official having custody of corporate records in the state or country under whose law the foreign corporation is incorporated stating that it has been dissolved or disappeared as the result of a merger.

§ 15.31 Procedure for and Effect of Revocation

(a) If the secretary of state determines that one or more grounds exist under section 15.30 for revocation of a certificate of authority, he shall serve the foreign corporation with written notice of his determination under section 15.10.

(b) If the foreign corporation does not correct each ground for revocation or demonstrate to the reasonable satisfaction of the secretary of state that each ground determined by the secretary of state does not exist within 60 days after service of the notice is perfected under section 15.10, the secretary of state may revoke the foreign corporation's certificate of authority by signing a certificate of revocation that recites the ground or grounds for revocation and its effective date. The secretary of state shall file the original of the certificate and serve a copy on the foreign corporation under section 15.10.

(c) The authority of a foreign corporation to transact business in this state ceases on the date shown on the certificate revoking its certificate of authority.

(d) The secretary of state's revocation of a foreign corporation's certificate of authority appoints the secretary of state the foreign corporation's agent for service of process in any proceeding based on a cause of action which arose during the time the foreign corporation was authorized to transact business in this state. Service of process on the secretary of state under this subsection is service on the foreign corporation. Upon receipt of process, the secretary of state shall mail a copy of the process to the secretary of the foreign corporation at its principal office shown in its most recent annual report or in any subsequent communication received from the corporation stating the current mailing address of its principal office, or, if none are on file, in its application for a certificate of authority.

(e) Revocation of a foreign corporation's certificate of authority does not terminate the authority of the registered agent of the corporation.

§ 15.32 Appeal From Revocation

(a) A foreign corporation may appeal the secretary of state's revocation of its certificate of authority to the [name or describe] court within 30 days after service of the certificate of revocation is perfected under section 15.10. The foreign corporation appeals by petitioning the court to set aside the revocation and attaching to the petition copies of its certificate of authority and the secretary of state's certificate of revocation.

(b) The court may summarily order the secretary of state to reinstate the certificate of authority or may take any other action the court considers appropriate.

(c) The court's final decision may be appealed as in other civil proceedings.

CHAPTER 16

RECORDS AND REPORTS

Subchapter A. Records

§ 16.01 Corporate Records

(a) A corporation shall keep as permanent records minutes of all meetings of its shareholders and board of directors, a record of all actions taken by the shareholders or board of directors without a meeting, and a record of all actions taken by a committee of the board of directors in place of the board of directors on behalf of the corporation.

(b) A corporation shall maintain appropriate accounting records.

(c) A corporation or its agent shall maintain a record of its shareholders, in a form that permits preparation of a list of the names and addresses of all shareholders, in alphabetical order by class of shares showing the number and class of shares held by each.

(d) A corporation shall maintain its records in written form or in another form capable of conversion into written form within a reasonable time.

(e) A corporation shall keep a copy of the following records at its principal office:

(1) its articles or restated articles of incorporation, all amendments to them currently in effect, and any notices to shareholders referred to in section 1.20(k)(5) regarding facts on which a filed document is dependent;

(2) its bylaws or restated bylaws and all amendments to them currently in effect;

(3) resolutions adopted by its board of directors creating one or more classes or series of shares, and fixing their relative rights, preferences, and limitations, if shares issued pursuant to those resolutions are outstanding;

(4) the minutes of all shareholders' meetings, and records of all action taken by shareholders without a meeting, for the past three years;

(5) all written communications to shareholders generally within the past three years, including the financial statements furnished for the past three years under section 16.20;

(6) a list of the names and business addresses of its current directors and officers; and

(7) its most recent annual report delivered to the secretary of state under section 16.21.

§ 16.02 Inspection of Records by Shareholders

(a) A shareholder of a corporation is entitled to inspect and copy, during regular business hours at the corporation's principal office, any of the records of the corporation described in section 16.01(e) if he gives the corporation written notice of his demand at least five business days before the date on which he wishes to inspect and copy.

(b) A shareholder of a corporation is entitled to inspect and copy, during regular business hours at a reasonable location specified by the corporation, any of the following records of the corporation if the shareholder meets the requirements of subsection (c) and gives the corporation written notice of his demand at least five business days before the date on which he wishes to inspect and copy:

(1) excerpts from minutes of any meeting of the board of directors, records of any action of a committee of the board of directors while acting in place of the board of directors on behalf of the corporation, minutes of any meeting of the shareholders, and records of action taken by the shareholders or board of directors without a meeting, to the extent not subject to inspection under section 16.02(a);

(2) accounting records of the corporation; and

(3) the record of shareholders.

(c) A shareholder may inspect and copy the records described in subsection (b) only if:

(1) his demand is made in good faith and for a proper purpose;

(2) he describes with reasonable particularity his purpose and the records he desires to inspect; and

(3) the records are directly connected with his purpose.

(d) The right of inspection granted by this section may not be abolished or limited by a corporation's articles of incorporation or bylaws.

(e) This section does not affect:

(1) the right of a shareholder to inspect records under section 7.20 or, if the shareholder is in litigation with the corporation, to the same extent as any other litigant;

(2) the power of a court, independently of this Act, to compel the production of corporate records for examination.

(f) For purposes of this section, "shareholder" includes a beneficial owner whose shares are held in a voting trust or by a nominee on his behalf.

§ 16.03 Scope of Inspection Right

(a) A shareholder's agent or attorney has the same inspection and copying rights as the shareholder represented.

(b) The right to copy records under section 16.02 includes, if reasonable, the right to receive copies by xerographic or other means, including copies through an electronic transmission if available and so requested by the shareholder.

(c) The corporation may comply at its expense with a shareholder's demand to inspect the record of shareholders under section 16.02(b)(3) by providing the shareholder with a list of shareholders that was compiled no earlier than the date of the shareholder's demand.

(d) The corporation may impose a reasonable charge, covering the costs of labor and material, for copies of any documents provided to the shareholder. The charge may not exceed the estimated cost of production, reproduction or transmission of the records.

§ 16.04 Court-Ordered Inspection

(a) If a corporation does not allow a shareholder who complies with section 16.02(a) to inspect and copy any records required by that subsection to be available for inspection, the [name or describe court] of the county where the corporation's principal office (or, if none in this state, its registered office) is located may summarily order inspection and copying of the records demanded at the corporation's expense upon application of the shareholder.

(b) If a corporation does not within a reasonable time allow a shareholder to inspect and copy any other record, the shareholder who complies with sections 16.02(b) and (c) may apply to the [name or describe court] in the county where the corporation's principal office (or, if none in this state, its registered office) is located for an order to permit inspection and copying of the records demanded. The court shall dispose of an application under this subsection on an expedited basis.

(c) If the court orders inspection and copying of the records demanded, it shall also order the corporation to pay the shareholder's costs (including reasonable counsel fees) incurred to obtain the order unless the corporation proves that it refused inspection in good faith because it had a reasonable basis for doubt about the right of the shareholder to inspect the records demanded.

(d) If the court orders inspection and copying of the records demanded, it may impose reasonable restrictions on the use or distribution of the records by the demanding shareholder.

§ 16.05 Inspection of Records by Directors

(a) A director of a corporation is entitled to inspect and copy the books, records and documents of the corporation at any reasonable time to the extent reasonably related to the performance of the director's duties as a director, including duties as a member of a committee, but not for any other purpose or in any manner that would violate any duty to the corporation.

(b) The [*name or describe the court*] of the county where the corporation's principal office (or if none in this state, its registered office) is located may order inspection and copying of the books, records and documents at the corporation's expense, upon application of a director who has been refused such inspection rights, unless the corporation establishes that the director is not entitled to such inspection rights. The court shall dispose of an application under this subsection on an expedited basis.

(c) If an order is issued, the court may include provisions protecting the corporation from undue burden or expense, and prohibiting the director from using information obtained upon exercise of the inspection rights in a manner that would violate a duty to the corporation, and may also order the corporation to reimburse the director for the director's costs (including reasonable counsel fees) incurred in connection with the application.

§ 16.06 Exception to Notice Requirement

(a) Whenever notice is required to be given under any provision of this Act to any shareholder, such notice shall not be required to be given if:

(i) Notice of two consecutive annual meetings, and all notices of meetings during the period between such two consecutive annual meetings, have been sent to such shareholder at such shareholder's address as shown on the records of the corporation and have been returned undeliverable; or

(ii) All, but not less than two, payments of dividends on securities during a twelve-month period, or two consecutive payments of dividends on securities during a period of more than twelve months, have been sent to such shareholder at such shareholder's address as shown on the records of the corporation and have been returned undeliverable.

(b) If any such shareholder shall deliver to the corporation a written notice setting forth such shareholder's then-current address, the requirement that notice be given to such shareholder shall be reinstated.

Subchapter B. Reports

§ 16.20 Financial Statements for Shareholders

(a) A corporation shall furnish its shareholders annual financial statements, which may be consolidated or combined statements of the corporation and one or more of its subsidiaries, as appropriate, that include a balance sheet as of the end of the fiscal year, an income statement for that year, and a statement of changes in shareholders' equity for the year unless that information appears elsewhere in the financial statements. If financial statements are prepared for the corporation on the basis of generally accepted accounting principles, the annual financial statements must also be prepared on that basis.

(b) If the annual financial statements are reported upon by a public accountant, his report must accompany them. If not, the statements must be accompanied by a statement of the president or the person responsible for the corporation's accounting records:

(1) stating his reasonable belief whether the statements were prepared on the basis of generally accepted accounting principles and, if not, describing the basis of preparation; and

(2) describing any respects in which the statements were not prepared on a basis of accounting consistent with the statements prepared for the preceding year.

(c) A corporation shall mail the annual financial statements to each shareholder within 120 days after the close of each fiscal year. Thereafter, on written request from a shareholder who was not mailed the statements, the corporation shall mail him the latest financial statements.

§ 16.21 Annual Report for Secretary of State

(a) Each domestic corporation, and each foreign corporation authorized to transact business in this state, shall deliver to the secretary of state for filing an annual report that sets forth:

(1) the name of the corporation and the state or country under whose law it is incorporated;

(2) the address of its registered office and the name of its registered agent at that office in this state;

(3) the address of its principal office;

(4) the names and business addresses of its directors and principal officers;

(5) a brief description of the nature of its business;

(6) the total number of authorized shares, itemized by class and series, if any, within each class; and

(7) the total number of issued and outstanding shares, itemized by class and series, if any, within each class.

(b) Information in the annual report must be current as of the date the annual report is executed on behalf of the corporation.

(c) The first annual report must be delivered to the secretary of state between January 1 and April 1 of the year following the calendar year in which a domestic corporation was incorporated or a foreign corporation was authorized to transact business. Subsequent annual reports must be delivered to the secretary of state between January 1 and April 1 of the following calendar years.

(d) If an annual report does not contain the information required by this section, the secretary of state shall promptly notify the reporting domestic or foreign corporation in writing and return the report to it for correction. If the report is corrected to contain the information required by this section and delivered to the secretary of state within 30 days after the effective date of notice, it is deemed to be timely filed.

CHAPTER 17

TRANSITION PROVISIONS

§ 17.01 Application to Existing Domestic Corporations

This Act applies to all domestic corporations in existence on its effective date that were incorporated under any general statute of this state providing for incorporation of corporations for profit if power to amend or repeal the statute under which the corporation was incorporated was reserved.

§ 17.02 Application to Qualified Foreign Corporations

A foreign corporation authorized to transact business in this state on the effective date of this Act is subject to this Act but is not required to obtain a new certificate of authority to transact business under this Act.

§ 17.03 Saving Provisions

(a) Except as provided in subsection (b), the repeal of a statute by this Act does not affect:

(1) the operation of the statute or any action taken under it before its repeal;

(2) any ratification, right, remedy, privilege, obligation, or liability acquired, accrued, or incurred under the statute before its repeal;

(3) any violation of the statute, or any penalty, forfeiture, or punishment incurred because of the violation, before its repeal;

(4) any proceeding, reorganization, or dissolution commenced under the statute before its repeal, and the proceeding, reorganization, or dissolution may be completed in accordance with the statute as if it had not been repealed.

(b) If a penalty or punishment imposed for violation of a statute repealed by this Act is reduced by this Act, the penalty or punishment if not already imposed shall be imposed in accordance with this Act.

§ 17.04 Severability

If any provision of this Act or its application to any person or circumstance is held invalid by a court of competent jurisdiction, the invalidity does not affect other provisions or applications of the Act that can be given effect without the invalid provision or application, and to this end the provisions of the Act are severable.

§ 17.05 Repeal

The following laws and parts of laws are repealed: [to be inserted].

§ 17.06 Effective Date

This Act takes effect ______.

*

MODEL STATUTORY CLOSE CORPORATION SUPPLEMENT

(Selected Provisions)

Table of Sections

§ 3. Definition and Election of Statutory Close Corporation Status

(a) A statutory close corporation is a corporation whose articles of incorporation contain a statement that the corporation is a statutory close corporation.

(b) A corporation having 50 or fewer shareholders may become a statutory close corporation by amending its articles of incorporation to include the statement required by subsection (a). The amendment must be approved by the holders of at least two-thirds of the votes of each class or series of shares of the corporation, voting as separate voting groups, whether or not otherwise entitled to vote on amendments. If the amendment is adopted, a shareholder who voted against the amendment is entitled to assert dissenters' rights under [MBCA ch. 13].

OFFICIAL COMMENT

1. 50–Shareholder Limit

With the exception of a corporation having more than 50 shareholders at the time it wishes to become a statutory close corporation, all corporations are potentially eligible to make the election. (See MBCA section 1.42 for the method of determining the number of shareholders.) The election is made by including in the articles of incorporation a statement that the corporation is a statutory close corporation. An electing corporation continues to be governed by the Supplement unless the shareholders revoke this election. Other terminating events, such as an increase in the number of shareholders beyond some arbitrary maximum or the making of a public share offering, commonly found in existing close corporation statutes, create the undesirable possibility of inadvertent terminations of close corporation status and do not seem to serve any purpose except to complicate the statutory framework.

The danger that a large corporation with numerous shareholders might attempt to elect close corporation status in order to operate without a board of directors, although highly unlikely as a practical matter, is the reason for the 50–shareholder limit in section 3(b). A new corporation that wishes to elect statutory close corporation status at the time of its initial incorporation is eligible, however, regardless of the number of subscribers. Likewise, a new or existing corporation that becomes a statutory close corporation at a time when it has fewer than 50 shareholders may continue to operate as a statutory close corporation even though it subsequently has more than 50 shareholders. The potential for abuse by evasion of the normal rules governing corporations is not considered to be sufficiently great to justify an absolute numerical limitation, which inevitably creates the possibility of an unknowing change in status, and complexity of statutory provisions designed to deal with those changes of status.

. . . .

3. Articles of Incorporation

The articles of incorporation contain the basic information about a corporation. They may also give notice to prospective shareholders and creditors of special or unusual contractual arrangements among the shareholders.

The only required difference between articles of incorporation for a statutory close corporation and for a regular corporation is the statement designating the corporation to be a statutory close corporation. . . .

. . . .

§ 14. Compulsory Purchase of Shares After Death of Shareholder

(a) This section, and sections 15 through 17, apply to a statutory close corporation only if so provided in its articles of incorporation. If these sections apply, the executor or administrator of the estate of a deceased shareholder may require the corporation to purchase or cause to be purchased all (but not less than all) of the decedent's shares or to be dissolved.

(b) The provisions of sections 15 through 17 may be modified only if the modification is set forth or referred to in the articles of incorporation.

(c) An amendment to the articles of incorporation to provide for application of sections 15 through 17, or to modify or delete the provisions of these sections, must be approved by the holders of at least two-thirds of the votes of each class or series of shares of the statutory close corporation, voting as separate voting groups, whether or not otherwise entitled to vote on amendments. If the corporation has no shareholders when the amendment is proposed, it must be approved by at least two-thirds of the subscribers for shares, if any, or, if none, by all of the incorporators.

(d) A shareholder who votes against an amendment to modify or delete the provisions of sections 15 through 17 is entitled to dissenters' rights under [MBCA chapter 13] if the amendment upon adoption terminates or substantially alters his existing rights under these sections to have his shares purchased.

(e) A shareholder may waive his and his estate's rights under sections 15 through 17 by a signed writing.

(f) Sections 15 through 17 do not prohibit any other agreement providing for the purchase of shares upon a shareholder's death, nor do they prevent a shareholder from enforcing any remedy he has independently of these sections.

OFFICIAL COMMENT

1. Introduction

Sections 14 through 17, which are operative only if the articles of incorporation specifically so provide, guarantee a buyout at the death of a shareholder. By including appropriate language in the articles of incorporation, the mandatory buyout authorized by this section may be limited to the death of one or more specified shareholders, or to shareholders holding a particular class of shares. It may also be expanded to cover other contingencies–for example, shareholders who retire or who are disabled. Moreover, the statutory language may be modified to change the type of buyout. Other commonly used buyout arrangements include an optional sell-optional purchase, mandatory sell-optional purchase, and mandatory sell-mandatory purchase, with the seller being a shareholder wishing to dispose of his shares and the purchaser being the corporation, the remaining shareholders, or a combination of the two. The optional sell-mandatory purchase option was chosen on the ground that it was the one most likely to be chosen by a shareholder in a closely held corporation, all other factors being equal.

The decision to utilize any kind of buyout arrangement should be made only after careful consideration of the factors involved in the particular situation. If sections 14 through 17 are used, the election must be made in the articles of incorporation by specifying that sections 14 through 17 apply. The articles of incorporation may also vary the statutory provisions in any desired manner.

. . . .

The statute grants the estate of a deceased shareholder the right to compel a purchase of the decedent's shares since this is the situation most often covered in privately drafted contractual buyouts. The problem of illiquidity of close corporation shares is most acute in this situation because the estate frequently needs cash for estate taxes and other purposes. At the same time the remaining shareholders are often concerned about having the decedent's spouse and children involved in the management of the corporation. A significant amount of shareholder litigation involving close corporations involves disputes between the surviving shareholders and the successors in interest of a deceased shareholder. Having a guaranteed market for the decedent's shares reduces the likelihood that disputes will arise. Life insurance may be used to fund part or all of the purchase obligation. In the absence of available cash, an installment arrangement may help to alleviate any financial strain on the corporation. The remaining shareholders may agree to purchase some or all of the shares or find a third-party purchaser if it is undesirable for the corporation to purchase all of the offered shares. Furthermore, if the parties do not have an existing agreement containing a binding price formula or other terms often contained in buyout agreements and are unable to agree voluntarily on the price or other terms, a court action may be brought in which a judge in his discretion may resolve the differences and structure a buyout plan that is realistic in light of the corporation's finances.

In summary, assuming some sort of mandatory buyout in a particular situation is desirable, the major advantage of electing sections 14 through 17 is that they provide basic protection in the event the shareholders have failed to enter into an appropriate private agreement, or have entered into a buyout agreement but have failed to agree upon a buyout price formula, or have agreed upon a formula but have neglected to provide other necessary terms such as interest rates or number of installments in the event deferred purchases are authorized or necessary. Sections 14 through 17 do not prevent the shareholders from having an all-inclusive buyout agreement. See section 14(f). An attorney drafting such an agreement, however, may use the provisions of sections 14 through 17 as the basis of the agreement, making any necessary additions and modifications. This procedure may substantially reduce the amount of drafting required.

2. Redemption Problems

The ability of a corporation to redeem its shares is subject to legal limitations. Section 6.40 of the Revised Model Business Corporation Act sets forth a clear set of principles dealing with permissible redemptions of shares. . . .

. . . .

4. Modification of Statutory Scheme

Sections 14(b) and (c) permit the modification of the provisions of sections 14 through 17 by a two-thirds vote of all the shares. Section 14(d) provides that a shareholder who votes against a modification that terminates or substantially alters buyout rights previously granted him under these sections has dissenters' rights to obtain the fair value of his shares. Authorization of dissenter's rights when statutory buyout rights are materially altered represents a compromise between requiring unanimous approval by all interested persons for the alteration and requiring less than unanimous approval but providing no statutory remedy for those opposed to the termination whose rights are adversely affected.

§ 15. Exercise of Compulsory Purchase Right

(a) A person entitled and desiring to exercise the compulsory purchase right described in section 14 must deliver a written notice to the corporation, within 120 days after the death of the shareholder, describing the number and class or series of shares beneficially owned by the decedent and requesting that the corporation offer to purchase the shares.

(b) Within 20 days after the effective date of the notice, the corporation shall call a special shareholders' meeting, to be held not more than 40 days after the call, to decide whether the corporation should offer to purchase the shares. A purchase offer must be approved by the affirmative vote of the holders of a majority of votes entitled to be cast at the meeting, excluding votes in respect of the shares covered by the notice.

(c) The corporation must deliver a purchase offer to the person requesting it within 75 days after the effective date of the request notice. A purchase offer must be accompanied by the corporation's balance sheet as of the end of a fiscal year ending not more than 16 months before the effective date of the request notice, an income statement for that year, a statement of changes in shareholders' equity for that year, and the latest available interim financial statements, if any. The person must accept the purchase offer in writing within 15 days after receiving it or the offer is rejected.

(d) A corporation agreeing to purchase shares under this section may allocate some or all of the shares to one or more of its shareholders or to other persons if all the shareholders voting in favor of the purchase offer approve the allocation. If the corporation has more than one class or series of shares, however, the remaining holders of the class or series of shares being purchased are entitled to a first option to purchase the shares not purchased by the corporation in proportion to their shareholdings or in some other proportion agreed to by all the shareholders participating in the purchase.

(e) If price and other terms of a compulsory purchase of shares are fixed or are to be determined by the articles of incorporation, bylaws, or a written agreement, the price and terms so fixed or determined govern the compulsory purchase unless the purchaser defaults, in which event the buyer is entitled to commence a proceeding for dissolution under section 16.

OFFICIAL COMMENT

Section 15 sets out the mechanics of exercising the buyout option.... [T]his section requires that the selling shareholder offer all of his shares for sale on the premise that a shareholder desiring to cash out his interest in the corporation ought to divest himself of all his equity interest in the business. If fewer than all [of] his shares are offered, the shareholder may pursue his rights, if any, under the corporation's share transfer restrictions.

§ 16. Court Action to Compel Purchase

(a) If an offer to purchase shares made under section 15 is rejected, or if no offer is made, the person exercising the compulsory purchase right may commence a proceeding against the corporation to compel the purchase in the [name or describe] court of the county where the corporation's principal office (or, if none in this state, its registered office) is located. The corporation at its expense shall notify in writing all of its shareholders, and any other person the court directs, of the commencement of the proceeding. The jurisdiction of the court in which the proceeding is commenced under this subsection is plenary and exclusive.

(b) The court shall determine the fair value of the shares subject to compulsory purchase in accordance with the standards set forth in section 42 together with terms for the purchase. Upon making these determinations the court shall order the corporation to purchase or cause the purchase of the shares or empower the person exercising the compulsory purchase right to have the corporation dissolved.

(c) After the purchase order is entered, the corporation may petition the court to modify the terms of purchase and the court may do so if it finds that changes in the financial or legal ability of the corporation or other purchaser to complete the purchase justify a modification.

(d) If the corporation or other purchaser does not make a payment required by the court's order within 30 days of its due date, the seller may petition the court to dissolve the corporation and, absent a showing of good cause for not making the payment, the court shall do so.

(e) A person making a payment to prevent or cure a default by the corporation or other purchaser is entitled to recover the payment from the defaulter.

OFFICIAL COMMENT

The rationale for a judicial proceeding to determine the fair value of shares and other terms of the buyout is explained in the Official Comment to section 15. The power of the court under section 17 to allocate all costs and counsel fees incurred in the suit should provide an adequate incentive for both sides to act in good faith. No court action will be necessary, however, if the buyout price and other terms are established pursuant to a written agreement among the shareholders or provisions in the articles of incorporation or bylaws. See section 15(e).

If a suit to determine the fair value of shares is brought, the court has discretion to include in its order any conditions it feels are justified on the basis of the financial and other needs of the selling shareholder and of the purchaser. The court, for example, may authorize an installment sale. The order may include a provision for interest and may require collateral to secure the unpaid installments.

If the purchase is not consummated or the purchasers default, the shareholder may petition for dissolution of the corporation. The court may deny the petition for good cause shown. The proceeding, however, affords the corporation an opportunity to be heard on the matter and an opportunity to avoid dissolution. Mandatory dissolution in the event the offered shares are not purchased provides a strong incentive for the corporation and the remaining shareholders either to purchase the shares or to find another purchaser. Presumably, the corporation and other shareholders would refuse to purchase if the corporation's financial prospects were bleak. If this is the case, then dissolution may be the appropriate solution. Under section 15 the other shareholders are given reasonable time to come up with a purchasing group and the court has power to authorize an installment purchase and any other terms that are necessary to enable the purchasing group to finance the purchase without undue financial strain on the corporation or other purchasers.

§ 17. Court Costs and Other Expenses

(a) The court in a proceeding commenced under section 16 shall determine the total costs of the proceeding, including the reasonable compensation and expenses of appraisers appointed by the court and of counsel and experts employed by the parties. Except as provided in subsection (b), the court shall assess these costs equally against the corporation and the party exercising the compulsory purchase right.

(b) The court may assess all or a portion of the total costs of the proceeding:

(1) against the person exercising the compulsory purchase right if the court finds that the fair value of the shares does not substantially exceed the corporation's last purchase offer made before commencement of the proceeding and that the person's failure to accept the offer was arbitrary, vexatious, or otherwise not in good faith; or

(2) against the corporation if the court finds that the fair value of the shares substantially exceeds the corporation's last sale offer made before commencement of the proceeding and that the offer was arbitrary, vexatious, or otherwise not made in good faith.

§ 20. Shareholder Agreements

(a) All the shareholders of a statutory close corporation may agree in writing to regulate the exercise of the corporate powers and the management of the business and affairs of the corporation or the relationship among the shareholders of the corporation.

(b) An agreement authorized by this section is effective although:

(1) it eliminates a board of directors;

(2) it restricts the discretion or powers of the board or authorizes director proxies or weighted voting rights;

(3) its effect is to treat the corporation as a partnership; or

(4) it creates a relationship among the shareholders or between the shareholders and the corporation that would otherwise be appropriate only among partners.

(c) If the corporation has a board of directors, an agreement authorized by this section restricting the discretion or powers of the board relieves directors of liability imposed by law, and imposes that liability on each person in whom the board's discretion or power is vested, to the extent that the discretion or powers of the board of directors are governed by the agreement.

(d) A provision eliminating a board of directors in an agreement authorized by this section is not effective unless the articles of incorporation contain a statement to that effect as required by section 21.

(e) A provision entitling one or more shareholders to dissolve the corporation under section 33 is effective only if a statement of this right is contained in the articles of incorporation.

(f) To amend an agreement authorized by this section, all the shareholders must approve the amendment in writing unless the agreement provides otherwise.

(g) Subscribers for shares may act as shareholders with respect to an agreement authorized by this section if shares are not issued when the agreement was made.

(h) This section does not prohibit any other agreement between or among shareholders in a statutory close corporation.

OFFICIAL COMMENT

This section authorizes the shareholders to make any agreement they wish regulating the business of the corporation and their relationship to one another and to the corporation. Examples of provisions that may be included in an agreement are:

(1) The management of the business and the affairs of the corporation in whole or part may be by or under the direction of all the shareholders of the corporation or by or under the direction of one or more shareholders or third parties selected by the shareholders.

(2) One or more shareholders may be given power to dissolve the corporation at will or upon the occurrence of a specified event or contingency.

(3) The manner of exercising or dividing voting power by the shareholders and directors may be established, and the use of director as well as shareholder proxies may be authorized.

(4) The terms and conditions of employment of any officer or employee by the corporation may be established, regardless of the length of employment.

(5) The identity of the directors and officers of the corporation may be established.

(6) The payment of dividends or division of profits may be established.

(7) Issues as to which the shareholders or directors are deadlocked may be made subject to arbitration, or arbitration may be required for any issue of disagreement between a shareholder in his capacity as a shareholder, director, officer, or employee and the corporation, or the other shareholders.

All the shareholders must enter into the agreement and, if the agreement specifies that the corporation is not to have a board of directors or that one or more shareholders is to have a special right to dissolve the corporation, the articles of incorporation must include appropriate language authorizing these provisions. See sections 21 and 33.

A shareholder agreement is valid and enforceable under this section even if it, in effect, permits the business to be operated essentially as a partnership without a board of directors. See subsection (b). Close corporations in which most or all of the shareholders are employees of the corporation are often referred to as "incorporated partnerships." This section gives legal sanction to the customary arrangements made by the shareholders of these corporations. Section 25 reinforces this concept by providing that shareholder limited liability is to be recognized in spite of an agreement that the corporation is to be operated essentially as a partnership.

. . . .

The requirement of unanimity for adoption and amendment is based on the unusual nature of an agreement that so radically alters the normal corporate structure.

Subsection (h) preserves the right of shareholders to enter into any other type of shareholder voting agreement or voting trust or similar agreement that is authorized in the state's general business corporation or professional corporation statutes. These statutes do not ordinarily require unanimous approval by the shareholders but in general they do not authorize as much flexibility, particularly with respect to restrictions on the normal powers of directors, as is permitted under this section. They also often contain time limitations and other restrictions that may be undesirable. See, e.g., MBCA section 7.30 (voting trust is valid for 10 years).

The shareholders of a statutory close corporation may choose to operate with or without a board of directors. Section 21 deals specifically with the requirements for making this election and the legal consequences of operating without a board of directors. If the corporation has a board of directors, any responsibilities required to be exercised by the board of directors may be delegated to one or more of the shareholders or to third parties selected by the shareholders.

If the shareholders exercise the traditional management rights and duties required by statute to be exercised by the board of directors or have delegated these rights and duties to others, they also assume the same liability as would otherwise be imposed on the directors for failure to exercise these rights or to carry out those duties in an appropriate fashion. The shareholders who assume the duties of directors would, however, be eligible for indemnification under chapter 8E of the Revised Model Act. See the Official Comment to section 21. If the corporation has a board of directors, the directors are responsible for the appropriate exercise of any management rights they have power to exercise and would be liable for their failure to carry out their duties.

. . . .

§ 21. Elimination of Board of Directors

(a) A statutory close corporation may operate without a board of directors if its articles of incorporation contain a statement to that effect.

(b) An amendment to articles of incorporation eliminating a board of directors must be approved by all the shareholders of the corporation, whether or not otherwise entitled to vote on amendments, or if no shares have been issued, by all the subscribers for shares, if any, or if none, by all the incorporators.

(c) While a corporation is operating without a board of directors as authorized by subsection (a):

(1) all corporate powers shall be exercised by or under the authority of, and the business and affairs of the corporation managed under the direction of, the shareholders;

(2) unless the articles of incorporation provide otherwise, (i) action requiring director approval or both director and shareholder approval is authorized if approved by the shareholders and (ii) action requiring a majority or greater percentage vote of the board of directors is authorized if approved by the majority or greater percentage of the votes of shareholders entitled to vote on the action;

(3) a shareholder is not liable for his act or omission, although a director would be, unless the shareholder was entitled to vote on the action;

(4) a requirement by a state or the United States that a document delivered for filing contain a statement that specified action has been taken by the board of directors is satisfied by a statement that the corporation is a statutory close corporation without a board of directors and that the action was approved by the shareholders;

(5) the shareholders by resolution may appoint one or more shareholders to sign documents as "designated directors."

(d) An amendment to articles of incorporation deleting the statement eliminating the board of directors must be approved by the holders of at least two-thirds of the votes of each class or series of shares of the corporation, voting as separate voting groups, whether or not otherwise entitled to vote on amendments. The amendment must also specify the number, names, and addresses of the corporation's directors or describe who will perform the duties of a board under [MBCA § 8.01].

OFFICIAL COMMENT

This section permits a statutory close corporation to dispense with a board of directors if a statement to that effect is included in its articles of incorporation. See the Official Comment to section 3. It also sets out the consequences of this election....

The shareholders of a statutory close corporation operating without a board of directors have the legal liability imposed by law on directors for managing the business and affairs of the corporation. They may appoint one or more persons to perform their duties but they are collectively liable for any mismanagement. They also have the usual duties of directors and must either hold a meeting or join in a written consent to initiate or to approve action required by statute to be taken by directors. If this option is exercised, it also is not necessary to call for an organizational meeting of directors or to hold other directors' meetings; the statutory requirements may be fulfilled by shareholders' meetings.

. . . .

Subsection (c)(2) provides that the shareholder vote on action normally requiring director approval is tallied in the same manner as at any meeting of shareholders, i.e., the vote is tallied by shares rather than per capita by individual shareholders. This rule may be changed by an appropriate provision in the articles of incorporation. For example, if the articles of incorporation so state, shareholders may vote on a one-vote-one-person basis (as is the normal rule for directors' votes) rather than the one-vote-per-share rule applicable to shareholders. The shareholder voting rule is utilized as the standard rule because it is the option most likely to be chosen. A weighted voting plan that gives one or more shareholders either a general veto power or the power to veto in designated cases is also permissible. If a corporation has different classes or series of shares with voting rights or the corporate statutes grant voting rights to all classes or series of shares on a particular issue, either together or as separate voting groups, the requisite vote of the various classes or series of shares must be obtained to validate the transaction. The vote under subsection (c)(2) only satisfies any requirement for director approval of proposed action.

Although unanimous approval is necessary to elect to dispense with a board of directors, the election can be terminated under subsection (d) by a two-thirds vote of all shares. Operating without a board of directors is such a radical departure from traditional corporate law that it should not be undertaken unless all the shareholders agree because additional liabilities may be incurred as a result of the election. Terminating the election, however, reinstates the statutory requirements for a board of directors; and a two-thirds vote, which is the voting standard used in this Supplement for most fundamental structural changes, seems sufficient. A corporation with 50 or fewer shareholders that elects not to have a board of directors under section 8.01 of the Revised Model Business Corporation Act, however, may make and terminate the election under that statute by majority vote.

If a corporation without a board of directors terminates its status as a statutory close corporation, it must immediately elect directors unless it has 50 or fewer shareholders and chooses to operate without a board under MBCA section 8.01.

§ 31. Termination of Statutory Close Corporation Status

(a) A statutory close corporation may terminate its statutory close corporation status by amending its articles of incorporation to delete the statement that it is a statutory close corporation. If the statutory close corporation has elected to operate without a board of directors under section 21, the amendment must either comply with [MBCA § 8.01] or delete the statement dispensing with the board of directors from its articles of incorporation.

(b) An amendment terminating statutory close corporation status must be approved by the holders of at least two-thirds of the votes of each class or series of shares of the corporation, voting as separate voting groups, whether or not the holders are otherwise entitled to vote on amendments.

(c) If an amendment to terminate statutory close corporation status is adopted, each shareholder who voted against the amendment is entitled to assert dissenters' rights under [MBCA ch. 13].

OFFICIAL COMMENT

Sections 31 and 32 deal with issues that arise when it is decided to terminate a corporation's status as a statutory close corporation.

Termination is accomplished by amendment of the articles of incorporation to eliminate the special designation required by section 3. This amendment must be approved by the same vote (two-thirds) that is necessary to elect close corporation status (unless the articles specify a higher vote); and shareholders who vote against the termination have dissenters' rights. This is consistent with the provisions in section 3(b) for election by an existing corporation to become a statutory close corporation.

If the status of a statutory close corporation that is operating without a board of directors is to be terminated, in addition to amending the articles of incorporation to delete the reference to the statutory close corporation election, the statement that it has no board of directors must also be deleted, and the corporation must immediately elect a board of directors. Or, if MBCA section 8.01(c) is applicable, the corporation must amend its articles of incorporation to describe who will perform some or all of the duties of the board of directors under that section.

In the absence of agreement upon rights and duties of the shareholders, the corporation upon termination automatically becomes subject to the state's general business corporation statute, or professional corporation act if the corporation was organized as a professional corporation. Further, except for transfer restrictions under section 11 and authority to operate without a board of directors under MBCA section 8.01(c), any existing rights of the shareholders established by agreement (cf. Uniform Commercial Code section 1–201(3)) between the shareholders or with the corporation and any rights granted to the shareholders in the articles of incorporation that are valid under the general business or professional corporation acts remain in effect.

. . . .

If the Revised Model Business Corporation Act and the Model Professional Corporation Supplement have been enacted, most of the special control and distribution arrangements among the shareholders and the optional provisions that may be included in the articles of incorporation are not affected by the termination. For example, if sections 14 through 17 have been elected, the buyout purchase option at the death of a shareholder continues to apply, unless the articles of incorporation are amended to terminate the option. See the Official Comment to section 14. Some provisions, however, may be of doubtful validity after termination. One that may be in this category is a provision in the articles of incorporation giving one or more minority shareholders the right to dissolve the corporation as authorized by section 33. At the time of termination, all relevant documents relating to the corporation and the shareholders should be carefully reviewed, and where necessary revised. This Supplement gives some automatic protection by providing in section 32(b) that the special control and contractual arrangements automatically continue in effect unless they are invalid under other applicable statutes or case law.

§ 33. Shareholder Option to Dissolve Corporation

(a) The articles of incorporation of a statutory close corporation may authorize one or more shareholders, or the holders of a specified number or percentage of shares of any class or series, to dissolve the corporation at will or upon the occurrence of a specified event or contingency. The shareholder or shareholders exercising this authority must give written notice of the intent to dissolve to all the other shareholders. Thirty-one days after the effective date of the notice, the corporation shall begin to wind up and liquidate its business and affairs and file articles of dissolution under [MBCA sections 14.03 through 14.07].

(b) Unless the articles of incorporation provide otherwise, an amendment to the articles of incorporation to add, change, or delete the authority to dissolve described in subsection (a) must be approved by the holders of all the outstanding shares, whether or not otherwise entitled to vote on amendments, or if no shares have been issued, by all the subscribers for shares if any, or if none, by all the incorporators.

OFFICIAL COMMENT

The purpose of this section is to give shareholders in a statutory close corporation, if they so elect, basically the same power to dissolve the business as general partners have under the Uniform Partnership

Act. The section applies only if it is elected in the corporation's original or amended articles of incorporation. The right may be given to a single shareholder or to any group of shareholders and may be exercisable at will or restricted to certain designated circumstances. Rights under this section are in addition to other rights a shareholder may have under the state's general business corporation or professional corporation acts or this Supplement to dissolve the corporation.

This section gives considerable leverage to the shareholder or group of shareholders having the power to dissolve over the other shareholders. It should therefore be utilized with caution. Investors may wish to alter the statutory language to provide that the remaining shareholders have an option to purchase the shares of the shareholder(s) giving notice of dissolution under this section.

. . . .

§ 40. Court Action to Protect Shareholders

(a) Subject to satisfying the conditions of subsections (c) and (d), a shareholder of a statutory close corporation may petition the [name or describe] court for any of the relief described in section 41, 42, or 43 if:

(1) the directors or those in control of the corporation have acted, are acting, or will act in a manner that is illegal, oppressive, fraudulent, or unfairly prejudicial to the petitioner, whether in his capacity as shareholder, director, or officer, of the corporation;

(2) management of the corporation's affairs, the shareholders are unable to break the deadlock, and the corporation is suffering or will suffer irreparable injury or the business and affairs of the corporation can no longer be conducted to the advantage of the shareholders generally because of the deadlock; or

(3) there exists one or more grounds for judicial dissolution of the corporation under [MBCA § 14.30].

(b) A shareholder must commence a proceeding under subsection (a) in the [name or describe] court of the county where the corporation's principal office (or, if none in this state, its registered office) is located. The jurisdiction of the court in which the proceeding is commenced is plenary and exclusive.

(c) If a shareholder has agreed in writing to pursue a nonjudicial remedy to resolve disputed matters, he may not commence a proceeding under this section with respect to the matters until he has exhausted the nonjudicial remedy.

(d) If a shareholder has dissenters' rights under this Act or [MBCA ch. 13] with respect to proposed corporate action, he must commence a proceeding under this section before he is required to give notice of his intent to demand payment under [MBCA § 13.21] or to demand payment under [MBCA § 13.23] or the proceeding is barred.

(e) Except as provided in subsections (c) and (d), a shareholder's right to commence a proceeding under this section and the remedies available under sections 41 through 43 are in addition to any other right or remedy he may have.

OFFICIAL COMMENT

1. Introduction

Sections 40 through 43 are derived from similar provisions in the California, Michigan, Minnesota, New Jersey, and South Carolina statutes.... There are two major differences ... (1) the statutes, either specifically or by implication, provide that a shareholder may obtain relief only if he has statutory grounds therefor, whereas section 43 does not tie relief either to a suit to compel dissolution or to the establishment of grounds for dissolution; and (2) the range of relief available to the court is spelled out in greater detail.

The primary danger in granting relief for oppression and related conduct by dissolution is that the remedy is drastic and courts have usually refused to order dissolution of a solvent corporation, except in extreme cases of fraudulent conduct. Moreover, even though authority may exist to grant relief other than dissolution, courts have often been reluctant to grant any relief unless the fact situation itself justifies dissolution. This approach makes the grounds for relief too narrow to protect in an adequate fashion the rights of minority shareholders. At the same time the threat of dissolution gives minority shareholders a powerful weapon to hold over the head of the majority. Under this Supplement, dissolution is one form of relief that may be ordered by the court, but it is appropriate only as a last resort after other possibilities of resolving the dispute have failed. If a shareholder is actually seeking liquidation of the corporation, he may bring an action for dissolution under the state's general business corporation act (assuming he qualifies to bring the proceeding) or under the option-to-dissolve provisions of section 33.

Although sections 40 through 43 probably will be invoked most frequently by minority shareholders, the ground for relief described in section 40(a)(2) may be used by the holders of the majority of shares to seek relief from deadlocks created by veto rights given minority shareholders which threaten the corporation's continued existence. Moreover, even in suits brought by minority shareholders, the court has power under section 42 to order the petitioning shareholders to sell their shares to the corporation or to the remaining shareholders, even if this is not the relief requested.

Relief available under sections 40 through 43 is circumscribed to minimize the danger of abuse by shareholders. No relief of any kind may be ordered unless the court affirmatively finds that one or more of the specific conditions listed in section 40(a)—fraud, oppression, unfairly prejudicial conduct, deadlock, or grounds for involuntary dissolution—exist. The petitioner has the burden of proof on this issue. The court may award expenses and counsel fees to either side under section 41(b) in order to discourage or punish the bringing of harassment suits. Finally, if the complaining shareholder has agreed to arbitrate the dispute in question or to resolve it in some other nonjudicial manner, these remedies must be exhausted under section 40(c) before a suit under this section may be filed.

2. Grounds for Relief

Only shareholders of record or beneficial owners of shares held by a voting trust may bring an action under section 40(a) (see the definition of "shareholder" in MBCA section 1.40). This parallels the limitations imposed on shareholder derivative proceedings by section 7.40 of the MBCA. Relief may be granted if any of the three categories of circumstances specified exist.

Section 40(a)(1) provides relief from oppression and related conduct that adversely affects a minority shareholder in any relationship with the corporation. Attempted squeeze-outs in close corporations often involve removing a shareholder from his various offices or diminishing his compensation. The subsection makes clear that relief is not limited to those situations in which the value of the shareholder's share interest has been adversely affected.

No attempt has been made to define oppression, fraud, or unfairly prejudicial conduct. These are elastic terms whose meaning varies with the circumstances presented in a particular case, and it is felt that existing case law provides sufficient guidelines for courts and litigants. See, e.g., Annotation, "What amounts to 'oppressive conduct' under statute authorizing dissolution of corporation at suit of minority shareholders," 56 A.L.R.3d 358 (1974).

Section 40(a)(2) allows relief when the corporation is deadlocked. Whether a deadlock is created by majority or minority shareholders is immaterial and either majority or minority shareholders may claim relief under this subsection. Relief may be granted even though the corporation's financial condition is not threatened with irreparable injury if the court finds that the interest of all the shareholders is being damaged by the deadlock.

Section 40(a)(3) permits a shareholder to claim relief under this section if grounds for involuntary dissolution exist (see MBCA section 14.30). By filing an action under this section, a greater range of relief is made available to the shareholder. For example, the petitioning shareholder may not wish the corporation dissolved, even though grounds for dissolution exist.

3. Prerequisites to Granting Relief

Under section 40(c), nonjudicial remedies that the petitioning shareholder has agreed to seek must be exhausted before a suit may be brought under this section. Arbitration clauses covering a wide variety of intracorporate disputes are commonly included in shareholder agreements. If a dispute is covered by an arbitration agreement, the shareholder must submit the claim to arbitration before filing suit under this section and the right to file under this section after the arbitration proceeding is commenced depends on the preclusive effect of the arbitration under state law independent of the corporation statutes.

The requirement in section 40(d) that a shareholder who has dissenters' rights with respect to a transaction must file suit challenging the transaction under this section before the time he is required to perfect his dissenters' rights is designed to prevent a shareholder who has forgone his dissenters' rights from filing suit under this section to prevent a proposed transaction from being consummated. If the complaining shareholder has not taken timely action to perfect his dissenters' rights, he is relegated to whatever other rights might be available to him under state or federal law. See, e.g., Official Comment to MBCA section 13.02. If the shareholder does file a timely proceeding under this section, the court must first determine whether relief under this section is warranted. If the court finds that a share purchase is the appropriate remedy, the proceeding should be treated as a valuation proceeding in a dissenters' rights case and consolidated with any other similar dissenters' rights proceedings involving the same transaction.

4. Relief is Cumulative

Section 40(e) makes clear that the remedies available under this and sections 41 through 43 are cumulative and are in addition to any other remedies the petitioner may have, except as otherwise provided in sections 40(c) and 40(d).

§ 41. Ordinary Relief

(a) If the court finds that one or more of the grounds for relief described in section 40(a) exist, it may order one or more of the following types of relief:

 (1) the performance, prohibition, alteration, or setting aside of any action of the corporation or of its shareholders, directors, or officers of or any other party to the proceeding;

 (2) the cancellation or alteration of any provision in the corporation's articles of incorporation or bylaws;

 (3) the removal from office of any director or officer;

 (4) the appointment of any individual as a director or officer;

 (5) an accounting with respect to any matter in dispute;

 (6) the appointment of a custodian to manage the business and affairs of the corporation;

(7) the appointment of a provisional director (who has all the rights, powers, and duties of a duly elected director) to serve for the term and under the conditions prescribed by the court;

(8) the payment of dividends;

(9) the award of damages to any aggrieved party.

(b) If the court finds that a party to the proceeding acted arbitrarily, vexatiously, or otherwise not in good faith, it may award one or more other parties their reasonable expenses, including counsel fees and the expenses of appraisers or other experts, incurred in the proceeding.

OFFICIAL COMMENT

The purpose of listing the types of relief available, in this section and in sections 42 and 43, is to overcome the reluctance some courts have shown in the past to ordering anything other than dissolution, or possibly a buyout. See, e.g., *Gruenberg v. Goldmine Plantation, Inc.*, 360 So.2d 884 (La. Ct. App. 1978); *Harkey v. Mobley*, 552 S.W.2d 79 (Mo. Ct. App. 1977); *White v. Perkins*, 213 Va. 129, 189 S.E.2d 315 (1972). A court should have broad discretion to fashion the most appropriate remedy to resolve the dispute. What works in one case may not work in another. Detailed standards are not provided since they might encourage litigation and also unduly restrict the court's discretion. The dangers of including detailed standards, however, outweigh the advantages. Existing cases applying principles of equity are, of course, precedents for the exercise of a judge's discretion under this section.

Although most close corporation statutes contain special provisions similar to sections 40(a)(6) and (7), authorizing the appointment of custodians and provisional directors, the number of actual cases in which appointments will be the most appropriate remedy are probably few. Usually the threat of an insider running the company or acting as a tie-breaker in a deadlock situation leads to a settlement of the controversy.

§ 42. Extraordinary Relief: Share Purchase

(a) If the court finds that the ordinary relief described in section 41(a) is or would be inadequate or inappropriate, it may order the corporation dissolved under section 43 unless the corporation or one or more of its shareholders purchases all the shares of the shareholder for their fair value and on terms determined under subsection (b).

(b) If the court orders a share purchase, it shall:

(1) determine the fair value of the shares, considering among other relevant evidence the going concern value of the corporation, any agreement among some or all of the shareholders fixing the price or specifying a formula for determining share value for any purpose, the recommendations of appraisers (if any) ap-

pointed by the court, and any legal constraints on the corporation's ability to purchase the shares;

(2) specify the terms of the purchase, including, if appropriate, terms for installment payments, subordination of the purchase obligation to the rights of the corporation's other creditors, security for a deferred purchase price, and a covenant not to compete or other restriction on the seller;

(3) require the seller to deliver all his shares to the purchaser upon receipt of the purchase price or the first installment of the purchase price;

(4) provide that after the seller delivers his shares he has no further claim against the corporation, its directors, officers, or shareholders, other than a claim to any unpaid balance of the purchase price and a claim under any agreement with the corporation or the remaining shareholders that is not terminated by the court; and

(5) provide that if the purchase is not completed in accordance with the specified terms, the corporation is to be dissolved under section 43.

(c) After the purchase order is entered, any party may petition the court to modify the terms of the purchase and the court may do so if it finds that changes in the financial or legal ability of the corporation or other purchaser to complete the purchase justify a modification.

(d) If the corporation is dissolved because the share purchase was not completed in accordance with the court's order, the selling shareholder has the same rights and priorities in the corporation's assets as if the sale had not been ordered.

OFFICIAL COMMENT

A court-ordered buyout is a drastic remedy, particularly if the shareholder ordered to sell his shares does not wish to sell. For this reason section 42 authorizes a share purchase order only if other relief short of liquidation will not, in the judge's opinion, resolve the dispute. If a buyout ordered by the court is not consummated, however, an order dissolving the corporation is authorized. This may place pressure on the remaining shareholders to obey the order but also gives them the option of dissolution if they think the order is too onerous.

If the court orders a buyout, it must also determine the fair value and other terms of the buyout in accordance with subsection (b). Fair value is to be determined under principles developed in dissenters' rights and other valuation cases. The court may require the selling shareholder to enter into a covenant not to compete and also may order an installment sale in order to protect the business and to minimize the financial strain on the purchasers. See also the Official Comment to section 14.

This section permits the designated purchasers either to consummate the purchase or to permit the corporation to be dissolved. Presumably the remaining shareholders will elect to have the corporation dissolved if its economic prospects are bleak. Leaving the choice to the remaining shareholders is fairer than ordering dissolution without giving the remaining shareholders the opportunity to buy out the complaining shareholder or requiring the shareholders to purchase the shares without giving them the option of voluntary dissolution (which they would not have unless they held sufficient voting shares to approve a dissolution).

If the remaining shareholders agree to comply with the court ordered buyout, the sale operates as a release of all claims the selling shareholder may have against the corporation, or its directors, officers, or shareholders. The selling shareholder may still pursue any contractual claim he might have against the corporation—for example, a claim for breach of a long-term employment contract—to the extent the claim is not dealt with in the court's order. Normally, however, the order should dispose of these contractual claims. The selling shareholder also retains the right to collect any unpaid balance due on the purchase price of his shares, including the right to realize on any collateral given as security for the unpaid balance. Quite frequently the shares being sold have been pledged as security; in these situations, if there is a default, the former shareholder has the choice of foreclosing on the note and again becoming a shareholder or suing to have the corporation dissolved under section 43.

Under section 42(c) the court has power to modify its final order at any time upon the petition of any party. For example, should financial or legal constraints prevent the purchasers from fulfilling the terms of a mandated buyout, the court might modify its order. See also the Official Comment to section 14.

Finally, the buyout and dissolution remedies provided by this section and section 43 are cumulative of ordinary remedies available under section 41; for example, a court may award damages in addition to compelling a buyout. See the Official Comment to section 40.

§ 43. Extraordinary Relief: Dissolution

(a) The court may dissolve the corporation if it finds:

(1) there are one or more grounds for judicial dissolution under [MBCA § 14.30]; or

(2) all other relief ordered by the court under section 41 or 42 has failed to resolve the matters in dispute.

(b) In determining whether to dissolve the corporation, the court shall consider among other relevant evidence the financial condition of the corporation but may not refuse to dissolve solely because the corporation has accumulated earnings or current operating profits.

*

AMERICAN LAW INSTITUTE PRINCIPLES OF CORPORATE GOVERNANCE

(Selected Provisions)

Table of Sections

---

§ 1.15 Disinterested Directors

A provision that gives a specified effect to action by "disinterested directors" requires the affirmative vote of a majority, but not less than two, of the directors on the board or on an appropriate committee who are not interested [§ 1.23] in the transaction or conduct in question.

§ 1.16 Disinterested Shareholders

A provision that gives a specified effect to action by "disinterested shareholders" requires approval by a majority of the votes cast by shareholders who are not interested [§ 1.23] in the transaction or conduct in question. In the case of § 5.15 (Transfer of Control in Which a Director or Principal Senior Executive Is Interested), such approval shall be deemed to have been given when there has been a tender offer and it has been accepted by a majority of the shares for which the tender offer has been made.

§ 1.23 Interested

(a) A director [§ 1.13] or officer [§ 1.27] is "interested" in a transaction or conduct if either:

(1) The director or officer, or an associate [§ 1.03] of the director or officer, is a party to the transaction or conduct;

(2) The director or officer has a business, financial, or familial relationship with a party to the transaction or conduct, and that relationship would reasonably be expected to affect the director's or officer's judgment with respect to the transaction or conduct in a manner adverse to the corporation;

(3) The director or officer, an associate of the director or officer, or a person with whom the director or officer has a business, financial, or familial relationship, has a material pecuniary interest in the transaction or conduct (other than usual and customary directors' fees and benefits) and that interest and (if present) that relationship would reasonably be expected to affect the director's or officer's judgment in a manner adverse to the corporation; or

(4) The director or officer is subject to a controlling influence by a party to the transaction or conduct or a person who has a material pecuniary interest in the transaction or conduct, and that controlling influence could reasonably be expected to affect the director's or officer's judgment with respect to the transaction or conduct in a manner adverse to the corporation.

(b) A shareholder is interested in a transaction or conduct if either the shareholder or, to the shareholder's knowledge, an associate of the shareholder is a party to the transaction or conduct, or the shareholder is also an interested director or officer with respect to the same transaction or conduct.

(c) A director is interested in an action within the meaning of Part VII, Chapter 1 (The Derivative Action), but not elsewhere in these Principles, if:

(1) The director is interested, within the meaning of Subsection (a), in the transaction or conduct that is the subject of the action, or

(2) The director is a defendant in the action, except that the fact a director is named as a defendant does not make the director interested under this section if the complaint against the director:

(A) is based only on the fact that the director approved of or acquiesced in the transaction or conduct that is the subject of the action, and

(B) does not otherwise allege with particularity facts that, if true, raise a significant prospect that the director would be adjudged liable to the corporation or its shareholders.

§ 1.27 Officer

"Officer" means (a) the chief executive, operating, financial, legal, and accounting officers of a corporation; (b) to the extent not encompassed by the foregoing, the chairman of the board of directors (unless the chairman neither performs a policymaking function other than as a director nor receives a material amount of compensation in excess of director's fees), president, treasurer, and secretary, and a vice-president or vice-chairman who is in charge of a principal business unit, division, or function (such as sales, administration, or finance) or performs a major policymaking function for the corporation; and (c) any other individual designated by the corporation as an officer.

§ 1.33 Senior Executive

"Senior executive" means an officer described in Subsection (a) or (b) of § 1.27 (Officer).

§ 2.01 The Objective and Conduct of the Corporation

(a) Subject to the provisions of Subsection (b) and § 6.02 (Action of Directors That Has the Foreseeable Effect of Blocking Unsolicited Tender Offers), a corporation [§ 1.12] should have as its objective the conduct of business activities with a view to enhancing corporate profit and shareholder gain.

(b) Even if corporate profit and shareholder gain are not thereby enhanced, the corporation, in the conduct of its business:

(1) Is obliged, to the same extent as a natural person, to act within the boundaries set by law;

(2) May take into account ethical considerations that are reasonably regarded as appropriate to the responsible conduct of business; and

(3) May devote a reasonable amount of resources to public welfare, humanitarian, educational, and philanthropic purposes.

§ 4.01 Duty of Care of Directors and Officers; the Business Judgment Rule

(a) A director or officer has a duty to the corporation to perform the director's or officer's functions in good faith, in a manner that he or she reasonably believes to be in the best interests of the corporation, and with the care that an ordinarily prudent person would reasonably be expected to exercise in a like position and under similar circumstances. This Subsection (a) is subject to the provisions of Subsection (c) (the business judgment rule) where applicable.

(1) The duty in Subsection (a) includes the obligation to make, or cause to be made, an inquiry when, but only when, the circumstances would alert a reasonable director or officer to the need therefor. The extent of such inquiry shall be such as the director or officer reasonably believes to be necessary.

(2) In performing any of his or her functions (including oversight functions), a director or officer is entitled to rely on materials and persons in accordance with §§ 4.02 and 4.03 (reliance on directors, officers, employees, experts, other persons, and committees of the board).

(b) Except as otherwise provided by statute or by a standard of the corporation [§ 1.36] and subject to the board's ultimate responsibility for oversight, in performing its functions (including oversight functions), the board may delegate, formally or informally by course of conduct, any function (including the function of identifying matters requiring the attention of the board) to committees of the board or to directors, officers, employees, experts, or other persons; a director may rely on such committees and persons in fulfilling the duty under this Section with respect to any delegated function if the reliance is in accordance with §§ 4.02 and 4.03.

(c) A director or officer who makes a business judgment in good faith fulfills the duty under this Section if the director or officer:

(1) is not interested [§ 1.23] in the subject of the business judgment;

(2) is informed with respect to the subject of the business judgment to the extent the director or officer reasonably believes to be appropriate under the circumstances; and

(3) rationally believes that the business judgment is in the best interests of the corporation.

(d) A person challenging the conduct of a director or officer under this Section has the burden of proving a breach of the duty of care, including the inapplicability of the provisions as to the fulfillment of duty under Subsection (b) or (c), and, in a damage action, the burden of proving that the breach was the legal cause of damage suffered by the corporation.

Comment:

a. General comparison with present law . . . .

. . . .

It should be noted that Subsections (a), (c), and (d) of § 4.01 deal with both directors and officers. Although most precedents and statutory provisions deal solely with directors, it is relatively well settled, through judicial precedents and statutory provisions in at least 18 states, that officers will be held to the same duty of care standards as directors. Sound public policy points in the direction of holding officers to the same duty of care and business judgment standards as directors, as does the little case authority that exists on the applicability of the business judgment standard to officers, and the views of most commentators support this position. See Reporter's Notes to § 4.01(a) and § 4.01(c). When it comes to the application of these formulations, of course, full-time officers will generally be expected to be more familiar with the affairs of a corporation than outside directors. Officers will be expected to be more familiar with business affairs under their direct supervision than officers who do not have such responsibility.

. . . .

d. Duty of care standards as applied to business judgments . . . .

If a director or officer acts in good faith and in accordance with § 4.01(c)(1) and (2) with respect to a business judgment, the standard in § 4.01(c)(3) will provide insulation from liability unless the director of officer does not rationally believe that the business judgment is in the best interests of the corporation. This standard is intended to provide directors and officers with a wide ambit of discretion. It is recognized that the word "rational," which is widely used by courts, has a close etymological tie to the word "reasonable" and that, at times, the words have been used almost interchangeably. But a sharp distinction is being drawn between the words here. The phrase "rationally believes" is intended to permit a significantly wider range of discretion than the term "reasonable," and to give a director or officer a safe harbor from liability for business judgments that might arguably fall outside the term "reasonable" but are not so removed from the realm of reason when made that liability should be incurred. Stated another way, the judgment of a director or officer will pass muster under § 4.01(c)(3) if the director or officer believes it to be in the best interests of the corporation and that belief is rational. See Comment *f* to § 4.01(c).

. . . .

g. Burden of proof. Under § 4.01, a person challenging the conduct of a director or officer has the burden of proving the failure of the director or officer to comply with the duty of care obligations under Subsection (a) and the inapplicability of the provisions concerning the fulfillment of duty under Subsection (b) or (c). The safe harbor provided by the business judgment rule in Subsection (c) may be inapplicable, for example, because a director was not informed in accordance with the standard of § 4.01(c)(2) or did not have a rational belief that a business judgment was in the best interests of the corporation.

Courts, when applying the business judgment rule, have often stated that a "presumption" exists in favor of the propriety or regularity of the actions of directors and officers. This correctly signifies that no inference of dereliction of duty can or should be drawn, for example, from the fact that a corporation has suffered a business reversal. These Principles agree with the observation that directors and officers generally act properly. Section 4.01 does not use the word "presumption," which is imprecise and subject to misinterpretation, because, for example, the concept might be misinterpreted so that it is thought to be irrebuttable or to establish a special evidentiary standard. Section 4.01 does, however, specifically recognize the general propriety of actions by directors and officers (including, in the case of the business judgment rule, an assumption that the directors or officers acted on an informed basis and met the other prerequisites of § 4.01(c)) by placing the burden of proof on persons challenging conduct under this Section. See Comment *a* to § 4.01(d).

. . . .

Comment to § 4.01(a), first paragraph:

. . . .

f. Subjective aspects of the duty of care standard. The terms "good faith," "reasonably believes," and "like position," in § 4.01(a), recognize that in determining whether reasonable care has been exercised, the special skills, background, or expertise of a director or officer are properly accorded weight. Special skills (e.g., in engineering, accounting, or law) may, for example, alert a director to a significant corporate problem before other directors would recognize it. Such a director, being obliged to act in the best interests of the corporation, cannot reasonably ignore this knowledge. The *Corporate Director's Guidebook* (p. 1601) "recognizes that the special background and qualifications of a particular director ... may place greater responsibility on that director."

. . . .

Comment to § 4.01(c):

. . . .

c. *Prerequisite of a conscious exercise of judgment.* Section 4.01(c) affords protection only to a "business judgment." This means that to be afforded protection a decision must have been consciously made and judgment must, in fact, have been exercised. For efficiency reasons, corporate decisionmakers should be permitted to act decisively and with relative freedom from a judge's or jury's subsequent second-guessing. It is desirable to encourage directors and officers to enter new markets, develop new products, innovate, and take other business risks.

There is, however, no reason to provide special protection where no business decisionmaking is to be found. If, for example, directors have failed to oversee the conduct of the corporation's business (§ 3.02(a)(2)) by not even considering the need for an effective audit process, and this permits an executive to abscond with corporate funds, business judgment rule protection would be manifestly undesirable. The same would be true where a director received but did not read basic financial information, over a period of time, and thus allowed his corporation to be looted. Cf. Hoye v. Meek, 795 F.2d 893 (10th Cir.1986); DePinto v. Provident Security Life Insur. Co., 374 F.2d 37 (9th Cir.), cert. denied, 389 U.S. 822, 88 S.Ct. 48, 19 L.Ed.2d 74 (1967); Francis v. United Jersey Bank, 87 N.J. 15, 432 A.2d 814 (Sup. Ct. 1981). In these and other "omission" situations, the director or officer would be judged under the reasonable care standards of § 4.01(a) and not protected by § 4.01(c). See, e.g., Aronson v. Lewis, 473 A.2d 805, 813 (Del.1984) ("the business judgment rule operates only in the context of director action.... It has no role where directors have either abdicated their functions, or absent a conscious decision, failed to act."); Arsht, The Business Judgment Rule Revisited, 8 Hofstra L. Rev. 93, 112 (1979); Block & Prussin, The Business Judgment Rule and Shareholder Derivative Actions: Viva Zapata?, 37 Bus. Law. 27, 33 (1981) ("The [business judgment] rule does not apply where the director has in fact made no decision").

Of course, whether there has been a conscious decision or inexcusable inattentiveness may, at times, not be readily discernible and may present close evidentiary questions. For example, in what might appear at first glance to be an "omission" situation, the directors might actually have carefully marshaled relevant information, appraised the risks, and then decided (with a rational belief) not to install a particular antitrust compliance program or a computer security program. In that event, assuming that they acted in good faith and were disinterested, the safe harbor provided by the business judgment rule would be available. Similarly, informed directors might have concluded that the effectiveness of a particular procedure or program need only be reviewed once every two years, and if they rationally believed that their decision was in the best interests of the corporation, the safe harbor provided by § 4.01(c) would again be available....

It is important to recognize that a business decision may involve a judgment either to act or to abstain from action. If the prerequisites of § 4.01(c) are met, the board of directors of a major computer manufacturer could, for example, decide to invest heavily, or abstain from investing, in a potentially profitable new computer product, and in either instance, the business judgment rule would be applicable.

....

f. The "rationally believes" requirement. If the requirements of "good faith" and § 4.01(c)(1)-(c)(2) are met, § 4.01(c)(3) will protect a director or officer from liability for a business judgment if the director or officer "rationally believes that the business judgment is in the best interests of the corporation." The term "rationally believes" has both an objective and a subjective content. A director or officer must actually believe that the business judgment is in the best interests of the corporation and that belief must be rational. This "rationally believes" test is the basis of the legal insulation provided by the formulation of the business judgment rule in Subsection (c)....

There have been varying approaches taken in the cases and by commentators to the proper standard for judicial review of business judgments. Some courts have stated that a director's or officer's business judgment must be "reasonable" to be upheld.... On the other hand, a few cases have simply said that a director's or officer's judgment would be upheld if made with disinterest, in an informed manner, and in good faith. Both a "reasonableness" test and the "good faith alone" approach have been rejected in § 4.01(c), for the reasons expressed below.

Sound public policy dictates that directors and officers be given greater protection than courts and commentators using a "reasonableness" test would afford. Indeed, some courts and commentators, even when using a "reasonableness" test, have expressly indicated that they do not intend that business judgments be given the rigorous review that the word "reasonable" may be read to imply....

The "rationally believes" standard set forth in § 4.01(c)(3) is intended to afford directors and officers wide latitude when making business decisions that meet the other prerequisites of Subsection (c). See Comment *d* to § 4.01. The approach taken in Subsection (c)(3) is consistent with the large majority of business judgment cases and with sound public policy. Many courts have used words like "reckless disregard" or "recklessness" to convey a similar sense of the wide latitude that directors or officers should be afforded....

On the other hand, courts that have articulated only a "good faith" test may, depending on the court's meaning, provide too much legal insulation for directors and officers. A "good faith" test could be interpreted broadly to achieve the same result as the "rationally believes" standard. For example, in Sam Wong & Son v. New York Mercantile Exchange, 735 F.2d 653, 671, 678 n.32 (2d Cir.1984), Judge Friendly held that the rationality of a decision by the Board of Governors of the Mercantile Exchange was relevant in determining whether the Board had acted in good faith, and concluded that "[a]bsent some basis in reason, action could hardly be in good faith even apart from ulterior motive." See also In re RJR Nabisco, Inc. Shareholders Litigation, 556 A.2d 1070 n.13 (Del.Ch.1989). Serious problems arise, however, if the phrase "good faith" is interpreted narrowly to mean only the absence of subjective "bad motives." There is no reason to insulate an objectively irrational business decision—one so removed from the realm of reason that it should not be sustained—solely on the basis that it was made in subjective good faith....

....

§ 5.04 Use by a Director or Senior Executive of Corporate Property, Material Non-Public Corporate Information, or Corporate Position

(a) *General Rule.* A director [§ 1.13] or senior executive [§ 1.33] may not use corporate property, material non-public corporate information, or corporate position to secure a pecuniary benefit, unless either:

(1) Value is given for the use and the transaction meets the standards of § 5.02 (Transactions with the Corporation);

(2) The use constitutes compensation and meets the standards of § 5.03 (Compensation of Directors and Senior Executives);

(3) The use is solely of corporate information, and is not in connection with trading of the corporation's securities, is not a use of proprietary information of the corporation, and does not harm the corporation;

(4) The use is subject neither to § 5.02 nor § 5.03 but is authorized in advance or ratified by disinterested directors [§ 1.15] or disinterested shareholders [§ 1.16], and meets the requirements and standards of disclosure and review set forth in § 5.02 as if that Section were applicable to the use; or

(5) The benefit is received as a shareholder and is made proportionately available to all other similarly situated shareholders,

and the use is not otherwise unlawful.

(b) *Burden of Proof.* A party who challenges the conduct of a director or senior executive under Subsection (a) has the burden of proof, except that if value was given for the benefit, the burden of proving whether the value was fair should be allocated as provided in § 5.02 in the case of a transaction with the corporation.

(c) *Special Rule on Remedies.* A director or senior executive is subject to liability under this Section only to the extent of any improper benefit received and retained, except to the extent that any foreseeable harm caused by the conduct of the director or senior executive exceeds the value of the benefit received, and multiple liability based on receipt of the same benefit is not to be imposed.

§ 5.05 Taking of Corporate Opportunities by Directors or Senior Executives

(a) *General Rule.* A director [§ 1.13] or senior executive [§ 1.33] may not take advantage of a corporate opportunity unless:

(1) The director or senior executive first offers the corporate opportunity to the corporation and makes disclosure concerning the conflict of interest [§ 1.14(a)] and the corporate opportunity [§ 1.14(b)];

(2) The corporate opportunity is rejected by the corporation; and

(3) Either:

(A) The rejection of the opportunity is fair to the corporation;

(B) The opportunity is rejected in advance, following such disclosure, by disinterested directors [§ 1.15], or, in the case of a senior executive who is not a director, by a disinterested superior, in a manner that satisfies the standards of the business judgment rule [§ 4.01(c)]; or

(C) The rejection is authorized in advance or ratified, following such disclosure, by disinterested shareholders [§ 1.16], and the rejection is not equivalent to a waste of corporate assets [§ 1.42].

(b) *Definition of a Corporate Opportunity.* For purposes of this Section, a corporate opportunity means:

(1) Any opportunity to engage in a business activity of which a director or senior executive becomes aware, either:

(A) In connection with the performance of functions as a director or senior executive, or under circumstances that should reasonably lead the director or senior executive to believe that the person offering the opportunity expects it to be offered to the corporation; or

(B) Through the use of corporate information or property, if the resulting opportunity is one that the director or senior executive should reasonably be expected to believe would be of interest to the corporation; or

(2) Any opportunity to engage in a business activity of which a senior executive becomes aware and knows is closely related to a business in which the corporation is engaged or expects to engage.

(c) *Burden of Proof.* A party who challenges the taking of a corporate opportunity has the burden of proof, except that if such party establishes that the requirements of Subsection (a)(3)(B) or (C) are not met, the director or the senior executive has the burden of proving that the rejection and the taking of the opportunity were fair to the corporation.

(d) *Ratification of Defective Disclosure.* A good faith but defective disclosure of the facts concerning the corporate opportunity may be cured if at any time (but no later than a reasonable time after suit is filed challenging the taking of the corporate opportunity) the original rejection of the corporate opportunity is ratified, following the required disclosure, by the board, the shareholders, or the corporate decisionmaker who initially approved the rejection of the corporate opportunity, or such decisionmaker's successor.

(e) *Special Rule Concerning Delayed Offering of Corporate Opportunities.* Relief based solely on failure to first offer an opportunity to the corporation under Subsection (a)(1) is not available if: (1) such failure resulted from a good faith belief that the business activity did not constitute a corporate opportunity, and (2) not later than a reasonable time after suit is filed challenging the taking of the corporate opportunity, the corporate opportunity is to the extent possible offered to the corporation and rejected in a manner that satisfies the standards of Subsection (a).

Comment:

a. Comparison with existing law. Existing judicial decisions offer a wide variety of tests for determining whether a director or a senior executive should be required to offer a corporate opportunity to the corporation. Some courts have given primary weight to whether the opportunity was related to or in the corporation's line of business. The doctrine has occasionally been limited to instances where the corporation has an interest already existing in the relevant property or an expectancy growing out of an existing right. Some courts have applied a so-called "two-step" approach, which seeks to combine the "line of business" test with a "fairness" test by first determining whether a corporate opportunity exists and then determining whether it is fair to require the director or senior executive to make it available to the corporation. Some courts have simply applied a general standard of fairness without articulating specific criteria to be utilized.

Section 5.05 sets forth a comprehensive statement of the doctrine of corporate opportunity that generally requires an opportunity to be offered to the corporation by a senior executive before it is taken by the senior executive. Directors other than those who are also senior executives are subjected to a significantly more limited duty to offer opportunities to the corporation than are senior executives. Section 5.05 reflects the general approach to what constitutes a corporate opportunity adopted by some courts and approved by the *Corporate Directors' Guidebook* (p. 6).

Section 5.05 permits the corporation to accept or reject an opportunity and treats the process of rejection as if it were a transaction between the director or principal senior executive and the corporation under § 5.02, except that if the rejection is approved in advance by disinterested directors or, in the case of a senior executive who is not a director, by a disinterested superior, after full disclosure, the rejection will be subject to review only under the business judgment rule. If the corporation rejects the opportunity, the director or senior executive is free to pursue the opportunity so long as it does not result in competition with the corporation in violation of § 5.06 (Competition with the Corporation). . . .

. . . .

c. General operation of § 5.05. Section 5.05 applies the doctrine of corporate opportunity to defined opportunities that come to directors or senior executives in either their individual or corporate capacity. In some cases, the director or senior executive is charged by the corporation with the responsibility for carrying out a particular activity that naturally leads to the generation of the opportunity in question. In such cases, when the opportunity has come to the director or senior executive in a corporate capacity, the duty to offer the opportunity to the corporation is obvious.

Illustration:

1. A, a senior executive of X Corporation, an oil exploration company, is charged with the responsibility for locating new drilling prospects. X Corporation's geologists give A the result of seismic surveys made by X Corporation in a particular area, and A thereupon personally acquires the most promising prospects. A is obliged to offer the prospects so acquired to X Corporation, and has therefore violated § 5.05.

The taking of a corporate opportunity that arises through use of material non-public corporate information may be potentially subject to review under both §§ 5.04 (Use by a Director or Senior Executive of Corporate Property, Material Non–Public Corporate Information, or Corporate Position) and 5.05. If the opportunity is offered to the corporation, then the director or senior executive will not have misused corporate position under § 5.04, and review of the conduct will occur only under § 5.05 (except for the obligation to reimburse the corporation for any significant use of corporate property or information, to the extent required by § 5.04, if the director or senior executive is properly allowed to take the opportunity). If the opportunity is not initially offered to the corporation because of a good faith belief that it did not constitute a corporate opportunity, then under § 5.05(e) the opportunity may still be subsequently offered to and rejected by disinterested directors or shareholders or, in the case of a senior executive who is not a director, by a disinterested superior.

Because of the importance of encouraging persons who are not employees of the corporation to serve as directors, and the likelihood that many such persons will be engaged in multiple business activities, under § 5.05 directors who are not senior executives have no obligation to offer an opportunity to the corporation simply because the opportunity is closely related to the corporation's business.

Comment to § 5.05(a):

Section 5.05(a) sets forth the general rule requiring a director or senior executive to first offer an opportunity to the corporation before taking it for personal advantage. If the opportunity is not offered to the corporation, the director or senior executive will not have satisfied § 5.05(a). Under § 5.05(a), a corporate opportunity should be promptly offered to the corporation, and the corporation should promptly accept or reject the opportunity. Failure to accept the opportunity within a reasonable time will be considered tantamount to a rejection. The process by which the corporation determines whether to accept or reject the opportunity will be governed by the same procedures set forth in § 5.02, as if the acceptance or rejection were a transaction subject to § 5.02. Accordingly, under § 5.05(a)(1) disclosure of all material facts known to the director or senior executive concerning the conflict of interest and the corporate opportunity should be made to the corporate decisionmaker reviewing the matter.

Under § 5.05(a)(3) the rejection should occur in a manner that meets the applicable standard provided in § 5.05(a)(3) (or § 5.12(a) (Taking of Corporate Opportunities by a Controlling Shareholder) if the director or senior executive is also a controlling shareholder [§ 1.10]). Rejection in the context of § 5.05(a)(3) may be based on one or more of a number of factors, such as lack of interest by the corporation in the opportunity, the corporation's financial inability to acquire the opportunity, legal restrictions on the corporation's ability to accept the opportunity, or unwillingness of a third party to deal with the corporation. Accordingly, § 5.05(a)(3)(B) provides that where disinterested directors reject the opportunity before it is taken, the propriety of rejecting the opportunity will be judged under the business judgment rule [§ 4.01(c)].

If a corporate opportunity is rejected, § 5.05(a) contemplates that the director or senior executive may then pursue the opportunity, subject to any limitations imposed by § 5.06 on the ability to compete with the corporation, and to the obligation of the director or senior executive to reimburse the corporation for any significant use of corporate property or information, to the extent required by § 5.04.

If an opportunity is offered to and rejected by the corporation, a director or principal senior executive who did not initially offer the opportunity to the corporation and who did not participate in the action of the corporation in rejecting the opportunity, may thereafter take the opportunity without again offering it to the corporation, unless the director or principal senior executive is aware of material facts concerning the opportunity not disclosed to the corporation when the opportunity was initially rejected.

Under § 5.05 it is not necessary to offer opportunities to the corporation where the amount involved would be de minimis.

Section 5.05 imposes upon directors or senior executives the obligation to offer a corporate opportunity to the corporation only if they wish to pursue it for their personal benefit, because the essential vice prohibited by § 5.05 is the taking of an opportunity for one's own benefit which should rightfully be offered to the corporation. However, directors or senior executives may under certain circumstances be liable for breach of the duty of care if they allow an opportunity to be forgone that they are charged with pursuing for the corporation. For example, if a senior executive is charged with the official duty to pursue an opportunity on behalf of the corporation and fails to do so, liability may be imposed under § 4.01(a) for failure to perform the undertaking of due care to the corporation.

Section 5.05 resolves the dilemma of a senior executive who has the duty to offer a corporate opportunity to more than one corporation by providing one of three alternatives—(1) refrain from offering the opportunity to any corporation (unless there is a duty to pursue the opportunity under § 4.01), and not pursue it for personal benefit; (2) offer the opportunity to each corporation and secure a rejection of the opportunity from each corporation before pursuing it for personal benefit; or (3) if there is an obligation, pursuant to § 4.01, to pursue the opportunity for one or more of the corporations, offer the opportunity to the corporation or corporations to whom the duty is owed, in which event the obligation under § 4.01 to each corporation is satisfied. The director or senior executive may secure advance rejection from one or more corporations to whom a duty is owed under § 5.05 in favor of another corporation in which a comparable position is held. If advance rejection cannot be obtained, the director or senior executive should consider terminating the relationship with one corporation or the other to resolve the conflict as to future opportunities. A director who is not a senior executive of a corporation will have an obligation under § 5.05 only with respect to opportunities of the kind described in § 5.05(b)(1). Accordingly, it is not anticipated that § 5.05 will impose conflicting duties of fair dealing on such a director.

Comment to § 5.05(b):

a. Definition of corporate opportunities. Section 5.05(b) defines a corporate opportunity as an opportunity to engage in a business activity of which a director or senior executive becomes aware and which meets the conditions specified in § 5.05(b)(1) or 5.05(b)(2). For this purpose, a business activity includes the acquisition or use of any contract rights or other tangible or intangible property.

b. Limitations imposed by § 5.05(b). Section 5.05 applies only to those business activities that fall within one of the categories described in § 5.05(b)(1) or 5.05(b)(2).

(1) *Corporate opportunities under § 5.05(b)(1).* Section 5.05(b)(1) covers the only situations in which § 5.05 applies with respect to both senior executives and directors who are not senior executives of the corporation. Section 5.05(b)(1)(A) treats as a corporate opportunity any opportunity that a director or the senior executive learns of in connection with the performance of directorial or executive functions and opportunities that are directed to the director or senior executive in that capacity and intercepted for personal benefit.

Use of information obtained by a director or senior executive through a corporate position, but not as a result of performance of corporate functions, will be subject to review under § 5.04.

Section 5.05(b)(1)(A) also covers opportunities that are presented to the senior executive or director under circumstances that should reasonably lead the senior executive or director to believe that the person offering the opportunity expects it to be offered to the corporation rather than taken personally. Accordingly, the focus under this provision is on whether a reasonable person in the position of the senior executive or director would assume that an opportunity was proffered for personal or corporate benefit. The director or senior executive has a duty of reasonable inquiry as to whether the opportunity was intended for the corporation.

Illustrations:

2. A is the chief executive officer of X Corporation, which is engaged in the steel manufacturing business. Although X Corporation has no present plans for diversifying its business, A is offered and accepts the opportunity, in connection with the performance of his functions as chief executive officer of X Corporation, to acquire all of the stock of Y Corporation, which is engaged in commercial development of solar energy. If A takes the opportunity for himself he will have taken a corporate opportunity under § 5.05(b)(1)(A) and will therefore have violated § 5.05.

3. The facts being otherwise as stated in Illustration 2, A is offered the opportunity to invest in stock in Y Corporation as part of a private placement of Y Corporation's stock, in his personal capacity and not in his capacity as a principal senior executive of X Corporation. A is not obliged to offer the opportunity to X Corporation under § 5.05(b)(1)(A).

4. The facts being otherwise as stated in Illustration 2, A is offered the opportunity in connection with the performance of his functions as chief executive officer of X Corporation to acquire the stock of Z Corporation, which is engaged in the production of iron ore pellets. A has received a corporate opportunity under § 5.05(b)(1)(A) which he must offer to X Corporation. Even if A were not offered the opportunity in connection with the performance of his functions as chief executive officer of X Corporation, he must offer the opportunity under § 5.05(b)(2).

. . . .

(2) *Corporate opportunities under § 5.05(b)(2).* Section 5.05(b)(2) makes § 5.05 applicable to those properties or activities that a senior executive knows are closely related to the business in which the corporation is engaged or expects to engage. Section 5.05(b)(2) expands the scope of corporate opportunity beyond the concept of an existing "line of business," which is utilized as a test in some decisions, to cover an existing or contemplated activity of the corporation. . . .

. . . .

Some older judicial decisions apply the doctrine of corporate opportunity to a contract right, property, or business activity in which the corporation has an "interest or expectancy." Section 5.05(b) does not expressly state this concept in the black-letter rule because § 5.05(b)(2) includes the concept of an interest or expectancy by covering a contemplated activity of a corporation.

. . . .

Section 5.05(b)(2) covers only those business activities that the senior executive knows are closely related to a business in which the corporation is engaged or expects to engage. If the senior executive has such knowledge, the opportunity must be offered to the corporation without regard to the senior executive's own judgment whether the corporation would be capable of or interested in pursuing the opportunity.

. . . .

Comment to § 5.05(e):

. . . .

If the director or senior executive acquires property that should have been offered to the corporation, the property will be required to be held in constructive trust for the corporation. See Restatement of Restitution §§ 194, 195. However, the director or senior executive will not be compelled to forfeit the amount paid for the property, and can be compelled to surrender the property only if reimbursed for the purchase price or the price for which it could have originally been obtained by the corporation, whichever is less. See Restatement of Restitution § 194, Comment *b*. The director or senior executive must also account to the corporation for any profit realized due to the use of corporate position or corporate property, and for any enhancement in value that creates a pecuniary benefit.

Illustration:

13. A, a senior executive of X Corporation, acquires for $500,000 a parcel of real property which A learns, prior to its acquisition and through A's position, that X Corporation may wish to acquire in order to build a new manufacturing facility. After A acquires the parcel, property values in the area increase for reasons unrelated to X Corporation's plans, so that the fair market value of A's parcel increases to $750,000. A had an obligation under § 5.05 to offer X Corporation the opportunity to buy the parcel, and therefore violated § 5.05. X Corporation may now acquire the parcel at A's purchase price of $500,000, rather than at its current fair market value of $750,000, which it would have to pay in an arm's-length transaction.

. . . .

[The "Reporter's Note" to § 5.05 states, in relevant part, the following: "The cases offer a variety of justifications for a corporation's rejection of an opportunity, including the corporation's financial inability to take the opportunity, a limitation in the corporation's charter which precludes incurring the debt required to take the opportunity, the absence of adequate physical facilities to permit the corporation to take the opportunity, and legal inhibitions on the corporation's engaging in the opportunity. In some of these cases, it is not clear that the opportunity was in fact offered to the corporation, and the court justified the taking by the director or senior executive on the ground that under the circumstances there was no "opportunity" to be proffered. Section 5.05 contemplates that whenever an opportunity, as defined in § 5.05(b), is present, it is to be offered to the corporation, which may then determine whether the obstacles to accepting the opportunity are insuperable or can be avoided. For example, charter limitations may be eliminated, and what are thought to be legal limitations may often be avoided with the assistance of counsel. If the opportunity is never offered to the corporation, the director or senior executive who takes the opportunity may not thereafter defend on the ground that there was no opportunity because the corporation was unable to accept it." Reporter's Note, No. 8].

§ 5.06 Competition with the Corporation

(a) *General Rule.* Directors [§ 1.13] and senior executives [§ 1.33] may not advance their pecuniary interests by engaging in competition with the corporation unless either:

(1) Any reasonably foreseeable harm to the corporation from such competition is outweighed by the benefit that the corporation may reasonably be expected to derive from allowing the competition to take place, or there is no reasonably foreseeable harm to the corporation from such competition;

(2) The competition is authorized in advance or ratified, following disclosure concerning the conflict of interest [§ 1.14(a)] and the competition [§ 1.14(b)], by disinterested directors [§ 1.15], or in the case of a senior executive who is not a director, is authorized in advance by a disinterested superior, in a manner that satisfies the standards of the business judgment rule [§ 4.01(c)]; or

(3) The competition is authorized in advance or ratified, following such disclosure, by disinterested shareholders [§ 1.16], and the shareholders' action is not equivalent to a waste of corporate assets [§ 1.42].

(b) *Burden of Proof.* A party who challenges a director or senior executive for advancing the director's or senior executive's pecuniary interest by competing with the corporation has the burden of proof, except that if such party establishes that neither Subsection (a)(2) nor (3) is satisfied, the director or the senior executive has the burden of proving that any reasonably foreseeable harm to the corporation from such competition is outweighed by the benefit that the corporation may reasonably be expected to derive from allowing the competition to take place, or that there is no reasonably foreseeable harm to the corporation.

§ 5.16 Disposition of Voting Equity Securities by a Controlling Shareholder to Third Parties

A controlling shareholder [§ 1.10] has the same right to dispose of voting equity securities [§ 1.40] as any other shareholder, including the right to dispose of those securities for a price that is not made proportionally available to other shareholders, but the controlling shareholder does not satisfy the duty of fair dealing to the other shareholders if:

(a) The controlling shareholder does not make disclosure concerning the transaction [§ 1.14(b)] to other shareholders with whom the controlling shareholder deals in connection with the transaction; or

(b) It is apparent from the circumstances that the purchaser is likely to violate the duty of fair dealing under Part V in such a way as to obtain a significant financial benefit for the purchaser or an associate [§ 1.03].

§ 7.01 Direct and Derivative Actions Distinguished

(a) A derivative action may be brought in the name or right of a corporation by a holder [§ 1.22], as provided in § 7.02 (Standing to Commence and Maintain a Derivative Action), to redress an injury sustained by, or enforce a duty owed to, a corporation. An action in which the holder can prevail only by showing an injury or breach of duty to the corporation should be treated as a derivative action.

(b) A direct action may be brought in the name and right of a holder to redress an injury sustained by, or enforce a duty owed to, the holder. An action in which the holder can prevail without showing an injury or breach of duty to the corporation should be treated as a direct action that may be maintained by the holder in an individual capacity.

(c) If a transaction gives rise to both direct and derivative claims, a holder may commence and maintain direct and derivative actions simultaneously, and any special restrictions or defenses pertaining to the maintenance, settlement, or dismissal of either action should not apply to the other.

(d) In the case of a closely held corporation [§ 1.06], the court in its discretion may treat an action raising derivative claims as a direct action, exempt it from those restrictions and defenses applicable only to derivative actions, and order an individual recovery, if it finds that to do so will not (i) unfairly expose the corporation or the defendants to a multiplicity of actions, (ii) materially prejudice the interests of creditors of the corporation, or (iii) interfere with a fair distribution of the recovery among all interested persons.

§ 7.22 Standards for Determining Fair Value

(a) The fair value of shares under § 7.21 (Corporate Transactions Giving Rise to Appraisal Rights) should be the value of the eligible holder's [§ 1.17] proportionate interest in the corporation, without any discount for minority status or, absent extraordinary circumstances, lack of marketability. Subject to Subsections (b) and (c), fair value should be determined using the customary valuation concepts and techniques generally employed in the relevant securities and financial markets for similar businesses in the context of the transaction giving rise to appraisal.

(b) In the case of a business combination that gives rise to appraisal rights, but does not fall within § 5.10 (Transactions by a Controlling Shareholder with the Corporation), § 5.15 (Transfer of Control in Which a Director or Principal Senior Executive Is Interested), or § 7.25 (Transactions in Control Involving Corporate Combinations to Which a Majority Shareholder Is a Party), the aggregate price accepted by the board of directors of the subject corporation should be presumed to represent the fair value of the corporation, or of the assets sold in the case of an asset sale, unless the plaintiff can prove otherwise by clear and convincing evidence.

(c) If the transaction giving rise to appraisal falls within § 5.10, § 5.15, or § 7.25, the court generally should give substantial weight to the highest realistic price that a willing, able, and fully informed buyer would pay for the corporation as an entirety. In determining what such a buyer would pay, the court may include a proportionate share of any gain reasonably to be expected to result from the combination, unless special circumstances would make such an allocation unreasonable.

Comment:

. . . .

e. Special valuation issues: "minority discounts," timing, and synergy gains. Some decisions have upheld the subtraction of a minority discount from the value of shares held by small stockholders on the theory that non-controlling stock is worth less than its proportionate share of the corporation's fair value. Other decisions have accepted a functionally similar adjustment to reflect the non-marketability of minority shares. However, both Delaware and Maine have recently and properly rejected the use of any such discount. Section 7.22(a) follows these jurisdictions in requiring the appraisal court to value the firm as a whole, not specific shares, and to allocate that value proportionately, absent extraordinary circumstances. Any contrary rule would require the court to undertake a complicated and ultimately speculative inquiry, which could produce disparate awards depending on the number of shares held by otherwise similarly situated dissenting shareholders. . . .

. . . .

Under a very limited exception to the principles set forth in § 7.22(a), the court may determine that a discount reflecting the lack of marketability of shares is appropriate in "extraordinary circumstances." Such circumstances require more than the absence of a trading market in the shares; rather, the court should apply this exception only when it finds that the dissenting shareholder has held out in order to exploit the transaction giving rise to appraisal so as to divert value to itself that could not be made available proportionately to other shareholders. For example, assume that a financially strained corporation with highly illiquid assets amends its charter to eliminate preemptive rights and authorize a new class of preferred stock in order to raise capital from a group of institutional investors, and that this charter amendment triggers appraisal. Because the corporation has highly illiquid assets and is financially troubled, fair value in an appraisal proceeding is likely to be significantly higher than the price that would actually be paid for a shareholder's stock in a market transaction. One shareholder dissents, solely because the shareholder had been unsuccessfully trying to induce the remaining shareholders to buy the shareholder out, and seeks to exploit the relatively minor certificate change as a mechanism to bail out of a troubled situation at a price that is much higher than any shareholder could obtain in a market transaction. On these facts, a court could find that the shareholder was opportunistically exploiting a change in the charter that was relatively minor, and to which the shareholder had no real objection. Here, unless a marketability discount was applied, there would be an unfair wealth transfer from the remaining shareholders to the dissenting shareholder. However, it would be inappropriate to apply a marketability discount, on otherwise identical facts, if the shareholder was dissenting to a fundamental corporate change, such as a merger, rather than a relatively minor matter.

. . . .

NEW YORK BUSINESS CORPORATION LAW

(Selected Provisions)

Table of Sections

---

§ 1002. Dissolution Under Provision in Certificate of Incorporation

(a) The certificate of incorporation may contain a provision that any shareholder, or the holders of any specified number or proportion of shares or votes of shares, or of any specified number or proportion of shares or votes of shares of any class or series thereof, may require the dissolution of the corporation at will or upon the occurrence of a specified event. If the certificate of incorporation contains such a provision, a certificate of dissolution under section 1003 (Certificate of dissolution; contents) may be signed, verified and delivered to the department of state as provided in section 104 (Certificate; requirements, signing, filing, effectiveness) when authorized by a holder or holders of the number or proportion of shares or votes of shares specified in such provision, given in such manner as may be specified therein, or if no manner is specified therein, when authorized on written consent signed by such holder or holders; or such certificate may be signed, verified and delivered to the department by such holder or holders or by such of them as are designated by them.

(b) An amendment of the certificate of incorporation which adds a provision permitted by this section, or which changes or strikes out such a provision, shall be authorized at a meeting of shareholders by vote of all outstanding shares, whether or not otherwise entitled to vote on any amendment, or of such lesser proportion of shares and of such class or series of shares, but not less than a majority of all outstanding shares entitled to vote on any amendment, as may be provided specifically in the certificate of incorporation for adding, changing or striking out a provision permitted by this section.

(c) If the certificate of incorporation of any corporation contains a provision authorized by this section, the existence of such provision shall be noted conspicuously on the face or back of every certificate for shares issued by such corporation.

§ 1104. Petition in Case of Deadlock Among Directors or Shareholders

(a) Except as otherwise provided in the certificate of incorporation under section 613 (Limitations on right to vote), the holders of shares representing one-half of the votes of all outstanding shares of a corporation entitled to vote in an election of directors may present a petition for dissolution on one or more of the following grounds:

(1) That the directors are so divided respecting the management of the corporation's affairs that the votes required for action by the board cannot be obtained.

(2) That the shareholders are so divided that the votes required for the election of directors cannot be obtained.

(3) That there is internal dissension and two or more factions of shareholders are so divided that dissolution would be beneficial to the shareholders.

(b) If the certificate of incorporation provides that the proportion of votes required for action by the board, or the proportion of votes of shareholders required for election of directors, shall be greater than that otherwise required by this chapter, such a petition may be presented by the holders of shares representing more than one-third of the votes of all outstanding shares entitled to vote on non-judicial dissolution under section 1001 (Authorization of dissolution).

(c) Notwithstanding any provision in the certificate of incorporation, any holder of shares entitled to vote at an election of directors of a corporation, may present a petition for its dissolution on the ground that the shareholders are so divided that they have failed, for a period which includes at least two consecutive annual meeting dates, to elect successors to directors whose terms have expired or would have expired upon the election and qualification of their successors.

§ 1104–a. Petition for Judicial Dissolution Under Special Circumstances

(a) The holders of shares representing twenty percent or more of the votes of all outstanding shares of a corporation, other than a corporation registered as an investment company under an act of congress entitled "Investment Company Act of 1940", no shares of which are listed on a national securities exchange or regularly quoted in an over-the-counter market by one or more members of a national or an affiliated securities association, entitled to vote in an election of directors may present a petition of dissolution on one or more of the following grounds:

(1) The directors or those in control of the corporation have been guilty of illegal, fraudulent or oppressive actions toward the complaining shareholders;

(2) The property or assets of the corporation are being looted, wasted, or diverted for non-corporate purposes by its directors, officers or those in control of the corporation.

(b) The court, in determining whether to proceed with involuntary dissolution pursuant to this section, shall take into account:

(1) Whether liquidation of the corporation is the only feasible means whereby the petitioners may reasonably expect to obtain a fair return on their investment; and

(2) Whether liquidation of the corporation is reasonably necessary for the protection of the rights and interests of any substantial number of shareholders or of the petitioners.

(c) In addition to all other disclosure requirements, the directors or those in control of the corporation, no later than thirty days after the filing of a petition hereunder, shall make available for inspection and copying to the petitioners under reasonable working conditions the corporate financial books and records for the three preceding years.

(d) The court may order stock valuations be adjusted and may provide for a surcharge upon the directors or those in control of the corporation upon a finding of wilful or reckless dissipation or transfer of assets or corporate property without just or adequate compensation therefor.

§ 1111. Judgment or Final Order of Dissolution

(a) In an action or special proceeding under this article if, in the court's discretion, it shall appear that the corporation should be dissolved, it shall make a judgment or final order dissolving the corporation.

(b) In making its decision, the court shall take into consideration the following criteria:

(1) In an action brought by the attorney-general, the interest of the public is of paramount importance.

(2) In a special proceeding brought by directors or shareholders, the benefit to the shareholders of a dissolution is of paramount importance.

(3) In a special proceeding brought under section 1104 (Petition in case of deadlock among directors or shareholders) or section 1104–a (Petition for judicial dissolution under special circumstances) dissolution is not to be denied merely because it is found that the corporate business has been or could be conducted at a profit.

(c) If the judgment or final order shall provide for a dissolution of the corporation, the court may, in its discretion, provide therein for the distribution of the property of the corporation to those entitled thereto according to their respective rights.

(d) The clerk of the court or such other person as the court may direct shall transmit certified copies of the judgment or final order of dissolution to the department of state and to the clerk of the county in which the office of the corporation was located at the date of the judgment or order. Upon filing by the department of state, the corporation shall be dissolved.

(e) The corporation shall promptly thereafter transmit a certified copy of the judgment or final order to the clerk of each other county in which its certificate of incorporation was filed.

§ 1118. Purchase of Petitioner's Shares; Valuation

(a) In any proceeding brought pursuant to section eleven hundred four-a of this chapter, any other shareholder or shareholders or the corporation may, at any time within ninety days after the filing of such petition or at such later time as the court in its discretion may allow, elect to purchase the shares owned by the petitioners at their fair value and upon such terms and conditions as may be approved by the court, including the conditions of paragraph (c) herein. An election pursuant to this section shall be irrevocable unless the court, in its discretion, for just and equitable considerations, determines that such election be revocable.

(b) If one or more shareholders or the corporation elect to purchase the shares owned by the petitioner but are unable to agree with the petitioner upon the fair value of such shares, the court, upon the application of such prospective purchaser or purchasers or the petitioner, may stay the proceedings brought pursuant to section 1104–a of this chapter and determine the fair value of the petitioner's shares as of the day prior to the date on which such petition was filed, exclusive of any element of value arising from such filing but giving effect to any adjustment or surcharge found to be appropriate in the proceeding under section 1104–a of this chapter. In determining the fair value of the petitioner's shares, the court, in its discretion, may award interest from the date the petition is filed to the date of payment for the petitioner's share at an equitable rate upon judicially determined fair value of his shares.

(c) In connection with any election to purchase pursuant to this section:

(1) If such election is made beyond ninety days after the filing of the petition, and the court allows such petition, the court, in its discretion, may award the petitioner his reasonable expenses incurred in the proceeding prior to such election, including reasonable attorneys' fees;

(2) The court, in its discretion, may require, at any time prior to the actual purchase of petitioner's shares, the posting of a bond or other acceptable security in an amount sufficient to secure petitioner for the fair value of his shares.

*

CALIFORNIA CORPORATIONS CODE

(Selected Provisions)

Table of Sections

---

§ 308. Deadlocked Board of Directors; Deadlocked Shareholders; Provisional Director; Appointment; Powers

(a) If a corporation has an even number of directors who are equally divided and cannot agree as to the management of its affairs, so that its business can no longer be conducted to advantage or so that there is danger that its property and business will be impaired or lost, the superior court of the proper county may, notwithstanding any provisions of the articles or bylaws and whether or not an action is pending for an involuntary winding up or dissolution of the corporation, appoint a provisional director pursuant to this section. Action for such appointment may be brought by any director or by the holders of not less than 33 1/3 percent of the voting power.

(b) If the shareholders of a corporation are deadlocked so that they cannot elect the directors to be elected at an annual meeting of shareholders, the superior court of the proper county may, notwithstanding any provisions of the articles or bylaws, upon petition of a shareholder or shareholders holding 50 percent of the voting power, appoint a provisional director or directors pursuant to this section or order such other equitable relief as the court deems appropriate.

(c) A provisional director shall be an impartial person, who is neither a shareholder nor a creditor of the corporation, nor related by consanguinity or affinity within the third degree according to the common law to any of the other directors of the corporation or to any judge of the court by which such provisional director is appointed. A provisional director shall have all the rights and powers of a director until the deadlock in the board or among shareholders is broken or until such provisional director is removed by order of the court or by approval of the outstanding shares (Section 152). Such person shall be entitled to such compensation as shall be fixed by the court unless otherwise agreed with the corporation.

(d) This section does not apply to corporations subject to the Public Utilities Act (Part 1 (commencing with Section 201) of Division 1 of the Public Utilities Code).

§ 1800. Verified Complaint; Plaintiffs; Grounds; Intervention by Shareholder or Creditor; Exempt Corporations

(a) A verified complaint for involuntary dissolution of a corporation on any one or more of the grounds specified in subdivision (b) may be filed in the superior court of the proper county by any of the following persons:

(1) One-half or more of the directors in office.

(2) A shareholder or shareholders who hold shares representing not less than 33 1/3 percent of (i) the total number of outstanding shares (assuming conversion of any preferred shares convertible into common shares) or (ii) the outstanding common shares or (iii) the equity of the corporation, exclusive in each case of shares owned by persons who have personally participated in any of the transactions enumerated in paragraph (4) of subdivision (b), or any shareholder or shareholders of a close corporation.

(3) Any shareholder if the ground for dissolution is that the period for which the corporation was formed has terminated without extension thereof.

(4) Any other person expressly authorized to do so in the articles.

(b) The grounds for involuntary dissolution are that:

(1) The corporation has abandoned its business for more than one year.

(2) The corporation has an even number of directors who are equally divided and cannot agree as to the management of its affairs, so that its business can no longer be conducted to advantage or so

that there is danger that its property and business will be impaired or lost, and the holders of the voting shares of the corporation are so divided into factions that they cannot elect a board consisting of an uneven number.

(3) There is internal dissension and two or more factions of shareholders in the corporation are so deadlocked that its business can no longer be conducted with advantage to its shareholders or the shareholders have failed at two consecutive annual meetings at which all voting power was exercised, to elect successors to directors whose terms have expired or would have expired upon election of their successors.

(4) Those in control of the corporation have been guilty of or have knowingly countenanced persistent and pervasive fraud, mismanagement or abuse of authority or persistent unfairness toward any shareholders or its property is being misapplied or wasted by its directors or officers.

(5) In the case of any corporation with 35 or fewer shareholders (determined as provided in Section 605), liquidation is reasonably necessary for the protection of the rights or interests of the complaining shareholder or shareholders.

(6) The period for which the corporation was formed has terminated without extension of such period.

(c) At any time prior to the trial of the action any shareholder or creditor may intervene therein.

(d) This section does not apply to any corporation subject to the Banking Law (Division 1 (commencing with Section 99) of the Financial Code), the Public Utilities Act (Part 1 (commencing with 201) of Division 1 of the Public Utilities Code), the Savings and Loan Association Law (Division 2 (commencing with Section 5000) of the Financial Code) or Article 14 (commencing with Section 1010) of Chapter 1 of Part 2 of Division 1 of the Insurance Code.

(e) For the purposes of this section, "shareholder" includes a beneficial owner of shares who has entered into an agreement under Section 300 or 706.

§ 1802. Provisional Director; Appointment; Deadlocked Board

If the ground for the complaint for involuntary dissolution of the corporation is a deadlock in the board as set forth in subdivision (b) (2) of Section 1800, the court may appoint a provisional director. The provisions of subdivision (c) of Section 308 apply to any such provisional director so appointed.

§ 1804. Decree for Winding Up and Dissolution; Other Judicial Relief

After hearing the court may decree a winding up and dissolution of the corporation if cause therefor is shown or, with or without winding up and dissolution, may make such orders and decrees and issue such injunctions in the case as justice and equity require.

§ 2000. Avoidance of Dissolution by Purchase of Plaintiffs' Shares; Valuation; Vote Required; Stay of Dissolution Proceedings; Appraisal Under Court Order; Confirmation by Court; Appeal

(a) Subject to any contrary provision in the articles, in any suit for involuntary dissolution, or in any proceeding for voluntary dissolution initiated by the vote of shareholders representing only 50 percent of the voting power, the corporation or, if it does not elect to purchase, the holders of 50 percent or more of the voting power of the corporation (the "purchasing parties") may avoid the dissolution of the corporation and the appointment of any receiver by purchasing for cash the shares owned by the plaintiffs or by the shareholders so initiating the proceeding (the "moving parties") at their fair value. The fair value shall be determined on the basis of the liquidation value as of the valuation date but taking into account the possibility, if any, of sale of the entire business as a going concern in a liquidation. In fixing the value, the amount of any damages resulting if the initiation of the dissolution is a breach by any moving party or parties of an agreement with the purchasing party or parties may be deducted from the amount payable to such moving party or parties, unless the ground for dissolution is that specified in paragraph (4) of subdivision (b) of Section 1800. The election of the corporation to purchase may be made by the approval of the outstanding shares (Section 152) excluding shares held by the moving parties.

(b) If the purchasing parties (1) elect to purchase the shares owned by the moving parties, and (2) are unable to agree with the moving parties upon the fair value of such shares, and (3) give bond with sufficient security to pay the estimated reasonable expenses (including attorneys' fees) of the moving parties if such expenses are recoverable under subdivision (c), the court upon application of the purchasing parties, either in the pending action or in a proceeding initiated in the superior court of the proper county by the purchasing parties in the case of a voluntary election to wind up and dissolve, shall stay the winding up and dissolution proceeding and shall proceed to ascertain and fix the fair value of the shares owned by the moving parties.

(c) The court shall appoint three disinterested appraisers to appraise the fair value of the shares owned by the moving parties, and shall make an order referring the matter to the appraisers so appointed for the purpose of ascertaining such value. The order shall prescribe the time and manner of producing evidence, if evidence is required. The award of the appraisers or of a majority of them, when confirmed by the court, shall be final and conclusive upon all parties. The court shall enter a decree which shall provide in the alternative for winding up and dissolution of the corporation unless payment is made for the shares within the time specified by the decree. If the purchasing parties do not make payment for the shares within the time specified, judgment shall be entered against them and the surety or sureties on the bond for the amount of the expenses (including attorneys' fees) of the moving parties. Any shareholder aggrieved by the action of the court may appeal therefrom.

(d) If the purchasing parties desire to prevent the winding up and dissolution, they shall pay to the moving parties the value of their shares ascertained and decreed within the time specified pursuant to this section, or, in case of an appeal, as fixed on appeal. On receiving such payment or the tender thereof, the moving parties shall transfer their shares to the purchasing parties.

(e) For the purposes of this section, "shareholder" includes a beneficial owner of shares who has entered into an agreement under Section 300 or 706.

(f) For the purposes of this section, the valuation date shall be (1) in the case of a suit for involuntary dissolution under Section 1800, the date upon which that action was commenced, or (2) in the case of a proceeding for voluntary dissolution initiated by the vote of shareholders representing only 50 percent of the voting power, the date upon which that proceeding was initiated. However, in either case the court may, upon the hearing of a motion by any party, and for good cause shown, designate some other date as the valuation date.

*

MINNESOTA STATUTES § 302A.751

§ 302A.751. Judicial Intervention; Equitable Remedies or Dissolution

Subdivision 1. When permitted. A court may grant any equitable relief it deems just and reasonable in the circumstances or may dissolve a corporation and liquidate its assets and business:

(a) In a supervised voluntary dissolution pursuant to section 302A.741;

(b) In an action by a shareholder when it is established that:

(1) the directors or the persons having the authority otherwise vested in the board are deadlocked in the management of the corporate affairs and the shareholders are unable to break the deadlock;

(2) the directors or those in control of the corporation have acted fraudulently or illegally toward one or more shareholders in their capacities as shareholders or directors, or as officers or employees of a closely held corporation;

(3) the directors or those in control of the corporation have acted in a manner unfairly prejudicial toward one or more shareholders in their capacities as shareholders or directors of a corporation that is not a publicly held corporation, or as officers or employees of a closely held corporation;

(4) the shareholders of the corporation are so divided in voting power that, for a period that includes the time when two consecutive regular meetings were held, they have failed to elect successors to directors whose terms have expired or would have expired upon the election and qualification of their successors;

(5) the corporate assets are being misapplied or wasted; or

(6) the period of duration as provided in the articles has expired and has not been extended as provided in section 302A.801;

(c) In an action by a creditor when:

(1) the claim of the creditor has been reduced to judgment and an execution thereon has been returned unsatisfied; or

(2) the corporation has admitted in writing that the claim of the creditor is due and owing and it is established that the corporation is unable to pay its debts in the ordinary course of business; or

(d) In an action by the attorney general to dissolve the corporation in accordance with section 302A.757 when it is established that a decree of dissolution is appropriate.

Subd. 2. Buy-out on motion. In an action under subdivision 1, clause (b), involving a corporation that is not a publicly held corporation at the time the action is commenced and in which one or more of the circumstances described in that clause is established, the court may, upon motion of a corporation or a shareholder or beneficial owner of shares of the corporation, order the sale by a plaintiff or a defendant of all shares of the corporation held by the plaintiff or defendant to either the corporation or the moving shareholders, whichever is specified in the motion, if the court determines in its discretion that an order would be fair and equitable to all parties under all of the circumstances of the case.

The purchase price of any shares so sold shall be the fair value of the shares as of the date of the commencement of the action or as of another date found equitable by the court, provided that, if the shares in question are then subject to sale and purchase pursuant to the bylaws of the corporation, a shareholder control agreement, the terms of the shares, or otherwise, the court shall order the sale for the price and on the terms set forth in them, unless the court determines that the price or terms are unreasonable under all the circumstances of the case.

Within five days after the entry of the order, the corporation shall provide each selling shareholder or beneficial owner with the information it is required to provide under section 302A.473, subdivision 5, paragraph (a).

If the parties are unable to agree on fair value within 40 days of entry of the order, the court shall determine the fair value of the shares under the provisions of section 302A.473, subdivision 7, and may allow interest or costs as provided in section 302A.473, subdivisions 1 and 8.

The purchase price shall be paid in one or more installments as agreed on by the parties, or, if no agreement can be reached within 40 days of entry of the order, as ordered by the court. Upon entry of an order for the sale of shares under this subdivision and provided that the corporation or the moving shareholders post a bond in adequate amount with sufficient sureties or otherwise satisfy the court that the full purchase price of the shares, plus such additional costs, expenses, and fees as may be awarded, will be paid when due and payable, the selling shareholders shall no longer have any rights or status as shareholders, officers, or directors, except the right to receive the fair value of their shares plus such other amounts as might be awarded.

Subd. 3. Condition of corporation. In determining whether to order equitable relief, dissolution, or a buy-out, the court shall take into consideration the financial condition of the corporation but shall not refuse to order equitable relief, dissolution, or a buy-out solely on the ground that the corporation has accumulated or current operating profits.

Subd. 3a. Considerations in granting relief involving closely held corporations. In determining whether to order equitable relief, dissolution, or a buy-out, the court shall take into consideration the duty which all shareholders in a closely held corporation owe one another to act in an honest, fair, and reasonable manner in the operation of the corporation and the reasonable expectations of all shareholders as they exist at the inception and develop during the course of the shareholders' relationship with the corporation and with each other. For purposes of this section, any written agreements, including employment agreements and buy-sell agreements, between or among shareholders or between or among one or more shareholders and the corporation are presumed to reflect the parties' reasonable expectations concerning matters dealt with in the agreements.

Subd. 3b. Dissolution as remedy. In deciding whether to order dissolution, the court shall consider whether lesser relief suggested by one or more parties, such as any form of equitable relief, a buy-out, or a partial liquidation, would be adequate to permanently relieve the circumstances established under subdivision 1, clause (b) or (c). Lesser relief may be ordered in any case where it would be appropriate under all the facts and circumstances of the case.

Subd. 4. Expenses. If the court finds that a party to a proceeding brought under this section has acted arbitrarily, vexatiously, or otherwise not in good faith, it may in its discretion award reasonable expenses, including attorneys' fees and disbursements, to any of the other parties.

Subd. 5. Venue; parties. Proceedings under this section shall be brought in a court within the county in which the registered office of the corporation is located. It is not necessary to make shareholders parties to the action or proceeding unless relief is sought against them personally.

*

SELECTED FEDERAL SECURITIES LAW PROVISIONS

SECURITIES EXCHANGE ACT (1934)

(15 U.S.C. § 78j)

§ 10. Manipulative and deceptive devices

It shall be unlawful for any person, directly or indirectly, by the use of any means or instrumentality of interstate commerce or of the mails, or of any facility of any national securities exchange—

(a)

(1) To effect a short sale, or to use or employ any stop-loss order in connection with the purchase or sale, of any security registered on a national securities exchange, in contravention of such rules and regulations as the Commission may prescribe as necessary or appropriate in the public interest or for the protection of investors.

(2) Paragraph (1) of this subsection shall not apply to security futures products.

(b) To use or employ, in connection with the purchase or sale of any security registered on a national securities exchange or any security not so registered, or any securities-based swap agreement (as defined in section 206B of the Gramm–Leach–Bliley Act), any manipulative or deceptive device or contrivance in contravention of such rules and regulations as the Commission may prescribe as necessary or appropriate in the public interest or for the protection of investors. . . .

CODE OF FEDERAL REGULATIONS

(17 C.F.R. § 240.10b-5)

Rule 10b–5. Employment of manipulative and deceptive devices

It shall be unlawful for any person, directly or indirectly, by the use of any means or instrumentality of interstate commerce, or of the mails or of any facility of any national securities exchange,

(a) To employ any device, scheme, or artifice to defraud,

(b) To make any untrue statement of a material fact or to omit to state a material fact necessary in order to make the statements made, in the light of the circumstances under which they were made, not misleading, or

(c) To engage in any act, practice, or course of business which operates or would operate as a fraud or deceit upon any person,

in connection with the purchase or sale of any security.

SELECTED DELAWARE CHANCERY COURT RULES

Rule 11. Signing of Pleadings, Motions, and Other Papers; Representations to Court; Sanctions

(a) Signature.—Every pleading, motion, and other paper shall be signed by at least 1 attorney of record in the attorney's individual name, or, if the party is not represented by an attorney, shall be signed by the party. Each paper shall state the signer's address and telephone number, if any. Except when otherwise specifically provided by statute or rule, pleadings need not be verified or accompanied by affidavit. An unsigned paper shall be stricken unless it is corrected promptly after the omission of the signature is called to the attention of the attorney of party.

(b) Representations to Court.—By presenting to the Court (whether by signing, filing, submitting, or later advocating) a pleading, written motion, or other paper, an attorney or unrepresented party is certifying that to the best of the person's knowledge, information, and belief, formed after an inquiry reasonable under the circumstances:

(1) it is not being presented for any improper purpose, such as to harass or to cause unnecessary delay or needless increase in the cost of litigation;

(2) the claims, defenses, and other legal contentions therein are warranted by existing law or by a nonfrivolous argument for the extension, modification, or reversal of existing law or the establishment of new law;

(3) the allegations and other factual contentions have evidentiary support or, if specifically so identified, are likely to have evidentiary support after a reasonable opportunity for further investigation or discovery; and

(4) the denials of factual contentions are warranted on the evidence or, if specifically so identified, are reasonably based on a lack of information or belief.

(c) Sanctions.—If, after notice and a reasonable opportunity to respond, the Court determines that subdivision (b) has been violated, the

Court may, subject to the conditions stated below, impose an appropriate sanction upon the attorneys, law firms, or parties that have violated subdivision (b) or are responsible for the violation.

(1) How initiated.

(A) By motion.—A motion for sanctions under this rule shall be made separately from other motions or requests and shall describe the specific conduct alleged to violate subdivision (b). It shall be served as provided in Rule 5, but shall not be filed with or presented to the Court unless, within 21 days after service of the motion (or such other period as the Court may prescribe), the challenged paper, claim, defense, contention, allegation, or denial is not withdrawn or appropriately corrected. If warranted, the Court may award to the party prevailing on the motion the reasonable expenses and attorney's fees incurred in presenting or opposing the motion. Absent exceptional circumstances, a law firm shall be held jointly responsible for violations committed by its partners, associates, and employees.

(B) On Court's initiative.—On its own initiative, the Court may enter an order describing the specific conduct that appears to violate subdivision (b) and directing an attorney, law firm, or party to show cause why it has not violated subdivision (b) with respect thereto.

(2) Nature of sanction; limitations.—A sanction imposed for violation of this rule shall be limited to what is sufficient to deter repetition of such conduct or comparable conduct by others similarly situated. Subject to the limitations in subparagraphs (A) and (B), the sanction may consist of, or include, directives of a nonmonetary nature, an order to pay a penalty into Court, or, if imposed on motion and warranted for effective deterrence, an order directing payment to the movant of some or all of the reasonable attorneys' fees and other expenses incurred as a direct result of the violation.

(A) Monetary sanctions may not be awarded against a represented party for a violation of subdivision (b)(2).

(B) Monetary sanctions may not be awarded on the Court's initiative unless the Court issues its order to show cause before a voluntary dismissal or settlement of the claims made by or against the party which is, or whose attorneys are, to be sanctioned.

(3) Order.—When imposing sanctions, the Court shall describe the conduct determined to constitute a violation of this rule and explain the basis for the sanction imposed.

(d) Inapplicability to discovery.—Subdivisions (a) through (c) of this rule do not apply to disclosures and discovery requests, responses, objections, and motions that are subject to the provisions of Rules 26 through 37.

Rule 23.1. Derivative Actions by Shareholders

In a derivative action brought by 1 or more shareholders or members to enforce a right of a corporation or of an unincorporated association, the corporation or association having failed to enforce a right which may properly be asserted by it, the complaint shall allege that the plaintiff was a shareholder or member at the time of the transaction of which the plaintiff complains or that the plaintiff's share or membership thereafter devolved on the plaintiff by operation of law. The complaint shall also allege with particularity the efforts, if any, made by the plaintiff to obtain the action the plaintiff desires from the directors or comparable authority and the reasons for the plaintiff's failure to obtain the action or for not making the effort. Subject to the provisions of Rule 15(aaa), the action shall not be dismissed or compromised without the approval of the Court, and notice by mail, publication or otherwise of the proposed dismissal or compromise shall be given to shareholders or members in such manner as the Court directs; except that if the dismissal is to be without prejudice or with prejudice to the plaintiff only, then such dismissal shall be ordered without notice thereof if there is a showing that no compensation in any form has passed directly or indirectly from any of the defendants to the plaintiff or plaintiff's attorney and that no promise to give any such compensation has been made.

*

REVISED UNIFORM LIMITED PARTNERSHIP ACT (1976) WITH 1985 AMENDMENTS

(The 1985 Amendments are Indicated by Underscore and Strikeout)

Table of Sections

ARTICLE 1. GENERAL PROVISIONS

ARTICLE 2. FORMATION: CERTIFICATE OF LIMITED PARTNERSHIP

ARTICLE 3. LIMITED PARTNERS

ARTICLE 4. GENERAL PARTNERS

ARTICLE 5. FINANCE

ARTICLE 6. DISTRIBUTIONS AND WITHDRAWAL

ARTICLE 7. ASSIGNMENT OF PARTNERSHIP INTERESTS

ARTICLE 8. DISSOLUTION

ARTICLE 9. FOREIGN LIMITED PARTNERSHIPS

ARTICLE 10. DERIVATIVE ACTIONS

ARTICLE 11. MISCELLANEOUS

ARTICLE 1
GENERAL PROVISIONS

§ 101. Definitions

As used in this [Act], unless the context otherwise requires:

(1) "Certificate of limited partnership" means the certificate referred to in Section 201, and the certificate as amended or restated.

(2) "Contribution" means any cash, property, services rendered, or a promissory note or other binding obligation to contribute cash or property or to perform services, which a partner contributes to a limited partnership in his capacity as a partner.

(3) "Event of withdrawal of a general partner" means an event that causes a person to cease to be a general partner as provided in Section 402.

(4) "Foreign limited partnership" means a partnership formed under the laws of any ~~State~~ state other than this State and having as partners one or more general partners and one or more limited partners.

(5) "General partner" means a person who has been admitted to a limited partnership as a general partner in accordance with the partnership agreement and named in the certificate of limited partnership as a general partner.

(6) "Limited partner" means a person who has been admitted to a limited partnership as a limited partner in accordance with the partnership agreement ~~and named in the certificate of limited partnership as a limited partner~~.

(7) "Limited partnership" and "domestic limited partnership" mean a partnership formed by two or more persons under the laws of

this State and having one or more general partners and one or more limited partners.

(8) "Partner" means a limited or general partner.

(9) "Partnership agreement" means any valid agreement, written or oral, of the partners as to the affairs of a limited partnership and the conduct of its business.

(10) "Partnership interest" means a partner's share of the profits and losses of a limited partnership and the right to receive distributions of partnership assets.

(11) "Person" means a natural person, partnership, limited partnership (domestic or foreign), trust, estate, association, or corporation.

(12) "State" means a state, territory, or possession of the United States, the District of Columbia, or the Commonwealth of Puerto Rico.

Comment

The definitions in this section clarify a number of uncertainties in the law existing law prior to the 1976 Act, and also make certain changes in such prior law. The 1985 Act makes very few additional changes in Section 101.

Contribution: this definition makes it clear that a present contribution of services and a promise to make a future payment of cash, contribution of property or performance of services are permissible forms for a contribution. Accordingly, the present Section 502 of the 1985 Act provides that a limited partner's promise to make a contribution is enforceable only when set out in a writing signed by the limited partner. (This result is not dissimilar from that under the 1976 Act, which required all promises of future contributions to be described in the certificate of limited partnership, which was to be signed by, among others, the partners making such promises.) The property or services contributed presently or promise promised to be contributed in the future must be accorded a value in the certificate of limited partnership (Section 201(5)) partnership agreement or the partnership records required to be kept pursuant to Section 105, and, in the case of a promise, that value may determine the liability of a partner who fails to honor his agreement (Section 502). Section 3 of the prior uniform law 1916 Act did not permit a limited partner's contribution to be in the form of services, although that inhibition did not apply to general partners.

Foreign limited partnership: the Act only deals with foreign limited partnerships formed under the laws of another "State" "state" of the United States (see subdivision 12 of Section 101), and any adopting State state that desires to deal by statute with the status of entities formed under the laws of foreign countries must make appropriate changes throughout the Act. The exclusion of such entities from the Act was not intended to suggest that their "limited partners" should not be accorded limited liability by the courts of a ~~State~~ state adopting the Act. That question would be resolved by the choice-of-law rules of the forum ~~State~~ state.

General partner: this definition recognizes the separate functions of the partnership agreement and the certificate of limited partnership. The partnership agreement establishes the basic grant of management power to the persons named as general partners; but because of the passive role played by the limited partners, the separate, formal step of ~~embodying~~ memorializing that grant of power in the certificate of limited partnership has been preserved to emphasize its importance and to provide notice of the identity of the partnership's general partners to persons dealing with the partnership.

Limited partner: ~~as in~~ unlike the ~~case of~~ definition of general partners, this definition provides for admission of limited partners through the partnership agreement ~~and solemnization in the certificate of limited partnership. In addition, the definition makes it clear that being named in the certificate of limited partnership is a prerequisite to limited partner status. Failure to file does not, however, mean that the participant is a general partner or that he has general liability. See Sections 202(e) and 303~~ alone and does not require identification of any limited partner in the certificate of limited partnership (Section 201). Under the 1916 and the 1976 Acts, being named as a limited partner in the certificate of limited partnership was a statutory requirement and, in most if not all cases, probably also a prerequisite to limited partner status. By eliminating the requirement that the certificate of limited partnership contain the name, address, and capital contribution of each limited partner, the 1985 Act all but eliminates any risk that a person intended to be a limited partner may be exposed to liability as a general partner as a result of the inadvertent omission of any of that information from the certificate of limited partnership, and also dispenses with the need to amend the certificate of limited partnership upon the admission or withdrawal of, transfer of an interest by, or change in the address or capital contribution of, any limited partner.

Partnership agreement: the ~~prior uniform law~~ 1916 Act did not refer to the partnership agreement, assuming that all important matters affecting limited partners would be set forth in the certificate of limited partnership. Under modern practice, however, it has been common for the partners to enter into a comprehensive partnership agreement, only part of which was required to be included or summarized in the certificate of limited partnership. As reflected in Section 201 of the 1985 Act, the certificate of limited partnership is confined principally to matters respecting the partnership itself and the ~~addition and withdrawal~~ identity of general partners ~~and of capital~~, and other important issues are left to the partnership agreement. Most of the information formerly provided by, but no longer required to be included in, the certificate of limited partnership is now required to be kept in the partnership records (Section 105).

Partnership interest: this definition ~~is new~~ first appeared in the 1976 Act and is intended to define what it is that is transferred when a partnership interest is assigned.

§ 102. Name

The name of each limited partnership as set forth in its certificate of limited partnership:

(1) shall contain without abbreviation the words "limited partnership";

(2) may not contain the name of a limited partner unless (i) it is also the name of a general partner or the corporate name of a corporate general partner, or (ii) the business of the limited partnership had been carried on under that name before the admission of that limited partner;

~~(3) may not contain any word or phrase indicating or implying that it is organized other than for a purpose stated in its certificate of limited partnership;~~

~~(4)~~ (3) may not be the same as, or deceptively similar to, the name of any corporation or limited partnership organized under the laws of this State or licensed or registered as a foreign corporation or limited partnership in this State; and

~~(5)~~ (4) may not contain the following words [here insert prohibited words].

Comment

Subdivision (2) of Section 102 has been carried over from Section 5 of the ~~prior uniform law~~ 1916 Act with certain editorial changes. The remainder of Section 102 ~~is new~~ first appeared in the 1976 Act and primarily reflects the intention to integrate the registration of limited partnership names with that of corporate names. Accordingly, Section 201 provides for central, ~~State-wide~~ state-wide filing of certificates of limited partnership, and subdivisions (3)~~,~~ and (4) ~~and (5)~~ of Section 102 contain standards to be applied by the filing officer in determining whether the certificate should be filed. Subdivision (1) requires that the proper name of a limited partnership contain the words "limited partnership" in full. Subdivision (3) of the 1976 Act has been deleted, to reflect the deletion from Section 201 of any requirement that the certificate of limited partnership describe the partnership's purposes or the character of its business.

§ 103. Reservation of Name

(a) The exclusive right to the use of a name may be reserved by:

(1) any person intending to organize a limited partnership under this [Act] and to adopt that name;

(2) any domestic limited partnership or any foreign limited partnership registered in this State which, in either case, intends to adopt that name;

(3) any foreign limited partnership intending to register in this State and adopt that name; and

(4) any person intending to organize a foreign limited partnership and intending to have it register in this State and adopt that name.

(b) The reservation shall be made by filing with the Secretary of State an application, executed by the applicant, to reserve a specified name. If the Secretary of State finds that the name is available for use by a domestic or foreign limited partnership, he [or she] shall reserve the name for the exclusive use of the applicant for a period of 120 days. Once having so reserved a name, the same applicant may not again reserve the same name until more than 60 days after the expiration of the last 120–day period for which that applicant reserved that name. The right to the exclusive use of a reserved name may be transferred to any other person by filing in the office of the Secretary of State a notice of the transfer, executed by the applicant for whom the name was reserved and specifying the name and address of the transferee.

Comment

Section 103 ~~is new~~ first appeared in the 1976 Act. The ~~prior uniform law~~ 1916 Act did not provide for registration of names.

§ 104. Specified Office and Agent

Each limited partnership shall continuously maintain in this State:

(1) an office, which may but need not be a place of its business in this State, at which shall be kept the records required by Section 105 to be maintained; and

(2) an agent for service of process on the limited partnership, which agent must be an individual resident of this State, a domestic corporation, or a foreign corporation authorized to do business in this State.

Comment

Section 104 ~~is new~~ first appeared in the 1976 Act. It requires that a limited partnership have certain minimum contacts with its State of organization, i.e., an office at which the constitutive documents and basic financial information is kept and an agent for service of process.

§ 105. Records to be Kept

(a) Each limited partnership shall keep at the office referred to in Section 104(1) the following:

(1) a current list of the full name and last known business address of each partner ~~set forth~~, separately identifying the general partners (in alphabetical order) and the limited partners (in alphabetical order~~,~~);

(2) a copy of the certificate of limited partnership and all certificates of amendment thereto, together with executed copies of any powers of attorney pursuant to which any certificate has been executed~~,~~;

(3) copies of the limited partnership's federal, state and local income tax returns and reports, if any, for the three most recent years~~, and~~;

(4) copies of any then effective written partnership agreements and of any financial statements of the limited partnership for the three most recent years; and

(5) unless contained in a written partnership agreement, a writing setting out:

(i) the amount of cash and a description and statement of the agreed value of the other property or services contributed by each partner and which each partner has agreed to contribute;

(ii) the times at which or events on the happening of which any additional contributions agreed to be made by each partner are to be made;

(iii) any right of a partner to receive, or of a general partner to make, distributions to a partner which include a return of all or any part of the partner's contribution; and

(iv) any events upon the happening of which the limited partnership is to be dissolved and its affairs wound up.

(b) ~~Those records~~ Records kept under this section are subject to inspection and copying at the reasonable request and at the expense of any partner during ordinary business hours.

Comment

Section 105 ~~is new~~ first appeared in the 1976 Act. In view of the passive nature of the limited partner's position, it has been widely felt that limited partners are entitled to access to certain basic documents and information, including the certificate of limited partnership ~~and~~, any partnership agreement, and a writing setting out certain important matters which, under the 1916 and 1976 Acts, were required to be set out in the certificate of limited partnership. In view of the great diversity among limited partnerships, it was thought inappropriate to require a standard form of financial report, and Section 105 does no more than require retention of tax returns and any other financial statements that are prepared. The names and addresses of the general partners are made available to the general public in the certificate of limited partnership.

§ 106. Nature of Business

A limited partnership may carry on any business that a partnership without limited partners may carry on except [here designate prohibited activities].

Comment

Section 106 is identical to Section 3 of the ~~prior uniform law~~ 1916 Act. Many states require that certain regulated industries, such as banking, may be carried on only by entities organized pursuant to special statutes, and it is contemplated that the prohibited activities would be confined to the matters covered by those statutes.

§ 107. Business Transactions of Partner with Partnership

Except as provided in the partnership agreement, a partner may lend money to and transact other business with the limited partnership and, subject to other applicable law, has the same rights and obligations with respect thereto as a person who is not a partner.

Comment

Section 107 makes a number of important changes in Section 13 of the ~~prior uniform law~~ 1916 Act. Section 13, in effect, created a special fraudulent conveyance provision applicable to the making of secured loans by limited partners and the repayment by limited partnerships of loans from limited partners. Section 107 leaves that question to a ~~State's~~ state's general fraudulent conveyance statute. In addition, Section 107 eliminates the prohibition in ~~former~~ Section 13 against a general ~~partner (as opposed to a limited partner)~~ partner's sharing pro rata with general creditors in the case of an unsecured loan. Of course, other doctrines developed under bankruptcy and insolvency laws may require the subordination of loans by partners under appropriate circumstances.

ARTICLE 2
FORMATION: CERTIFICATE OF LIMITED PARTNERSHIP

§ 201. Certificate of Limited Partnership

(a) In order to form a limited partnership, ~~two or more persons must execute~~ a certificate of limited partnership~~. The certificate shall be~~ must be executed and filed in the office of the Secretary of State. ~~and~~ The certificate shall set forth:

(1) the name of the limited partnership;

~~(2) the general character of its business;~~

~~(3)~~ (2) the address of the office and the name and address of the agent for service of process required to be maintained by Section 104;

~~(4)~~ (3) the name and the business address of each general partner ~~(specifying separately the general partners and limited partners)~~;

~~(5) the amount of cash and a description and statement of the agreed value of the other property or services contributed by each partner and which each partner has agreed to contribute in the future;~~

~~(6) the times at which or events on the happening of which any additional contributions agreed to be made by each partner are to be made;~~

~~(7) any power of a limited partner to grant the right to become a limited partner to an assignee of any part of his partnership interest, and the terms and conditions of the power;~~

~~(8) if agreed upon, the time at which or the events on the happening of which a partner may terminate his membership in the limited partnership and the amount of, or the method of determining, the distribution to which he may be entitled respecting his partnership interest, and the terms and conditions of the termination and distribution;~~

~~(9) any right of a partner to receive distributions of property, including cash from the limited partnership;~~

~~(10) any right of a partner to receive, or of a general partner to make, distributions to a partner which include a return of all or any part of the partner's contribution;~~

~~(11) any time at which or events upon the happening of which the limited partnership is to be dissolved and its affairs wound up;~~

~~(12) any right of the remaining general partners to continue the business on the happening of an event of withdrawal of a general partner; and~~

(4) the latest date upon which the limited partnership is to dissolve; and

~~(13)~~ (5) any other matters the general partners determine to include therein.

(b) A limited partnership is formed at the time of the filing of the certificate of limited partnership in the office of the Secretary of State or at any later time specified in the certificate of limited partnership if, in either case, there has been substantial compliance with the requirements of this section.

Comment

The 1985 Act requires far fewer matters required to be set forth in the certificate of limited partnership are not different in kind from those required by than did Section 2 of the prior uniform law, although certain additions and deletions have been made and the description has been revised to conform with the rest of the Act. In general, the certificate is intended to serve two functions: first, to place creditors on notice of the 1916 Act and Section 201 of the 1976 Act. This is in recognition of the fact that the partnership agreement, not the certificate of limited partnership, has become the authoritative and comprehensive document for most limited partnerships, and that creditors and potential creditors of the partnership do and should refer to the partnership agreement and to other information furnished to them directly by the partnership and by others, not to the certificate of limited partnership, to obtain facts concerning the capital and finances of the partnership and the rules regarding additional contributions to and withdrawals from the partnership; second, to clearly delineate the time at which persons become general partners and limited partners other matters of concern. Subparagraph (b), which is based upon the prior uniform law 1916 Act, has been retained to make it clear that the existence of the limited partnership depends only upon compliance with this section. Its continued existence is not dependent upon compliance with other provisions of this Act.

§ 202. Amendment to Certificate

(a) A certificate of limited partnership is amended by filing a certificate of amendment thereto in the office of the Secretary of State. The certificate shall set forth:

(1) the name of the limited partnership;

(2) the date of filing the certificate; and

(3) the amendment to the certificate.

(b) Within 30 days after the happening of any of the following events, an amendment to a certificate of limited partnership reflecting the occurrence of the event or events shall be filed:

(1) a change in the amount or character of the contribution of any partner, or in any partner's obligation to make a contribution;

(2) (1) the admission of a new general partner;

(3) (2) the withdrawal of a general partner; or

(4) (3) the continuation of the business under Section 801 after an event of withdrawal of a general partner.

(c) A general partner who becomes aware that any statement in a certificate of limited partnership was false when made or that any arrangements or other facts described have changed, making the certificate inaccurate in any respect, shall promptly amend the certificate, but

~~an amendment to show a change of address of a limited partner need be filed only once every 12 months~~.

(d) A certificate of limited partnership may be amended at any time for any other proper purpose the general partners determine.

(e) No person has any liability because an amendment to a certificate of limited partnership has not been filed to reflect the occurrence of any event referred to in subsection (b) of this ~~Section~~ section if the amendment is filed within the 30–day period specified in subsection (b).

(f) A restated certificate of limited partnership may be executed and filed in the same manner as a certificate of amendment.

Comment

Section 202 ~~makes~~ of the 1976 Act made substantial changes in Section 24 of the ~~prior uniform law~~ 1916 Act. Further changes in this section are made by the 1985 Act. Paragraph (b) lists the basic events—the addition or withdrawal of ~~partners or capital or capital obligations~~ a general partner—that are so central to the function of the certificate of limited partnership that they require prompt amendment. With the elimination of the requirement that the certificate of limited partnership include the names of all limited partners and the amount and character of all capital contributions, the requirement of the 1916 and 1976 Acts that the certificate be amended upon the admission or withdrawal of limited partners or on any change in the partnership capital must also be eliminated. This change should greatly reduce the frequency and complexity of amendments to the certificate of limited partnership. Paragraph (c) makes it clear, as it was not clear under ~~subdivision (2)(g) of former~~ Section ~~24~~ 24(2)(g) of the 1916 Act, that the certificate of limited partnership is intended to be an accurate description of the facts to which it relates at all times and does not speak merely as of the date it is executed.

Paragraph (e) provides a "safe harbor" against claims of creditors or others who assert that they have been misled by the failure to amend the certificate of limited partnership to reflect changes in any of the important facts referred to in paragraph (b); if the certificate of limited partnership is amended within 30 days of the occurrence of the event, no creditor or other person can recover for damages sustained during the interim. Additional protection is afforded by the provisions of Section 304. The elimination of the requirement that the certificate of limited partnership identify all limited partners and their respective capital contributions may have rendered paragraph (e) an obsolete and unnecessary vestige. The principal, if not the sole, purpose of paragraph (e) in the 1976 Act was to protect limited partners newly admitted to a partnership from being held liable as general partners when an amendment to the certificate identifying them as limited partners and describing their contributions was not filed contemporaneously with their admission to the partnership. Such liability cannot arise under the 1985 Act because such information is not required to be stated in the certificate. Nevertheless, the 1985 Act retains paragraph (e) because it is protective of partners, shielding them from liability to the extent its provisions apply, and does not create or impose any liability.

Paragraph (f) is added in the 1985 Act to provide explicit statutory recognition of the common practice of restating an amended certificate of limited partnership. While a limited partnership seeking to amend its certificate of limited partnership may do so by recording a restated certificate which incorporates the amendment, that is by no means the only purpose or function of a restated certificate, which may be filed for the sole purpose of restating in a single integrated instrument all the provisions of a limited partnership's certificate of limited partnership which are then in effect.

§ 203. Cancellation of Certificate

A certificate of limited partnership shall be cancelled upon the dissolution and the commencement of winding up of the partnership or at any other time there are no limited partners. A certificate of cancellation shall be filed in the office of the Secretary of State and set forth:

(1) the name of the limited partnership;

(2) the date of filing of its certificate of limited partnership;

(3) the reason for filing the certificate of cancellation;

(4) the effective date (which shall be a date certain) of cancellation if it is not to be effective upon the filing of the certificate; and

(5) any other information the general partners filing the certificate determine.

Comment

Section 203 changes Section 24 of the ~~prior uniform law~~ 1916 Act by making it clear that the certificate of cancellation should be filed upon the commencement of winding up of the limited partnership. Section 24 provided for cancellation "when the partnership is dissolved."

§ 204. Execution of Certificates

(a) Each certificate required by this Article to be filed in the office of the Secretary of State shall be executed in the following manner:

(1) an original certificate of limited partnership must be signed by all general partners ~~named therein~~;

(2) a certificate of amendment must be signed by at least one general partner and by each other general partner designated in the certificate as a new general partner ~~or whose contribution is described as having been increased~~; and

(3) a certificate of cancellation must be signed by all general partners~~;~~.

(b) Any person may sign a certificate by an attorney-in-fact, but a power of attorney to sign a certificate relating to the admission~~, or increased contribution,~~ of a general partner must specifically describe the admission ~~or increase~~.

(c) The execution of a certificate by a general partner constitutes an affirmation under the penalties of perjury that the facts stated therein are true.

Comment

Section 204 collects in one place the formal requirements for the execution of certificates which were set forth in Sections 2 and 25 of the ~~prior uniform law~~ 1916 Act. Those sections required that each certificate be signed by all partners, and there developed an unnecessarily cumbersome practice of having each limited partner sign powers of attorney to authorize the general partners to execute certificates of amendment on their behalf. ~~Section 204 insures that each partner must sign a certificate when he becomes a partner or when the certificates reflect any increase in his obligation to make contributions.~~ The 1976 Act, while simplifying the execution requirements, nevertheless required that an original certificate of limited partnership be signed by all partners and a certificate of amendment by all new partners being admitted to the limited partnership. However, the certificate of limited partnership is no longer required to include the name or capital contribution of any limited partner. Therefore, while the 1985 Act still requires all general partners to sign the original certificate of limited partnership, no limited partner is required to sign any certificate. Certificates of amendment are required to be signed by only one general partner and all general partners must sign certificates of cancellation. ~~Section 204 prohibits blanket powers of attorney for the execution of certificates in many cases, since those conditions under which a partner is required to sign have been narrowed to circumstances of special importance to that partner.~~ The ~~former~~ requirement in the 1916 Act that all certificates be sworn ~~has been confined to statements by the general partners, recognizing that the limited partner's role is a limited one~~ was deleted in the 1976 and 1985 Acts as potentially an unfair trap for the unwary (see, e.g., Wisniewski v. Johnson, 223 Va. 141, 286 S.E.2d 223 (1982)); in its place, paragraph (c) now provides, as a matter of law, that the execution of a certificate by a general partner subjects him to the penalties of perjury for inaccuracies in the certificate.

§ 205. ~~Amendment or Cancellation~~ Execution by Judicial Act

If a person required by Section 204 to execute ~~a~~ any certificate ~~of amendment or cancellation~~ fails or refuses to do so, any other ~~partner,~~

~~and any assignee of a partnership interest,~~ person who is adversely affected by the failure or refusal~~,~~ may petition the [designate the appropriate court] to direct the ~~amendment or cancellation~~ execution of the certificate. If the court finds that ~~the amendment or cancellation is proper~~ it is proper for the certificate to be executed and that any person so designated has failed or refused to execute the certificate, it shall order the Secretary of State to record an appropriate certificate ~~of amendment or cancellation~~.

Comment

Section 205 ~~changes~~ of the 1976 Act changed subdivisions (3) and (4) of Section 25 of the ~~prior uniform law~~ 1916 Act by confining the persons who have standing to seek judicial intervention to partners and to those assignees who ~~are~~ were adversely affected by the failure or refusal of the appropriate persons to file a certificate of amendment or cancellation. Section 205 of the 1985 Act reverses that restriction, and provides that any person adversely affected by a failure or refusal to file any certificate (not only a certificate of cancellation or amendment) has standing to seek judicial intervention.

§ 206. Filing in Office of Secretary of State

(a) Two signed copies of the certificate of limited partnership and of any certificates of amendment or cancellation (or of any judicial decree of amendment or cancellation) shall be delivered to the Secretary of State. A person who executes a certificate as an agent or fiduciary need not exhibit evidence of his [or her] authority as a prerequisite to filing. Unless the Secretary of State finds that any certificate does not conform to law, upon receipt of all filing fees required by law he [or she] shall:

(1) endorse on each duplicate original the word "Filed" and the day, month and year of the filing thereof;

(2) file one duplicate original in his [or her] office; and

(3) return the other duplicate original to the person who filed it or his [or her] representative.

(b) Upon the filing of a certificate of amendment (or judicial decree of amendment) in the office of the Secretary of State, the certificate of limited partnership shall be amended as set forth therein, and upon the effective date of a certificate of cancellation (or a judicial decree thereof), the certificate of limited partnership is cancelled.

Comment

Section 206 ~~is new~~ first appeared in the 1976 Act. In addition to providing mechanics for the central filing system, the second sentence of this section does away with the requirement, formerly imposed by some local filing officers, that persons who have executed certificates under a power of attorney exhibit executed copies of the power of attorney itself. Paragraph (b) changes subdivision (5) of Section 25 of the ~~prior uniform law~~ 1916 Act by providing that certificates of cancellation are effective upon their effective date under Section 203.

§ 207. Liability for False Statement in Certificate

If any certificate of limited partnership or certificate of amendment or cancellation contains a false statement, one who suffers loss by reliance on the statement may recover damages for the loss from:

(1) any person who executes the certificate, or causes another to execute it on his behalf, and knew, and any general partner who knew or should have known, the statement to be false at the time the certificate was executed; and

(2) any general partner who thereafter knows or should have known that any arrangement or other fact described in the certificate has changed, making the statement inaccurate in any respect within a sufficient time before the statement was relied upon reasonably to have enabled that general partner to cancel or amend the certificate, or to file a petition for its cancellation or amendment under Section 205.

Comment

Section 207 changes Section 6 of the ~~prior uniform law~~ 1916 Act by providing explicitly for the liability of persons who sign a certificate as agent under a power of attorney and by confining the obligation to amend a certificate of limited partnership in light of future events to general partners.

§ 208. Scope of Notice

The fact that a certificate of limited partnership is on file in the office of the Secretary of State is notice that the partnership is a limited partnership and the persons designated therein as ~~limited~~ general partners are ~~limited~~ general partners, but it is not notice of any other fact.

Comment

Section 208 ~~is new~~ first appeared in the 1976 Act, and referred to the certificate's providing constructive notice of the status as limited partners of those so identified therein. The 1985 Act's deletion of any requirement that the certificate name limited partners required that Section 208 be modified accordingly.

By stating that the filing of a certificate of limited partnership only results in notice of the ~~limited~~ general liability of the ~~limited~~ general partners, ~~it~~ Section 208 obviates the concern that third parties may be held to have notice of special provisions set forth in the certificate. While this section is designed to preserve by implication the limited liability of limited partners, the ~~notice~~ implicit protection provided is not intended to change any liability of a limited partner which may be created by his action or inaction under the law of estoppel, agency, fraud, or the like.

§ 209. Delivery of Certificates to Limited Partners

Upon the return by the Secretary of State pursuant to Section 206 of a certificate marked "Filed", the general partners shall promptly deliver or mail a copy of the certificate of limited partnership and each certificate of amendment or cancellation to each limited partner unless the partnership agreement provides otherwise.

Comment

This section ~~is new~~ first appeared in the 1976 Act.

ARTICLE 3
LIMITED PARTNERS

§ 301. Admission of ~~Additional~~ Limited Partners

(a) A person becomes a limited partner:

(1) at the time the limited partnership is formed; or

(2) at any later time specified in the records of the limited partnership for becoming a limited partner.

~~(a)~~ (b) After the filing of a limited partnership's original certificate of limited partnership, a person may be admitted as an additional limited partner:

(1) in the case of a person acquiring a partnership interest directly from the limited partnership, upon compliance with the partnership agreement or, if the partnership agreement does not so provide, upon the written consent of all partners; and

(2) in the case of an assignee of a partnership interest of a partner who has the power, as provided in Section 704, to grant the assignee the right to become a limited partner, upon the exercise of that power and compliance with any conditions limiting the grant or exercise of the power.

~~(b) In each case under subsection (a), the person acquiring the partnership interest becomes a limited partner only upon amendment of the certificate of limited partnership reflecting that fact.~~

Comment

Section 301(a) is new; no counterpart was found in the 1916 or 1976 Acts. This section imposes on the partnership an obligation to maintain in its records the date each limited partner becomes a limited partner. Under the 1976 Act, one could not become a limited partner until an appropriate certificate reflecting his status as such was filed with the Secretary of State. Because the 1985 Act eliminates the need to name limited partners in the certificate of limited partnership, an alternative mechanism had to be established to evidence the fact and date of a limited partner's admission. The partnership records required to be maintained under Section 105 now serve that function, subject to the limitation that no person may become a limited partner before the partnership is formed (Section 201(b)).

Subdivision (1) of Section ~~301(a)~~ 301(b) adds to Section 8 of the ~~prior uniform law~~ 1916 Act an explicit recognition of the fact that unanimous consent of all partners is required for admission of new limited partners unless the partnership agreement provides otherwise. Subdivision (2) is derived from Section 19 of the ~~prior uniform law~~ 1916 Act but abandons the former terminology of "substituted limited partner."

§ 302. Voting

Subject to Section 303, the partnership agreement may grant to all or a specified group of the limited partners the right to vote (on a per capita or other basis) upon any matter.

Comment

Section 302 ~~is new~~ first appeared in the 1976 Act, and must be read together with subdivision ~~(b)(5)~~ (b)(6) of Section 303. Although the ~~prior uniform law~~ 1916 Act did not speak specifically of the voting powers of limited partners, it ~~is~~ was not uncommon for partnership agreements to grant such ~~power~~ powers to limited partners. Section 302 is designed only to make it clear that the partnership agreement may grant such power to limited partners. If such powers are granted to limited partners beyond the "safe harbor" of subdivision (6) or (8) of Section ~~303(b)(5)~~ 303(b), a court may (but of course need not) hold that, under the circumstances, the limited partners have participated in "control of the business" within the meaning of Section 303(a). Section 303(c) ~~simply means~~ makes clear that the exercise of powers beyond the ambit of Section 303(b) is not ipso facto to be taken as taking part in the control of the business.

§ 303. Liability to Third Parties

(a) Except as provided in subsection (d), a limited partner is not liable for the obligations of a limited partnership unless he [or she] is also a general partner or, in addition to the exercise of his [or her] rights and powers as a limited partner, he [or she] ~~takes part~~ participates in the control of the business. However, if the limited ~~partner's partic-~~

~~ipation~~ partner participates in the control of the business ~~is not substantially the same as the exercise of the powers of a general partner~~, he [or she] is liable only to persons who transact business with the limited partnership ~~with actual knowledge of his participation in control~~ reasonably believing, based upon the limited partner's conduct, that the limited partner is a general partner.

(b) A limited partner does not participate in the control of the business within the meaning of subsection (a) solely by doing one or more of the following:

(1) being a contractor for or an agent or employee of the limited partnership or of a general partner or being an officer, director, or shareholder of a general partner that is a corporation;

(2) consulting with and advising a general partner with respect to the business of the limited partnership;

(3) acting as surety for the limited partnership or guaranteeing or assuming one or more specific obligations of the limited partnership;

(4) ~~approving or disapproving an amendment to the partnership agreement~~ taking any action required or permitted by law to bring or pursue a derivative action in the right of the limited partnership; ~~or~~

~~(5) voting on one or more of the following matters:~~

(5) requesting or attending a meeting of partners;

(6) proposing, approving, or disapproving, by voting or otherwise, one or more of the following matters:

(i) the dissolution and winding up of the limited partnership;

(ii) the sale, exchange, lease, mortgage, pledge, or other transfer of all or substantially all of the assets of the limited partnership ~~other than in the ordinary course of its business~~;

(iii) the incurrence of indebtedness by the limited partnership other than in the ordinary course of its business;

(iv) a change in the nature of the business; ~~or~~

(v) the admission or removal of a general partner~~.~~;

(vi) the admission or removal of a limited partner;

(vii) a transaction involving an actual or potential conflict of interest between a general partner and the limited partnership or the limited partners;

(viii) an amendment to the partnership agreement or certificate of limited partnership; or

(ix) matters related to the business of the limited partnership not otherwise enumerated in this subsection (b), which the partnership agreement states in writing may be subject to the approval or disapproval of limited partners;

(7) winding up the limited partnership pursuant to Section 803; or

(8) exercising any right or power permitted to limited partners under this [Act] and not specifically enumerated in this subsection (b).

(c) The enumeration in subsection (b) does not mean that the possession or exercise of any other powers by a limited partner constitutes participation by him [or her] in the business of the limited partnership.

(d) A limited partner who knowingly permits his [or her] name to be used in the name of the limited partnership, except under circumstances permitted by Section 102(2), is liable to creditors who extend credit to the limited partnership without actual knowledge that the limited partner is not a general partner.

Comment

Section 303 makes several important changes in Section 7 of the ~~prior uniform law~~ 1916 Act. The first sentence of Section 303(a) ~~carries over the basic test from former Section 7—whether the limited partner "takes part in the control of the business"—in order to insure that judicial decisions under the prior uniform law remain applicable to the extent not expressly changed~~ differs from the text of Section 7 of the 1916 Act in that it speaks of participating (rather than taking part) in the control of the business; this was done for the sake of consistency with the second sentence of Section 303(a), not to change the meaning of the text. It is intended that judicial decisions interpreting the phrase "takes part in the control of the business" under the prior uniform law will remain applicable to the extent that a different result is not called for by other provisions of Section 303 and other provisions of the Act. The second sentence of Section 303(a) reflects a wholly new concept~~. Because~~ in the 1976 Act that has been further modified in the 1985 Act. It was adopted partly because of the difficulty of determining when the "control" line has been overstepped, ~~it was thought it unfair to impose general partner's liability on a limited partner except to the extent that a third party had knowledge of his participation in control of the business. On the other hand, in order to avoid permitting a limited partner to exercise all of the powers of a general partner while avoiding any direct dealings with third parties, the "is not substantially the same as" test was introduced~~ but also (and more importantly) because of a determination that it is not sound public policy to hold a limited partner who is not also a general partner liable for the obligations of the partnership except to persons who have done business with the limited partnership reasonably believing, based on the limited partner's conduct, that he is a general partner. Paragraph (b) is intended to provide a "safe harbor" by enumerating certain activities which a limited partner may carry on for the partnership without being deemed to have taken part in control of the business. This "safe harbor" list has been expanded beyond that set out in the 1976 Act to reflect case law and statutory developments and more clearly to assure that limited partners are not subjected to general liability where such liability is inappropriate. Paragraph (d) is derived from Section 5 of the ~~prior uniform law~~ 1916 Act, but adds as a condition to the limited partner's liability the ~~fact~~ requirement that a limited partner must have knowingly permitted his name to be used in the name of the limited partnership.

§ 304. Person Erroneously Believing Himself [or Herself] Limited Partner

(a) Except as provided in subsection (b), a person who makes a contribution to a business enterprise and erroneously but in good faith believes that he [or she] has become a limited partner in the enterprise is not a general partner in the enterprise and is not bound by its obligations by reason of making the contribution, receiving distributions from the enterprise, or exercising any rights of a limited partner, if, on ascertaining the mistake, he [or she]:

(1) causes an appropriate certificate of limited partnership or a certificate of amendment to be executed and filed; or

(2) withdraws from future equity participation in the enterprise by executing and filing in the office of the Secretary of State a certificate declaring withdrawal under this section.

(b) A person who makes a contribution of the kind described in subsection (a) is liable as a general partner to any third party who transacts business with the enterprise (i) before the person withdraws and an appropriate certificate is filed to show withdrawal, or (ii) before an appropriate certificate is filed to show ~~his status as a limited partner and, in the case of an amendment, after expiration of the 30-day period for filing an amendment relating to the person as a limited partner under Section 202~~ that he [or she] is not a general partner, but in either case only if the third party actually believed in good faith that the person was a general partner at the time of the transaction.

Comment

Section 304 is derived from Section 11 of the ~~prior uniform law~~ 1916 Act. The "good faith" requirement has been added in the first sentence of Section 304(a). The provisions of subdivision (2) of Section 304(a) are intended to clarify an ambiguity in the prior law by providing that a person who chooses to withdraw from the enterprise in order to protect himself from liability is not required to renounce any of his then current interest in the enterprise so long as he has no further participation as an equity participant. Paragraph (b) preserves the liability of the equity participant prior to withdrawal (and after the time for appropriate amendment in the case of a limited partnership) by such person from the limited partnership or amendment to the certificate demonstrating that such person is not a general partner to any third party who has transacted business with the person believing in good faith that he was a general partner.

Evidence strongly suggests that Section 11 of the 1916 Act and Section 304 of the 1976 Act were rarely used, and one might expect that Section 304 of the 1985 Act may never have to be used. Section 11 of the 1916 Act and Section 304 of the 1976 Act could have been used by a person who invested in a limited partnership believing he would be a limited partner but who was not identified as a limited partner in the certificate of limited partnership. However, because the 1985 Act does not require limited partners to be named in the certificate, the only situation to which Section 304 would now appear to be applicable is one in which a person intending to be a limited partner was erroneously identified as a general partner in the certificate.

§ 305. Information

Each limited partner has the right to:

(1) inspect and copy any of the partnership records required to be maintained by Section 105; and

(2) obtain from the general partners from time to time upon reasonable demand (i) true and full information regarding the state of the business and financial condition of the limited partnership, (ii) promptly after becoming available, a copy of the limited partnership's federal, state and local income tax returns for each year, and (iii) other information regarding the affairs of the limited partnership as is just and reasonable.

Comment

Section 305 changes and restates the rights of limited partners to information about the partnership formerly provided by Section 10 of the prior uniform law 1916 Act. Its importance has increased as a result of the 1985 Act's substituting the records of the partnership for the certificate of limited partnership as the place where certain categories of information are to be kept.

Section 305, which should be read together with Section 105(b), provides a mechanism for limited partners to obtain information about the partnership useful to them in making decisions concerning the partnership and their investments in it. Its purpose is not to provide a mechanism for competitors of the partnership or others having interests or agendas adverse to the partnership's to subvert the partnership's business. It is assumed that courts will protect limited partnerships from abuses and attempts to misuse Section 305 for improper purposes.

ARTICLE 4
GENERAL PARTNERS

§ 401. Admission of Additional General Partners

After the filing of a limited partnership's original certificate of limited partnership, additional general partners may be admitted ~~only~~ as provided in writing in the partnership agreement or, if the partnership agreement does not provide in writing for the admission of additional general partners, with the ~~specific~~ written consent of ~~each partner~~ all partners.

Comment

Section 401 is derived from, but represents a significant departure from, Section 9(1)(e) of the ~~prior law and carries over the unwaivable requirement that all limited partners must consent~~ 1916 Act and Section 401 of the 1976 Act, which required, as a condition to the admission of an additional general partner, that all limited partners consent and that such consent ~~must~~ specifically identify the general partner involved. Section 401 of the 1985 Act provides that the written partnership agreement determines the procedure for authorizing the admission of additional general partners, and that the written consent of all partners is required only when the partnership agreement fails to address the question.

§ 402. Events of Withdrawal

Except as approved by the specific written consent of all partners at the time, a person ceases to be a general partner of a limited partnership upon the happening of any of the following events:

(1) the general partner withdraws from the limited partnership as provided in Section 602;

(2) the general partner ceases to be a member of the limited partnership as provided in Section 702;

(3) the general partner is removed as a general partner in accordance with the partnership agreement;

(4) unless otherwise provided in writing in the ~~certificate of limited~~ partnership agreement, the general partner: (i) makes an assignment for the benefit of creditors; (ii) files a voluntary petition in bankruptcy; (iii) is adjudicated a bankrupt or insolvent; (iv) files a petition or answer seeking for himself [or herself] any reorganization, arrangement, composition, readjustment, liquidation, dissolution or similar relief under any statute, law, or regulation; (v) files

an answer or other pleading admitting or failing to contest the material allegations of a petition filed against him [or her] in any proceeding of this nature; or (vi) seeks, consents to, or acquiesces in the appointment of a trustee, receiver, or liquidator of the general partner or of all or any substantial part of his [or her] properties;

(5) unless otherwise provided in writing in the ~~certificate of limited~~ partnership agreement, [120] days after the commencement of any proceeding against the general partner seeking reorganization, arrangement, composition, readjustment, liquidation, dissolution or similar relief under any statute, law, or regulation, the proceeding has not been dismissed, or if within [90] days after the appointment without his [or her] consent or acquiescence of a trustee, receiver, or liquidator of the general partner or of all or any substantial part of his [or her] properties, the appointment is not vacated or stayed or within [90] days after the expiration of any such stay, the appointment is not vacated;

(6) in the case of a general partner who is a natural person,

(i) his [or her] death; or

(ii) the entry of an order by a court of competent jurisdiction adjudicating him [or her] incompetent to manage his [or her] person or his [or her] estate;

(7) in the case of a general partner who is acting as a general partner by virtue of being a trustee of a trust, the termination of the trust (but not merely the substitution of a new trustee);

(8) in the case of a general partner that is a separate partnership, the dissolution and commencement of winding up of the separate partnership;

(9) in the case of a general partner that is a corporation, the filing of a certificate of dissolution, or its equivalent, for the corporation or the revocation of its charter; or

(10) in the case of an estate, the distribution by the fiduciary of the estate's entire interest in the partnership.

Comment

Section 402 expands considerably the provisions of Section 20 of the ~~prior uniform law~~ 1916 Act which provided for dissolution in the event of the retirement, death or insanity of a general partner. Subdivisions (1), (2) and (3) recognize that the general partner's agency relationship is terminable at will, although it may result in a breach of the partnership agreement giving rise to an action for damages. Subdivisions (4) and (5) reflect a judgment that, unless the limited partners agree otherwise, they ought to have the power to rid themselves of a general partner who is in such dire financial straits that he is the subject of proceedings under the National Bankruptcy ~~Act~~ Code or a similar provision of law. Subdivisions

(6) through (10) simply elaborate on the notion of death in the case of a general partner who is not a natural person. Of course, the addition of the words "and in the partnership statement" was not intended to suggest that liabilities to third parties could be affected by provisions in the partnership agreement. Subdivisions (4) and (5) differ from their counterparts in the 1976 Act, reflecting the policy underlying the 1985 revision of Section 201, that the partnership agreement, not the certificate of limited partnership, is the appropriate document for setting out most provisions relating to the respective powers, rights, and obligations of the partners inter se. Although the partnership agreement need not be written, the 1985 Act provides that, to protect the partners from fraud, these and certain other particularly significant provisions must be set out in a written partnership agreement to be effective for the purposes described in the Act.

§ 403. General Powers and Liabilities

(a) Except as provided in this [Act] or in the partnership agreement, a general partner of a limited partnership has the rights and powers and is subject to the restrictions of a partner in a partnership without limited partners.

(b) Except as provided in this [Act], a general partner of a limited partnership has the liabilities of a partner in a partnership without limited partners to persons other than the partnership and the other partners. Except as provided in this [Act] or in the partnership agreement, a general partner of a limited partnership has the liabilities of a partner in a partnership without limited partners to the partnership and to the other partners.

Comment

Section 403 is derived from Section 9(1) of the prior uniform law 1916 Act.

§ 404. Contributions by General Partner

A general partner of a limited partnership may make contributions to the partnership and share in the profits and losses of, and in distributions from, the limited partnership as a general partner. A general partner also may make contributions to and share in profits, losses, and distributions as a limited partner. A person who is both a general partner and a limited partner has the rights and powers, and is subject to the restrictions and liabilities, of a general partner and, except as provided in the partnership agreement, also has the powers, and is subject to the restrictions, of a limited partner to the extent of his [or her] participation in the partnership as a limited partner.

Comment

Section 404 is derived from Section 12 of the ~~prior uniform law~~ 1916 Act and makes clear that the partnership agreement may provide that a general partner who is also a limited partner may exercise all of the powers of a limited partner.

§ 405. Voting

The partnership agreement may grant to all or certain identified general partners the right to vote (on a per capita or any other basis), separately or with all or any class of the limited partners, on any matter.

Comment

Section 405 ~~is new~~ first appeared in the 1976 Act and is intended to make it clear that the Act does not require that the limited partners have any right to vote on matters as a separate class.

ARTICLE 5
FINANCE

§ 501. Form of Contribution

The contribution of a partner may be in cash, property, or services rendered, or a promissory note or other obligation to contribute cash or property or to perform services.

Comment

As noted in the comment to Section 101, the explicit permission to make contributions of services expands Section 4 of the ~~prior uniform law~~ 1916 Act.

§ 502. Liability for Contribution

(a) A promise by a limited partner to contribute to the limited partnership is not enforceable unless set out in a writing signed by the limited partner.

~~(a)~~ (b) Except as provided in the ~~certificate of limited~~ partnership agreement, a partner is obligated to the limited partnership to perform any enforceable promise to contribute cash or property or to perform services, even if he [or she] is unable to perform because of death, disability, or any other reason. If a partner does not make the required contribution of property or services, he [or she] is obligated at the option of the limited partnership to contribute cash equal to that portion of the value, as stated in the ~~certificate of limited~~ partnership records required to be kept pursuant to Section 105, of the stated contribution which has not been made.

~~(b)~~ (c) Unless otherwise provided in the partnership agreement, the obligation of a partner to make a contribution or return money or other property paid or distributed in violation of this [Act] may be compromised only by consent of all partners. Notwithstanding the compromise, a creditor of a limited partnership who extends credit~~,~~ or ~~whose claim arises,~~ otherwise acts in reliance on that obligation after the ~~filing of the certificate of limited partnership or an amendment thereto~~ partner signs a writing which~~, in either case,~~ reflects the obligation~~,~~ and before the amendment or cancellation thereof to reflect the compromise~~,~~ may enforce the original obligation.

Comment

Section 502(a) is new; it has no counterpart in the 1916 or 1976 Act. Because, unlike the prior uniform acts, the 1985 Act does not require that promises to contribute cash, property, or services be described in the limited partnership certificate, to protect against fraud it requires instead that such important promises be in a signed writing.

Although Section 17(1) of the ~~prior uniform law~~ 1916 Act required a partner to fulfill his promise to make contributions, the addition of contributions in the form of a promise to render services means that a partner who is unable to perform those services because of death or disability as well as because of an intentional default is required to pay the cash value of the services unless the ~~certificate of limited partnership~~ partnership agreement provides otherwise.

Subdivision ~~(b)~~ (c) is derived from, but expands upon, Section 17(3) of the ~~prior uniform law~~ 1916 Act.

§ 503. Sharing of Profits and Losses

The profits and losses of a limited partnership shall be allocated among the partners, and among classes of partners, in the manner provided in writing in the partnership agreement. If the partnership agreement does not so provide in writing, profits and losses shall be allocated on the basis of the value, as stated in the ~~certificate of limited~~ partnership records required to be kept pursuant to Section 105, of the contributions made by each partner to the extent they have been received by the partnership and have not been returned.

Comment

Section 503 ~~is new~~ first appeared in the 1976 Act. The ~~prior uniform law~~ 1916 Act did not provide ~~for~~ the basis on which partners would share profits and losses in the absence of agreement. The 1985 Act differs from its counterpart in the 1976 Act by requiring that, to be effective, the partnership agreement provisions concerning allocation of profits and losses be in writing, and by its reference to records required to be kept pursuant to Section 105, the latter reflecting the 1985 changes in Section 201.

§ 504. Sharing of Distributions

Distributions of cash or other assets of a limited partnership shall be allocated among the partners and among classes of partners in the manner provided in writing in the partnership agreement. If the partnership agreement does not so provide in writing, distributions shall be made on the basis of the value, as stated in the ~~certificate of limited~~ partnership records required to be kept pursuant to Section 105, of the contributions made by each partner to the extent they have been received by the partnership and have not been returned.

Comment

Section 504 ~~is new~~ first appeared in the 1976 Act. The ~~prior uniform law~~ 1916 Act did not provide ~~for~~ the basis on which partners would share distributions in the absence of agreement. Section 504 also differs from its counterpart in the 1976 Act by requiring that, to be effective, the partnership agreement provisions concerning allocation of distributions be in writing, and in its reference to records required to be kept pursuant to Section 105, the latter reflecting the 1985 changes in Section 201. This section also recognizes that partners may choose to share in ~~distribution~~ distributions on a ~~different~~ basis ~~than~~ different from that on which they share in profits and losses.

ARTICLE 6
DISTRIBUTIONS AND WITHDRAWAL

§ 601. Interim Distributions

Except as provided in this Article, a partner is entitled to receive distributions from a limited partnership before his [or her] withdrawal from the limited partnership and before the dissolution and winding up thereof~~:~~

~~(1)~~ to the extent and at the times or upon the happening of the events specified in the partnership agreement~~; and~~

~~(2) if any distribution constitutes a return of any part of his contribution under Section 608(c), to the extent and at the times or upon the happening of the events specified in the certificate of limited partnership~~.

Comment

Section 601 ~~is new~~ first appeared in the 1976 Act. The 1976 Act provisions have been modified to reflect the 1985 changes made in Section 201.

§ 602. Withdrawal of General Partner

A general partner may withdraw from a limited partnership at any time by giving written notice to the other partners, but if the withdrawal violates the partnership agreement, the limited partnership may recover from the withdrawing general partner damages for breach of the partnership agreement and offset the damages against the amount otherwise distributable to him [or her].

Comment

Section 602 ~~is new~~ first appeared in the 1976 Act, but is generally derived from Section 38 of the Uniform Partnership Act.

§ 603. Withdrawal of Limited Partner

A limited partner may withdraw from a limited partnership at the time or upon the happening of events specified ~~in the certificate of limited partnership and in accordance with~~ in writing in the partnership agreement. If the ~~certificate~~ agreement does not specify in writing the time or the events upon the happening of which a limited partner may withdraw or a definite time for the dissolution and winding up of the limited partnership, a limited partner may withdraw upon not less than six months' prior written notice to each general partner at his [or her] address on the books of the limited partnership at its office in this State.

Comment

Section 603 is derived from Section ~~16(c)~~ 16 of the ~~prior uniform law~~ 1916 Act. The 1976 Act provision has been modified to reflect the 1985 changes made in Section 201. This section additionally reflects the policy determination, also embodied in certain other sections of the 1985 Act, that to avoid fraud, agreements concerning certain matters of substantial importance to the partners will be enforceable only if in writing. If the partnership agreement does provide, in writing, whether a limited partner may withdraw and, if he may, when and on what terms and conditions, those provisions will control.

§ 604. Distribution Upon Withdrawal

Except as provided in this Article, upon withdrawal any withdrawing partner is entitled to receive any distribution to which he [or she] is entitled under the partnership agreement and, if not otherwise provided in the agreement, he [or she] is entitled to receive, within a reasonable time after withdrawal, the fair value of his [or her] interest in the limited partnership as of the date of withdrawal based upon his [or her] right to share in distributions from the limited partnership.

Comment

Section 604 ~~is new~~ first appeared in the 1976 Act. It fixes the distributive share of a withdrawing partner in the absence of an agreement among the partners.

§ 605. Distribution in Kind

Except as provided in writing in the ~~certificate of limited~~ partnership agreement, a partner, regardless of the nature of his [or her] contribution, has no right to demand and receive any distribution from a limited partnership in any form other than cash. Except as provided in writing in the partnership agreement, a partner may not be compelled to accept a distribution of any asset in kind from a limited partnership to the extent that the percentage of the asset distributed to him [or her] exceeds a percentage of that asset which is equal to the percentage in which he [or she] shares in distributions from the limited partnership.

Comment

The first sentence of Section 605 is derived from Section 16(3) of the ~~prior uniform law~~ 1916 Act; it also differs from its counterpart in the 1976 Act, reflecting the 1985 changes made in Section 201. The second sentence ~~is new~~ first appeared in the 1976 Act, and is intended to protect a limited partner (and the remaining partners) against a distribution in kind of more than his share of particular assets.

§ 606. Right to Distribution

At the time a partner becomes entitled to receive a distribution, he [or she] has the status of, and is entitled to all remedies available to, a creditor of the limited partnership with respect to the distribution.

Comment

Section 606 ~~is new~~ first appeared in the 1976 Act and is intended to make it clear that the right of a partner to receive a distribution, as between the partners, is not subject to the equity risks of the enterprise. On the other hand, since partners entitled to distributions have creditor status, there did not seem to be a need for the extraordinary remedy of Section 16(4)(a) of the ~~prior uniform law~~ 1916 Act, which granted a limited partner the right to seek dissolution of the partnership if he was unsuccessful in demanding the return of his contribution. It is more appropriate for the partner to simply sue as an ordinary creditor and obtain a judgment.

§ 607. Limitations on Distribution

A partner may not receive a distribution from a limited partnership to the extent that, after giving effect to the distribution, all liabilities of the limited partnership, other than liabilities to partners on account of their partnership interests, exceed the fair value of the partnership assets.

Comment

Section 607 is derived from Section 16(1)(a) of the ~~prior uniform law~~ 1916 Act.

§ 608. Liability Upon Return of Contribution

(a) If a partner has received the return of any part of his [or her] contribution without violation of the partnership agreement or this [Act], he [or she] is liable to the limited partnership for a period of one year thereafter for the amount of the returned contribution, but only to the extent necessary to discharge the limited partnership's liabilities to creditors who extended credit to the limited partnership during the period the contribution was held by the partnership.

(b) If a partner has received the return of any part of his [or her] contribution in violation of the partnership agreement or this [Act], he [or she] is liable to the limited partnership for a period of six years thereafter for the amount of the contribution wrongfully returned.

(c) A partner receives a return of his [or her] contribution to the extent that a distribution to him [or her] reduces his [or her] share of the fair value of the net assets of the limited partnership below the value, as set forth in the ~~certificate of limited~~ partnership records required to be kept pursuant to Section 105, of his contribution which has not been distributed to him [or her].

Comment

Paragraph (a) is derived from Section 17(4) of the ~~prior uniform law~~ 1916 Act, but the one year statute of limitations has been added. Paragraph (b) is derived from Section 17(2)(b) of the ~~prior uniform law~~ 1916 Act but, again, a statute of limitations has been added.

Paragraph (c) ~~is new~~ first appeared in the 1976 Act. The provisions of former Section 17(2) that referred to the partner holding as "trustee" any money or specific property wrongfully returned to him have been eliminated. Paragraph (c) in the 1985 Act also differs from its counterpart in the 1976 Act to reflect the 1985 changes made in Sections 105 and 201.

ARTICLE 7
ASSIGNMENT OF PARTNERSHIP INTERESTS

§ 701. Nature of Partnership Interest

A partnership interest is personal property.

Comment

This section is derived from Section 18 of the ~~prior uniform law~~ 1916 Act.

§ 702. Assignment of Partnership Interest

Except as provided in the partnership agreement, a partnership interest is assignable in whole or in part. An assignment of a partnership interest does not dissolve a limited partnership or entitle the assignee to become or to exercise any rights of a partner. An assignment entitles the assignee to receive, to the extent assigned, only the distribution to which the assignor would be entitled. Except as provided in the partnership agreement, a partner ceases to be a partner upon assignment of all his [or her] partnership interest.

Comment

Section 19(1) of the ~~prior uniform law~~ 1916 Act provided simply that "a limited partner's interest is assignable," raising a question whether any limitations on the right of assignment were permitted. While the first sentence of Section 702 recognizes that the power to assign may be restricted in the partnership agreement, there was no intention to affect in any way the usual rules regarding restraints on alienation of personal property. The second and third sentences of Section 702 are derived from Section 19(3) of the ~~prior uniform law~~ 1916 Act. The last sentence ~~is new~~ first appeared in the 1976 Act.

§ 703. Rights of Creditor

On application to a court of competent jurisdiction by any judgment creditor of a partner, the court may charge the partnership interest of the partner with payment of the unsatisfied amount of the judgment with interest. To the extent so charged, the judgment creditor has only the rights of an assignee of the partnership interest. This [Act] does not deprive any partner of the benefit of any exemption laws applicable to his [or her] partnership interest.

Comment

Section 703 is derived from Section 22 of the ~~prior uniform law~~ 1916 Act but has not carried over some provisions that were thought to be superfluous. For example, references in Section 22(1) to specific remedies have been omitted, as has a prohibition in Section 22(2) against discharge of the lien with partnership property. Ordinary rules governing the remedies available to a creditor and the fiduciary obligations of general partners will determine those matters.

§ 704. Right of Assignee to Become Limited Partner

(a) An assignee of a partnership interest, including an assignee of a general partner, may become a limited partner if and to the extent that ~~(1)~~ (i) the assignor gives the assignee that right in accordance with authority described in the ~~certificate of limited~~ partnership agreement, or ~~(2)~~ (ii) all other partners consent.

(b) An assignee who has become a limited partner has, to the extent assigned, the rights and powers, and is subject to the restrictions and liabilities, of a limited partner under the partnership agreement and this [Act]. An assignee who becomes a limited partner also is liable for the obligations of his [or her] assignor to make and return contributions as provided in ~~Article~~ Articles 5 and 6. However, the assignee is not obligated for liabilities unknown to the assignee at the time he [or she] became a limited partner ~~and which could not be ascertained from the certificate of limited partnership~~.

(c) If an assignee of a partnership interest becomes a limited partner, the assignor is not released from his [or her] liability to the limited partnership under Sections 207 and 502.

Comment

Section 704 is derived from Section 19 of the ~~prior uniform law~~ 1916 Act, but paragraph (b) defines more narrowly than Section 19 the obligations of the assignor that are automatically assumed by the assignee. Section 704 of the 1985 Act also differs from the 1976 Act to reflect the 1985 changes made in Section 201.

§ 705. Power of Estate of Deceased or Incompetent Partner

If a partner who is an individual dies or a court of competent jurisdiction adjudges him [or her] to be incompetent to manage his [or her] person or his [or her] property, the partner's executor, administrator, guardian, conservator, or other legal representative may exercise all the partner's rights for the purpose of settling his [or her] estate or administering his [or her] property, including any power the partner had to give an assignee the right to become a limited partner. If a partner is a corporation, trust, or other entity and is dissolved or terminated, the powers of that partner may be exercised by its legal representative or successor.

Comment

Section 705 is derived from Section 21(1) of the ~~prior uniform law~~ 1916 Act. Former Section 21(2), making a deceased limited partner's estate liable for his liabilities as a limited partner was deleted as superfluous, with no intention of changing the liability of the estate.

ARTICLE 8
DISSOLUTION

§ 801. Nonjudicial Dissolution

A limited partnership is dissolved and its affairs shall be wound up upon the happening of the first to occur of the following:

(1) at the time specified in the certificate of limited partnership;

(2) ~~or~~ upon the happening of events specified in writing in the ~~certificate of limited~~ partnership agreement;

~~(2)~~ (3) written consent of all partners;

~~(3)~~ (4) an event of withdrawal of a general partner unless at the time there is at least one other general partner and the ~~certificate of limited~~ written provisions of the partnership agreement ~~permits~~ permit the business of the limited partnership to be carried on by the remaining general partner and that partner does so, but the limited partnership is not dissolved and is not required to be wound up by reason of any event of withdrawal~~,~~ if, within 90 days after the withdrawal, all partners agree in writing to continue the business of the limited partnership and to the appointment of one or more additional general partners if necessary or desired; or

~~(4)~~ (5) entry of a decree of judicial dissolution under Section 802.

Comment

Section 801 merely collects in one place all of the events causing dissolution. Paragraph (3) is derived from Sections 9(1)(g) and 20 of the ~~prior uniform law~~ 1916 Act, but adds the 90–day grace period. Section 801 also differs from its counterpart in the 1976 Act to reflect the 1985 changes made in Section 201.

§ 802. Judicial Dissolution

On application by or for a partner the [designate the appropriate court] court may decree dissolution of a limited partnership whenever it is not reasonably practicable to carry on the business in conformity with the partnership agreement.

Comment

Section 802 ~~is new~~ first appeared in the 1976 Act.

§ 803. Winding Up

Except as provided in the partnership agreement, the general partners who have not wrongfully dissolved a limited partnership or, if none, the limited partners, may wind up the limited partnership's affairs; but the [designate the appropriate court] court may wind up the limited partnership's affairs upon application of any partner, his [or her] legal representative, or assignee.

Comment

Section 803 ~~is new~~ first appeared in the 1976 Act and is derived in part from Section 37 of the Uniform ~~General~~ Partnership Act.

§ 804. Distribution of Assets

Upon the winding up of a limited partnership, the assets shall be distributed as follows:

(1) to creditors, including partners who are creditors, to the extent permitted by law, in satisfaction of liabilities of the limited partnership other than liabilities for distributions to partners under Section 601 or 604;

(2) except as provided in the partnership agreement, to partners and former partners in satisfaction of liabilities for distributions under Section 601 or 604; and

(3) except as provided in the partnership agreement, to partners first for the return of their contributions and secondly respecting their partnership interests, in the proportions in which the partners share in distributions.

Comment

Section 804 revises Section 23 of the ~~prior uniform law~~ 1916 Act by providing that (1) to the extent partners are also creditors, other than in respect of their interests in the partnership, they share with other creditors, (2) once the partnership's obligation to make a distribution accrues, it must be paid before any other distributions of an "equity" nature are made, and (3) general and limited partners rank on the same level except as otherwise provided in the partnership agreement.

ARTICLE 9
FOREIGN LIMITED PARTNERSHIPS

§ 901. Law Governing

Subject to the Constitution of this State, (i) the laws of the state under which a foreign limited partnership is organized govern its organization and internal affairs and the liability of its limited partners, and (ii) a foreign limited partnership may not be denied registration by reason of any difference between those laws and the laws of this State.

Comment

Section 901 ~~is new~~ first appeared in the 1976 Act.

§ 902. Registration

Before transacting business in this State, a foreign limited partnership shall register with the Secretary of State. In order to register, a foreign limited partnership shall submit to the Secretary of State, in duplicate, an application for registration as a foreign limited partnership, signed and sworn to by a general partner and setting forth:

(1) the name of the foreign limited partnership and, if different, the name under which it proposes to register and transact business in this State;

(2) the ~~state~~ State and date of its formation;

~~(3) the general character of the business it proposes to transact in this State;~~

~~(4)~~ (3) the name and address of any agent for service of process on the foreign limited partnership whom the foreign limited partnership elects to appoint; the agent must be an individual resident of this ~~state~~ State, a domestic corporation, or a foreign corporation having a place of business in, and authorized to do business in, this State;

~~(5)~~ (4) a statement that the Secretary of State is appointed the agent of the foreign limited partnership for service of process if no agent has been appointed under paragraph ~~(4)~~ (3) or, if appointed, the agent's authority has been revoked or if the agent cannot be found or served with the exercise of reasonable diligence;

~~(6)~~ (5) the address of the office required to be maintained in the ~~State~~ state of its organization by the laws of that ~~State~~ state or, if not so required, of the principal office of the foreign limited partnership; ~~and~~

~~(7) if the certificate of limited partnership filed in the foreign limited partnership's state of organization is not required to include the names and business addresses of the partners, a list of the names and addresses.~~

(6) the name and business address of each general partner; and

(7) the address of the office at which is kept a list of the names and addresses of the limited partners and their capital contributions, together with an undertaking by the foreign limited partnership to keep those records until the foreign limited partnership's registration in this State is cancelled or withdrawn.

Comment

Section 902 ~~is new~~ first appeared in the 1976 Act. It was thought that requiring a full copy of the certificate of limited partnership and all amendments thereto to be filed in each state in which the partnership does business would impose an unreasonable burden on interstate limited partnerships and that the information ~~on file was~~ Section 902 required to be filed would be sufficient to tell interested persons where they could write to obtain copies of those basic documents. Subdivision (3) of the 1976 Act has been omitted, and subdivisions (6) and (7) differ from their counterparts in the 1976 Act, to conform these provisions relating to the registration of foreign limited partnerships to the corresponding changes made by the Act in the provisions relating to domestic limited partnerships. The requirement that an application for registration be sworn to by a general partner is simply intended to produce the same result as is provided for in Section 204(c) with respect to certificates of domestic limited partnerships; the acceptance and endorsement by the Secretary of State (or equivalent authority) of an application which was not sworn by a general partner should be deemed a mere technical and insubstantial shortcoming, and should not result in the limited partners' being subjected to general liability for the obligations of the foreign limited partnership (see Section 907(c)).

§ 903. Issuance of Registration

(a) If the Secretary of State finds that an application for registration conforms to law and all requisite fees have been paid, he [or she] shall:

(1) endorse on the application the word "Filed," and the month, day and year of the filing thereof;

(2) file in his [or her] office a duplicate original of the application; and

(3) issue a certificate of registration to transact business in this State.

(b) The certificate of registration, together with a duplicate original of the application, shall be returned to the person who filed the application or his [or her] representative.

Comment

Section 903 first appeared in the 1976 Act.

§ 904. Name

A foreign limited partnership may register with the Secretary of State under any name, whether or not it is the name under which it is registered in its state of organization, that includes without abbreviation the words "limited partnership" and that could be registered by a domestic limited partnership.

Comment

Section 904 ~~is new~~ first appeared in the 1976 Act.

§ 905. Changes and Amendments

If any statement in the application for registration of a foreign limited partnership was false when made or any arrangements or other facts described have changed, making the application inaccurate in any respect, the foreign limited partnership shall promptly file in the office of the Secretary of State a certificate, signed and sworn to by a general partner, correcting such statement.

Comment

Section 905 ~~is new~~ first appeared in the 1976 Act. It corresponds to the provisions of Section 202(c) relating to domestic limited partnerships.

§ 906. Cancellation of Registration

A foreign limited partnership may cancel its registration by filing with the Secretary of State a certificate of cancellation signed and sworn to by a general partner. A cancellation does not terminate the authority of the Secretary of State to accept service of process on the foreign limited partnership with respect to [claims for relief] [causes of action] arising out of the transactions of business in this State.

Comment

Section 906 ~~is new~~ first appeared in the 1976 Act.

§ 907. Transaction of Business Without Registration

(a) A foreign limited partnership transacting business in this State may not maintain any action, suit, or proceeding in any court of this State until it has registered in this State.

(b) The failure of a foreign limited partnership to register in this State does not impair the validity of any contract or act of the foreign limited partnership or prevent the foreign limited partnership from defending any action, suit, or proceeding in any court of this State.

(c) A limited partner of a foreign limited partnership is not liable as a general partner of the foreign limited partnership solely by reason of having transacted business in this State without registration.

(d) A foreign limited partnership, by transacting business in this State without registration, appoints the Secretary of State as its agent for service of process with respect to [claims for relief] [causes of action] arising out of the transaction of business in this State.

Comment

Section 907 ~~is new~~ first appeared in the 1976 Act.

§ 908. Action by [Appropriate Official]

The [designate the appropriate official] may bring an action to restrain a foreign limited partnership from transacting business in this State in violation of this Article.

Comment

Section 908 ~~is new~~ first appeared in the 1976 Act.

ARTICLE 10
DERIVATIVE ACTIONS

§ 1001. Right of Action

A limited partner may bring an action in the right of a limited partnership to recover a judgment in its favor if general partners with authority to do so have refused to bring the action or if an effort to cause those general partners to bring the action is not likely to succeed.

Comment

Section 1001 ~~is new~~ first appeared in the 1976 Act.

§ 1002. Proper Plaintiff

In a derivative action, the plaintiff must be a partner at the time of bringing the action and (i) must have been a partner at the time of the transaction of which he [or she] complains or (ii) his [or her] status as a partner ~~had~~ must have devolved upon him [or her] by operation of law or pursuant to the terms of the partnership agreement from a person who was a partner at the time of the transaction.

Comment

Section 1002 ~~is new~~ first appeared in the 1976 Act.

§ 1003. Pleading

In a derivative action, the complaint shall set forth with particularity the effort of the plaintiff to secure initiation of the action by a general partner or the reasons for not making the effort.

Comment

Section 1003 ~~is new~~ first appeared in the 1976 Act.

§ 1004. Expenses

If a derivative action is successful, in whole or in part, or if anything is received by the plaintiff as a result of a judgment, compromise or settlement of an action or claim, the court may award the plaintiff reasonable expenses, including reasonable attorney's fees, and shall direct him [or her] to remit to the limited partnership the remainder of those proceeds received by him [or her].

Comment

Section 1004 ~~is new~~ first appeared in the 1976 Act.

ARTICLE 11
MISCELLANEOUS

§ 1101. Construction and Application

This [Act] shall be so applied and construed to effectuate its general purpose to make uniform the law with respect to the subject of this [Act] among states enacting it.

Comment

Because the principles set out in Sections 28(1) and 29 of the 1916 Act have become so universally established, it was felt that the 1976 and 1985 Acts need not contain express provisions to the same effect. However, it is intended that the principles enunciated in those provisions of the 1916 Act also apply to this Act.

§ 1102. Short Title

This [Act] may be cited as the Uniform Limited Partnership Act.

§ 1103. Severability

If any provision of this [Act] or its application to any person or circumstance is held invalid, the invalidity does not affect other provisions or applications of the [Act] which can be given effect without the invalid provision or application, and to this end the provisions of this [Act] are severable.

§ 1104. Effective Date, Extended Effective Date and Repeal

Except as set forth below, the effective date of this [Act] is ______ and the following acts [list ~~prior~~ existing limited partnership acts] are hereby repealed:

(1) The existing provisions for execution and filing of certificates of limited partnerships and amendments thereunder and can-

cellations thereof continue in effect until [specify time required to create central filing system], the extended effective date, and Sections 102, 103, 104, 105, 201, 202, 203, 204 and 206 are not effective until the extended effective date.

(2) Section 402, specifying the conditions under which a general partner ceases to be a member of a limited partnership, is not effective until the extended effective date, and the applicable provisions of existing law continue to govern until the extended effective date.

(3) Sections 501, 502 and 608 apply only to contributions and distributions made after the effective date of this [Act].

(4) Section 704 applies only to assignments made after the effective date of this [Act].

(5) Article 9, dealing with registration of foreign limited partnerships, is not effective until the extended effective date.

(6) Unless otherwise agreed by the partners, the applicable provisions of existing law governing allocation of profits and losses (rather than the provisions of Section 503), distributions to a withdrawing partner (rather than the provisions of Section 604), and distribution of assets upon the winding up of a limited partnership (rather than the provisions of Section 804) govern limited partnerships formed before the effective date of this [Act].

Comment

Subdivisions (6) and (7) did not appear in Section 1104 of the 1976 Act. They are included in the 1985 Act to ensure that the application of the Act to limited partnerships formed and existing before the Act becomes effective would not violate constitutional prohibitions against the impairment of contracts.

§ 1105. Rules for Cases not Provided for in this [Act]

In any case not provided for in this [Act] the provisions of the Uniform Partnership Act govern.

Comment

The result provided for in Section 1105 would obtain even in its absence in a jurisdiction which had adopted the Uniform Partnership Act, by operation of Section 6 of that act.

§ 1106. Savings Clause

The repeal of any statutory provision by this [Act] does not impair, or otherwise affect, the organization or the continued existence of a limited partnership existing at the effective date of this [Act], nor does the repeal of any existing statutory provision by this [Act] impair any contract or affect any right accrued before the effective date of this [Act].

Comment

Section 1106 did not appear in the 1976 Act. It was included in the 1985 Act to ensure that the application of the Act to limited partnerships formed and existing before the Act becomes effective would not violate constitutional prohibitions against the impairment of contracts.

UNIFORM LIMITED PARTNERSHIP ACT (2001)

Table of Sections

[ARTICLE] 1. GENERAL PROVISIONS

[ARTICLE] 2. FORMATION; CERTIFICATE OF LIMITED PARTNERSHIP AND OTHER FILINGS

[ARTICLE] 11. CONVERSION AND MERGER

[ARTICLE] 12. MISCELLANEOUS PROVISIONS

UNIFORM LIMITED PARTNERSHIP ACT (2001)

PREFATORY NOTE

The Act's Overall Approach

The new Limited Partnership Act is a "stand alone" act, "de-linked" from both the original general partnership act ("UPA") and the Revised Uniform Partnership Act ("RUPA"). To be able to stand alone, the Limited Partnership incorporates many provisions from RUPA and some from the Uniform Limited Liability Company Act ("ULLCA"). As a result, the new Act is far longer and more complex than its immediate predecessor, the Revised Uniform Limited Partnership Act ("RULPA").

The new Act has been drafted for a world in which limited liability partnerships and limited liability companies can meet many of the needs formerly met by limited partnerships. This Act therefore targets two types of enterprises that seem largely beyond the scope of LLPs and LLCs: (i) sophisticated, manager-entrenched commercial deals whose participants commit for the long term, and (ii) estate planning arrangements (family limited partnerships). This Act accordingly assumes that, more often than not, people utilizing it will want:

- strong centralized management, strongly entrenched, and
- passive investors with little control over or right to exit the entity

The Act's rules, and particularly its default rules, have been designed to reflect these assumptions.

The Decision to "De-Link" and Create a Stand Alone Act

Unlike this Act, RULPA is not a stand alone statute. RULPA was drafted to rest on and link to the UPA. RULPA Section 1105 states that "In any case not provided for in this [Act] the provisions of the Uniform Partnership Act govern." UPA Section 6(2) in turn provides that "this Act shall apply to limited partnerships except in so far as the statutes relating to such partnerships are inconsistent herewith." More particularly, RULPA Section 403 defines the rights, powers, restrictions and liabilities of a "general partner of a limited partnership" by equating them to the rights, powers, restrictions and liabilities of "a partner in a partnership without limited partners."

This arrangement has not been completely satisfactory, because the consequences of linkage are not always clear. *See, e.g., Frye v. Manacare Ltd.*, 431 So.2d 181, 183–84 (Fla. Dist. Ct. App. 1983) (applying UPA Section 42 in favor of a limited partner), *Porter v. Barnhouse*, 354 N.W.2d 227, 232–33 (Iowa 1984) (declining to apply UPA Section 42 in favor of a limited partner) and *Baltzell-Wolfe Agencies, Inc. v. Car Wash Investments No. 1, Ltd.*, 389 N.E.2d 517, 518–20 (Ohio App. 1978) (holding that neither the specific provisions of the general partnership statute nor those of the limited partnership statute determined the liability of a person who had withdrawn as general partner of a limited partnership). Moreover, in some instances the "not inconsistent" rules of the UPA can be inappropriate for the fundamentally different relations involved in a limited partnership.

In any event, the promulgation of RUPA unsettled matters. RUPA differs substantially from the UPA, and the drafters of RUPA expressly declined to decide whether RUPA provides a suitable base and link for the limited partnership statute. According to RUPA's Prefatory Note:

> Partnership law no longer governs limited partnerships pursuant to the provisions of RUPA itself. First, limited partnerships are not "partnerships" within the RUPA definition. Second, UPA Section 6(2), which provides that the UPA governs limited partnerships in cases not provided for in the Uniform Limited Partnership Act (1976) (1985) ("RULPA") has been deleted. No substantive change in result is intended, however. Section 1105 of RULPA already provides that the UPA governs in any case not provided for in RULPA, and thus the express linkage in RUPA is unnecessary. Structurally, it is more appropriately left to RULPA to determine the applicability of RUPA to limited partnerships. It is contemplated

that the Conference will review the linkage question carefully, although no changes in RULPA may be necessary despite the many changes in RUPA.

The linkage question was the first major issue considered and decided by this Act's Drafting Committee. Since the Conference has recommended the repeal of the UPA, it made no sense to recommend retaining the UPA as the base and link for a revised or new limited partnership act. The Drafting Committee therefore had to choose between recommending linkage to the new general partnership act (i.e., RUPA) or recommending de-linking and a stand alone act.

The Committee saw several substantial advantages to de-linking. A stand alone statute would:

- be more convenient, providing a single, self-contained source of statutory authority for issues pertaining to limited partnerships;
- eliminate confusion as to which issues were solely subject to the limited partnership act and which required reference (i.e., linkage) to the general partnership act; and
- rationalize future case law, by ending the automatic link between the cases concerning partners in a general partnership and issues pertaining to general partners in a limited partnership.

Thus, a stand alone act seemed likely to promote efficiency, clarity, and coherence in the law of limited partnerships.

In contrast, recommending linkage would have required the Drafting Committee to (1) consider each provision of RUPA and determine whether the provision addressed a matter provided for in RULPA; (2) for each RUPA provision which addressed a matter not provided for in RULPA, determine whether the provision stated an appropriate rule for limited partnerships; and (3) for each matter addressed both by RUPA and RULPA, determine whether RUPA or RULPA stated the better rule for limited partnerships.

That approach was unsatisfactory for at least two reasons. No matter how exhaustive the Drafting Committee's analysis might be, the Committee could not guarantee that courts and practitioners would reach the same conclusions. Therefore, in at least some situations linkage would have produced ambiguity. In addition, the Drafting Committee could not guarantee that all currently appropriate links would remain appropriate as courts begin to apply and interpret RUPA. Even if the Committee recommended linkage, RUPA was destined to be interpreted primarily in the context of general partnerships. Those interpretations might not make sense for limited partnership law, because the modern limited partnership involves fundamentally different relations than those involved in "the small, often informal, partnership" that is "[t]he primary focus of RUPA." RUPA, Prefatory Note.

The Drafting Committee therefore decided to draft and recommend a stand alone act.

Availability of LLLP Status

Following the example of a growing number of States, this Act provides for limited liability limited partnerships. In a limited liability limited partnership ("LLLP"), no partner—whether general or limited—is liable on account of partner status for the limited partnership's obligations. Both general and limited partners benefit from a full, status-based liability shield that is equivalent to the shield enjoyed by corporate shareholders, LLC members, and partners in an LLP.

This Act is designed to serve preexisting limited partnerships as well as limited partnerships formed after the Act's enactment. Most of those preexisting limited partnership will not be LLLPs, and accordingly the Act does not prefer or presume LLLP status. Instead, the Act makes LLLP status available through a simple statement in the certificate of limited partnership. See Sections 102(9), 201(a)(4) and 404(c).

Liability Shield for Limited Partners

RULPA provides only a restricted liability shield for limited partners. The shield is at risk for any limited partner who "participates in the control of the business." RULPA Section 303(a). Although this "control rule" is subject to a lengthy list of safe harbors, RULPA Section 303(b), in a world with LLPs, LLCs and, most importantly, LLLPs, the rule is an anachronism. This Act therefore eliminates the control rule and provides a full, status-based shield against limited partner liability for entity obligations. The shield applies whether or not the limited partnership is an LLLP. See Section 303.

Transition Issues

Following RUPA's example, this Act provides (i) an effective date, after which all newly formed limited partnerships are subject to this Act; (ii) an optional period, during which limited partnerships formed under a predecessor statute may elect to become subject to this Act; and (iii) a mandatory date, on which all preexisting limited partnerships become subject to this Act by operation of law.

A few provisions of this Act differ so substantially from prior law that they should not apply automatically to a preexisting limited partnership. Section 1206(c) lists these provisions and states that each remains inapplicable to a preexisting limited partnership, unless the limited partnership elects for the provision to apply.

Comparison of RULPA and this Act

The following table compares some of the major characteristics of RULPA and this Act. In most instances, the rules involved are "default" rules—i.e., subject to change by the partnership agreement.

Characteristic	RULPA	this Act
relationship to general partnership act	linked, Sections 1105, 403; UPA Section 6(2)	de-linked (but many RUPA provisions incorporated)

Characteristic	RULPA	this Act
permitted purposes	subject to any specified exceptions, "any business that a partnership without limited partners may carry on, "Section 106	any lawful purpose, Section 104(b)
constructive notice via publicly filed documents	only that limited partnership exists and that designated general partners are general partners, Section 208	RULPA constructive notice provisions carried forward, Section 103(c), plus constructive notice, 90 days after appropriate filing, of: general partner dissociation and of limited partnership dissolution, termination, merger and conversion, Section 103(d)
duration	specified in certificate of limited partnership, Section 201(a)(4)	perpetual, Section 104(c); subject to change in partnership agreement
use of limited partner name in entity name	prohibited, except in unusual circumstances, Section 102(2)	permitted, Section108(a)
annual report	none	required, Section 210
limited partner liability for entity debts	none unless limited partner "participates in the control of the business" and person "transact[s] business with the limited partnership reasonably believing . . . that the limited partner is a general partner," Section 303(a); safe harbor lists many activities that do not constitute participating in the control of the business, Section 303(b)	none, regardless of whether the limited partnership is an LLLP, "even if the limited partner participates in the management and control of the limited partnership," Section 303
limited partner duties	none specified	no fiduciary duties "solely by reason of being a limited partner," Section 305(a); each limited partner is obliged to "discharge duties . . . and exercise rights consistently with the obligation of good faith and fair dealing," Section 305(b)
partner access to information–required records/ information	all partners have right of access; no requirement of good cause; Act does not state whether partnership agreement may limit access; Sections 105(b) and 305(1)	list of required information expanded slightly; Act expressly states that partner does not have to show good cause; Sections 304(a), 407(a); however, the partnership agreement may set reasonable restrictions on access to and use of required information, Section

Characteristic	RULPA	this Act
		110(b)(4), and limited partnership may impose reasonable restrictions on the use of information, Sections 304(g) and 407(f)
partner access to information–other information	limited partners have the right to obtain other relevant information "upon reasonable demand," Section 305(2); general partner rights linked to general partnership act, Section 403	for limited partners, RULPA approach essentially carried forward, with procedures and standards for making a reasonable demand stated in greater detail, plus requirement that limited partnership supply known material information when limited partner consent sought, Section 304; general partner access rights made explicit, following ULLCA and RUPA, including obligation of limited partnership and general partners to volunteer certain information, Section 407; access rights provided for former partners, Sections 304 and 407
general partner liability for entity debts	complete, automatic and formally inescapable, Section 403(b) (n.b.–in practice, most modern limited partnerships have used a general partner that has its own liability shield; *e.g.*, a corporation or limited liability company)	LLLP status available via a simple statement in the certificate of limited partnership, Sections 102(9), 201(a)(4); LLLP status provides a full liability shield to all general partners, Section 404(c); if the limited partnership is not an LLLP, general partners are liable just as under RULPA, Section 404(a)
general partner duties	linked to duties of partners in a general partnership, Section 403	RUPA general partner duties imported, Section 408; general partner's noncompete duty continues during winding up, Section 408(b)(3)
allocation of profits, losses and distributions	provides separately for sharing of profits and losses, Section 503, and for sharing of distributions, Section 504; allocates each according to contributions made and not returned	eliminates as unnecessary the allocation rule for profits and losses; allocates distributions according to contributions made, Section 503 (n.b.–in the default mode, the Act's formulation produces the same result as RULPA formulation)
partner liability for distributions	recapture liability if distribution involved "the return	following ULLCA Sections 406 and 407, the Act adopts

Characteristic	RULPA	this Act
	of ... contribution"; one year recapture liability if distribution rightful, Section 608(a); six year recapture liability if wrongful, Section 608(b)	the RMBCA approach to improper distributions, Sections 508 and 509
limited partner voluntary dissociation	theoretically, limited partner may withdraw on six months notice unless partnership agreement specifies a term for the limited partnership or withdrawal events for limited partner, Section 603; practically, virtually every partnership agreement specifies a term, thereby eliminating the right to withdraw (n.b.–due to estate planning concerns, several States have amended RULPA to prohibit limited partner withdrawal unless otherwise provided in the partnership agreement)	no "right to dissociate as a limited partner before the termination of the limited partnership," Section 601(a); power to dissociate expressly recognized, Section 601(b)(1), but can be eliminated by the partnership agreement
limited partner involuntary dissociation	not addressed	lengthy list of causes, Section 601(b), taken with some modification from RUPA
limited partner dissociation–payout	"fair value ... based upon [the partner's] right to share in distributions," Section 604	no payout; person becomes transferee of its own transferable interest, Section 602(3)
general partner voluntary dissociation	right exists unless otherwise provided in partnership agreement, Section 602; power exists regardless of partnership agreement, Section 602	RULPA rule carried forward, although phrased differently, Section 604(a); dissociation before termination of the limited partnership is defined as wrongful, Section 604(b)(2)
general partner involuntary dissociation	Section 402 lists causes	following RUPA, Section 603 expands the list of causes, including expulsion by court order, Section 603(5)
general partner dissociation–payout	"fair value ... based upon [the partner's] right to share in distributions," Section 604, subject to offset for damages caused by wrongful withdrawal, Section 602	no payout; person becomes transferee of its own transferable interest, Section 605(5)
transfer of partner interest–nomenclature	"Assignment of Partnership Interest," Section 702	"Transfer of Partner's Transferable Interest," Section 702

Characteristic	RULPA	this Act
transfer of partner interest–substance	economic rights fully transferable, but management rights and partner status are not transferable, Section 702	same rule, but Sections 701 and 702 follow RUPA's more detailed and less oblique formulation
rights of creditor of partner	limited to charging order, Section 703	essentially the same rule, but, following RUPA and ULLCA, the Act has a more elaborate provision that expressly extends to creditors of transferees, Section 703
dissolution by partner consent	requires unanimous written consent, Section 801(3)	requires consent of "all general partners and of limited partners owning a majority of the rights to receive distributions as limited partners at the time the consent is to be effective," Section 801(2)
dissolution following dissociation of a general partner	occurs automatically unless all partners agree to continue the business and, if there is no remaining general partner, to appoint a replacement general partner, Section 801(4)	if at least one general partner remains, no dissolution unless "within 90 days after the dissociation . . . partners owning a majority of the rights to receive distributions as partners" consent to dissolve the limited partnership; Section 801(3)(A); if no general partner remains, dissolution occurs upon the passage of 90 days after the dissociation, unless before that deadline limited partners owning a majority of the rights to receive distributions owned by limited partners consent to continue the business and admit at least one new general partner and a new general partner is admitted, Section 801(3)(B)
filings related to entity termination	certificate of limited partnership to be cancelled when limited partnership dissolves and begins winding up, Section 203	limited partnership may amend certificate to indicate dissolution, Section 803(b)(1), and may file statement of termination indicating that winding up has been completed and the limited partnership is terminated, Section 203
procedures for barring claims against dissolved	none	following ULLCA Sections 807 and 808, the Act adopts the RMBCA approach pro-

Characteristic	RULPA	this Act
limited partnership		viding for giving notice and barring claims, Sections 806 and 807
conversions and mergers	no provision	Article 11 permits conversions to and from and mergers with any "organization," defined as "a general partnership, including a limited liability partnership; limited partnership, including a limited liability limited partnership; limited liability company; business trust; corporation; or any other entity having a governing statute . . . [including] domestic and foreign entities regardless of whether organized for profit." Section 1101(8)
writing requirements	some provisions pertain only to written understandings; *see, e.g.*, Sections 401 (partnership agreement may "provide in writing for the admission of additional general partners"; such admission also permitted "with the written consent of all partners"), 502(a) (limited partner's promise to contribute "is not enforceable unless set out in a writing signed by the limited partner"), 801(2) and (3) (dissolution occurs "upon the happening of events specified in writing in the partnership agreement" and upon "written consent of all partners"), 801(4) (dissolution avoided following withdrawal of a general partner if "all partners agree in writing")	removes virtually all writing requirements; but does require that certain information be maintained in record form, Section 111

[ARTICLE] 1. GENERAL PROVISIONS

§ 101. Short Title

This [Act] may be cited as the Uniform Limited Partnership Act [year of enactment].

§ 102. Definitions

In this [Act]:

(1) "Certificate of limited partnership" means the certificate required by Section 201. The term includes the certificate as amended or restated.

(2) "Contribution", except in the phrase "right of contribution," means any benefit provided by a person to a limited partnership in order to become a partner or in the person's capacity as a partner.

(3) "Debtor in bankruptcy" means a person that is the subject of:

(A) an order for relief under Title 11 of the United States Code or a comparable order under a successor statute of general application; or

(B) a comparable order under federal, state, or foreign law governing insolvency.

(4) "Designated office" means:

(A) with respect to a limited partnership, the office that the limited partnership is required to designate and maintain under Section 114; and

(B) with respect to a foreign limited partnership, its principal office.

(5) "Distribution" means a transfer of money or other property from a limited partnership to a partner in the partner's capacity as a partner or to a transferee on account of a transferable interest owned by the transferee.

(6) "Foreign limited liability limited partnership" means a foreign limited partnership whose general partners have limited liability for the obligations of the foreign limited partnership under a provision similar to Section 404(c).

(7) "Foreign limited partnership" means a partnership formed under the laws of a jurisdiction other than this State and required by those laws to have one or more general partners and one or more limited partners. The term includes a foreign limited liability limited partnership.

(8) "General partner" means:

(A) with respect to a limited partnership, a person that:

(i) becomes a general partner under Section 401; or

(ii) was a general partner in a limited partnership when the limited partnership became subject to this [Act] under Section 1206(a) or (b); and

(B) with respect to a foreign limited partnership, a person that has rights, powers, and obligations similar to those of a general partner in a limited partnership.

(9) "Limited liability limited partnership", except in the phrase "foreign limited liability limited partnership", means a limited partnership whose certificate of limited partnership states that the limited partnership is a limited liability limited partnership.

(10) "Limited partner" means:

(A) with respect to a limited partnership, a person that:

(i) becomes a limited partner under Section 301; or

(ii) was a limited partner in a limited partnership when the limited partnership became subject to this [Act] under Section 1206(a) or (b); and

(B) with respect to a foreign limited partnership, a person that has rights, powers, and obligations similar to those of a limited partner in a limited partnership.

(11) "Limited partnership", except in the phrases "foreign limited partnership" and "foreign limited liability limited partnership", means an entity, having one or more general partners and one or more limited partners, which is formed under this [Act] by two or more persons or becomes subject to this [Act] under [Article] 11 or Section 1206(a) or (b). The term includes a limited liability limited partnership.

(12) "Partner" means a limited partner or general partner.

(13) "Partnership agreement" means the partners' agreement, whether oral, implied, in a record, or in any combination, concerning the limited partnership. The term includes the agreement as amended.

(14) "Person" means an individual, corporation, business trust, estate, trust, partnership, limited liability company, association, joint venture, government; governmental subdivision, agency, or instrumentality; public corporation, or any other legal or commercial entity.

(15) "Person dissociated as a general partner" means a person dissociated as a general partner of a limited partnership.

(16) "Principal office" means the office where the principal executive office of a limited partnership or foreign limited partnership is located, whether or not the office is located in this State.

(17) "Record" means information that is inscribed on a tangible medium or that is stored in an electronic or other medium and is retrievable in perceivable form.

(18) "Required information" means the information that a limited partnership is required to maintain under Section 111.

(19) "Sign" means:

(A) to execute or adopt a tangible symbol with the present intent to authenticate a record; or

(B) to attach or logically associate an electronic symbol, sound, or process to or with a record with the present intent to authenticate the record.

(20) "State" means a State of the United States, the District of Columbia, Puerto Rico, the United States Virgin Islands, or any territory or insular possession subject to the jurisdiction of the United States.

(21) "Transfer" includes an assignment, conveyance, deed, bill of sale, lease, mortgage, security interest, encumbrance, gift, and transfer by operation of law.

(22) "Transferable interest" means a partner's right to receive distributions.

(23) "Transferee" means a person to which all or part of a transferable interest has been transferred, whether or not the transferor is a partner.

Comment

This section contains definitions applicable throughout the Act. Section 1101 provides additional definitions applicable within Article 11.

Paragraph 8(A)(i) [General partner]—A partnership agreement may vary Section 401 and provide a process or mechanism for becoming a general partner which is different from or additional to the rules stated in that section. For the purposes of this definition, a person who becomes a general partner pursuant to a provision of the partnership agreement "becomes a general partner under Section 401."

Paragraph 10(A)(i) [Limited partner]—The Comment to Paragraph 8(A)(i) applies here as well. For the purposes of this definition, a person who becomes a limited partner pursuant to a provision of the partnership agreement "becomes a limited partner under Section 301."

Paragraph (11) [Limited partnership]—This definition pertains to what is commonly termed a "domestic" limited partnership. The definition encompasses: (i) limited partnerships originally formed under this Act, including limited partnerships formed under Section 1101(11) to be the surviving organization in a merger; (ii) any entity that becomes subject to this Act by converting into a limited partnership under Article 11; (iii) any preexisting domestic limited partnership that elects pursuant to Section 1206(a) to become subject to this Act; and (iv) all other preexisting domestic limited partnerships when they become subject to this Act under Section 1206(b).

Following the approach of predecessor law, RULPA Section 101(7), this definition contains two substantive requirements. First, it is of the essence of a limited partnership to have two classes of partners. Accordingly, under Section 101(11) a limited partnership must have at least one general and one limited partner. Section 801(3)(B) and (4) provide that a limited partnership dissolves if its sole general partner or sole limited partner dissociates and the limited partnership fails to admit a replacement within 90 days of the dissociation. The 90 day limitation is a default rule, but, in light of Section 101(11), a limited partnership may not indefinitely delay "having one or more general partners and one or more limited partners."

It is also of the essence of a limited partnership to have at least two partners. Section 101(11) codifies this requirement by referring to a limited partnership as "an entity . . . which is formed under this [Act] by two or more persons." Thus, while the same person may be both a general and limited partner, Section 113 (Dual Capacity), one person alone cannot be the "two persons" contemplated by this definition. However, nothing in this definition prevents two closely affiliated persons from satisfying the two person requirement.

Paragraph (13) [Partnership agreement]—Section 110 is essential to understanding the significance of the partnership agreement. See also Section 201(d) (resolving inconsistencies between the certificate of limited partnership and the partnership agreement).

Paragraph (21) [Transfer]—Following RUPA, this Act uses the words "transfer" and "transferee" rather than the words "assignment" and "assignee." See RUPA Section 503.

The reference to "transfer by operation of law" is significant in connection with Section 702 (Transfer of Partner's Transferable Interest). That section severely restricts a transferee's rights (absent the consent of the partners), and this definition makes those restrictions applicable, for example, to transfers ordered by a family court as part of a divorce proceeding and transfers resulting from the death of a partner.

Paragraph (23) [Transferee]—See comment to Paragraph 21 for an explanation of why this Act refers to "transferee" rather than "assignee."

§ 103. Knowledge and Notice

(a) A person knows a fact if the person has actual knowledge of it.

(b) A person has notice of a fact if the person:

(1) knows of it;

(2) has received a notification of it;

(3) has reason to know it exists from all of the facts known to the person at the time in question; or

(4) has notice of it under subsection (c) or (d).

(c) A certificate of limited partnership on file in the [office of the Secretary of State] is notice that the partnership is a limited partnership and the persons designated in the certificate as general partners are general partners. Except as otherwise provided in subsection (d), the certificate is not notice of any other fact.

(d) A person has notice of:

(1) another person's dissociation as a general partner, 90 days after the effective date of an amendment to the certificate of limited partnership which states that the other person has dissociated or 90 days after the effective date of a statement of dissociation pertaining to the other person, whichever occurs first;

(2) a limited partnership's dissolution, 90 days after the effective date of an amendment to the certificate of limited partnership stating that the limited partnership is dissolved;

(3) a limited partnership's termination, 90 days after the effective date of a statement of termination;

(4) a limited partnership's conversion under [Article] 11, 90 days after the effective date of the articles of conversion; or

(5) a merger under [Article] 11, 90 days after the effective date of the articles of merger.

(e) A person notifies or gives a notification to another person by taking steps reasonably required to inform the other person in ordinary course, whether or not the other person learns of it.

(f) A person receives a notification when the notification:

(1) comes to the person's attention; or

(2) is delivered at the person's place of business or at any other place held out by the person as a place for receiving communications.

(g) Except as otherwise provided in subsection (h), a person other than an individual knows, has notice, or receives a notification of a fact for purposes of a particular transaction when the individual conducting the transaction for the person knows, has notice, or receives a notification of the fact, or in any event when the fact would have been brought to the individual's attention if the person had exercised reasonable diligence. A person other than an individual exercises reasonable diligence if it maintains reasonable routines for communicating significant information to the individual conducting the transaction for the person and there is reasonable compliance with the routines. Reasonable diligence does not require an individual acting for the person to communicate information unless the communication is part of the individual's regular duties or the individual has reason to know of the transaction and that the transaction would be materially affected by the information.

(h) A general partner's knowledge, notice, or receipt of a notification of a fact relating to the limited partnership is effective immediately as knowledge of, notice to, or receipt of a notification by the limited partnership, except in the case of a fraud on the limited partnership committed by or with the consent of the general partner. A limited partner's knowledge, notice, or receipt of a notification of a fact relating to the limited partnership is not effective as knowledge of, notice to, or receipt of a notification by the limited partnership.

Comment

Source—RUPA Section 102; RULPA Section 208.

Notice and the relationship among subsections (b), (c) and (d)–These subsections provide separate and independent avenues through which a person can have notice of a fact. A person has notice of a fact as soon as any of the avenues applies.

> **Example:** A limited partnership dissolves and amends its certificate of limited partnership to indicate dissolution. The amendment is effective on March 1. On March 15, Person #1 has reason to know of the dissolution and therefore has "notice" of the dissolution under Section 103(b)(3) even though Section 103(d)(2) does not yet apply. Person #2 does not have actual knowledge of the dissolution until June 15. Nonetheless, under Section 103(d)(2) Person #2 has "notice" of the dissolution on May 30.

Subsection (c)—This subsection provides what is commonly called constructive notice and comes essentially verbatim from RULPA Section 208. As for the significance of constructive notice "that the partnership is a limited partnership," see *Water, Waste & Land, Inc. v. Lanham*, 955 P.2d 997, 1001–1003 (Colo. 1998) (interpreting a comparable provision of the Colorado LLC statute and holding the provision ineffective to change common law agency principles, including the rules relating to the liability of an agent that transacts business for an undisclosed principal).

As for constructive notice that "the persons designated in the certificate as general partners are general partners," Section 201(a)(3) requires the initial certificate of limited partnership to name each general partner, and Section 202(b) requires a limited partnership to promptly amend its certificate of limited partnership to reflect any change in the identity of its general partners. Nonetheless, it will be possible, albeit improper, for a person to be designated in the certificate of limited partnership as a general partner without having become a general partner as contemplated by Section 401. Likewise, it will be possible for a person to have become a general partner under Section 401 without being designated as a general partner in the certificate of limited partnership. According to the last clause of this subsection, the fact that a person is **not** listed ... in the certificate as a general partner is **not** notice that the person is **not** a general partner. For further discussion of this point, see the Comment to Section 401.

If the partnership agreement and the public record are inconsistent, Section 201(d) applies (partnership agreement controls *inter se*; public record controls as to third parties who have relied). See also Section

202(b) (requiring the limited partnership to amend its certificate of limited partnership to keep accurate the listing of general partners), 202(c) (requiring a general partner to take corrective action when the general partner knows that the certificate of limited partnership contains false information), and 208 (imposing liability for false information in *inter alia* the certificate of limited partnership).

Subsection (d)—This subsection also provides what is commonly called constructive notice and works in conjunction with other sections of this Act to curtail the power to bind and personal liability of general partners and persons dissociated as general partners. See Sections 402, 606, 607, 804, 805, 1111, and 1112. Following RUPA (in substance, although not in form), the constructive notice begins 90 days after the effective date of the filed record. For the Act's rules on delayed effective dates, see Section 206(c).

The 90–day delay applies only to the constructive notice and not to the event described in the filed record.

> **Example:** On March 15, X dissociates as a general partner from XYZ Limited Partnership by giving notice to XYZ. See Section 603(1). On March 20, XYZ amends its certificate of limited partnership to remove X's name from the list of general partners. See Section 202(b)(2).
>
> X's **dissociation** is effective March 15. If on March 16 X purports to be a general partner of XYZ and under Section 606(a) binds XYZ to some obligation, X will be liable under Section 606(b) as a "person dissociated as a general partner."
>
> On June 13 (90 days after March 15), the world has constructive notice of X's dissociation as a general partner. Beginning on that date, X will lack the power to bind XYZ. See Section 606(a)(2)(B) (person dissociated as a general partner can bind the limited partnership only if, *inter alia*, "at the time the other party enters into the transaction ... the other party does not have notice of the dissociation").

Constructive notice under this subsection applies to partners and transferees as well as other persons.

Subsection (e)—The phrase "person learns of it" in this subsection is equivalent to the phrase "knows of it" in subsection (b)(1).

Subsection (h)—Under this subsection and Section 302, information possessed by a person that is only a limited partner is not attributable to the limited partnership. However, information possessed by a person that is both a general partner and a limited partner is attributable to the limited partnership. See Section 113 (Dual Capacity).

§ 104. Nature, Purpose, and Duration of Entity

(a) A limited partnership is an entity distinct from its partners. A limited partnership is the same entity regardless of whether its certificate states that the limited partnership is a limited liability limited partnership.

(b) A limited partnership may be organized under this [Act] for any lawful purpose.

(c) A limited partnership has a perpetual duration.

Comment

Subsection (a)—Acquiring or relinquishing an LLLP shield changes only the rules governing a general partner's liability for subsequently incurred obligations of the limited partnership. The underlying entity is unaffected.

Subsection (b)—In contrast with RULPA Section 106, this Act does not require a limited partnership to have a business purpose. However, many of the Act's default rules presuppose at least a profit-making purpose. See, e.g., Section 503 (providing for the sharing of distributions in proportion to the value of contributions), 701 (defining a transferable interest in terms of the right to receive distributions), 801 (allocating the right to consent to cause or avoid dissolution in proportion to partners' rights to receive distributions), and 812 (providing that, after a dissolved limited partnership has paid its creditors, "[a]ny surplus remaining ... must be paid in cash as a distribution" to partners and transferees). If a limited partnership is organized for an essentially non-pecuniary purpose, the organizers should carefully review the Act's default rules and override them as necessary via the partnership agreement.

Subsection (c)—The partnership agreement has the power to vary this subsection, either by stating a definite term or by specifying an event or events which cause dissolution. Sections 110(a) and 801(1). Section 801 also recognizes several other occurrences that cause dissolution. Thus, the public record pertaining to a limited partnership will not necessarily reveal whether the limited partnership actually has a perpetual duration.

The public record might also fail to reveal whether the limited partnership has in fact dissolved. A dissolved limited partnership may amend its certificate of limited partnership to indicate dissolution but is not required to do so. Section 803(b)(1).

Predecessor law took a somewhat different approach. RULPA Section 201(4) required the certificate of limited partnership to state "the latest date upon which the limited partnership is to dissolve." Although RULPA Section 801(2) provided for a limited partnership to dissolve "upon the happening of events specified in writing in the partnership agreement," RULPA Section 203 required the limited partnership to file a certificate of cancellation to indicate that dissolution had occurred.

§ 105. Powers

A limited partnership has the powers to do all things necessary or convenient to carry on its activities, including the power to sue, be sued, and defend in its own name and to maintain an action against a partner for harm caused to the limited partnership by a breach of the partnership agreement or violation of a duty to the partnership.

Comment

This Act omits as unnecessary any detailed list of specific powers. The power to sue and be sued is mentioned specifically so that Section 110(b)(1) can prohibit the partnership agreement from varying that power. The power to maintain an action against a partner is mentioned specifically to establish that the limited partnership itself has standing to enforce the partnership agreement.

§ 106. Governing Law

The law of this State governs relations among the partners of a limited partnership and between the partners and the limited partnership and the liability of partners as partners for an obligation of the limited partnership.

Comment

To partially define its scope, this section uses the phrase "relations among the partners of a limited partnership and between the partners and the limited partnership." Section 110(a) uses essentially identical language in defining the proper realm of the partnership agreement: "relations among the partners and between the partners and the partnership."

Despite the similarity of language, this section has no bearing on the power of a partnership agreement to vary other provisions of this Act. It is quite possible for a provision of this Act to involve "relations among the partners of a limited partnership and between the partners and the limited partnership" and thus come within this section, and yet not be subject to variation by the partnership agreement. Although Section 110(a) grants plenary authority to the partnership agreement to regulate "relations among the partners and between the partners and the partnership," that authority is subject to Section 110(b).

For example, Section 408 (General Standards of General Partner's Conduct) certainly involves "relations among the partners of a limited partnership and between the partners and the limited partnership." Therefore, according to this section, Section 408 applies to a limited partnership formed or otherwise subject to this Act. Just as certainly, Section 408 pertains to "relations among the partners and between the partners and the partnership" for the purposes of Section 110(a), and therefore the partnership agreement may properly address matters covered by Section 408. However, Section 110(b)(5), (6), and (7) limit the power of the partnership agreement to vary the rules stated in Section 408. See also, e.g., Section 502(c) (stating creditor's rights, which are protected under Section 110(b)(13) from being restricted by the partnership agreement) and Comment to Section 509.

This section also applies to "the liability of partners as partners for an obligation of a limited partnership." The phrase "as partners" contemplates the liability shield for limited partners under Section 303 and the rules for general partner liability stated in Section 404. Other grounds for liability can be supplied by other law, including the law of some other jurisdiction. For example, a partner's contractual guaranty of a limited partnership obligation might well be governed by the law of some other jurisdiction.

Transferees derive their rights and status under this Act from partners and accordingly this section applies to the relations of a transferee to the limited partnership.

The partnership agreement may not vary the rule stated in this section. See Section 110(b)(2).

§ 107. Supplemental Principles of Law; Rate of Interest

(a) Unless displaced by particular provisions of this [Act], the principles of law and equity supplement this [Act].

(b) If an obligation to pay interest arises under this [Act] and the rate is not specified, the rate is that specified in [applicable statute].

Comment

Subsection (a)—This language comes from RUPA Section 104 and does not address an important question raised by the de-linking of this Act from the UPA and RUPA–namely, to what extent is the case law of general partnerships relevant to limited partnerships governed by this Act?

Predecessor law, RULPA Section 403, expressly equated the rights, powers, restrictions, and liabilities of a general partner in a limited partnership with the rights, powers, restrictions, and liabilities of a partner in a general partnership. This Act has no comparable provision. See Prefatory Note. Therefore, a court should not assume that a case concerning a general partnership is automatically relevant to a limited partnership governed by this Act. A general partnership case may be relevant by analogy, especially if (1) the issue in dispute involves a provision of this Act for which a comparable provision exists under the law of general partnerships; and (2) the fundamental differences between a general partnership and limited partnership are immaterial to the disputed issue.

§ 108. Name

(a) The name of a limited partnership may contain the name of any partner.

(b) The name of a limited partnership that is not a limited liability limited partnership must contain the phrase "limited partnership" or the abbreviation "L.P."or "LP" and may not contain the phrase "limited liability limited partnership" or the abbreviation "LLLP" or "L.L.L.P."

(c) The name of a limited liability limited partnership must contain the phrase "limited liability limited partnership" or the abbreviation "LLLP" or "L.L.L.P." and must not contain the abbreviation "L.P."or "LP."

(d) Unless authorized by subsection (e), the name of a limited partnership must be distinguishable in the records of the [Secretary of State] from:

(1) the name of each person other than an individual incorporated, organized, or authorized to transact business in this State; and

(2) each name reserved under Section 109 [or other state laws allowing the reservation or registration of business names, including fictitious name statutes].

(e) A limited partnership may apply to the [Secretary of State] for authorization to use a name that does not comply with subsection (d). The [Secretary of State] shall authorize use of the name applied for if, as to each conflicting name:

(1) the present user, registrant, or owner of the conflicting name consents in a signed record to the use and submits an undertaking in a form satisfactory to the [Secretary of State] to change the conflicting name to a name that complies with subsection (d) and is distinguishable in the records of the [Secretary of State] from the name applied for;

(2) the applicant delivers to the [Secretary of State] a certified copy of the final judgment of a court of competent jurisdiction establishing the applicant's right to use in this State the name applied for; or

(3) the applicant delivers to the [Secretary of State] proof satisfactory to the [Secretary of State] that the present user, registrant, or owner of the conflicting name:

(A) has merged into the applicant;

(B) has been converted into the applicant; or

(C) has transferred substantially all of its assets, including the conflicting name, to the applicant.

(f) Subject to Section 905, this section applies to any foreign limited partnership transacting business in this State, having a certificate of authority to transact business in this State, or applying for a certificate of authority.

Comment

Subsection (a)—Predecessor law, RULPA Section 102, prohibited the use of a limited partner's name in the name of a limited partnership except in unusual circumstances. That approach derived from the 1916 Uniform Limited Partnership Act and has become antiquated. In 1916, most business organizations were either unshielded (*e.g.*, general partnerships) or partially shielded (*e.g.*, limited partnerships), and it was reasonable for third parties to believe that an individual whose own name appeared in the name of a business would "stand behind" the business. Today most businesses have a full shield (*e.g.*, corporations, limited liability companies, most limited liability partnerships), and corporate, LLC and LLP statutes generally pose no barrier to the use of an owner's name in the name of the entity. This Act eliminates RULPA's restriction and puts limited partnerships on equal footing with these other "shielded" entities.

Subsection (d)(1)—If a sole proprietor registers or reserves a business name under a fictitious name statute, that name comes within this provision. For the purposes of this provision, a sole proprietor doing business under a registered or reserved name is a "person other than an individual."

Subsection (f)—Section 905 permits a foreign limited partnership to obtain a certificate of authority under an alternate name if the foreign limited partnership's actual name does not comply with this section.

§ 109. Reservation of Name

(a) The exclusive right to the use of a name that complies with Section 108 may be reserved by:

(1) a person intending to organize a limited partnership under this [Act] and to adopt the name;

(2) a limited partnership or a foreign limited partnership authorized to transact business in this State intending to adopt the name;

(3) a foreign limited partnership intending to obtain a certificate of authority to transact business in this State and adopt the name;

(4) a person intending to organize a foreign limited partnership and intending to have it obtain a certificate of authority to transact business in this State and adopt the name;

(5) a foreign limited partnership formed under the name; or

(6) a foreign limited partnership formed under a name that does not comply with Section 108(b) or (c), but the name reserved under this paragraph may differ from the foreign limited partnership's name only to the extent necessary to comply with Section 108(b) and (c).

(b) A person may apply to reserve a name under subsection (a) by delivering to the [Secretary of State] for filing an application that states the name to be reserved and the paragraph of subsection (a) which applies. If the [Secretary of State] finds that the name is available for use by the applicant, the [Secretary of State] shall file a statement of name reservation and thereby reserve the name for the exclusive use of the applicant for a 120 days.

(c) An applicant that has reserved a name pursuant to subsection (b) may reserve the same name for additional 120–day periods. A person having a current reservation for a name may not apply for another 120–day period for the same name until 90 days have elapsed in the current reservation.

(d) A person that has reserved a name under this section may deliver to the [Secretary of State] for filing a notice of transfer that states the reserved name, the name and street and mailing address of some other person to which the reservation is to be transferred, and the paragraph of subsection (a) which applies to the other person. Subject to Section 206(c), the transfer is effective when the [Secretary of State] files the notice of transfer.

§ 110. Effect of Partnership Agreement; Nonwaivable Provisions

(a) Except as otherwise provided in subsection (b), the partnership agreement governs relations among the partners and between the partners and the partnership. To the extent the partnership agreement does not otherwise provide, this [Act] governs relations among the partners and between the partners and the partnership.

(b) A partnership agreement may not:

(1) vary a limited partnership's power under Section 105 to sue, be sued, and defend in its own name;

(2) vary the law applicable to a limited partnership under Section 106;

(3) vary the requirements of Section 204;

(4) vary the information required under Section 111 or unreasonably restrict the right to information under Sections 304 or 407, but the partnership agreement may impose reasonable restrictions on the availability and use of information obtained under those sections and may define appropriate remedies, including liquidated damages, for a breach of any reasonable restriction on use;

(5) eliminate the duty of loyalty under Section 408, but the partnership agreement may:

(A) identify specific types or categories of activities that do not violate the duty of loyalty, if not manifestly unreasonable; and

(B) specify the number or percentage of partners which may authorize or ratify, after full disclosure to all partners of all material facts, a specific act or transaction that otherwise would violate the duty of loyalty;

(6) unreasonably reduce the duty of care under Section 408(c);

(7) eliminate the obligation of good faith and fair dealing under Sections 305(b) and 408(d), but the partnership agreement may prescribe the standards by which the performance of the obligation is to be measured, if the standards are not manifestly unreasonable;

(8) vary the power of a person to dissociate as a general partner under Section 604(a) except to require that the notice under Section 603(1) be in a record;

(9) vary the power of a court to decree dissolution in the circumstances specified in Section 802;

(10) vary the requirement to wind up the partnership's business as specified in Section 803;

(11) unreasonably restrict the right to maintain an action under [Article] 10;

(12) restrict the right of a partner under Section 1110(a) to approve a conversion or merger or the right of a general partner under Section 1110(b) to consent to an amendment to the certificate of limited partnership which deletes a statement that the limited partnership is a limited liability limited partnership; or

(13) restrict rights under this [Act] of a person other than a partner or a transferee.

Comment

Source—RUPA Section 103.

Subject only to subsection (b), the partnership agreement has plenary power to structure and regulate the relations of the partners *inter se.* Although the certificate of limited partnership is a limited partnership's foundational document, among the partners the partnership agreement controls. See Section 201(d).

The partnership agreement has the power to control the manner of its own amendment. In particular, a provision of the agreement prohibiting oral modifications is enforceable, despite any common law antagonism to "no oral modification" provisions. Likewise, a partnership agreement can impose "made in a record" requirements on other aspects of the partners' relationship, such as requiring consents to be made in a record and signed, or rendering unenforceable oral promises to make contributions or oral understandings as to "events upon the happening of which the limited partnership is to be dissolved," Section 111(9)(D). See also Section 801(1).

Subsection (b)(3)—The referenced section states who must sign various documents.

Subsection (b)(4)—In determining whether a restriction is reasonable, a court might consider: (i) the danger or other problem the restriction seeks to avoid; (ii) the purpose for which the information is sought; and (iii) whether, in light of both the problem and the purpose, the restriction is reasonably tailored. Restricting access to or use of the names and addresses of limited partners is not per se unreasonable.

Under this Act, general and limited partners have sharply different roles. A restriction that is reasonable as to a limited partner is not necessarily reasonable as to a general partner.

Sections 304(g) and 407(f) authorize the limited partnership (as distinguished from the partnership agreement) to impose restrictions on the use of information. For a comparison of restrictions contained in the partnership agreement and restrictions imposed unilaterally by the limited partnership, see the Comment to Section 304(g).

Subsection (b)(5)(A)—It is not per se manifestly unreasonable for the partnership agreement to permit a general partner to compete with the limited partnership.

Subsection (b)(5)(B)—The Act does not require that the authorization or ratification be by **disinterested** partners, although the partnership agreement may so provide. The Act does require that the disclosure be made to all partners, even if the partnership agreement excludes some partners from the authorization or ratification process. An interested partner that participates in the authorization or ratification process is subject to the obligation of good faith and fair dealing. Sections 305(b) and 408(d).

Subsection (b)(8)—This restriction applies only to the power of a person to dissociate as a general partner. The partnership agreement may eliminate the power of a person to dissociate as a limited partner.

Subsection (b)(9)—This provision should not be read to limit a partnership agreement's power to provide for arbitration. For example, an agreement to arbitrate all disputes–including dissolution disputes–is enforceable. Any other interpretation would put this Act at odds with federal law. *See Southland Corp. v. Keating*, 465 U.S. 1 (1984) (holding that the Federal Arbitration Act preempts state statutes that seek to invalidate agreements to arbitrate) and *Allied-Bruce Terminix Cos., Inc. v. Dobson*, 513 U.S. 265 (1995) (same). This provision does prohibit any narrowing of the substantive grounds for judicial dissolution as stated in Section 802.

Example: A provision of a partnership agreement states that no partner may obtain judicial dissolution without showing that a general partner is in material breach of the partnership agreement. The provision is ineffective to prevent a court from ordering dissolution under Section 802.

Subsection (b)(11)—Section 1001 codifies a partner's right to bring a direct action, and the rest of Article 10 provides for derivative actions. The partnership agreement may not restrict a partner's right to bring either type of action if the effect is to undercut or frustrate the duties and rights protected by Section 110(b).

The reasonableness of a restriction on derivative actions should be judged in light of the history and purpose of derivative actions. They originated as an equitable remedy, intended to protect passive owners against management abuses. A partnership agreement may not provide that all derivative claims will be subject to final determination by a special litigation committee appointed by the limited partnership, because that provision would eliminate, not merely restrict, a partner's right to bring a derivative *action*.

Subsection (b)(12)—Section 1110 imposes special consent requirements with regard to transactions that might make a partner personally liable for entity debts.

Subsection (b)(13)—The partnership agreement is a contract, and this provision reflects a basic notion of contract law—namely, that a contract can **directly** restrict rights only of parties to the contract and of persons who derive their rights from the contract. A provision of a partnership agreement can be determined to be unenforceable against third parties under paragraph (b)(13) without therefore and automatically being unenforceable *inter se* the partners and any transferees. How the former determination affects the latter question is a matter of other law.

§ 111. Required Information

A limited partnership shall maintain at its designated office the following information:

(1) a current list showing the full name and last known street and mailing address of each partner, separately identifying the general partners, in alphabetical order, and the limited partners, in alphabetical order;

(2) a copy of the initial certificate of limited partnership and all amendments to and restatements of the certificate, together with signed copies of any powers of attorney under which any certificate, amendment, or restatement has been signed;

(3) a copy of any filed articles of conversion or merger;

(4) a copy of the limited partnership's federal, state, and local income tax returns and reports, if any, for the three most recent years;

(5) a copy of any partnership agreement made in a record and any amendment made in a record to any partnership agreement;

(6) a copy of any financial statement of the limited partnership for the three most recent years;

(7) a copy of the three most recent annual reports delivered by the limited partnership to the [Secretary of State] pursuant to Section 210;

(8) a copy of any record made by the limited partnership during the past three years of any consent given by or vote taken of any partner pursuant to this [Act] or the partnership agreement; and

(9) unless contained in a partnership agreement made in a record, a record stating:

(A) the amount of cash, and a description and statement of the agreed value of the other benefits, contributed and agreed to be contributed by each partner;

(B) the times at which, or events on the happening of which, any additional contributions agreed to be made by each partner are to be made;

(C) for any person that is both a general partner and a limited partner, a specification of what transferable interest the person owns in each capacity; and

(D) any events upon the happening of which the limited partnership is to be dissolved and its activities wound up.

Comment

Source—RULPA Section 105.

Sections 304 and 407 govern access to the information required by this section, as well as to other information pertaining to a limited partnership.

Paragraph (5)—This requirement applies to superseded as well as current agreements and amendments. An agreement or amendment is "made in a record "to the extent the agreement is "integrated" into a record and consented to in that memorialized form. It is possible for a partnership agreement to be made in part in a record and in part otherwise. See Comment to Section 110. An oral agreement that is subsequently inscribed in a record (but not consented to as such) was not "made in a record" and is not covered by paragraph (5). However, if the limited partnership happens to have such a record, Section 304(b) might and Section 407(a)(2) will provide a right of access.

Paragraph (8)—This paragraph does not require a limited partnership to make a record of consents given and votes taken. However, if the limited partnership has made such a record, this paragraph requires that the limited partnership maintain the record for three years. The requirement applies to any record made by the limited partnership, not just to records made contemporaneously with the giving of consent or voting. The three year period runs from when the record was made and not from when the consent was given or vote taken.

Paragraph (9)—Information is "contained in a partnership agreement made in a record" only to the extent that the information is "integrated" into a record and, in that memorialized form, has been consented to as part of the partnership agreement.

This paragraph is not a statute of frauds provision. For example, failure to comply with paragraph (9)(A) or (B) does not render unenforceable an oral promise to make a contribution. Likewise, failure to comply with paragraph (9)(D) does not invalidate an oral term of the partnership specifying "events upon the happening of which the limited partnership is to be dissolved and its activities wound up." See also Section 801(1).

Obversely, the mere fact that a limited partnership maintains a record in purported compliance with paragraph (9)(A) or (B) does not prove that a person has actually promised to make a contribution. Likewise, the mere fact that a limited partnership maintains a record in purported compliance with paragraph (9)(D) does not prove that the partnership agreement actually includes the specified events as causes of dissolution.

Consistent with the partnership agreement's plenary power to structure and regulate the relations of the partners *inter se*, a partnership agreement can impose "made in a record" requirements which render unenforceable oral promises to make contributions or oral understandings as to "events upon the happening of which the limited partnership is to be dissolved." See Comment to Section 110.

Paragraph (9)(A) and (B)—Often the partnership agreement will state in record form the value of contributions made and promised to be made. If not, these provisions require that the value be stated in a record maintained as part of the limited partnership's required information. The Act does not authorize the limited partnership or the general partners to set the value of a contribution without the concurrence of the person who has made or promised the contribution, although the partnership agreement itself can grant that authority.

Paragraph (9)(C)—The information required by this provision is essential for determining what happens to the transferable interests of a person that is both a general partner and a limited partner and that dissociates in one of those capacities but not the other. See Sections 602(3) and 605(5).

§ 112. Business Transactions of Partner with Partnership

A partner may lend money to and transact other business with the limited partnership and has the same rights and obligations with respect to the loan or other transaction as a person that is not a partner.

Comment

Source—RULPA Section 107. See also RUPA Section 404(f) and ULLCA Section 409(f).

This section has no impact on a general partner's duty under Section 408(b)(2) (duty of loyalty includes refraining from acting as or for an adverse party) and means rather that this Act does not discriminate against a creditor of a limited partnership that happens also to be a partner. *See, e.g., BT-I v. Equitable Life Assurance Society of the United States*, 75 Cal.App.4th 1406, 1415, 89 Cal.Rptr.2d 811, 814 (Cal.App. 4 Dist.1999). and *SEC v. DuPont, Homsey & Co.*, 204 F. Supp. 944, 946 (D. Mass. 1962), vacated and remanded on other grounds, 334 F.2d 704 (1st Cir. 1964). This section does not, however, override other law, such as fraudulent transfer or conveyance acts.

§ 113. Dual Capacity

A person may be both a general partner and a limited partner. A person that is both a general and limited partner has the rights, powers, duties, and obligations provided by this [Act] and the partnership agreement in each of those capacities. When the person acts as a general partner, the person is subject to the obligations, duties and restrictions under this [Act] and the partnership agreement for general partners. When the person acts as a limited partner, the person is subject to the obligations, duties and restrictions under this [Act] and the partnership agreement for limited partners.

Comment

Source—RULPA Section 404, redrafted for reasons of style.

§ 114. Office and Agent for Service of Process

(a) A limited partnership shall designate and continuously maintain in this State:

(1) an office, which need not be a place of its activity in this State; and

(2) an agent for service of process.

(b) A foreign limited partnership shall designate and continuously maintain in this State an agent for service of process.

(c) An agent for service of process of a limited partnership or foreign limited partnership must be an individual who is a resident of this State or other person authorized to do business in this State.

Comment

Subsection (a)—The initial designation occurs in the original certificate of limited partnership. Section 201(a)(2). A limited partnership may change the designation in any of three ways: a statement of change, Section 115, an amendment to the certificate, Section 202, and the annual report, Section 210(e). If a limited partnership fails to maintain an agent for service of process, substituted service may be made on the Secretary of State. Section 117(b). Although a limited partnership's failure to maintain an agent for service of process is not immediate grounds for administrative dissolution, Section 809(a), the failure will prevent the limited partnership from delivering to the Secretary of State for filing an annual report that complies with Section 210(a)(2). Failure to deliver a proper annual report is grounds for administrative dissolution. Section 809(a)(2).

Subsection (b)—The initial designation occurs in the application for a certificate of authority. See Section 902(a)(4). A foreign limited partnership may change the designation in either of two ways: a statement of change, Section 115, and the annual report, Section 210(e). If a foreign limited partnership fails to maintain an agent for service of process, substituted service may be made on the Secretary of State. Section 117(b). A foreign limited partnership's failure to maintain an agent for service of process is grounds for administrative revocation of the certificate of authority. Section 906(a)(3).

A foreign limited partnership need not maintain an office in this State.

§ 115. Change of Designated Office or Agent for Service of Process

(a) In order to change its designated office, agent for service of process, or the address of its agent for service of process, a limited partnership or a foreign limited partnership may deliver to the [Secretary of State] for filing a statement of change containing:

(1) the name of the limited partnership or foreign limited partnership;

(2) the street and mailing address of its current designated office;

(3) if the current designated office is to be changed, the street and mailing address of the new designated office;

(4) the name and street and mailing address of its current agent for service of process; and

(5) if the current agent for service of process or an address of the agent is to be changed, the new information.

(b) Subject to Section 206(c), a statement of change is effective when filed by the [Secretary of State].

Comment

Source—ULLCA Section 109.

Subsection (a)—The Act uses "may" rather than "shall" here because other avenues exist. A limited partnership may also change the information by an amendment to its certificate of limited partnership, Section 202, or through its annual report. Section 210(e). A foreign limited partnership may use its annual report. Section 210(e). However, neither a limited partnership nor a foreign limited partnership may wait for the annual report if the information described in the public record becomes inaccurate. See Sections 208 (imposing liability for false information in record) and 117(b) (providing for substitute service).

§ 116. Resignation of Agent for Service of Process

(a) In order to resign as an agent for service of process of a limited partnership or foreign limited partnership, the agent must deliver to the [Secretary of State] for filing a statement of resignation containing the name of the limited partnership or foreign limited partnership.

(b) After receiving a statement of resignation, the [Secretary of State] shall file it and mail a copy to the designated office of the limited partnership or foreign limited partnership and another copy to the principal office if the address of the office appears in the records of the [Secretary of State] and is different from the address of the designated office.

(c) An agency for service of process is terminated on the 31st day after the [Secretary of State] files the statement of resignation.

Comment

Source—ULLCA Section 110.

This section provides the only way an agent can resign without cooperation from the limited partnership or foreign limited partnership and the only way the agent, rather than the limited partnership or foreign limited partnership, can effect a change in the public record. See Sections 115(a) (Statement of Change), 202 (Amendment or Restatement of Certificate), and 210(e) (Annual Report), all of which involve the limited partnership or foreign limited partnership designating a replacement agent for service of process.

Subsection (c)—In contrast to most records authorized or required to be delivered to the filing officer for filing under this Act, a statement of resignation may not provide for a delayed effective date. This subsection mandates the effective date, and an effective date included in a statement of resignation is disregarded. See also Section 206(c).

§ 117. Service of Process

(a) An agent for service of process appointed by a limited partnership or foreign limited partnership is an agent of the limited partnership or foreign limited partnership for service of any process, notice, or demand required or permitted by law to be served upon the limited partnership or foreign limited partnership.

(b) If a limited partnership or foreign limited partnership does not appoint or maintain an agent for service of process in this State or the agent for service of process cannot with reasonable diligence be found at the agent's address, the [Secretary of State] is an agent of the limited partnership or foreign limited partnership upon whom process, notice, or demand may be served.

(c) Service of any process, notice, or demand on the [Secretary of State] may be made by delivering to and leaving with the [Secretary of State] duplicate copies of the process, notice, or demand. If a process, notice, or demand is served on the [Secretary of State], the [Secretary of State] shall forward one of the copies by registered or certified mail, return receipt requested, to the limited partnership or foreign limited partnership at its designated office.

(d) Service is effected under subsection (c) at the earliest of:

(1) the date the limited partnership or foreign limited partnership receives the process, notice, or demand;

(2) the date shown on the return receipt, if signed on behalf of the limited partnership or foreign limited partnership; or

(3) five days after the process, notice, or demand is deposited in the mail, if mailed postpaid and correctly addressed.

(e) The [Secretary of State] shall keep a record of each process, notice, and demand served pursuant to this section and record the time of, and the action taken regarding, the service.

(f) This section does not affect the right to serve process, notice, or demand in any other manner provided by law.

Comment

Source—ULLCA Section 111.

Requiring a foreign limited partnership to name an agent for service of process is a change from RULPA. See RULPA Section 902(3).

§ 118. Consent and Proxies of Partners

Action requiring the consent of partners under this [Act] may be taken without a meeting, and a partner may appoint a proxy to consent or otherwise act for the partner by signing an appointment record, either personally or by the partner's attorney in fact.

Comment

Source—ULLCA Section 404(d) and (e).

This Act imposes no meeting requirement and does not distinguish among oral, record, express and tacit consent. The partnership agreement may establish such requirements and make such distinctions.

[ARTICLE] 2. FORMATION; CERTIFICATE OF LIMITED PARTNERSHIP AND OTHER FILINGS

§ 201. Formation of Limited Partnership; Certificate of Limited Partnership

(a) In order for a limited partnership to be formed, a certificate of limited partnership must be delivered to the [Secretary of State] for filing. The certificate must state:

(1) the name of the limited partnership, which must comply with Section 108;

(2) the street and mailing address of the initial designated office and the name and street and mailing address of the initial agent for service of process;

(3) the name and the street and mailing address of each general partner;

(4) whether the limited partnership is a limited liability limited partnership; and

(5) any additional information required by [Article] 11.

(b) A certificate of limited partnership may also contain any other matters but may not vary or otherwise affect the provisions specified in Section 110(b) in a manner inconsistent with that section.

(c) If there has been substantial compliance with subsection (a), subject to Section 206(c) a limited partnership is formed when the [Secretary of State] files the certificate of limited partnership.

(d) Subject to subsection (b), if any provision of a partnership agreement is inconsistent with the filed certificate of limited partnership or with a filed statement of dissociation, termination, or change or filed articles of conversion or merger:

(1) the partnership agreement prevails as to partners and transferees; and

(2) the filed certificate of limited partnership, statement of dissociation, termination, or change or articles of conversion or

merger prevail as to persons, other than partners and transferees, that reasonably rely on the filed record to their detriment.

Comment

Source—RULPA Section 201.

A limited partnership is a creature of statute, and this section governs how a limited partnership comes into existence. A limited partnership is formed only if (i) a certificate of limited partnership is prepared and delivered to the specified public official for filing, (ii) the public official files the certificate, and (iii) the certificate, delivery and filing are in "substantial compliance" with the requirements of subsection (a). Section 206(c) governs when a limited partnership comes into existence.

Despite its foundational importance, a certificate of limited partnership is far less powerful than a corporation's articles of incorporation. Among partners and transferees, for example, the partnership agreement is paramount. See Section 201(d).

Subsection (a)(1)—Section 108 contains name requirements. To be acceptable for filing, a certificate of limited partnership must state a name for the limited partnership which complies with Section 108.

Subsection (a)(3)—This provision should be read in conjunction with Section 103(c) and Section 401. See the Comment to those sections.

Subsection (a)(4)—This Act permits a limited partnership to be a limited liability limited partnership ("LLLP"), and this provision requires the certificate of limited partnership to state whether the limited partnership is an LLLP. The requirement is intended to force the organizers of a limited partnership to decide whether the limited partnership is to be an LLLP.

Subject to Sections 406(b)(2) and 1110, a limited partnership may amend its certificate of limited partnership to add or delete a statement that the limited partnership is a limited liability limited partnership. An amendment deleting such a statement must be accompanied by an amendment stating that the limited partnership is **not** a limited liability limited partnership. Section 201(a)(4) does not permit a certificate of limited partnership to be silent on this point, except for pre-existing partnerships that become subject to this Act under Section 1206. See Section 1206(c)(2).

Subsection (d)—Source: ULLCA Section 203(c).

A limited partnership is a creature of contract as well as a creature of statute. It will be possible, albeit improper, for the partnership agreement to be inconsistent with the certificate of limited partnership or other specified public filings relating to the limited partnership. For those circumstances, this subsection provides the rule for determining which source of information prevails.

For partners and transferees, the partnership agreement is paramount. For third parties seeking to invoke the public record, actual knowledge of that record is necessary and notice under Section 103(c) or (d) is irrelevant. A third party wishing to enforce the public record over the partnership agreement must show reasonable reliance on the public record, and reliance presupposes knowledge.

This subsection does not expressly cover a situation in which (i) one of the specified filed records contains information in addition to, but not inconsistent with, the partnership agreement, and (ii) a person, other than a partner or transferee, detrimentally relies on the additional information. However, the policy reflected in this subsection seems equally applicable to that situation.

Responsibility for maintaining a limited partnership's public record rests with the general partner or partners. Section 202(c). A general partner's failure to meet that responsibility can expose the general partner to liability to third parties under Section 208(a)(2) and might constitute a breach of the general partner's duties under Section 408. In addition, an aggrieved person may seek a remedy under Section 205 (Signing and Filing Pursuant to Judicial Order).

§ 202. Amendment or Restatement of Certificate

(a) In order to amend its certificate of limited partnership, a limited partnership must deliver to the [Secretary of State] for filing an amendment or, pursuant to [Article] 11, articles of merger stating:

(1) the name of the limited partnership;

(2) the date of filing of its initial certificate; and

(3) the changes the amendment makes to the certificate as most recently amended or restated.

(b) A limited partnership shall promptly deliver to the [Secretary of State] for filing an amendment to a certificate of limited partnership to reflect:

(1) the admission of a new general partner;

(2) the dissociation of a person as a general partner; or

(3) the appointment of a person to wind up the limited partnership's activities under Section 803(c) or (d).

(c) A general partner that knows that any information in a filed certificate of limited partnership was false when the certificate was filed or has become false due to changed circumstances shall promptly:

(1) cause the certificate to be amended; or

(2) if appropriate, deliver to the [Secretary of State] for filing a statement of change pursuant to Section 115 or a statement of correction pursuant to Section 207.

(d) A certificate of limited partnership may be amended at any time for any other proper purpose as determined by the limited partnership.

(e) A restated certificate of limited partnership may be delivered to the [Secretary of State] for filing in the same manner as an amendment.

(f) Subject to Section 206(c), an amendment or restated certificate is effective when filed by the [Secretary of State].

Comment

Source—RULPA Section 202.

Subsection (b)—This subsection lists changes in circumstances which require an amendment to the certificate. Neither a statement of change, Section 115, nor the annual report, Section 210(e), suffice to report the addition or deletion of a general partner or the appointment of a person to wind up a limited partnership that has no general partner.

This subsection states an obligation of the limited partnership. However, so long as the limited partnership has at least one general partner, the general partner or partners are responsible for managing the limited partnership's activities. Section 406(a). That management responsibility includes maintaining accuracy in the limited partnership's public record. Moreover, subsection (c) imposes direct responsibility on any general partner that knows that the filed certificate of limited partnership contains false information.

Acquiring or relinquishing LLLP status also requires an amendment to the certificate. See Sections 201(a)(4), 406(b)(2), and 1110(b)(2).

Subsection (c)—This provision imposes an obligation directly on the general partners rather than on the limited partnership. A general partner's failure to meet that responsibility can expose the general partner to liability to third parties under Section 208(a)(2) and might constitute a breach of the general partner's duties under Section 408. In addition, an aggrieved person may seek a remedy under Section 205 (Signing and Filing Pursuant to Judicial Order).

Subsection (d)—A limited partnership that desires to change its name will have to amend its certificate of limited partnership. The new name will have to comply with Section 108. See Section 201(a)(1).

§ 203. Statement of Termination

A dissolved limited partnership that has completed winding up may deliver to the [Secretary of State] for filing a statement of termination that states:

(1) the name of the limited partnership;

(2) the date of filing of its initial certificate of limited partnership; and

(3) any other information as determined by the general partners filing the statement or by a person appointed pursuant to Section 803(c) or (d).

Comment

Under Section 103(d)(3), a filed statement of termination provides constructive notice, 90 days after the statement's effective date, that the limited partnership is terminated. That notice effectively terminates any apparent authority to bind the limited partnership.

However, this section is permissive. Therefore, it is not possible to use Section 205 (Signing and Filing Pursuant to Judicial Order) to cause a statement of termination to be filed.

This section differs from predecessor law, RULPA Section 203, which required the filing of a certificate of cancellation when a limited partnership dissolved.

§ 204. Signing of Records

(a) Each record delivered to the [Secretary of State] for filing pursuant to this [Act] must be signed in the following manner:

(1) An initial certificate of limited partnership must be signed by all general partners listed in the certificate.

(2) An amendment adding or deleting a statement that the limited partnership is a limited liability limited partnership must be signed by all general partners listed in the certificate.

(3) An amendment designating as general partner a person admitted under Section 801(3)(B) following the dissociation of a limited partnership's last general partner must be signed by that person.

(4) An amendment required by Section 803(c) following the appointment of a person to wind up the dissolved limited partnership's activities must be signed by that person.

(5) Any other amendment must be signed by:

(A) at least one general partner listed in the certificate;

(B) each other person designated in the amendment as a new general partner; and

(C) each person that the amendment indicates has dissociated as a general partner, unless:

(i) the person is deceased or a guardian or general conservator has been appointed for the person and the amendment so states; or

(ii) the person has previously delivered to the [Secretary of State] for filing a statement of dissociation.

(6) A restated certificate of limited partnership must be signed by at least one general partner listed in the certificate, and, to the extent the restated certificate effects a change under any other paragraph of this subsection, the certificate must be signed in a manner that satisfies that paragraph.

(7) A statement of termination must be signed by all general partners listed in the certificate or, if the certificate of a dissolved limited partnership lists no general partners, by the person appointed pursuant to Section 803(c) or (d) to wind up the dissolved limited partnership's activities.

(8) Articles of conversion must be signed by each general partner listed in the certificate of limited partnership.

(9) Articles of merger must be signed as provided in Section 1108(a).

(10) Any other record delivered on behalf of a limited partnership to the [Secretary of State] for filing must be signed by at least one general partner listed in the certificate.

(11) A statement by a person pursuant to Section 605(a)(4) stating that the person has dissociated as a general partner must be signed by that person.

(12) A statement of withdrawal by a person pursuant to Section 306 must be signed by that person.

(13) A record delivered on behalf of a foreign limited partnership to the [Secretary of State] for filing must be signed by at least one general partner of the foreign limited partnership.

(14) Any other record delivered on behalf of any person to the [Secretary of State] for filing must be signed by that person.

(b) Any person may sign by an attorney in fact any record to be filed pursuant to this [Act].

Comment

Source—ULLCA Section 205.

This section pertains only to signing requirements and implies nothing about approval requirements. For example, Section 204(a)(2) requires that an amendment changing a limited partnership's LLLP status be signed by all **general** partners listed in the certificate, but under Section 406(b)(2) **all** partners must consent to that change unless otherwise provided in the partnership agreement.

A person who signs a record without ascertaining that the record has been properly authorized risks liability under Section 208.

Subsection (a)—The recurring reference to general partners "listed in the certificate" recognizes that a person might be admitted as a general partner under Section 401 without immediately being listed in the certificate of limited partnership. Such persons may have rights, powers and obligations despite their unlisted status, but they cannot act as general partners for the purpose of affecting the limited partnership's public record. See the Comment to Section 103(c) and the Comment to Section 401.

§ 205. Signing and Filing Pursuant to Judicial Order

(a) If a person required by this [Act] to sign a record or deliver a record to the [Secretary of State] for filing does not do so, any other person that is aggrieved may petition the [appropriate court] to order:

(1) the person to sign the record;

(2) deliver the record to the [Secretary of State] for filing; or

(3) the [Secretary of State] to file the record unsigned.

(b) If the person aggrieved under subsection (a) is not the limited partnership or foreign limited partnership to which the record pertains, the aggrieved person shall make the limited partnership or foreign limited partnership a party to the action. A person aggrieved under subsection (a) may seek the remedies provided in subsection (a) in the same action in combination or in the alternative.

(c) A record filed unsigned pursuant to this section is effective without being signed.

Comment

Source—RULPA Section 205.

§ 206. Delivery to and Filing of Records by [Secretary of State]; Effective Time and Date

(a) A record authorized or required to be delivered to the [Secretary of State] for filing under this [Act] must be captioned to describe the record's purpose, be in a medium permitted by the [Secretary of State], and be delivered to the [Secretary of State]. Unless the [Secretary of State] determines that a record does not comply with the filing requirements of this [Act], and if all filing fees have been paid, the [Secretary of State] shall file the record and:

(1) for a statement of dissociation, send:

(A) a copy of the filed statement and a receipt for the fees to the person which the statement indicates has dissociated as a general partner; and

(B) a copy of the filed statement and receipt to the limited partnership;

(2) for a statement of withdrawal, send:

(A) a copy of the filed statement and a receipt for the fees to the person on whose behalf the record was filed; and

(B) if the statement refers to an existing limited partnership, a copy of the filed statement and receipt to the limited partnership; and

(3) for all other records, send a copy of the filed record and a receipt for the fees to the person on whose behalf the record was filed.

(b) Upon request and payment of a fee, the [Secretary of State] shall send to the requester a certified copy of the requested record.

(c) Except as otherwise provided in Sections 116 and 207, a record delivered to the [Secretary of State] for filing under this [Act] may specify an effective time and a delayed effective date. Except as otherwise provided in this [Act], a record filed by the [Secretary of State] is effective:

(1) if the record does not specify an effective time and does not specify a delayed effective date, on the date and at the time the record is filed as evidenced by the [Secretary of State's] endorsement of the date and time on the record;

(2) if the record specifies an effective time but not a delayed effective date, on the date the record is filed at the time specified in the record;

(3) if the record specifies a delayed effective date but not an effective time, at 12:01 a.m. on the earlier of:

(A) the specified date; or

(B) the 90th day after the record is filed; or

(4) if the record specifies an effective time and a delayed effective date, at the specified time on the earlier of:

(A) the specified date; or

(B) the 90th day after the record is filed.

Comment

Source—ULLCA Section 206.

In order for a record prepared by a private person to become part of the public record under this Act, (i) someone must put a properly prepared version of the record into the possession of the public official specified in the Act as the appropriate filing officer, and (ii) that filing officer must determine that the record complies with the filing requirements of this Act and then officially make the record part of the public record. This Act refers to the first step as *delivery to the [Secretary of State] for filing* and refers to the second step as *filing*. Thus, under this Act "filing" is an official act.

Subsection (a)—The caption need only indicate the title of the record; *e.g.*, Certificate of Limited Partnership, Statement of Change for Limited Partnership.

Filing officers typically note on a filed record the fact, date and time of filing. The copies provided by the filing officer under this subsection should contain that notation.

This Act does not provide a remedy if the filing officer wrongfully fails or refuses to file a record.

Subsection (c)—This subsection allows most records to have a delayed effective date, up to 90 days after the date the record is filed by the filing officer. A record specifying a longer delay will **not** be rejected. Instead, under paragraph (c)(3) and (4), the delayed effective date is adjusted by operation of law to the "90th day after the record is filed." The Act does not require the filing officer to notify anyone of the adjustment.

§ 207. Correcting Filed Record

(a) A limited partnership or foreign limited partnership may deliver to the [Secretary of State] for filing a statement of correction to correct a record previously delivered by the limited partnership or foreign limited partnership to the [Secretary of State] and filed by the [Secretary of State], if at the time of filing the record contained false or erroneous information or was defectively signed.

(b) A statement of correction may not state a delayed effective date and must:

(1) describe the record to be corrected, including its filing date, or attach a copy of the record as filed;

(2) specify the incorrect information and the reason it is incorrect or the manner in which the signing was defective; and

(3) correct the incorrect information or defective signature.

(c) When filed by the [Secretary of State], a statement of correction is effective retroactively as of the effective date of the record the statement corrects, but the statement is effective when filed:

(1) for the purposes of Section 103(c) and (d); and

(2) as to persons relying on the uncorrected record and adversely affected by the correction.

Comment

Source—ULLCA Section 207.

A statement of correction is appropriate only to correct inaccuracies that existed or signatures that were defective "at the time of filing." A statement of correction may not be used to correct a record that was accurate when filed but has become inaccurate due to subsequent events.

Subsection (c)—Generally, a statement of correction "relates back." However, there is no retroactive effect: (1) for the purposes of constructive notice under Section 103(c) and (d); and (2) against persons who have relied on the uncorrected record and would be adversely affected if the correction related back.

§ 208. Liability for False Information in Filed Record

(a) If a record delivered to the [Secretary of State] for filing under this [Act] and filed by the [Secretary of State] contains false information, a person that suffers loss by reliance on the information may recover damages for the loss from:

(1) a person that signed the record, or caused another to sign it on the person's behalf, and knew the information to be false at the time the record was signed; and

(2) a general partner that has notice that the information was false when the record was filed or has become false because of changed circumstances, if the general partner has notice for a reasonably sufficient time before the information is relied upon to enable the general partner to effect an amendment under Section 202, file a petition pursuant to Section 205, or deliver to the [Secretary of State] for filing a statement of change pursuant to Section 115 or a statement of correction pursuant to Section 207.

(b) Signing a record authorized or required to be filed under this [Act] constitutes an affirmation under the penalties of perjury that the facts stated in the record are true.

Comment

This section pertains to both limited partnerships and foreign limited partnerships.

LLLP status is irrelevant to this section. The LLLP shield protects only to the extent that (i) the obligation involved is an obligation of the limited partnership or foreign limited partnership, and (ii) a partner is claimed to be liable for that obligation by reason of being a partner. This section does not address the obligations of a limited partnership or foreign limited partnership and instead imposes direct liability on signers and general partners.

Subsection (a)—This subsection's liability rules apply only to records (i) created by private persons ("delivered to the [Secretary of State] for filing"), (ii) which actually become part of the public record ("filed by the [Secretary of State]"). This subsection does not preempt other law, which might provide remedies for misleading information contained, for example, in a record that is delivered to the filing officer for filing but withdrawn before the filing officer takes the official action of filing the record.

Records filed under this Act are signed subject to the penalties for perjury. See subsection (b). This subsection therefore does not require a party who relies on a record to demonstrate that the reliance was reasonable. Contrast Section 201(d)(2), which provides that, if the partnership agreement is inconsistent with the public record, the public record prevails in favor of a person that is neither a partner nor a transferee and that reasonably relied on the record.

§ 209. Certificate of Existence or Authorization

(a) The [Secretary of State], upon request and payment of the requisite fee, shall furnish a certificate of existence for a limited partnership if the records filed in the [office of the Secretary of State] show that the [Secretary of State] has filed a certificate of limited partnership and has not filed a statement of termination. A certificate of existence must state:

(1) the limited partnership's name;

(2) that it was duly formed under the laws of this State and the date of formation;

(3) whether all fees, taxes, and penalties due to the [Secretary of State] under this [Act] or other law have been paid;

(4) whether the limited partnership's most recent annual report required by Section 210 has been filed by the [Secretary of State];

(5) whether the [Secretary of State] has administratively dissolved the limited partnership;

(6) whether the limited partnership's certificate of limited partnership has been amended to state that the limited partnership is dissolved;

(7) that a statement of termination has not been filed by the [Secretary of State]; and

(8) other facts of record in the [office of the Secretary of State] which may be requested by the applicant.

(b) The [Secretary of State], upon request and payment of the requisite fee, shall furnish a certificate of authorization for a foreign limited partnership if the records filed in the [office of the Secretary of State] show that the [Secretary of State] has filed a certificate of authority, has not revoked the certificate of authority, and has not filed a notice of cancellation. A certificate of authorization must state:

(1) the foreign limited partnership's name and any alternate name adopted under Section 905(a) for use in this State;

(2) that it is authorized to transact business in this State;

(3) whether all fees, taxes, and penalties due to the [Secretary of State] under this [Act] or other law have been paid;

(4) whether the foreign limited partnership's most recent annual report required by Section 210 has been filed by the [Secretary of State];

(5) that the [Secretary of State] has not revoked its certificate of authority and has not filed a notice of cancellation; and

(6) other facts of record in the [office of the Secretary of State] which may be requested by the applicant.

(c) Subject to any qualification stated in the certificate, a certificate of existence or authorization issued by the [Secretary of State] may be relied upon as conclusive evidence that the limited partnership or foreign limited partnership is in existence or is authorized to transact business in this State.

Comment

Source—ULLCA Section 208.

A certificate of existence can reveal only information present in the public record, and under this Act significant information bearing on the status of a limited partnership may be outside the public record. For example, while this Act provides for a limited partnership to have a perpetual duration, Section 104(c), the partnership agreement may set a definite term or designate particular events whose occurrence will cause dissolution. Section 801(1). Dissolution is also possible by consent, Section 801(2), and, absent a contrary provision in the partnership agreement, will at least be at issue whenever a general partner dissociates. Section 801(3). Nothing in this Act requires a limited partnership to deliver to the filing officer for filing a record indicating that the limited partnership has dissolved.

A certificate of authorization furnished under this section is different than a certificate of authority filed under Section 904.

§ 210. Annual Report for [Secretary of State]

(a) A limited partnership or a foreign limited partnership authorized to transact business in this State shall deliver to the [Secretary of State] for filing an annual report that states:

(1) the name of the limited partnership or foreign limited partnership;

(2) the street and mailing address of its designated office and the name and street and mailing address of its agent for service of process in this State;

(3) in the case of a limited partnership, the street and mailing address of its principal office; and

(4) in the case of a foreign limited partnership, the State or other jurisdiction under whose law the foreign limited partnership is formed and any alternate name adopted under Section 905(a).

(b) Information in an annual report must be current as of the date the annual report is delivered to the [Secretary of State] for filing.

(c) The first annual report must be delivered to the [Secretary of State] between [January 1 and April 1] of the year following the calendar year in which a limited partnership was formed or a foreign limited partnership was authorized to transact business. An annual report must be delivered to the [Secretary of State] between [January 1 and April 1] of each subsequent calendar year.

(d) If an annual report does not contain the information required in subsection (a), the [Secretary of State] shall promptly notify the reporting limited partnership or foreign limited partnership and return the report to it for correction. If the report is corrected to contain the information required in subsection (a) and delivered to the [Secretary of State] within 30 days after the effective date of the notice, it is timely delivered.

(e) If a filed annual report contains an address of a designated office or the name or address of an agent for service of process which differs from the information shown in the records of the [Secretary of State] immediately before the filing, the differing information in the annual report is considered a statement of change under Section 115.

Comment

Source—ULLCA Section 211.

Subsection (d)—This subsection's rule affects only Section 809(a)(2) (late filing of annual report grounds for administrative dissolution) and any late fees that the filing officer might have the right to impose. For the purposes of subsection (e), the annual report functions as a statement of change only when "filed" by the filing officer. Likewise, a person cannot rely on subsection (d) to escape liability arising under Section 208.

[ARTICLE] 3. LIMITED PARTNERS

§ 301. Becoming Limited Partner

A person becomes a limited partner:

(1) as provided in the partnership agreement;

(2) as the result of a conversion or merger under [Article] 11; or

(3) with the consent of all the partners.

Comment

Source—RULPA Section 301.

Although Section 801(4) contemplates the admission of a limited partner to avoid dissolution, that provision does not itself authorize the admission. Instead, this section controls. Contrast Section 801(3)(B), which itself authorizes the admission of a general partner in order to avoid dissolution.

§ 302. No Right or Power as Limited Partner to Bind Limited Partnership

A limited partner does not have the right or the power as a limited partner to act for or bind the limited partnership.

Comment

In this respect a limited partner is analogous to a shareholder in a corporation; status as owner provides neither the right to manage nor a reasonable appearance of that right.

The phrase "as a limited partner" is intended to recognize that: (i) this section does not disable a general partner that also owns a limited partner interest; (ii) the partnership agreement may as a matter of contract allocate managerial rights to one or more limited partners; and (iii) a separate agreement can empower and entitle a person that is a limited partner to act for the limited partnership in another capacity; *e.g.*, as an agent. See Comment to Section 305.

The fact that a limited partner *qua* limited partner has no power to bind the limited partnership means that, subject to Section 113 (Dual Capacity), information possessed by a limited partner is not attributed to the limited partnership. See Section 103(h).

This Act specifies various circumstances in which limited partners have consent rights, including:

- admission of a limited partner, Section 301(3)
- admission of a general partner, Section 401(4)
- amendment of the partnership agreement, Section 406(b)(1)
- the decision to amend the certificate of limited partnership so as to obtain or relinquish LLLP status, Section 406(b)(2)
- the disposition of all or substantially all of the limited partnership's property, outside the ordinary course, Section 406(b)(3)
- the compromise of a partner's obligation to make a contribution or return an improper distribution, Section 502(c)
- expulsion of a limited partner by consent of the other partners, Section 601(b)(4)

- expulsion of a general partner by consent of the other partners, Section 603(4)
- redemption of a transferable interest subject to charging order, using limited partnership property, Section 703(c)(3)
- causing dissolution by consent, Section 801(2)
- causing dissolution by consent following the dissociation of a general partner, when at least one general partner remains, Section 801(3)(A)
- avoiding dissolution and appointing a successor general partner, following the dissociation of the sole general partner, Section 801(3)(B)
- appointing a person to wind up the limited partnership when there is no general partner, Section 803(C)
- approving, amending or abandoning a plan of conversion, Section 1103(a) and (b)(2)
- approving, amending or abandoning a plan of merger, Section 1107(a) and (b)(2).

§ 303. No Liability as Limited Partner for Limited Partnership Obligations

An obligation of a limited partnership, whether arising in contract, tort, or otherwise, is not the obligation of a limited partner. A limited partner is not personally liable, directly or indirectly, by way of contribution or otherwise, for an obligation of the limited partnership solely by reason of being a limited partner, even if the limited partner participates in the management and control of the limited partnership.

Comment

This section provides a full, status-based liability shield for each limited partner, "even if the limited partner participates in the management and control of the limited partnership." The section thus eliminates the so-called "control rule" with respect to personal liability for entity obligations and brings limited partners into parity with LLC members, LLP partners and corporate shareholders.

The "control rule" first appeared in an uniform act in 1916, although the concept is much older. Section 7 of the original Uniform Limited Partnership Act provided that "A limited partner shall not become liable as a general partner [i.e., for the obligations of the limited partnership] unless ... he takes part in the control of the business." The 1976 Uniform Limited Partnership Act (ULPA–1976) "carrie[d] over the basic test from former Section 7," but recognized "the difficulty of determining when the 'control' line has been overstepped." Comment to ULPA–1976, Section 303. Accordingly, ULPA–1976 tried to buttress the limited partner's shield by (i) providing a safe harbor for a lengthy list of activities deemed not to constitute participating in control, ULPA–1976, Section 303(b), and (ii) limiting a limited partner's "control rule" liability "only to persons who transact business with the limited partnership with actual knowledge of [the limited partner's] participation in control." ULPA–1976, Section 303(a). However, these protections were complicated by a countervailing rule which made a limited partner generally liable for the limited partnership's obligations "if the limited partner's participation in the control of the business is ... substantially the same as the exercise of the powers of a general partner." ULPA–1976, Section 303(a).

The 1985 amendments to ULPA–1976 (i.e., RULPA) further buttressed the limited partner's shield, removing the "substantially the same" rule, expanding the list of safe harbor activities and limiting "control rule" liability "only to persons who transact business with the limited partnership reasonably believing, based upon the limited partner's conduct, that the limited partner is a general partner."

In a world with LLPs, LLCs and, most importantly, LLLPs, the control rule has become an anachronism. This Act therefore takes the next logical step in the evolution of the limited partner's liability shield and renders the control rule extinct.

The shield established by this section protects only against liability for the limited partnership's obligations and only to the extent that the limited partner is claimed to be liable on account of being a limited partner. Thus, a person that is both a general and limited partner will be liable as a general partner for the limited partnership's obligations. Moreover, this section does not prevent a limited partner from being liable as a result of the limited partner's own conduct and is therefore inapplicable when a third party asserts that a limited partner's own wrongful conduct has injured the third party. This section is likewise inapplicable to claims by the limited partnership or another partner that a limited partner has breached a duty under this Act or the partnership agreement.

This section does not eliminate a limited partner's liability for promised contributions, Section 502 or improper distributions. Section 509. That liability pertains to a person's status as a limited partner but is **not** liability for an obligation of the limited partnership.

The shield provided by this section applies whether or not a limited partnership is a limited liability limited partnership.

§ 304. Right of Limited Partner and Former Limited Partner to Information

(a) On 10 days' demand, made in a record received by the limited partnership, a limited partner may inspect and copy required information during regular business hours in the limited partnership's designated office. The limited partner need not have any particular purpose for seeking the information.

(b) During regular business hours and at a reasonable location specified by the limited partnership, a limited partner may obtain from the limited partnership and inspect and copy true and full information regarding the state of the activities and financial condition of the limited partnership and other information regarding the activities of the limited partnership as is just and reasonable if:

(1) the limited partner seeks the information for a purpose reasonably related to the partner's interest as a limited partner;

(2) the limited partner makes a demand in a record received by the limited partnership, describing with reasonable particularity the information sought and the purpose for seeking the information; and

(3) the information sought is directly connected to the limited partner's purpose.

(c) Within 10 days after receiving a demand pursuant to subsection (b), the limited partnership in a record shall inform the limited partner that made the demand:

(1) what information the limited partnership will provide in response to the demand;

(2) when and where the limited partnership will provide the information; and

(3) if the limited partnership declines to provide any demanded information, the limited partnership's reasons for declining.

(d) Subject to subsection (f), a person dissociated as a limited partner may inspect and copy required information during regular business hours in the limited partnership's designated office if:

(1) the information pertains to the period during which the person was a limited partner;

(2) the person seeks the information in good faith; and

(3) the person meets the requirements of subsection (b).

(e) The limited partnership shall respond to a demand made pursuant to subsection (d) in the same manner as provided in subsection (c).

(f) If a limited partner dies, Section 704 applies.

(g) The limited partnership may impose reasonable restrictions on the use of information obtained under this section. In a dispute concerning the reasonableness of a restriction under this subsection, the limited partnership has the burden of proving reasonableness.

(h) A limited partnership may charge a person that makes a demand under this section reasonable costs of copying, limited to the costs of labor and material.

(i) Whenever this [Act] or a partnership agreement provides for a limited partner to give or withhold consent to a matter, before the consent is given or withheld, the limited partnership shall, without demand, provide the limited partner with all information material to the limited partner's decision that the limited partnership knows.

(j) A limited partner or person dissociated as a limited partner may exercise the rights under this section through an attorney or other agent. Any restriction imposed under subsection (g) or by the partnership agreement applies both to the attorney or other agent and to the limited partner or person dissociated as a limited partner.

(k) The rights stated in this section do not extend to a person as transferee, but may be exercised by the legal representative of an individual under legal disability who is a limited partner or person dissociated as a limited partner.

Comment

This section balances two countervailing concerns relating to information: the need of limited partners and former limited partners for access versus the limited partnership's need to protect confidential business data and other intellectual property. The balance must be understood in the context of fiduciary duties. The general partners are obliged through their duties of care and loyalty to protect information whose confidentiality is important to the limited partnership or otherwise inappropriate for dissemination. See Section 408 (general standards of general partner conduct). A limited partner, in contrast, "does not have any fiduciary duty to the limited partnership or to any other partner solely by reason of being a limited partner." Section 305(a). (Both general partners and limited partners are subject to a duty of good faith and fair dealing. Section 305(b) and 408(d)).

Like predecessor law, this Act divides limited partner access rights into two categories—required information and other information. However, this Act builds on predecessor law by:

- expanding slightly the category of required information and stating explicitly that a limited partner may have access to that information without having to show cause
- specifying a procedure for limited partners to follow when demanding access to other information
- specifying how a limited partnership must respond to such a demand and setting a time limit for the response
- retaining predecessor law's "just and reasonable" standard for determining a limited partner's right to other information, while recognizing that, to be "just and reasonable," a limited partner's demand for other information must meet at minimum standards of relatedness and particularity

- expressly requiring the limited partnership to volunteer known, material information when seeking or obtaining consent from limited partners
- codifying (while limiting) the power of the partnership agreement to vary limited partner access rights
- permitting the limited partnership to establish other reasonable limits on access
- providing access rights for former limited partners.

The access rights stated in this section are personal to each limited partner and are enforceable through a direct action under Section 1001(a). These access rights are in addition to whatever discovery rights a party has in a civil suit.

Subsection (a)—The phrase "required information" is a defined term. See Sections 102(18) and 111. This subsection's broad right of access is subject not only to reasonable limitations in the partnership agreement, Section 110(b)(4), but also to the power of the limited partnership to impose reasonable limitations on use. Unless the partnership agreement provides otherwise, it will be the general partner or partners that have the authority to use that power. See Section 406(a).

Subsection (b)—The language describing the information to be provided comes essentially verbatim from RULPA Section 305(a)(2)(i) and (iii). The procedural requirements derive from RMBCA Section 16.02(c). This subsection does not impose a requirement of good faith, because Section 305(b) contains a generally applicable obligation of good faith and fair dealing for limited partners.

Subsection (d)—The notion that former owners should have information rights comes from RUPA Section 403(b) and ULLCA Section 408(a). The access is limited to the required information and is subject to certain conditions.

> **Example:** A person dissociated as a limited partner seeks data which the limited partnership has compiled, which relates to the period when the person was a limited partner, but which is beyond the scope of the information required by Section 111. No matter how reasonable the person's purpose and how well drafted the person's demand, the limited partnership is not obliged to provide the data.
>
> **Example:** A person dissociated as a limited partner seeks access to required information pertaining to the period during which the person was a limited partner. The person makes a bald demand, merely stating a desire to review the required information at the limited partnership's designated office. In particular, the demand does not describe "with reasonable particularity the information sought and the purpose for seeking the information." See subsection (b)(2). The limited partnership is not obliged to allow access. The person must first comply with subsection (d), which incorporates by reference the requirements of subsection (b).

Subsection (f) and Section 704 provide greater access rights for the estate of a deceased limited partner.

Subsection (d)(2)—A duty of good faith is needed here, because a person claiming access under this subsection is no longer a limited partner and is no longer subject to Section 305(b). See Section 602(a)(2) (dissociation as a limited partner terminates duty of good faith as to subsequent events).

Subsection (g)—This subsection permits the limited partnership–as distinguished from the partnership agreement–to impose use limitations. Contrast Section 110(b)(4). Under Section 406(a), it will be the general partner or partners that decide whether the limited partnership will impose use restrictions.

The limited partnership bears the burden of proving the reasonableness of any restriction imposed under this subsection. In determining whether a restriction is reasonable, a court might consider: (i) the danger or other problem the restriction seeks to avoid; (ii) the purpose for which the information is sought; and (iii) whether, in light of both the problem and the purpose, the restriction is reasonably tailored. Restricting use of the names and addresses of limited partners is not per se unreasonable.

The following table compares the limitations available through the partnership agreement with those available under this subsection.

	partnership agreement	**Section 304(g)**
how restrictions adopted	by the consent of partners when they adopt or amend the partnership agreement, unless the partnership agreement provides another method of amendment	by the general partners, acting under Section 406(a)
what restrictions may be imposed	"reasonable restrictions on the availability and use of information obtained," Section 110(b)(4)	"reasonable restrictions on the use of information obtained"
burden of proof	the person challenging the restriction must prove that the restriction will "unreasonably restrict the right of information," Section 110(b)(4)	"the limited partnership has the burden of proving reasonableness"

Subsection (h)—Source: RUPA Section 403(b) and ULLCA Section 408(a).

Subsection (i)—Source: ULLCA Section 408(b).

The duty stated in this subsection is at the core of the duties owed the limited partners by a limited partnership and its general partners.

This subsection imposes an affirmative duty to volunteer information, but that obligation is limited to information which is both material and known by the limited partnership. The duty applies to known, material information, even if the limited partnership does not know that the information is material.

A limited partnership will "know" what its general partners know. Section 103(h). A limited partnership may also know information known by the "individual conducting the transaction for the [limited partnership]." Section 103(g).

A limited partner's right to information under this subsection is enforceable through the full panoply of "legal or equitable relief" provided by Section 1001(a), including in appropriate circumstances the withdrawal or invalidation of improperly obtained consent and the invalidation or recision of action taken pursuant to that consent.

Subsection (k)—Section 304 provides no information rights to a transferee as transferee. Transferee status brings only the very limited information rights stated in Section 702(c).

It is nonetheless possible for a person that happens to be a transferee to have rights under this section. For example, under Section 602(a)(3) a person dissociated as a limited partner becomes a "mere transferee" of its own transferable interest. While that status provides the person no rights under this section, the status of person dissociated as a limited partner triggers rights under subsection (d).

§ 305. Limited Duties of Limited Partners

(a) A limited partner does not have any fiduciary duty to the limited partnership or to any other partner solely by reason of being a limited partner.

(b) A limited partner shall discharge the duties to the partnership and the other partners under this [Act] or under the partnership agreement and exercise any rights consistently with the obligation of good faith and fair dealing.

(c) A limited partner does not violate a duty or obligation under this [Act] or under the partnership agreement merely because the limited partner's conduct furthers the limited partner's own interest.

Comment

Subsection (a)—Fiduciary duty typically attaches to a person whose status or role creates significant power for that person over the interests of another person. Under this Act, limited partners have very limited power of any sort in the regular activities of the limited partnership and no power whatsoever justifying the imposition of fiduciary duties either to the limited partnership or fellow partners. It is possible for a partnership agreement to allocate significant managerial authority and power to a limited partner, but in that case the power exists not as a matter of status or role but rather as a matter of contract. The proper limit on such contract-based power is the obligation of good faith and fair dealing, not fiduciary duty, unless the partnership agreement itself expressly imposes a fiduciary duty or creates a role for a limited partner which, as a matter of other law, gives rise to a fiduciary duty. For example, if the partnership agreement makes a limited partner an agent for the limited partnership as to particular matters, the law of agency will impose fiduciary duties on the limited partner with respect to the limited partner's role as agent.

Subsection (b)—Source: RUPA Section 404(d). The same language appears in Section 408(d), pertaining to general partners.

The obligation of good faith and fair dealing is *not* a fiduciary duty, does not command altruism or self-abnegation, and does not prevent a partner from acting in the partner's own self-interest. Courts should not use the obligation to change *ex post facto* the parties' or this Act's allocation of risk and power. To the contrary, in light of the nature of a limited partnership, the obligation should be used only to protect agreed-upon arrangements from conduct that is manifestly beyond what a reasonable person could have contemplated when the arrangements were made.

The partnership agreement or this Act may grant discretion to a partner, and that partner may properly exercise that discretion even though another partner suffers as a consequence. Conduct does not violate the obligation of good faith and fair dealing merely because that conduct substantially prejudices a party. Indeed, parties allocate risk precisely because prejudice may occur. The exercise of discretion constitutes a breach of the obligation of good faith and fair dealing only when the party claiming breach shows that the conduct has no honestly-held purpose that legitimately comports with the parties' agreed-upon arrangements. Once such a purpose appears, courts should not second guess a party's choice of method in serving that purpose, unless the party invoking the obligation of good faith and fair dealing shows that the choice of method itself lacks any honestly-held purpose that legitimately comports with the parties' agreed-upon arrangements.

In sum, the purpose of the obligation of good faith and fair dealing is to protect the arrangement the partners have chosen for themselves, not to restructure that arrangement under the guise of safeguarding it.

§ 306. Person Erroneously Believing Self to be Limited Partner

(a) Except as otherwise provided in subsection (b), a person that makes an investment in a business enterprise and erroneously but in good faith believes that the person has become a limited partner in the enterprise is not liable for the enterprise's obligations by reason of making the investment, receiving distributions from the enterprise, or exercising any rights of or appropriate to a limited partner, if, on ascertaining the mistake, the person:

(1) causes an appropriate certificate of limited partnership, amendment, or statement of correction to be signed and delivered to the [Secretary of State] for filing; or

(2) withdraws from future participation as an owner in the enterprise by signing and delivering to the [Secretary of State] for filing a statement of withdrawal under this section.

(b) A person that makes an investment described in subsection (a) is liable to the same extent as a general partner to any third party that enters into a transaction with the enterprise, believing in good faith that the person is a general partner, before the [Secretary of State] files a statement of withdrawal, certificate of limited partnership, amendment, or statement of correction to show that the person is not a general partner.

(c) If a person makes a diligent effort in good faith to comply with subsection (a)(1) and is unable to cause the appropriate certificate of limited partnership, amendment, or statement of correction to be signed and delivered to the [Secretary of State] for filing, the person has the right to withdraw from the enterprise pursuant to subsection (a)(2) even if the withdrawal would otherwise breach an agreement with others that are or have agreed to become co-owners of the enterprise.

Comment

Source—RULPA Section 304, substantially redrafted for reasons of style.

Subsection (a)(2)—The requirement that a person "withdraw[] from future participation as an owner in the enterprise" means, in part, that the person refrain from taking any further profit from the enterprise. The requirement does not mean, however, that the person is required to return previously obtained profits or forfeit any investment.

[ARTICLE] 4. GENERAL PARTNERS

§ 401. Becoming General Partner

A person becomes a general partner:

(1) as provided in the partnership agreement;

(2) under Section 801(3)(B) following the dissociation of a limited partnership's last general partner;

(3) as the result of a conversion or merger under [Article] 11; or

(4) with the consent of all the partners.

Comment

This section does not make a person's status as a general partner dependent on the person being so designated in the certificate of limited partnership. If a person does become a general partner under this section without being so designated:

- the limited partnership is obligated to promptly and appropriately amend the certificate of limited partnership, Section 202(b)(1);
- each general partner that knows of the anomaly is personally obligated to cause the certificate to be promptly and appropriately amended, Section 202(c)(1), and is subject to liability for failing to do so, Section 208(a)(2);
- the "non-designated" general partner has:
  - — all the rights and duties of a general partner to the limited partnership and the other partners, and
  - — the powers of a general partner to bind the limited partnership under Sections 402 and 403, but
  - — no power to sign records which are to be filed on behalf of the limited partnership under this Act

Example: By consent of the partners of XYZ Limited Partnership, G is admitted as a general partner. However, XYZ's certificate of limited partnership is not amended accordingly. Later, G—acting without actual authority—purports to bind XYZ to a transaction with Third Party. Third Party does not review the filed certificate of limited partnership before entering into the transaction. XYZ might be bound under Section 402.

Section 402 attributes to a limited partnership "[a]n act of a general partner . . . for apparently carrying on in the ordinary course the limited partnership's activities or activities of the kind carried on by the limited partnership." The limited partnership's liability under Section 402 does not depend on the "act of a general partner" being the act of a general partner designated in the certificate of limited partnership. Moreover, the notice provided by Section 103(c) does not undercut G's appearance of authority. Section 402 refers only to notice under Section 103(d) and, in any event, according to the second sentence of Section 103(c), the fact that a person is **not** listed as in the certificate as a general partner is **not** notice that the person is **not** a general partner. See Comment to Section 103(c).

Example: Same facts, except that Third Party does review the certificate of limited partnership before entering into the transaction. The result might still be the same.

The omission of a person's name from the certificate's list of general partners is **not** notice that the person is **not** a general partner. Therefore, Third Party's review of the certificate does not mean that Third Party knew, had received a notification or had notice that G lacked authority. At most, XYZ could argue that, because Third Party knew that G was not listed in the certificate, a transaction entered into by G could not appear to Third Party to be for apparently carrying on the limited partnership's activities in the ordinary course.

§ 402. General Partner Agent of Limited Partnership

(a) Each general partner is an agent of the limited partnership for the purposes of its activities. An act of a general partner, including the signing of a record in the partnership's name, for apparently carrying on in the ordinary course the limited partnership's activities or activities of the kind carried on by the limited partnership binds the limited partnership, unless the general partner did not have authority to act for the limited partnership in the particular matter and the person with which the general partner was dealing knew, had received a notification, or had notice under Section 103(d) that the general partner lacked authority.

(b) An act of a general partner which is not apparently for carrying on in the ordinary course the limited partnership's activities or activities of the kind carried on by the limited partnership binds the limited partnership only if the act was actually authorized by all the other partners.

Comment

Source—RUPA Section 301. For the meaning of "authority" in subsection (a) and "authorized" in subsection (b), see RUPA Section 301, Comment 3 (stating that "Subsection (2) [of RUPA Section 301] makes it clear that the partnership is bound by a partner's *actual* authority, even if the partner has no apparent authority"; emphasis added).

The fact that a person is not listed in the certificate of limited partnership as a general partner is **not** notice that the person is **not** a partner and is **not** notice that the person lacks authority to act for the limited partnership. See Comment to Section 103(c) and Comment to Section 401.

Section 103(f) defines receipt of notification. Section 103(d) lists various public filings, each of which provides notice 90 days after its effective date.

> **Example:** For the past ten years, X has been a general partner of XYZ Limited Partnership and has regularly conducted the limited partnership's business with Third Party. However, 100 days ago the limited partnership expelled X as a general partner and the next day delivered for filing an amendment to XYZ's certificate of limited partnership which stated that X was no longer a general partner. On that same day, the filing officer filed the amendment.

> Today X approaches Third Party, purports [to still be] a general partner of XYZ and purports to enter into a transaction with Third Party on XYZ's behalf. Third Party is unaware that X has been expelled and has no reason to doubt . . . X's bona fides. Nonetheless, XYZ is not liable on the transaction. Under Section 103(d), Third Party has notice that X is dissociated and perforce has notice that X is not a general partner authorized to bind XYZ.

§ 403. Limited Partnership Liable for General Partner's Actionable Conduct

(a) A limited partnership is liable for loss or injury caused to a person, or for a penalty incurred, as a result of a wrongful act or omission, or other actionable conduct, of a general partner acting in the ordinary course of activities of the limited partnership or with authority of the limited partnership.

(b) If, in the course of the limited partnership's activities or while acting with authority of the limited partnership, a general partner receives or causes the limited partnership to receive money or property of a person not a partner, and the money or property is misapplied by a general partner, the limited partnership is liable for the loss.

Comment

Source—RUPA Section 305. For the meaning of "authority" in subsections (a) and (b), see RUPA Section 305, Comment. The third-to-last paragraph of that Comment states:

> The partnership is liable for the actionable conduct or omission of a partner acting in the ordinary course of its business or "with the authority of the partnership." This is intended to include a partner's apparent, as well as actual, authority, thereby bringing within Section 305(a) the situation covered in UPA Section 14(a).

The last paragraph of that Comment states:

> Section 305(b) is drawn from UPA Section 14(b), but has been edited to improve clarity. It imposes strict liability on the partnership for the misapplication of money or property received by a partner in the course of the partnership's business or otherwise within the scope of the partner's actual authority.

Section 403(a) of this Act is taken essentially verbatim from RUPA Section 305(a), and Section 403(b) of this Act is taken essentially verbatim from RUPA Section 305(b).

This section makes the limited partnership vicariously liable for a partner's misconduct. That vicarious[] liability in no way discharges or diminishes the partner's direct liability for the partner's own misconduct.

A general partner can cause a limited partnership to be liable under this section, even if the general partner is not designated as a general partner in the certificate of limited partnership. See Comment to Section 401.

§ 404. General Partner's Liability

(a) Except as otherwise provided in subsections (b) and (c), all general partners are liable jointly and severally for all obligations of the limited partnership unless otherwise agreed by the claimant or provided by law.

(b) A person that becomes a general partner of an existing limited partnership is not personally liable for an obligation of a limited partnership incurred before the person became a general partner.

(c) An obligation of a limited partnership incurred while the limited partnership is a limited liability limited partnership, whether arising in contract, tort, or otherwise, is solely the obligation of the limited partnership. A general partner is not personally liable, directly or indirectly, by way of contribution or otherwise, for such an obligation solely by reason of being or acting as a general partner. This subsection applies despite anything inconsistent in the partnership agreement that existed immediately before the consent required to become a limited liability limited partnership under Section 406(b)(2).

Comment

Source—RUPA Section 306.

Following RUPA and the UPA, this Act leaves to other law the question of when a limited partnership obligation is incurred.

Subsection (c)—For an explanation of the decision to provide for limited liability limited partnerships, see the Prefatory Note.

§ 405. Actions by and Against Partnership and Partners

(a) To the extent not inconsistent with Section 404, a general partner may be joined in an action against the limited partnership or named in a separate action.

(b) A judgment against a limited partnership is not by itself a judgment against a general partner. A judgment against a limited partnership may not be satisfied from a general partner's assets unless there is also a judgment against the general partner.

(c) A judgment creditor of a general partner may not levy execution against the assets of the general partner to satisfy a judgment based on a claim against the limited partnership, unless the partner is personally liable for the claim under Section 404 and:

(1) a judgment based on the same claim has been obtained against the limited partnership and a writ of execution on the judgment has been returned unsatisfied in whole or in part;

(2) the limited partnership is a debtor in bankruptcy;

(3) the general partner has agreed that the creditor need not exhaust limited partnership assets;

(4) a court grants permission to the judgment creditor to levy execution against the assets of a general partner based on a finding that limited partnership assets subject to execution are clearly insufficient to satisfy the judgment, that exhaustion of limited partnership assets is excessively burdensome, or that the grant of permission is an appropriate exercise of the court's equitable powers; or

(5) liability is imposed on the general partner by law or contract independent of the existence of the limited partnership.

Comment

Source—RUPA Section 307.

If a limited partnership is a limited liability limited partnership throughout its existence, this section will bar a creditor of a limited partnership from impleading, suing or reaching the assets of a general partner unless the creditor can satisfy subsection (c)(5).

§ 406. Management Rights of General Partner

(a) Each general partner has equal rights in the management and conduct of the limited partnership's activities. Except as expressly provided in this [Act], any matter relating to the activities of the limited partnership may be exclusively decided by the general partner or, if there is more than one general partner, by a majority of the general partners.

(b) The consent of each partner is necessary to:

(1) amend the partnership agreement;

(2) amend the certificate of limited partnership to add or, subject to Section 1110, delete a statement that the limited partnership is a limited liability limited partnership; and

(3) sell, lease, exchange, or otherwise dispose of all, or substantially all, of the limited partnership's property, with or without the good will, other than in the usual and regular course of the limited partnership's activities.

(c) A limited partnership shall reimburse a general partner for payments made and indemnify a general partner for liabilities incurred by the general partner in the ordinary course of the activities of the partnership or for the preservation of its activities or property.

(d) A limited partnership shall reimburse a general partner for an advance to the limited partnership beyond the amount of capital the general partner agreed to contribute.

(e) A payment or advance made by a general partner which gives rise to an obligation of the limited partnership under subsection (c) or (d) constitutes a loan to the limited partnership which accrues interest from the date of the payment or advance.

(f) A general partner is not entitled to remuneration for services performed for the partnership.

Comment

Source—RUPA Section 401 and ULLCA Section 404.

Subsection (a)—As explained in the Prefatory Note, this Act assumes that, more often than not, people utilizing the Act will want (i) strong centralized management, strongly entrenched, and (ii) passive investors with little control over the entity. Section 302 essentially excludes limited partners from the ordinary management of a limited partnership's activities. This subsection states affirmatively the general partners' commanding role. Only the partnership agreement and the express provisions of this Act can limit that role.

The authority granted by this subsection includes the authority to delegate. Delegation does not relieve the delegating general partner or partners of their duties under Section 408. However, the fact of delegation is a fact relevant to any breach of duty analysis.

Example: A sole general partner personally handles all "important paperwork" for a limited partnership. The general partner neglects to renew the fire insurance coverage on the a building owned by the limited partnership, despite having received and read a warning notice from the insurance company. The building subsequently burns to the ground and is a total loss. The general partner might be liable for breach of the duty of care under Section 408(c) (gross negligence).

Example: A sole general partner delegates responsibility for insurance renewals to the limited partnership's office manager, and that manager neglects to renew the fire insurance coverage on the building. Even assuming that the office manager has been grossly negligent, the general partner is not necessarily liable under Section 408(c). The office manager's gross negligence is not automatically attributed to the general partner. Under Section 408(c), the question is whether the general partner was grossly negligent (or worse) in selecting the general manager, delegating insurance renewal matters to the general manager and supervising the general manager after the delegation.

For the consequences of delegating authority to a person that is a limited partner, see the Comment to Section 305.

The partnership agreement may also provide for delegation and, subject to Section 110(b)(5)–(7), may modify a general partner's Section 408 duties.

Subsection (b)—This subsection limits the managerial rights of the general partners, requiring the consent of each general and limited partner for the specified actions. The subsection is subject to change by the partnership agreement, except as provided in Section 110(b)(12) (pertaining to consent rights established by Section 1110).

Subsection (c)—This Act does not include any parallel provision for limited partners, because they are assumed to be passive. To the extent that by contract or other arrangement a limited partner has authority to act on behalf of the limited partnership, agency law principles will create an indemnity obligation. In other situations, principles of restitution might apply.

Subsection (f)—Unlike RUPA Section 401(h), this subsection provides no compensation for winding up efforts. In a limited partnership, winding up is one of the tasks for which the limited partners depend on the general partner. There is no reason for the Act to single out this particular task as giving rise to compensation.

§ 407. Right of General Partner and Former General Partner to Information

(a) A general partner, without having any particular purpose for seeking the information, may inspect and copy during regular business hours:

(1) in the limited partnership's designated office, required information; and

(2) at a reasonable location specified by the limited partnership, any other records maintained by the limited partnership regarding the limited partnership's activities and financial condition.

(b) Each general partner and the limited partnership shall furnish to a general partner:

(1) without demand, any information concerning the limited partnership's activities and activities reasonably required for the proper exercise of the general partner's rights and duties under the partnership agreement or this [Act]; and

(2) on demand, any other information concerning the limited partnership's activities, except to the extent the demand or the information demanded is unreasonable or otherwise improper under the circumstances.

(c) Subject to subsection (e), on 10 days' demand made in a record received by the limited partnership, a person dissociated as a general partner may have access to the information and records described in subsection (a) at the location specified in subsection (a) if:

(1) the information or record pertains to the period during which the person was a general partner;

(2) the person seeks the information or record in good faith; and

(3) the person satisfies the requirements imposed on a limited partner by Section 304(b).

(d) The limited partnership shall respond to a demand made pursuant to subsection (c) in the same manner as provided in Section 304(c).

(e) If a general partner dies, Section 704 applies.

(f) The limited partnership may impose reasonable restrictions on the use of information under this section. In any dispute concerning the reasonableness of a restriction under this subsection, the limited partnership has the burden of proving reasonableness.

(g) A limited partnership may charge a person dissociated as a general partner that makes a demand under this section reasonable costs of copying, limited to the costs of labor and material.

(h) A general partner or person dissociated as a general partner may exercise the rights under this section through an attorney or other agent. Any restriction imposed under subsection (f) or by the partnership agreement applies both to the attorney or other agent and to the general partner or person dissociated as a general partner.

(i) The rights under this section do not extend to a person as transferee, but the rights under subsection (c) of a person dissociated as a general may be exercised by the legal representative of an individual who dissociated as a general partner under Section 603(7)(B) or (C).

Comment

This section's structure parallels the structure of Section 304 and the Comment to that section may be helpful in understanding this section.

Subsection (b)—Source: RUPA Section 403(c).

Subsection (b)(1)—If a particular item of material information is apparent in the limited partnership's records, whether a general partner is obliged to disseminate that information to fellow general partners depends on the circumstances.

Example: A limited partnership has two general partners: each of which is regularly engaged in conducting the limited partnership's activities; both of which are aware of and have regular access to all significant limited partnership records; and neither of which has special responsibility for or knowledge about any particular aspect of those activities or the partnership records pertaining to any particular aspect of those activities. Most likely, neither general partner is obliged to draw the other general partner's attention to information apparent in the limited partnership's records.

Example: Although a limited partnership has three general partners, one is the managing partner with day-to-day responsibility for running the limited partnership's activities. The other two meet periodically with the managing general partner, and together with that partner function in a manner analogous to a corporate board of directors. Most likely, the managing general partner has a duty to draw the attention of the other general partners to important information, even if that information would be apparent from a review of the limited partnership's records.

In all events under subsection (b)(1), the question is whether the disclosure by one general partner is "reasonably required for the proper exercise" of the other general partner's rights and duties.

Subsection (f)—This provision is identical to Section 304(g) and the Comment to Section 304(g) is applicable here. Under this Act, general and limited partners have sharply different roles. A restriction that is reasonable as to a limited partner is not necessarily reasonable as to a general partner.

Subsection (g)—No charge is allowed for current general partners, because in almost all cases they would be entitled to reimbursement under Section 406(c). Contrast Section 304(h), which authorizes charges to current limited partners.

Subsection (i)—The Comment to Section 304(k) is applicable here.

§ 408. General Standards of General Partner's Conduct

(a) The only fiduciary duties that a general partner has to the limited partnership and the other partners are the duties of loyalty and care under subsections (b) and (c).

(b) A general partner's duty of loyalty to the limited partnership and the other partners is limited to the following:

(1) to account to the limited partnership and hold as trustee for it any property, profit, or benefit derived by the general partner in the conduct and winding up of the limited partnership's activities or derived from a use by the general partner of limited partnership property, including the appropriation of a limited partnership opportunity;

(2) to refrain from dealing with the limited partnership in the conduct or winding up of the limited partnership's activities as or on behalf of a party having an interest adverse to the limited partnership; and

(3) to refrain from competing with the limited partnership in the conduct or winding up of the limited partnership's activities.

(c) A general partner's duty of care to the limited partnership and the other partners in the conduct and winding up of the limited partnership's activities is limited to refraining from engaging in grossly negligent or reckless conduct, intentional misconduct, or a knowing violation of law.

(d) A general partner shall discharge the duties to the partnership and the other partners under this [Act] or under the partnership agreement and exercise any rights consistently with the obligation of good faith and fair dealing.

(e) A general partner does not violate a duty or obligation under this [Act] or under the partnership agreement merely because the general partner's conduct furthers the general partner's own interest.

Comment

Source—RUPA Section 404.

This section does not prevent a general partner from delegating one or more duties, but delegation does not discharge the duty. For further discussion, see the Comment to Section 406(a).

If the partnership agreement removes a particular responsibility from a general partner, that general partner's fiduciary duty must be judged according to the rights and powers the general partner retains. For example, if the partnership agreement denies a general partner the right to act in a particular matter, the general partner's compliance with the partnership agreement cannot be a breach of fiduciary duty. However, the general partner may still have a duty to provide advice with regard to the matter. That duty could arise from the fiduciary duty of care under Section 408(c) and the duty to provide information under Sections 304(i) and 407(b).

For the partnership agreement's power directly to circumscribe a general partner's fiduciary duty, see Section 110(b)(5) and (6).

Subsection (a)—The reference to "the other partners" does not affect the distinction between direct and derivative claims. See Section 1001(b) (prerequisites for a partner bringing a direct claim).

Subsection (b)—A general partner's duty under this subsection continues through winding up, since the limited partners' dependence on the general partner does not end at dissolution. See Comment to Section 406(f) (explaining why this Act provides no remuneration for a general partner's winding up efforts).

Subsection (d)—This provision is identical to Section 305(b) and the Comment to Section 305(b) is applicable here.

[ARTICLE] 5. CONTRIBUTIONS AND DISTRIBUTIONS

§ 501. Form of Contribution

A contribution of a partner may consist of tangible or intangible property or other benefit to the limited partnership, including money, services performed, promissory notes, other agreements to contribute cash or property, and contracts for services to be performed.

Comment

Source—ULLCA Section 401.

§ 502. Liability for Contribution

(a) A partner's obligation to contribute money or other property or other benefit to, or to perform services for, a limited partnership is not excused by the partner's death, disability, or other inability to perform personally.

(b) If a partner does not make a promised non-monetary contribution, the partner is obligated at the option of the limited partnership to contribute money equal to that portion of the value, as stated in the required information, of the stated contribution which has not been made.

(c) The obligation of a partner to make a contribution or return money or other property paid or distributed in violation of this [Act] may be compromised only by consent of all partners. A creditor of a limited partnership which extends credit or otherwise acts in reliance on an obligation described in subsection (a), without notice of any compromise under this subsection, may enforce the original obligation.

Comment

In contrast with predecessor law, RULPA Section 502(a), this Act does not include a statute of frauds provision covering promised contributions. Section 111(9)(A) does require that the value of a promised contribution be memorialized, but that requirement does not affect enforceability. See Comment to Section 111(9).

Subsection (a)—Source: RULPA Section 502(b).

Under common law principles of impracticability, an individual's death or incapacity will sometimes discharge a duty to render performance. Restatement (Second) of Contracts, Sections 261 and 262. This subsection overrides those principles.

Subsection (b)—RULPA Section 502(b).

This subsection is a statutory liquidated damage provision, exercisable at the option of the limited partnership, with the damage amount set according to the value of the promised, non-monetary contribution as stated in the required information.

Example: In order to become a limited partner, a person promises to contribute to the limited partnership various assets which the partnership agreement values at $150,000. In return for the person's promise, and in light of the agreed value, the limited partnership admits the person as a limited partner with a right to receive 25% of the limited partnership's distributions.

The promised assets are subject to a security agreement, but the limited partner promises to contribute them "free and clear." Before the limited partner can contribute the assets, the secured party forecloses on the security interest and sells the assets at a public sale for $75,000. Even if the $75,000 reflects the actual fair market value of the assets, under this subsection the limited partnership has a claim against the limited partner for "the value, as stated in the required information, of the stated contribution which has not been made"—i.e, $150,000.

This section applies "at the option of the limited partnership" and does not affect other remedies which the limited partnership may have under other law.

Example: Same facts as the previous example, except that the public sale brings $225,000. The limited partnership is not obliged to invoke this subsection and may instead sue for breach of the promise to make the contribution, asserting the $225,000 figure as evidence of the actual loss suffered as a result of the breach.

Subsection (c)—Source: ULLCA Section 402(b); RULPA Section 502(c). The first sentence of this subsection applies not only to promised contributions but also to improper distributions. See Sections 508 and 509. The second sentence, pertaining to creditor's rights, applies only to promised contributions.

§ 503. Sharing of Distributions

A distribution by a limited partnership must be shared among the partners on the basis of the value, as stated in the required records when the limited partnership decides to make the distribution, of the contributions the limited partnership has received from each partner.

Comment

This Act has no provision allocating profits and losses among the partners. Instead, the Act directly apportions the right to receive distributions.

Nearly all limited partnerships will choose to allocate profits and losses in order to comply with applicable tax, accounting and other regulatory requirements. Those requirements, rather than this Act, are the proper source of guidance for that profit and loss allocation.

Unlike predecessor law, this section apportions distributions in relation to the value of contributions received from each partner without regard to whether the limited partnership has returned any of those contributions. Compare RULPA Sections 503 and 504. This Act's approach produces the same result as predecessor law, so long as the limited partnership does not vary this section's approach to apportioning distributions.

This section's rule for sharing distributions is subject to change under Section 110. A limited partnership that does vary the rule should be careful to consider not only the tax and accounting consequences but also the "ripple" effect on other provisions of this Act. See, e.g., Sections 801 and 803(c) (apportioning consent power in relation to the right to receive distributions).

§ 504. Interim Distributions

A partner does not have a right to any distribution before the dissolution and winding up of the limited partnership unless the limited partnership decides to make an interim distribution.

Comment

Under Section 406(a), the general partner or partners make this decision for the limited partnership.

§ 505. No Distribution on Account of Dissociation

A person does not have a right to receive a distribution on account of dissociation.

Comment

This section varies substantially from predecessor law. RULPA Sections 603 and 604 permitted a limited partner to withdraw on six months notice and receive the fair value of the limited partnership interest, unless the partnership agreement provided the limited partner with some exit right or stated a definite duration for the limited partnership.

Under this Act, a partner that dissociates becomes a transferee of its own transferable interest. See Sections 602(a)(3) (person dissociated as a limited partner) and 605(a)(5) (person dissociated as a general partner).

§ 506. Distribution in Kind

A partner does not have a right to demand or receive any distribution from a limited partnership in any form other than cash. subject to Section 812(b), a limited partnership may distribute an asset in kind to the extent each partner receives a percentage of the asset equal to the partner's share of distributions.

Comment

Source—RULPA Section 605.

§ 507. Right to Distribution

When a partner or transferee becomes entitled to receive a distribution, the partner or transferee has the status of, and is entitled to all remedies available to, a creditor of the limited partnership with respect to the distribution. However, the limited partnership's obligation to make a distribution is subject to offset for any amount owed to the limited partnership by the partner or dissociated partner on whose account the distribution is made.

Comment

Source—RULPA Section 606.

This section's first sentence refers to distributions generally. Contrast Section 508(e), which refers to indebtedness issued as a distribution.

The reference in the second sentence to "dissociated partner" encompasses circumstances in which the partner is gone and the dissociated partner's transferable interest is all that remains.

§ 508. Limitations on Distribution

(a) A limited partnership may not make a distribution in violation of the partnership agreement.

(b) A limited partnership may not make a distribution if after the distribution:

(1) the limited partnership would not be able to pay its debts as they become due in the ordinary course of the limited partnership's activities; or

(2) the limited partnership's total assets would be less than the sum of its total liabilities plus the amount that would be needed, if the limited partnership were to be dissolved, wound up, and terminated at the time of the distribution, to satisfy the preferential rights upon dissolution, winding up, and termination of partners whose preferential rights are superior to those of persons receiving the distribution.

(c) A limited partnership may base a determination that a distribution is not prohibited under subsection (b) on financial statements prepared on the basis of accounting practices and principles that are reasonable in the circumstances or on a fair valuation or other method that is reasonable in the circumstances.

(d) Except as otherwise provided in subsection (g), the effect of a distribution under subsection (b) is measured:

(1) in the case of distribution by purchase, redemption, or other acquisition of a transferable interest in the limited partnership, as of the date money or other property is transferred or debt incurred by the limited partnership; and

(2) in all other cases, as of the date:

(A) the distribution is authorized, if the payment occurs within120 days after that date; or

(B) the payment is made, if payment occurs more than120 days after the distribution is authorized.

(e) A limited partnership's indebtedness to a partner incurred by reason of a distribution made in accordance with this section is at parity with the limited partnership's indebtedness to its general, unsecured creditors.

(f) A limited partnership's indebtedness, including indebtedness issued in connection with or as part of a distribution, is not considered a liability for purposes of subsection (b) if the terms of the indebtedness provide that payment of principal and interest are made only to the extent that a distribution could then be made to partners under this section.

(g) If indebtedness is issued as a distribution, each payment of principal or interest on the indebtedness is treated as a distribution, the effect of which is measured on the date the payment is made.

Comment

Source—ULLCA Section 406. See also RMBCA Section 6.40.

Subsection (c)—This subsection appears to impose a standard of ordinary care, in contrast with the general duty of care stated in Section 408(c). For a reconciliation of these two provisions, see Comment to Section 509(a).

§ 509. Liability for Improper Distributions

(a) A general partner that consents to a distribution made in violation of Section 508 is personally liable to the limited partnership for the amount of the distribution which exceeds the amount that could have been distributed without the violation if it is established that in consenting to the distribution the general partner failed to comply with Section 408.

(b) A partner or transferee that received a distribution knowing that the distribution to that partner or transferee was made in violation of Section 508 is personally liable to the limited partnership but only to the extent that the distribution received by the partner or transferee exceeded the amount that could have been properly paid under Section 508.

(c) A general partner against which an action is commenced under subsection (a) may:

(1) implead in the action any other person that is liable under subsection (a) and compel contribution from the person; and

(2) implead in the action any person that received a distribution in violation of subsection (b) and compel contribution from the person in the amount the person received in violation of subsection (b).

(d) An action under this section is barred if it is not commenced within two years after the distribution.

Comment

Source—ULLCA Section 407. See also RMBCA Section 8.33.

In substance and effect this section protects the interests of creditors of the limited partnership. Therefore, according to Section 110(b)(13), the partnership agreement may not change this section in a way that restricts the rights of those creditors. As for a limited partnership's power to compromise a claim under this section, see Section 502(c).

Subsection (a)—This subsection refers both to Section 508, which includes in its subsection (c) a standard of ordinary care ("reasonable in the circumstances"), and to Section 408, which includes in its subsection (c) a general duty of care that is limited to "refraining from engaging in grossly negligent or reckless conduct, intentional misconduct, or a knowing violation of law."

A limited partnership's failure to meet the standard of Section 508(c) cannot by itself cause a general partner to be liable under Section 509(a). *Both* of the following would have to occur before a failure to satisfy Section 508(c) could occasion personal liability for a general partner under Section 509(a):

- the limited partnership "base[s] a determination that a distribution is not prohibited . . . on financial statements prepared on the basis of accounting practices and principles that are [not] reasonable in the circumstances or on a [not] fair valuation or other method that is [not] reasonable in the circumstances" [Section 508(c)]

AND

- the general partner's decision to rely on the improper methodology in consenting to the distribution constitutes "grossly negligent or reckless conduct, intentional misconduct, or a knowing violation of law" [Section 408(c)] or breaches some other duty under Section 408.

To serve the protective purpose of Sections 508 and 509, in this subsection "consent" must be understood as encompassing any form of approval, assent or acquiescence, whether formal or informal, express or tacit.

Subsection (d)—The subsection's limitation applies to the commencement of an action under subsection (a) or (b) and not to subsection (c), under which a general partner may implead other persons.

[ARTICLE] 6. DISSOCIATION

§ 601. Dissociation as Limited Partner

(a) A person does not have a right to dissociate as a limited partner before the termination of the limited partnership.

(b) A person is dissociated from a limited partnership as a limited partner upon the occurrence of any of the following events:

(1) the limited partnership's having notice of the person's express will to withdraw as a limited partner or on a later date specified by the person;

(2) an event agreed to in the partnership agreement as causing the person's dissociation as a limited partner;

(3) the person's expulsion as a limited partner pursuant to the partnership agreement;

(4) the person's expulsion as a limited partner by the unanimous consent of the other partners if:

(A) it is unlawful to carry on the limited partnership's activities with the person as a limited partner;

(B) there has been a transfer of all of the person's transferable interest in the limited partnership, other than a transfer for security purposes, or a court order charging the person's interest, which has not been foreclosed;

(C) the person is a corporation and, within 90 days after the limited partnership notifies the person that it will be expelled as a limited partner because it has filed a certificate of dissolution or the equivalent, its charter has been revoked, or its right to conduct business has been suspended by the jurisdiction of its incorporation, there is no revocation of the certificate of dissolution or no reinstatement of its charter or its right to conduct business; or

(D) the person is a limited liability company or partnership that has been dissolved and whose business is being wound up;

(5) on application by the limited partnership, the person's expulsion as a limited partner by judicial order because:

(A) the person engaged in wrongful conduct that adversely and materially affected the limited partnership's activities;

(B) the person willfully or persistently committed a material breach of the partnership agreement or of the obligation of good faith and fair dealing under Section 305(b); or

(C) the person engaged in conduct relating to the limited partnership's activities which makes it not reasonably practicable to carry on the activities with the person as limited partner;

(6) in the case of a person who is an individual, the person's death;

(7) in the case of a person that is a trust or is acting as a limited partner by virtue of being a trustee of a trust, distribution of the trust's entire transferable interest in the limited partnership, but not merely by reason of the substitution of a successor trustee;

(8) in the case of a person that is an estate or is acting as a limited partner by virtue of being a personal representative of an estate, distribution of the estate's entire transferable interest in the limited partnership, but not merely by reason of the substitution of a successor personal representative;

(9) termination of a limited partner that is not an individual, partnership, limited liability company, corporation, trust, or estate;

(10) the limited partnership's participation in a conversion or merger under [Article] 11, if the limited partnership:

(A) is not the converted or surviving entity; or

(B) is the converted or surviving entity but, as a result of the conversion or merger, the person ceases to be a limited partner.

Comment

Source—RUPA Section 601.

This section adopts RUPA's dissociation provision essentially verbatim, except for provisions inappropriate to limited partners. For example, this section does not provide for the dissociation of a person as a limited partner on account of bankruptcy, insolvency or incompetency.

This Act refers to *a person's dissociation as a limited partner* rather than to the *dissociation of a limited partner*, because the same person may be both a general and a limited partner. See Section 113 (Dual Capacity). It is possible for a dual capacity partner to dissociate in one capacity and not in the other.

Subsection (a)—This section varies substantially from predecessor law. See Comment to Section 505.

Subsection (b)(1)—This provision gives a person the power to dissociate as a limited partner even though the dissociation is wrongful under subsection (a). See, however, Section 110(b)(8) (prohibiting the partnership agreement from eliminating the power of a person to dissociate as a *general* partner but imposing no comparable restriction with regard to a person's dissociation as a *limited* partner).

Subsection (b)(5)—In contrast to RUPA, this provision may be varied or even eliminated by the partnership agreement.

§ 602. Effect of Dissociation as Limited Partner

(a) Upon a person's dissociation as a limited partner:

(1) subject to Section 704, the person does not have further rights as a limited partner;

(2) the person's obligation of good faith and fair dealing as a limited partner under Section 305(b) continues only as to matters arising and events occurring before the dissociation; and

(3) subject to Section 704 and [Article] 11, any transferable interest owned by the person in the person's capacity as a limited partner immediately before dissociation is owned by the person as a mere transferee.

(b) A person's dissociation as a limited partner does not of itself discharge the person from any obligation to the limited partnership or the other partners which the person incurred while a limited partner.

Comment

Source—RUPA Section 603(b).

Subsection (a)(1)—In general, when a person dissociates as a limited partner, the person's rights as a limited partner disappear and, subject to Section 113 (Dual Status), the person's status degrades to that of a mere transferee. However, Section 704 provides some special rights when dissociation is caused by an individual's death.

Subsection (a)(3)—For any person that is both a general partner and a limited partner, the required records must state which transferable interest is owned in which capacity. Section 111(9)(C).

Article 11 provides for conversions and mergers. A plan of conversion or merger may provide for the dissociation of a person as a limited partner and may override the rule stated in this paragraph.

§ 603. Dissociation as General Partner

A person is dissociated from a limited partnership as a general partner upon the occurrence of any of the following events:

(1) the limited partnership's having notice of the person's express will to withdraw as a general partner or on a later date specified by the person;

(2) an event agreed to in the partnership agreement as causing the person's dissociation as a general partner;

(3) the person's expulsion as a general partner pursuant to the partnership agreement;

(4) the person's expulsion as a general partner by the unanimous consent of the other partners if:

(A) it is unlawful to carry on the limited partnership's activities with the person as a general partner;

(B) there has been a transfer of all or substantially all of the person's transferable interest in the limited partnership, other than a transfer for security purposes, or a court order charging the person's interest, which has not been foreclosed;

(C) the person is a corporation and, within 90 days after the limited partnership notifies the person that it will be expelled as a general partner because it has filed a certificate of dissolution or the equivalent, its charter has been revoked, or its right to conduct business has been suspended by the jurisdiction of its incorporation, there is no revocation of the certificate of dissolution or no reinstatement of its charter or its right to conduct business; or

(D) the person is a limited liability company or partnership that has been dissolved and whose business is being wound up;

(5) on application by the limited partnership, the person's expulsion as a general partner by judicial determination because:

(A) the person engaged in wrongful conduct that adversely and materially affected the limited partnership activities;

(B) the person willfully or persistently committed a material breach of the partnership agreement or of a duty owed to the partnership or the other partners under Section 408; or

(C) the person engaged in conduct relating to the limited partnership's activities which makes it not reasonably practicable to carry on the activities of the limited partnership with the person as a general partner;

(6) the person's:

(A) becoming a debtor in bankruptcy;

(B) execution of an assignment for the benefit of creditors;

(C) seeking, consenting to, or acquiescing in the appointment of a trustee, receiver, or liquidator of the person or of all or substantially all of the person's property; or

(D) failure, within 90 days after the appointment, to have vacated or stayed the appointment of a trustee, receiver, or liquidator of the general partner or of all or substantially all of the person's property obtained without the person's consent or acquiescence, or failing within 90 days after the expiration of a stay to have the appointment vacated;

(7) in the case of a person who is an individual:

(A) the person's death;

(B) the appointment of a guardian or general conservator for the person; or

(C) a judicial determination that the person has otherwise become incapable of performing the person's duties as a general partner under the partnership agreement;

(8) in the case of a person that is a trust or is acting as a general partner by virtue of being a trustee of a trust, distribution of the trust's entire transferable interest in the limited partnership, but not merely by reason of the substitution of a successor trustee;

(9) in the case of a person that is an estate or is acting as a general partner by virtue of being a personal representative of an estate, distribution of the estate's entire transferable interest in the limited partnership, but not merely by reason of the substitution of a successor personal representative;

(10) termination of a general partner that is not an individual, partnership, limited liability company, corporation, trust, or estate; or

(11) the limited partnership's participation in a conversion or merger under [Article] 11, if the limited partnership:

(A) is not the converted or surviving entity; or

(B) is the converted or surviving entity but, as a result of the conversion or merger, the person ceases to be a general partner.

Comment

Source—RUPA Section 601.

This section adopts RUPA's dissociation provision essentially verbatim. This Act refers to *a person's dissociation as a general partner* rather than to the *dissociation of a general partner*, because the same person may be both a general and a limited partner. See Section 113 (Dual Capacity). It is possible for a dual capacity partner to dissociate in one capacity and not in the other.

Paragraph (1)—The partnership agreement may not eliminate this power to dissociate. See Section 110(b)(8).

Paragraph (5)—In contrast to RUPA, this provision may be varied or even eliminated by the partnership agreement.

§ 604. Person's Power to Dissociate as General Partner; Wrongful Dissociation

(a) A person has the power to dissociate as a general partner at any time, rightfully or wrongfully, by express will pursuant to Section 603(1).

(b) A person's dissociation as a general partner is wrongful only if:

(1) it is in breach of an express provision of the partnership agreement; or

(2) it occurs before the termination of the limited partnership, and:

(A) the person withdraws as a general partner by express will;

(B) the person is expelled as a general partner by judicial determination under Section 603(5);

(C) the person is dissociated as a general partner by becoming a debtor in bankruptcy; or

(D) in the case of a person that is not an individual, trust other than a business trust, or estate, the person is expelled or otherwise dissociated as a general partner because it willfully dissolved or terminated.

(c) A person that wrongfully dissociates as a general partner is liable to the limited partnership and, subject to Section 1001, to the other partners for damages caused by the dissociation. The liability is in addition to any other obligation of the general partner to the limited partnership or to the other partners.

Comment

Source—RUPA Section 602.

Subsection (a)—The partnership agreement may not eliminate this power. See Section 110(b)(8).

Subsection (b)(1)—The reference to "an express provision of the partnership agreement" means that a person's dissociation as a general partner in breach of the obligation of good faith and fair dealing is not wrongful dissociation for the purposes of this section. The breach might be actionable on other grounds.

Subsection (b)(2)—The reference to "before the termination of the limited partnership" reflects the expectation that each general partner will shepherd the limited partnership through winding up. See Comment to Section 406(f). A person's obligation to remain as general partner through winding up continues even if another general partner dissociates and even if that dissociation leads to the limited partnership's premature dissolution under Section 801(3)(A).

Subsection (c)—The language "subject to Section 1001" is intended to preserve the distinction between direct and derivative claims.

§ 605. Effect of Dissociation as General Partner

(a) Upon a person's dissociation as a general partner:

(1) the person's right to participate as a general partner in the management and conduct of the partnership's activities terminates;

(2) the person's duty of loyalty as a general partner under Section 408(b)(3) terminates;

(3) the person's duty of loyalty as a general partner under Section 408(b)(1) and (2) and duty of care under Section 408(c) continue only with regard to matters arising and events occurring before the person's dissociation as a general partner;

(4) the person may sign and deliver to the [Secretary of State] for filing a statement of dissociation pertaining to the person and, at the request of the limited partnership, shall sign an amendment to the certificate of limited partnership which states that the person has dissociated; and

(5) subject to Section 704 and [Article] 11, any transferable interest owned by the person immediately before dissociation in the person's capacity as a general partner is owned by the person as a mere transferee.

(b) A person's dissociation as a general partner does not of itself discharge the person from any obligation to the limited partnership or the other partners which the person incurred while a general partner.

Comment

Source—RUPA Section 603(b).

Subsection (a)(1)—Once a person dissociates as a general partner, the person loses all management rights as a general partner regardless of what happens to the limited partnership. This rule contrasts with RUPA Section 603(b)(1), which permits a dissociated general partner to participate in winding up in some circumstances.

Subsection (a)(4)—Both records covered by this paragraph have the same effect under Section 103(d)–namely, to give constructive notice that the person has dissociated as a general partner. The notice benefits the person by curtailing any further personal liability under Sections 607, 805, and 1111. The notice benefits the limited partnership by curtailing any lingering power to bind under Sections 606, 804, and 1112.

The limited partnership is in any event obligated to amend its certificate of limited partnership to reflect the dissociation of a person as general partner. See Section 202(b)(2). In most circumstances, the amendment requires the signature of the person that has dissociated. Section 204(a)(5)(C). If that signature is required and the person refuses or fails to sign, the limited partnership may invoke Section 205 (Signing and Filing Pursuant to Judicial Order).

Subsection (a)(5)—In general, when a person dissociates as a general partner, the person's rights as a general partner disappear and, subject to Section 113 (Dual Status), the person's status degrades to that of a mere transferee. For any person that is both a general partner and a limited partner, the required records must state which transferable interest is owned in which capacity. Section 111(9)(C).

Section 704 provides some special rights when an individual dissociates by dying. Article 11 provides for conversions and mergers. A plan of conversion or merger may provide for the dissociation of a person as a general partner and may override the rule stated in this paragraph.

§ 606. Power to Bind and Liability to Limited Partnership Before Dissolution of Partnership of Person Dissociated as General Partner

(a) After a person is dissociated as a general partner and before the limited partnership is dissolved, converted under [Article] 11, or merged out of existence under [Article 11], the limited partnership is bound by an act of the person only if:

(1) the act would have bound the limited partnership under Section 402 before the dissociation; and

(2) at the time the other party enters into the transaction:

(A) less than two years has passed since the dissociation; and

(B) the other party does not have notice of the dissociation and reasonably believes that the person is a general partner.

(b) If a limited partnership is bound under subsection (a), the person dissociated as a general partner which caused the limited partnership to be bound is liable:

(1) to the limited partnership for any damage caused to the limited partnership arising from the obligation incurred under subsection (a); and

(2) if a general partner or another person dissociated as a general partner is liable for the obligation, to the general partner or other person for any damage caused to the general partner or other person arising from the liability.

Comment

Source—RUPA Section 702.

This Act contains three sections pertaining to the lingering power to bind of a person dissociated as a general partner:

- this section, which applies until the limited partnership dissolves, converts to another form of organization under Article 11, or is merged out of existence under Article 11;
- Section 804(b), which applies after a limited partnership dissolves; and

• Section 1112(b), which applies after a conversion or merger.

Subsection (a)(2)(B)—A person might have notice under Section 103(d)(1) as well as under Section 103(b).

Subsection (b)—The liability provided by this subsection is not exhaustive. For example, if a person dissociated as a general partner causes a limited partnership to be bound under subsection (a) and, due to a guaranty, some other person is liable on the resulting obligation, that other person may have a claim under other law against the person dissociated as a general partner.

§ 607. Liability to Other Persons of Person Dissociated as General Partner

(a) A person's dissociation as a general partner does not of itself discharge the person's liability as a general partner for an obligation of the limited partnership incurred before dissociation. Except as otherwise provided in subsections (b) and (c), the person is not liable for a limited partnership's obligation incurred after dissociation.

(b) A person whose dissociation as a general partner resulted in a dissolution and winding up of the limited partnership's activities is liable to the same extent as a general partner under Section 404 on an obligation incurred by the limited partnership under Section 804.

(c) A person that has dissociated as a general partner but whose dissociation did not result in a dissolution and winding up of the limited partnership's activities is liable on a transaction entered into by the limited partnership after the dissociation only if:

(1) a general partner would be liable on the transaction; and

(2) at the time the other party enters into the transaction:

(A) less than two years has passed since the dissociation; and

(B) the other party does not have notice of the dissociation and reasonably believes that the person is a general partner.

(d) By agreement with a creditor of a limited partnership and the limited partnership, a person dissociated as a general partner may be released from liability for an obligation of the limited partnership.

(e) A person dissociated as a general partner is released from liability for an obligation of the limited partnership if the limited partnership's creditor, with notice of the person's dissociation as a general partner but without the person's consent, agrees to a material alteration in the nature or time of payment of the obligation.

Comment

Source—RUPA Section 703.

A person's dissociation as a general partner does not categorically prevent the person from being liable as a general partner for subsequently incurred obligations of the limited partnership. If the dissociation results in dissolution, subsection (b) applies and the person will be liable as a general partner on any partnership obligation incurred under Section 804. In these circumstances, neither filing a statement of dissociation nor amending the certificate of limited partnership to state that the person has dissociated as a general partner will curtail the person's lingering exposure to liability.

If the dissociation does not result in dissolution, subsection (c) applies. In this context, filing a statement of dissociation or amending the certificate of limited partnership to state that the person has dissociated as a general partner will curtail the person's lingering liability. See subsection (c)(2)(B).

If the limited partnership subsequently dissolves as the result of some other occurrence (i.e., not a result of the person's dissociation as a general partner), subsection (c) continues to apply. In that situation, Section 804 will determine whether, for the purposes of subsection (c), the limited partnership has entered into a transaction after dissolution.

If the limited partnership is a limited liability limited partnership, these liability rules are moot.

Subsection (a)—The phrase "liability as a general partner for an obligation of the limited partnership" refers to liability under Section 404. Following RUPA and the UPA, this Act leaves to other law the question of when a limited partnership obligation is incurred.

Subsection (c)(2)(B)—A person might have notice under Section 103(d)(1) as well as under Section 103(b).

[ARTICLE] 7. TRANSFERABLE INTERESTS AND RIGHTS OF TRANSFEREES AND CREDITORS

§ 701. Partner's Transferable Interest

The only interest of a partner which is transferable is the partner's transferable interest. A transferable interest is personal property.

Comment

Source—RUPA Section 502.

Like all other partnership statutes, this Act dichotomizes each partner's rights into economic rights and other rights. The former are freely transferable, as provided in Section 702. The latter are not transferable at all, unless the partnership agreement so provides.

Although a partner or transferee owns a transferable interest as a present right, that right only entitles the owner to distributions if and when made. See Sections 504 (subject to any contrary provision in the partnership agreement, no right to interim distribution unless the limited partnership decides to make an interim distribution) and the Comment to Section 812 (subject to any contrary provision in the partnership agreement, no partner obligated to contribute for the purpose of equalizing or otherwise allocating capital losses).

§ 702. Transfer of Partner's Transferable Interest

(a) A transfer, in whole or in part, of a partner's transferable interest:

(1) is permissible;

(2) does not by itself cause the partner's dissociation or a dissolution and winding up of the limited partnership's activities; and

(3) does not, as against the other partners or the limited partnership, entitle the transferee to participate in the management or conduct of the limited partnership's activities, to require access to information concerning the limited partnership's transactions except as otherwise provided in subsection (c), or to inspect or copy the required information or the limited partnership's other records.

(b) A transferee has a right to receive, in accordance with the transfer:

(1) distributions to which the transferor would otherwise be entitled; and

(2) upon the dissolution and winding up of the limited partnership's activities the net amount otherwise distributable to the transferor.

(c) In a dissolution and winding up, a transferee is entitled to an account of the limited partnership's transactions only from the date of dissolution.

(d) Upon transfer, the transferor retains the rights of a partner other than the interest in distributions transferred and retains all duties and obligations of a partner.

(e) A limited partnership need not give effect to a transferee's rights under this section until the limited partnership has notice of the transfer.

(f) A transfer of a partner's transferable interest in the limited partnership in violation of a restriction on transfer contained in the partnership agreement is ineffective as to a person having notice of the restriction at the time of transfer.

(g) A transferee that becomes a partner with respect to a transferable interest is liable for the transferor's obligations under Sections 502 and 509. However, the transferee is not obligated for liabilities unknown to the transferee at the time the transferee became a partner.

Comment

Source—RUPA Section 503, except for subsection (g), which derives from RULPA Section 704(b). Following RUPA, this Act uses the words "transfer" and "transferee" rather than the words "assignment" and "assignee." See RUPA Section 503.

Subsection (a)(2)—The phrase "by itself" is significant. A transfer of all of a person's transferable interest could lead to dissociation via expulsion, Sections 601(b)(4)(B) and 603(4)(B).

Subsection (a)(3)—Mere transferees have no right to intrude as the partners carry on their activities as partners. Moreover, a partner's obligation of good faith and fair dealing under Sections 305(b) and 408(d) is framed in reference to "the limited partnership and the other partners." See also Comment to Section 1102(b)(3) and Comment to Section 1106(b)(3).

§ 703. Rights of Creditor of Partner or Transferee

(a) On application to a court of competent jurisdiction by any judgment creditor of a partner or transferee, the court may charge the transferable interest of the judgment debtor with payment of the unsatisfied amount of the judgment with interest. To the extent so charged, the judgment creditor has only the rights of a transferee. The court may appoint a receiver of the share of the distributions due or to become due to the judgment debtor in respect of the partnership and make all other orders, directions, accounts, and inquiries the judgment debtor might have made or which the circumstances of the case may require to give effect to the charging order.

(b) A charging order constitutes a lien on the judgment debtor's transferable interest. The court may order a foreclosure upon the interest subject to the charging order at any time. The purchaser at the foreclosure sale has the rights of a transferee.

(c) At any time before foreclosure, an interest charged may be redeemed:

(1) by the judgment debtor;

(2) with property other than limited partnership property, by one or more of the other partners; or

(3) with limited partnership property, by the limited partnership with the consent of all partners whose interests are not so charged.

(d) This [Act] does not deprive any partner or transferee of the benefit of any exemption laws applicable to the partner's or transferee's transferable interest.

(e) This section provides the exclusive remedy by which a judgment creditor of a partner or transferee may satisfy a judgment out of the judgment debtor's transferable interest.

Comment

Source—RUPA Section 504 and ULLCA Section 504.

This section balances the needs of a judgment creditor of a partner or transferee with the needs of the limited partnership and non-debtor partners and transferees. The section achieves that balance by allowing the judgment creditor to collect on the judgment through the transferable interest of the judgment debtor while prohibiting interference in the management and activities of the limited partnership.

Under this section, the judgment creditor of a partner or transferee is entitled to a charging order against the relevant transferable interest. While in effect, that order entitles the judgment creditor to whatever distributions would otherwise be due to the partner or transferee whose interest is subject to the order. The creditor has no say in the timing or amount of those distributions. The charging order does not entitle the creditor to accelerate any distributions or to otherwise interfere with the management and activities of the limited partnership.

Foreclosure of a charging order effects a permanent transfer of the charged transferable interest to the purchaser. The foreclosure does not, however, create any rights to participate in the management and conduct of the limited partnership's activities. The purchaser obtains nothing more than the status of a transferee.

Subsection (a)—The court's power to appoint a receiver and "make all other orders, directions, accounts, and inquiries the judgment debtor might have made or which the circumstances of the case may require" must be understood in the context of the balance described above. In particular, the court's power to make orders "which the circumstances may require" is limited to "giv[ing] effect to the charging order."

> **Example:** A judgment creditor with a charging order believes that the limited partnership should invest less of its surplus in operations, leaving more funds for distributions. The creditor moves the court for an order directing the general partners to restrict reinvestment. This section does not authorize the court to grant the motion.

> **Example:** A judgment creditor with a judgment for $10,000 against a partner obtains a charging order against the partner's transferable interest. The limited partnership is duly served with the order. However, the limited partnership subsequently fails to comply with the order and makes a $3000 distribution to the partner. The court has the power to order the limited partnership to turn over $3000 to the judgment creditor to "give effect to the charging order."

The court also has the power to decide whether a particular payment is a distribution, because this decision determines whether the payment is part of a transferable interest subject to a charging order. (To the extent a payment is not a distribution, it is not part of the transferable interest and is not subject to subsection (e). The payment is therefore subject to whatever other creditor remedies may apply.)

Subsection (c)(3)—This provision requires the consent of all the limited as well as general partners.

§ 704. Power of Estate of Deceased Partner

If a partner dies, the deceased partner's personal representative or other legal representative may exercise the rights of a transferee as provided in section 702 and, for the purposes of settling the estate, may exercise the rights of a current limited partner under section 304.

Comment

Section 702 strictly limits the rights of transferees. In particular, a transferee has no right to participate in management in any way, no voting rights and, except following dissolution, no information rights. Even after dissolution, a transferee's information rights are limited. See Section 702(c).

This section provides special informational rights for a deceased partner's legal representative for the purposes of settling the estate. For those purposes, the legal representative may exercise the informational rights of a current limited partner under Section 304. Those rights are of course subject to the limitations and obligations stated in that section—*e.g.*, Section 304 (g) (restrictions on use) and (h) (charges for copies)—as well as any generally applicable limitations stated in the partnership agreement.

[ARTICLE] 8. DISSOLUTION

§ 801. Nonjudicial Dissolution

Except as otherwise provided in Section 802, a limited partnership is dissolved, and its activities must be wound up, only upon the occurrence of any of the following:

(1) the happening of an event specified in the partnership agreement;

(2) the consent of all general partners and of limited partners owning a majority of the rights to receive distributions as limited partners at the time the consent is to be effective;

(3) after the dissociation of a person as a general partner:

(A) if the limited partnership has at least one remaining general partner, the consent to dissolve the limited partnership given within 90 days after the dissociation by partners owning a majority of the rights to receive distributions as partners at the time the consent is to be effective; or

(B) if the limited partnership does not have a remaining general partner, the passage of 90 days after the dissociation, unless before the end of the period:

(i) consent to continue the activities of the limited partnership and admit at least one general partner is given by limited partners owning a majority of the rights to receive distributions as limited partners at the time the consent is to be effective; and

(ii) at least one person is admitted as a general partner in accordance with the consent;

(4) the passage of 90 days after the dissociation of the limited partnership's last limited partner, unless before the end of the period the limited partnership admits at least one limited partner; or

(5) the signing and filing of a declaration of dissolution by the [Secretary of State] under Section 809(c).

Comment

This Act does not require that any of the consents referred to in this section be given in the form of a signed record. The partnership agreement has the power to impose that requirement. See Comment to Section 110.

In several provisions, this section provides for consent in terms of rights to receive distributions. Distribution rights of non-partner transferees are not relevant. Mere transferees have no consent rights, and their distribution rights are not counted in determining whether majority consent has been obtained.

Paragraph (1)—There is no requirement that the relevant provision of the partnership agreement be made in a record, unless the partnership agreement creates that requirement. However, if the relevant provision is not "contained in a partnership agreement made in a record," Section 111(9)(D) includes among the limited partnership's required information "a record stating ... any events upon the happening of which the limited partnership is to be dissolved and its activities wound up."

Paragraph (2)—Rights to receive distributions owned by a person that is both a general and a limited partner figure into the limited partner determination only to the extent those rights are owned in the person's capacity as a limited partner. See Section 111(9)(C).

Example: XYZ is a limited partnership with three general partners, each of whom is also a limited partner, and 5 other limited partners. Rights to receive distributions are allocated as follows:

Partner #1 as general partner–3%
Partner #2 as general partner–2%

Partner #3 as general partner–1%
Partner #1 as limited partner–7%
Partner #2 as limited partner–3%
Partner #3 as limited partner–4%
Partner #4 as limited partner–5%
Partner #5 as limited partner–5%
Partner #6 as limited partner–5%
Partner #7 as limited partner–5%
Partner #8 as limited partner–5%
Several non-partner transferees, in the aggregate–55%

Distribution rights owned by persons as limited partners amount to 39% of total distribution rights. A majority is therefore anything greater than 19.5%. If only Partners 1, 2, 3 and 4 consent to dissolve, the limited partnership is not dissolved. Together these partners own as limited partners 19% of the distribution rights owned by persons as limited partners–just short of the necessary majority. For purposes of this calculation, distribution rights owned by non-partner transferees are irrelevant. So, too, are distribution rights owned by persons as general partners. (However, dissolution under this provision requires "the consent of all general partners.")

Paragraph (3)(A)—Unlike paragraph (2), this paragraph makes no distinction between distribution rights owned by persons as general partners and distribution rights owned by persons as limited partners. Distribution rights owned by non-partner transferees are irrelevant.

§ 802. Judicial Dissolution

On application by a partner the [appropriate court] may order dissolution of a limited partnership if it is not reasonably practicable to carry on the activities of the limited partnership in conformity with the partnership agreement.

Comment

Source—RULPA Section 802.

Section 110(b)(9) limits the power of the partnership agreement with regard to this section.

§ 803. Winding Up

(a) A limited partnership continues after dissolution only for the purpose of winding up its activities.

(b) In winding up its activities, the limited partnership:

(1) may amend its certificate of limited partnership to state that the limited partnership is dissolved, preserve the limited partnership business or property as a going concern for a reasonable time, prosecute and defend actions and proceedings, whether civil,

criminal, or administrative, transfer the limited partnership's property, settle disputes by mediation or arbitration, file a statement of termination as provided in Section 203, and perform other necessary acts; and

(2) shall discharge the limited partnership's liabilities, settle and close the limited partnership's activities, and marshal and distribute the assets of the partnership.

(c) If a dissolved limited partnership does not have a general partner, a person to wind up the dissolved limited partnership's activities may be appointed by the consent of limited partners owning a majority of the rights to receive distributions as limited partners at the time the consent is to be effective. A person appointed under this subsection:

(1) has the powers of a general partner under Section 804; and

(2) shall promptly amend the certificate of limited partnership to state:

(A) that the limited partnership does not have a general partner;

(B) the name of the person that has been appointed to wind up the limited partnership; and

(C) the street and mailing address of the person.

(d) On the application of any partner, the [appropriate court] may order judicial supervision of the winding up, including the appointment of a person to wind up the dissolved limited partnership's activities, if:

(1) a limited partnership does not have a general partner and within a reasonable time following the dissolution no person has been appointed pursuant to subsection (c); or

(2) the applicant establishes other good cause.

Comment

Source—RUPA Sections 802 and 803.

Subsection (b)(2)—A limited partnership may satisfy its duty to "discharge" a liability either by paying or by making an alternative arrangement satisfactory to the creditor.

Subsection (c)—The method for determining majority consent is analogous to the method applicable under Section 801(2). See the Comment to that paragraph.

A person appointed under this subsection is **not** a general partner and therefore is not subject to Section 408.

§ 804. Power of General Partner and Person Dissociated as General Partner to Bind Partnership After Dissolution

(a) A limited partnership is bound by a general partner's act after dissolution which:

(1) is appropriate for winding up the limited partnership's activities; or

(2) would have bound the limited partnership under Section 402 before dissolution, if, at the time the other party enters into the transaction, the other party does not have notice of the dissolution.

(b) A person dissociated as a general partner binds a limited partnership through an act occurring after dissolution if:

(1) at the time the other party enters into the transaction:

(A) less than two years has passed since the dissociation; and

(B) the other party does not have notice of the dissociation and reasonably believes that the person is a general partner; and

(2) the act:

(A) is appropriate for winding up the limited partnership's activities; or

(B) would have bound the limited partnership under Section 402 before dissolution and at the time the other party enters into the transaction the other party does not have notice of the dissolution.

Comment

Subsection (a)—Source: RUPA Section 804.

Subsection (a)(2)—A person might have notice under Section 103(d)(2) (amendment of certificate of limited partnership to indicate dissolution) as well as under Section 103(b).

Subsection (b)—This subsection deals with the post-dissolution power to bind of a person dissociated as a general partner. Paragraph (1) replicates the provisions of Section 606, pertaining to the pre-dissolution power to bind of a person dissociated as a general partner. Paragraph (2) replicates the provisions of subsection (a), which state the post-dissolution power to bind of a general partner. For a person dissociated as a general partner to bind a dissolved limited partnership, the person's act will have to satisfy both paragraph (1) and paragraph (2).

Subsection (b)(1)(B)—A person might have notice under Section 103(d)(1) as well as under Section 103(b).

Subsection (b)(2)(B)—A person might have notice under Section 103(d)(2) (amendment of certificate of limited partnership to indicate dissolution) as well as under Section 103(b).

§ 805. Liability After Dissolution of General Partner and Person Dissociated as General Partner to Limited Partnership, Other General Partners, and Persons Dissociated as General Partner

(a) If a general partner having knowledge of the dissolution causes a limited partnership to incur an obligation under Section 804(a) by an act that is not appropriate for winding up the partnership's activities, the general partner is liable:

(1) to the limited partnership for any damage caused to the limited partnership arising from the obligation; and

(2) if another general partner or a person dissociated as a general partner is liable for the obligation, to that other general partner or person for any damage caused to that other general partner or person arising from the liability.

(b) If a person dissociated as a general partner causes a limited partnership to incur an obligation under Section 804(b), the person is liable:

(1) to the limited partnership for any damage caused to the limited partnership arising from the obligation; and

(2) if a general partner or another person dissociated as a general partner is liable for the obligation, to the general partner or other person for any damage caused to the general partner or other person arising from the liability.

Comment

Source—RUPA Section 806.

It is possible for more than one person to be liable under this section on account of the same limited partnership obligation. This Act does not provide any rule for apportioning liability in that circumstance.

Subsection (a)(2)—If the limited partnership is not a limited liability limited partnership, the liability created by this paragraph includes liability under Sections 404(a), 607(b), and 607(c). The paragraph also applies when a partner or person dissociated as a general partner suffers damage due to a contract of guaranty.

§ 806. Known Claims Against Dissolved Limited Partnership

(a) A dissolved limited partnership may dispose of the known claims against it by following the procedure described in subsection (b).

(b) A dissolved limited partnership may notify its known claimants of the dissolution in a record. The notice must:

(1) specify the information required to be included in a claim;

(2) provide a mailing address to which the claim is to be sent;

(3) state the deadline for receipt of the claim, which may not be less than 120 days after the date the notice is received by the claimant;

(4) state that the claim will be barred if not received by the deadline; and

(5) unless the limited partnership has been throughout its existence a limited liability limited partnership, state that the barring of a claim against the limited partnership will also bar any corresponding claim against any general partner or person dissociated as a general partner which is based on Section 404.

(c) A claim against a dissolved limited partnership is barred if the requirements of subsection (b) are met and:

(1) the claim is not received by the specified deadline; or

(2) in the case of a claim that is timely received but rejected by the dissolved limited partnership, the claimant does not commence an action to enforce the claim against the limited partnership within 90 days after the receipt of the notice of the rejection.

(d) This section does not apply to a claim based on an event occurring after the effective date of dissolution or a liability that is contingent on that date.

Comment

Source—ULLCA Section 807. See also RMBCA Section 14.06.

Paragraph (b)(5)—If the limited partnership has always been a limited liability limited partnership, there can be no liability under Section 404 for any general partner or person dissociated as a general partner.

§ 807. Other Claims Against Dissolved Limited Partnership

(a) A dissolved limited partnership may publish notice of its dissolution and request persons having claims against the limited partnership to present them in accordance with the notice.

(b) The notice must:

(1) be published at least once in a newspaper of general circulation in the [county] in which the dissolved limited partnership's principal office is located or, if it has none in this State, in the [county] in which the limited partnership's designated office is or was last located;

(2) describe the information required to be contained in a claim and provide a mailing address to which the claim is to be sent;

(3) state that a claim against the limited partnership is barred unless an action to enforce the claim is commenced within five years after publication of the notice; and

(4) unless the limited partnership has been throughout its existence a limited liability limited partnership, state that the barring of a claim against the limited partnership will also bar any corresponding claim against any general partner or person dissociated as a general partner which is based on Section 404.

(c) If a dissolved limited partnership publishes a notice in accordance with subsection (b), the claim of each of the following claimants is barred unless the claimant commences an action to enforce the claim against the dissolved limited partnership within five years after the publication date of the notice:

(1) a claimant that did not receive notice in a record under Section 806;

(2) a claimant whose claim was timely sent to the dissolved limited partnership but not acted on; and

(3) a claimant whose claim is contingent or based on an event occurring after the effective date of dissolution.

(d) A claim not barred under this section may be enforced:

(1) against the dissolved limited partnership, to the extent of its undistributed assets;

(2) if the assets have been distributed in liquidation, against a partner or transferee to the extent of that person's proportionate share of the claim or the limited partnership's assets distributed to the partner or transferee in liquidation, whichever is less, but a person's total liability for all claims under this paragraph does not exceed the total amount of assets distributed to the person as part of the winding up of the dissolved limited partnership; or

(3) against any person liable on the claim under Section 404.

Comment

Source—ULLCA Section 808. See also RMBCA Section 14.07.

Paragraph (b)(4)—If the limited partnership has always been a limited liability limited partnership, there can be no liability under Section 404 for any general partner or person dissociated as a general partner.

§ 808. Liability of General Partner and Person Dissociated as General Partner When Claim Against Limited Partnership Barred

If a claim against a dissolved limited partnership is barred under Section 806 or 807, any corresponding claim under Section 404 is also barred.

Comment

The liability under Section 404 of a general partner or person dissociated as a general partner is merely liability for the obligations of the limited partnership.

§ 809. Administrative Dissolution

(a) The [Secretary of State] may dissolve a limited partnership administratively if the limited partnership does not, within 60 days after the due date:

(1) pay any fee, tax, or penalty due to the [Secretary of State] under this [Act] or other law; or

(2) deliver its annual report to the [Secretary of State].

(b) If the [Secretary of State] determines that a ground exists for administratively dissolving a limited partnership, the [Secretary of State] shall file a record of the determination and serve the limited partnership with a copy of the filed record.

(c) If within 60 days after service of the copy the limited partnership does not correct each ground for dissolution or demonstrate to the reasonable satisfaction of the [Secretary of State] that each ground determined by the [Secretary of State] does not exist, the [Secretary of State] shall administratively dissolve the limited partnership by preparing, signing and filing a declaration of dissolution that states the grounds for dissolution. The [Secretary of State] shall serve the limited partnership with a copy of the filed declaration.

(d) A limited partnership administratively dissolved continues its existence but may carry on only activities necessary to wind up its activities and liquidate its assets under Sections 803 and 812 and to notify claimants under Sections 806 and 807.

(e) The administrative dissolution of a limited partnership does not terminate the authority of its agent for service of process.

Comment

Source—ULLCA Sections 809 and 810. See also RMBCA Sections 14.20 and 14.21.

Subsection (a)(1)—This provision refers solely to money due the specified filing officer and does not apply to other money due to the State.

Subsection (c)—The filing of a declaration of dissolution does not provide notice under Section 103(d).

§ 810. Reinstatement Following Administrative Dissolution

(a) A limited partnership that has been administratively dissolved may apply to the [Secretary of State] for reinstatement within two years after the effective date of dissolution. The application must be delivered to the [Secretary of State] for filing and state:

(1) the name of the limited partnership and the effective date of its administrative dissolution;

(2) that the grounds for dissolution either did not exist or have been eliminated; and

(3) that the limited partnership's name satisfies the requirements of Section 108.

(b) If the [Secretary of State] determines that an application contains the information required by subsection (a) and that the information is correct, the [Secretary of State] shall prepare a declaration of reinstatement that states this determination, sign, and file the original of the declaration of reinstatement, and serve the limited partnership with a copy.

(c) When reinstatement becomes effective, it relates back to and takes effect as of the effective date of the administrative dissolution and the limited partnership may resume its activities as if the administrative dissolution had never occurred.

Comment

Source—ULLCA Section 811. See also RMBCA Section 14.22.

§ 811. Appeal From Denial of Reinstatement

(a) If the [Secretary of State] denies a limited partnership's application for reinstatement following administrative dissolution, the [Secretary of State] shall prepare, sign and file a notice that explains the reason or reasons for denial and serve the limited partnership with a copy of the notice.

(b) Within 30 days after service of the notice of denial, the limited partnership may appeal from the denial of reinstatement by petitioning the [appropriate court] to set aside the dissolution. The petition must be served on the [Secretary of State] and contain a copy of the [Secretary of State's] declaration of dissolution, the limited partnership's application for reinstatement, and the [Secretary of State's] notice of denial.

(c) The court may summarily order the [Secretary of State] to reinstate the dissolved limited partnership or may take other action the court considers appropriate.

Comment

Source—ULLCA Section 812.

§ 812. Disposition of Assets; When Contributions Required

(a) In winding up a limited partnership's activities, the assets of the limited partnership, including the contributions required by this section, must be applied to satisfy the limited partnership's obligations to creditors, including, to the extent permitted by law, partners that are creditors.

(b) Any surplus remaining after the limited partnership complies with subsection (a) must be paid in cash as a distribution.

(c) If a limited partnership's assets are insufficient to satisfy all of its obligations under subsection (a), with respect to each unsatisfied obligation incurred when the limited partnership was not a limited liability limited partnership, the following rules apply:

(1) Each person that was a general partner when the obligation was incurred and that has not been released from the obligation under Section 607 shall contribute to the limited partnership for the purpose of enabling the limited partnership to satisfy the obligation. The contribution due from each of those persons is in proportion to the right to receive distributions in the capacity of general partner in effect for each of those persons when the obligation was incurred.

(2) If a person does not contribute the full amount required under paragraph (1) with respect to an unsatisfied obligation of the limited partnership, the other persons required to contribute by paragraph (1) on account of the obligation shall contribute the additional amount necessary to discharge the obligation. The additional contribution due from each of those other persons is in proportion to the right to receive distributions in the capacity of general partner in effect for each of those other persons when the obligation was incurred.

(3) If a person does not make the additional contribution required by paragraph (2), further additional contributions are determined and due in the same manner as provided in that paragraph.

(d) A person that makes an additional contribution under subsection (c)(2) or (3) may recover from any person whose failure to contribute under subsection (c)(1) or (2) necessitated the additional contribution. A person may not recover under this subsection more than the amount additionally contributed. A person's liability under this subsection may not exceed the amount the person failed to contribute.

(e) The estate of a deceased individual is liable for the person's obligations under this section.

(f) An assignee for the benefit of creditors of a limited partnership or a partner, or a person appointed by a court to represent creditors of a limited partnership or a partner, may enforce a person's obligation to contribute under subsection (c).

Comment

In some circumstances, this Act requires a partner to make payments to the limited partnership. See, e.g., Sections 502(b), 509(a), 509(b), and 812(c). In other circumstances, this Act requires a partner to make payments to other partners. See, e.g., Sections 509(c) and 812(d). In no circumstances does this Act require a partner to make a payment for the purpose of equalizing or otherwise reallocating capital losses incurred by partners.

Example: XYZ Limited Partnership ("XYZ") has one general partner and four limited partners. According to XYZ's required information, the value of each partner's contributions to XYZ are:

General partner–$5,000
Limited partner #1–$10,000
Limited partner #2–$15,000
Limited partner #3–$20,000
Limited partner #4–$25,000

XYZ is unsuccessful and eventually dissolves without ever having made a distribution to its partners. XYZ lacks any assets with which to return to the partners the value of their respective contributions. No partner is obliged to make any payment either to the limited partnership or to fellow partners to adjust these capital losses. These losses are not part of "the limited partnership's obligations to creditors." Section 812(a).

Example: Same facts, except that Limited Partner #4 loaned $25,000 to XYZ when XYZ was not a limited liability limited partnership, and XYZ lacks the assets to repay the loan. The general partner must contribute to the limited partnership whatever funds are necessary to enable XYZ to satisfy the obligation owned to Limited Partner #4 on account of the loan. Section 812(a) and (c).

Subsection (c)—Following RUPA and the UPA, this Act leaves to other law the question of when a limited partnership obligation is incurred.

[ARTICLE] 9. FOREIGN LIMITED PARTNERSHIPS

§ 901. Governing Law

(a) The laws of the State or other jurisdiction under which a foreign limited partnership is organized govern relations among the partners of the foreign limited partnership and between the partners and the foreign limited partnership and the liability of partners as partners for an obligation of the foreign limited partnership.

(b) A foreign limited partnership may not be denied a certificate of authority by reason of any difference between the laws of the jurisdiction under which the foreign limited partnership is organized and the laws of this State.

(c) A certificate of authority does not authorize a foreign limited partnership to engage in any business or exercise any power that a limited partnership may not engage in or exercise in this State.

Comment

Source—ULLCA Section 1001 for subsections (b) and (c).

Subsection (a)—This subsection parallels and is analogous in scope and effect to Section 106 (choice of law for domestic limited partnerships).

§ 902. Application for Certificate of Authority

(a) A foreign limited partnership may apply for a certificate of authority to transact business in this State by delivering an application to the [Secretary of State] for filing. The application must state:

(1) the name of the foreign limited partnership and, if the name does not comply with Section 108, an alternate name adopted pursuant to Section 905(a).

(2) the name of the State or other jurisdiction under whose law the foreign limited partnership is organized;

(3) the street and mailing address of the foreign limited partnership's principal office and, if the laws of the jurisdiction under which the foreign limited partnership is organized require the foreign limited partnership to maintain an office in that jurisdiction, the street and mailing address of the required office;

(4) the name and street and mailing address of the foreign limited partnership's initial agent for service of process in this State;

(5) the name and street and mailing address of each of the foreign limited partnership's general partners; and

(6) whether the foreign limited partnership is a foreign limited liability limited partnership.

(b) A foreign limited partnership shall deliver with the completed application a certificate of existence or a record of similar import signed by the [Secretary of State] or other official having custody of the foreign limited partnership's publicly filed records in the State or other jurisdiction under whose law the foreign limited partnership is organized.

Comment

Source—ULLCA Section 1002.

A certificate of authority applied for under this section is different than a certificate of authorization furnished under Section 209.

§ 903. Activities not Constituting Transacting Business

(a) Activities of a foreign limited partnership which do not constitute transacting business in this State within the meaning of this [article] include:

(1) maintaining, defending, and settling an action or proceeding;

(2) holding meetings of its partners or carrying on any other activity concerning its internal affairs;

(3) maintaining accounts in financial institutions;

(4) maintaining offices or agencies for the transfer, exchange, and registration of the foreign limited partnership's own securities or maintaining trustees or depositories with respect to those securities;

(5) selling through independent contractors;

(6) soliciting or obtaining orders, whether by mail or electronic means or through employees or agents or otherwise, if the orders require acceptance outside this State before they become contracts;

(7) creating or acquiring indebtedness, mortgages, or security interests in real or personal property;

(8) securing or collecting debts or enforcing mortgages or other security interests in property securing the debts, and holding, protecting, and maintaining property so acquired;

(9) conducting an isolated transaction that is completed within 30 days and is not one in the course of similar transactions of a like manner; and

(10) transacting business in interstate commerce.

(b) For purposes of this [article], the ownership in this State of income-producing real property or tangible personal property, other than property excluded under subsection (a), constitutes transacting business in this State.

(c) This section does not apply in determining the contacts or activities that may subject a foreign limited partnership to service of process, taxation, or regulation under any other law of this State.

Comment

Source—ULLCA Section 1003.

§ 904. Filing of Certificate of Authority

Unless the [Secretary of State] determines that an application for a certificate of authority does not comply with the filing requirements of this [Act], the [Secretary of State], upon payment of all filing fees, shall file the application, prepare, sign and file a certificate of authority to transact business in this state, and send a copy of the filed certificate, together with a receipt for the fees, to the foreign limited partnership or its representative.

Comment

Source—ULLCA Section 1004 and RULPA Section 903.

A certificate of authority filed under this section is different than a certificate of authorization furnished under Section 209.

§ 905. Noncomplying Name of Foreign Limited Partnership

(a) A foreign limited partnership whose name does not comply with Section 108 may not obtain a certificate of authority until it adopts, for the purpose of transacting business in this State, an alternate name that complies with Section 108. A foreign limited partnership that adopts an alternate name under this subsection and then obtains a certificate of authority with the name need not comply with [fictitious name statute]. After obtaining a certificate of authority with an alternate name, a foreign limited partnership shall transact business in this State under the name unless the foreign limited partnership is authorized under [fictitious name statute] to transact business in this State under another name.

(b) If a foreign limited partnership authorized to transact business in this State changes its name to one that does not comply with Section 108, it may not thereafter transact business in this State until it complies with subsection (a) and obtains an amended certificate of authority.

Comment

Source—ULLCA Section 1005.

§ 906. Revocation of Certificate of Authority

(a) A certificate of authority of a foreign limited partnership to transact business in this State may be revoked by the [Secretary of

State] in the manner provided in subsections (b) and (c) if the foreign limited partnership does not:

(1) pay, within 60 days after the due date, any fee, tax or penalty due to the [Secretary of State] under this [Act] or other law;

(2) deliver, within 60 days after the due date, its annual report required under Section 210;

(3) appoint and maintain an agent for service of process as required by Section 114(b); or

(4) deliver for filing a statement of a change under Section 115 within 30 days after a change has occurred in the name or address of the agent.

(b) In order to revoke a certificate of authority, the [Secretary of State] must prepare, sign, and file a notice of revocation and send a copy to the foreign limited partnership's agent for service of process in this State, or if the foreign limited partnership does not appoint and maintain a proper agent in this State, to the foreign limited partnership's designated office. The notice must state:

(1) the revocation's effective date, which must be at least 60 days after the date the [Secretary of State] sends the copy; and

(2) the foreign limited partnership's failures to comply with subsection (a) which are the reason for the revocation.

(c) The authority of the foreign limited partnership to transact business in this State ceases on the effective date of the notice of revocation unless before that date the foreign limited partnership cures each failure to comply with subsection (a) stated in the notice. If the foreign limited partnership cures the failures, the [Secretary of State] shall so indicate on the filed notice.

Comment

Source—ULLCA Section 1006.

§ 907. Cancellation of Certificate of Authority; Effect of Failure to Have Certificate

(a) In order to cancel its certificate of authority to transact business in this State, a foreign limited partnership must deliver to the [Secretary of State] for filing a notice of cancellation. The certificate is canceled when the notice becomes effective under Section 206.

(b) A foreign limited partnership transacting business in this State may not maintain an action or proceeding in this State unless it has a certificate of authority to transact business in this State.

(c) The failure of a foreign limited partnership to have a certificate of authority to transact business in this State does not impair the validity of a contract or act of the foreign limited partnership or prevent the foreign limited partnership from defending an action or proceeding in this State.

(d) A partner of a foreign limited partnership is not liable for the obligations of the foreign limited partnership solely by reason of the foreign limited partnership's having transacted business in this State without a certificate of authority.

(e) If a foreign limited partnership transacts business in this State without a certificate of authority or cancels its certificate of authority, it appoints the [Secretary of State] as its agent for service of process for rights of action arising out of the transaction of business in this State.

Comment

Source—RULPA Section 907(d); ULLCA Section 1008.

§ 908. Action by [Attorney General]

The [Attorney General] may maintain an action to restrain a foreign limited partnership from transacting business in this state in violation of this [article].

Comment

Source—RULPA Section 908; ULLCA Section 1009.

[ARTICLE] 10. ACTIONS BY PARTNERS

§ 1001. Direct Action by Partner

(a) Subject to subsection (b), a partner may maintain a direct action against the limited partnership or another partner for legal or equitable relief, with or without an accounting as to the partnership's activities, to enforce the rights and otherwise protect the interests of the partner, including rights and interests under the partnership agreement or this [Act] or arising independently of the partnership relationship.

(b) A partner commencing a direct action under this section is required to plead and prove an actual or threatened injury that is not solely the result of an injury suffered or threatened to be suffered by the limited partnership.

(c) The accrual of, and any time limitation on, a right of action for a remedy under this section is governed by other law. A right to an accounting upon a dissolution and winding up does not revive a claim barred by law.

Comment

Subsection (a)—Source: RUPA Section 405(b).

Subsection (b)—In ordinary contractual situations it is axiomatic that each party to a contract has standing to sue for breach of that contract. Within a limited partnership, however, different circumstances may exist. A partner does not have a direct claim against another partner merely because the other partner has breached the partnership agreement. Likewise a partner's violation of this Act does not automatically create a direct claim for every other partner. To have standing in his, her, or its own right, a partner plaintiff must be able to show a harm that occurs independently of the harm caused or threatened to be caused to the limited partnership.

The reference to "threatened" harm is intended to encompass claims for injunctive relief and does not relax standards for proving injury.

§ 1002. Derivative Action

A partner may maintain a derivative action to enforce a right of a limited partnership if:

(1) the partner first makes a demand on the general partners, requesting that they cause the limited partnership to bring an action to enforce the right, and the general partners do not bring the action within a reasonable time; or

(2) a demand would be futile.

Comment

Source—RULPA Section 1001.

§ 1003. Proper Plaintiff

A derivative action may be maintained only by a person that is a partner at the time the action is commenced and:

(1) that was a partner when the conduct giving rise to the action occurred; or

(2) whose status as a partner devolved upon the person by operation of law or pursuant to the terms of the partnership agreement from a person that was a partner at the time of the conduct.

Comment

Source—RULPA Section 1002.

§ 1004. Pleading

In a derivative action, the complaint must state with particularity:

(1) the date and content of plaintiff's demand and the general partners' response to the demand; or

(2) why demand should be excused as futile.

Comment

Source—RULPA Section 1003.

§ 1005. Proceeds and Expenses

(a) Except as otherwise provided in subsection (b):

(1) any proceeds or other benefits of a derivative action, whether by judgment, compromise, or settlement, belong to the limited partnership and not to the derivative plaintiff;

(2) if the derivative plaintiff receives any proceeds, the derivative plaintiff shall immediately remit them to the limited partnership.

(b) If a derivative action is successful in whole or in part, the court may award the plaintiff reasonable expenses, including reasonable attorney's fees, from the recovery of the limited partnership.

Comment

Source—RULPA Section 1004.

[ARTICLE] 11. CONVERSION AND MERGER

§ 1101. Definitions

In this [article]:

(1) "Constituent limited partnership" means a constituent organization that is a limited partnership.

(2) "Constituent organization" means an organization that is party to a merger.

(3) "Converted organization" means the organization into which a converting organization converts pursuant to Sections 1102 through 1105.

(4) "Converting limited partnership" means a converting organization that is a limited partnership.

(5) "Converting organization" means an organization that converts into another organization pursuant to Section 1102.

(6) "General partner" means a general partner of a limited partnership.

(7) "Governing statute" of an organization means the statute that governs the organization's internal affairs.

(8) "Organization" means a general partnership, including a limited liability partnership; limited partnership, including a limited liability

limited partnership; limited liability company; business trust; corporation; or any other person having a governing statute. The term includes domestic and foreign organizations whether or not organized for profit.

(9) "Organizational documents" means:

(A) for a domestic or foreign general partnership, its partnership agreement;

(B) for a limited partnership or foreign limited partnership, its certificate of limited partnership and partnership agreement;

(C) for a domestic or foreign limited liability company, its articles of organization and operating agreement, or comparable records as provided in its governing statute;

(D) for a business trust, its agreement of trust and declaration of trust;

(E) for a domestic or foreign corporation for profit, its articles of incorporation, bylaws, and other agreements among its shareholders which are authorized by its governing statute, or comparable records as provided in its governing statute; and

(F) for any other organization, the basic records that create the organization and determine its internal governance and the relations among the persons that own it, have an interest in it, or are members of it.

(10) "Personal liability" means personal liability for a debt, liability, or other obligation of an organization which is imposed on a person that co-owns, has an interest in, or is a member of the organization:

(A) by the organization's governing statute solely by reason of the person co-owning, having an interest in, or being a member of the organization; or

(B) by the organization's organizational documents under a provision of the organization's governing statute authorizing those documents to make one or more specified persons liable for all or specified debts, liabilities, and other obligations of the organization solely by reason of the person or persons co-owning, having an interest in, or being a member of the organization.

(11) "Surviving organization" means an organization into which one or more other organizations are merged. A surviving organization may preexist the merger or be created by the merger.

Comment

This section contains definitions specific to this Article.

§ 1102. Conversion

(a) An organization other than a limited partnership may convert to a limited partnership, and a limited partnership may convert to another organization pursuant to this section and Sections 1103 through 1105 and a plan of conversion, if:

(1) the other organization's governing statute authorizes the conversion;

(2) the conversion is not prohibited by the law of the jurisdiction that enacted the governing statute; and

(3) the other organization complies with its governing statute in effecting the conversion.

(b) A plan of conversion must be in a record and must include:

(1) the name and form of the organization before conversion;

(2) the name and form of the organization after conversion; and

(3) the terms and conditions of the conversion, including the manner and basis for converting interests in the converting organization into any combination of money, interests in the converted organization, and other consideration; and

(4) the organizational documents of the converted organization.

Comment

In a statutory conversion an existing entity changes its form, the jurisdiction of its governing statute or both. For example, a limited partnership organized under the laws of one jurisdiction might convert to:

- a limited liability company (or other form of entity) organized under the laws of the same jurisdiction,
- a limited liability company (or other form of entity) organized under the laws of another jurisdiction, or
- a limited partnership organized under the laws of another jurisdiction (referred to in some statutes as "domestication").

In contrast to a merger, which involves at least two entities, a conversion involves only one. The converting and converted organization are the same entity. See Section 1105(a). For this Act to apply to a conversion, either the converting or converted organization must be a limited partnership subject to this Act. If the converting organization is a limited partnership subject to this Act, the partners of the converting organization are subject to the duties and obligations stated in this Act, including Sections 304 (informational rights of limited partners), 305(b) (limited partner's obligation of good faith and fair dealing), 407 (informational rights of general partners), and 408 (general partner duties).

Subsection (a)(2)—Given the very broad definition of "organization," Section 1101(8), this Act authorizes conversions involving nonprofit organizations. This provision is intended as an additional safeguard for that context.

Subsection (b)(3)—A plan of conversion may provide that some persons with interests in the converting organization will receive interests in the converted organization while other persons with interests in the converting organization will receive some other form of consideration. Thus, a "squeeze out" conversion is possible. As noted above, if the converting organization is a limited partnership subject to this Act, the partners of the converting organization are subject to the duties and obligations stated in this Act. Those duties would apply to the process and terms under which a squeeze out conversion occurs.

If the converting organization is a limited partnership, the plan of conversion will determine the fate of any interests held by mere transferees. This Act does not state any duty or obligation owed by a converting limited partnership or its partners to mere transferees. That issue is a matter for other law.

§ 1103. Action on Plan of Conversion by Converting Limited Partnership

(a) Subject to Section 1110, a plan of conversion must be consented to by all the partners of a converting limited partnership.

(b) Subject to Section 1110 and any contractual rights, after a conversion is approved, and at any time before a filing is made under Section 1104, a converting limited partnership may amend the plan or abandon the planned conversion:

(1) as provided in the plan; and

(2) except as prohibited by the plan, by the same consent as was required to approve the plan.

Comment

Section 1110 imposes special consent requirements for transactions which might cause a partner to have "personal liability," as defined in Section 1101(10) for entity debts. The partnership agreement may not restrict the rights provided by Section 1110. See Section 110(b)(12).

Subsection (a)—Like many of the rules stated in this Act, this subsection's requirement of unanimous consent is a default rule. Subject only to Section 1110, the partnership agreement may state a different quantum of consent or provide a completely different approval mechanism. Varying this subsection's rule means that a partner might be subject to a conversion (including a "squeeze out" conversion) without consent and with no appraisal remedy. If the converting organization is a limited partnership subject to this Act, the partners of the converting organization are subject to the duties and obligations stated in this Act. Those duties would apply to the process and terms under which the conversion occurs. However, if the partnership agreement allows for a conversion with less than unanimous consent, the mere fact a partner objects to a conversion does not mean that the partners favoring, arranging, consenting to or effecting the conversation have breached a duty under this Act.

§ 1104. Filings Required for Conversion; Effective Date

(a) After a plan of conversion is approved:

(1) a converting limited partnership shall deliver to the [Secretary of State] for filing articles of conversion, which must include:

(A) a statement that the limited partnership has been converted into another organization;

(B) the name and form of the organization and the jurisdiction of its governing statute;

(C) the date the conversion is effective under the governing statute of the converted organization;

(D) a statement that the conversion was approved as required by this [Act];

(E) a statement that the conversion was approved as required by the governing statute of the converted organization; and

(F) if the converted organization is a foreign organization not authorized to transact business in this State, the street and mailing address of an office which the [Secretary of State] may use for the purposes of Section 1105(c); and

(2) if the converting organization is not a converting limited partnership, the converting organization shall deliver to the [Secretary of State] for filing a certificate of limited partnership, which must include, in addition to the information required by Section 201:

(A) a statement that the limited partnership was converted from another organization;

(B) the name and form of the organization and the jurisdiction of its governing statute; and

(C) a statement that the conversion was approved in a manner that complied with the organization's governing statute.

(b) A conversion becomes effective:

(1) if the converted organization is a limited partnership, when the certificate of limited partnership takes effect; and

(2) if the converted organization is not a limited partnership, as provided by the governing statute of the converted organization.

Comment

Subsection (b)—The effective date of a conversion is determined under the governing statute of the converted organization.

§ 1105. Effect of Conversion

(a) An organization that has been converted pursuant to this [article] is for all purposes the same entity that existed before the conversion.

(b) When a conversion takes effect:

(1) all property owned by the converting organization remains vested in the converted organization;

(2) all debts, liabilities, and other obligations of the converting organization continue as obligations of the converted organization;

(3) an action or proceeding pending by or against the converting organization may be continued as if the conversion had not occurred;

(4) except as prohibited by other law, all of the rights, privileges, immunities, powers, and purposes of the converting organization remain vested in the converted organization;

(5) except as otherwise provided in the plan of conversion, the terms and conditions of the plan of conversion take effect; and

(6) except as otherwise agreed, the conversion does not dissolve a converting limited partnership for the purposes of [Article] 8.

(c) A converted organization that is a foreign organization consents to the jurisdiction of the courts of this State to enforce any obligation owed by the converting limited partnership, if before the conversion the converting limited partnership was subject to suit in this State on the obligation. A converted organization that is a foreign organization and not authorized to transact business in this State appoints the [Secretary of State] as its agent for service of process for purposes of enforcing an obligation under this subsection. Service on the [Secretary of State] under this subsection is made in the same manner and with the same consequences as in Section 117(c) and (d).

Comment

Subsection (a)—A conversion changes an entity's legal type, but does not create a new entity.

Subsection (b)—Unlike a merger, a conversion involves a single entity, and the conversion therefore does not transfer any of the entity's rights or obligations.

§ 1106. Merger

(a) A limited partnership may merge with one or more other constituent organizations pursuant to this section and Sections 1107 through 1109 and a plan of merger, if:

(1) the governing statute of each the other organizations authorizes the merger;

(2) the merger is not prohibited by the law of a jurisdiction that enacted any of those governing statutes; and

(3) each of the other organizations complies with its governing statute in effecting the merger.

(b) A plan of merger must be in a record and must include:

(1) the name and form of each constituent organization;

(2) the name and form of the surviving organization and, if the surviving organization is to be created by the merger, a statement to that effect;

(3) the terms and conditions of the merger, including the manner and basis for converting the interests in each constituent organization into any combination of money, interests in the surviving organization, and other consideration;

(4) if the surviving organization is to be created by the merger, the surviving organization's organizational documents; and

(5) if the surviving organization is not to be created by the merger, any amendments to be made by the merger to the surviving organization's organizational documents.

Comment

For this Act to apply to a merger, at least one of the constituent organizations must be a limited partnership subject to this Act. The partners of any such limited partnership are subject to the duties and obligations stated in this Act, including Sections 304 (informational rights of limited partners), 305(b) (limited partner's obligation of good faith and fair dealing), 407 (informational rights of general partners), and 408 (general partner duties).

Subsection (a)(2)—Given the very broad definition of "organization," Section 1101(8), this Act authorizes mergers involving non-profit organizations. This provision is intended as an additional safeguard for that context.

Subsection (b)(3)—A plan of merger may provide that some persons with interests in a constituent organization will receive interests in the surviving organization, while other persons with interests in the same constituent organization will receive some other form of consideration. Thus, a "squeeze out" merger is possible. As noted above, the duties and obligations stated in this Act apply to the partners of a constituent organization that is a limited partnership subject to this Act. Those duties would apply to the process and terms under which a squeeze out merger occurs.

If a constituent organization is a limited partnership, the plan of merger will determine the fate of any interests held by mere transferees. This Act does not state any duty or obligation owed by a constituent limited partnership or its partners to mere transferees. That issue is a matter for other law.

§ 1107. Action on Plan of Merger by Constituent Limited Partnership

(a) Subject to Section 1110, a plan of merger must be consented to by all the partners of a constituent limited partnership.

(b) Subject to Section 1110 and any contractual rights, after a merger is approved, and at any time before a filing is made under Section 1108, a constituent limited partnership may amend the plan or abandon the planned merger:

(1) as provided in the plan; and

(2) except as prohibited by the plan, with the same consent as was required to approve the plan.

Comment

Section 1110 imposes special consent requirements for transactions which might make a partner personally liable for entity debts. The partnership agreement may not restrict the rights provided by Section 1110. See Section 110(b)(12).

Subsection (a)—Like many of the rules stated in this Act, this subsection's requirement of unanimous consent is a default rule. Subject only to Section 1110, the partnership agreement may state a different quantum of consent or provide a completely different approval mechanism. Varying this subsection's rule means that a partner might be subject to a merger (including a "squeeze out" merger) without consent and with no appraisal remedy. The partners of a constituent limited partnership are subject to the duties and obligations stated in this Act, and those duties would apply to the process and terms under which the merger occurs. However, if the partnership agreement allows for a merger with less than unanimous consent, the mere fact a partner objects to a merger does not mean that the partners favoring, arranging, consenting to or effecting the merger have breached a duty under this Act.

§ 1108. Filings Required for Merger; Effective Date

(a) After each constituent organization has approved a merger, articles of merger must be signed on behalf of:

(1) each preexisting constituent limited partnership, by each general partner listed in the certificate of limited partnership; and

(2) each other preexisting constituent organization, by an authorized representative.

(b) The articles of merger must include:

(1) the name and form of each constituent organization and the jurisdiction of its governing statute;

(2) the name and form of the surviving organization, the jurisdiction of its governing statute, and, if the surviving organization is created by the merger, a statement to that effect;

(3) the date the merger is effective under the governing statute of the surviving organization;

(4) if the surviving organization is to be created by the merger:

(A) if it will be a limited partnership, the limited partnership's certificate of limited partnership; or

(B) if it will be an organization other than a limited partnership, the organizational document that creates the organization;

(5) if the surviving organization preexists the merger, any amendments provided for in the plan of merger for the organizational document that created the organization;

(6) a statement as to each constituent organization that the merger was approved as required by the organization's governing statute;

(7) if the surviving organization is a foreign organization not authorized to transact business in this State, the street and mailing address of an office which the [Secretary of State] may use for the purposes of Section 1109(b); and

(8) any additional information required by the governing statute of any constituent organization.

(c) Each constituent limited partnership shall deliver the articles of merger for filing in the [office of the Secretary of State].

(d) A merger becomes effective under this [article]:

(1) if the surviving organization is a limited partnership, upon the later of:

(i) compliance with subsection (c); or

(ii) subject to Section 206(c), as specified in the articles of merger; or

(2) if the surviving organization is not a limited partnership, as provided by the governing statute of the surviving organization.

Comment

Subsection (b)—The effective date of a merger is determined under the governing statute of the surviving organization.

§ 1109. Effect of Merger

(a) When a merger becomes effective:

(1) the surviving organization continues or comes into existence;

(2) each constituent organization that merges into the surviving organization ceases to exist as a separate entity;

(3) all property owned by each constituent organization that ceases to exist vests in the surviving organization;

(4) all debts, liabilities, and other obligations of each constituent organization that ceases to exist continue as obligations of the surviving organization;

(5) an action or proceeding pending by or against any constituent organization that ceases to exist may be continued as if the merger had not occurred;

(6) except as prohibited by other law, all of the rights, privileges, immunities, powers, and purposes of each constituent organization that ceases to exist vest in the surviving organization;

(7) except as otherwise provided in the plan of merger, the terms and conditions of the plan of merger take effect; and

(8) except as otherwise agreed, if a constituent limited partnership ceases to exist, the merger does not dissolve the limited partnership for the purposes of [Article] 8;

(9) if the surviving organization is created by the merger:

(A) if it is a limited partnership, the certificate of limited partnership becomes effective; or

(B) if it is an organization other than a limited partnership, the organizational document that creates the organization becomes effective; and

(10) if the surviving organization preexists the merger, any amendments provided for in the articles of merger for the organizational document that created the organization become effective.

(b) A surviving organization that is a foreign organization consents to the jurisdiction of the courts of this State to enforce any obligation owed by a constituent organization, if before the merger the constituent organization was subject to suit in this State on the obligation. A surviving organization that is a foreign organization and not authorized to transact business in this State appoints the [Secretary of State] as its agent for service of process for the purposes of enforcing an obligation under this subsection. Service on the [Secretary of State] under this subsection is made in the same manner and with the same consequences as in Section 117(c) and (d).

§ 1110. Restrictions on Approval of Conversions and Mergers and on Relinquishing LLLP Status

(a) If a partner of a converting or constituent limited partnership will have personal liability with respect to a converted or surviving organization, approval and amendment of a plan of conversion or merger are ineffective without the consent of the partner, unless:

(1) the limited partnership's partnership agreement provides for the approval of the conversion or merger with the consent of fewer than all the partners; and

(2) the partner has consented to the provision of the partnership agreement.

(b) An amendment to a certificate of limited partnership which deletes a statement that the limited partnership is a limited liability limited partnership is ineffective without the consent of each general partner unless:

(1) the limited partnership's partnership agreement provides for the amendment with the consent of less than all the general partners; and

(2) each general partner that does not consent to the amendment has consented to the provision of the partnership agreement.

(c) A partner does not give the consent required by subsection (a) or (b) merely by consenting to a provision of the partnership agreement which permits the partnership agreement to be amended with the consent of fewer than all the partners.

Comment

This section imposes special consent requirements for transactions that might make a partner personally liable for entity debts. The partnership agreement may not restrict the rights provided by this section. See Section 110(b)(12).

Subsection (c)—This subsection prevents circumvention of the consent requirements of subsections (a) and (b).

Example: As initially ... consented to, the partnership agreement of a limited partnership leaves in place the Act's rule requiring unanimous consent for a conversion or merger. The partnership agreement does provide, however, that the agreement may be amended with the affirmative vote of general partners owning 2/3 of the rights to receive distributions as general partners and of limited partners owning 2/3 of the rights to receive distributions as limited partners. The required vote is obtained for an amendment that permits approval of a conversion or merger by the same vote necessary to amend the partnership agreement. Partner X votes for the amendment. Partner Y votes against. Partner Z does not vote.

Subsequently the limited partnership proposes to convert to a limited partnership (not an LLLP) organized under the laws of another state, with Partners X, Y and Z each receiving interests as general partners. Under the amended partnership agreement, approval of the conversion does not require unanimous consent. However, since after the conversion, Partners X, Y and Z will each have "personal liability with respect to [the] converted ... organization," Section 1110(a) applies.

As a result, the approval of the plan of conversion will require the consent of Partner Y and Partner Z. They did not consent to the amendment that provided for non-unanimous approval of a conversion or merger. Their initial consent to the partnership agreement, with its provision permitting non-unanimous consent for amendments, does not satisfy the consent requirement of Subsection 1110(a)(2).

In contrast, Partner X's consent is not required. Partner X lost its Section 1110(a) veto right by consenting directly to the amendment to the partnership agreement which permitted non-unanimous consent to a conversion or merger.

§ 1111. Liability of General Partner After Conversion or Merger

(a) A conversion or merger under this [article] does not discharge any liability under Sections 404 and 607 of a person that was a general partner in or dissociated as a general partner from a converting or constituent limited partnership, but:

(1) the provisions of this [Act] pertaining to the collection or discharge of the liability continue to apply to the liability;

(2) for the purposes of applying those provisions, the converted or surviving organization is deemed to be the converting or constituent limited partnership; and

(3) if a person is required to pay any amount under this subsection:

(A) the person has a right of contribution from each other person that was liable as a general partner under Section 404 when the obligation was incurred and has not been released from the obligation under Section 607; and

(B) the contribution due from each of those persons is in proportion to the right to receive distributions in the capacity of general partner in effect for each of those persons when the obligation was incurred.

(b) In addition to any other liability provided by law:

(1) a person that immediately before a conversion or merger became effective was a general partner in a converting or constituent limited partnership that was not a limited liability limited partnership is personally liable for each obligation of the converted or surviving organization arising from a transaction with a third party after the conversion or merger becomes effective, if, at the time the third party enters into the transaction, the third party:

(A) does not have notice of the conversion or merger; and

(B) reasonably believes that:

(i) the converted or surviving business is the converting or constituent limited partnership;

(ii) the converting or constituent limited partnership is not a limited liability limited partnership; and

(iii) the person is a general partner in the converting or constituent limited partnership; and

(2) a person that was dissociated as a general partner from a converting or constituent limited partnership before the conversion or merger became effective is personally liable for each obligation of the converted or surviving organization arising from a transaction with a third party after the conversion or merger becomes effective, if:

(A) immediately before the conversion or merger became effective the converting or surviving limited partnership was a not a limited liability limited partnership; and

(B) at the time the third party enters into the transaction less than two years have passed since the person dissociated as a general partner and the third party:

(i) does not have notice of the dissociation;

(ii) does not have notice of the conversion or merger; and

(iii) reasonably believes that the converted or surviving organization is the converting or constituent limited partnership, the converting or constituent limited partnership is not a limited liability limited partnership, and the person is a general partner in the converting or constituent limited partnership.

Comment

This section extrapolates the approach of Section 607 into the context of a conversion or merger involving a limited partnership.

Subsection (a)—This subsection pertains to general partner liability for obligations which a limited partnership incurred before a conversion or merger. Following RUPA and the UPA, this Act leaves to other law the question of when a limited partnership obligation is incurred.

If the converting or constituent limited partnership was a limited liability limited partnership at all times before the conversion or merger, this subsection will not apply because no person will have any liability under Section 404 or 607.

Subsection (b)—This subsection pertains to entity obligations incurred after a conversion or merger and creates lingering exposure to personal liability for general partners and persons previously dissociated as general partners. In contrast to subsection (a)(3), this subsection does not provide for contribution among persons personally liable under this section for the same entity obligation. That issue is left for other law.

Subsection (b)(1)—If the converting or constituent limited partnership was a limited liability limited partnership immediately before the conversion or merger, there is no lingering exposure to personal liability under this subsection.

Subsection (b)(1)(A)—A person might have notice under Section 103(d)(4) or (5) as well as under Section 103(b).

Subsection (b)(2)(B)(i)—A person might have notice under Section 103(d)(1) as well as under Section 103(b).

Subsection (b)(2)(B)(ii)—A person might have notice under Section 103(d)(4) or (5) as well as under Section 103(b).

§ 1112. Power of General Partners and Persons Dissociated as General Partners to Bind Organization After Conversion or Merger

(a) An act of a person that immediately before a conversion or merger became effective was a general partner in a converting or constituent limited partnership binds the converted or surviving organization after the conversion or merger becomes effective, if:

(1) before the conversion or merger became effective, the act would have bound the converting or constituent limited partnership under Section 402; and

(2) at the time the third party enters into the transaction, the third party:

(A) does not have notice of the conversion or merger; and

(B) reasonably believes that the converted or surviving business is the converting or constituent limited partnership and that the person is a general partner in the converting or constituent limited partnership.

(b) An act of a person that before a conversion or merger became effective was dissociated as a general partner from a converting or constituent limited partnership binds the converted or surviving organization after the conversion or merger becomes effective, if:

(1) before the conversion or merger became effective, the act would have bound the converting or constituent limited partnership under Section 402 if the person had been a general partner; and

(2) at the time the third party enters into the transaction, less than two years have passed since the person dissociated as a general partner and the third party:

(A) does not have notice of the dissociation;

(B) does not have notice of the conversion or merger; and

(C) reasonably believes that the converted or surviving organization is the converting or constituent limited partnership and that the person is a general partner in the converting or constituent limited partnership.

(c) If a person having knowledge of the conversion or merger causes a converted or surviving organization to incur an obligation under subsection (a) or (b), the person is liable:

(1) to the converted or surviving organization for any damage caused to the organization arising from the obligation; and

(2) if another person is liable for the obligation, to that other person for any damage caused to that other person arising from the liability.

Comment

This section extrapolates the approach of Section 606 into the context of a conversion or merger involving a limited partnership.

Subsection (a)(2)(A)—A person might have notice under Section 103(d)(4) or (5) as well as under Section 103(b).

Subsection (b)(2)(A)—A person might have notice under Section 103(d)(1) as well as under Section 103(b).

Subsection (b)(2)(B)—A person might have notice under Section 103(d)(4) or (5) as well as under Section 103(b).

§ 1113. [Article] not Exclusive

This [article] does not preclude an entity from being converted or merged under other law.

[ARTICLE] 12. MISCELLANEOUS PROVISIONS

§ 1201. Uniformity of Application and Construction

In applying and construing this Uniform Act, consideration must be given to the need to promote uniformity of the law with respect to its subject matter among States that enact it.

§ 1202. Severability Clause

If any provision of this [Act] or its application to any person or circumstance is held invalid, the invalidity does not affect other provisions or applications of this [Act] which can be given effect without the invalid provision or application, and to this end the provisions of this [Act] are severable.

§ 1203. Relation to Electronic Signatures in Global and National Commerce Act

This [Act] modifies, limits, or supersedes the federal Electronic Signatures in Global and National Commerce Act, 15 U.S.C. Section 7001 et seq., but this [Act] does not modify, limit, or supersede Section 101(c) of that Act or authorize electronic delivery of any of the notices described in Section 103(b) of that act.

§ 1204. Effective Date

This [Act] takes effect [effective date].

Comment

Section 1206 specifies how this Act affects domestic limited partnerships, with special provisions pertaining to domestic limited partnerships formed before the Act's effective date. Section 1206 contains no comparable provisions for foreign limited partnerships. Therefore, once this Act is effective, it applies immediately to all foreign limited partnerships, whether formed before or after the Act's effective date.

§ 1205. Repeals

Effective [all-inclusive date], the following acts and parts of acts are repealed: [the State Limited Partnership Act as amended and in effect immediately before the effective date of this [Act]].

§ 1206. Application to Existing Relationships

(a) Before [all-inclusive date], this [Act] governs only:

(1) a limited partnership formed on or after [the effective date of this [Act]]; and

(2) except as otherwise provided in subsections (c) and (d), a limited partnership formed before [the effective date of this [Act]] which elects, in the manner provided in its partnership agreement or by law for amending the partnership agreement, to be subject to this [Act].

(b) Except as otherwise provided in subsection (c), on and after [all-inclusive date] this [Act] governs all limited partnerships.

(c) With respect to a limited partnership formed before [the effective date of this [Act]], the following rules apply except as the partners otherwise elect in the manner provided in the partnership agreement or by law for amending the partnership agreement:

(1) Section 104(c) does not apply and the limited partnership has whatever duration it had under the law applicable immediately before [the effective date of this [Act]].

(2) the limited partnership is not required to amend its certificate of limited partnership to comply with Section 201(a)(4).

(3) Sections 601 and 602 do not apply and a limited partner has the same right and power to dissociate from the limited partnership, with the same consequences, as existed immediately before [the effective date of this [Act]].

(4) Section 603(4) does not apply.

(5) Section 603(5) does not apply and a court has the same power to expel a general partner as the court had immediately before [the effective date of this [Act]].

(6) Section 801(3) does not apply and the connection between a person's dissociation as a general partner and the dissolution of the limited partnership is the same as existed immediately before [the effective date of this [Act]].

(d) With respect to a limited partnership that elects pursuant to subsection (a)(2) to be subject to this [Act], after the election takes effect the provisions of this [Act] relating to the liability of the limited partnership's general partners to third parties apply:

(1) before [all-inclusive date], to:

(A) a third party that had not done business with the limited partnership in the year before the election took effect; and

(B) a third party that had done business with the limited partnership in the year before the election took effect only if the third party knows or has received a notification of the election; and

(2) on and after [all-inclusive date], to all third parties, but those provisions remain inapplicable to any obligation incurred while those provisions were inapplicable under paragraph (1)(B).

Legislative Note: In a State that has previously amended its existing limited partnership statute to provide for limited liability limited partnerships (LLLPs), this Act should include transition provisions specifically applicable to preexisting limited liability limited partnerships. The precise wording of those provisions must depend on the wording of the State's previously enacted LLLP provisions. However, the following principles apply generally:

1. In Sections 806(b)(5) and 807(b)(4) (notice by dissolved limited partnership to claimants), the phrase "the limited partnership has been throughout its existence a limited liability limited partnership" should be revised to encompass a limited partnership that was a limited liability limited partnership under the State's previously enacted LLLP provisions.

2. Section 1206(d) should provide that, if a preexisting limited liability limited partnership elects to be subject to this Act, this Act's provisions relating to the liability of general partners to third parties apply immediately to all third parties, regardless of whether a third party has previously done business with the limited liability limited partnership.

3. A preexisting limited liability limited partnership that elects to be subject to this Act should have to comply with Sections 201(a)(4) (requiring the certificate of limited partnership to state whether the limited partnership is a limited liability limited partnership) and 108(c) (establishing name requirements for a limited liability limited partnership).

4. As for Section 1206(b) (providing that, after a transition period, this Act applies to all preexisting limited partnerships):

a. if a State's previously enacted LLLP provisions have requirements essentially the same as Sections 201(a)(4) and 108(c), preexisting limited liability limited partnerships should automatically retain LLLP status under this Act.

b. if a State's previously enacted LLLP provisions have name requirements essentially the same as Section 108(c) and provide that a public filing other than the certificate of limited partnership establishes a limited partnership's status as a limited liability limited partnership:

i. that filing can be deemed to an amendment to the certificate of limited partnership to comply with Section 201(a)(4), and

ii. preexisting limited liability limited partnerships should automatically retain LLLP status under this Act.

c. if a State's previously enacted LLLP provisions do not have name requirements essentially the same as Section 108(c), it will be impossible both to enforce Section 108(c) and provide for automatic transition to LLLP status under this Act.

Comment

Source: RUPA Section 1206.

This section pertains exclusively to domestic limited partnerships–i.e., to limited partnerships formed under this Act or a predecessor statute enacted by the same jurisdiction. For foreign limited partnerships, see the Comment to Section 1204.

This Act governs all limited partnerships formed on or after the Act's effective date. As for pre-existing limited partnerships, this section establishes an optional "elect in" period and a mandatory, all-inclusive date. The "elect in" period runs from the effective date, stated in Section 1204, until the all-inclusive date, stated in both subsection(a) and (b).

During the "elect in" period, a pre-existing limited partnership may elect to become subject to this Act. Subsection (d) states certain important consequences for a limited partnership that elects in. Beginning on the all-inclusive date, each pre-existing limited partnership that has not previously elected in becomes subject to this Act by operation of law.

Subsection (c)—This subsection specifies six provisions of this Act which never automatically apply to any pre-existing limited partnership. Except for subsection (c)(2), the list refers to provisions governing the relationship of the partners *inter se* and considered too different than predecessor law to be fairly applied to a preexisting limited partnership without the consent of its partners. Each of these *inter se* provisions is subject to change in the partnership agreement. However, many pre-existing limited partnerships may have taken for granted the analogous provisions of predecessor law and may therefore not have addressed the issues in their partnership agreements.

Subsection (c)(1)—Section 104(c) provides that a limited partnership has a perpetual duration.

Subsection (c)(2)—Section 201(a)(4) requires the certificate of limited partnership to state "whether the limited partnership is a limited liability limited partnership." The requirement is intended to force the organizers of a limited partnership to decide whether the limited partnership is to be an LLLP and therefore is inapposite to pre-existing limited partnerships. Moreover, applying the requirement to pre-existing limited partnerships would create a significant administrative burden both for limited partnerships and the filing officer and probably would result in many pre-existing limited partnerships being in violation of the requirement.

Subsection (c)(3)—Section 601 and 602 concern a person's dissociation as a limited partner.

Subsection (c)(4)—Section 603(4) provides for the expulsion of a general partner by the unanimous consent of the other partners in specified circumstances.

Subsection (c)(5)—Section 603(5) provides for the expulsion of a general partner by a court in specified circumstances.

Subsection (c)(6)—Section 801(3) concerns the continuance or dissolution of a limited partnership following a person's dissociation as a general partner.

Subsection (d)—Following RUPA Section 1206(c), this subsection limits the efficacy of the Act's liability protections for partners of an "electing in" limited partnership. The limitation:

- applies only to the benefit of "a third party that had done business with the limited partnership in the year before the election took effect," and
- ceases to apply when "the third party knows or has received a notification of the election" or on the "all-inclusive" date, whichever occurs first.

If the limitation causes a provision of this Act to be inapplicable with regard to a third party, the comparable provision of predecessor law applies.

Example: A pre-existing limited partnership elects to be governed by this Act before the "all-inclusive" date. Two months before the election, Third Party provided services to the limited partnership. Third Party neither knows nor has received a notification of the election. Until the "all inclusive" date, with regard to Third Party, Section 303's full liability shield does not apply to each limited partner. Instead, each limited partner has the liability shield applicable under predecessor law.

Subsection (d)(2)—To the extent subsection (d) causes a provision of this Act to be inapplicable when an obligation is incurred, the inapplicability continues as to that obligation even after the "all inclusive" date.

§ 1207. Savings Clause

This [Act] does not affect an action commenced, proceeding brought, or right accrued before this [Act] takes effect.

DELAWARE REVISED UNIFORM LIMITED PARTNERSHIP ACT

(Delaware Code, Title 6, Chapter 17)

Table of Sections

SUBCHAPTER I. GENERAL PROVISIONS

SUBCHAPTER II. FORMATION; CERTIFICATE OF LIMITED PARTNERSHIP

SUBCHAPTER VII. ASSIGNMENT OF PARTNERSHIP INTERESTS

SUBCHAPTER VIII. DISSOLUTION

SUBCHAPTER IX. FOREIGN LIMITED PARTNERSHIPS

SUBCHAPTER X. DERIVATIVE ACTIONS

SUBCHAPTER XI. MISCELLANEOUS

SUBCHAPTER I. GENERAL PROVISIONS

§ 17–101. Definitions

As used in this chapter unless the context otherwise requires:

(1) "Certificate of limited partnership" means the certificate referred to in § 17–201 of this title, and the certificate as amended.

(2) "Contribution" means any cash, property, services rendered or a promissory note or other obligation to contribute cash or property or to perform services, which a partner contributes to a limited partnership in the capacity as a partner.

(3) "Event of withdrawal of a general partner" means an event that causes a person to cease to be a general partner as provided in § 17–402 of this title.

(4) "Foreign limited partnership" includes a partnership formed under the laws of any state or under the laws of any foreign country or other foreign jurisdiction and having as partners 1 or more general partners and 1 or more limited partners.

(5) "General partner" means a person who has been admitted to a limited partnership as a general partner in accordance with the partnership agreement and so named in the certificate of limited partnership or similar instrument under which the limited partnership is organized if so required.

(6) "Knowledge" means a person's actual knowledge of a fact, rather than the person's constructive knowledge of the fact.

(7) "Limited liability limited partnership" means a limited partnership complying with § 17–214 of this title.

(8) "Limited partner" means a person who has been admitted to a limited partnership as a limited partner as provided in § 17–301 of this title or, in the case of a foreign limited partnership, in accordance with the laws of the state or foreign country or other foreign jurisdiction under which the limited partnership is organized.

(9) "Limited partnership" and "domestic limited partnership" mean a partnership formed by 2 or more persons under the laws of the State of Delaware and having 1 or more general partners and 1 or more limited partners, and includes, for all purposes of the laws of the State of Delaware, a limited liability limited partnership.

(10) "Liquidating trustee" means a person, other than a general partner, but including a limited partner, carrying out the winding up of a limited partnership.

(11) "Partner" means a limited or general partner.

(12) "Partnership agreement" means any agreement, written or oral, of the partners as to the affairs of a limited partnership and the conduct of its business. A partner of a limited partnership or an assignee of a partnership interest is bound by the partnership agreement whether or not the partner or assignee executes the partnership agreement. A limited partnership is not required to execute its partnership agreement. A limited partnership is bound by its partnership agreement whether or not the limited partnership executes the partnership agreement. A partnership agreement may provide rights to any person, including a person who is not a party to the partnership agreement, to the extent set forth therein. A written partnership agreement or another written agreement or writing:

a. May provide that a person shall be admitted as a limited partner of a limited partnership, or shall become an assignee of a partnership interest or other rights or powers of a limited partner to the extent assigned (i) if such person (or a representative authorized by such person orally, in writing or by other action such as payment for a partnership interest) executes the partnership agreement or any other writing evidencing the intent of such person to become a limited partner or assignee, or (ii) without such execution, if such person (or a representative authorized by such person orally, in writing or by other action such as payment for a partnership interest) complies with the conditions for becoming a limited partner or assignee as set forth in the partnership agreement or any other writing; and

b. Shall not be unenforceable by reason of its not having been signed by a person being admitted as a limited partner or becoming an assignee as provided in paragraph a. of this subdivision, or by reason of its having been signed by a representative as provided in this title.

(13) "Partnership interest" means a partner's share of the profits and losses of a limited partnership and the right to receive distributions of partnership assets.

(14) "Person" means a natural person, partnership (whether general or limited), limited liability company, trust, estate, association (including any group, organization, co-tenancy, plan, board, council or committee), corporation, government (including a country, state, county or any other governmental subdivision, agency or instrumentality), custodian, nominee or any other individual or entity (or series thereof) in its own or any representative capacity, in each case, whether domestic or foreign.

(15) "Personal representative" means, as to a natural person, the executor, administrator, guardian, conservator or other legal representative thereof and, as to a person other than a natural person, the legal representative or successor thereof.

(16) "State" means the District of Columbia or the Commonwealth of Puerto Rico or any state, territory, possession, or other jurisdiction of the United States other than the State of Delaware.

§ 17–102. Name Set Forth in Certificate

The name of each limited partnership as set forth in its certificate of limited partnership:

(1) Shall contain the words "Limited Partnership" or the abbreviation "L.P." or the designation "LP" or, in the case of a limited partnership that is formed as or becomes a limited liability limited partnership, shall contain the words, abbreviation or designation required by § 17–214(a) of this title;

(2) May contain the name of a partner;

(3) Must be such as to distinguish it upon the records in the office of the Secretary of State from the name on such records of any corporation, partnership, limited partnership, statutory trust or limited liability company reserved, registered or organized under the laws of the State of Delaware or qualified to do business or registered as a foreign corporation, foreign limited partnership, foreign statutory trust, foreign partnership or foreign limited liability company in the State of Delaware; provided, however, that a limited partnership may register under any name which is not such as to distinguish it upon the records in the office of the Secretary of State from the name on such records of any domestic or foreign corporation, partnership, limited partnership, statutory trust, or limited liability company reserved, registered or organized under the laws of the State of Delaware with the written consent of the other corpora-

tion, partnership, statutory trust, or limited liability company, which written consent shall be filed with the Secretary of State; and

(4) May contain the following words: "Company," "Association," "Club," "Foundation," "Fund," "Institute," "Society," "Union," "Syndicate," "Limited" or "Trust" (or abbreviations of like import).

§ 17-103. Reservation of Name

(a) The exclusive right to the use of a name may be reserved by:

(1) Any person intending to organize a limited partnership under this chapter and to adopt that name;

(2) Any domestic limited partnership or any foreign limited partnership registered in the State of Delaware which, in either case, proposes to change its name;

(3) Any foreign limited partnership intending to register in the State of Delaware and adopt that name; and

(4) Any person intending to organize a foreign limited partnership and intending to have it register in the State of Delaware and adopt that name.

(b) The reservation of a specified name shall be made by filing with the Secretary of State an application, executed by the applicant, specifying the name to be reserved and the name and address of the applicant. If the Secretary of State finds that the name is available for use by a domestic or foreign limited partnership, the Secretary shall reserve the name for the exclusive use of the applicant for a period of 120 days. Once having so reserved a name, the same applicant may again reserve the same name for successive 120 day periods. The right to the exclusive use of a reserved name may be transferred to any other person by filing in the Office of the Secretary of State a notice of the transfer, executed by the applicant for whom the name was reserved, specifying the name to be transferred and the name and address of the transferee. The reservation of a specified name may be cancelled by filing with the Secretary of State a notice of cancellation, executed by the applicant or transferee, specifying the name reservation to be cancelled and the name and address of the applicant or transferee. Unless the Secretary of State finds that any application, notice of transfer, or notice of cancellation filed with the Secretary of State as required by this subsection does not conform to law, upon receipt of all filing fees required by law, the Secretary shall prepare and return to the person who filed such instrument a copy of the filed instrument with a notation thereon of the action taken by the Secretary of State.

(c) A fee as set forth in § 17-1107(a)(1) of this title shall be paid at the time of the initial reservation of any name, at the time of the renewal of any such reservation and at the time of the filing of a notice of the transfer or cancellation of any such reservation.

§ 17-104. Registered Office; Registered Agent [Effective Until Jan. 1, 2007]

(a) Each limited partnership shall have and maintain in the State of Delaware:

(1) A registered office, which may but need not be a place of its business in the State of Delaware; and

(2) A registered agent for service of process on the limited partnership, which agent may be either an individual resident of the State of Delaware whose business office is identical with the limited partnership's registered office, or a domestic corporation, or a domestic limited partnership, or a domestic limited liability company, or a domestic statutory trust, or a foreign corporation, or a foreign limited partnership or a foreign limited liability company authorized to do business in the State of Delaware having a business office identical with such registered office, which is generally open during normal business hours to accept service of process and otherwise perform the functions of a registered agent, or the limited partnership itself.

(b) A registered agent may change the address of the registered office of the limited partnership(s) for which it is registered agent to another address in the State by paying a fee as set forth in § 17-1107(a)(2) of this title and filing with the Secretary of State a certificate, executed by such registered agent, setting forth the address at which such registered agent has maintained the registered office for each of the limited partnerships for which it is a registered agent, and further certifying to the new address to which each such registered office will be changed on a given day, and at which new address such registered agent will thereafter maintain the registered office for each of the limited partnerships for which it is a registered agent. Upon the filing of such certificate, the Secretary of State shall furnish to the registered agent a certified copy of the same under the Secretary's hand and seal of office, and thereafter, or until further change of address, as authorized by law, the registered office in the State of Delaware of each of the limited partnerships for which the agent is a registered agent shall be located at the new address of the registered agent thereof as given in the certificate. In the event of a change of name of any person acting as a registered agent of a limited partnership, such registered agent shall file with the Secretary of State a certificate, executed by such registered agent, setting forth the new name of such registered agent, the name of such registered agent before it was changed, and the address at which such registered agent has maintained the registered office for each of the limited partnerships for which it is a registered agent, and shall pay a fee as set forth in § 17-1107(a)(2) of this title. Upon the filing of such certificate, the Secretary of State shall furnish to the registered agent a certified copy of the certificate under his or her hand and seal of office. A change of name of any person acting as a registered agent of a limited partnership as a result of a merger or consolidation of the registered agent, with or into another person which succeeds to its assets and liabilities by operation of law, shall be deemed a change of name for purposes of this section. Filing a certificate under this section shall be deemed to be an amendment of the certificate of limited partnership of each limited partnership affected thereby and each such limited partnership shall not be required to take any further action with respect thereto, to amend its certificate of limited partnership under § 17-202 of this title. Any registered agent filing a certificate under this section shall promptly, upon such filing, deliver a copy of any such certificate to each limited partnership affected thereby.

(c) The registered agent of 1 or more limited partnerships may resign and appoint a successor registered agent by paying a fee as set forth in § 17-1107(a)(2) of this title and filing a certificate with the Secretary of State stating that it resigns and the name and address of the successor registered agent. There shall be attached to such certificate a statement of each affected limited partnership ratifying and approving such change of registered agent. Upon such filing, the successor registered agent shall become the registered agent of such limited partnerships as have ratified and approved such substitution and the successor registered agent's address, as stated in such certificate, shall become the address of each such limited partnership's registered office in the State of Delaware. The Secretary of State shall then issue a certificate that the successor registered agent has become the registered agent of the limited partnerships so ratifying and approving such change and setting out the names of such limited partnerships. Filing of such certificate of resignation shall be deemed to be an amendment of the certificate of limited partnership of each limited partnership affected thereby and each such limited partnership shall not be required to take any further action with respect thereto to amend its certificate of limited partnership under § 17-202 of this title.

(d) The registered agent of 1 or more limited partnerships may resign without appointing a successor registered agent by paying a fee as set forth in § 17-1107(a)(2) of this title and filing a certificate of resignation with the Secretary of State, but such resignation shall not become effective until 30 days after the certificate is filed. The certificate shall contain a statement that written notice of resignation was given to each affected limited partnership at least 30 days prior to the filing of the certificate by mailing or delivering such notice to the limited partnership at its address last known to the registered agent and shall set forth the date of such notice. After receipt of the notice of the resignation of its registered agent, the limited partnership for which such registered agent was acting shall obtain and designate a new registered agent to take the place of the registered agent so resigning. If such limited partnership fails to obtain and designate a new registered agent as aforesaid prior to the expiration of the period of 30 days after the filing by the registered agent of the certificate of resignation, the certificate of such limited partnership shall be deemed to be canceled. After the resignation of the registered agent shall have become effective as provided in this section and if no new registered agent shall have been obtained and designated in the time and manner aforesaid, service of legal process against each limited partnership for which the resigned registered agent had been acting shall thereafter be upon the Secretary of State in accordance with § 17-105 of this title.

§ 17-104. Registered Office; Registered Agent [Effective Jan. 1, 2007]

(a) Each limited partnership shall have and maintain in the State of Delaware:

(1) A registered office, which may but need not be a place of its business in the State of Delaware; and

(2) A registered agent for service of process on the limited partnership, which agent may be any of

a. The limited partnership itself,

b. An individual resident in the State of Delaware,

c. A domestic limited liability company, a domestic corporation, a domestic partnership (whether general (including a limited liability partnership) or limited (other than the limited partnership itself, including a limited liability limited partnership)), or a domestic statutory trust, or

d. A foreign corporation, a foreign partnership (whether general (including a limited liability partnership) or limited (including a limited liability limited partnership)), a foreign limited liability company, or a foreign statutory trust.

(b) A registered agent may change the address of the registered office of the limited partnership(s) for which it is registered agent to another address in the State by paying a fee as set forth in § 17-1107(a)(2) of this title and filing with the Secretary of State a certificate, executed by such registered agent, setting forth the address at which such registered agent has maintained the registered office for each of the limited partnerships for which it is a registered agent, and further certifying to the new address to which each such registered office will be changed on a given day, and at which new address such registered agent will thereafter maintain the registered office for each of the limited partnerships for which it is a registered agent. Upon the filing of such certificate, the Secretary of State shall furnish to the registered agent a certified copy of the same under the Secretary's hand and seal of office, and thereafter, or until further change of address, as authorized by law, the registered office in the State of Delaware of each of the limited partnerships for which the agent is a registered agent shall be located at the new address of the registered agent thereof as given in the certificate. In the event of a change of name of any person acting as a registered agent of a limited partnership, such registered agent shall file with the Secretary of State a certificate, executed by such registered agent, setting forth the new name of such registered agent, the name of such registered agent before it was changed, and the address at which such registered agent has maintained the registered office for each of the limited partnerships for which it is a registered agent, and shall pay a fee as set forth in § 17-1107(a)(2) of this title. Upon the filing of such certificate, the Secretary of State shall furnish to the registered agent a certified copy of the certificate under his or her hand and seal of office. A change of name of any person acting as a registered agent of a limited partnership as a result of a merger or consolidation of the registered agent, with or into another person which succeeds to its assets and liabilities by operation of law, shall be deemed a change of name for purposes of this section. Filing a certificate under this section shall be deemed to be an amendment of the certificate of limited partnership of each limited partnership affected thereby and each such limited partnership shall not be required to take any further action with respect thereto, to amend its certificate of limited partnership under § 17-202 of this title. Any registered agent filing a certificate under this section shall promptly, upon such filing, deliver a copy of any such certificate to each limited partnership affected thereby.

(c) The registered agent of 1 or more limited partnerships may resign and appoint a successor registered agent by paying a fee as set forth in § 17-1107(a)(2) of this title and filing a certificate with the Secretary of State stating that it resigns and the name and address of the successor registered agent. There shall be attached to such certificate a statement of each affected limited partnership ratifying and approving such change of registered agent. Upon such filing, the successor registered agent shall become the registered agent of such limited partnerships as have ratified and approved such substitution and the successor registered agent's address, as stated in such certificate, shall become the address of each such limited partnership's registered office in the State of Delaware. The Secretary of State shall then issue a certificate that the successor registered agent has become the registered agent of the limited partnerships so ratifying and approving such change and setting out the names of such limited partnerships. Filing of such certificate of resignation shall be deemed to be an amendment of the certificate of limited partnership of each limited partnership affected thereby and each such limited partnership shall not be required to take any further action with respect thereto to amend its certificate of limited partnership under § 17-202 of this title.

(d) The registered agent of 1 or more limited partnerships may resign without appointing a successor registered agent by paying a fee as set forth in § 17-1107(a)(2) of this title and filing a certificate of resignation with the Secretary of State, but such resignation shall not become effective until 30 days after the certificate is filed. The certificate shall contain a statement that written notice of resignation was given to each affected limited partnership at least 30 days prior to the filing of the certificate by mailing or delivering such notice to the limited partnership at its address last known to the registered agent and shall set forth the date of such notice. After receipt of the notice of the resignation of its registered agent, the limited partnership for which such registered agent was acting shall obtain and designate a new registered agent to take the place of the registered agent so resigning. If such limited partnership fails to obtain and designate a new registered agent as aforesaid prior to the expiration of the period of 30 days after the filing by the registered agent of the certificate of resignation, the certificate of such limited partnership shall be deemed to be canceled. After the resignation of the registered agent shall have become effective as provided in this section and if no new registered agent shall have been obtained and designated in the time and manner aforesaid, service of legal process against each limited partnership for which the resigned registered agent had been acting shall thereafter be upon the Secretary of State in accordance with § 17-105 of this title.

(e) Every registered agent shall:

(1) If an entity, maintain a business office in the State of Delaware which is generally open, or if an individual, be generally present at a designated location in the State of Delaware, at sufficiently frequent times to accept service of process and otherwise perform the functions of a registered agent;

(2) If a foreign entity, be authorized to transact business in the State of Delaware;

(3) Accept service of process and other communications directed to the limited partnerships for which it serves as registered agent and forward same to the limited partnership to which the service or communication is directed; and

(4) Forward to the limited partnerships for which it serves as registered agent the statement for the annual tax described in § 17-1109 of this title or an electronic notification of same in a form satisfactory to the Secretary of State.

(f) Any registered agent, who at any time serves as registered agent for more than 50 entities (a "commercial registered agent"), whether domestic or foreign, shall satisfy and comply with the following qualifications.

(1) A natural person serving as a commercial registered agent shall:

a. Maintain a principal residence or a principal place of business in the State of Delaware;

b. Maintain a Delaware business license;

c. Be generally present at a designated location within the State of Delaware during normal business hours to accept service of process and otherwise perform the functions of a registered agent as specified in subsection (e) of this section; and

d. Provide the Secretary of State upon request with such information identifying and enabling communication with such commercial registered agent as the Secretary of State shall require.

(2) A domestic or foreign corporation, a domestic or foreign partnership (whether general (including a limited liability partnership) or limited (including a limited liability limited partnership)), a domestic or foreign limited liability company, or a domestic or foreign statutory trust serving as a commercial registered agent shall:

a. Have a business office within the State of Delaware which is generally open during normal business hours to accept service of process and otherwise perform the functions of a registered agent as specified in subsection (e) of this section;

b. Maintain a Delaware business license;

c. Have generally present at such office during normal business hours an officer, director or managing agent who is a natural person; and

d. Provide the Secretary of State upon request with such information identifying and enabling communication with such commercial registered agent as the Secretary of State shall require.

(3) For purposes of this subsection and paragraph (i)(2)a. of this section, a "commercial registered agent" shall also include any registered agent which has an officer, director or managing agent in common with any other registered agent or agents if such registered agents at any time during such common service as officer, director or managing agent collectively served as registered agents for more than 50 entities, whether domestic or foreign.

(g) Every limited partnership formed under the laws of the State of Delaware or qualified to do business in the State of Delaware shall provide to its registered agent and update from time to time as necessary the name, business address and business telephone number of a natural person who is a partner, officer, employee or designated agent of the limited partnership, who is then authorized to receive communications from the registered agent. Such person shall be deemed the communications contact for the limited partnership. Every registered agent shall retain (in paper or electronic form) the above information concerning the current communications contact for each limited partnership for which he, she, or it serves as registered agent. If the limited partnership fails to provide the registered agent with a current communications contact, the registered agent may resign as the registered agent for such limited partnership pursuant to this section.

(h) The Secretary of State is authorized to issue such rules and regulations as may be necessary or appropriate to carry out the enforcement of subsections (e), (f) and (g) of this section, and to take actions reasonable and necessary to assure registered agents' compliance with subsections (e), (f) and (g) of this section. Such actions may include refusal to file documents submitted by a registered agent.

(i) Upon application of the Secretary of State, the Court of Chancery may enjoin any person or entity from serving as a registered agent or as an officer, director or managing agent of a registered agent.

(1) Upon the filing of a complaint by the Secretary of State pursuant to this section, the court may make such orders respecting such proceeding as it deems appropriate, and may enter such orders granting interim or final relief as it deems proper under the circumstances.

(2) Any 1 or more of the following grounds shall be a sufficient basis to grant an injunction pursuant to this section:

a. With respect to any registered agent who at any time within 1 year immediately prior to the filing of the Secretary of State's complaint is a commercial registered agent, failure after notice and warning to comply with the qualifications set forth in subsection (e) of this section and/or the requirements of subsections (f) or (g) of this section above;

b. The person serving as a registered agent, or any person who is an officer, director or managing agent of an entity registered agent, has been convicted of a felony or any crime which includes an element of dishonesty or fraud or involves moral turpitude; or

c. The registered agent has engaged in conduct in connection with acting as a registered agent that is intended to or likely to deceive or defraud the public.

(3) With respect to any order the court enters pursuant to this section with respect to an entity that has acted as a registered agent, the court may also direct such order to any person who has served as an officer, director or managing agent of such registered agent. Any person who, on or after January 1, 2007, serves as an officer, director or managing agent of an entity acting as a registered agent in the State of Delaware shall be deemed thereby to have consented to the appointment of such registered agent as agent upon whom service of process may be made in any action brought pursuant to this section, and service as an officer, director or managing agent of an entity acting as a registered agent in the State of Delaware shall be a signification of the consent of such person that any process when so served shall be of the same legal force and validity as if

served upon such person within the State of Delaware, and such appointment of the registered agent shall be irrevocable.

(4) Upon the entry of an order by the court enjoining any person or entity from acting as a registered agent, the Secretary of State shall mail or deliver notice of such order to each general partner of each affected limited partnership at the address of such general partner specified in the affected limited partnership's certificate of limited partnership. If such a limited partnership is a domestic limited partnership and fails to obtain and designate a new registered agent within 30 days after such notice is given, the certificate of limited partnership of such limited partnership shall be deemed to be cancelled. If such a limited partnership is a foreign limited partnership and fails to obtain and designate a new registered agent within 30 days after such notice is given, such foreign limited partnership shall not be permitted to do business in the State of Delaware and its registration shall be deemed to be cancelled. If the court enjoins a person or entity from acting as a registered agent as provided in this section and no new registered agent shall have been obtained and designated in the time and manner aforesaid by an affected limited partnership, service of legal process against the limited partnership for which the registered agent had been acting shall thereafter be upon the Secretary of State in accordance with § 17-105 or § 17-911 of this title. The Court of Chancery may, upon application of the Secretary of State on notice to the former registered agent, enter such orders as it deems appropriate to give the Secretary of State access to information in the former registered agent's possession in order to facilitate communication with the limited partnerships the former registered agent served.

(j) The Secretary of State is authorized to make a list of registered agents available to the public, and to establish such qualifications and issue such rules and regulations with respect to such listing as the Secretary of State deems necessary or appropriate.

§ 17-105. Service of Process on Domestic Limited Partnerships

(a) Service of legal process upon any domestic limited partnership shall be made by delivering a copy personally to any managing or general agent or general partner of the limited partnership in the State of Delaware or the registered agent of the limited partnership in the State of Delaware, or by leaving it at the dwelling house or usual place of abode in the State of Delaware of any such managing or general agent, general partner or registered agent (if the registered agent be an individual), or at the registered office or other place of business of the limited partnership in the State of Delaware. If the registered agent be a corporation, service of process upon it as such may be made by serving, in the State of Delaware, a copy thereof on the president, vice-president, secretary, assistant secretary or any director of the corporate registered agent. Service by copy left at the dwelling house or usual place of abode of an officer, managing or general agent, general partner or registered agent, or at the registered office or other place of business of the limited partnership in the State of Delaware, to be effective, must be delivered thereat at least 6 days before the return date of the process, and in the presence of an adult person, and the officer serving the process shall distinctly state the manner of service in his or her return thereto. Process returnable forthwith must be delivered personally to the officer, managing or general agent, general partner or registered agent.

(b) In case the officer whose duty it is to serve legal process cannot by due diligence serve the process in any manner provided for by subsection (a) of this section, it shall be lawful to serve the process against the limited partnership upon the Secretary of State, and such service shall be as effectual for all intents and purposes as if made in any of the ways provided for in subsection (a) hereof. In the event that service is effected through the Secretary of State in accordance with this subsection, the Secretary of State shall forthwith notify the limited partnership by letter, certified mail, return receipt requested, directed to the limited partnership at the address of a general partner as it appears on the records relating to such limited partnership on file with the Secretary of State or, if no such address appears, at its last registered office. Such letter shall enclose a copy of the process and any other papers served on the Secretary of State pursuant to this subsection. It shall be the duty of the plaintiff in the event of such service to serve process and any other papers in duplicate, to notify the Secretary of State that service is being effected pursuant to this subsection, and to pay the Secretary of State the sum of $50 for the use of the State of Delaware, which sum shall be taxed as part of the costs in the proceeding if the plaintiff shall prevail therein. The Secretary of State shall maintain an alphabetical record of any such service setting forth the name of the plaintiff and defendant, the title, docket number and nature of the proceeding in which process has been served upon the Secretary, the fact that service has been effected pursuant to this subsection, the return date thereof, and the day and hour when the service was made. The Secretary of State shall not be required to retain such information for a period longer than 5 years from the receipt of the service of process.

§ 17-106. Nature of Business Permitted; Powers

(a) A limited partnership may carry on any lawful business, purpose or activity, whether or not for profit, with the exception of the business of banking as defined in § 126 of Title 8.

(b) A limited partnership shall possess and may exercise all the powers and privileges granted by this chapter or by any other law or by its partnership agreement, together with any powers incidental thereto, including such powers and privileges as are necessary or convenient to the conduct, promotion or attainment of the business, purposes or activities of the limited partnership.

(c) Notwithstanding any provision of this chapter to the contrary, without limiting the general powers enumerated in subsection (b) above, a limited partnership shall, subject to such standards and restrictions, if any, as are set forth in its partnership agreement, have the power and authority to make contracts of guaranty and suretyship and enter into interest rate, basis, currency, hedge or other swap agreements or cap, floor, put, call, option, exchange or collar agreements, derivative agreements or other agreements similar to any of the foregoing.

§ 17–107. Business Transactions of Partner with the Partnership

Except as provided in the partnership agreement, a partner may lend money to, borrow money from, act as a surety, guarantor or endorser for, guarantee or assume 1 or more specific obligations of, provide collateral for and transact other business with, the limited partnership and, subject to other applicable law, has the same rights and obligations with respect thereto as a person who is not a partner.

§ 17–108. Indemnification

Subject to such standards and restrictions, if any, as are set forth in its partnership agreement, a limited partnership may, and shall have the power to, indemnify and hold harmless any partner or other person from and against any and all claims and demands whatsoever.

§ 17–109. Service of Process on Partners and Liquidating Trustees

(a) A general partner or a liquidating trustee of a limited partnership may be served with process in the manner prescribed in this section in all civil actions or proceedings brought in the State of Delaware involving or relating to the business of the limited partnership or a violation by the general partner or the liquidating trustee of a duty to the limited partnership, or any partner of the limited partnership, whether or not the general partner or the liquidating trustee is a general partner or a liquidating trustee at the time suit is commenced. The filing in the Office of the Secretary of State of a certificate of limited partnership executed, and the execution thereof, by a resident or nonresident of the State of Delaware which names such person as a general partner or a liquidating trustee of a limited partnership, or the acceptance by a general partner or a liquidating trustee after August 1, 1999, of election or appointment as a general partner or a liquidating trustee of a limited partnership, or a general partner or a liquidating trustee of a limited partnership serving in such capacity after August 1, 1999, constitute such person's consent to the appointment of the registered agent of the limited partnership (or, if there is none, the Secretary of State) as such person's agent upon whom service of process may be made as provided in this section. Such execution and filing, or such acceptance or service, shall signify the consent of such general partner or liquidating trustee that any process when so served shall be of the same legal force and validity as if served upon such general partner or liquidating trustee within the State of Delaware and such appointment of the registered agent (or, if there is none, the Secretary of State) shall be irrevocable.

(b) Service of process shall be effected by serving the registered agent (or, if there is none, the Secretary of State) with 1 copy of such process in the manner provided by law for service of writs of summons. In the event service is made under this subsection upon the Secretary of State, the plaintiff shall pay to the Secretary of State the sum of $50 for the use of the State of Delaware, which sum shall be taxed as part of the costs of the proceeding if the plaintiff shall prevail therein. In addition, the Prothonotary or the Register in Chancery of the court in which the civil action or proceeding is pending shall, within 7 days of such service, deposit in the United States mails, by registered mail, postage prepaid, true and attested copies of the process, together with a statement that service is being made pursuant to this section, addressed to such general partner or liquidating trustee at the same address that appears in the certificate of limited partnership of the limited partnership, or, if no such address appears, at his or her address last known to the party desiring to make such service.

(c) In any action in which any such general partner or liquidating trustee has been served with process as hereinabove provided, the time in which a defendant shall be required to appear and file a responsive pleading shall be computed from the date of mailing by the Prothonotary or the Register in Chancery as provided in subsection (b) of this section; however, the court in which such action has been commenced may order such continuance or continuances as may be necessary to afford such general partner or liquidating trustee reasonable opportunity to defend the action.

(d) In a written partnership agreement or other writing, a partner may consent to be subject to the nonexclusive jurisdiction of the courts of, or arbitration in, a specified jurisdiction, or the exclusive jurisdiction of the courts of the State of Delaware, or the exclusivity of arbitration in a specified jurisdiction or the State of Delaware, and to be served with legal process in the manner prescribed in such partnership agreement or other writing. Except by agreeing to arbitrate any arbitrable matter in a specified jurisdiction or in the State of Delaware, a limited partner may not waive its right to maintain a legal action or proceeding in the courts of the State of Delaware with respect to matters relating to the organization or internal affairs of a limited partnership.

(e) Nothing herein contained limits or affects the right to serve process in any other manner now or hereafter provided by law. This section is an extension of and not a limitation upon the right otherwise existing of service of legal process upon nonresidents.

(f) The Court of Chancery and the Superior Court may make all necessary rules respecting the form of process, the manner of issuance and return thereof and such other rules which may be necessary to implement this section and are not inconsistent with this section.

§ 17–110. Contested Matters Relating to General Partners; Contested Votes

(a) Upon application of any partner, the Court of Chancery may hear and determine the validity of any admission, election, appointment or removal or other withdrawal of a general partner of a limited partnership, and the right of any person to become or continue to be a general partner of a limited partnership, and, in case the right to serve as a general partner is claimed by more than 1 person, may determine the person or persons entitled to serve as general partners; and to that end make such order or decree in any such case as may be just and proper, with power to enforce the production of any books, papers and records of the limited partnership relating to the issue. In any such application, the limited partnership shall be named as a party and service of copies of the application upon the registered agent of the limited partnership shall be deemed to be service upon the limited partnership and upon the person or persons whose right to serve as a general partner is contested and upon the person or persons, if any, claiming to be a general partner or claiming the right to be a general partner; and the registered agent shall forward immediately a copy of the application to the limited partnership and to the person or persons whose right to serve as a general partner is contested and to the person or persons, if any, claiming to be a general partner or the right to be a general partner, in a postpaid, sealed, registered letter addressed to such limited partnership and such person or persons at their post-office addresses last known to the registered agent or furnished to the registered agent by the applicant partner. The Court may make such order respecting further or other notice of such application as it deems proper under the circumstances.

(b) Upon application of any partner, the Court of Chancery may hear and determine the result of any vote of partners upon matters as to which the partners of the limited partnership, or any class or group of partners, have the right to vote pursuant to the partnership agreement or other agreement or this chapter (other than the admission, election, appointment or removal or other withdrawal of general partners). In any such application, the limited partnership shall be named as a party and service of the application upon the registered agent of the limited partnership shall be deemed to be service upon the limited partnership, and no other party need be joined in order for the Court to adjudicate the result of the vote. The Court may make such order respecting further or other notice of such application as it deems proper under the circumstances.

(c) Nothing herein contained limits or affects the right to serve process in any other manner now or hereafter provided by law. This section is an extension of and not a limitation upon the right otherwise existing of service of legal process upon nonresidents.

§ 17-111. Interpretation and Enforcement of Partnership Agreement

Any action to interpret, apply or enforce the provisions of a partnership agreement, or the duties, obligations or liabilities of a limited partnership to the partners of the limited partnership, or the duties, obligations or liabilities among partners or of partners to the limited partnership, or the rights or powers of, or restrictions on, the limited partnership or partners, may be brought in the Court of Chancery.

SUBCHAPTER II. FORMATION; CERTIFICATE OF LIMITED PARTNERSHIP

§ 17-201. Certificate of Limited Partnership

(a) In order to form a limited partnership, 1 or more persons (but not less than all of the general partners) must execute a certificate of limited partnership. The certificate of limited partnership shall be filed in the Office of the Secretary of State and set forth:

(1) The name of the limited partnership;

(2) The address of the registered office and the name and address of the registered agent for service of process required to be maintained by § 17-104 of this title;

(3) The name and the business, residence or mailing address of each general partner; and

(4) Any other matters the partners determine to include therein.

(b) A limited partnership is formed at the time of the filing of the initial certificate of limited partnership in the Office of the Secretary of State or at any later date or time specified in the certificate of limited partnership if, in either case, there has been substantial compliance with the requirements of this section. A limited partnership formed under this chapter shall be a separate legal entity, the existence of which as a separate legal entity shall continue until cancellation of the limited partnership's certificate of limited partnership.

(c) The filing of the certificate of limited partnership in the Office of the Secretary of State shall make it unnecessary to file any other documents under Chapter 31 of this title.

§ 17–202. Amendment to Certificate

(a) A certificate of limited partnership is amended by filing a certificate of amendment thereto in the Office of the Secretary of State. The certificate of amendment shall set forth:

(1) The name of the limited partnership; and

(2) The amendment to the certificate.

(b) A general partner who becomes aware that any statement in a certificate of limited partnership was false when made, or that any matter described has changed making the certificate false in any material respect, shall promptly amend the certificate.

(c) Notwithstanding the requirements of subsection (b) of this section, no later than 90 days after the happening of any of the following events an amendment to a certificate of limited partnership reflecting the occurrence of the event or events shall be filed by a general partner:

(1) The admission of a new general partner;

(2) The withdrawal of a general partner; or

(3) A change in the name of the limited partnership, or, except as provided in § 17–104(b) and (c) of this title, a change in the address of the registered office or a change in the name or address of the registered agent of the limited partnership.

(d) A certificate of limited partnership may be amended at any time for any other proper purpose the general partners may determine.

(e) Unless otherwise provided in this chapter or in the certificate of amendment, a certificate of amendment shall be effective at the time of its filing with the Secretary of State.

(f) If after the dissolution of a limited partnership but prior to the filing of a certificate of cancellation as provided in § 17–203 of this title:

(1) A certificate of limited partnership has been amended to reflect the withdrawal of all general partners of a limited partnership, the certificate of limited partnership shall be amended to set forth the name and the business, residence or mailing address of each person winding up the limited partnership's affairs, each of whom shall execute and file such certificate of amendment, and each of whom shall not be subject to liability as a general partner by reason of such amendment; or

(2) A person shown on a certificate of limited partnership as a general partner is not winding up the limited partnership's affairs, the certificate of limited partnership shall be amended to add the name and the business, residence or mailing address of each person winding up the limited partnership's affairs, each of whom shall execute and file such certificate of amendment, and each of whom shall not be subject to liability as a general partner by reason of such amendment. A person shown on a certificate of limited partner-

ship as a general partner who is not winding up a limited partnership's affairs need not execute a certificate of amendment which is being executed and filed as required under this subsection.

§ 17-203. Cancellation of Certificate [Effective Until Jan. 1, 2007]

A certificate of limited partnership shall be cancelled upon the dissolution and the completion of winding up of the partnership, or as provided in § 17-104(d) or § 17-1110 of this title, or upon the filing of a certificate of merger or consolidation if the limited partnership is not the surviving or resulting entity in a merger or consolidation, or upon the filing of a certificate of transfer, or upon the filing of a certificate of conversion to a non-Delaware entity. A certificate of cancellation shall be filed in the Office of the Secretary of State to accomplish the cancellation of a certificate of limited partnership upon the dissolution and the completion of winding up of a limited partnership and shall set forth:

(1) The name of the limited partnership;

(2) The date of filing of its certificate of limited partnership;

(3) The future effective date or time (which shall be a date or time certain) of cancellation if it is not to be effective upon the filing of the certificate; and

(4) Any other information the person filing the certificate of cancellation determines.

§ 17-203. Cancellation of Certificate [Effective Jan. 1, 2007]

A certificate of limited partnership shall be cancelled upon the dissolution and the completion of winding up of the partnership, or as provided in § 17-104(d) or § 17-104(i)(4) or § 17-1110 of this title, or upon the filing of a certificate of merger or consolidation if the limited partnership is not the surviving or resulting entity in a merger or consolidation, or upon the filing of a certificate of transfer, or upon the filing of a certificate of conversion to a non-Delaware entity. A certificate of cancellation shall be filed in the Office of the Secretary of State to accomplish the cancellation of a certificate of limited partnership upon the dissolution and the completion of winding up of a limited partnership and shall set forth:

(1) The name of the limited partnership;

(2) The date of filing of its certificate of limited partnership;

(3) The future effective date or time (which shall be a date or time certain) of cancellation if it is not to be effective upon the filing of the certificate; and

(4) Any other information the person filing the certificate of cancellation determines.

§ 17–204. Execution

(a) Each certificate required by this subchapter to be filed in the Office of the Secretary of State shall be executed in the following manner:

(1) An initial certificate of limited partnership, a certificate of limited partnership domestication, a certificate of conversion to limited partnership, a certificate of conversion to a non-Delaware entity, a certificate of transfer and a certificate of transfer and continuance must be signed by all general partners;

(2) A certificate of amendment or a certificate of correction must be signed by at least 1 general partner and by each other general partner designated in the certificate of amendment or a certificate of correction as a new general partner, but if the certificate of amendment or a certificate of correction reflects the withdrawal of a general partner as a general partner, it need not be signed by that former general partner;

(3) A certificate of cancellation must be signed by all general partners or, if the general partners are not winding up the limited partnership's affairs, then by all liquidating trustees; provided, however, that if the limited partners are winding up the limited partnership's affairs, a certificate of cancellation shall be signed by the limited partners or, if there is more than 1 class or group of limited partners, then by each class or group of limited partners, in either case, by limited partners who own more than 50 percent of the then current percentage or other interest in the profits of the limited partnership owned by all of the limited partners or by the limited partners in each class or group, as appropriate;

(4) If a domestic limited partnership is filing a certificate of merger or consolidation, the certificate of merger or consolidation must be signed by at least 1 general partner of the domestic limited partnership, or if the certificate of merger or consolidation is being filed by another business entity (as defined in § 17–211(a) of this title), the certificate of merger or consolidation, must be signed by a person authorized by such other business entity;

(5) A certificate of revival must be signed by at least 1 general partner; and

(6) A certificate of termination of a certificate with a future effective date or time or a certificate of amendment of a certificate with a future effective date or time being filed in accordance with § 17–206(c) of this title shall be signed in the same manner as the certificate with a future effective date or time being amended or terminated is required to be signed under this chapter.

(b) Unless otherwise provided in the partnership agreement, any person may sign any certificate or amendment thereof or enter into a partnership agreement or amendment thereof by an agent, including an attorney-in-fact. An authorization, including a power of attorney, to sign any certificate or amendment thereof or to enter into a partnership agreement or amendment thereof need not be in writing, need not be sworn to, verified or acknowledged, and need not be filed in the Office of the Secretary of State, but if in writing, must be retained by a general partner.

(c) The execution of a certificate by a general partner constitutes an oath or affirmation, under the penalties of perjury in the third degree, that, to the best of the general partner's knowledge and belief, the facts stated therein are true.

§ 17-205. Execution, Amendment or Cancellation by Judicial Order

(a) If a person required by § 17-204 of this title to execute any certificate fails or refuses to do so, any other person who is adversely affected by the failure or refusal may petition the Court of Chancery to direct the execution of the certificate. If the Court finds that the execution of the certificate is proper and that any person so designated has failed or refused to execute the certificate, it shall order the Secretary of State to record an appropriate certificate.

(b) If a person required to execute a partnership agreement or amendment thereof fails or refuses to do so, any other person who is adversely affected by the failure or refusal may petition the Court of Chancery to direct the execution of the partnership agreement or amendment thereof. If the Court finds that the partnership agreement or amendment thereof should be executed and that any person so designated has failed or refused to do so, it shall enter an order granting appropriate relief.

§ 17-206. Filing [Effective Until Jan. 1, 2007]

(a) The signed copy of the certificate of limited partnership and of any certificates of amendment, correction, amendment of a certificate with a future effective date or time, termination of a certificate with a future effective date or time or cancellation (or of any judicial decree of amendment or cancellation), and of any certificate of merger or consolidation, any restated certificate, any corrected certificate, any certificate of conversion to limited partnership, any certificate of conversion to a non-Delaware entity, any certificate of transfer, any certificate of transfer and continuance, any certificate of limited partnership domestication, and any certificate of revival shall be delivered to the Secretary of State. A person who executes a certificate as an agent or fiduciary need not exhibit evidence of that person's authority as a prerequisite to filing. Any signature on any certificate authorized to be filed with the Secretary of State under any provision of this chapter may be a facsimile, a conformed signature or an electronically transmitted signature. Upon delivery of any certificate, the Secretary of State shall record the date and time of its delivery. Unless the Secretary of State finds that any certificate does not conform to law, upon receipt of all filing fees required by law the Secretary of State shall:

(1) Certify that the certificate of limited partnership, the certificate of amendment, the certificate of correction, the certificate of amendment of a certificate with a future effective date or time, the certificate of termination of a certificate with a future effective date or time, the certificate of cancellation (or of any judicial decree of amendment or cancellation), the certificate of merger or consolidation, restated certificate, the corrected certificate, the certificate of conversion to limited partnership, the certificate of conversion to a non-Delaware entity, the certificate of transfer, the certificate of transfer and continuance, the certificate of limited partnership domestication or certificate of revival has been filed in the Secretary of State's office by endorsing upon the signed certificate the word "Filed," and the date and time of the filing. This endorsement is conclusive of the date and time of its filing in the absence of actual fraud. Except as provided in subdivision (a)(5) or (a)(6) of this section, such date and time of filing of a certificate shall be the date and time of delivery of the certificate;

(2) File and index the endorsed certificate;

(3) Prepare and return to the person who filed it or that person's representative a copy of the signed certificate, similarly endorsed, and shall certify such copy as a true copy of the signed certificate; and

(4) Cause to be entered such information from the certificate as the Secretary of State deems appropriate into the Delaware Corporation Information System or any system which is a successor thereto in the office of the Secretary of State, and such information and a copy of such certificate shall be permanently maintained as a public record on a suitable medium. The Secretary of State is authorized to grant direct access to such system to registered agents subject to the execution of an operating agreement between the Secretary of State and such registered agent. Any registered agent granted such access shall demonstrate the existence of policies to ensure that information entered into the system accurately reflects the content of certificates in the possession of the registered agent at the time of entry.

(5) Upon request made upon or prior to delivery, the Secretary of State may, to the extent deemed practicable, establish as the date and time of filing of a certificate a date and time after its delivery. If the Secretary of State refuses to file any certificate due to an error, omission or other imperfection, the Secretary of State may hold such certificate in suspension, and in such event, upon delivery of a replacement certificate in proper form for filing and tender of the required fees within 5 business days after notice of such suspension

is given to the filer, the Secretary of State shall establish as the date and time of filing of such certificate the date and time that would have been the date and time of filing of the rejected certificate had it been accepted for filing. The Secretary of State shall not issue a certificate of good standing with respect to any limited partnership with a certificate held in suspension pursuant to this subsection. The Secretary of State may establish as the date and time of filing of a certificate the date and time at which information from such certificate is entered pursuant to subdivision (a)(4) of this section if such certificate is delivered on the same date and within 4 hours after such information is entered.

(6) If:

a. Together with the actual delivery of a certificate and tender of the required fees, there is delivered to the Secretary of State a separate affidavit (which in its heading shall be designated as an affidavit of extraordinary condition) attesting, on the basis of personal knowledge of the affiant or a reliable source of knowledge identified in the affidavit, that an earlier effort to deliver such certificate and tender such fees was made in good faith, specifying the nature, date and time of such good faith effort and requesting that the Secretary of State establish such date and time as the date and time of filing of such certificate; or

b. Upon the actual delivery of a certificate and tender of the required fees, the Secretary of State in his or her discretion provides a written waiver of the requirement for such an affidavit stating that it appears to the Secretary of State that an earlier effort to deliver such certificate and tender such fees was made in good faith and specifying the date and time of such effort; and

c. The Secretary of State determines that an extraordinary condition existed at such date and time, that such earlier effort was unsuccessful as a result of the existence of such extraordinary condition, and that such actual delivery and tender were made within a reasonable period (not to exceed 2 business days) after the cessation of such extraordinary condition, then the Secretary of State may establish such date and time as the date and time of filing of such certificate. No fee shall be paid to the Secretary of State for receiving an affidavit of extraordinary condition. For purposes of this subsection, an extraordinary condition means: any emergency resulting from an attack on, invasion or occupation by foreign military forces of, or disaster, catastrophe, war or other armed conflict, revolution or insurrection, or rioting or civil commotion in, the United States or a locality in which the Secretary of State conducts its business or in which the good faith effort to deliver the certificate and tender the required fees is made, or the immediate threat of any of the foregoing; or any malfunction or outage of the electrical or telephone service to the Secretary of State's office, or weather or other condition in or about a locality in which the Secretary of State conducts its business, as a result of which the Secretary of State's office is not open for the purpose of the filing of certificates under this chapter or such filing cannot be effected without extraordinary effort. The Secretary of State may require such proof as it deems necessary to make the determination required under this subparagraph c. of this subdivision, and any such determination shall be conclusive in the absence of actual fraud. If the Secretary of State establishes the date and time of filing of a certificate pursuant to this subsection, the date and time of delivery of the affidavit of extraordinary condition or the date and time of the Secretary of State's written waiver of such affidavit shall be endorsed on such affidavit or waiver and such affidavit or waiver, so endorsed, shall be attached to the filed certificate to which it relates. Such filed certificate shall be effective as of the date and time established as the date and time of filing by the Secretary of State pursuant to this subsection, except as to those persons who are substantially and adversely affected by such establishment and, as to those persons, the certificate shall be effective from the date and time endorsed on the affidavit of extraordinary condition or written waiver attached thereto.

(b) Upon the filing of a certificate of amendment (or judicial decree of amendment), certificate of correction, corrected certificate or restated certificate in the Office of the Secretary of State, or upon the future effective date or time of a certificate of amendment (or judicial decree thereof) or restated certificate, as provided for therein, the certificate of limited partnership shall be amended, corrected or restated as set forth therein. Upon the filing of a certificate of cancellation (or a judicial decree thereof), or a certificate of merger or consolidation which acts as a certificate of cancellation, or a certificate of transfer, or a certificate of conversion to a non-Delaware entity, or upon the future effective date or time of a certificate of cancellation (or a judicial decree thereof) or of a certificate of merger or consolidation which acts as a certificate of cancellation, or a certificate of transfer, or a certificate of conversion to a non-Delaware entity, as provided for therein, or as specified in § 17-104(d) of this title, the certificate of limited partnership is cancelled. Upon the filing of a certificate of limited partnership domestication, or upon the future effective date or time of a certificate of limited partnership domestication, the entity filing the certificate of limited partnership domestication is domesticated as a limited partnership with the effect provided in § 17-215 of this title. Upon the filing of a certificate of conversion to limited partnership, or upon the future effective date or time of a certificate of conversion to limited partnership, the entity filing the certificate of conversion to limited partnership is converted to a limited partnership with the effect provided in § 17–217 of this title. Upon the filing of a certificate of revival, the limited partnership shall be revived with the effect provided in § 17–1111 of this title. Upon the filing of a certificate of transfer and continuance, or upon the future effective date or time of a certificate of transfer and continuance, as provided for therein, the limited partnership filing the certificate of transfer and continuance shall continue to exist as a limited partnership of the State of Delaware with the effect provided in § 17–216 of this title.

(c) If any certificate filed in accordance with this chapter provides for a future effective date or time and if, prior to such future effective date or time set forth in such certificate, the transaction is terminated or its terms are amended to change the future effective date or time or any other matter described in such certificate so as to make such certificate false or inaccurate in any respect, such certificate shall, prior to the future effective date or time set forth in such certificate, be terminated or amended by the filing of a certificate of termination or certificate of amendment of such certificate, executed in accordance with § 17–204 of this title, which shall identify the certificate which has been terminated or amended and shall state that the certificate has been terminated or the manner in which it has been amended. Upon the filing of a certificate of amendment of a certificate with a future effective date or time, the certificate identified in such certificate of amendment is amended. Upon the filing of a certificate of termination of a certificate with a future effective date or time, the certificate identified in such certificate of termination is terminated.

(d) A fee as set forth in § 17–1107(a)(3) of this title shall be paid at the time of the filing of a certificate of limited partnership, a certificate of amendment, a certificate of correction, a certificate of amendment of a certificate with a future effective date or time, a certificate of termination of a certificate with a future effective date of time, a certificate of termination of a merger or consolidation, a certificate of cancellation, a certificate of merger or consolidation, a restated certificate, a corrected certificate, a certificate of conversion to limited partnership, a certificate of conversion to a non-Delaware entity, a certificate of transfer, certificate of transfer and continuance, a certificate of limited partnership domestication or a certificate of revival.

(e) A fee as set forth in § 17–1107(a)(4) of this title shall be paid for a certified copy of any paper on file as provided for by this chapter, and a fee as set forth in § 17–1107(a)(5) of this title shall be paid for each page copied.

§ 17–206. Filing [Effective Jan. 1, 2007]

(a) The signed copy of the certificate of limited partnership and of any certificates of amendment, correction, amendment of a certificate with a future effective date or time, termination of a certificate with a future effective date or time or cancellation (or of any judicial decree of amendment or cancellation), and of any certificate of merger or consolidation, any restated certificate, any corrected certificate, any certificate of conversion to limited partnership, any certificate of conversion to a non-Delaware entity, any certificate of transfer, any certificate of transfer and continuance, any certificate of limited partnership domestication, and any certificate of revival shall be delivered to the Secretary of State. A person who executes a certificate as an agent or fiduciary need not exhibit evidence of that person's authority as a prerequisite to filing. Any signature on any certificate authorized to be filed with the Secretary of State under any provision of this chapter may be a facsimile, a conformed signature or an electronically transmitted signature. Upon delivery of any certificate, the Secretary of State shall record the date and time of its delivery. Unless the Secretary of State finds that any certificate does not conform to law, upon receipt of all filing fees required by law the Secretary of State shall:

(1) Certify that the certificate of limited partnership, the certificate of amendment, the certificate of correction, the certificate of amendment of a certificate with a future effective date or time, the certificate of termination of a certificate with a future effective date or time, the certificate of cancellation (or of any judicial decree of amendment or cancellation), the certificate of merger or consolidation, restated certificate, the corrected certificate, the certificate of conversion to limited partnership, the certificate of conversion to a non-Delaware entity, the certificate of transfer, the certificate of transfer and continuance, the certificate of limited partnership domestication or certificate of revival has been filed in the Secretary of State's office by endorsing upon the signed certificate the word "Filed," and the date and time of the filing. This endorsement is conclusive of the date and time of its filing in the absence of actual fraud. Except as provided in subdivision (a)(5) or (a)(6) of this section, such date and time of filing of a certificate shall be the date and time of delivery of the certificate;

(2) File and index the endorsed certificate;

(3) Prepare and return to the person who filed it or that person's representative a copy of the signed certificate, similarly endorsed, and shall certify such copy as a true copy of the signed certificate; and

(4) Cause to be entered such information from the certificate as the Secretary of State deems appropriate into the Delaware Corporation Information System or any system which is a successor thereto in the office of the Secretary of State, and such information and a copy of such certificate shall be permanently maintained as a public record on a suitable medium. The Secretary of State is authorized to grant direct access to such system to registered agents subject to the

execution of an operating agreement between the Secretary of State and such registered agent. Any registered agent granted such access shall demonstrate the existence of policies to ensure that information entered into the system accurately reflects the content of certificates in the possession of the registered agent at the time of entry.

(5) Upon request made upon or prior to delivery, the Secretary of State may, to the extent deemed practicable, establish as the date and time of filing of a certificate a date and time after its delivery. If the Secretary of State refuses to file any certificate due to an error, omission or other imperfection, the Secretary of State may hold such certificate in suspension, and in such event, upon delivery of a replacement certificate in proper form for filing and tender of the required fees within 5 business days after notice of such suspension is given to the filer, the Secretary of State shall establish as the date and time of filing of such certificate the date and time that would have been the date and time of filing of the rejected certificate had it been accepted for filing. The Secretary of State shall not issue a certificate of good standing with respect to any limited partnership with a certificate held in suspension pursuant to this subsection. The Secretary of State may establish as the date and time of filing of a certificate the date and time at which information from such certificate is entered pursuant to subdivision (a)(4) of this section if such certificate is delivered on the same date and within 4 hours after such information is entered.

(6) If:

a. Together with the actual delivery of a certificate and tender of the required fees, there is delivered to the Secretary of State a separate affidavit (which in its heading shall be designated as an affidavit of extraordinary condition) attesting, on the basis of personal knowledge of the affiant or a reliable source of knowledge identified in the affidavit, that an earlier effort to deliver such certificate and tender such fees was made in good faith, specifying the nature, date and time of such good faith effort and requesting that the Secretary of State establish such date and time as the date and time of filing of such certificate; or

b. Upon the actual delivery of a certificate and tender of the required fees, the Secretary of State in his or her discretion provides a written waiver of the requirement for such an affidavit stating that it appears to the Secretary of State that an earlier effort to deliver such certificate and tender such fees was made in good faith and specifying the date and time of such effort; and

c. The Secretary of State determines that an extraordinary condition existed at such date and time, that such earlier effort was unsuccessful as a result of the existence of such extraordinary condition, and that such actual delivery and tender were made within a reasonable period (not to exceed 2 business days) after the cessation of such extraordinary condition, then the Secretary of State may establish such date and time as the date and time of filing of such certificate. No fee shall be paid to the Secretary of State for receiving an affidavit of extraordinary condition. For purposes of this subsection, an extraordinary condition means: any emergency resulting from an attack on, invasion or occupation by foreign military forces of, or disaster, catastrophe, war or other armed conflict, revolution or insurrection, or rioting or civil commotion in, the United States or a locality in which the Secretary of State conducts its business or in which the good faith effort to deliver the certificate and tender the required fees is made, or the immediate threat of any of the foregoing; or any malfunction or outage of the electrical or telephone service to the Secretary of State's office, or weather or other condition in or about a locality in which the Secretary of State conducts its business, as a result of which the Secretary of State's office is not open for the purpose of the filing of certificates under this chapter or such filing cannot be effected without extraordinary effort. The Secretary of State may require such proof as it deems necessary to make the determination required under this subparagraph c. of this subdivision, and any such determination shall be conclusive in the absence of actual fraud. If the Secretary of State establishes the date and time of filing of a certificate pursuant to this subsection, the date and time of delivery of the affidavit of extraordinary condition or the date and time of the Secretary of State's written waiver of such affidavit shall be endorsed on such affidavit or waiver and such affidavit or waiver, so endorsed, shall be attached to the filed certificate to which it relates. Such filed certificate shall be effective as of the date and time established as the date and time of filing by the Secretary of State pursuant to this subsection, except as to those persons who are substantially and adversely affected by such establishment and, as to those persons, the certificate shall be effective from the date and time endorsed on the affidavit of extraordinary condition or written waiver attached thereto.

(b) Upon the filing of a certificate of amendment (or judicial decree of amendment), certificate of correction, corrected certificate or restated certificate in the Office of the Secretary of State, or upon the future effective date or time of a certificate of amendment (or judicial decree thereof) or restated certificate, as provided for therein, the certificate of limited partnership shall be amended, corrected or restated as set forth therein. Upon the filing of a certificate of cancellation (or a judicial decree thereof), or a certificate of merger or consolidation which acts as a certificate of cancellation, or a certificate of transfer, or a certificate of conversion to a non-Delaware entity, or upon the future effective date or time of a certificate of cancellation (or a judicial decree thereof) or of a certificate of merger or consolidation which acts as a certificate of cancellation, or a certificate of transfer, or a certificate of conversion to a non-Delaware entity, as provided for therein, or as specified in § 17-104(d) or § 17-104(i)(4) of this title, the certificate of limited partnership is cancelled. Upon the filing of a certificate of limited partnership domestication, or upon the future effective date or time of a certificate of limited partnership domestication, the entity filing the certificate of limited partnership domestication is domesticated as a limited partnership with the effect provided in § 17-215 of this title. Upon the filing of a certificate of conversion to limited partnership, or upon the future effective date or time of a certificate of conversion to limited partnership, the entity filing the certificate of conversion to limited partnership is converted to a limited partnership with the effect provided in § 17-217 of this title. Upon the filing of a certificate of revival, the limited partnership shall be revived with the effect provided in § 17-1111 of this title. Upon the filing of a certificate of transfer and continuance, or upon the future effective date or time of a certificate of transfer and continuance, as provided for therein, the limited partnership filing the certificate of transfer and continuance shall continue to exist as a limited partnership of the State of Delaware with the effect provided in § 17-216 of this title.

(c) If any certificate filed in accordance with this chapter provides for a future effective date or time and if, prior to such future effective date or time set forth in such certificate, the transaction is terminated or its terms are amended to change the future effective date or time or any other matter described in such certificate so as to make such certificate false or inaccurate in any respect, such certificate shall, prior to the future effective date or time set forth in such certificate, be terminated or amended by the filing of a certificate of termination or certificate of amendment of such certificate, executed in accordance with § 17-204 of this title, which shall identify the certificate which has been terminated or amended and shall state that the certificate has been terminated or the manner in which it has been amended. Upon the filing of a certificate of amendment of a certificate with a future effective date or time, the certificate identified in such certificate of amendment is amended. Upon the filing of a certificate of termination of a certificate with a future effective date or time, the certificate identified in such certificate of termination is terminated.

(d) A fee as set forth in § 17-1107(a)(3) of this title shall be paid at the time of the filing of a certificate of limited partnership, a certificate of amendment, a certificate of correction, a certificate of amendment of a certificate with a future effective date or time, a certificate of termination of a certificate with a future effective date of time, a certificate of termination of a merger or consolidation, a certificate of cancellation, a certificate of merger or consolidation, a restated certificate, a corrected certificate, a certificate of conversion to limited partnership, a certificate of conversion to a non-Delaware entity, a certificate of transfer, certificate of transfer and continuance, a certificate of limited partnership domestication or a certificate of revival.

(e) A fee as set forth in § 17–1107(a)(4) of this title shall be paid for a certified copy of any paper on file as provided for by this chapter, and a fee as set forth in § 17–1107(a)(5) of this title shall be paid for each page copied.

§ 17–207. Liability for False Statement

(a) If any certificate of limited partnership or certificate of amendment, correction, revival or cancellation or certificate of conversion to limited partnership, or certificate of conversion to a non-Delaware entity, certificate of transfer, certificate of transfer and continuance, or certificate of limited partnership domestication contains a materially false statement, one who suffers loss by reasonable reliance on the statement may recover damages for the loss from:

(1) Any general partner who executes the certificate and knew or should have known the statement to be false in any material respect at the time the certificate was executed; and

(2) Any general partner who thereafter knows that any arrangement or other fact described in the certificate is false in any material respect or has changed, making the statement false in any material respect, if that general partner had sufficient time to amend, correct or cancel the certificate, or to file a petition for its amendment, correction or cancellation, before the statement was reasonably relied upon.

(b) No general partner shall have any liability for failing to cause the amendment, correction or cancellation of a certificate to be filed or failing to file a petition for its amendment, correction or cancellation pursuant to subsection (a) of this section if the certificate of amendment, certificate of correction, certificate of cancellation or petition is filed within 90 days of when that general partner knew or should have known to the extent provided in subsection (a) of this section that the statement in the certificate was false in any material respect.

§ 17–208. Notice

The fact that a certificate of limited partnership is on file in the Office of the Secretary of State is notice that the partnership is a limited partnership and is notice of all other facts set forth therein which are required to be set forth in a certificate of limited partnership by § 17–201(a)(1)-(3) and by § 17–202(f) of this title and which are permitted to be set forth in a certificate of limited partnership by § 17–218(b) of this title.

§ 17–209. Delivery of Certificates to Limited Partners

Upon the return by the Secretary of State pursuant to § 17–206 of this title of a certificate marked "Filed," the general partners shall promptly deliver or mail a copy of the certificate to each limited partner if the partnership agreement so requires.

§ 17–210. Restated Certificate

(a) A limited partnership may, whenever desired, integrate into a single instrument all of the provisions of its certificate of limited partnership which are then in effect and operative as a result of there having theretofore been filed with the Secretary of State 1 or more certificates or other instruments pursuant to any of the sections referred to in this subchapter and it may at the same time also further amend its certificate of limited partnership by adopting a restated certificate of limited partnership.

(b) If the restated certificate of limited partnership merely restates and integrates but does not further amend the initial certificate of limited partnership, as theretofore amended or supplemented by any instrument that was executed and filed pursuant to any of the sections in this subchapter, it shall be specifically designated in its heading as a "Restated Certificate of Limited Partnership" together with such other words as the partnership may deem appropriate and shall be executed by a general partner and filed as provided in § 17–206 of this title in the Office of the Secretary of State. If the restated certificate restates and integrates and also further amends in any respect the certificate of limited partnership, as theretofore amended or supplemented, it shall be specifically designated in its heading as an "Amended and Restated Certificate of Limited Partnership" together with such other words as the partnership may deem appropriate and shall be executed by at least 1 general partner and by each other general partner designated in the restated certificate of limited partnership as a new general partner, but if the restated certificate reflects the withdrawal of a general partner as a general partner, such restated certificate of limited partnership need not be signed by that former general partner, and filed as provided in § 17–206 of this title in the Office of the Secretary of State.

(c) A restated certificate of limited partnership shall state, either in its heading or in an introductory paragraph, the limited partnership's present name, and, if it has been changed, the name under which it was originally filed, and the date of filing of its original certificate of limited partnership with the Secretary of State, and the future effective date or time (which shall be a date or time certain) of the restated certificate if it is not to be effective upon the filing of the restated certificate. A restated certificate shall also state that it was duly executed and is being filed in accordance with this section. If the restated certificate only restates and integrates and does not further amend the limited partnership's certificate of limited partnership as theretofore amended or supplemented and there is no discrepancy between those provisions and the restated certificate, it shall state that fact as well.

(d) Upon the filing of the restated certificate of limited partnership with the Secretary of State, or upon the future effective date or time of a restated certificate of limited partnership as provided for therein, the initial certificate of limited partnership, as theretofore amended or supplemented, shall be superseded; thenceforth, the restated certificate of limited partnership, including any further amendment or changes made thereby, shall be the certificate of limited partnership of the limited partnership, but the original effective date of formation shall remain unchanged.

(e) Any amendment or change effected in connection with the restatement and integration of the certificate of limited partnership shall be subject to any other provision of this chapter, not inconsistent with this section, which would apply if a separate certificate of amendment were filed to effect such amendment or change.

§ 17–211. Merger and Consolidation

(a) As used in this section, "other business entity" means a corporation, a statutory trust, a business trust or association, a real estate investment trust, a common-law trust, a limited liability company, or an unincorporated business, including a partnership (whether general (including a limited liability partnership) or limited (including a foreign limited liability limited partnership), but excluding a domestic limited partnership).

(b) Pursuant to an agreement of merger or consolidation, 1 or more domestic limited partnerships may merge or consolidate with or into 1 or more domestic limited partnerships or 1 or more other business entities formed or organized under the laws of the State of Delaware or any other state or the United States or any foreign country or other foreign jurisdiction, or any combination thereof, with such domestic limited partnership or other business entity as the agreement shall provide being the surviving or resulting domestic limited partnership or other business entity. Unless otherwise provided in the partnership agreement, a merger or consolidation shall be approved by each domestic limited partnership which is to merge or consolidate (1) by all general partners, and (2) by the limited partners or, if there is more than 1 class or group of limited partners, then by each class or group of limited partners, in either case, by limited partners who own more than 50 percent of the then current percentage or other interest in the profits of the domestic limited partnership owned by all of the limited partners or by the limited partners in each class or group, as appropriate. In connection with a merger or consolidation hereunder, rights or securities of, or interests in, a limited partnership or other business entity which is a constituent party to the merger or consolidation may be exchanged for or converted into cash, property, rights or securities of, or interests in, the surviving or resulting limited partnership or other business entity or, in addition to or in lieu thereof, may be exchanged for or converted into cash, property, rights or securities of, or interests in, a limited partnership or other business entity which is not the surviving or resulting limited partnership or other business entity in the merger or consolidation or may be cancelled. Notwithstanding prior approval, an agreement of merger or consolidation may be terminated or amended pursuant to a provision for such termination or amendment contained in the agreement of merger or consolidation.

(c) If a domestic limited partnership is merging or consolidating under this section, the domestic limited partnership or other business entity surviving or resulting in or from the merger or consolidation shall file a certificate of merger or consolidation executed by at least 1 general partner on behalf of the domestic limited partnership when it is the surviving or resulting entity in the office of the Secretary of State. The certificate of merger or consolidation shall state:

(1) The name and jurisdiction of formation or organization of each of the domestic limited partnerships and other business entities which is to merge or consolidate;

(2) That an agreement of merger or consolidation has been approved and executed by each of the domestic limited partnerships and other business entities which is to merge or consolidate;

(3) The name of the surviving or resulting domestic limited partnership or other business entity;

(4) In the case of a merger in which a domestic limited partnership is the surviving entity, such amendments, if any, to the certificate of limited partnership of the surviving domestic limited partnership (and in the case of a surviving domestic limited partnership that is a limited liability limited partnership, to the statement of qualification of such surviving domestic limited partnership filed under § 15-1001 of this title) to change its name as are desired to be effected by the merger;

(5) The future effective date or time (which shall be a date or time certain) of the merger or consolidation if it is not to be effective upon the filing of the certificate of merger or consolidation;

(6) That the agreement of merger or consolidation is on file at a place of business of the surviving or resulting domestic limited partnership or other business entity, and shall state the address thereof;

(7) That a copy of the agreement of merger or consolidation will be furnished by the surviving or resulting domestic limited partnership or other business entity, on request and without cost, to any partner of any domestic limited partnership or any person holding

an interest in any other business entity which is to merge or consolidate; and

(8) If the surviving or resulting entity is not a domestic limited partnership or corporation or limited liability company organized under the laws of the State of Delaware or a statutory trust organized under Chapter 38 of Title 12, a statement that such surviving or resulting other business entity agrees that it may be served with process in the State of Delaware in any action, suit or proceeding for the enforcement of any obligation of any domestic limited partnership which is to merge or consolidate, irrevocably appointing the Secretary of State as its agent to accept service of process in any such action, suit or proceeding and specifying the address to which a copy of such process shall be mailed to it by the Secretary of State. In the event of service hereunder upon the Secretary of State, the procedures set forth in § 17-911(c) of this title shall be applicable, except that the plaintiff in any such action, suit or proceeding shall furnish the Secretary of State with the address specified in the certificate of merger or consolidation provided for in this section and any other address which the plaintiff may elect to furnish, together with copies of such process as required by the Secretary of State, and the Secretary of State shall notify such surviving or resulting other business entity at all such addresses furnished by the plaintiff in accordance with the procedures set forth in § 17-911(c) of this title.

(d) Any failure to file a certificate of merger or consolidation in connection with a merger or consolidation pursuant to this section which was effective prior to September 1, 1988, shall not affect the validity or effectiveness of any such merger or consolidation.

(e) Unless a future effective date or time is provided in a certificate of merger or consolidation, in which event a merger or consolidation shall be effective at any such future effective date or time, a merger or consolidation shall be effective upon the filing in the Office of the Secretary of State of a certificate of merger or consolidation.

(f) A certificate of merger or consolidation shall act as a certificate of cancellation for a domestic limited partnership which is not the surviving or resulting entity in the merger or consolidation. A certificate of merger that sets forth any amendment in accordance with subsection (c)(4) of this section shall be deemed to be an amendment to the certificate of limited partnership (and if applicable to the statement of qualification) of the limited partnership, and the limited partnership shall not be required to take any further action to amend its certificate of limited partnership under § 17-202 of this title (or if applicable its statement of qualification under § 15-105 of this title) with respect to such amendments set forth in the certificate of merger. Whenever this section requires the filing of a certificate of merger or consolidation, such requirement shall be deemed satisfied by the filing of an agreement of merger or consolidation containing the information required by this section to be set forth in the certificate of merger or consolidation.

(g) An agreement of merger or consolidation approved in accordance with subsection (b) of this section may (1) effect any amendment to the partnership agreement or (2) effect the adoption of a new partnership agreement for a limited partnership if it is the surviving or resulting limited partnership in the merger or consolidation. Any amendment to a partnership agreement or adoption of a new partnership agreement made pursuant to the foregoing sentence shall be effective at the effective time or date of the merger or consolidation. The provisions of this subsection shall not be construed to limit the accomplishment of a merger or of any of the matters referred to herein by any other means provided for in a partnership agreement or other agreement or as otherwise permitted by law, including that the partnership agreement of any constituent limited partnership to the merger or consolidation (including a limited partnership formed for the purpose of consummating a merger or consolidation) shall be the partnership agreement of the surviving or resulting limited partnership. Unless otherwise provided in a partnership agreement, a limited partnership whose original certificate of limited partnership was filed with the Secretary of State and effective on or prior to July 31, 2005, shall continue to be governed by this subsection as in effect on July 31, 2005.

(h) When any merger or consolidation shall have become effective under this section, for all purposes of the laws of the State of Delaware, all of the rights, privileges and powers of each of the domestic limited partnerships and other business entities that have merged or consolidated, and all property, real, personal and mixed, and all debts due to any of said domestic limited partnerships and other business entities, as well as all other things and causes of action belonging to each of such domestic limited partnerships and other business entities, shall be vested in the surviving or resulting domestic limited partnership or other business entity, and shall thereafter be the property of the surviving or resulting domestic limited partnership or other business entity as they were of each of the domestic limited partnerships and other business entities that have merged or consolidated, and the title to any real property vested by deed or otherwise, under the laws of the State of Delaware, in any of such domestic limited partnerships and other business entities, shall not revert or be in any way impaired by reason of this chapter; but all rights of creditors and all liens upon any property of any of said domestic limited partnerships and other business entities shall be preserved unimpaired, and all debts, liabilities and duties of each of the said domestic limited partnerships and other business entities that have merged or consolidated shall thenceforth attach to the surviving or resulting domestic limited partnership or other business entity, and may be enforced against it to the same extent as if said debts, liabilities and duties had been incurred or contracted by it. Unless otherwise agreed, a merger or consolidation of a domestic limited partnership, including a domestic limited partnership which is not the surviving or resulting entity in the merger or consolidation, shall not require such domestic limited partnership to wind up its affairs under § 17-803 of this title or pay its liabilities and distribute its assets under § 17-804 of this title.

(i) Except as provided by agreement with a person to whom a general partner of a limited partnership is obligated, a merger or consolidation of a limited partnership that has become effective shall not affect any obligation or liability existing at the time of such merger or consolidation of a general partner of a limited partnership which is merging or consolidating.

(j) If a limited partnership is a constituent party to a merger or consolidation that shall have become effective, but the limited partnership is not the surviving or resulting entity of the merger or consolidation, then a judgment creditor of a general partner of such limited partnership may not levy execution against the assets of the general partner to satisfy a judgment based on a claim against the surviving or resulting entity of the merger or consolidation unless:

(1) A judgment based on the same claim has been obtained against the surviving or resulting entity of the merger or consolidation and a writ of execution on the judgment has been returned unsatisfied in whole or in part;

(2) The surviving or resulting entity of the merger or consolidation is a debtor in bankruptcy;

(3) The general partner has agreed that the creditor need not exhaust the assets of the limited partnership that was not the surviving or resulting entity of the merger or consolidation;

(4) The general partner has agreed that the creditor need not exhaust the assets of the surviving or resulting entity of the merger or consolidation;

(5) A court grants permission to the judgment creditor to levy execution against the assets of the general partner based on a finding that the assets of the surviving or resulting entity of the merger or consolidation that are subject to execution are clearly insufficient to satisfy the judgment, that exhaustion of the assets of the surviving or resulting entity of the merger or consolidation is excessively burdensome, or that the grant of permission is an appropriate exercise of the court's equitable powers; or

(6) Liability is imposed on the general partner by law or contract independent of the existence of the surviving or resulting entity of the merger or consolidation.

§ 17-212. Contractual Appraisal Rights

A partnership agreement or an agreement of merger or consolidation may provide that contractual appraisal rights with respect to a partnership interest or another interest in a limited partnership shall be available for any class or group of partners or partnership interests in connection with any amendment of a partnership agreement, any merger or consolidation in which the limited partnership is a constituent party to the merger or consolidation, any conversion of the limited partnership to another business form, any transfer to or domestication in any jurisdiction by the limited partnership, or the sale of all or substantially all of the limited partnership's assets. The Court of Chancery shall have jurisdiction to hear and determine any matter relating to any such appraisal rights.

§ 17–213. Certificate of Correction

(a) Whenever any certificate authorized to be filed with the office of the Secretary of State under any provision of this chapter has been so filed and is an inaccurate record of the action therein referred to, or was defectively or erroneously executed, such certificate may be corrected by filing with the office of the Secretary of State a certificate of correction of such certificate. The certificate of correction shall specify the inaccuracy or defect to be corrected, shall set forth the portion of the certificate in corrected form and shall be executed and filed as required by this chapter. The certificate of correction shall be effective as of the date the original certificate was filed except as to those persons who are substantially and adversely affected by the correction, and as to those persons, the certificate of correction shall be effective from the filing date.

(b) In lieu of filing a certificate of correction, a certificate may be corrected by filing with the Secretary of State a corrected certificate which shall be executed and filed as if the corrected certificate were the certificate being corrected, and a fee equal to the fee payable to the Secretary of State if the certificate being corrected were then being filed shall be paid to and collected by the Secretary of State for the use of the State of Delaware in connection with the filing of the corrected certificate. The corrected certificate shall be specifically designated as such in its heading, shall specify the inaccuracy or defect to be corrected and shall set forth the entire certificate in corrected form. A certificate corrected in accordance with this section shall be effective as of the date the original certificate was filed except as to those persons who are substantially and adversely affected by the correction and, as to those persons, the certificate as corrected shall be effective from the filing date.

§ 17–214. Limited Partnerships as Limited Liability Limited Partnerships

(a) A limited partnership may be formed as, or may become, a limited liability limited partnership pursuant to this section. A limited partnership may become a limited liability limited partnership as permitted by the limited partnership's partnership agreement or, if the limited partnership's partnership agreement does not provide for the limited partnership's becoming a limited liability limited partnership, with the approval (i) by all general partners, and (ii) by the limited partners, or, if there is more than 1 class or group of limited partners, then by each class or group of limited partners, in either case, by limited partners who own more than 50 percent of the then current percentage or other interest in the profits of the limited partnership owned by all of the limited partners or by the limited partners in each class or group, as appropriate. To be formed or to become, and to continue as, a limited liability limited partnership, a limited partnership shall, in addition to complying with the requirements of this chapter:

(1) File a statement of qualification as provided in § 15-1001 of this title and thereafter an annual report as provided in § 15-1003 of this title; and

(2) Have as the last words or letters of its name the words "Limited Liability Limited Partnership," or the abbreviation "L.L.L.P.," or the designation "LLLP."

(b) In applying the Delaware Revised Uniform Partnership Act [Chapter 15 of this title] to a limited liability limited partnership for the purposes of subsections (a) and (c) of this section:

(1) Any statement shall be executed by at least 1 general partner of the limited partnership; and

(2) All references to partners mean general partners only.

(c) If a limited partnership is a limited liability limited partnership, (i) its partners who are liable for the debts, liabilities and other obligations of the limited partnership shall have the limitation on liability afforded to partners of limited liability partnerships under the Delaware Revised Uniform Partnership Act [Chapter 15 of this title], and (ii) no limited partner of the limited partnership shall have any liability for the obligations of the limited partnership under § 17-303(a) of this title.

(d) Except as provided in subsections (a), (b) and (c) of this section, a limited liability limited partnership shall be governed by this chapter, including, without limitation, § 17-1105 of this chapter.

(e) Notwithstanding anything in this chapter to the contrary, a limited partnership having, on December 31, 1999, the status of a registered limited liability limited partnership under predecessor law shall have the status of a limited liability limited partnership under this chapter as of January 1, 2000, and to the extent such limited partnership has not filed a statement of qualification pursuant to § 15-1001 of the Delaware Revised Uniform Partnership Act, the latest application or renewal application filed by such limited partnership under such predecessor law shall constitute a statement of qualification filed under § 15-1001 of the Delaware Revised Uniform Partnership Act.

§ 17–215. Domestication of non-United States Entities

(a) As used in this section, "non-United States entity" means a foreign limited partnership (other than one formed under the laws of a state)(including a foreign limited liability limited partnership (other than one formed under the laws of a state)), or a corporation, a statutory trust, a business trust, an association, a real estate investment trust, a common-law trust or any other unincorporated business or entity, including a general partnership (including a limited liability partnership) or a limited liability company, formed, incorporated, created or that otherwise came into being under the laws of any foreign country or other foreign jurisdiction (other than any state).

(b) Any non-United States entity may become domesticated as a limited partnership in the State of Delaware by complying with subsection (g) of this section and filing in the office of the Secretary of State in accordance with § 17–206 of this title:

(1) A certificate of limited partnership domestication that has been executed in accordance with § 17–204 of this title; and

(2) A certificate of limited partnership that complies with § 17–201 of this title and has been executed in accordance with § 17–204 of this title.

(c) The certificate of limited partnership domestication shall state:

(1) The date on which and jurisdiction where the non-United States entity was first formed, incorporated, created or otherwise came into being;

(2) The name of the non-United States entity immediately prior to the filing of the certificate of limited partnership domestication;

(3) The name of the limited partnership as set forth in the certificate of limited partnership filed in accordance with subsection (b) of this section;

(4) The future effective date or time (which shall be a date or time certain) of the domestication as a limited partnership if it is not to be effective upon the filing of the certificate of limited partnership domestication and the certificate of limited partnership;

(5) The jurisdiction that constituted the seat, siege social, or principal place of business or central administration of the non-United States entity, or any other equivalent thereto under applicable law, immediately prior to the filing of the certificate of limited partnership domestication; and

(6) That the domestication has been approved in the manner provided for by the document, instrument, agreement or other writing, as the case may be, governing the internal affairs of the non-United States entity and the conduct of its business or by applicable non-Delaware law, as appropriate.

(d) Upon the filing in the office of the Secretary of State of the certificate of limited partnership domestication and the certificate of limited partnership or upon the future effective date or time of the certificate of limited partnership domestication and the certificate of limited partnership, the non-United States entity shall be domesticated as a limited partnership in the State of Delaware and the limited partnership shall thereafter be subject to all of the provisions of this chapter, except that notwithstanding § 17–201 of this title, the existence of the limited partnership shall be deemed to have commenced on the date the non-United States entity commenced its existence in the jurisdiction in which the non-United States entity was first formed, incorporated, created or otherwise came into being.

(e) The domestication of any non-United States entity as a limited partnership in the State of Delaware shall not be deemed to affect any obligations or liabilities of the non-United States entity incurred prior to its domestication as a limited partnership in the State of Delaware, or the personal liability of any person therefor.

(f) The filing of a certificate of limited partnership domestication shall not affect the choice of law applicable to the non-United States entity, except that from the effective date or time of the domestication, the law of the State of Delaware, including the provisions of this chapter, shall apply to the non-United States entity to the same extent as if the non-United States entity had been formed as a limited partnership on that date.

(g) Prior to the filing of a certificate of limited partnership domestication with the office of the Secretary of State, the domestication shall be approved in the manner provided for by the document, instrument, agreement or other writing, as the case may be, governing the internal affairs of the non-United States entity and the conduct of its business or by applicable non-Delaware law, as appropriate, and a partnership agreement shall be approved by the same authorization required to approve the domestication; provided that, in any event, such approval shall include the approval of any person who, at the effective date or time of the domestication, shall be a general partner of the limited partnership.

(h) When any domestication shall have become effective under this section, for all purposes of the laws of the State of Delaware, all of the rights, privileges and powers of the non-United States entity that has been domesticated, and all property, real, personal and mixed, and all debts due to such non-United States entity, as well as all other things and causes of action belonging to such non-United States entity, shall remain vested in the domestic limited partnership to which such non-United States entity has been domesticated (and also in the non-United States entity, if and for so long as the non-United States entity continues its existence in the foreign jurisdiction in which it was existing immediately prior to the domestication) and shall be the property of such domestic limited partnership (and also of the non-United States entity, if and for so long as the non-United States entity continues its existence in the foreign jurisdiction in which it was existing immediately prior to the domestication), and the title to any real property vested by deed or otherwise in such non-United States entity shall not revert or be in any way impaired by reason of this chapter; but all rights of creditors and all liens upon any property of such non-United States entity shall be preserved unimpaired, and all debts, liabilities and duties of the non-United States entity that has been domesticated shall remain attached to the domestic limited partnership to which such non-United States entity has been domesticated (and also to the non-United States entity, if and for so long as the non-United States entity continues its existence in the foreign jurisdiction in which it was existing immediately prior to the domestication), and may be enforced against it to the same extent as if said debts, liabilities and duties had originally been incurred or contracted by it in its capacity as a domestic limited partnership. The rights, privileges, powers and interests in property of the non-United States entity, as well as the debts, liabilities and duties of the non-United States entity, shall not be deemed, as a consequence of the domestication, to have been transferred to the domestic limited partnership to which such non-United States entity has domesticated for any purpose of the laws of the State of Delaware.

(i) When a non-United States entity has become domesticated as a limited partnership pursuant to this section, for all purposes of the laws of the State of Delaware the limited partnership shall,, be deemed to be the same entity as the domesticating non-United States entity and the domestication shall constitute a continuation of the existence of the domesticating non-United States entity in the form of a domestic limited partnership. Unless otherwise agreed, for all purposes of the laws of the State of Delaware, the domesticating non-United States entity shall not be required to wind up its affairs or pay its liabilities and distribute its assets, and the domestication shall not be deemed to constitute a dissolution of such non-United States entity. If, following domestication, a non-United States entity that has become domesticated as a limited partnership continues its existence in the foreign country or other foreign jurisdiction in which it was existing immediately prior to domestication, the limited partnership and such non-United States entity shall, for all purposes of the laws of the State of Delaware, constitute a single entity formed, incorporated, created or otherwise having come into being, as applicable, and existing under the laws of the State of Delaware and the laws of such foreign country or other foreign jurisdiction.

(j) In connection with a domestication hereunder, rights or securities of, or interests in, the non-United States entity that is to be domesticated as a domestic limited partnership may be exchanged for or converted into cash, property, rights or securities of, or interests in, such domestic limited partnership or, in addition to or in lieu thereof, may be exchanged for or converted into cash, property, rights or securities of, or interests in, another domestic limited partnership or other entity or may be cancelled.

§ 17-216. Transfer or Continuance of Domestic Limited Partnerships

(a) Upon compliance with the provisions of this section, any limited partnership may transfer to or domesticate or continue in any jurisdiction, other than any state, and, in connection therewith, may elect to continue its existence as a limited partnership in the State of Delaware.

(b) If the partnership agreement specifies the manner of authorizing a transfer or domestication or continuance described in subsection (a) of this section, the transfer or domestication or continuance shall be authorized as specified in the partnership agreement. If the partnership agreement does not specify the manner of authorizing a transfer or domestication or continuance described in subsection (a) of this section and does not prohibit such a transfer or domestication or continuance, the transfer or domestication or continuance shall be authorized in the same manner as is specified in the partnership agreement for authorizing a merger or consolidation that involves the limited partnership as a constituent party to the merger or consolidation. If the partnership agreement does not specify the manner of authorizing a transfer or domestication or continuance described in subsection (a) of this section or a merger or consolidation that involves the limited partnership as a constituent party and does not prohibit such a transfer or domestication or continuance, the transfer or domestication or continuance shall be authorized by the approval by (1) all general partners and (2) the limited partners or, if there is more than 1 class or group of limited partners, then by each class or group of limited partners, in either case, by limited partners who own more than 50 percent of the then current percentage or other interest in the profits of the domestic limited partnership owned by all of the limited partners or by the limited partners in each class or group, as appropriate. If a transfer or domestication or continuance described in subsection (a) of this section shall be authorized as provided in this subsection (b), a certificate of transfer if the limited partnership's existence as a limited partnership of the State of Delaware is to cease or a certificate of transfer and domestic continuance if the limited partnership's existence as a limited partnership in the State of Delaware is to continue, executed in accordance with § 17-204 of this title, shall be filed in the office of the Secretary of State in accordance with § 17-206 of this title. The certificate of transfer or the certificate of transfer and domestic continuance shall state:

(1) The name of the limited partnership and, if it has been changed, the name under which its certificate of limited partnership was originally filed;

(2) The date of the filing of its original certificate of limited partnership with the Secretary of State;

(3) The jurisdiction to which the limited partnership shall be transferred or in which it shall be domesticated or continued and the name of the entity or business form formed, incorporated, created or that otherwise comes into being as a consequence of the transfer of the limited partnership to, or its domestication or continuance in, such foreign jurisdiction;

(4) The future effective date or time (which shall be a date or time certain) of the transfer to or domestication or continuance in the jurisdiction specified in subsection (b)(3) of this section if it is not to be effective upon the filing of the certificate of transfer or the certificate of transfer and domestic continuance;

(5) That the transfer or domestication or continuance of the limited partnership has been approved in accordance with the provisions of this section;

(6) In the case of a certificate of transfer, (i) that the existence of the limited partnership as a limited partnership of the State of Delaware shall cease when the certificate of transfer becomes effective and (ii) the agreement of the limited partnership that it may be served with process in the State of Delaware in any action, suit or proceeding for enforcement of any obligation of the limited partnership arising while it was a limited partnership of the State, and that it irrevocably appoints the Secretary of State as its agent to accept service of process in any such action, suit or proceeding;

(7) The address to which a copy of the process referred to in subsection (b)(6) of this section shall be mailed to it by the Secretary of State. In the event of service hereunder upon the Secretary of State, the procedures set forth in § 17-911(c) of this title shall be applicable, except that the plaintiff in any such action, suit or proceeding shall furnish the Secretary of State with the address specified in this subsection and any other address that the plaintiff may elect to furnish, together with copies of such process as required by the Secretary of State, and the Secretary of State shall notify the limited partnership that has transferred or domesticated or continued out of the State of Delaware at all such addresses furnished by the plaintiff in accordance with the procedures set forth in § 17-911(c) of this title; and

(8) In the case of a certificate of transfer and domestic continuance, that the limited partnership will continue to exist as a limited partnership of the State of Delaware after the certificate of transfer and domestic continuance becomes effective.

(c) Upon the filing in the office of the Secretary of State of the certificate of transfer or upon the future effective date or time of the certificate of transfer and payment to the Secretary of State of all fees prescribed in this chapter, the Secretary of State shall certify that the limited partnership has filed all documents and paid all fees required by this chapter and thereupon the limited partnership shall cease to exist as a limited partnership of the State of Delaware. Such certificate of the Secretary of State shall be prima facie evidence of the transfer or domestication or continuance by such limited partnership out of the State of Delaware.

(d) The transfer or domestication or continuance of a limited partnership out of the State of Delaware in accordance with this section and the resulting cessation of its existence as a limited partnership of the State of Delaware pursuant to a certificate of transfer shall not be deemed to affect any obligations or liabilities of the limited partnership incurred prior to such transfer or domestication or continuance or the personal liability of any person incurred prior to such transfer or domestication or continuance, nor shall it be deemed to affect the choice of law applicable to the limited partnership with respect to matters arising prior to such transfer or domestication or continuance. Unless otherwise agreed, the transfer or domestication or continuance of a limited partnership out of the State of Delaware in accordance with this section shall not require such limited partnership to wind up its affairs under § 17–803 of this title or pay its liabilities and distribute its assets under § 17–804 of this title and shall not be deemed to constitute a dissolution of such limited partnership.

(e) If a limited partnership files a certificate of transfer and domestic continuance, after the time the certificate of transfer and domestic continuance becomes effective, the limited partnership shall continue to exist as a limited partnership of the State of Delaware, and the laws of the State of Delaware, including the provisions of this chapter, shall apply to the limited partnership, to the same extent as prior to such time. So long as a limited partnership continues to exist as a limited partnership of the State of Delaware following the filing of a certificate of transfer and domestic continuance, the continuing domestic limited partnership and the entity or business form formed, incorporated, created or that otherwise came into being as a consequence of the transfer of the limited partnership to, or its domestication or continuance in, a foreign country or other foreign jurisdiction shall, for all purposes of the laws of the State of Delaware, constitute a single entity formed, incorporated, created or otherwise having come into being, as applicable, and existing under the laws of the State of Delaware and the laws of such foreign country or other foreign jurisdiction.

(f) In connection with a transfer or domestication or continuance of a domestic limited partnership to or in another jurisdiction pursuant to subsection (a) of this section, rights or securities of, or interests in, such limited partnership may be exchanged for or converted into cash, property, rights or securities of, or interests in, the entity or business form in which the limited partnership will exist in such other jurisdiction as a consequence of the transfer or domestication or continuance or, in addition to or in lieu thereof, may be exchanged for or converted into cash, property, rights or securities of, or interests in, another entity or business form or may be cancelled.

(g) When a limited partnership has transferred or domesticated or continued out of the State of Delaware pursuant to this section, the transferred or domesticated or continued entity or business form shall, for all purposes of the laws of the State of Delaware, be deemed to be the same entity as the limited partnership and shall constitute a continuation of the existence of such limited partnership in the form of the transferred or domesticated or continued entity or business form. When any transfer or domestication or continuance of a limited partnership out of the State of Delaware shall have become effective under this section, for all purposes of the laws of the State of Delaware, all of the rights, privileges and powers of the limited partnership that has transferred or domesticated or continued, and all property, real, personal and mixed, and all debts due to such limited partnership, as well as all other things and causes of action belonging to such limited partnership, shall remain vested in the transferred or domesticated or continued entity or business form (and also in the limited partnership that has transferred, domesticated or continued, if and for so long as such limited partnership continues its existence as a domestic limited partnership) and shall be the property of such transferred or domesticated or continued entity or business form (and also of the limited partnership that has transferred, domesticated or continued, if and for so long as such limited partnership continues its existence as a domestic limited partnership), and the title to any real property vested by deed or otherwise in such limited partnership shall not revert or be in any way impaired by reason of this chapter; but all rights of creditors and all liens upon any property of such limited partnership shall be preserved unimpaired, and all debts, liabilities and duties of the limited partnership that has transferred or domesticated or continued shall remain attached to the transferred or domesticated or continued entity or business form (and also to the limited partnership that has transferred, domesticated or continued, if and for so long as such limited partnership continues its existence as a domestic limited partnership), and may be enforced against it to the same extent as if said debts, liabilities and duties had originally been incurred or contracted by it in its capacity as the transferred or domesticated or continued entity or business form. The rights, privileges, powers and interests in property of the limited partnership that has transferred or domesticated or continued, as well as the debts, liabilities and duties of such limited partnership, shall not be deemed, as a consequence of the transfer or domestication or continuation out of the State of Delaware, to have been transferred to the transferred or domesticated or continued entity or business form for any purpose of the laws of the State of Delaware.

§ 17-217. Conversion of Certain Entities to a Limited Partnership

(a) As used in this section, the term "other entity" means a corporation, a statutory trust, a business trust, an association, a real estate investment trust, a common-law trust, or any other unincorporated business or entity, including a general partnership (including a limited liability partnership) or a foreign limited partnership (including a foreign limited liability limited partnership) or a limited liability company.

(b) Any other entity may convert to a domestic limited partnership (including a limited liability limited partnership) by complying with subsection (h) of this section and filing in the office of the Secretary of State in accordance with § 17–206 of this title:

(1) A certificate of conversion to limited partnership that has been executed in accordance with § 17–204 of this title;

(2) A certificate of limited partnership that complies with § 17–201 of this title and has been executed in accordance with § 17–204 of this title; and

(3) In the case of a conversion to a limited liability limited partnership, a statement of qualification in accordance with subsection (c) of § 15–1001 of this title.

(c) The certificate of conversion to limited partnership shall state:

(1) The date on which and jurisdiction where the other entity was first created, incorporated, formed or otherwise came into being and, if it has changed, its jurisdiction immediately prior to its conversion to a domestic limited partnership;

(2) The name of the other entity immediately prior to the filing of the certificate of conversion to limited partnership;

(3) The name of the limited partnership as set forth in its certificate of limited partnership filed in accordance with subsection (b) of this section; and

(4) The future effective date or time (which shall be a date or time certain) of the conversion to a limited partnership if it is not to be effective upon the filing of the certificate of conversion to limited partnership and the certificate of limited partnership.

(d) Upon the filing in the office of the Secretary of State of the certificate of conversion to limited partnership, the certificate of limited partnership and the statement of qualification (if applicable), or upon the future effective date or time of the certificate of conversion to limited partnership, the certificate of limited partnership and the statement of qualification (if applicable), the other entity shall be converted into a domestic limited partnership (including a limited liability limited partnership, if applicable) and the limited partnership shall thereafter be subject to all of the provisions of this chapter, except that notwithstanding § 17–201 of this title, the existence of the limited partnership shall be deemed to have commenced on the date the other entity commenced its existence in the jurisdiction in which the other entity was first created, formed, incorporated or otherwise came into being.

(e) The conversion of any other entity into a domestic limited partnership (including a limited liability limited partnership) shall not be deemed to affect any obligations or liabilities of the other entity incurred prior to its conversion to a domestic limited partnership, or the personal liability of any person incurred prior to such conversion.

(f) When any conversion shall have become effective under this section, for all purposes of the laws of the State of Delaware, all of the rights, privileges and powers of the other entity that has converted, and all property, real, personal and mixed, and all debts due to such other entity, as well as all other things and causes of action belonging to such other entity, shall remain vested in the domestic limited partnership to which such other entity has converted and shall be the property of such domestic limited partnership, and the title to any real property vested by deed or otherwise in such other entity shall not revert or be in any way impaired by reason of this chapter; but all rights of creditors and all liens upon any property of such other entity shall be preserved unimpaired, and all debts, liabilities and duties of the other entity that has converted shall remain attached to the domestic limited partnership to which such other entity has converted, and may be enforced against it to the same extent as if said debts, liabilities and duties had originally been incurred or contracted by it in its capacity as a domestic limited partnership. The rights, privileges, powers and interests in property of the other entity, as well as the debts, liabilities and duties of the other entity, shall not be deemed, as a consequence of the conversion, to have been transferred to the domestic limited partnership to which such other entity has converted for any purpose of the laws of the State of Delaware.

(g) Unless otherwise agreed, for all purposes of the laws of the State of Delaware, the converting other entity shall not be required to wind up its affairs or pay its liabilities and distribute its assets, and the conversion shall not be deemed to constitute a dissolution of such other entity. When an other entity has been converted to a limited partnership pursuant to this section, for all purposes of the laws of the State of Delaware, the limited partnership shall be deemed to be the same entity as the converting other entity and the conversion shall constitute a continuation of the existence of the converting other entity in the form of a domestic limited partnership.

(h) Prior to filing a certificate of conversion to limited partnership with the office of the Secretary of State, the conversion shall be approved in the manner provided for by the document, instrument, agreement or other writing, as the case may be, governing the internal affairs of the other entity and the conduct of its business or by applicable law, as appropriate, and a partnership agreement shall be approved by the same authorization required to approve the conversion; provided, that in any event, such approval shall include the approval of any person who, at the effective date or time of the conversion, shall be a general partner of the limited partnership.

(i) In connection with a conversion hereunder, rights or securities of, or interests in, the other entity which is to be converted to a domestic limited partnership may be exchanged for or converted into cash, property, rights or securities of, or interests in, such domestic limited partnership or, in addition to or in lieu thereof, may be exchanged for or converted into cash, property, rights or securities of, or interests in, another domestic limited partnership or other entity or may be cancelled.

(j) The provisions of this section shall not be construed to limit the accomplishment of a change in the law governing, or the domicile of, an other entity to the State of Delaware by any other means provided for in a partnership agreement or other agreement or as otherwise permitted by law, including by the amendment of a partnership agreement or other agreement.

§ 17–218. Series of Limited Partners, General Partners or Partnership Interests

(a) A partnership agreement may establish or provide for the establishment of 1 or more designated series of limited partners, general partners or partnership interests having separate rights, powers or duties with respect to specified property or obligations of the limited partnership or profits and losses associated with specified property or obligations, and any such series may have a separate business purpose or investment objective.

(b) Notwithstanding anything to the contrary set forth in this chapter or under other applicable law, in the event that a partnership agreement establishes or provides for the establishment of 1 or more series or states that the liabilities of a general partner are limited to the liabilities of a designated series, and if separate and distinct records are maintained for any such series and the assets associated with any such series are held in such separate and distinct records (directly or indirectly, including through a nominee or otherwise) and accounted for in such separate and distinct records separately from the other assets of the limited partnership, or any other series thereof, and if the partnership agreement so provides, and if notice of the limitation on liabilities of a series or a general partner as referenced in this subsection is set forth in the certificate of limited partnership, then the debts, liabilities, obligations and expenses incurred, contracted for or otherwise existing with respect to a particular series or general partner shall be enforceable only against the assets of such series or a general partner associated with such series and not against the assets of the limited partnership generally, any other series thereof, or any general partner not associated with such series, and, unless otherwise provided in the partnership agreement, none of the debts, liabilities, obligations and expenses incurred, contracted for or otherwise existing with respect to the limited partnership generally or any other series thereof shall be enforceable against the assets of such series or a general partner associated with such series.

(c) Notice in a certificate of limited partnership of the limitation on liabilities of a series as referenced in subsection (b) of this section shall be sufficient for all purposes of subsection (b) of this section whether or not the limited partnership has established any series when such notice is included in the certificate of limited partnership, and there shall be no requirement that any specific series of the limited partnership be referenced in such notice. The fact that a certificate of limited partnership that contains the notice of the limitation on liabilities of a series or a general partner as referenced in subsection (b) of this section is on file in the office of the Secretary of State shall constitute notice of such limitation on liabilities.

(d) A limited partner may possess or exercise any of the rights and powers or act or attempt to act in 1 or more of the capacities as permitted under § 17–303 of this title, with respect to any series, without participating in the control of the business of the limited partnership or with respect to any series thereof within the meaning of § 17–303(a) of this title. A partnership agreement may provide for classes or groups of general partners or limited partners associated with a series having such relative rights, powers and duties as the partnership agreement may provide, and may make provision for the future creation in the manner provided in the partnership agreement of additional classes or groups of general partners or limited partners associated with the series having such relative rights, powers and duties as may from time to time be established, including rights, powers and duties senior to existing classes and groups of general partners or limited partners associated with the series. A partnership agreement may provide for the taking of an action, including the amendment of the partnership agreement, without the vote or approval of any general partner or limited partner or class or group of general partners or limited partners, including an action to create under the provisions of the partnership agreement a class or group of the series of partnership interests that was not previously outstanding.

(e) A partnership agreement may grant to all or certain identified general partners or limited partners or a specified class or group of the general partners or limited partners associated with a series the right to vote separately or with all or any class or group of the general partners or limited partners associated with the series, on any matter. Voting by general partners or limited partners associated with a series may be on a per capita, number, financial interest, class, group or any other basis.

(f) Section 17–603 of this title shall apply to a limited partner with respect to any series with which the limited partner is associated. Except as otherwise provided in a partnership agreement, any event under this subsection or in a partnership agreement that causes a limited partner to cease to be associated with a series shall not, in itself, cause such limited partner to cease to be associated with any other series or to be a limited partner of the limited partnership or cause the termination of the series, regardless of whether such limited partner was the last remaining limited partner associated with such series. A limited partner shall cease to be a limited partner with respect to a series and to have the power to exercise any rights or powers of a limited partner with respect to such series upon the happening of either of the following events:

(1) The limited partner withdraws with respect to the series in accordance with § 17–603 of this title; or

(2) Except as otherwise provided in the partnership agreement, the limited partner assigns all of his or her partnership interest with respect to the series.

(g) Section 17–602 of this title shall apply to a general partner with respect to any series with which the general partner is associated. A general partner shall cease to be a general partner with respect to a series and to have the power to exercise any rights or powers of a general partner with respect to such series upon an event of withdrawal of the general partner with respect to such series. Except as otherwise provided in a partnership agreement, either of the following events or any event in a partnership agreement that causes a general partner to cease to be associated with a series shall not, in itself, cause such general partner to cease to be associated with any other series or to be a general partner of the limited partnership:

(1) The general partner withdraws with respect to the series in accordance with § 17–602 of this title; or

(2) The general partner assigns all of the general partner's partnership interest with respect to the series.

(h) Notwithstanding § 17–606 of this title, but subject to subsections (i) and (k) of this section, and unless otherwise provided in a partnership agreement, at the time a partner associated with a series that has been established in accordance with subsection (b) of this section becomes entitled to receive a distribution with respect to such series, the partner has the status of, and is entitled to all remedies available to, a creditor of the series, with respect to the distribution. A partnership agreement may provide for the establishment of a record date with respect to allocations and distributions with respect to a series.

(i) Notwithstanding § 17–607(a) of this title, a limited partnership may make a distribution with respect to a series that has been established in accordance with subsection (b) of this section. A limited partnership shall not make a distribution with respect to a series that has been established in accordance with subsection (b) of this section to a partner to the extent that at the time of the distribution, after giving effect to the distribution, all liabilities of such series, other than liabilities to partners on account of their partnership interests with respect to such series and liabilities for which the recourse of creditors is limited to specified property of such series, exceed the fair value of the assets associated with such series, except that the fair value of property of the series that is subject to a liability for which the recourse of creditors is limited shall be included in the assets associated with such series only to the extent that the fair value of that property exceeds that liability. For purposes of the immediately preceding sentence, the term "distribution" shall not include amounts constituting reasonable compensation for present or past services or reasonable payments made in the ordinary course of business pursuant to a bona fide retirement plan or other benefits program. A limited partner who receives a distribution in violation of this subsection, and who knew at the time of the distribution that the distribution violated this subsection, shall be liable to a series for the amount of the distribution. A limited partner who receives a distribution in violation of this subsection, and who did not know at the time of the distribution that the distribution violated this subsection, shall not be liable for the amount of the distribution. Subject to § 17-607(c) of this title, which shall apply to any distribution made with respect to a series under this subsection, this subsection shall not affect any obligation or liability of a limited partner under an agreement or other applicable law for the amount of a distribution.

(j) Subject to § 17-801 of this title, except to the extent otherwise provided in the partnership agreement, a series may be terminated and its affairs wound up without causing the dissolution of the limited partnership. The termination of a series established in accordance with subsection (b) of this section shall not affect the limitation on liabilities of such series provided by subsection (b) of this section. A series is terminated and its affairs shall be wound up upon the dissolution of the limited partnership under § 17-801 of this chapter or otherwise upon the first to occur of the following:

(1) At the time specified in the partnership agreement;

(2) Upon the happening of events specified in the partnership agreement;

(3) Unless otherwise provided in the partnership agreement, upon the affirmative vote or written consent of (i) all general partners associated with such series and (ii) the limited partners associated with such series or, if there is more than 1 class or group of limited partners associated with such series, then by each class or group of limited partners associated with such series, in either case, by limited partners associated with such series who own more than two-thirds of the then-current percentage or other interest in the profits of the limited partnership associated with such series owned by all of the limited partners associated with such series or by the limited partners in each class or group associated with such series, as appropriate;

(4) An event of withdrawal of a general partner associated with the series unless at the time there is at least 1 other general partner associated with the series and the partnership agreement permits the business of the series to be carried on by the remaining general partner and that partner does so, but the series is not terminated and is not required to be wound up by reason of any event of withdrawal if (i) within 90 days or such other period as is provided for in the partnership agreement after the withdrawal either (A) if provided for in the partnership agreement, the then-current percentage or other interest in the profits of the series specified in the partnership agreement owned by the remaining partners associated with the series agree, in writing or vote, to continue the business of the series and to appoint, effective as of the date of withdrawal, 1 or more additional general partners for the series if necessary or desired, or (B) if no such right to agree or vote to continue the business of the series of the limited partnership and to appoint 1 or more additional general partners for such series is provided for in the partnership agreement, then more than 50% of the then-current percentage or other interest in the profits of the series owned by the remaining partners associated with the series or, if there is more than 1 class or group of remaining partners associated with the series, then more than 50% of the then-current percentage or other interest in the profits of the series owned by each class or classes or group or groups of remaining partners associated with the series agree, in writing or vote, to continue the business of the series and to appoint, effective as of the date of withdrawal, 1 or more additional general partners for the series if necessary or desired, or (ii) the business of the series is continued pursuant to a right to continue stated in the partnership agreement and the appointment, effective as of the date of withdrawal, of 1 or more additional general partners to be associated with the series if necessary or desired; or

(5) The termination of such series under subsection (*l*) of this section.

(k) Notwithstanding § 17–803(a) of this title, unless otherwise provided in the partnership agreement, a general partner associated with a series who has not wrongfully terminated the series or, if none, the limited partners associated with the series or a person approved by the limited partners associated with the series or, if there is more than one class or group of limited partners associated with the series, then by each class or group of limited partners associated with the series, in either case, by limited partners who own more than 50 percent of the then current percentage or other interest in the profits of the series owned by all of the limited partners associated with the series or by the limited partners in each class or group associated with the series, as appropriate, may wind up the affairs of the series; but, if the series has been established in accordance with subsection (b) of this section, the Court of Chancery, upon cause shown, may wind up the affairs of the series upon application of any partner associated with the series, the partner's personal representative or assignee, and in connection therewith, may appoint a liquidating trustee. The persons winding up the affairs of a series may, in the name of the limited partnership and for and on behalf of the limited partnership and such series, take all actions with respect to the series as are permitted under § 17–803(b) of this title. The persons winding up the affairs of a series shall provide for the claims and obligations of the series and distribute the assets of the series as provided in § 17–804 of this title, which section shall apply to the winding up and distribution of assets of a series. Actions taken in accordance with this subsection shall not affect the liability of limited partners and shall not impose liability on a liquidating trustee.

(l) On application by or for a partner associated with a series established in accordance with subsection (b) of this section, the Court of Chancery may decree termination of such series whenever it is not reasonably practicable to carry on the business of the series in conformity with a partnership agreement.

(m) If a foreign limited partnership that is registering to do business in the State of Delaware in accordance with § 17–902 of this chapter is governed by a partnership agreement that establishes or provides for the establishment of designated series of limited partners, general partners or partnership interests having separate rights, powers or duties with respect to specified property or obligations of the foreign limited partnership or profits and losses associated with specified property or obligations, that fact shall be so stated on the application for registration as a foreign limited partnership. In addition, the foreign limited partnership shall state on such application whether the debts, liabilities and obligations incurred, contracted for or otherwise existing with respect to a particular series, if any, or general partner associated with such series shall be enforceable only against the assets of such series or any general partner associated with such series and not against the assets of the foreign limited partnership generally, any other series thereof, or any general partner not associated with such series, and, unless otherwise provided in the partnership agreement, none of the debts, liabilities, obligations and expenses incurred, contracted for or otherwise existing with respect to the foreign limited partnership generally or any other series thereof shall be enforceable against the assets of such series or a general partner associated with such series.

§ 17–219. Approval of Conversion of a Limited Partnership

(a) Upon compliance with this section, a domestic limited partnership may convert to a corporation, a statutory trust, a business trust, an association, a real estate investment trust, a common-law trust or any other unincorporated business or entity, including a general partnership (including a limited liability partnership) or a foreign limited partnership (including a foreign limited liability limited partnership) or a limited liability company.

(b) If the partnership agreement specifies the manner of authorizing a conversion of the limited partnership, the conversion shall be authorized as specified in the partnership agreement. If the partnership agreement does not specify the manner of authorizing a conversion of the limited partnership and does not prohibit a conversion of the limited partnership, the conversion shall be authorized in the same manner as is specified in the partnership agreement for authorizing a merger or consolidation that involves the limited partnership as a constituent party to the merger or consolidation. If the partnership agreement does not specify the manner of authorizing a conversion of the limited partnership or a merger or consolidation that involves the limited partnership as a constituent party and does not prohibit a conversion of the limited partnership, the conversion shall be authorized by the approval (1) by all general partners, and (2) by the limited partners or, if there is more than 1 class or group of limited partners, then by each class or group of limited partners, in either case, by limited partners who own more than 50 percent of the then current percentage or other interest in the profits of the domestic limited partnership owned by all of the limited partners or by the limited partners in each class or group, as appropriate.

(c) Unless otherwise agreed, the conversion of a domestic limited partnership to another entity or business form pursuant to this section shall not require such limited partnership to wind up its affairs under § 17-803 of this title or pay its liabilities and distribute its assets under § 17-804 of this title, and the conversion shall not constitute a dissolution of such limited partnership. When a limited partnership has converted to another entity or business form pursuant to this Section, for all purposes of the laws of the State of Delaware, the other entity or business form shall be deemed to be the same entity as the converting limited partnership and the conversion shall constitute a continuation of the existence of the limited partnership in the form of such other entity or business form.

(d) In connection with a conversion of a domestic limited partnership to another entity or business form pursuant to this section, rights or securities of or interests in the domestic limited partnership which is to be converted may be exchanged for or converted into cash, property, rights or securities of or interests in the entity or business form into which the domestic limited partnership is being converted or, in addition to or in lieu thereof, may be exchanged for or converted into cash, property, rights or securities of or interests in another entity or business form or may be cancelled.

(e) If a limited partnership shall convert in accordance with this section to another entity or business form organized, formed or created under the laws of a jurisdiction other than the State of Delaware, a certificate of conversion to non-Delaware entity executed in accordance with § 17–204 of this title shall be filed in the office of the Secretary of State in accordance with § 17–206 of this title. The certificate of conversion to non-Delaware entity shall state:

(1) The name of the limited partnership and, if it has been changed, the name under which its certificate of limited partnership was originally filed;

(2) The date of filing of its original certificate of limited partnership with the Secretary of State;

(3) The jurisdiction in which the entity or business form, to which the limited partnership shall be converted, is organized, formed or created, and the name of such entity or business form;

(4) The future effective date or time (which shall be a date or time certain) of the conversion if it is not to be effective upon the filing of the certificate of conversion to non-Delaware entity;

(5) That the conversion has been approved in accordance with this section;

(6) The agreement of the limited partnership that it may be served with process in the State of Delaware in any action, suit or proceeding for enforcement of any obligation of the limited partnership arising while it was a limited partnership of the State of Delaware, and that it irrevocably appoints the Secretary of State as its agent to accept service of process in any such action, suit or proceeding;

(7) The address to which a copy of the process referred to in subdivision (e)(6) of this section shall be mailed to it by the Secretary of State. In the event of service hereunder upon the Secretary of State, the procedures set forth in § 17–911(c) of this title shall be applicable, except that the plaintiff in any such action, suit or proceeding shall furnish the Secretary of State with the address specified in this subdivision and any other address that the plaintiff may elect to furnish, together with copies of such process as required by the Secretary of State, and the Secretary of State shall notify the limited partnership that has converted out of the State of Delaware at all such addresses furnished by the plaintiff in accordance with the procedures set forth in § 17–911(c) of this title.

(f) Upon the filing in the office of the Secretary of State of the certificate of conversion to non-Delaware entity or upon the future effective date or time of the certificate of conversion to non-Delaware entity and payment to the Secretary of State of all fees prescribed in this chapter, the Secretary of State shall certify that the limited partnership has filed all documents and paid all fees required by this chapter, and thereupon the limited partnership shall cease to exist as a limited partnership of the State of Delaware. Such certificate of the Secretary of State shall be prima facie evidence of the conversion by such limited partnership out of the State of Delaware.

(g) The conversion of a limited partnership out of the State of Delaware in accordance with this section and the resulting cessation of its existence as a limited partnership of the State of Delaware pursuant to a certificate of conversion to non-Delaware entity shall not be deemed to affect any obligations or liabilities of the limited partnership incurred prior to such conversion or the personal liability of any person incurred prior to such conversion, nor shall it be deemed to affect the choice of law applicable to the limited partnership with respect to matters arising prior to such conversion.

(h) When a limited partnership has been converted to another entity or business form pursuant to this section, the other entity or business form shall, for all purposes of the laws of the State of Delaware, be deemed to be the same entity as the limited partnership. When any conversion shall have become effective under this section, for all purposes of the laws of the State of Delaware, all of the rights, privileges and powers of the limited partnership that has converted, and all property, real, personal and mixed, and all debts due to such limited partnership, as well as all other things and causes of action belonging to such limited partnership, shall remain vested in the other entity or business form to which such limited partnership has converted and shall be the property of such other entity or business form, and the title to any real property vested by deed or otherwise in such limited partnership shall not revert or be in any way impaired by reason of this chapter; but all rights of creditors and all liens upon any property of such limited partnership shall be preserved unimpaired, and all debts, liabilities and duties of the limited partnership that has converted shall remain attached to the other entity or business form to which such limited partnership has converted, and may be enforced against it to the same extent as if said debts, liabilities and duties had originally been incurred or contracted by it in its capacity as such other entity or business form. The rights, privileges, powers and interests in property of the limited partnership that has converted, as well as the debts, liabilities and duties of such limited partnership, shall not be deemed, as a consequence of the conversion, to have been transferred to the other entity or business form to which such limited partnership has converted for any purpose of the laws of the State of Delaware.

SUBCHAPTER III. LIMITED PARTNERS

§ 17-301. Admission of Limited Partners

(a) In connection with the formation of a limited partnership, a person is admitted as a limited partner of the limited partnership upon the later to occur of:

(1) The formation of the limited partnership; or

(2) The time provided in and upon compliance with the partnership agreement or, if the partnership agreement does not so provide,

when the person's admission is reflected in the records of the limited partnership.

(b) After the formation of a limited partnership, a person is admitted as a limited partner of the limited partnership:

(1) In the case of a person who is not an assignee of a partnership interest, including a person acquiring a partnership interest directly from the limited partnership and a person to be admitted as a limited partner of the limited partnership without acquiring a partnership interest in the limited partnership, at the time provided in and upon compliance with the partnership agreement or, if the partnership agreement does not so provide, upon the consent of all partners and when the person's admission is reflected in the records of the limited partnership;

(2) In the case of an assignee of a partnership interest, as provided in § 17-704(a) of this title and at the time provided in and upon compliance with the partnership agreement or, if the partnership agreement does not so provide, when any such person's permitted admission is reflected in the records of the limited partnership; or

(3) In the case of a person being admitted as a partner of a surviving or resulting limited partnership pursuant to a merger or consolidation approved in accordance with § 17-211(b) of this title, as provided in the partnership agreement of the surviving or resulting limited partnership or in the agreement of merger or consolidation, and in the event of any inconsistency, the terms of the agreement of merger or consolidation shall control; and in the case of a person being admitted as a partner of a limited partnership pursuant to a merger or consolidation in which such limited partnership is not the surviving or resulting limited partnership in the merger or consolidation, as provided in the partnership agreement of such limited partnership.

(c) In connection with the domestication of a non-United States entity (as defined in § 17-215 of this title) as a limited partnership in the State of Delaware in accordance with § 17-215 of this title or the conversion of an other entity (as defined in § 17-217 of this title) to a domestic limited partnership in accordance with § 17-217 of this title, a person is admitted as a limited partner of the limited partnership as provided in the partnership agreement.

(d) A person may be admitted to a limited partnership as a limited partner of the limited partnership and may receive a partnership interest in the limited partnership without making a contribution or being obligated to make a contribution to the limited partnership. Unless otherwise provided in a partnership agreement, a person may be admitted to a limited partnership as a limited partner of the limited partnership without acquiring a partnership interest in the limited partnership. Unless otherwise provided in a partnership agreement, a person may be admitted as the sole limited partner of a limited partnership without making a contribution or being obligated to make a contribution to the limited partnership or without acquiring a partnership interest in the limited partnership.

(e) Unless otherwise provided in a partnership agreement or another agreement, a limited partner shall have no preemptive right to subscribe to any additional issue of partnership interests or another interest in a limited partnership.

§ 17–302. Classes and Voting

(a) A partnership agreement may provide for classes or groups of limited partners having such relative rights, powers and duties as the partnership agreement may provide, and may make provision for the future creation in the manner provided in the partnership agreement of additional classes or groups of limited partners having such relative rights, powers and duties as may from time to time be established, including rights, powers and duties senior to existing classes and groups of limited partners.

A partnership agreement may provide for the taking of an action, including the amendment of the partnership agreement, without the vote or approval of any limited partner or class or group of limited partners, including an action to create under the provisions of the partnership agreement a class or group of partnership interests that was not previously outstanding.

(b) Subject to § 17–303 of this title, the partnership agreement may grant to all or certain identified limited partners or a specified class or group of the limited partners the right to vote separately or with all or any class or group of the limited partners or the general partners, on any matter. Voting by limited partners may be on a per capita, number, financial interest, class, group or any other basis.

(c) A partnership agreement may set forth provisions relating to notice of the time, place or purpose of any meeting at which any matter is to be voted on by any limited partners, waiver of any such notice, action by consent without a meeting, the establishment of a record date, quorum requirements, voting in person or by proxy, or any other matter with respect to the exercise of any such right to vote.

(d) Any right or power, including voting rights, granted to limited partners as permitted under § 17–303 of this title shall be deemed to be permitted by this section.

(e) Unless otherwise provided in a partnership agreement, meetings of limited partners may be held by means of conference telephone or other communications equipment by means of which all persons participating in the meeting can hear each other, and participation in a meeting pursuant to this subsection shall constitute presence in person at the meeting. Unless otherwise provided in a partnership agreement, on any matter that is to be voted on, consented to or approved by limited partners, the limited partners may take such action without a meeting, without prior notice and without a vote if a consent or consents in writing, setting forth the action so taken, shall be signed by the limited partners having not less than the minimum number of votes that would be necessary to authorize or take such action at a meeting at which all limited partners entitled to vote thereon were present and voted. Unless otherwise provided in a partnership agreement, on any matter that is to be voted on by limited partners, the limited partners may vote in person or by proxy, and such proxy may be granted in writing, by means of electronic transmission or as otherwise permitted by applicable law. Unless otherwise provided in a partnership agreement, a consent transmitted by electronic transmission by a limited partner or by a person or persons authorized to act for a limited partner shall be deemed to be written and signed for purposes of this subsection. For purposes of this subsection, the term "electronic transmission" means any form of communication not directly involving the physical transmission of paper that creates a record that may be retained, retrieved and reviewed by a recipient thereof and that may be directly reproduced in paper form by such a recipient through an automated process.

(f) If a partnership agreement provides for the manner in which it may be amended, including by requiring the approval of a person who is not a party to the partnership agreement or the satisfaction of conditions, it may be amended only in that manner or as otherwise permitted by law (provided that the approval of any person may be waived by such person and that any such conditions may be waived by all persons for whose benefit such conditions were intended). If a partnership agreement does not provide for the manner in which it may be amended, the partnership agreement may be amended with the approval of all the partners or as otherwise permitted by law. A limited partner and any class or group of limited partners have the right to vote only on matters as specifically set forth in this chapter, on matters specifically provided by agreement, including a partnership agreement, and on any matter with respect to which a general partner may determine in its discretion to seek a vote of a limited partner or a class or group of limited partners if a vote on such matter is not contrary to a partnership agreement or another agreement to which a general partner or the limited partnership is a party. A limited partner and any class or group of limited partners have no other voting rights. A partnership agreement may provide that any limited partner or class or group of limited partners shall have no voting rights.

§ 17-303. Liability to Third Parties

(a) A limited partner is not liable for the obligations of a limited partnership unless he or she is also a general partner or, in addition to the exercise of the rights and powers of a limited partner, he or she participates in the control of the business. However, if the limited partner does participate in the control of the business, he or she is liable only to persons who transact business with the limited partnership reasonably believing, based upon the limited partner's conduct, that the limited partner is a general partner.

(b) A limited partner does not participate in the control of the business within the meaning of subsection (a) of this section by virtue of possessing or, regardless of whether or not the limited partner has the rights or powers, exercising or attempting to exercise 1 or more of the following rights or powers or having or, regardless of whether or not the limited partner has the rights or powers, acting or attempting to act in 1 or more of the following capacities:

(1) To be an independent contractor for or to transact business with, including being a contractor for, or to be an agent or employee of, the limited partnership or a general partner, or to be an officer, director or stockholder of a corporate general partner, or to be a partner of a partnership that is a general partner of the limited partnership, or to be a trustee, administrator, executor, custodian or other fiduciary or beneficiary of an estate or trust which is a general partner, or to be a trustee, officer, advisor, stockholder or beneficiary of a business trust or a statutory trust which is a general partner or to be a member, manager, agent or employee of a limited liability company which is a general partner;

(2) To consult with or advise a general partner or any other person with respect to any matter, including the business of the limited partnership, or to act or cause a general partner or any other person to take or refrain from taking any action, including by proposing, approving, consenting or disapproving, by voting or otherwise, with respect to any matter, including the business of the limited partnership;

(3) To act as surety, guarantor or endorser for the limited partnership or a general partner, to guaranty or assume 1 or more obligations of the limited partnership or a general partner, to borrow money from the limited partnership or a general partner, to lend money to the limited partnership or a general partner, or to provide collateral for the limited partnership or a general partner;

(4) To call, request, or attend or participate at a meeting of the partners or the limited partners;

(5) To wind up a limited partnership pursuant to § 17-803 of this title;

(6) To take any action required or permitted by law to bring, pursue or settle or otherwise terminate a derivative action in the right of the limited partnership;

(7) To serve on a committee of the limited partnership or the limited partners or partners or to appoint, elect or otherwise participate in the choice of a representative or another person to serve on

any such committee, and to act as a member of any such committee directly or by or through any such representative or other person;

(8) To act or cause the taking or refraining from the taking of any action, including by proposing, approving, consenting or disapproving, by voting or otherwise, with respect to 1 or more of the following matters:

a. The dissolution and winding up of the limited partnership or an election to continue the limited partnership or an election to continue the business of the limited partnership;

b. The sale, exchange, lease, mortgage, assignment, pledge or other transfer of, or granting of a security interest in, any asset or assets of the limited partnership;

c. The incurrence, renewal, refinancing or payment or other discharge of indebtedness by the limited partnership;

d. A change in the nature of the business;

e. The admission, removal or retention of a general partner;

f. The admission, removal or retention of a limited partner;

g. A transaction or other matter involving an actual or potential conflict of interest;

h. An amendment to the partnership agreement or certificate of limited partnership;

i. The merger or consolidation of a limited partnership;

j. In respect of a limited partnership which is registered as an investment company under the Investment Company Act of 1940, as amended [15 U.S.C. § 80a-1 et seq.], any matter required by the Investment Company Act of 1940, as amended, or the rules and regulations of the Securities and Exchange Commission thereunder, to be approved by the holders of beneficial interests in an investment company, including the electing of directors or trustees of the investment company, the approving or terminating of investment advisory or underwriting contracts and the approving of auditors;

k. The indemnification of any partner or other person;

l. The making of, or calling for, or the making of other determinations in connection with, contributions;

m. The making of, or the making of other determinations in connection with or concerning, investments, including investments in property, whether real, personal or mixed, either directly or indirectly, by the limited partnership; or

n. Such other matters as are stated in the partnership agreement or in any other agreement or in writing;

(9) To serve on the board of directors or a committee of, to consult with or advise, to be an officer, director, stockholder, partner, member, manager, trustee, agent or employee of, or to be a fiduciary or contractor for, any person in which the limited partnership has an interest or any person providing management, consulting, advisory, custody or other services or products for, to or on behalf of, or otherwise having a business or other relationship with, the limited partnership or a general partner of the limited partnership; or

(10) Any right or power granted or permitted to limited partners under this chapter and not specifically enumerated in this subsection.

(c) The enumeration in subsection (b) of this section does not mean that the possession or exercise of any other powers or having or acting in other capacities by a limited partner constitutes participation by him or her in the control of the business of the limited partnership.

(d) A limited partner does not participate in the control of the business within the meaning of subsection (a) of this section by virtue of the fact that all or any part of the name of such limited partner is included in the name of the limited partnership.

(e) This section does not create rights or powers of limited partners. Such rights and powers may be created only by a certificate of limited partnership, a partnership agreement or any other agreement or in writing, or other sections of this chapter.

(f) A limited partner does not participate in the control of the business within the meaning of subsection (a) of this section regardless of the nature, extent, scope, number or frequency of the limited partner's possessing or, regardless of whether or not the limited partner has the rights or powers, exercising or attempting to exercise 1 or more of the rights or powers or having or, regardless of whether or not the limited partner has the rights or powers, acting or attempting to act in 1 or more of the capacities which are permitted under this section.

§ 17–304. Person Erroneously Believing Himself or Herself Limited Partner

(a) Except as provided in subsection (b) of this section, a person who makes a contribution to a partnership and erroneously but in good faith believes that he or she has become a limited partner in the partnership is not a general partner in the partnership and is not bound by its obligations by reason of making the contribution, receiving distributions from the partnership or exercising any rights of a limited partner, if, within a reasonable time after ascertaining the mistake:

(1) In the case of a person who wishes to be a limited partner, he or she causes an appropriate certificate to be executed and filed; or

(2) In the case of a person who wishes to withdraw from the partnership, that person takes such action as may be necessary to withdraw.

(b) A person who makes a contribution under the circumstances described in subsection (a) of this section is liable as a general partner to any third party who transacts business with the partnership prior to the occurrence of either of the events referred to in subsection (a) of this section:

(1) If such person knew or should have known either that no certificate has been filed or that the certificate inaccurately refers to the person as a general partner; and

(2) If the third party actually believed in good faith that such person was a general partner at the time of the transaction, acted in reasonable reliance on such belief and extended credit to the partnership in reasonable reliance on the credit of such person.

§ 17–305. Access to and Confidentiality of Information; Records

(a) Each limited partner has the right, subject to such reasonable standards (including standards governing what information and documents are to be furnished, at what time and location and at whose expense) as may be set forth in the partnership agreement or otherwise established by the general partners, to obtain from the general partners from time to time upon reasonable demand for any purpose reasonably related to the limited partner's interest as a limited partner:

(1) True and full information regarding the status of the business and financial condition of the limited partnership;

(2) Promptly after becoming available, a copy of the limited partnership's federal, state and local income tax returns for each year;

(3) A current list of the name and last known business, residence or mailing address of each partner;

(4) A copy of any written partnership agreement and certificate of limited partnership and all amendments thereto, together with executed copies of any written powers of attorney pursuant to which the partnership agreement and any certificate and all amendments thereto have been executed;

(5) True and full information regarding the amount of cash and a description and statement of the agreed value of any other property or services contributed by each partner and which each partner has agreed to contribute in the future, and the date on which each became a partner; and

(6) Other information regarding the affairs of the limited partnership as is just and reasonable.

(b) A general partner shall have the right to keep confidential from limited partners for such period of time as the general partner deems reasonable, any information which the general partner reasonably believes to be in the nature of trade secrets or other information the disclosure of which the general partner in good faith believes is not in the best interest of the limited partnership or could damage the limited partnership or its business or which the limited partnership is required by law or by agreement with a third party to keep confidential.

(c) A limited partnership may maintain its records in other than a written form if such form is capable of conversion into written form within a reasonable time.

(d) Any demand under this section shall be in writing and shall state the purpose of such demand.

(e) Any action to enforce any right arising under this section shall be brought in the Court of Chancery. If a general partner refuses to permit a limited partner to obtain from the general partner the information described in subsection (a)(3) of this section or does not reply to the demand that has been made within 5 business days after the demand has been made, the limited partner may apply to the Court of Chancery for an order to compel such disclosure. The Court of Chancery is hereby vested with exclusive jurisdiction to determine whether or not the person seeking such information is entitled to the information sought. The Court of Chancery may summarily order the general partner to permit the limited partner to obtain the information described in subsection (a)(3) of this section and to make copies or abstracts therefrom, or the Court of Chancery may summarily order the general partner to furnish to the limited partner the information described in subsection (a)(3) of this section on the condition that the limited partner first pay to the limited partnership the reasonable cost of obtaining and furnishing such information and on such other conditions as the Court of Chancery deems appropriate. When a limited partner seeks to obtain the information described in subsection (a)(3) of this section, the limited partner shall first establish (1) that the limited partner has complied with the provisions of this section respecting the form and manner of making demand for obtaining such information, and (2) that the information the limited partner seeks is reasonably related to the limited partner's interest as a limited partner. The Court of Chancery may, in its discretion, prescribe any limitations or conditions with reference to the obtaining of information, or award such other or further relief as the Court of Chancery may deem just and proper. The Court of Chancery may order books, documents and records, pertinent extracts therefrom, or duly authenticated copies thereof, to be brought within the State of Delaware and kept in the State of Delaware upon such terms and conditions as the order may prescribe.

(f) The rights of a limited partner to obtain information as provided in this section may be restricted in an original partnership agreement or in any subsequent amendment approved or adopted by all of the partners and in compliance with any applicable requirements of the partnership agreement. The provisions of this subsection shall not be construed to limit the ability to impose restrictions on the rights of a limited partner to obtain information by any other means permitted under this section.

§ 17–306. Remedies for Breach of Partnership Agreement by Limited Partner

A partnership agreement may provide that:

(1) A limited partner who fails to perform in accordance with, or to comply with the terms and conditions of, the partnership agreement shall be subject to specified penalties or specified consequences; and

(2) At the time or upon the happening of events specified in the partnership agreement, a limited partner shall be subject to specified penalties or specified consequences.

Such specified penalties or specified consequences may include and take the form of any penalty or consequence set forth in § 17–502(c) of this title.

SUBCHAPTER IV. GENERAL PARTNERS

§ 17–401. Admission of General Partners

(a) A person may be admitted to a limited partnership as a general partner of the limited partnership and may receive a partnership interest in the limited partnership without making a contribution or being obligated to make a contribution to the limited partnership. Unless otherwise provided in a partnership agreement, a person may be admitted to a limited partnership as a general partner of the limited partnership without acquiring a partnership interest in the limited partnership. Unless otherwise provided in a partnership agreement, a person may be admitted as the sole general partner of a limited partnership without making a contribution or being obligated to make a contribution to the limited partnership or without acquiring a partnership interest in the limited partnership. Nothing contained in this subsection shall affect the first sentence of § 17–403(b) of this title.

(b) After the filing of a limited partnership's initial certificate of limited partnership, unless otherwise provided in the partnership agreement, additional general partners may be admitted only with the written consent of each partner.

(c) Unless otherwise provided in a partnership agreement or another agreement, a general partner shall have no preemptive right to subscribe to any additional issue of partnership interests or another interest in a limited partnership.

§ 17–402. Events of Withdrawal

(a) A person ceases to be a general partner of a limited partnership upon the happening of any of the following events:

(1) The general partner withdraws from the limited partnership as provided in § 17–602 of this title;

(2) The general partner ceases to be a general partner of the limited partnership as provided in § 17–702 of this title;

(3) The general partner is removed as a general partner in accordance with the partnership agreement;

(4) Unless otherwise provided in the partnership agreement, or with the written consent of all partners, the general partner:

a. Makes an assignment for the benefit of creditors;

b. Files a voluntary petition in bankruptcy;

c. Is adjudged a bankrupt or insolvent, or has entered against him or her an order for relief in any bankruptcy or insolvency proceeding;

d. Files a petition or answer seeking for himself or herself any reorganization, arrangement, composition, readjustment, liquidation, dissolution or similar relief under any statute, law or regulation;

e. Files an answer or other pleading admitting or failing to contest the material allegations of a petition filed against him or her in any proceeding of this nature; or

f. Seeks, consents to or acquiesces in the appointment of a trustee, receiver or liquidator of the general partner or of all or any substantial part of his properties;

(5) Unless otherwise provided in the partnership agreement, or with the written consent of all partners, 120 days after the commencement of any proceeding against the general partner seeking reorganization, arrangement, composition, readjustment, liquidation, dissolution or similar relief under any statute, law or regulation, the proceeding has not been dismissed, or if within 90 days after the appointment without the general partner's consent or acquiescence of a trustee, receiver or liquidator of the general partner or of all or any substantial part of his or her properties, the appointment is not vacated or stayed, or within 90 days after the expiration of any such stay, the appointment is not vacated;

(6) In the case of a general partner who is a natural person:

a. The general partner's death; or

b. The entry by a court of competent jurisdiction adjudicating the general partner incompetent to manage his or her person or property;

(7) In the case of a general partner who is acting as a general partner by virtue of being a trustee of a trust, the termination of the trust (but not merely the substitution of a new trustee);

(8) In the case of a general partner that is a separate partnership, the dissolution and commencement of winding up of the separate partnership;

(9) In the case of a general partner that is a corporation, the filing of a certificate of dissolution, or its equivalent, for the corporation or the revocation of its charter and the expiration of 90 days after the date of notice to the corporation of revocation without a reinstatement of its charter;

(10) Unless otherwise provided in the partnership agreement, or with the written consent of all partners, in the case of a general partner that is an estate, the distribution by the fiduciary of the estate's entire interest in the limited partnership;

(11) In the case of a general partner that is a limited liability company, the dissolution and commencement of winding up of the limited liability company; or

(12) In the case of a general partner who is not an individual, partnership, limited liability company, corporation, trust or estate, the termination of the general partner.

(b) A general partner who suffers an event that with the passage of the specified period becomes an event of withdrawal under subsection (a)(4) or (5) of this section shall notify each other general partner, or in the event that there is no other general partner, each limited partner, of the occurrence of the event within 30 days after the date of occurrence of the event of withdrawal.

§ 17–403. General Powers and Liabilities

(a) Except as provided in this chapter or in the partnership agreement, a general partner of a limited partnership has the rights and powers and is subject to the restrictions of a partner in a partnership that is governed by the Delaware Uniform Partnership Law in effect on July 11, 1999 (6 Del. C. § 1501, et seq.).

(b) Except as provided in this chapter, a general partner of a limited partnership has the liabilities of a partner in a partnership that is governed by the Delaware Uniform Partnership Law in effect on July 11, 1999 (6 Del. C. § 1501, et seq.) to persons other than the partnership and the other partners. Except as provided in this chapter or in the partnership agreement, a general partner of a limited partnership has the liabilities of a partner in a partnership that is governed by the Delaware Uniform Partnership Law in effect on July 11, 1999 (6 Del. C. § 1501, et seq.) to the partnership and to the other partners.

(c) Unless otherwise provided in the partnership agreement, a general partner of a limited partnership has the power and authority to delegate to 1 or more other persons the general partner's rights and powers to manage and control the business and affairs of the limited partnership, including to delegate to agents, officers and employees of the general partner or the limited partnership, and to delegate by a management agreement or another agreement with, or otherwise to, other persons. Unless otherwise provided in the partnership agreement, such delegation by a general partner of a limited partnership shall not cause the general partner to cease to be a general partner of the limited partnership or cause the person to whom any such rights and powers have been delegated to be a general partner of the limited partnership.

(d) A judgment creditor of a general partner of a limited partnership may not levy execution against the assets of the general partner to satisfy a judgment based on a claim against the limited partnership unless:

(1) A judgment based on the same claim has been obtained against the limited partnership and a writ of execution on the judgment has been returned unsatisfied in whole or in part;

(2) The limited partnership is a debtor in bankruptcy;

(3) The general partner has agreed that the creditor need not exhaust the assets of the limited partnership;

(4) A court grants permission to the judgment creditor to levy execution against the assets of the general partner based on a finding that the assets of the limited partnership that are subject to execution are clearly insufficient to satisfy the judgment, that exhaustion of the assets of the limited partnership is excessively burdensome, or that the grant of permission is an appropriate exercise of the court's equitable powers; or

(5) Liability is imposed on the general partner by law or contract independent of the existence of the limited partnership.

§ 17–404. Contributions by a General Partner

A general partner of a limited partnership may make contributions to the limited partnership and share in the profits and losses of, and in distributions from, the limited partnership as a general partner. A general partner also may make contributions to and share in profits, losses and distributions as a limited partner. A person who is both a general partner and a limited partner has the rights and powers, and is subject to the restrictions and liabilities, of a general partner and, except as provided in the partnership agreement, also has the rights and powers, and is subject to the restrictions, of a limited partner to the extent of his or her participation in the partnership as a limited partner.

§ 17–405. Classes and Voting

(a) A partnership agreement may provide for classes or groups of general partners having such relative rights, powers and duties as the partnership agreement may provide, and may make provision for the future creation in the manner provided in the partnership agreement of additional classes or groups of general partners having such relative rights, powers and duties as may from time to time be established, including rights, powers and duties senior to existing classes and groups of general partners.

A partnership agreement may provide for the taking of an action, including the amendment of the partnership agreement, without the vote or approval of any general partner or class or group of general partners, including an action to create under the provisions of the partnership agreement a class or group of partnership interests that was not previously outstanding.

(b) The partnership agreement may grant to all or certain identified general partners or a specified class or group of the general partners the right to vote, separately or with all or any class or group of the limited partners or the general partners, on any matter. Voting by general partners may be on a per capita, number, financial interest, class, group or any other basis.

(c) A partnership agreement may set forth provisions relating to notice of the time, place or purpose of any meeting at which any matter is to be voted on by any general partner, waiver of any such notice, action by consent without a meeting, the establishment of a record date, quorum requirements, voting in person or by proxy, or any other matter with respect to the exercise of any such right to vote.

(d) Unless otherwise provided in a partnership agreement, meetings of general partners may be held by means of conference telephone or other communications equipment by means of which all persons participating in the meeting can hear each other, and participation in a meeting pursuant to this subsection shall constitute presence in person at the meeting. Unless otherwise provided in a partnership agreement, on any matter that is to be voted on, consented to or approved by general partners, the general partners may take such action without a meeting, without prior notice and without a vote if a consent or consents in writing, setting forth the action so taken, shall be signed by the general partners having not less than the minimum number of votes that would be necessary to authorize or take such action at a meeting at which all general partners entitled to vote thereon were present and voted. Unless otherwise provided in a partnership agreement, on any matter that is to be voted on by general partners, the general partners may vote in person or by proxy, and such proxy may be granted in writing, by means of electronic transmission or as otherwise permitted by applicable law. Unless otherwise provided in a partnership agreement, a consent transmitted by electronic transmission by a general partner or by a person or persons authorized to act for a general partner shall be deemed to be written and signed for purposes of this subsection (d). For purposes of this subsection (d), the term "electronic transmission" means any form of communication not directly involving the physical transmission of paper that creates a record that may be retained, retrieved and reviewed by a recipient thereof and that may be directly reproduced in paper form by such a recipient through an automated process.

§ 17-406. Remedies for Breach of Partnership Agreement by General Partner

A partnership agreement may provide that (1) a general partner who fails to perform in accordance with, or to comply with the terms and conditions of, the partnership agreement shall be subject to specified penalties or specified consequences, and (2) at the time or upon the happening of events specified in the partnership agreement, a general partner shall be subject to specified penalties or specified consequences. Such specified penalties or specified consequences may include and take the form of any penalty or consequence set forth in § 17-502(c) of this title.

§ 17-407. Reliance on Reports and Information by Limited Partners, Liquidating Trustees, and General Partners

(a) A limited partner or liquidating trustee of a limited partnership shall be fully protected in relying in good faith upon the records of the limited partnership and upon information, opinions, reports or statements presented by a general partner of the limited partnership, an officer or employee of a general partner of the limited partnership, another liquidating trustee, or committees of the limited partnership, limited partners or partners, or by any other person as to matters the limited partner or liquidating trustee reasonably believes are within such other person's professional or expert competence, including information, opinions, reports or statements as to the value and amount of the assets, liabilities, profits or losses of the limited partnership, or the value and amount of assets or reserves or contracts, agreements or other undertakings that would be sufficient to pay claims and obligations of the limited partnership or to make reasonable provision to pay such claims and obligations, or any other facts pertinent to the existence and amount of assets from which distributions to partners or creditors might properly be paid.

(b) A general partner of a limited liability limited partnership shall be fully protected in relying in good faith upon the records of the limited partnership and upon information, opinions, reports or statements presented by another general partner of the limited partnership, an officer or employee of the limited partnership, a liquidating trustee, or committees of the limited partnership, limited partners or partners, or by any other person as to matters the general partner reasonably believes are within such other person's professional or expert competence, including information, opinions, reports or statements as to the value and amount of the assets, liabilities, profits or losses of the limited partnership, or the value and amount of assets or reserves or contracts, agreements or other undertakings that would be sufficient to pay claims and obligations of the limited partnership or to make reasonable provision to pay such claims and obligations, or any other facts pertinent to the existence and amount of assets from which distributions to partners or creditors might properly be paid.

(c) A general partner of a limited partnership that is not a limited liability limited partnership shall be fully protected from liability to the limited partnership, its partners or other persons party to or otherwise bound by the partnership agreement in relying in good faith upon the records of the limited partnership and upon information, opinions, reports or statements presented by another general partner of the limited partnership, an officer or employee of the limited partnership, a liquidating trustee, or committees of the limited partnership, limited partners or partners, or by any other person as to matters the general partner reasonably believes are within such other person's professional or expert competence, including information, opinions, reports or statements as to the value and amount of the assets, liabilities, profits or losses of the limited partnership, or the value and amount of assets or reserves or contracts, agreements or other undertakings that would be sufficient to pay claims and obligations of the limited partnership or to make reasonable provision to pay such claims and obligations, or any other facts pertinent to the existence and amount of assets from which distributions to partners or creditors might properly be paid.

SUBCHAPTER V. FINANCE

§ 17-501. Form of Contribution

The contribution of a partner may be in cash, property or services rendered, or a promissory note or other obligation to contribute cash or property or to perform services.

§ 17-502. Liability for Contribution

(a)(1) Except as provided in the partnership agreement, a partner is obligated to the limited partnership to perform any promise to contribute cash or property or to perform services, even if that partner is unable to perform because of death, disability or any other reason. If a partner does not make the required contribution of property or services, he or she is obligated at the option of the limited partnership to contribute cash equal to that portion of the agreed value (as stated in the records of the limited partnership) of the contribution that has not been made.

(2) The foregoing option shall be in addition to, and not in lieu of, any other rights, including the right to specific performance, that

the limited partnership may have against such partner under the partnership agreement or applicable law.

(b)(1) Unless otherwise provided in the partnership agreement, the obligation of a partner to make a contribution or return money or other property paid or distributed in violation of this chapter may be compromised only by consent of all the partners. Notwithstanding the compromise, a creditor of a limited partnership who extends credit, after the entering into of a partnership agreement or an amendment thereto which, in either case, reflects the obligation, and before the amendment thereof to reflect the compromise, may enforce the original obligation to the extent that, in extending credit, the creditor reasonably relied on the obligation of a partner to make a contribution or return.

(2) A conditional obligation of a partner to make a contribution or return money or other property to a limited partnership may not be enforced unless the conditions to the obligation have been satisfied or waived as to or by such partner. Conditional obligations include contributions payable upon a discretionary call of a limited partnership or a general partner prior to the time the call occurs.

(c) A partnership agreement may provide that the interest of any partner who fails to make any contribution that he or she is obligated to make shall be subject to specified penalties for, or specified consequences of, such failure. Such penalty or consequence may take the form of reducing or eliminating the defaulting partner's proportionate interest in the limited partnership, subordinating the partnership interest to that of nondefaulting partners, a forced sale of his or her partnership interest, forfeiture of that partnership interest, the lending by other partners of the amount necessary to meet his or her commitment, a fixing of the value of that partnership interest by appraisal or by formula and redemption or sale of the partnership interest at such value, or other penalty or consequence.

§ 17–503. Allocation of Profits and Losses

The profits and losses of a limited partnership shall be allocated among the partners, and among classes or groups of partners, in the manner provided in the partnership agreement. If the partnership agreement does not so provide, profits and losses shall be allocated on the basis of the agreed value (as stated in the records of the limited partnership) of the contributions made by each partner to the extent they have been received by the limited partnership and have not been returned.

§ 17–504. Allocation of Distributions

Distributions of cash or other assets of a limited partnership shall be allocated among the partners, and among classes or groups of partners, in the manner provided in the partnership agreement. If the partnership agreement does not so provide, distributions shall be made on the basis of the agreed value (as stated in the records of the limited partnership) of the contributions made by each partner to the extent they have been received by the limited partnership and have not been returned.

§ 17-505. Defense of Usury not Available

No obligation of a partner of a limited partnership to the limited partnership arising under the partnership agreement or a separate agreement or writing, and no note, instrument or other writing evidencing any such obligation of a partner, shall be subject to the defense of usury, and no partner shall interpose the defense of usury with respect to any such obligation in any action.

SUBCHAPTER VI. DISTRIBUTIONS AND WITHDRAWAL

§ 17-601. Interim Distributions

Except as provided in this subchapter, to the extent and at the times or upon the happening of the events specified in the partnership agreement, a partner is entitled to receive from a limited partnership distributions before withdrawing from the limited partnership and before the dissolution and winding up thereof.

§ 17-602. Withdrawal of General Partner and Assignment of General Partner's Partnership Interest

(a) A general partner may withdraw from a limited partnership at the time or upon the happening of events specified in the partnership agreement and in accordance with the partnership agreement. A partnership agreement may provide that a general partner shall not have the right to withdraw as a general partner of a limited partnership. Notwithstanding that a partnership agreement provides that a general partner does not have the right to withdraw as a general partner of a limited partnership, a general partner may withdraw from a limited partnership at any time by giving written notice to the other partners. If the withdrawal of a general partner violates a partnership agreement, in addition to any remedies otherwise available under applicable law, the limited partnership may recover from the withdrawing general partner damages for breach of the partnership agreement and offset the damages against the amount otherwise distributable to the withdrawing general partner.

(b) Notwithstanding anything to the contrary set forth in this chapter, a partnership agreement may provide that a general partner may not assign a partnership interest in a limited partnership prior to the dissolution and winding up of the limited partnership.

§ 17-603. Withdrawal of Limited Partner

A limited partner may withdraw from a limited partnership only at the time or upon the happening of events specified in the partnership agreement and in accordance with the partnership agreement. Notwithstanding anything to the contrary under applicable law, unless a partnership agreement provides otherwise, a limited partner may not withdraw from a limited partnership prior to the dissolution and winding up of the limited partnership. Notwithstanding anything to the contrary under applicable law, a partnership agreement may provide that a partnership interest may not be assigned prior to the dissolution and winding up of the limited partnership.

Unless otherwise provided in a partnership agreement, a limited partnership whose original certificate of limited partnership was filed with the Secretary of State and effective on or prior to July 31, 1996, shall continue to be governed by this section as in effect on July 31, 1996, and shall not be governed by this section.

§ 17-604. Distribution Upon Withdrawal

Except as provided in this subchapter, upon withdrawal any withdrawing partner is entitled to receive any distribution to which such partner is entitled under a partnership agreement and, if not otherwise provided in a partnership agreement, such partner is entitled to receive, within a reasonable time after withdrawal, the fair value of such partner's partnership interest in the limited partnership as of the date of withdrawal based upon such partner's right to share in distributions from the limited partnership.

§ 17-605. Distribution in Kind

Except as provided in the partnership agreement, a partner, regardless of the nature of the partner's contribution, has no right to demand and receive any distribution from a limited partnership in any form other than cash. Except as provided in the partnership agreement, a partner may not be compelled to accept a distribution of any asset in kind from a limited partnership to the extent that the percentage of the asset distributed exceeds a percentage of that asset which is equal to the percentage in which the partner shares in distributions from the limited partnership. Except as provided in the partnership agreement, a partner may be compelled to accept a distribution of any asset in kind from a limited partnership to the extent that the percentage of the asset distributed is equal to a percentage of that asset which is equal to the percentage in which the partner shares in distributions from the limited partnership.

§ 17-606. Right to Distribution

(a) Subject to §§ 17-607 and 17-804 of this title, and unless otherwise provided in the partnership agreement, at the time a partner becomes entitled to receive a distribution, he or she has the status of, and is entitled to all remedies available to, a creditor of the limited partnership with respect to the distribution.

(b) A partnership agreement may provide for the establishment of a record date with respect to allocations and distributions by a limited partnership.

§ 17-607. Limitations on Distribution

(a) A limited partnership shall not make a distribution to a partner to the extent that at the time of the distribution, after giving effect to the distribution, all liabilities of the limited partnership, other than liabilities to partners on account of their partnership interests and liabilities for which the recourse of creditors is limited to specified property of the limited partnership, exceed the fair value of the assets of the limited partnership, except that the fair value of property that is subject to a liability for which the recourse of creditors is limited shall be included in the assets of the limited partnership only to the extent that the fair value of that property exceeds that liability. For purposes of this subsection (a), the term "distribution" shall not include amounts constituting reasonable compensation for present or past services or reasonable payments made in the ordinary course of business pursuant to a bona fide retirement plan or other benefits program.

(b) A limited partner who receives a distribution in violation of subsection (a) of this section, and who knew at the time of the distribution that the distribution violated subsection (a) of this section, shall be liable to the limited partnership for the amount of the distribution. A limited partner who receives a distribution in violation of subsection (a) of this section, and who did not know at the time of the distribution that the distribution violated subsection (a) of this section, shall not be liable for the amount of the distribution. Subject to subsection (c) of this section, this subsection shall not affect any obligation or liability of a limited partner under an agreement or other applicable law for the amount of a distribution.

(c) Unless otherwise agreed, a limited partner who receives a distribution from a limited partnership shall have no liability under this chapter or other applicable law for the amount of the distribution after the expiration of 3 years from the date of the distribution.

§ 17-608. Liability Upon Return of Contribution

Repealed by 66 Del. Laws, c. 316, § 56, eff. Sept. 1, 1988.

SUBCHAPTER VII. ASSIGNMENT OF PARTNERSHIP INTERESTS

§ 17-701. Nature of Partnership Interest

A partnership interest is personal property. A partner has no interest in specific limited partnership property.

§ 17-702. Assignment of Partnership Interest

(a) Unless otherwise provided in the partnership agreement:

(1) A partnership interest is assignable in whole or in part;

(2) An assignment of a partnership interest does not dissolve a limited partnership or entitle the assignee to become or to exercise any rights or powers of a partner;

(3) An assignment of a partnership interest entitles the assignee to share in such profits and losses, to receive such distribution or distributions, and to receive such allocation of income, gain, loss, deduction, or credit or similar item to which the assignor was entitled, to the extent assigned; and

(4) A partner ceases to be a partner and to have the power to exercise any rights or powers of a partner upon assignment of all partnership interests. Unless otherwise provided in a partnership agreement, the pledge of, or granting of a security interest, lien or other encumbrance in or against, any or all of the partnership interest of a partner shall not cause the partner to cease to be a partner or to have the power to exercise any rights or powers of a partner.

(b) Unless otherwise provided in a partnership agreement, a partner's interest in a limited partnership may be evidenced by a certificate of partnership interest issued by the limited partnership. A partnership agreement may provide for the assignment or transfer of any partnership interest represented by such a certificate and make other provisions with respect to such certificates.

(c) Unless otherwise provided in a partnership agreement and except to the extent assumed by agreement, until an assignee of a partnership interest becomes a partner, the assignee shall have no liability as a partner solely as a result of the assignment.

(d) Unless otherwise provided in the partnership agreement, a limited partnership may acquire, by purchase, redemption or otherwise, any partnership interest or other interest of a partner in the limited partnership. Unless otherwise provided in the partnership agreement, any such interest so acquired by the limited partnership shall be deemed canceled.

§ 17-703. Partner's Partnership Interest Subject to Charging Order

(a) On application by a judgment creditor of a partner or of a partner's assignee, a court having jurisdiction may charge the partnership interest of the judgment debtor to satisfy the judgment. To the extent so charged, the judgment creditor has only the right to receive any distribution or distributions to which the judgment debtor would otherwise have been entitled in respect of such partnership interest.

(b) A charging order constitutes a lien on the judgment debtor's partnership interest.

(c) This chapter does not deprive a partner or partner's assignee of a right under exemption laws with respect to the judgment debtor's partnership interest.

(d) The entry of a charging order is the exclusive remedy by which a judgment creditor of a partner or of a partner's assignee may satisfy a judgment out of the judgment debtor's partnership interest.

(e) No creditor of a partner or of a partner's assignee shall have any right to obtain possession of, or otherwise exercise legal or equitable remedies with respect to, the property of the limited partnership.

(f) The Court of Chancery shall have jurisdiction to hear and determine any matter relating to any such charging order.

§ 17-704. Right of Assignee to Become Limited Partner

(a) An assignee of a partnership interest, including an assignee of a general partner, may become a limited partner if and to the extent that:

(1) The partnership agreement so provides; or

(2) All partners consent.

(b) An assignee who has become a limited partner has, to the extent assigned, the rights and powers, and is subject to the restrictions and liabilities, of a limited partner under the partnership agreement and this chapter. Notwithstanding the foregoing, unless otherwise provided in the partnership agreement, an assignee who becomes a limited partner is liable for the obligations of his or her assignor to make contributions as provided in § 17-502 of this title, but shall not be liable for the obligations of the assignor under subchapter VI of this chapter. However, the assignee is not obligated for liabilities, including the obligations of the assignor to make contributions as provided in § 17-502 of this title, unknown to the assignee at the time the assignee became a limited partner and which could not be ascertained from the partnership agreement.

(c) Whether or not an assignee of a partnership interest becomes a limited partner, the assignor is not released from liability to the limited partnership under subchapters V and VI of this chapter.

§ 17-705. Powers of Estate of Deceased or Incompetent Partner

If a partner who is an individual dies or a court of competent jurisdiction adjudges the partner to be incompetent to manage the partner's person or property, the partner's personal representative may exercise all of the partner's rights for the purpose of settling the partner's estate or administering the partner's property, including any power under the partnership agreement of an assignee to become a limited partner. If a partner is a corporation, trust or other entity and is dissolved or terminated, the powers of that partner may be exercised by its personal representative.

SUBCHAPTER VIII. DISSOLUTION

§ 17–801. Nonjudicial Dissolution

A limited partnership is dissolved and its affairs shall be wound up upon the first to occur of the following:

(1) At the time specified in a partnership agreement, but if no such time is set forth in the partnership agreement, then the limited partnership shall have a perpetual existence;

(2) Unless otherwise provided in a partnership agreement, upon the affirmative vote or written consent of (i) all general partners and (ii) the limited partners of a limited partnership or, if there is more than 1 class or group of limited partners, then by each class or group of limited partners, in either case, by limited partners who own more than two-thirds of the then-current percentage or other interest in the profits of the limited partnership owned by all of the limited partners or by the limited partners in each class or group, as appropriate.

(3) An event of withdrawal of a general partner unless at the time there is at least 1 other general partner and the partnership agreement permits the business of the limited partnership to be carried on by the remaining general partner and that partner does so, but the limited partnership is not dissolved and is not required to be wound up by reason of any event of withdrawal if (i) within 90 days or such other period as is provided for in a partnership agreement after the withdrawal either (A) if provided for in the partnership agreement, the then-current percentage or other interest in the profits of the limited partnership specified in the partnership agreement owned by the remaining partners agree, in writing or vote, to continue the business of the limited partnership and to appoint, effective as of the date of withdrawal, 1 or more additional general partners if necessary or desired, or (B) if no such right to agree or vote to continue the business of the limited partnership and to appoint 1 or more additional general partners is provided for in the partnership agreement, then more than 50% of the then-current percentage or other interest in the profits of the limited partnership owned by the remaining partners or, if there is more than 1 class or group of remaining partners, then more than 50% of the then-current percentage or other interest in the profits of the limited partnership owned by each class or classes or group or groups of remaining partners agree, in writing or vote, to continue the business of the limited partnership and to appoint, effective as of the

date of withdrawal, 1 or more additional general partners if necessary or desired, or (ii) the business of the limited partnership is continued pursuant to a right to continue stated in the partnership agreement and; the appointment, effective as of the date of withdrawal, of 1 or more additional general partners if necessary or desired;

(4) At the time there are no limited partners; provided, that the limited partnership is not dissolved and is not required to be wound up if:

a. Unless otherwise provided in a partnership agreement, within 90 days or such other period as is provided for in the partnership agreement after the occurrence of the event that caused the last remaining limited partner to cease to be a limited partner, the personal representative of the last remaining limited partner and all of the general partners agree, in writing or by vote, to continue the business of the limited partnership and to the admission of the personal representative of such limited partner or its nominee or designee to the limited partnership as a limited partner, effective as of the occurrence of the event that caused the last remaining limited partner to cease to be a limited partner; provided, that a partnership agreement may provide that the general partners or the personal representative of the last remaining limited partner shall be obligated to agree in writing to continue the business of the limited partnership and to the admission of the personal representative of such limited partner or its nominee or designee to the limited partnership as a limited partner, effective as of the occurrence of the event that caused the last limited partner to cease to be a limited partner; or

b. A limited partner is admitted to the limited partnership in the manner provided for in the partnership agreement, effective as of the occurrence of the event that caused the last remaining limited partner to cease to be a limited partner, within 90 days or such other period as is provided for in the partnership agreement after the occurrence of the event that caused the last remaining limited partner to cease to be a limited partner, pursuant to a provision of the partnership agreement that specifically provides for the admission of a limited partner to the limited partnership after there is no longer a remaining limited partner of the limited partnership.

(5) Upon the happening of events specified in a partnership agreement; or

(6) Entry of a decree of judicial dissolution under § 17-802 of this title.

§ 17–802. Judicial Dissolution

On application by or for a partner the Court of Chancery may decree dissolution of a limited partnership whenever it is not reasonably practicable to carry on the business in conformity with the partnership agreement.

§ 17–803. Winding Up

(a) Unless otherwise provided in the partnership agreement, the general partners who have not wrongfully dissolved a limited partnership or, if none, the limited partners, or a person approved by the limited partners or, if there is more than 1 class or group of limited partners, then by each class or group of limited partners, in either case, by limited partners who own more than 50 percent of the then current percentage or other interest in the profits of the limited partnership owned by all of the limited partners or by the limited partners in each class or group, as appropriate may wind up the limited partnership's affairs; but the Court of Chancery, upon cause shown, may wind up the limited partnership's affairs upon application of any partner, the partner's personal representative or assignee, and in connection therewith, may appoint a liquidating trustee.

(b) Upon dissolution of a limited partnership and until the filing of a certificate of cancellation as provided in § 17–203 of this title, the persons winding up the limited partnership's affairs may, in the name of, and for and on behalf of, the limited partnership, prosecute and defend suits, whether civil, criminal or administrative, gradually settle and close the limited partnership's business, dispose of and convey the limited partnership's property, discharge or make reasonable provision for the limited partnership's liabilities, and distribute to the partners any remaining assets of the limited partnership, all without affecting the liability of limited partners and without imposing the liability of a general partner on a liquidating trustee.

§ 17–804. Distribution of Assets

(a) Upon the winding up of a limited partnership, the assets shall be distributed as follows:

(1) To creditors, including partners who are creditors, to the extent otherwise permitted by law, in satisfaction of liabilities of the limited partnership (whether by payment or the making of reasonable provision for payment thereof) other than liabilities for which reasonable provision for payment has been made and liabilities for distributions to partners and former partners under § 17–601 or § 17–604 of this title;

(2) Unless otherwise provided in the partnership agreement, to partners and former partners in satisfaction of liabilities for distributions under § 17–601 or § 17–604 of this title; and

(3) Unless otherwise provided in the partnership agreement, to partners first for the return of their contributions and second respecting their partnership interests, in the proportions in which the partners share in distributions.

(b) A limited partnership which has dissolved:

(1) Shall pay or make reasonable provision to pay all claims and obligations, including all contingent, conditional or unmatured contractual claims, known to the limited partnership;

(2) Shall make such provision as will be reasonably likely to be sufficient to provide compensation for any claim against the limited partnership which is the subject of a pending action, suit or proceeding to which the limited partnership is a party and

(3) Shall make such provision as will be reasonably likely to be sufficient to provide compensation for claims that have not been made known to the limited partnership or that have not arisen but that, based on facts known to the limited partnership, are likely to arise or to become known to the limited partnership within 10 years after the date of dissolution.

If there are sufficient assets, such claims and obligations shall be paid in full and any such provision for payment made shall be made in full. If there are insufficient assets, such claims and obligations shall be paid or provided for according to their priority and, among claims of equal priority, ratably to the extent of assets available therefor. Unless otherwise provided in the partnership agreement, any remaining assets shall be distributed as provided in this chapter. Any liquidating trustee winding up a limited partnership's affairs who has complied with this section shall not be personally liable to the claimants of the dissolved limited partnership by reason of such person's actions in winding up the limited partnership.

(c) A limited partner who receives a distribution in violation of subsection (a) of this section, and who knew at the time of the distribution that the distribution violated subsection (a) of this section, shall be liable to the limited partnership for the amount of the distribution. For purposes of the immediately preceding sentence, the term "distribution" shall not include amounts constituting reasonable compensation for present or past services or reasonable payments made in the ordinary course of business pursuant to a bona fide retirement plan or other benefits program. A limited partner who receives a distribution in violation of subsection (a) of this section, and who did not know at the time of the distribution that the distribution violated subsection (a) of this section, shall not be liable for the amount of the distribution. Subject to subsection (d) of this section, this subsection shall not affect any obligation or liability of a limited partner under an agreement or other applicable law for the amount of a distribution.

(d) Unless otherwise agreed, a limited partner who receives a distribution from a limited partnership to which this section applies shall have no liability under this chapter or other applicable law for the amount of the distribution after the expiration of 3 years from the date of the distribution.

(e) Section 17-607 of this title shall not apply to a distribution to which this section applies.

§ 17-805. Trustees or Receivers for Limited Partnerships; Appointment; Powers; Duties

When the certificate of limited partnership of any limited partnership formed under this chapter shall be canceled by the filing of a certificate of cancellation pursuant to § 17-203 of this title, the Court of Chancery, on application of any creditor or partner of the limited partnership, or any other person who shows good cause therefor, at any time, may either appoint 1 or more of the general partners of the limited partnership to be trustees, or appoint 1 or more persons to be receivers, of and for the limited partnership, to take charge of the limited partnership's property, and to collect the debts and property due and belonging to the limited partnership, with the power to prosecute and defend, in the name of the limited partnership, or otherwise, all such suits as may be necessary or proper for the purposes aforesaid, and to appoint an agent or agents under them, and to do all other acts which might be done by the limited partnership, if in being, that may be necessary for the final settlement of the unfinished business of the limited partnership. The powers of the trustees or receivers may be continued as long as the Court of Chancery shall think necessary for the purposes aforesaid.

§ 17-806. Revocation of Dissolution

Notwithstanding the occurrence of an event set forth in § 17-801(1), (2), (3), (4) or (5) of this title, the limited partnership shall not be dissolved and its affairs shall not be wound up if, prior to the filing of a certificate of cancellation in the office of the Secretary of State, the business of the limited partnership is continued, effective as of the occurrence of such event, pursuant to the affirmative vote or written consent of (1) all remaining general partners and all remaining limited partners of the limited partnership, (2) all remaining general partners and the personal representative of the last remaining limited partner of the limited partnership if there is no remaining limited partner, (3) all remaining limited partners if there is no remaining general partner or (4) the personal representative of the last remaining limited partner if there is no remaining limited partner and no remaining general partner (and, in each instance, any other person whose approval is required under the partnership agreement to revoke a dissolution pursuant to this section), provided, however, if the dissolution was caused by a vote or written consent, the dissolution shall not be revoked unless each general partner and limited partner and other person (or their respective personal representatives) who voted in favor of, or consented to, the dissolution has voted or consented in writing to continue the business of the limited partnership. If there is no remaining general partner of the limited partnership and all remaining limited partners or, if there is no remaining limited partner, the personal representative of the last remaining limited partner, vote in favor of or consent to the continuation of the business of the limited partnership, such limited partners or personal representative, as applicable, shall be required to agree in writing to appoint 1 or more general partners effective as of the date of withdrawal of the last general partner, and if there is no remaining limited partner of the limited partnership and the personal representative of the last remaining limited partner votes in favor of or consents to the continuation of the business of the limited partnership, such personal representative shall be required to agree in writing to the admission of the personal representative of such limited partner or its nominee or designee to the limited partnership as a limited partner, effective as of the occurrence of the event that caused the last remaining limited partner to cease to be a limited partner.

SUBCHAPTER IX. FOREIGN LIMITED PARTNERSHIPS

§ 17–901. Law Governing

(a) Subject to the Constitution of the State of Delaware:

(1) The laws of the State of Delaware, territory, possession, or other jurisdiction or country under which a foreign limited partnership is organized govern its organization and internal affairs and the liability of its limited partners; and

(2) A foreign limited partnership may not be denied registration by reason of any difference between those laws and the laws of the State of Delaware.

(b) A foreign limited partnership shall be subject to § 17–106 of this title.

§ 17–902. Registration Required; Application

Before doing business in the State of Delaware, a foreign limited partnership shall register with the Secretary of State. In order to register, a foreign limited partnership shall submit to the Secretary of State:

(1) A copy executed by a general partner of an application for registration as a foreign limited partnership, setting forth:

a. The name of the foreign limited partnership and, if different, the name under which it proposes to register and do business in the State of Delaware;

b. The State, territory, possession or other jurisdiction or country where organized, the date of its organization and a statement from a general partner that, as of the date of filing, the foreign limited partnership validly exists as a limited partnership under the laws of the jurisdiction of its organization;

c. The nature of the business or purposes to be conducted or promoted in the State of Delaware;

d. The address of the registered office and the name and address of the registered agent for service of process required to be maintained by § 17–904(b) of this title;

e. A statement that the Secretary of State is appointed the agent of the foreign limited partnership for service of process under the circumstances set forth in § 17–910(b) of this title;

f. The name and business, residence or mailing addresses of each of the general partners; and

g. The date on which the foreign limited partnership first did, or intends to do, business in the State of Delaware.

(2) A fee as set forth in § 17–1107(a)(6) of this title shall be paid.

§ 17–903. Issuance of Registration

(a) If the Secretary of State finds that an application for registration conforms to law and all requisite fees have been paid, the Secretary shall:

(1) Certify that the application has been filed in the Secretary's office by endorsing upon the original application the word "Filed," and the date and hour of the filing. This endorsement is conclusive of the date and time of its filing in the absence of actual fraud;

(2) File and index the endorsed application.

(b) The Secretary of State shall prepare and return to the person who filed the application or the person's representative a copy of the original signed application, similarly endorsed, and shall certify such copy as a true copy of the original signed application.

(c) The filing of the application with the Secretary of State shall make it unnecessary to file any other documents under Chapter 31 of this title.

§ 17–904. Name; Registered Office; Registered Agent

(a) A foreign limited partnership may register with the Secretary of State under any name (whether or not it is the name under which it is registered in the jurisdiction of its organization) that includes the words "Limited Partnership" or the abbreviation "L.P." or the designation

"LP" and that could be registered by a domestic limited partnership; provided, however, that a foreign limited partnership may register under any name which is not such as to distinguish it upon the records in the Office of the Secretary of State from the name on such records of any domestic or foreign corporation, partnership, statutory trust, limited liability company or limited partnership reserved, registered, formed or organized under the laws of the State of Delaware with the written consent of the other corporation, partnership, statutory trust, limited liability company or limited partnership, which written consent shall be filed with the Secretary of State.

(b) Each foreign limited partnership shall have and maintain in the State of Delaware:

(1) A registered office which may but need not be a place of its business in the State of Delaware; and

(2) A registered agent for service of process on the limited partnership, which agent may be either an individual resident of the State of Delaware whose business office is identical with the limited partnership's registered office, or a domestic corporation, or a domestic limited partnership, or a domestic limited liability company, or a domestic statutory trust, or a foreign corporation, or a foreign limited partnership, or a foreign limited liability company authorized to do business in the State of Delaware having a business office identical with such registered office, which is generally open during normal business hours to accept service of process and otherwise perform the functions of a registered agent.

(c) A registered agent may change the address of the registered office of the foreign limited partnership(s) for which the agent is registered agent to another address in the State of Delaware by paying a fee as set forth in § 17-1107(a)(7) of this title and filing with the Secretary of State a certificate, executed by such registered agent, setting forth the address at which such registered agent has maintained the registered office for each of the foreign limited partnerships for which it is a registered agent, and further certifying to the new address to which each such registered office will be changed on a given day, and at which new address such registered agent will thereafter maintain the registered office for each of the foreign limited partnerships for which it is a registered agent. Upon the filing of such certificate, the Secretary of State shall furnish to the registered agent a certified copy of the same under the Secretary's hand and seal of office, and thereafter, or until further change of address, as authorized by law, the registered office in the State of Delaware of each of the foreign limited partnerships for which the agent is a registered agent shall be located at the new address of the registered agent thereof as given in the certificate. In the event of a change of name of any person acting as a registered agent of a foreign limited partnership, such registered agent shall file with the Secretary of State a certificate, executed by such registered agent, setting forth the new name of such registered agent, the name of such registered agent before it was changed and the address at which such registered agent has maintained the registered office for each of the foreign limited partnerships for which it is a registered agent, and shall pay a fee as set forth in § 17–1107(a)(7) of this title. Upon the filing of such certificate, the Secretary of State shall furnish to the registered agent a certified copy of the certificate under his or her hand and seal of office. A change of name of any person acting as a registered agent of a foreign limited partnership as a result of a merger or consolidation of the registered agent with or into another person which succeeds to its assets and liabilities by operation of law shall be deemed a change of name for purposes of this section. Filing a certificate under this section shall be deemed to be an amendment of the application of each foreign limited partnership affected thereby and each such foreign limited partnership shall not be required to take any further action with respect thereto to amend its application under § 17–905 of this title. Any registered agent filing a certificate under this section shall promptly, upon such filing, deliver a copy of any such certificate to each foreign limited partnership affected thereby.

(d) The registered agent of 1 or more foreign limited partnerships may resign and appoint a successor registered agent by paying a fee as set forth in § 17–1107(a)(7) of this title and filing a certificate with the Secretary of State stating that it resigns and the name and address of the successor registered agent. There shall be attached to such certificate a statement of each affected foreign limited partnership ratifying and approving such change of registered agent. Upon such filing, the successor registered agent shall become the registered agent of such foreign limited partnerships as have ratified and approved such substitution and the successor registered agent's address, as stated in such certificate, shall become the address of each such foreign limited partnership's registered office in the State of Delaware. The Secretary of State shall then issue a certificate that the successor registered agent has become the registered agent of the foreign limited partnerships so ratifying and approving such change and setting out the names of such foreign limited partnerships. Filing of such certificate of resignation shall be deemed to be an amendment of the application of each foreign limited partnership affected thereby and each such foreign limited partnership shall not be required to take any further action with respect thereto to amend its application under § 17–905 of this title.

(e) The registered agent of 1 or more foreign limited partnerships may resign without appointing a successor registered agent by paying a fee as set forth in § 17–1107(a)(7) of this title and filing a certificate of resignation with the Secretary of State, but such resignation shall not become effective until 30 days after the certificate is filed. The certificate shall contain a statement that written notice of resignation was given to each affected foreign limited partnership at least 30 days prior to the filing of the certificate by mailing or delivering such notice to the foreign limited partnership at its address last known to the registered agent and shall set forth the date of such notice. After receipt of the notice of the resignation of its registered agent, the foreign limited partnership for which such registered agent was acting shall obtain and designate a new registered agent to take the place of the registered agent so resigning. If such foreign limited partnership fails to obtain and designate a new registered agent as aforesaid prior to the expiration of the period of 30 days after the filing by the registered agent of the certificate of resignation, such foreign limited partnership shall not be permitted to do business in the State of Delaware and its registration shall be deemed to be cancelled. After the resignation of the registered agent shall have become effective as provided in this section and if no new registered agent shall have been obtained and designated in the time and manner aforesaid, service of legal process against each foreign limited partnership for which the resigned registered agent had been acting shall thereafter be upon the Secretary of State in accordance with § 17-911 of this title.

§ 17-905. Amendments to Application

If any statement in the application for registration of a foreign limited partnership was false when made or any arrangements or other facts described have changed, making the application false in any respect, the foreign limited partnership shall promptly file in the Office of the Secretary of State a certificate, executed by a general partner, correcting such statement, together with a fee as set forth in § 17-1107(a)(6) of this title.

§ 17-906. Cancellation of Registration [Effective Until Jan. 1, 2007]

A foreign limited partnership may cancel its registration by filing with the Secretary of State a certificate of cancellation executed by a general partner, together with a fee as set forth in § 17-1107(a)(6) of this title. A cancellation does not terminate the authority of the Secretary of State to accept service of process on the foreign limited partnership with respect to causes of action arising out of the doing of business in the State of Delaware.

§ 17-906. Cancellation of Registration [Effective Jan. 1, 2007]

A foreign limited partnership may cancel its registration by filing with the Secretary of State a certificate of cancellation executed by a general partner, together with a fee as set forth in § 17-1107(a)(6) of this title. The registration of a foreign limited partnership shall be cancelled as provided in § 17-104(i)(4) and § 17-904(e) of this title. A cancellation does not terminate the authority of the Secretary of State to accept service of process on the foreign limited partnership with respect to causes of action arising out of the doing of business in the State of Delaware.

§ 17-907. Doing Business Without Registration

(a) A foreign limited partnership doing business in the State of Delaware may not maintain any action, suit or proceeding in the State of Delaware until it has registered in the State of Delaware, and has paid to the State of Delaware all fees and penalties for the years or parts thereof during which it did business in the State of Delaware without having registered.

(b) The failure of a foreign limited partnership to register in the State of Delaware does not impair:

(1) The validity of any contract or act of the foreign limited partnership;

(2) The right of any other party to the contract to maintain any action, suit or proceeding on the contract; or

(3) Prevent the foreign limited partnership from defending any action, suit or proceeding in any court of the State of Delaware.

(c) A limited partner of a foreign limited partnership is not liable as a general partner of the foreign limited partnership solely by reason of the foreign limited partnership's having done business in the State of Delaware without registration.

(d) Any foreign limited partnership doing business in the State of Delaware without first having registered shall be fined and shall pay to the Secretary of State $200 for each year or part thereof during which the foreign limited partnership failed to register in the State of Delaware.

§ 17-908. Foreign Limited Partnerships Doing Business Without Having Qualified; Injunctions

The Court of Chancery shall have jurisdiction to enjoin any foreign limited partnership, or any agent thereof, from doing any business in the State of Delaware if such foreign limited partnership has failed to register under this subchapter or if such foreign limited partnership has secured a certificate of the Secretary of State under § 17-903 of this title on the basis of false or misleading representations. The Attorney General shall, upon the Attorney General's own motion or upon the relation of proper parties, proceed for this purpose by complaint in any county in which such foreign limited partnership is doing or has done business.

§ 17-909. Execution; Liability

Sections 17-204(c) and 17-207 of this title shall be applicable to foreign limited partnerships as if they were domestic limited partnerships.

§ 17-910. Service of Process on Registered Foreign Limited Partnerships

(a) Service of legal process upon any foreign limited partnership shall be made by delivering a copy personally to any managing or general agent or general partner of the foreign limited partnership in the State of Delaware or the registered agent of the foreign limited partnership in the State of Delaware, or by leaving it at the dwelling house or usual place of abode in the State of Delaware of any such managing or general agent, general partner or registered agent (if the registered agent be an individual), or at the registered office or other place of business of the foreign limited partnership in the State of Delaware. If the registered agent be a corporation, service of process upon it as such may be made by serving, in the State of Delaware, a copy thereof on the president, vice-president, secretary, assistant secretary or any director of the corporate registered agent. Service by copy left at the dwelling house or usual place of abode of any officer, managing or general agent, general partner or registered agent, or at the registered office or other place of business of the foreign limited partnership in the State of Delaware, to be effective must be delivered thereat at least 6 days before the return date of the process, and in the presence of an adult person, and the officer serving the process shall distinctly state the manner of service in the return thereto. Process returnable forthwith must be delivered personally to the officer, managing or general agent, general partner or registered agent.

(b) In case the officer whose duty it is to serve legal process cannot by due diligence serve the process in any manner provided for by subsection (a) of this section, it shall be lawful to serve the process against the foreign limited partnership upon the Secretary of State, and such service shall be as effectual for all intents and purposes as if made in any of the ways provided for in subsection (a) hereof. In the event service is effected through the Secretary of State in accordance with this subsection, the Secretary of State shall forthwith notify the foreign limited partnership by letter, certified mail, return receipt requested, directed to the foreign limited partnership at the address of a general partner as it appears on the records relating to such foreign limited partnership on file with the Secretary of State or, if no such address appears, at its last registered office. Such letter shall enclose a copy of the process and any other papers served on the Secretary of State pursuant to this subsection. It shall be the duty of the plaintiff in the event of such service to serve process and any other papers in duplicate, to notify the Secretary of State that service is being effected pursuant to this subsection, and to pay to the Secretary of State the sum of $50 for the use of the State of Delaware, which sum shall be taxed as a part of the costs in the proceeding if the plaintiff shall prevail therein. The Secretary of State shall maintain an alphabetical record of any such service setting forth the name of the plaintiff and defendant, the title, docket number and nature of the proceeding in which process has been served upon the Secretary, the fact that service has been effected pursuant to this subsection, the return date thereof and the day and hour when the service was made. The Secretary of State shall not be required to retain such information for a period longer than 5 years from receipt of the service of process.

§ 17-911. Service of Process on Unregistered Foreign Limited Partnerships

(a) Any foreign limited partnership which shall do business in the State of Delaware without having registered under § 17-902 of this title shall be deemed to have thereby appointed and constituted the Secretary of State of the State of Delaware its agent for the acceptance of legal process in any civil action, suit or proceeding against it in any state or federal court in the State of Delaware arising or growing out of any business done by it within the State of Delaware. The doing of business in the State of Delaware by such foreign limited partnership shall be a signification of the agreement of such foreign limited partnership that any such process when so served shall be of the same legal force and validity as if served upon an authorized general partner or agent personally within the State of Delaware.

(b) Whenever the words "doing business," "the doing of business" or "business done in the State," by any such foreign limited partnership are used in this section, they shall mean the course or practice of carrying on any business activities in the State of Delaware, including, without limiting the generality of the foregoing, the solicitation of business or orders in the State of Delaware.

(c) In the event of service upon the Secretary of State in accordance with subsection (a) of this section, the Secretary of State shall forthwith notify the foreign limited partnership thereof by letter, certified mail, return receipt requested, directed to the foreign limited partnership at the address furnished to the Secretary of State by the plaintiff in such action, suit or proceeding. Such letter shall enclose a copy of the process and any other papers served upon the Secretary of State. It shall be the duty of the plaintiff in the event of such service to serve process and any other papers in duplicate, to notify the Secretary of State that service is being made pursuant to this subsection, and to pay to the Secretary of State the sum of $50 for the use of the State of Delaware, which sum shall be taxed as part of the costs in the proceeding, if the plaintiff shall prevail therein. The Secretary of State shall maintain an alphabetical record of any such process setting forth the name of the plaintiff and defendant, the title, docket number and nature of the proceeding in which process has been served upon the Secretary, the return date thereof, and the day and hour when the service was made. The Secretary of State shall not be required to retain such information for a period longer than 5 years from receipt of the service of process.

§ 17–912. Activities not Constituting Doing Business

(a) Activities of a foreign limited partnership in the State of Delaware that do not constitute doing business for the purpose of this subchapter include:

(1) Maintaining, defending or settling an action or proceeding;

(2) Holding meetings of its partners or carrying on any other activity concerning its internal affairs;

(3) Maintaining bank accounts;

(4) Maintaining offices or agencies for the transfer, exchange or registration of the limited partnership's own securities or maintaining trustees or depositories with respect to those securities;

(5) Selling through independent contractors;

(6) Soliciting or obtaining orders, whether by mail or through employees or agents or otherwise, if the orders require acceptance outside the State of Delaware before they become contracts;

(7) Selling, by contract consummated outside the State of Delaware, and agreeing, by the contract, to deliver into the State of Delaware, machinery, plants or equipment, the construction, erection or installation of which within the State of Delaware requires the supervision of technical engineers or skilled employees performing services not generally available, and as part of the contract of sale agreeing to furnish such services, and such services only, to the vendee at the time of construction, erection or installation;

(8) Creating, as borrower or lender, or acquiring indebtedness with or without a mortgage or other security interest in property;

(9) Collecting debts or foreclosing mortgages or other security interests in property securing the debts, and holding, protecting and maintaining property so acquired;

(10) Conducting an isolated transaction that is not one in the course of similar transactions;

(11) Doing business in interstate commerce; and

(12) Doing business in the State of Delaware as an insurance company.

(b) A person shall not be deemed to be doing business in the State of Delaware solely by reason of being a partner of a domestic limited partnership or a foreign limited partnership.

(c) This section does not apply in determining whether a foreign limited partnership is subject to service of process, taxation or regulation under any other law of the State of Delaware.

SUBCHAPTER X. DERIVATIVE ACTIONS

§ 17–1001. Right to Bring Action

A limited partner or an assignee of a partnership interest may bring an action in the Court of Chancery in the right of a limited partnership to recover a judgment in its favor if general partners with authority to do so have refused to bring the action or if an effort to cause those general partners to bring the action is not likely to succeed.

§ 17–1002. Proper Plaintiff

In a derivative action, the plaintiff must be a partner or an assignee of a partnership interest at the time of bringing the action and:

(1) At the time of the transaction of which the plaintiff complains; or

(2) The plaintiff's status as a partner or an assignee of a partnership interest had devolved upon the plaintiff by operation of law or pursuant to the terms of the partnership agreement from a person who was a partner or an assignee of a partnership interest at the time of the transaction.

§ 17–1003. Complaint

In a derivative action, the complaint shall set forth with particularity the effort, if any, of the plaintiff to secure initiation of the action by a general partner or the reasons for not making the effort.

§ 17–1004. Expenses

If a derivative action is successful, in whole or in part, as a result of a judgment, compromise or settlement of any such action, the court may award the plaintiff reasonable expenses, including reasonable attorney's fees, from any recovery in any such action or from a limited partnership.

SUBCHAPTER XI. MISCELLANEOUS

§ 17–1101. Construction and Application of Chapter and Partnership Agreement

(a) This chapter shall be so applied and construed to effectuate its general purpose to make uniform the law with respect to the subject of this chapter among states enacting it.

(b) The rule that statutes in derogation of the common law are to be strictly construed shall have no application to this chapter.

(c) It is the policy of this chapter to give maximum effect to the principle of freedom of contract and to the enforceability of partnership agreements.

(d) To the extent that, at law or in equity, a partner or other person has duties (including fiduciary duties) to a limited partnership or to another partner or to another person that is a party to or is otherwise bound by a partnership agreement, the partner's or other person's duties may be expanded or restricted or eliminated by provisions in the partnership agreement; provided that the partnership agreement may not eliminate the implied contractual covenant of good faith and fair dealing.

(e) Unless otherwise provided in a partnership agreement, a partner or other person shall not be liable to a limited partnership or to another partner or to another person that is a party to or is otherwise bound by a partnership agreement for breach of fiduciary duty for the partner's or other person's good faith reliance on the provisions of the partnership agreement.

(f) A partnership agreement may provide for the limitation or elimination of any and all liabilities for breach of contract and breach of duties (including fiduciary duties) of a partner or other person to a limited partnership or to another partner or to an other person that is a party to or is otherwise bound by a partnership agreement; provided, that a partnership agreement may not limit or eliminate liability for any act or omission that constitutes a bad faith violation of the implied contractual covenant of good faith and fair dealing.

(g) Sections 9–406 and 9–408 of this title do not apply to any interest in a limited partnership, including all rights, powers and interests arising under a partnership agreement or this chapter. This provision prevails over §§ 9–406 and 9–408 of this title.

§ 17–1102. Short Title

This chapter may be cited as the "Delaware Revised Uniform Limited Partnership Act".

§ 17–1103. Severability

If any provision of this chapter or its application to any person or circumstances is held invalid, the invalidity does not affect other provisions or applications of the chapter which can be given effect without the invalid provision or application, and to this end the provisions of this chapter are severable.

§ 17–1104. Effective Date and Extended Effective Date

(a) All limited partnerships formed on or after January 1, 1983, the "effective date," shall be governed by this chapter.

(b) Except as provided in subsections (e) and (f) of this section, all limited partnerships formed on or after July 1, 1973, and prior to the effective date, under Chapter 17 of this title as hereby repealed, shall continue to be governed by that chapter until January 1, 1985, the "extended effective date," at which time such limited partnerships shall be governed by this chapter.

(c) Except as provided in subsection (e) of this section, a limited partnership formed prior to July 1, 1973, shall continue to be governed by Chapter 17 of this title in effect prior to the adoption of Chapter 17 of this title as hereby repealed, except that such limited partnership shall not be renewed except under this chapter.

(d) Except as provided in subsection (e) of this section, subchapter IX of this chapter, dealing with foreign limited partnerships, is not effective until the extended effective date.

(e) Any limited partnership formed prior to the effective date, and any foreign limited partnership, may elect to be governed by this chapter before the extended effective date by filing with the Secretary of State a certificate of limited partnership or an application for registration as a foreign limited partnership which complies with this chapter or a certificate of amendment which would cause its certificate of limited partnership to comply with this chapter and which specifically states that it is electing to be so bound.

(f) With respect to a limited partnership formed on or after July 1, 1973, and prior to the effective date:

(1) On and after the extended effective date, such limited partnership need not file with the Secretary of State a certificate of amendment which would cause its certificate of limited partnership to comply with this chapter until the occurrence of an event which, under this chapter, requires the filing of a certificate of amendment;

(2) Sections 17–501 and 17–502 of this title shall apply only to contributions and distributions made after the effective date; and

(3) Section 17–704 of this title shall apply only to assignments made after the effective date.

§ 17–1105. Cases not Provided for in this Chapter

In any case not provided for in this chapter, the Delaware Uniform Partnership Law in effect on July 11, 1999 (6 Del. C. § 1501, et seq.) and the rules of law and equity, including the Law Merchant, shall govern.

§ 17–1106. Prior Law

Except as set forth in § 17–1104 of this title, Chapter 17 of this title is hereby repealed.

§ 17–1107. Fees

(a) No document required to be filed under this chapter shall be effective until the applicable fee required by this section is paid. The following fees shall be paid to and collected by the Secretary of State for the use of the State of Delaware:

(1) Upon the receipt for filing of an application for reservation of name, an application for renewal of reservation or a notice of transfer or cancellation of reservation pursuant to § 17–103(b) of this title, a fee in the amount of $75.

(2) Upon the receipt for filing of a certificate under § 17–104(b) of this title, a fee in the amount of $50, upon the receipt for filing of a certificate under § 17–104(c) of this title, a fee in the amount of $50 and a further fee of $2 for each limited partnership affected by such certificate, and upon the receipt for filing of a certificate under § 17–104(d) of this title, a fee in the amount of $2.50.

(3) Upon the receipt for filing of a certificate of limited partnership domestication under § 17–215 of this title, a certificate of transfer or a certificate of transfer and continuance under § 17–216 of this title, a certificate of conversion to limited partnership under § 17–217 of this title, a certificate of conversion to a non-Delaware entity under § 17–219 of this title, a certificate of limited partnership under § 17–201 of this title, a certificate of amendment under § 17–202 of this title, a certificate of cancellation under § 17–203 of this title, a certificate of merger or consolidation under § 17–211 of this title, a restated certificate of limited partnership under § 17–210 of this title, a certificate of amendment of a certificate with a future effective date or time under § 17–206(c) of this title, a certificate of termination of a certificate with a future effective date or time under § 17–206(c) of this title, a certificate of correction under § 17–213 of this title, or a certificate of revival under § 17–1111 of this title, a fee in the amount of $200.

(4) For certifying copies of any paper on file as provided for by this chapter, a fee in the amount of $30 for each copy certified.

(5) The Secretary of State may issue photocopies or electronic image copies of instruments on file, as well as instruments, documents and other papers not on file, and for all such photocopies or electronic image copies, whether certified or not, a fee of $10 shall be paid for the first page and $2 for each additional page. The Secretary of State may also issue microfiche copies of instruments on file as well as instruments, documents and other papers not on file, and for each such microfiche a fee of $2 shall be paid therefor. Notwithstanding the State of Delaware's Freedom of Information Act [Chapter 100 of Title 29] or other provision of this Code granting access to public records, the Secretary of State shall issue only photocopies, microfiche or electronic image copies of records in exchange for the fees described above.

(6) Upon the receipt for filing of an application for registration as a foreign limited partnership under § 17–902 of this title, a certificate under § 17–905 of this title or a certificate of cancellation under § 17–906 of this title, a fee in the amount of $200.

(7) Upon the receipt for filing of a certificate under § 17–904(c) of this title, a fee in the amount of $50, upon the receipt for filing of a certificate under § 17–904(d) of this title, a fee in the amount of $50 and a further fee of $2 for each foreign limited partnership affected by such certificate, and upon the receipt for filing of a certificate under § 17–904(e) of this title, a fee in the amount of $10.

(8) For preclearance of any document for filing, a fee in the amount of $250.

(9) For preparing and providing a written report of a record search, a fee in the amount of $30.

(10) For issuing any certificate of the Secretary of State, including but not limited to a certificate of good standing, other than a certification of a copy under paragraph (4) of this subsection, a fee in the amount of $30, except that for issuing any certificate of the Secretary of State that recites all of a limited partnership's filings with the Secretary of State, a fee of $125 shall be paid for each such certificate.

(11) For receiving and filing and/or indexing any certificate, affidavit, agreement or any other paper provided for by this chapter, for which no different fee is specifically prescribed, a fee in the amount of $50.

(12) The Secretary of State may in his or her discretion charge a fee of $60 for each check received for payment of any fee that is returned due to insufficient funds or the result of a stop payment order.

(b) In addition to those fees charged under subsection (a) of this section, there shall be collected by and paid to the Secretary of State the following:

(1) For all services described in subsection (a) of this section that are requested to be completed within 1 hour on the same day as the day of the request, an additional sum of up to $1,000 and for all services described in subsection (a) of this section that are requested to be completed within 2 hours on the same day of the request, an additional sum of $200;

(2) For all services described in subsection (a) of this section that are requested to be completed within the same day as the day of the request, an additional sum of up to $200; and

(3) For all services described in subsection (a) of this section that are requested to be completed within a 24–hour period from the time of the request, an additional sum of up to $100.

The Secretary of State shall establish (and may from time to time amend) a schedule of specific fees payable pursuant to this subsection.

(c) The Secretary of State may in his or her discretion permit the extension of credit for the fees required by this section upon such terms as the secretary shall deem to be appropriate.

(d) The Secretary of State shall retain from the revenue collected from the fees required by this section a sum sufficient to provide at all times a fund of at least $500, but not more than $1,500, from which the secretary may refund any payment made pursuant to this section to the extent that it exceeds the fees required by this section. The funds shall be deposited in a financial institution which is a legal depository of State of Delaware moneys to the credit of the Secretary of State and shall be disbursable on order of the Secretary of State.

(e) Except as provided in this section, the fees of the Secretary of State shall be as provided in § 2315 of Title 29.

§ 17-1108. Reserved Power of State of Delaware to Alter or Repeal Chapter

All provisions of this chapter may be altered from time to time or repealed and all rights of partners are subject to this reservation. Unless expressly stated to the contrary in this chapter, all amendments of this chapter shall apply to limited partnerships and partners whether or not existing as such at the time of the enactment of any such amendment.

§ 17-1109. Annual Tax of Domestic Limited Partnership and Foreign Limited Partnership

(a) Every domestic limited partnership and every foreign limited partnership registered to do business in the State of Delaware shall pay an annual tax, for the use of the State of Delaware, in the amount of $200.

(b) The annual tax shall be due and payable on the 1st day of June following the close of the calendar year or upon the cancellation of a certificate of limited partnership. The Secretary of State shall receive the annual tax and pay over all taxes collected to the Department of Finance of the State of Delaware. If the annual tax remains unpaid after the due date established by subsection (d) of this section, the tax shall bear interest at the rate of 11/2% for each month or portion thereof until fully paid.

(c) The Secretary of State shall, at least 60 days prior to the 1st day of June of each year, cause to be mailed to each domestic limited partnership and foreign limited partnership required to comply with the provisions of this section in care of its registered agent in the State of Delaware an annual statement for the tax to be paid hereunder.

(d) In the event of neglect, refusal or failure on the part of any domestic limited partnership or foreign limited partnership to pay the annual tax to be paid hereunder on or before the 1st day of June in any year, such domestic limited partnership or foreign limited partnership shall pay the sum of $100 to be recovered by adding that amount to the annual tax, and such additional sum shall become a part of the tax and shall be collected in the same manner and subject to the same penalties.

(e) In case any domestic limited partnership or foreign limited partnership shall fail to pay the annual tax due within the time required by this section, and in case the agent in charge of the registered office of any domestic limited partnership or foreign limited partnership upon whom process against such domestic limited partnership or foreign limited partnership may be served shall die, resign, refuse to act as such, remove from the State of Delaware or cannot with due diligence be found, it shall be lawful while default continues to serve process against such domestic limited partnership or foreign limited partnership upon the Secretary of State. Such service upon the Secretary of State shall be made in the manner and shall have the effect stated in § 17-105 of this title in the case of a domestic limited partnership and § 17-910 of this title in the case of a foreign limited partnership and shall be governed in all respects by said sections.

(f) The annual tax shall be a debt due from a domestic limited partnership or foreign limited partnership to the State of Delaware, for which an action at law may be maintained after the same shall have been in arrears for a period of 1 month. The tax shall also be a preferred debt in the case of insolvency.

(g) A domestic limited partnership or foreign limited partnership that neglects, refuses or fails to pay the annual tax when due shall cease to be in good standing as a domestic limited partnership or registered as a foreign limited partnership in the State of Delaware.

(h) A domestic limited partnership that has ceased to be in good standing or a foreign limited partnership that has ceased to be registered by reason of the failure to pay an annual tax shall be restored to and have the status of a domestic limited partnership in good standing or a foreign limited partnership that is registered in the State of Delaware upon the payment of the annual tax and all penalties and interest thereon for each year for which such domestic limited partnership or foreign limited partnership neglected, refused or failed to pay an annual tax.

(i) The Attorney General, either on the Attorney General's own motion or upon request of the Secretary of State, whenever any annual tax due under this chapter from any domestic limited partnership or foreign limited partnership shall have remained in arrears for a period of 3 months after the tax shall have become payable, may apply to the Court of Chancery, by petition in the name of the State of Delaware, on 5 days' notice to such domestic limited partnership or foreign limited partnership, which notice may be served in such manner as the Court may direct, for an injunction to restrain such domestic limited partnership or foreign limited partnership from the transaction of any business within the State of Delaware or elsewhere, until the payment of the annual tax, and all penalties and interest due thereon and the cost of the application, which shall be fixed by the Court. The Court of Chancery may grant the injunction, if a proper case appears, and upon granting and service of the injunction, such domestic limited partnership or foreign limited partnership thereafter shall not transact any business until the injunction shall be dissolved.

(j) A domestic limited partnership that has ceased to be in good standing by reason of its neglect, refusal or failure to pay an annual tax shall remain a domestic limited partnership formed under this chapter. The Secretary of State shall not accept for filing any certificate (except a certificate of resignation of a registered agent when a successor registered agent is not being appointed) required or permitted by this chapter to be filed in respect of any domestic limited partnership or foreign limited partnership which has neglected, refused or failed to pay an annual tax, and shall not issue any certificate of good standing with respect to such domestic limited partnership or foreign limited partnership, unless and until such domestic limited partnership or foreign limited partnership shall have been restored to and have the status of a domestic limited partnership in good standing or a foreign limited partnership duly registered in the State of Delaware.

(k) A domestic limited partnership that has ceased to be in good standing or a foreign limited partnership that has ceased to be registered in the State of Delaware by reason of its neglect, refusal or failure to pay an annual tax may not maintain any action, suit or proceeding in any court of the State of Delaware until such domestic limited partnership or foreign limited partnership has been restored to and has the status of a domestic limited partnership or foreign limited partnership in good standing or duly registered in the State of Delaware. An action, suit or proceeding may not be maintained in any court of the State of Delaware by any successor or assignee of such domestic limited partnership or foreign limited partnership on any right, claim or demand arising out of the transaction of business by such domestic limited partnership after it has ceased to be in good standing or a foreign limited partnership that has ceased to be registered in the State of Delaware until such domestic limited partnership or foreign limited partnership, or any person that has acquired all or substantially all of its assets, has paid any annual tax then due and payable, together with penalties and interest thereon.

(l) The neglect, refusal or failure of a domestic limited partnership or foreign limited partnership to pay an annual tax shall not impair the validity of any contract, deed, mortgage, security interest, lien or act of such domestic limited partnership or foreign limited partnership or prevent such domestic limited partnership or foreign limited partnership from defending any action, suit or proceeding in any court of the State of Delaware.

(m) A limited partner of a domestic limited partnership or foreign limited partnership is not liable as a general partner of such domestic limited partnership or foreign limited partnership solely by reason of the neglect, refusal or failure of such domestic limited partnership or foreign limited partnership to pay an annual tax or by reason of such domestic limited partnership or foreign limited partnership ceasing to be in good standing or duly registered.

§ 17-1110. Cancellation of Certificate of Limited Partnership for Failure to Pay Annual Tax

(a) The certificate of limited partnership of a domestic limited partnership shall be deemed to be canceled if the limited partnership shall fail to pay the annual tax due under § 17-1109 of this title for a period of 3 years from the date it is due, such cancellation to be effective on the 3rd anniversary of such due date.

(b) A list of those domestic limited partnerships whose certificates of limited partnership were canceled on June 1 of such calendar year pursuant to § 17-1110(a) of this title shall be filed in the office of the Secretary of State. On or before October 31 of each calendar year, the Secretary of State shall publish such list on the Internet or on a similar medium for a period of 1 week and shall advertise the website or other address where such list can be accessed in at least 1 newspaper of general circulation in the State of Delaware.

§ 17-1111. Revival of Domestic Limited Partnership [Effective Until Jan. 1, 2007]

(a) A domestic limited partnership whose certificate of limited partnership has been canceled pursuant to § 17-104(d) or § 17-1110(a) of this title may be revived by filing in the office of the Secretary of State a certificate of revival accompanied by the payment of the fee required by § 17-1107(a)(3) of this title and payment of the annual tax due under § 17-1109 of this title and all penalties and interest thereon for each year for which such domestic limited partnership neglected, refused or failed to pay such annual tax, including each year between the cancellation of its certificate of limited partnership and its revival. The certificate of revival shall set forth:

(1) The name of the limited partnership at the time its certificate of limited partnership was canceled and, if such name is not available at the time of revival, the name under which the limited partnership is to be revived;

(2) The date of filing of the original certificate of limited partnership of the limited partnership;

(3) The address of the limited partnership's registered office in the State of Delaware and the name and address of the limited partnership's registered agent in the State of Delaware;

(4) A statement that the certificate of revival is filed by 1 or more general partners of the limited partnership authorized to execute and file the certificate of revival to revive the limited partnership; and

(5) Any other matters the general partner or general partners executing the certificate of revival determine to include therein.

(b) The certificate of revival shall be deemed to be an amendment to the certificate of limited partnership of the limited partnership, and the limited partnership shall not be required to take any further action to amend its certificate of limited partnership under § 17-202 of this title with respect to the matters set forth in the certificate of revival.

(c) Upon the filing of a certificate of revival, a limited partnership shall be revived with the same force and effect as if its certificate of limited partnership had not been canceled pursuant to § 17-104(d) or § 17-1110(a) of this title. Such revival shall validate all contracts, acts, matters and things made, done and performed by the limited partnership, its partners, employees and agents during the time when its certificate of limited partnership was canceled pursuant to § 17-104(d) or § 17-1110(a) of this title, with the same force and effect and to all intents and purposes as if the certificate of limited partnership had remained in full force and effect. All real and personal property, and all rights and interests, which belonged to the limited partnership at the time its certificate of limited partnership was canceled pursuant to § 17-104(d) or § 17-1110(a) of this title, or which were acquired by the limited partnership following the cancellation of its certificate of limited partnership pursuant to § 17-104(d) or § 17-1110(a) of this title, and which were not disposed of prior to the time of its revival, shall be vested in the limited partnership after its revival as fully as they were held by the limited partnership at, and after, as the case may be, the time its certificate of limited partnership was canceled pursuant to § 17-104(d) or § 17-1110(a) of this title. After its revival, the limited partnership and its partners shall have the same liability for all contracts, acts, matters and things made, done or performed in the limited partnership's name and on its behalf by its partners, employees and agents as the limited partnership and its partners would have had if the limited partnership's certificate of limited partnership had at all times remained in full force and effect.

§ 17-1111. Revival of Domestic Limited Partnership [Effective Jan. 1, 2007]

(a) A domestic limited partnership whose certificate of limited partnership has been canceled pursuant to § 17-104(d) or § 17-104(i)(4) or § 17-1110(a) of this title may be revived by filing in the office of the

Secretary of State a certificate of revival accompanied by the payment of the fee required by § 17-1107(a)(3) of this title and payment of the annual tax due under § 17-1109 of this title and all penalties and interest thereon for each year for which such domestic limited partnership neglected, refused or failed to pay such annual tax, including each year between the cancellation of its certificate of limited partnership and its revival. The certificate of revival shall set forth:

(1) The name of the limited partnership at the time its certificate of limited partnership was canceled and, if such name is not available at the time of revival, the name under which the limited partnership is to be revived;

(2) The date of filing of the original certificate of limited partnership of the limited partnership;

(3) The address of the limited partnership's registered office in the State of Delaware and the name and address of the limited partnership's registered agent in the State of Delaware;

(4) A statement that the certificate of revival is filed by 1 or more general partners of the limited partnership authorized to execute and file the certificate of revival to revive the limited partnership; and

(5) Any other matters the general partner or general partners executing the certificate of revival determine to include therein.

(b) The certificate of revival shall be deemed to be an amendment to the certificate of limited partnership of the limited partnership, and the limited partnership shall not be required to take any further action to amend its certificate of limited partnership under § 17-202 of this title with respect to the matters set forth in the certificate of revival.

(c) Upon the filing of a certificate of revival, a limited partnership shall be revived with the same force and effect as if its certificate of limited partnership had not been canceled pursuant to § 17-104(d) or § 17-104(i)(4) or § 17-1110(a) of this title. Such revival shall validate all contracts, acts, matters and things made, done and performed by the limited partnership, its partners, employees and agents during the time when its certificate of limited partnership was canceled pursuant to § 17-104(d) or § 17-104(i)(4) or § 17-1110(a) of this title, with the same force and effect and to all intents and purposes as if the certificate of limited partnership had remained in full force and effect. All real and personal property, and all rights and interests, which belonged to the limited partnership at the time its certificate of limited partnership was canceled pursuant to § 17-104(d) or § 17-104(i)(4) or § 17-1110(a) of this title, or which were acquired by the limited partnership following the cancellation of its certificate of limited partnership pursuant to § 17-104(d) or § 17-104(i)(4) or § 17-1110(a) of this title, and which were not disposed of prior to the time of its revival, shall be vested in the limited partnership after its revival as fully as they were held by the limited partnership at, and after, as the case may be, the time its certificate of limited partnership was canceled pursuant to § 17–104(d) or § 17–104(i)(4) or § 17–1110(a) of this title. After its revival, the limited partnership and its partners shall have the same liability for all contracts, acts, matters and things made, done or performed in the limited partnership's name and on its behalf by its partners, employees and agents as the limited partnership and its partners would have had if the limited partnership's certificate of limited partnership had at all times remained in full force and effect.

TEXAS REVISED CIVIL STATUTES

Table of Sections

ART. 6132b. TEXAS REVISED PARTNERSHIP ACT
(Selected Provisions)

ART. 6132a–1. TEXAS REVISED LIMITED PARTNERSHIP ACT
(Selected Provisions)

ART. 1528e. PROFESSIONAL CORPORATION ACT

ART. 1528f. PROFESSIONAL ASSOCIATION ACT

ART. 6132b. TEXAS REVISED PARTNERSHIP ACT

§ 3.08. Liability in and Registration of Registered Limited Liability Partnership

(a) Liability of Partner. (1) Except as provided in Subsection (a)(2), a partner in a registered limited liability partnership is not individually liable, directly or indirectly, by contribution, indemnity, or otherwise, for debts and obligations of the partnership incurred while the partnership is a registered limited liability partnership.

(2) A partner in a registered limited liability partnership is not individually liable, directly or indirectly, by contribution, indemnity, or

otherwise, for debts and obligations of the partnership arising from errors, omissions, negligence, incompetence, or malfeasance committed while the partnership is a registered limited liability partnership and in the course of the partnership business by another partner or a representative of the partnership not working under the supervision or direction of the first partner unless the first partner:

(A) was directly involved in the specific activity in which the errors, omissions, negligence, incompetence, or malfeasance were committed by the other partner or representative; or

(B) had notice or knowledge of the errors, omissions, negligence, incompetence, or malfeasance by the other partner or representative at the time of occurrence and then failed to take reasonable steps to prevent or cure the errors, omissions, negligence, incompetence, or malfeasance.

(3) Subsections (a)(1) and (a)(2) do not affect:

(A) the liability of a partnership to pay its debts and obligations out of partnership property;

(B) the liability of a partner, if any, imposed by law or contract independently of the partner's status as a partner; or

(C) the manner in which service of citation or other civil process may be served in an action against a partnership.

(4) In this subsection, "representative" includes an agent, servant, or employee of a registered limited liability partnership.

(5) In the case of a registered limited liability partnership, Subsection (a) prevails over the other parts of this Act regarding the liability of partners, their chargeability for the debts and obligations of the partnership, and their obligations regarding contributions and indemnity.

(b) Registration. (1) In addition to complying with subsections (c) and (d)(1), to become a registered limited liability partnership, a partnership must file with the secretary of state an application stating:

(A) the name of the partnership;

(B) the federal tax identification number of the partnership;

(C) the street address of the partnership's principal office in this state and outside this state, as applicable;

(D) the number of partners at the date of application; and

(E) in brief, the partnership's business.

(2) The application must be executed by a majority-in-interest of the partners or by one or more partners authorized by a majority-in-interest of the partners.

(3) Two copies of the application must be filed, accompanied by a fee of $200 for each partner.

(4) A partnership is registered as a registered limited liability partnership on filing a completed initial or renewal application, in duplicate with the required fee, or on a later date specified in the application. A registration is not affected by later changes in the partners of the partnership.

(5) An initial application filed under this subsection and registered by the secretary of state expires one year after the date of registration or later effective date unless earlier withdrawn or revoked or unless renewed in accordance with Subdivision (7).

(6) A registration may be withdrawn by filing in duplicate with the secretary of state a written withdrawal notice executed by a majority-in-interest of the partners or by one or more partners authorized by a majority-in-interest of the partners. A withdrawal notice must include the name of the partnership, the federal tax identification number of the partnership, the date of registration of the partnership's last application under this section, and a current street address of the partnership's principal office in this state and outside this state, if applicable. A withdrawal notice terminates the status of the partnership as a registered limited liability partnership as of the date of filing the notice or a later date specified in the notice, but not later than the expiration date under Subdivision (5).

(7) An effective registration may be renewed before its expiration by filing in duplicate with the secretary of state an application containing current information of the kind required in an initial application and the most recent date of registration of the partnership. The renewal application must be accompanied by a fee of $200 for each partner on the date of renewal. A renewal application filed under this section continues an effective registration for one year after the date the effective registration would otherwise expire.

(8) The secretary of state may remove from its active records the registration of a partnership whose registration has been withdrawn or revoked or has expired and not been renewed.

(9) The secretary of state may revoke the filing of a document filed under this subsection if the secretary of state determines that the filing fee for the document was paid by an instrument that was dishonored when presented by the state for payment. The secretary of state shall return the document and give notice of revocation to the filing party by regular mail. Failure to give or receive notice does not invalidate the revocation. A revocation of a filing does not affect an earlier filing.

(10) The secretary of state may provide forms for application for or renewal of registration.

(11) A document filed under this subsection may be amended or corrected by filing in duplicate with the secretary of state articles of amendment executed by a majority-in-interest of the partners or by one or more partners authorized by a majority-in-interest of the partners.

The articles of amendment must contain the name of the partnership, the tax identification number of the partnership, the identity of the document being amended, the date on which the document being amended was filed, the part of the document being amended, and the amendment or correction. Two copies of the articles of amendment must be filed, accompanied by a fee of $10 plus, if the amendment increases the number of partners, $200 for each partner added by amendment of the number of partners.

(12) A document filed under this subsection may be a photographic, facsimile, or similar reproduction of a signed document. A signature on a document filed under this section may be a facsimile, the mark made by a person unable to write, in electronic format permitted by the rules of the secretary of state or any symbol executed or adopted by a person with the intent to authenticate a writing.

(13) A person commits an offense if the person signs a document the person knows is false in any material respect with the intent that the document be delivered on behalf of a partnership to the secretary of state for filing. An offense under this subdivision is a Class A misdemeanor.

(14) The secretary of state is not responsible for determining if a partnership is in compliance with the requirements of Subsection (d)(1).

(15) The secretary of state may adopt procedural rules on filing documents under this subsection.

(16) If permitted by the rules of the secretary of state, any document authorized to be filed with the secretary of state under this subsection may be transmitted for filing electronically. If the document conforms to the requirements of this subsection and the rules promulgated by the secretary of state, the secretary shall file the document by acceptance into the filing system adopted by the secretary and assigning to the document a date of filing. An electronic acknowledgment of the filing, together with an electronically transmitted confirmation copy of the document, shall be provided by the secretary of state to the partnership or its representative.

(17) This subsection does not require any document authorized to be filed with the secretary of state under this subsection or any certificate issued by the secretary of state concerning any such document to be on paper or reduced to printed form.

(18) All electronic acknowledgments and certificates required to be issued by the secretary of state under this Act shall be considered issued or provided by the secretary of state on the initial transmission by the secretary of state of the acknowledgment or certificate required to be issued.

(c) Name. A registered limited liability partnership's name must contain the words "registered limited liability partnership" or "limited liability partnership" or the abbreviation "LLP" or "L.L.P." as the last words or letters of its name.

(d) Insurance or Financial Responsibility. (1) A registered limited liability partnership must:

(A) carry at least $100,000 of liability insurance of a kind that is designed to cover the kinds of errors, omissions, negligence, incompetence, or malfeasance for which liability is limited by Subsection (a)(2); or

(B) provide $100,000 of funds specifically designated and segregated for the satisfaction of judgments against the partnership based on the kinds of errors, omissions, negligence, incompetence, or malfeasance for which liability is limited by Subsection (a)(2) by:

(i) deposit in trust or in bank escrow of cash, bank certificates of deposit, or United States Treasury obligations; or

(ii) a bank letter of credit or insurance company bond.

(2) If the registered limited liability partnership is in compliance with Subdivision (1), the requirements of this subsection shall not be admissible or in any way be made known to the jury in determining an issue of liability for or extent of the debt or obligation or damages in question.

(3) If compliance with Subdivision (1) is disputed:

(A) compliance must be determined separately from the trial or proceeding to determine the partnership debt or obligation in question, its amount, or partner liability for the debt or obligation; and

(B) the burden of proof of compliance is on the person claiming limitation of liability under Subsection (a)(2).

(e) Limited Partnership. A limited partnership may become a registered limited liability partnership by complying with applicable provisions of the Texas Revised Limited Partnership Act (Article 6132a–1, Vernon's Texas Civil Statutes) and its subsequent amendments.

ART. 6132a–1. TEXAS REVISED LIMITED PARTNERSHIP ACT

§ 2.14. Limited Partnership as Registered Limited Liability Partnership

(a) A limited partnership is a registered limited liability partnership as well as a limited partnership if it:

(1) registers as a registered limited liability partnership as provided by Section 3.08(b), Texas Revised Partnership Act, as permitted by its partnership agreement or, if its partnership agreement does not include provisions for becoming a registered limited

liability partnership, with the consent of partners required to amend its partnership agreement;

(2) complies with Section 3.08(d), Texas Revised Partnership Act; and

(3) has as the last words or letters of its name the words "Limited Partnership" or the abbreviation "Ltd." followed by the words "registered limited liability partnership" or "limited liability partnership" or the abbreviation "LLP" or "L.L.P."

(b) In applying Section 3.08(b), Texas Revised Partnership Act, to a limited partnership:

(1) an application to become a registered limited liability partnership or to withdraw a registration must be executed by at least one general partner; and

(2) all other references to partners mean general partners only.

(c) If a limited partnership is a registered limited liability partnership, Section 3.08(a), Texas Revised Partnership Act, applies to its general partners and to any of its limited partners who, under other provisions of this Act, are liable for the debts or obligations of the limited partnership.

ART. 1528e. PROFESSIONAL CORPORATION ACT

§ 1. Title

This Act shall be known and may be cited as "The Texas Professional Corporation Act."

§ 2. Sections, Subsections and Captions

The division of this Act into sections and subsections and the use of captions in connection therewith are solely for convenience and shall have no legal effect in construing the provisions of this Act.

§ 3. Definitions

As used in this Act, unless the context otherwise requires, the term:

(a) "Professional Service" means any type of personal service which requires as a condition precedent to the rendering of such service, the obtaining of a license, permit, certificate of registration or other legal authorization, and which prior to the passage of this Act and by reason of law, could not be performed by a corporation, including by way of example and not in limitation of the generality of the foregoing provisions of this definition, the personal services rendered by architects, attorneys-at-law, certified public accountants, dentists, public accountants, and veterinarians; provided, however, that physicians, surgeons and other doctors of medicine are specifically excluded from the operations of this Act, since there are established precedents allowing them to associate for the practice of medicine in joint stock companies.

(b) "Professional Corporation" means a corporation organized under this Act for the sole and specific purpose of rendering professional service and which has as its shareholders only individuals who themselves are duly licensed or otherwise duly authorized within this state to render the same professional service as the corporation.

(c) "Professional Legal Service" means any type of personal service rendered by attorneys-at-law which requires as a condition precedent to the rendering of such service within this state, the obtaining of a license, permit, certificate of registration, or other legal authorization and which prior to the passage of this Act and by reason of law could not be performed within this state by a corporation.

(d) "Professional Legal Corporation" means a corporation organized under this Act for the sole and specific purpose of rendering professional legal service and which has as its shareholders only individuals, professional legal corporations and foreign professional legal corporations each of which is duly licensed or otherwise duly authorized to render professional legal service; provided, however, any individual shareholder, director, officer, employee or agent of a professional legal corporation who renders professional legal service within this state must be duly licensed to render professional legal service within this state.

(e) "Foreign Professional Legal Corporation" means a professional corporation organized in a jurisdiction other than this state for the sole specific purpose of rendering professional legal service and which has as its shareholders only individuals, professional legal corporations and foreign legal professional corporations each of which is duly licensed or otherwise duly authorized to render professional legal service.

§ 4. Articles of Incorporation

(a) One or more individuals may incorporate a professional corporation by filing the original and a copy of Articles of Incorporation with the Secretary of State. One or more individuals may incorporate a professional legal corporation by filing the original and a copy of Articles of Incorporation with the Secretary of State. Except as provided by Subsection (b) of this section, no professional corporation organized under this Act shall render more than one kind of professional service. In addition to other provisions required or permitted by law, the Articles of Incorporation shall set forth:

(1) A statement that the corporation is a professional corporation; and

(2) A statement of the professional service to be rendered by the corporation.

(b) Professionals, other than physicians, engaged in related mental health fields such as psychology, clinical social work, licensed professional counseling, and licensed marriage and family therapy may form a professional corporation under this Act to perform professional services that fall within the scope of practice of those practitioners. When professionals engaged in related mental health fields form a corporation under this Act, the authority of each of the practitioners is limited by the scope of practice of the respective practitioner, and none can exercise control over the others' clinical authority granted by their respective licenses, whether through agreements, bylaws, directives, financial incentives, or other arrangements that would assert control over treatment decisions made by a practitioner. The state agencies exercising regulatory control over professions to which this subsection applies continue to exercise regulatory authority over the respective licenses of the professionals.

§ 5. Applicability of Texas Business Corporation Act

The Texas Business Corporation Act shall be applicable to professional corporations, except to the extent that the provisions of the Texas Business Corporation Act conflict with the provisions of this Act; and professional corporations shall enjoy the powers and privileges and be subject to the duties, restrictions and liabilities of other business corporations except insofar as the same may be limited or enlarged by this Act. A shareholder of a professional corporation, as such, shall have no duty to supervise the manner or means whereby the officers or employees of the corporation perform their respective duties. Shareholders of a professional corporation, as such, shall have no greater liability than do shareholders, as such, of other business corporations. This Act shall take precedence in the event of any conflict with the provisions of the Texas Business Corporation Act or the law. The filing fee for a document under this Act is the same as the filing fee for a similar document filed under the Texas Business Corporation Act.

§ 6. Purpose

A professional corporation may be organized under this Act only for the purpose of rendering one specific type of professional service and services ancillary thereto.

§ 7. Deleted by Acts 1991, 72nd Leg., ch. 901, § 49, eff. Aug. 26, 1991.

§ 8. Name

A professional corporation may adopt any name that is not contrary to the law or ethics regulating the practice of the professional service rendered through the professional corporation. A professional corporation may use the initials "P.C." in its corporate name in lieu of the word, or in lieu of the abbreviation of the word, "corporation," "company," or "incorporated."

§ 9. Board of Directors

No person not duly licensed or otherwise duly authorized to render the professional service of the corporation shall be a member of the Board of Directors.

§ 10. Officers

No person not duly licensed or otherwise duly authorized to render the professional service of the professional corporation may hold an office.

§ 11. Repealed by Acts 1991, 72nd Leg., ch. 901, § 52, eff. Aug. 26, 1991.

§ 12. Issuance and Transfer of Shares

A professional corporation may issue shares representing ownership of the capital of the professional corporation only to individuals, and in the case of a professional legal corporation, individuals, professional legal corporations and foreign professional legal corporations, which are duly licensed or otherwise legally authorized to render the same type of professional service as that for which the corporation was organized. Except to the extent provided in the Articles of Incorporation, the bylaws or any applicable stock purchase or redemption agreement, shares representing ownership of professional corporation capital shall be freely transferable by any shareholder to any other shareholder, or to the professional corporation which issued such shares or to any person, and in the case of a professional legal corporation, to any professional legal corporation or foreign professional legal corporation, who or which is not a shareholder, provided such person is duly licensed or qualified under the laws of this state, or in the case of a professional legal corporation, such person, professional legal corporation or foreign professional legal corporation is duly licensed or otherwise duly authorized to render professional legal service, and such transferee shall thereupon become a shareholder and be entitled to participate in the management, affairs, and profits of the professional corporation. Any restriction on the transfer of shares imposed by the Articles of Incorporation, the bylaws or any stock purchase or redemption agreement shall be written or printed on all certificates representing shares issued to shareholders, unless such restrictions are incorporated by reference pursuant to the provisions of the Texas Business Corporation Act.

§ 13. Redemption of Shares

A professional corporation shall have the power to redeem the shares of any shareholder, or the shares of a deceased shareholder, upon such terms as may be agreed upon by the Board of Directors and such shareholder or his personal representative, or at such price and upon such terms as may be provided in the Articles of Incorporation, the bylaws, or any applicable stock purchase or redemption agreement.

§ 14. Legal Disqualification

If any shareholder, officer or director of a professional corporation, or any agent or employee thereof who has been rendering professional service for or with it of the same type which such professional corporation was organized to render, becomes legally disqualified to render such professional service, he shall sever all employment with such professional corporation and shall terminate all financial interest therein forthwith; and such corporation shall thereupon purchase or cause to be purchased from him all shares owned by him in such professional corporation, at such price and upon such terms as may be provided in the Articles of Incorporation, the bylaws or any applicable stock purchase or redemption agreement; provided, however, that if he was the sole shareholder of the professional corporation, he may continue to act as officer, director and shareholder for the purposes of winding up the affairs of the corporation and effecting its dissolution, selling the assets of the corporation, or selling the outstanding shares of the corporation, but not for rendering any professional service. Likewise, if any person who is not licensed or duly authorized to render the professional service which a professional corporation was organized to render should succeed to the interest of any shareholder of such professional corporation, the person holding such interest shall terminate all financial interest in such professional corporation forthwith; and such corporation shall thereupon purchase or cause to be purchased from such person all shares owned by such person in such professional corporation, at such price and upon such terms as may be provided in the Articles of Incorporation, the bylaws or any applicable stock purchase or redemption agreement; provided, however, that if such person has succeeded to all of the shares of the professional corporation, such person may act as officer, director and shareholder for the purposes of winding up the affairs of the corporation and effecting its dissolution, selling the assets of the corporation, or selling the outstanding shares of the corporation, but not for rendering any professional service.

§ 15. Rendering of Professional Services

A professional corporation may render professional service in this state only through its officers, employees and individual agents who are duly licensed to render such professional service in this state or through agents of the professional corporation that are themselves professional corporations that render such professional service only through officers and employees of the agent who are so licensed, and a professional legal corporation may render professional legal service in this state only through its officers, employees and individual agents who are duly licensed to render professional legal service in this state or through agents of the professional legal corporation that are themselves professional legal corporations or foreign professional legal corporations that render professional legal service in this state only through officers, employees and agents who are duly licensed to render professional legal service in this state; provided, however, that this provision shall not be interpreted to include within such prohibition employees such as clerks, secretaries, bookkeepers, technicians, nurses, assistants and other individuals who are not usually and ordinarily considered by custom and practice to be rendering professional service for which a license or other legal authorization is required; and further provided, that no person shall, under the guise of employment, practice a profession in this state unless duly licensed or otherwise legally authorized to practice that profession under the laws of this state.

§ 16. Professional Relationships not Affected

The provisions of this Act shall not be construed to alter or affect the professional relationship between a person rendering professional service and a person receiving such service, and all such confidential relationships enjoyed under this state shall remain unchanged. Nothing in this Act shall remove or diminish any rights at law that a person receiving professional service shall have against a person rendering professional service for errors, omissions, negligence, incompetence or malfeasance. The corporation (but not the individual shareholders, officers or directors) shall be jointly and severally liable with the officer, employee or agent rendering professional service for such professional errors, omissions, negligence, incompetence or malfeasance on the part of such officer, employee or agent when such officer, employee or agent is in the course of his employment for the corporation.

§ 17. Continuity of Existence

Unless the Articles of Incorporation expressly provide otherwise, a professional corporation shall continue as a separate entity for all purposes and for such period of time as is provided in the Articles of Incorporation until dissolved by a vote of its shareholders. A professional corporation shall continue to exist regardless of the death, incompetency, bankruptcy, resignation, withdrawal, retirement or expulsion of any one or more of its shareholders or the transfer of any of its shares to any new holder or the happening of any other event which under the laws of this state and under like circumstances would cause a dissolution of a partnership, it being the intent of this Section that such professional corporation shall have continuity of life independent of the life or status of its shareholders. No shareholder shall have power to dissolve the professional corporation by his independent act of any kind.

§ 18. Repealed by Acts 2001, 77th Leg., ch. 757, § 17, eff. Sept. 1, 2001.

§ 19. Exemption from Securities Laws

The sale, issuance or offering of any capital stock of a professional corporation to persons permitted by the provisions of this Act to own such capital stock are hereby exempted from all provisions of the laws of this state, other than this Act, which provide for supervision, registration or regulation in connection with the sale, issuance or offering of securities; and the sale, issuance or offering of any such capital stock to such persons shall be legal without any action or approval whatsoever on the part of any official or state regulatory agency authorized to license, regulate, or supervise the sale, issuance or offering of securities.

§ 19A. Foreign Professional Corporations

(a) A foreign professional legal corporation may apply for a certificate of authority to perform professional legal service in this state by filing an application in accordance with the Texas Business Corporation Act. The Secretary of State may not issue the certificate unless the name of the corporation or the name the corporation elects in this state meets the requirements of Section 8 of this Act. The corporation may not exercise in this state powers other than the powers provided by Section 7 of this Act. A shareholder, director, officer, employee, or agent of the corporation who renders professional legal service in this state on behalf of the corporation must be licensed or otherwise authorized to render professional legal service in this state.

(b) A certificate may not be issued to a corporation under this section unless the application for such certificate of authority includes a statement that the jurisdiction in which the corporation is incorporated would permit reciprocal admission of such corporation if it were incorporated in this state.

§ 20. Effective Date

This Act shall be effective on and after January 1, 1970.

§ 21. Applicability; Expiration

(a) Except as provided by Title 8, Business Organizations Code, this Act does not apply to a professional corporation to which the Business Organizations Code applies.

(b) This Act expires January 1, 2010.

ART. 1528f. PROFESSIONAL ASSOCIATION ACT

§ 1. Short Title

Sec. 1. This Act may be cited as the Texas Professional Association Act.

§ 2. Authority

(A) Formation. Any one or more persons duly licensed to practice a profession, including podiatry, dentistry, optometry, therapeutic optometry, chiropractic, or veterinary medicine, under the laws of this state may, by complying with this Act, form a professional association, as distinguished from either a partnership or a corporation, by associating themselves for the purpose of performing professional services and dividing the gains therefrom as stated in articles of association or bylaws.

(B) Licenses. (1) Except as provided by this subsection, all members of the association shall be licensed to perform the type of professional service for which the association is formed.

(2) Doctors of medicine and osteopathy licensed by the Texas State Board of Medical Examiners and podiatrists licensed by the Texas State Board of Podiatric Medical Examiners may form an association that is jointly owned by those practitioners to perform a professional service that falls within the scope of practice of those practitioners.

(3) Professionals, other than physicians, engaged in related mental health fields such as psychology, clinical social work, licensed professional counseling, and licensed marriage and family therapy may form an association that is jointly owned by those practitioners to perform professional services that fall within the scope of practice of those practitioners.

(4) When doctors of medicine, osteopathy, and podiatry or mental health professionals form an association that is jointly owned by those practitioners, the authority of each of the practitioners is limited by the scope of practice of the respective practitioners and none can exercise control over the other's clinical authority granted by their respective licenses, either through agreements, bylaws, directives, financial incentives, or other arrangements that would assert control over treatment decisions made by the practitioner. The state agencies exercising regulatory control over professions to which this subdivision applies continue to exercise regulatory authority over their respective licenses.

§ 3. Definitions

As used in this Act, the term "professional service" means any type of personal service to the public which requires as a condition precedent to the rendering of such service the obtaining of a license, and which service by law cannot be performed by a corporation. The term "license" includes a license, certificate of registration or any other evidence of the satisfaction of state requirements.

§ 4. Name

A professional association shall adopt a name which shall be followed by the word or words "Associated," "Association," "Professional Association," "and Associates," or the abbreviation "Assoc." or "P.A."; provided, and except, however, a professional association shall not adopt or make use of any name which is contrary to or in conflict with any law or ethics regulating the practice or practitioners of any professional service rendered through or in connection with the professional association.

§ 5. Powers Concerning Property and Suits

(A) Property. A professional association may in its own name invest its funds in real estate, mortgages, stocks, bonds, or any other type of investment, and may own real or personal property necessary or appropriate for rendering its professional service. Any investment or property so owned may be transferred in the association name by action of the Board of Directors or Executive Committee.

(B) Suits. An association shall have power to sue and be sued, complain and defend in its association name.

§ 6. Licensed Individuals as Employees of Association—Prohibition

Each individual licensed in this state to perform professional services who is employed by a professional association shall remain subject to reprimand or discipline for his conduct under the provisions of the licensing statute pursuant to which he is licensed.

§ 7. Professional Relations

This Act does not alter any law applicable to the relationship between a person furnishing professional service and a person receiving such professional service including liability arising out of such professional service.

§ 8. Articles of Association

(A) Required provisions. The articles of association shall set forth:

(1) The name and address of the association

(2) The period of duration

(3) The type of professional service to be performed

(4) The names and addresses of each of the original members

(5) A statement that each of the original members is licensed to perform the type of professional service for which the association is formed.

(B) Continuity. Articles of association may provide that a professional association

(1) shall continue as a separate entity independent of its members, for all purposes, for such period of time as provided in the articles, or until dissolved by a vote of two-thirds of the members, and

(2) shall continue notwithstanding the death, insanity, incompetency, conviction for felony, resignation, withdrawal, transfer of membership, retirement, or expulsion of any one or more of the members (except the last surviving member), the admission of or transfer of membership to any new member or members, or the happening of any other event, which under the law of this state and under like circumstances, would work a dissolution of a partnership.

(C) Power to dissolve. The articles shall provide that no member of a professional association shall have the power to dissolve the association by his independent act of any kind.

(D) Optional provisions. The articles of association may set forth any other provision, not inconsistent with the law, which the members elect to set forth for the regulation of the internal affairs of the association.

(E) Execution. The articles of association shall be signed by each of the members.

§ 9. Governing Body; Officers

(A) Board or committee. A professional association organized pursuant to the provisions of this Act shall be governed by, and the business and affairs of a professional association shall be managed under the direction of, a Board of Directors or an Executive Committee elected by the members, and represented by officers elected by the Board of Directors or Executive Committee, so that centralization of management will be assured.

(B) Member's power to bind. No member shall have the power to bind the association within the scope of the association's business or profession merely by virtue of his being a member of the association.

(C) Qualification of officers and board or committee members. Officers and members of the Board of Directors or Executive Committee shall be members of the professional association. Officers need not be members of the Board of Directors or Executive Committee except that the President shall be a member of the Board of Directors or Executive Committee.

(D) Bylaws. The members may adopt such bylaws as they may deem proper, or the power to promulgate bylaws of the association may be delegated by the articles of association to the Board of Directors or Executive Committee, as the members may decide.

(E) Members' voting rights. Each member shall have power to cast such vote or votes at the meeting of the members as the articles of association shall provide.

(F) Agents and employees. The officers of the professional association may employ such agents or employees of the association as they may deem advisable.

(G) Officers. The officers of the association shall include a President, Vice–President, Secretary, Treasurer, and such other officers as the Board of Directors or Executive Committee may determine. Any one person may serve in more than one office provided that the President and the Secretary of the professional association shall not be the same person unless the association has only one member.

§ 10. Shares or Units of Ownership—Transfer

Shares or units of ownership in a professional association shall be transferable to persons licensed to perform the same type of professional service as that for which the professional association was formed.

§ 11. Regulation of Practice of Law

The manner in which lawyers practice law under this Act is subject to the powers of the Supreme Court to regulate the practice of law.

§ 12. Filing of Articles of Association

(A) The original and a copy of the articles of association shall be delivered to the Secretary of State. If the Secretary of State finds that the articles of association conform to law, he shall, when all fees have been paid as required by law:

(1) Endorse on the original and the copy the word "Filed," and the month, day, and year of the filing thereof.

(2) File the original in his office.

(3) Issue a certificate of association to which he shall affix the copy.

(B) The certificate of association, together with the copy of the articles of association affixed thereto by the Secretary of State, shall be delivered to the members or their representatives.

§ 13. Effect of Issuance of Certificate of Association

Upon the issuance of the certificate of association, the association's existence shall begin.

§ 14. Amendment of Articles of Association

(A) Authority to amend. A professional association may amend its articles of association, from time to time, in accordance with the procedure for amendment stated therein or if none is stated therein, by two-thirds vote of its members.

(B) Acts not requiring amendment. Changes in membership or transfer of shares or units of ownership shall not require amendment.

§ 15. Articles of Amendment

The articles of amendment shall be executed on behalf of the association by an officer and shall set forth:

(1) The name and address of the association;

(2) If the amendment alters any provision of the original or amended articles of association, an identification by reference or description of the altered provision and a statement of its text as it is amended to read. If the amendment is an addition to the original or amended articles of association, a statement of that fact and the full text of each provision added;

(3) The date of the adoption of the amendment; and

(4) A statement that the amendment was adopted in accordance with the procedure for amendment stated in the articles of association, or, if none is stated therein, a statement that the amendment was adopted by two-thirds vote of its members.

§ 16. Filing of Articles of Amendment

(A) The original and a copy of the articles of amendment shall be delivered to the Secretary of State. If the Secretary of State finds that the articles of amendment conform to law, he shall, when all fees have been paid as required by law:

(1) Endorse on the original and the copy the word "Filed," and the month, day, and year of the filing thereof.

(2) File the original in his office.

(3) Issue a certificate of amendment to which he shall affix the copy.

(B) The certificate of amendment, together with the copy of the articles of amendment affixed thereto by the Secretary of State, shall be delivered to the association or its representatives.

§ 17. Effect of Certificate of Amendment

(A) Issuance. Upon the issuance of the certificate of amendment by the Secretary of State, the amendment shall become effective and the articles of association shall be deemed to be amended accordingly.

(B) Prior rights. No amendment shall affect any existing cause of action in favor of or against the association, or any pending suit to which the association shall be a party, or the existing rights of persons other than members. If the association name is changed by amendment, no suit brought by or against the association under its former name shall abate for that reason.

§ 18. Articles of Dissolution

The articles of dissolution shall be executed on behalf of the association by an officer. If there are no living officers of the association, the articles shall be executed by the legal representative of the last surviving officer. The articles of dissolution shall set forth:

(1) The name and address of the association;

(2) The names and respective addresses of its officers;

(3) The names and respective addresses of the members of its Board of Directors or Executive Committee; and

(4) A statement that the association is dissolving in accordance with its articles of association or, if there is no dissolution provision in the articles, by two-thirds vote of its members.

§ 19. Filing of Articles of Dissolution

(A) The original and a copy of the articles of dissolution shall be delivered to the Secretary of State. If the Secretary of State finds that the articles of dissolution conform to law, he shall, when all fees have been paid as required by law:

(1) Endorse on the original and the copy the word "Filed," and the month, day, and year of the filing thereof.

(2) File the original in his office.

(3) Issue a certificate of dissolution to which he shall affix the copy.

(B) The certificate of dissolution, together with the copy of the articles of dissolution affixed thereto by the Secretary of State, shall be delivered to the association or its representatives.

§ 20. Effect of Certificate of Dissolution

Upon the issuance of the certificate of dissolution by the Secretary of State, the dissolution shall become effective and the existence of the association shall cease except for the purpose of suits, other proceedings and acts necessary for the winding up of the association.

§ 21. Annual Statement

A professional association shall in June of each year file with the Secretary of State a statement showing the name and address of the association; the names and addresses of all members of the association, and all officers and all members of the Board of Directors or Executive Committee; and shall state that all members are licensed to perform the type of professional service for which the association is formed. The statement shall be on such form as the Secretary of State shall prescribe and furnish. It shall be executed on behalf of the association by an officer.

§ 22. Fees

The Secretary of State is authorized and required to collect for the use of the state the following fees:

(1) Filing articles of association and issuing a certificate of association, Two Hundred Dollars ($200.00)

(2) Filing annual statement, Thirty–Five Dollars ($35.00)

(3) Filing any other document, the fee provided for the filing of a similar document under the Texas Business Corporation Act.

§ 23. Existing Associations

Any existing association may become subject to this Act by complying with its terms and filing requirements.

§ 24. Association Liability

Nothing in this Act shall remove or diminish any rights at law that a person receiving professional services shall have against a person furnishing professional services for errors, omissions, negligence, incompetence or malfeasance. The association (but not the individual members, officers or directors) shall be jointly and severally liable with the officer or employee furnishing professional services for such professional errors, omissions, negligence, incompetence or malfeasance on the part of such officer or employee when such officer or employee is in the course of his employment for the association.

§ 25. Applicability of Business Corporation Act

The Texas Business Corporation Act shall be applicable to professional associations, except to the extent that the provisions of the Texas Business Corporation Act conflict with the provisions of this Act; and professional associations shall enjoy the powers and privileges and be subject to the duties, restrictions and liabilities of business corporations except insofar as the same may be limited or enlarged by this Act. This Act shall take precedence in the event of any conflict with the provisions of the Texas Business Corporation Act or the law.

§ 26. Penalty for Signing False Document

(A) A person commits an offense if the person signs a document the person knows is false in any material respect with intent that the document be delivered on behalf of a professional association to the Secretary of State for filing.

(B) An offense under this section is a Class A misdemeanor.

§ 27. Applicability; Expiration

(a) Except as provided by Title 8, Business Organizations Code, this Act does not apply to a professional association to which the Business Organizations Code applies.

(b) This Act expires January 1, 2010.

*

UNIFORM LIMITED LIABILITY COMPANY ACT (1996)

Table of Sections

ARTICLE 1. GENERAL PROVISIONS

ARTICLE 2. ORGANIZATION

ARTICLE 3. RELATIONS OF MEMBERS AND MANAGERS TO PERSONS DEALING WITH LIMITED LIABILITY COMPANY

UNIFORM LIMITED LIABILITY COMPANY ACT (1996)

PREFATORY NOTE

Borrowing from abroad, Wyoming initiated a national movement in 1977 by enacting this country's first limited liability company act. The movement started slowly as the Internal Revenue Service took more than ten years to announce finally that a Wyoming limited liability company would be taxed like a partnership. Since that time, every State has adopted or is considering its own distinct limited liability company act, many of which have already been amended one or more times.

The allure of the limited liability company is its unique ability to bring together in a single business organization the best features of all other business forms—properly structured, its owners obtain both a corporate-styled liability shield and the pass-through tax benefits of a partnership. General and limited partnerships do not offer their partners a corporate-styled liability shield. Corporations, including those having made a Subchapter Selection, do not offer their shareholders all the pass-through tax benefits of a partnership. All state limited liability company acts contain provisions for a liability shield and partnership tax status.

Despite these two common themes, state limited liability company acts display a dazzling array of diversity. Multistate activities of businesses are widespread. Recognition of out-of-state limited liability companies varies. Unfortunately, this lack of uniformity manifests itself in basic but fundamentally important questions, such as: may a company be formed and operated by only one owner; may it be formed for purposes other than to make a profit; whether owners have the power and right to withdraw from a company and receive a distribution of the fair value of their interests; whether a member's dissociation threatens a dissolution of the company; who has the apparent authority to bind the company and the limits of that authority; what are the fiduciary duties of owners and managers to a company and each other; how are the rights to manage a company allocated among its owners and managers; do the owners have the right to sue a company and its other owners in their own right as well as derivatively on behalf of the company; may general and limited partnerships be converted to limited liability companies and may limited liability companies merge with other limited liability companies and other business organizations; what is the law governing foreign limited liability companies; and are any or all of these and other rules simply default rules that may be modified by agreement or are they nonwaivable.

Practitioners and entrepreneurs struggle to understand the law governing limited liability companies organized in their own State and to understand the burgeoning law of other States. Simple questions concerning where to organize are increasingly complex. Since most state limited liability company acts are in their infancy, little if any interpretative case law exists. Even when case law develops, it will have limited precedential value because of the diversity of the state acts.

Accordingly, uniform legislation in this area of the law appeared to have become urgent.

After a Study Committee appointed by the National Conference of Commissioners in late 1991 recommended that a comprehensive project be undertaken, the Conference appointed a Drafting Committee which worked on a Uniform Limited Liability Company Act (ULLCA) from early 1992 until its adoption by the Conference at its Annual Meeting in August 1994. The Drafting Committee was assisted by a blue ribbon panel of national experts and other interested and affected parties and organizations. Many, if not all, of those assisting the Committee brought substantial experience from drafting limited liability company legislation in their own States. Many are also authors of leading treatises and articles in the field. Those represented in the drafting process included an American Bar Association (ABA) liaison, four advisors representing the three separate ABA Sections of Business Law, Taxation, and Real Property, Trust and Probate, the United States Treasury Department, the Internal Revenue Service, and many observers representing several other organizations, including the California Bar Association, the New York City Bar Association, the American College of Real Estate Lawyers, the National Association of Certified Public Accountants, the National Association of Secretaries of State, the Chicago and Lawyers Title Companies, the American Land Title Association, and several university law and business school faculty members.

The Committee met nine times and engaged in numerous national telephonic conferences to discuss policies, review over fifteen drafts, evaluate legal developments and consider comments by our many knowledgeable advisers and observers, as well as an ABA subcommittee's earlier work on a prototype. In examining virtually every aspect of each state limited liability company act, the Committee maintained a single policy vision—to draft a flexible act with a comprehensive set of default rules designed to substitute as the essence of the bargain for small entrepreneurs and others.

This Act is flexible in the sense that the vast majority of its provisions may be modified by the owners in a private agreement. Only limited and specific fundamental matters may not be altered by private agreement. To simplify, those nonwaivable provisions are set forth in a single subsection. Helped thereby, sophisticated parties will negotiate their own deal with the benefit of counsel.

The Committee also recognized that small entrepreneurs without the benefit of counsel should also have access to the Act. To that end, the great bulk of the Act sets forth default rules designed to operate a limited liability company without sophisticated agreements and to recognize that members may also modify the default rules by oral agreements defined in part by their own conduct. Uniquely, the Act combines two simple default structures which depend upon the presence of designations in the articles of organization. All default rules under the Act flow from these two designations.

First, unless the articles reflect that a limited liability company is a term company and the duration of that term, the company will be an at-will company. Generally, the owners of an at-will company may demand a payment of the fair value of their interests at any time. Owners of a term company must generally wait until the expiration of the term to obtain the value of their interests. Secondly, unless the articles reflect that a company will be managed by managers, the company will be managed by its members. This designation controls whether the members or managers have apparent agency authority, management authority, and the nature of fiduciary duties in the company.

In January of 1995 the Executive Committee of the Conference adopted an amendment to harmonize the Act with new and important Internal Revenue Service announcements, and the amendment was ratified by the National Conference at its Annual Meeting in August of 1995. Those Internal Revenue Service announcements generally provide that a limited liability company will not be taxed like a corporation regardless of its organizational structure. Freed from the old tax classification restraints, the amendment modifies the Act's dissolution provision by eliminating member dissociation as a dissolution event. This important amendment significantly increases the stability of a limited liability company and places greater emphasis on a limited liability company's required purchase of a dissociated member's interest.

The adoption of ULLCA will provide much needed consistency among the States, with flexible default rules, and multistate recognition of limited liability on the part of company owners. It will also promote the development of precedential case law.

[ARTICLE] 1

GENERAL PROVISIONS

§ 101. Definitions

In this [Act]:

(1) "Articles of organization" means initial, amended, and restated articles of organization and articles of merger. In the case of a foreign limited liability company, the term includes all records serving a similar function required to be filed in the office of the [Secretary of State] or other official having custody of company records in the State or country under whose law it is organized.

(2) "At-will company" means a limited liability company other than a term company.

(3) "Business" includes every trade, occupation, profession, and other lawful purpose, whether or not carried on for profit.

(4) "Debtor in bankruptcy" means a person who is the subject of an order for relief under Title 11 of the United States Code or a comparable order under a successor statute of general application or a comparable order under federal, state, or foreign law governing insolvency.

(5) "Distribution" means a transfer of money, property, or other benefit from a limited liability company to a member in the member's capacity as a member or to a transferee of the member's distributional interest.

(6) "Distributional interest" means all of a member's interest in distributions by the limited liability company.

(7) "Entity" means a person other than an individual.

(8) "Foreign limited liability company" means an unincorporated entity organized under laws other than the laws of this State which afford limited liability to its owners comparable to the liability under Section 303 and is not required to obtain a certificate of authority to transact business under any law of this State other than this [Act].

(9) "Limited liability company" means a limited liability company organized under this [Act].

(10) "Manager" means a person, whether or not a member of a manager-managed company, who is vested with authority under Section 301.

(11) "Manager-managed company" means a limited liability company which is so designated in its articles of organization.

(12) "Member-managed company" means a limited liability company other than a manager-managed company.

(13) "Operating agreement" means the agreement under Section 103 concerning the relations among the members, managers, and limited liability company. The term includes amendments to the agreement.

(14) "Person" means an individual, corporation, business trust, estate, trust, partnership, limited liability company, association, joint venture, government, governmental subdivision, agency, or instrumentality, or any other legal or commercial entity.

(15) "Principal office" means the office, whether or not in this State, where the principal executive office of a domestic or foreign limited liability company is located.

(16) "Record" means information that is inscribed on a tangible medium or that is stored in an electronic or other medium and is retrievable in perceivable form.

(17) "Sign" means to identify a record by means of a signature, mark, or other symbol, with intent to authenticate it.

(18) "State" means a State of the United States, the District of Columbia, the Commonwealth of Puerto Rico, or any territory or insular possession subject to the jurisdiction of the United States.

(19) "Term company" means a limited liability company in which its members have agreed to remain members until the expiration of a term specified in the articles of organization.

(20) "Transfer" includes an assignment, conveyance, deed, bill of sale, lease, mortgage, security interest, encumbrance, and gift.

Comment

Uniform Limited Liability Company Act ("ULLCA") definitions, like the rest of the Act, are a blend of terms and concepts derived from the Uniform Partnership Act ("UPA"), the Uniform Partnership Act (1994) ("UPA 1994", also previously known as the Revised Uniform Partnership Act or "RUPA"), the Revised Uniform Limited Partnership Act ("RULPA"), the Uniform Commercial Code ("UCC"), and the Model Business Corporation Act ("MBCA"), or their revisions from time to time; some are tailored specially for this Act.

"Business." A limited liability company may be organized to engage in an activity either for or not for profit. The extent to which contributions to a nonprofit company may be deductible for Federal income tax purposes is determined by federal law. Other state law determines the extent of exemptions from state and local income and property taxes.

"Debtor in bankruptcy." The filing of a voluntary petition operates immediately as an "order for relief." See Sections 601(7)(i) and 602(b)(2)(iii).

"Distribution." This term includes all sources of a member's distributions including the member's capital contributions, undistributed profits, and residual interest in the assets of the company after all claims, including those of third parties and debts to members, have been paid.

"Distributional interest." The term does not include a member's broader rights to participate in the management of the company. See Comments to Article 5.

"Foreign limited liability company." The term is not restricted to companies formed in the United States.

"Manager." The rules of agency apply to limited liability companies. Therefore, managers may designate agents with whatever titles, qualifications, and responsibilities they desire. For example, managers may designate an agent as "President."

"Manager-managed company." The term includes only a company designated as such in the articles of organization. In a manager-managed company agency authority is vested exclusively in one or more managers and not in the members. See Sections 101(10) (manager), 203(a)(6) (articles designation), and 301(b) (agency authority of members and managers).

"Member-managed limited liability company." The term includes every company not designated as "manager-managed" under Section 203(a)(6) in its articles of organization.

"Operating agreement." This agreement may be oral. Members may agree upon the extent to which their relationships are to be governed by writings.

"Principal office." The address of the principal office must be set forth in the annual report required under Section 211(a)(3).

"Record." This Act is the first Uniform Act promulgated with a definition of this term. The definition brings this Act in conformity with the present state of technology and accommodates prospective future technology in the communication and storage of information other than by human memory. Modern methods of communicating and storing information employed in commercial practices are no longer confined to physical documents.

The term includes any writing. A record need not be permanent or indestructible, but an oral or other unwritten communication must be stored or preserved on some medium to qualify as a record. Information that has not been retained other than through human memory does not qualify as a record. A record may be signed or may be created without the knowledge or intent of a particular person. Other law must be consulted to determine admissibility in evidence, the applicability of statute of frauds, and other questions regarding the use of records. Under Section 206(a), electronic filings may be permitted and even encouraged.

§ 102. Knowledge and Notice

(a) A person knows a fact if the person has actual knowledge of it.

(b) A person has notice of a fact if the person:

(1) knows the fact;

(2) has received a notification of the fact; or

(3) has reason to know the fact exists from all of the facts known to the person at the time in question.

(c) A person notifies or gives a notification of a fact to another by taking steps reasonably required to inform the other person in ordinary course, whether or not the other person knows the fact.

(d) A person receives a notification when the notification:

(1) comes to the person's attention; or

(2) is duly delivered at the person's place of business or at any other place held out by the person as a place for receiving communications.

(e) An entity knows, has notice, or receives a notification of a fact for purposes of a particular transaction when the individual conducting the transaction for the entity knows, has notice, or receives a notification of the fact, or in any event when the fact would have been brought to the individual's attention had the entity exercised reasonable diligence. An entity exercises reasonable diligence if it maintains reasonable routines for communicating significant information to the individual conducting the transaction for the entity and there is reasonable compliance with the routines. Reasonable diligence does not require an individual acting for the entity to communicate information unless the communication is part of the individual's regular duties or the individual has reason to know of the transaction and that the transaction would be materially affected by the information.

Comment

Knowledge requires cognitive awareness of a fact, whereas notice is based on a lesser degree of awareness. The Act imposes constructive knowledge under limited circumstances. See Comments to Sections 301(c), 703, and 704.

§ 103. Effect of Operating Agreement; Nonwaivable Provisions

(a) Except as otherwise provided in subsection (b), all members of a limited liability company may enter into an operating agreement, which need not be in writing, to regulate the affairs of the company and the conduct of its business, and to govern relations among the members, managers, and company. To the extent the operating agreement does not otherwise provide, this [Act] governs relations among the members, managers, and company.

(b) The operating agreement may not:

(1) unreasonably restrict a right to information or access to records under Section 408;

(2) eliminate the duty of loyalty under Section 409(b) or 603(b)(3), but the agreement may:

(i) identify specific types or categories of activities that do not violate the duty of loyalty, if not manifestly unreasonable; and

(ii) specify the number or percentage of members or disinterested managers that may authorize or ratify, after full disclosure of all material facts, a specific act or transaction that otherwise would violate the duty of loyalty;

(3) unreasonably reduce the duty of care under Section 409(c) or 603(b)(3);

(4) eliminate the obligation of good faith and fair dealing under Section 409(d), but the operating agreement may determine the

standards by which the performance of the obligation is to be measured, if the standards are not manifestly unreasonable;

(5) vary the right to expel a member in an event specified in Section 601(6);

(6) vary the requirement to wind up the limited liability company's business in a case specified in Section 801(3) or (4); or

(7) restrict rights of a person, other than a manager, member, and transferee of a member's distributional interest, under this [Act].

Comment

The operating agreement is the essential contract that governs the affairs of a limited liability company. Since it is binding on all members, amendments must be approved by all members unless otherwise provided in the agreement. Although many agreements will be in writing, the agreement and any amendments may be oral or may be in the form of a record. Course of dealing, course of performance and usage of trade are relevant to determine the meaning of the agreement unless the agreement provides that all amendments must be in writing.

This section makes clear that the only matters an operating agreement may not control are specified in subsection (b). Accordingly, an operating agreement may modify or eliminate any rule specified in any section of this Act except matters specified in subsection (b). To the extent not otherwise mentioned in subsection (b), every section of this Act is simply a default rule, regardless of whether the language of the section appears to be otherwise mandatory. This approach eliminates the necessity of repeating the phrase "unless otherwise agreed" in each section and its commentary.

Under subsection (b)(1), an operating agreement may not unreasonably restrict the right to information or access to any records under Section 408. This does not create an independent obligation beyond Section 408 to maintain any specific records. Under subsections (b)(2) to (4), an irreducible core of fiduciary responsibilities survive any contrary provision in the operating agreement. Subsection (b)(2)(i) authorizes an operating agreement to modify, but not eliminate, the three specific duties of loyalty set forth in Section 409(b)(1) to (3) provided the modification itself is not manifestly unreasonable, a question of fact. Subsection (b)(2)(ii) preserves the common law right of the members to authorize future or ratify past violations of the duty of loyalty provided there has been a full disclosure of all material facts. The authorization or ratification must be unanimous unless otherwise provided in an operating agreement, because the authorization or ratification itself constitutes an amendment to the agreement. The authorization or ratification of specific past or future conduct may sanction conduct that would have been manifestly unreasonable under subsection (b)(2)(i).

§ 104. Supplemental Principles of Law

(a) Unless displaced by particular provisions of this [Act], the principles of law and equity supplement this [Act].

(b) If an obligation to pay interest arises under this [Act] and the rate is not specified, the rate is that specified in [applicable statute].

Comment

Supplementary principles include, but are not limited to, the law of agency, estoppel, law merchant, and all other principles listed in UCC Section 1–103, including the law relative to the capacity to contract, fraud, misrepresentation, duress, coercion, mistake, bankruptcy, and other validating and invalidating clauses. Other principles such as those mentioned in UCC Section 1–205 (Course of Dealing and Usage of Trade) apply as well as course of performance. As with UPA 1994 Section 104, upon which this provision is based, no substantive change from either the UPA or the UCC is intended. Section 104(b) establishes the applicable rate of interest in the absence of an agreement among the members.

§ 105. Name

(a) The name of a limited liability company must contain "limited liability company" or "limited company" or the abbreviation "L.L.C.", "LLC", "L.C.", or "LC". "Limited" may be abbreviated as "Ltd.", and "company" may be abbreviated as "Co.".

(b) Except as authorized by subsections (c) and (d), the name of a limited liability company must be distinguishable upon the records of the [Secretary of State] from:

(1) the name of any corporation, limited partnership, or company incorporated, organized or authorized to transact business, in this State;

(2) a name reserved or registered under Section 106 or 107;

(3) a fictitious name approved under Section 1005 for a foreign company authorized to transact business in this State because its real name is unavailable.

(c) A limited liability company may apply to the [Secretary of State] for authorization to use a name that is not distinguishable upon the records of the [Secretary of State] from one or more of the names described in subsection (b). The [Secretary of State] shall authorize use of the name applied for if:

(1) the present user, registrant, or owner of a reserved name consents to the use in a record and submits an undertaking in form satisfactory to the [Secretary of State] to change the name to a name

that is distinguishable upon the records of the [Secretary of State] from the name applied for; or

(2) the applicant delivers to the [Secretary of State] a certified copy of the final judgment of a court of competent jurisdiction establishing the applicant's right to use the name applied for in this State.

(d) A limited liability company may use the name, including a fictitious name, of another domestic or foreign company which is used in this State if the other company is organized or authorized to transact business in this State and the company proposing to use the name has:

(1) merged with the other company;

(2) been formed by reorganization with the other company; or

(3) acquired substantially all of the assets, including the name, of the other company.

§ 106. Reserved Name

(a) A person may reserve the exclusive use of the name of a limited liability company, including a fictitious name for a foreign company whose name is not available, by delivering an application to the [Secretary of State] for filing. The application must set forth the name and address of the applicant and the name proposed to be reserved. If the [Secretary of State] finds that the name applied for is available, it must be reserved for the applicant's exclusive use for a nonrenewable 120–day period.

(b) The owner of a name reserved for a limited liability company may transfer the reservation to another person by delivering to the [Secretary of State] a signed notice of the transfer which states the name and address of the transferee.

Comment

A foreign limited liability company that is not presently authorized to transact business in the State may reserve a fictitious name for a nonrenewable 120–day period. When its actual name is available, a company will generally register that name under Section 107 because the registration is valid for a year and may be extended indefinitely.

§ 107. Registered Name

(a) A foreign limited liability company may register its name subject to the requirements of Section 1005, if the name is distinguishable upon the records of the [Secretary of State] from names that are not available under Section 105(b).

(b) A foreign limited liability company registers its name, or its name with any addition required by Section 1005, by delivering to the [Secretary of State] for filing an application:

(1) setting forth its name, or its name with any addition required by Section 1005, the State or country and date of its organization, and a brief description of the nature of the business in which it is engaged; and

(2) accompanied by a certificate of existence, or a record of similar import, from the State or country of organization.

(c) A foreign limited liability company whose registration is effective may renew it for successive years by delivering for filing in the office of the [Secretary of State] a renewal application complying with subsection (b) between October 1 and December 31 of the preceding year. The renewal application renews the registration for the following calendar year.

(d) A foreign limited liability company whose registration is effective may qualify as a foreign company under its name or consent in writing to the use of its name by a limited liability company later organized under this [Act] or by another foreign company later authorized to transact business in this State. The registered name terminates when the limited liability company is organized or the foreign company qualifies or consents to the qualification of another foreign company under the registered name.

§ 108. Designated Office and Agent for Service of Process

(a) A limited liability company and a foreign limited liability company authorized to do business in this State shall designate and continuously maintain in this State:

(1) an office, which need not be a place of its business in this State; and

(2) an agent and street address of the agent for service of process on the company.

(b) An agent must be an individual resident of this State, a domestic corporation, another limited liability company, or a foreign corporation or foreign company authorized to do business in this State.

Comment

Limited liability companies organized under Section 202 or authorized to transact business under Section 1004 are required to designate and continuously maintain an office in the State. Although the designated office need not be a place of business, it most often will be the only place of business of the company. The company must also designate an agent for service of process within the State and the agent's street address. The agent's address need not be the same as the company's designated office address. The initial office and agent designations must be set forth in the articles of organization, including the address of the designated office. See Section 203(a)(2) to (3). The current office and agent designations must be set forth in the company's annual report. See Section 211(a)(2). See also Section 109 (procedure for changing the office or agent designations), Section 110 (procedure for an agent to resign), and Section 111(b) (the filing officer is the service agent for the company if it fails to maintain its own service agent).

§ 109. Change of Designated Office or Agent for Service of Process

A limited liability company may change its designated office or agent for service of process by delivering to the [Secretary of State] for filing a statement of change which sets forth:

(1) the name of the company;

(2) the street address of its current designated office;

(3) if the current designated office is to be changed, the street address of the new designated office;

(4) the name and address of its current agent for service of process; and

(5) if the current agent for service of process or street address of that agent is to be changed, the new address or the name and street address of the new agent for service of process.

§ 110. Resignation of Agent for Service of Process

(a) An agent for service of process of a limited liability company may resign by delivering to the [Secretary of State] for filing a record of the statement of resignation.

(b) After filing a statement of resignation, the [Secretary of State] shall mail a copy to the designated office and another copy to the limited liability company at its principal office.

(c) An agency is terminated on the 31st day after the statement is filed in the office of the [Secretary of State].

§ 111. Service of Process

(a) An agent for service of process appointed by a limited liability company or a foreign limited liability company is an agent of the company for service of any process, notice, or demand required or permitted by law to be served upon the company.

(b) If a limited liability company or foreign limited liability company fails to appoint or maintain an agent for service of process in this State or the agent for service of process cannot with reasonable diligence be found at the agent's address, the [Secretary of State] is an agent of the company upon whom process, notice, or demand may be served.

(c) Service of any process, notice, or demand on the [Secretary of State] may be made by delivering to and leaving with the [Secretary of State], the [Assistant Secretary of State], or clerk having charge of the limited liability company department of the [Secretary of State's] office duplicate copies of the process, notice, or demand. If the process, notice, or demand is served on the [Secretary of State], the [Secretary of State] shall forward one of the copies by registered or certified mail, return receipt requested, to the company at its designated office. Service is effected under this subsection at the earliest of:

(1) the date the company receives the process, notice, or demand;

(2) the date shown on the return receipt, if signed on behalf of the company; or

(3) five days after its deposit in the mail, if mailed postpaid and correctly addressed.

(d) The [Secretary of State] shall keep a record of all processes, notices, and demands served pursuant to this section and record the time of and the action taken regarding the service.

(e) This section does not affect the right to serve process, notice, or demand in any manner otherwise provided by law.

Comment

Service of process on a limited liability company and a foreign company authorized to transact business in the State must be made on the company's agent for service of process whose name and address should be on file with the filing office. If for any reason a company fails to appoint or maintain an agent for service of process or the agent cannot be found with reasonable diligence at the agent's address, the filing officer will be deemed the proper agent.

§ 112. Nature of Business and Powers

(a) A limited liability company may be organized under this [Act] for any lawful purpose, subject to any law of this State governing or regulating business.

(b) Unless its articles of organization provide otherwise, a limited liability company has the same powers as an individual to do all things necessary or convenient to carry on its business or affairs, including power to:

(1) sue and be sued, and defend in its name;

(2) purchase, receive, lease, or otherwise acquire, and own, hold, improve, use, and otherwise deal with real or personal property, or any legal or equitable interest in property, wherever located;

(3) sell, convey, mortgage, grant a security interest in, lease, exchange, and otherwise encumber or dispose of all or any part of its property;

(4) purchase, receive, subscribe for, or otherwise acquire, own, hold, vote, use, sell, mortgage, lend, grant a security interest in, or otherwise dispose of and deal in and with, shares or other interests in or obligations of any other entity;

(5) make contracts and guarantees, incur liabilities, borrow money, issue its notes, bonds, and other obligations, which may be convertible into or include the option to purchase other securities of the limited liability company, and secure any of its obligations by a mortgage on or a security interest in any of its property, franchises, or income;

(6) lend money, invest and reinvest its funds, and receive and hold real and personal property as security for repayment;

(7) be a promoter, partner, member, associate, or manager of any partnership, joint venture, trust, or other entity;

(8) conduct its business, locate offices, and exercise the powers granted by this [Act] within or without this State;

(9) elect managers and appoint officers, employees, and agents of the limited liability company, define their duties, fix their compensation, and lend them money and credit;

(10) pay pensions and establish pension plans, pension trusts, profit sharing plans, bonus plans, option plans, and benefit or incentive plans for any or all of its current or former members, managers, officers, employees, and agents;

(11) make donations for the public welfare or for charitable, scientific, or educational purposes; and

(12) make payments or donations, or do any other act, not inconsistent with law, that furthers the business of the limited liability company.

Comment

A limited liability company may be organized for any lawful purpose unless the State has specifically prohibited a company from engaging in a specific activity. For example, many States require that certain regulated industries, such as banking and insurance, be conducted only by organizations that meet the special requirements. Also, many States impose restrictions on activities in which a limited liability company may engage. For example, the practice of certain professionals is often subject to special conditions.

A limited liability company has the power to engage in and perform important and necessary acts related to its operation and function. A company's power to enter into a transaction is distinguishable from the authority of an agent to enter into the transaction. See Section 301 (agency rules).

[ARTICLE] 2

ORGANIZATION

§ 201. Limited Liability Company as Legal Entity

A limited liability company is a legal entity distinct from its members.

Comment

A limited liability company is legally distinct from its members who are not normally liable for the debts, obligations, and liabilities of the company. See Section 303. Accordingly, members are not proper parties to suits against the company unless an object of the proceeding is to enforce members' rights against the company or to enforce their liability to the company.

§ 202. Organization

(a) One or more persons may organize a limited liability company, consisting of one or more members, by delivering articles of organization to the office of the [Secretary of State] for filing.

(b) Unless a delayed effective date is specified, the existence of a limited liability company begins when the articles of organization are filed.

(c) The filing of the articles of organization by the [Secretary of State] is conclusive proof that the organizers satisfied all conditions precedent to the creation of a limited liability company.

Comment

Any person may organize a limited liability company by performing the ministerial act of signing and filing the articles of organization. The person need not be a member. As a matter of flexibility, a company may be organized and operated with only one member to enable sole proprietors to obtain the benefit of a liability shield. New and important Internal Revenue Service announcements clarify that a one-member limited liability company will not be taxed like a corporation. Nor will it be taxed like a partnership since it lacks at least two members. Rather, a one-member limited liability company is disregarded for Federal tax purposes and its operations are reported on the return of its single owner.

The existence of a company begins when the articles are filed. Therefore, the filing of the articles of organization is conclusive as to the existence of the limited liability shield for persons who enter into transactions on behalf of the company. Until the articles are filed, a firm is not organized under this Act and is not a "limited liability company" as defined in Section 101(9). In that case, the parties' relationships are not governed by this Act unless they have expressed a contractual intent to be bound by the provisions of the Act. Third parties would also not be governed by the provisions of this Act unless they have expressed a contractual intent to extend a limited liability shield to the members of the would-be limited liability company.

§ 203. Articles of Organization

(a) Articles of organization of a limited liability company must set forth:

(1) the name of the company;

(2) the address of the initial designated office;

(3) the name and street address of the initial agent for service of process;

(4) the name and address of each organizer;

(5) whether the company is to be a term company and, if so, the term specified;

(6) whether the company is to be manager-managed, and, if so, the name and address of each initial manager; and

manager notice

(7) whether one or more of the members of the company are to be liable for its debts and obligations under Section 303(c).

(b) Articles of organization of a limited liability company may set forth:

(1) provisions permitted to be set forth in an operating agreement; or

(2) other matters not inconsistent with law.

(c) Articles of organization of a limited liability company may not vary the nonwaivable provisions of Section 103(b). As to all other matters, if any provision of an operating agreement is inconsistent with the articles of organization:

(1) the operating agreement controls as to managers, members, and members' transferees; and

(2) the articles of organization control as to persons, other than managers, members and their transferees, who reasonably rely on the articles to their detriment.

Comment

The articles serve primarily a notice function and generally do not reflect the substantive agreement of the members regarding the business affairs of the company. Those matters are generally reserved for an operating agreement which may be unwritten. Under Section 203(b), the articles may contain provisions permitted to be set forth in an operating agreement. Where the articles and operating agreement conflict, the operating agreement controls as to members but the articles control as to third parties. The articles may also contain any other matter not inconsistent with law. The most important is a Section 301(c) limitation on the authority of a member or manager to transfer interests in the company's real property.

A company will be at-will unless it is designated as a term company and the duration of its term is specified in its articles under Section 203(a)(5). The duration of a term company may be specified in any manner which sets forth a specific and final date for the dissolution of the company. For example, the period specified may be in the form of "50 years from the date of filing of the articles" or "the period ending on January 1, 2020." Mere specification of a particular undertaking of an uncertain business duration is not sufficient unless the particular undertaking is within a longer fixed period. An example of this type of designation would include "2020 or until the building is completed, whichever occurs first." When the specified period is incorrectly specified, the company will be an at-will company. Notwithstanding the correct specification of a term in the articles, a company will be an at-will company among the members under Section 203(c)(1) if an operating agreement so provides. A term company that continues after the expiration of its term specified in its articles will also be an at-will company.

A term company possesses several important default rule characteristics that differentiate it from an at-will company. An operating agreement may alter any of these rules. Generally, a member of an at-will company may rightfully dissociate at any time whereas a dissociation from a term company prior to the expiration of the specified term is wrongful. See Comments to Section 602(b). Accordingly, a dissociated member of an at-will company is entitled to have the company purchase that member's interest for its fair value determined as of the date of the member's dissociation. A dissociated member of a term company must generally await the expiration of the agreed term to withdraw the fair value of the interest determined at as of the date of the expiration of the agreed term. Thus, a dissociated member in an at-will company receives the fair value of their interest sooner than in a term company and also does not bear the risk of valuation changes for the remainder of the specified term. See Comments to Section 701(a).

A company will be member-managed unless it is designated as manager-managed under Section 203(a)(6). Absent further designation in the articles, a company will be a member-managed at-will company. The designation of a limited liability company as either member-or manager-managed is important because it defines who are agents and have the apparent authority to bind the company under Section 301. In a member-managed company, the members have the agency authority to bind the company. In a manager-managed company only the managers have that authority. New and important Internal Revenue Service announcements clarify that the agency structure of a limited liability company will not cause it to be taxed like a corporation. The agency designation relates only to agency and does not preclude members of a manager-managed company from participating in the actual management of company business. See Comments to Section 404(b).

§ 204. Amendment or Restatement of Articles of Organization

(a) Articles of organization of a limited liability company may be amended at any time by delivering articles of amendment to the [Secretary of State] for filing. The articles of amendment must set forth the:

(1) name of the limited liability company;

(2) date of filing of the articles of organization; and

(3) amendment to the articles.

(b) A limited liability company may restate its articles of organization at any time. Restated articles of organization must be signed and filed in the same manner as articles of amendment. Restated articles of organization must be designated as such in the heading and state in the heading or in an introductory paragraph the limited liability company's present name and, if it has been changed, all of its former names and the date of the filing of its initial articles of organization.

Comment

An amendment to the articles requires the consent of all the members unless an operating agreement provides for a lesser number. See Section 404(c)(3).

§ 205. Signing of Records

(a) Except as otherwise provided in this [Act], a record to be filed by or on behalf of a limited liability company in the office of the [Secretary of State] must be signed in the name of the company by a:

(1) manager of a manager-managed company;

(2) member of a member-managed company;

(3) person organizing the company, if the company has not been formed; or

(4) fiduciary, if the company is in the hands of a receiver, trustee, or other court-appointed fiduciary.

(b) A record signed under subsection (a) must state adjacent to the signature the name and capacity of the signer.

(c) Any person may sign a record to be filed under subsection (a) by an attorney-in-fact. Powers of attorney relating to the signing of records to be filed under subsection (a) by an attorney-in-fact need not be filed in the office of the [Secretary of State] as evidence of authority by the person filing but must be retained by the company.

Comment

Both a writing and a record may be signed. An electronic record is signed when a person adds a name to the record with the intention to authenticate the record. See Sections 101(16) ("record" definition) and 101(17) ("signed" definition).

Other provisions of this Act also provide for the filing of records with the filing office but do not require signing by the persons specified in clauses (1) to (3). Those specific sections prevail.

§ 206. Filing in Office of [Secretary of State]

(a) Articles of organization or any other record authorized to be filed under this [Act] must be in a medium permitted by the [Secretary of State] and must be delivered to the office of the [Secretary of State]. Unless the [Secretary of State] determines that a record fails to comply as to form with the filing requirements of this [Act], and if all filing fees have been paid, the [Secretary of State] shall file the record and send a receipt for the record and the fees to the limited liability company or its representative.

(b) Upon request and payment of a fee, the [Secretary of State] shall send to the requester a certified copy of the requested record.

(c) Except as otherwise provided in subsection (d) and Section 207(c), a record accepted for filing by the [Secretary of State] is effective:

(1) at the time of filing on the date it is filed, as evidenced by the [Secretary of State's] date and time endorsement on the original record; or

(2) at the time specified in the record as its effective time on the date it is filed.

(d) A record may specify a delayed effective time and date, and if it does so the record becomes effective at the time and date specified. If a delayed effective date but no time is specified, the record is effective at the close of business on that date. If a delayed effective date is later than the 90th day after the record is filed, the record is effective on the 90th day.

Comment

The definition and use of the term "record" permits filings with the filing office under this Act to conform to technological advances that have been adopted by the filing office. However, since Section 206(a) provides that the filing "must be in a medium permitted by the [Secretary of State]", the Act simply conforms to filing changes as they are adopted.

§ 207. Correcting Filed Record

(a) A limited liability company or foreign limited liability company may correct a record filed by the [Secretary of State] if the record contains a false or erroneous statement or was defectively signed.

(b) A record is corrected:

(1) by preparing articles of correction that:

(i) describe the record, including its filing date, or attach a copy of it to the articles of correction;

(ii) specify the incorrect statement and the reason it is incorrect or the manner in which the signing was defective; and

(iii) correct the incorrect statement or defective signing; and

(2) by delivering the corrected record to the [Secretary of State] for filing.

(c) Articles of correction are effective retroactively on the effective date of the record they correct except as to persons relying on the uncorrected record and adversely affected by the correction. As to those persons, articles of correction are effective when filed.

§ 208. Certificate of Existence or Authorization

(a) A person may request the [Secretary of State] to furnish a certificate of existence for a limited liability company or a certificate of authorization for a foreign limited liability company.

(b) A certificate of existence for a limited liability company must set forth:

(1) the company's name;

(2) that it is duly organized under the laws of this State, the date of organization, whether its duration is at-will or for a specified term, and, if the latter, the period specified;

(3) if payment is reflected in the records of the [Secretary of State] and if nonpayment affects the existence of the company, that all fees, taxes, and penalties owed to this State have been paid;

(4) whether its most recent annual report required by Section 211 has been filed with the [Secretary of State];

(5) that articles of termination have not been filed; and

(6) other facts of record in the office of the [Secretary of State] which may be requested by the applicant.

(c) A certificate of authorization for a foreign limited liability company must set forth:

(1) the company's name used in this State;

(2) that it is authorized to transact business in this State;

(3) if payment is reflected in the records of the [Secretary of State] and if nonpayment affects the authorization of the company, that all fees, taxes, and penalties owed to this State have been paid;

(4) whether its most recent annual report required by Section 211 has been filed with the [Secretary of State];

(5) that a certificate of cancellation has not been filed; and

(6) other facts of record in the office of the [Secretary of State] which may be requested by the applicant.

(d) Subject to any qualification stated in the certificate, a certificate of existence or authorization issued by the [Secretary of State] may be relied upon as conclusive evidence that the domestic or foreign limited liability company is in existence or is authorized to transact business in this State.

§ 209. Liability for False Statement in Filed Record

If a record authorized or required to be filed under this [Act] contains a false statement, one who suffers loss by reliance on the statement may recover damages for the loss from a person who signed the record or caused another to sign it on the person's behalf and knew the statement to be false at the time the record was signed.

§ 210. Filing by Judicial Act

If a person required by Section 205 to sign any record fails or refuses to do so, any other person who is adversely affected by the failure or refusal may petition the [designate the appropriate court] to direct the signing of the record. If the court finds that it is proper for the record to be signed and that a person so designated has failed or refused to sign the record, it shall order the [Secretary of State] to sign and file an appropriate record.

§ 211. Annual Report for [Secretary of State]

(a) A limited liability company, and a foreign limited liability company authorized to transact business in this State, shall deliver to the [Secretary of State] for filing an annual report that sets forth:

(1) the name of the company and the State or country under whose law it is organized;

(2) the address of its designated office and the name and address of its agent for service of process in this State;

(3) the address of its principal office; and

(4) the names and business addresses of any managers.

(b) Information in an annual report must be current as of the date the annual report is signed on behalf of the limited liability company.

(c) The first annual report must be delivered to the [Secretary of State] between [January 1 and April 1] of the year following the calendar year in which a limited liability company was organized or a foreign company was authorized to transact business. Subsequent annual reports must be delivered to the [Secretary of State] between [January 1 and April 1] of the ensuing calendar years.

(d) If an annual report does not contain the information required in subsection (a), the [Secretary of State] shall promptly notify the reporting limited liability company or foreign limited liability company and return the report to it for correction. If the report is corrected to contain the information required in subsection (a) and delivered to the [Secretary of State] within 30 days after the effective date of the notice, it is timely filed.

Comment

Failure to deliver the annual report within 60 days after its due date is a primary ground for administrative dissolution of the company under Section 809. See Comments to Sections 809 to 812.

[ARTICLE] 3

RELATIONS OF MEMBERS AND MANAGERS TO PERSONS DEALING WITH LIMITED LIABILITY COMPANY

§ 301. Agency of Members and Managers

(a) Subject to subsections (b) and (c):

(1) Each member is an agent of the limited liability company for the purpose of its business, and an act of a member, including the signing of an instrument in the company's name, for apparently carrying on in the ordinary course the company's business or business of the kind carried on by the company binds the company, unless the member had no authority to act for the company in the particular matter and the person with whom the member was dealing knew or had notice that the member lacked authority.

(2) An act of a member which is not apparently for carrying on in the ordinary course the company's business or business of the kind carried on by the company binds the company only if the act was authorized by the other members.

(b) Subject to subsection (c), in a manager-managed company:

(1) A member is not an agent of the company for the purpose of its business solely by reason of being a member. Each manager is an agent of the company for the purpose of its business, and an act of a manager, including the signing of an instrument in the company's name, for apparently carrying on in the ordinary course the company's business or business of the kind carried on by the company binds the company, unless the manager had no authority to act for the company in the particular matter and the person with whom the manager was dealing knew or had notice that the manager lacked authority.

(2) An act of a manager which is not apparently for carrying on in the ordinary course the company's business or business of the kind carried on by the company binds the company only if the act was authorized under Section 404.

(c) Unless the articles of organization limit their authority, any member of a member-managed company or manager of a manager-managed company may sign and deliver any instrument transferring or affecting the company's interest in real property. The instrument is conclusive in favor of a person who gives value without knowledge of the lack of the authority of the person signing and delivering the instrument.

Comment

Members of a member-managed and managers of manager-managed company, as agents of the firm, have the apparent authority to bind a company to third parties. Members of a manager-managed company are not as such agents of the firm and do not have the apparent authority, as members, to bind a company. Members and managers with apparent authority possess actual authority by implication unless the actual authority is restricted in an operating agreement. Apparent authority extends to acts for carrying on in the ordinary course the company's business and business of the kind carried on by the company. Acts beyond this scope bind the company only where supported by actual authority created before the act or ratified after the act.

Ordinarily, restrictions on authority in an operating agreement do not affect the apparent authority of members and managers to bind the company to third parties without notice of the restriction. However, the restriction may make a member or manager's conduct wrongful and create liability to the company for the breach. This rule is subject to three important exceptions. First, under Section 301(c), a limitation reflected in the articles of organization on the authority of any member or manager to sign and deliver an instrument affecting an interest in company real property is effective when filed, even to persons without knowledge of the agent's lack of authority. New and important Internal Revenue Service announcements clarify that the agency structure of a limited liability company will not cause it to be taxed like a corporation.

Secondly, under Section 703, a dissociated member's apparent authority terminates two years after dissociation, even to persons without knowledge of the dissociation. Thirdly, under Section 704, a dissociated member's apparent authority may be terminated earlier than the two years by filing a statement of dissociation. The statement is effective 90 days after filing, even to persons without knowledge of the filing. Together, these three provisions provide constructive knowledge to the world of the lack of apparent authority of an agent to bind the company.

§ 302. Limited Liability Company Liable for Member's or Manager's Actionable Conduct

A limited liability company is liable for loss or injury caused to a person, or for a penalty incurred, as a result of a wrongful act or omission, or other actionable conduct, of a member or manager acting in the ordinary course of business of the company or with authority of the company.

Comment

Since a member of a manager-managed company is not as such an agent, the acts of the member are not imputed to the company unless the member is acting under actual or apparent authority created by circumstances other than membership status.

§ 303. Liability of Members and Managers

(a) Except as otherwise provided in subsection (c), the debts, obligations, and liabilities of a limited liability company, whether arising in contract, tort, or otherwise, are solely the debts, obligations, and liabilities of the company. A member or manager is not personally liable for a debt, obligation, or liability of the company solely by reason of being or acting as a member or manager.

(b) The failure of a limited liability company to observe the usual company formalities or requirements relating to the exercise of its company powers or management of its business is not a ground for imposing personal liability on the members or managers for liabilities of the company.

(c) All or specified members of a limited liability company are liable in their capacity as members for all or specified debts, obligations, or liabilities of the company if:

(1) a provision to that effect is contained in the articles of organization; and

(2) a member so liable has consented in writing to the adoption of the provision or to be bound by the provision.

Comment

A member or manager, as an agent of the company, is not liable for the debts, obligations, and liabilities of the company simply because of the agency. A member or manager is responsible for acts or omissions to the extent those acts or omissions would be actionable in contract or tort against the member or manager if that person were acting in an individual capacity. Where a member or manager delegates or assigns the authority or duty to exercise appropriate company functions, the member or manager is ordinarily not personally liable for the acts or omissions of the officer, employee, or agent if the member or manager has complied with the duty of care set forth in Section 409(c).

Under Section 303(c), the usual liability shield may be waived, in whole or in part, provided the waiver is reflected in the articles of organization and the member has consented in writing to be bound by the waiver. The importance and unusual nature of the waiver consent requires that the consent be evidenced by a writing and not merely an unwritten record. See Comments to Section 205. New and important Internal Revenue Service announcements clarify that the owner liability structure of a limited liability company (other than a foreign limited liability company formed outside the United States) will not cause it to be taxed like a corporation.

[ARTICLE] 4

RELATIONS OF MEMBERS TO EACH OTHER AND TO LIMITED LIABILITY COMPANY

§ 401. Form of Contribution

A contribution of a member of a limited liability company may consist of tangible or intangible property or other benefit to the company, including money, promissory notes, services performed, or other agreements to contribute cash or property, or contracts for services to be performed.

Comment

Unless otherwise provided in an operating agreement, admission of a member and the nature and valuation of a would-be member's contribution are matters requiring the consent of all of the other members. See Section 404(c)(7). An agreement to contribute to a company is controlled by the operating agreement and therefore may not be created or modified without amending that agreement through the unanimous consent of all the members, including the member to be bound by the new contribution terms. See 404(c)(1).

§ 402. Member's Liability for Contributions

(a) A member's obligation to contribute money, property, or other benefit to, or to perform services for, a limited liability company is not excused by the member's death, disability, or other inability to perform personally. If a member does not make the required contribution of property or services, the member is obligated at the option of the company to contribute money equal to the value of that portion of the stated contribution which has not been made.

(b) A creditor of a limited liability company who extends credit or otherwise acts in reliance on an obligation described in subsection (a), and without notice of any compromise under Section 404(c)(5), may enforce the original obligation.

Comment

An obligation need not be in writing to be enforceable. Given the informality of some companies, a writing requirement may frustrate reasonable expectations of members based on a clear oral agreement. Obligations may be compromised with the consent of all of the members under Section 404(c)(5), but the compromise is generally effective only among the consenting members. Company creditors are bound by the compromise only as provided in Section 402(b).

§ 403. Member's and Manager's Rights to Payments and Reimbursement

(a) A limited liability company shall reimburse a member or manager for payments made and indemnify a member or manager for liabilities incurred by the member or manager in the ordinary course of the business of the company or for the preservation of its business or property.

(b) A limited liability company shall reimburse a member for an advance to the company beyond the amount of contribution the member agreed to make.

(c) A payment or advance made by a member which gives rise to an obligation of a limited liability company under subsection (a) or (b) constitutes a loan to the company upon which interest accrues from the date of the payment or advance.

(d) A member is not entitled to remuneration for services performed for a limited liability company, except for reasonable compensation for services rendered in winding up the business of the company.

default rule

Comment

The presence of a liability shield will ordinarily prevent a member or manager from incurring personal liability on behalf of the company in the ordinary course of the company's business. Where a member of a member-managed or a manager of a manager-managed company incurs such liabilities, Section 403(a) provides that the company must indemnify the member or manager where that person acted in the ordinary course of the company's business or the preservation of its property. A member or manager is therefore entitled to indemnification only if the act was within the member or manager's actual authority. A member or manager is therefore not entitled to indemnification for conduct that violates the duty of care set forth in Section 409(c) or for tortious conduct against a third party. Since members of a manager-managed company do not possess the apparent authority to bind the company, it would be more unusual for such a member to incur a liability for indemnification in the ordinary course of the company's business.

§ 404. Management of Limited Liability Company

(a) In a member-managed company:

(1) each member has equal rights in the management and conduct of the company's business; and

(2) except as otherwise provided in subsection (c), any matter relating to the business of the company may be decided by a majority of the members.

(b) In a manager-managed company:

(1) each manager has equal rights in the management and conduct of the company's business;

(2) except as otherwise provided in subsection (c), any matter relating to the business of the company may be exclusively decided by the manager or, if there is more than one manager, by a majority of the managers; and

(3) a manager:

(i) must be designated, appointed, elected, removed, or replaced by a vote, approval, or consent of a majority of the members; and

(ii) holds office until a successor has been elected and qualified, unless the manager sooner resigns or is removed.

Unanimous

(c) The only matters of a member or manager-managed company's business requiring the consent of all of the members are:

(1) the amendment of the operating agreement under Section 103;

CoI

(2) the authorization or ratification of acts or transactions under Section 103(b)(2)(ii) which would otherwise violate the duty of loyalty;

(3) an amendment to the articles of organization under Section 204;

(4) the compromise of an obligation to make a contribution under Section 402(b);

(5) the compromise, as among members, of an obligation of a member to make a contribution or return money or other property paid or distributed in violation of this [Act];

(6) the making of interim distributions under Section 405(a), including the redemption of an interest;

(7) the admission of a new member;

(8) the use of the company's property to redeem an interest subject to a charging order;

(9) the consent to dissolve the company under Section 801(b)(2);

(10) a waiver of the right to have the company's business wound up and the company terminated under Section 802(b);

(11) the consent of members to merge with another entity under Section 904(c)(1); and

(12) the sale, lease, exchange, or other disposal of all, or substantially all, of the company's property with or without goodwill.

(d) Action requiring the consent of members or managers under this [Act] may be taken without a meeting.

(e) A member or manager may appoint a proxy to vote or otherwise act for the member or manager by signing an appointment instrument, either personally or by the member's or manager's attorney-in-fact.

Comment

In a member-managed company, each member has equal rights in the management and conduct of the company's business unless otherwise provided in an operating agreement. For example, an operating agreement may allocate voting rights based upon capital contributions rather than the subsection (a) per capita rule. Also, member disputes as to any matter relating to the company's business may be resolved by a majority of the members unless the matter relates to a matter specified in subsection (c) (unanimous consent required). Regardless of how the members allocate management rights, each member is an agent of the company with the apparent authority to bind the company in the ordinary course of its business. See Comments to Section 301(a). A member's right to participate in management terminates upon dissociation. See Section 603(b)(1).

In a manager-managed company, the members, unless also managers, have no rights in the management and conduct of the company's business unless otherwise provided in an operating agreement. If there is more than one manager, manager disputes as to any matter relating to the company's business may be resolved by a majority of the managers unless the matter relates to a matter specified in subsection (c) (unanimous member consent required). Managers must be designated, appointed, or elected by a majority of the members. A manager need not be a member and is an agent of the company with the apparent authority to bind the company in the ordinary course of its business. See Sections 101(10) and 301(b).

To promote clarity and certainty, subsection (c) specifies those exclusive matters requiring the unanimous consent of the members, whether the company is member-or manager-managed. For example, interim distributions, including redemptions, may not be made without the unanimous consent of all the members. Unless otherwise agreed, all other company matters are to be determined under the majority of members or managers rules of subsections (a) and (b).

§ 405. Sharing of and Right to Distributions

(a) Any distributions made by a limited liability company before its dissolution and winding up must be in equal shares.

(b) A member has no right to receive, and may not be required to accept, a distribution in kind.

(c) If a member becomes entitled to receive a distribution, the member has the status of, and is entitled to all remedies available to, a creditor of the limited liability company with respect to the distribution.

Comment

Recognizing the informality of many limited liability companies, this section creates a simple default rule regarding interim distributions. Any interim distributions made must be in equal shares and approved by all members. See Section 404(c)(6). The rule assumes that: profits will be shared equally; some distributions will constitute a return of contributions that should be shared equally rather than a distribution of profits; and property contributors should have the right to veto any distribution that threatens their return of contributions on liquidation. In the simple case where the members make equal contributions of property or equal contributions of services, those assumptions avoid the necessity of maintaining a complex capital account or determining profits. Where some members contribute services and others property, the unanimous vote necessary to approve interim distributions protects against unwanted distributions of contributions to service contributors. Consistently, Section 408(a) does not require the company to maintain a separate account for each member, the Act does not contain a default rule for allocating profits and losses, and Section 806(b) requires that liquidating distributions to members be made in equal shares after the return of contributions not previously returned. See Comments to Section 806(b).

Section 405(c) governs distributions declared or made when the company was solvent. Section 406 governs distributions declared or made when the company is insolvent.

§ 406. Limitations on Distributions

(a) A distribution may not be made if:

(1) the limited liability company would not be able to pay its debts as they become due in the ordinary course of business; or

(2) the company's total assets would be less than the sum of its total liabilities plus the amount that would be needed, if the company were to be dissolved, wound up, and terminated at the time of the distribution, to satisfy the preferential rights upon dissolution, winding up, and termination of members whose preferential rights are superior to those receiving the distribution.

(b) A limited liability company may base a determination that a distribution is not prohibited under subsection (a) on financial statements prepared on the basis of accounting practices and principles that are reasonable in the circumstances or on a fair valuation or other method that is reasonable in the circumstances.

(c) Except as otherwise provided in subsection (e), the effect of a distribution under subsection (a) is measured:

(1) in the case of distribution by purchase, redemption, or other acquisition of a distributional interest in a limited liability company, as of the date money or other property is transferred or debt incurred by the company; and

(2) in all other cases, as of the date the:

(i) distribution is authorized if the payment occurs within 120 days after the date of authorization; or

(ii) payment is made if it occurs more than 120 days after the date of authorization.

(d) A limited liability company's indebtedness to a member incurred by reason of a distribution made in accordance with this section is at parity with the company's indebtedness to its general, unsecured creditors.

(e) Indebtedness of a limited liability company, including indebtedness issued in connection with or as part of a distribution, is not considered a liability for purposes of determinations under subsection (a) if its terms provide that payment of principal and interest are made only if and to the extent that payment of a distribution to members could then be made under this section. If the indebtedness is issued as a distribution, each payment of principal or interest on the indebtedness is treated as a distribution, the effect of which is measured on the date the payment is made.

Comment

This section establishes the validity of company distributions, which in turn determines the potential liability of members and managers for improper distributions under Section 407. Distributions are improper if the company is insolvent under subsection (a) at the time the distribution is measured under subsection (c). In recognition of the informality of many limited liability companies, the solvency determination under subsection (b) may be made on the basis of a fair valuation or other method reasonable under the circumstances.

The application of the equity insolvency and balance sheet tests present special problems in the context of the purchase, redemption, or other acquisition of a company's distributional interests. Special rules establish the time of measurement of such transfers. Under Section 406(c)(1), the time for measuring the effect of a distribution to purchase a distributional interest is the date of payment. The company may make payment either by transferring property or incurring a debt to transfer property in the future. In the latter case, subsection (c)(1) establishes a clear rule that the legality of the distribution is tested when the debt is actually incurred, not later when the debt is actually paid. Under Section 406(e), indebtedness is not considered a liability for purposes of subsection (a) if the terms of the indebtedness itself provide that payments can be made only if and to the extent that a payment of a distribution could then be made under this section. The effect makes the holder of the indebtedness junior to all other creditors but senior to members in their capacity as members.

§ 407. Liability for Unlawful Distributions

(a) A member of a member-managed company or a member or manager of a manager-managed company who votes for or assents to a distribution made in violation of Section 406, the articles of organization, or the operating agreement is personally liable to the company for the amount of the distribution which exceeds the amount that could have been distributed without violating Section 406, the articles of organization, or the operating agreement if it is established that the member or manager did not perform the member's or manager's duties in compliance with Section 409.

(b) A member of a manager-managed company who knew a distribution was made in violation of Section 406, the articles of organization, or the operating agreement is personally liable to the company, but only to the extent that the distribution received by the member exceeded the amount that could have been properly paid under Section 406.

(c) A member or manager against whom an action is brought under this section may implead in the action all:

(1) other members or managers who voted for or assented to the distribution in violation of subsection (a) and may compel contribution from them; and

(2) members who received a distribution in violation of subsection (b) and may compel contribution from the member in the amount received in violation of subsection (b).

(d) A proceeding under this section is barred unless it is commenced within two years after the distribution.

Comment

Whenever members or managers fail to meet the standards of conduct of Section 409 and vote for or assent to an unlawful distribution, they are personally liable to the company for the portion of the distribution that exceeds the maximum amount that could have been lawfully distributed. The recovery remedy under this section extends only to the company, not the company's creditors. Under subsection (a), members and managers are not liable for an unlawful distribution provided their vote in favor of the distribution satisfies the duty of care of Section 409(c).

Subsection (a) creates personal liability in favor of the company against members or managers who approve an unlawful distribution for the entire amount of a distribution that could not be lawfully distributed. Subsection (b) creates personal liability against only members who knowingly received the unlawful distribution, but only in the amount measured by the portion of the actual distribution received that was not lawfully made. Members who both vote for or assent to an unlawful distribution and receive a portion or all of the distribution will be liable, at the election of the company, under either but not both subsections.

A member or manager who is liable under subsection (a) may seek contribution under subsection (c)(1) from other members and managers who also voted for or assented to the same distribution and may also seek recoupment under subsection (c)(2) from members who received the distribution, but only if they accepted the payments knowing they were unlawful.

The two-year statute of limitations of subsection (d) is measured from the date of the distribution. The date of the distribution is determined under Section 406(c).

§ 408. Member's Right to Information

(a) A limited liability company shall provide members and their agents and attorneys access to its records, if any, at the company's principal office or other reasonable locations specified in the operating agreement. The company shall provide former members and their agents and attorneys access for proper purposes to records pertaining to the period during which they were members. The right of access provides the opportunity to inspect and copy records during ordinary business hours. The company may impose a reasonable charge, limited to the costs of labor and material, for copies of records furnished.

(b) A limited liability company shall furnish to a member, and to the legal representative of a deceased member or member under legal disability:

(1) without demand, information concerning the company's business or affairs reasonably required for the proper exercise of the member's rights and performance of the member's duties under the operating agreement or this [Act]; and

(2) on demand, other information concerning the company's business or affairs, except to the extent the demand or the information demanded is unreasonable or otherwise improper under the circumstances.

(c) A member has the right upon written demand given to the limited liability company to obtain at the company's expense a copy of any written operating agreement.

Comment

Recognizing the informality of many limited liability companies, subsection (a) does not require a company to maintain any records. In general, a company should maintain records necessary to enable members to determine their share of profits and losses and their rights on dissociation. If inadequate records are maintained to determine those and other critical rights, a member may maintain an action for an accounting under Section 410(a). Normally, a company will maintain at least records required by state or federal authorities regarding tax and other filings.

The obligation to furnish access includes the obligation to insure that all records, if any, are accessible in intelligible form. For example, a company that switches computer systems has an obligation either to convert the records from the old system or retain at least one computer capable of accessing the records from the old system.

The right to inspect and copy records maintained is not conditioned on a member or former member's purpose or motive. However, an abuse of the access and copy right may create a remedy in favor of the other members as a violation of the requesting member or former member's obligation of good faith and fair dealing. See Section 409(d).

Although a company is not required to maintain any records under subsection (a), it is nevertheless subject to a disclosure duty to furnish specified information under subsection (b)(1). A company must therefore furnish to members, without demand, information reasonably needed for members to exercise their rights and duties as members. A member's exercise of these duties justifies an unqualified right of access to the company's records. The member's right to company records may not be unreasonably restricted by the operating agreement. See Section 103(b)(1).

§ 409. General Standards of Member's and Manager's Conduct

(a) The only fiduciary duties a member owes to a member-managed company and its other members are the duty of loyalty and the duty of care imposed by subsections (b) and (c).

(b) A member's duty of loyalty to a member-managed company and its other members is limited to the following:

(1) to account to the company and to hold as trustee for it any property, profit, or benefit derived by the member in the conduct or winding up of the company's business or derived from a use by the member of the company's property, including the appropriation of a company's opportunity;

(2) to refrain from dealing with the company in the conduct or winding up of the company's business as or on behalf of a party having an interest adverse to the company; and

(3) to refrain from competing with the company in the conduct of the company's business before the dissolution of the company.

(c) A member's duty of care to a member-managed company and its other members in the conduct of and winding up of the company's business is limited to refraining from engaging in grossly negligent or reckless conduct, intentional misconduct, or a knowing violation of law.

(d) A member shall discharge the duties to a member-managed company and its other members under this [Act] or under the operating agreement and exercise any rights consistently with the obligation of good faith and fair dealing.

(e) A member of a member-managed company does not violate a duty or obligation under this [Act] or under the operating agreement merely because the member's conduct furthers the member's own interest.

(f) A member of a member-managed company may lend money to and transact other business with the company. As to each loan or transaction, the rights and obligations of the member are the same as those of a person who is not a member, subject to other applicable law.

(g) This section applies to a person winding up the limited liability company's business as the personal or legal representative of the last surviving member as if the person were a member.

(h) In a manager-managed company:

(1) a member who is not also a manager owes no duties to the company or to the other members solely by reason of being a member;

(2) a manager is held to the same standards of conduct prescribed for members in subsections (b) through (f);

(3) a member who pursuant to the operating agreement exercises some or all of the rights of a manager in the management and conduct of the company's business is held to the standards of conduct in subsections (b) through (f) to the extent that the member exercises the managerial authority vested in a manager by this [Act]; and

(4) a manager is relieved of liability imposed by law for violation of the standards prescribed by subsections (b) through (f) to the extent of the managerial authority delegated to the members by the operating agreement.

Comment

Under subsections (a), (c), and (h), members and managers, and their delegatees, owe to the company and to the other members and managers only the fiduciary duties of loyalty and care set forth in subsections (b) and (c) and the obligation of good faith and fair dealing set forth in subsection (d). An operating agreement may not waive or eliminate the duties or obligation, but may, if not manifestly unreasonable, identify activities and determine standards for measuring the performance of them. See Section 103(b)(2) to (4).

Upon a member's dissociation, the duty to account for personal profits under subsection (b)(1), the duty to refrain from acting as or representing adverse interests under subsection (b)(2), and the duty of care under subsection (c) are limited to those derived from matters arising or events occurring before the dissociation unless the member participates in winding up the company's business. Also, the duty not to compete terminates upon dissociation. See Section 603(b)(3) and (b)(2). However, a dissociated member is not free to use confidential company information after dissociation. For example, a dissociated member of a company may immediately compete with the company for new clients but must exercise care in completing on-going client transactions and must account to the company for any fees from the old clients on account of those transactions. Subsection (c) adopts a gross negligence standard for the duty of care, the standard actually used in most partnerships and corporations.

Subsection (b)(2) prohibits a member from acting adversely or representing an adverse party to the company. The rule is based on agency principles and seeks to avoid the conflict of opposing interests in the mind of the member agent whose duty is to act for the benefit of the principal company. As reflected in subsection (f), the rule does not prohibit the member from dealing with the company other than as an adversary. A member may generally deal with the company under subsection (f) when the transaction is approved by the company.

Subsection (e) makes clear that a member does not violate the obligation of good faith under subsection (d) merely because the member's conduct furthers that member's own interest. For example, a member's refusal to vote for an interim distribution because of negative tax implications to that member does not violate that member's obligation of good faith to the other members. Likewise, a member may vote against a proposal by the company to open a shopping center that would directly compete with another shopping center in which the member owns an interest.

§ 410. Actions by Members

(a) A member may maintain an action against a limited liability company or another member for legal or equitable relief, with or without an accounting as to the company's business, to enforce:

(1) the member's rights under the operating agreement;

(2) the member's rights under this [Act]; and

(3) the rights and otherwise protect the interests of the member, including rights and interests arising independently of the member's relationship to the company.

(b) The accrual, and any time limited for the assertion, of a right of action for a remedy under this section is governed by other law. A right to an accounting upon a dissolution and winding up does not revive a claim barred by law.

Comment

During the existence of the company, members have under this section access to the courts to resolve claims against the company and other members, leaving broad judicial discretion to fashion appropriate legal remedies. A member pursues only that member's claim against the company or another member under this section. Article 11 governs a member's derivative pursuit of a claim on behalf of the company.

A member may recover against the company and the other members under subsection (a)(3) for personal injuries or damage to the member's property caused by another member. One member's negligence is therefore not imputed to bar another member's action.

§ 411. Continuation of Term Company After Expiration of Specified Term

(a) If a term company is continued after the expiration of the specified term, the rights and duties of the members and managers remain the same as they were at the expiration of the term except to the extent inconsistent with rights and duties of members and managers of an at-will company.

(b) If the members in a member-managed company or the managers in a manager-managed company continue the business without any winding up of the business of the company, it continues as an at-will company.

Comment

A term company will generally dissolve upon the expiration of its term unless either its articles are amended before the expiration of the original specified term to provide for an additional specified term or the members or managers simply continue the company as an at-will company under this section. Amendment of the articles specifying an additional term requires the unanimous consent of the members. See Section 404(c)(3). Therefore, any member has the right to block the amendment. Absent an amendment to the articles, a company may only be continued under subsection (b) as an at-will company. The decision to continue a term company as an at-will company does not require the unanimous consent of the members and is treated as an ordinary business matter with disputes resolved by a simple majority vote of either the members or managers. See Section 404. In that case, subsection (b) provides that the members' conduct amends or becomes part of an operating agreement to "continue" the company as an at-will company. The amendment to the operating agreement does not alter the rights of creditors who suffer detrimental reliance because the company does not liquidate after the expiration of its specified term. See Section 203(c)(2).

Preexisting operating-agreement provisions continue to control the relationship of the members under subsection (a) except to the extent inconsistent with the rights and duties of members of an at-will company with an operating agreement containing the same provisions. However, the members could agree in advance that, if the company's business continues after the expiration of its specified term, the company continues as a company with a new specified term or that the provisions of its operating agreement survive the expiration of the specified term.

[ARTICLE] 5

TRANSFEREES AND CREDITORS OF MEMBER

§ 501. Member's Distributional Interest

(a) A member is not a co-owner of, and has no transferable interest in, property of a limited liability company.

(b) A distributional interest in a limited liability company is personal property and, subject to Sections 502 and 503, may be transferred in whole or in part.

(c) An operating agreement may provide that a distributional interest may be evidenced by a certificate of the interest issued by the limited liability company and, subject to Section 503, may also provide for the transfer of any interest represented by the certificate.

Comment

Members have no property interest in property owned by a limited liability company. A distributional interest is personal property and is defined under Section 101(6) as a member's interest in distributions only and does not include the member's broader rights to participate in management under Section 404 and to inspect company records under Section 408.

Under Section 405(a), distributions are allocated in equal shares unless otherwise provided in an operating agreement. Whenever it is desirable to allocate distributions in proportion to contributions rather than per capita, certification may be useful to reduce valuation issues. New and important Internal Revenue Service announcements clarify that certification of a limited liability company will not cause it to be taxed like a corporation.

§ 502. Transfer of Distributional Interest

A transfer of a distributional interest does not entitle the transferee to become or to exercise any rights of a member. A transfer entitles the transferee to receive, to the extent transferred, only the distributions to which the transferor would be entitled.

Comment

Under Sections 501(b) and 502, the only interest a member may freely transfer is that member's distributional interest. A member's transfer of all of a distributional interest constitutes an event of dissociation. See Section 601(3). A transfer of less than all of a member's distributional interest is not an event of dissociation. A member ceases to be a member upon the transfer of all that member's distributional interest and that transfer is also an event of dissociation under Section 601(3). Relating the event of dissociation to the member's transfer of all of the member's distributional interest avoids the need for the company to track potential future dissociation events associated with a member no longer financially interested in the company. Also, all the remaining members may expel a member upon the transfer of "substantially all" the member's distributional interest. The expulsion is an event of dissociation under Section 601(5)(ii).

§ 503. Rights of Transferee

(a) A transferee of a distributional interest may become a member of a limited liability company if and to the extent that the transferor gives the transferee the right in accordance with authority described in the operating agreement or all other members consent.

(b) A transferee who has become a member, to the extent transferred, has the rights and powers, and is subject to the restrictions and liabilities, of a member under the operating agreement of a limited liability company and this [Act]. A transferee who becomes a member also is liable for the transferor member's obligations to make contributions under Section 402 and for obligations under Section 407 to return unlawful distributions, but the transferee is not obligated for the transferor member's liabilities unknown to the transferee at the time the transferee becomes a member.

(c) Whether or not a transferee of a distributional interest becomes a member under subsection (a), the transferor is not released from liability to the limited liability company under the operating agreement or this [Act].

(d) A transferee who does not become a member is not entitled to participate in the management or conduct of the limited liability company's business, require access to information concerning the company's transactions, or inspect or copy any of the company's records.

(e) A transferee who does not become a member is entitled to:

(1) receive, in accordance with the transfer, distributions to which the transferor would otherwise be entitled;

(2) receive, upon dissolution and winding up of the limited liability company's business:

(i) in accordance with the transfer, the net amount otherwise distributable to the transferor;

(ii) a statement of account only from the date of the latest statement of account agreed to by all the members;

(3) seek under Section 801(5) a judicial determination that it is equitable to dissolve and wind up the company's business.

(f) A limited liability company need not give effect to a transfer until it has notice of the transfer.

Comment

The only interest a member may freely transfer is the member's distributional interest. A transferee may acquire the remaining rights of a member only by being admitted as a member of the company by all of the remaining members. New and important Internal Revenue Service announcements clarify that the transferability of membership interests of a limited liability company in excess of these default rules will not cause it to be taxed like a corporation. In many cases a limited liability company will be organized and operated with only a few members. These default rules were chosen in the interest of preserving the right of existing members in such companies to determine whether a transferee will become a member.

A transferee not admitted as a member is not entitled to participate in management, require access to information, or inspect or copy company records. The only rights of a transferee are to receive the distributions the transferor would otherwise be entitled, receive a limited statement of account, and seek a judicial dissolution under Section 801(a)(5).

Subsection (e) sets forth the rights of a transferee of an existing member. Although the rights of a dissociated member to participate in the future management of the company parallel the rights of a transferee, a dissociated member retains additional rights that accrued from that person's membership such as the right to enforce Article 7 purchase rights. See and compare Sections 603(b)(1) and 801(a)(4) and Comments.

§ 504. Rights of Creditor

(a) On application by a judgment creditor of a member of a limited liability company or of a member's transferee, a court having jurisdiction may charge the distributional interest of the judgment debtor to satisfy the judgment. The court may appoint a receiver of the share of the distributions due or to become due to the judgment debtor and make all other orders, directions, accounts, and inquiries the judgment debtor might have made or which the circumstances may require to give effect to the charging order.

(b) A charging order constitutes a lien on the judgment debtor's distributional interest. The court may order a foreclosure of a lien on a distributional interest subject to the charging order at any time. A purchaser at the foreclosure sale has the rights of a transferee.

(c) At any time before foreclosure, a distributional interest in a limited liability company which is charged may be redeemed:

(1) by the judgment debtor;

(2) with property other than the company's property, by one or more of the other members; or

(3) with the company's property, but only if permitted by the operating agreement.

(d) This [Act] does not affect a member's right under exemption laws with respect to the member's distributional interest in a limited liability company.

(e) This section provides the exclusive remedy by which a judgment creditor of a member or a transferee may satisfy a judgment out of the judgment debtor's distributional interest in a limited liability company.

Comment

A charging order is the only remedy by which a judgment creditor of a member or a member's transferee may reach the distributional interest of a member or member's transferee. Under Section 503(e), the distributional interest of a member or transferee is limited to the member's right to receive distributions from the company and to seek judicial liquidation of the company.

[ARTICLE] 6

MEMBER'S DISSOCIATION

§ 601. Events Causing Member's Dissociation

A member is dissociated from a limited liability company upon the occurrence of any of the following events:

(1) the company's having notice of the member's express will to withdraw upon the date of notice or on a later date specified by the member;

(2) an event agreed to in the operating agreement as causing the member's dissociation;

(3) upon transfer of all of a member's distributional interest, other than a transfer for security purposes or a court order charging the member's distributional interest which has not been foreclosed;

(4) the member's expulsion pursuant to the operating agreement;

(5) the member's expulsion by unanimous vote of the other members if:

(i) it is unlawful to carry on the company's business with the member;

(ii) there has been a transfer of substantially all of the member's distributional interest, other than a transfer for security purposes or a court order charging the member's distributional interest which has not been foreclosed;

(iii) within 90 days after the company notifies a corporate member that it will be expelled because it has filed a certificate of dissolution or the equivalent, its charter has been revoked, or its right to conduct business has been suspended by the jurisdiction of its incorporation, the member fails to obtain a revocation of the certificate of dissolution or a reinstatement of its charter or its right to conduct business; or

(iv) a partnership or a limited liability company that is a member has been dissolved and its business is being wound up;

(6) on application by the company or another member, the member's expulsion by judicial determination because the member:

(i) engaged in wrongful conduct that adversely and materially affected the company's business;

(ii) willfully or persistently committed a material breach of the operating agreement or of a duty owed to the company or the other members under Section 409; or

(iii) engaged in conduct relating to the company's business which makes it not reasonably practicable to carry on the business with the member;

(7) the member's:

(i) becoming a debtor in bankruptcy;

(ii) executing an assignment for the benefit of creditors;

(iii) seeking, consenting to, or acquiescing in the appointment of a trustee, receiver, or liquidator of the member or of all or substantially all of the member's property; or

(iv) failing, within 90 days after the appointment, to have vacated or stayed the appointment of a trustee, receiver, or liquidator of the member or of all or substantially all of the member's property obtained without the member's consent or acquiescence, or failing within 90 days after the expiration of a stay to have the appointment vacated;

(8) in the case of a member who is an individual:

(i) the member's death;

(ii) the appointment of a guardian or general conservator for the member; or

(iii) a judicial determination that the member has otherwise become incapable of performing the member's duties under the operating agreement;

(9) in the case of a member that is a trust or is acting as a member by virtue of being a trustee of a trust, distribution of the trust's entire rights to receive distributions from the company, but not merely by reason of the substitution of a successor trustee;

(10) in the case of a member that is an estate or is acting as a member by virtue of being a personal representative of an estate, distribution of the estate's entire rights to receive distributions from the company, but not merely the substitution of a successor personal representative; or

(11) termination of the existence of a member if the member is not an individual, estate, or trust other than a business trust.

Comment

The term "dissociation" refers to the change in the relationships among the dissociated member, the company and the other members caused by a member's ceasing to be associated in the carrying on of the company's business. Member dissociation from either an at-will or term company, whether member-or manager-managed is not an event of dissolution of the company unless otherwise specified in an operating agreement. See Section 801(a)(1). However, member dissociation will generally trigger the obligation of the company to purchase the dissociated member's interest under Article 7.

A member may be expelled from the company under paragraph (5)(ii) by the unanimous vote of the other members upon a transfer of "substantially all" of the member's distributional interest other than for a transfer as security for a loan. A transfer of "all" of the member's distributional interest is an event of dissociation under paragraph (3).

Although a member is dissociated upon death, the effect of the dissociation where the company does not dissolve depends upon whether the company is at-will or term. Only the decedent's distributional interest transfers to the decedent's estate which does not acquire the decedent member's management rights. See Section 603(b)(1). Unless otherwise agreed, if the company was at-will, the estate's distributional interest must be purchased by the company at fair value determined at the date of death. However, if a term company, the estate and its transferees continue only as the owner of the distributional interest with no management rights until the expiration of the specified term that existed on the date of death. At the expiration of that term, the company must purchase the interest of a dissociated member if the company continues for an additional term by amending its articles or simply continues as an at-will company. See Sections 411 and 701(a)(2) and Comments. Before that time, the estate and its transferees have the right to make application for a judicial dissolution of the company under Section 801(b)(5) as successors in interest to a dissociated member. See Comments to Sections 801, 411, and 701. Where the members have allocated management rights on the basis of contributions rather than simply the number of members, a member's death will result in a transfer of management rights to the remaining members on a proportionate basis. This transfer of rights may be avoided by a provision in an operating agreement extending the Section 701(a)(1) at-will purchase right to a decedent member of a term company.

§ 602. Member's Power to Dissociate; Wrongful Dissociation

(a) Unless otherwise provided in the operating agreement, a member has the power to dissociate from a limited liability company at any time, rightfully or wrongfully, by express will pursuant to Section 601(1).

(b) If the operating agreement has not eliminated a member's power to dissociate, the member's dissociation from a limited liability company is wrongful only if:

(1) it is in breach of an express provision of the agreement; or

(2) before the expiration of the specified term of a term company:

(i) the member withdraws by express will;

(ii) the member is expelled by judicial determination under Section 601(6);

(iii) the member is dissociated by becoming a debtor in bankruptcy; or

(iv) in the case of a member who is not an individual, trust other than a business trust, or estate, the member is expelled or otherwise dissociated because it willfully dissolved or terminated its existence.

(c) A member who wrongfully dissociates from a limited liability company is liable to the company and to the other members for damages caused by the dissociation. The liability is in addition to any other obligation of the member to the company or to the other members.

(d) If a limited liability company does not dissolve and wind up its business as a result of a member's wrongful dissociation under subsection (b), damages sustained by the company for the wrongful dissociation must be offset against distributions otherwise due the member after the dissociation.

Comment

A member has the power to withdraw from both an at-will company and a term company although the effects of the withdrawal are remarkably different. See Comments to Section 601. At a minimum, the exercise of a power to withdraw enables members to terminate their continuing duties of loyalty and care. See Section 603(b)(2) to (3).

A member's power to withdraw by express will may be eliminated by an operating agreement. New and important Internal Revenue Service announcements clarify that alteration of a member's power to withdraw will not cause the limited liability company to be taxed like a corporation. An operating agreement may eliminate a member's power to withdraw by express will to promote the business continuity of an at-will company by removing member's right to force the company to purchase the member's distributional interest. See Section 701(a)(1). However, such a member retains the ability to seek a judicial dissolution of the company. See Section 801(a)(4).

If a member's power to withdraw by express will is not eliminated in an operating agreement, the withdrawal may nevertheless be made wrongful under subsection (b). All dissociations, including withdrawal by express will, may be made wrongful under subsection (b)(1) in both an at-will and term company by the inclusion of a provision in an operating agreement. Even where an operating agreement does not eliminate the power to withdraw by express will or make any dissociation wrongful, the dissociation of a member of a term company for the reasons specified under subsection (b)(2) is wrongful. The member is liable to the company and other members for damages caused by a wrongful dissociation under subsection (c) and, under subsection (d), the damages may be offset against all distributions otherwise due the member after the dissociation. Section 701(f) provides a similar rule permitting damages for wrongful dissociation to be offset against any company purchase of the member's distributional interest.

§ 603. Effect of Member's Dissociation

(a) Upon a member's dissociation:

(1) in an at-will company, the company must cause the dissociated member's distributional interest to be purchased under [Article] 7; and

(2) in a term company:

(i) if the company dissolves and winds up its business on or before the expiration of its specified term, [Article] 8 applies to determine the dissociated member's rights to distributions; and

(ii) if the company does not dissolve and wind up its business on or before the expiration of its specified term, the company must cause the dissociated member's distributional interest to be purchased under [Article] 7 on the date of the expiration of the term specified at the time of the member's dissociation.

(b) Upon a member's dissociation from a limited liability company:

(1) the member's right to participate in the management and conduct of the company's business terminates, except as otherwise provided in Section 803, and the member ceases to be a member and is treated the same as a transferee of a member;

(2) the member's duty of loyalty under Section 409(b)(3) terminates; and

(3) the member's duty of loyalty under Section 409(b)(1) and (2) and duty of care under Section 409(c) continue only with regard to matters arising and events occurring before the member's dissociation, unless the member participates in winding up the company's business pursuant to Section 803.

Comment

Member dissociation is not an event of dissolution of a company unless otherwise specified in an operating agreement. See Section 801(a)(1). Dissociation from an at-will company that does not dissolve the company causes the dissociated member's distributional interest to be immediately purchased under Article 7. See Comments to Sections 602 and 603. Dissociation from a term company that does not dissolve the company does not cause the dissociated member's distributional interest to be purchased under Article 7 until the expiration of the specified term that existed on the date of dissociation.

Subsection (b)(1) provides that a dissociated member forfeits the right to participate in the future conduct of the company's business.

Dissociation does not however forfeit that member's right to enforce the Article 7 rights that accrue by reason of the dissociation. Similarly, where dissociation occurs by death, the decedent member's successors in interest may enforce that member's Article 7 rights. See and compare Comments to Section 503(e).

Dissociation terminates the member's right to participate in management, including the member's actual authority to act for the company under Section 301, and begins the two-year period after which a member's apparent authority conclusively ends. See Comments to Section 703. Dissociation also terminates a member's continuing duties of loyalty and care, except with regard to continuing transactions, to the company and other members unless the member participates in winding up the company's business. See Comments to Section 409.

[ARTICLE] 7

MEMBER'S DISSOCIATION WHEN BUSINESS NOT WOUND UP

§ 701. Company Purchase of Distributional Interest

(a) A limited liability company shall purchase a distributional interest of a:

(1) member of an at-will company for its fair value determined as of the date of the member's dissociation if the member's dissociation does not result in a dissolution and winding up of the company's business under Section 801; or

(2) member of a term company for its fair value determined as of the date of the expiration of the specified term that existed on the date of the member's dissociation if the expiration of the specified term does not result in a dissolution and winding up of the company's business under Section 801.

(b) A limited liability company must deliver a purchase offer to the dissociated member whose distributional interest is entitled to be purchased not later than 30 days after the date determined under subsection (a). The purchase offer must be accompanied by:

(1) a statement of the company's assets and liabilities as of the date determined under subsection (a);

(2) the latest available balance sheet and income statement, if any; and

(3) an explanation of how the estimated amount of the payment was calculated.

(c) If the price and other terms of a purchase of a distributional interest are fixed or are to be determined by the operating agreement, the price and terms so fixed or determined govern the purchase unless the purchaser defaults. If a default occurs, the dissociated member is entitled to commence a proceeding to have the company dissolved under Section 801(4)(iv).

(d) If an agreement to purchase the distributional interest is not made within 120 days after the date determined under subsection (a), the dissociated member, within another 120 days, may commence a proceeding against the limited liability company to enforce the purchase. The company at its expense shall notify in writing all of the remaining members, and any other person the court directs, of the commencement of the proceeding. The jurisdiction of the court in which the proceeding is commenced under this subsection is plenary and exclusive.

(e) The court shall determine the fair value of the distributional interest in accordance with the standards set forth in Section 702 together with the terms for the purchase. Upon making these determinations, the court shall order the limited liability company to purchase or cause the purchase of the interest.

(f) Damages for wrongful dissociation under Section 602(b), and all other amounts owing, whether or not currently due, from the dissociated member to a limited liability company, must be offset against the purchase price.

Comment

This section sets forth default rules regarding an otherwise mandatory company purchase of a distributional interest. Even though a dissociated member's rights to participate in the future management of the company are equivalent to those of a transferee of a member, the dissociation does not forfeit that member's right to enforce the Article 7 purchase right. Similarly, if the dissociation occurs by reason of death, the decedent member's successors in interest may enforce the Article 7 rights. See Comments to Sections 503(e) and 603(b)(1).

An at-will company must purchase a dissociated member's distributional interest under subsection (a)(1) when that member's dissociation does not result in a dissolution of the company under Section 801(a)(1). The purchase price is equal to the fair value of the interest determined as of the date of dissociation. Any damages for wrongful dissociation must be offset against the purchase price.

Dissociation from a term company does not require an immediate purchase of the member's interest but the operating agreement may specify that dissociation is an event of dissolution. See Section 801(a)(1). A term company must only purchase the dissociated member's distributional interest under subsection (a)(2) on the expiration of the specified term that existed on the date of the member's dissociation. The purchase price is equal to the fair value of the interest determined as of the date of the expiration of that specified term. Any damages for wrongful dissociation must be offset against the purchase price.

The valuation dates differ between subsections (a)(1) and (a)(2) purchases. The former is valued on the date of member dissociation whereas the latter is valued on the date of the expiration of the specified term that existed on the date of dissociation. A subsection (a)(2) dissociated member therefore assumes the risk of loss between the date of dissociation and the expiration of the then stated specified term. See Comments to Section 801 (dissociated member may file application to dissolve company under Section 801(a)(4)).

The default valuation standard is fair value. See Comments to Section 702. An operating agreement may fix a method or formula for determining the purchase price and the terms of payment. The purchase right may be modified. For example, an operating agreement may eliminate a member's power to withdraw from an at-will company which narrows the dissociation events contemplated under subsection (a)(1). See Comments to Section 602(a). However, a provision in an operating agreement providing for complete forfeiture of the purchase right may be unenforceable where the power to dissociate has not also been eliminated. See Section 104(a).

The company must deliver a purchase offer to the dissociated member within 30 days after the date determined under subsection (a). The offer must be accompanied by information designed to enable the dissociated member to evaluate the fairness of the offer. The subsection (b)(3) explanation of how the offer price was calculated need not be elaborate. For example, a mere statement of the basis of the calculation, such as "book value," may be sufficient.

The company and the dissociated member must reach an agreement on the purchase price and terms within 120 days after the date determined under subsection (a). Otherwise, the dissociated member may file suit within another 120 days to enforce the purchase under subsection (d). The court will then determine the fair value and terms of purchase under subsection (e). See Section 702. The member's lawsuit is not available under subsection (c) if the parties have previously agreed to price and terms in an operating agreement.

§ 702. Court Action to Determine Fair Value of Distributional Interest

(a) In an action brought to determine the fair value of a distributional interest in a limited liability company, the court shall:

(1) determine the fair value of the interest, considering among other relevant evidence the going concern value of the company, any agreement among some or all of the members fixing the price or specifying a formula for determining value of distributional interests for any other purpose, the recommendations of any appraiser appointed by the court, and any legal constraints on the company's ability to purchase the interest;

(2) specify the terms of the purchase, including, if appropriate, terms for installment payments, subordination of the purchase obligation to the rights of the company's other creditors, security for a deferred purchase price, and a covenant not to compete or other restriction on a dissociated member; and

(3) require the dissociated member to deliver an assignment of the interest to the purchaser upon receipt of the purchase price or the first installment of the purchase price.

(b) After the dissociated member delivers the assignment, the dissociated member has no further claim against the company, its members, officers, or managers, if any, other than a claim to any unpaid balance of the purchase price and a claim under any agreement with the company or the remaining members that is not terminated by the court.

(c) If the purchase is not completed in accordance with the specified terms, the company is to be dissolved upon application under Section 801(b)(5)(iv). If a limited liability company is so dissolved, the dissociated member has the same rights and priorities in the company's assets as if the sale had not been ordered.

(d) If the court finds that a party to the proceeding acted arbitrarily, vexatiously, or not in good faith, it may award one or more other parties their reasonable expenses, including attorney's fees and the expenses of appraisers or other experts, incurred in the proceeding. The finding may be based on the company's failure to make an offer to pay or to comply with Section 701(b).

(e) Interest must be paid on the amount awarded from the date determined under Section 701(a) to the date of payment.

Comment

The default valuation standard is fair value. Under this broad standard, a court is free to determine the fair value of a distributional interest on a fair market, liquidation, or any other method deemed appropriate under the circumstances. A fair market value standard is not used because it is too narrow, often inappropriate, and assumes a fact not contemplated by this section—a willing buyer and a willing seller.

The court has discretion under subsection (a)(2) to include in its order any conditions the court deems necessary to safeguard the interests of the company and the dissociated member or transferee. The discretion may be based on the financial and other needs of the parties.

If the purchase is not consummated or the purchaser defaults, the dissociated member or transferee may make application for dissolution of the company under subsection (c). The court may deny the petition for good cause but the proceeding affords the company an opportunity to be heard on the matter and avoid dissolution. See Comments to Section 801(a)(4).

The power of the court to award all costs and attorney's fees incurred in the suit under subsection (d) is an incentive for both parties to act in good faith. See Section 701(c).

§ 703. Dissociated Member's Power to Bind Limited Liability Company

For two years after a member dissociates without the dissociation resulting in a dissolution and winding up of a limited liability company's business, the company, including a surviving company under [Article] 9, is bound by an act of the dissociated member which would have bound the company under Section 301 before dissociation only if at the time of entering into the transaction the other party:

(1) reasonably believed that the dissociated member was then a member;

(2) did not have notice of the member's dissociation; and

(3) is not deemed to have had notice under Section 704.

Comment

Member dissociation will not dissolve the company unless otherwise specified in an operating agreement. See Section 801(a)(1). A dissociated member of a member-managed company does not have actual authority to act for the company. See Section 603(b)(1). Under Section 301(a), a dissociated member of a member-managed company has apparent authority to bind the company in ordinary course transactions except as to persons who knew or had notice of the dissociation. This section modifies that rule by requiring the person to show reasonable reliance on the member's status as a member provided a Section 704 statement has not been filed within the previous 90 days. See also Section 804 (power to bind after dissolution).

§ 704. Statement of Dissociation

(a) A dissociated member or a limited liability company may file in the office of the [Secretary of State] a statement of dissociation stating the name of the company and that the member is dissociated from the company.

(b) For the purposes of Sections 301 and 703, a person not a member is deemed to have notice of the dissociation 90 days after the statement of dissociation is filed.

[ARTICLE] 8

WINDING UP COMPANY'S BUSINESS

§ 801. Events Causing Dissolution and Winding Up of Company's Business

A limited liability company is dissolved, and its business must be wound up, upon the occurrence of any of the following events:

(1) an event specified in the operating agreement;

(2) consent of the number or percentage of members specified in the operating agreement;

(3) an event that makes it unlawful for all or substantially all of the business of the company to be continued, but any cure of illegality within 90 days after notice to the company of the event is effective retroactively to the date of the event for purposes of this section;

(4) on application by a member or a dissociated member, upon entry of a judicial decree that:

(i) the economic purpose of the company is likely to be unreasonably frustrated;

(ii) another member has engaged in conduct relating to the company's business that makes it not reasonably practicable to carry on the company's business with that member;

(iii) it is not otherwise reasonably practicable to carry on the company's business in conformity with the articles of organization and the operating agreement;

(iv) the company failed to purchase the petitioner's distributional interest as required by Section 701; or

(v) the managers or members in control of the company have acted, are acting, or will act in a manner that is illegal, oppressive, fraudulent, or unfairly prejudicial to the petitioner;

(5) on application by a transferee of a member's interest, a judicial determination that it is equitable to wind up the company's business:

(i) after the expiration of the specified term, if the company was for a specified term at the time the applicant became a transferee by member dissociation, transfer, or entry of a charging order that gave rise to the transfer; or

(ii) at any time, if the company was at will at the time the applicant became a transferee by member dissociation, transfer, or entry of a charging order that gave rise to the transfer; or

(6) the expiration of the term specified in the articles of organization.

Comment

The dissolution rules of this section are mostly default rules and may be modified by an operating agreement. However, an operating agreement may not modify or eliminate the dissolution events specified in subsection (a)(3) (illegal business) or subsection (a)(4) (member application). See Section 103(b)(6).

The relationship between member dissociation and company dissolution is set forth under subsection (a)(1). Unless member dissociation is specified as an event of dissolution in the operating agreement, such dissociation does not dissolve the company. New and important Internal Revenue Service announcements clarify that the failure of member dissociation to cause or threaten dissolution of a limited liability company will not cause the company to be taxed like a corporation.

A member or dissociated member whose interest is not required to be purchased by the company under Section 701 may make application under subsection (a)(4) for the involuntary dissolution of both an at-will company and a term company. A transferee may make application under subsection (a)(5). A transferee's application right, but not that of a member or dissociated member, may be modified by an operating agreement. See Section 103(b)(6). A dissociated member is not treated as a transferee for purposes of an application under subsections (a)(4) and (a)(5). See Section 603(b)(1). For example, this affords reasonable protection to a dissociated member of a term company to make application under subsection (a)(4) before the expiration of the term that existed at the time of dissociation. For purposes of a subsection (a)(4) application, a dissociated member includes a successor in interest, e.g., surviving spouse. See Comments to Section 601.

In the case of applications under subsections (a)(4) and (a)(5), the applicant has the burden of proving either the existence of one or more of the circumstances listed under subsection (a)(4) or that it is equitable to wind up the company's business under subsection (a)(5). Proof of the existence of one or more of the circumstances in subsection (a)(4), may be the basis of a subsection (a)(5) application. Even where the burden of proof is met, the court has the discretion to order relief other than the dissolution of the company. Examples include an accounting, a declaratory judgment, a distribution, the purchase of the distributional interest of the applicant or another member, or the appointment of a receiver. See Section 410.

A court has the discretion to dissolve a company under subsection (a)(4)(i) when the company has a very poor financial record that is not likely to improve. In this instance, dissolution is an alternative to placing the company in bankruptcy. A court may dissolve a company under subsections (a)(4)(ii), (a)(4)(iii), and (a)(4)(iv) for serious and protracted misconduct by one or more members. Subsection (a)(4)(v) provides a specific remedy for an improper squeeze-out of a member.

In determining whether and what type of relief to order under subsections (a)(4) and (a)(5) involuntary dissolution suits, a court should take into account other rights and remedies of the applicant. For example, a court should not grant involuntary dissolution of an at-will company if the applicant member has the right to dissociate and force the company to purchase that member's distributional interest under Sections 701 and 702. In other cases, involuntary dissolution or some other remedy such as a buy-out might be appropriate where, for example, one or more members have (i) engaged in fraudulent or unconscionable conduct, (ii) improperly expelled a member seeking an unfair advantage of a provision in an operating agreement that provides for a significantly lower price on expulsion than would be payable in the event of voluntary dissociation, or (iii) engaged in serious misconduct and the applicant member is a member of a term company and would not have a right to have the company purchase that member's distributional interest upon dissociation until the expiration of the company's specified term.

§ 802. Limited Liability Company Continues After Dissolution

(a) Subject to subsection (b), a limited liability company continues after dissolution only for the purpose of winding up its business.

(b) At any time after the dissolution of a limited liability company and before the winding up of its business is completed, the members, including a dissociated member whose dissociation caused the dissolution, may unanimously waive the right to have the company's business wound up and the company terminated. In that case:

(1) the limited liability company resumes carrying on its business as if dissolution had never occurred and any liability incurred by the company or a member after the dissolution and before the waiver is determined as if the dissolution had never occurred; and

(2) the rights of a third party accruing under Section 804(a) or arising out of conduct in reliance on the dissolution before the third party knew or received a notification of the waiver are not adversely affected.

Comment

The liability shield continues in effect for the winding up period because the legal existence of the company continues under subsection (a). The company is terminated on the filing of articles of termination. See Section 805.

§ 803. Right to Wind Up Limited Liability Company's Business

(a) After dissolution, a member who has not wrongfully dissociated may participate in winding up a limited liability company's business, but on application of any member, member's legal representative, or transferee, the [designate the appropriate court], for good cause shown, may order judicial supervision of the winding up.

(b) A legal representative of the last surviving member may wind up a limited liability company's business.

(c) A person winding up a limited liability company's business may preserve the company's business or property as a going concern for a reasonable time, prosecute and defend actions and proceedings, whether civil, criminal, or administrative, settle and close the company's business, dispose of and transfer the company's property, discharge the company's liabilities, distribute the assets of the company pursuant to Section 806, settle disputes by mediation or arbitration, and perform other necessary acts.

§ 804. Member's or Manager's Power and Liability as Agent After Dissolution

(a) A limited liability company is bound by a member's or manager's act after dissolution that:

(1) is appropriate for winding up the company's business; or

(2) would have bound the company under Section 301 before dissolution, if the other party to the transaction did not have notice of the dissolution.

(b) A member or manager who, with knowledge of the dissolution, subjects a limited liability company to liability by an act that is not appropriate for winding up the company's business is liable to the company for any damage caused to the company arising from the liability.

Comment

After dissolution, members and managers continue to have the authority to bind the company that they had prior to dissolution provided that the third party did not have notice of the dissolution. See Section 102(b) (notice defined). Otherwise, they have only the authority appropriate for winding up the company's business. See Section 703 (agency power of member after dissociation).

§ 805. Articles of Termination

(a) At any time after dissolution and winding up, a limited liability company may terminate its existence by filing with the [Secretary of State] articles of termination stating:

(1) the name of the company;

(2) the date of the dissolution; and

(3) that the company's business has been wound up and the legal existence of the company has been terminated.

(b) The existence of a limited liability company is terminated upon the filing of the articles of termination, or upon a later effective date, if specified in the articles of termination.

Comment

The termination of legal existence also terminates the company's liability shield. See Comments to Section 802 (liability shield continues in effect during winding up). It also ends the company's responsibility to file an annual report. See Section 211.

§ 806. Distribution of Assets in Winding Up Limited Liability Company's Business

(a) In winding up a limited liability company's business, the assets of the company must be applied to discharge its obligations to creditors, including members who are creditors. Any surplus must be applied to pay in money the net amount distributable to members in accordance with their right to distributions under subsection (b).

(b) Each member is entitled to a distribution upon the winding up of the limited liability company's business consisting of a return of all contributions which have not previously been returned and a distribution of any remainder in equal shares.

§ 807. Known Claims Against Dissolved Limited Liability Company

(a) A dissolved limited liability company may dispose of the known claims against it by following the procedure described in this section.

(b) A dissolved limited liability company shall notify its known claimants in writing of the dissolution. The notice must:

(1) specify the information required to be included in a claim;

(2) provide a mailing address where the claim is to be sent;

(3) state the deadline for receipt of the claim, which may not be less than 120 days after the date the written notice is received by the claimant; and

(4) state that the claim will be barred if not received by the deadline.

(c) A claim against a dissolved limited liability company is barred if the requirements of subsection (b) are met, and:

(1) the claim is not received by the specified deadline; or

(2) in the case of a claim that is timely received but rejected by the dissolved company, the claimant does not commence a proceed-

ing to enforce the claim within 90 days after the receipt of the notice of the rejection.

(d) For purposes of this section, "claim" does not include a contingent liability or a claim based on an event occurring after the effective date of dissolution.

Comment

A known claim will be barred when the company provides written notice to a claimant that a claim must be filed with the company no later than at least 120 days after receipt of the written notice and the claimant fails to file the claim. If the claim is timely received but is rejected by the company, the claim is nevertheless barred unless the claimant files suit to enforce the claim within 90 days after the receipt of the notice of rejection. A claim described in subsection (d) is not a "known" claim and is governed by Section 808. This section does not extend any other applicable statutes of limitation. See Section 104. Depending on the management of the company, members or managers must discharge or make provision for discharging all of the company's known liabilities before distributing the remaining assets to the members. See Sections 806(a), 406, and 407.

§ 808. Other Claims Against Dissolved Limited Liability Company

(a) A dissolved limited liability company may publish notice of its dissolution and request persons having claims against the company to present them in accordance with the notice.

(b) The notice must:

(1) be published at least once in a newspaper of general circulation in the [county] in which the dissolved limited liability company's principal office is located or, if none in this State, in which its designated office is or was last located;

(2) describe the information required to be contained in a claim and provide a mailing address where the claim is to be sent; and

(3) state that a claim against the limited liability company is barred unless a proceeding to enforce the claim is commenced within five years after publication of the notice.

(c) If a dissolved limited liability company publishes a notice in accordance with subsection (b), the claim of each of the following claimants is barred unless the claimant commences a proceeding to enforce the claim against the dissolved company within five years after the publication date of the notice:

(1) a claimant who did not receive written notice under Section 807;

(2) a claimant whose claim was timely sent to the dissolved company but not acted on; and

(3) a claimant whose claim is contingent or based on an event occurring after the effective date of dissolution.

(d) A claim not barred under this section may be enforced:

(1) against the dissolved limited liability company, to the extent of its undistributed assets; or

(2) if the assets have been distributed in liquidation, against a member of the dissolved company to the extent of the member's proportionate share of the claim or the company's assets distributed to the member in liquidation, whichever is less, but a member's total liability for all claims under this section may not exceed the total amount of assets distributed to the member.

Comment

An unknown claim will be barred when the company publishes notice requesting claimants to file claims with the company and stating that claims will be barred unless the claimant files suit to enforce the claim within five years after the date of publication. The procedure also bars known claims where the claimant either did not receive written notice described in Section 807 or received notice, mailed a claim, but the company did not act on the claim.

Depending on the management of the company, members or managers must discharge or make provision for discharging all of the company's known liabilities before distributing the remaining assets to the members. See Comment to Section 807. This section does not contemplate that a company will postpone member distributions until all unknown claims are barred under this section. In appropriate cases, the company may purchase insurance or set aside funds permitting a distribution of the remaining assets. Where winding up distributions have been made to members, subsection (d)(2) authorizes recovery against those members. However, a claimant's recovery against a member is limited to the lesser of the member's proportionate share of the claim or the amount received in the distribution. This section does not extend any other applicable statutes of limitation. See Section 104.

§ 809. Grounds for Administrative Dissolution

The [Secretary of State] may commence a proceeding to dissolve a limited liability company administratively if the company does not:

(1) pay any fees, taxes, or penalties imposed by this [Act] or other law within 60 days after they are due; or

(2) deliver its annual report to the [Secretary of State] within 60 days after it is due.

Comment

Administrative dissolution is an effective enforcement mechanism for a variety of statutory obligations under this Act and it avoids the more expensive judicial dissolution process. When applicable, administrative dissolution avoids wasteful attempts to compel compliance by a company abandoned by its members.

§ 810. Procedure for and Effect of Administrative Dissolution

(a) If the [Secretary of State] determines that a ground exists for administratively dissolving a limited liability company, the [Secretary of State] shall enter a record of the determination and serve the company with a copy of the record.

(b) If the company does not correct each ground for dissolution or demonstrate to the reasonable satisfaction of the [Secretary of State] that each ground determined by the [Secretary of State] does not exist within 60 days after service of the notice, the [Secretary of State] shall administratively dissolve the company by signing a certification of the dissolution that recites the ground for dissolution and its effective date. The [Secretary of State] shall file the original of the certificate and serve the company with a copy of the certificate.

(c) A company administratively dissolved continues its existence but may carry on only business necessary to wind up and liquidate its business and affairs under Section 802 and to notify claimants under Sections 807 and 808.

(d) The administrative dissolution of a company does not terminate the authority of its agent for service of process.

Comment

A company's failure to comply with a ground for administrative dissolution may simply occur because of oversight. Therefore, subsections (a) and (b) set forth a mandatory notice by the filing officer to the company of the ground for dissolution and a 60 day grace period for correcting the ground.

§ 811. Reinstatement Following Administrative Dissolution

(a) A limited liability company administratively dissolved may apply to the [Secretary of State] for reinstatement within two years after the effective date of dissolution. The application must:

(1) recite the name of the company and the effective date of its administrative dissolution;

(2) state that the ground for dissolution either did not exist or have been eliminated;

(3) state that the company's name satisfies the requirements of Section 105; and

(4) contain a certificate from the [taxing authority] reciting that all taxes owed by the company have been paid.

(b) If the [Secretary of State] determines that the application contains the information required by subsection (a) and that the information is correct, the [Secretary of State] shall cancel the certificate of dissolution and prepare a certificate of reinstatement that recites this determination and the effective date of reinstatement, file the original of the certificate, and serve the company with a copy of the certificate.

(c) When reinstatement is effective, it relates back to and takes effect as of the effective date of the administrative dissolution and the company may resume its business as if the administrative dissolution had never occurred.

§ 812. Appeal From Denial of Reinstatement

(a) If the [Secretary of State] denies a limited liability company's application for reinstatement following administrative dissolution, the [Secretary of State] shall serve the company with a record that explains the reason or reasons for denial.

(b) The company may appeal the denial of reinstatement to the [name appropriate] court within 30 days after service of the notice of denial is perfected. The company appeals by petitioning the court to set aside the dissolution and attaching to the petition copies of the [Secretary of State's] certificate of dissolution, the company's application for reinstatement, and the [Secretary of State's] notice of denial.

(c) The court may summarily order the [Secretary of State] to reinstate the dissolved company or may take other action the court considers appropriate.

(d) The court's final decision may be appealed as in other civil proceedings.

[ARTICLE] 9

CONVERSIONS AND MERGERS

§ 901. Definitions

In this [article]:

(1) "Corporation" means a corporation under [the State Corporation Act], a predecessor law, or comparable law of another jurisdiction.

(2) "General partner" means a partner in a partnership and a general partner in a limited partnership.

(3) "Limited partner" means a limited partner in a limited partnership.

(4) "Limited partnership" means a limited partnership created under [the State Limited Partnership Act], a predecessor law, or comparable law of another jurisdiction.

(5) "Partner" includes a general partner and a limited partner.

(6) "Partnership" means a general partnership under [the State Partnership Act], a predecessor law, or comparable law of another jurisdiction.

(7) "Partnership agreement" means an agreement among the partners concerning the partnership or limited partnership.

(8) "Shareholder" means a shareholder in a corporation.

Comment

Section 907 makes clear that the provisions of Article 9 are not mandatory. Therefore, a partnership or a limited liability company may convert or merge in any other manner provided by law. However, if the requirements of Article 9 are followed, the conversion or merger is legally valid. Article 9 is not restricted to domestic business entities.

§ 902. Conversion of Partnership or Limited Partnership to Limited Liability Company

(a) A partnership or limited partnership may be converted to a limited liability company pursuant to this section.

(b) The terms and conditions of a conversion of a partnership or limited partnership to a limited liability company must be approved by all of the partners or by a number or percentage of the partners required for conversion in the partnership agreement.

(c) An agreement of conversion must set forth the terms and conditions of the conversion of the interests of partners of a partnership or of a limited partnership, as the case may be, into interests in the converted limited liability company or the cash or other consideration to be paid or delivered as a result of the conversion of the interests of the partners, or a combination thereof.

(d) After a conversion is approved under subsection (b), the partnership or limited partnership shall file articles of organization in the office of the [Secretary of State] which satisfy the requirements of Section 203 and contain:

(1) a statement that the partnership or limited partnership was converted to a limited liability company from a partnership or limited partnership, as the case may be;

(2) its former name;

(3) a statement of the number of votes cast by the partners entitled to vote for and against the conversion and, if the vote is less than unanimous, the number or percentage required to approve the conversion under subsection (b); and

(4) in the case of a limited partnership, a statement that the certificate of limited partnership is to be canceled as of the date the conversion took effect.

(e) In the case of a limited partnership, the filing of articles of organization under subsection (d) cancels its certificate of limited partnership as of the date the conversion took effect.

(f) A conversion takes effect when the articles of organization are filed in the office of the [Secretary of State] or at any later date specified in the articles of organization.

(g) A general partner who becomes a member of a limited liability company as a result of a conversion remains liable as a partner for an obligation incurred by the partnership or limited partnership before the conversion takes effect.

(h) A general partner's liability for all obligations of the limited liability company incurred after the conversion takes effect is that of a member of the company. A limited partner who becomes a member as a result of a conversion remains liable only to the extent the limited partner was liable for an obligation incurred by the limited partnership before the conversion takes effect.

Comment

Subsection (b) makes clear that the terms and conditions of the conversion of a general or limited partnership to a limited liability company must be approved by all of the partners unless the partnership agreement specifies otherwise.

§ 903. Effect of Conversion; Entity Unchanged

(a) A partnership or limited partnership that has been converted pursuant to this [article] is for all purposes the same entity that existed before the conversion.

(b) When a conversion takes effect:

(1) all property owned by the converting partnership or limited partnership vests in the limited liability company;

(2) all debts, liabilities, and other obligations of the converting partnership or limited partnership continue as obligations of the limited liability company;

(3) an action or proceeding pending by or against the converting partnership or limited partnership may be continued as if the conversion had not occurred;

(4) except as prohibited by other law, all of the rights, privileges, immunities, powers, and purposes of the converting partnership or limited partnership vest in the limited liability company; and

(5) except as otherwise provided in the agreement of conversion under Section 902(c), all of the partners of the converting partnership continue as members of the limited liability company.

Comment

A conversion is not a conveyance or transfer and does not give rise to claims of reverter or impairment of title based on a prohibited conveyance or transfer. Under subsection (b)(1), title to all partnership property, including real estate, vests in the limited liability company as a matter of law without reversion or impairment.

§ 904. Merger of Entities

(a) Pursuant to a plan of merger approved under subsection (c), a limited liability company may be merged with or into one or more limited liability companies, foreign limited liability companies, corporations, foreign corporations, partnerships, foreign partnerships, limited partnerships, foreign limited partnerships, or other domestic or foreign entities.

(b) A plan of merger must set forth:

(1) the name of each entity that is a party to the merger;

(2) the name of the surviving entity into which the other entities will merge;

(3) the type of organization of the surviving entity;

(4) the terms and conditions of the merger;

(5) the manner and basis for converting the interests of each party to the merger into interests or obligations of the surviving entity, or into money or other property in whole or in part; and

(6) the street address of the surviving entity's principal place of business.

(c) A plan of merger must be approved:

(1) in the case of a limited liability company that is a party to the merger, by all of the members or by a number or percentage of members specified in the operating agreement;

(2) in the case of a foreign limited liability company that is a party to the merger, by the vote required for approval of a merger by the law of the State or foreign jurisdiction in which the foreign limited liability company is organized;

(3) in the case of a partnership or domestic limited partnership that is a party to the merger, by the vote required for approval of a conversion under Section 902(b); and

(4) in the case of any other entities that are parties to the merger, by the vote required for approval of a merger by the law of this State or of the State or foreign jurisdiction in which the entity is organized and, in the absence of such a requirement, by all the owners of interests in the entity.

(d) After a plan of merger is approved and before the merger takes effect, the plan may be amended or abandoned as provided in the plan.

(e) The merger is effective upon the filing of the articles of merger with the [Secretary of State], or at such later date as the articles may provide.

Comment

This section sets forth a "safe harbor" for cross-entity mergers of limited liability companies with both domestic and foreign: corporations, general and limited partnerships, and other limited liability companies. Subsection (c) makes clear that the terms and conditions of the plan of merger must be approved by all of the partners unless applicable state law specifies otherwise for the merger.

§ 905. Articles of Merger

(a) After approval of the plan of merger under Section 904(c), unless the merger is abandoned under Section 904(d), articles of merger must be signed on behalf of each limited liability company and other entity that is a party to the merger and delivered to the [Secretary of State] for filing. The articles must set forth:

(1) the name and jurisdiction of formation or organization of each of the limited liability companies and other entities that are parties to the merger;

(2) for each limited liability company that is to merge, the date its articles of organization were filed with the [Secretary of State];

(3) that a plan of merger has been approved and signed by each limited liability company and other entity that is to merge;

(4) the name and address of the surviving limited liability company or other surviving entity;

(5) the effective date of the merger;

(6) if a limited liability company is the surviving entity, such changes in its articles of organization as are necessary by reason of the merger;

(7) if a party to a merger is a foreign limited liability company, the jurisdiction and date of filing of its initial articles of organization

and the date when its application for authority was filed by the [Secretary of State] or, if an application has not been filed, a statement to that effect; and

(8) if the surviving entity is not a limited liability company, an agreement that the surviving entity may be served with process in this State and is subject to liability in any action or proceeding for the enforcement of any liability or obligation of any limited liability company previously subject to suit in this State which is to merge, and for the enforcement, as provided in this [Act], of the right of members of any limited liability company to receive payment for their interest against the surviving entity.

(b) If a foreign limited liability company is the surviving entity of a merger, it may not do business in this State until an application for that authority is filed with the [Secretary of State].

(c) The surviving limited liability company or other entity shall furnish a copy of the plan of merger, on request and without cost, to any member of any limited liability company or any person holding an interest in any other entity that is to merge.

(d) Articles of merger operate as an amendment to the limited liability company's articles of organization.

§ 906. Effect of Merger

(a) When a merger takes effect:

(1) the separate existence of each limited liability company and other entity that is a party to the merger, other than the surviving entity, terminates;

(2) all property owned by each of the limited liability companies and other entities that are party to the merger vests in the surviving entity;

(3) all debts, liabilities, and other obligations of each limited liability company and other entity that is party to the merger become the obligations of the surviving entity;

(4) an action or proceeding pending by or against a limited liability company or other party to a merger may be continued as if the merger had not occurred or the surviving entity may be substituted as a party to the action or proceeding; and

(5) except as prohibited by other law, all the rights, privileges, immunities, powers, and purposes of every limited liability company and other entity that is a party to a merger vest in the surviving entity.

(b) The [Secretary of State] is an agent for service of process in an action or proceeding against the surviving foreign entity to enforce an obligation of any party to a merger if the surviving foreign entity fails to appoint or maintain an agent designated for service of process in this

State or the agent for service of process cannot with reasonable diligence be found at the designated office. Upon receipt of process, the [Secretary of State] shall send a copy of the process by registered or certified mail, return receipt requested, to the surviving entity at the address set forth in the articles of merger. Service is effected under this subsection at the earliest of:

(1) the date the company receives the process, notice, or demand;

(2) the date shown on the return receipt, if signed on behalf of the company; or

(3) five days after its deposit in the mail, if mailed postpaid and correctly addressed.

(c) A member of the surviving limited liability company is liable for all obligations of a party to the merger for which the member was personally liable before the merger.

(d) Unless otherwise agreed, a merger of a limited liability company that is not the surviving entity in the merger does not require the limited liability company to wind up its business under this [Act] or pay its liabilities and distribute its assets pursuant to this [Act].

(e) Articles of merger serve as articles of dissolution for a limited liability company that is not the surviving entity in the merger.

§ 907. [Article] not Exclusive

This [article] does not preclude an entity from being converted or merged under other law.

[ARTICLE] 10

FOREIGN LIMITED LIABILITY COMPANIES

§ 1001. Law Governing Foreign Limited Liability Companies

(a) The laws of the State or other jurisdiction under which a foreign limited liability company is organized govern its organization and internal affairs and the liability of its managers, members, and their transferees.

(b) A foreign limited liability company may not be denied a certificate of authority by reason of any difference between the laws of another jurisdiction under which the foreign company is organized and the laws of this State.

(c) A certificate of authority does not authorize a foreign limited liability company to engage in any business or exercise any power that a limited liability company may not engage in or exercise in this State.

Comment

The law where a foreign limited liability company is organized, rather than this Act, governs that company's internal affairs and the liability of its owners. Accordingly, any difference between the laws of the foreign jurisdiction and this Act will not constitute grounds for denial of a certificate of authority to transact business in this State. However, a foreign limited liability company transacting business in this State by virtue of a certificate of authority is limited to the business and powers that a limited liability company may lawfully pursue and exercise under Section 112.

§ 1002. Application for Certificate of Authority

(a) A foreign limited liability company may apply for a certificate of authority to transact business in this State by delivering an application to the [Secretary of State] for filing. The application must set forth:

(1) the name of the foreign company or, if its name is unavailable for use in this State, a name that satisfies the requirements of Section 1005;

(2) the name of the State or country under whose law it is organized;

(3) the street address of its principal office;

(4) the address of its initial designated office in this State;

(5) the name and street address of its initial agent for service of process in this State;

(6) whether the duration of the company is for a specified term and, if so, the period specified;

(7) whether the company is manager-managed, and, if so, the name and address of each initial manager; and

(8) whether the members of the company are to be liable for its debts and obligations under a provision similar to Section 303(c).

(b) A foreign limited liability company shall deliver with the completed application a certificate of existence or a record of similar import authenticated by the secretary of state or other official having custody of company records in the State or country under whose law it is organized.

Comment

As with articles of organization, the application must be signed and filed with the filing office. See Sections 105, 107 (name registration), 205, 206, 209 (liability for false statements), and 1005.

§ 1003. Activities not Constituting Transacting Business

(a) Activities of a foreign limited liability company that do not constitute transacting business in this State within the meaning of this [article] include:

(1) maintaining, defending, or settling an action or proceeding;

(2) holding meetings of its members or managers or carrying on any other activity concerning its internal affairs;

(3) maintaining bank accounts;

(4) maintaining offices or agencies for the transfer, exchange, and registration of the foreign company's own securities or maintaining trustees or depositories with respect to those securities;

(5) selling through independent contractors;

(6) soliciting or obtaining orders, whether by mail or through employees or agents or otherwise, if the orders require acceptance outside this State before they become contracts;

(7) creating or acquiring indebtedness, mortgages, or security interests in real or personal property;

(8) securing or collecting debts or enforcing mortgages or other security interests in property securing the debts, and holding, protecting, and maintaining property so acquired;

(9) conducting an isolated transaction that is completed within 30 days and is not one in the course of similar transactions of a like manner; and

(10) transacting business in interstate commerce.

(b) For purposes of this [article], the ownership in this State of income-producing real property or tangible personal property, other than property excluded under subsection (a), constitutes transacting business in this State.

(c) This section does not apply in determining the contacts or activities that may subject a foreign limited liability company to service of process, taxation, or regulation under any other law of this State.

§ 1004. Issuance of Certificate of Authority

Unless the [Secretary of State] determines that an application for a certificate of authority fails to comply as to form with the filing requirements of this [Act], the [Secretary of State], upon payment of all filing fees, shall file the application and send a receipt for it and the fees to the limited liability company or its representative.

§ 1005. Name of Foreign Limited Liability Company

(a) If the name of a foreign limited liability company does not satisfy the requirements of Section 105, the company, to obtain or maintain a certificate of authority to transact business in this State, must use a fictitious name to transact business in this State if its real name is unavailable and it delivers to the [Secretary of State] for filing a copy of the resolution of its managers, in the case of a manager-managed company, or of its members, in the case of a member-managed company, adopting the fictitious name.

(b) Except as authorized by subsections (c) and (d), the name, including a fictitious name to be used to transact business in this State, of a foreign limited liability company must be distinguishable upon the records of the [Secretary of State] from:

(1) the name of any corporation, limited partnership, or company incorporated, organized, or authorized to transact business in this State;

(2) a name reserved or registered under Section 106 or 107; and

(3) the fictitious name of another foreign limited liability company authorized to transact business in this State.

(c) A foreign limited liability company may apply to the [Secretary of State] for authority to use in this State a name that is not distinguishable upon the records of the [Secretary of State] from a name described in subsection (b). The [Secretary of State] shall authorize use of the name applied for if:

(1) the present user, registrant, or owner of a reserved name consents to the use in a record and submits an undertaking in form satisfactory to the [Secretary of State] to change its name to a name that is distinguishable upon the records of the [Secretary of State] from the name of the foreign applying limited liability company; or

(2) the applicant delivers to the [Secretary of State] a certified copy of a final judgment of a court establishing the applicant's right to use the name applied for in this State.

(d) A foreign limited liability company may use in this State the name, including the fictitious name, of another domestic or foreign entity that is used in this State if the other entity is incorporated, organized, or authorized to transact business in this State and the foreign limited liability company:

(1) has merged with the other entity;

(2) has been formed by reorganization of the other entity; or

(3) has acquired all or substantially all of the assets, including the name, of the other entity.

(e) If a foreign limited liability company authorized to transact business in this State changes its name to one that does not satisfy the requirements of Section 105, it may not transact business in this State under the name as changed until it adopts a name satisfying the requirements of Section 105 and obtains an amended certificate of authority.

§ 1006. Revocation of Certificate of Authority

(a) A certificate of authority of a foreign limited liability company to transact business in this State may be revoked by the [Secretary of State] in the manner provided in subsection (b) if:

(1) the company fails to:

(i) pay any fees, taxes, and penalties owed to this State;

(ii) deliver its annual report required under Section 211 to the [Secretary of State] within 60 days after it is due;

(iii) appoint and maintain an agent for service of process as required by this [article]; or

(iv) file a statement of a change in the name or business address of the agent as required by this [article]; or

(2) a misrepresentation has been made of any material matter in any application, report, affidavit, or other record submitted by the company pursuant to this [article].

(b) The [Secretary of State] may not revoke a certificate of authority of a foreign limited liability company unless the [Secretary of State] sends the company notice of the revocation, at least 60 days before its effective date, by a record addressed to its agent for service of process in this State, or if the company fails to appoint and maintain a proper agent in this State, addressed to the office required to be maintained by Section 108. The notice must specify the cause for the revocation of the certificate of authority. The authority of the company to transact business in this State ceases on the effective date of the revocation unless the foreign limited liability company cures the failure before that date.

§ 1007. Cancellation of Authority

A foreign limited liability company may cancel its authority to transact business in this State by filing in the office of the [Secretary of State] a certificate of cancellation. Cancellation does not terminate the authority of the [Secretary of State] to accept service of process on the company for [claims for relief] arising out of the transactions of business in this State.

§ 1008. Effect of Failure to Obtain Certificate of Authority

(a) A foreign limited liability company transacting business in this State may not maintain an action or proceeding in this State unless it has a certificate of authority to transact business in this State.

(b) The failure of a foreign limited liability company to have a certificate of authority to transact business in this State does not impair the validity of a contract or act of the company or prevent the foreign limited liability company from defending an action or proceeding in this State.

(c) Limitations on personal liability of managers, members, and their transferees are not waived solely by transacting business in this State without a certificate of authority.

(d) If a foreign limited liability company transacts business in this State without a certificate of authority, it appoints the [Secretary of State] as its agent for service of process for [claims for relief] arising out of the transaction of business in this State.

§ 1009. Action by [Attorney General]

The [Attorney General] may maintain an action to restrain a foreign limited liability company from transacting business in this State in violation of this [article].

[ARTICLE] 11

DERIVATIVE ACTIONS

§ 1101. Right of Action

A member of a limited liability company may maintain an action in the right of the company if the members or managers having authority to do so have refused to commence the action or an effort to cause those members or managers to commence the action is not likely to succeed.

Comment

A member may bring an action on behalf of the company when the members or managers having the authority to pursue the company recovery refuse to do so or an effort to cause them to pursue the recovery is not likely to succeed. See Comments to Section 411(a) (personal action of member against company or another member).

§ 1102. Proper Plaintiff

In a derivative action for a limited liability company, the plaintiff must be a member of the company when the action is commenced; and:

(1) must have been a member at the time of the transaction of which the plaintiff complains; or

(2) the plaintiff's status as a member must have devolved upon the plaintiff by operation of law or pursuant to the terms of the operating agreement from a person who was a member at the time of the transaction.

§ 1103. Pleading

In a derivative action for a limited liability company, the complaint must set forth with particularity the effort of the plaintiff to secure initiation of the action by a member or manager or the reasons for not making the effort.

Comment

There is no obligation of the company or its members or managers to respond to a member demand to bring an action to pursue a company recovery. However, if a company later decides to commence the demanded action or assume control of the derivative litigation, the member's right to commence or control the proceeding ordinarily ends.

§ 1104. Expenses

If a derivative action for a limited liability company is successful, in whole or in part, or if anything is received by the plaintiff as a result of a judgment, compromise, or settlement of an action or claim, the court may award the plaintiff reasonable expenses, including reasonable attorney's fees, and shall direct the plaintiff to remit to the limited liability company the remainder of the proceeds received.

[ARTICLE] 12

MISCELLANEOUS PROVISIONS

§ 1201. Uniformity of Application and Construction

This [Act] shall be applied and construed to effectuate its general purpose to make uniform the law with respect to the subject of this [Act] among States enacting it.

§ 1202. Short Title

This [Act] may be cited as the Uniform Limited Liability Company Act (1996).

§ 1203. Severability Clause

If any provision of this [Act] or its application to any person or circumstance is held invalid, the invalidity does not affect other provisions or applications of this [Act] which can be given effect without the invalid provision or application, and to this end the provisions of this [Act] are severable.

§ 1204. Effective Date

This [Act] takes effect [______].

§ 1205. Transitional Provisions

(a) Before January 1, 199__, this [Act] governs only a limited liability company organized:

(1) after the effective date of this [Act], unless the company is continuing the business of a dissolved limited liability company under [Section of the existing Limited Liability Company Act]; and

(2) before the effective date of this [Act], which elects, as provided by subsection (c), to be governed by this [Act].

(b) On and after January 1, 199__, this [Act] governs all limited liability companies.

(c) Before January 1, 199__, a limited liability company voluntarily may elect, in the manner provided in its operating agreement or by law for amending the operating agreement, to be governed by this [Act].

Comment

Under subsection (a)(1), the application of the Act is mandatory for all companies formed after the effective date of the Act determined under Section 1204. Under subsection (a)(2), the application of the Act is permissive, by election under subsection (c), for existing companies for a period of time specified in subsection (b) after which application becomes mandatory. This affords existing companies and their members an opportunity to consider the changes effected by this Act and to amend their operating agreements, if appropriate. If no election is made, the Act becomes effective after the period specified in subsection (b). The period specified by adopting States may vary, but a period of five years is a common period in similar cases.

§ 1206. Savings Clause

This [Act] does not affect an action or proceeding commenced or right accrued before the effective date of this [Act].

*

DELAWARE LIMITED LIABILITY COMPANY ACT

(Delaware Code, Title 6, Chapter 18)

Table of Sections

SUBCHAPTER I. GENERAL PROVISIONS

SUBCHAPTER II. FORMATION; CERTIFICATE OF FORMATION

SUBCHAPTER III. MEMBERS

SUBCHAPTER IV. MANAGERS

SUBCHAPTER V. FINANCE

SUBCHAPTER VI. DISTRIBUTIONS AND RESIGNATION

SUBCHAPTER VII. ASSIGNMENT OF LIMITED LIABILITY COMPANY INTERESTS

SUBCHAPTER I. GENERAL PROVISIONS

§ 18–101. Definitions

As used in this chapter unless the context otherwise requires:

(1) "Bankruptcy" means an event that causes a person to cease to be a member as provided in § 18–304 of this title.

(2) "Certificate of formation" means the certificate referred to in § 18–201 of this title, and the certificate as amended.

(3) "Contribution" means any cash, property, services rendered or a promissory note or other obligation to contribute cash or property or to perform services, which a person contributes to a limited liability company in the person's capacity as a member.

(4) "Foreign limited liability company" means a limited liability company formed under the laws of any state or under the laws of any foreign country or other foreign jurisdiction and denominated as such under the laws of such state or foreign country or other foreign jurisdiction.

(5) "Knowledge" means a person's actual knowledge of a fact, rather than the person's constructive knowledge of the fact.

(6) "Limited liability company" and "domestic limited liability company" means a limited liability company formed under the laws of the State of Delaware and having 1 or more members.

(7) "Limited liability company agreement" means any agreement (whether referred to as a limited liability company agreement, operating agreement or otherwise), written or oral, of the member or members as to the affairs of a limited liability company and the conduct of its business. A member or manager of a limited liability company or an assignee of a limited liability company interest is bound by the limited liability company agreement whether or not the member or manager or assignee executes the limited liability company agreement. A limited liability company is not required to execute its limited liability company agreement. A limited liability

company is bound by its limited liability company agreement whether or not the limited liability company executes the limited liability company agreement. A limited liability company agreement of a limited liability company having only 1 member shall not be unenforceable by reason of there being only 1 person who is a party to the limited liability company agreement. A limited liability company agreement may provide rights to any person, including a person who is not a party to the limited liability company agreement, to the extent set forth therein. A written limited liability company agreement or another written agreement or writing:

a. May provide that a person shall be admitted as a member of a limited liability company, or shall become an assignee of a limited liability company interest or other rights or powers of a member to the extent assigned:

1. If such person (or a representative authorized by such person orally, in writing or by other action such as payment for a limited liability company interest) executes the limited liability company agreement or any other writing evidencing the intent of such person to become a member or assignee; or

2. Without such execution, if such person (or a representative authorized by such person orally, in writing or by other action such as payment for a limited liability company interest) complies with the conditions for becoming a member or assignee as set forth in the limited liability company agreement or any other writing; and

b. Shall not be unenforceable by reason of its not having been signed by a person being admitted as a member or becoming an assignee as provided in subparagraph a. of this paragraph, or by reason of its having been signed by a representative as provided in this chapter.

(8) "Limited liability company interest" means a member's share of the profits and losses of a limited liability company and a member's right to receive distributions of the limited liability company's assets.

(9) "Liquidating trustee" means a person carrying out the winding up of a limited liability company.

(10) "Manager" means a person who is named as a manager of a limited liability company in, or designated as a manager of a limited liability company pursuant to, a limited liability company agreement or similar instrument under which the limited liability company is formed.

(11) "Member" means a person who has been admitted to a limited liability company as a member as provided in § 18–301 of this title or, in the case of a foreign limited liability company, in

accordance with the laws of the state or foreign country or other foreign jurisdiction under which the foreign limited liability company is organized.

(12) "Person" means a natural person, partnership (whether general or limited), limited liability company, trust, estate, association (including any group, organization, co-tenancy, plan, board, council or committee), corporation, government (including a country, state, county or any other governmental subdivision, agency or instrumentality), custodian, nominee or any other individual or entity (or series thereof) in its own or any representative capacity, in each case, whether domestic or foreign.

(13) "Personal representative" means, as to a natural person, the executor, administrator, guardian, conservator or other legal representative thereof and, as to a person other than a natural person, the legal representative or successor thereof.

(14) "State" means the District of Columbia or the Commonwealth of Puerto Rico or any state, territory, possession or other jurisdiction of the United States other than the State of Delaware.

§ 18–102. Name Set Forth in Certificate

The name of each limited liability company as set forth in its certificate of formation:

(1) Shall contain the words "Limited Liability Company" or the abbreviation "L.L.C." or the designation "LLC";

(2) May contain the name of a member or manager;

(3) Must be such as to distinguish it upon the records in the office of the Secretary of State from the name on such records of any corporation, partnership, limited partnership, statutory trust or limited liability company reserved, registered, formed or organized under the laws of the State of Delaware or qualified to do business or registered as a foreign corporation, foreign limited partnership, foreign statutory trust, foreign partnership, or foreign limited liability company in the State of Delaware; provided however, that a limited liability company may register under any name which is not such as to distinguish it upon the records in the office of the Secretary of State from the name on such records of any domestic or foreign corporation, partnership, limited partnership, statutory trust or limited liability company reserved, registered, formed or organized under the laws of the State of Delaware with the written consent of the other corporation, partnership, limited partnership, statutory trust or limited liability company, which written consent shall be filed with the Secretary of State; and

(4) May contain the following words: "Company," "Association," "Club," "Foundation," "Fund," "Institute," "Society," "Un-

ion," "Syndicate," "Limited" or "Trust" (or abbreviations of like import).

§ 18–103. Reservation of Name

(a) The exclusive right to the use of a name may be reserved by:

(1) Any person intending to organize a limited liability company under this chapter and to adopt that name;

(2) Any domestic limited liability company or any foreign limited liability company registered in the State of Delaware which, in either case, proposes to change its name;

(3) Any foreign limited liability company intending to register in the State of Delaware and adopt that name; and

(4) Any person intending to organize a foreign limited liability company and intending to have it register in the State of Delaware and adopt that name.

(b) The reservation of a specified name shall be made by filing with the Secretary of State an application, executed by the applicant, specifying the name to be reserved and the name and address of the applicant. If the Secretary of State finds that the name is available for use by a domestic or foreign limited liability company, the Secretary shall reserve the name for the exclusive use of the applicant for a period of 120 days. Once having so reserved a name, the same applicant may again reserve the same name for successive 120–day periods. The right to the exclusive use of a reserved name may be transferred to any other person by filing in the office of the Secretary of State a notice of the transfer, executed by the applicant for whom the name was reserved, specifying the name to be transferred and the name and address of the transferee. The reservation of a specified name may be cancelled by filing with the Secretary of State a notice of cancellation, executed by the applicant or transferee, specifying the name reservation to be cancelled and the name and address of the applicant or transferee. Unless the Secretary of State finds that any application, notice of transfer, or notice of cancellation filed with the Secretary of State as required by this subsection does not conform to law, upon receipt of all filing fees required by law the Secretary shall prepare and return to the person who filed such instrument a copy of the filed instrument with a notation thereon of the action taken by the Secretary of State.

(c) A fee as set forth in § 18–1105(a)(1) of this title shall be paid at the time of the initial reservation of any name, at the time of the renewal of any such reservation and at the time of the filing of a notice of the transfer or cancellation of any such reservation.

§ 18–104. Registered Office; Registered Agent [Effective Until Jan. 1, 2007]

(a) Each limited liability company shall have and maintain in the State of Delaware:

(1) A registered office, which may but need not be a place of its business in the State of Delaware; and

(2) A registered agent for service of process on the limited liability company, which agent may be either an individual resident of the State of Delaware whose business office is identical with the limited liability company's registered office, or a domestic corporation, or a domestic limited partnership, or a domestic limited liability company, or a domestic statutory trust, or a foreign corporation, or a foreign limited partnership, or a foreign limited liability company authorized to do business in the State of Delaware having a business office identical with such registered office, which is generally open during normal business hours to accept service of process and otherwise perform the functions of a registered agent, or the limited liability company itself.

(b) A registered agent may change the address of the registered office of the limited liability company(ies) for which it is registered agent to another address in the State of Delaware by paying a fee as set forth in § 18-1105(a)(2) of this title and filing with the Secretary of State a certificate, executed by such registered agent, setting forth the address at which such registered agent has maintained the registered office for each of the limited liability companies for which it is a registered agent, and further certifying to the new address to which each such registered office will be changed on a given day, and at which new address such registered agent will thereafter maintain the registered office for each of the limited liability companies for which it is a registered agent. Upon the filing of such certificate, the Secretary of State shall furnish to the registered agent a certified copy of the same under the Secretary's hand and seal of office, and thereafter, or until further change of address, as authorized by law, the registered office in the State of Delaware of each of the limited liability companies for which the agent is a registered agent shall be located at the new address of the registered agent thereof as given in the certificate. In the event of a change of name of any person acting as a registered agent of a limited liability company, such registered agent shall file with the Secretary of State a certificate executed by such registered agent setting forth the new name of such registered agent, the name of such registered agent before it was changed, and the address at which such registered agent has maintained the registered office for each of the limited liability companies for which it is a registered agent, and shall pay a fee as set forth in § 18-1105(a)(2) of this title. Upon the filing of such certificate, the Secretary of State shall furnish to the registered agent a certified copy of the certificate under the Secretary of State's own hand and seal of office. A change of name of any person acting as a registered agent of a limited liability company as a result of a merger or consolidation of the registered agent with or into another person which succeeds to its assets and liabilities by operation of law shall be deemed a change of name for purposes of this section. Filing a certificate under this section shall be deemed to be an amendment of the certificate of formation of each limited liability company affected thereby, and each such limited liability company shall not be required to take any further action with respect thereto to amend its certificate of formation under § 18–202 of this title. Any registered agent filing a certificate under this section shall promptly, upon such filing, deliver a copy of any such certificate to each limited liability company affected thereby.

(c) The registered agent of 1 or more limited liability companies may resign and appoint a successor registered agent by paying a fee as set forth in § 18–1105(a)(2) of this title and filing a certificate with the Secretary of State stating that it resigns and the name and address of the successor registered agent. There shall be attached to such certificate a statement of each affected limited liability company ratifying and approving such change of registered agent. Upon such filing, the successor registered agent shall become the registered agent of such limited liability companies as have ratified and approved such substitution, and the successor registered agent's address, as stated in such certificate, shall become the address of each such limited liability company's registered office in the State of Delaware. The Secretary of State shall then issue a certificate that the successor registered agent has become the registered agent of the limited liability companies so ratifying and approving such change and setting out the names of such limited liability companies. Filing of such certificate of resignation shall be deemed to be an amendment of the certificate of formation of each limited liability company affected thereby, and each such limited liability company shall not be required to take any further action with respect thereto to amend its certificate of formation under § 18–202 of this title.

(d) The registered agent of 1 or more limited liability companies may resign without appointing a successor registered agent by paying a fee as set forth in § 18–1105(a)(2) of this title and filing a certificate of resignation with the Secretary of State, but such resignation shall not become effective until 30 days after the certificate is filed. The certificate shall contain a statement that written notice of resignation was given to each affected limited liability company at least 30 days prior to the filing of the certificate by mailing or delivering such notice to the limited liability company at its address last known to the registered agent and shall set forth the date of such notice. After receipt of the notice of the resignation of its registered agent, the limited liability company for which such registered agent was acting shall obtain and designate a new registered agent, to take the place of the registered agent so resigning. If such limited liability company fails to obtain and designate a new registered agent as aforesaid prior to the expiration of the period of 30 days after the filing by the registered agent of the certificate of resignation, the certificate of formation of such limited liability company shall be deemed to be canceled. After the resignation of the registered agent shall have become effective as provided in this section and if no new registered agent shall have been obtained and designated in the time and manner aforesaid, service of legal process against each limited liability company for which the resigned registered agent had been acting shall thereafter be upon the Secretary of State in accordance with § 18–105 of this title.

§ 18–104. Registered Office; Registered Agent [Effective Jan. 1, 2007]

(a) Each limited liability company shall have and maintain in the State of Delaware:

(1) A registered office, which may but need not be a place of its business in the State of Delaware; and

(2) A registered agent for service of process on the limited liability company, which agent may be any of:

a. The limited liability company itself,

b. An individual resident in the State of Delaware,

c. A domestic limited liability company (other than the limited liability company itself), a domestic corporation, a domestic partnership (whether general (including a limited liability partnership) or limited (including a limited liability limited partnership)), or a domestic statutory trust, or

d. A foreign corporation, a foreign partnership (whether general (including a limited liability partnership) or limited (including a limited liability limited partnership)), a foreign limited liability company, or a foreign statutory trust.

(b) A registered agent may change the address of the registered office of the limited liability company(ies) for which it is registered agent to another address in the State of Delaware by paying a fee as set forth in § 18–1105(a)(2) of this title and filing with the Secretary of State a certificate, executed by such registered agent, setting forth the address at which such registered agent has maintained the registered office for each of the limited liability companies for which it is a registered agent, and further certifying to the new address to which each such registered office will be changed on a given day, and at which new address such registered agent will thereafter maintain the registered office for each of the limited liability companies for which it is a registered agent. Upon the filing of such certificate, the Secretary of State shall furnish to the registered agent a certified copy of the same under the Secretary's hand and seal of office, and thereafter, or until further change of address, as authorized by law, the registered office in the State of Delaware of each of the limited liability companies for which the agent is a registered agent shall be located at the new address of the registered agent thereof as given in the certificate. In the event of a change of name of any person acting as a registered agent of a limited liability company, such registered agent shall file with the Secretary of State a certificate executed by such registered agent setting forth the new name of such registered agent, the name of such registered agent before it was changed, and the address at which such registered agent has maintained the registered office for each of the limited liability companies for which it is a registered agent, and shall pay a fee as set forth in § 18–1105(a)(2) of this title. Upon the filing of such certificate, the Secretary of State shall furnish to the registered agent a certified copy of the certificate under the Secretary of State's own hand and seal of office. A change of name of any person acting as a registered agent of a limited liability company as a result of a merger or consolidation of the registered agent with or into another person which succeeds to its assets and liabilities by operation of law shall be deemed a change of name for purposes of this section. Filing a certificate under this section shall be deemed to be an amendment of the certificate of formation of each limited liability company affected thereby, and each such limited liability company shall not be required to take any further action with respect thereto to amend its certificate of formation under § 18–202 of this title. Any registered agent filing a certificate under this section shall promptly, upon such filing, deliver a copy of any such certificate to each limited liability company affected thereby.

(c) The registered agent of 1 or more limited liability companies may resign and appoint a successor registered agent by paying a fee as set forth in § 18–1105(a)(2) of this title and filing a certificate with the Secretary of State stating that it resigns and the name and address of the successor registered agent. There shall be attached to such certificate a statement of each affected limited liability company ratifying and approving such change of registered agent. Upon such filing, the successor registered agent shall become the registered agent of such limited liability companies as have ratified and approved such substitution, and the successor registered agent's address, as stated in such certificate, shall become the address of each such limited liability company's registered office in the State of Delaware. The Secretary of State shall then issue a certificate that the successor registered agent has become the registered agent of the limited liability companies so ratifying and approving such change and setting out the names of such limited liability companies. Filing of such certificate of resignation shall be deemed to be an amendment of the certificate of formation of each limited liability company affected thereby, and each such limited liability company shall not be required to take any further action with respect thereto to amend its certificate of formation under § 18–202 of this title.

(d) The registered agent of 1 or more limited liability companies may resign without appointing a successor registered agent by paying a fee as set forth in § 18–1105(a)(2) of this title and filing a certificate of resignation with the Secretary of State, but such resignation shall not become effective until 30 days after the certificate is filed. The certificate shall contain a statement that written notice of resignation was given to each affected limited liability company at least 30 days prior to the filing of the certificate by mailing or delivering such notice to the limited liability company at its address last known to the registered agent and shall set forth the date of such notice. After receipt of the notice of the resignation of its registered agent, the limited liability company for which such registered agent was acting shall obtain and designate a new registered agent, to take the place of the registered agent so resigning. If such limited liability company fails to obtain and designate a new registered agent as aforesaid prior to the expiration of the period of 30 days after the filing by the registered agent of the certificate of resignation, the certificate of formation of such limited liability company shall be deemed to be canceled. After the resignation of the registered agent shall have become effective as provided in this section and if no new registered agent shall have been obtained and designated in the time and manner aforesaid, service of legal process against each limited liability company for which the resigned registered agent had been acting shall thereafter be upon the Secretary of State in accordance with § 18–105 of this title.

(e) Every registered agent shall:

(1) If an entity, maintain a business office in the State of Delaware which is generally open, or if an individual, be generally present at a designated location in the State of Delaware, at sufficiently frequent times to accept service of process and otherwise perform the functions of a registered agent;

(2) If a foreign entity, be authorized to transact business in the State of Delaware;

(3) Accept service of process and other communications directed to the limited liability companies for which it serves as registered agent and forward same to the limited liability company to which the service or communication is directed; and

(4) Forward to the limited liability companies for which it serves as registered agent the statement for the annual tax described in § 18–1107 of this title or an electronic notification of same in a form satisfactory to the Secretary of State.

(f) Any registered agent who at any time serves as registered agent for more than 50 entities (a "commercial registered agent"), whether domestic or foreign, shall satisfy and comply with the following qualifications:

(1) A natural person serving as a commercial registered agent shall:

a. Maintain a principal residence or a principal place of business in the State of Delaware;

b. Maintain a Delaware business license;

c. Be generally present at a designated location within the State of Delaware during normal business hours to accept service of process and otherwise perform the functions of a registered agent as specified in subsection (e) of this section; and

d. Provide the Secretary of State upon request with such information identifying and enabling communication with such commercial registered agent as the Secretary of State shall require.

(2) A domestic or foreign corporation, a domestic or foreign partnership (whether general (including a limited liability partnership) or limited (including a limited liability limited partnership)), a domestic or foreign limited liability company, or a domestic or foreign statutory trust serving as a commercial registered agent shall:

a. Have a business office within the State of Delaware which is generally open during normal business hours to accept service of process and otherwise perform the functions of a registered agent as specified in subsection (e) of this section;

b. Maintain a Delaware business license;

c. Have generally present at such office during normal business hours an officer, director or managing agent who is a natural person; and

d. Provide the Secretary of State upon request with such information identifying and enabling communication with such commercial registered agent as the Secretary of State shall require.

(3) For purposes of this subsection and subsection (i)(2)a. of this section, a commercial registered agent shall also include any registered agent which has an officer, director or managing agent in common with any other registered agent or agents if such registered agents at any time during such common service as officer, director or managing agent collectively served as registered agents for more than 50 entities, whether domestic or foreign.

(g) Every limited liability company formed under the laws of the State of Delaware or qualified to do business in the State of Delaware shall provide to its registered agent and update from time to time as necessary the name, business address and business telephone number of a natural person who is a member, manager, officer, employee or designated agent of the limited liability company, who is then authorized to receive communications from the registered agent. Such person shall be deemed the communications contact for the limited liability company. Every registered agent shall retain (in paper or electronic form) the above information concerning the current communications contact for each limited liability company for which that registered agent serves as registered agent. If the limited liability company fails to provide the registered agent with a current communications contact, the registered agent may resign as the registered agent for such limited liability company pursuant to this section.

(h) The Secretary of State is authorized to issue such rules and regulations as may be necessary or appropriate to carry out the enforcement of subsections (e), (f) and (g) of this section, and to take actions reasonable and necessary to assure registered agents' compliance with subsections (e), (f) and (g) of this section. Such actions may include refusal to file documents submitted by a registered agent.

(i) Upon application of the Secretary of State, the Court of Chancery may enjoin any person or entity from serving as a registered agent or as an officer, director or managing agent of a registered agent.

(1) Upon the filing of a complaint by the Secretary of State pursuant to this section, the court may make such orders respecting such proceeding as it deems appropriate, and may enter such orders granting interim or final relief as it deems proper under the circumstances.

(2) Any 1 or more of the following grounds shall be a sufficient basis to grant an injunction pursuant to this section:

a. With respect to any registered agent who at any time within 1 year immediately prior to the filing of the Secretary of State's complaint is a commercial registered agent, failure after notice and warning to comply with the qualifications set forth in subsection (e) of this section and/or the requirements of subsections (f) or (g) of this section above;

b. The person serving as a registered agent, or any person who is an officer, director or managing agent of an entity registered agent, has been convicted of a felony or any crime which includes an element of dishonesty or fraud or involves moral turpitude; or

c. The registered agent has engaged in conduct in connection with acting as a registered agent that is intended to or likely to deceive or defraud the public.

(3) With respect to any order the court enters pursuant to this section with respect to an entity that has acted as a registered agent, the court may also direct such order to any person who has served as an officer, director or managing agent of such registered agent. Any person who, on or after January 1, 2007, serves as an officer, director or managing agent of an entity acting as a registered agent in the State of Delaware shall be deemed thereby to have consented to the appointment of such registered agent as agent upon whom service of process may be made in any action brought pursuant to this section, and service as an officer, director or managing agent of an entity acting as a registered agent in the State of Delaware shall be a signification of the consent of such person that any process when so served shall be of the same legal force and validity as if

served upon such person within the State of Delaware, and such appointment of the registered agent shall be irrevocable.

(4) Upon the entry of an order by the court enjoining any person or entity from acting as a registered agent, the Secretary of State shall mail or deliver notice of such order to each affected limited liability company:

a. That has specified the address of a place of business in a record of the Secretary of State, to the address specified, or

b. An address of which the Secretary of State has obtained from the limited liability company's former registered agent, to the address obtained.

If such a limited liability company is a domestic limited liability company and fails to obtain and designate a new registered agent within 30 days after such notice is given, the certificate of formation of such limited liability company shall be deemed to be cancelled. If such a limited liability company is a foreign limited liability company and fails to obtain and designate a new registered agent within 30 days after such notice is given, such foreign limited liability company shall not be permitted to do business in the State of Delaware and its registration shall be deemed to be cancelled. If any other affected limited liability company is a domestic limited liability company and fails to obtain and designate a new registered agent within 60 days after entry of an order by the court enjoining such limited liability company's registered agent from acting as a registered agent, the certificate of formation of such limited liability company shall be deemed to be cancelled. If any other affected limited liability company is a foreign limited liability company and fails to obtain and designate a new registered agent within 60 days after entry of an order by court enjoining such limited liability company's registered agent from acting as a registered agent, such foreign limited liability company shall not be permitted to do business in the State of Delaware and its registration shall be deemed to be cancelled. If the court enjoins a person or entity from acting as a registered agent as provided in this section and no new registered agent shall have been obtained and designated in the time and manner aforesaid, service of legal process against the limited liability company for which the registered agent had been acting shall thereafter be upon the Secretary of State in accordance with § 18–105 or § 18–911 of this title. The Court of Chancery may, upon application of the Secretary of State on notice to the former registered agent, enter such orders as it deems appropriate to give the Secretary of State access to information in the former registered agent's possession in order to facilitate communication with the limited liability companies the former registered agent served.

(j) The Secretary of State is authorized to make a list of registered agents available to the public, and to establish such qualifications and issue such rules and regulations with respect to such listing as the Secretary of State deems necessary or appropriate.

§ 18–105. Service of Process on Domestic Limited Liability Companies

(a) Service of legal process upon any domestic limited liability company shall be made by delivering a copy personally to any manager of the limited liability company in the State of Delaware or the registered agent of the limited liability company in the State of Delaware, or by leaving it at the dwelling house or usual place of abode in the State of Delaware of any such manager or registered agent (if the registered agent be an individual), or at the registered office or other place of business of the limited liability company in the State of Delaware. If the registered agent be a corporation, service of process upon it as such may be made by serving, in the State of Delaware, a copy thereof on the president, vice-president, secretary, assistant secretary or any director of the corporate registered agent. Service by copy left at the dwelling house or usual place of abode of a manager or registered agent, or at the registered office or other place of business of the limited liability company in the State of Delaware, to be effective, must be delivered thereat at least 6 days before the return date of the process, and in the presence of an adult person, and the officer serving the process shall distinctly state the manner of service in the officer's return thereto. Process returnable forthwith must be delivered personally to the manager or registered agent.

(b) In case the officer whose duty it is to serve legal process cannot by due diligence serve the process in any manner provided for by subsection (a) of this section, it shall be lawful to serve the process against the limited liability company upon the Secretary of State, and such service shall be as effectual for all intents and purposes as if made in any of the ways provided for in subsection (a) of this section. In the event that service is effected through the Secretary of State in accordance with this subsection, the Secretary of State shall forthwith notify the limited liability company by letter, certified mail, return receipt requested, directed to the limited liability company at its address as it appears on the records relating to such limited liability company on file with the Secretary of State or, if no such address appears, at its last registered office. Such letter shall enclose a copy of the process and any other papers served on the Secretary of State pursuant to this subsection. It shall be the duty of the plaintiff in the event of such service to serve process and any other papers in duplicate, to notify the Secretary of State that service is being effected pursuant to this subsection, and to pay the Secretary of State the sum of $50 for the use of the State of Delaware, which sum shall be taxed as part of the costs in the proceeding if the plaintiff shall prevail therein. The Secretary of State shall maintain an alphabetical record of any such service setting forth the name of the plaintiff and defendant, the title, docket number and nature of the proceeding in which process has been served upon the Secretary, the fact that service has been effected pursuant to this subsection, the return date thereof, and the day and hour when the service was made. The

Secretary of State shall not be required to retain such information for a period longer than 5 years from the Secretary's receipt of the service of process.

§ 18–106. Nature of Business Permitted; Powers

(a) A limited liability company may carry on any lawful business, purpose or activity, whether or not for profit, with the exception of the business of banking as defined in § 126 of Title 8.

(b) A limited liability company shall possess and may exercise all the powers and privileges granted by this chapter or by any other law or by its limited liability company agreement, together with any powers incidental thereto, including such powers and privileges as are necessary or convenient to the conduct, promotion or attainment of the business, purposes or activities of the limited liability company.

(c) Notwithstanding any provision of this chapter to the contrary, without limiting the general powers enumerated in subsection (b) of this section, a limited liability company shall, subject to such standards and restrictions, if any, as are set forth in its limited liability company agreement, have the power and authority to make contracts of guaranty and suretyship and enter into interest rate, basis, currency, hedge or other swap agreements or cap, floor, put, call, option, exchange or collar agreements, derivative agreements, or other agreements similar to any of the foregoing.

§ 18–107. Business Transactions of Member or Manager with the Limited Liability Company

Except as provided in a limited liability company agreement, a member or manager may lend money to, borrow money from, act as a surety, guarantor or endorser for, guarantee or assume 1 or more obligations of, provide collateral for, and transact other business with, a limited liability company and, subject to other applicable law, has the same rights and obligations with respect to any such matter as a person who is not a member or manager.

§ 18–108. Indemnification

Subject to such standards and restrictions, if any, as are set forth in its limited liability company agreement, a limited liability company may, and shall have the power to, indemnify and hold harmless any member or manager or other person from and against any and all claims and demands whatsoever.

§ 18–109. Service of Process on Managers and Liquidating Trustees

(a) A manager or a liquidating trustee of a limited liability company may be served with process in the manner prescribed in this section in all civil actions or proceedings brought in the State of Delaware involving or relating to the business of the limited liability company or a violation by the manager or the liquidating trustee of a duty to the limited liability company, or any member of the limited liability company, whether or not the manager or the liquidating trustee is a manager or a liquidating trustee at the time suit is commenced. A manager's or a liquidating trustee's serving as such constitutes such person's consent to the appointment of the registered agent of the limited liability company (or, if there is none, the Secretary of State) as such person's agent upon whom service of process may be made as provided in this section. Such service as a manager or a liquidating trustee shall signify the consent of such manager or liquidating trustee that any process when so served shall be of the same legal force and validity as if served upon such manager or liquidating trustee within the State of Delaware and such appointment of the registered agent (or, if there is none, the Secretary of State) shall be irrevocable. As used in this subsection (a) and in subsections (b), (c) and (d) of this section, the term "manager" refers (i) to a person who is a manager as defined in § 18-101(10) of this title and (ii) to a person, whether or not a member of a limited liability company, who, although not a manager as defined in § 18-101(10) of this title, participates materially in the management of the limited liability company; provided however, that the power to elect or otherwise select or to participate in the election or selection of a person to be a manager as defined in § 18-101(10) of this title shall not, by itself, constitute participation in the management of the limited liability company.

(b) Service of process shall be effected by serving the registered agent (or, if there is none, the Secretary of State) with 1 copy of such process in the manner provided by law for service of writs of summons. In the event service is made under this subsection upon the Secretary of State, the plaintiff shall pay to the Secretary of State the sum of $50 for the use of the State of Delaware, which sum shall be taxed as part of the costs of the proceeding if the plaintiff shall prevail therein. In addition, the Prothonotary or the Register in Chancery of the court in which the civil action or proceeding is pending shall, within 7 days of such service, deposit in the United States mails, by registered mail, postage prepaid, true and attested copies of the process, together with a statement that service is being made pursuant to this section, addressed to such manager or liquidating trustee at the registered office of the limited liability company and at the manager's or liquidating trustee's address last known to the party desiring to make such service.

(c) In any action in which any such manager or liquidating trustee has been served with process as hereinabove provided, the time in which a defendant shall be required to appear and file a responsive pleading shall be computed from the date of mailing by the Prothonotary or the Register in Chancery as provided in subsection (b) of this section; however, the court in which such action has been commenced may order such continuance or continuances as may be necessary to afford such manager or liquidating trustee reasonable opportunity to defend the action.

(d) In a written limited liability company agreement or other writing, a manager or member may consent to be subject to the nonexclusive jurisdiction of the courts of, or arbitration in, a specified jurisdiction, or the exclusive jurisdiction of the courts of the State of Delaware, or the exclusivity of arbitration in a specified jurisdiction or the State of Delaware, and to be served with legal process in the manner prescribed in such limited liability company agreement or other writing. Except by agreeing to arbitrate any arbitrable matter in a specified jurisdiction or in the State of Delaware, a member who is not a manager may not waive its right to maintain a legal action or proceeding in the courts of the State of Delaware with respect to matters relating to the organization or internal affairs of a limited liability company.

(e) Nothing herein contained limits or affects the right to serve process in any other manner now or hereafter provided by law. This section is an extension of and not a limitation upon the right otherwise existing of service of legal process upon nonresidents.

(f) The Court of Chancery and the Superior Court may make all necessary rules respecting the form of process, the manner of issuance and return thereof and such other rules which may be necessary to implement this section and are not inconsistent with this section.

§ 18–110. Contested Matters Relating to Managers; Contested Votes

(a) Upon application of any member or manager, the Court of Chancery may hear and determine the validity of any admission, election, appointment, removal or resignation of a manager of a limited liability company, and the right of any person to become or continue to be a manager of a limited liability company, and, in case the right to serve as a manager is claimed by more than 1 person, may determine the person or persons entitled to serve as managers; and to that end make such order or decree in any such case as may be just and proper, with power to enforce the production of any books, papers and records of the limited liability company relating to the issue. In any such application, the limited liability company shall be named as a party and service of copies of the application upon the registered agent of the limited liability company shall be deemed to be service upon the limited liability company and upon the person or persons whose right to serve as a manager is contested and upon the person or persons, if any, claiming to be a manager or claiming the right to be a manager; and the registered agent shall forward immediately a copy of the application to the limited liability company and to the person or persons whose right to serve as a manager is contested and to the person or persons, if any, claiming to be a manager or the right to be a manager, in a postpaid, sealed, registered letter addressed to such limited liability company and such person or persons at their post-office addresses last known to the registered agent or furnished to the registered agent by the applicant member or manager. The Court may make such order respecting further or other notice of such application as it deems proper under these circumstances.

(b) Upon application of any member or manager, the Court of Chancery may hear and determine the result of any vote of members or managers upon matters as to which the members or managers of the limited liability company, or any class or group of members or managers, have the right to vote pursuant to the limited liability company agreement or other agreement or this chapter (other than the admission, election, appointment, removal or resignation of managers). In any such application, the limited liability company shall be named as a party and service of the application upon the registered agent of the limited liability company shall be deemed to be service upon the limited liability company, and no other party need be joined in order for the Court to adjudicate the result of the vote. The Court may make such order respecting further or other notice of such application as it deems proper under these circumstances.

(c) Nothing herein contained limits or affects the right to serve process in any other manner now or hereafter provided by law. This section is an extension of and not a limitation upon the right otherwise existing of service of legal process upon nonresidents.

§ 18–111. Interpretation and Enforcement of Limited Liability Company Agreement

Any action to interpret, apply or enforce the provisions of a limited liability company agreement, or the duties, obligations or liabilities of a limited liability company to the members or managers of the limited liability company, or the duties, obligations or liabilities among members or managers and of members or managers to the limited liability company, or the rights or powers of, or restrictions on, the limited liability company, members or managers, may be brought in the Court of Chancery.

SUBCHAPTER II. FORMATION; CERTIFICATE OF FORMATION

§ 18–201. Certificate of Formation

(a) In order to form a limited liability company, 1 or more authorized persons must execute a certificate of formation. The certificate of formation shall be filed in the office of the Secretary of State and set forth:

(1) The name of the limited liability company;

(2) The address of the registered office and the name and address of the registered agent for service of process required to be maintained by § 18-104 of this title; and

(3) Any other matters the members determine to include therein.

(b) A limited liability company is formed at the time of the filing of the initial certificate of formation in the office of the Secretary of State or at any later date or time specified in the certificate of formation if, in either case, there has been substantial compliance with the requirements of this section. A limited liability company formed under this chapter shall be a separate legal entity, the existence of which as a separate legal entity shall continue until cancellation of the limited liability company's certificate of formation.

(c) The filing of the certificate of formation in the office of the Secretary of State shall make it unnecessary to file any other documents under Chapter 31 of this title.

(d) A limited liability company agreement may be entered into either before, after or at the time of the filing of a certificate of formation and, whether entered into before, after or at the time of such filing, may be made effective as of the formation of the limited liability company or at such other time or date as provided in the limited liability company agreement.

§ 18-202. Amendment to Certificate of Formation

(a) A certificate of formation is amended by filing a certificate of amendment thereto in the office of the Secretary of State. The certificate of amendment shall set forth:

(1) The name of the limited liability company; and

(2) The amendment to the certificate of formation.

(b) A manager or, if there is no manager, then any member who becomes aware that any statement in a certificate of formation was false when made, or that any matter described has changed making the certificate of formation false in any material respect, shall promptly amend the certificate of formation.

(c) A certificate of formation may be amended at any time for any other proper purpose.

(d) Unless otherwise provided in this chapter or unless a later effective date or time (which shall be a date or time certain) is provided for in the certificate of amendment, a certificate of amendment shall be effective at the time of its filing with the Secretary of State.

§ 18-203. Cancellation of Certificate [Effective Until Jan. 1, 2007]

A certificate of formation shall be cancelled upon the dissolution and the completion of winding up of a limited liability company, or as provided in § 18–104(d) or § 18–1108 of this title, or upon the filing of a certificate of merger or consolidation if the limited liability company is not the surviving or resulting entity in a merger or consolidation or upon the filing of a certificate of transfer, or upon the filing of a certificate of conversion to a non-Delaware entity. A certificate of cancellation shall be filed in the office of the Secretary of State to accomplish the cancellation of a certificate of formation upon the dissolution and the completion of winding up of a limited liability company and shall set forth:

(1) The name of the limited liability company;

(2) The date of filing of its certificate of formation;

(3) The future effective date or time (which shall be a date or time certain) of cancellation if it is not to be effective upon the filing of the certificate; and

(4) Any other information the person filing the certificate of cancellation determines.

§ 18–203. Cancellation of Certificate [Effective Jan. 1, 2007]

A certificate of formation shall be cancelled upon the dissolution and the completion of winding up of a limited liability company, or as provided in § 18–104(d) or § 18–104(i)(4) or § 18–1108 of this title, or upon the filing of a certificate of merger or consolidation if the limited liability company is not the surviving or resulting entity in a merger or consolidation or upon the filing of a certificate of transfer, or upon the filing of a certificate of conversion to a non-Delaware entity. A certificate of cancellation shall be filed in the office of the Secretary of State to accomplish the cancellation of a certificate of formation upon the dissolution and the completion of winding up of a limited liability company and shall set forth:

(1) The name of the limited liability company;

(2) The date of filing of its certificate of formation;

(3) The future effective date or time (which shall be a date or time certain) of cancellation if it is not to be effective upon the filing of the certificate; and

(4) Any other information the person filing the certificate of cancellation determines.

§ 18–204. Execution

(a) Each certificate required by this subchapter to be filed in the office of the Secretary of State shall be executed by 1 or more authorized persons.

(b) Unless otherwise provided in a limited liability company agreement, any person may sign any certificate or amendment thereof or enter into a limited liability company agreement or amendment thereof by an agent, including an attorney-in-fact. An authorization, including a power of attorney, to sign any certificate or amendment thereof or to enter into a limited liability company agreement or amendment thereof need not be in writing, need not be sworn to, verified or acknowledged, and need not be filed in the office of the Secretary of State, but if in writing, must be retained by the limited liability company.

(c) The execution of a certificate by an authorized person constitutes an oath or affirmation, under the penalties of perjury in the third degree, that, to the best of the authorized person's knowledge and belief, the facts stated therein are true.

§ 18-205. Execution, Amendment or Cancellation by Judicial Order

(a) If a person required to execute a certificate required by this subchapter fails or refuses to do so, any other person who is adversely affected by the failure or refusal may petition the Court of Chancery to direct the execution of the certificate. If the Court finds that the execution of the certificate is proper and that any person so designated has failed or refused to execute the certificate, it shall order the Secretary of State to record an appropriate certificate.

(b) If a person required to execute a limited liability company agreement or amendment thereof fails or refuses to do so, any other person who is adversely affected by the failure or refusal may petition the Court of Chancery to direct the execution of the limited liability company agreement or amendment thereof. If the Court finds that the limited liability company agreement or amendment thereof should be executed and that any person required to execute the limited liability company agreement or amendment thereof has failed or refused to do so, it shall enter an order granting appropriate relief.

§ 18-206. Filing [Effective Until Jan. 1, 2007]

(a) The signed copy of the certificate of formation and of any certificates of amendment, correction, amendment of a certificate with a future effective date or time, termination of a certificate with a future effective date or time or cancellation (or of any judicial decree of amendment or cancellation), and of any certificate of merger or consolidation, any restated certificate, any corrected certificate, any certificate of conversion to limited liability company, any certificate of conversion to a non-Delaware entity, any certificate of transfer, any certificate of transfer and continuance, any certificate of limited liability company domestication, and of any certificate of revival shall be delivered to the Secretary of State. A person who executes a certificate as an agent or fiduciary need not exhibit evidence of that person's authority as a prerequisite to filing. Any signature on any certificate authorized to be filed with the Secretary of State under any provision of this chapter may be a facsimile, a conformed signature or an electronically transmitted signature. Upon delivery of any certificate, the Secretary of State shall record the date and time of its delivery. Unless the Secretary of State finds that any certificate does not conform to law, upon receipt of all filing fees required by law the Secretary of State shall:

(1) Certify that the certificate of formation, the certificate of amendment, the certificate of correction, the certificate of amendment of a certificate with a future effective date or time, the certificate of termination of a certificate with a future effective date or time, the certificate of cancellation (or of any judicial decree of amendment or cancellation), the certificate of merger or consolidation, the restated certificate, the corrected certificate, the certificate of conversion to limited liability company, the certificate of conversion to a non-Delaware entity, the certificate of transfer, the certificate of transfer and continuance, the certificate of limited liability company domestication or the certificate of revival has been filed in the Secretary of State's office by endorsing upon the signed certificate the word "Filed," and the date and time of the filing. This endorsement is conclusive of the date and time of its filing in the absence of actual fraud. Except as provided in subdivision (a)(5) or (a)(6) of this section, such date and time of filing of a certificate shall be the date and time of delivery of the certificate;

(2) File and index the endorsed certificate;

(3) Prepare and return to the person who filed it or that person's representative a copy of the signed certificate, similarly endorsed, and shall certify such copy as a true copy of the signed certificate; and

(4) Cause to be entered such information from the certificate as the Secretary of State deems appropriate into the Delaware Corporation Information System or any system which is a successor thereto in the office of the Secretary of State, and such information and a copy of such certificate shall be permanently maintained as a public record on a suitable medium. The Secretary of State is authorized to grant direct access to such system to registered agents subject to the execution of an operating agreement between the Secretary of State and such registered agent. Any registered agent granted such access shall demonstrate the existence of policies to ensure that information entered into the system accurately reflects the content of certificates in the possession of the registered agent at the time of entry.

(5) Upon request made upon or prior to delivery, the Secretary of State may, to the extent deemed practicable, establish as the date and time of filing of a certificate a date and time after its delivery. If the Secretary of State refuses to file any certificate due to an error, omission or other imperfection, the Secretary of State may hold such certificate in suspension, and in such event, upon delivery of a replacement certificate in proper form for filing and tender of the

required fees within 5 business days after notice of such suspension is given to the filer, the Secretary of State shall establish as the date and time of filing of such certificate the date and time that would have been the date and time of filing of the rejected certificate had it been accepted for filing. The Secretary of State shall not issue a certificate of good standing with respect to any limited liability company with a certificate held in suspension pursuant to this subsection. The Secretary of State may establish as the date and time of filing of a certificate the date and time at which information from such certificate is entered pursuant to subdivision (a)(4) of this section if such certificate is delivered on the same date and within 4 hours after such information is entered.

(6) If:

a. Together with the actual delivery of a certificate and tender of the required fees, there is delivered to the Secretary of State a separate affidavit (which in its heading shall be designated as an affidavit of extraordinary condition) attesting, on the basis of personal knowledge of the affiant or a reliable source of knowledge identified in the affidavit, that an earlier effort to deliver such certificate and tender such fees was made in good faith, specifying the nature, date and time of such good faith effort and requesting that the Secretary of State establish such date and time as the date and time of filing of such certificate; or

b. Upon the actual delivery of a certificate and tender of the required fees, the Secretary of State in the Secretary of State's own discretion provides a written waiver of the requirement for such an affidavit stating that it appears to the Secretary of State that an earlier effort to deliver such certificate and tender such fees was made in good faith and specifying the date and time of such effort; and

c. The Secretary of State determines that an extraordinary condition existed at such date and time, that such earlier effort was unsuccessful as a result of the existence of such extraordinary condition, and that such actual delivery and tender were made within a reasonable period (not to exceed 2 business days) after the cessation of such extraordinary condition, then the Secretary of State may establish such date and time as the date and time of filing of such certificate. No fee shall be paid to the Secretary of State for receiving an affidavit of extraordinary condition. For purposes of this subsection, an extraordinary condition means: any emergency resulting from an attack on, invasion or occupation by foreign military forces of, or disaster, catastrophe, war or other armed conflict, revolution or insurrection or rioting or civil commotion in, the United States or a locality in which the Secretary of State conducts its business or in which the good faith effort to deliver the certificate and tender the required fees is made, or the immediate threat of any of the foregoing; or any malfunction or outage of the electrical or telephone service to the Secretary of State's office, or weather or other condition in or about a locality in which the Secretary of State conducts its business, as a result of which the Secretary of State's office is not open for the purpose of the filing of certificates under this chapter or such filing cannot be effected without extraordinary effort. The Secretary of State may require such proof as it deems necessary to make the determination required under this subparagraph of subdivision (a)(6), and any such determination shall be conclusive in the absence of actual fraud. If the Secretary of State establishes the date and time of filing of a certificate pursuant to this subsection, the date and time of delivery of the affidavit of extraordinary condition or the date and time of the Secretary of State's written waiver of such affidavit shall be endorsed on such affidavit or waiver and such affidavit or waiver, so endorsed, shall be attached to the filed certificate to which it relates. Such filed certificate shall be effective as of the date and time established as the date and time of filing by the Secretary of State pursuant to this subsection, except as to those persons who are substantially and adversely affected by such establishment and, as to those persons, the certificate shall be effective from the date and time endorsed on the affidavit of extraordinary condition or written waiver attached thereto.

(b) Upon the filing of a certificate of amendment (or judicial decree of amendment), certificate of correction, corrected certificate or restated certificate in the office of the Secretary of State, or upon the future effective date or time of a certificate of amendment (or judicial decree thereof) or restated certificate, as provided for therein, the certificate of formation shall be amended, corrected or restated as set forth therein. Upon the filing of a certificate of cancellation (or a judicial decree thereof), or a certificate of merger or consolidation which acts as a certificate of cancellation or a certificate of transfer, or a certificate of conversion to a non-Delaware entity, or upon the future effective date or time of a certificate of cancellation (or a judicial decree thereof) or of a certificate of merger or consolidation which acts as a certificate of cancellation or a certificate of transfer, or a certificate of conversion to a non-Delaware entity, as provided for therein, or as specified in § 18-104(d) of this title, the certificate of formation is cancelled. Upon the filing of a certificate of limited liability company domestication or upon the future effective date or time of a certificate of limited liability company domestication, the entity filing the certificate of limited liability company domestication is domesticated as a limited liability company with the effect provided in § 18-212 of this title. Upon the filing of a certificate of conversion to limited liability company or upon the future effective date or time of a certificate of conversion to limited liability company, the entity filing the certificate of conversion to limited liability company is converted to a limited liability company with the effect provided in § 18–214 of this title. Upon the filing of a certificate of revival, the limited liability company is revived with the effect provided in § 18–1109 of this title. Upon the filing of a certificate of transfer and continuance, or upon the future effective date or time of a certificate of transfer and continuance, as provided for therein, the limited liability company filing the certificate of transfer and continuance shall continue to exist as a limited liability company of the State of Delaware with the effect provided in § 18–213 of this title.

(c) If any certificate filed in accordance with this chapter provides for a future effective date or time and if, prior to such future effective date or time set forth in such certificate, the transaction is terminated or its terms are amended to change the future effective date or time or any other matter described in such certificate so as to make such certificate false or inaccurate in any respect, such certificate shall, prior to the future effective date or time set forth in such certificate, be terminated or amended by the filing of a certificate of termination or certificate of amendment of such certificate, executed in accordance with § 18–204 of this title, which shall identify the certificate which has been terminated or amended and shall state that the certificate has been terminated or the manner in which it has been amended. Upon the filing of a certificate of amendment of a certificate with a future effective date or time, the certificate identified in such certificate of amendment is amended. Upon the filing of a certificate of termination of a certificate with a future effective date or time, the certificate identified in such certificate of termination is terminated.

(d) A fee as set forth in § 18–1105(a)(3) of this title shall be paid at the time of the filing of a certificate of formation, a certificate of amendment, a certificate of correction, a certificate of amendment of a certificate with a future effective date or time, a certificate of termination of a certificate with a future effective date or time, a certificate of cancellation, a certificate of merger or consolidation, a restated certificate, a corrected certificate, a certificate of conversion to limited liability company, a certificate of conversion to a non-Delaware entity, a certificate of transfer, a certificate of transfer and continuance, a certificate of limited liability company domestication or a certificate of revival.

(e) The Secretary of State, acting as agent, shall collect and deposit in a separate account established exclusively for that purpose, a courthouse municipality fee with respect to each filed instrument and shall thereafter monthly remit funds from such account to the treasuries of the municipalities designated in § 301 of Title 10. Said fees shall be for the purposes of defraying certain costs incurred by such municipalities in hosting the primary locations for the Delaware Courts. The fee to such municipalities shall be $20 for each instrument filed with the Secretary of State in accordance with this section. The municipality to receive the fee shall be the municipality designated in § 301 of Title 10 in the county in which the limited liability company's registered office in this State is, or is to be, located, except that a fee shall not be charged for a document filed in accordance with subchapter IX of this chapter.

(f) A fee as set forth in § 18–1105(a)(4) of this title shall be paid for a certified copy of any paper on file as provided for by this chapter, and a fee as set forth in § 18–1105(a)(5) of this title shall be paid for each page copied.

§ 18–206. Filing [Effective Jan. 1, 2007]

(a) The signed copy of the certificate of formation and of any certificates of amendment, correction, amendment of a certificate with a future effective date or time, termination of a certificate with a future effective date or time or cancellation (or of any judicial decree of amendment or cancellation), and of any certificate of merger or consolidation, any restated certificate, any corrected certificate, any certificate of conversion to limited liability company, any certificate of conversion to a non-Delaware entity, any certificate of transfer, any certificate of transfer and continuance, any certificate of limited liability company domestication, and of any certificate of revival shall be delivered to the Secretary of State. A person who executes a certificate as an agent or fiduciary need not exhibit evidence of that person's authority as a prerequisite to filing. Any signature on any certificate authorized to be filed with the Secretary of State under any provision of this chapter may be a facsimile, a conformed signature or an electronically transmitted signature. Upon delivery of any certificate, the Secretary of State shall record the date and time of its delivery. Unless the Secretary of State finds that any certificate does not conform to law, upon receipt of all filing fees required by law the Secretary of State shall:

(1) Certify that the certificate of formation, the certificate of amendment, the certificate of correction, the certificate of amendment of a certificate with a future effective date or time, the certificate of termination of a certificate with a future effective date or time, the certificate of cancellation (or of any judicial decree of amendment or cancellation), the certificate of merger or consolidation, the restated certificate, the corrected certificate, the certificate of conversion to limited liability company, the certificate of conversion to a non-Delaware entity, the certificate of transfer, the certificate of transfer and continuance, the certificate of limited liability company domestication or the certificate of revival has been filed in the Secretary of State's office by endorsing upon the signed certificate the word "Filed," and the date and time of the filing. This endorsement is conclusive of the date and time of its filing in the absence of actual fraud. Except as provided in subdivision (a)(5) or (a)(6) of this section, such date and time of filing of a certificate shall be the date and time of delivery of the certificate;

(2) File and index the endorsed certificate;

(3) Prepare and return to the person who filed it or that person's representative a copy of the signed certificate, similarly endorsed, and shall certify such copy as a true copy of the signed certificate; and

(4) Cause to be entered such information from the certificate as the Secretary of State deems appropriate into the Delaware Corporation Information System or any system which is a successor thereto in the office of the Secretary of State, and such information and a copy of such certificate shall be permanently maintained as a public record on a suitable medium. The Secretary of State is authorized to grant direct access to such system to registered agents subject to the execution of an operating agreement between the Secretary of State and such registered agent. Any registered agent granted such access shall demonstrate the existence of policies to ensure that information entered into the system accurately reflects the content of certificates in the possession of the registered agent at the time of entry.

(5) Upon request made upon or prior to delivery, the Secretary of State may, to the extent deemed practicable, establish as the date and time of filing of a certificate a date and time after its delivery. If the Secretary of State refuses to file any certificate due to an error, omission or other imperfection, the Secretary of State may hold such certificate in suspension, and in such event, upon delivery of a replacement certificate in proper form for filing and tender of the required fees within 5 business days after notice of such suspension is given to the filer, the Secretary of State shall establish as the date and time of filing of such certificate the date and time that would have been the date and time of filing of the rejected certificate had it been accepted for filing. The Secretary of State shall not issue a certificate of good standing with respect to any limited liability company with a certificate held in suspension pursuant to this subsection. The Secretary of State may establish as the date and time of filing of a certificate the date and time at which information from such certificate is entered pursuant to subdivision (a)(4) of this section if such certificate is delivered on the same date and within 4 hours after such information is entered.

(6) If:

a. Together with the actual delivery of a certificate and tender of the required fees, there is delivered to the Secretary of State a separate affidavit (which in its heading shall be designated as an affidavit of extraordinary condition) attesting, on the basis of personal knowledge of the affiant or a reliable source of knowledge identified in the affidavit, that an earlier effort to deliver such certificate and tender such fees was made in good faith, specifying the nature, date and time of such good faith effort and requesting that the Secretary of State establish such date and time as the date and time of filing of such certificate; or

b. Upon the actual delivery of a certificate and tender of the required fees, the Secretary of State in the Secretary of State's own discretion provides a written waiver of the requirement for such an affidavit stating that it appears to the Secretary of State that an earlier effort to deliver such certificate and tender such fees was made in good faith and specifying the date and time of such effort; and

c. The Secretary of State determines that an extraordinary condition existed at such date and time, that such earlier effort was unsuccessful as a result of the existence of such extraordinary condition, and that such actual delivery and tender were made within a reasonable period (not to exceed 2 business days) after the cessation of such extraordinary condition, then the Secretary of State may establish such date and time as the date and time of filing of such certificate. No fee shall be paid to the Secretary of State for receiving an affidavit of extraordinary condition. For purposes of this subsection, an extraordinary condition means: any emergency resulting from an attack on, invasion or occupation by foreign military forces of, or disaster, catastrophe, war or other armed conflict, revolution or insurrection or rioting or civil commotion in, the United States or a locality in which the Secretary of State conducts its business or in which the good faith effort to deliver the certificate and tender the required fees is made, or the immediate threat of any of the foregoing; or any malfunction or outage of the electrical or telephone service to the Secretary of State's office, or weather or other condition in or about a locality in which the Secretary of State conducts its business, as a result of which the Secretary of State's office is not open for the purpose of the filing of certificates under this chapter or such filing cannot be effected without extraordinary effort. The Secretary of State may require such proof as it deems necessary to make the determination required under this subparagraph of subdivision (a)(6), and any such determination shall be conclusive in the absence of actual fraud. If the Secretary of State establishes the date and time of filing of a certificate pursuant to this subsection, the date and time of delivery of the affidavit of extraordinary condition or the date and time of the Secretary of State's written waiver of such affidavit shall be endorsed on such affidavit or waiver and such affidavit or waiver, so endorsed, shall be attached to the filed certificate to which it relates. Such filed certificate shall be effective as of the date and time established as the date and time of filing by the Secretary of State pursuant to this subsection, except as to those persons who are substantially and adversely affected by such establishment and, as to those persons, the certificate shall be effective from the date and time endorsed on the affidavit of extraordinary condition or written waiver attached thereto.

(b) Upon the filing of a certificate of amendment (or judicial decree of amendment), certificate of correction, corrected certificate or restated certificate in the office of the Secretary of State, or upon the future effective date or time of a certificate of amendment (or judicial decree thereof) or restated certificate, as provided for therein, the certificate of formation shall be amended, corrected or restated as set forth therein. Upon the filing of a certificate of cancellation (or a judicial decree thereof), or a certificate of merger or consolidation which acts as a certificate of cancellation or a certificate of transfer, or a certificate of conversion to a non-Delaware entity, or upon the future effective date or time of a certificate of cancellation (or a judicial decree thereof) or of a certificate of merger or consolidation which acts as a certificate of cancellation or a certificate of transfer, or a certificate of conversion to a non-Delaware entity, as provided for therein, or as specified in § 18–104(d) or § 18–104(i)(4) of this title, the certificate of formation is cancelled. Upon the filing of a certificate of limited liability company domestication or upon the future effective date or time of a certificate of limited liability company domestication, the entity filing the certificate of limited liability company domestication is domesticated as a limited liability company with the effect provided in § 18–212 of this title. Upon the filing of a certificate of conversion to limited liability company or upon the future effective date or time of a certificate of conversion to limited liability company, the entity filing the certificate of conversion to limited liability company is converted to a limited liability company with the effect provided in § 18–214 of this title. Upon the filing of a certificate of revival, the limited liability company is revived with the effect provided in § 18–1109 of this title. Upon the filing of a certificate of transfer and continuance, or upon the future effective date or time of a certificate of transfer and continuance, as provided for therein, the limited liability company filing the certificate of transfer and continuance shall continue to exist as a limited liability company of the State of Delaware with the effect provided in § 18–213 of this title.

(c) If any certificate filed in accordance with this chapter provides for a future effective date or time and if, prior to such future effective date or time set forth in such certificate, the transaction is terminated or its terms are amended to change the future effective date or time or any other matter described in such certificate so as to make such certificate false or inaccurate in any respect, such certificate shall, prior to the future effective date or time set forth in such certificate, be terminated or amended by the filing of a certificate of termination or certificate of amendment of such certificate, executed in accordance with § 18–204 of this title, which shall identify the certificate which has been terminated or amended and shall state that the certificate has been terminated or the manner in which it has been amended. Upon the filing of a certificate of amendment of a certificate with a future effective date or time, the certificate identified in such certificate of amendment is amended. Upon the filing of a certificate of termination of a certificate with a future effective date or time, the certificate identified in such certificate of termination is terminated.

(d) A fee as set forth in § 18–1105(a)(3) of this title shall be paid at the time of the filing of a certificate of formation, a certificate of amendment, a certificate of correction, a certificate of amendment of a certificate with a future effective date or time, a certificate of termination of a certificate with a future effective date or time, a certificate of cancellation, a certificate of merger or consolidation, a restated certificate, a corrected certificate, a certificate of conversion to limited liability company, a certificate of conversion to a non-Delaware entity, a certificate of transfer, a certificate of transfer and continuance, a certificate of limited liability company domestication or a certificate of revival.

(e) The Secretary of State, acting as agent, shall collect and deposit in a separate account established exclusively for that purpose, a courthouse municipality fee with respect to each filed instrument and shall thereafter monthly remit funds from such account to the treasuries of the municipalities designated in § 301 of Title 10. Said fees shall be for the purposes of defraying certain costs incurred by such municipalities in hosting the primary locations for the Delaware Courts. The fee to such municipalities shall be $20 for each instrument filed with the Secretary of State in accordance with this section. The municipality to receive the fee shall be the municipality designated in § 301 of Title 10 in the county in which the limited liability company's registered office in this State is, or is to be, located, except that a fee shall not be charged for a document filed in accordance with subchapter IX of this chapter.

(f) A fee as set forth in § 18–1105(a)(4) of this title shall be paid for a certified copy of any paper on file as provided for by this chapter, and a fee as set forth in § 18–1105(a)(5) of this title shall be paid for each page copied.

§ 18–207. Notice

The fact that a certificate of formation is on file in the office of the Secretary of State is notice that the entity formed in connection with the filing of the certificate of formation is a limited liability company formed under the laws of the State of Delaware and is notice of all other facts set forth therein which are required to be set forth in a certificate of formation by § 18–201(a)(1) and (2) of this title and which are permitted to be set forth in a certificate of formation by § 18–215(b) of this title.

§ 18–208. Restated Certificate

(a) A limited liability company may, whenever desired, integrate into a single instrument all of the provisions of its certificate of formation which are then in effect and operative as a result of there having theretofore been filed with the Secretary of State 1 or more certificates or other instruments pursuant to any of the sections referred to in this subchapter, and it may at the same time also further amend its certificate of formation by adopting a restated certificate of formation.

(b) If a restated certificate of formation merely restates and integrates but does not further amend the initial certificate of formation, as theretofore amended or supplemented by any instrument that was executed and filed pursuant to any of the sections in this subchapter, it shall be specifically designated in its heading as a "Restated Certificate of Formation" together with such other words as the limited liability company may deem appropriate and shall be executed by an authorized person and filed as provided in § 18-206 of this title in the office of the Secretary of State. If a restated certificate restates and integrates and also further amends in any respect the certificate of formation, as theretofore amended or supplemented, it shall be specifically designated in its heading as an "Amended and Restated Certificate of Formation" together with such other words as the limited liability company may deem appropriate and shall be executed by at least 1 authorized person, and filed as provided in § 18-206 of this title in the office of the Secretary of State.

(c) A restated certificate of formation shall state, either in its heading or in an introductory paragraph, the limited liability company's present name, and, if it has been changed, the name under which it was originally filed, and the date of filing of its original certificate of formation with the Secretary of State, and the future effective date or time (which shall be a date or time certain) of the restated certificate if it is not to be effective upon the filing of the restated certificate. A restated certificate shall also state that it was duly executed and is being filed in accordance with this section. If a restated certificate only restates and integrates and does not further amend a limited liability company's certificate of formation as theretofore amended or supplemented and there is no discrepancy between those provisions and the restated certificate, it shall state that fact as well.

(d) Upon the filing of a restated certificate of formation with the Secretary of State, or upon the future effective date or time of a restated certificate of formation as provided for therein, the initial certificate of formation, as theretofore amended or supplemented, shall be superseded; thenceforth, the restated certificate of formation, including any further amendment or changes made thereby, shall be the certificate of formation of the limited liability company, but the original effective date of formation shall remain unchanged.

(e) Any amendment or change effected in connection with the restatement and integration of the certificate of formation shall be subject to any other provision of this chapter, not inconsistent with this section, which would apply if a separate certificate of amendment were filed to effect such amendment or change.

§ 18–209. Merger and Consolidation

(a) As used in this section, "other business entity" means a corporation, a statutory trust, or a business trust or association, a real estate investment trust, a common-law trust, or any other unincorporated business, including a partnership (whether general (including a limited liability partnership) or limited (including a limited liability limited partnership)), and a foreign limited liability company, but excluding a domestic limited liability company.

(b) Pursuant to an agreement of merger or consolidation, 1 or more domestic limited liability companies may merge or consolidate with or into 1 or more domestic limited liability companies or 1 or more other business entities formed or organized under the laws of the State of Delaware or any other state or the United States or any foreign country or other foreign jurisdiction, or any combination thereof, with such domestic limited liability company or other business entity as the agreement shall provide being the surviving or resulting domestic limited liability company or other business entity. Unless otherwise provided in the limited liability company agreement, a merger or consolidation shall be approved by each domestic limited liability company which is to merge or consolidate by the members or, if there is more than one class or group of members, then by each class or group of members, in either case, by members who own more than 50 percent of the then current percentage or other interest in the profits of the domestic limited liability company owned by all of the members or by the members in each class or group, as appropriate. In connection with a merger or consolidation hereunder, rights or securities of, or interests in, a domestic limited liability company or other business entity which is a constituent party to the merger or consolidation may be exchanged for or converted into cash, property, rights or securities of, or interests in, the surviving or resulting domestic limited liability company or other business entity or, in addition to or in lieu thereof, may be exchanged for or converted into cash, property, rights or securities of, or interests in, a domestic limited liability company or other business entity which is not the surviving or resulting limited liability company or other business entity in the merger or consolidation or may be cancelled. Notwithstanding prior approval, an agreement of merger or consolidation may be terminated or amended pursuant to a provision for such termination or amendment contained in the agreement of merger or consolidation.

(c) If a domestic limited liability company is merging or consolidating under this section, the domestic limited liability company or other business entity surviving or resulting in or from the merger or consolidation shall file a certificate of merger or consolidation executed by 1 or more authorized persons on behalf of the domestic limited liability company when it is the surviving or resulting entity in the office of the Secretary of State. The certificate of merger or consolidation shall state:

(1) The name and jurisdiction of formation or organization of each of the domestic limited liability companies and other business entities which is to merge or consolidate;

(2) That an agreement of merger or consolidation has been approved and executed by each of the domestic limited liability companies and other business entities which is to merge or consolidate;

(3) The name of the surviving or resulting domestic limited liability company or other business entity;

(4) In the case of a merger in which a domestic limited liability company is the surviving entity, such amendments, if any, to the certificate of formation of the surviving domestic limited liability company to change its name as are desired to be effected by the merger;

(5) The future effective date or time (which shall be a date or time certain) of the merger or consolidation if it is not to be effective upon the filing of the certificate of merger or consolidation;

(6) That the agreement of merger or consolidation is on file at a place of business of the surviving or resulting domestic limited liability company or other business entity, and shall state the address thereof;

(7) That a copy of the agreement of merger or consolidation will be furnished by the surviving or resulting domestic limited liability company or other business entity, on request and without cost, to any member of any domestic limited liability company or any person holding an interest in any other business entity which is to merge or consolidate; and

(8) If the surviving or resulting entity is not a domestic limited liability company, or a corporation or limited partnership organized under the laws of the State of Delaware, or a statutory trust organized under Chapter 38 of Title 12, a statement that such surviving or resulting other business entity agrees that it may be served with process in the State of Delaware in any action, suit or proceeding for the enforcement of any obligation of any domestic limited liability company which is to merge or consolidate, irrevocably appointing the Secretary of State as its agent to accept service of process in any such action, suit or proceeding and specifying the address to which a copy of such process shall be mailed to it by the Secretary of State. In the event of service hereunder upon the Secretary of State, the procedures set forth in § 18-911(c) of this title shall be applicable, except that the plaintiff in any such action, suit or proceeding shall furnish the Secretary of State with the address specified in the certificate of merger or consolidation provid-

ed for in this section and any other address which the plaintiff may elect to furnish, together with copies of such process as required by the Secretary of State, and the Secretary of State shall notify such surviving or resulting other business entity at all such addresses furnished by the plaintiff in accordance with the procedures set forth in § 18-911(c) of this title.

(d) Unless a future effective date or time is provided in a certificate of merger or consolidation, in which event a merger or consolidation shall be effective at any such future effective date or time, a merger or consolidation shall be effective upon the filing in the office of the Secretary of State of a certificate of merger or consolidation.

(e) A certificate of merger or consolidation shall act as a certificate of cancellation for a domestic limited liability company which is not the surviving or resulting entity in the merger or consolidation. A certificate of merger that sets forth any amendment in accordance with subsection (c)(4) of this section shall be deemed to be an amendment to the certificate of formation of the limited liability company, and the limited liability company shall not be required to take any further action to amend its certificate of formation under § 18-202 of this title with respect to such amendments set forth in the certificate of merger. Whenever this section requires the filing of a certificate of merger or consolidation, such requirement shall be deemed satisfied by the filing of an agreement of merger or consolidation containing the information required by this section to be set forth in the certificate of merger or consolidation.

(f) An agreement of merger or consolidation approved in accordance with subsection (b) of this section may:

(1) Effect any amendment to the limited liability company agreement; or

(2) Effect the adoption of a new limited liability company agreement, for a limited liability company if it is the surviving or resulting limited liability company in the merger or consolidation.

Any amendment to a limited liability company agreement or adoption of a new limited liability company agreement made pursuant to the foregoing sentence shall be effective at the effective time or date of the merger or consolidation. The provisions of this subsection shall not be construed to limit the accomplishment of a merger or of any of the matters referred to herein by any other means provided for in a limited liability company agreement or other agreement or as otherwise permitted by law, including that the limited liability company agreement of any constituent limited liability company to the merger or consolidation (including a limited liability company formed for the purpose of consummating a merger or consolidation) shall be the limited liability company agreement of the surviving or resulting limited liability company.

(g) When any merger or consolidation shall have become effective under this section, for all purposes of the laws of the State of Delaware, all of the rights, privileges and powers of each of the domestic limited liability companies and other business entities that have merged or consolidated, and all property, real, personal and mixed, and all debts due to any of said domestic limited liability companies and other business entities, as well as all other things and causes of action belonging to each of such domestic limited liability companies and other business entities, shall be vested in the surviving or resulting domestic limited liability company or other business entity, and shall thereafter be the property of the surviving or resulting domestic limited liability company or other business entity as they were of each of the domestic limited liability companies and other business entities that have merged or consolidated, and the title to any real property vested by deed or otherwise, under the laws of the State of Delaware, in any of such domestic limited liability companies and other business entities, shall not revert or be in any way impaired by reason of this chapter; but all rights of creditors and all liens upon any property of any of said domestic limited liability companies and other business entities shall be preserved unimpaired, and all debts, liabilities and duties of each of the said domestic limited liability companies and other business entities that have merged or consolidated shall thenceforth attach to the surviving or resulting domestic limited liability company or other business entity, and may be enforced against it to the same extent as if said debts, liabilities and duties had been incurred or contracted by it. Unless otherwise agreed, a merger or consolidation of a domestic limited liability company, including a domestic limited liability company which is not the surviving or resulting entity in the merger or consolidation, shall not require such domestic limited liability company to wind up its affairs under § 18-803 of this title or pay its liabilities and distribute its assets under § 18-804 of this title.

§ 18-210. Contractual Appraisal Rights

A limited liability company agreement or an agreement of merger or consolidation may provide that contractual appraisal rights with respect to a limited liability company interest or another interest in a limited liability company shall be available for any class or group of members or limited liability company interests in connection with any amendment of a limited liability company agreement, any merger or consolidation in which the limited liability company is a constituent party to the merger or consolidation, any conversion of the limited liability company to another business form, any transfer to or domestication in any jurisdiction by the limited liability company, or the sale of all or substantially all of the limited liability company's assets. The Court of Chancery shall have jurisdiction to hear and determine any matter relating to any such appraisal rights.

§ 18-211. Certificate of Correction

(a) Whenever any certificate authorized to be filed with the office of the Secretary of State under any provision of this chapter has been so filed and is an inaccurate record of the action therein referred to, or was defectively or erroneously executed, such certificate may be corrected by filing with the office of the Secretary of State a certificate of correction of such certificate. The certificate of correction shall specify the inaccuracy or defect to be corrected, shall set forth the portion of the certificate in corrected form, and shall be executed and filed as required by this chapter. The certificate of correction shall be effective as of the date the original certificate was filed, except as to those persons who are substantially and adversely affected by the correction, and as to those persons the certificate of correction shall be effective from the filing date.

(b) In lieu of filing a certificate of correction, a certificate may be corrected by filing with the Secretary of State a corrected certificate which shall be executed and filed as if the corrected certificate were the certificate being corrected, and a fee equal to the fee payable to the Secretary of State if the certificate being corrected were then being filed shall be paid and collected by the Secretary of State for the use of the State of Delaware in connection with the filing of the corrected certificate. The corrected certificate shall be specifically designated as such in its heading, shall specify the inaccuracy or defect to be corrected and shall set forth the entire certificate in corrected form. A certificate corrected in accordance with this section shall be effective as of the date the original certificate was filed, except as to those persons who are substantially and adversely affected by the correction and as to those persons the certificate as corrected shall be effective from the filing date.

§ 18-212. Domestication of non-United States Entities

(a) As used in this section, "non-United States entity" means a foreign limited liability company (other than one formed under the laws of a state) or a corporation, a statutory trust, a business trust, an association, a real estate investment trust, a common-law trust or any other unincorporated business or entity, including a partnership (whether general (including a limited liability partnership) or limited (including a limited liability limited partnership)) formed, incorporated, created or that otherwise came into being under the laws of any foreign country or other foreign jurisdiction (other than any state).

(b) Any non-United States entity may become domesticated as a limited liability company in the State of Delaware by complying with subsection (g) of this section and filing in the office of the Secretary of State in accordance with § 18-206 of this title:

(1) A certificate of limited liability company domestication that has been executed by 1 or more authorized persons in accordance with § 18-204 of this title; and

(2) A certificate of formation that complies with § 18–201 of this title and has been executed by 1 or more authorized persons in accordance with § 18–204 of this title.

(c) The certificate of limited liability company domestication shall state:

(1) The date on which and jurisdiction where the non-United States entity was first formed, incorporated, created or otherwise came into being;

(2) The name of the non-United States entity immediately prior to the filing of the certificate of limited liability company domestication;

(3) The name of the limited liability company as set forth in the certificate of formation filed in accordance with subsection (b) of this section;

(4) The future effective date or time (which shall be a date or time certain) of the domestication as a limited liability company if it is not to be effective upon the filing of the certificate of limited liability company domestication and the certificate of formation;

(5) The jurisdiction that constituted the seat, siege social, or principal place of business or central administration of the non-United States entity, or any other equivalent thereto under applicable law, immediately prior to the filing of the certificate of limited liability company domestication; and

(6) That the domestication has been approved in the manner provided for by the document, instrument, agreement or other writing, as the case may be, governing the internal affairs of the non-United States entity and the conduct of its business or by applicable non-Delaware law, as appropriate.

(d) Upon the filing in the office of the Secretary of State of the certificate of limited liability company domestication and the certificate of formation or upon the future effective date or time of the certificate of limited liability company domestication and the certificate of formation, the non-United States entity shall be domesticated as a limited liability company in the State of Delaware and the limited liability company shall thereafter be subject to all of the provisions of this chapter, except that notwithstanding § 18–201 of this title, the existence of the limited liability company shall be deemed to have commenced on the date the non-United States entity commenced its existence in the jurisdiction in which the non-United States entity was first formed, incorporated, created or otherwise came into being.

(e) The domestication of any non-United States entity as a limited liability company in the State of Delaware shall not be deemed to affect any obligations or liabilities of the non-United States entity incurred prior to its domestication as a limited liability company in the State of Delaware, or the personal liability of any person therefor.

(f) The filing of a certificate of limited liability company domestication shall not affect the choice of law applicable to the non-United States entity, except that from the effective date or time of the domestication, the law of the State of Delaware, including the provisions of this chapter, shall apply to the non-United States entity to the same extent as if the non-United States entity had been formed as a limited liability company on that date.

(g) Prior to the filing of a certificate of limited liability company domestication with the Office of the Secretary of State, the domestication shall be approved in the manner provided for by the document, instrument, agreement or other writing, as the case may be, governing the internal affairs of the non-United States entity and the conduct of its business or by applicable non-Delaware law, as appropriate, and a limited liability company agreement shall be approved by the same authorization required to approve the domestication.

(h) When any domestication shall have become effective under this section, for all purposes of the laws of the State of Delaware, all of the rights, privileges and powers of the non-United States entity that has been domesticated, and all property, real, personal and mixed, and all debts due to such non-United States entity, as well as all other things and causes of action belonging to such non-United States entity, shall remain vested in the domestic limited liability company to which such non-United States entity has been domesticated (and also in the non-United States entity, if and for so long as the non-United States entity continues its existence in the foreign jurisdiction in which it was existing immediately prior to the domestication) and shall be the property of such domestic limited liability company (and also of the non-United States entity, if and for so long as the non-United States entity continues its existence in the foreign jurisdiction in which it was existing immediately prior to the domestication), and the title to any real property vested by deed or otherwise in such non-United States entity shall not revert or be in any way impaired by reason of this chapter; but all rights of creditors and all liens upon any property of such non-United States entity shall be preserved unimpaired, and all debts, liabilities and duties of the non-United States entity that has been domesticated shall remain attached to the domestic limited liability company to which such non-United States entity has been domesticated (and also to the non-United States entity, if and for so long as the non-United States entity continues its existence in the foreign jurisdiction in which it was existing immediately prior to the domestication), and may be enforced against it to the same extent as if said debts, liabilities and duties had originally been incurred or contracted by it in its capacity as a domestic limited liability company. The rights, privileges, powers and interests in property of the non-United States entity, as well as the debts, liabilities and duties of the non-United States entity, shall not be deemed, as a consequence of the domestication, to have been transferred to the domestic limited liability company to which such non-United States entity has domesticated for any purpose of the laws of the State of Delaware.

(i) When a non-United States entity has become domesticated as a limited liability company pursuant to this section, for all purposes of the laws of the State of Delaware, the limited liability company shall be deemed to be the same entity as the domesticating non-United States entity and the domestication shall constitute a continuation of the existence of the domesticating non-United States entity in the form of a domestic limited liability company. Unless otherwise agreed, for all purposes of the laws of the State of Delaware, the domesticating non-United States entity shall not be required to wind up its affairs or pay its liabilities and distribute its assets, and the domestication shall not be deemed to constitute a dissolution of such non-United States entity. If, following domestication, a non-United States entity that has become domesticated as a limited liability company continues its existence in the foreign country or other foreign jurisdiction in which it was existing immediately prior to domestication, the limited liability company and such non-United States entity shall, for all purposes of the laws of the State of Delaware, constitute a single entity formed, incorporated, created or otherwise having come into being, as applicable, and existing under the laws of the State of Delaware and the laws of such foreign country or other foreign jurisdiction.

(j) In connection with a domestication hereunder, rights or securities of, or interests in, the non-United States entity that is to be domesticated as a domestic limited liability company may be exchanged for or converted into cash, property, rights or securities of, or interests in, such domestic limited liability company or, in addition to or in lieu thereof, may be exchanged for or converted into cash, property, rights or securities of, or interests in, another domestic limited liability company or other entity or may be cancelled.

§ 18–213. Transfer or Continuance of Domestic Limited Liability Companies

(a) Upon compliance with this section, any limited liability company may transfer to or domesticate or continue in any jurisdiction, other than any state, and, in connection therewith, may elect to continue its existence as a limited liability company in the State of Delaware.

(b) If the limited liability company agreement specifies the manner of authorizing a transfer or domestication or continuance described in subsection (a) of this section, the transfer or domestication or continuance shall be authorized as specified in the limited liability company agreement. If the limited liability company agreement does not specify the manner of authorizing a transfer or domestication or continuance described in subsection (a) of this section and does not prohibit such a transfer or domestication or continuance, the transfer or domestication or continuance shall be authorized in the same manner as is specified in the limited liability company agreement for authorizing a merger or consolidation that involves the limited liability company as a constituent party to the merger or consolidation. If the limited liability company agreement does not specify the manner of authorizing a transfer or domestication or continuance described in subsection (a) of this section or a merger or consolidation that involves the limited liability company as a constituent party and does not prohibit such a transfer or domestication or continuance, the transfer or domestication or continuance shall be authorized by the approval by the members or, if there is more than 1 class or group of members, then by each class or group of members, in either case, by the members who own more than 50% of the then current percentage or other interest in the profits of the domestic limited liability company owned by all of the members or by the members in each class or group, as appropriate. If a transfer or domestication or continuance described in subsection (a) of this section shall be authorized as provided in this subsection (b), a certificate of transfer if the limited liability company's existence as a limited liability company of the State of Delaware is to cease, or a certificate of transfer and domestic continuance if the limited liability company's existence as a limited liability company in the State of Delaware is to continue, executed in accordance with § 18–204 of this title, shall be filed in the office of the Secretary of State in accordance with § 18–206 of this title. The certificate of transfer or the certificate of transfer and domestic continuance shall state:

(1) The name of the limited liability company and, if it has been changed, the name under which its certificate of formation was originally filed;

(2) The date of the filing of its original certificate of formation with the Secretary of State;

(3) The jurisdiction to which the limited liability company shall be transferred or in which it shall be domesticated or continued and the name of the entity or business form formed, incorporated, created or that otherwise comes into being as a consequence of the transfer of the limited liability company to, or its domestication or continuance in, such foreign jurisdiction;

(4) The future effective date or time (which shall be a date or time certain) of the transfer to or domestication or continuance in the jurisdiction specified in subsection (b)(3) of this section if it is not to be effective upon the filing of the certificate of transfer or the certificate of transfer and domestic continuance;

(5) That the transfer or domestication or continuance of the limited liability company has been approved in accordance with this section;

(6) In the case of a certificate of transfer, (i) that the existence of the limited liability company as a limited liability company of the State of Delaware shall cease when the certificate of transfer be-

comes effective, and (ii) the agreement of the limited liability company that it may be served with process in the State of Delaware in any action, suit or proceeding for enforcement of any obligation of the limited liability company arising while it was a limited liability company of the State of Delaware, and that it irrevocably appoints the Secretary of State as its agent to accept service of process in any such action, suit or proceeding;

(7) The address to which a copy of the process referred to in subsection (b)(6) of this section shall be mailed to it by the Secretary of State. In the event of service hereunder upon the Secretary of State, the procedures set forth in § 18–911(c) of this title shall be applicable, except that the plaintiff in any such action, suit or proceeding shall furnish the Secretary of State with the address specified in this subsection and any other address that the plaintiff may elect to furnish, together with copies of such process as required by the Secretary of State, and the Secretary of State shall notify the limited liability company that has transferred or domesticated or continued out of the State of Delaware at all such addresses furnished by the plaintiff in accordance with the procedures set forth in § 18–911(c) of this title; and

(8) In the case of a certificate of transfer and domestic continuance, that the limited liability company will continue to exist as a limited liability company of the State of Delaware after the certificate of transfer and domestic continuance becomes effective.

(c) Upon the filing in the office of the Secretary of State of the certificate of transfer or upon the future effective date or time of the certificate of transfer and payment to the Secretary of State of all fees prescribed in this chapter, the Secretary of State shall certify that the limited liability company has filed all documents and paid all fees required by this chapter, and thereupon the limited liability company shall cease to exist as a limited liability company of the State of Delaware. Such certificate of the Secretary of State shall be prima facie evidence of the transfer or domestication or continuance by such limited liability company out of the State of Delaware.

(d) The transfer or domestication or continuance of a limited liability company out of the State of Delaware in accordance with this section and the resulting cessation of its existence as a limited liability company of the State of Delaware pursuant to a certificate of transfer shall not be deemed to affect any obligations or liabilities of the limited liability company incurred prior to such transfer or domestication or continuance or the personal liability of any person incurred prior to such transfer or domestication or continuance, nor shall it be deemed to affect the choice of law applicable to the limited liability company with respect to matters arising prior to such transfer or domestication or continuance. Unless otherwise agreed, the transfer or domestication or continuance of a limited liability company out of the State of Delaware in accordance with this section shall not require such limited liability company to wind up its affairs under § 18–803 of this title or pay its liabilities and distribute its assets under § 18–804 of this title and shall not be deemed to constitute a dissolution of such limited liability company.

(e) If a limited liability company files a certificate of transfer and domestic continuance, after the time the certificate of transfer and domestic continuance becomes effective, the limited liability company shall continue to exist as a limited liability company of the State of Delaware, and the laws of the State of Delaware, including this chapter, shall apply to the limited liability company to the same extent as prior to such time. So long as a limited liability company continues to exist as a limited liability company of the State of Delaware following the filing of a certificate of transfer and domestic continuance, the continuing domestic limited liability company and the entity or business form formed, incorporated, created or that otherwise came into being as a consequence of the transfer of the limited liability company to, or its domestication or continuance in, a foreign country or other foreign jurisdiction shall, for all purposes of the laws of the State of Delaware, constitute a single entity formed, incorporated, created or otherwise having come into being, as applicable, and existing under the laws of the State and the laws of such foreign country or other foreign jurisdiction.

(f) In connection with a transfer or domestication or continuance of a domestic limited liability company to or in another jurisdiction pursuant to subsection (a) of this section, rights or securities of, or interests in, such limited liability company may be exchanged for or converted into cash, property, rights or securities of, or interests in, the entity or business form in which the limited liability company will exist in such other jurisdiction as a consequence of the transfer or domestication or continuance or, in addition to or in lieu thereof, may be exchanged for or converted into cash, property, rights or securities of, or interests in, another entity or business form or may be cancelled.

(g) When a limited liability company has transferred or domesticated or continued out of the State of Delaware pursuant to this section, the transferred or domesticated or continued entity or business form shall, for all purposes of the laws of the State of Delaware, be deemed to be the same entity as the limited liability company and shall constitute a continuation of the existence of such limited liability company in the form of the transferred or domesticated or continued entity or business form. When any transfer or domestication or continuance of a limited liability company out of the State of Delaware shall have become effective under this section, for all purposes of the laws of the State of Delaware, all of the rights, privileges and powers of the limited liability company that has transferred or domesticated or continued, and all property, real, personal and mixed, and all debts due to such limited liability company, as well as all other things and causes of action belonging to such limited liability company, shall remain vested in the transferred or domesticated or continued entity or business form (and also in the limited liability company that has transferred, domesticated or continued, if and for so long as such limited liability company continues its existence as a domestic limited liability company) and shall be the property of such transferred or domesticated or continued entity or business form (and also of the limited liability company that has transferred, domesticated or continued, if and for so long as such limited liability company continues its existence as a domestic limited liability company), and the title to any real property vested by deed or otherwise in such limited liability company shall not revert or be in any way impaired by reason of this chapter; but all rights of creditors and all liens upon any property of such limited liability company shall be preserved unimpaired, and all debts, liabilities and duties of the limited liability company that has transferred or domesticated or continued shall remain attached to the transferred or domesticated or continued entity or business form (and also to the limited liability company that has transferred, domesticated or continued, if and for so long as such limited liability company continues its existence as a domestic limited liability company), and may be enforced against it to the same extent as if said debts, liabilities and duties had originally been incurred or contracted by it in its capacity as the transferred or domesticated or continued entity or business form. The rights, privileges, powers and interests in property of the limited liability company that has transferred or domesticated or continued, as well as the debts, liabilities and duties of such limited liability company, shall not be deemed, as a consequence of the transfer or domestication or continuation out of the State of Delaware, to have been transferred to the transferred or domesticated or continued entity or business form for any purpose of the laws of the State of Delaware.

§ 18–214. Conversion of Certain Entities to a Limited Liability Company

(a) As used in this section, the term "other entity" means a corporation, a statutory trust, a business trust, an association, a real estate investment trust, a common-law trust or any other unincorporated business or entity, including a partnership (whether general (including a limited liability partnership) or limited (including a limited liability limited partnership)) or a foreign limited liability company.

(b) Any other entity may convert to a domestic limited liability company by complying with subsection (h) of this section and filing in the office of the Secretary of State in accordance with § 18–206 of this title:

(1) A certificate of conversion to limited liability company that has been executed by 1 or more authorized persons in accordance with § 18–204 of this title; and

(2) A certificate of formation that complies with § 18–201 of this title and has been executed by 1 or more authorized persons in accordance with § 18–204 of this title.

(c) The certificate of conversion to limited liability company shall state:

(1) The date on which and jurisdiction where the other entity was first created, incorporated, formed or otherwise came into being and, if it has changed, its jurisdiction immediately prior to its conversion to a domestic limited liability company;

(2) The name of the other entity immediately prior to the filing of the certificate of conversion to limited liability company;

(3) The name of the limited liability company as set forth in its certificate of formation filed in accordance with subsection (b) of this section; and

(4) The future effective date or time (which shall be a date or time certain) of the conversion to a limited liability company if it is not to be effective upon the filing of the certificate of conversion to limited liability company and the certificate of formation.

(d) Upon the filing in the office of the Secretary of State of the certificate of conversion to limited liability company and the certificate of formation or upon the future effective date or time of the certificate of conversion to limited liability company and the certificate of formation, the other entity shall be converted into a domestic limited liability company and the limited liability company shall thereafter be subject to all of the provisions of this chapter, except that notwithstanding § 18–201 of this title, the existence of the limited liability company shall be deemed to have commenced on the date the other entity commenced its existence in the jurisdiction in which the other entity was first created, formed, incorporated or otherwise came into being.

(e) The conversion of any other entity into a domestic limited liability company shall not be deemed to affect any obligations or liabilities of the other entity incurred prior to its conversion to a domestic limited liability company or the personal liability of any person incurred prior to such conversion.

(f) When any conversion shall have become effective under this section, for all purposes of the laws of the State of Delaware, all of the rights, privileges and powers of the other entity that has converted, and all property, real, personal and mixed, and all debts due to such other entity, as well as all other things and causes of action belonging to such other entity, shall remain vested in the domestic limited liability company to which such other entity has converted and shall be the property of such domestic limited liability company, and the title to any real property vested by deed or otherwise in such other entity shall not revert or be in any way impaired by reason of this chapter; but all rights of creditors and all liens upon any property of such other entity shall be preserved unimpaired, and all debts, liabilities and duties of the other entity that has converted shall remain attached to the domestic limited liability company to which such other entity has converted, and may be enforced against it to the same extent as if said debts, liabilities and duties had originally been incurred or contracted by it in its capacity as a domestic limited liability company. The rights, privileges, powers and interests in property of the other entity, as well as the debts, liabilities and duties of the other entity, shall not be deemed, as a consequence of the conversion, to have been transferred to the domestic limited liability company to which such other entity has converted for any purpose of the laws of the State of Delaware.

(g) Unless otherwise agreed, for all purposes of the laws of the State of Delaware, the converting other entity shall not be required to wind up its affairs or pay its liabilities and distribute its assets, and the conversion shall not be deemed to constitute a dissolution of such other entity. When an other entity has been converted to a limited liability company pursuant to this section, for all purposes of the laws of the State of Delaware, the limited liability company shall be deemed to be the same entity as the converting other entity and the conversion shall constitute a continuation of the existence of the converting other entity in the form of a domestic limited liability company.

(h) Prior to filing a certificate of conversion to limited liability company with the office of the Secretary of State, the conversion shall be approved in the manner provided for by the document, instrument, agreement or other writing, as the case may be, governing the internal affairs of the other entity and the conduct of its business or by applicable law, as appropriate and a limited liability company agreement shall be approved by the same authorization required to approve the conversion.

(i) In connection with a conversion hereunder, rights or securities of or interests in the other entity which is to be converted to a domestic limited liability company may be exchanged for or converted into cash, property, or rights or securities of or interests in such domestic limited liability company or, in addition to or in lieu thereof, may be exchanged for or converted into cash, property, or rights or securities of or interests in another domestic limited liability company or other entity or may be cancelled.

(j) The provisions of this section shall not be construed to limit the accomplishment of a change in the law governing, or the domicile of, an other entity to the State of Delaware by any other means provided for in a limited liability company agreement or other agreement or as otherwise permitted by law, including by the amendment of a limited liability company agreement or other agreement.

§ 18-215. Series of Members, Managers or Limited Liability Company Interests

(a) A limited liability company agreement may establish or provide for the establishment of 1 or more designated series of members, managers or limited liability company interests having separate rights, powers or duties with respect to specified property or obligations of the limited liability company or profits and losses associated with specified property or obligations, and any such series may have a separate business purpose or investment objective.

(b) Notwithstanding anything to the contrary set forth in this chapter or under other applicable law, in the event that a limited liability company agreement establishes or provides for the establishment of 1 or more series, and if separate and distinct records are maintained for any such series and the assets associated with any such series are held in such separate and distinct records (directly or indirectly, including through a nominee or otherwise) and accounted for in such separate and distinct records separately from the other assets of the limited liability company, or any other series thereof, and if the limited liability company agreement so provides, and if notice of the limitation on liabilities of a series as referenced in this subsection is set forth in the certificate of formation of the limited liability company, then the debts, liabilities, obligations and expenses incurred, contracted for or otherwise existing with respect to a particular series shall be enforceable against the assets of such series only, and not against the assets of the limited liability company generally or any other series thereof, and, unless otherwise provided in the limited liability company agreement, none of the debts, liabilities, obligations and expenses incurred, contracted for or otherwise existing with respect to the limited liability company generally or any other series thereof shall be enforceable against the assets of such series. Notice in a certificate of formation of the limitation on liabilities of a series as referenced in this subsection shall be sufficient for all purposes of this subsection whether or not the limited liability company has established any series when such notice is included in the certificate of formation, and there shall be no requirement that any specific series of the limited liability company be referenced in such notice. The fact that a certificate of formation that contains the foregoing notice of the limitation on liabilities of a series is on file in the office of the Secretary of State shall constitute notice of such limitation on liabilities of a series.

(c) Notwithstanding § 18–303(a) of this title, under a limited liability company agreement or under another agreement, a member or manager may agree to be obligated personally for any or all of the debts, obligations and liabilities of one or more series.

(d) A limited liability company agreement may provide for classes or groups of members or managers associated with a series having such relative rights, powers and duties as the limited liability company agreement may provide, and may make provision for the future creation in the manner provided in the limited liability company agreement of additional classes or groups of members or managers associated with the series having such relative rights, powers and duties as may from time to time be established, including rights, powers and duties senior to existing classes and groups of members or managers associated with the series. A limited liability company agreement may provide for the taking of an action, including the amendment of the limited liability company agreement, without the vote or approval of any member or manager or class or group of members or managers, including an action to create under the provisions of the limited liability company agreement a class or group of the series of limited liability company interests that was not previously outstanding. A limited liability company agreement may provide that any member or class or group of members associated with a series shall have no voting rights.

(e) A limited liability company agreement may grant to all or certain identified members or managers or a specified class or group of the members or managers associated with a series the right to vote separately or with all or any class or group of the members or managers associated with the series, on any matter. Voting by members or managers associated with a series may be on a per capita, number, financial interest, class, group or any other basis.

(f) Unless otherwise provided in a limited liability company agreement, the management of a series shall be vested in the members associated with such series in proportion to the then current percentage or other interest of members in the profits of the series owned by all of the members associated with such series, the decision of members owning more than 50 percent of the said percentage or other interest in the profits controlling; provided, however, that if a limited liability company agreement provides for the management of the series, in whole or in part, by a manager, the management of the series, to the extent so provided, shall be vested in the manager who shall be chosen in the manner provided in the limited liability company agreement. The manager of the series shall also hold the offices and have the responsibilities accorded to the manager as set forth in a limited liability company agreement. A series may have more than 1 manager. Subject to § 18–602 of this title, a manager shall cease to be a manager with respect to a series as provided in a limited liability company agreement. Except as otherwise provided in a limited liability company agreement, any event under this chapter or in a limited liability company agreement that causes a manager to cease to be a manager with respect to a series shall not, in itself, cause such manager to cease to be a manager of the limited liability company or with respect to any other series thereof.

(g) Notwithstanding § 18–606 of this title, but subject to subsections (h) and (k) of this section, and unless otherwise provided in a limited liability company agreement, at the time a member associated with a series that has been established in accordance with subsection (b) of this section becomes entitled to receive a distribution with respect to such series, the member has the status of, and is entitled to all remedies available to, a creditor of the series, with respect to the distribution. A limited liability company agreement may provide for the establishment of a record date with respect to allocations and distributions with respect to a series.

(h) Notwithstanding § 18–607(a) of this title, a limited liability company may make a distribution with respect to a series that has been established in accordance with subsection (b) of this section. A limited liability company shall not make a distribution with respect to a series that has been established in accordance with subsection (b) of this section to a member to the extent that at the time of the distribution, after giving effect to the distribution, all liabilities of such series, other than liabilities to members on account of their limited liability company interests with respect to such series and liabilities for which the recourse of creditors is limited to specified property of such series, exceed the fair value of the assets associated with such series, except that the fair value of property of the series that is subject to a liability for which the recourse of creditors is limited shall be included in the assets associated with such series only to the extent that the fair value of that property exceeds that liability. For purposes of the immediately preceding sentence, the term "distribution" shall not include amounts constituting reasonable compensation for present or past services or reasonable payments made in the ordinary course of business pursuant to a bona fide retirement plan or other benefits program. A member who receives a distribution in violation of this subsection, and who knew at the time of the distribution that the distribution violated this subsection, shall be liable to a series for the amount of the distribution. A member who receives a distribution in violation of this subsection, and who did not know at the time of the distribution that the distribution violated this subsection, shall not be liable for the amount of the distribution. Subject to § 18–607(c) of this title, which shall apply to any distribution made with respect to a series under this subsection, this subsection shall not affect any obligation or liability of a member under an agreement or other applicable law for the amount of a distribution.

(i) Unless otherwise provided in the limited liability company agreement, a member shall cease to be associated with a series and to have the power to exercise any rights or powers of a member with respect to such series upon the assignment of all of the member's limited liability company interest with respect to such series. Except as otherwise provided in a limited liability company agreement, any event under this chapter or a limited liability company agreement that causes a member to cease to be associated with a series shall not, in itself, cause such member to cease to be associated with any other series or terminate the continued membership of a member in the limited liability company or cause the termination of the series, regardless of whether such member was the last remaining member associated with such series.

(j) Subject to § 18–801 of this title, except to the extent otherwise provided in the limited liability company agreement, a series may be terminated and its affairs wound up without causing the dissolution of the limited liability company. The termination of a series established in accordance with subsection (b) of this section shall not affect the limitation on liabilities of such series provided by subsection (b) of this section. A series is terminated and its affairs shall be wound up upon the dissolution of the limited liability company under § 18–801 of this title or otherwise upon the first to occur of the following:

(1) At the time specified in the limited liability company agreement;

(2) Upon the happening of events specified in the limited liability company agreement;

(3) Unless otherwise provided in the limited liability company agreement, upon the affirmative vote or written consent of the members of the limited liability company associated with such series or, if there is more than 1 class or group of members associated with such series, then by each class or group of members associated with such series, in either case, by members associated with such series who own more than two-thirds of the then-current percentage or other interest in the profits of the series of the limited liability company owned by all of the members associated with such series or by the members in each class or group of such series, as appropriate; or

(4) The termination of such series under subsection (l) of this section.

(k) Notwithstanding § 18–803(a) of this title, unless otherwise provided in the limited liability company agreement, a manager associated with a series who has not wrongfully terminated the series or, if none, the members associated with the series or a person approved by the members associated with the series or, if there is more than 1 class or group of members associated with the series, then by each class or group of members associated with the series, in either case, by members who own more than 50 percent of the then current percentage or other interest in the profits of the series owned by all of the members associated with the series or by the members in each class or group associated with the series, as appropriate, may wind up the affairs of the series; but, if the series has been established in accordance with subsection (b) of this section, the Court of Chancery, upon cause shown, may wind up the affairs of the series upon application of any member associated with the series, the member's personal representative or assignee, and in connection therewith, may appoint a liquidating trustee. The persons winding up the affairs of a series may, in the name of the limited liability company and for and on behalf of the limited liability company and such series, take all actions with respect to the series as are permitted under § 18–803(b) of this title. The persons winding up the affairs of a series shall provide for the claims and obligations of the series and distribute the assets of the series as provided in § 18–804 of this title, which section shall apply to the winding up and distribution of assets of a series. Actions taken in accordance with this subsection shall not affect the liability of members and shall not impose liability on a liquidating trustee.

(l) On application by or for a member or manager associated with a series established in accordance with subsection (b) of this section, the Court of Chancery may decree termination of such series whenever it is not reasonably practicable to carry on the business of the series in conformity with a limited liability company agreement.

(m) If a foreign limited liability company that is registering to do business in the State of Delaware in accordance with § 18-902 of this title is governed by a limited liability company agreement that establishes or provides for the establishment of designated series of members, managers or limited liability company interests having separate rights, powers or duties with respect to specified property or obligations of the foreign limited liability company or profits and losses associated with specified property or obligations, that fact shall be so stated on the application for registration as a foreign limited liability company. In addition, the foreign limited liability company shall state on such application whether the debts, liabilities and obligations incurred, contracted for or otherwise existing with respect to a particular series, if any, shall be enforceable against the assets of such series only, and not against the assets of the foreign limited liability company generally or any other series thereof, and, unless otherwise provided in the limited liability company agreement, none of the debts, liabilities, obligations and expenses incurred, contracted for or otherwise existing with respect to the foreign limited liability company generally or any other series thereof shall be enforceable against the assets of such series.

§ 18-216. Approval of Conversion of a Limited Liability Company

(a) Upon compliance with this section, a domestic limited liability company may convert to a corporation, a statutory trust, a business trust, an association, a real estate investment trust, a common-law trust or any other unincorporated business or entity, including a partnership (whether general (including a limited liability partnership) or limited (including a limited liability limited partnership)) or a foreign limited liability company.

(b) If the limited liability company agreement specifies the manner of authorizing a conversion of the limited liability company, the conversion shall be authorized as specified in the limited liability company agreement. If the limited liability company agreement does not specify the manner of authorizing a conversion of the limited liability company and does not prohibit a conversion of the limited liability company, the conversion shall be authorized in the same manner as is specified in the limited liability company agreement for authorizing a merger or consolidation that involves the limited liability company as a constituent party to the merger or consolidation. If the limited liability company agreement does not specify the manner of authorizing a conversion of the limited liability company or a merger or consolidation that involves the limited liability company as a constituent party and does not prohibit a conversion of the limited liability company, the conversion shall be authorized by the approval by the members or, if there is more than 1 class or group of members, then by each class or group of members, in either case, by members who own more than 50 percent of the then current percentage or other interest in the profits of the domestic limited liability company owned by all of the members or by the members in each class or group, as appropriate.

(c) Unless otherwise agreed, the conversion of a domestic limited liability company to another entity or business form pursuant to this section shall not require such limited liability company to wind up its affairs under § 18–803 of this title or pay its liabilities and distribute its assets under § 18–804 of this title, and the conversion shall not constitute a dissolution of such limited liability company. When a limited liability company has converted to another entity or business form pursuant to this section, for all purposes of the laws of the State of Delaware, the other entity or business form shall be deemed to be the same entity as the converting limited liability company and the conversion shall constitute a continuation of the existence of the limited liability company in the form of such other entity or business form.

(d) In connection with a conversion of a domestic limited liability company to another entity or business form pursuant to this section, rights or securities of or interests in the domestic limited liability company which is to be converted may be exchanged for or converted into cash, property, rights or securities of or interests in the entity or business form into which the domestic limited liability company is being converted or, in addition to or in lieu thereof, may be exchanged for or converted into cash, property, rights or securities of or interests in another entity or business form or may be cancelled.

(e) If a limited liability company shall convert in accordance with this section to another entity or business form organized, formed or created under the laws of a jurisdiction other than the State of Delaware, a certificate of conversion to non-Delaware entity executed in accordance with § 18–204 of this title, shall be filed in the office of the Secretary of State in accordance with § 18–206 of this title. The certificate of conversion to non-Delaware entity shall state:

(1) The name of the limited liability company and, if it has been changed, the name under which its certificate of formation was originally filed;

(2) The date of filing of its original certificate of formation with the Secretary of State;

(3) The jurisdiction in which the entity or business form, to which the limited liability company shall be converted, is organized, formed or created, and the name of such entity or business form;

(4) The future effective date or time (which shall be a date or time certain) of the conversion if it is not to be effective upon the filing of the certificate of conversion to non-Delaware entity;

(5) That the conversion has been approved in accordance with this section;

(6) The agreement of the limited liability company that it may be served with process in the State of Delaware in any action, suit or proceeding for enforcement of any obligation of the limited liability company arising while it was a limited liability company of the State of Delaware, and that it irrevocably appoints the Secretary of State as its agent to accept service of process in any such action, suit or proceeding;

(7) The address to which a copy of the process referred to in paragraph (6) of this subsection shall be mailed to it by the Secretary of State. In the event of service hereunder upon the Secretary of State, the procedures set forth in § 18-911(c) of this title shall be applicable, except that the plaintiff in any such action, suit or proceeding shall furnish the Secretary of State with the address specified in this subdivision and any other address that the plaintiff may elect to furnish, together with copies of such process as required by the Secretary of State, and the Secretary of State shall notify the limited liability company that has converted out of the State of Delaware at all such addresses furnished by the plaintiff in accordance with the procedures set forth in § 18-911(c) of this title.

(f) Upon the filing in the office of the Secretary of State of the certificate of conversion to non-Delaware entity or upon the future effective date or time of the certificate of conversion to non-Delaware entity and payment to the Secretary of State of all fees prescribed in this chapter, the Secretary of State shall certify that the limited liability company has filed all documents and paid all fees required by this chapter, and thereupon the limited liability company shall cease to exist as a limited liability company of the State of Delaware. Such certificate of the Secretary of State shall be prima facie evidence of the conversion by such limited liability company out of the State of Delaware.

(g) The conversion of a limited liability company out of the State of Delaware in accordance with this section and the resulting cessation of its existence as a limited liability company of the State of Delaware pursuant to a certificate of conversion to non-Delaware entity shall not be deemed to affect any obligations or liabilities of the limited liability company incurred prior to such conversion or the personal liability of any person incurred prior to such conversion, nor shall it be deemed to affect the choice of law applicable to the limited liability company with respect to matters arising prior to such conversion.

(h) When a limited liability company has been converted to another entity or business form pursuant to this section, the other entity or business form shall, for all purposes of the laws of the State of Delaware, be deemed to be the same entity as the limited liability company. When any conversion shall have become effective under this section, for all purposes of the laws of the State of Delaware, all of the rights, privileges and powers of the limited liability company that has converted, and all property, real, personal and mixed, and all debts due to such limited liability company, as well as all other things and causes of action belonging to such limited liability company, shall remain vested in the other entity or business form to which such limited liability company has converted and shall be the property of such other entity or business form, and the title to any real property vested by deed or otherwise in such limited liability company shall not revert or be in any way impaired by reason of this chapter; but all rights of creditors and all liens upon any property of such limited liability company shall be preserved unimpaired, and all debts, liabilities and duties of the limited liability company that has converted shall remain attached to the other entity or business form to which such limited liability company has converted, and may be enforced against it to the same extent as if said debts, liabilities and duties had originally been incurred or contracted by it in its capacity as such other entity or business form. The rights, privileges, powers and interests in property of the limited liability company that has converted, as well as the debts, liabilities and duties of such limited liability company, shall not be deemed, as a consequence of the conversion, to have been transferred to the other entity or business form to which such limited liability company has converted for any purpose of the laws of the State of Delaware.

SUBCHAPTER III. MEMBERS

§ 18–301. Admission of Members

(a) In connection with the formation of a limited liability company, a person is admitted as a member of the limited liability company upon the later to occur of:

(1) The formation of the limited liability company; or

(2) The time provided in and upon compliance with the limited liability company agreement or, if the limited liability company agreement does not so provide, when the person's admission is reflected in the records of the limited liability company.

(b) After the formation of a limited liability company, a person is admitted as a member of the limited liability company:

(1) In the case of a person who is not an assignee of a limited liability company interest, including a person acquiring a limited liability company interest directly from the limited liability company and a person to be admitted as a member of the limited liability company without acquiring a limited liability company interest in the limited liability company at the time provided in and upon compliance with the limited liability company agreement or, if the

limited liability company agreement does not so provide, upon the consent of all members and when the person's admission is reflected in the records of the limited liability company;

(2) In the case of an assignee of a limited liability company interest, as provided in § 18-704(a) of this title and at the time provided in and upon compliance with the limited liability company agreement or, if the limited liability company agreement does not so provide, when any such person's permitted admission is reflected in the records of the limited liability company; or

(3) In the case of a person being admitted as a member of a surviving or resulting limited liability company pursuant to a merger or consolidation approved in accordance with § 18-209(b) of this title, as provided in the limited liability company agreement of the surviving or resulting limited liability company or in the agreement of merger or consolidation, and in the event of any inconsistency, the terms of the agreement of merger or consolidation shall control; and in the case of a person being admitted as a member of a limited liability company pursuant to a merger or consolidation in which such limited liability company is not the surviving or resulting limited liability company in the merger or consolidation, as provided in the limited liability company agreement of such limited liability company.

(c) In connection with the domestication of a non-United States entity (as defined in § 18-212 of this title) as a limited liability company in the State of Delaware in accordance with § 18-212 of this title or the conversion of an other entity (as defined in § 18-214 of this title) to a domestic limited liability company in accordance with § 18-214 of this title, a person is admitted as a member of the limited liability company as provided in the limited liability company agreement.

(d) A person may be admitted to a limited liability company as a member of the limited liability company and may receive a limited liability company interest in the limited liability company without making a contribution or being obligated to make a contribution to the limited liability company. Unless otherwise provided in a limited liability company agreement, a person may be admitted to a limited liability company as a member of the limited liability company without acquiring a limited liability company interest in the limited liability company. Unless otherwise provided in a limited liability company agreement, a person may be admitted as the sole member of a limited liability company without making a contribution or being obligated to make a contribution to the limited liability company or without acquiring a limited liability company interest in the limited liability company.

(e) Unless otherwise provided in a limited liability company agreement or another agreement, a member shall have no preemptive right to subscribe to any additional issue of limited liability company interests or another interest in a limited liability company.

§ 18–302. Classes and Voting

(a) A limited liability company agreement may provide for classes or groups of members having such relative rights, powers and duties as the limited liability company agreement may provide, and may make provision for the future creation in the manner provided in the limited liability company agreement of additional classes or groups of members having such relative rights, powers and duties as may from time to time be established, including rights, powers and duties senior to existing classes and groups of members. A limited liability company agreement may provide for the taking of an action, including the amendment of the limited liability company agreement, without the vote or approval of any member or class or group of members, including an action to create under the provisions of the limited liability company agreement a class or group of limited liability company interests that was not previously outstanding. A limited liability company agreement may provide that any member or class or group of members shall have no voting rights.

(b) A limited liability company agreement may grant to all or certain identified members or a specified class or group of the members the right to vote separately or with all or any class or group of the members or managers, on any matter. Voting by members may be on a per capita, number, financial interest, class, group or any other basis.

(c) A limited liability company agreement may set forth provisions relating to notice of the time, place or purpose of any meeting at which any matter is to be voted on by any members, waiver of any such notice, action by consent without a meeting, the establishment of a record date, quorum requirements, voting in person or by proxy, or any other matter with respect to the exercise of any such right to vote.

(d) Unless otherwise provided in a limited liability company agreement, meetings of members may be held by means of conference telephone or other communications equipment by means of which all persons participating in the meeting can hear each other, and participation in a meeting pursuant to this subsection shall constitute presence in person at the meeting. Unless otherwise provided in a limited liability company agreement, on any matter that is to be voted on, consented to or approved by members, the members may take such action without a meeting, without prior notice and without a vote if a consent or consents in writing, setting forth the action so taken, shall be signed by the members having not less than the minimum number of votes that would be necessary to authorize or take such action at a meeting at which all members entitled to vote thereon were present and voted. Unless otherwise provided in a limited liability company agreement, on any matter that is to be voted on by members, the members may vote in person or by proxy, and such proxy may be granted in writing, by means of electronic transmission or as otherwise permitted by applicable law. Unless otherwise provided in a limited liability company agreement, a consent transmitted by electronic transmission by a member or by a person or persons authorized to act for a member shall be deemed to be written and signed for purposes of this subsection. For purposes of this subsection, the term "electronic transmission" means any form of communication not directly involving the physical transmission of paper that creates a record that may be retained, retrieved and reviewed by a recipient thereof and that may be directly reproduced in paper form by such a recipient through an automated process.

(e) If a limited liability company agreement provides for the manner in which it may be amended, including by requiring the approval of a person who is not a party to the limited liability company agreement or the satisfaction of conditions, it may be amended only in that manner or as otherwise permitted by law (provided that the approval of any person may be waived by such person and that any such conditions may be waived by all persons for whose benefit such conditions were intended).

§ 18-303. Liability to 3rd Parties

(a) Except as otherwise provided by this chapter, the debts, obligations and liabilities of a limited liability company, whether arising in contract, tort or otherwise, shall be solely the debts, obligations and liabilities of the limited liability company, and no member or manager of a limited liability company shall be obligated personally for any such debt, obligation or liability of the limited liability company solely by reason of being a member or acting as a manager of the limited liability company.

(b) Notwithstanding the provisions of subsection (a) of this section, under a limited liability company agreement or under another agreement, a member or manager may agree to be obligated personally for any or all of the debts, obligations and liabilities of the limited liability company.

§ 18-304. Events of Bankruptcy

A person ceases to be a member of a limited liability company upon the happening of any of the following events:

(1) Unless otherwise provided in a limited liability company agreement, or with the written consent of all members, a member:

a. Makes an assignment for the benefit of creditors;

b. Files a voluntary petition in bankruptcy;

c. Is adjudged a bankrupt or insolvent, or has entered against the member an order for relief, in any bankruptcy or insolvency proceeding;

d. Files a petition or answer seeking for the member any reorganization, arrangement, composition, readjustment, liquidation, dissolution or similar relief under any statute, law or regulation;

e. Files an answer or other pleading admitting or failing to contest the material allegations of a petition filed against the member in any proceeding of this nature;

f. Seeks, consents to or acquiesces in the appointment of a trustee, receiver or liquidator of the member or of all or any substantial part of the member's properties; or

(2) Unless otherwise provided in a limited liability company agreement, or with the written consent of all members, 120 days after the commencement of any proceeding against the member seeking reorganization, arrangement, composition, readjustment, liquidation, dissolution or similar relief under any statute, law or regulation, if the proceeding has not been dismissed, or if within 90 days after the appointment without the member's consent or acquiescence of a trustee, receiver or liquidator of the member or of all or any substantial part of the member's properties, the appointment is not vacated or stayed, or within 90 days after the expiration of any such stay, the appointment is not vacated.

§ 18–305. Access to and Confidentiality of Information; Records

(a) Each member of a limited liability company has the right, subject to such reasonable standards (including standards governing what information and documents are to be furnished at what time and location and at whose expense) as may be set forth in a limited liability company agreement or otherwise established by the manager or, if there is no manager, then by the members, to obtain from the limited liability company from time to time upon reasonable demand for any purpose reasonably related to the member's interest as a member of the limited liability company:

(1) True and full information regarding the status of the business and financial condition of the limited liability company;

(2) Promptly after becoming available, a copy of the limited liability company's federal, state and local income tax returns for each year;

(3) A current list of the name and last known business, residence or mailing address of each member and manager;

(4) A copy of any written limited liability company agreement and certificate of formation and all amendments thereto, together with executed copies of any written powers of attorney pursuant to which the limited liability company agreement and any certificate and all amendments thereto have been executed;

(5) True and full information regarding the amount of cash and a description and statement of the agreed value of any other property or services contributed by each member and which each

member has agreed to contribute in the future, and the date on which each became a member; and

(6) Other information regarding the affairs of the limited liability company as is just and reasonable.

(b) Each manager shall have the right to examine all of the information described in subsection (a) of this section for a purpose reasonably related to the position of manager.

(c) The manager of a limited liability company shall have the right to keep confidential from the members, for such period of time as the manager deems reasonable, any information which the manager reasonably believes to be in the nature of trade secrets or other information the disclosure of which the manager in good faith believes is not in the best interest of the limited liability company or could damage the limited liability company or its business or which the limited liability company is required by law or by agreement with a 3rd party to keep confidential.

(d) A limited liability company may maintain its records in other than a written form if such form is capable of conversion into written form within a reasonable time.

(e) Any demand by a member under this section shall be in writing and shall state the purpose of such demand.

(f) Any action to enforce any right arising under this section shall be brought in the Court of Chancery. If the limited liability company refuses to permit a member to obtain or a manager to examine the information described in subsection (a)(3) of this section or does not reply to the demand that has been made within 5 business days after the demand has been made, the demanding member or manager may apply to the Court of Chancery for an order to compel such disclosure. The Court of Chancery is hereby vested with exclusive jurisdiction to determine whether or not the person seeking such information is entitled to the information sought. The Court of Chancery may summarily order the limited liability company to permit the demanding member to obtain or manager to examine the information described in subsection (a)(3) of this section and to make copies or abstracts therefrom, or the Court of Chancery may summarily order the limited liability company to furnish to the demanding member or manager the information described in subsection (a)(3) of this section on the condition that the demanding member or manager first pay to the limited liability company the reasonable cost of obtaining and furnishing such information and on such other conditions as the Court of Chancery deems appropriate. When a demanding member seeks to obtain or a manager seeks to examine the information described in subsection (a)(3) of this section, the demanding member or manager shall first establish (1) that the demanding member or manager has complied with the provisions of this section respecting the form and manner of making demand for obtaining or examining of such information, and (2) that the information the demanding member or manager seeks is reasonably related to the member's interest as a member or the manager's position as a manager, as the case may be. The Court of Chancery may, in its discretion, prescribe any limitations or conditions with reference to the obtaining or examining of information, or award such other or further relief as the Court of Chancery may deem just and proper. The Court of Chancery may order books, documents and records, pertinent extracts therefrom, or duly authenticated copies thereof, to be brought within the State of Delaware and kept in the State of Delaware upon such terms and conditions as the order may prescribe.

(g) The rights of a member or manager to obtain information as provided in this section may be restricted in an original limited liability company agreement or in any subsequent amendment approved or adopted by all of the members and in compliance with any applicable requirements of the limited liability company agreement. The provisions of this subsection shall not be construed to limit the ability to impose restrictions on the rights of a member or manager to obtain information by any other means permitted under this section.

§ 18-306. Remedies for Breach of Limited Liability Company Agreement by Member

A limited liability company agreement may provide that:

(1) A member who fails to perform in accordance with, or to comply with the terms and conditions of, the limited liability company agreement shall be subject to specified penalties or specified consequences; and

(2) At the time or upon the happening of events specified in the limited liability company agreement, a member shall be subject to specified penalties or specified consequences.

Such specified penalties or specified consequences may include and take the form of any penalty or consequence set forth in § 18-502(c) of this title.

SUBCHAPTER IV. MANAGERS

§ 18-401. Admission of Managers

A person may be named or designated as a manager of the limited liability company as provided in § 18-101(10) of this title.

§ 18-402. Management of Limited Liability Company

Unless otherwise provided in a limited liability company agreement, the management of a limited liability company shall be vested in its members in proportion to the then current percentage or other interest of members in the profits of the limited liability company owned by all of the members, the decision of members owning more than 50 percent of the said percentage or other interest in the profits controlling; provided however, that if a limited liability company agreement provides for the management, in whole or in part, of a limited liability company by a manager, the management of the limited liability company, to the extent so provided, shall be vested in the manager who shall be chosen in the manner provided in the limited liability company agreement. The manager shall also hold the offices and have the responsibilities accorded to the manager by or in the manner provided in a limited liability company agreement. Subject to § 18–602 of this title, a manager shall cease to be a manager as provided in a limited liability company agreement. A limited liability company may have more than 1 manager. Unless otherwise provided in a limited liability company agreement, each member and manager has the authority to bind the limited liability company.

both can bind

§ 18–403. Contributions by a Manager

A manager of a limited liability company may make contributions to the limited liability company and share in the profits and losses of, and in distributions from, the limited liability company as a member. A person who is both a manager and a member has the rights and powers, and is subject to the restrictions and liabilities, of a manager and, except as provided in a limited liability company agreement, also has the rights and powers, and is subject to the restrictions and liabilities, of a member to the extent of the manager's participation in the limited liability company as a member.

§ 18–404. Classes and Voting

(a) A limited liability company agreement may provide for classes or groups of managers having such relative rights, powers and duties as the limited liability company agreement may provide, and may make provision for the future creation in the manner provided in the limited liability company agreement of additional classes or groups of managers having such relative rights, powers and duties as may from time to time be established, including rights, powers and duties senior to existing classes and groups of managers. A limited liability company agreement may provide for the taking of an action, including the amendment of the limited liability company agreement, without the vote or approval of any manager or class or group of managers, including an action to create under the provisions of the limited liability company agreement a class or group of limited liability company interests that was not previously outstanding.

(b) A limited liability company agreement may grant to all or certain identified managers or a specified class or group of the managers the right to vote, separately or with all or any class or group of managers or members, on any matter. Voting by managers may be on a per capita, number, financial interest, class, group or any other basis.

(c) A limited liability company agreement may set forth provisions relating to notice of the time, place or purpose of any meeting at which any matter is to be voted on by any manager or class or group of managers, waiver of any such notice, action by consent without a meeting, the establishment of a record date, quorum requirements, voting in person or by proxy, or any other matter with respect to the exercise of any such right to vote.

(d) Unless otherwise provided in a limited liability company agreement, meetings of managers may be held by means of conference telephone or other communications equipment by means of which all persons participating in the meeting can hear each other, and participation in a meeting pursuant to this subsection shall constitute presence in person at the meeting. Unless otherwise provided in a limited liability company agreement, on any matter that is to be voted on, consented to or approved by managers, the managers may take such action without a meeting, without prior notice and without a vote if a consent or consents in writing, setting forth the action so taken, shall be signed by the managers having not less than the minimum number of votes that would be necessary to authorize or take such action at a meeting at which all managers entitled to vote thereon were present and voted. Unless otherwise provided in a limited liability company agreement, on any matter that is to be voted on by managers, the managers may vote in person or by proxy, and such proxy may be granted in writing, by means of electronic transmission or as otherwise permitted by applicable law. Unless otherwise provided in a limited liability company agreement, a consent transmitted by electronic transmission by a manager or by a person or persons authorized to act for a manager shall be deemed to be written and signed for purposes of this subsection. For purposes of this subsection, the term "electronic transmission" means any form of communication not directly involving the physical transmission of paper that creates a record that may be retained, retrieved and reviewed by a recipient thereof and that may be directly reproduced in paper form by such a recipient through an automated process.

§ 18–405. Remedies for Breach of Limited Liability Company Agreement by Manager

A limited liability company agreement may provide that:

(1) A manager who fails to perform in accordance with, or to comply with the terms and conditions of, the limited liability company agreement shall be subject to specified penalties or specified consequences; and

(2) At the time or upon the happening of events specified in the limited liability company agreement, a manager shall be subject to specified penalties or specified consequences.

§ 18–406. Reliance on Reports and Information by Member or Manager

A member, manager or liquidating trustee of a limited liability company shall be fully protected in relying in good faith upon the records of the limited liability company and upon information, opinions, reports or statements presented by another manager, member or liquidating trustee, an officer or employee of the limited liability company, or committees of the limited liability company, members or managers, or by any other person as to matters the member, manager or liquidating trustees reasonably believes are within such other person's professional or expert competence, including information, opinions, reports or statements as to the value and amount of the assets, liabilities, profits or losses of the limited liability company, or the value and amount of assets or reserves or contracts, agreements or other undertakings that would be sufficient to pay claims and obligations of the limited liability company or to make reasonable provision to pay such claims and obligations, or any other facts pertinent to the existence and amount of assets from which distributions to members or creditors might properly be paid.

§ 18–407. Delegation of Rights and Powers to Manage

Unless otherwise provided in the limited liability company agreement, a member or manager of a limited liability company has the power and authority to delegate to 1 or more other persons the member's or manager's, as the case may be, rights and powers to manage and control the business and affairs of the limited liability company, including to delegate to agents, officers and employees of a member or manager or the limited liability company, and to delegate by a management agreement or another agreement with, or otherwise to, other persons. Unless otherwise provided in the limited liability company agreement, such delegation by a member or manager of a limited liability company shall not cause the member or manager to cease to be a member or manager, as the case may be, of the limited liability company or cause the person to whom any such rights and powers have been delegated to be a member or manager, as the case may be, of the limited liability company.

SUBCHAPTER V. FINANCE

§ 18–501. Form of Contribution

The contribution of a member to a limited liability company may be in cash, property or services rendered, or a promissory note or other obligation to contribute cash or property or to perform services.

§ 18–502. Liability for Contribution

(a) Except as provided in a limited liability company agreement, a member is obligated to a limited liability company to perform any promise to contribute cash or property or to perform services, even if the member is unable to perform because of death, disability or any other reason. If a member does not make the required contribution of property or services, the member is obligated at the option of the limited liability company to contribute cash equal to that portion of the agreed value (as stated in the records of the limited liability company) of the contribution that has not been made. The foregoing option shall be in addition to, and not in lieu of, any other rights, including the right to specific performance, that the limited liability company may have against such member under the limited liability company agreement or applicable law.

(b) Unless otherwise provided in a limited liability company agreement, the obligation of a member to make a contribution or return money or other property paid or distributed in violation of this chapter may be compromised only by consent of all the members. Notwithstanding the compromise, a creditor of a limited liability company who extends credit, after the entering into of a limited liability company agreement or an amendment thereto which, in either case, reflects the obligation, and before the amendment thereof to reflect the compromise, may enforce the original obligation to the extent that, in extending credit, the creditor reasonably relied on the obligation of a member to make a contribution or return. A conditional obligation of a member to make a contribution or return money or other property to a limited liability company may not be enforced unless the conditions of the obligation have been satisfied or waived as to or by such member. Conditional obligations include contributions payable upon a discretionary call of a limited liability company prior to the time the call occurs.

(c) A limited liability company agreement may provide that the interest of any member who fails to make any contribution that the member is obligated to make shall be subject to specified penalties for, or specified consequences of, such failure. Such penalty or consequence may take the form of reducing or eliminating the defaulting member's proportionate interest in a limited liability company, subordinating the member's limited liability company interest to that of nondefaulting members, a forced sale of that limited liability company interest, forfeiture of the defaulting member's limited liability company interest, the lending by other members of the amount necessary to meet the defaulting member's commitment, a fixing of the value of the defaulting member's limited liability company interest by appraisal or by formula and redemption or sale of the limited liability company interest at such value, or other penalty or consequence.

§ 18-503. Allocation of Profits and Losses

The profits and losses of a limited liability company shall be allocated among the members, and among classes or groups of members, in the manner provided in a limited liability company agreement. If the limited liability company agreement does not so provide, profits and losses shall be allocated on the basis of the agreed value (as stated in the records of the limited liability company) of the contributions made by each member to the extent they have been received by the limited liability company and have not been returned.

§ 18-504. Allocation of Distributions

Distributions of cash or other assets of a limited liability company shall be allocated among the members, and among classes or groups of members, in the manner provided in a limited liability company agreement. If the limited liability company agreement does not so provide, distributions shall be made on the basis of the agreed value (as stated in the records of the limited liability company) of the contributions made by each member to the extent they have been received by the limited liability company and have not been returned.

§ 18–505. Defense of Usury not Available

No obligation of a member or manager of a limited liability company to the limited liability company arising under the limited liability company agreement or a separate agreement or writing, and no note, instrument or other writing evidencing any such obligation of a member or manager, shall be subject to the defense of usury, and no member or manager shall interpose the defense of usury with respect to any such obligation in any action.

SUBCHAPTER VI. DISTRIBUTIONS AND RESIGNATION

§ 18–601. Interim Distributions

Except as provided in this subchapter, to the extent and at the times or upon the happening of the events specified in a limited liability company agreement, a member is entitled to receive from a limited liability company distributions before the member's resignation from the limited liability company and before the dissolution and winding up thereof.

§ 18–602. Resignation of Manager

A manager may resign as a manager of a limited liability company at the time or upon the happening of events specified in a limited liability company agreement and in accordance with the limited liability company agreement. A limited liability company agreement may provide that a manager shall not have the right to resign as a manager of a limited liability company. Notwithstanding that a limited liability company agreement provides that a manager does not have the right to resign as a manager of a limited liability company, a manager may resign as a manager of a limited liability company at any time by giving written notice to the members and other managers. If the resignation of a manager violates a limited liability company agreement, in addition to any remedies otherwise available under applicable law, a limited liability company may recover from the resigning manager damages for breach of the limited liability company agreement and offset the damages against the amount otherwise distributable to the resigning manager.

§ 18–603. Resignation of Member

A member may resign from a limited liability company only at the time or upon the happening of events specified in a limited liability company agreement and in accordance with the limited liability company agreement. Notwithstanding anything to the contrary under applicable law, unless a limited liability company agreement provides otherwise, a member may not resign from a limited liability company prior to the dissolution and winding up of the limited liability company. Notwithstanding anything to the contrary under applicable law, a limited liability company agreement may provide that a limited liability company interest may not be assigned prior to the dissolution and winding up of the limited liability company.

Unless otherwise provided in a limited liability company agreement, a limited liability company whose original certificate of formation was filed with the Secretary of State and effective on or prior to July 31, 1996, shall continue to be governed by this section as in effect on July 31, 1996, and shall not be governed by this section.

§ 18-604. Distribution Upon Resignation

Except as provided in this subchapter, upon resignation any resigning member is entitled to receive any distribution to which such member is entitled under a limited liability company agreement and, if not otherwise provided in a limited liability company agreement, such member is entitled to receive, within a reasonable time after resignation, the fair value of such member's limited liability company interest as of the date of resignation based upon such member's right to share in distributions from the limited liability company.

§ 18-605. Distribution in Kind

Except as provided in a limited liability company agreement, a member, regardless of the nature of the member's contribution, has no right to demand and receive any distribution from a limited liability company in any form other than cash. Except as provided in a limited liability company agreement, a member may not be compelled to accept a distribution of any asset in kind from a limited liability company to the extent that the percentage of the asset distributed exceeds a percentage of that asset which is equal to the percentage in which the member shares in distributions from the limited liability company. Except as provided in the limited liability company agreement, a member may be compelled to accept a distribution of any asset in kind from a limited liability company to the extent that the percentage of the asset distributed is equal to a percentage of that asset which is equal to the percentage in which the member shares in distributions from the limited liability company.

§ 18-606. Right to Distribution

Subject to §§ 18-607 and 18-804 of this title, and unless otherwise provided in a limited liability company agreement, at the time a member becomes entitled to receive a distribution, the member has the status of, and is entitled to all remedies available to, a creditor of a limited liability company with respect to the distribution. A limited liability company agreement may provide for the establishment of a record date with respect to allocations and distributions by a limited liability company.

§ 18–607. Limitations on Distribution

(a) A limited liability company shall not make a distribution to a member to the extent that at the time of the distribution, after giving effect to the distribution, all liabilities of the limited liability company, other than liabilities to members on account of their limited liability company interests and liabilities for which the recourse of creditors is limited to specified property of the limited liability company, exceed the fair value of the assets of the limited liability company, except that the fair value of property that is subject to a liability for which the recourse of creditors is limited shall be included in the assets of the limited liability company only to the extent that the fair value of that property exceeds that liability. For purposes of this subsection (a), the term "distribution" shall not include amounts constituting reasonable compensation for present or past services or reasonable payments made in the ordinary course of business pursuant to a bona fide retirement plan or other benefits program.

(b) A member who receives a distribution in violation of subsection (a) of this section, and who knew at the time of the distribution that the distribution violated subsection (a) of this section, shall be liable to a limited liability company for the amount of the distribution. A member who receives a distribution in violation of subsection (a) of this section, and who did not know at the time of the distribution that the distribution violated subsection (a) of this section, shall not be liable for the amount of the distribution. Subject to subsection (c) of this section, this subsection shall not affect any obligation or liability of a member under an agreement or other applicable law for the amount of a distribution.

(c) Unless otherwise agreed, a member who receives a distribution from a limited liability company shall have no liability under this chapter or other applicable law for the amount of the distribution after the expiration of 3 years from the date of the distribution unless an action to recover the distribution from such member is commenced prior to the expiration of the said 3–year period and an adjudication of liability against such member is made in the said action.

SUBCHAPTER VII. ASSIGNMENT OF LIMITED LIABILITY COMPANY INTERESTS

§ 18–701. Nature of Limited Liability Company Interest

A limited liability company interest is personal property. A member has no interest in specific limited liability company property.

§ 18–702. Assignment of Limited Liability Company Interest

(a) A limited liability company interest is assignable in whole or in part except as provided in a limited liability company agreement. The assignee of a member's limited liability company interest shall have no right to participate in the management of the business and affairs of a limited liability company except as provided in a limited liability company agreement and upon:

(1) The approval of all of the members of the limited liability company other than the member assigning the limited liability company interest; or

(2) Compliance with any procedure provided for in the limited liability company agreement.

(b) Unless otherwise provided in a limited liability company agreement:

(1) An assignment of a limited liability company interest does not entitle the assignee to become or to exercise any rights or powers of a member;

(2) An assignment of a limited liability company interest entitles the assignee to share in such profits and losses, to receive such distribution or distributions, and to receive such allocation of income, gain, loss, deduction, or credit or similar item to which the assignor was entitled, to the extent assigned; and

(3) A member ceases to be a member and to have the power to exercise any rights or powers of a member upon assignment of all of the member's limited liability company interest. Unless otherwise provided in a limited liability company agreement, the pledge of, or granting of a security interest, lien or other encumbrance in or against, any or all of the limited liability company interest of a member shall not cause the member to cease to be a member or to have the power to exercise any rights or powers of a member.

(c) Unless otherwise provided in a limited liability company agreement, a member's interest in a limited liability company may be evidenced by a certificate of limited liability company interest issued by the limited liability company. A limited liability company agreement may provide for the assignment or transfer of any limited liability company interest represented by such a certificate and make other provisions with respect to such certificates.

(d) Unless otherwise provided in a limited liability company agreement and except to the extent assumed by agreement, until an assignee of a limited liability company interest becomes a member, the assignee shall have no liability as a member solely as a result of the assignment.

(e) Unless otherwise provided in the limited liability company agreement, a limited liability company may acquire, by purchase, redemption or otherwise, any limited liability company interest or other interest of a member or manager in the limited liability company. Unless otherwise provided in the limited liability company agreement, any such interest so acquired by the limited liability company shall be deemed canceled.

§ 18–703. Member's Limited Liability Company Interest Subject to Charging Order

(a) On application by a judgment creditor of a member or of a member's assignee, a court having jurisdiction may charge the limited liability company interest of the judgment debtor to satisfy the judgment. To the extent so charged, the judgment creditor has only the right to receive any distribution or distributions to which the judgment debtor would otherwise have been entitled in respect of such limited liability company interest.

(b) A charging order constitutes a lien on the judgment debtor's limited liability company interest.

(c) This chapter does not deprive a member or member's assignee of a right under exemption laws with respect to the judgment debtor's limited liability company interest.

(d) The entry of a charging order is the exclusive remedy by which a judgment creditor of a member or of a member's assignee may satisfy a judgment out of the judgment debtor's limited liability company interest.

(e) No creditor of a member or of a member's assignee shall have any right to obtain possession of, or otherwise exercise legal or equitable remedies with respect to, the property of the limited liability company.

(f) The Court of Chancery shall have jurisdiction to hear and determine any matter relating to any such charging order.

§ 18–704. Right of Assignee to Become Member

(a) An assignee of a limited liability company interest may become a member as provided in a limited liability company agreement and upon:

(1) The approval of all of the members of the limited liability company other than the member assigning limited liability company interest; or

(2) Compliance with any procedure provided for in the limited liability company agreement.

(b) An assignee who has become a member has, to the extent assigned, the rights and powers, and is subject to the restrictions and liabilities, of a member under a limited liability company agreement and this chapter. Notwithstanding the foregoing, unless otherwise provided in a limited liability company agreement, an assignee who becomes a member is liable for the obligations of the assignor to make contributions as provided in § 18–502 of this title, but shall not be liable for the obligations of the assignor under subchapter VI of this chapter. However, the assignee is not obligated for liabilities, including the obligations of the assignor to make contributions as provided in § 18–502 of this title, unknown to the assignee at the time the assignee became a member and which could not be ascertained from a limited liability company agreement.

(c) Whether or not an assignee of a limited liability company interest becomes a member, the assignor is not released from liability to a limited liability company under subchapters V and VI of this chapter.

§ 18–705. Powers of Estate of Deceased or Incompetent Member

If a member who is an individual dies or a court of competent jurisdiction adjudges the member to be incompetent to manage the member's person or property, the member's personal representative may exercise all of the member's rights for the purpose of settling the member's estate or administering the member's property, including any power under a limited liability company agreement of an assignee to become a member. If a member is a corporation, trust or other entity and is dissolved or terminated, the powers of that member may be exercised by its personal representative.

SUBCHAPTER VIII. DISSOLUTION

§ 18–801. Dissolution

(a) A limited liability company is dissolved and its affairs shall be wound up upon the first to occur of the following:

(1) At the time specified in a limited liability company agreement, but if no such time is set forth in the limited liability company agreement, then the limited liability company shall have a perpetual existence;

(2) Upon the happening of events specified in a limited liability company agreement;

(3) Unless otherwise provided in a limited liability company agreement, upon the affirmative vote or written consent of the members of the limited liability company or, if there is more than 1 class or group of members, then by each class or group of members, in either case, by members who own more than two-thirds of the then-current percentage or other interest in the profits of the limited liability company owned by all of the members or by the members in each class or group, as appropriate;

(4) At any time there are no members; provided, that the limited liability company is not dissolved and is not required to be wound up if:

a. Unless otherwise provided in a limited liability company agreement, within 90 days or such other period as is provided for in the limited liability company agreement after the occurrence of the event that terminated the continued membership of the last remaining member, the personal representative of the last remaining member agrees in writing to continue the limited liability company and to the admission of the personal representative of such member or its nominee or designee to the limited liability company as a member, effective as of the occurrence of the event that terminated the continued membership of the last remaining member; provided, that a limited liability company agreement may provide that the personal representative of the last remaining member shall be obligated to agree in writing to continue the limited liability company and to the admission of the personal representative of such member or its nominee or designee to the limited liability company as a member, effective as of the occurrence of the event that terminated the continued membership of the last remaining member, or

b. A member is admitted to the limited liability company in the manner provided for in the limited liability company agreement, effective as of the occurrence of the event that terminated the continued membership of the last remaining member, within 90 days or such other period as is provided for in the limited liability company agreement after the occurrence of the event that terminated the continued membership of the last remaining member, pursuant to a provision of the limited liability company agreement that specifically provides for the admission of a member to the limited liability company after there is no longer a remaining member of the limited liability company.

(5) The entry of a decree of judicial dissolution under § 18-802 of this title.

(b) Unless otherwise provided in a limited liability company agreement, the death, retirement, resignation, expulsion, bankruptcy or dissolution of any member or the occurrence of any other event that terminates the continued membership of any member shall not cause the limited liability company to be dissolved or its affairs to be wound up, and upon the occurrence of any such event, the limited liability company shall be continued without dissolution.

§ 18-802. Judicial Dissolution

On application by or for a member or manager the Court of Chancery may decree dissolution of a limited liability company whenever it is not reasonably practicable to carry on the business in conformity with a limited liability company agreement.

§ 18-803. Winding Up

(a) Unless otherwise provided in a limited liability company agreement, a manager who has not wrongfully dissolved a limited liability company or, if none, the members or a person approved by the members or, if there is more than 1 class or group of members, then by each class or group of members, in either case, by members who own more than 50 percent of the then current percentage or other interest in the profits of the limited liability company owned by all of the members or by the members in each class or group, as appropriate, may wind up the limited liability company's affairs; but the Court of Chancery, upon cause shown, may wind up the limited liability company's affairs upon application of any member or manager, the member's or manager's personal representative or assignee, and in connection therewith, may appoint a liquidating trustee.

(b) Upon dissolution of a limited liability company and until the filing of a certificate of cancellation as provided in § 18–203 of this title, the persons winding up the limited liability company's affairs may, in the name of, and for and on behalf of, the limited liability company, prosecute and defend suits, whether civil, criminal or administrative, gradually settle and close the limited liability company's business, dispose of and convey the limited liability company's property, discharge or make reasonable provision for the limited liability company's liabilities, and distribute to the members any remaining assets of the limited liability company, all without affecting the liability of members and managers and without imposing liability on a liquidating trustee.

§ 18–804. Distribution of Assets

(a) Upon the winding up of a limited liability company, the assets shall be distributed as follows:

(1) To creditors, including members and managers who are creditors, to the extent otherwise permitted by law, in satisfaction of liabilities of the limited liability company (whether by payment or the making of reasonable provision for payment thereof) other than liabilities for which reasonable provision for payment has been made and liabilities for distributions to members and former members under § 18–601 or § 18–604 of this title;

(2) Unless otherwise provided in a limited liability company agreement, to members and former members in satisfaction of liabilities for distributions under § 18–601 or § 18–604 of this title; and

(3) Unless otherwise provided in a limited liability company agreement, to members first for the return of their contributions and second respecting their limited liability company interests, in the proportions in which the members share in distributions.

(b) A limited liability company which has dissolved:

(1) Shall pay or make reasonable provision to pay all claims and obligations, including all contingent, conditional or unmatured contractual claims, known to the limited liability company;

(2) Shall make such provision as will be reasonably likely to be sufficient to provide compensation for any claim against the limited liability company which is the subject of a pending action, suit or proceeding to which the limited liability company is a party; and

(3) Shall make such provision as will be reasonably likely to be sufficient to provide compensation for claims that have not been made known to the limited liability company or that have not arisen but that, based on facts known to the limited liability company, are likely to arise or to become known to the limited liability company within 10 years after the date of dissolution.

If there are sufficient assets, such claims and obligations shall be paid in full and any such provision for payment made shall be made in full. If there are insufficient assets, such claims and obligations shall be paid or provided for according to their priority and, among claims of equal priority, ratably to the extent of assets available therefor. Unless otherwise provided in the limited liability company agreement, any remaining assets shall be distributed as provided in this chapter. Any liquidating trustee winding up a limited liability company's affairs who has complied with this section shall not be personally liable to the claimants of the dissolved limited liability company by reason of such person's actions in winding up the limited liability company.

(c) A member who receives a distribution in violation of subsection (a) of this section, and who knew at the time of the distribution that the distribution violated subsection (a) of this section, shall be liable to the limited liability company for the amount of the distribution. For purposes of the immediately preceding sentence, the term "distribution" shall not include amounts constituting reasonable compensation for present or past services or reasonable payments made in the ordinary course of business pursuant to a bona fide retirement plan or other benefits program. A member who receives a distribution in violation of subsection (a) of this section, and who did not know at the time of the distribution that the distribution violated subsection (a) of this section, shall not be liable for the amount of the distribution. Subject to subsection (d) of this section, this subsection shall not affect any obligation or liability of a member under an agreement or other applicable law for the amount of a distribution.

(d) Unless otherwise agreed, a member who receives a distribution from a limited liability company to which this section applies shall have no liability under this chapter or other applicable law for the amount of the distribution after the expiration of 3 years from the date of the distribution unless an action to recover the distribution from such member is commenced prior to the expiration of the said 3-year period and an adjudication of liability against such member is made in the said action.

(e) Section 18-607 of this title shall not apply to a distribution to which this section applies.

§ 18–805. Trustees or Receivers for Limited Liability Companies; Appointment; Powers; Duties

When the certificate of formation of any limited liability company formed under this chapter shall be canceled by the filing of a certificate of cancellation pursuant to § 18–203 of this title, the Court of Chancery, on application of any creditor, member or manager of the limited liability company, or any other person who shows good cause therefor, at any time, may either appoint 1 or more of the managers of the limited liability company to be trustees, or appoint 1 or more persons to be receivers, of and for the limited liability company, to take charge of the limited liability company's property, and to collect the debts and property due and belonging to the limited liability company, with the power to prosecute and defend, in the name of the limited liability company, or otherwise, all such suits as may be necessary or proper for the purposes aforesaid, and to appoint an agent or agents under them, and to do all other acts which might be done by the limited liability company, if in being, that may be necessary for the final settlement of the unfinished business of the limited liability company. The powers of the trustees or receivers may be continued as long as the Court of Chancery shall think necessary for the purposes aforesaid.

§ 18–806. Revocation of Dissolution

Notwithstanding the occurrence of an event set forth in § 18–801(a)(1), (2), (3) or (4) of this title, the limited liability company shall not be dissolved and its affairs shall not be wound up if, prior to the filing of a certificate of cancellation in the office of the Secretary of State, the limited liability company is continued, effective as of the occurrence of such event, pursuant to the affirmative vote or written consent of all remaining members of the limited liability company or the personal representative of the last remaining member of the limited liability company if there is no remaining member (and any other person whose approval is required under the limited liability company agreement to revoke a dissolution pursuant to this section); provided, however, if the dissolution was caused by a vote or written consent, the dissolution shall not be revoked unless each member and other person (or their respective personal representatives) who voted in favor of, or consented to, the dissolution has voted or consented in writing to continue the limited liability company. If there is no remaining member of the limited liability company and the personal representative of the last remaining member votes in favor of or consents to the continuation of the limited liability company, such personal representative shall be required to agree in writing to the admission of the personal representative of such member or its nominee or designee to the limited liability company as a member, effective as of the occurrence of the event that terminated the continued membership of the last remaining member.

SUBCHAPTER IX. FOREIGN LIMITED LIABILITY COMPANIES

§ 18-901. Law Governing

(a) Subject to the Constitution of the State of Delaware:

(1) The laws of the state, territory, possession, or other jurisdiction or country under which a foreign limited liability company is organized govern its organization and internal affairs and the liability of its members and managers; and

(2) A foreign limited liability company may not be denied registration by reason of any difference between those laws and the laws of the State of Delaware.

(b) A foreign limited liability company shall be subject to § 18-106 of this title.

§ 18-902. Registration Required; Application

Before doing business in the State of Delaware, a foreign limited liability company shall register with the Secretary of State. In order to register, a foreign limited liability company shall submit to the Secretary of State:

(1) A copy executed by an authorized person of an application for registration as a foreign limited liability company, setting forth:

a. The name of the foreign limited liability company and, if different, the name under which it proposes to register and do business in the State of Delaware;

b. The state, territory, possession or other jurisdiction or country where formed, the date of its formation and a statement from an authorized person that, as of the date of filing, the foreign limited liability company validly exists as a limited liability company under the laws of the jurisdiction of its formation;

c. The nature of the business or purposes to be conducted or promoted in the State of Delaware;

d. The address of the registered office and the name and address of the registered agent for service of process required to be maintained by § 18-904(b) of this title;

e. A statement that the Secretary of State is appointed the agent of the foreign limited liability company for service of process under the circumstances set forth in § 18-910(b) of this title; and

f. The date on which the foreign limited liability company first did, or intends to do, business in the State of Delaware.

(2) A fee as set forth in § 18–1105(a)(6) of this title shall be paid.

§ 18–903. Issuance of Registration

(a) If the Secretary of State finds that an application for registration conforms to law and all requisite fees have been paid, the Secretary shall:

(1) Certify that the application has been filed by endorsing upon the original application the word "Filed", and the date and hour of the filing. This endorsement is conclusive of the date and time of its filing in the absence of actual fraud;

(2) File and index the endorsed application.

(b) The Secretary of State shall prepare and return to the person who filed the application or the person's representative a copy of the original signed application, similarly endorsed, and shall certify such copy as a true copy of the original signed application.

(c) The filing of the application with the Secretary of State shall make it unnecessary to file any other documents under Chapter 31 of this title.

§ 18–904. Name; Registered Office; Registered Agent

(a) A foreign limited liability company may register with the Secretary of State under any name (whether or not it is the name under which it is registered in the jurisdiction of its formation) that includes the words "Limited Liability Company" or the abbreviation "L.L.C." or the designation "LLC" and that could be registered by a domestic limited liability company; provided however, that a foreign limited liability company may register under any name which is not such as to distinguish it upon the records in the office of the Secretary of State from the name on such records of any domestic or foreign corporation, partnership, statutory trust, limited liability company or limited partnership reserved, registered, formed or organized under the laws of the State of Delaware with the written consent of the other corporation, partnership, statutory trust, limited liability company or limited partnership, which written consent shall be filed with the Secretary of State.

(b) Each foreign limited liability company shall have and maintain in the State of Delaware:

(1) A registered office which may but need not be a place of its business in the State of Delaware; and

(2) A registered agent for service of process on the foreign limited liability company, which agent may be either an individual resident of the State of Delaware whose business office is identical with the foreign limited liability company's registered office, or a

domestic corporation, or a domestic limited partnership, or a domestic limited liability company, or a domestic statutory trust, or a foreign corporation, or a foreign limited partnership, or a foreign limited liability company authorized to do business in the State of Delaware having a business office identical with such registered office, which is generally open during normal business hours to accept service of process and otherwise perform the functions of a registered agent.

(c) A registered agent may change the address of the registered office of the foreign limited liability company or companies for which the agent is registered agent to another address in the State of Delaware by paying a fee as set forth in § 18-1105(a)(7) of this title and filing with the Secretary of State a certificate, executed by such registered agent, setting forth the address at which such registered agent has maintained the registered office for each of the foreign limited liability companies for which it is a registered agent, and further certifying to the new address to which each such registered office will be changed on a given day, and at which new address such registered agent will thereafter maintain the registered office for each of the foreign limited liability companies for which it is registered agent. Upon the filing of such certificate, the Secretary of State shall furnish to the registered agent a certified copy of the same under the Secretary's hand and seal of office, and thereafter, or until further change of address, as authorized by law, the registered office in the State of Delaware of each of the foreign limited liability companies for which the agent is a registered agent shall be located at the new address of the registered agent thereof as given in the certificate. In the event of a change of name of any person acting as a registered agent of a foreign limited liability company, such registered agent shall file with the Secretary of State a certificate, executed by such registered agent, setting forth the new name of such registered agent, the name of such registered agent before it was changed and the address at which such registered agent has maintained the registered office for each of the foreign limited liability companies for which it is registered agent, and shall pay a fee as set forth in § 18-1105(a)(7) of this title. Upon the filing of such certificate, the Secretary of State shall furnish to the registered agent a certified copy of the same under the Secretary of State's own hand and seal of office. A change of name of any person acting as a registered agent of a foreign limited liability company as a result of the merger or consolidation of the registered agent with or into another person which succeeds to its assets and liabilities by operation of law shall be deemed a change of name for purposes of this section. Filing a certificate under this section shall be deemed to be an amendment of the application of each foreign limited liability company affected thereby and each such foreign limited liability company shall not be required to take any further action with respect thereto to amend its application under § 18-905 of this title. Any registered agent filing a certificate under this section shall promptly, upon such filing, deliver a copy of any such certificate to each foreign limited liability company affected thereby.

(d) The registered agent of 1 or more foreign limited liability companies may resign and appoint a successor registered agent by paying a fee as set forth in § 18-1105(a)(7) of this title and filing a certificate with the Secretary of State stating that it resigns and the name and address of the successor registered agent. There shall be attached to such certificate a statement of each affected foreign limited liability company ratifying and approving such change of registered agent. Upon such filing, the successor registered agent shall become the registered agent of such foreign limited liability companies as have ratified and approved such substitution and the successor registered agent's address, as stated in such certificate, shall become the address of each such foreign limited liability company's registered office in the State of Delaware. The Secretary of State shall then issue a certificate that the successor registered agent has become the registered agent of the foreign limited liability companies so ratifying and approving such change and setting out the names of such foreign limited liability companies. Filing of such certificate of resignation shall be deemed to be an amendment of the application of each foreign limited liability company affected thereby and each such foreign limited liability company shall not be required to take any further action with respect thereto to amend its application under § 18-905 of this title.

(e) The registered agent of 1 or more foreign limited liability companies may resign without appointing a successor registered agent by paying a fee as set forth in § 18-1105(a)(7) of this title and filing a certificate of resignation with the Secretary of State, but such resignation shall not become effective until 30 days after the certificate is filed. The certificate shall contain a statement that written notice of resignation was given to each affected foreign limited liability company at least 30 days prior to the filing of the certificate by mailing or delivering such notice to the foreign limited liability company at its address last known to the registered agent and shall set forth the date of such notice. After receipt of the notice of the resignation of its registered agent, the foreign limited liability company for which such registered agent was acting shall obtain and designate a new registered agent to take the place of the registered agent so resigning. If such foreign limited liability company fails to obtain and designate a new registered agent as aforesaid prior to the expiration of the period of 30 days after the filing by the registered agent of the certificate of resignation, such foreign limited liability company shall not be permitted to do business in the State of Delaware and its registration shall be deemed to be cancelled. After the resignation of the registered agent shall have become effective as provided in this section and if no new registered agent shall have been obtained and designated in the time and manner aforesaid, service of legal process against each foreign limited liability company for which the resigned registered agent had been acting shall thereafter be upon the Secretary of State in accordance with § 18–911 of this title.

§ 18–905. Amendments to Application

If any statement in the application for registration of a foreign limited liability company was false when made or any arrangements or other facts described have changed, making the application false in any respect, the foreign limited liability company shall promptly file in the office of the Secretary of State a certificate, executed by an authorized person, correcting such statement, together with a fee as set forth in § 18–1105(a)(6) of this title.

§ 18–906. Cancellation of Registration [Effective Until Jan. 1, 2007]

A foreign limited liability company may cancel its registration by filing with the Secretary of State a certificate of cancellation, executed by an authorized person, together with a fee as set forth in § 18–1105(a)(6) of this title. A cancellation does not terminate the authority of the Secretary of State to accept service of process on the foreign limited liability company with respect to causes of action arising out of the doing of business in the State of Delaware.

§ 18–906. Cancellation of Registration [Effective Jan. 1, 2007]

A foreign limited liability company may cancel its registration by filing with the Secretary of State a certificate of cancellation, executed by an authorized person, together with a fee as set forth in § 18–1105(a)(6) of this title. The registration of a foreign limited liability company shall be cancelled as provided in §§ 18–104(i)(4) and 18–904(e) of this title. A cancellation does not terminate the authority of the Secretary of State to accept service of process on the foreign limited liability company with respect to causes of action arising out of the doing of business in the State of Delaware.

§ 18–907. Doing Business Without Registration

(a) A foreign limited liability company doing business in the State of Delaware may not maintain any action, suit or proceeding in the State of Delaware until it has registered in the State of Delaware, and has paid to the State of Delaware all fees and penalties for the years or parts thereof, during which it did business in the State of Delaware without having registered.

(b) The failure of a foreign limited liability company to register in the State of Delaware does not impair:

(1) The validity of any contract or act of the foreign limited liability company;

(2) The right of any other party to the contract to maintain any action, suit or proceeding on the contract; or

(3) Prevent the foreign limited liability company from defending any action, suit or proceeding in any court of the State of Delaware.

(c) A member or a manager of a foreign limited liability company is not liable for the obligations of the foreign limited liability company solely by reason of the limited liability company's having done business in the State of Delaware without registration.

(d) Any foreign limited liability company doing business in the State of Delaware without first having registered shall be fined and shall pay to the Secretary of State $200 for each year or part thereof during which the foreign limited liability company failed to register in the State of Delaware.

§ 18-908. Foreign Limited Liability Companies Doing Business Without Having Qualified; Injunctions.

The Court of Chancery shall have jurisdiction to enjoin any foreign limited liability company, or any agent thereof, from doing any business in the State of Delaware if such foreign limited liability company has failed to register under this subchapter or if such foreign limited liability company has secured a certificate of the Secretary of State under § 18-903 of this title on the basis of false or misleading representations. Upon the motion of the Attorney General or upon the relation of proper parties, the Attorney General shall proceed for this purpose by complaint in any county in which such foreign limited liability company is doing or has done business.

§ 18-909. Execution; Liability

Section 18-204(c) of this title shall be applicable to foreign limited liability companies as if they were domestic limited liability companies.

§ 18-910. Service of Process on Registered Foreign Limited Liability Companies

(a) Service of legal process upon any foreign limited liability company shall be made by delivering a copy personally to any managing or general agent or manager of the foreign limited liability company in the State of Delaware or the registered agent of the foreign limited liability company in the State of Delaware, or by leaving it at the dwelling house or usual place of abode in the State of Delaware of any such managing or general agent, manager or registered agent (if the registered agent be an individual), or at the registered office or other place of business of the foreign limited liability company in the State of Delaware. If the registered agent be a corporation, service of process upon it as such may be made by serving, in the State of Delaware, a copy thereof on the president, vice-president, secretary, assistant secretary or any director of the corporate registered agent. Service by copy left at the dwelling house or usual place of abode of any managing or general agent, manager or registered agent, or at the registered office or other place of business of the foreign limited liability company in the State of Delaware, to be effective must be delivered thereat at least 6 days before the return date of the process, and in the presence of an adult person, and the officer serving the process shall distinctly state the manner of service in the officer's return thereto. Process returnable forthwith must be delivered personally to the managing or general agent, manager or registered agent.

(b) In case the officer whose duty it is to serve legal process cannot by due diligence serve the process in any manner provided for by subsection (a) of this section, it shall be lawful to serve the process against the foreign limited liability company upon the Secretary of State, and such service shall be as effectual for all intents and purposes as if made in any of the ways provided for in subsection (a) of this section. In the event service is effected through the Secretary of State in accordance with this subsection, the Secretary of State shall forthwith notify the foreign limited liability company by letter, certified mail, return receipt requested, directed to the foreign limited liability company at its last registered office. Such letter shall enclose a copy of the process and any other papers served on the Secretary of State pursuant to this subsection. It shall be the duty of the plaintiff in the event of such service to serve process and any other papers in duplicate, to notify the Secretary of State that service is being effected pursuant to this subsection, and to pay to the Secretary of State the sum of $50 for the use of the State of Delaware, which sum shall be taxed as a part of the costs in the proceeding if the plaintiff shall prevail therein. The Secretary of State shall maintain an alphabetical record of any such service setting forth the name of the plaintiff and defendant, the title, docket number and nature of the proceeding in which process has been served upon the Secretary, the fact that service has been effected pursuant to this subsection, the return date thereof and the day and hour when the service was made. The Secretary of State shall not be required to retain such information for a period longer than 5 years from the Secretary's receipt of the service of process.

§ 18–911. Service of Process on Unregistered Foreign Limited Liability Companies

(a) Any foreign limited liability company which shall do business in the State of Delaware without having registered under § 18–902 of this title shall be deemed to have thereby appointed and constituted the Secretary of State of the State of Delaware its agent for the acceptance of legal process in any civil action, suit or proceeding against it in any state or federal court in the State of Delaware arising or growing out of any business done by it within the State of Delaware. The doing of business in the State of Delaware by such foreign limited liability company shall be a signification of the agreement of such foreign limited liability company that any such process when so served shall be of the same legal force and validity as if served upon an authorized manager or agent personally within the State of Delaware.

(b) Whenever the words "doing business," "the doing of business" or "business done in this State," by any such foreign limited liability company are used in this section, they shall mean the course or practice of carrying on any business activities in the State of Delaware, including, without limiting the generality of the foregoing, the solicitation of business or orders in the State of Delaware.

(c) In the event of service upon the Secretary of State in accordance with subsection (a) of this section, the Secretary of State shall forthwith notify the foreign limited liability company thereof by letter, certified mail, return receipt requested, directed to the foreign limited liability company at the address furnished to the Secretary of State by the plaintiff in such action, suit or proceeding. Such letter shall enclose a copy of the process and any other papers served upon the Secretary of State. It shall be the duty of the plaintiff in the event of such service to serve process and any other papers in duplicate, to notify the Secretary of State that service is being made pursuant to this subsection, and to pay to the Secretary of State the sum of $50 for the use of the State of Delaware, which sum shall be taxed as part of the costs in the proceeding, if the plaintiff shall prevail therein. The Secretary of State shall maintain an alphabetical record of any such process setting forth the name of the plaintiff and defendant, the title, docket number and nature of the proceeding in which process has been served upon the Secretary, the return date thereof, and the day and hour when the service was made. The Secretary of State shall not be required to retain such information for a period longer than 5 years from the receipt of the service of process.

§ 18–912. Activities not Constituting Doing Business

(a) Activities of a foreign limited liability company in the State of Delaware that do not constitute doing business for the purpose of this subchapter include:

(1) Maintaining, defending or settling an action or proceeding;

(2) Holding meetings of its members or managers or carrying on any other activity concerning its internal affairs;

(3) Maintaining bank accounts;

(4) Maintaining offices or agencies for the transfer, exchange or registration of the limited liability company's own securities or maintaining trustees or depositories with respect to those securities;

(5) Selling through independent contractors;

(6) Soliciting or obtaining orders, whether by mail or through employees or agents or otherwise, if the orders require acceptance outside the State of Delaware before they become contracts;

(7) Selling, by contract consummated outside the State of Delaware, and agreeing, by the contract, to deliver into the State of Delaware, machinery, plants or equipment, the construction, erection or installation of which within the State of Delaware requires the supervision of technical engineers or skilled employees performing services not generally available, and as part of the contract of sale agreeing to furnish such services, and such services only, to the vendee at the time of construction, erection or installation;

(8) Creating, as borrower or lender, or acquiring indebtedness with or without a mortgage or other security interest in property;

(9) Collecting debts or foreclosing mortgages or other security interests in property securing the debts, and holding, protecting and maintaining property so acquired;

(10) Conducting an isolated transaction that is not 1 in the course of similar transactions;

(11) Doing business in interstate commerce; and

(12) Doing business in the State of Delaware as an insurance company.

(b) A person shall not be deemed to be doing business in the State of Delaware solely by reason of being a member or manager of a domestic limited liability company or a foreign limited liability company.

(c) This section does not apply in determining whether a foreign limited liability company is subject to service of process, taxation or regulation under any other law of the State of Delaware.

SUBCHAPTER X. DERIVATIVE ACTIONS

§ 18–1001. Right to Bring Action

A member or an assignee of a limited liability company interest may bring an action in the Court of Chancery in the right of a limited liability company to recover a judgment in its favor if managers or members with authority to do so have refused to bring the action or if an effort to cause those managers or members to bring the action is not likely to succeed.

§ 18–1002. Proper Plaintiff

In a derivative action, the plaintiff must be a member or an assignee of a limited liability company interest at the time of bringing the action and:

(1) At the time of the transaction of which the plaintiff complains; or

(2) The plaintiff's status as a member or an assignee of a limited liability company interest had devolved upon the plaintiff by operation of law or pursuant to the terms of a limited liability company agreement from a person who was a member or an assignee of a limited liability company interest at the time of the transaction.

§ 18–1003. Complaint

In a derivative action, the complaint shall set forth with particularity the effort, if any, of the plaintiff to secure initiation of the action by a manager or member or the reasons for not making the effort.

§ 18–1004. Expenses

If a derivative action is successful, in whole or in part, as a result of a judgment, compromise or settlement of any such action, the court may award the plaintiff reasonable expenses, including reasonable attorney's fees, from any recovery in any such action or from a limited liability company.

SUBCHAPTER XI. MISCELLANEOUS

§ 18–1101. Construction and Application of Chapter and Limited Liability Company Agreement

(a) The rule that statutes in derogation of the common law are to be strictly construed shall have no application to this chapter.

(b) It is the policy of this chapter to give the maximum effect to the principle of freedom of contract and to the enforceability of limited liability company agreements.

(c) To the extent that, at law or in equity, a member or manager or other person has duties (including fiduciary duties) to a limited liability company or to another member or manager or to another person that is a party to or is otherwise bound by a limited liability company agreement, the member's or manager's or other person's duties may be expanded or restricted or eliminated by provisions in the limited liability company agreement; provided, that the limited liability company agreement may not eliminate the implied contractual covenant of good faith and fair dealing.

(d) Unless otherwise provided in a limited liability company agreement, a member or manager or other person shall not be liable to a limited liability company or to another member or manager or to another person that is a party to or is otherwise bound by a limited liability company agreement for breach of fiduciary duty for the member's or manager's or other person's good faith reliance on the provisions of the limited liability company agreement.

(e) A limited liability company agreement may provide for the limitation or elimination of any and all liabilities for breach of contract and breach of duties (including fiduciary duties) of a member, manager or other person to a limited liability company or to another member or manager or to another person that is a party to or is otherwise bound by a limited liability company agreement; provided, that a limited liability company agreement may not limit or eliminate liability for any act or omission that constitutes a bad faith violation of the implied contractual covenant of good faith and fair dealing.

(f) Unless the context otherwise requires, as used herein, the singular shall include the plural and the plural may refer to only the singular. The use of any gender shall be applicable to all genders. The captions contained herein are for purposes of convenience only and shall not control or affect the construction of this chapter.

(g) Sections 9–406 and 9–408 of this title do not apply to any interest in a limited liability company, including all rights, powers and interests arising under a limited liability company agreement or this chapter. This provision prevails over §§ 9–406 and 9–408 of this title.

§ 18–1102. Short Title

This chapter may be cited as the "Delaware Limited Liability Company Act."

§ 18–1103. Severability

If any provision of this chapter or its application to any person or circumstances is held invalid, the invalidity does not affect other provisions or applications of the chapter which can be given effect without the invalid provision or application, and to this end, the provisions of this chapter are severable.

§ 18–1104. Cases not Provided for in this Chapter

In any case not provided for in this chapter, the rules of law and equity, including the law merchant, shall govern.

§ 18–1105. Fees

(a) No document required to be filed under this chapter shall be effective until the applicable fee required by this section is paid. The following fees shall be paid to and collected by the Secretary of State for the use of the State of Delaware:

(1) Upon the receipt for filing of an application for reservation of name, an application for renewal of reservation or a notice of

transfer or cancellation of reservation pursuant to § 18–103(b) of this title, a fee in the amount of $75.

(2) Upon the receipt for filing of a certificate under § 18–104(b) of this title, a fee in the amount of $50, upon the receipt for filing of a certificate under § 18–104(c) of this title, a fee in the amount of $50 and a further fee of $2 for each limited liability company affected by such certificate, and upon the receipt for filing of a certificate under § 18–104(d) of this title, a fee in the amount of $2.50.

(3) Upon the receipt for filing of a certificate of limited liability company domestication under § 18–212 of this title, a certificate of transfer or a certificate of transfer and continuance under § 18–213 of this title, a certificate of conversion to limited liability company under § 18–214 of this title, a certificate of conversion to a non-Delaware entity under § 18–216 of this title, a certificate of formation under § 18–201 of this title, a fee in the amount of $70; and upon the receipt for filing of a certificate of amendment under § 18–202 of this title, a certificate of cancellation under § 18–203 of this title, a certificate of merger or consolidation under § 18–209 of this title, a restated certificate of formation under § 18–208 of this title, a certificate of amendment of a certificate with a future effective date or time under § 18–206(c) of this title, a certificate of termination of a certificate with a future effective date or time under § 18–206(c) of this title, a certificate of correction under § 18–211 of this title, or a certificate of revival under § 18–1109 of this title, a fee in the amount of $80.

(4) For certifying copies of any paper on file as provided for by this chapter, a fee in the amount of $30 for each copy certified.

(5) The Secretary of State may issue photocopies or electronic image copies of instruments on file, as well as instruments, documents and other papers not on file, and for all such photocopies or electronic image copies, whether certified or not, a fee of $10 shall be paid for the 1st page and $2 for each additional page. The Secretary of State may also issue microfiche copies of instruments on file as well as instruments, documents and other papers not on file, and for each such microfiche a fee of $2 shall be paid therefor. Notwithstanding the State of Delaware's Freedom of Information Act [Chapter 100 of Title 29] or other provision of this Code granting access to public records, the Secretary of State shall issue only photocopies, microfiche or electronic image copies of records in exchange for the fees described above.

(6) Upon the receipt for filing of an application for registration as a foreign limited liability company under § 18–902 of this title, a certificate under § 18–905 of this title or a certificate of cancellation under § 18–906 of this title, a fee in the amount of $100.

(7) Upon the receipt for filing of a certificate under § 18–904(c) of this title, a fee in the amount of $50, upon the receipt for filing of a certificate under § 18–904(d) of this title, a fee in the amount of $50 and a further fee of $2 for each foreign limited liability company affected by such certificate, and upon the receipt for filing of a certificate under § 18–904(e) of this title, a fee in the amount of $2.50.

(8) For preclearance of any document for filing, a fee in the amount of $250.

(9) For preparing and providing a written report of a record search, a fee in the amount of $30.

(10) For issuing any certificate of the Secretary of State, including but not limited to a certificate of good standing, other than a certification of a copy under paragraph (4) of this subsection, a fee in the amount of $30, except that for issuing any certificate of the Secretary of State that recites all of a limited liability company's filings with the Secretary of State, a fee of $125 shall be paid for each such certificate.

(11) For receiving and filing and/or indexing any certificate, affidavit, agreement or any other paper provided for by this chapter, for which no different fee is specifically prescribed, a fee in the amount of $50.

(12) The Secretary of State may in the Secretary of State's own discretion charge a fee of $60 for each check received for payment of any fee that is returned due to insufficient funds or the result of a stop payment order.

(b) In addition to those fees charged under subsection (a) of this section, there shall be collected by and paid to the Secretary of State the following:

(1) For all services described in subsection (a) of this section that are requested to be completed within 1 hour on the same day as the day of the request, an additional sum of up to $1,000 and for all services described in subsection (a) of this section that are requested to be completed within 2 hours on the same day of the request, an additional sum of up to $500;

(2) For all services described in subsection (a) of this section that are requested to be completed within the same day as the day of the request, an additional sum of up to $200; and

(3) For all services described in subsection (a) of this section that are requested to be completed within a 24–hour period from the time of the request, an additional sum of up to $100.

The Secretary of State shall establish (and may from time to time amend) a schedule of specific fees payable pursuant to this subsection.

(c) The Secretary of State may in his or her discretion permit the extension of credit for the fees required by this section upon such terms as the secretary shall deem to be appropriate.

(d) The Secretary of State shall retain from the revenue collected from the fees required by this section a sum sufficient to provide at all times a fund of at least $500, but not more than $1,500, from which the secretary may refund any payment made pursuant to this section to the extent that it exceeds the fees required by this section. The funds shall be deposited in a financial institution which is a legal depository of State of Delaware moneys to the credit of the Secretary of State and shall be disbursable on order of the Secretary of State.

(e) Except as provided in this section, the fees of the Secretary of State shall be as provided in § 2315 of Title 29.

§ 18–1106. Reserved Power of State of Delaware to Alter or Repeal Chapter

All provisions of this chapter may be altered from time to time or repealed and all rights of members and managers are subject to this reservation. Unless expressly stated to the contrary in this chapter, all amendments of this chapter shall apply to limited liability companies and members and managers whether or not existing as such at the time of the enactment of any such amendment.

§ 18–1107. Taxation of Limited Liability Companies

(a) For purposes of any tax imposed by the State of Delaware or any instrumentality, agency or political subdivision of the State of Delaware, a limited liability company formed under this chapter or qualified to do business in the State of Delaware as a foreign limited liability company shall be classified as a partnership unless classified otherwise for federal income tax purposes, in which case the limited liability company shall be classified in the same manner as it is classified for federal income tax purposes. For purposes of any tax imposed by the State of Delaware or any instrumentality, agency or political subdivision of the State of Delaware, a member or an assignee of a member of a limited liability company formed under this chapter or qualified to do business in the State of Delaware as a foreign limited liability company shall be treated as either a resident or nonresident partner unless classified otherwise for federal income tax purposes, in which case the member or assignee of a member shall have the same status as such member or assignee of a member has for federal income tax purposes.

(b) Every domestic limited liability company and every foreign limited liability company registered to do business in the State of Delaware shall pay an annual tax, for the use of the State of Delaware, in the amount of $200.

(c) The annual tax shall be due and payable on the first day of June following the close of the calendar year or upon the cancellation of a certificate of formation. The Secretary of State shall receive the annual tax and pay over all taxes collected to the Department of Finance of the State of Delaware. If the annual tax remains unpaid after the due date, the tax shall bear interest at the rate of 1 and one-half percent for each month or portion thereof until fully paid.

(d) The Secretary of State shall, at least 60 days prior to the first day of June of each year, cause to be mailed to each domestic limited liability company and each foreign limited liability company required to comply with the provisions of this section in care of its registered agent in the State of Delaware an annual statement for the tax to be paid hereunder.

(e) In the event of neglect, refusal or failure on the part of any domestic limited liability company or foreign limited liability company to pay the annual tax to be paid hereunder on or before the 1st day of June in any year, such domestic limited liability company or foreign limited liability company shall pay the sum of $100 to be recovered by adding that amount to the annual tax and such additional sum shall become a part of the tax and shall be collected in the same manner and subject to the same penalties.

(f) In case any domestic limited liability company or foreign limited liability company shall fail to pay the annual tax due within the time required by this section, and in case the agent in charge of the registered office of any domestic limited liability company or foreign limited liability company upon whom process against such domestic limited liability company or foreign limited liability company may be served shall die, resign, refuse to act as such, remove from the State of Delaware or cannot with due diligence be found, it shall be lawful while default continues to serve process against such domestic limited liability company or foreign limited liability company upon the Secretary of State. Such service upon the Secretary of State shall be made in the manner and shall have the effect stated in § 18–105 of this title in the case of a domestic limited liability company and § 18–910 of this title in the case of a foreign limited liability company and shall be governed in all respects by said sections.

(g) The annual tax shall be a debt due from a domestic limited liability company or foreign limited liability company to the State of Delaware, for which an action at law may be maintained after the same shall have been in arrears for a period of 1 month. The tax shall also be a preferred debt in the case of insolvency.

(h) A domestic limited liability company or foreign limited liability company that neglects, refuses or fails to pay the annual tax when due shall cease to be in good standing as a domestic limited liability company or registered as a foreign limited liability company in the State of Delaware.

(i) A domestic limited liability company that has ceased to be in good standing or a foreign limited liability company that has ceased to be registered by reason of the failure to pay an annual tax shall be restored to and have the status of a domestic limited liability company in good standing or a foreign limited liability company that is registered in the State of Delaware upon the payment of the annual tax and all penalties and interest thereon for each year for which such domestic limited liability company or foreign limited liability company neglected, refused or failed to pay an annual tax.

(j) On the motion of the Attorney General or upon request of the Secretary of State, whenever any annual tax due under this chapter from any domestic limited liability company or foreign limited liability company shall have remained in arrears for a period of 3 months after the tax shall have become payable, the Attorney General may apply to the Court of Chancery, by petition in the name of the State of Delaware, on 5 days' notice to such domestic limited liability company or foreign limited liability company, which notice may be served in such manner as the Court may direct, for an injunction to restrain such domestic limited liability company or foreign limited liability company from the transaction of any business within the State of Delaware or elsewhere, until the payment of the annual tax, and all penalties and interest due thereon and the cost of the application which shall be fixed by the Court. The Court of Chancery may grant the injunction, if a proper case appears, and upon granting and service of the injunction, such domestic limited liability company or foreign limited liability company thereafter shall not transact any business until the injunction shall be dissolved.

(k) A domestic limited liability company that has ceased to be in good standing by reason of its neglect, refusal or failure to pay an annual tax shall remain a domestic limited liability company formed under this chapter. The Secretary of State shall not accept for filing any certificate (except a certificate of resignation of a registered agent when a successor registered agent is not being appointed) required or permitted by this chapter to be filed in respect of any domestic limited liability company or foreign limited liability company which has neglected, refused or failed to pay an annual tax, and shall not issue any certificate of good standing with respect to such domestic limited liability company or foreign limited liability company, unless or until such domestic limited liability company or foreign limited liability company shall have been restored to and have the status of a domestic limited liability company in good standing or a foreign limited liability company duly registered in the State of Delaware.

(l) A domestic limited liability company that has ceased to be in good standing or a foreign limited liability company that has ceased to be registered in the State of Delaware by reason of its neglect, refusal or failure to pay an annual tax may not maintain any action, suit or proceeding in any court of the State of Delaware until such domestic limited liability company or foreign limited liability company has been restored to and has the status of a domestic limited liability company or foreign limited liability company in good standing or duly registered in the State of Delaware. An action, suit or proceeding may not be maintained in any court of the State of Delaware by any successor or assignee of such domestic limited liability company or foreign limited liability company on any right, claim or demand arising out the transaction of business by such domestic limited liability company after it has ceased to be in good standing or a foreign limited liability company that has ceased to be registered in the State of Delaware until such domestic limited liability company or foreign limited liability company, or any person that has acquired all or substantially all of its assets, has paid any annual tax then due and payable, together with penalties and interest thereon.

(m) The neglect, refusal or failure of a domestic limited liability company or foreign limited liability company to pay an annual tax shall not impair the validity on any contract, deed, mortgage, security interest, lien or act or such domestic limited liability company or foreign limited liability company or prevent such domestic limited liability company or foreign limited liability company from defending any action, suit or proceeding with any court of the State of Delaware.

(n) A member or manager of a domestic limited liability company or foreign limited liability company is not liable for the debts, obligations or liabilities of such domestic limited liability company or foreign limited liability company solely by reason of the neglect, refusal or failure of such domestic limited liability company or foreign limited liability company to pay an annual tax or by reason of such domestic limited liability company or foreign limited liability company ceasing to be in good standing or duly registered.

§ 18–1108. Cancellation of Certificate of Formation for Failure to Pay Taxes

(a) The certificate of formation of a domestic limited liability company shall be deemed to be canceled if the domestic limited liability company shall fail to pay the annual tax due under § 18–1107 of this title for a period of 3 years from the date it is due, such cancellation to be effective on the third anniversary of such due date.

(b) A list of those domestic limited liability companies whose certificates of formation were canceled on June 1 of such calendar year pursuant to § 18–1108(a) of this title shall be filed in the office of the Secretary of State. On or before October 31 of each calendar year, the Secretary of State shall publish such list on the Internet or on a similar medium for a period of 1 week and shall advertise the website or other address where such list can be accessed in at least 1 newspaper of general circulation in the State of Delaware.

§ 18–1109. Revival of Domestic Limited Liability Company [Effective Until Jan. 1, 2007]

(a) A domestic limited liability company whose certificate of formation has been canceled pursuant to § 18–104(d) or § 18–1108(a) of this title may be revived by filing in the office of the Secretary of State a certificate of revival accompanied by the payment of the fee required by § 18–1105(a)(3) of this title and payment of the annual tax due under § 18–1107 of this title and all penalties and interest thereon for each year for which such domestic limited liability company neglected, refused or failed to pay such annual tax, including each year between the cancellation of its certificate of formation and its revival. The certificate of revival shall set forth:

(1) The name of the limited liability company at the time its certificate of formation was canceled and, if such name is not available at the time of revival, the name under which the limited liability company is to be revived;

(2) The date of filing of the original certificate of formation of the limited liability company;

(3) The address of the limited liability company's registered office in the State of Delaware and the name and address of the limited liability company's registered agent in the State of Delaware;

(4) A statement that the certificate of revival is filed by 1 or more persons authorized to execute and file the certificate of revival to revive the limited liability company; and

(5) Any other matters the persons executing the certificate of revival determine to include therein.

(b) The certificate of revival shall be deemed to be an amendment to the certificate of formation of the limited liability company, and the limited liability company shall not be required to take any further action to amend its certificate of formation under § 18–202 of this title with respect to the matters set forth in the certificate of revival.

(c) Upon the filing of a certificate of revival, a limited liability company shall be revived with the same force and effect as if its certificate of formation had not been canceled pursuant to § 18–104(d) or § 18–1108(a) of this title. Such revival shall validate all contracts, acts, matters and things made, done and performed by the limited liability company, its members, managers, employees and agents during the time when its certificate of formation was canceled pursuant to § 18–104(d) or § 18–1108(a) of this title, with the same force and effect and to all intents and purposes as if the certificate of formation had remained in full force and effect. All real and personal property, and all rights and interests, which belonged to the limited liability company at the time its certificate of formation was canceled pursuant to § 18–104(d) or § 18–1108(a) of this title or which were acquired by the limited liability company following the cancellation of its certificate of formation pursuant to § 18–104(d) or § 18–1108(a) of this title, and which were not disposed of prior to the time of its revival, shall be vested in the limited liability company after its revival as fully as they were held by the limited liability company at, and after, as the case may be, the time its certificate of formation was canceled pursuant to § 18–104(d) or § 18–1108(a) of this title. After its revival, the limited liability company shall be as exclusively liable for all contracts, acts, matters and things made, done or performed in its name and on its behalf by its members, managers, employees and agents prior to its revival as if its certificate of formation had at all times remained in full force and effect.

§ 18–1109. Revival of Domestic Limited Liability Company [Effective Jan. 1, 2007]

(a) A domestic limited liability company whose certificate of formation has been canceled pursuant to § 18–104(d) or § 18–104(i)(4) or § 18–1108(a) of this title may be revived by filing in the office of the Secretary of State a certificate of revival accompanied by the payment of the fee required by § 18–1105(a)(3) of this title and payment of the annual tax due under § 18–1107 of this title and all penalties and interest thereon for each year for which such domestic limited liability company neglected, refused or failed to pay such annual tax, including each year between the cancellation of its certificate of formation and its revival. The certificate of revival shall set forth:

(1) The name of the limited liability company at the time its certificate of formation was canceled and, if such name is not available at the time of revival, the name under which the limited liability company is to be revived;

(2) The date of filing of the original certificate of formation of the limited liability company;

(3) The address of the limited liability company's registered office in the State of Delaware and the name and address of the limited liability company's registered agent in the State of Delaware;

(4) A statement that the certificate of revival is filed by 1 or more persons authorized to execute and file the certificate of revival to revive the limited liability company; and

(5) Any other matters the persons executing the certificate of revival determine to include therein.

(b) The certificate of revival shall be deemed to be an amendment to the certificate of formation of the limited liability company, and the limited liability company shall not be required to take any further action to amend its certificate of formation under § 18–202 of this title with respect to the matters set forth in the certificate of revival.

(c) Upon the filing of a certificate of revival, a limited liability company shall be revived with the same force and effect as if its certificate of formation had not been canceled pursuant to § 18–104(d) or § 18–104(i)(4) or § 18–1108(a) of this title. Such revival shall validate all contracts, acts, matters and things made, done and performed by the limited liability company, its members, managers, employees and agents during the time when its certificate of formation was canceled pursuant to § 18–104(d) or § 18–104(i)(4) or § 18–1108(a) of this title, with the same force and effect and to all intents and purposes as if the certificate of formation had remained in full force and effect. All real and personal property, and all rights and interests, which belonged to the limited liability company at the time its certificate of formation was canceled pursuant to § 18–104(d) or § 18–104(i)(4) or § 18–1108(a) of this title or which were acquired by the limited liability company following the cancellation of its certificate of formation pursuant to § 18–104(d) or § 18–104(i)(4) or § 18–1108(a) of this title, and which were not disposed of prior to the time of its revival, shall be vested in the limited liability company after its revival as fully as they were held by the limited liability company at, and after, as the case may be, the time its certificate of formation was canceled pursuant to § 18–104(d) or § 18–104(i)(4) or § 18–1108(a) of this title. After its revival, the limited liability company shall be as exclusively liable for all contracts, acts, matters and things made, done or performed in its name and on its behalf by its members, managers, employees and agents prior to its revival as if its certificate of formation had at all times remained in full force and effect.

*

DELAWARE PROFESSIONAL SERVICE CORPORATION ACT

(Delaware Code, Title 8, Chapter 6)

Table of Sections

---

§ 601. Legislative Intent

It is the legislative intent to provide for the incorporation of an individual, or group of individuals who render the same professional service to the public, for which such individuals are required by law to be licensed or to obtain other legal authorization.

§ 602. Short Title

This chapter may be cited as "The Professional Service Corporation Act."

§ 603. Definitions

As used in this chapter the following words shall have the meaning indicated:

(1) The term "professional service" shall mean any type of personal service to the public which requires as a condition precedent to the rendering of the service the obtaining of a license or other legal authorization, and which, by reason of law, prior to June 7, 1969, could not be performed by a corporation. In addition, and by way of example without limiting the generality thereof, the personal services which come within this chapter are the personal services rendered by architects, certified or other public accountants, chiropodists, chiropractors, doctors of dentistry, doctors of medicine, optometrists, osteopaths, professional engineers, veterinarians, and, subject to the Rules of the Supreme Court, attorneys-at-law.

(2) The term "professional corporation" means a corporation which is organized, under this chapter, for the sole and specific purpose of rendering professional service, and which has as its shareholders only individuals who themselves are duly licensed or otherwise legally authorized within this State to render the same professional service as the corporation.

§ 604. Exemptions

This chapter shall not apply to any individual or groups of individuals within this State who, prior to June 7, 1969, were permitted to organize a corporation and perform personal services to the public by the means of a corporation, and this chapter shall not apply to any corporations organized by any individual or group of individuals prior to June 7, 1969, unless, any such individual, or group of individuals, or any such corporation bring themselves and such corporation within this chapter by amending the certificate of incorporation, in a manner so as to be consistent with all the provisions of this chapter, and by affirmatively stating in the amended certificate of incorporation that the shareholders have elected to bring the corporation within this chapter, or be incorporated initially under this chapter.

§ 605. Authority to Organize; Law Governing

One or more persons, each of whom is duly licensed or otherwise legally authorized to render the same professional services within this

State, may organize and become a shareholder or shareholders of a professional corporation for pecuniary profit, under this title, for the sole and specific purpose of rendering the same professional services.

§ 606. Number of Directors; Officers

A professional corporation which has only 1 shareholder need have only 1 director, who shall be the shareholder. The 1 shareholder shall also serve as the president of the corporation. The other officers of the corporation, in such a case, need not be licensed or otherwise legally authorized to render the same professional service within this State, as the 1 shareholder. A professional corporation which has only 2 shareholders need have only 2 directors who shall be such shareholders. The 2 shareholders shall, between them, fill all the offices of the professional corporation.

§ 607. Rendition of Professional Services Through Licensed Officers, Employees and Agents

No corporation organized and incorporated under this chapter, may render professional services except through its officers, employees and agents who are duly licensed or otherwise legally authorized to render such professional services within this State; provided, however, this provision shall not be interpreted to include in the term "employee" as used in this chapter, clerks, secretaries, nurses, administrators, bookkeepers, technicians and other assistants who are not usually and ordinarily considered by law, custom and practice to be rendering professional services to the public for which a license, or other legal authorization, is required in connection with the profession to be practiced, nor does the term "employee" include any other person who performs all of such person's employment under the direct supervision and control of an officer, employee or agent who renders professional service to the public on behalf of the professional corporation; provided that, no person shall, under the guise of employment, practice a profession unless duly licensed to practice that profession under the laws of this State. Notwithstanding any other or contrary provisions of the laws of this State, a professional corporation, organized under this chapter, may charge for the services of its officers, employees and agents, may collect such charges, and may compensate those who render such professional services.

§ 608. Chapter not to Affect Professional Relationship; Legal Liabilities and Standards for Professional Conduct; Negligence; Attachment of Assets

Nothing contained in this chapter shall be interpreted to abolish, repeal, modify, restrict or limit the law now in effect in this State, applicable to the professional relationship and the contract, tort, and other legal liabilities between the person furnishing the professional services and the person receiving the professional service, and to the standards for professional conduct, including the confidential relationship between the person rendering the professional services and the person receiving such professional service, if any; and all confidential relationships previously enjoyed under the laws of this State or hereafter enacted shall remain inviolate. Any officer, employee, agent or shareholder of a corporation, organized under this chapter, shall remain personally and fully liable and accountable for any negligent, wrongful acts, or misconduct committed by such person, or by any person under such person's direct supervision and control, while rendering professional service on behalf of the corporation to the person for whom such professional services were being rendered. The corporation shall be liable up to the full value of its property for any negligent, wrongful acts, or misconduct committed by any of its officers, employees, agents or shareholders while they are engaged in behalf of the corporation in the rendering of professional services. The assets of a professional corporation shall not be liable to attachment for the individual debts of its shareholders. Notwithstanding the foregoing, the relationship of an individual to a professional corporation, organized under this chapter, with which such individual is or may be associated, whether as officer, employee, agent, or shareholder director, shall in no way modify, extend, or diminish the jurisdiction over such individual, of and by whatever state agency, or office which licensed or otherwise legally authorized such person for or to render service in a particular field of endeavor.

§ 609. Engaging in Other Business Prohibited

No corporation organized under this chapter shall engage in any business other than the rendering of the professional services for which it was specifically incorporated; provided, however, nothing in this chapter or in any other provisions of existing law applicable to corporations shall be interpreted to prohibit such corporation from investing its funds in real estate, mortgages, stocks, bonds, or any other type of investments, or from owning real or personal property necessary for, or appropriate or desirable in, the fulfillment or rendering of its professional services.

§ 610. Issuance of Capital Stock to Licensed Individuals; Voting Trust Agreements Prohibited; Holding of Stock by Shareholder's Estate

No corporation, organized under this chapter, may issue any of its capital stock to anyone other than an individual who is duly licensed or otherwise legally authorized to render the same specific professional services as those for which the corporation was incorporated. No shareholder of a corporation, organized under this chapter, shall enter into a voting trust agreement, proxy, or any other type of agreement vesting another person with the authority to exercise the voting power of any or all of such shareholder's stock. Subject to the corporation's certificate of incorporation, the estate of a shareholder who was a person duly licensed or otherwise legally authorized to render the same professional service as that for which the professional corporation was organized may continue to hold stock pursuant to the certificate of incorporation for a reasonable period of administration of the estate, but shall not be authorized to participate in any decisions concerning the rendering of professional service.

§ 611. Disqualification of Officer, Shareholder, Agent or Employee

If any officer, employee, agent or shareholder of a corporation, organized under this chapter, becomes legally disqualified to render such professional services within this State, or either (a) is elected to a public office that, or (b) accepts employment that, pursuant to existing law, places restrictions or limitations upon such person's continued rendering of such professional services, such person shall sever all employment with, and financial interests in, the corporation, forthwith. A corporation's failure to require compliance with this provision shall constitute a ground for the forfeiture of its charter and its dissolution. When a corporation's failure to comply with this provision is brought to the attention of the office of the Secretary of State, the Secretary of State shall forthwith certify that fact to the Attorney General for appropriate action to dissolve the corporation.

§ 612. Sale or Transfer of Shares

Except as provided in § 616 of this title, no shareholder of a corporation, organized under this chapter, may sell or transfer such shareholder's shares in the corporation, except to the corporation, or to another individual who is eligible to be a shareholder of such corporation, and the sale or transfer may be made only after the same shall have been approved, at a stockholders' meeting specially called for such purpose, or at an annual meeting with 10 days' notice of such additional purpose, by such proportion, not less than a majority, of the outstanding stock entitled to be voted on that question as may be provided in the certificate of incorporation or in the bylaws. At such shareholders' meeting the shares of stock held by the shareholder proposing to sell or transfer such shareholder's shares may not be voted or counted for any purpose. The certificate of incorporation may provide specifically for additional restraints on the alienation of shares, and may require the redemption or purchase of such shares by the corporation at prices and in a specific manner, or authorize the corporation's board of directors or its shareholders to adopt bylaws restraining the alienation of shares and providing for the purchase or redemption by the corporation of its shares; provided, however, such provisions, dealing with the purchase or redemption by the corporation of its shares, may not be invoked at a time or in a manner that would impair the capital of the corporation.

§ 613. Price for Shares

If the certificate of incorporation or bylaws of a professional corporation fail to fix a price at which a professional corporation or its shareholders may purchase the shares of a deceased, retired, expelled or disqualified shareholder, and if the certificate of incorporation or bylaws do not otherwise provide, then the price for the share or shares shall be the book value at the end of the month immediately preceding the death or disqualification of the shareholder. Book value shall be determined by an independent certified public accountant employed by the professional corporation. The determination by the certified public accountant of book value shall be conclusive on the professional corporation and its shareholders.

§ 614. Perpetual Corporate Existence

A corporation under this chapter shall have perpetual existence until dissolved in accordance with other provisions of this chapter.

§ 615. Conversion into Business Corporation

Whenever all shareholders of a corporation, licensed under this chapter, cease at any time, and for any reason, to be licensed, certified or registered in the particular field of endeavor for which such corporation was organized, the corporation shall thereupon be treated as converted into and shall operate henceforth solely as a business corporation under applicable provisions of Chapter 1 of this title, exclusive of this chapter.

§ 616. Time for Transfer of Shares Upon Death or Disqualification

Within 375 days following the date of death of a shareholder, or within 30 days following such shareholder's disqualification to own shares in the corporation, as provided in this chapter, all of the shares of such shareholder shall be transferred to, and acquired by, the corporation or persons qualified to own such shares. If no other provision to accomplish such transfer and acquisition is in effect and carried out within said period, the corporation shall thereafter purchase and redeem all of such shareholder's shares of its stock at the book value thereof, determined as of the end of the month immediately preceding death or disqualification. For this purpose, the book value shall be determined from the books and records of the corporation in accordance with the regular methods of accounting used by it for the purposes of determining its net taxable income for federal income tax purposes; and no subsequent adjustment of such income, whether by the corporation itself, by federal income tax audit made and agreed to, or by a court decision which has become final, shall alter the redemption price. Nothing contained in this section shall prevent the parties involved from making any other arrangement or provision in the certificate of incorporation, bylaws, or by contract to transfer the shares of a deceased or disqualified shareholder to the corporation or to persons qualified to own the same, whether made before or after the death or disqualification of the shareholder, provided that within the period specified by this section, all the stock involved shall have been so transferred.

§ 617. Corporate Name

The corporate name of a corporation organized under this chapter shall contain either a word or words descriptive of the professional service to be rendered by the corporation or shall contain the last names of 1 or more of its present, prospective or former shareholders or of persons who were associated with a predecessor person, partnership, corporation or other organization or whose name or names appeared in the name of such predecessor organization. The corporate name shall also contain the words "chartered" or "professional association" or abbreviation "P.A." The use of the word "company," "corporation" or "incorporated" or any other word, words, abbreviations, affix or prefix indicating that it is a corporation, in the corporate name of a corporation organized under this chapter, is specifically prohibited. However, it shall be permissible for the professional service corporation and its shareholders to render professional services and to exercise the corporation's authorized powers under a name which is identical to its corporate name except for the omission of the words "chartered" or "professional association" or the omission of the abbreviation "P.A."

§ 618. Applicability of General Corporation Law; Consolidation or Merger of Corporations; Annual Report

This title shall be applicable to a corporation organized pursuant to this chapter, except to the extent that any of the provisions of this chapter are interpreted to be in conflict with the provisions of this title, and in such event the provisions and sections of this chapter shall take precedence with respect to a corporation organized pursuant to this chapter. A professional corporation, organized under this chapter, may consolidate or merge only with another professional corporation organized under this chapter, empowered to render the same specific professional service; and a merger or consolidation with any foreign corporation is prohibited. Sections 501–518 of this title shall be applicable to a corporation organized pursuant to this chapter; but in addition to the information called for on the annual report of all corporations by those provisions, the annual report of a corporation organized pursuant to this chapter shall certify that its shareholders, directors and officers listed on such report are duly licensed, certified, registered or otherwise legally authorized to render the same professional or other personal service in this State.

§ 619. Construction of Chapter

This chapter shall not be construed as repealing, modifying or restricting the applicable provisions of law relating to incorporations, sales of securities, or regulating the several professions enumerated in this chapter, except insofar as such laws conflict with this chapter.

DELAWARE STATUTORY TRUST ACT

(Delaware Code, Title 12, Chapter 38)

Table of Sections

SUBCHAPTER I. GENERAL PROVISIONS

SUBCHAPTER II. FOREIGN STATUTORY TRUSTS

SUBCHAPTER I. DOMESTIC STATUTORY TRUSTS

§ 3801. Definitions

(a) "Statutory trust" means an unincorporated association which:

(1) Is created by a governing instrument under which property is or will be held, managed, administered, controlled, invested, reinvested and/or operated, or business or professional activities for profit are carried on or will be carried on, by a trustee or trustees or as otherwise provided in the governing instrument for the benefit of such person or persons as are or may become beneficial owners or as otherwise provided in the governing instrument, including but not limited to a trust of the type known at common law as a "business trust," or "Massachusetts trust," or a trust qualifying as a real estate investment trust under § 856 et seq. of the United States Internal Revenue Code of 1986 [26 U.S.C. § 856 et seq., as amended, or under any successor provision, or a trust qualifying as a real estate mortgage investment conduit under § 860D of the United States Internal Revenue Code of 1986 26 U.S.C. § 860D], as amended, or under any successor provision; and

(2) Files a certificate of trust pursuant to § 3810 of this title.

Any such association heretofore or hereafter organized shall be a statutory trust and a separate legal entity. The term "statutory trust" shall be deemed to include each trust formed under this chapter prior to September 1, 2002, as a "business trust" (as such term was then defined in this subsection). A statutory trust may be organized to carry on any lawful business or activity, whether or not conducted for profit, and/or for any of the purposes referred to paragraph (a)(1) of this section (including, without limitation, for the purpose of holding or otherwise taking title to property, whether in an active or custodial capacity). Neither use of the designation "business trust" nor a statement in a certificate of trust or governing instrument executed prior to September 1, 2002, to the effect that the trust formed thereby is or will qualify as a Delaware business trust within the meaning of or pursuant to this chapter, shall create a presumption or an inference that the trust so formed is a "business trust" for purposes of Title 11 of the United States Code.

(b) "Beneficial owner" means any owner of a beneficial interest in a statutory trust, the fact of ownership to be determined and evidenced (whether by means of registration, the issuance of certificates or otherwise) in conformity to the applicable provisions of the governing instrument of the statutory trust.

(c) "Trustee" means the person or persons appointed as a trustee in accordance with the governing instrument of a statutory trust, and may include the beneficial owners or any of them.

(d) "Person" means a natural person, partnership (whether general or limited), limited liability company, trust, estate, association (including any group, organization, co-tenancy, plan, board, council or committee), corporation, government (including a country, state, county or any other governmental subdivision, agency or instrumentality), custodian, nominee or any other individual or entity (or series thereof) in its own or any representative capacity, in each case, whether domestic or foreign, and a statutory trust or foreign statutory trust.

(e) "Other business entity" means a corporation, a partnership (whether general or limited), a limited liability company, a common-law trust, a foreign statutory trust or any other unincorporated business, excluding a statutory trust.

(f) "Governing instrument" means any instrument (whether referred to as a trust agreement, declaration of trust or otherwise) which creates a statutory trust or provides for the governance of the affairs of the statutory trust and the conduct of its business. A governing instrument:

(1) May provide that a person shall become a beneficial owner or a trustee if such person (or, in the case of a beneficial owner, a representative authorized by such person orally, in writing or by other action such as payment for a beneficial interest) complies with the conditions for becoming a beneficial owner or a trustee set forth in the governing instrument or any other writing and, in the case of a beneficial owner, acquires a beneficial interest;

(2) May consist of 1 or more agreements, instruments or other writings and may include or incorporate bylaws containing provisions relating to the business of the statutory trust, the conduct of its affairs and its rights or powers or the rights or powers of its trustees, beneficial owners, agents or employees; and

(3) May contain any provision that is not inconsistent with law or with the information contained in the certificate of trust.

A statutory trust is not required to execute its governing instrument. A statutory trust is bound by its governing instrument whether or not it executes the governing instrument. A beneficial owner or a trustee is bound by the governing instrument whether or not such beneficial owner or trustee executes the governing instrument.

(g) "Foreign statutory trust" means a business trust or statutory trust formed under the laws of any state or under the laws of any foreign country or other foreign jurisdiction and denominated as such under the laws of such state or foreign country or other foreign jurisdiction.

(h) "Independent trustee" means, solely with respect to a statutory trust that is registered as an investment company under the Investment Company Act of 1940, as amended (15 U.S.C. § 80a–1 et seq.), or any successor statute thereto (the "1940 Act"), any trustee who is not an "interested person" (as such term is defined below) of the statutory trust; provided that the receipt of compensation for service as an independent trustee of the statutory trust and also for service as an independent trustee of 1 or more other investment companies managed by a single investment adviser (or an "affiliated person" (as such term is defined below) of such investment adviser) shall not affect the status of a trustee as an independent trustee under this chapter. An independent trustee as defined hereunder shall be deemed to be independent and disinterested for all purposes. For purposes of this definition, the terms "affiliated person" and "interested person" have the meanings set forth in the 1940 Act or any rule adopted thereunder.

§ 3802. Contributions by Beneficial Owners

(a) A contribution of a beneficial owner to the statutory trust may be in cash, property or services rendered, or a promissory note or other obligation to contribute cash or property or to perform services; provided however, that a person may become a beneficial owner of a statutory trust and may receive a beneficial interest in a statutory trust without making a contribution or being obligated to make a contribution to the statutory trust.

(b) Except as provided in the governing instrument, a beneficial owner is obligated to the statutory trust to perform any promise to contribute cash, property or to perform services, even if the beneficial owner is unable to perform because of death, disability or any other reason. If a beneficial owner does not make the required contribution of property or services, the beneficial owner is obligated at the option of the statutory trust to contribute cash equal to that portion of the agreed value (as stated in the records of the statutory trust) of the contribution that has not been made. The foregoing option shall be in addition to, and not in lieu of, any other rights, including the right to specific performance, that the statutory trust may have against such beneficial owner under the governing instrument of applicable law.

(c) A governing instrument may provide that the interest of any beneficial owner who fails to make any contribution that the beneficial owner is obligated to make shall be subject to specific penalties for, or specified consequences of, such failure. Such penalty or consequence may take the form of reducing or eliminating the defaulting beneficial owner's proportionate interest in the statutory trust, subordinating the beneficial interest to that of nondefaulting beneficial owners, a forced sale of the beneficial interest, forfeiture of the beneficial interest, the lending by other beneficial owners of the amount necessary to meet the beneficiary's commitment, a fixing of the value of the defaulting beneficial owner's beneficial interest by appraisal or by formula and redemption or sale of the beneficial interest at such value, or any other penalty or consequence.

§ 3803. Liability of Beneficial Owners and Trustees

(a) Except to the extent otherwise provided in the governing instrument of the statutory trust, the beneficial owners shall be entitled to the same limitation of personal liability extended to stockholders of private corporations for profit organized under the general corporation law of the State.

(b) Except to the extent otherwise provided in the governing instrument of a statutory trust, a trustee, when acting in such capacity, shall not be personally liable to any person other than the statutory trust or a beneficial owner for any act, omission or obligation of the statutory trust or any trustee thereof.

(c) Except to the extent otherwise provided in the governing instrument of a statutory trust, an officer, employee, manager or other person acting pursuant to § 3806(b)(7) of this title, when acting in such capacity, shall not be personally liable to any person other than the statutory trust or a beneficial owner for any act, omission or obligation of the statutory trust or any trustee thereof.

(d) No obligation of a beneficial owner or trustee of a statutory trust to the statutory trust arising under the governing instrument or a separate agreement in writing, and no note, instrument or other writing evidencing any such obligation of a beneficial owner or trustee, shall be subject to the defense of usury, and no beneficial owner or trustee shall interpose the defense of usury with respect to any such obligation in any action.

§ 3804. Legal Proceedings

(a) A statutory trust may sue and be sued, and service of process upon 1 of the trustees shall be sufficient. In furtherance of the foregoing, a statutory trust may be sued for debts and other obligations or liabilities contracted or incurred by the trustees, or by the duly authorized agents of such trustees, in the performance of their respective duties under the governing instrument of the statutory trust, and for any damages to persons or property resulting from the negligence of such trustees or agents acting in the performance of such respective duties. The property of a statutory trust shall be subject to attachment and execution as if it were a corporation, subject to § 3502 of Title 10. Notwithstanding the foregoing provisions of this section, in the event that the governing instrument of a statutory trust, including a statutory trust which is a registered investment company under the Investment Company Act of 1940, as amended (15 U.S.C. § 80a–1 et seq.), creates 1 or more series as provided in § 3806(b)(2) of this title, and if separate and distinct records are maintained for any such series and the assets associated with any such series are held in such separate and distinct records (directly or indirectly, including through a nominee or otherwise) and accounted for in such separate and distinct records separately from the other assets of the statutory trust, or any other series thereof, and if the governing instrument so provides, and notice of the limitation on liabilities of a series as referenced in this sentence is set forth in the certificate of trust of the statutory trust, then the debts, liabilities, obligations and expenses incurred, contracted for or otherwise existing with respect to a particular series shall be enforceable against the assets of such series only, and not against the assets of the statutory trust generally or any other series thereof, and, unless otherwise provided in the governing instrument, none of the debts, liabilities, obligations and expenses incurred, contracted for or otherwise existing with respect to the statutory trust generally or any other series thereof shall be enforceable against the assets of such series.

(b) A trustee of a statutory trust may be served with process in the manner prescribed in subsection (c) of this section in all civil actions or proceedings brought in the State involving or relating to the activities of the statutory trust or a violation by a trustee of a duty to the statutory trust, or any beneficial owner, whether or not the trustee is a trustee at the time suit is commenced. Every resident or nonresident of the State who accepts election or appointment or serves as a trustee of a statutory trust shall, by such acceptance or service, be deemed thereby to have consented to the appointment of the Delaware trustee or registered agent of such statutory trust required by § 3807 of this title (or, if there is none, the Secretary of State) as such person's agent upon whom service of process may be made as provided in this section. Such acceptance or service shall signify the consent of such trustee that any process when so served shall be of the same legal force and validity as if served upon such trustee within the State and such appointment of such Delaware trustee or registered agent (or, if there is none, the Secretary of State) shall be irrevocable.

(c) Service of process shall be effected by serving the Delaware trustee or registered agent of such statutory trust required by § 3807 of this title (or, if there is none, the Secretary of State) with 1 copy of such process in the manner provided by law for service of writs of summons. In the event service is made under this subsection upon the Secretary of State, the plaintiff shall pay to the Secretary of State the sum of $50 for the use of the State, which sum shall be taxed as part of the costs of the proceeding if the plaintiff shall prevail therein. In addition, the Prothonotary or the Register in Chancery of the court in which the civil action or proceeding is pending shall, within 7 days of such service, deposit in the United States mails, by registered mail, postage prepaid, true and attested copies of the process, together with a statement that service is being made pursuant to this section, addressed to the defendant at the defendant's address last known to and furnished by the party desiring to make such service.

(d) In any action in which any such trustee has been served with process as hereinafter provided, the time in which a defendant shall be required to appear and file a responsive pleading shall be computed from the date of mailing by the Prothonotary or the Register in Chancery as provided in subsection (c) of this section; provided however, the court in which such action has been commenced may order such continuance or continuances as may be necessary to afford such trustee reasonable opportunity to defend the action.

(e) In the governing instrument of the statutory trust or other writing, a trustee or beneficial owner or other person may consent to be subject to the nonexclusive jurisdiction of the courts of, or arbitration in, a specified jurisdiction, or the exclusive jurisdiction of the courts of the State, or the exclusivity of arbitration in a specified jurisdiction or the State, and to be served with legal process in the manner prescribed in such governing instrument of the statutory trust or other writing. Except by agreeing to arbitrate any arbitrable matter in a specified jurisdiction or in the State, a beneficial owner who is not a trustee may not waive its right to maintain a legal action or proceeding in the courts of the State with respect to matters relating to the organization or internal affairs of a statutory trust.

(f) Nothing herein contained limits or affects the right to serve process in any other manner now or hereafter provided by law. This section is an extension of and not a limitation upon the right otherwise existing of service of legal process upon nonresidents.

(g) The Court of Chancery and the Superior Court may make all necessary rules respecting the form of process, the manner of issuance and return thereof and such other rules which may be necessary to implement this section and are not inconsistent with this section. The Court of Chancery shall have jurisdiction over statutory trusts to the same extent as it has jurisdiction over common law trusts formed under the laws of the State.

(h) [Repealed.]

§ 3805. Rights of Beneficial Owners and Trustees in Trust Property

(a) Except to the extent otherwise provided in the governing instrument of the statutory trust, a beneficial owner shall have an undivided beneficial interest in the property of the statutory trust and shall share in the profits and losses of the statutory trust in the proportion (expressed as a percentage) of the entire undivided beneficial interest in the statutory trust owned by such beneficial owner. The governing instrument of a statutory trust may provide that the statutory trust or the trustees, acting for and on behalf of the statutory trust, shall be deemed to hold beneficial ownership of any income earned on securities of the statutory trust issued by any business entities formed, organized, or existing under the laws of any jurisdiction, including the laws of any foreign country.

(b) No creditor of the beneficial owner shall have any right to obtain possession of, or otherwise exercise legal or equitable remedies with respect to, the property of the statutory trust.

(c) A beneficial owner's beneficial interest in the statutory trust is personal property notwithstanding the nature of the property of the trust. Except to the extent otherwise provided in the governing instrument of a statutory trust, a beneficial owner has no interest in specific statutory trust property.

(d) A beneficial owner's beneficial interest in the statutory trust is freely transferable except to the extent otherwise provided in the governing instrument of the statutory trust.

(e) Except to the extent otherwise provided in the governing instrument of a statutory trust, at the time a beneficial owner becomes entitled to receive a distribution, the beneficial owner has the status of, and is entitled to all remedies available to, a creditor of the statutory trust with respect to the distribution. A governing instrument may provide for the establishment of record dates with respect to allocations and distributions by a statutory trust.

(f) Except to the extent otherwise provided in the governing instrument of the statutory trust, legal title to the property of the statutory trust or any part thereof may be held in the name of any trustee of the statutory trust, in its capacity as such, with the same effect as if such property were held in the name of the statutory trust.

(g) No creditor of the trustee shall have any right to obtain possession of, or otherwise exercise legal or equitable remedies with respect to, the property of the statutory trust with respect to any claim against, or obligation of, such trustee in its individual capacity and not related to the statutory trust.

(h) Except to the extent otherwise provided in the governing instrument of the statutory trust, where the statutory trust is a registered investment company under the Investment Company Act of 1940, as amended (15 U.S.C. § 80a–1 et seq.), any class, group or series of beneficial interests established by the governing instrument with respect to such statutory trust shall be a class, group or series preferred as to distribution of assets or payment of dividends over all other classes, groups or series in respect to assets specifically allocated to the class, group or series as contemplated by § 18 (or any amendment or successor provision) of the Investment Company Act of 1940 [15 U.S.C. § 80a–18], as amended, and any regulations issued thereunder, provided that this section is not intended to affect in any respect the provisions of § 3804(a) of this title.

(i) Unless otherwise provided in the governing instrument of a statutory trust or another agreement, a beneficial owner shall have no preemptive right to subscribe to any additional issue of beneficial interests or another interest in a statutory trust.

§ 3806. Management of Statutory Trust

(a) Except to the extent otherwise provided in the governing instrument of a statutory trust, the business and affairs of a statutory trust shall be managed by or under the direction of its trustees. To the extent provided in the governing instrument of a statutory trust, any person (including a beneficial owner) shall be entitled to direct the trustees or other persons in the management of the statutory trust. Except to the extent otherwise provided in the governing instrument of a statutory trust, neither the power to give direction to a trustee or other persons nor the exercise thereof by any person (including a beneficial owner) shall cause such person to be a trustee. To the extent provided in the governing instrument of a statutory trust, neither the power to give direction to a trustee or other persons nor the exercise thereof by any person (including a beneficial owner) shall cause such person to have duties (including fiduciary duties) or liabilities relating thereto to the statutory trust or to a beneficial owner thereof.

(b) A governing instrument may contain any provision relating to the management of the business and affairs of the statutory trust, and the rights, duties and obligations of the trustees, beneficial owners and other persons, which is not contrary to any provision or requirement of this subchapter and, without limitation:

(1) May provide for classes, groups or series of trustees or beneficial owners, or classes, groups or series of beneficial interests, having such relative rights, powers and duties as the governing instrument may provide, and may make provision for the future creation in the manner provided in the governing instrument of additional classes, groups or series of trustees, beneficial owners or beneficial interests, having such relative rights, powers and duties as may from time to time be established, including rights, powers and duties senior or subordinate to existing classes, groups or series of trustees, beneficial owners or beneficial interests;

(2) May establish or provide for the establishment of designated series of trustees, beneficial owners or beneficial interests having separate rights, powers or duties with respect to specified property or obligations of the statutory trust or profits and losses associated with specified property or obligations, and, to the extent provided in the governing instrument, any such series may have a separate business purpose or investment objective;

(3) May provide for the taking of any action, including the amendment of the governing instrument, the accomplishment of a merger, conversion or consolidation, the appointment of one or more trustees, the sale, lease, exchange, transfer, pledge or other disposition of all or any part of the assets of the statutory trust or the assets of any series, or the dissolution of the statutory trust, or may provide for the taking of any action to create under the provisions of the governing instrument a class, group or series of beneficial interests that was not previously outstanding, in any such case without the vote or approval of any particular trustee or beneficial owner, or class, group or series of trustees or beneficial owners;

(4) May grant to (or withhold from) all or certain trustees or beneficial owners, or a specified class, group or series of trustees or beneficial owners, the right to vote, separately or with any or all other classes, groups or series of the trustees or beneficial owners, on any matter, such voting being on a per capita, number, financial interest, class, group, series or any other basis;

(5) May, if and to the extent that voting rights are granted under the governing instrument, set forth provisions relating to notice of the time, place or purpose of any meeting at which any matter is to be voted on, waiver of any such notice, action by consent without a meeting, the establishment of record dates, quorum requirements, voting in person, by proxy or in any other manner, or any other matter with respect to the exercise of any such right to vote;

(6) May provide for the present or future creation of more than 1 statutory trust, including the creation of a future statutory trust to which all or any part of the assets, liabilities, profits or losses of any existing statutory trust will be transferred, and for the conversion of beneficial interests in an existing statutory trust, or series thereof, into beneficial interests in the separate statutory trust, or series thereof;

(7) May provide for the appointment, election or engagement, either as agents or independent contractors of the statutory trust or as delegatees of the trustees, of officers, employees, managers or other persons who may manage the business and affairs of the statutory trust and may have such titles and such relative rights, powers and duties as the governing instrument shall provide. Except to the extent otherwise provided in the governing instrument of a

statutory trust, the trustees shall choose and supervise such officers, managers, employees and other persons;

(8) May provide rights to any person, including a person who is not a party to the governing instrument, to the extent set forth therein; or

(9) May provide for the manner in which it may be amended, including by requiring the approval of a person who is not a party to the governing instrument or the satisfaction of conditions, and to the extent the governing instrument provides for the manner in which it may be amended such governing instrument may be amended only in that manner or as otherwise permitted by law (provided that the approval of any person may be waived by such person and that any such conditions may be waived by all persons for whose benefit such conditions were intended).

(c) To the extent that, at law or in equity, a trustee or beneficial owner or other person has duties (including fiduciary duties) to a statutory trust or to another trustee or beneficial owner or to another person that is a party to or is otherwise bound by a governing instrument, the trustee's or beneficial owner's or other person's duties may be expanded or restricted or eliminated by provisions in the governing instrument; provided, that the governing instrument may not eliminate the implied contractual covenant of good faith and fair dealing.

(d) Unless otherwise provided in a governing instrument, a trustee or beneficial owner or other person shall not be liable to a statutory trust or to another trustee or beneficial owner or to another person that is a party to or is otherwise bound by a governing instrument for breach of fiduciary duty for the trustee's or beneficial owner's or other person's good faith reliance on the provisions of the governing instrument.

(e) A governing instrument may provide for the limitation or elimination of any and all liabilities for breach of contract and breach of duties (including fiduciary duties) of a trustee, beneficial owner or other person to a statutory trust or to another trustee or beneficial owner or to another person that is a party to or is otherwise bound by a governing instrument; provided, that a governing instrument may not limit or eliminate liability for any act or omission that constitutes a bad faith violation of the implied contractual covenant of good faith and fair dealing.

(f) Unless otherwise provided in the governing instrument of a statutory trust, meetings of beneficial owners may be held by means of conference telephone or other communications equipment by means of which all persons participating in the meeting can hear each other, and participation in a meeting pursuant to this subsection shall constitute presence in person at the meeting. Unless otherwise provided in the governing instrument of a statutory trust, on any matter that is to be voted on by the beneficial owners, (i) the beneficial owners may take such action without a meeting, without a prior notice and without a vote if a consent or consents in writing, setting forth the action so taken, shall be signed by the beneficial owners having not less than the minimum number of votes that would be necessary to authorize or take such action at a meeting at which all interests in the statutory trust entitled to vote thereon were present and voted and (ii) the beneficial owners may vote in person or by proxy, and such proxy may be granted in writing, by means of electronic transmission; or as otherwise permitted by applicable law. Unless otherwise provided in a governing instrument, a consent transmitted by electronic transmission by a beneficial owner or by a person or persons authorized to act for a beneficial owner shall be deemed to be written and signed for purposes of this subsection. For purposes of this subsection, the term "electronic transmission" means any form of communication not directly involving the physical transmission of paper that creates a record that may be retained, retrieved and reviewed by a recipient thereof and that may be directly reproduced in paper form by such a recipient through an automated process.

(g) Unless otherwise provided in the governing instrument of a statutory trust, meetings of trustees may be held by means of conference telephone or other communications equipment by means of which all persons participating in the meeting can hear each other, and participation in a meeting pursuant to this subsection shall constitute presence in person at the meeting. Unless otherwise provided in the governing instrument of a statutory trust, on any matter that is to be voted on by the trustees, (i) the trustees may take such action without a meeting, without a prior notice and without a vote if a consent or consents in writing, setting forth the action so taken, shall be signed by the trustees having not less than the minimum number of votes that would be necessary to authorize or take such action at a meeting at which all trustees entitled to vote thereon were present and voted and (ii) the trustee may vote in person or by proxy, and such proxy may be granted in writing, by means of electronic transmission, or as otherwise permitted by applicable law. Unless otherwise provided in a governing instrument, a consent transmitted by electronic transmission by a trustee or by a person or persons authorized to act for a trustee shall be deemed to be written and signed for purposes of this subsection. For purposes of this subsection, the term "electronic transmission" means any form of communication not directly involving the physical transmission of paper that creates a record that may be retained, retrieved and reviewed by a recipient thereof and that may be directly reproduced in paper form by such a recipient through an automated process.

(h) Except to the extent otherwise provided in the governing instrument of a statutory trust, a beneficial owner, trustee, officer, employee or manager may lend money to, borrow money from, act as a surety, guarantor or endorser for, guarantee or assume 1 or more obligations of, provide collateral for, and transact other business with a statutory trust and, subject to other applicable law, has the same rights and obligations with respect to any such matter as a person who is not a beneficial owner, trustee, officer, employee or manager.

(i) Except to the extent otherwise provided in the governing instrument of a statutory trust, a trustee of a statutory trust has the power and authority to delegate to 1 or more other persons the trustee's rights and powers to manage and control the business and affairs of the statutory trust, including to delegate to agents, officers and employees of the trustee or the statutory trust, and to delegate by management agreement or other agreement with, or otherwise to, other persons. Except to the extent otherwise provided in the governing instrument of a statutory trust, such delegation by a trustee of a statutory trust shall not cause the trustee to cease to be a trustee of the statutory trust or cause the person to whom any such rights and powers have been delegated to be a trustee of the statutory trust.

(j) The governing instrument of a statutory trust may provide that:

(1) A beneficial owner who fails to perform in accordance with, or to comply with the terms and conditions of, the governing instrument shall be subject to specified penalties or specified consequences;

(2) At the time or upon the happening of events specified in the governing instrument, a beneficial owner shall be subject to specified penalties or specified consequences; and

(3) The specified penalties or specified consequences under paragraphs (1) and (2) of this subsection may include and take the form of any penalty or consequence set forth in § 3802(c) of this title.

(k) A trustee, beneficial owner or an officer, employee, manager or other person designated in accordance with paragraph (b)(7) of this section shall be fully protected in relying in good faith upon the records of the statutory trust and upon information, opinions, reports or statements presented by another trustee, beneficial owner or officer, employee, manager or other person designated in accordance with paragraph (b)(7) of this section, or by any other person as to matters the trustee, beneficial owner or officer, employee, manager or other person designated in accordance with paragraph (b)(7) of this section reasonably believes are within such other person's professional or expert competence, including information, opinions, reports or statements as to the value and amount of the assets, liabilities, profits or losses of the statutory trust, or the value and amount of assets or reserves or contracts, agreements or other undertakings that would be sufficient to pay claims and obligations of the statutory trust or to make reasonable provision to pay such claims and obligations, or any other facts pertinent to the existence and amount of assets from which distributions to beneficial owners or creditors might properly be paid.

§ 3807. Trustee in State

(a) Every statutory trust shall at all times have at least 1 trustee which, in the case of a natural person, shall be a person who is a resident of this State or which, in all other cases, has its principal place of business in this State.

(b) Notwithstanding the provisions of subsection (a) of this section, if a statutory trust is, becomes, or will become prior to or within 180 days following the first issuance of beneficial interests, a registered investment company under the Investment Company Act of 1940, as amended (15 U.S.C. §§ 80a–1 et seq.), such statutory trust shall not be required to have a trustee who is a resident of this State or who has a principal place of business in this State if notice that the statutory trust is or will become an investment company as referenced in this sentence is set forth in the certificate of trust of the statutory trust and if and for so long as such statutory trust shall have and maintain in this State:

(1) A registered office, which may but need not be a place of business in this State; and

(2) A registered agent for service of process on the statutory trust, which agent may be either an individual resident in this State whose business office is identical with such statutory trust's registered office, or a domestic corporation, limited partnership, limited liability company or statutory trust, or a foreign corporation, limited partnership, limited liability company or statutory trust authorized to transact business in this State, having a business office identical with such registered office.

(c) Any statutory trust maintaining a registered office and registered agent in this State under subsection (b) of this section may change the location of its registered office in this State to any other place in this State, or may change the registered agent to any other person or corporation (meeting the requirements contained in subsection (b) of this section), by filing an amendment to its certificate of trust in accordance with the applicable provisions of this subchapter. If a statutory trust which is an investment company registered as aforesaid maintains a registered office and registered agent in this State as herein provided, then the reference in § 3810(a)(1)b. of this title to the "name and the business address of at least 1 of the trustees meeting the requirements of § 3807 of this title" shall be deemed a reference to the name and the business address of the registered agent and registered office maintained under this section, and the certificate of trust filed under § 3810 of this title shall reflect such information in lieu of the information otherwise required by § 3810(a)(1)b. of this title.

(d) Service of process upon a registered agent maintained by a statutory trust pursuant to subsection (b) of this section shall be as effective as if served upon one of the trustees of the statutory trust pursuant to § 3804 of this title.

(e) A trustee or registered agent of a statutory trust whose address, as set forth in a certificate of trust pursuant to § 3810(a)(1)b. of this title, has changed may change such address in the certificates of trust of all statutory trusts for which such trustee or registered agent is appointed to another address in the State by paying a fee as set forth in § 3813(a)(5) of this title and filing with the Secretary of State a certificate, executed by such trustee or registered agent, setting forth the address of such trustee or registered agent before it was changed, and further certifying as to the new address of such trustee or registered agent for each of the statutory trusts for which it is trustee or registered agent. Upon the filing of such certificate, the Secretary of State shall furnish to the trustee or registered agent a certified copy of the same under the Secretary's hand and seal of office, and thereafter, or until further change of address, as authorized by law, the address of such trustee or registered agent in the State for each of the statutory trusts for which it is trustee or registered agent shall be located at the new address of the trustee or registered agent thereof as given in the certificate. A trustee or registered agent of a statutory trust whose name, as set forth in a certificate of trust pursuant to § 3810(a)(1)b. of this title, has changed may change such name in the certificates of trust of all statutory trusts for which such trustee or registered agent is appointed to its new name by paying a fee as set forth in § 3813(a)(5) of this title and filing with the Secretary of State a certificate, executed by such trustee or registered agent, setting forth the name of such trustee or registered agent before it was changed and further certifying as to the new name of such trustee or registered agent for each of the statutory trusts for which it is a trustee or registered agent. Upon the filing of such certificate and payment of such fee, the Secretary of State shall furnish to the trustee or registered agent a certified copy of the certificate under the Secretary's hand and seal of office. A change of name of any person acting as a trustee or registered agent of a statutory trust as a result of a merger or consolidation of the trustee or registered agent with another person who succeeds to its assets and liabilities by operation of law shall be deemed a change of name for purposes of this section. Filing a certificate under this section shall be deemed to be an amendment of the certificate of trust of each statutory trust affected thereby, and no further action with respect thereto to amend its certificate of trust under § 3810 of this title shall be required. Any trustee or registered agent filing a certificate under this section shall promptly, upon such filing, deliver a copy of any such certificate to each statutory trust affected thereby.

§ 3808. Existence of Statutory Trust

(a) Except to the extent otherwise provided in the governing instrument of the statutory trust, a statutory trust shall have perpetual existence, and a statutory trust may not be terminated or revoked by a beneficial owner or other person except in accordance with the terms of its governing instrument.

(b) Except to the extent otherwise provided in the governing instrument of a statutory trust, the death, incapacity, dissolution, termination or bankruptcy of a beneficial owner shall not result in the termination or dissolution of a statutory trust.

(c) In the event that a statutory trust does not have perpetual existence, a statutory trust is dissolved and its affairs shall be wound up at the time or upon the happening of events specified in the governing instrument. Notwithstanding the happening of events specified in the governing instrument, the statutory trust shall not be dissolved and its affairs shall not be wound up if, prior to the filing of a certificate of cancellation as provided in § 3810 of this title, the statutory trust is continued, effective as of the happening of such event, pursuant to the affirmative vote or written consent of all remaining beneficial owners of the statutory trust (and any other person whose approval is required under the governing instrument to revoke a dissolution pursuant to this section), provided, however, if the dissolution was caused by a vote or written consent, the dissolution shall not be revoked unless each beneficial owner and other person (or their respective personal representatives) who voted in favor of, or consented to, the dissolution has voted or consented in writing to continue the statutory trust.

(d) Upon dissolution of a statutory trust and until the filing of a certificate of cancellation as provided in § 3810 of this title, the persons who, under the governing instrument of the statutory trust, are responsible for winding up the statutory trust's affairs may, in the name of and for and on behalf of the statutory trust, prosecute and defend suits, whether civil, criminal or administrative, gradually settle and close the statutory trust business, dispose of and convey the statutory trust property, discharge or make reasonable provision for the statutory trust liabilities and distribute to the beneficial owners any remaining assets of the statutory trust.

(e) A statutory trust which has dissolved shall pay or make reasonable provision to pay all claims and obligations, including all contingent, conditional or unmatured claims and obligations, known to the statutory trust and all claims and obligations which are known to the statutory trust but for which the identity of the claimant is unknown and claims and obligations that have not been made known to the statutory trust or that have not arisen but that, based on the facts known to the statutory trust, are likely to arise or to become known to the statutory trust within 10 years after the date of dissolution. If there are sufficient assets, such claims and obligations shall be paid in full and any such provision for payment shall be made in full. If there are insufficient assets, such claims and obligations shall be paid or provided for according to their priority and, among claims and obligations of equal priority, ratably to the extent of assets available therefor. Unless otherwise provided in the governing instrument of a statutory trust, any remaining assets shall be distributed to the beneficial owners. Any person, including any trustee, who under the governing instrument of the statutory trust is responsible for winding up a statutory trust's affairs who has complied with this subsection shall not be personally liable to the claimants of the dissolved statutory trust by reason of such person's actions in winding up the statutory trust.

(f) Except to the extent otherwise provided in the governing instrument of the statutory trust, a series established in accordance with § 3804(a) of this title may be dissolved and its affairs wound up without causing the dissolution of the statutory trust or any other series thereof. Unless otherwise provided in the governing instrument of the statutory trust, the dissolution, winding up, liquidation or termination of the statutory trust or any series thereof shall not affect the limitation of liability with respect to a series established in accordance with § 3804(a) of this title. A series established in accordance with § 3804(a) of this title is dissolved and its affairs shall be wound up at the time or upon the happening of events specified in the governing instrument of the statutory trust. Except to the extent otherwise provided in the governing instrument of a statutory trust, the death, incapacity, dissolution, termination or bankruptcy of a beneficial owner of such series shall not result in the termination or dissolution of such series and such series may not be terminated or revoked by a beneficial owner of such series or other person except in accordance with the terms of the governing instrument of the statutory trust.

(g) Upon dissolution of a series of a statutory trust, the persons who under the governing instrument of the statutory trust are responsible for winding up such series" affairs may, in the name of the statutory trust and for and on behalf of the statutory trust and such series, take all actions with respect to the series as are permitted under subsection (d) of this section and shall provide for the claims and obligations of the series and distribute the assets of the series as provided under subsection (e) of this section. Any person, including any trustee, who under the governing instrument is responsible for winding up such series" affairs who has complied with subsection (e) of this section shall not be personally liable to the claimants of the dissolved series by reason of such person's actions in winding up the series.

§ 3809. Applicability of Trust Law

Except to the extent otherwise provided in the governing instrument of a statutory trust or in this subchapter, the laws of this State pertaining to trusts are hereby made applicable to statutory trusts; provided however, that for purposes of any tax imposed by this State or any instrumentality, agency or political subdivision of this State a statutory trust shall be classified as a corporation, an association, a partnership, a trust or otherwise, as shall be determined under the

United States Internal Revenue Code of 1986 [26 U.S. Code § 1 et seq.], as amended, or under any successor provision.

§ 3810. Certificate of Trust; Amendment; Restatement; Cancellation

(a)(1) Every statutory trust shall file a certificate of trust in the office of the Secretary of State. The certificate of trust shall set forth:

a. The name of the statutory trust;

b. The name and the business address of at least 1 of the trustees meeting the requirements of § 3807 of this title;

c. The future effective date or time (which shall be a date or time certain) of effectiveness of the certificate if it is not to be effective upon the filing of the certificate; and

d. Any other information the trustees determine to include therein.

(2) A statutory trust is formed at the time of the filing of the initial certificate of trust in the office of the Secretary of State or at any later date or time specified in the certificate of trust if, in either case, there has been substantial compliance with the requirements of this section. A statutory trust formed under this chapter shall be a separate legal entity, the existence of which as a separate legal entity shall continue until cancellation of the statutory trust's certificate of trust.

(3) The filing of a certificate of trust in the office of the Secretary of State shall make it unnecessary to file any other documents under Chapter 31 of Title 6.

(b)(1) A certificate of trust may be amended by filing a certificate of amendment thereto in the office of the Secretary of State. The certificate of amendment shall set forth:

a. The name of the statutory trust;

b. The amendment to the certificate; and

c. The future effective date or time (which shall be a date or time certain) of effectiveness of the certificate if it is not to be effective upon the filing of the certificate.

(2) Except to the extent otherwise provided in the certificate of trust or in the governing instrument of a statutory trust, a certificate of trust may be amended at any time for any purpose as the trustees may determine. A trustee who becomes aware that any statement in a certificate of trust was false when made or that any matter described has changed making the certificate false in any material respect shall promptly file a certificate of amendment.

(c)(1) A certificate of trust may be restated by integrating into a single instrument all of the provisions of the certificate of trust which are then in effect and operative as a result of there having been theretofore filed 1 or more certificates of amendment pursuant to subsection (b) of this section, and the certificate of trust may be amended or further amended by the filing of a restated certificate of trust. The restated certificate of trust shall be specifically designated as such in its heading and shall set forth:

a. The present name of the statutory trust, and if it has been changed, the name under which the statutory trust was originally formed;

b. The date of filing of the original certificate of trust with the Secretary of State;

c. The information required to be included pursuant to subsection (a) of this section; and

d. Any other information the trustees determine to include therein.

(2) A certificate of trust may be restated at any time for any purpose as the trustees may determine. A trustee who becomes aware that any statement in a restated certificate of trust was false when made or that any matter described has changed making the restated certificate false in any material respect shall promptly file a certificate of amendment or a restated certificate of trust.

(d) A certificate of trust shall be cancelled upon the dissolution and the completion of winding up of a statutory trust, or shall be deemed to be cancelled upon the filing of a certificate of merger or consolidation if the statutory trust is not the surviving or resulting entity in a merger or consolidation, or upon the filing of a certificate of transfer, or upon the filing of a certificate of conversion to a non-Delaware other business entity. A certificate of cancellation shall be filed in the office of the Secretary of State and set forth:

(1) The name of the statutory trust;

(2) The date of filing of its certificate of trust;

(3) The future effective date or time (which shall be a date or time certain) of cancellation if it is not to be effective upon the filing of the certificate; and

(4) Any other information the trustee determines to include therein.

(e) Whenever any certificate authorized to be filed with the office of the Secretary of State under this subchapter has been so filed and is an inaccurate record of the action therein referred to or was defectively or erroneously executed, such certificate may be corrected by filing with the office of the Secretary of State a certificate of correction of such certificate. The certificate of correction shall specify the inaccuracy or defect to be corrected, shall set forth the portion of the certificate in corrected form and shall be executed and filed as required by this subchapter. In lieu of filing a certificate of correction, the certificate may be corrected by filing with the office of the Secretary of State a corrected certificate which shall be executed and filed in accordance with this subchapter. The corrected certificate shall be specifically designated as such in its heading, shall specify the inaccuracy or defect to be corrected and shall set forth the entire certificate in corrected form. The corrected certificate shall be effective as of the date the original certificate was filed, except as to those persons who are substantially and adversely affected by the corrections, and as to those persons the corrected certificate shall be effective from the filing date.

(f) If any certificate filed in accordance with this subchapter provides for a future effective date or time and if the transaction is terminated or amended to change the future effective date or time prior to the future effective date or time, the certificate shall be terminated or amended by the filing, prior to the future effective date or time set forth in such original certificate, of a certificate of termination or amendment of the original certificate, executed and filed in accordance with this subchapter, which shall identify the original certificate which has been terminated or amended and shall state that the original certificate has been terminated or amended.

§ 3811. Execution of Certificate

(a) Each certificate required by this subchapter to be filed in the office of the Secretary of State shall be executed in the following manner:

(1) A certificate of trust must be signed by all of the trustees;

(2) A certificate of amendment, a certificate of correction, a corrected certificate, a certificate of termination or amendment, and a restated certificate of trust must be signed by at least one of the trustees;

(3) A certificate of cancellation must be signed by all of the trustees or as otherwise provided in the governing instrument of the statutory trust; and

(4) If a statutory trust is filing a certificate of merger or consolidation, certificate of conversion, certificate of transfer, certificate of transfer and continuance, certificate of statutory trust domestication or certificate of termination or amendment to any such certificate, the certificate of merger or consolidation, certificate of conversion, certificate of transfer, certificate of transfer and continuance, certificate of statutory trust domestication or certificate of termination or amendment to any such certificate must be signed by all of the trustees or as otherwise provided in the governing instrument of the statutory trust, or if the certificate of merger or consolidation, certificate of conversion, certificate of transfer, certificate of transfer and continuance, certificate of statutory trust domestication or certificate of termination or amendment to any such certificate is being filed by another business entity, the certificate of

merger or consolidation, certificate of conversion, certificate of transfer, certificate of transfer and continuance, certificate of statutory trust domestication or certificate of termination or amendment to any such certificate must be signed by a person authorized to execute the certificate on behalf of the other business entity.

(b) Unless otherwise provided in the governing instrument, any person may sign any certificate or amendment thereof or enter into a governing instrument or amendment thereof by any agent, including any attorney-in-fact. An authorization, including a power of attorney, to sign any certificate or amendment thereof or to enter into a governing instrument or amendment thereof need not be in writing, need not be sworn to, verified or acknowledged and need not be filed in the office of the Secretary of State, but if in writing, must be retained by the statutory trust or a trustee or other person authorized to manage the business and affairs of the statutory trust.

(c) The execution of a certificate by a trustee constitutes an oath or affirmation, under the penalties of perjury in the third degree, that, to the best of the trustee's knowledge and belief, the facts stated therein are true.

§ 3812. Filing of Certificate

(a) Any certificate authorized to be filed with the office of the Secretary of State under this subchapter (or any judicial decree of amendment or cancellation) shall be delivered to the office of the Secretary of State for filing. A person who executes a certificate as an agent or fiduciary need not exhibit evidence of the person's authority as a prerequisite to filing. Unless the Secretary of State finds that any certificate does not conform to law, upon receipt of all filing fees required by law the Secretary of State shall:

(1) Certify that the certificate (or any judicial decree of amendment or cancellation) has been filed in the Secretary of State's office by endorsing upon the filed certificate (or judicial decree) the word "filed," and the date and hour of the filing. This endorsement is conclusive of the date and time of its filing in the absence of actual fraud;

(2) File and index the endorsed certificate (or judicial decree);

(3) Prepare and return to the person who filed it or the person's representative a copy of the filed certificate (or judicial decree), similarly endorsed, and shall certify such copy as a true copy of the filed certificate (or judicial decree); and

(4) Enter such information from the certificate as the Secretary of State deems appropriate into the Delaware Corporation Information System or any system which is a successor thereto in the office of the Secretary of State, and such information shall be permanently maintained as a public record. A copy of each certificate shall be

permanently maintained on optical disk or by other suitable medium.

(b) Upon the filing of a certificate of trust in the office of the Secretary of State, or upon the future effective date or time of a certificate of trust as provided for therein, the certificate of trust shall be effective. Upon the filing of a certificate of amendment (or judicial decree of amendment), certificate of correction, corrected certificate or restated certificate in the office of the Secretary of State, or upon the future effective date or time of a certificate of amendment (or judicial decree of amendment) or restated certificate as provided for therein, the certificate of trust shall be amended or restated as set forth therein. Upon the filing of a certificate of cancellation (or a judicial decree thereof) or a certificate of merger or consolidation which acts as a certificate of cancellation or a certificate of transfer or a certificate of conversion to a non-Delaware entity in the office of the Secretary of State, or upon the future effective date or time of a certificate of cancellation (or a judicial decree thereof) or a certificate of merger or consolidation which acts as a certificate of cancellation or a certificate of transfer or a certificate of conversion to a non-Delaware entity, as provided for therein, the certificate of trust shall be canceled. Upon the filing of a certificate of termination or amendment, the original certificate identified in the certificate of termination or amendment shall be terminated or amended, as the case may be.

(c) A fee as set forth in § 3813(a)(2) of this title shall be paid at the time of the filing of a certificate of trust, a certificate of amendment, a certificate of correction, a corrected certificate, a certificate of termination or amendment, a certificate of cancellation, a certificate of merger or consolidation, a certificate of conversion, a certificate of transfer, a certificate of transfer and continuance, a certificate of statutory trust domestication or a restated certificate.

(d) A fee as set forth in § 3813(a)(3) of this title shall be paid for a certified copy of any certificate on file as provided for by this subchapter and a fee as set forth in § 3813(a)(4) of this title shall be paid for each page copied.

(e) Any signature on any certificate authorized to be filed with the Secretary of State under any provision of this subchapter may be a facsimile, a conformed signature or an electronically transmitted signature. Any such certificate may be filed by telecopy, fax or similar electronic transmission; provided, however, that the Secretary of State shall have no obligation to accept such filing if such certificate is illegible or otherwise unsuitable for processing.

(f) The fact that a certificate of trust is on file in the office of the Secretary of State is notice that the entity formed in connection with the filing of the certificate of trust is a statutory trust formed under the laws of the State and is notice of all other facts set forth therein which are required to be set forth in a certificate of trust by § 3810(a)(1) of this title and is notice of the limitation on liability of a series of a statutory trust which is permitted to be set forth in a certificate of trust by § 3804(a) of this title.

§ 3813. Fees [Effective Until July 1, 2008]

(a) No documents required to be filed under this subchapter shall be effective until the applicable fee required by this section is paid. The following fees shall be paid to and collected by the Secretary of State for the use of this State:

(1) Upon the receipt for filing of an application for reservation of name, and application for renewal of reservation, or notice of transfer or cancellation of reservation pursuant to § 3814 of this title, a fee in the amount of $75.

(2) Upon the receipt for filing of a certificate of trust, a certificate of amendment, a certificate of cancellation or a certificate of merger or consolidation, a certificate of correction, a corrected certificate, a certificate of conversion, a certificate of transfer, a certificate of transfer and continuance, a certificate of statutory trust domestication, a certificate of termination or amendment or a restated certificate, a fee in the amount of $200.

(3) For certifying copies of any paper on file as provided for by this subchapter, a fee in the amount of $30 for each copy certified.

(4) For issuing further copies of instruments on file, whether certified or not, a fee in the amount of $10 for the first page and $2 for each additional page.

(5) Upon the receipt for filing of a certificate under § 3807(e) of this title, a fee in the amount of $50.

(6) For issuing any certificate of the Secretary of State, including but not limited to a certificate of good standing, other than a certification of a copy under subdivision (3) of this subsection, a fee in the amount of $30, except that for issuing any certificate of the Secretary of State that recites all of a statutory trust's filings with the Secretary of State, a fee of $125 shall be paid for each such certificate.

(b) In addition to those fees charged under subsection (a) of this section, there shall be collected by and paid to the Secretary of State the following:

(1) For all services described in subsection (a) of this section that are requested to completed within 1 hour on the same day as the day of the request, an additional sum of up to $1,000 and for all services described in subsection (a) of this section that are requested to be completed within 2 hours on the same day as the day of the request, an additional sum of up to $500; and

(2) For all services described in subsection (a) of this section that are requested to be completed within the same day as the day of the request, an additional sum of up to $200; and

(3) For all services described in subsection (a) of this section that are requested to be completed within a 24–hour period from the time of the request, an additional sum of up to $100.

The Secretary of State shall establish (and may from time to time alter or amend) a schedule of specific fees payable pursuant to this subsection.

(c) Except as provided by this section, all other fees for the Secretary of State shall be as provided for in § 2315 of Title 29.

§ 3813. Fees [Effective July 1, 2008]

(a) No documents required to be filed under this subchapter shall be effective until the applicable fee required by this section is paid. The following fees shall be paid to and collected by the Secretary of State for the use of this State:

(1) Upon the receipt for filing of an application for reservation of name, and application for renewal of reservation, or notice of transfer or cancellation of reservation pursuant to § 3814 of this title, a fee in the amount of $75.

(2) Upon the receipt for filing of a certificate of trust, a certificate of amendment, a certificate of cancellation or a certificate of merger or consolidation, a certificate of correction, a corrected certificate, a certificate of conversion, a certificate of transfer, a certificate of transfer and continuance, a certificate of statutory trust domestication, a certificate of termination or amendment or a restated certificate, a fee in the amount of up to $300.

(3) For certifying copies of any paper on file as provided for by this subchapter, a fee in the amount of $30 for each copy certified.

(4) For issuing further copies of instruments on file, whether certified or not, a fee in the amount of $10 for the first page and $2 for each additional page.

(5) Upon the receipt for filing of a certificate under § 3807(e) of this title, a fee in the amount of $50.

(6) For issuing any certificate of the Secretary of State, including but not limited to a certificate of good standing, other than a certification of a copy under subdivision (3) of this subsection, a fee in the amount of $30, except that for issuing any certificate of the Secretary of State that recites all of a statutory trust's filings with the Secretary of State, a fee of $125 shall be paid for each such certificate.

(b) In addition to those fees charged under subsection (a) of this section, there shall be collected by and paid to the Secretary of State the following:

(1) For all services described in subsection (a) of this section that are requested to completed within 1 hour on the same day as the day of the request, an additional sum of up to $1,000 and for all services described in subsection (a) of this section that are requested to be completed within 2 hours on the same day as the day of the request, an additional sum of up to $500; and

(2) For all services described in subsection (a) of this section that are requested to be completed within the same day as the day of the request, an additional sum of up to $200; and

(3) For all services described in subsection (a) of this section that are requested to be completed within a 24–hour period from the time of the request, an additional sum of up to $100.

The Secretary of State shall establish (and may from time to time alter or amend) a schedule of specific fees payable pursuant to this subsection.

(c) Except as provided by this section, all other fees for the Secretary of State shall be as provided for in § 2315 of Title 29.

§ 3814. Use of Names Regulated

(a) The name of each statutory trust as set forth in its certificate of trust must be such as to distinguish it upon the records of the office of the Secretary of State from the name of any corporation, partnership, limited partnership, statutory trust or limited liability company reserved, registered, formed or organized under the laws of this State or qualified to do business or registered as a foreign corporation, foreign partnership, foreign limited partnership, foreign statutory trust or foreign limited liability company in this State; provided however, that a statutory trust may register under any name which is not such as to distinguish it upon the records of the office of the Secretary of State from the name of any domestic or foreign corporation, partnership, limited partnership, statutory trust or limited liability company reserved, registered, formed or organized under the laws of this State with the written consent of the other corporation, partnership, limited partnership, statutory trust or limited liability company, which written consent shall be filed with the Secretary of State.

(b) The name of each statutory trust as set forth in its certificate of trust may contain the name of a beneficial owner, a trustee or any other person.

(c) The name of each statutory trust, as set forth in its certificate of trust, may contain the following words: "company," "association," "club," "foundation," "fund," "institute," "society," "union," "syndicate," "limited" or "trust" (or abbreviations of like import).

(d) The exclusive right to the use of a name may be reserved by:

(1) Any person intending to form a statutory trust and to adopt that name; and

(2) Any statutory trust registered in this State which proposes to change its name.

(e) The reservation of a specified name shall be made by filing with the Secretary of State an application, executed by the applicant, together with a duplicate copy, which may either be a signed or conformed copy, specifying the name to be reserved and the name and address of the applicant. If the Secretary of State finds that the name is available for use by a statutory trust, the Secretary shall reserve the name for the exclusive use of the applicant for a period of 120 days. Once having so reserved a name, the same applicant may again reserve the same name for successive 120–day periods. The right to the exclusive use of a reserved name may be transferred to any other person by filing in the office of the Secretary of State a notice of the transfer, executed by the applicant for whom the name was reserved, together with a duplicate copy, which may be either a signed or conformed copy, specifying the name to be transferred and the name and address of the transferee. The reservation of a specified name may be cancelled by filing with the Secretary of State a notice of cancellation, executed by the applicant or transferee, together with a duplicate copy, which may be either a signed or conformed copy, specifying the name reservation to be cancelled and the name and address of the applicant or transferee. Any duplicate copy filed with the Secretary of State, as required by this subsection, shall be returned by the Secretary of State to the person who filed it or that person's representative with a notation thereon of the action taken with respect to the original copy thereof by the Secretary of State.

(f) Fees as set forth in § 3813 of this title shall be paid at the time of the initial reservation of any name, at the time of the renewal of any such reservation and at the time of the filing of a notice of the transfer or cancellation of any such reservation.

§ 3815. Merger and Consolidation

(a) Pursuant to an agreement of merger or consolidation, a statutory trust may merge or consolidate with or into 1 or more statutory trusts or other business entities formed or organized or existing under the laws of the State or any other state or the United States or any foreign country or other foreign jurisdiction, with such statutory trust or other business entity as the agreement shall provide being the surviving or resulting statutory trust or other business entity. Unless otherwise provided in the governing instrument of a statutory trust, a merger or consolidation shall be approved by each statutory trust which is to merge or consolidate by all of the trustees and the beneficial owners of such statutory trust. In connection with a merger or consolidation hereunder, rights or securities of, or interests in, a statutory trust or other business entity which is a constituent party to the merger or consolidation may be exchanged for or converted into cash, property, rights or securities of, or interests in, the surviving or resulting statutory trust or other business entity or, in addition to or in lieu thereof, may be exchanged for or converted into cash, property, rights or securities of, or interests in, a statutory trust or other business entity which is not the surviving or resulting statutory trust or other business entity in the merger or consolidation or may be cancelled. Notwithstanding prior approval, an agreement of merger or consolidation may be terminated or amended pursuant to a provision for such termination or amendment contained in the agreement of merger or consolidation.

(b) If a statutory trust is merging or consolidating under this section, the statutory trust or other business entity surviving or resulting in or from the merger or consolidation shall file a certificate of merger or consolidation in the office of the Secretary of State. The certificate of merger or consolidation shall state:

(1) The name and jurisdiction of formation or organization of each of the statutory trust or other business entities which is to merge or consolidate;

(2) That an agreement of merger or consolidation has been approved and executed by each of the statutory trusts or other business entities which is to merge or consolidate;

(3) The name of the surviving or resulting statutory trust or other business entity;

(4) In the case of a merger in which a statutory trust is the surviving entity, such amendments, if any, to the certificate of trust of the surviving statutory trust to change its name as are desired to be effected by the merger;

(5) The future effective date or time (which shall be a date or time certain) of the merger or consolidation if it is not to be effective upon the filing of the certificate of merger or consolidation;

(6) That the executed agreement of merger or consolidation is on file at the principal place of business of the surviving or resulting statutory trust or other business entity, and shall state the address thereof;

(7) That a copy of the agreement of merger or consolidation will be furnished by the surviving or resulting statutory trust or other business entity, on request and without cost, to any beneficial owner of any statutory trust or any person holding an interest in any other business entity which is to merge or consolidate; and

(8) If the surviving or resulting entity is not a statutory trust or other business entity formed or organized or existing under the laws of the State of Delaware, a statement that such surviving or resulting other business entity agrees that it may be served with process in the State in any action, suit or proceeding for the enforcement of any obligation of any statutory trust which is to merge or consolidate, irrevocably appointing the Secretary of State as its agent to accept service of process in any such action, suit or proceeding and specifying the address to which a copy of such process shall be

mailed to it by the Secretary of State. In the event of service hereunder upon the Secretary of State, the plaintiff in any such action, suit or proceeding shall furnish the Secretary of State with the address specified in the certificate of merger or consolidation provided for in this section and any other address which the plaintiff may elect to furnish, together with copies of such process as required by the Secretary of State, and the Secretary of State shall notify such surviving or resulting other business entity thereof at all such addresses furnished by the plaintiff by letter, certified mail, return receipt requested. Such letter shall enclose a copy of the process and any other papers served upon the Secretary of State. It shall be the duty of the plaintiff in the event of such service to serve process and any other papers in duplicate, to notify the Secretary of State that service is being made pursuant to this subsection, and to pay the Secretary of State the sum of $50 for use of the State, which sum shall be taxed as part of the costs in the proceeding, if the plaintiff shall prevail therein. The Secretary of State shall maintain an alphabetical record of any such process setting forth the name of the plaintiff and defendant, the title, docket number and nature of the proceedings in which process has been served upon the Secretary, the return date thereof, and the day and hour when the service was made. The Secretary of State shall not be required to retain such information for a period longer than 5 years from the Secretary's receipt of the service of process.

(c) Any failure to file a certificate of merger or consolidation in connection with a merger or consolidation which was effective prior to July 5, 1990 shall not affect the validity or effectiveness of any such merger or consolidation.

(d) Unless a future effective date or time is provided in a certificate of merger or consolidation, in which event a merger or consolidation shall be effective at any such future effective date or time, a merger or consolidation shall be effective upon the filing in the office of the Secretary of State of a certificate of merger or consolidation.

(e) A certificate of merger or consolidation shall act as a certificate of cancellation for a statutory trust which is not the surviving or resulting entity in the merger or consolidation. A certificate of merger that sets forth any amendment in accordance with subsection (b)(4) of this section shall be deemed to be an amendment to the certificate of trust of the statutory trust, and the statutory trust shall not be required to take any further action to amend its certificate of trust under § 3810 of this title with respect to such amendments set forth in the certificate of merger. Whenever this section requires the filing of a certificate of merger or consolidation, such requirement shall be deemed satisfied by the filing of an agreement of merger or consolidation containing the information required by this section to be set forth in the certificate of merger or consolidation.

(f) Notwithstanding anything to the contrary contained in the governing instrument of a statutory trust, a governing instrument of a statutory trust containing a specific reference to this subsection may provide that an agreement of merger or consolidation approved in accordance with subsection (a) of this section may:

(1) Effect any amendment to the governing instrument of the statutory trust; or

(2) Effect the adoption of a new governing instrument of the statutory trust if it is the surviving or resulting statutory trust in the merger or consolidation.

Any amendment to the governing instrument of a statutory trust or adoption of a new governing instrument of the statutory trust made pursuant to the foregoing sentence shall be effective at the effective time or date of the merger or consolidation. The provisions of this subsection shall not be construed to limit the accomplishment of a merger or consolidation or of any of the matters referred to herein by any other means provided for in the governing instrument of a statutory trust or other agreement or as otherwise permitted by law, including that the governing instrument of any constituent statutory trust to the merger or consolidation (including a statutory trust formed for the purpose of consummating a merger or consolidation) shall be the governing instrument of the surviving or resulting statutory trust.

(g) When any merger or consolidation shall have become effective under this section, for all purposes of the laws of the State, all of the rights, privileges and powers of each of the statutory trusts and other business entities that have merged or consolidated, and all property, real, personal and mixed, and all debts due to any of said statutory trusts and other business entities, as well as all other things and causes of action belonging to each of such statutory trusts and other business entities, shall be vested in the surviving or resulting statutory trust or other business entity, and shall thereafter be the property of the surviving or resulting statutory trust or other business entity as they were of each of the statutory trusts and other business entities that have merged or consolidated, and the title to any real property vested by deed or otherwise, under the laws of the State, in any of such statutory trusts and other business entities, shall not revert or be in any way impaired by reason of this subchapter; but all rights of creditors and all liens upon any property of any of said statutory trusts and other business entities shall be preserved unimpaired, and all debts, liabilities and duties of each of the said statutory trusts and other business entities that have merged or consolidated shall thenceforth attach to the surviving or resulting statutory trust or other business entity, and may be enforced against it to the same extent as if said debts, liabilities and duties had been incurred or contracted by it.

(h) A governing instrument or an agreement of merger or consolidation may provide that contractual appraisal rights with respect to a beneficial interest or another interest in a statutory trust shall be available for any class or group of beneficial owners or beneficial interests in connection with any amendment of a governing instrument, any merger or consolidation in which the statutory trust is a constituent party to the merger or consolidation or the sale of all or substantially all of the statutory trust's assets. The Court of Chancery shall have jurisdiction to hear and determine any matter relating to any such appraisal rights.

§ 3816. Derivative Actions

(a) A beneficial owner may bring an action in the Court of Chancery in the right of a statutory trust to recover a judgment in its favor if trustees with authority to do so have refused to bring the action or if an effort to cause those trustees to bring the action is not likely to succeed.

(b) In a derivative action, the plaintiff must be a beneficial owner at the time of bringing the action and:

(1) At the time of the transaction of which the plaintiff complains; or

(2) Plaintiff's status as a beneficial owner had devolved upon plaintiff by operation of law or pursuant to the terms of the governing instrument of the statutory trust from a person who was a beneficial owner at the time of the transaction.

(c) In a derivative action, the complaint shall set forth with particularity the effort, if any, of the plaintiff to secure initiation of the action by the trustees, or the reasons for not making the effort.

(d) If a derivative action is successful, in whole or in part, or if anything is received by a statutory trust as a result of a judgment, compromise or settlement of any such action, the Court may award the plaintiff reasonable expenses, including reasonable attorney's fees. If anything is so received by the plaintiff, the Court shall make such award of plaintiff's expenses payable out of those proceeds and direct plaintiff to remit to the statutory trust the remainder thereof, and if those proceeds are insufficient to reimburse plaintiff's reasonable expenses, the Court may direct that any such award of plaintiff's expenses or a portion thereof be paid by the statutory trust.

(e) A beneficial owner's right to bring a derivative action may be subject to such additional standards and restrictions, if any, as are set forth in the governing instrument of the statutory trust, including, without limitation, the requirement that beneficial owners owning a specified beneficial interest in the statutory trust join in the bringing of the derivative action.

§ 3817. Indemnification

(a) Subject to such standards and restrictions, if any, as are set forth in the governing instrument of a statutory trust, a statutory trust shall have the power to indemnify and hold harmless any trustee or beneficial owner or other person from and against any and all claims and demands whatsoever.

(b) The absence of a provision for indemnity in the governing instrument of a statutory trust shall not be construed to deprive any trustee or beneficial owner or other person of any right to indemnity which is otherwise available to such person under the laws of this State.

§ 3818. Treasury Interests

Except to the extent otherwise provided in the governing instrument of a statutory trust, a statutory trust may acquire, by purchase, redemption or otherwise, any beneficial interest in the statutory trust held by a beneficial owner of the statutory trust. Except to the extent otherwise provided in the governing instrument of a statutory trust, any such interest so acquired by a statutory trust shall be deemed canceled.

§ 3819. Access to and Confidentiality of Information; Records

(a) Except to the extent otherwise provided in the governing instrument of a statutory trust, each beneficial owner of a statutory trust has the right, subject to such reasonable standards (including standards governing what information and documents are to be furnished at what time and location and at whose expense) as may be established by the trustees, to obtain from the statutory trust from time to time upon reasonable demand for any purpose reasonably related to the beneficial owner's interest as a beneficial owner of the statutory trust:

(1) A copy of the governing instrument and certificate of trust and all amendments thereto, together with copies of any written powers of attorney pursuant to which the governing instrument and any certificate and any amendments thereto have been executed;

(2) A current list of the name and last known business, residence or mailing address of each beneficial owner and trustee;

(3) Information regarding the business and financial condition of the statutory trust; and

(4) Other information regarding the affairs of the statutory trust as is just and reasonable.

(b) Except to the extent otherwise provided in the governing instrument of a statutory trust, each trustee shall have the right to examine all the information described in subsection (a) of this section for any purpose reasonably related to the trustee's position as a trustee.

(c) Except to the extent otherwise provided in the governing instrument of a statutory trust, the trustees of a statutory trust shall have the right to keep confidential from the beneficial owners, for such period of time as the trustees deem reasonable, any information that the trustees reasonably believe to be in the nature of trade secrets or other information, the disclosure of which the trustees in good faith believe is not in the best interest of the statutory trust or could damage the statutory trust or its business or which the statutory trust is required by law or by agreement with a third party to keep confidential.

(d) A statutory trust may maintain its records in other than a written form if such form is capable of conversion into a written form within a reasonable time.

(e) Any demand by a beneficial owner or trustee under this section shall be in writing and shall state the purpose of such demand.

§ 3820. Conversion of Other Business Entities to a Statutory Trust

(a) Any other business entity formed or organized or existing under the laws of the State or any other state or the United States or any foreign country or other foreign jurisdiction may convert to a statutory trust by complying with subsection (g) of this section and filing in the Office of the Secretary of State in accordance with § 3812 of this title:

(1) A certificate of conversion to statutory trust that has been executed by the trustees in accordance with § 3811 of this title; and

(2) A certificate of trust that complies with § 3810 of this title and has been executed by the trustees in accordance with § 3811 of this title.

(b) The certificate of conversion to statutory trust shall state:

(1) The date on which and jurisdiction where the other business entity was first formed or organized or otherwise came into being and, if it has changed, its jurisdiction immediately prior to its conversion to a statutory trust;

(2) The name of the other business entity immediately prior to the filing of the certificate of conversion to statutory trust;

(3) The name of the statutory trust as set forth in its certificate of trust filed in accordance with subsection (a) of this section; and

(4) The future effective date or time (which shall be a date or time certain) of the conversion to a statutory trust if it is not to be effective upon the filing of the certificate of conversion to statutory trust and the certificate of trust.

(c) Upon the filing in the Office of the Secretary of State of the certificate of conversion to statutory trust and the certificate of trust or upon the future effective date or time of the certificate of conversion to statutory trust and the certificate of trust, the other business entity shall be converted into a statutory trust and the statutory trust shall thereafter be subject to all of the provisions of this chapter, except that notwithstanding § 3810(a)(2) of this title, the existence of the statutory trust shall be deemed to have commenced on the date the other business entity commenced its existence in the jurisdiction in which the other business entity was first formed or organized or otherwise came into being.

(d) The conversion of any other business entity into a statutory trust shall not be deemed to affect any obligations or liabilities of the other business entity incurred prior to its conversion to a statutory trust, or the personal liability of any person incurred prior to such conversion.

(e) When any conversion shall have become effective under this section, for all purposes of the laws of the State, all of the rights, privileges and powers of the other business entity that has converted, and all property, real, personal and mixed, and all debts due to such other business entity, as well as all other things and causes of action belonging to such other business entity, shall remain vested in the statutory trust to which such other business entity has converted and shall be the property of such statutory trust, and the title to any real property vested by deed or otherwise in such other business entity shall not revert or be in any way impaired by reason of this chapter; but all rights of creditors and all liens upon any property of such other business entity shall be preserved unimpaired, and all debts, liabilities and duties of the other business entity that has converted shall remain attached to the statutory trust to which such other business entity has converted, and may be enforced against it to the same extent as if said debts, liabilities and duties had been incurred or contracted by it in its capacity as a statutory trust. The rights, privileges, powers and interests in property of the other business entity, as well as the debts, liabilities and duties of the other business entity, shall not be deemed, as a consequence of the conversion, to have been transferred to the statutory trust to which such other business entity has converted for any purpose of the laws of the State.

(f) Unless otherwise agreed, for all purposes of the laws of the State of Delaware, the converting other business entity shall not be required to wind up its affairs or pay its liabilities and distribute its assets, and the conversion shall not be deemed to constitute a dissolution of such other business entity and shall constitute a continuation of the existence of the converting other business entity in the form of a statutory trust. When the other business entity has been converted to a statutory trust pursuant to this section, the statutory trust shall, for all purposes of the laws of the State, be deemed to be the same entity as the converting other business entity.

(g) Prior to filing a certificate of conversion to statutory trust with the Office of the Secretary of State, the conversion shall be approved in the manner provided for by the document, instrument, agreement or other writing, as the case may be, governing the internal affairs of the other business entity and the conduct of its business or by applicable law, as appropriate, and a governing instrument shall be approved by the same authorization required to approve the conversion.

(h) This section shall not be construed to limit the accomplishment of a change in the law governing, or the domicile of, any other business entity to the State by any other means provided for in an agreement governing the internal affairs of the other business entity or as otherwise permitted by law, including by the amendment of an agreement governing the internal affairs of the other business entity.

(i) In connection with a conversion hereunder, rights or securities of or interests in the other business entity which is to be converted to a statutory trust may be exchanged for or converted into cash, property, rights or securities of, or interests in, such statutory trust or, in addition to or in lieu thereof, may be exchanged for or converted into cash, property, rights or securities of, or interests in, another statutory trust or other business entity or may be cancelled.

§ 3821. Conversion of a Statutory Trust

(a) Upon compliance with this section, a statutory trust may convert to another business entity.

(b) If the governing instrument specifies the manner of authorizing a conversion of the statutory trust, the conversion shall be authorized as specified in the governing instrument. If the governing instrument does not specify the manner of authorizing a conversion of the statutory trust and does not prohibit a conversion of the statutory trust, the conversion shall be authorized in the same manner as is specified in the governing instrument for authorizing a merger or consolidation that involves the statutory trust as a constituent party to the merger or consolidation. If the governing instrument does not specify the manner of authorizing a conversion of the statutory trust or a merger or consolidation that involves the statutory trust as a constituent party and does not prohibit a conversion of the statutory trust, the conversion shall be authorized by the approval by all of the beneficial owners and all of the trustees.

(c) Unless otherwise agreed, the conversion of a statutory trust to another business entity pursuant to this section shall not require such statutory trust to wind up its affairs under § 3808 of this title or pay its liabilities and distribute its assets under § 3808 of this title.

(d) In connection with a conversion of a statutory trust to an other business entity pursuant to this section, rights or securities of, or interests in, the statutory trust which is to be converted may be exchanged for or converted into cash, property, rights or securities of, or interests in, the other business entity into which the statutory trust is being converted or, in addition to or in lieu thereof, may be exchanged for or converted into cash, property, rights or securities of, or interests in, any other business entity or may be cancelled.

(e) If a statutory trust shall convert in accordance with this section to an other business entity organized, formed or created under the laws of a jurisdiction other than the State of Delaware, a certificate of conversion to a non-Delaware entity executed in accordance with § 3811 of this title, shall be filed in the Office of the Secretary of State in accordance with § 3812 of this title. The certificate of conversion to a non-Delaware entity shall state:

(1) The name of the statutory trust and, if it has been changed, the name under which its certificate of trust was originally filed;

(2) The date of filing of its original certificate of trust with the Secretary of State;

(3) The jurisdiction in which the other business entity, to which the statutory trust shall be converted, is organized, formed or created;

(4) The future effective date or time (which shall be a date or time certain) of the conversion if it is not to be effective upon the filing of the certificate of conversion to a non-Delaware entity;

(5) That the conversion has been approved in accordance with this section;

(6) The agreement of the statutory trust that it may be served with process in the State of Delaware in any action, suit or proceeding for enforcement of any obligation of the statutory trust arising while it was a statutory trust of the State of Delaware, and that it irrevocably appoints the Secretary of State as its agent to accept service of process in any such action, suit or proceeding;

(7) The address to which a copy of the process referred to in subsection (e)(6) of this section shall be mailed to it by the Secretary of State. In the event of service under this section upon the Secretary of State, the procedures set forth in § 3861(c) of this title shall be applicable, except that the plaintiff in any such action, suit or proceeding shall furnish the Secretary of State with the address specified in this subsection and any other address that the plaintiff may elect to furnish, together with copies of such process as required by the Secretary of State, and the Secretary of State shall notify the statutory trust that has converted out of the State of Delaware at all such addresses furnished by the plaintiff in accordance with the procedures set forth in § 3861(c) of this title.

(f) Upon the filing in the Office of the Secretary of State of the certificate of conversion to a non-Delaware entity or upon the future effective date or time of the certificate of conversion to a non-Delaware entity and payment to the Secretary of State of all fees prescribed in this chapter, the Secretary of State shall certify that the statutory trust has filed all documents and paid all fees required by this chapter, and thereupon the statutory trust shall cease to exist as a statutory trust of the State of Delaware. Such certificate of the Secretary of State shall be prima facie evidence of the conversion by such statutory trust out of the State of Delaware.

(g) The conversion of a statutory trust out of the State of Delaware in accordance with this section and the resulting cessation of its existence as a statutory trust of the State of Delaware pursuant to a certificate of conversion to a non-Delaware entity shall not be deemed to affect any obligations or liabilities of the statutory trust incurred prior to such conversion or the personal liability of any person incurred prior to such conversion, nor shall it be deemed to affect the choice of law applicable to the statutory trust with respect to matters arising prior to such conversion.

(h) When a statutory trust has been converted to an other business entity pursuant to this section, the other business entity shall, for all purposes of the laws of the State of Delaware, be deemed to be the same entity as the statutory trust. When any conversion becomes effective under this section, for all purposes of the laws of the State of Delaware, all of the rights, privileges and powers of the statutory trust that has converted, and all property, real, personal and mixed, and all debts due to such statutory trust, as well as all other things and causes of action belonging to such statutory trust, shall remain vested in the other business entity to which such statutory trust has converted and shall be the property of such other business entity, and the title to any real property vested by deed or otherwise in such statutory trust shall not revert or be in any way impaired by reason of this chapter; but all rights of creditors and all liens upon any property of such statutory trust shall be preserved unimpaired, and all debts, liabilities and duties of the statutory trust that has converted shall remain attached to the other business entity to which such statutory trust has converted, and may been forced against it to the same extent as if said debts, liabilities and duties had originally been incurred or contracted by it in its capacity as such other business entity. The rights, privileges, powers and interests in property of the statutory trust that has converted, as well as the debts, liabilities and duties of such statutory trust, shall not be deemed, as a consequence of the conversion, to have been transferred to the other business entity to which such statutory trust has converted for any purpose of the laws of the State of Delaware.

§ 3822. Domestication of non-United States Entities

(a) As used in this section, "non-United States entity" means a foreign statutory trust (other than one formed under the laws of a state), or a corporation, a limited liability company, a business trust or association, a real estate investment trust, a common-law trust, or any other unincorporated business, including a partnership (whether general (including a limited liability partnership) or limited (including a limited liability limited partnership)), formed, incorporated, created or that otherwise came into being under the laws of any foreign country or other foreign jurisdiction (other than any state).

(b) Any non-United States entity may become domesticated as a statutory trust in the State of Delaware by complying with subsection (g) of this section and filing in the Office of the Secretary of State in accordance with § 3812 of this title:

(1) A certificate of statutory trust domestication that has been executed in accordance with § 3811 of this title; and

(2) A certificate of trust that complies with § 3810 of this title and has been executed in accordance with § 3811 of this title.

(c) The certificate of statutory trust domestication shall state:

(1) The date on which and jurisdiction where the non-United States entity was first formed, incorporated, created or otherwise came into being;

(2) The name of the non-United States entity immediately prior to the filing of the certificate of statutory trust domestication;

(3) The name of the statutory trust as set forth in the certificate of trust filed in accordance with subsection (b) of this section;

(4) The future effective date or time (which shall be a date or time certain) of the domestication as a statutory trust if it is not to be effective upon the filing of the certificate of statutory trust domestication and the certificate of trust; and

(5) The jurisdiction that constituted the seat, siege social, or principal place of business or central administration of the non-United States entity, or any other equivalent thereto under applicable law, immediately prior to the filing of the certificate of statutory trust domestication.

(d) Upon the filing in the Office of the Secretary of State of the certificate of statutory trust domestication and the certificate of trust or upon the future effective date or time of the certificate of statutory trust domestication and the certificate of trust, the non-United States entity shall be domesticated as a statutory trust in the State of Delaware and the statutory trust shall thereafter be subject to all of the provisions of this chapter, except that notwithstanding § 3810(a)(2) of this title, the existence of the statutory trust shall be deemed to have commenced on the date the non-United States entity commenced its existence in the jurisdiction in which the non-United States entity was first formed, incorporated, created or otherwise came into being.

(e) The domestication of any non-United States entity as a statutory trust in the State of Delaware shall not be deemed to affect any obligations or liabilities of the non-United States entity incurred prior to its domestication as a statutory trust in the State of Delaware, or the personal liability of any person therefor.

(f) The filing of a certificate of statutory trust domestication shall not affect the choice of law applicable to the non-United States entity, except that from the effective date or time of the domestication, the law of the State of Delaware, including the provisions of this chapter, shall apply to the non-United States entity to the same extent as if the non-United States entity had been formed as a statutory trust on that date.

(g) Prior to filing a certificate of statutory trust domestication with the Office of the Secretary of State, the domestication shall be approved in the manner provided for by the document, instrument, agreement or other writing, as the case may be, governing the internal affairs of the non-United States entity and the conduct of its business or by applicable non-Delaware law, as appropriate, and a governing instrument shall be approved by the same authorization required to approve the domestication.

(h) When any domestication shall have become effective under this section, for all purposes of the laws of the State of Delaware, all of the rights, privileges and powers of the non-United States entity that has been domesticated, and all property, real, personal and mixed, and all debts due to such non-United States entity, as well as all other things and causes of action belonging to such non-United States entity, shall remain vested in the domestic statutory trust to which such non-United States entity has been domesticated and shall be the property of such domestic statutory trust, and the title to any real property vested by deed or otherwise in such non-United States entity shall not revert or be in any way impaired by reason of this chapter; but all rights of creditors and all liens upon any property of such non-United States entity shall be preserved unimpaired, and all debts, liabilities and duties of the non-United States entity that has been domesticated shall remain attached to the domestic statutory trust to which such non-United States entity has been domesticated, and may be enforced against it to the same extent as if said debts, liabilities and duties had originally been incurred or contracted by it in its capacity as a domestic statutory trust. The rights, privileges, powers and interests in property of the non-United States entity, as well as the debts, liabilities and duties of the non-United States entity, shall not be deemed, as a consequence of the domestication, to have been transferred to the domestic statutory trust to which such non-United States entity has domesticated for any purpose of the laws of the State of Delaware.

(i) When a non-United States entity has become domesticated as a statutory trust pursuant to this section, the statutory trust shall, for all purposes of the laws of the State of Delaware, be deemed to be the same entity as the domesticating non-United States entity. Unless otherwise agreed, for all purposes of the laws of the State of Delaware, the domesticating non-United States entity shall not be required to wind up its affairs or pay its liabilities and distribute its assets, and the domestication shall not be deemed to constitute a dissolution of such non-United States entity and shall constitute a continuation of the existence of the domesticating non-United States entity in the form of a domestic statutory trust. If, following domestication, a non-United States entity that has become domesticated as a statutory trust continues its existence in the foreign country or other foreign jurisdiction in which it was existing immediately prior to domestication, the statutory trust and such non-United States entity shall, for all purposes of the laws of the State of Delaware, constitute a single entity formed, incorporated, created or otherwise having come into being, as applicable, and existing under the laws of the State of Delaware and the laws of such foreign country or other foreign jurisdiction.

(j) In connection with a domestication hereunder, rights or securities of, or interests in, the non-United States entity that is to be domesticated as a domestic statutory trust may be exchanged for or converted into cash, property, rights or securities of, or interests in, such domestic statutory trust or, in addition to or in lieu thereof, may be exchanged for or converted into cash, property, rights or securities of, or interests in, an other domestic statutory trust or other entity or may be cancelled.

§ 3823. Transfer or Continuance of Domestic Statutory Trusts

(a) Upon compliance with the provisions of this section, any statutory trust may transfer to or domesticate in any jurisdiction, other than any state, and, in connection therewith, may elect to continue its existence as a statutory trust in the State of Delaware.

(b) If the governing instrument specifies the manner of authorizing a transfer or domestication or continuance described in subsection (a) of this section, the transfer or domestication or continuance shall be authorized as specified in the governing instrument. If the governing instrument does not specify the manner of authorizing a transfer or domestication or continuance described in subsection (a) of this section and does not prohibit such a transfer or domestication or continuance, the transfer or domestication or continuance shall be authorized in the same manner as is specified in the governing instrument for authorizing a merger or consolidation that involves the statutory trust as a constituent party to the merger or consolidation. If the governing instrument does not specify the manner of authorizing a transfer or domestication or continuance described in subsection (a) of this section or a merger or consolidation that involves the statutory trust as a constituent party and does not prohibit such a transfer or domestication or continuance, the transfer or domestication or continuance shall be authorized by the approval by all of the beneficial owners and all of the trustees. If a transfer or domestication or continuance described in subsection (a) of this section shall be approved as provided in this subsection (b) of this section, a certificate of transfer if the statutory trust's existence as a statutory trust of the State of Delaware is to cease, or a certificate of transfer and continuance if the statutory trust's existence as a statutory trust in the State of Delaware is to continue, executed in accordance with § 3811 of this title, shall be filed in the Office of the Secretary of

State in accordance with § 3812 of this title. The certificate of transfer or the certificate of transfer and continuance shall state:

(1) The name of the statutory trust and, if it has been changed, the name under which its certificate of trust was originally filed;

(2) The date of the filing of its original certificate of trust with the Secretary of State;

(3) The jurisdiction to which the statutory trust shall be transferred or in which it shall be domesticated;

(4) The future effective date or time (which shall be a date or time certain) of the transfer or domestication to the jurisdiction specified in subsection (b)(3) of this section if it is not to be effective upon the filing of the certificate of transfer or the certificate of transfer and continuance;

(5) That the transfer or domestication or continuance of the statutory trust has been approved in accordance with the provisions of this section;

(6) In the case of a certificate of transfer:

a. That the existence of the statutory trust as a statutory trust of the State of Delaware shall cease when the certificate of transfer becomes effective; and

b. The agreement of the statutory trust that it may be served with process in the State of Delaware in any action, suit or proceeding for enforcement of any obligation of the statutory trust arising while it was a statutory trust of the State of Delaware, and that it irrevocably appoints the Secretary of State as its agent to accept service of process in any such action, suit or proceeding;

(7) The address to which a copy of the process referred to in subsection (b)(6) of this section shall be mailed to it by the Secretary of State. In the event of service under this section upon the Secretary of State, the procedures set forth in § 3861(c) of this title shall be applicable, except that the plaintiff in any such action, suit or proceeding shall furnish the Secretary of State with the address specified in this subsection and any other address that the plaintiff may elect to furnish, together with copies of such process as required by the Secretary of State, and the Secretary of State shall notify the statutory trust that has transferred or domesticated out of the State of Delaware at all such addresses furnished by the plaintiff in accordance with the procedures set forth in § 3861(c) of this title; and

(8) In the case of a certificate of transfer and continuance, that the statutory trust will continue to exist as a statutory trust of the State of Delaware after the certificate of transfer and continuance becomes effective.

(c) Upon the filing in the Office of the Secretary of State of the certificate of transfer or upon the future effective date or time of the certificate of transfer and payment to the Secretary of State of all fees prescribed in this chapter, the Secretary of State shall certify that the statutory trust has filed all documents and paid all fees required by this chapter, and thereupon the statutory trust shall cease to exist as a statutory trust of the State of Delaware. Such certificate of the Secretary of State shall be prima facie evidence of the transfer or domestication by such statutory trust out of the State of Delaware.

(d) The transfer or domestication of a statutory trust out of the State of Delaware in accordance with this section and the resulting cessation of its existence as a statutory trust of the State of Delaware pursuant to a certificate of transfer shall not be deemed to affect any obligations or liabilities of the statutory trust incurred prior to such transfer or domestication or the personal liability of any person incurred prior to such transfer or domestication, nor shall it be deemed to affect the choice of law applicable to the statutory trust with respect to matters arising prior to such transfer or domestication. Unless otherwise agreed, the transfer or domestication of a statutory trust out of the State of Delaware in accordance with this section shall not require such statutory trust to wind up its affairs or pay its liabilities and distribute its assets under § 3808 of this title.

(e) If a statutory trust files a certificate of transfer and continuance, after the time the certificate of transfer and continuance becomes effective, the statutory trust shall continue to exist as a statutory trust of the State of Delaware, and the laws of the State of Delaware, including the provisions of this chapter, shall apply to the statutory trust, to the same extent as prior to such time. So long as a statutory trust continues to exist as a statutory trust of the State of Delaware following the filing of a certificate of transfer and continuance, the continuing statutory trust and the other business entity formed, incorporated, created or that otherwise came into being as a consequence of the transfer of the statutory trust to, or its domestication in, a foreign country or other foreign jurisdiction shall, for all purposes of the laws of the State of Delaware, constitute a single entity formed, incorporated, created or otherwise having come into being, as applicable, and existing under the laws of the State of Delaware and the laws of such foreign country or other foreign jurisdiction.

(f) In connection with a transfer or domestication of a statutory trust to or in an other jurisdiction pursuant to subsection (a) of this section, rights or securities of, or interests in, such statutory trust may be exchanged for or converted into cash, property, rights or securities of, or interests in, the other business entity in which the statutory trust will exist in such other jurisdiction as a consequence of the transfer or domestication or, in addition to or in lieu thereof, may be exchanged for or converted into cash, property, rights or securities of, or interests in, any other business entity or may be cancelled.

(g) When a statutory trust has transferred or domesticated out of the State of Delaware pursuant to this section, the transferred or domesticated other business entity shall, for all purposes of the laws of the State of Delaware, be deemed to be the same entity as the statutory trust. When any transfer or domestication of a statutory trust out of the State of Delaware shall have become effective under this section, for all purposes of the laws of the State of Delaware, all of the rights, privileges and powers of the statutory trust that has transferred or domesticated, and all property, real, personal and mixed, and all debts due to such statutory trust, as well as all other things and causes of action belonging to such statutory trust, shall remain vested in the transferred or domesticated other business entity and shall be the property of such transferred or domesticated other business entity, and the title to any real property vested by deed or otherwise in such statutory trust shall not revert or be in any way impaired by reason of this chapter; but all rights of creditors and all liens upon any property of such statutory trust shall be preserved unimpaired, and all debts, liabilities and duties of the statutory trust that has transferred or domesticated shall remain attached to the transferred or domesticated other business entity, and may be enforced against it to the same extent as if said debts, liabilities and duties had originally been incurred or contracted by it in its capacity as the transferred or domesticated other business entity. The rights, privileges, powers and interests in property of the statutory trust that has transferred or domesticated, as well as the debts, liabilities and duties of such statutory trust, shall not be deemed, as a consequence of the transfer or domestication out of the State of Delaware, to have been transferred to the transferred or domesticated other business entity for any purpose of the laws of the State of Delaware.

§ 3824. Reserved Power of State to Amend or Repeal Chapter

All provisions of this subchapter may be altered from time to time or repealed and all rights of statutory trusts, trustees, beneficial owners and other persons are subject to this reservation. Unless expressly stated to the contrary in this chapter, all amendments of this chapter shall apply to statutory trusts, trustees, beneficial owners and other persons whether or not existing as at the time of the enactment of any such amendment.

§ 3825. Construction and Application of Chapter and Governing Instrument

(a) The rule that statutes in derogation of the common law are to be strictly construed shall have no application to this subchapter.

(b) It is the policy of this subchapter to give maximum effect to the principle of freedom of contract and to the enforceability of governing instruments.

§ 3826. Short Title

This subchapter may be cited as the "Delaware Statutory Trust Act."

SUBCHAPTER II. FOREIGN STATUTORY TRUSTS

§ 3851. Law Governing

Subject to the Constitution of the State:

(1) The laws of the state, territory, possession or other jurisdiction or country under which a foreign statutory trust is organized govern its organization and internal affairs and the liability of its beneficial owners and trustees; and

(2) A foreign statutory trust may not be denied registration by reason of any difference between those laws and the laws of the State.

§ 3852. Registration Required; Application

(a) Before doing business in the State, a foreign statutory trust shall register with the Secretary of State. In order to register, a foreign statutory trust shall submit to the Secretary of State:

(1) A copy executed by a trustee or other authorized person of an application for registration as a foreign statutory trust, setting forth:

a. The name of the foreign statutory trust and, if different, the name under which it proposes to register and do business in the State;

b. The state, territory, possession or other jurisdiction or country where formed, the date of its formation and a statement from a trustee or other authorized person that, as of the date of filing, the foreign statutory trust validly exists as a statutory trust under the laws of the jurisdiction of its formation;

c. The nature of the business or purposes to be conducted or promoted in the State;

d. The address of the registered office and the name and address of the registered agent for service of process required to be maintained by § 3854(b) of this title;

e. A statement that the Secretary of State is appointed the agent of the trust for service of process under the circumstances set forth in § 3860(b) of this title; and

f. The date on which the foreign statutory trust first did, or intends to do, business in the State.

(2) A fee as set forth in § 3862 of this title shall be paid.

(b) [Repealed.]

§ 3853. Issuance of Registration

(a) If the Secretary of State finds that an application for registration conforms to law and all requisite fees have been paid, the Secretary of State shall:

(1) Certify that the application has been filed in the Secretary of State's office by endorsing upon the original application the word "Filed," and the date and hour of the filing. This endorsement is conclusive of the date and time of its filing in the absence of actual fraud;

(2) File and index the endorsed application.

(b) The Secretary of State shall prepare and return to the person who filed the application or the person's representative a copy of the original signed application, similarly endorsed, and shall certify such copy as a true copy of the original signed application.

(c) The filing of the application with the Secretary of State shall make it unnecessary to file any other documents under Chapter 31 of this title.

§ 3854. Name; Registered Office; Registered Agent

(a) A foreign statutory trust may register with the Secretary of State under any name (whether or not it is the name under which it is registered in the jurisdiction of its formation) that could be registered by a domestic statutory trust; provided however, that a foreign statutory trust may register under any name which is not such as to distinguish it upon the records in the Office of the Secretary of State from the name on such records of any domestic or foreign corporation, partnership, statutory trust, limited liability company or limited partnership reserved, registered, formed or organized under the laws of the State with the written consent of the other corporation, partnership, statutory trust, limited liability company or limited partnership, which written consent shall be filed with the Secretary of State.

(b) Each foreign statutory trust shall have and maintain in the State:

(1) A registered office which may but need not be a place of its business in the State; and

(2) A registered agent for service of process on the foreign statutory trust, which agent may be either an individual resident of the State whose business office is identical with the foreign statutory trust's registered office, or a domestic corporation, or a domestic limited partnership, or a statutory trust, or a domestic limited liability company, or a foreign corporation, or a foreign limited partnership, or a foreign statutory trust, or a foreign limited liability company authorized to do business in the State having a business office identical with such registered office, which is generally open

during normal business hours to accept service of process and otherwise perform the functions of a registered agent.

(c) A registered agent may change the address of the registered office of the foreign statutory trust(s) for which he is registered agent to another address in the State by paying a fee as set forth in § 3862 of this title and filing with the Secretary of State a certificate, executed by such registered agent, setting forth the address at which such registered agent has maintained the registered office for each of the foreign statutory trusts for which it is a registered agent and further certifying to the new address to which each such registered office will be changed on a given day and at which new address such registered agent will thereafter maintain the registered office for each of the foreign statutory trusts for which it is registered agent. Upon the filing of such certificate, the Secretary of State shall furnish to the registered agent a certified copy of the same under the Secretary's hand and seal of office, and thereafter, or until further change of address, as authorized by law the registered offices in the State each of the foreign statutory trusts for which the agent is registered agent shall be located at the new address of the registered agent thereof as given in the certificate. In the event of a change of name of any person acting as a registered agent of a foreign statutory trust, such registered agent shall file with the Secretary of State a certificate, executed by such registered agent, setting forth the new name of such registered agent, the name of such registered agent before it was changed, and the address at which such registered agent has maintained the registered office for each of the foreign statutory trusts for which it is registered agent, and shall pay a fee as set forth in § 3862 of this title. Upon the filing of such certificate, the Secretary of State shall furnish to the registered agent a certified copy of the same under the Secretary's hand and seal of office. A change of name of any person acting as a registered agent of a foreign statutory trust as a result of the merger or consolidation of the registered agent, with or into another person which succeeds to its assets and liabilities by operation of law, shall be deemed a change of name for purposes of this section. Filing a certificate under this section shall be deemed to be an amendment of the application of each foreign statutory trust affected thereby, and each foreign statutory trust shall not be required to take any further action with respect thereto to amend its application under § 3855 of this title. Any registered agent filing a certificate under this section shall promptly, upon such filing, deliver a copy of any such certificate to each foreign statutory trust affected thereby.

(d) The registered agent of 1 or more foreign statutory trusts may resign and appoint a successor registered agent by paying a fee as set forth in § 3862 of this title and filing a certificate with the Secretary of State stating that it resigns and the name and address of the successor registered agent. There shall be attached to such certificate a statement of each affected foreign statutory trust ratifying and approving such change of registered agent. Upon such filing, the successor registered agent shall become the registered agent of such foreign statutory trust as has ratified and approved such substitution and the successor registered agent's address, as stated in such certificate, shall become the address of each such foreign statutory trust's registered office in the State. The Secretary of State shall then issue a certificate that the successor registered agent has become the registered agent of the foreign statutory trusts so ratifying and approving such change and setting out the names of such foreign statutory trusts. Filing of such certificate of resignation shall be deemed to be an amendment of the application of each foreign statutory trust affected thereby, and each such foreign statutory trust shall not be required to take any further action with respect thereto to amend its application under § 3855 of this title.

(e) The registered agent of 1 or more foreign statutory trusts may resign without appointing a successor registered agent by paying a fee as set forth in § 3862 of this title and filing a certificate of resignation with the Secretary of State, but such resignation shall not become effective until 30 days after the certificate is filed. The certificate shall contain a statement that written notice of resignation was given to each affected foreign statutory trust at least 30 days prior to the filing of the certificate by mailing or delivering such notice to the foreign statutory trust at its address last known to the registered agent and shall set forth the date of such notice. After receipt of the notice of the resignation of its registered agent, the foreign statutory trust for which such registered agent was acting shall obtain and designate a new registered agent to take the place of the registered agent so resigning. If such foreign statutory trust fails to obtain and designate a new registered agent as aforesaid prior to the expiration of the period of 30 days after the filing by the registered agent of the certificate of resignation, such foreign statutory trust shall not be permitted to do business in the State and its registration shall be deemed to be canceled. After the resignation of the registered agent shall have become effective as provided in this section and if no new registered agent shall have been obtained and designated in the time and manner aforesaid, service of legal process against the foreign statutory trust for which the resigned registered agent had been acting shall thereafter be upon the Secretary of State in accordance with § 3861 of this title.

§ 3855. Amendments to Application

If any statement in the application for registration of a foreign statutory trust was false when made or any arrangements or other facts described have changed, making the application false in any respect, the foreign statutory trust shall promptly file in the Office of the Secretary of State a certificate, executed by a trustee or other authorized person, correcting such statement, together with a fee as set forth in § 3862 of this title.

§ 3856. Cancellation of Registration

A foreign statutory trust may cancel its registration by filing with the Secretary of State a certificate of cancellation, executed by a trustee or other authorized person, together with a fee as set forth in § 3862 of this title. A cancellation does not terminate the authority of the Secretary of State to accept service of process on the foreign statutory trust with respect to causes of action arising out of the doing of business in the State.

§ 3857. Doing Business Without Registration

(a) A foreign statutory trust doing business in the State may not maintain any action, suit or proceeding in the State until it has registered in the State, and has paid to the State all fees and penalties for the years or parts thereof, during which it did business in the State without having registered.

(b) The failure of a foreign statutory trust to register in the State does not:

(1) Impair the validity of any contract or act of the foreign statutory trust;

(2) Impair the right of any other party to the contract to maintain any action, suit or proceeding on the contract; or

(3) Prevent the foreign statutory trust from defending any action, suit or proceeding in any court of the State.

(c) A beneficial owner or a trustee of a foreign statutory trust is not liable for the obligations of the foreign statutory trust solely by reason of the statutory trust's having done business in the State without registration.

(d) Any foreign statutory trust doing business in the State without first having registered shall be fined and shall pay to the Secretary of State $200 for each year or part thereof during which the foreign statutory trust failed to register in the State.

§ 3858. Foreign Statutory Trusts Doing Business Without Having Qualified; Injunctions

The Court of Chancery shall have jurisdiction to enjoin any foreign statutory trust, or any agent thereof, from doing any business in the State if such foreign statutory trust has failed to register under this subchapter or if such foreign statutory trust has secured a certificate of the Secretary of State under § 3853 of this title on the basis of false or misleading representations. The Attorney General shall, upon the Attorney General's own motion or upon the relation of proper parties, proceed for this purpose by complaint in any county in which such foreign statutory trust is doing or has done business.

§ 3859. Execution—Liability

Section 3811(c) of this title shall be applicable to foreign statutory trusts as if they were domestic statutory trusts.

§ 3860. Service of Process on Registered Foreign Statutory Trusts

(a) Service of legal process upon any foreign statutory trust shall be made by delivering a copy personally to any trustee of the foreign statutory trust in the State or the registered agent of the foreign statutory trust in the State, or by leaving it at the dwelling house or usual place of abode in the State of any such trustee or registered agent (if the registered agent be an individual), or at the registered office or other place of business of the foreign statutory trust in the State. If the registered agent be a corporation, service of process upon it as such may be made by serving, in the State, a copy thereof on the president, vice-president, secretary, assistant secretary or any director of the corporate registered agent. Service by copy left at the dwelling house or usual place of abode of any trustee or registered agent, or at the registered office or other place of business of the foreign statutory trust in the State, to be effective must be delivered thereat at least 6 days before the return date of the process, and in the presence of an adult person, and the officer serving the process shall distinctly state the manner of service in the officer's return thereto. Process returnable forthwith must be delivered personally to the trustee or registered agent.

(b) In case the officer whose duty it is to serve legal process cannot by due diligence serve the process in any manner provided for by subsection (a) of this section, it shall be lawful to serve the process against the foreign statutory trust upon the Secretary of State, and such service shall be as effectual for all intents and purposes as if made in any of the ways provided for in subsection (a) of this section. In the event service is effected through the Secretary of State in accordance with this subsection, the Secretary of State shall forthwith notify the foreign statutory trust by letter, certified mail, return receipt requested, directed to the foreign statutory trust at its last registered office. Such letter shall enclose a copy of the process and any other papers served on the Secretary of State pursuant to this subsection. It shall be the duty of the plaintiff in the event of such service to serve process and any other papers in duplicate, to notify the Secretary of State that service is being effected pursuant to this subsection, and to pay to the Secretary of State the sum of $50 for the use of the State, which sum shall be taxed as a part of the costs in the proceeding if the plaintiff shall prevail therein. The Secretary of State shall maintain an alphabetical record of any such service setting forth the name of the plaintiff and defendant, the title, docket number and nature of the proceeding in which process has been served upon the Secretary of State, the fact that service has been effected pursuant to this subsection, the return date thereof and the day and hour when the service was made. The Secretary of State shall not be required to retain such information for a period longer than 5 years from receipt of the service of process.

§ 3861. Service of Process on Unregistered Foreign Statutory Trusts

(a) Any foreign statutory trust which shall do business in the State without having registered under § 3852 of this title shall be deemed to have thereby appointed and constituted the Secretary of State of the State its agent for the acceptance of legal process in any civil action, suit or proceeding against it in any state or federal court in the State arising or growing out of any business done by it within the State. The doing of business in the State by such foreign statutory trust shall be a signification of the agreement of such foreign statutory trust that any such process when so served shall be of the same legal force and validity as if served upon an authorized manager or agent personally within the State.

(b) Whenever the words "doing business," "the doing of business" or "business done in this State" by any such foreign statutory trust are used in this section, they shall mean the course or practice of carrying on any business activities in the State, including, without limiting the generality of the foregoing, the solicitation of business or orders in the State; provided, however such words shall be deemed to have the same meaning as similar words of like import in § 371 of Title 8, but the requirement of such foreign statutory trust to register under § 3852 of this title shall be subject to the same exceptions as are set forth in § 373 of Title 8.

(c) In the event of service upon the Secretary of State in accordance with subsection (a) of this section, the Secretary of State shall forthwith notify the foreign statutory trust thereof by letter, certified mail, return receipt requested, directed to the foreign statutory trust at the address furnished to the Secretary of State by the plaintiff in such action, suit or proceeding. Such letter shall enclose a copy of the process and any other papers served upon the Secretary of State. It shall be the duty of the plaintiff in the event of such service to serve process and any other papers in duplicate, to notify the Secretary of State that service is being made pursuant to this subsection, and to pay to the Secretary of State the sum of $50 for the use of the State, which sum shall be taxed as part of the costs in the proceeding, if the plaintiff shall prevail therein. The Secretary of State shall maintain an alphabetical record of any such process setting forth the name of the plaintiff and defendant, the title, docket number and nature of the proceeding in which process has been served upon the Secretary of State, the return date thereof, and the day and hour when the service was made. The Secretary of State shall not be required to retain such information for a period longer than 5 years from receipt of the service of process.

§ 3862. Fees [Effective Until July 1, 2008]

No document required to be filed under this subchapter shall be effective until the applicable fee required by this section is paid. The following fees shall be paid to and collected by the Secretary of State for the use of the State:

(1) Upon receipt for filing of an application for registration as a foreign statutory trust under § 3852 of this title, a certificate under § 3855 of this title or a certificate of cancellation under § 3856 of this title, a fee in amount of $200 together with such fees for services as may be authorized pursuant to § 3813(b) of this title.

(2) Upon the receipt for filing of a certificate under § 3854(c) of this title, a fee in the amount of $50, upon the receipt for filing of a certificate under § 3854(d) of this title, a fee in the amount of $50 and a further fee of $2 for each foreign statutory trust affected by such certificate, and upon the receipt for filing of a certificate under § 3854(e) of this title, a fee in the amount of $2.50.

§ 3862. Fees [Effective July 1, 2008]

No document required to be filed under this subchapter shall be effective until the applicable fee required by this section is paid. The following fees shall be paid to and collected by the Secretary of State for the use of the State:

(1) Upon receipt for filing of an application for registration as a foreign statutory trust under § 3852 of this title, a certificate under § 3855 of this title or a certificate of cancellation under § 3856 of this title, a fee in amount of up to $300 together with such fees for services as may be authorized pursuant to § 3813(b) of this title.

(2) Upon the receipt for filing of a certificate under § 3854(c) of this title, a fee in the amount of $50, upon the receipt for filing of a certificate under § 3854(d) of this title, a fee in the amount of $50 and a further fee of $2 for each foreign statutory trust affected by such certificate, and upon the receipt for filing of a certificate under § 3854(e) of this title, a fee in the amount of $2.50.

§ 3863. Activities not Constituting Doing Business

(a) Activities of a foreign statutory trust in the State of Delaware that do not constitute doing business for the purpose of this chapter include:

(1) Maintaining, defending or settling an action or proceeding;

(2) Holding meetings of its beneficial owners or trustees or carrying on any other activity concerning its internal affairs;

(3) Maintaining bank accounts;

(4) Maintaining offices or agencies for the transfer, exchange or registration of the statutory trust's own securities or maintaining trustees or depositories with respect to those securities;

(5) Selling through independent contractors;

(6) Soliciting or obtaining orders, whether by mail or through employees or agents or otherwise, if the orders require acceptance outside the State of Delaware before they become contracts;

(7) Selling, by contract consummated outside the State of Delaware, and agreeing, by the contract, to deliver into the State of Delaware, machinery, plants or equipment, the construction, erection or installation of which within the State of Delaware requires the supervision of technical engineers or skilled employees performing services not generally available, and as part of the contract of sale agreeing to furnish such services, and such services only, to the vendee at the time of construction, erection or installation;

(8) Creating, as borrower or lender, or acquiring indebtedness with or without a mortgage or other security interest in property;

(9) Collecting debts or foreclosing mortgages or other security interests in property securing the debts, and holding, protecting and maintaining property so acquired;

(10) Conducting an isolated transaction that is not one in the course of similar transactions;

(11) Doing business in interstate commerce; and

(12) Doing business in the State of Delaware as an insurance company.

(b) A person shall not be deemed to be doing business in the State of Delaware solely by reason of being a beneficial owner or trustee of a domestic statutory trust or a foreign statutory trust.

(c) This section does not apply in determining whether a foreign statutory trust is subject to service or process, taxation or regulation under any other law of the State of Delaware.

†